PAGE 40 ON THE ROAD

YOUR COMPLETE DESTINATION GUIDE
In-depth reviews, detailed listings
and insider tips

**Orkney &
Shetland Islands**
p416

EAST GREENWICH FREE LIBRARY

**Northern Highlands
& Islands**
p363

**Inverness & the
Central Highlands**
p318

**Northeast
Scotland**
p234

**Central
Scotland**
p186

**Southern Highlands
& Islands**
p270

Edinburgh
p42

Glasgow
p102

**Southern
Scotland**
p141

PAGE 479 SURVIVAL GUIDE

VITAL PRACTICAL INFORMATION TO
HELP YOU HAVE A SMOOTH TRIP

THIS EDITION WRITTEN AND RESEARCHED BY

Neil Wilson

Andy Symington

welcome to Scotland

Outdoor Adventure

Scotland harbours some of the largest areas of wilderness left in Western Europe, a wildlife haven where you can see golden eagles soar above the lochs and mountains of the northern Highlands, spot otters tumbling in the kelp along the shores of the Outer Hebrides, and watch minke whales breach through shoals of mackerel off the coast of Mull. It's also an adventure playground where you can tramp the tundra plateaus of the Cairngorms, balance along tightrope ridges strung between the rocky peaks of the Cuillin, sea-kayak among the seal-haunted isles of the Outer Hebrides, and take a speed-boat ride into the surging white water of the Corryvreckan

whirlpool. And it's a place that changes with the seasons, offering something new each time you visit. Spring means a lilac haze of bluebells in the woods around Loch Lomond, while in summer the Hebridean beaches flaunt their golden sands and turquoise waters like Caribbean imposters. October brings a riot of autumn colour to the Perthshire forests, and in winter a fresh layer of crisp snow lends grandeur to the mountains of Glen Coe.

Deep History

Scotland is a land with a rich, multilayered history, a place where every corner of the landscape is steeped in the past – a deserted croft on an island shore, a moor

Like a fine single malt, Scotland is a connoisseur's delight – an intoxicating blend of stunning scenery and sophisticated cities, of salt-tanged sea air and dark peaty waters, of outdoor adventure and deep history.

(left) Loch Tummel (p225), Perthshire
(below) A busker on the Royal Mile (p48), Edinburgh

that was once a battlefield, a beach where Vikings hauled their boats ashore, a cave that once sheltered Bonnie Prince Charlie. Hundreds of castles, from the plain but forbidding tower houses of Hermitage and Smailholm to the elaborate machicolated fortresses of Caerlaverock and Craigmillar, testify to the country's often turbulent past. Battles that played a pivotal part in the building of a nation are remembered and brought to life at sites such as Bannockburn and Culloden. And museums and galleries such as Glasgow's Kelvingrove, Dundee's Discovery Point and Aberdeen's Maritime Museum recall the influence of Scottish engineers, artists, explorers, writers and inventors in shaping the modern world.

A Taste of Scotland

But it's not just connoisseurs of history and adrenalin who flock to Scotland's misty shores. An increasing number of visitors have discovered that its restaurants have shaken off their old reputation for deep-fried food and unsmiling service and can now compete with the best in Europe. A new-found respect for top-quality local produce means that you can feast on fresh seafood mere hours after it was caught, beef and venison that was raised just a few miles away from your table, and vegetables that were grown in your hotel's own organic garden. And top it all off with a dram of single malt whisky – rich, evocative and complex, the true taste of Scotland.

⟩ Scotland

Top Experiences ⟩

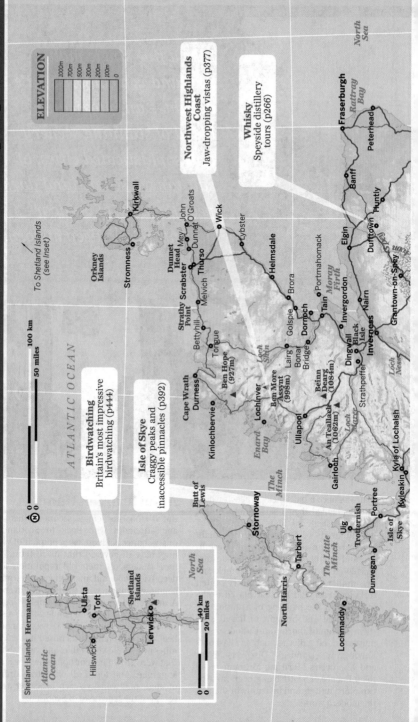

ELEVATION

1000m
700m
500m
300m
200m
100m
0

Northwest Highlands Coast (p377)
Jaw-dropping vistas

Whisky
Speyside distillery tours (p266)

Birdwatching
Britain's most impressive birdwatching (p444)

Isle of Skye (p392)
Craggy peaks and inaccessible pinnacles

ATLANTIC OCEAN

North Sea

Rattray Bay

0 ———— 100 km
0 ———— 50 miles

To Shetland Islands (see inset)

Shetland Islands Hermaness

Atlantic Ocean

Hillswick
Toft
Ulsta
Shetland Islands
Lerwick

North Sea

0 ——— 40 km
0 ——— 20 miles

Orkney Islands
Kirkwall
Stromness

Dunnet Head
Dunnet Mey John O'Groats
Strathy Point Scrabster Thurso Wick
Melvich Lybster
Bettyhill Helmsdale
Tongue Brora
Cape Wrath Ben Hope (927m) Golspie
Durness Lairg Dornoch Portmahomack
Kinlochbervie Loch Shin Bonat Bridge Tain
Ben More Assynt (998m) Invergordon
Enard Bay Lochinver Beinn Dearg (1084m) Dingwall Nairn
Ullapool An Teallach (1062m) Strathpeffel Inverness
Loch Maree Black Isle
Gairloch Loch Ness Grantown-on-Spey
Butt of Lewis Kyle of Lochalsh Elgin Dufftown
The Minch Kyleakin Nairn Huntly
Stornoway Trotternish Banff
Uig Portree Fraserburgh
North Harris Isle of Skye Peterhead
Tarbert The Little Minch
Dunvegan
Lochmaddy

Moray Firth

Loch Shin

Elgin Dufftown

Banff
Fraserburgh
Peterhead

North Sea

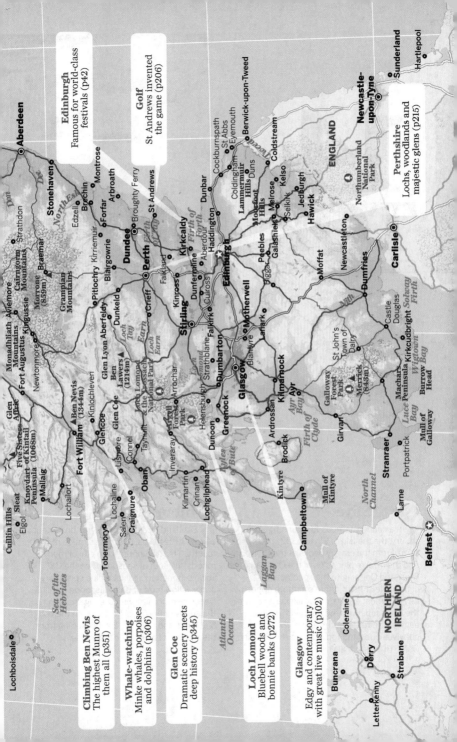

Edinburgh
Famous for world-class festivals (p42)

Golf
St Andrews invented the game (p206)

Perthshire
Lochs, woodlands and majestic glens (p215)

Climbing Ben Nevis
The highest Munro of them all (p351)

Whale-watching
Minke whales, porpoises and dolphins (p306)

Glen Coe
Dramatic scenery meets deep history (p345)

Loch Lomond
Bluebell woods and bonnie banks (p272)

Glasgow
Edgy and contemporary with great live music (p102)

14 TOP EXPERIENCES

Isle of Skye

1 In a country famous for stunning scenery, the the Isle of Skye (p392) takes top prize. From the craggy peaks of the Cuillins and the bizarre pinnacles of the Old Man of Storr and Quiraing to the spectacular sea cliffs of Neist Point, there's a photo opportunity at almost every turn. Walkers can share the landscape with red deer and golden eagles, and refuel at the end of the day in convivial pubs and top seafood restaurants.
Cuillin Hills, Isle of Skye

Edinburgh

2 Scotland's capital (p42) may be famous for its festivals, but there's much more to it than that. Edinburgh is a city of many moods: visit out of season to see the Old Town silhouetted against a blue spring sky and a yellow haze of daffodils; or on a chill December morning with the fog snagging the spires of the Royal Mile, rain on the cobblestones and a warm glow beckoning from the window of a pub. The Royal Mile

Loch Lomond

3 Despite being less than an hour's drive from the bustle and sprawl of Glasgow, the bonnie banks and bonnie braes of Loch Lomond (p272) – immortalised in the words of one of Scotland's best-known songs – comprise one of the most scenic parts of the country. At the heart of Scotland's first national park, the loch begins as a broad, island-peppered lake in the south, its shores clothed in bluebell woods, narrowing in the north to a fjordlike trench ringed by 900m-high mountains.

Walking the West Highland Way

4 The best way to really get inside Scotland's landscapes is to walk them. Despite the wind, midges and drizzle, walking here is a pleasure, with numerous short- and long-distance trails, hills and mountains begging to be tramped. Top of the wish list for many hikers is the 95-mile West Highland Way (p30) from Milngavie (near Glasgow) to Fort William, a challenging week-long walk through some of the country's finest scenery, finishing in the shadow of its highest peak, Ben Nevis.

Hikers on the West Highland Way, near Glen Coe

3

JOE CORNISH / GETTY IMAGES ©

Climbing Ben Nevis

5 The allure of Britain's highest peak (p351) is strong – around 100,000 people a year set off up the summit trail, though not all make it to the top. Nevertheless, the highest Munro of them all is within the reach of anyone who's reasonably fit. Treat Ben Nevis with respect and your reward (weather permitting) will be a truly magnificent view and a great sense of achievement. Real walking enthusiasts can warm up by hiking the 95-mile West Highland Way first.

Marine Wildlife Watching

6 Scotland is one of the best places in Europe for seeing marine wildlife. In the high season (July and August) many cruise operators on the west coast can almost guarantee sightings of minke whales and porpoises, and the Moray Firth is famous for its resident population of bottlenose dolphins (p268). Basking sharks – at up to 12m, the biggest fish to be found in British waters – make another common sighting. Tobermory (p306) and Easdale (p303; near Oban) are top departure points. Bottlenose dolphin in Moray Firth

PANORAMIC IMAGES / GETTY IMAGES ©

VISITBRITAIN / BRITAIN ON VIEW / GETTY IMAGES ©

Glasgow

7 Scotland's biggest city (p102) lacks Edinburgh's classical beauty, but more than makes up for it with a barrelful of things to do and a warmth and energy that leave every visitor impressed. Edgy and contemporary, it's a great spot to browse art galleries and – despite the deep-fried-Mars-bar reputation – Scotland's best place to eat. Add to this what is perhaps Britain's best pub culture and one of the world's best live-music scenes, and the only thing to do is live it. Ashton Lane, Glasgow

Northwest Highlands

8 The Highlands abound in breathtaking views, but the far northwest is truly awe-inspiring. The coastal road between Durness and Kyle of Lochalsh (p381) offers jaw-dropping scenes at every turn: the rugged mountains of Assynt, the desolate beauty of Torridon and the remote cliffs of Cape Wrath. These and the nooks of warm Highland hospitality found in classic rural pubs make this an unforgettable corner of the country. Kyle of Durness

Golf

9 Scotland invented the game of golf (p33) and is still revered as its spiritual home by hackers and champions alike. Links courses are the classic experience here – bumpy coastal affairs where the rough is heather and machair and the main enemy is the wind, which can make a disaster of a promising round in an instant. St Andrews (p206), the historic Fife university town, is golf's headquarters, and an alluring destination for anyone who loves the sport. St Andrews Old Course

Perthshire – Big Tree Country

10 Blue-grey lochs shimmer, reflecting the changing moods of the weather; swaths of noble woodland clothe the hills; majestic glens scythe their way into remote wildernesses; and salmon leap upriver to the place of their birth. In Perthshire (p215), the heart of the country, picturesque towns bloom with flowers, distilleries emit tempting malty odours and sheep graze in impossibly green meadows. There's a feeling of the bounty of nature that no other place in Scotland can replicate. Loch Tummel

Glen Coe

11 Scotland's most famous glen (p345) combines those two essential qualities of Highlands landscape: dramatic scenery and deep history. The peacefulness and beauty of this valley today belie the fact that it was the scene of a ruthless 17th-century massacre, when the local MacDonalds were murdered by soldiers of the Campbell clan. Some of the glen's finest walks – to the Lost Valley, for example – follow the routes used by the clanspeople trying to flee their attackers, and where many perished in the snow.

Whisky

12 Scotland's national drink (p463) – from the Gaelic *uisge bagh*, meaning 'water of life' – has been distilled here for more than 500 years. More than 100 distilleries are still in operation, producing hundreds of varieties of single malt; learning to distinguish the smoky, peaty whiskies of Islay from, say, the flowery, sherried malts of Speyside has become a hugely popular pastime. Many distilleries offer guided tours (p266), rounded off with a tasting session, and ticking off the local varieties is a great way to explore the whisky-making regions. Copper whisky stills

DAVID FORMAN / GETTY IMAGES ©

MARCUS BROOKE / GETTY IMAGES ©

MINT IMAGES / FRANS LANTING / GETTY IMAGES ©

JONATHAN SMITH / GETTY IMAGES ©

Birdwatching in Shetland

13 Sparsely populated, and with large areas of wild land, Scotland is an important sanctuary for all sorts of wildlife. Amazing birdwatching is on offer throughout the country, but the seabird cities of the Shetland Islands (p444) take first prize for spectacle. From their first arrival in late spring to the raucous feeding frenzies of high summer, the vast colonies of gannets, guillemots, puffins and kittiwakes at Hermaness, Noss and Sumburgh Head provide one of British birdwatching's most impressive experiences.
Atlantic puffins in the Outer Hebrides

Castles

14 Desolate stone fortresses looming in the mist, majestic castles towering over historic towns, or luxurious palaces built on expansive grounds by lairds more concerned with pampering than with defence: Scotland has a full range of castles that reflect its turbulent history and tense relations with its southern neighbour. Most castles have a story (or 10) to tell of plots, intrigues, imprisonments and treachery – as well as a ghost rumoured to stalk their halls. Dunnottar Castle

need to know

Currency
» Pounds Sterling (£)

Language
» English
» Gaelic & Lallans

When to Go

Cool to mild summers, cold winters

Lerwick
GO mid-May–mid July

Stornoway
• GO May

Inverness
• GO May–Sep

Fort William
GO May–Sep

• Edinburgh
GO Aug

High Season
Jul & Aug
» Accommodation prices 10%–20% higher (book in advance if possible)
» Warmest time of year, but often wet
» Midges at their worst in Highlands and islands

Shoulder Season
May, Jun & Sep
» Wildflowers and rhododendrons bloom in May and June
» Statistically, best chance of dry weather, minus midges
» June evenings have daylight till 11pm

Low Season
Oct-Apr
» Rural attractions and accommodation often closed
» Snow on hills November to March
» Gets dark at 4pm in December
» Can be very cold and wet November to March

Your Daily Budget

Less than £30
» Dorm beds: £10–20
» Wild camping is free
» Cheap supermarkets for self-caterers
» Lots of free museums and galleries

Midrange £30–100
» Double room at mid-range B&B: £50–90
» B&Bs often better value than midrange hotels
» Bar lunch: £10; dinner at midrange restaurant: £25
» Car hire: £30 per day
» Petrol costs: around 12p per mile

Top end over £100
» Double room at high-end hotel: £120–250
» Dinner at high-end restaurant: £40–60
» Flights to islands: £60–120 each way

Money

» ATMs widely available; credit cards widely accepted.

Visas

» Generally not needed for stays of up to six months. Not a member of the Schengen Zone.

Mobile Phones

» Uses the GSM 900/1800 network. Local SIM cards can be used in European and Australian phones.

Driving

» Drive on the left; steering wheel on right-hand side of car.

Websites

» **Lonely Planet** (lonelyplanet.com /scotland) Destination information, forums, hotel bookings.

» **VisitScotland** (www .visitscotland.com) Offical tourism site; booking services.

» **Internet Guide to Scotland** (www .scotland-info.co.uk) Best online tourist guide to Scotland.

» **Traveline** (www .travelinescotland. com) Up-to-date public transport timetables.

» **ScotlandsPeople** (www.scotlandspeople .gov.uk) Official, search-able genealogical website; pay-per-view.

Exchange Rates

Australia	A$1	£0.62
Canada	C$1	£0.62
Euro zone	€1	£0.85
Japan	Y100	£0.75
New Zealand	NZ$1	£0.48
USA	US$1	£0.62

For current exchange rates, see www.xe.com.

Important Numbers

Country code	+44
International access code	00
Ambulance	112 or 999
Fire	112 or 999
Police	112 or 999

Arriving in Scotland

» **Edinburgh Airport**
Buses – to Edinburgh city centre every 10 to 15 minutes from 4.30am to midnight (£3.50)
Night buses – every 30 minutes from 12.30am to 4am (£3.50)
Taxis – £15–£20; about 20 minutes to the city centre

» **Glasgow Airport**
Buses – to Glasgow city centre every 10 to 15 minutes from 6am to 11pm (£5)
Night buses – hourly 11pm to 4am, half-hourly 4am to 6pm (£5)
Taxis – £20–£25; about 30 minutes to city centre

Midges

If you've never been to the Scottish Highlands and islands before, be prepared for an encounter with the dreaded midge. These tiny, 2mm-long blood-sucking flies appear in huge swarms in summer, and can completely ruin a holiday if you're not prepared to deal with them.

They proliferate from late May to mid-September, but especially mid-June to mid-August – which unfortunately coincides with the main tourist season – and are most common in the western and northern Highlands. Midges are at their worst during the twilight hours, and on still, overcast days – strong winds and bright sunshine tend to discourage them.

The only way to combat them is to cover up, particularly in the evening. Wear long-sleeved, light-coloured clothing (midges are attracted to dark colours) and, most importantly, use a reliable insect repellent.

first time

Everyone needs a helping hand when they visit a country for the first time. There are phrases to learn, customs to get used to and etiquette to understand. The following section will help demystify Scotland so your first trip goes as smoothly as your fifth.

Top Tips for Your Trip

» Quality rather than quantity should be your goal: instead of a hair-raising race to see everything, pick a handful of destinations and give yourself time to linger. The most memorable experiences in Scotland are often the ones where you're doing very little at all.

» If you're driving, get off the main roads when you can. Some of the country's most stunning scenery is best enjoyed on secondary or tertiary roads that wind their narrow way through standout photo ops.

» Make the effort to greet the locals. The best experiences of Scotland are to be had courtesy of the Scots themselves, whose helpfulness, friendliness and fun has not been exaggerated.

Booking Ahead

If you're planning to visit Scotland in the high season, the sooner you book your accommodation the better – up to two months in advance for an Easter or July/August visit. Activities should also be booked in advance – cooking courses, organised tours, etc.

A month before you travel, book your hire car and reserve a table in whatever top-end restaurants you plan to dine at. Now is also the time to make theatre reservations, especially for new productions.

Two weeks before you arrive, check attraction opening hours and prices. A week before, get the weather forecast. Then ignore it.

What to Wear

Scotland is a fairly casual destination and you can wear pretty much whatever you like all the time. For fancy dinners, smart casual is all that's required. No restaurant will insist on jackets or ties, nor will any theatre or concert hall.

Summer days can be warm but rarely hot, so you'll always want something around your legs and shoulders when the inevitable cool sets in. If you plan to be in the Highlands during midge season, make sure you have long-sleeved shirts and long trousers – anyone in shorts and T-shirt will be eaten alive.

In the end, the factor that will determine your outfits the most is the weather, which also means that a light, waterproof jacket should always be close at hand, preferably one that you can fold away and keep in a shoulder bag.

What to Pack

» Passport
» Credit card
» Drivers licence
» Good walking shoes or boots
» Waterproof jacket
» Camera
» UK electrical adaptor
» Insect repellent
» Binoculars
» Hangover cure (all that whisky, you know)

Checklist

» Make sure your passport is valid for at least six months past your arrival date

» Make all necessary bookings (for accommodation, events and travel)

» Check the airline baggage restrictions

» Inform your debit-/credit-card company of your travels

» Arrange appropriate travel insurance

» Check if you can use your mobile/cell phone

Etiquette

Although largely informal in their everyday dealings, the Scots do observe some rules of etiquette.

» **Greetings**
Shake hands with men, women and children when meeting for the first time and when saying goodbye. Scots expect a firm handshake with eye contact.

» **Conversation**
Generally friendly but often reserved, Scots avoid conversations that might embarrass.

» **Language**
The Scots speak English with an accent that varies in strength – in places such as Glasgow and Aberdeen it can often be indecipherable. Oddly, native Gaelic speakers often have the most easily understood accent when speaking English.

» **Buying your round at the pub**
Like the English, Welsh and Irish, Scots generally take it in turns to buy a round of drinks for the whole group, and everyone is expected to take part. The next round should always be bought before the first round is finished.

Tipping

» **Hotels**
One pound per bag is standard; gratuity for cleaning staff completely at your discretion.

» **Pubs**
Not expected unless table service is provided, then £1 for a round of drinks.

» **Restaurants**
For decent service 10% and up to 15% at more expensive places. Check to see if service has been added to the bill already (most likely for large groups).

» **Taxis**
Taxis are expensive, and locals rarely tip; generally rounded up to nearest pound.

Money

ATMs can generally be found throughout Scotland. If not, it's often possible to get 'cash back' at a hotel or shop in remote areas – ie make a payment by debit card and get some cash back (the cash amount is added to the transaction).

Usually, you should have no problem withdrawing money with your bank's own card – but be sure to check with your bank before you travel.

Credit and debit cards can be used almost everywhere except for some rural B&Bs that only accept cash. Make sure bars or restaurants will accept cards before you order as some don't. The most popular cards are Visa and MasterCard; American Express is only accepted by the major chains, and virtually no one will accept Diners or JCB. Chip-and-PIN is the norm for card transactions; only a few places will accept a signature.

Banks, post offices and some of the larger hotels will change cash and travellers cheques.

what's new

For this new edition of Scotland, our authors have hunted down the fresh, the transformed, the hot and the happening. These are some of our favourites. For up-to-the-minute recommendations, see lonelyplanet.com/scotland.

Riverside Museum

1 Glasgow's rapidly developing waterfront has been graced with a magnificent new home for the collections of the former Museum of Transport. Designed by Iraqi architect Zaha Hadid, the Riverside Museum is an extraordinary building with a sinuous metallic roof intended to evoke a series of waves, symbolising the city's historic link with shipbuilding. The three-masted sailing ship *Glenlee*, built in 1896, is now moored outside the museum. (p111)

National Museum of Scotland

2 Closed for two years, Edinburgh's leading museum reopened its doors in 2011 after a major reconstruction that saw its exhibition space extended, and the Grand Gallery restored to its original Victorian splendour. (p58)

Robert Burns Birthplace Museum

3 Located in Burns' home village of Alloway, this new museum showcases an impressive collection of manuscripts and personal possessions, including the pistols Burns carried when he was employed as an excise man. (p169)

Castle Terrace

4 TV chef Tom Kitchin has added to the success of his Leith restaurant by opening Castle Terrace in the shadow of Edinburgh Castle. Within a year of opening in 2010 it had garnered its first Michelin star. (p82)

South Loch Ness Trail

5 The latest addition to Scotland's collection of waymarked hiking trails wends its way for 28 miles along the southern side of Loch Ness, allowing walkers and cyclists to explore this little-visted part of the country. (p331)

Auberge Carnish

6 The white sands and turquoise waters of Uig Bay (Traighe Uig) on the remote west coast of Lewis are famous for their beauty. Guests at this new, ecofriendly hotel (just five rooms) can wake up to that view every morning. (p409)

Starfish

7 This new seafood restaurant in the pretty fishing village of Tarbert ticks all our boxes – a friendly welcome, relaxed atmosphere, and fresh, top-quality seafood. (p287)

Mareel

8 Shetland finally got the spectacular new cinema and live-music venue it had been waiting for when this dramatic modern building on the edge of Lerwick Harbour opened in 2012. (p438)

Red Roof Café

9 The Isle of Skye's newest (and most remote) eating place has proved a hit, serving lunch platters of fresh local produce (some grown just across the road) and hosting live music events. (p401)

if you like...

Castles

The clash and conflict of Scotland's colourful history has left a legacy of military strongholds scattered across the country, from the border castles raised against English incursions to the island fortresses that controlled the seaways for the Lords of the Isles.

Edinburgh Castle The biggest, the most popular, the Scottish capital's reason for being (p49)

Stirling Castle Perched on a volcanic crag at the top of the town, this historic royal fortress and palace has the lot (p187)

Craigievar Castle The epitome of the Scottish Baronial style, all towers and turrets (p262)

Culzean Castle Enormous, palatial 18th-century mansion in a romantic coastal setting (p170)

Eilean Donan Perfect lochside location conveniently located just by the main road to Skye makes this the Highlands' most photographed fortress (p390)

Hermitage Castle Bleak and desolate borderland fortress speaking of turbulent times with England (p150)

Wild Beaches

Nothing clears a whisky hangover like a walk along a wind-whipped shoreline, and Scotland is blessed with a profusion of wild beaches. The west coast in particular has many fine strands of blinding white sands and turquoise waters that could pass for Caribbean beaches if it wasn't for the weather.

Kiloran Bay A perfect curve of deep-golden sand – the perfect vantage point for stunning sunsets (p296)

Bosta A beautiful and remote cove filled with white sand beside an Iron Age house (p408)

Durness A series of pristine sandy coves and duney headlands surrounds this northwestern village (p379)

Scousburgh Sands Shetland's finest beach is a top spot for birdwatching as well as a bracing walk (p441)

Orkney's Northern Islands Most of these islands, especially Sanday, Westray and North Ronaldsay, have spectacular stretches of white sand with seabirds galore and seals lazing on the rocks (p431)

Good Food

Scotland's chefs have an enviable range of quality meat, game, seafood and vegetables at their disposal. The country has shaken off its once-dismal culinary reputation as the land of deep-fried Mars Bars, and now boasts countless regional specialities, farmers markets, artisan cheesemakers, smokeries and microbreweries.

Ondine Sustainably sourced fish in one of Edinburgh's finest restaurants (p82)

Contrast Brasserie French culinary art meets quality Highland produce in Inverness (p324)

Café Fish Perched on Tobermory waterfront, and serving fresh seafood and shellfish straight off the boat (p308)

Monachyle Mhor Utterly romantic location deep in the Trossachs and utterly wonderful food with sound sustainable principles (p202)

Peat Inn One of Scotland's most acclaimed restaurants sits in a hamlet amid the peaceful Fife countryside (p212)

The Albannach Fabulous gourmet retreat in the northwest; a real haven for relaxation (p382)

» Music fans at the RockNess Music Festival (p332), Loch Ness

Outdoor Adventures

Scotland is one of Europe's finest outdoor adventure playgrounds. The rugged mountain terrain and convoluted coastline of the Highlands and islands offer unlimited opportunities for hiking, mountain biking, surfing and snowboarding.

Fort William The self-styled Outdoor Capital of the UK, centre for hiking, climbing, mountain biking, winter sports... (p348)

Shetland One of Scotland's top coastlines for sea kayaking, with an abundance of bird and sea life to observe from close quarters (p435)

7 Stanes Mountain-biking trails for all abilities in the forests of southern Scotland (p181)

Cairngorms Winter skiing and summer walking amid the epic beauty of this high, subarctic plateau (p336)

Thurso Right up the top of Scotland, this is an unlikely surfing mecca, but once you've got the wetsuit on the waves are pretty good (p375)

Live Music & Festivals

Scotland's festival calendar has seen an explosion of events in the last decade, with music festivals especially springing up in the most unlikely corners. The ones that have stood the test of time are full of character with superb settings and a smaller, more convivial scale than monster gigs like Glastonbury and Reading.

RockNess Regularly praised as the most beautiful festival in the world, held in June with scenic Loch Ness as a backdrop (p332)

Arran Folk Festival June sees the fiddles pulled out all over this scenic island (p162)

T in the Park The country's biggest rock festival kicks off in mid-July near the town of Kinross (p216)

King Tut's Wah Wah Hut Live music nightly at this legendary Glasgow venue. Perhaps the best thing about it is that it's one of many great places in the city (p133)

Orkney Folk Festival Stromness vibrates to the wail of the fiddle and the stamping of feet in this good-natured, late-partying island festival (p429)

Rural Museums

Every bit as interesting and worthy of study as the 'big picture' history involving Mary Queen of Scots and Bonnie Prince Charlie – especially if you're investigating your Scottish ancestry – the history of rural communities is preserved in a wide range of fascinating museums, often in original farm buildings and historic houses.

Arnol Blackhouse Preserved in peat smoke since its last inhabitant left in the 1960s, a genuine slice of 'living history' (p407)

Highland Folk Museum Fascinating outdoor museum populated with real historic buildings reassembled here on site (p341)

Scottish Crannog Centre Head back to the Bronze Age in this excellent archaeological reconstruction of a fortified loch house (p224)

Tain Through Time Really entertaining local museum with a comprehensive display on Scottish history and Tain's silversmithing tradition (p367)

Stromness Museum Delightful small-town museum has details and artefacts about the Orkney fishing industry, the World Wars, and local marine wildlife (p428)

If you like... unusual jewellery, take a look at the innovative, colourful items created by Heathergems

Pubs

No visit to Scotland is complete without a night in a traditional Scottish hostelry, supping real ales, sipping whisky and tapping your toes to traditional music. The choice of pubs is huge, but in our opinion the old ones are the best.

Drovers Inn A classic Highland hostelry with kilted staff, candlelight and a stuffed bear (p276)

Sandy Bell's A stalwart of the Edinburgh folk scene, with real ale and live trad music (p89)

Glenelg Inn The beer garden here *is* actually a garden. What's more, it's got sensational views across the water to Skye (p391)

Horse Shoe This place – all real ales and polished brass – is Glasgow's best traditional pub (p129)

Stein Inn A lochside pub in Skye with fine ales, fresh seafood and a view to die for (p402)

Captain Flint's Don't plan on a quiet pint in this boisterous harbourside Shetland pub; a great place for a chat with locals (p438)

Shopping

Scotland offers countless opportunities for shoppers to indulge in retail therapy, from designer frocks and shoes in city malls to local art, handmade pottery and traditional textiles in Highland and island workshops.

Glasgow The centre of Glasgow is a shopper's paradise, with everything from designer boutiques to secondhand records (p134)

Barras Glasgow's legendary flea market is a boisterous and intriguing place to browse for a taste of the city (p134)

Edinburgh Competes with Glasgow as the country's shopping epicentre, with its Harvey Nicks, malls, cashmere, tartan and quirky little gift shops (p92)

Wigtown An amazing array of secondhand and specialist bookshops cluster around the square in this small, out-of-the-way village (p182)

Isle of Skye It seems as if every second cottage on Skye is home to a workshop or an artist's studio, making the island a great place to find quality handmade arts and crafts (p392)

Classic Walks

Scotland's wild, dramatic scenery and varied landscape has made hiking a hugely popular pastime. There's something for all levels of fitness and enthusiasm, but the really keen hiker will want to tick off some (or all) of the classic walks.

West Highland Way The granddaddy of Scottish long-distance walks, the one everyone wants to do (p30)

Glen Affric to Shiel Bridge A classic two-day cross-country hike, with a night in a remote hostel (p328)

Southern Upland Way Crosses Southern Scotland's hills from coast to coast; longer and harder than the WHW (p152)

Ben Lawers One of central Scotland's classic hill walks, with super views over Loch Tay (p224)

Fife Coastal Path Seascapes and clifftops galore on this picturesque route right around the 'Kingdom' (p204)

Cape Wrath Trail Head for the northwest corner from Fort William through some of Scotland's remotest scenery (p381)

Hidden Gems

For those who enjoy exploring off the beaten track, Scotland is littered with hidden corners, remote road-ends and quiet cul-de-sacs where you can feel as if you are discovering the place for the first time.

Fossil Grove This strange fossilised forest is a relaxing place to escape Glasgow's bustle (p113)

Falls of Clyde Normally associated with shipbuilding, the River Clyde reveals the bucolic side of its character further upstream (p157)

Benmore Botanic Gardens Tucked away in a fold of the hills in the heart of the Cowal peninsula, this Victorian garden is a riot of colour in spring and early summer (p281)

Scotland's Secret Bunker It's back to the Cold War in this chilling but fascinating nuclear hideout hidden beneath a field in the middle of rural Fife (p215)

Cape Wrath A curious boat-minibus combo grinds you through a missile range to this spectacular headland at Britain's northwest tip (p381000)

Islands

Scotland has more than 700 islands scattered around its shore. While the vast majority of visitors stick to the larger, better-known ones such as Arran, Skye, Mull and Lewis, it's often the smaller, lesser-known islands that provide the real highlights.

Iona Beautiful, peaceful (once the day-trippers have left) and of huge historic and cultural importance, Iona is the jewel of the Hebrides (p310)

Eigg The most intriguing of the Small Isles, with its miniature mountain, massacre cave and singing sands (p360)

Jura Wild and untamed, with more deer than people, and a dangerous whirlpool at its northern end (p293)

Isle of May Just a mile long, this spot off the Fife coast erupts to the clamour of tens of thousands of puffins in spring and summer (p214)

Westray & Papa Westray There's something magical about these adjacent islands at the north end of the Orkney archipelago. Great accommodation and eating options, plenty of coastal scenery, birdwatching and historic sights (p433 & p434)

Natural Wonders

Scotland's stunning landscapes harbour many awe-inspiring natural features, including spectacular sea stacks and rock formations, thundering waterfalls, impressive gorges and swirling tidal whirlpools.

Old Man of Hoy While most of the Orkneys is fairly flat, Hoy is rugged and rocky; its spectacular west coast includes Britain's tallest sea stack (p430)

Corryvreckan Whirlpool One of the world's three most powerful tidal whirlpools, squeezed between Jura and Scarba (p294)

Falls of Measach A trembling suspension bridge provides a scary viewpoint for one of Scotland's most impressive waterfalls (p385)

Fossil Grove Ponder the immensity of geological time among 350-million-year-old fossilised trees (p113)

Fingal's Cave Accessible only by boat, this columnar sea cave inspired Mendelssohn's *Hebrides Overture* (p311)

month by month

January

The nation shakes off its Hogmanay hangover and gets back to work, but only until Burns Night comes along. It's still cold and dark, but the skiing can be good.

🏃 Burns Night

Suppers all over the country (and the world for that matter) are held on 25 January to celebrate the anniversary of national poet Robert Burns, with much eating of haggis, drinking of whisky and reciting of poetry.

✸ Celtic Connections

Glasgow hosts the world's largest winter music festival, a celebration of Celtic music, dance and culture, with participants arriving from all over the globe. Held mid- to late January. See www.celticconnections.com.

✸ Up Helly Aa

Half of Shetland dresses up with horned helmets and battleaxes in this spectacular re-enactment of a Viking fire festival, with a torchlit procession leading the burning of a full-size Viking longship. Held in Lerwick on the last Tuesday in January. See www.up hellyaa.org.

February

The coldest month of the year is usually the best for hill walking, ice-climbing and skiing. The days are getting longer now, and snowdrops begin to bloom.

🏃 Six Nations Rugby Tournament

Scotland, England, Wales, Ireland, France and Italy battle it out in this prestigious tournament, held February to March; home games played at Murrayfield, Edinburgh. See www.rbs6nations.com.

✸ Fort William Mountain Festival

The UK's Outdoor Capital celebrates the peak of the winter season with ski and snowboard learning workshops, talks by famous climbers, kids events and a festival of mountaineering films. See www.mountainfilmfestival.co.uk.

April

The bluebell woods on the shores of Loch Lomond come into flower, ospreys arrive at their Loch Garten nest. Weather improving, though heavy showers are still common.

🏃 Rugby Sevens

A series of weekend, seven-a-side rugby tournaments held throughout the Borders region in April and May, kicking off with Melrose in early April. Fast and furious rugby (sevens was invented here), crowded pubs and great craic. See www.melrose7s.com.

May

Wildflowers on the Hebridean machair, hawthorn hedges in bloom and cherry blossom in city parks – Scottish weather is often at its best in May.

✸ Burns an' a' That

Ayrshire towns see performances of poetry and music, childrens events, exhibitions and more in celebration of the Scottish bard. See www.burnsfestival.com.

Spirit of Speyside

Based in the Moray town of Dufftown, this festival of whisky, food and music involves five days of distillery tours, knocking back the 'water of life', cooking, art and outdoor activities; held late April to early May in Moray and Speyside. See www.spiritofspeyside.com.

June

Argyllshire is ablaze with pink rhododendron blooms as the long summer evenings stretch on till 11pm. Border towns are strung with bunting to mark gala days and Common Ridings.

Common Ridings

Following the age-old tradition that commemorates the ancient conflict with England, horsemen and -women ride the old boundaries of common lands, along with parades, marching bands and street parties. Held in various Border towns; Jedburgh (www.jethartcallantsfestival.com) is one of the biggest and best.

Glasgow Festivals

June is Glasgow's version of the Edinburgh festival, when the city hosts three major events – West End Festival (www.westendfestival.co.uk), Glasgow's biggest music and arts event; Glasgow International Jazz Festival (www.jazzfest.co.uk); and Glasgow Mela (www.glasgowmela.com), a celebration of the city's Asian community.

July

School holidays begin, as does the busiest time of year for resort towns. High season for Shetland birdwatchers.

T in the Park

Held annually since 1994, and headlined by world-class acts such as The Who, REM, Eminem and Kasabian, this major music festival is Scotland's answer to Glastonbury; held over a mid-July weekend at Balado, by Kinross. See www.tinthepark.com.

August

Festival time in Edinburgh and the city is crammed with visitors. On the west coast, this is the peak month for sighting Minke whales and basking sharks.

Edinburgh Festivals

You name it, Edinburgh has a festival event that covers it – books, art, theatre, music, comedy, dance, and the Military Tattoo (www.edintattoo.co.uk). The overlapping International Festival and Fringe keep the city jumping from the first week in August to the first week in September. See www.edinburghfestivals.co.uk.

September

School holidays are over, midges are dying off, wild brambles are ripe for picking in the hedgerows, and the weather is often dry and mild – an excellent time of year for outdoor pursuits.

Braemar Gathering

The biggest and most famous Highland Games in the Scottish calendar, traditionally attended by members of the Royal Family. Highland dancing, bagpipe-playing and caber-tossing; held early September in Braemar, Royal Deeside. See www.braemargathering.org.

December

Darkness falls mid-afternoon as the shortest day approaches. The often cold and wet weather is relieved by Christmas and New Year festivities.

Hogmanay

Christmas celebrations in Edinburgh (www.edinburghschristmas.com) culminate in a huge street party on Hogmanay (31 December). The fishing town of Stonehaven echoes an ancient, pre-Christian tradition with its procession of fireball-swinging locals who parade to the harbour and fling their blazing orbs into the sea (www.stonehavenfireballs.co.uk).

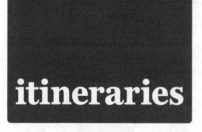

itineraries

Whether you've got five days or 15, these itineraries provide a starting point for the trip of a lifetime. Want more inspiration? Head online to lonelyplanet .com/thorntree to chat with other travellers.

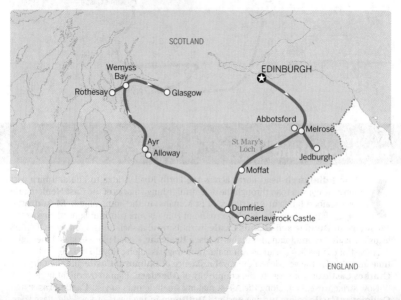

Five Days
Border Raid

From **Edinburgh** your first objective should be a visit to Sir Walter Scott's former home at **Abbotsford**, followed by a traipse around the beautiful Border abbeys of **Melrose** and nearby Dryburgh; Melrose is a charming place to stay the night, with a choice of good hotels and eating places.

Next morning head west along the A708 to **Moffat**, passing through glorious scenery around St Mary's Loch. Continue to **Dumfries** (and stop for the night), where you can visit the first of several sights related to Scotland's national poet Robert Burns, and make a short side trip to see spectacular **Caerlaverock Castle**.

Take the A76 northwest towards Ayr, and spend the rest of day three in **Alloway** visiting the birthplace of Robert Burns (and other Burns-related sites); nearby **Ayr** has plenty of accommodation options.

North now to **Wemyss Bay** and the ferry to **Rothesay** on the Isle of Bute, where you can visit stunning Mount Stuart, one of Scotland's most impressive stately homes. Spend the night on the island, then return to the mainland and head east to **Glasgow**.

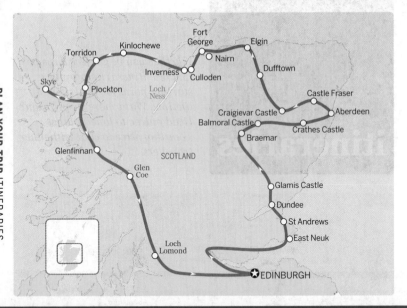

Two Weeks
Best of Scotland

From **Edinburgh** head north across the Forth Road Bridge to Fife and turn east along the coastal road through the delightful fishing villages of the **East Neuk** (pause for a seafood lunch at Anstruther or St Monans) to the home of golf, **St Andrews**. Stay a night or two – heck, play a round of golf – before continuing north across the Tay Bridge to **Dundee** and **Glamis Castle**, with its royal associations. From here the A93 leads through the Grampian Mountains to reach **Braemar**, a good place to spend the night.

A feast of castles lies ahead as you make your way east along Royal Deeside – take your time and visit (at the very least) the royal residence of **Balmoral Castle** and the fairy-tale **Crathes Castle** on your way to the granite city of **Aberdeen**. Plan to overnight here.

Now strike west again along the A944, making small detours to visit **Castle Fraser** and **Craigievar Castle** before turning north to **Dufftown** in the heart of Speyside. Base yourself here for at least a day while you explore the many **whisky distilleries** nearby – there are two excellent restaurants to try, plus the Quaich whisky bar at the nearby Craigellachie Hotel.

Head northwest to **Elgin** and its magnificent ruined cathedral, then west on the A96 visiting **Fort George** and **Culloden** on the way to Inverness (you'll probably need a stopover in Nairn). **Inverness** itself is worth a night or two – there are some excellent hotels and restaurants, and the opportunity for a side trip to **Loch Ness** (Drumnadrochit for monster-spotters, Dores Inn for foodies).

Now for a glorious drive from Inverness to **Torridon** via **Kinlochewe** through some of the country's finest mountain scenery; try to spend a night at the Torridon hotel. Then head south via Applecross and the pretty village of **Plockton** to Kyle of Lochalsh and the bridge to **Skye**.

Spend two days exploring Scotland's most famous island before taking the ferry from Armadale to Mallaig, and follow the **Road to the Isles** in reverse, stopping to visit **Glenfinnan**, where Bonnie Prince Charlie raised his Highland army in 1745. Overnight at Fort William, and drive back to Edinburgh via the scenic road through **Glen Coe** and and along the bonnie banks of **Loch Lomond**.

MALCOLM FIFE / GETTY IMAGES ©

JOE CORNISH / GETTY IMAGES ©

» (above) Autumn in the Trossachs (p198)
» (left) Melrose Abbey (p146)

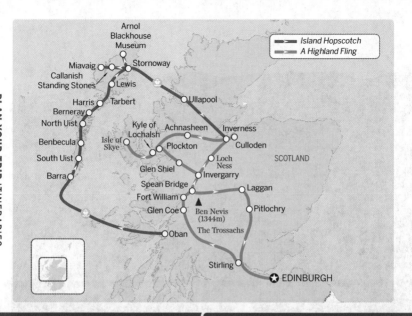

Arnol
Blackhouse
Museum
Stornoway
Miavaig
Callanish
Standing Stones
Lewis
Harris
Tarbert
Berneray
North Uist
Kyle of
Lochalsh
Achnasheen
Inverness
Benbecula
Isle of
Skye
Plockton
Culloden
South Uist
Glen Shiel
Loch
Ness
SCOTLAND
Barra
Invergarry
Spean Bridge
Laggan
Fort William
Ben Nevis
(1344m)
Pitlochry
Glen Coe
The Trossachs
Oban
Stirling
EDINBURGH
Ullapool

Island Hopscotch
A Highland Fling

One Week
A Highland Fling

No trip to Scotland would be complete without a visit to **Edinburgh**, and even if your Scottish trip lasts only a week the capital is worth two days of your time. On day three, head northwest to **Stirling** to see Scotland's other great castle, then on to the **Trossachs** for your first taste of Highland scenery (overnight in Callander).

Day four starts with a scenic drive north via Crianlarich, **Glen Coe** and **Fort William**, then along the Great Glen to **Loch Ness** in time for an afternoon visiting Urquhart Castle and the Loch Ness Centre & Exhibition. An evening cruise on Loch Ness rounds off the day before spending the night in **Inverness** on picturesque River Ness.

On day five, spend the morning visiting **Culloden Battlefield**, then drive west via **Achnasheen** and **Plockton** to **Kyle of Lochalsh** and cross the bridge to the **Isle of Skye**. Devote day six to exploring Skye – there will be time for a visit to Dunvegan Castle and a tour of the Trotternish peninsula.

Day seven is the long drive back south – the scenic route goes via **Glen Shiel**, **Invergarry**, **Spean Bridge** (pause at the Commando Monument), **Laggan** and then south on the A9 to Edinburgh, with a stop in **Pitlochry**.

One Week
Island Hopscotch

This route is usually done by car, but it also makes a brilliant cycling tour (270 miles, including the 60 miles from Ullapool to Inverness train station, making both start and finish accessible by rail).

From **Oban** it's a five-hour ferry crossing to **Barra**; plan to spend the night here (book ahead). On day two, after a visit to Kisimul Castle and a tour around the island, take the ferry to **South Uist**. Walk the wild beaches of the west coast, sample the local seafood and perhaps go fishing on the island's trout lochs.

Overnight at Lochmaddy on North Uist then continue through **North Uist** and **Benbecula**, prime birdwatching country. If you're camping or hostelling, a night at **Berneray** is a must before taking the ferry to **Harris**, whose west coast has some of the most spectacular beaches in Scotland. The road continues north from **Tarbert** (good hotels) through rugged hills to **Lewis**.

Don't go directly to Stornoway, but loop west via the **Callanish Standing Stones** and **Arnol Blackhouse museum**. Spend your final night in **Stornoway** (eat at Digby Chick), then take the ferry to **Ullapool** for a scenic drive to **Inverness**.

Walking in Scotland

Scotland's wild, dramatic scenery and varied landscape has made walking a hugely popular pastime for locals and tourists alike. There really is something for everyone, from after-breakfast strolls to the popular sport of Munro bagging.

Essential Hill-Walking Gear

Good waterproofs
Spare warm clothing
Map and compass
Mobile phone (but don't rely on it)
First-aid kit
Head torch
Whistle (for emergencies)
Spare food and drink
Bivvy bag

Planning

Highland hikers should be properly equipped and cautious, as the weather can become vicious at any time of year. After rain, peaty soil can become boggy so always wear stout shoes or boots and carry extra food and drink – many unsuspecting walkers have had to survive an unplanned night in the open. Don't depend on mobile phones (although carrying one with you is a good idea, and can be a lifesaver if you get a signal). If necessary, leave a note with your route and expected time of return on the dashboard of your car.

When to Go

The best time of year for hill walking is usually May to September, although snow can fall on the highest summits even in midsummer. Winter walking on the higher hills of Scotland requires the use of an ice axe and crampons and is for experienced mountaineers only.

Access & Rights of Way

There is a tradition of relatively free access to open country in Scotland, a tradition that was enshrined in law in the 2003 Land Reform (Scotland) Bill, popularly known as 'the right to roam'. The **Scottish Outdoor Access Code** (www.outdooraccess-scotland .com) states that everyone has the right to be on most land and inland waters, providing they act responsibly. You should avoid areas where you might disrupt or disturb wildlife, lambing (generally mid-April to the end of May), grouse shooting (from 12 August to the third week in October) or deer stalking (1 July to 15 February, but the peak period is August to October). You can get up-to-date information on deer stalking in various areas through the **Heading for the Scottish Hills** (www.outdooraccess-scotland.com/hftsh) service. You are also free to pitch a tent almost anywhere that doesn't cause inconvenience to others or damage to property, as long as you stay no longer than two or three nights in any one spot, take all litter away with you, and keep well away from houses and roads. (Note that this right does not extend to the use of motorised vehicles.)

Local authorities aren't required to list and map rights of way, so they're not shown on Ordnance Survey (OS) maps of Scotland, as they are in England and Wales. However, the **Scottish Rights of Way & Access Society** (📞0131-558 1222; www.scotways.com; 24 Annandale St, Edinburgh EH7 4AN) keeps records of these routes, provides and maintains signposting, and publicises them in its guidebook, *Scottish Hill Tracks*.

Where to Walk
West Highland Way

This classic hike – the country's most popular long-distance path – stretches for 96 miles through some of Scotland's most spectacular scenery, from Milngavie (mull-guy), on the northwestern fringes of Glasgow, to Fort William.

The route begins in the Lowlands but the greater part of the trail is among the mountains, lochs and fast-flowing rivers of the western Highlands. After following the eastern shore of Loch Lomond and passing Crianlarich and Tyndrum, the route crosses the vast wilderness of Rannoch Moor and reaches Fort William via Glen Nevis, in the shadow of Britain's highest peak, Ben Nevis.

The path is easy to follow, making use of old drovers roads (along which Highland cattle were once driven to Lowland markets), an old military road (built by troops to help subdue the Highlands in the 18th century) and disused railway lines.

Best done from south to north, the walk takes about six or seven days. Many people round it off with an ascent of Ben Nevis.

OFFICIAL LONG-DISTANCE FOOTPATHS

WALK	DISTANCE	FEATURES	DURATION	DIFFICULTY
Fife Coastal Path (p204)	78 miles	Firth of Forth, undulating country	5-6 days	easy
Great Glen Way (p331)	73 miles	Loch Ness, canal paths, forest tracks	4 days	easy
Pilgrims Way (p152)	25 miles	Machars peninsula, standing stones, burial mounds	2-3 days	easy
St Cuthbert's Way (p152)	62 miles	follows the path of a famous saint	6-7 days	medium
South Loch Ness Trail (p331)	28 miles	low hills, forests, lochs, waterfalls	2-3 days	easy
Southern Upland Way (p152)	212 miles	remote hills & moorlands	9-14 days	medium-hard
Speyside Way (p31)	66 miles	follows river, whisky distilleries	3-4 days	easy-medium
West Highland Way (p30)	96 miles	spectacular scenery, mountains & lochs	6-8 days	medium

TOP 10 SHORT WALKS

Quiraing (p402; Isle of Skye) One to two hours; bizarre rock pinnacles.

Steall Meadows (p351; Glen Nevis) One to two hours; waterfall beneath Ben Nevis.

Lost Valley (p345; Glen Coe) Three hours; impressive mountain scenery.

Conic Hill (p277; Loch Lomond) Two hours; views over Loch Lomond.

Loch an Eilein (p336; Aviemore) One hour; lovely lochan amid Scots pines.

Linn of Quoich (p262; Braemar) One hour; rocky gorge and waterfall.

Plodda Falls (p329; Cannich) One hour; dizzying viewpoint above waterfall.

Duncansby Head (p374; John O'Groats) One hour; spectacular sea stacks.

Stac Pollaidh (p383; Coigach) Two to four hours; ascent of miniature mountain.

Old Man of Hoy (p430; Orkney) Three hours; Britain's tallest sea stack.

You need to be properly equipped with good boots, waterproofs, maps, a compass, and food and drink for the northern part of the walk. Midge repellent is also essential.

It's possible to do just a day's hike along part of the trail. For example, the Loch Lomond Water Bus allows you to walk the section from Rowardennan to Inversnaid, returning to your starting point by boat.

The West Highland Way Official Guide by Bob Aitken and Roger Smith is the most comprehensive guidebook, while the Harveys map *West Highland Way* shows the entire route in a single waterproof map sheet.

Accommodation shouldn't be too difficult to find, though between Bridge of Orchy and Kinlochleven it's limited. At peak times (May, July and August), book accommodation in advance. There are some youth hostels and bunkhouses on or near the path, and it's possible to camp in some parts. A list of accommodation is available from tourist offices.

For more information check out the website www.west-highland-way.co.uk.

Speyside Way

This long-distance footpath follows the course of the River Spey, one of Scotland's most famous salmon-fishing rivers. It starts at Buckie and first follows the coast to Spey Bay, east of Elgin, then runs inland along the river to Aviemore in the Cairngorms (with branches to Tomintoul and Dufftown).

The 66-mile route has been dubbed the 'Whisky Trail' as it passes near a number of distilleries, including The Glenlivet and Glenfiddich, both open to the public. If you stop at them all, the walk may take a lot longer than the usual three or four days! The first 11 miles from Buckie to Fochabers make a good half-day hike (four to five hours).

The Speyside Way, a guidebook by Jacquetta Megarry and Jim Strachan, describes the route in detail. Check out the route at www.speysideway.org.

Isle of Skye

Skye is a walker's paradise, criss-crossed with trails both easy and strenuous that lead you through some of the country's most spectacular scenery.

The Quiraing (3.5 miles; two to three hours) Start at the parking area at the highest point of the minor road between Staffin and Uig. A clear path leads northeast towards the obvious pinnacles, but after 200m or so strike north up the hill to reach another path that leads across the summit of Meall na Suiramach with fantastic views down into the Quiraing. The path continues to a saddle and break in the cliffs where you can descend and return to your starting point through the midst of the pinnacles.

Kilmarie to Coruisk (11 miles; at least six hours) This is one of the most spectacular and challenging of Skye's low-level walks. Begin at a parking area just south of Kilmarie, on the Broadford to Elgol road. A stony track leads over a hill pass to the gorgeous bay of Camasunary, and continues on the far side of the Camasunary River – at low tide you can cross on stepping stones, but if the tide is high you'll have to splash across further upstream. The notorious Bad Step is opposite the north end of the little island in Loch ni Cuilce; it's a rock slab that drops straight into the sea, where you scramble out onto a shelf and along a rising crack (the

STEVEN FALLON: CHAMPION MUNRO BAGGER

Steven Fallon, a hill walker, fell runner and qualified Mountain Leader who lives in Edinburgh, is the world's most prolific Munro bagger, having climbed all of Scotland's 283 Munros (peaks of 3000ft and higher) no fewer than 14 times.

Do you have a favourite Munro? Practically anything in the northwest Highlands – they tend to be pointy with great views. I'd single out Slioch by Loch Maree; Beinn Alligin, Liathach and Beinn Eighe in Torridon; the Five Sisters of Kintail; and all of the mountains in the Cuillin of Skye. However, my most-most-favourite has to be Ladhar Bheinn in the Knoydart Peninsula. It's pretty remote and to reach it requires a long walk-in along the southern shore of Loch Hourn. It's just so beautiful there. The mountain itself is complex with corries and ridges, and the summit has great views over Eigg to Skye and beyond.

Which is the easiest Munro, and which is the hardest? With only 430m of ascent over 5km, the easiest Munros have to be the Cairnwell and Carn Aosda from the Glenshee ski resort. Good paths and ski-tows make for simple navigation over these two peaks, and if you time it right, you'll be back at the cafe in time for something to eat. The most technically difficult has to be the aptly named Inaccessible Pinnacle in the Cuillin Hills on Skye. It's a clamber up a long fin of rock with sensational, tremble-inducing exposure, followed by an abseil down a short but vertical drop. Most Munro-baggers will have to enlist the help of their rock-climbing friends or hire a guide.

Check out Steven's website (www.stevenfallon.co.uk) for the 10 easiest Munro walks (click on Hill Lists and Maps/Munros/Easiest Munros).

secret is to drop down leftward when you reach a niche in the crack). There are no further obstacles, and 15 minutes later you arrive at Loch Coruisk, one of the most remote spots in Scotland. Return by the same route.

Munro Bagging

At the end of the 19th century an eager hill walker, Sir Hugh Munro, published a list of Scottish mountains over 3000ft (914m) – a height at which he believed they gained a special significance. He couldn't have realised that in time his name would be used to describe any Scottish mountain over 3000ft. Many keen hill walkers now set themselves the target of reaching the summit of (or bagging) all of Scotland's 283 Munros.

To the uninitiated it may seem odd that Munro baggers see venturing into mist, cloud and driving rain as time well spent. However, for those who can add one or more ticks to their list, the vagaries of the weather are part of the enjoyment, at least in retrospect. Munro bagging is, of course, more than merely ticking off a list – it takes you to some of the wildest and most beautiful corners of Scotland.

Once you've bagged all the Munros you can move on to the Corbetts – hills over 2500ft (700m), with a drop of at least 500ft (150m) on all sides – and the Donalds, low-land hills over 2000ft (610m). And then there are the McPhies: 'eminences in excess of 300ft (90m)' on the Isle of Colonsay.

Further Information

Every tourist office has leaflets (free or for a nominal charge) of suggested walks that take in local points of interest. Lonely Planet's *Walking in Scotland* is a comprehensive resource, covering short walks and long-distance paths; its *Walking in Britain* guide covers Scottish walks, too. For general advice, VisitScotland produces a **Walking Scotland** (http://walking.visitscotland.com) website that describes numerous routes in various parts of the country, and also offers safety tips and other useful information.

Other useful resources:

Mountaineering Council of Scotland (www.mcofs.org.uk)

Ordnance Survey (www.ordnancesurvey.co.uk)

Ramblers' Association Scotland (www.ramblers.org.uk/scotland)

Scottish Mountaineering Club (www.smc.org.uk)

WalkHighlands (www.walkhighlands.co.uk) Online database of more than 1500 walks complete with maps and detailed descriptions.

Golf

When to Play

Summer is most enjoyable – long daylight hours mean you can tee off at 6am or 7pm and play a full round. Courses are busy at this time, and a good compromise is to play in May or September.

Resources

www.visitscotland.com/golf Useful resource, and also details discount golf passes. VisitScotland also publishes Golf in Scotland, a free annual brochure listing course details, costs and clubs with information on where to stay.
www.scotlands-golf-courses.com Another good place to start investigating courses to play.

Costs

A round at an unfashionable rural course may cost as little as £10. Showpiece courses charge green fees of £150 to £200 in high season. It's more economical in winter, it's often cheaper midweek, and its worth looking out for 'twilight' rates. Teeing off after 4pm can save you up to 50% at some clubs.

Golf is part of the fabric of Scotland: playing here is an experience like no other in the world. Whether taking the challenge of one of the classic courses or hacking your way around a rustic island half-course, you're just about guaranteed heart-stopping scenery. And Scotland's tradition of public courses means that more often than not, outstanding golf goes hand in hand with sociable moments and warm hospitality.

History

The first mention of golf in the historical record is from 1457, when James II banned it to prevent archery, which was crucial for military reasons, being ignored as an activity.

Scotland's (and the world's) oldest course is at Musselburgh and its oldest club is the Honourable Company of Edinburgh Golfers at Muirfield, founded in 1744. The Royal and Ancient of St Andrews, which became the game's governing body, was founded in 1754.

Golf as we know it today really evolved in the late 19th and early 20th centuries. Legendary figures such as James Braid and Old Tom Morris designed courses all around the country; the latter was a founding figure of the Open Championship and won it four times.

What are Links?

Most of Scotland's courses are known as links. These seaside courses where modern golf was born present unique challenges with their undulating fairways, rough, vertical bunkers and enormous greens that can look like the Scottish Highlands in miniature.

There's one sound you won't hear in links golf – that demoralising thud as your otherwise perfect drive meets a tree hazard. They're usually treeless, with gorse, heather and machair making up the vegetation. But that's not to say that these typical, historic, seaside courses are easy. Far from it.

These largely unplanned courses lie on sandy uncultivable ground between the fields and the sea and follow the contours of the land. They are at the mercy of the weather: on a sunny day you can post flattering scores, but a healthy sea breeze means that your approach into that green had better be well planned. It pays to listen to locals.

Where to Play

With more golf courses per capita than any other country, Scotland offers a bewildering choice of venues. A selection of golf's most iconic courses offers some of the sport's most famous holes, with deep, challenging bunkers where you might only get out backwards, if at all. But there's also great pleasure to be had on simpler, local fairways eked out by small communities, where you have to hope the sheep or deer nibbling at the green understand your cry of 'Fore!'.

Practical Tips

» On many courses, a handicap certificate is not needed, but bring one just in case, along with a letter of introduction from your home club if you plan to play any of the more upmarket clubs. Some courses have a minimum handicap requirement.

» Dress regulations aren't generally too rigorous – think smart casual as a norm. Most places prohibit jeans, trainers and T-shirts, and several don't look kindly on shorts. In general, mobile phone use on the course is frowned upon. Stricter dress regulations may apply for parts of the clubhouse.

» Club hire is available at most courses, but it's not cheap (up to £60 on elite courses), so it may be worth bringing your own bag.

» Motorised golf carts are available at many courses, but aren't used as much as in the USA or Australia, for example. In Scotland, they tend to be hired only by people with mobility difficulties. They are prohibited on some courses.

CATRIONA MATTHEW, SCOTTISH PROFESSIONAL GOLFER, WINNER OF THE 2009 WOMEN'S BRITISH OPEN

What is your favourite course in Scotland? And why? St Andrews is my favourite. The course gets better every time you play it. It is easy to appreciate how naturally it fits into the land with bunkers that are positioned perfectly and the history associated with the course makes it a thrill to play for every level of golfer.

What's different about golf in Scotland compared with other countries? Golf in Scotland is all about playing courses that fit into the natural landscape, that are designed to be played in all types of weather conditions. The welcome is always second to none and virtually every course in the country is accessible to visitors.

What's the most scenic course in Scotland? I believe the most scenic course in Scotland is North Berwick West Links. It also happens to be my home course and the views in my opinion are even better than Pebble Beach in California.

Where would you recommend playing for a high handicapper who wants to experience Scottish golf without posting 130? An ideal course for a high handicapper is Gullane number 3. It is a great little course with par around 65. The views are as good as the main course (Gullane number 1) and it is still challenging.

Any advice for someone who's never played a links course? Take a local caddie to help you. Most clubs have members who caddy in the summer and they are very knowledgeable and make the round both more interesting and fun.

What would be your one golden tip to an amateur to help us reach the clubhouse in better shape? Don't try and swing any harder when playing in wind. The golden rule is to take one club more than you think and swing it easier.

Any etiquette tips for someone who's never played in Britain? Please take your hats off when you go into the clubhouse after your round. Let quicker groups behind you play through. Those two tips will make you popular both on and off the course!

Where's the best 19th hole in Scotland? The old clubhouse in Gullane is great after a round at Gullane or North Berwick. A friendly pub with great food.

TEN OF THE BEST

St Andrews (p207) The public Old Course is the spiritual home of the game and you can't help but be awed by the history and sense of occasion here. The 17th – the Road Hole – is famous for its blind drive, nasty bunker and seriously sloping green. Several other courses for all abilities make this Scotland's premium golfing destination.

Turnberry (p170) Marvellous views out to the island of Ailsa Craig make this resort one of Scotland's finest. Pack an extra ball or two for the nasty 9th on the Ailsa course, where your ball will sleep with the fish unless you manage the 200-yard carry off the tee. Luckily there's the renowned Halfway Hut for a stiff drink before taking on the 10th.

Carnoustie (☎01241-802270; www.carnoustiegolflinks.co.uk; 20 Links Parade, Carnoustie, Angus) Widely known as Scotland's toughest challenge and nicknamed Car-nasty, as much for the almost constant winds as for the course itself. It ain't over till it's over here: the Barry Burn on the 18th hole has undone many a prospective winner in social games and Open Championships alike.

Loch Lomond (☎01436-655555; www.lochlomond.com; Luss) On the shores of the famous loch, this has a picturesque, romantic location – including Scotland's most impressive clubhouse and a ruined castle by the 18th green – but is a real test, with plenty of water hazards and cunningly placed sand traps. Not a links course.

Royal Troon (p169) This classic seaside venue along the dunes could define a links course. The short 8th is known as the Postage Stamp for its tiny, protected green.

Royal Dornoch (p369) A long way up north, the sumptuous Championship course rewards the journey with picture-perfect links scenery and a quieter pace. If this was near the southern population centres, many would rate it Scotland's best course.

Machrihanish (www.machrihanishdunes.com) On the Kintyre peninsula, this is one of Scotland's most scenic courses. There's no easing into your round here; strike long and clean on the 1st or you'll be on the beach – literally.

Muirfield (☎01620-842123; www.muirfield.org.uk; Duncur Rd, Muirfield, Gullane) In easy striking distance of Edinburgh, this course on land reclaimed from the sea is private but allocates some tee times to the public. Hosts the British Open in 2013.

Gleneagles (p220) Three brilliant courses and a five-star hotel with truly excellent service make this a top destination for a golfing break. Hosts the Ryder Cup in 2014.

Trump International Golf Links (☎01358-743300; www.trumpgolfscotland.com; Balmedie, Aberdeenshire) Donald Trump's environmentally controversial new course near Aberdeen features spectacular high-dune scenery.

» It's worth booking rounds at desirable courses well ahead – many months ahead in the case of prestige links like the Old Course at St Andrews.

» If you're looking to post a competitive score, caddies can help greatly. They know the layout, and will advise when to attack the pin and when caution is better. Their local lore and inexhaustable fund of anecdotes can also make for a special Scottish experience. Caddies should be booked ahead, though you may be able to hire one on the day. Think around £50 plus tip for the round.

» Some courses will have a starter, whose job is to get your group out on time. It's worth chatting to these savvy folk, who'll give you a few tips on not embarrassing yourself off the 1st tee.

» Some of the busier courses won't allow solo players to book, allocating places in existing groups on a first-come, first-served basis.

Accommodation

In golf-crazy places like St Andrews, you can bet that all accommodation is more or less golfer friendly, but in other locations it's worth finding out beforehand. VisitScotland has a 'golfer-friendly' criterion, which means that early breakfasts (and maybe late snacks) are available, as well as club storage and washing facilities, and there's a tolerant attitude to grass clippings and mud on the carpets.

regions at a glance

Edinburgh

Culture ✓✓✓
History ✓✓✓
Food ✓✓✓

Culture
Dubbed the Athens of the North, the Scottish capital is a city of high culture and lofty ideals, art and literature, philosophy and science. It is here that each summer the world's biggest arts festival rises, phoenixlike, from the ashes of its rave reviews and box-office records to evoke yet another string of superlatives. Outside festival time, there's plenty to enjoy in the city's many theatres and world-class art galleries and museums.

History
Perched on a brooding black crag overlooking the city centre, Edinburgh Castle has played a pivotal role in Scottish history. The growth of the city from its medieval Old Town to the Georgian elegance of the New Town and the parallel development of Scottish nationhood is well documented in its excellent museums and historic buildings. And on the edge of the city lies medieval Rosslyn Chapel, Scotland's most beautiful and enigmatic church.

Food
Edinburgh has more restaurants per head of population than any city in the UK. Eating out is commonplace, not just for special occasions, and the eateries range from stylish but inexpensive bistros and cafes to gourmet restaurants with Michelin stars. Scottish cuisine has been given a makeover too, with inventive chefs using top-quality local produce and adding contemporary twists to traditional favourites.

p42

Glasgow

Museums ✓✓✓
Music ✓✓✓
Design ✓✓

Museums & Art Galleries
Glasgow's mercantile, industrial and academic history has left the city with a wonderful legacy of museums and art galleries, dominated by the grand Victorian cathedral of culture, Kelvingrove, boasting a bewildering variety of exhibits.

Live Music
Scotland's liveliest nightlife is found in the din and roar of Glasgow's drinking dens, from traditional Victorian pubs to its famed style bars. It's also the star of Scotland's live-music scene, with many venues and bands, from top international acts to local start-ups.

Design
From Charles Rennie Mackintosh's iconic buildings and interiors and the centre's grand Victorian architecture, to the fashion boutiques of the Italian Centre and design exhibitions at the Lighthouse, Glasgow stakes its claim as Scotland's most stylish city.

p102

Southern Scotland

Historic Abbeys ✓✓✓
Stately Homes ✓✓
Activities ✓✓

Historic Abbeys
Rolling countryside and ru-ined abbeys dot Scotland's southern border. The Gothic ruins of Melrose, Jedburgh, Dryburgh and Sweetheart and the martial towers of Hermitage Castle, Caerlav-erock Castle and Smailholm are eloquent testimony to a turbulent past.

Stately Homes
This region is rich in Adam-designed mansions such as Culzean Castle, Paxton House, Floors Castle and Mellerstain House, but the almost perfectly preserved Chippendale time-capsule Dumfries House takes top place.

Outdoor Activities
The rounded, heather-clad hills of the Southern Up-lands can't compete with the Highlands for scenery, but the granite hills of Gal-loway and Arran are prime hill walking country, and the 7stanes trail centres offer some of the UK's best and most challenging mountain biking.

p141

Central Scotland

Golf ✓✓✓
Scenery ✓✓
Castles ✓✓

Golf
Scotland is the home of golf, and the Old Course at St Andrews – the oldest in the world – is on every golfer's wish list. The game has been played here for more than 600 years; the Royal & Ancient Golf Club, the game's governing body, was founded in 1754.

Scenery
From the picturesque Fife coastline, dotted with quaint fishing villages, and the wood-fringed lochs and hills of the Trossachs, to the big-tree country of Perth-shire and the epic mountain scenery of Glen Lyon and Glenshee, central Scotland displays the full range of classic Scottish landscapes.

Castles
Some say that Stirling has the finest castle in the country, but the region has plenty of others worth visit-ing, including Scone Palace, Blair Castle, Kellie Castle, Doune Castle and St Andrews Castle.

p186

Northeast Scotland

Whisky ✓✓✓
Castles ✓✓✓
Royalty ✓✓

Whisky
Don't leave Scotland without visiting a whisky distillery; the Speyside re-gion, around Dufftown in Moray, is the epicentre of the industry. More than 50 distilleries open their doors during the twice-yearly Spirit of Speyside festival; many open year-round.

Castles
Aberdeenshire and Moray have the greatest concentra-tion of Scottish Baronial castles in the country, from the turreted splendour of Craigievar and Fyvie to the restrained elegance of Crathie and Balmoral.

Royalty
The valley of the River Dee (often called Royal Dee-side) has been associated with the royal family since Queen Victoria acquired her holiday home, Balmoral Castle. Besides royal links with Balmoral and Ballater, there's Glamis Castle, fam-ily home of the late Queen Mother and birthplace of Princess Margaret.

p234

Southern Highlands & Islands

Wildlife ✓✓✓
Islands ✓✓✓
Food ✓✓✓

Wildlife
This region is home to some of Scotland's most spectacular wildlife, from magnificent white-tailed sea eagles at Mull, to majestic minke whales and basking sharks cruising the west coast. It's also where the beaver – extinct here for centuries – has been reintroduced into the wild.

Islands
Island-hopping is one of the best ways to explore the western seaboard, and the cluster of islands here – Islay with its whisky distilleries, wild and mountainous Jura, scenic Mull and the little jewel of Iona, and the gorgeous beaches of Colonsay, Coll and Tiree – provide a brilliant introduction.

Seafood
Whether you dine at a top restaurant in Oban or Tobermory, or eat with your fingers on the harbourside, the rich harvest of the sea is one of the region's biggest drawcards.

p270

Inverness & the Central Highlands

Activities ✓✓✓
Scenery ✓✓✓
Legends ✓✓

Activities
The Cairngorm towns of Aviemore and Fort William offer outdoor adventure galore. Be it climbing Ben Nevis, walking the West Highland Way, biking the trails around Loch Morlich or skiing the slopes of Cairngorm, there's something for everyone.

Scenery
Photographers are spoiled with classic views here, from the rugged beauty of Glen Coe and snow-patched Cairngorms summits to the Caledonian pine forests around Loch Affric and the golden beaches and island views of Arisaig and Morar.

Legends
Scotland's most iconic legend, the Loch Ness monster, lurks in the heart of this region. You might not spot Nessie, but the magnificent scenery of the Great Glen makes a visit worthwhile, as does Culloden battlefield, the undoing of another Scottish legend, Bonnie Prince Charlie.

p318

Northern Highlands & Islands

Scenery ✓✓✓
Activities ✓✓✓
History ✓✓

Scenery
From the peaks of Assynt and Torridon to the jagged rock pinnacles of the Cuillin Hills, to the dazzling beaches of the Outer Hebrides, the big skies and lonely landscapes of the northern Highlands and islands are the very essence of Scotland, a wilderness of sea and mountains that remains one of Europe's most unspoilt regions.

Activities
The northwest's vast spaces are one huge adventure playground for hikers, bikers, climbers and kayakers, providing the chance to see some of the UK's most spectacular wildlife.

History
The abandoned rural communities of the north teach much about the Clearances, especially Arnol Blackhouse and Skye Museum of Island Life. The region is also rich in prehistoric remains, including the famous standing stones of Callanish.

p363

Orkney & Shetland Islands

History ✓✓✓
Birdwatching ✓✓✓
Music ✓

History
These treeless, cliff-bound islands have a fascinating Viking heritage and unique prehistoric villages, tombs and stone circles. Predating the pyramids of Egypt, Skara Brae is northern Europe's best-preserved prehistoric village; Maes Howe is one of Britain's finest Neolithic tombs.

Birdwatching
Shetland is a birdwatcher's paradise, its cliffs teeming in summer with gannets, fulmars, kittiwakes, razorbills and puffins, and Europe's largest colony of Arctic terns. Several nature reserves include Hermaness on Unst, Scotland's northernmost inhabited island.

Music
The pubs of Kirkwall, Stromness and Lerwick are fertile ground for exploring the traditional-music scene, with impromptu sessions of fiddle, bodhrán and guitar music. Both Orkney and Shetland host annual festivals of folk music.

p416

> Every listing is recommended by our authors, and their favourite places are listed first.

> Look out for these icons:

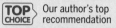 Our author's top recommendation

A green or sustainable option

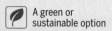 No payment required

On the Road

Edinburgh

POP 430,000

Best Places to Eat

» The Dogs (p85)
» Ondine (p82)
» Castle Terrace (p82)
» Porto & Fi (p82)
» Tower (p81)

Best Places to Stay

» Witchery by the Castle (p77)
» Hotel Missoni (p77)
» Sheridan Guest House (p78)
» Southside Guest House (p79)
» Prestonfield House Hotel (p79)

Why Go?

Edinburgh is a city that begs to be explored. From the vaults and wynds (narrow lanes) that riddle the Old Town to the urban villages of Stockbridge and Cramond, it's filled with quirky, come-hither nooks that tempt you to walk just a little bit further. And every corner turned reveals sudden views and unexpected vistas – green sunlit hills, a glimpse of rust-red crags, a blue flash of distant sea.

But there's more to Edinburgh than sightseeing – there are top shops, world-class restaurants and a bacchanalia of bars to enjoy. This is a city of pub crawls and impromptu music sessions, mad-for-it clubbing and all-night parties, overindulgence, late nights and wanders home through cobbled streets at dawn.

All these superlatives come together in August at festival time, when it seems as if half the world descends on Edinburgh for one enormous party. If you can possibly manage it, join them.

When to Go
Edinburgh

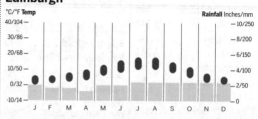

May Good weather (usually), flowers and cherry blossoms everywhere and (gasp!) no crowds.

Aug Festival time! Crowded and mad but irresistible.

Dec Christmas decorations, cosy pubs with open fires, ice skating in Princes Street Gardens.

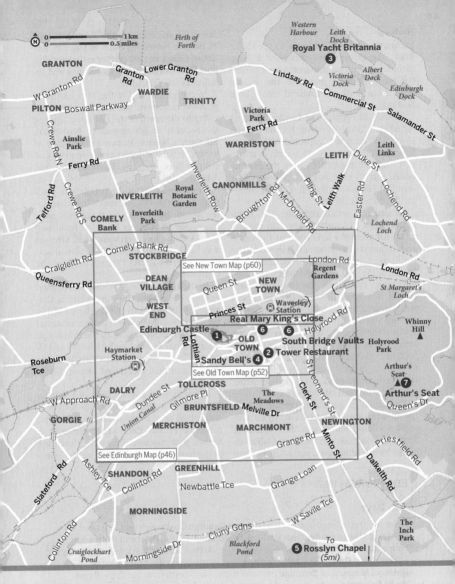

Edinburgh Highlights

1 Taking in the views from the battlements of **Edinburgh Castle** (p49)

2 Feasting on steak and oysters at the **Tower** (p81) restaurant as the sun sets over the city

3 Nosing around the Queen's private quarters on the former **Royal Yacht Britannia** (p65) at Leith

4 Listening to live folk music at **Sandy Bell's** (p89)

5 Trying to decipher the Da Vinci Code at mysterious **Rosslyn Chapel** (p97)

6 Exploring Edinburgh's subterranean history in the haunted vaults of **South Bridge** and **Real Mary King's Close** (p55)

7 Climbing to the summit of the city's miniature mountain, **Arthur's Seat** (p58)

History

Edinburgh owes its existence to the Castle Rock, the glacier-worn stump of a long-extinct volcano that provided a near-perfect defensive position guarding the coastal route from northeast England into central Scotland.

In the 7th century the Castle Rock was called Dun Eiden (meaning 'Fort on the Hill Slope'). When it was captured by invaders from the kingdom of Northumbria in northeast England in 638, they took the existing Gaelic name 'Eiden' and tacked it onto their own Old English word for fort, 'burh', to create the name Edinburgh.

Originally a purely defensive site, Edinburgh began to expand in the 12th century when King David I held court at the castle and founded the abbey at Holyrood. The royal court came to prefer Edinburgh to Dunfermline and, as parliament followed the king, Edinburgh became Scotland's capital. The city's first effective town wall was constructed around 1450, enclosing the Old Town as far east as Netherbow and south to the Grassmarket. This overcrowded area – by then the most populous town in Scotland – became a medieval Manhattan, forcing its densely packed inhabitants to build upwards instead of outwards, creating tenements five and six storeys high.

The capital played an important role in the Reformation (1560–1690), led by the Calvinist firebrand John Knox. Mary, Queen of Scots held court in the Palace of Holyroodhouse for six brief years, but when her son James VI succeeded to the English throne in 1603 he moved his court to London. The Act of Union in 1707 further reduced Edinburgh's importance, but its cultural and intellectual life flourished.

In the second half of the 18th century a planned new town was created across the valley to the north of the Old Town. During the Scottish Enlightenment (c 1740–1830), Edinburgh became known as 'a hotbed of genius', inhabited by leading scientists and philosophers such as David Hume and Adam Smith.

In the 19th century the population quadrupled to 400,000, not much less than today's, and the Old Town's tenements were taken over by refugees from the Irish famines. A new ring of crescents and circuses was built to the north of New Town, and grey Victorian terraces spread south of the Old Town.

In the 1920s the city's borders expanded again to encompass Leith in the north, Cramond in the west and the Pentland Hills in the south. Following WWII the city's cultural life blossomed, stimulated by the Edinburgh International Festival and its fellow traveller, the Fringe, both held for the first time in 1947 and now recognised as world-class arts festivals.

Edinburgh entered a new era following the 1997 referendum vote in favour of a devolved Scottish parliament, which first convened in July 1999. The parliament is housed in a controversial modern building at the foot of the Royal Mile. The 2007 elec-

EDINBURGH IN...

Two Days

A two-day trip to Edinburgh should start at **Edinburgh Castle**, followed by a stroll down the **Royal Mile** to the **Scottish Parliament Building** and the **Palace of Holyroodhouse**. You can work up an appetite by climbing **Arthur's Seat**, then satisfy your hunger with dinner at **Ondine** or **Castle Terrace**. On day two spend the morning in the **National Museum of Scotland** then catch the bus to **Leith** for a visit to the **Royal Yacht Britannia**. In the evening have dinner at one of Leith's many excellent restaurants, or scare yourself silly on a guided **ghost tour**.

Four Days

Two more days will give you time for a morning stroll around the **Royal Botanic Garden**, followed by a trip to the enigmatic and beautiful **Rosslyn Chapel**, or a relaxing afternoon visit to the seaside village of **Cramond** – bring binoculars (for birdwatching and yacht-spotting) and a book (to read in the sun). Dinner at the **Cafe Royal Oyster Bar** could be before or after your sunset walk to the summit of **Calton Hill**. On day four head out to the pretty harbour village of **Queensferry**, nestled beneath the **Forth Bridges**, and take a cruise to **Inchcolm** island.

UNDERGROUND EDINBURGH

As Edinburgh expanded in the late 18th and early 19th centuries, many old tenements were demolished and new bridges were built to link the Old Town to the newly built areas to its north and south. South Bridge (built between 1785 and 1788) and George IV Bridge (built between 1829 and 1834) lead south from the Royal Mile over the deep valley of Cowgate, but so many buildings have been constructed around them you can hardly tell they are bridges – George IV Bridge has a total of nine arches but only two are visible; South Bridge has no less than 18 hidden arches.

These **subterranean vaults** were originally used as storerooms, workshops and drinking dens. But as Edinburgh's population swelled in the early 19th century with an influx of penniless Highlanders cleared from their lands, and Irish refugees from the potato famine, the dark, dripping chambers were given over to slum accommodation and abandoned to poverty, filth and crime.

The vaults were eventually cleared in the late 19th century, then lay forgotten until 1994 when the **South Bridge vaults** were opened to guided tours. Certain chambers are said to be haunted and one particular vault was investigated by paranormal researchers in 2001.

Nevertheless, the most ghoulish aspect of Edinburgh's hidden history dates from much earlier – from the plague that struck the city in 1645. Legend has it that the disease-ridden inhabitants of **Mary King's Close** (a lane on the northern side of the Royal Mile, on the site of the City Chambers – you can still see its blocked-off northern end from Cockburn St) were walled up in their houses and left to perish. When the lifeless bodies were eventually cleared from the houses, they were so stiff that workmen had to hack off limbs to get them through the small doorways and narrow, twisting stairs.

From that day on, the close was said to be haunted by the spirits of the plague victims. The few people who were prepared to live there reported seeing apparitions of severed heads and limbs, and the largely abandoned close fell into ruin. When the Royal Exchange (now the City Chambers) was constructed between 1753 and 1761, it was built over the lower levels of Mary King's Close, which were left intact and sealed off beneath the building.

Interest in the close revived in the 20th century when Edinburgh's city council began to allow occasional guided tours to enter. Visitors have reported many supernatural experiences – the most famous ghost is 'Sarah', a little girl whose sad tale has prompted people to leave gifts of dolls in a corner of one of the rooms. In 2003 the close was opened to the public as the Real Mary King's Close (p55).

tions saw the Scottish National Party, whose long-term aim is independence for Scotland, take power for the first time.

⊙ Sights

Edinburgh's main attractions are concentrated in the city centre – on and around the Old Town's Royal Mile between the castle and Holyrood, and in the New Town. A major exception is the Royal Yacht *Britannia,* which is in the redeveloped docklands district of Leith, 2 miles northeast of the centre.

If you tire of sightseeing, good areas for aimless wandering include the posh suburbs of Stockbridge and Morningside, the pretty riverside village of Cramond and the winding footpaths of Calton Hill and Arthur's Seat.

Old Town

Edinburgh's Old Town stretches along a ridge to the east of the castle, and tumbles down Victoria St to the broad expanse of the Grassmarket. It's a jagged and jumbled maze of masonry riddled with closes (alleys) and wynds, stairs and vaults, and cleft along its spine by the cobbled ravine of the Royal Mile.

Until the founding of the New Town in the 18th century, old Edinburgh was an overcrowded and insanitary hive of humanity squeezed between the boggy ground of the Nor' Loch (North Loch, now drained and occupied by Princes Street Gardens) to the north and the city walls to the south and east. The only way for the town to expand was upwards, and the five- and six-storey tenements that were raised along the Royal Mile in the 16th and 17th centuries were

Edinburgh

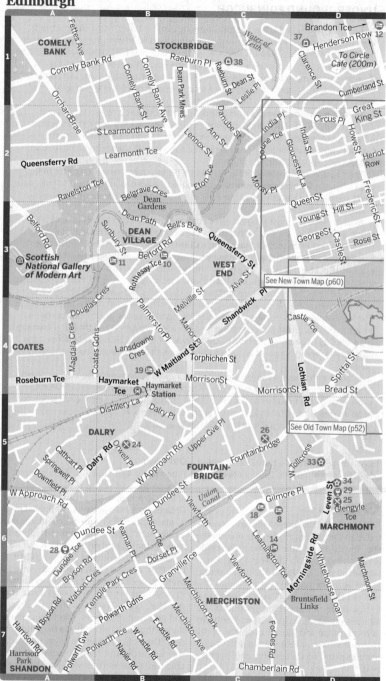

COMELY BANK

STOCKBRIDGE

Brandon Tce
37
Henderson Row
12

To Circle Cafe (200m)

Comely Bank Rd
Comely Bank Ave
Comely Bank St

Raeburn Pl
Raeburn St
Dean St
Leslie Pl

38

Clarence St

Cumberland St

Fettes Ave

Orchard Brae

S Learmonth Gdns

Dean Park Mews

Danube St

India Pl
Doune Tce
India St

Circus Pl
Great King St

Howe St

Queensferry Rd

Learmonth Tce

Lennox St

Ann St

Gloucester La

Moray Pl

Queen St

Heriot Row

Frederick St

Ravelston Tce

Belgrave Cres

Dean Gardens

Eton Tce

Young St
Hill St

George St
Castle St

Rose St

Belford Rd

Dean Path

Bell's Brae

Queensferry St

Dean Village

Sunbury St
Belford Rd
11
Rothesay Tce
10

WEST END

Alva St

Shandwick Pl

See New Town Map (p60)

Scottish National Gallery of Modern Art

Douglas Cres

Magdala Cres

Coates Gdns

Palmerston Pl

Melville St

Manor

Castle Tce

COATES

Lansdowne Cres

W Maitland St

Torphichen St

Lothian Rd

Spittal St

Roseburn Tce

Haymarket Tce

Haymarket Station

Morrison St

Morrison St

Bread St

Distillery La

Dalry Pl

DALRY

Dalry Rd
Orwell Pl
24

W Approach Rd

Upper Gve Pl

Fountainbridge

26

W Tollcross

33

Cathcart Pl

19

Springwell Pl

Downfield Pl

W Approach Rd

Dundee St

FOUNTAIN-BRIDGE

Union Canal

Gilmore Pl

18
8

Leven St
34
29
25

Glengyle Tce

MARCHMONT

28

Dundee Tce
Bryson Rd

Dundee St

Yeaman Pl

Dorset Pl

Gibson Tce

Viewforth

Viewforth

Leamington Tce

14

Bruntsfield Links

Morningside Rd

Whitehouse Loan

Marchmont St

W Bryson Rd

Watson Cres

Temple Park Cres

Granville Tce

Polwarth Gdns

Merchiston Park

MERCHISTON

Merchiston Ave

See Old Town Map (p52)

Harrison Rd

Harrison Park

SHANDON

Polwarth Gve

Polwarth Tce

W Castle Rd

Napier Rd

E Castle Rd

Forbes Rd

Chamberlain Rd

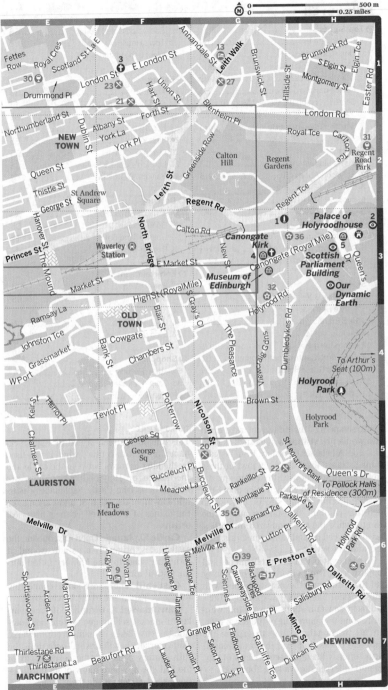

Edinburgh

the skyscrapers of their day, remarked upon with wonder by visiting writers such as Daniel Defoe. All classes of society, from beggars to magistrates, lived cheek by jowl in these urban ant nests, the wealthy occupying the middle floors – high enough to be above the noise and stink of the streets, but not so high that climbing the stairs would be too tiring – while the poor squeezed into attics, basements, cellars and vaults amid rats, rubbish and raw sewage.

The renovated Old Town tenements still support a thriving city-centre community, and today the street level is crammed with cafes, restaurants, bars, backpacker hostels and tacky souvenir shops. Few visitors wander beyond the main drag of the Royal Mile, but it's worth taking time to explore the countless closes that lead into quiet courtyards, often with unexpected views of city, sea and hills (see the Walking Tour, p66).

THE ROYAL MILE

This mile-long street earned its regal nickname in the 16th century when it was used by the king to travel between the castle and the Palace of Holyroodhouse. There are five sections (the Castle Esplanade, Castlehill, Lawnmarket, High St and Canongate), the names of which reflect their historical origins.

Castle Esplanade Open area outside the castle gates; originally a parade ground, it forms the stage for the Military Tattoo during festival time.

Castlehill The short slope connecting the Castle Esplanade to the Lawnmarket.

Lawnmarket A corruption of 'Landmarket', a market selling goods from land outside the city. Takes its name from the large cloth market that flourished here until the 18th century. This was the poshest part of the Old Town, where many of its most distinguished citizens made their homes.

High St Stretches from George IV Bridge down to the Netherbow at St Mary's St. It's the heart and soul of the Old Town, home to the city's main church, the law courts, the city council and – until 1707 – the Scottish parliament.

Canongate The stretch of the Royal Mile from Netherbow to Holyrood takes its name from the Augustinian canons (monks) of Holyrood Abbey. From the 16th century it was home to aristocrats attracted to the Palace of Holyroodhouse. Originally governed by the monks, Canongate was an independent burgh separate from Edinburgh until 1856.

Edinburgh Castle   CASTLE
(Map p52; www.edinburghcastle.gov.uk; adult/child incl audioguide £16/9.20; ☺9.30am-6pm Apr-Sep, to 5pm Oct-Mar, last admission 45min before closing) The brooding, black crags of Castle Rock, rising above the western end of Princes St, are the very reason for Edinburgh's existence. This rocky hill was the most easily defended hilltop on the invasion route between England and central Scotland, a route followed by countless armies from the Roman legions of the 1st and 2nd centuries AD to the Jacobite troops of Bonnie Prince Charlie in 1745.

Edinburgh Castle has played a pivotal role in Scottish history, both as a royal residence – King Malcolm Canmore (r 1058–93) and Queen Margaret first made their home here in the 11th century – and as a military stronghold. The castle last saw military action in 1745; from then until the 1920s it served as the British army's main base in Scotland. Today it is one of Scotland's most atmospheric, most popular – and most expensive – tourist attractions.

The **Entrance Gateway**, flanked by statues of Robert the Bruce and William Wallace, opens to a cobbled lane that leads up beneath the 16th-century **Portcullis Gate** to the cannons ranged along the Argyle and Mills Mount batteries. The battlements here have great views over New Town to the Firth of Forth.

At the far end of Mills Mount Battery is the famous **One O'Clock Gun**, where crowds gather to watch a gleaming WWII 25-pounder fire an ear-splitting time signal at exactly 1pm (every day except Sunday, Christmas Day and Good Friday).

South of Mills Mount, the road curls up leftwards through **Foog's Gate** to the highest part of Castle Rock, crowned by the tiny,

THE STONE OF DESTINY

On St Andrew's Day 1996 a block of sandstone – 26.5 inches by 16.5 inches by 11 inches in size, with rusted iron hoops at either end – was installed with much pomp and ceremony in Edinburgh Castle. For the previous 700 years it had lain in London, beneath the Coronation Chair in Westminster Abbey. Almost all English, and later British, monarchs from Edward II in 1307 to Elizabeth II in 1953 have parked their backsides firmly over this stone during their coronation ceremony.

The legendary Stone of Destiny – said to have originated in the Holy Land, and on which Scottish kings placed their feet during their coronation (not their bums; the English got that bit wrong) – was stolen from Scone Abbey near Perth by King Edward I of England in 1296. It was taken to London and there it remained for seven centuries – except for a brief removal to Gloucester during WWII air raids, and a three-month sojourn in Scotland after it was stolen by Scottish Nationalist students at Christmas in 1950 – as an enduring symbol of Scotland's subjugation by England.

The Stone of Destiny returned to the political limelight in 1996, when the then Scottish Secretary and Conservative Party MP Michael Forsyth arranged for the return of the sandstone block to Scotland. A blatant attempt to boost the flagging popularity of the Conservative Party in Scotland prior to a general election, Forsyth's publicity stunt failed miserably. The Scots said thanks very much for the stone and then, in May 1997, voted every Conservative MP in Scotland into oblivion.

Many people, however, believe Edward I was fobbed off with a shoddy imitation in 1296 and that the true Stone of Destiny remains safely hidden somewhere in Scotland. This is not impossible – some descriptions of the original stone state that it was made of black marble and decorated with elaborate carvings. Interested parties should read *Scotland's Stone of Destiny* by Nick Aitchinson, which details the history and cultural significance of Scotland's most famous lump of rock.

Royal Mile

A GRAND DAY OUT

Planning your own procession along the Royal Mile involves some tough decisions – it would be impossible to see everything in a single day, so it's wise to decide in advance what you don't want to miss and shape your visit around that. Remember to leave time for lunch, for exploring some of the Mile's countless side alleys and, during festival time, for enjoying the street theatre that is bound to be happening in High St.

The most pleasant way to reach the Castle Esplanade at the start of the Royal Mile is to hike up the zigzag path from the footbridge behind the Ross Bandstand in Princes Street Gardens (in springtime you'll be knee-deep in daffodils). Starting at **Edinburgh Castle 1** means that the rest of your walk is downhill. For a superb view up and down the length of the Mile, climb the **Camera Obscura's Outlook Tower 2** before visiting **Gladstone's Land 3** and **St Giles**

Royal Visits to the Royal Mile

1561: Mary, Queen of Scots arrives from France and holds an audience with John Knox.
1745: Bonnie Prince Charlie fails to capture Edinburgh Castle, and instead sets up court in Holyroodhouse.
2004: Queen Elizabeth II officially opens the Scottish Parliament building.

Edinburgh Castle

If you're pushed for time, visit the Great Hall, the Honours of Scotland and the Prisons of War exhibit. Head for the Half Moon Battery for a photo looking down the length of the Royal Mile.

Royal Scottish Academy
Scott Monument
Heart of Midlothian
City Chambers
NORTH BRIDGE
National Gallery of Scotland
Princes Street Gardens
THE MOUND
HIGH ST
5
4
3
2
GEORGE IV BRIDGE
CASTLEHILL
1
Scotch Whisky Experience

Gladstone's Land

The 1st floor houses a faithful recreation of how a wealthy Edinburgh merchant lived in the 17th century. Check out the beautiful Painted Bedchamber, with its ornately decorated walls and wooden ceilings.

Lunch Break

Pie and a pint at **Royal Mile Tavern**; soup and a sandwich at **Always Sunday**; bistro nosh at **Café Marlayne**.

Cathedral 4 . If history's your thing, you'll want to add **Real Mary King's Close** 5 , **John Knox House** 6 and the **Museum of Edinburgh** 7 to your must-see list.

At the foot of the mile, choose between modern and ancient seats of power – the **Scottish Parliament** 8 or the **Palace of Holyroodhouse** 9 . Round off the day with an evening ascent of Arthur's Seat or, slightly less strenuously, Calton Hill. Both make great sunset viewpoints.

TAKING YOUR TIME

Minimum time needed for each attraction:
- » **Edinburgh Castle:** two hours
- » **Gladstone's Land:** 45 minutes
- » **St Giles Cathedral:** 30 minutes
- » **Real Mary King's Close:** one hour (tour)
- » **Scottish Parliament:** one hour (tour)
- » **Palace of Holyroodhouse:** one hour

Real Mary King's Close
The guided tour is heavy on ghost stories, but a highlight is standing in an original 17th-century room with tufts of horsehair poking from the crumbling plaster, and breathing in the ancient scent of stone, dust and history.

Canongate Kirk

CANONGATE

ST MARY'S ST

SOUTH BRIDGE

Tron Kirk

Our Dynamic Earth

Palace of Holyroodhouse
Find the secret staircase joining Mary, Queen of Scots' bedchamber with that of her husband, Lord Darnley, who restrained the queen while his henchmen stabbed to death her secretary (and possible lover), David Rizzio.

Scottish Parliament
Don't have time for the guided tour? Pick up a 'Discover the Scottish Parliament Building' leaflet from reception and take a self-guided tour of the exterior, then hike up to Salisbury Crags for a great view of the complex.

St Giles Cathedral
Look out for the Burne-Jones stained-glass window (1873) at the west end, showing the crossing of the River Jordan, and the bronze memorial to Robert Louis Stevenson in the Moray Aisle.

EUROPHOTOS/ALAMY ©

COLIN PALMER PHOTOGRAPHY/ALAMY ©

JEAN-CHRISTOPHE GODET/ALAMY ©

Old Town

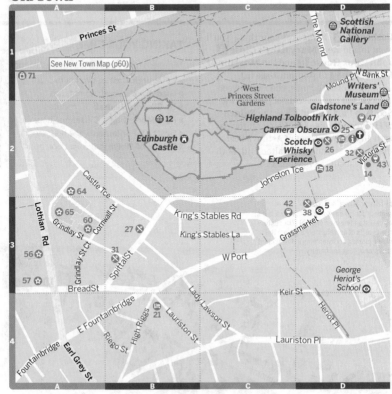

See New Town Map (p60)

Romanesque **St Margaret's Chapel**, the oldest surviving building in Edinburgh. It was probably built by David I or Alexander I in memory of their mother, Queen Margaret, sometime around 1130 (she was canonised in 1250). Beside the chapel stands **Mons Meg**, a giant 15th-century siege gun built at Mons (in what is now Belgium) in 1449.

DON'T MISS

CASTLE HIT LIST

If you're pushed for time, here are the top things to see at Edinburgh Castle:

» Views from Argyle Battery
» One O'Clock Gun
» Great Hall
» Honours of Scotland
» Prisons of War

The main group of buildings on the summit of Castle Rock is ranged around Crown Sq, dominated by the shrine of the **Scottish National War Memorial**. Opposite is the **Great Hall**, built for James IV (r 1488–1513) as a ceremonial hall and used as a meeting place for the Scottish parliament until 1639. Its most remarkable feature is the original, 16th-century hammer-beam roof.

The **Castle Vaults** beneath the Great Hall (entered from Crown Sq via the Prisons of War exhibit) were used variously as storerooms, bakeries and a prison. The vaults have been renovated to resemble 18th- and early-19th-century **prisons**, where graffiti carved by French and American prisoners can be seen on the ancient wooden doors.

On the eastern side of the square is the **Royal Palace**, built during the 15th and 16th centuries, where a series of historical tableaux leads to the highlight of the castle – a strongroom housing the **Honours of**

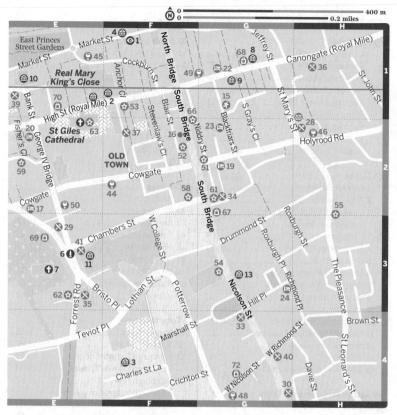

Scotland (the Scottish crown jewels), the oldest surviving crown jewels in Europe. Locked away in a chest following the Act of Union in 1707, the crown (made in 1540 from the gold of Robert the Bruce's 14th-century coronet), sword and sceptre lay forgotten until they were unearthed at the instigation of the novelist Sir Walter Scott in 1818. Also on display here is the **Stone of Destiny**.

Among the neighbouring **Royal Apartments** is the bedchamber where Mary, Queen of Scots gave birth to her son James VI, who was to unite the crowns of Scotland and England in 1603.

National War Museum of Scotland   MUSEUM
(Map p52; www.nms.ac.uk; admission incl in Edinburgh Castle ticket; ⊙9.45am-5.45pm Apr-Oct, to 4.45pm Nov-Mar) At the western end of the castle, to the left of the castle restaurant, a road leads down to the National War Museum of Scotland, which brings Scotland's military history vividly to life. The exhibits

have been personalised by telling the stories of the original owners of the objects on display, making it easier to empathise with the experiences of war than any dry display of dusty weaponry ever could.

FREE Highland Tolbooth Kirk   CHURCH
(Map p52; Castlehill; ⊙9.30am-7pm) Edinburgh's tallest spire (71.7m) is at the foot of Castlehill and is a prominent feature of the Old Town's skyline. The interior has been refurbished and it now houses the Hub (p76), the ticket office and the information centre for the Edinburgh Festival. There's also a good cafe here.

Scotch Whisky Experience   EXHIBITION
(Map p52; www.scotchwhiskyexperience.co.uk; 354 Castlehill; adult/child incl tour & tasting £12.50/6.50; ⊙10am-6.30pm Jun-Aug, to 6pm Sep-May) A former school houses this multimedia centre explaining the making of whisky from barley to bottle in a series of

Old Town

exhibits, demonstrations and tours that combine sight, sound and smell, including the world's largest collection of malt whiskies; look out for Peat the distillery cat! There's also a restaurant that serves traditional Scottish dishes with, where possible, a dash of whisky thrown in. It's a short distance downhill from the Castle Esplanade.

Camera Obscura
EXHIBITION

(Map p52; www.camera-obscura.co.uk; Castlehill; adult/child £10.95/7.95; ⊙9.30am-9pm Jul & Aug, 9.30am-7pm Apr-Jun, Sep & Oct, 10am-6pm Nov-Mar) Edinburgh's camera obscura is a curious 19th-century device – in constant use since 1853 – that uses lenses and mirrors to throw a live image of the city onto a large horizontal screen. The accompanying commentary is entertaining and the whole experience has a quirky charm, complemented by an intriguing exhibition dedicated to illusions of all kinds. Stairs lead up through various displays to the **Outlook Tower**, which offers great views over the city.

Gladstone's Land
HISTORIC BUILDING

(NTS; Map p52; www.nts.org.uk; 477 Lawnmarket; adult/child £6/5; ⊙10am-6.30pm Jul & Aug, to 5pm Apr-Jun, Sep & Oct) One of Edinburgh's most prominent 17th-century merchants was Thomas Gledstanes, who in 1617 purchased the tenement later known as Gladstone's Land. It contains fine painted ceilings, walls and beams, and some splendid furniture from the 17th and 18th centuries. The volunteer guides provide a wealth of anecdotes and a detailed history.

FREE Writers' Museum
MUSEUM

(Map p52; www.edinburghmuseums.org.uk; Lady Stair's Close, Lawnmarket; ⊙10am-5pm Mon-Sat year-round, 2-5pm Sun Aug) Tucked down a close just east of Gladstone's Land you'll find Lady Stair's House (1622), home to this museum that contains manuscripts and memorabilia belonging to three of Scotland's most famous writers: Robert Burns, Sir Walter Scott and Robert Louis Stevenson.

St Giles Cathedral
CHURCH

(Map p52; www.stgilescathedral.org.uk; High St; £3 donation suggested; ⊙9am-7pm Mon-Fri, to 5pm Sat, 1-5pm Sun May-Sep, 9am-5pm Mon-Sat, 1-5pm Sun Oct-Apr) Dominating the High St is the great grey bulk of St Giles Cathedral. Properly called the High Kirk of Edinburgh (it was only a true cathedral – the seat of a bishop – from 1633 to 1638 and from 1661

to 1689), St Giles Cathedral was named after the patron saint of cripples and beggars. A Norman-style church was built here in 1126 but was destroyed by English invaders in 1385; the only substantial remains are the central piers that support the tower.

The present church dates largely from the 15th century – the beautiful **crown spire** was completed in 1495 – but much of it was restored in the 19th century. The interior lacks grandeur but is rich in history: St Giles was at the heart of the Scottish Reformation, and John Knox served as minister here from 1559 to 1572. One of the most interesting corners of the kirk is the **Thistle Chapel**, built in 1911 for the Knights of the Most Ancient & Most Noble Order of the Thistle. The elaborately carved Gothic-style stalls have canopies topped with the helms and arms of the 16 knights – look out for the bagpipe-playing angel amid the vaulting.

By the side of the street, outside the western door of St Giles, is the **Heart of Midlothian**, set into the cobblestone paving. This marks the site of the Tolbooth. Built in the 15th century and demolished in the early 19th century, the Tolbooth served variously as a meeting place for parliament, the town council and the General Assembly of the Reformed Kirk, before becoming law courts and, finally, a notorious prison and place of execution. Passers-by traditionally spit on the heart for luck (don't stand downwind!).

At the other end of St Giles is the **Mercat Cross**, a 19th-century copy of the 1365 original, where merchants and traders met to transact business and royal proclamations were read.

Real Mary King's Close
HISTORIC BUILDING

(Map p52; ☎0845 070 6244; www.realmarykings close.com; 2 Warriston's Close, High St; adult/child £12.95/7.45; ⊙10am-9pm Mar-Oct, to 11pm Aug, to 5pm Sun-Thu & to 9pm Fri & Sat Nov-Mar) Across from St Giles are the City Chambers, originally built by John Adam (brother of Robert) between 1753 and 1761 to serve as the Royal Exchange – a covered meeting place for city merchants. However, the merchants preferred their old stamping ground in the street and the building became the city council offices in 1811.

Part of the Royal Exchange was built over the sealed-off remains of Mary King's Close, and the lower levels of this medieval Old Town alley have survived almost unchanged in the foundations of the City Chambers for 250 years. Now open to the public as the

Real Mary King's Close, this spooky, subterranean labyrinth gives a fascinating insight into the daily life of 16th- and 17th-century Edinburgh. Costumed characters give tours through a 16th-century town house and the plague-stricken home of a 17th-century gravedigger. Advance booking recommended.

FREE **Museum of Childhood** MUSEUM
(Map p52; www.edinburghmuseums.org.uk; 42 High St; ☉10am-5pm Mon-Sat, 2-5pm Sun) Halfway down the Royal Mile is 'the noisiest museum in the world'. Often filled with the chatter of excited children, it covers serious issues related to childhood – health, education, upbringing etc – but also has an enormous collection of toys, dolls, games and books, recordings of school lessons from the 1930s, and film of kids playing street games in 1950s Edinburgh.

John Knox House HISTORIC BUILDING
(Map p52; www.scottishstorytellingcentre.co.uk; 43-45 High St; adult/child £4.25/1; ☉10am-6pm Mon-Sat year-round, noon-6pm Sun Jul & Aug) The Royal Mile narrows at the foot of High St beside the jutting facade of John Knox House. This is the oldest surviving tenement in Edinburgh, dating from around 1490. John Knox, an influential church reformer and leader of the Protestant Reformation in Scotland, is thought to have lived here from 1561 to 1572. The labyrinthine interior has some beautiful painted-timber ceilings and an interesting display on Knox's life and work.

FREE **People's Story** MUSEUM
(Map p46; www.edinburghmuseums.org.uk; 163 Canongate; ☉10am-5pm Mon-Sat year-round, 2-5pm Sun Aug) One of the surviving symbols of Canongate's former independence is the **Canongate Tolbooth**. Built in 1591 it served successively as a collection point for tolls (taxes), a council house, a courtroom and a jail. With picturesque turrets and a projecting clock, it's an interesting example of 16th-century architecture. It now houses a fascinating museum called the People's Story, which covers the life, work and pastimes of ordinary Edinburgh folk from the 18th century to today.

FREE **Museum of Edinburgh** MUSEUM
(Map p46; www.edinburghmuseums.org.uk; 142 Canongate; ☉10am-5pm Mon-Sat year-round, 2-5pm Sun Aug) You can't miss the colourful facade of Huntly House, newly renovated in bright red and yellow ochre, opposite the Tolbooth clock. Built in 1570, it houses a museum covering Edinburgh from its prehistory to the present. Exhibits of national importance include an original copy of the National Covenant of 1638, but the crowd-pleaser is the dog collar and feeding bowl that once belonged to **Greyfriars Bobby**, the city's most famous canine citizen.

Canongate Kirk CHURCH
(Map p46) Downhill from Huntly House is the attractive curved gable of the Canongate Kirk, built in 1688. The kirkyard contains the graves of several famous people, including the economist **Adam Smith**, author of *The Wealth of Nations;* Mrs Agnes MacLehose (the 'Clarinda' of Robert Burns' love poems); and poet **Robert Fergusson** (1750–74; there's a statue of him on the street outside the church). Fergusson was much admired by Robert Burns, who paid for the gravestone and penned the epitaph – take a look at the inscription on the back. (An information board just inside the gate lists famous graves and their locations.)

HOLYROOD

Palace of Holyroodhouse PALACE
(Map p46; www.royalcollection.org.uk; adult/child £10.75/6.50; ☉9.30am-6pm Apr-Oct, to 4.30pm Nov-Mar) This palace is the royal family's official residence in Scotland, but is more famous as the 16th-century home of the ill-fated Mary, Queen of Scots. The palace developed from a guest house, attached to Holyrood Abbey, which was extended by King James IV in 1501. The oldest surviving part of the building, the northwestern tower, was built in 1529 as a royal apartment for James V and his wife, Mary of Guise. Mary, Queen of Scots spent six turbulent years here, during which time she debated with John Knox, married both her first and second husbands, and witnessed the murder of her secretary David Rizzio. The palace is closed to the public when the royal family is visiting and during state functions (usually in mid-May, and mid-June to early July; check the website for exact dates).

The self-guided audio tour leads you through a series of impressive royal apartments, ending in the **Great Gallery**. The 89 portraits of Scottish kings were commissioned by Charles II and supposedly record his unbroken lineage from Scota, the Egyptian pharaoh's daughter who discovered the infant Moses in a reed basket on the banks of the Nile.

But the highlight of the tour is **Mary, Queen of Scots' Bed Chamber**, home to the unfortunate Mary from 1561 to 1567, and connected by a secret stairway to her husband's bedchamber. It was here that her jealous first husband, Lord Darnley, restrained the pregnant queen while his henchmen murdered her secretary – and favourite – Rizzio. A plaque in the neighbouring room marks the spot where he bled to death.

Holyrood Abbey ABBEY
(Map p46; admission incl in palace ticket; ☉9.30am-6pm Apr-Oct, to 4.30pm Nov-Mar) King David I founded the abbey here in the shadow of Salisbury Crags in 1128. It was probably named after a fragment of the True Cross (*rood* is an old Scots word for cross), said to have been brought to Scotland by his mother, St Margaret. Most of the surviving ruins date from the 12th and 13th centuries, although a doorway in the far southeastern corner has survived from the original Norman church.

Queen's Gallery GALLERY
(Map p46; www.royalcollection.org.uk; adult/child £6/3, joint ticket incl admission to palace £15.10/8.55; ☉same as palace) This stunning modern gallery, which occupies the shell of a former church and school, was opened in 2002 as a showcase for exhibitions of art from the Royal Collections. The exhibitions change every six months or so; for details of the latest, check the website.

Our Dynamic Earth EXHIBITION
(Map p46; www.dynamicearth.co.uk; Holyrood Rd; adult/child £11.50/7.50; ☉10am-6pm Jul & Aug, to 5.30pm Apr-Jun, Sep & Oct, to 5pm Wed-Sun Nov-Mar, last admission 90min before closing; 🚼) The modernistic white marquee pitched beneath Salisbury Crags marks Our Dynamic Earth, billed as an interactive, multimedia journey of discovery through Earth's history from the Big Bang to the present day. Hugely popular with kids of all ages, it's a slick extravaganza of whiz-bang special effects and 3-D movies cleverly designed to fire up young

SCOTTISH PARLIAMENT BUILDING

The Scottish parliament building (Map p46; 📞0131-348 5200; www.scottish.parliament. uk; admission free; ☉9am-6.30pm Tue-Thu, 10am-5.30pm Mon & Fri in session, to 6pm Mon-Fri in recess Apr-Oct, to 4pm in recess Nov-Mar), built on the site of a former brewery close to the Palace of Holyroodhouse, was officially opened by HM the Queen in October 2005.

The public areas of the building – the Main Hall, where there is an exhibition, shop and cafe; and the **public gallery** in the Debating Chamber – are open to visitors (tickets needed for public gallery – see website for details). You can also take a free, one-hour **guided tour** (advance booking recommended) that includes a visit to the Debating Chamber, a committee room, the Garden Lobby and, when possible, the office of an MSP (Member of the Scottish Parliament). If you want to see the **parliament in session**, check the website for sitting times – business days are normally Tuesday to Thursday year-round.

Enric Miralles (1955–2000), the architect who conceived the Scottish parliament building, believed that a building could be a work of art. However, the weird concrete confection that has sprouted at the foot of Salisbury Crags has left the good people of Edinburgh staring and scratching their heads in confusion. What does it all mean? The strange forms of the exterior are all symbolic in some way, from the oddly shaped windows on the west wall (inspired by the silhouette of the *Reverend Robert Walker Skating on Duddingston Loch,* one of Scotland's most famous paintings), to the ground plan of the whole complex, which represents a 'flower of democracy rooted in Scottish soil' (best seen looking down from Salisbury Crags).

The **Main Hall**, inside the public entrance, has a low, triple-arched ceiling of polished concrete, like a cave, or cellar, or castle vault. It is a dimly lit space, the starting point for a metaphorical journey from this relative darkness up to the **Debating Chamber** (sitting directly above the Main Hall), which is, in contrast, a palace of light – the light of democracy. This magnificent chamber is the centrepiece of the parliament, designed not to glorify but to humble the politicians who sit within it. The windows face Calton Hill, allowing MSPs to look up to its monuments (reminders of the Scottish Enlightenment), while the massive, pointed oak beams of the roof are suspended by steel threads above the MSPs' heads like so many Damoclean swords.

minds with curiosity about all things geological and environmental. Its true purpose, of course, is to disgorge you into a gift shop where you can buy model dinosaurs and souvenir T-shirts.

Holyrood Park   PARK

(Map p46) In Holyrood Park Edinburgh is blessed with a little bit of wilderness in the heart of the city. The former hunting ground of Scottish monarchs, the park covers 263 hectares of varied landscape, including crags, moorland and a loch. The highest point is the 251m summit of **Arthur's Seat**, the deeply eroded remnant of a long-extinct volcano. Holyrood Park can be circumnavigated by car or bike along Queen's Dr, and you can hike from Holyrood to the summit in around 45 minutes.

NORTH OF THE ROYAL MILE

FREE Fruitmarket Gallery   GALLERY

(Map p52; www.fruitmarket.co.uk; 45 Market St; ⊙11am-6pm Mon-Sat, noon-5pm Sun) One of Edinburgh's most innovative and popular galleries, the Fruitmarket showcases contemporary Scottish and international artists, and has an excellent arts bookshop and cafe.

FREE City Art Centre   ART CENTRE

(Map p52; www.edinburghmuseums.org.uk; 2 Market St; fee for temporary exhibitions; ⊙10am-5pm Mon-Sat, noon-5pm Sun) Across the street from the Fruitmarket Gallery, this art centre comprises six floors of exhibitions with a variety of themes, including an extensive collection of Scottish art.

SOUTH OF THE ROYAL MILE

FREE National Museum of Scotland   MUSEUM

(Map p52; www.nms.ac.uk; Chambers St; fee for special exhibitions; ⊙10am-5pm) Broad, elegant Chambers St is dominated by the long facade of the National Museum of Scotland. Its extensive collections are spread between two buildings, one modern, one Victorian. The museum reopened to the public in 2011 after two years of major renovation and reconstruction.

The golden stone and striking modern architecture of the museum's new building, opened in 1998, is one of the city's most distinctive landmarks. The five floors of the museum trace the history of Scotland from geological beginnings to the 1990s, with many imaginative and stimulating exhibits – audio guides are available in several languages.

The new building connects with the original Victorian museum, dating from 1861, the stolid, grey exterior of which gives way to a bright and airy, glass-roofed hall. The museum houses an eclectic collection covering natural history, archaeology, scientific and industrial technology, and the decorative arts of ancient Egypt, Islam, China, Japan, Korea and the West.

FREE Greyfriars Kirk & Kirkyard   CHURCH

(Map p52; www.greyfriarskirk.com; Candlemaker Row; ⊙10.30am-4.30pm Mon-Fri & 11am-2pm Sat Apr-Oct, 1.30-3.30pm Thu only Nov-Mar) One of Edinburgh's most famous churches, Greyfriars Kirk was built on the site of a Franciscan friary and opened for worship on Christmas Day 1620. In 1638 the **National Covenant** was signed here, rejecting Charles I's attempts to impose episcopacy and a new English prayer book on the Scots, and affirming the independence of the Scottish Church. Many who signed were later executed at the Grassmarket and, in 1679, 1200 Covenanters were held prisoner in terrible conditions in the southwestern corner of the kirkyard. There's a small exhibition inside the church.

Surrounding the church, hemmed in by high walls and overlooked by the brooding presence of the castle, **Greyfriars Kirkyard** is one of Edinburgh's most evocative cemeteries, a peaceful green oasis dotted with elaborate monuments. Many famous Edinburgh names are buried here, including the poet Allan Ramsay (1686–1758), architect William Adam (1689–1748) and William Smellie (1740–95), the editor of the first edition of the *Encyclopedia Britannica*.

If you want to experience the graveyard at its scariest – inside a burial vault, in the dark, at night – go on one of Black Hart Storytellers' guided tours (p72).

Greyfriars Bobby Statue   MONUMENT

(Map p52) The memorials inside Greyfriars Kirkyard are interesting, but the one that draws the biggest crowds is outside, opposite the pub beside the kirkyard gate. It's the tiny statue of Greyfriars Bobby, a Skye terrier who, from 1858 to 1872, maintained a vigil over the grave of his master, an Edinburgh police officer. The story was immortalised in a novel by Eleanor Atkinson in 1912, and in 1963 was made into a movie by Walt Disney. Bobby's own grave, marked by a small, pink granite stone, is just inside the kirkyard entrance. You can see his original collar and bowl in the Museum of Edinburgh (p56).

Grassmarket   STREET

(Map p52) The site of a cattle market from the 15th century until the start of the 20th century, the Grassmarket has always been a focal point of the Old Town. It was also the city's main **place of execution**, and over 100 martyred Covenanters are commemorated by a monument at the eastern end, where the gallows used to stand. The notorious murderers Burke and Hare (p71) operated from a now-vanished close off the western end.

Nowadays the broad, open square, lined by tall tenements and dominated by the

NATIONAL MUSEUM OF SCOTLAND: HIGHLIGHTS

Begin at the main entrance in the middle of Chambers St, rather than the modern tower at the west end of the street. This opens into an atmospheric entrance hall occupying what used to be the museum cellars where you'll find an information desk with museum maps and leaflets, a cloakroom, toilets and a cafe-restaurant. Stairs lead up into the light of the **Grand Gallery**, a spectacular glass-roofed atrium lined with cast-iron pillars and balconies that is the centrepiece of the original Victorian museum.

This half of the building is devoted to the natural world, art and design, and world cultures. A door at the east end of the gallery leads into **Animal World**, one of the most impressive of the museum's new exhibits. No dusty, static regiments of stuffed creatures here, but a beautiful and dynamic display of animals apparently caught in the act of bounding, leaping or pouncing, arranged in groups that illustrate different means of locomotion, methods of feeding, and modes of reproduction. Extinct creatures mingle with the living, including a full-size skeleton of *Tyrannosausus rex*.

Take some time to explore the exhibits ranged around the balconies of the Grand Gallery, billed as a **Window on the World** that showcases more than 800 items from the museum's collections, ranging from the world's largest scrimshaw carving, occupying two full-size sperm whale jawbones, to a four-seat racing bicycle dating from 1898.

Return to the ground floor of the Grand Gallery and go through the Connect exhibit at the western end – where **Dolly the Sheep**, the world's first mammal cloned from an adult cell, is on display – to emerge into Hawthornden Court, the soaring central atrium of the modern half of the museum, graced by the **Formula 1 racing car** driven by Sir Jackie Stewart in the 1970s. This half of the building is devoted to Scottish history and culture.

Stairs at the far end lead down to the Early Peoples galleries on level 0, decorated with intriguing humanoid sculptures by Sir Eduardo Paolozzi. Look for the **Cramond Lioness**, a Roman sculpture of a lion gripping a human head in her jaws that was discovered in the River Almond in 1997, and the 20kg of 5th-century silver that makes up the **Traprain Treasure**.

From here, you work your way upwards through the the history of Scotland. Highlights of the medieval Kingdom of the Scots galleries, on levels 1 and 2, include the **Monymusk Reliquary**, a tiny silver casket dating from AD 750, which is said to have been carried into battle with Robert the Bruce at Bannockburn in 1314; and the famous **Lewis Chessmen**, a set of charming 12th-century chess pieces carved from walrus ivory, that was discovered on Uig beach on the Isle of Lewis.

Continue up through levels 3 and 4, which follow Scotland's progress through the Industrial Revolution, potently symbolised by the towering **Newcomen atmospheric engine** that once pumped water from flooded Ayrshire coal mines. The Ways of Death exhibit on level 5 – a Goth's paradise of jet jewellery and mourning bracelets made from human hair – contains several fascinating objects, including the tiny and mysterious **Arthur's Seat coffins** that were discovered in Holyrood Park in 1836, and which featured in Ian Rankin's Inspector Rebus novel *The Falls*.

Level 6 is given over to the 20th century, with galleries devoted to war and industry, and a particularly affecting exhibition called **Leaving Scotland**, containing stories of the Scottish diaspora that emigrated to begin new lives in Canada, Australia, the USA and other places.

Finally, find the elevator in the corner near the war gallery and go up to the **Roof Terrace** to enjoy a fantastic view across the city and the castle.

New Town

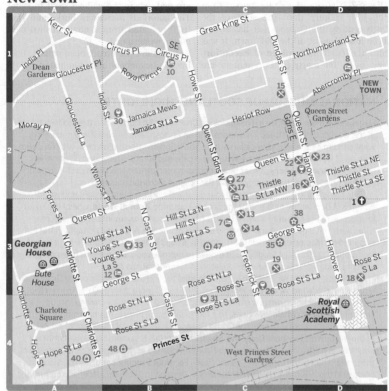

looming castle, has many lively pubs and restaurants, including the **White Hart Inn**, which was once patronised by Robert Burns. Claiming to be the city's oldest pub in continuous use (since 1516), it also hosted William Wordsworth in 1803. **Cowgate** – the long, dark ravine leading eastwards from the Grassmarket – was once the road along which cattle were driven from the pastures around Arthur's Seat to the safety of the city walls. Today it is the heart of Edinburgh's nightlife, with around two dozen clubs and bars within five minutes' walk of each other.

New Town

Edinburgh's New Town lies north of the Old Town, on a ridge running parallel to the Royal Mile and separated from it by the valley of Princes Street Gardens. Its grid of elegant Georgian terraces is a complete contrast to the chaotic tangle of tenements and wynds that characterise the Old Town.

Between the end of the 14th century and the start of the 18th, the population of Edinburgh – still confined within the walls of the Old Town – increased from 2000 to 50,000. The tottering tenements were unsafe and occasionally collapsed, fire was an ever-present danger, and the overcrowding and squalor became unbearable.

When the Act of Union in 1707 brought the prospect of long-term stability, the upper classes were keen to find healthier, more spacious living quarters, and in 1766 the lord provost of Edinburgh announced an architectural competition to design an extension to the city. It was won by an unknown 23-year-old, James Craig, a self-taught architect whose simple and elegant plan envisaged a main axis along George St, with grand squares at either end, and with building restricted to one side only of Princes and Queen Sts so that the houses enjoyed views

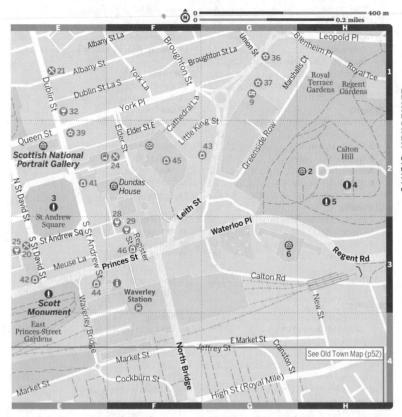

over the Firth of Forth to the north and to the castle and Old Town to the south.

During the 18th and 19th centuries the New Town continued to sprout squares, circuses, parks and terraces, with some of its finest neoclassical architecture designed by Robert Adam. Today Edinburgh's New Town remains the world's most complete and unspoilt example of Georgian architecture and town planning. Along with the Old Town, it was declared a Unesco World Heritage Site in 1995.

PRINCES STREET

Princes St is one of the world's most spectacular shopping streets. Built up on the north side only, it catches the sun in summer and allows expansive views across Princes Street Gardens to the castle and the crowded skyline of the Old Town.

The western end of Princes St is dominated by the red-sandstone edifice of the Caledonian Hilton Hotel and the tower of

St John's Church, worth visiting for its fine Gothic Revival interior. It overlooks **St Cuthbert's Parish Church**, built in the 1890s on a site of great antiquity – there has been a church here since at least the 12th century, and perhaps since the 7th century. There is a circular **watchtower** in the graveyard – a reminder of the Burke and Hare days when graves had to be guarded against robbers.

At the eastern end is the prominent clock tower – traditionally three minutes fast so you don't miss your train – of the **Balmoral Hotel** (originally the North British Hotel, built by the railway company of the same name in 1902) and the beautiful 1788 **Register House**, designed by Robert Adam, with a statue of the Duke of Wellington on horseback in front. It houses the National Archives of Scotland and the Scotlands People genealogical research centre.

Princes Street Gardens lie in a valley that was once occupied by the Nor' Loch,

New Town

a boggy depression that was drained in the early 19th century. The gardens are split in the middle by **The Mound**, which was created from around two million cartloads of earth excavated from the foundations of the New Town and dumped here to provide a road link across the valley to the Old Town. It was completed in 1830.

Scott Monument   MONUMENT
(Map p60; www.edinburghmuseums.org.uk; East Princes Street Gardens; admission £3; ⊙10am-7pm Mon-Sat Apr-Sep, 9am-4pm Mon-Sat Oct-Mar, 10am-6pm Sun year-round) The eastern half of Princes Street Gardens is dominated by the massive Gothic spire of the Scott Monument, built by public subscription in memory of the novelist Sir Walter Scott after his death in 1832. The exterior is decorated with carvings of characters from his novels; inside you can see an exhibition on Scott's life, and climb the 287 steps to the top for a superb view of the city.

FREE **Scottish National Gallery**   GALLERY
(Map p52; www.nationalgalleries.org; The Mound; fee for special exhibitions; ⊙10am-5pm Fri-Wed, to 7pm Thu) Designed by William Playfair, this imposing classical building with its Ionic porticoes dates from the 1850s. Its octagonal rooms, lit by skylights, have been restored to their original Victorian decor of deep-green carpets and dark-red walls.

The gallery houses an important collection of **European art** from the Renaissance to post-Impressionism, with works by Verrocchio (Leonardo da Vinci's teacher), Tintoretto, Titian, Holbein, Rubens, Van Dyck,

Vermeer, El Greco, Poussin, Rembrandt, Gainsborough, Turner, Constable, Monet, Pissarro, Gauguin and Cézanne. Each January the gallery exhibits its collection of **Turner watercolours**, bequeathed by Henry Vaughan in 1900. Room X is graced by Antonio Canova's white marble sculpture, **The Three Graces**; it is owned jointly with London's Victoria & Albert Museum.

The upstairs galleries house portraits by Sir Joshua Reynolds and Sir Henry Raeburn, and a clutch of **Impressionist** paintings, including Monet's luminous *Haystacks,* Van Gogh's demonic *Olive Trees* and Gauguin's hallucinatory *Vision After the Sermon*. But the painting that really catches your eye is the gorgeous portrait, *Lady Agnew of Lochnaw*, by John Singer Sargent.

The basement galleries dedicated to **Scottish art** include glowing portraits by Allan Ramsay and Sir Henry Raeburn, rural scenes by Sir David Wilkie and Impressionistic landscapes by William MacTaggart. Look out for Raeburn's iconic *Reverend Robert Walker Skating on Duddingston Loch,* and Sir George Harvey's hugely entertaining *A Schule Skailin* (A School Emptying) – a stern dominie (teacher) looks on as the boys stampede for the classroom door, one reaching for a confiscated spinning top. Kids will love the fantasy paintings of Sir Joseph Noel Paton in room B5; the incredibly detailed canvases are crammed with hundreds of tiny fairies, goblins and elves.

FREE Royal Scottish Academy   GALLERY
(Map p60; www.royalscottishacademy.org; The Mound; fee for special exhibitions; ☉10am-5pm Mon-Sat, 2-5pm Sun) The distinguished Greek Doric temple at the corner of The Mound and Princes St, its northern pediment crowned by a seated figure of Queen Victoria, is the home of the Royal Scottish Academy. Designed by William Playfair and built between 1823 and 1836, it was originally called the Royal Institution; the RSA took over the building in 1910. The galleries display a collection of paintings, sculptures and architectural drawings by academy members dating from 1831, and they also host temporary exhibitions throughout the year.

The RSA and the National Gallery of Scotland are linked via an underground mall – the **Weston Link** – which gives them twice the temporary exhibition space of the Prado in Madrid and three times that of the Royal Academy in London, as well as

housing cloakrooms, a lecture theatre and a restaurant.

GEORGE STREET & CHARLOTTE SQUARE
Until the 1990s George St – the major axis of New Town – was the centre of Edinburgh's financial industry and Scotland's equivalent of Wall St. Today the big financial firms have moved to premises in the Exchange office district west of Lothian Rd, and George St's former banks and offices house upmarket shops, pubs and restaurants.

At the western end of George St is Charlotte Sq, the architectural jewel of New Town, designed by Robert Adam shortly before his death in 1791. The northern side of the square is Adam's masterpiece and one of the finest examples of Georgian architecture anywhere. **Bute House**, in the centre at No 6, is the official residence of Scotland's first minister, the equivalent of London's 10 Downing St.

Georgian House   HISTORIC BUILDING
(NTS; Map p60; 7 Charlotte Sq; adult/child £6/5; ☉10am-6pm Jul & Aug, to 5pm Apr-Jun, Sep & Oct, 11am-4pm Mar, to 3pm Nov) The National Trust for Scotland's Georgian House has been beautifully restored and furnished to show how Edinburgh's wealthy elite lived at the end of the 18th century. The walls are decorated with paintings by Allan Ramsay, Sir Henry Raeburn and Sir Joshua Reynolds.

ST ANDREW SQUARE
Not as architecturally distinguished as its sister at the opposite end of George St, St Andrew Sq is dominated by the fluted column of the Melville Monument (Map p60), commemorating Henry Dundas, 1st Viscount Melville (1742–1811). Dundas was the most powerful Scottish politician of his time, often referred to when alive as 'Harry IX, the Uncrowned King of Scotland'. The impressive Palladian mansion of **Dundas House**, built between 1772 and 1774, on the eastern side of the square, was built for Sir Laurence Dundas (1712–81) – no relation to Viscount Melville. It has been the head office of the Royal Bank of Scotland since 1825 and has a spectacular domed banking hall dating from 1857 (you can nip inside for a look).

A short distance along George St is the Church of St Andrew & St George (Map p60), built in 1784 with an unusual oval nave. It was the scene of the Disruption of 1843, when 451 dissenting ministers left the Church of Scotland to form the Free Church.

FREE Scottish National
Portrait Gallery   GALLERY
(Map p60; www.nationalgalleries.org; 1 Queen St; ⊙10am-5pm Fri-Wed, to 7pm Thu) The Venetian Gothic palace of the Scottish National Portrait Gallery reopened its doors in 2011 after a two-year renovation, emerging as one of the city's top attractions. Its galleries illustrate Scottish history through paintings, photographs and sculptures, putting faces to famous names from Scotland's past and present, from Robert Burns, Mary, Queen of Scots and Bonnie Prince Charlie to Sean Connery, Billy Connolly and poet Jackie Kay.

CALTON HILL

Calton Hill (100m), rising dramatically above the eastern end of Princes St, is Edinburgh's acropolis, its summit scattered with grandiose memorials dating mostly from the first half of the 19th century. It is also one of the best viewpoints in the city, with a panorama that takes in the castle, Holyrood, Arthur's Seat, the Firth of Forth, New Town and the full length of Princes St.

On the southern side of the hill, on Regent Rd, is the modernist facade of St Andrew's House (Map p60), built between 1936 and 1939 and housing the civil servants of the Westminster government's Scottish Office until they were moved to the new Scottish Executive building in Leith in 1996.

Just beyond St Andrew's House, and on the opposite side of the road, is the imposing **Royal High School** building, dating from 1829 and modelled on the Temple of Theseus in Athens. Former pupils include Robert Adam, Alexander Graham Bell and Sir Walter Scott. It now stands empty. To its east, on the other side of Regent Rd, is the 1830 Burns Monument (Map p46), a Greek-style memorial to Robert Burns.

You can reach the summit of Calton Hill via the road beside the Royal High School or by the stairs at the eastern end of Waterloo Pl. The largest structure on the summit is the National Monument (Map p60), an overambitious attempt to replicate the Parthenon in Athens and intended to honour Scotland's dead in the Napoleonic Wars. Construction – paid for by public subscription – began in 1822, but funds ran dry when only 12 columns had been completed.

Looking like an upturned telescope – the similarity is intentional – and offering even better views, the Nelson Monument (Map p60; admission £3; ⊙10am-7pm Mon-Sat & noon-5pm Sun Apr-Sep, 10am-3pm Mon-Sat Oct-Mar;

⊟all Leith St buses) was built to commemorate Admiral Lord Nelson's victory at Trafalgar in 1805.

The design of the City Observatory (Map p60), built in 1818, was based on the ancient Greek Temple of the Winds in Athens. Its original function was to provide a precise, astronomical time-keeping service for marine navigators, but smoke from Waverley train station forced the astronomers to move to Blackford Hill in the south of Edinburgh in 1895.

Dean Village

If you follow Queensferry St northwards from the western end of Princes St, you come to **Dean Bridge**, designed by Thomas Telford and built between 1829 and 1832. Down in the valley, just west of the bridge, is **Dean Village** (from 'dene', a Scots word for valley). It was founded as a milling community by the canons of Holyrood Abbey in the 12th century and by 1700 there were 11 watermills here operated by the Incorporation of Baxters (the bakers' trade guild). One of the old mill buildings has been converted into flats, and the village is now an attractive residential area.

FREE Scottish National
Gallery of Modern Art   GALLERY
(Map p46; www.nationalgalleries.org; 75 Belford Rd; fee for special exhibitions; ⊙10am-5pm) Set in an impressive neoclassical building surrounded by a landscaped sculpture park some 500m west of Dean Village is the Scottish National Gallery of Modern Art.

The main collection, known as **Modern One**, concentrates on 20th-century art, with various European movements represented by the likes of Matisse, Picasso, Kirchner, Magritte, Miró, Mondrian and Giacometti. American and English artists are also represented, but most space is given to Scottish painters – from the Scottish colourists of the early 20th century to contemporary artists such as Peter Howson and Ken Currie.

There's an excellent **cafe** downstairs, and the surrounding **park** features sculptures by Henry Moore, Rachel Whiteread and Barbara Hepworth, among others, as well as a 'landform artwork' by Charles Jencks.

A footpath and stairs at the rear of the gallery lead down to the **Water of Leith Walkway**, which you can follow along the river for 4 miles to Leith. This takes you past **6 Times**, a sculptural project by Anthony Gormley consisting of six human figures

EXPLORING YOUR SCOTTISH ANCESTRY

Genealogy is a hugely popular pastime, and many visitors to Scotland take the opportunity to do some detective work on their Scottish ancestry.

One of the best guides is *Tracing Your Scottish Ancestry* by Kathleen B Cory, and there are many useful websites; GenUKI (www.genuki.org.uk) is a good starting point. Ancestry (www.ancestry.co.uk) is another.

At the excellent ScotlandsPeople (www.scotlandspeople.gov.uk) website you can search the indexes to Old Parish Registers and Statutory Registers as well as census returns, on a pay-per-view basis. FamilySearch (familysearch.org) includes freely searchable records of Scottish baptisms and marriages.

The following places in Edinburgh can help out:

ScotlandsPeople Centre (☑0131-314 4300; www.scotlandspeoplehub.gov.uk; 2 Princes St; ☉9am-4.30pm Mon-Fri) The main records used in Scottish genealogical research – the Statutory Registers of births, marriages and deaths (1855 to the present), the Old Parish Registers (1533–1854) and the 10-yearly census returns from 1841 to 1901 – are held here. The registration of births, marriages and deaths became compulsory in Scotland on 1 January 1855; before that date, the ministers of the Church of Scotland kept registers of baptisms and marriages. The oldest surviving parish registers date back to 1553, but these records are far from complete, and many births and marriages before 1855 went unrecorded. Records of wills and testaments, valuation rolls and coats of arms can also be searched. Daily search fee is £15 and there are tutorial sessions available.

Scottish Genealogy Society Library (☑0131-220 3677; www.scotsgenealogy.com; 15 Victoria Tce; guests/members £5/free; ☉10am-5pm Mon-Thu & Sat) Maintains the world's largest library of Scottish gravestone inscriptions and a comprehensive records and family history collection.

standing at various points along the river. (The statues are designed to fall over in flood conditions, so some of them may not be visible after heavy rain.)

Directly across Belford Rd from Modern One, another neoclassical mansion (formerly an orphanage) houses its annexe, **Modern Two**, which houses a large collection of sculpture and graphic art created by the Edinburgh-born artist Sir Eduardo Paolozzi. One of the 1st-floor rooms houses a recreation of Paolozzi's studio, while the rest of the building stages temporary exhibitions of modern art.

Leith

Two miles northeast of the city centre, Leith has been Edinburgh's seaport since the 14th century and remained an independent burgh with its own town council until it was incorporated by the city in the 1920s. Like many of Britain's dockland areas, it fell into decay in the decades following WWII but has been undergoing a revival since the late 1980s. Old warehouses have been turned into luxury flats, and a lush crop of trendy bars and restaurants has sprouted along the waterfront. The area was given an addi-

tional boost in the late 1990s when the Scottish Executive (a government department) moved to a new building on Leith docks.

The city council has formulated a major redevelopment plan for the entire Edinburgh waterfront from Leith to Granton, the first phase of which is Ocean Terminal (☑555 8888; www.oceanterminal.com; Ocean Dr; ☉10am-8pm Mon-Fri, to 7pm Sat, 11am-6pm Sun; ☐1, 11, 22, 34, 35 or 36), a shopping and leisure complex that includes the former Royal Yacht *Britannia* and a berth for visiting cruise liners. Parts of Leith are still a bit rough but it's a distinctive corner of the city and well worth exploring.

Royal Yacht Britannia   HISTORIC VESSEL
(www.royalyachtbritannia.co.uk; Ocean Terminal; adult/child £11.75/7.50; ☉9.30am-4.30pm Jul-Sep, to 4pm Apr-Jun & Oct, 10am-3.30pm Nov-Mar, last admission 90min before closing) One of Scotland's biggest tourist attractions is the former Royal Yacht *Britannia*. She was the British royal family's floating home during their foreign travels from the time of her launch in 1953 until her decommissioning in 1997, and is now moored permanently in front of Ocean Terminal.

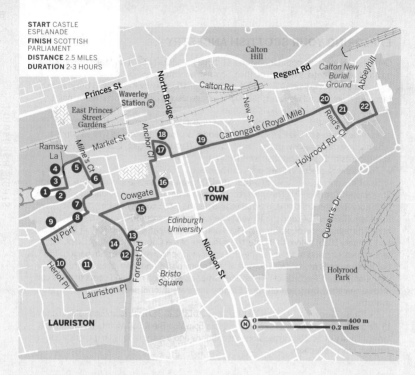

Walking Tour
Old Town Alleys

❯ This walk explores the alleys and side streets around the the Royal Mile, and involves a bit of climbing up and down steep stairs.

Begin on the ❶ **Castle Esplanade**, which provides a grandstand view south over the Grassmarket; the prominent quadrangular building with all the turrets is George Heriot's School, which you'll be passing later on. Head towards Castlehill and the start of the Royal Mile.

The 17th-century house on the right is known as ❷ **Cannonball House** because of the iron ball lodged in the wall (look between, and slightly below, the two largest windows on the wall facing the castle). It was not fired in anger, but marks the gravitation height to which water would flow naturally from the city's first piped water supply.

The low, rectangular building across the street (now a touristy tartan-weaving mill) was originally the reservoir that held the Old Town's water supply. On its west wall is the ❸ **Witches Well**, where a bronze fountain

commemorates around 4000 people (mostly women) who were executed between 1479 and 1722 on suspicion of witchcraft.

Go past the reservoir and turn left down Ramsay Lane. Take a look at ❹ **Ramsay Garden** – one of Edinburgh's most desirable addresses – where late-19th-century apartments were built around the octagonal Ramsay Lodge, once home to poet Allan Ramsay. The cobbled street continues around to the right below student residences, to the towers of the ❺ **New College**, home to Edinburgh University's Faculty of Divinity. Nip into the courtyard to see the statue of John Knox (a firebrand preacher who led the Protestant Reformation in Scotland, and was instrumental in the creation of the Church of Scotland in 1560).

Just past New College turn right and climb the stairs into Milne's Court, a student residence belonging to Edinburgh University. Exit into Lawnmarket, cross the street (bearing slightly left) and duck into ❻ **Riddell's Court**, a typical Old Town close at No 322–8.

You'll find yourself in a small courtyard, but the house in front of you (built in 1590) was originally the edge of the street (the building you just walked under was added in 1726 – look for the inscription in the doorway on the right). The arch with the inscription *Vivendo discimus* (we live and learn) leads into the original 16th-century courtyard.

Go back into the street, turn right and right again down Fisher's Close, which leads to the delightful Victoria Terrace, strung above the cobbled curve of shop-lined Victoria St. Wander right, enjoying the view – **7 Maxie's Bistro**, at the far end of the terrace, is a great place to stop for a drink – then descend the stairs at the foot of Upper Bow and continue downhill to the Grassmarket. At the east end, outside Maggie Dickson's pub, is the **8 Covenanters Monument**, which marks the site of the gallows where more than 100 Covenanters were martyred in the 17th century.

If you're feeling peckish, the Grassmarket has several good places to eat and a couple of good pubs – Robert Burns once stayed at the **9 White Hart Inn**. Go to the west end of the Grassmarket and turn left up the stairs known as The Vennel. At the top, on the left, you'll find the **10 Flodden Wall**, one of the few surviving fragments of the city wall that was built in the early 16th century as protection against a feared English invasion. Follow its extension, the Telfer Wall, to Lauriston Pl and turn left along the impressive facade of **11 George Heriot's School**, built in the 17th century with funds bequeathed by George Heriot (goldsmith and banker to King James VI). It was originally a school and home for orphaned children, but became a fee-paying public school in 1886. Note this is the back of the building – the front was designed to face the castle and impress the inhabitants of the Grassmarket.

Turn left at Forrest Rd and, if it's a Sunday afternoon, pop into **12 Sandy Bell's** for a pint and some Scottish folk music; otherwise, pause for a photo oppurtunity with the statue of **13 Greyfriars Bobby**, then take a stroll through atmospheric **14 Greyfriars Kirkyard**. Descend Candlemakers Row and turn right at the bottom of the hill into the Cowgate.

Pass under the arch of George IV Bridge – the buildings to your right are the new law courts, while high up to the left you can see the complex of buildings behind Parliament Sq. Past the courts, on the right, is **15 Tailors Hall** (built 1621, extended 1757), now a hotel and bar but formerly the meeting place of the Companie of Tailzeours (Tailors' Guild).

Turn left and climb up Old Fishmarket Close, and perhaps stop for lunch at the little brasserie, **16 Passepartout**. Emerge once more onto the Royal Mile – across the street and slightly downhill is **17 Anchor Close**, named for a tavern that once stood there. It hosted the Crochallan Fencibles, an 18th-century drinking club that provided its patrons with an agreeable blend of intellectual debate and intoxicating liquor. The club was founded by William Smellie, editor of the first edition of the *Encyclopedia Brittanica*; its best-known member was the poet Robert Burns.

Go down Anchor Close, which leads to Cockburn St, one of the city's coolest shopping streets, lined with record shops and clothes boutiques. The street was cut through Old Town tenements in the 1850s to provide an easy route between Waverley Station and the Royal Mile. Turn right and head uphill. Look up high on **18 55-7 Cockburn Street** (on the left) – on either side of the gable are the carved figures of an owl and a grotesque catlike creature with huge claws and vampirelike fangs. Their origin and meaning are unknown.

At the top of Cockburn St turn left along the Royal Mile, and pause at **19 Paisley Close**, beneath a protruding castellated window. Above the entrance is a carving of a young man's head, and the words 'Heave awa' chaps, I'm no dead yet'. This is a monument to a young man who survived a tenement collapse in 1861; his rescuers heard him yell these words from beneath a pile of debris.

Continue down the Royal Mile and look for the first alley on the left after Canongate Kirk. This is **20 Dunbar's Close**, which leads to a hidden garden laid out in 17th-century style. Across the street and slightly downhill (beside Starbucks), follow Crichton's Close past the **21 Scottish Poetry Library**, an architectural-award-winning modern building, to Holyrood Rd. Turn left to finish outside the **22 Scottish Parliament Building**, beneath the imposing skyline of Salisbury Crags.

EDINBURGH FOR CHILDREN

Edinburgh has a multitude of attractions for children, and most things to see and do are child-friendly. Kids under five travel for free on Edinburgh buses, and five- to 15-year-olds pay a flat fare of 70p.

The Edinburgh Information Centre (p94) has lots of info on childrens events, and the handy guidebook Edinburgh for Under Fives (www.edinburghforunderfives.co.uk) can be found in most bookshops. The List (p93) magazine has a special kids section listing children's activities and events in and around Edinburgh. The week-long Imaginate Festival (p73) of childrens theatre, dance and puppetry takes place each year in late May/early June.

There are good, safe **playgrounds** in most Edinburgh parks, including Princes Street Gardens West, Inverleith Park (opposite the Royal Botanic Garden), George V Park (New Town), the Meadows and Bruntsfield Links.

Some more ideas for outdoor activities include exploring the Royal Botanic Garden (p69), going to see the animals at Edinburgh Zoo (p69), visiting the statue of Greyfriars Bobby (p58) and feeding the swans and playing on the beach at Cramond (p69). During the Edinburgh and Fringe Festivals there is also plenty of **street theatre** for kids, especially on the High St and at the foot of The Mound, and in December there's an open-air ice rink and fairground rides in Princes Street Gardens.

If it's raining, you can visit the Discovery Centre, a hands-on activity zone on level 3 of the National Museum of Scotland (p58), play on the flumes at the Royal Commonwealth Pool (p70), try out the earthquake simulator at Our Dynamic Earth (p57), or take a tour of the haunted Real Mary King's Close (p55).

You should be aware that the majority of Scottish pubs, even those that serve bar meals, are forbidden by law to admit children under the age of 14. Even in the family-friendly pubs (ie those in possession of a Children's Certificate), under-14s are only admitted between the hours of 11am and 8pm for a meal, and only when accompanied by an adult. Sixteen- and 17-year-olds can buy and drink beer and wine with a meal in a restaurant.

Childminding Services

For information on government-approved childminding services, contact Edinburgh Childcare Information Service (☎0800 032 0323) The following are reliable Edinburgh agencies that charge from £8 an hour for babysitting:

Super Mums (☎0131-225 1744; www.supermums.co.uk; 6 Glencairn Cres)

Panda's Nanny Agency (☎0131-663 3967; www.pandasnannyagency.co.uk; 22 Durham Pl)

The tour, which you take at your own pace with an audioguide (available in 20 languages), gives an intriguing insight into the Queen's private tastes – *Britannia* was one of the few places where the royal family could enjoy true privacy. The entire ship is a monument to 1950s decor and technology, and the accommodation reveals Her Majesty's preference for simple, unfussy surroundings – the Queen's own bed is surprisingly tiny and plain.

There was nothing simple or unfussy, however, about the running of the ship. When the Queen travelled, with her went 45 members of the royal household, five tons of luggage and a Rolls-Royce that was carefully squeezed into a specially built garage on the deck. The ship's company consisted of an admiral, 20 officers and 220 yachtsmen. The decks (of Burmese teak) were scrubbed daily, but all work near the royal accommodation was carried out in complete silence and had to be finished by 8am. A thermometer was kept in the Queen's bathroom to make sure the water was the correct temperature, and when in harbour one yachtsman was charged with ensuring that the angle of the gangway never exceeded 12 degrees. Note the mahogany windbreak that was added to the balcony deck in front of the bridge. It was put there to stop wayward breezes from blowing up skirts and inadvertently revealing the royal undies.

Britannia was joined in 2010 by the 1930s racing yacht **Bloodhound**, which was owned by the Queen in the 1960s. She is moored alongside *Britannia* (except in July and August, when she is away cruising) as part of an exhibition about the Royal Family's love of all things nautical.

The Majestic Tour bus runs from Waverley Bridge to *Britannia* during opening times. Alternatively, take Lothian Bus 11, 22 or 35 to Ocean Terminal.

Greater Edinburgh

Edinburgh Zoo   ZOO
(www.edinburghzoo.org.uk; 134 Corstorphine Rd; adult/child £15.50/11; ☉9am-6pm Apr-Sep, to 5pm Oct & Mar, to 4.30pm Nov-Feb) Opened in 1913, Edinburgh Zoo is one of the world's leading conservation zoos. Edinburgh's captive breeding program has helped save many endangered species, including Siberian tigers, pygmy hippos and red pandas. The main attractions are the **penguin parade** (the penguins go for a walk every day at 2.15pm), the **sea lion** training session (daily at 11.15am), and the two **giant pandas**, Tian Tian and Yang Guang.

The zoo is 2.5 miles west of the city centre; take Lothian Bus 12, 26 or 31, First Bus 16, 18, 80 or 86, or the Airlink Bus 100 westbound from Princes St.

FREE **Royal Botanic Garden**   GARDEN
(www.rbge.org.uk; 20a Inverleith Row; admission to glasshouses £4.50; ☉10am-6pm Mar-Sep, to 5pm Feb & Oct, to 4pm Nov-Jan) Just north of Stockbridge is the lovely Royal Botanic Garden. Twenty-eight beautifully landscaped hectares include splendid Victorian **palm houses**, colourful swaths of rhododendrons and azaleas, and a world-famous **rock garden**. The Terrace Cafe offers good views towards the city centre.

Take Lothian Bus 8, 17, 23 or 27 to the East Gate, or the Majestic Tour bus.

Cramond   NEIGHBOURHOOD
With its moored yachts, stately swans and whitewashed houses spilling down the hillside at the mouth of the River Almond, Cramond is the most picturesque corner of Edinburgh. It is also rich in history. The Romans built a fort here in the 2nd century AD, but recent archaeological excavations have revealed evidence of a Bronze Age settlement dating from 8500 BC, the oldest-known site in Scotland.

Cramond, which was originally a mill village, has a historic 17th-century church and a 15th-century tower house, as well as some rather unimpressive Roman remains,

but most people come to enjoy the walks along the river to the ruined mills and to stroll along the seafront. On the riverside, opposite the cottage on the far bank, is the Maltings (☎0131-312 6034; www.cramondasso ciation.org.uk; Riverside, Cramond; admission free; ☉2-5pm Sat & Sun Apr-Sep, daily during Edinburgh Festival), which hosts an interesting exhibition on Cramond's history.

Cramond is 5 miles northwest of the city centre; take bus 41 from George St (westbound) or Queensferry St to Cramond Glebe Rd, then walk north for 400m.

Craigmillar Castle   CASTLE
(HS; Craigmillar Castle Rd; adult/child £5/3; ☉9.30am-5.30pm Apr-Sep, to 4.30pm Oct, to 4.30pm Sat-Wed Nov-Mar) If you want to explore a Scottish fortress away from the crowds that throng Edinburgh Castle, try Craigmillar. Dating from the 15th century, the tower house rises above two sets of machicolated curtain walls. Mary, Queen of Scots took refuge here after the murder of Rizzio; it was here too that plans to murder her husband Darnley were laid. Look for the prison cell complete with built-in sanitation, something some 'modern' British prisons only finally managed in 1996.

The castle is 2.5 miles southeast of the city centre. Take bus 33 (eastbound) from Princes St to Old Dalkeith Rd and walk 500m up Craigmillar Castle Rd.

🏃 Activities

Walking
Edinburgh is lucky to have several good walking areas within the city boundary, including Arthur's Seat, Calton Hill, Blackford Hill, Hermitage of Braid, Corstorphine Hill and the coast and river at Cramond. The **Pentland Hills**, which rise to over 500m, stretch southwest from the city for 15 miles, offering excellent high- and low-level walking.

You can follow the **Water of Leith Walkway** from the city centre to Balerno (8 miles), and continue across the Pentlands to Silverburn (6.5 miles) or Carlops (8 miles), and return to Edinburgh by bus. Another good walk is along the **Union Canal towpath**, which begins in Fountainbridge and runs all the way to Falkirk (31 miles). You can return to Edinburgh by bus at Ratho (8.5 miles) or Broxburn (12 miles), and by bus or train from Linlithgow (21 miles).

Cycling
Edinburgh and its surroundings offer many excellent opportunities for cycling (see

www.cyclingedinburgh.info and www.cycling-edinburgh.org.uk). The main off-road routes from the city to the countryside follow the **Union Canal towpath** then the **Water of Leith Walkway** from Tollcross southwest to Balerno (7.5 miles) on the edge of the Pentland Hills, and the **Innocent Railway Cycle Path** from the southern side of Arthur's Seat east to Musselburgh (5 miles) on to Ormiston and Pencaitland.

There are several routes through the **Pentland Hills** that are suitable for mountain bikes. For details ask at any bike shop or check out the Pentland Hills Regional Park (www.pentlandhills.org) website. The Spokes *Edinburgh Cycle Map* (www.spokes.org.uk; available from cycle shops for £6) shows all the city's cycle routes.

Cycle Scotland
BICYCLE RENTAL

(Map p52; ✆0131-556 5560; www.cyclescotland.co.uk; 29 Blackfriars St; per day £15-20, per week £70-90; ☉10am-6pm Mon-Sat) The friendly and helpful folk here rent out top-quality bikes; rates include helmet, lock and repair kit. You can hire tents and touring equipment too. The company also organises cycle tours in Edinburgh and all over Scotland – check the website for details.

Golf

There are no fewer than 19 golf courses in Edinburgh – the following are two of the best city courses.

Braid Hills Public Golf Course
GOLF

(www.edinburghleisuregolf.co.uk; Braid Hills Approach; green fees weekday/weekend £21/24.25) A scenic but challenging course to the south of the city centre.

Lothianburn Golf Course
GOLF

(www.lothianburngc.co.uk; 106a Biggar Rd; green fees weekday/weekend £25/35) Enjoys a scenic setting at the foot of the Pentland Hills, south of the city.

Swimming

The Firth of Forth is a bit on the chilly side for enjoyable swimming, but there are several indoor alternatives.

Royal Commonwealth Pool
SWIMMING

(Map p46; www.thecommiepool.co.uk; 21 Dalkeith Rd; adult/child £5.50/2.80; ☉5.30am-9.30pm Mon-Fri, to 5pm Sat, 7.30am-5pm Sun) Edinburgh's main facility – built for the 1970 Commonwealth Games, and serving as a venue for the 2014 Glasgow games – is affectionately known as the 'Commie Pool'.

Recently refurbished, it has a 50m eight-lane pool, diving pool, teaching/childrens pool, fitness centre and kids soft play area.

Warrender Swim Centre
SWIMMING

(Map p46; www.edinburghleisure.co.uk; Thirlestane Rd; adult/child £4.20/2.10; ☉7am-10pm Mon-Fri, 9am-6pm Sat & Sun) Beautiful Victorian-era 25-yard (23m) pool, with gym and sauna.

Water Sports

The sheltered waters of the Firth of Forth host all kinds of water sports. Port Edgar Marina & Sailing School (www.edinburghleisure.co.uk; Shore Rd; ☉9am-4.30pm) offers a wide range of courses in sailing, canoeing and power-boating. You can also hire sailing dinghies for £15 to £20 an hour.

Horse Riding

There are many scenic bridleways suitable for horse riding in the countryside around Edinburgh, and a number of riding schools offer two- and three-hour treks as well as tuition, including Tower Farm Riding Stables (✆0131 664 3375; www.towerfarm.org; 85 Liberton Dr; per hr £26.50) in the south of the city.

Quirky Edinburgh

Edinburgh is full of unusual attractions and out-of-the-way corners that most visitors never see – even though they may be standing just a few metres away. Here are a few of the city's less-mainstream attractions.

Surgeons' Hall Museums
MUSEUM

(Map p52; www.museum.rcsed.ac.uk; Nicolson St; adult/child £5/3; ☉noon-4pm Mon-Fri, plus Sat & Sun Apr-Oct) The **History of Surgery Museum** is a fascinating look at surgery in Scotland from the 15th century – when barbers supplemented their income with bloodletting, amputations and other surgical procedures – to the present day. The highlight is the exhibit on **Burke and Hare**, which includes Burke's death mask and a pocketbook bound in his skin. The adjacent **Dental Collection**, with its wince-inducing collections of extraction tools, covers the history of dentistry. The **Pathology Museum** houses a gruesome but compelling 19th-century collection of diseased organs and massive tumours pickled in formaldehyde.

Gilmerton Cove
HISTORIC SITE

(www.gilmertoncove.org.uk; 16 Drum St; adult/child £5/4; ☉10am-7pm) While ghost tours of Edinburgh's underground vaults and haunted graveyards have become a mainstream attraction, few tourists have yet explored Gilmerton Cove. Hidden in the southern suburbs, the mysterious cove is a series of manmade subterranean caverns hacked out of the rock, their origin and function unknown. Advance booking essential through Rosslyn Tours (☑0131-440 3293; www.rosslyn tours.co.uk).

Mansfield Place Church CHURCH
(Map p46; www.mansfieldtraquair.org.uk; Mansfield Pl; ⊙1-4pm 2nd Sun of the month, 11am-1pm Sun-Thu during Edinburgh Festival Fringe) In complete contrast to the austerity of most of Edinburgh's religious buildings, this 19th-century, neo-Romanesque church at the foot of Broughton St contains a remarkable series of Renaissance-style frescos, which were painted in the 1890s by Irish-born artist Phoebe Anna Traquair (1852–1936). The murals have been restored and are on view to the public (check the website for any changes to viewing times).

FREE Museum on the Mound MUSEUM
(Map p52; www.museumonthemound.com; The Mound; ⊙10am-5pm Tue-Fri, 1-5pm Sat & Sun) Housed in the Bank of Scotland's splendid Georgian HQ, this museum is a treasure trove of gold coins, bullion chests, safes, banknotes, forgeries, cartoons and lots of fascinating old documents and photographs charting the history of Scotland's oldest bank.

FREE Edinburgh University Collection of Historic Musical Instruments MUSEUM
(Map p52; www.music.ed.ac.uk/euchmi; Reid Concert Hall, Teviot Pl; ⊙3-5pm Wed, 10am-1pm Sat year-round, 2-5pm Mon-Fri during Edinburgh Festival) Musicians will enjoy this collection, which contains more than 1000 instruments, ranging from a 400-year-old lute to a 1959 synthesiser.

THE RESURRECTION MEN

In 1505 Edinburgh's newly founded Royal College of Surgeons was officially allocated the corpse of one executed criminal per year for the purposes of dissection. But this was not nearly enough to satisfy the curiosity of the city's anatomists, and in the following centuries an illegal trade in dead bodies emerged, which reached its culmination in the early 19th century when the anatomy classes of famous surgeons such as Professor Robert Knox drew audiences of up to 500.

The readiest supply of corpses was to be found in the city's graveyards, especially Greyfriars. Grave robbers – who came to be known as 'resurrection men' – plundered newly buried coffins and sold the cadavers to the anatomists, who turned a blind eye to the source of their research material.

This gruesome trade led to a series of countermeasures, including the mort-safe – a metal cage that was placed over a coffin until the corpse had begun to decompose; you can see examples in Greyfriars Kirkyard and on level 5 of the National Museum of Scotland. Watchtowers, where a sexton, or relatives of the deceased, would keep watch over new graves, survive in St Cuthbert's and Duddingston kirkyards.

The notorious William Burke and William Hare, who kept a lodging house in Tanner's Close at the west end of the Grassmarket, took the body-snatching business a step further. When an elderly lodger died without paying his rent, Burke and Hare stole his body from the coffin and sold it to the famous Professor Knox. Seeing a lucrative business opportunity, they figured that rather than waiting for someone else to die, they could create their own supply of fresh cadavers by resorting to murder.

Burke and Hare preyed on the poor and weak of Edinburgh's Grassmarket, luring them back to Hare's lodging house, plying them with drink and then suffocating their victims. Between December 1827 and October 1828, they murdered at least 16 people, selling their bodies to Professor Knox. When the law finally caught up with them, Hare turned King's evidence and testified against Burke.

Burke was hanged outside St Giles Cathedral in January 1829 and, in an ironic twist, his body was given to the anatomy school for public dissection. His skeleton, and a wallet made from his flayed skin, are still on display in Surgeons' Hall Museums (p70).

It was as a result of the Burke and Hare case that the Anatomy Act of 1832 – regulating the supply of cadavers for dissection, and still in force today – was passed.

Burry Man
CULTURAL

If you're in Edinburgh on the first Friday of August, head west to the village of Queensferry to see the bizarre Burry Man. As part of the village gala day, a local man spends nine hours roaming the streets wearing a woolly suit, which has been laboriously covered from head to toe in big, green, prickly burrs. One glance at his costume – he looks like a child's drawing of a Martian, with added prickles – would make you think he's suffering a medieval punishment, but it's actually a great honour to be selected.

☞ Tours

Bus Tours

Open-topped buses leave from Waverley Bridge, outside the main train station, and offer hop-on, hop-off tours of the main sights, taking in New Town, the Grassmarket and the Royal Mile. They're a good way to get your bearings, although with a bus map and a Day Saver bus ticket (£3.50) you could do much the same thing (but without the commentary). Tours run daily, year-round, except for 24 and 25 December.

Tickets for the following three tours are valid for 24 hours.

City Sightseeing
BUS TOUR

(www.edinburghtour.com; adult/child £12/5) Bright-red, open-top buses depart every 20 minutes from Waverley Bridge.

MacTours
BUS TOUR

(www.edinburghtour.com; adult/child £12/5) Similar tours to City Sightseeing, but in a vintage bus.

Majestic Tour
BUS TOUR

(www.edinburghtour.com; adult/child £12/5) Runs every 30 minutes (every 20 minutes in July and August) from Waverley Bridge to the Royal Yacht *Britannia* at Ocean Terminal via the New Town, Royal Botanic Garden and Newhaven, returning via Leith Walk, Holyrood and the Royal Mile.

Walking Tours

There are plenty of organised walks around Edinburgh, many of them related to ghosts, murders and witches. For starting times of individual walks, check the websites.

Black Hart Storytellers
WALKING TOUR

(www.blackhart.uk.com; adult/concession £10/5) Not suitable for young children. The 'City of the Dead' tour of Greyfriars Kirkyard is probably the scariest of Edinburgh's 'ghost' tours. Many people have reported encounters with the 'McKenzie Poltergeist', the ghost of a 17th-century judge who persecuted the Covenanters, and now haunts their former prison in a corner of the kirkyard.

Cadies & Witchery Tours
WALKING TOUR

(Map p52; www.witcherytours.com; adult/child £8.50/6) The becloaked Adam Lyal (deceased) leads a 'Murder & Mystery' tour of the Old Town's darker corners. These tours are famous for their 'jumper-ooters' – actors who 'jump oot' when you least expect it.

Edinburgh Literary Pub Tour
WALKING TOUR

(www.edinburghliterarypubtour.co.uk; adult/student £10/8) An enlightening two-hour trawl through Edinburgh's literary history – and

---

LOCAL KNOWLEDGE

ADAM LYAL (DECEASED): GHOST

Adam Lyal (deceased) – aka Andrew Henderson – is the ghost of an Edinburgh highwayman who was hanged at the Tolbooth in 1811, and a tour leader with Cadies & Witchery Tours.

What are Edinburgh's spookiest places? The graveyards, though I would hesitate to recommend that anyone go to visit them at night! The spookiest by far is undoubtedly the Old Calton Burial Ground on Waterloo Rd, home to such departed notables as philosopher David Hume.

Where would a hard-working ghoul go to slake his thirst? We tend to do our carousing in some of the Old Town's marvellous little howffs (pubs), such as the Jolly Judge (p87), and we can often be found in the Bow Bar (p87).

Can you recommend any good off-the-beaten-track places? The wonderful thing about Edinburgh's Old Town is that so much of it is off the beaten track! One of my favourite venues is Whistle Binkie's (p89). It's quite hard to spot, being located under the actual street, with only a doorway on the pavement leading down, but it's well worth finding. Of course, there are other tours in Edinburgh, and the one I'd recommend to anyone is the Literary Pub Tour (p72). Booze, history and Scottish literature? It's a work of genius!

EDINBURGH'S HOGMANAY

Traditionally, the New Year has always been a more important celebration for Scots than Christmas. In towns, cities and villages all over the country, people fill the streets at midnight on 31 December to wish each other a Guid New Year and, yes, to knock back a dram or six to keep the cold at bay.

In 1993 Edinburgh's city council had the excellent idea of spicing up Hogmanay by organising some events, laying on some live music in Princes St and issuing an open invitation to the rest of the world. Most of them turned up, or so it seemed, and had such a good time that they told all their pals and came back again the next year.

Now Edinburgh's Hogmanay (www.edinburghshogmanay.com) is the biggest winter festival in Europe. Events run from 29 December to 1 January, and include a torchlight procession, huge street party and a New Year's Day triathlon. To get into the main party area in the city centre after 8pm on 31 December you'll need a ticket – book well in advance.

its associated howffs (pubs) – in the entertaining company of Messrs Clart and McBrain. One of the city's best walking tours.

Mercat Tours   WALKING TOUR
(Map p52; www.mercattours.com; adult/child £10/5) Mercat offers a wide range of fascinating tours, including history walks in the Old Town and Leith, 'Ghosts & Ghouls' tours and visits to haunted underground vaults.

Rebus Tours   WALKING TOUR
(www.rebustours.com; adult/student £10/9) Tours of the 'hidden Edinburgh' frequented by novelist Ian Rankin's fictional detective, John Rebus. Not recommended for children under 10.

Trainspotting Tours   WALKING TOUR
(www.leithwalks.co.uk; per person £8) A tour of locations from Irvine Welsh's notorious 1993 novel *Trainspotting,* delivered with wit and enthusiasm. Not suitable for kids.

✩ Festivals & Events

Edinburgh hosts an amazing number of festivals throughout the year, notably the Edinburgh International Festival, the Edinburgh Festival Fringe and the Military Tattoo, which are all held around the same time in August. Hogmanay, Scotland's New Year's celebrations, is also a peak party time.

April
**Edinburgh International
Science Festival**   SCIENCE FESTIVAL
(www.sciencefestival.co.uk) First held in 1987, it hosts a wide range of events, including talks, lectures, exhibitions, demonstrations, guided tours and interactive experiments designed to stimulate, inspire and challenge. From dinosaurs to ghosts to alien life forms,

there's something to interest everyone. The festival runs over two weeks.

May
Imaginate Festival   ARTS FESTIVAL
(www.imaginate.org.uk) This is Britain's biggest festival of performing arts for children, with events suitable for kids from three to 12. Groups from around the world perform classic tales like *Hansel and Gretel,* as well as new material written specially for children. The festival takes place annually in the last week of May.

June
**Scottish Real
Ale Festival**   FOOD & DRINK FESTIVAL
(www.scottishbeerfestival.org.uk) A celebration of all things fermented and yeasty, Scotland's biggest beer-fest gives you the opportunity to sample a wide range of traditionally brewed beers from Scotland and around the world. Froth-topped bliss. The festival is held over a weekend in June.

Royal Highland Show   AGRICULTURE SHOW
(www.royalhighlandshow.org; Royal Highland Centre) Scotland's hugely popular national agricultural show is a four-day feast of all things rural, with everything from showjumping and tractor driving to sheep shearing and falconry. Countless pens are filled with coiffed show cattle and pedicured prize ewes. The show is held over a long weekend (Thursday to Sunday) in late June.

**Edinburgh International
Film Festival**   FILM FESTIVAL
(Map p52; www.edfilmfest.org.uk) One of the original Edinburgh Festival trinity, having first been staged in 1947 along with the International Festival and the Fringe, the two-week

1. Festival City (p76)
Edinburgh is a frenzy of festivals in August, including the Edinburgh International Festival and Edinburgh Festival Fringe.

2. Six Nations Rugby Tournament (p23)
Scotland, England, Wales, Ireland, France and Italy battle it out in this prestigious tournament.

3. Burns Night (p23)
On 25 January, across the country and the world, Scots gather with haggis, pipes and whisky to celebrate the poet Robert Burns.

FESTIVAL CITY

August in Edinburgh sees a frenzy of festivals, with half-a-dozen world-class events running at the same time.

Edinburgh Festival Fringe

When the first Edinburgh Festival was held in 1947, there were eight theatre companies who didn't make it onto the main program. Undeterred, they grouped together and held their own mini-festival, on the fringe, and an Edinburgh institution was born. Today the Edinburgh Festival Fringe (Map p52; ✆0131-226 0026; www.edfringe.com; 180 High St) is the biggest festival of the performing arts anywhere in the world.

Since 1990 the Fringe has been dominated by stand-up comedy, but the sheer variety of shows on offer is staggering – everything from chainsaw juggling to performance poetry to Tibetan yak-milk gargling. So how do you decide what to see? There are daily reviews in the *Scotsman* newspaper – one good *Scotsman* review and a show sells out in hours – but the best recommendation is word of mouth. If you have the time, go to at least one unknown show – it may be crap, but at least you'll have your obligatory 'worst show I ever saw' story.

The big names play at megavenues organised by big agencies such as Assembly (Map p60; www.assemblyfestival.com) and the Gilded Balloon (www.gildedballoon.co.uk), and charge megaprices (£15 a ticket and up, with some famous comedians notoriously charging more than £30), but there are plenty of good shows in the £5 to £10 range and, best of all, lots of free stuff. **Fringe Sunday** – usually the second Sunday – is a smorgasbord of free performances, staged in the Meadows park to the south of the city centre.

The Fringe takes place over 3½ weeks, the last two weeks overlapping with the first two of the Edinburgh International Festival.

Edinburgh International Festival

First held in 1947 to mark a return to peace after the ordeal of WWII, the Edinburgh International Festival (✆0131-473 2099; www.eif.co.uk) is festooned with superlatives – the oldest, the biggest, the most famous, the best in the world. The original was a modest affair, but today hundreds of the world's top musicians and performers congregate in Edinburgh for three weeks of diverse and inspirational music, opera, theatre and dance.

The festival takes place over the three weeks ending on the first Saturday in September; the program is usually available from April. Tickets for popular events – especially music and opera – sell out quickly, so it's best to book as far in advance as possible. You can buy tickets in person at the Hub (✆01131-473 2000; www.thehub-edinburgh.com; Castlehill; admission free; ⏰ticket center 10am-5pm Mon-Sat), or by phone or internet.

Edinburgh Military Tattoo

August kicks off with the Edinburgh Military Tattoo (✆0131-225 1188; www.edintattoo.co.uk; Tattoo Office, 32 Market St), a spectacular display of military marching bands, massed pipes and drums, acrobats, cheerleaders and motorcycle display teams, all played out in front of the magnificent backdrop of the floodlit castle. Each show traditionally finishes with a lone piper, dramatically lit, playing a lament on the battlements. The Tattoo takes place over the first three weeks of August (from a Friday to a Saturday); there's one show at 9pm Monday to Friday and two (at 7.30pm and 10.30pm) on Saturday, but no performance on Sunday.

Edinburgh International Book Festival

Held in a little village of marquees in the middle of Charlotte Sq, the Edinburgh International Book Festival (✆0845 373 5888; www.edbookfest.co.uk) is a fun fortnight of talks, readings, debates, lectures, book signings and meet-the-author events, with a cafe-bar and tented bookshop thrown in. The festival lasts for two weeks (usually the first two weeks of the Edinburgh International Festival).

film festival is a major international event, serving as a showcase for new British and European films, and staging the European premieres of one or two Hollywood blockbusters.

July

Edinburgh International Jazz & Blues Festival   MUSIC FESTIVAL
(www.edinburghjazzfestival.com) Held annually since 1978, the Jazz & Blues Festival pulls in top talent from all over the world. The festival runs for nine days, beginning on a Friday, a week before the Fringe and Tattoo begin. The first weekend sees a Mardi Gras–style festival in the Grassmarket on Saturday, and a Sunday carnival on Princes St and Princes Street Gardens, with an afternoon of free, open-air music. On the Sunday there's a series of free concerts at the Ross Bandstand in Princes Street Gardens.

August

See the boxed text, for details of August's festivals.

December

Edinburgh's Hogmanay is the biggest winter festival in Europe.

Edinburgh's Christmas   ENTERTAINMENT
(www.edinburghschristmas.com) The youngest of the Scottish capital's festivals, first held in 2000, the Christmas bash includes a big street parade, a fairground and Ferris wheel, and an open-air ice rink in Princes Street Gardens. The celebrations are held over the three weeks before Christmas Day.

🛏 Sleeping

A boom in hotel building saw Edinburgh's tourist capacity swell significantly since 2000, but you can guarantee the city will still be packed to the gills during the festival period (August) and over Hogmanay (New Year). If you want a room during these periods, book as far in advance as possible – a year ahead if possible. In general, it's best to book at least a few months ahead for accommodation at Easter and from mid-May to mid-September.

Hotels and hostels are found throughout the Old and New Towns; midrange B&Bs and guest houses are concentrated outside the centre in the suburbs of Tollcross, Bruntsfield, Newington and Pilrig.

If you're driving, don't even think about staying in the city centre unless your hotel has its own private car park – parking in the centre is a nightmare. Instead, look for somewhere in a suburb like Newington, where there's a chance of finding free on-street parking (even then, don't bet on getting a parking space outside the front door). Alternatively, stay outside the city and travel in by bus or train.

Edinburgh accommodation is slightly more expensive than the rest of Scotland, so the price breakdown here is as follows: – budget is less than £60, midrange £60 to £150, and top end is more than £150, based on the cost of a double room with bed and breakfast.

Accommodation Agencies

If you arrive in Edinburgh without a room, the Edinburgh Information Centre (p94) booking service will try to find a room to suit you (and will charge a £5 fee if successful). If you have the time, pick up the tourist office's accommodation brochure and ring around yourself.

You can also try VisitScotland's **booking hotline** (☎0845 859 1006), which has a £3 surcharge; or search for accommodation on the Edinburgh & Lothians Tourist Board (p93) website.

Old Town

Most of the interesting accommodation in the Old Town is either backpacker hostels or expensive hotels. For midrange options you'll have to resort to chain hotels – check the websites of Travelodge, Ibis etc.

TOP CHOICE Hotel Missoni   BOUTIQUE HOTEL £££
(Map p52; ☎0131-220 6666; www.hotelmissoni.com; 1 George IV Bridge; r £90-225; 📶) The Italian fashion house has established a style icon in the heart of the medieval Old Town with this bold statement of a hotel – modernistic architecture, black-and-white decor with well-judged splashes of colour, impeccably mannered staff and, most importantly, very comfortable bedrooms and bathrooms with lots of nice little touches, from fresh milk in the minibar to plush bathrobes.

TOP CHOICE Witchery by the Castle   B&B £££
(Map p52; ☎0131-225 5613; www.thewitchery.com; Castlehill, Royal Mile; ste £325-350) Set in a 16th-century Old Town house in the shadow of Edinburgh Castle, the Witchery's eight lavish Gothic suites are extravagantly furnished with antiques, oak panelling, tapestries, open fires, four-poster beds and roll-top baths, and supplied with flowers, chocolates and complimentary champagne.

Overwhelmingly popular – you'll have to book several months in advance to be sure of getting a room.

Knight Residence
APARTMENTS £££
(Map p52; ✆0131-622 8120; www.theknight residence.co.uk; 12 Lauriston St; d/2-bedroom apt £250/437; ☎) Works by contemporary artists adorn these modern one- and two-bedroom apartments (available by the night; the latter sleep up to four adults and one child), each with fully equipped kitchen and comfortable lounge with cable TV, video and stereo. It has a good central location in a quiet street only a few minutes' walk from the Grassmarket.

Ten Hill Place
HOTEL ££
(Map p52; ✆0131-662 2080; www.tenhillplace .com; 10 Hill Pl; r from £110; ☎) This attractive modern hotel offers good-value accommodation close to the city centre. The standard bedrooms are comfortable and stylish with a sober but sophisticated colour scheme in rich browns, purples and tweedy greens, and appealing modern bathrooms. For a special weekend, ask for one of the four 'skyline' rooms on the top floor, with king-size beds and panoramic views of Salisbury Crags.

Smart City Hostel
HOSTEL £
(Map p52; ✆0870 892 3000; www.smartcityhos tels.com; 50 Blackfriars St; dm from £22, tr £107; @☎) A big (620 beds), bright, modern hostel that feels more like a hotel, with a convivial cafe where you can buy breakfast, and mod cons such as keycard access and secure charging stations for mobile phones, MP3 players and laptops. Lockers in every room, a huge bar and a central location just off the Royal Mile make this a favourite place to stay for the young, party-mad crowd – don't expect a quiet night!

Castle Rock Hostel
HOSTEL £
(Map p52; ✆0131-225 9666; www.scotlands-top hostels.com; 15 Johnston Tce; dm/d £22/50; @☎) With its bright, spacious, single-sex dorms, superb views and friendly staff, the 200-bed Castle Rock has lots to like. It has a great location – the only way to get closer to the castle would be to pitch a tent on the esplanade – a games room, reading lounge and big-screen video nights.

Budget Backpackers
HOSTEL £
(Map p52; ✆0131-226 6351; www.budgetback packers.com; 9 Cowgate; dm from £16, tw £54; @) This fun spot piles on the extras, with bike

storage, pool tables, laundry and a colourful chill-out lounge. You'll pay a little more for four-bunk dorms, but larger dorms are great value. The only downside is that prices increase at weekends, but otherwise a brilliant spot to doss.

Edinburgh Metro
HOSTEL £
(SYHA; Map p52; ✆0131-556 8718; 11/2 Robertson's Close, Cowgate; s £42; ☼Jul & Aug) Summer only; all single rooms in student accommodation.

Royal Mile Backpackers
HOSTEL £
(Map p52; ✆0131-557 6120; www.royalmileback packers.com; 105 High St; dm £25; ☎) Small, cosy and quaint.

New Town & Around

TOP CHOICE Sheridan Guest House
B&B ££
(✆0131-554 4107; www.sheridanedinburgh.co.uk; 1 Bonnington Tce, Newhaven Rd; s/d from £55/70; ☎) Flowerpots filled with colourful blooms line the steps of this little haven hidden away to the north of the New Town. The eight bedrooms (all en suite) blend crisp colours with contemporary furniture, stylish lighting and colourful paintings, which complement the house's clean-cut Georgian lines, while the breakfast menu adds omelettes, pancakes with maple syrup, and scrambled eggs with smoked salmon to the usual offerings. Take bus 11 from the city centre.

One Royal Circus
B&B £££
(Map p60; ✆0131-625 6669; www.oneroyalcircus. com; 1 Royal Circus; r £180-260; ☎) Live the New Town dream at this incredibly chic Georgian mansion where genuine antiques and parquet floors sit comfortably alongside slate bathrooms and Philippe Starck furniture. Bedrooms are kitted out with Egyptian cotton sheets, iPod docks and Arran Aromatics toiletries, and there are foosball and pool tables in the drawing room.

Gerald's Place
B&B ££
(Map p60; ✆0131-558 7017; www.geraldsplace. com; 21b Abercromby Pl; d £119-149; @☎) Gerald is an unfailingly charming and helpful host, and his lovely Georgian garden flat (just two guest bedrooms) has a great location across from a peaceful park, an easy stroll from the city centre.

Tigerlily
BOUTIQUE HOTEL £££
(Map p60; ✆0131-225 5005; www.tigerlilyedin burgh.co.uk; 125 George St; r from £175; ☎) Georgian meets gorgeous at this glamorous, glittering boutique hotel (complete with its own

nightclub) decked out in mirror mosaics, beaded curtains, swirling Timorous Beasties textiles and wall coverings and atmospheric pink uplighting. Book the Georgian Suite (from £310) for a truly special romantic getaway.

B+B Edinburgh
HOTEL **££**

(Map p46; ☏0131-225 5084; www.bb-edinburgh. com; 3 Rothesay Tce; s/d £99/140; ☏) Built in 1883 as a grand home for the proprietor of the *Scotsman* newspaper, this Victorian extravaganza of carved oak, parquet floors, stained glass and elaborate fireplaces was given a designer makeover in 2011 to create a striking contemporary hotel. Rooms on the 2nd floor are the most spacious, but the smaller top-floor rooms enjoy the finest views – those at the front can see Edinburgh Castle, those at the back look across the Water of Leith to the Firth of Forth.

Rick's
BOUTIQUE HOTEL **£££**

(Map p60; ☏0131-622 7800; www.ricksedinburgh .co.uk; 55a Frederick St; r from £175; ☏) One of the first boutique hotels to appear in Edinburgh, Rick's offers sharp styling and a laidback atmosphere, though the furniture is beginning to show its age. The bedrooms boast walnut headboards and designer fabrics, with fluffy bathrobes, well-stocked minibars and Molton Brown toiletries.

Glasshouse
HOTEL **£££**

(Map p60; ☏0131-525 8200; www.theetoncollec tion.com; 2 Greenside Pl; r/ste from £165/245; P☏) A palace of cutting-edge design perched atop the Omni Centre at the foot of Calton Hill, and entered through the preserved facade of a 19th-century church, the Glasshouse sports luxury rooms with floor-to-ceiling windows, leather sofas, marble bathrooms and a rooftop garden.

Dene Guest House
B&B **££**

(Map p46; ☏0131-556 2700; www.deneguesthouse .com; 7 Eyre Pl; per person £25-50) The Dene is a friendly and informal place, set in a charming Georgian town house, with a welcoming owner and spacious bedrooms. The inexpensive single rooms make it ideal for solo travellers; children under 10 staying in their parents' room pay half price.

West End Hostel
HOSTEL **£**

(Map p46; ☏0131-202 6107; www.hosteledinburgh .co.uk; 3 Clifton Tce; dm £18-22; ☏) This relatively new hostel is clean and bright, with six- to 16-bed dorms (including female-only ones),

a coffee lounge with pool table, and a pleasant garden terrace. Handy for train travellers (Haymarket station is across the road), and just 10 minutes' walk from Princes St.

Belford Hostel
HOSTEL **£**

(Map p46; ☏0131-220 2200; www.hoppo.com; 6/8 Douglas Gardens; dm £14-29, d £50-70; @☏) An unusual hostel housed in a converted church. Although some people complain about noise – there are only thin partitions between dorms, and no ceilings – it's cheerful and well run with good facilities. This hostel is about 20 minutes' walk west of Waverley train station. If you're arriving by train from Glasgow or the north, get off at Haymarket station, which is much closer.

Frederick House Hotel
HOTEL **££**

(Map p60; ☏0131-226 1999; www.frederickhouse hotel.com; 42 Frederick St; s/d £110/130; ☏) This well-positioned, good-value hotel has roomy double beds and large baths to soak away the day's walking aches. It's also one of few options in this price range that has a lift, which is ideal is you've got lots of baggage. Breakfast is served in the cafe across the street.

South Edinburgh

There are lots of guest houses in the South Edinburgh suburbs of Tollcross, Morningside, Marchmont and Newington, especially on and around Minto St and Mayfield Gardens (the continuation of North Bridge and Nicolson St) in Newington. This is the main traffic artery from the south and a main bus route into the city centre.

TOP CHOICE Southside Guest House
B&B **££**

(Map p46; ☏0131-668 4422; www.southsideguest house.co.uk; 8 Newington Rd; s/d £70/90; ☏) Though set in a typical Victorian terrace, the Southside transcends the traditional guesthouse category and feels more like a modern boutique hotel. Its eight stylish rooms ooze interior design, standing out from other Newington B&Bs through the clever use of bold colours and modern furniture.

TOP CHOICE Prestonfield
House Hotel
BOUTIQUE HOTEL **£££**

(☏0131-668 3346; www.prestonfield.com; Priestfield Rd; r/ste from £221/274; P☏) If the blonde wood, brown leather and brushed steel of modern boutique hotels leave you cold, then this is the place for you. A 17th-century mansion set in 8 hectares of parkland (complete with peacocks and Highland cattle),

Prestonfield House is draped in damask, packed with antiques and decorated in red, black and gold – look out for original tapestries, 17th-century embossed-leather panels, and £500-a-roll hand-painted wallpaper. The hotel's rooms are supplied with all mod cons, including Bose sound systems, DVD players and plasma-screen TVs. The hotel is southeast of the city centre, east of Dalkeith Rd.

45 Gilmour Rd
B&B ££

(☎0131-667 3536; www.edinburghbedbreakfast.com; 45 Gilmour Rd; s/d £70/140) A peaceful setting, large garden and friendly owners contribute to the appeal of this Victorian terraced house, which overlooks the local bowling green. The decor is a blend of 19th- and 20th-century influences, with bold Victorian reds, pine floors and period fireplace in the lounge, a rocking horse and art-nouveau lamp in the hallway, and a 1930s vibe in the three spacious bedrooms. Located 1 mile southeast of the city centre.

Aonach Mor Guest House
B&B ££

(☎0131-667 8694; www.aonachmor.com; 14 Kilmaurs Tce; r per person £33-70; @🤶) This elegant Victorian terraced house is located on a quiet back street and has seven bedrooms, beautifully decorated, with many original period features. Our favourite is the four-poster bedroom with polished mahogany furniture and period fireplace. Located 1 mile southeast of the city centre.

Sherwood Guest House
B&B ££

(Map p46; ☎0131-667 1200; www.sherwood-edinburgh.com; 42 Minto St; s £65-85, d £75-100; P🤶) One of the most attractive guest houses on Minto St's B&B strip, the Sherwood is a refurbished Georgian terraced house decked out with hanging baskets and shrubs. Inside are six en suite rooms that combine Regency-style striped wallpaper with modern fabrics and pine furniture.

Town House
B&B ££

(Map p46; ☎0131-229 1985; www.thetownhouse.com; 65 Gilmore Pl; per person £45-60; P🤶) The five-room Town House is a plush little place, offering the sort of quality and comfort you might expect from a much larger and more expensive hotel. It's an elegant Victorian terraced house with big bay windows, spacious bedrooms (all en suite) and a breakfast menu that includes salmon fishcakes and kippers alongside the more usual offerings.

Amaryllis Guest House
B&B ££

(Map p46; ☎0131-229 3293; www.amaryllisguesthouse.com; 21 Upper Gilmore Pl; s/d £60/80; 🤶) The Amaryllis is a cute little Georgian town house on a quiet back street. There are five bedrooms, including a spacious family room that can take two adults and up to four kids. Princes St is only 10 minutes' walk away.

Argyle Backpackers
HOSTEL £

(Map p46; ☎0131-667 9991; www.argyle-backpackers.co.uk; 14 Argyle Pl; dm £17-22, d & tw £45-65; 🤶) The Argyle, spread across three adjacent terraced houses, is a quiet and relaxed hostel offering double and twin rooms as well as four- to 10-bed dorms (mixed sex). There is a comfortable TV lounge, an attractive little conservatory and a pleasant walled garden at the back where you can sit outside in summer.

Pollock Halls of Residence
STUDENT ACCOMMODATION ££

(☎0131-651 2007; www.edinburghfirst.co.uk; 18 Holyrood Park Rd; s/tw from £45/85; ☺Jun-Aug; P) This is a modern student complex belonging to the University of Edinburgh, with 2000 rooms (500 with en suite bathroom). It's busy and often noisy, but close to the city centre, with Arthur's Seat as a backdrop. Available during summer vacation only (see website for dates).

Salisbury Hotel
HOTEL ££

(Map p46; ☎0131-667 1264; www.the-salisbury.co.uk; 45 Salisbury Rd; s/d/f from £80/115/135; P🤶) Boutique-style guest house set in a quiet, comfortable Georgian villa with large garden.

Menzies Guest House
B&B £

(Map p46; ☎0131-229 4629; www.menzies-guesthouse.co.uk; 33 Leamington Tce; per person £25-50) Clean, friendly and well-run place with seven high-ceilinged Victorian rooms spread over three floors. The cheaper rooms, with shared bathroom, are small but offer excellent value.

Kenvie Guest House
B&B ££

(☎0131-668 1964; www.kenvie.co.uk; 16 Kilmaurs Rd; r per person £30-45; 🤶) Top value, warm welcome. Situated in a quiet side street but close to a main bus route.

Leith Walk & Pilrig St

Northeast of the New Town, the area around Leith Walk and Pilrig St has lots of guest houses, all within about a mile of the centre. To get there, take bus 11 from Princes St.

Millers 64
B&B ££

(📞0131-454 3666; www.millers64.com; 64 Pilrig St; s from £80, d £90-150; 🛜) Luxury textiles, colourful cushions, stylish bathrooms and fresh flowers added to a warm Edinburgh welcome make this Victorian town house a highly desirable address. There are just two bedrooms (and a minimum three-night stay during festival periods) so book well in advance.

Wallace's Arthouse
B&B ££

(📞0131-538 3320; www.wallacesarthousescotland .com; 41/4 Constitution St; s/d £95/105; 🛜) This Georgian flat, housed in the neoclassical Leith Assembly Rooms (a grade A listed building), offers B&B in two beautifully nostalgic bedrooms, styled by former fashion designer Wallace, who comes as part of the package – your charming host and breakfast chef is an unfailing source of colourful anecdote and local knowledge.

Ardmor House
B&B ££

(📞0131-554 4944; www.ardmorhouse.com; 74 Pilrig St; s £60-85, d £85-170; 🛜) The 'gay-owned, straight-friendly' Ardmor is a stylishly renovated Victorian house with five en suite bedrooms, and all those little touches that make a place special – an open fire, thick towels, crisp white bedlinen and free newspapers at breakfast.

Sandaig Guest House
B&B ££

(📞0131-554 7357; www.sandaigguesthouse.co.uk; 5 East Hermitage Pl, Leith Links; s/d £90/110; 🛜) From the welcoming tot of whisky liqueur to the cheerful goodbye wave from the doorstep, the owners of the Sandaig know a thing or two about hospitality. There are plenty of other things that make staying at the Sandaig a pleasure, from the boldly coloured decor to the crisp cotton sheets, big fluffy bath towels and refreshing power showers, and a breakfast menu that includes porridge with cream and maple syrup.

Edinburgh Central Youth Hostel
HOSTEL £

(SYHA; Map p46; 📞0131-524 2090; www.edin burghcentral.org; 9 Haddington Pl, Leith Walk; dm £25, s/tw £49/74; @🛜) This modern, purpose-built hostel, about a half mile north of Waverley train station, is a big (300 beds), flashy, five-star establishment with its own cafe-bistro as well as self-catering kitchen, smart and comfortable eight-bed dorms and private rooms, and mod cons including keycard entry and plasma- screen TVs.

Balmoral Guest House
B&B ££

(📞0131-554 1857; www.balmoralguesthouse.co.uk; 32 Pilrig St; r per person £45-65; 🛜) A deservedly popular B&B set in an elegant, flower-bedecked, Victorian terraced house dating from 1856. The owners have a good eye for antiques (including, unusually, antique radios), and period furniture gives the bedrooms a pleasantly retro atmosphere.

Outside the Centre

Mortonhall Caravan Park
CAMPGROUND £

(📞0131-664 1533; www.meadowhead.co.uk; 38 Mortonhall Gate, Frogston Rd East; tent site incl 1 car & 2 people £20-26) Located in attractive parkland 5 miles southeast of the centre, Mortonhall has an on-site shop, bar and restaurant. Note: the one-person tent rate (£11.50) is not available during the Edinburgh International Festival. Take bus 11 from Princes St (westbound).

✗ Eating

Edinburgh has more restaurants per head of population than any other UK city. Eating out has become a commonplace event rather than something reserved for special occasions, and the choice of eateries ranges from stylish but inexpensive bistros and cafes to Michelin-starred gourmet restaurants.

In addition most pubs also serve food, offering either bar meals or a more formal restaurant or both, but be aware that pubs without a Children's Certificate are not allowed to serve children under the age of 14.

If you want more listings than we can provide here, the excellent *Edinburgh & Glasgow Eating & Drinking Guide* (www .list.co.uk/food-and-drink), published annually by *List* magazine, contains reviews of around 800 restaurants, cafes and bars.

Old Town & Around

TOP CHOICE Tower
SCOTTISH £££

(Map p52; 📞0131-225 3003; www.tower-restaurant .com; National Museum of Scotland, Chambers St; mains £16-30; ⏲noon-11pm) Chic and sleek, with a great view of the castle, Tower is perched in a turret atop the National Museum of Scotland building. A star-studded guest list of celebrities has enjoyed its menu of quality Scottish food, simply prepared – try half a dozen oysters followed by roast partridge with chestnut stuffing. A two-/ three-course pretheatre menu (£16/22) is available from 5pm to 6.30pm, and afternoon tea (£16) is served from 3pm to 5pm.

TOP CHOICE Ondine   SEAFOOD £££

(Map p52; ☑0131-226 1888; www.ondinerestaurant
.co.uk; 2 George IV Bridge; mains £15-25; ☉lunch &
dinner) Ondine is one of Edinburgh's finest
seafood restaurants, with a menu based on
sustainably sourced fish. Take an octopus-
inspired seat at the curved Crustacean Bar
and tuck into oysters Kilpatrick, lobster
thermidor, a roast shellfish platter or just
good old haddock and chips (with minted
pea purée, just to keep things posh). The
two-course lunch (noon to 2.30pm) and
pretheatre (5pm to 6.30pm) menu costs £17.

TOP CHOICE Porto & Fi   CAFE £

(Map p52; www.portofi.com; 9 North Bank St; mains
£4-8; ☉10am-11pm Mon-Sat, to 9pm Sun) With its
designer decor, a prime location overlooking
The Mound, and a suprisingly sophisticated
menu built around quality Scottish produce,
this cafe is hard to beat for a breakfast of
eggs Benedict or Stornoway black pudding
(served till noon, all day Sunday), or lunch of
smoked salmon cannelloni or roast fig and
asparagus salad.

TOP CHOICE Castle Terrace   MODERN SCOTTISH £££

(Map p52; ☑0131-229 1222; www.castleterracer
estaurant.com; 33-35 Castle Tce; mains £25-28,
3-course lunch £24; ☉lunch & dinner Tue-Sat) It
was little more than a year after opening
in 2010 that TV chef Tom Kitchin's second
Edinburgh restaurant was awarded a Michelin star. The menu is seasonal and applies
sharply whetted Parisian skills to the finest
of local produce, be it Ayrshire pork, Aberdeenshire lamb or Newhaven crab – even
the cheese in the sauces is Scottish.

Leven's   FUSION ££

(Map p46; ☑0131-229 8988; 30-32 Leven St; mains
£12-19; ☉lunch & dinner Sun-Thu, noon-10.30pm Fri
& Sat) From the spectacular chandeliers and
slowly pulsing blue/purple mood lighting to
the designer colour palette and Villeroy &
Boch tableware, everything about this restaurant oozes style. The food lives up to the
surroundings, with clever and unexpected
combinations of flavours, colours and tex-
tures in dishes such as beef sirloin Panang
curry, with peanuts and lime leaves.

BEST VALUE BISTROS

Urban Angel (Map p60; ☑0131-225 6215; www.urban-angel.co.uk; 121 Hanover St; mains
£8-14; ☉9am-10pm Mon-Sat, 10am-5pm Sun; ☑⊞) A wholesome deli that puts the emphasis on fair-trade, organic and locally sourced produce, Urban Angel is also a delightfully
informal cafe-bistro that serves all-day brunch (porridge with honey, French toast, eggs
Benedict), tapas and a wide range of light, snacky meals.

First Coast (Map p46; ☑0131-313 4404; www.first-coast.co.uk; 99-101 Dalry Rd; mains £10-
19; ☉lunch & dinner Mon-Sat) Our favourite neighbourhood bistro, First Coast has a striking main dining area with pale-grey wood panelling, stripped stone walls and Victorian
cornices, and a short and simple menu offering hearty comfort food such as Thai mari-
nated chicken salad, or glazed ham hough with mustard mash. At lunch, and from 5pm
to 6.30pm, you can have an excellent two-course meal for £12.

Daniel's Bistro (☑0131-553 5933; www.daniels-bistro.co.uk; 88 Commercial St; mains £8-15;
☉10am-10pm) This popular Leith bistro combines top Scottish and French produce with
Gallic know-how to create a wide range of delicious dishes. The Provençal fish soup is
excellent, and main courses range from boeuf bourguignon to cassoulet. A seriously
filling two-course business lunch is £8.75.

La P'tite Folie (Map p60; ☑0131-225 7983; www.laptitefolie.co.uk; 61 Frederick St; mains
£16-25; ☉lunch & dinner) This is a delightful little restaurant with a Breton owner whose
menu includes French classics – onion soup, moules marinières – alongside steaks,
seafood and a range of plats du jour. The two-course lunch is a bargain at £9.95.

Petit Paris (Map p52; ☑0131-226 2442; www.petitparis-restaurant.co.uk; 38-40 Grassmarket;
mains £14-18; ☉noon-3pm & 5.30-11pm, closed Mon Oct-Mar) Like the name says, this is a
little piece of Paris, complete with checked tablecloths, friendly waiters and good-value
grub – the moules-frîtes (mussels and chips) are excellent. There's a lunch/pretheatre
deal (noon to 3pm and 5.30pm to 7pm) offering the plat du jour and a coffee for £7.90;
add a starter and it's £11.90.

TOP VEGETARIAN RESTAURANTS

Many Edinburgh restaurants offer vegetarian options on the menu, some good, some bad, some indifferent. The places listed here are all 100% veggie and fall into the 'good' category.

David Bann (Map p52; ☎0131-556 5888; www.davidbann.com; 56-58 St Mary's St; mains £9-13; ☺noon-10pm Mon-Fri, 11am-10pm Sat & Sun; ✔) If you want to convince a carnivorous friend that cuisine à la veg can be as tasty and inventive as a meat-muncher's menu, take them to David Bann's stylish restaurant – dishes such as beetroot, apple and Dunsyre blue cheese pudding, and Thai fritter of spiced broccoli and smoked tofu, are guaranteed to win converts.

Ann Purna (Map p46; ☎0131-662 1807; www.annpurna-edinburgh.co.uk; 45 St Patrick Sq; mains £6-9; ☺lunch & dinner; ✔) This little gem of an Indian restaurant serves exclusively vegetarian dishes from southern India, delivered with a smile by the family team who run the place. If you're new to this kind of food, opt for a thali (£16) – a self-contained platter that has about half a dozen different dishes, including a dessert. You can get a light lunch for £6 or £7.

Kalpna (Map p52; ☎0131-667 9890; www.kalpnarestaurant.com; 2-3 St Patrick Sq; mains £6-11; ☺lunch & dinner Mon-Sat year-round, plus dinner Sun May-Sep; ✔) A long-standing Edinburgh favourite, Kalpna is one of the best Indian restaurants in the country, vegetarian or otherwise. The cuisine is mostly Gujarati, with a smattering of dishes from other parts of India. The all-you-can-eat lunch buffet (£8) is superb value.

Engine Shed (Map p46; www.theengineshed.org; 19 St Leonard's Lane; mains £4-7; ☺10am-4pm Mon-Sat; ✔🖶) This fair-trade, organic vegetarian cafe is an ideal spot for a healthy lunch, or a cuppa and a bakery-fresh scone after climbing Arthur's Seat. It's been set up to provide employment and training for special-needs adults, and as well as having its own bakery it also makes its own tofu, which is used plentifully in its tasty curries.

Henderson's (Map p60; ☎0131-225 2131; www.hendersonsofedinburgh.co.uk; 94 Hanover St; mains £6-8; ☺8am-10pm Mon-Sat year-round, 11am-4pm Sun Aug & Dec; ✔) Established in 1962, Henderson's is the grandmother of Edinburgh's vegetarian restaurants. The food is mostly organic and guaranteed GM-free, and special dietary requirements can be catered for. The place still has a 1970s feel to it (in a good way), and the daily salads and hot dishes are as popular as ever. Two-course set lunch is £8.95.

Mums CAFE £
(Map p52; www.monstermashcafe.co.uk; 4a Forrest Rd; mains £6-9; ☺9am-10pm Mon-Sat, 10am-10pm Sun) This nostalgia-fuelled cafe serves up classic British comfort food that wouldn't look out of place on a 1950s menu – bacon and eggs, bangers and mash, shepherd's pie, fish and chips. But there's a twist – the food is all top-quality nosh freshly prepared from local produce, including Crombie's gourmet sausages. There's even a wine list, though we prefer the real ales and Scottish-brewed cider.

Passepartout INTERNATIONAL £
(Map p52; ☎0131-629 0252; 7 Old Fishmarket Close; platters for two £12-13) Hidden down a steep cobbled alley off the Royal Mile, with three indoor seating areas (including a 'cinema room' screening old movies) and a lovely little sun trap of an outdoor terrace, this French-owned, Indian-inspired bistro offers an eclectic menu of dishes – from lobster with mussels to chickpea curry to kebabs – served as sharing platters for two, which you eat with your fingers. Good fun, and good value.

Kanpai JAPANESE ££
(Map p52; ☎0131-228 1602; www.kanpaisushi.co.uk; 8-10 Grindlay St; mains £8-14, sushi per piece £4-7; ☺lunch & dinner Tue-Sun) The latest sushi restaurant to open in Edinburgh goes straight to the top of the charts with its minimalist interior, fresh, top-quality fish and elegantly presented dishes – the squid tempura comes in a delicate woven basket, while the sashimi combo is presented as a flower arrangement in an ice-filled stoneware bowl.

Mosque Kitchen   INDIAN £
(Map p52; www.mosquekitchen.com; 31 Nicolson Sq; mains £3-6; ⊙11.30am-12.50pm & 1.50-11pm; ☑) Sophisticated it ain't - expect shared tables and disposable plates - but this is the place to go for cheap, authentic and delicious homemade curries, kebabs, pakoras and naan bread washed down with lassi or mango juice. Caters to Edinburgh's Central Mosque, but welcomes all - local students have taken to it big time. No alcohol.

Maxie's Bistro   BISTRO ££
(Map p52; ☑0131-226 7770; www.maxiesbistro.com; 5b Johnston Tce; mains £8-18; ⊙11am-11pm) Maxie's candlelit bistro, with its cushion-lined nooks set amid stone walls and wooden beams, is a pleasant enough setting for a cosy dinner, but at summer lunchtimes people queue for the outdoor tables on the terrace overlooking Victoria St. The food is dependable - Maxie's

has been in the food business for more than 20 years - ranging from pastas, steaks and stir-fries to seafood platters and daily specials. Best to book, especially in summer.

Mother India   INDIAN ££
(Map p52; ☑0131-524 9801; www.motherindiaglas gow.co.uk; 3-5 Infirmary St; tapas £4-5; ⊙lunch & dinner Mon-Thu, noon-10pm Fri-Sun) A simple concept pioneered in Glasgow has captured hearts and minds - and stomachs - in Edinburgh: Indian food served in tapas-size portions, so that you can sample a greater variety of different dishes without busting your gut. Hugely popular, so book a table to avoid disappointment.

Pancho Villa's   MEXICAN ££
(Map p52; ☑0131-557 4416; www.panchovillas. co.uk; 240 Canongate; mains £11-13; ⊙lunch & dinner Mon-Fri, noon-10pm Sat, 5-10pm Sun; ☑) With a Mexican-born owner and lots of Latin

---

TOP FIVE EDINBURGH CAFES

Cafe culture is firmly ensconced in Edinburgh, and it is as easy to get your daily caffeine fix here as it is in New York or Paris. Most cafes offer some kind of food, from cakes and sandwiches to full-on meals.

Loudon's Café & Bakery (Map p46; www.loudons-cafe.co.uk; 94b Fountainbridge; mains £3-7; ⊙8am-6pm Mon-Fri, 9am-6pm Sat & Sun; ☎❧) A cafe that bakes its own organic bread and cakes on the premises, ethically sourced coffee, daily and weekend newspapers scattered about, even some outdoor tables - what's not to like? All-day brunch (9am to 3pm) served at weekends includes eggs Benedict, warm spiced quinoa with dried fruit, and specials such as blueberry pancakes with fruit salad.

Circle Cafe (www.thecirclecafe.com; 1 Brandon Tce; mains £6-9; ⊙8.30am-4.30pm Mon-Sat, 9am-4.30pm Sun) A great place for breakfast or a good-value lunch, Circle is a bustling neighbourhood cafe serving great coffee and cakes, and fresh, tasty lunch dishes ranging from chunky, home-baked quiches to smoked haddock fishcakes.

Glass & Thompson (Map p60; 2 Dundas St; mains £7-11; ⊙8am-6pm Mon-Sat, 10.30am-4.30pm Sun) Grab a table in this spick-and-span New Town deli and sip a double espresso as you ogle the cheeses in the cold counter or watch the world go by through the floor-to-ceiling windows (the cafe is featured in the novels of Alexander McCall Smith). Munchies include tasty platters such as dolmades and falafel, or Parma ham and parmesan.

Valvona & Crolla Caffé Bar (www.valvonacrolla.co.uk; 19 Elm Row, Leith Walk; mains £10-16; ⊙8.30am-5.30pm Mon-Thu, 8am-6pm Fri & Sat, 10.30am-3.30pm Sun; ☎) Try breakfast (served till 11.30am) with an Italian flavour - full *paesano* (meat) or *verdure* (veggie) fry-ups, or deliciously light and crisp *panettone* in *carrozza* (sweet brioche dipped in egg and fried) - or choose from almond croissants, muesli, yogurt and fruit, freshly squeezed orange juice and perfect Italian coffee. There's also a tasty lunch menu (noon to 3.30pm) of classic Italian dishes.

Elephant House (Map p52; www.elephanthouse.biz; 21 George IV Bridge; mains £6-9; ⊙8am-10pm Mon-Fri, 9am-10pm Sat & Sun; ☎) Here you'll find counters at the front, tables and views of the castle at the back (where JK Rowling famously wrote in the days before Harry Potter was published), and little effigies and images of elephants everywhere. Excellent coffee and tasty, homemade food - pizzas, quiches, pies, sandwiches and cakes - at reasonable prices.

American and Spanish staff, it's not surprising that this colourful and lively restaurant is one of the most authentic-feeling Mexican places in town. The dinner menu includes delicious steak fajitas and great vegetarian spinach enchiladas. It's often busy, so book ahead.

Amber
SCOTTISH **££**

(Map p52; ☑0131-477 8477; www.amber-restaurant.co.uk; 354 Castlehill; mains £10-25; ⊙lunch daily, dinner Tue-Sat) You've got to love a place where the waiter greets you with the words, 'My name is Craig, and I'll be your whisky adviser for this evening'. Located in the Scotch Whisky Experience (p53), this whisky-themed restaurant manages to avoid the tourist clichés and creates genuinely interesting and flavoursome dishes such as mussels in a cream, leek and Islay whisky sauce, and sirloin steak with thyme-roasted potatoes and whisky butter.

New Town

TOP CHOICE The Dogs
BRITISH **££**

(Map p60; ☑0131-220 1208; www.thedogsonline.co.uk; 110 Hanover St; mains £9-13; ⊙noon-4pm & 5-10pm) One of the coolest tables in town, this bistro-style place uses cheaper cuts of meat and less-well-known, more-sustainable species of fish to create hearty, no-nonsense dishes such as lamb sweetbreads on toast, baked coley with *skirlie* (fried oatmeal and onion), and devilled liver with bacon and onions.

Café Marlayne
FRENCH **££**

(Map p60; ☑0131-226 2230; www.cafemarlayne.com; 76 Thistle St; mains £12-15; ⊙noon-10pm) All weathered wood and candlelit tables, Café Marlayne is a cosy nook offering French farmhouse cooking – *brandade de morue* (salt cod) with green salad, slow-roast rack of lamb, *boudin noir* (black pudding) with scallops and sautéed potato – at very reasonable prices. Booking recommended.

Escargot Bleu
FRENCH **££**

(Map p46; ☑0131-556 1600; www.lescargotbleu.co.uk; 56 Broughton St; mains £13-18; ⊙lunch & dinner Mon-Sat) As with its sister restaurant, l'Escargot Blanc on Queensferry St, this cute little bistro is as Gallic as garlic but makes fine use of quality Scottish produce – the French-speaking staff will lead you knowledgeably through a menu that includes authentic Savoyard *tartiflette, quenelle* of pike

with lobster sauce, and pigs cheeks braised in red wine with roast winter vegetables.

Valvona & Crolla VinCaffè
ITALIAN **££**

(Map p60; ☑0131-557 0088; www.valvonacrolla.co.uk; 11 Multrees Walk, St Andrew Sq; mains £9-17; ⊙8am-11pm Mon-Sat, noon-5pm Sun; 🛜) Foodie colours dominate the decor at this delightful Italian bistro – bottle-green pillars and banquettes, chocolate-and-cream-coloured walls, espresso-black tables – a perfect backdrop for VinCaffè's superb antipasto (£17.50 for two), washed down with a bottle of pink Pinot Grigio.

Mussel Inn
SEAFOOD **££**

(Map p60; www.mussel-inn.com; 61-65 Rose St; mains £9-23; ⊙noon-10pm; ⓐ) Owned by west-coast shellfish farmers, the Mussel Inn provides a direct outlet for fresh Scottish seafood. The busy restaurant, decorated indoors with bright beechwood, spills out onto the pavement in summer. A 1kg pot of mussels with a choice of sauces – try leek, Dijon mustard and cream – costs £12.20.

Cafe Royal Oyster Bar
SEAFOOD **£££**

(Map p60; ☑0131-556 4124; www.caferoyal.org.uk; 17a West Register St; mains £11-28; ⊙lunch & dinner) Pass through the revolving doors on the corner of West Register St and you're transported back to Victorian times – a palace of glinting mahogany, polished brass, marble floors, stained glass, Doulton tiles, gilded cornices and starched table linen so thick it creaks when you fold it. The menu is mostly classic seafood, from oysters on ice to scallops with chorizo, to lobster with Cafe Royal sauce, augmented by a handful of beef and lamb dishes.

Eteaket
CAFE **£**

(Map p60; www.eteaket.co.uk; 41 Frederick St; mains £4-7; ⊙8am-7pm Mon-Fri, 10am-7pm Sat & Sun; 🛜🛗) A 'tea boutique' serving more than 40 varieties of leaf tea, this cosy cafe also offers tempting breakfasts (bagels, toasted crois-sants, scrambled eggs), fresh sandwiches (ciabatta with hummus, feta cheese and sunblush tomatoes) and afternoon tea (scones with jam and clotted cream).

Blue Moon Cafe
CAFE **£**

(Map p46; ☑0131-556 2788; 1 Barony St; mains £7-10; ⊙11am-10pm Mon-Fri, 10am-10pm Sat & Sun) The Blue Moon is the focus of Broughton St's gay social life, always busy, always friendly and serving up delicious nachos, salads, sandwiches and baked potatoes. It's famous for its homemade burgers (beef, chicken or falafel), which come with a range of toppings, and delicious daily specials.

Stac Polly   SCOTTISH £££
(Map p60; ✆0131-556 2231; www.stacpolly.com; 29-33 Dublin St; mains £16-23; ☺lunch Mon-Fri, dinner daily) Named after a mountain in northwestern Scotland, this rustic cellar restaurant adds sophisticated twists to fresh Highland produce. Dishes such as haggis in filo parcels with plum sauce might have Robert Burns spinning in his grave, but keep satisfied customers coming back for more. Orkney Brewery beers available.

Leith

TOP
CHOICE **Fishers Bistro**   SEAFOOD ££
(✆0131-554 5666; www.fishersbistros.co.uk; 1 The Shore; mains £10-23; ☺noon-10.30pm Mon-Sat, 12.30-10pm Sun) This cosy little restaurant, tucked beneath a 17th-century signal tower, is one of the city's best seafood places. The menu ranges widely in price, from cheaper dishes such as classic fishcakes with lemon and chive mayonnaise, to more expensive delights such as North Berwick lobster thermidor.

Plumed Horse   MODERN SCOTTISH £££
(✆0131-554 5556; www.plumedhorse.co.uk; 50-54 Henderson St; 3-course dinner £49; ☺lunch & dinner Tue-Sat) Smartly suited and booted staff welcome you to this quiet corner of understated elegance, where the muted decor of pale blues and greens, cream leather chairs and crisp white linen places the focus firmly on the exquisitely prepared and presented food. Eight-course tasting menu £65, plus £45 for matching wines.

Chop Chop   CHINESE £
(✆0131-553 1818; www.chop-chop.co.uk; 76 Commercial St; mains £8-10; ☺dinner daily, lunch Sat & Sun) Chop Chop is a Chinese restaurant with a difference, in that it serves dishes popular in China rather than Britain – as its slogan says, 'Can a billion people be wrong?'. No sweet-and-sour pork here, but a range of delicious dumplings filled with pork and coriander, beef and chilli, or lamb and leek, and unusual vegetarian dishes such as aubergine fried with garlic and Chinese spices.

Diner 7   CAFE ££
(www.diner7.co.uk; 7 Commercial St; mains £7-12; ☺4-11pm Mon-Sat, 11am-11pm Sun) A neat local eatery with rust-coloured leather booths and banquettes, black and copper tables, and local art on the walls, this diner has a menu of succulent Aberdeen Angus steaks and homemade burgers, but also offers more unusual fare such as chicken and chorizo kebabs, or smoked haddock with black-pudding stovies.

Self-Catering
There are grocery stores and food shops all over the city, many of them open 9am to 10pm daily. Many petrol stations also have late-opening shops that sell groceries.

Valvona & Crolla   DELI
(Map p46; ✆0131-556 6066; www.valvonacrolla .co.uk; 19 Elm Row; ☺8.30am-6pm Mon-Thu, 8am-6.30pm Fri & Sat, 10.30am-4pm Sun) The acknowledged queen of Edinburgh delicatessens, established during the 1930s, Valvona & Crolla is packed with Mediterranean goodies, including an excellent choice of fine wines. It also has a good cafe where the menu is based on family recipes from central and southern Italy, such as *rigatoni all'amatriciana* (pasta with Italian smoked bacon and tomato sauce) and *frittata con fava* (omelette made with broad beans, fresh herbs and Parmigiano Reggiano).

Sainsbury's   SUPERMARKET
(Map p60; 9-10 St Andrew Sq; ☺7am-10pm Mon-Sat, 9am-8pm Sun) Convenient city-centre supermarket.

Tesco Metro   SUPERMARKET
(Map p52; 94 Nicolson St; ☺6am-1am) Early- and late-opening supermarket.

Marks & Spencer   FOOD HALL
(Map p60; 54 Princes St; ☺8am-8pm Mon-Sat, 10am-6pm Sun) The food hall here sells high-quality ready-cooked meals.

🍸 Drinking
Edinburgh has more than 700 bars, which are as varied as the population – everything from Victorian palaces to rough-and-ready drinking dens, and from bearded, real-ale howffs to trendy cocktail bars.

Old Town
The pubs in the Grassmarket have outdoor tables on sunny summer afternoons, but in the evenings are favoured by boozed-up lads on the pull, so steer clear if that's not your thing. The Cowgate – the Grassmarket's extension to the east – is Edinburgh's clubland.

Bow Bar   PUB
(Map p52; 80 West Bow) One of the city's best traditional-style pubs (it's not as old as it looks), serving a range of excellent real ales and a vast selection of malt whiskies, the Bow Bar often has standing room only on Friday and Saturday evenings.

Jolly Judge   PUB
(Map p52; www.jollyjudge.co.uk; 7a James Ct; 🕱) A snug little howff tucked away down a close, the Judge exudes a cosy 17th-century atmosphere (low, timber-beamed painted ceilings) and has the added attraction of a cheering open fire in cold weather. No music or gaming machines, just the buzz of conversation.

BrewDog   BAR
(Map p52; www.brewdog.com; 143 Cowgate; 🕱) A new bar from Scotland's self-styled 'punk brewery', BrewDog stands out among the grimy, sticky-floored dives that line the Cowgate, with its cool, industrial-chic designer look. As well as its own highly rated beers, there's a choice of four guest real ales.

Ecco Vino   WINE BAR
(Map p52; www.eccovinoedinburgh.com; 19 Cockburn St; 🕱) With outdoor tables on sunny afternoons, and cosy candlelit intimacy in the evenings, this comfortably cramped Tuscan-style wine bar offers a tempting range of Italian wines, though not all are available by the glass – best to share a bottle.

Villager   BAR
(Map p52; www.villagerbar.com; 49-50 George IV Bridge; 🕱) A cross between a traditional pub and a preclub bar, Villager has a comfortable, laid-back vibe. It can be standing room only in the main bar in the evenings (the cocktails are excellent), but the side room, with its brown leather sofas and subtropical pot plants, comes into its own for a lazy Sunday afternoon with the papers.

Royal Mile Tavern   PUB
(Map p52; www.royalmiletavern.com; 127 High St) An elegant, traditional bar lined with polished wood, mirrors and brass, Royal Mile serves real ale (Deuchars IPA and Caledonian 80/-), good wines and decent pub grub – fish and chips, steak and Guinness pie, sausage and mash etc.

Holyrood 9A   PUB
(Map p52; www.fullerthomson.com; 9a Holyrood Rd; 🕱) Candlelight flickering off hectares of polished wood creates an atmospheric setting for this superb real-ale bar, with no fewer than 20 taps pouring craft beers from all corners of the country. If you're peckish, it serves excellent gourmet burgers, too.

Beehive Inn   PUB
(Map p52; 18-20 Grassmarket) The historic Beehive, a former coaching inn, is a big, buzzing party pub, with a range of real ales, but the main attraction is sitting out the back in the Grassmarket's only beer garden, with views up to the castle.

Pear Tree House   PUB
(Map p52; www.pear-tree-house.co.uk; 38 West Nicolson St; 🕱) Set in an 18th-century house with cobbled courtyard, the Pear Tree is a student favourite with an open fire in winter, comfy sofas and board games inside, plus the city's biggest and most popular beer garden in summer.

New Town
Rose St (between Princes St and George St) was once a famous pub crawl, where generations of students, sailors and rugby fans would try to visit every pub on the street (around 17 of them) and down a pint of beer in each one.

Oxford Bar   PUB
(Map p60; www.oxfordbar.co.uk; 8 Young St) The Oxford is that rarest of things: a real pub for real people, with no 'theme', no music, no frills and no pretensions. 'The Ox' has been immortalised by Ian Rankin, author of the Inspector Rebus novels, whose fictional detective is a regular here.

Cumberland Bar   PUB
(Map p46; www.cumberlandbar.co.uk; 1-3 Cumberland St; 🕱) Immortalised as the stereotypical New Town pub in Alexander McCall Smith's serialised novel *44 Scotland Street,* the Cumberland has an authentic, traditional wood-brass-and-mirrors look (despite being relatively new) and serves well-looked-after, cask-conditioned ales and a wide range of malt whiskies. There's also a pleasant little beer garden outside.

Guildford Arms   PUB
(Map p60; www.guildfordarms.com; 1 West Register St) Located next door to the Cafe Royal Circle Bar, the Guildford is another classic Victorian pub full of polished mahogany, brass and ornate cornices. The range of real ales is excellent – try to get a table in the unusual upstairs gallery, with a view over the sea of drinkers below.

Bramble
COCKTAIL BAR

(Map p60; www.bramblebar.co.uk; 16a Queen St; ☺4pm-1am) One of those places that easily earns the sobriquet 'best-kept secret', Bramble is an unmarked cellar bar where a maze of stone and brick hideaways conceals what is arguably the city's best cocktail bar. No beer taps, no fuss, just expertly mixed drinks.

Kenilworth
PUB

(Map p60; 152-154 Rose St) A gorgeous, Edwardian drinking palace, complete with original fittings – from the tile floors, mahogany circle bar and gantry, to the ornate mirrors and gas lamps – the Kenilworth was Edinburgh's original gay bar back in the 1970s. Today it attracts a mixed crowd of all ages, and serves a good range of real ales and malt whiskies.

Underdogs
COCKTAIL BAR

(Map p60; 104 Hanover St; ☎) A cellar furnished with stone-slab floors and a fire sale of battered, mismatched sofas and armchairs makes an unlikely setting for one of Edinburgh's best cocktail bars, but the relaxed atmosphere and friendly welcome here can't be beat. Excellent mixed drinks and some unusual bottled beers, but no brews on tap.

Kay's Bar
PUB

(Map p60; www.kaysbar.co.uk; 39 Jamaica St) Housed in a former wine merchant's office, tiny Kay's Bar is a cosy haven with a coal fire and a fine range of real ales. Good food is served in the back room at lunchtime, but you'll have to book a table – Kay's is a popular spot.

Amicus Apple
COCKTAIL BAR

(Map p60; www.amicusapple.com; 15 Frederick St; ☎) This laid-back cocktail lounge is the hippest hang-out in the New Town. The drinks menu ranges from retro classics such as Bloody Marys and mojitos, to original and unusual concoctions such as the Cuillin martini (Tanqueray No 10 gin, Talisker malt whisky and smoked rosemary).

TOP FIVE TRADITIONAL PUBS

Edinburgh is blessed with a large number of traditional 19th- and early-20th-century pubs, which have preserved much of their original Victorian or Edwardian decoration and serve cask-conditioned real ales and a staggering range of malt whiskies.

Athletic Arms (Diggers; Map p46; 1-3 Angle Park Tce) Nicknamed after the cemetery across the street – the gravediggers used to nip in and slake their thirst after a hard day's interring – the Diggers dates from the 1890s. It's still staunchly traditional – the decor has barely changed in 100 years – and has recently revived its reputation as a real-ale drinker's mecca by serving locally brewed Diggers' 80-shilling ale. Packed to the gills with football and rugby fans on match days.

Abbotsford (Map p60; www.theabbotsford.com; 3 Rose St) One of the few pubs in Rose St that has retained its Edwardian splendour, the Abbotsford has long been a hang-out for writers, actors, journalists and media people, and has many loyal regulars. Dating from 1902, and named after Sir Walter Scott's country house, the pub's centrepiece is a splendid mahogany island bar. Good selection of Scottish and English real ales.

Bennet's Bar (Map p46; 8 Leven St) Situated beside the King's Theatre, Bennet's has managed to hang on to almost all of its beautiful Victorian fittings, from the leaded stained-glass windows and ornate mirrors to the wooden gantry and the brass water taps on the bar (for your whisky – there are over 100 malts from which to choose).

Cafe Royal Circle Bar (Map p60; www.caferoyal.org.uk; 17 West Register St) Perhaps *the* classic Edinburgh bar, the Cafe Royal's main claims to fame are its magnificent oval bar and the series of Doulton tile portraits of famous Victorian inventors. Check out the bottles on the gantry – staff line them up to look like there's a mirror there, and many a drink-befuddled customer has been seen squinting and wondering why he can't see his reflection.

Sheep Heid (www.sheepheid.co.uk; 43-45 The Causeway) Possibly the oldest inn in Edinburgh (with a licence dating back to 1360), the Sheep Heid feels more like a country pub than an Edinburgh bar. Set in the semirural shadow of Arthur's Seat, it's famous for its 19th-century skittles alley and the lovely little beer garden.

Leith

Roseleaf
CAFE-BAR
(www.roseleaf.co.uk; 23-24 Sandport Pl; ⊘10am-1am; 🕾) Cute and quaint and verging on chintzy, the Roseleaf could hardly be further from the average Leith bar. Decked out in flowered wallpaper, old furniture and rose-patterned china (cocktails are served in teapots), the real ales and bottled beers are complemented by a range of speciality teas, coffees and fruit drinks (including rose lemonade) and well-above-average pub grub (served 10am to 10pm).

Teuchter's Landing
PUB
(www.aroomin.co.uk; 1 Dock Pl; 🕾) A cosy warren of timber-lined nooks and crannies housed in a single-storey red-brick building (once a waiting room for ferries across the Firth of Forth), this real-ale and malt-whisky bar also has outdoor tables on a floating terrace in the dock.

Port O'Leith
PUB
(www.portoleithpub.com; 58 Constitution St) This is a good, old-fashioned, friendly local boozer, swathed with flags and cap bands left behind by visiting sailors – Leith docks are just down the road. Pop in for a pint and you'll probably stay until closing time.

Starbank Inn
PUB
(www.starbankinn.co.uk; 64 Laverockbank Rd) The Starbank is an oasis of fine ales and good, homemade food on Edinburgh's windswept waterfront. In summer there's a sunny conservatory, and in winter a blazing fire.

Entertainment

Edinburgh has a number of fine theatres and concert halls, and there are independent art-house cinemas as well as mainstream movie theatres. Many pubs offer entertainment ranging from live Scottish folk music to pop, rock and jazz as well as karaoke and quiz nights, while a range of stylish modern bars purvey house, dance and hip-hop to the preclubbing crowd.

The comprehensive source for what's-on info is *The List* (www.list.co.uk), an excellent listings magazine covering both Edinburgh and Glasgow. It's available from most newsagents, and is published fortnightly on a Thursday.

Live Music

Check out the *List* and the *Gig Guide* (www.gigguide.co.uk), a free email newsletter and listings website, to see who's playing where.

JAZZ, BLUES & ROCK

Bannerman's
LIVE MUSIC
(Map p52; www.bannermanslive.co.uk; 212 Cowgate) A long-established favourite – it seems like every Edinburgh student for the last four decades spent half their youth here – Bannerman's straggles through a warren of old vaults beneath South Bridge. It pulls in crowds of students, locals and backpackers alike with live rock, punk and indie bands.

Henry's Cellar
LIVE MUSIC
(Map p52; www.musicglue.com/theraft; 8a Morrison St) One of Edinburgh's most eclectic live-music venues, Henry's has something going on most nights of the week, from rock and indie to 'Balkan-inspired folk', funk to hip-hop to hardcore, staging both local bands and acts from around the world. Open till 3am at weekends.

Whistle Binkie's
LIVE MUSIC
(Map p52; www.whistlebinkies.com; 4-6 South Bridge) This crowded cellar bar, just off the Royal Mile, has live music every night till 3am, from rock and blues to folk and jazz. Open-mic night on Monday and breaking bands on Tuesday are showcases for new talent.

Jazz Bar
JAZZ
(Map p52; www.thejazzbar.co.uk; 1a Chambers St; 🕾) This atmospheric cellar bar, with its polished parquet floors, bare stone walls, candlelit tables and stylish steel-framed chairs, is owned and operated by jazz musicians. There's live music every night from 9pm to 3am, and on Saturday from 3pm.

Liquid Room
CLUB, LIVE MUSIC
(Map p52; www.liquidroom.com; 9c Victoria St) Set in a subterranean vault deep beneath Victoria St, the Liquid Room is a superb club venue with a thundering sound system. There are regular club nights Wednesday to Saturday as well as live bands.

TRADITIONAL

The capital is a great place to hear traditional Scottish (and Irish) folk music, with a mix of regular spots and impromptu sessions.

Sandy Bell's
TRADITIONAL MUSIC
(Map p52; 25 Forrest Rd) This unassuming pub is a stalwart of the traditional music scene (the founder's wife sang with The Corries). There's music almost every evening at 9pm, and from 3pm Saturday and Sunday, plus lots of impromptu sessions.

Royal Oak   TRADITIONAL MUSIC

(Map p52; www.royal-oak-folk.com; 1 Infirmary St) This popular folk pub is tiny, so get there early (9pm start weekdays, 2.30pm Saturday) if you want to be sure of a place. Sundays from 4pm to 7pm is open session – bring your own instruments (or a good singing voice).

Edinburgh Folk Club   TRADITIONAL MUSIC

(Map p52; www.edinburghfolkclub.co.uk; Pleasance Cabaret Bar, 60 The Pleasance) The Pleasance Cabaret Bar is the home venue of the Edinburgh Folk Club, which runs a program of visiting bands and singers at 8pm on Wednesday nights.

Nightclubs

Edinburgh's club scene has some fine DJ talent and is well worth exploring; there are club-night listings in the *List*. Most of the venues are concentrated in and around the twin sumps of Cowgate and Calton Rd – so it's downhill all the way...

Bongo Club   ARTS VENUE

(Map p46; www.thebongoclub.co.uk; Moray House, Paterson's Land, 37 Holyrood Rd) The weird and wonderful Bongo Club boasts a long history of hosting everything from wild club nights to performance art to kids' comedy shows, and is open as a cafe and exhibition space during the day. May shift to new premises in 2013 – check website for latest news.

Cabaret Voltaire   CLUB, LIVE MUSIC

(Map p52; www.thecabaretvoltaire.com; 36 Blair St) An atmospheric warren of stone-lined vaults houses Edinburgh's most 'alternative' club, which eschews huge dance floors and egotistical DJ worship in favour of a 'creative crucible' hosting an eclectic mix of DJs, live acts, comedy, theatre, visual arts and the spoken word. Well worth a look.

Studio 24   CLUB

(Map p46; www.studio24.me; 24 Calton Rd) Studio 24 is the dark heart of Edinburgh's underground music scene, with a program that covers all bases, from house to nu metal via punk, ska, reggae, crossover, tribal, electro, techno and dance.

Opal Lounge   CLUB

(Map p60; www.opallounge.co.uk; 51 George St) The Opal Lounge is jammed at weekends with affluent 20-somethings who've spent £200 and two hours in front of a mirror to achieve that artlessly scruffy look. During the week, when the air-kissing crowds thin out, it's a good place to relax with an expensive but expertly mixed cocktail. Expect to queue on weekend evenings.

Lulu   CLUB

(Map p60; www.luluedinburgh.co.uk; 125 George St) Lush leather sofas, red satin cushions, fetishistic steel-mesh curtains and dim red lighting all help to create a decadent atmosphere in this drop-dead-gorgeous club venue beneath the Tigerlily boutique hotel. Resident and guest DJs show a bit more originality than your average club.

Cinemas

Film buffs will find plenty to keep them happy in Edinburgh's art-house cinemas, while popcorn munchers can choose from a range of multiplexes.

Filmhouse   CINEMA

(Map p52; www.filmhousecinema.com; 88 Lothian Rd; ☎) The Filmhouse is the main venue for the annual Edinburgh International Film Festival and screens a full program of art-house, classic, foreign and second-run films, with lots of themes, retrospectives and 70mm screenings. It has wheelchair access to all three screens.

Cameo   CINEMA

(Map p46; www.picturehouses.co.uk; 38 Home St) The three-screen, independently owned Cameo is a good, old-fashioned cinema showing an imaginative mix of mainstream and art-house movies. There is a good program of midnight movies and Sunday matinees, and the seats in screen 1 are big enough to get lost in.

Classical Music, Opera & Ballet

The following are the main venues for classical music.

Edinburgh Festival Theatre   BALLET, OPERA

(Map p52; www.edtheatres.com/festival; 13-29 Nicolson St; ☺box office 10am-6pm Mon-Sat, to 8pm show nights, 4pm-showtime Sun) A beautifully restored art-deco theatre with a modern frontage, the Festival is the city's main venue for opera, dance and ballet, but also stages musicals, concerts, drama and childrens shows.

Usher Hall   CLASSICAL MUSIC

(Map p52; www.usherhall.co.uk; Lothian Rd; ☺box office 10.30am-5.30pm, to 8pm show nights) The architecturally impressive Usher Hall hosts concerts by the Royal Scottish National Orchestra (RSNO) and performances of popular music.

Queen's Hall　　　　CLASSICAL MUSIC
(Map p46; www.thequeenshall.net; Clerk St; ☺box office 10am-5.30pm Mon-Sat, or till 15min after show begins) The home of the Scottish Chamber Orchestra also stages jazz, blues, folk, rock and comedy.

St Giles Cathedral　　　　CLASSICAL MUSIC
(Map p52; www.stgilescathedral.org.uk; High St) The big kirk on the Royal Mile plays host to a regular and varied program of classical music, including popular lunchtime and evening concerts and organ recitals. The cathedral choir sings at the 10am and 11.30am Sunday services.

Sport

Edinburgh is home to two rival **football** teams playing in the Scottish Premier League: **Heart of Midlothian** (aka Hearts) and **Hibernian** (aka Hibs). The domestic football season lasts from August to May, and most matches are played at 3pm on Saturday or 7.30pm on Tuesday or Wednesday.

Hearts has its home ground at Tynecastle Stadium (www.heartsfc.co.uk; Gorgie Rd), southwest of the city centre in Gorgie. Hibernian's home ground is northeast of the city centre at Easter Road Stadium (www .hibernianfc.co.uk; 12 Albion Pl).

Each year, from January to March, Scotland's national **rugby** team takes part in the Six Nations Rugby Union Championship. The most important fixture is the clash against England for the Calcutta Cup. At club level the season runs from September to May. Murrayfield Stadium (www.scottishrugby.org; 112 Roseburn St), about 1.5 miles west of the city centre, is the venue for international matches.

Most other **sporting events**, including athletics and cycling, are held at Meadowbank Sports Centre (www.edinburghleisure .co.uk; 139 London Rd), Scotland's main sports arena.

Horse-racing enthusiasts should head 6 miles east to Musselburgh Racecourse (☏0131 665 2859; www.musselburgh-racecourse. co.uk; Linkfield Rd; admission £15-20), Scotland's oldest racecourse (founded 1816), where meetings are held throughout the year.

Theatre, Musicals & Comedy

Royal Lyceum Theatre　　　　DRAMA, MUSICALS
(Map p52; www.lyceum.org.uk; 30b Grindlay St; ☺box office 10am-6pm Mon-Sat, to 8pm show nights) A grand Victorian theatre located

GAY & LESBIAN EDINBURGH

Edinburgh has a small – but perfectly formed – gay and lesbian scene, centred on the area around Broughton St (known affectionately as the 'Pink Triangle') at the eastern end of New Town. Blue Moon Cafe (p85), at the foot of Broughton St, is a friendly G&L caff offering good food and good company. It's also a good place to pick up on what's happening on the local scene.

Scotsgay (www.scotsgay.co.uk) is the local monthly magazine covering gay and lesbian issues, with listings of gay-friendly pubs and clubs. See also www.edinburghgay scene.com for online listings.

Useful contacts:

Edinburgh LGBT Centre (www.lgbthealth.org.uk; 9 Howe St)

Lothian LGBT Helpline (☏0131-556 4049; ☺12.30-7pm Wed)

Pubs & Clubs

CC Blooms (Map p60; ☏556 9331; www.bebo.com/ccbloomsnightclub; 23 Greenside Pl; admission free; ☺6pm-3am Mon-Sat, 7pm-3am Sun) New owners have given the raddled old queen of Edinburgh's gay scene a shot in the arm, with two floors of deafening dance and disco every night. It's overcrowded and drinks are a bit overpriced but it's worth a visit – go early, or sample the wild karaoke on Sunday nights.

Regent (Map p46; 2 Montrose Tce; ☺11am-1am Mon-Sat, 12.30pm-1am Sun) This is a pleasant gay local with a relaxed atmosphere (no loud music), serving coffee and croissants as well as excellent real ales, including Deuchars IPA and Caledonian 80/-. Meeting place for the Lesbian and Gay Real Ale Drinkers club (first Monday of month, 9pm).

Newtown Bar (Map p60; www.newtownbar.co.uk; 26b Dublin St; ☺noon-1am Sun-Thu, to 2am Fri & Sat) Stylish modern bar serving good food and drink, and basement club with resident DJ that hosts regular men-only events.

beside the Usher Hall, the Lyceum stages drama, concerts, musicals and ballet.

Traverse Theatre
DRAMA, DANCE

(Map p52; www.traverse.co.uk; 10 Cambridge St; box office 10am-6pm Mon-Sat, to 8pm on show nights) The Traverse is the main focus for new Scottish writing and stages an adventurous program of contemporary drama and dance. The box office is only open on Sunday (from 4pm) when there's a show on.

King's Theatre
DRAMA, MUSICALS

(Map p46; www.edtheatres.com/kings; 2 Leven St; box office open 1hr before show) King's is a traditional theatre with a program of musicals, drama, comedy and its famous Christmas pantomimes.

Edinburgh Playhouse
MUSICALS

(Map p60; www.edinburgh-playhouse.co.uk; 18-22 Greenside Pl; box office 10am-6pm Mon-Sat, to 8pm show nights) This restored theatre at the top of Leith Walk stages Broadway musicals, dance, opera and popular-music concerts.

Stand Comedy Club
COMEDY

(Map p60; www.thestand.co.uk; 5 York Pl) The Stand, founded in 1995, is Edinburgh's main independent comedy venue. It's an intimate cabaret bar with performances every night and a free Sunday lunchtime show.

🔒 Shopping

Princes St is Edinburgh's principal shopping street, lined with all the big high-street stores, with many smaller shops along pedestrianised Rose St, and more expensive designer boutiques on George St. There are also two big shopping centres in the New Town – **Princes Mall**, at the eastern end of Princes St, and the nearby **St James Centre** at the top of Leith St, plus **Multrees Walk**, a designer shopping complex with a Harvey Nichols store on the eastern side of St Andrew Sq. The huge **Ocean Terminal** in Leith is the biggest shopping centre in the city.

For more off-beat shopping – including fashion, music, crafts, gifts and jewellery – head for the cobbled lanes of Cockburn, Victoria and St Mary's Sts, all near the Royal Mile in the Old Town; William St in the western part of the New Town; and the Stockbridge district, immediately north of the New Town.

Bookshops

Blackwell's Bookshop
BOOKS

(Map p52; www.blackwell.co.uk; 53-62 South Bridge; 9am-8pm Mon & Wed-Fri, 9.30am-8pm

Tue, 9am-6pm Sat, noon-6pm Sun) The city's principal bookstore; big selection of academic books.

Waterstone's
BOOKS

(www.waterstones.com) East End (Map p60; 13 Princes St; 9am-8pm Mon-Fri, to 7.30pm Sat, 10am-7pm Sun); George St (Map p60; 83 George St; 9.30am-9pm Mon-Fri, to 8pm Sat, 11am-6pm Sun); West End (Map p60; 226 2666; 128 Princes St; 8.30am-8pm Mon-Sat, 10.30am-7pm Sun; all Princes St buses) The West End branch has an in-store cafe with great views.

Word Power
BOOKS

(Map p52; www.word-power.co.uk; 43 West Nicolson St; 10am-6pm Mon-Sat, noon-5pm Sun) Radical, independent bookshop with wide range of political, gay and feminist literature.

Cashmere & Wool

Woollen textiles and knitwear are one of Scotland's classic exports. Scottish cashmere – a fine, soft wool sourced from young goats and lambs – provides the most luxurious and expensive knitwear and has been seen gracing the torsos of pop star Robbie Williams and England footballer David Beckham.

Kinross Cashmere
FASHION

(Map p52; 2 St Giles St) Wide range of traditional and modern knitwear.

Joyce Forsyth Designer Knitwear
FASHION

(Map p52; www.joyceforsyth.co.uk; 42 Candlemaker Row; Tue-Sat) Colourful designs that will drag your ideas about woollens firmly into the 21st century.

Edinburgh Woollen Mill
FASHION

(Map p60; www.ewm.co.uk; 139 Princes St) A stalwart of the tourist trade, with a good selection of traditional jerseys, cardigans, scarves, shawls and rugs.

Crafts & Gifts

Galerie Mirages
JEWELLERY

(Map p46; www.galeriemirages.co.uk; 46a Raeburn Pl) An Aladdin's cave packed with jewellery, textiles and handicrafts from all over the world, best known for its silver, amber and gemstone jewellery in both ethnic and contemporary designs.

One World Shop
HANDICRAFTS

(Map p52; www.oneworldshop.co.uk; St John's Church, Princes St) Stocks a wide range of handmade crafts from developing countries, including paper goods, rugs, textiles, jewellery, ceramics, accessories, food and drink, all from accredited fair-trade suppliers. During the festival period (when the shop stays open till 6pm) there's a crafts fair in the churchyard outside.

Meadows Pottery   HANDICRAFTS
(Map p46; www.themeadowspottery.com; 11a Summerhall Pl) Sells colourful stoneware, all hand-thrown on the premises.

Adam Pottery   HANDICRAFTS
(Map p46; www.adampottery.co.uk; 76 Henderson Row) Produces its own ceramics, mostly decorative, in a wide range of styles.

Department Stores

Jenners   DEPARTMENT STORE
(Map p60; 48 Princes St) Founded in 1838, Jenners is the grande dame of Scottish department stores. It stocks a wide range of quality goods, both classic and contemporary.

Harvey Nichols   DEPARTMENT STORE
(Map p60; www.harveynichols.com; 30-34 St Andrew Sq) The jewel in the crown of Edinburgh's shopping scene has four floors of designer labels and eye-popping price tags.

John Lewis   DEPARTMENT STORE
(Map p60; www.johnlewis.com; St James Centre) The place to go for good-value clothes and household goods.

Tartan & Highland Dress

There are dozens of shops along the Royal Mile and Princes St where you can buy kilts and tartan goods.

Kinloch Anderson   FASHION
(www.kinlochanderson.com; 4 Dock St, Leith) One of the best, this was founded in 1868 and is still family run. Kinloch Anderson is a supplier of kilts and Highland dress to the royal family.

Geoffrey (Tailor) Inc   FASHION
(Map p52; www.geoffreykilts.co.uk; 57-59 High St) Can fit you out in traditional Highland dress, or run up a kilt in your own clan tartan. Its offshoot, 21st Century Kilts, offers modern fashion kilts in a variety of fabrics.

ⓘ Information

Emergency

In an emergency, dial 999 or 112 (free from public phones) and ask for police, ambulance, fire brigade or coastguard.

Edinburgh Rape Crisis Centre (☑08088 01 03 02; www.rapecrisisscotland.org.uk)

Lothian & Borders Police HQ (☑non-emergency 0131-311 3131; www.lbp.police.uk; Fettes Ave)

Lothian & Borders Police Information Centre (☑0131-226 6966; 188 High St; ☺10am-1pm & 2-5.30pm, to 9.30pm during Fringe Festival) Report a crime or make lost-property inquiries here.

Internet Access

There are several internet-enabled telephone boxes (10p a minute, 50p minimum) scattered around the city centre, and countless wi-fi hot spots – search on www.jiwire.com. Internet cafes are spread around the city. Some convenient ones:

e-corner (www.e-corner.co.uk; 54 Blackfriars St; per 20min £1; ☺7.30am-9pm Mon-Fri, 8am-9pm Sat & Sun; ☎)

G-Tec (www.grassmarket-technologies.com; 67 Grassmarket; per 20min £1; ☺10am-6pm Mon-Fri, to 5.30pm Sat)

Coffee Home (www.coffeehome.co.uk; 28 Crighton Pl, Leith Walk; per 20min 60p; ☺10am-10pm Mon-Sat, noon-10pm Sun)

Internet Resources

Edinburgh & Lothians Tourist Board (www.edinburgh.org) Official tourist-board site, with listings of accommodation, sights, activities and events.

Edinburgh Architecture (www.edinburgharchitecture.co.uk) Informative site dedicated to the city's modern architecture.

Edinburgh Festival Guide (www.edinburghfestivals.co.uk) Everything you need to know about Edinburgh's many festivals.

Events Edinburgh (www.eventsedinburgh.org.uk) The city council's official events guide.

The List (www.list.co.uk) Listings of restaurants, pubs, clubs and nightlife.

Media

Edinburgh's home-grown daily newspapers include the *Scotsman* (www.scotsman.com), a quality daily covering Scottish, UK and international news, sport and current affairs; and the *Edinburgh Evening News* (www.edinburghnews.com), covering news and entertainment in the city and its environs. *Scotland on Sunday* is the weekend newspaper from the same publisher.

Medical Services

For urgent medical advice you can call the **NHS 24 Helpline** (☑08454 24 24 24; www.nhs24.com). Chemists (pharmacists) can advise you on minor ailments. At least one local chemist remains open round the clock – its location will be displayed in the windows of other chemists.

For urgent dental treatment you can visit the walk-in **Chalmers Dental Centre** (3 Chalmers

St; ⊙9am-4.45pm Mon-Thu, to 4.15pm Fri). In the case of a dental emergency in the evenings or at weekends, call **Lothian Dental Advice Line** (☑0131-536 4800).

Boots (48 Shandwick Pl; ⊙8am-9pm Mon-Fri, 8am-6pm Sat, 10.30am-4.30pm Sun) Chemist open longer hours than most.

Royal Hospital for Sick Children (☑0131-536 0000; www.nhslothian.scot.nhs.uk; 9 Sciennes Rd) Casualty department for children aged under 13 years; located in Marchmont.

Royal Infirmary of Edinburgh (☑0131-536 1000; www.nhslothian.scot.nhs.uk; 51 Little France Cres, Old Dalkeith Rd) Edinburgh's main general hospital; has 24-hour accident and emergency department.

Western General Hospital (☑0131-537 1330; www.nhslothian.scot.nhs.uk; Crewe Rd South; ⊙9am-9pm) For non-life-threatening injuries and ailments, you can attend the Minor Injuries Unit without having to make an appointment.

Post

Main Post Office (St James Centre, Leith St; ⊙8.30am-5.30pm Mon-Fri, to 6pm Sat) Hidden away inside a shopping centre.

Tourist Information

Edinburgh Information Centre (☑0131-473 3868; www.edinburgh.org; Princes Mall, 3 Princes St; ⊙9am-9pm Mon-Sat, 10am-8pm Sun Jul & Aug, 9am-7pm Mon-Sat, 10am-7pm Sun May, Jun & Sep, 9am-5pm Mon-Wed, 9am-6pm Thu-Sun Oct-Apr) Includes an accommodation booking service, currency exchange, gift

CITY MAPS

For coverage of the whole city in detail, the best maps are Nicolson's *Edinburgh Citymap* and the Ordnance Survey's (OS) *Edinburgh Street Atlas*. You can buy these at the Edinburgh Information Centre (p94), bookshops and newsagents. Note that long streets may be known by different names along their length. For example, the southern end of Leith Walk is variously called Union Pl and Antigua St on one side, and Elm Row and Greenside Pl on the other.

The OS's 1:50,000 Landranger map *Edinburgh, Penicuik & North Berwick* (sheet No 66) covers the city and the surrounding region to the south and east at a scale of 1.25 inches to 1 mile; it's useful for walking in the Pentland Hills and exploring Edinburgh's fringes and East Lothian.

and bookshop, internet access and counters selling tickets for Edinburgh city tours and Scottish Citylink bus services.

Edinburgh Airport Information Centre (☑0131-344 3120; Main Concourse, Edinburgh Airport; ⊙7.30am-9pm)

ⓘ Getting There & Away

Air

Edinburgh Airport (☑0131-333 1000; www.edinburghairport.com), 8 miles west of the city, has numerous flights to other parts of Scotland and the UK, Ireland and mainland Europe.

FlyBe/Loganair (☑0871 700 2000; www.loganair.co.uk) operates daily flights to Inverness, Wick, Orkney, Shetland and Stornoway.

Bus

Edinburgh bus station is at the northeast corner of St Andrew Sq, with pedestrian entrances from the square and from Elder St. For timetable information, call **Traveline** (☑0871 200 22 33; www.travelinescotland.com).

Scottish Citylink (☑0871 266 3333; www.citylink.co.uk) buses connect Edinburgh with all of Scotland's cities and major towns. The following are sample one-way fares departing from Edinburgh.

DESTINATION	FARE
Aberdeen	£28
Dundee	£15
Fort William	£33
Glasgow	£6.80
Inverness	£28
Portree	£47
Stirling	£7.50

It's also worth checking with **Megabus** (☑0900 160 0900; www.megabus.com) for cheap intercity bus fares (from as little as £5) from Edinburgh to Aberdeen, Dundee, Glasgow, Inverness and Perth.

There are various buses to Edinburgh from London and the rest of the UK.

Car & Motorcycle

Arriving in or leaving Edinburgh by car during the morning and evening rush hours (7.30am to 9.30am and 4.30pm to 6.30pm Monday to Friday) is an experience you can live without. Try to time your journey to avoid these periods.

Train

The main terminus in Edinburgh is Waverley train station, located in the heart of the city. Trains arriving from, and departing for, the west also stop at Haymarket station, which is more convenient for the West End.

You can buy tickets, make reservations and get travel information at the **Edinburgh Rail Travel Centre** (◷4.45am-12.30am Mon-Sat, 7am-12.30am Sun) in Waverley station. For fare and timetable information, phone the **National Rail Enquiry Service** (☏08457 48 49 50; www .nationalrail.co.uk) or use the journey planner on the website.

First ScotRail (☏08457 55 00 33; www .scotrail.co.uk) operates a regular shuttle service between Edinburgh and Glasgow (£12.90, 50 minutes, every 15 minutes), and frequent daily services to all Scottish cities, including Aberdeen (£45, 2½ hours), Dundee (£23, 1¼ hours) and Inverness (£40, 3½ hours).

ⓘ Getting Around
To/From the Airport
The Lothian Buses **Airlink** (www.flybybus.com) service 100 runs from Waverley Bridge, outside the train station, to the airport (£3.50/6 one way/return, 30 minutes, every 10 to 15 minutes) via the West End and Haymarket.

An airport taxi to the city centre costs around £16 and takes about 20 minutes. Both buses and taxis depart from outside the arrivals hall; go out through the main doors and turn left.

Bicycle
Thanks to the efforts of local cycling campaign group Spokes and a bike-friendly city council, Edinburgh is well equipped with bike lanes and dedicated cycle tracks. You can buy a map of the city's cycle routes from most bike shops.

Biketrax (☏0131-228 6633; www.biketrax .co.uk; 11 Lochrin Pl; ◷9.30am-6pm Mon-Fri, to 5.30pm Sat, noon-5pm Sun; ▣all Tollcross buses) rents out a wide range of cycles and equipment, including kids bikes, tandems, recumbents, pannier bags and child seats. A mountain bike costs £16 for 24 hours, £12 for extra days, and £70 for one week. You'll need a £100 cash or credit-card deposit and photographic ID.

Car & Motorcycle
Though useful for day trips beyond the city, a car in central Edinburgh is more of a liability than a convenience. The streets have been in chaos for years as the city's controversial tram system gets built. There is restricted access on Princes St, George St and Charlotte Sq, many streets are one way and finding a parking place in the city centre is like striking gold. Queen's Dr around Holyrood Park is closed to motorised traffic on Sunday.

CAR RENTAL
All the big, international car-rental agencies have offices in Edinburgh.

There are many smaller, local agencies that offer better rates. **Arnold Clark** (☏0131-657 9120; www.arnoldclarkrental.co.uk; 20 Seafield Rd East), near Portobello, charges from £30 a day, or £180 a week for a small car, including VAT and insurance.

PARKING
There's no parking on main roads into the city from 7.30am to 6.30pm Monday to Saturday. Also, parking in the city centre can be a nightmare. **On-street parking** is controlled by self-service ticket machines from 8.30am to 6.30pm Monday to Saturday, and costs £1 to £2 per hour, with a 30-minute to four-hour maximum. If you break the rules, you'll get a fine, often within minutes of your ticket expiring – Edinburgh's parking wardens are both numerous and notorious. The fine is £60, reduced to £30 if you pay up within 14 days. Cars parked illegally will be towed away. There are large, long-stay car parks at the St James Centre, Greenside Pl, New St, Castle Tce and Morrison St. Motorcycles can be parked free at designated areas in the city centre.

Public Transport
For the moment, Edinburgh's public-transport system consists entirely of buses (a tram network is under construction, due to come into operation in 2014). The main operators are **Lothian Buses** (www.lothianbuses.com) and **First** (☏0131-663 9233; www.firstedinburgh .co.uk); for timetable information contact Traveline (p94).

Bus timetables, route maps and fare guides are posted at all main bus stops, and you can pick up a copy of the free *Lothian Buses Route Map* from **Lothian Buses Travelshops**.

Adult **fares** are £1.40; purchase from the driver. Children aged under five travel free and those aged five to 15 pay a flat fare of 70p. On Lothian Buses you must pay the driver the exact fare, but First buses will give change. Lothian Bus drivers also sell a Daysaver ticket (£3.50) that gives unlimited travel (on Lothian Buses only, excluding night buses) for a day. **Night-service buses** (www.nightbuses.com), which run hourly between midnight and 5am, charge a flat fare of £3.

You can also buy a **Ridacard** (from Travelshops; not available from bus drivers) that gives unlimited travel for one week for £17.

The Lothian Buses lost-property office is in the Hanover St Travelshop.

Hanover St Travelshop (27 Hanover St; ◷9am-6pm Mon-Fri, 10am-6pm Sat)

Shandwick Pl Travelshop (7 Shandwick Pl; ◷9am-6pm Mon-Fri, 10am-6pm Sat)

Waverley Bridge Travelshop (31 Waverley Bridge; ◷9am-6pm Mon-Fri, 10am-6pm Sat, 10am-5.15pm Sun)

Taxi

Edinburgh's black taxis can be hailed in the street, ordered by phone (extra 80p charge), or picked up at one of the many central ranks. The minimum charge is £2 (£3 at night) for the first 450m, then 25p for every subsequent 195m or 42 seconds – a typical 2-mile trip across the city centre will cost around £6 to £7. Tipping is up to you – because of the high fares local people rarely tip on short journeys, but occasionally round up to the nearest 50p on longer ones. Some taxi companies:

Central Taxis (☎0131-229 2468)

City Cabs (☎0131-228 1211)

ComCab (☎0131-272 8000)

AROUND EDINBURGH

Edinburgh is small enough that, when you need a break from the city, the beautiful surrounding countryside isn't far away and is easily accessible by public transport, or even by bike. The old counties around Edinburgh are called Midlothian, West Lothian and East Lothian, often referred to collectively as 'the Lothians'.

Midlothian

QUEENSFERRY

Queensferry is at the narrowest part of the Firth of Forth, where ferries have crossed to Fife from the earliest times. The village takes its name from Queen Margaret (1046–93), who gave pilgrims free passage across the firth on their way to St Andrews. Ferries continued to operate until 1964 when the graceful **Forth Road Bridge** was opened. Construction work has started on a second road bridge, scheduled to open in 2016.

Predating the road bridge by 74 years, the magnificent **Forth Bridge** – only outsiders ever call it the Forth Rail Bridge – is one of the finest engineering achievements of the 19th century. Completed in 1890 after seven years' work, its three huge cantilevers span 1447m and took 59,000 tonnes of steel, eight million rivets and the lives of 58 men to build.

In the pretty, terraced High St in Queensferry is the small Queensferry Museum (53 High St; admission free; ⊙10am-1pm & 2.15-5pm Mon & Thu-Sat, noon-5pm Sun). It contains some interesting background information on the bridges, and a fascinating exhibit on the Burry Man (p72), part of the village's summer gala festivities.

There are several good places to eat and drink along the High St, including the stylish Orocco Pier (www.oroccopier.co.uk; 17 High St; mains £15-24; ⊙9am-10pm; ⊕), which has a modern dining area and outdoor terrace with a stunning view of the Forth Bridge.

The atmospheric Hawes Inn (☎0131-331 1990; www.vintageinn.co.uk; Newhalls Rd; mains £7-16; ⊙food served noon-10pm; ⊡First Edinburgh 43), famously mentioned in Robert Louis Stevenson's novel *Kidnapped*, serves excellent pub grub; it's opposite the Inchcolm ferry, right beside the railway bridge.

❶ Getting There & Away

Queensferry lies on the southern bank of the Firth of Forth, 8 miles west of Edinburgh city centre. To get there, take First bus 43 (£3.30, 30 minutes, three hourly) westbound from St Andrew Sq. It's a 10-minute walk from the bus stop to the Hawes Inn and the Inchcolm ferry.

Trains go from Edinburgh's Waverley and Haymarket stations to Dalmeny station (£4, 15 minutes, two to four hourly). From the station exit, the Hawes Inn is five minutes' walk along a footpath (across the road, behind the bus stop) that leads north beside the railway and then downhill under the Forth Bridge.

INCHCOLM

Known as the 'Iona of the East', the island of Inchcolm (meaning 'St Columba's Island') lies east of the Forth bridges, less than a mile off the coast of Fife. Only 800m long, it is home to the ruins of Inchcolm Abbey (HS; adult/child £5/3; ⊙9.30am-5.30pm Apr-Sep, to 4.30pm Oct), one of Scotland's best-preserved medieval abbeys, founded by Augustinian priors in 1123.

The ferry boat Maid of the Forth (www .maidoftheforth.co.uk) sails to Inchcolm from Hawes Pier in Queensferry. There are one to four sailings most days from May to October. The return fare is £16/7 per adult/child, including admission to Inchcolm Abbey. It's a half-hour sail to Inchcolm and you get 1½ hours ashore. As well as the abbey, the trip gives you the chance to see the island's grey seals, puffins and other seabirds.

HOPETOUN HOUSE

One of Scotland's finest stately homes, Hopetoun House (www.hopetoun.co.uk; adult/child £9.20/4.90; ⊙10.30am-5pm Easter-Sep, last admission 4pm; Stables Tearoom 11am-4.30pm Easter-Sep) has a superb location in lovely grounds beside the Firth of Forth. There are two parts – the older built to Sir William Bruce's plans between 1699 and 1702

WORTH A TRIP

ROSSLYN CHAPEL

The success of Dan Brown's novel *The Da Vinci Code* and the subsequent Hollywood film has seen a flood of visitors descend on Scotland's most beautiful and enigmatic church Rosslyn Chapel (Collegiate Church of St Matthew; www.rosslynchapel.org.uk; adult/child £9/free; ⊙9.30am-6pm Mon-Sat, noon-4.45pm Sun). The chapel was built in the mid-15th century for William St Clair, third earl of Orkney, and the ornately carved interior – at odds with the architectural fashion of its time – is a monument to the mason's art, rich in symbolic imagery. As well as flowers, vines, angels and biblical figures, the carved stones include many examples of the pagan 'Green Man'; other figures are associated with Freemasonry and the Knights Templar. Intriguingly, there are also carvings of plants from the Americas that predate Columbus' voyage of discovery. The symbolism of these images has led some researchers to conclude that Rosslyn is some kind of secret Templar repository, and it has been claimed that hidden vaults beneath the chapel could conceal anything from the Holy Grail or the head of John the Baptist to the body of Christ himself. The chapel is owned by the Episcopal Church of Scotland and services are still held here on Sunday mornings.

The chapel is on the eastern edge of the village of Roslin, 7 miles south of Edinburgh's centre. Lothian Bus 15 (not 15A) runs from the west end of Princes St in Edinburgh to Roslin (£1.40, 30 minutes, every 30 minutes) via Penicuik (it may be faster to catch any bus to Penicuik, then the 15 to Roslin).

A refreshing alternative to the mainstream tours is offered by Celtic Trails (www.celtictrails.co.uk), whose knowledgeable owner, Jackie Queally, leads guided tours of Rosslyn Chapel and other ancient and sacred sites covering subjects such as Celtic mythology, geomancy, sacred geometry and the Knights Templar. A half-day tour of the chapel and surrounding area costs £130 for up to three people, plus £33 per additional person, not including admission fees.

and dominated by a splendid stairwell with (modern) trompe l'oeil paintings; and the newer, designed between 1720 and 1750 by three members of the Adam family, William and sons Robert and John. The highlights are the red and yellow **Adam drawing rooms**, lined in silk damask, and the view from the roof terrace.

Britain's most elegant equine accommodation – where the marquis once housed his pampered racehorses – is now the stylish Stables Tearoom (☏0131 331 3661; mains £6-8, afternoon tea £12.75; ⊙11am-4.30pm Easter-Sep), a delightful spot for lunch or afternoon tea.

Hopetoun House is 2 miles west of Queensferry along the coast road. Driving from Edinburgh, turn off the A90 onto the A904 just before the Forth Bridge and follow the signs.

PENTLAND HILLS

Rising on the southern edge of Edinburgh, the Pentland Hills (www.edinburgh.gov.uk/phrp) stretch 16 miles southwest to near Carnwath in Lanarkshire. The hills rise to 579m at their highest point and offer excellent, not-too-strenuous walking with great views.

There are several access points along the A702 road on the southern side of the hills. MacEwan's bus 100 runs four times daily along the A702 from Princes St in Edinburgh to Biggar.

East Lothian

Beyond the former coalfields of Dalkeith and Musselburgh, the fertile farmland of East Lothian stretches eastwards along the coast to the seaside resort of North Berwick and the fishing harbour of Dunbar. In the middle lies the prosperous market town of Haddington.

NORTH BERWICK & AROUND
POP 6220

North Berwick is an attractive Victorian seaside resort with long sandy beaches, three golf courses and a small harbour. The tourist office (☏01620-892197; Quality St; ⊙9am-6pm Mon-Sat, 11am-4pm Sun Jun-Sep, 9am-6pm Mon-Sat Apr & May, to 5pm Mon-Sat Oct-Mar) is two blocks inland from the harbour.

Off High St, a short steep path climbs **North Berwick Law** (184m), a conical hill

Rosslyn Chapel

DECIPHERING ROSSLYN

Rosslyn Chapel is a small building, but the density of decoration inside can be overwhelming. It's well worth buying the official guidebook by the Earl of Rosslyn first; find a bench in the gardens and have a skim through before going into the chapel – the background information will make your visit all the more interesting. The book also offers a useful self-guided tour of the chapel, and explains the legend of the Master Mason and the Apprentice.

Entrance is through the north door **1**. Take a pew and sit for a while to allow your eyes to adjust to the dim interior; then look up at the ceiling vault, decorated with engraved roses, lilies and stars, (Can you spot the sun and the moon?). Walk left along the north aisle to reach the Lady Chapel, separated from the rest of the church by the **Mason's Pillar 2** and the **Apprentice Pillar 3**. Here you'll find carvings of **Lucifer 4**, the Fallen Angel, and the **Green Man 5**. Nearby are carvings **6** that appear to resemble Indian corn (maize). Finally, go to the western end and look up at the wall – in the left corner is the head of the **Apprentice 7**; to the right is the (rather worn) head of the **Master Mason 8**.

ROSSLYN CHAPEL & THE DA VINCI CODE

» Dan Brown was referencing Rosslyn Chapel's alleged links to the Knights Templar and the Freemasons – unusual symbols found among the carvings, and the fact that a descendant of its founder, William St Clair, was a Grand Master Mason – when he chose it as the setting for his novel's denouement. Rosslyn is indeed a coded work, written in stone, but its meaning depends on your point of view. See *The Rosslyn Hoax?* by Robert LD Cooper (www.rosslynhoax.com) for an alternative interpretation of the chapel's symbolism.

Explore Some More

After visiting the chapel, head downhill to see the spectacularly sited ruins of Roslin Castle, then take a walk along leafy Roslin Glen.

Lucifer, the Fallen Angel
At head height, to the left of the second window from the left, is an upside-down angel bound with rope, a symbol often associated with Freemasonry. The arch above is decorated with the Dance of Death.

The Apprentice
High in the corner, beneath an empty statue niche, is the head of the murdered Apprentice, with a deep wound in his forehead above the right eye. Legend says the Apprentice was murdered in a jealous rage by the Master Mason. The worn head on the side wall to the left of the Apprentice is that of his mother.

North Door

The Master Mason **8**

Baptistery

Practical Tips

Buy your tickets in advance through the chapel's website (except in August, when no bookings are taken). No photography is allowed inside the chapel.

Green Man

On a boss at the base of the arch between the second and third windows from the left is the finest example of more than a hundred 'green man' carvings in the chapel, pagan symbols of spring, fertility and rebirth.

Sacristy

4

2　**Mason's Pillar**

5　Lady Chapel

3

rth Aisle

Altar

Choir

South Aisle

1

6

7

The Apprentice Pillar

This is perhaps the chapel's most beautiful carving. Four vines spiral up the pillar, issuing from the mouths of eight dragons at its base. At the top is Isaac, son of Abraham, lying bound upon the altar.

Indian Corn

The frieze around the second window on the south wall is said to represent Indian corn (maize), but it predates Columbus' discovery of the New World in 1492. Other carvings seem to resemble aloe vera.

that dominates the town. When the weather's fine there are great views to spectacular **Bass Rock**, iced white in spring and summer with guano from thousands of nesting gannets. Sula II (☑01620-880770; www.sulaboattrips .co.uk) runs boat trips (adult/child £12.50/7, daily April to September) around Bass Rock, departing from North Berwick's harbour.

◉ Sights

Scottish Seabird Centre WILDLIFE CENTRE
(www.seabird.org; The Harbour; adult/child £7.95/ 4.95; ⊙10am-6pm Apr-Aug, to 5pm Feb, Mar, Sep & Oct, to 4pm Nov-Jan) Top marks to the bright spark who came up with the idea for this centre, an ornithologist's paradise that uses remote-control video cameras sited on Bass Rock and other islands to relay live images of nesting gannets and other seabirds – you can control the cameras yourself, and zoom in on scenes of cosy gannet domesticity.

Dirleton Castle CASTLE
(HS; adult/child £5/3; ⊙9.30am-5.30pm Apr-Sep, to 4.30pm Oct-Mar) Two miles west of North Berwick is this impressive medieval fortress with massive round towers, a drawbridge and a horrific pit dungeon, surrounded rather incongruously by beautiful, manicured gardens.

Tantallon Castle CASTLE
(HS; adult/child £5/3; ⊙9.30am-5.30pm Apr-Sep, to 4.30pm Oct-Mar) Perched on a cliff 3 miles east of North Berwick is the spectacular ruin of Tantallon Castle. Built around 1350, it was the fortress residence of the Douglas earls of Angus (the Red Douglases), defended on one side by a series of ditches and on the other by an almost sheer drop into the sea.

⌸ Sleeping & Eating

North Berwick has plenty of places to stay, though they can fill up quickly at weekends, when golfers are in town. Recommended B&Bs include Glebe House (☑01620- 892608; www.glebehouse-nb.co.uk; Law Rd; r per person £55), a beautiful Georgian country house with three spacious bedrooms.

The top eating places in the area are the Grange (☑01620-893344; www.grangenorthber wick.co.uk; 35 High St; mains £12-15; ⊙lunch & dinner) in the centre of town, and the delightful Deveau's Brasserie (www.openarmshotel.com; Open Arms Hotel, Dirleton; mains £10-18; ⊙lunch & dinner) in the village of Dirleton.

❶ Getting There & Away

North Berwick is 24 miles east of Edinburgh. First bus 124 runs between Edinburgh and North

Berwick (1¼ hours, every 20 minutes). There are frequent trains between North Berwick and Edinburgh (£5.70, 35 minutes, hourly).

DUNBAR
POP 6350

Dunbar was an important Scottish fortress town in the Middle Ages, but little remains of its past, save for the tottering ruins of **Dunbar Castle** overlooking the harbour. Today the town survives as a fishing port and seaside resort, famed in the USA as the birthplace of John Muir (1838–1914), pioneer conservationist and father of the US national park system.

The tourist office (☑01368-863353; 143 High St; ⊙9am-5pm Mon-Sat, 11am-4pm Sun Jun-Sep, 9am-5pm Mon-Sat Apr, May & Oct) is near the town hall.

The town centre is home to John Muir House (www.jmbt.org.uk; 126 High St; admission free; ⊙10am-5pm Mon-Sat, 1-5pm Sun, closed Mon & Tue Nov-Mar), the birthplace and childhood home of the great man himself. The nearby Dunbar Town House Museum (www.dun barmuseum.org; High St; admission free; ⊙1-5pm Apr-Oct, Sat & Sun only Nov-Mar) provides an introduction to local history and archaeology.

From the castle, a scenic 2-mile clifftop trail follows the coastline west to the sands of Belhaven Bay and **John Muir Country Park**.

First bus X6 (one hour, hourly) runs between Edinburgh and Dunbar. Trains from Edinburgh's Waverley train station serve Dunbar (£6.90, 20 minutes) every hour or so.

West Lothian

LINLITHGOW
POP 13,400

This ancient royal burgh is one of Scotland's oldest towns, though much of it 'only' dates from the 15th to 17th centuries. Its centre retains a certain charm, despite some ugly modern buildings and occasional traffic congestion, and the town makes an excellent day trip from Edinburgh.

The tourist office (☑01506-282720; Burgh Halls, The Cross; ⊙9am-5pm Mon-Sat, 11am-5pm Sun) is close to the palace entrance.

◉ Sights & Activities

Linlithgow Palace HISTORIC BUILDING
(HS; Church Peel; adult/child £5.50/3.30; ⊙9.30am-5.30pm Apr-Sep, to 4.30pm Oct-Mar) The town's main attraction is this magnificent palace, begun by James I in 1425. The building of the palace continued for over

a century and it became a favourite royal residence – James V was born here in 1512, as was his daughter Mary (later Queen of Scots) in 1542, and Bonnie Prince Charlie visited briefly in 1745. The elaborately carved **King's Fountain**, the centrepiece of the palace courtyard, flowed with wine during Charlie's stay. The fountain, commissioned by James V in 1537, is the oldest in Britain, and was restored to working order in 2005.

FREE St Michael's Church   CHURCH
(www.stmichaelsparish.org.uk; Church Peel; ☉10.30am-4pm May-Sep, to 1pm Oct-Apr) Built between the 1420s and 1530s, the Gothic St Michael's Church is topped by a controversial aluminium spire that was added in 1964. The church is said to be haunted by a ghost that foretold King James IV of his impending defeat at Flodden in 1513.

Linlithgow Canal Centre   CANAL CENTRE
(www.lucs.org.uk; Manse Rd; admission free; ☉1.30-5pm Easter-Sep) Just 150m south of the town centre lies the Union Canal and the pretty canal centre, where a little museum records the history of the canal. The centre runs three-hour canal-boat trips (adult/child £8/5) west to the Avon Aqueduct, departing at 2pm Saturday and Sunday, Easter to September, and occasionally to the **Falkirk Wheel** (p197). Shorter 20-minute cruises (adult/child £4/2) leave every half hour during the centre's opening times.

✖ Eating & Drinking

Four Marys   PUB £
(www.thefourmarys.co.uk; 65-76 High St; mains £7-10; ☉lunch & dinner Mon-Fri, noon-9pm Sat, 12.30-8.30pm Sun) The Four Marys is an attractive traditional pub (opposite the palace entrance) that serves real ales and excellent pub grub, including haggis, neeps and tatties (haggis, mashed turnip and mashed potato).

Champany Inn   SCOTTISH £££
(☎01506-834532; www.champany.com; 3-course lunch/dinner £23/43; ☉lunch Mon-Fri, dinner Mon-Sat) This rustic inn is a trencherman's delight, famous for its excellent Aberdeen Angus steaks and Scottish lobsters (booking recommended). The neighbouring Chop & Ale House (mains £10-18) is a less-expensive alternative to the main dining room, offering delicious homemade burgers and steaks. The inn is 2 miles northeast of Linlithgow, on the A803/A904 road towards Bo'ness and Queensferry.

❶ Getting There & Away

Linlithgow is 15 miles west of Edinburgh, and is served by frequent trains from the capital (£4.60, 20 minutes, four every hour); the train station is 250m east of the town centre.

You can also cycle from Edinburgh to Linlithgow along the Union Canal towpath (21 miles); allow two hours.

EDINBURGH WEST LOTHIAN

Glasgow

POP 634,700

Includes »

Best Places to Stay

» Brunswick Hotel (p119)
» Malmaison (p120)
» Hotel du Vin (p122)
» Glasgow SYHA (p122)
» Blythswood Square (p120)

Best Places to Eat

» The Ubiquitous Chip (p125)
» Stravaigin (p125)
» The Inn at Kippen (p140)
» Mother India (p128)
» Café Gandolfi (p123)

Why Go?

Displaying a disarming blend of sophistication and earthiness, Scotland's biggest city has evolved over the last couple of decades to become one of Britain's most intriguing metropolises.

Its Victorian architectural legacy is now swamped with stylish bars, top-notch restaurants and a hedonistic club culture that will bring out your nocturnal instincts. Glasgow's pounding live-music scene is one of the best in Britain, accessible through countless venues dedicated to home-grown beats.

Museums and galleries abound, and the city's proud industrial and artistic heritage is innovatively displayed. Charles Rennie Mackintosh's sublime works dot the town, while the River Clyde, traditionally associated with the city's earthier side, is now a symbol of the its renaissance.

Glaswegians are proud of their working-class background, black humour and leftist traditions. Glasgow combines style, edgy urbanity and the residents' legendary friendliness in a captivating blend that will leave you wanting more.

When to Go

Glasgow

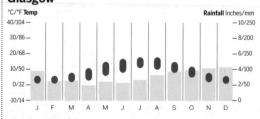

Feb The drizzle won't lift? Maroon yourself in one of Glasgow's fabulous pubs or clubs.

Jun The West End Festival and the Jazz Festival make the city a music heaven.

Aug Glasgow is friendly at any time, but when the sun is shining there's no happier city in Britain.

History

Glasgow grew around the cathedral founded by St Kertigan, later to become St Mungo, in the 6th century. Unfortunately, with the exception of the cathedral, virtually nothing of the medieval city remains. It was swept away by the energetic people of a new age – the age of capitalism, the Industrial Revolution and the British Empire.

In the 18th century, much of the tobacco trade between Europe and the USA was routed through Glasgow and provided a great source of wealth. Even after the tobacco trade declined in the 19th century, the city continued to prosper as a centre of textile manufacturing, shipbuilding and the coal and steel industries. The outward appearance of prosperity, however, was tempered by the dire working conditions in the factories.

In the first half of the 20th century Glasgow was the centre of Britain's munitions industry, supplying arms and ships for the two world wars, in the second of which the city was carpet-bombed. In the postwar years, however, the port and heavy industries began to dwindle, and by the early 1970s the city looked doomed. Unlike in Edinburgh, the working-class residents of Glasgow had few alternatives when recession hit, and the city became synonymous with unemployment, economic depression and urban violence, centred around high-rise housing schemes such as the infamous Gorbals. More recently, urban development and a booming cultural sector have injected style and confidence into the city; though the standard of living remains low for Britain and life continues to be tough for many, the ongoing regeneration process gives grounds for optimism.

◉ Sights

Glasgow's major sights are fairly evenly dispersed, with many found along the Clyde (the focus of a long-term regeneration program), in the leafy cathedral precinct in the East End and in the museum-rich South Side. Many museums are free. The centre also contains a variety of attractions, particularly Mackintoshania, while the trendy West End swarms with students during term time.

City Centre

The grid layout and pedestrian streets of the city centre make it easy to get around, and there are many cafes and pubs that make good pit stops between attractions.

Glasgow School of Art   MACKINTOSH BUILDING
(Map p106; ☎0141-353 4526; www.gsa.ac.uk/tours; 167 Renfrew St; adult/child/family £8.75/7/24; ☺9.30am-6.30pm Apr-Sep, 10.30am-5pm Oct-Mar) Mackintosh's greatest building, the Glasgow School of Art, still fulfils its original function, so just follow the steady stream of eclectically dressed students up the hill to find it. It's hard not to be impressed by the thoroughness of the design; the architect's pencil seems to have shaped everything inside and outside the building. The interior is strikingly austere, with simple colour combinations (often just black and cream) and the uncomfortable-looking high-backed chairs for which Mackintosh is famous. The library, designed as an addition in 1907, is a masterpiece. The visitor entrance is at the side of the building on Dalhousie St; here you'll find a shop with a small but useful interpretative display. Excellent hour-long guided tours (roughly hourly in summer; 11am, 1pm and 3pm in winter) run by architecture students leave from here; this is the only way (apart from enrolling) you can visit the building's interior. They're worth booking by phone at busy times. Multilingual translations are available.

FREE Gallery of Modern Art   GALLERY
(GoMA; Map p106; www.glasgowmuseums.com; Royal Exchange Sq; ☺10am-5pm Mon-Wed & Sat, to 8pm Thu, 11am-5pm Fri & Sun) Scotland's most popular contemporary art gallery features modern works from international artists, housed in a graceful neoclassical building. The original interior is used to make a daring, inventive art display. Social issues are a focal point of the museum but it's not all heavy going: there's a big effort made to keep the kids entertained.

FREE Willow Tearooms   MACKINTOSH BUILDING
(Map p106; www.willowtearooms.co.uk; Mackintosh Building, 217 Sauchiehall St; ☺9am-5pm Mon-Sat, 11am-5pm Sun) Admirers of the great Mackintosh will love the Willow Tearooms, an authentic reconstruction of tearooms Mackintosh designed and furnished in the early 20th century for restaurateur Kate Cranston. You can relive the original splendour of this unique tearoom while admiring the architect's distinctive touch in just about every element; he had a free rein and even

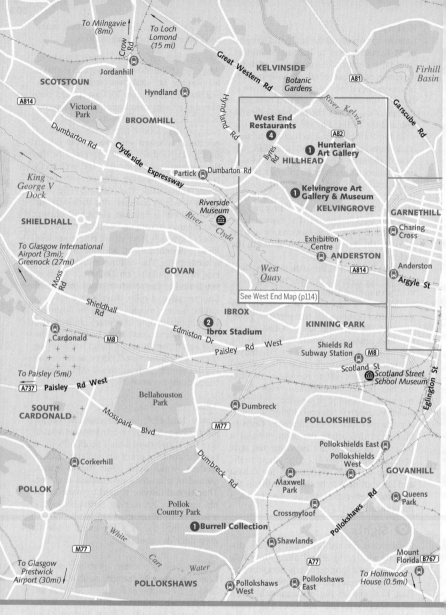

Glasgow Highlights

❶ Gazing at the city's fabulous wealth of paintings in the **Burrell Collection** (p114), the **Kelvingrove Art Gallery & Museum** (p112) and the **Hunterian Art Gallery** (p112)

❷ Catching a match in one of **Celtic** (p134) or **Rangers'** (p134) cauldrons of football

❸ Showing your latest dance moves among Glasgow's plethora of **nightclubs** (p131)

where the country's best DJs strut their stuff

❹ Deciding which one of the West End's excellent **restaurants** (p125) you are going to dine at next

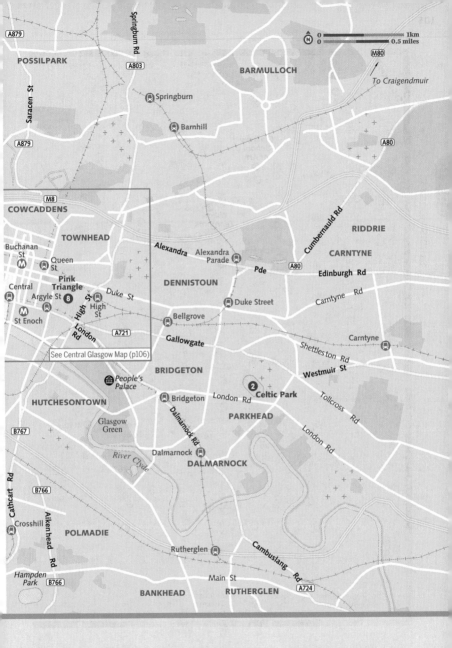

0 | 1km
0 | 0.5 miles

To Craigendmuir

POSSILPARK

Springburn Rd

A879

A803

BARMULLOCH

M80

A879

Springburn

Barnhill

A80

COWCADDENS

M8

TOWNHEAD

RIDDRIE

Cumbernauld Rd

Buchanan St

Queen St

Alexandra

Alexandra Parade

Pde

CARNTYNE

Edinburgh Rd

A80

Pink Triangle

DENNISTOUN

Central

Argyle St

Duke St

8

St Enoch

High St

High St

Duke Street

Carntyne Rd

London Rd

A721

Bellgrove

Carntyne

See Central Glasgow Map (p106)

Gallowgate

Shettleston Rd

Westmuir St

People's Palace

BRIDGETON

Celtic Park

2

Tollcross Rd

HUTCHESONTOWN

Bridgeton

London Rd

PARKHEAD

B767

Glasgow Green

Dalmarnock Rd

London Rd

River Clyde

Dalmarnock

DALMARNOCK

B766

Cathcart Rd

Crosshill

POLMADIE

Rutherglen

Cambuslang Rd

Aikenhead Rd

Hampden Park

B766

Main St

A724

BANKHEAD

RUTHERGLEN

⑤ Discovering the work of **Charles Rennie Mackintosh** (p120) – 'genius' is an overused word, but few would argue with it here

⑥ Plunging into the legendary and diverse **live-music scene** (p132) in one of the city's legendary pubs

⑦ Exploring Glasgow's industrial heritage and green surroundings on one of the great **cycle routes** (p117)

⑧ Immersing yourself in Glasgow's friendly gay culture in one of the bars of the **Pink Triangle** (p132)

Central Glasgow

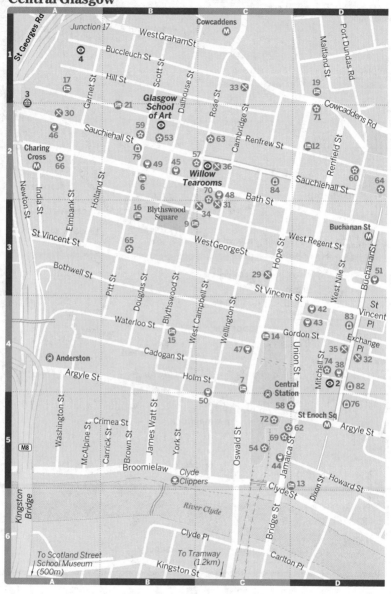

GLASGOW SIGHTS

the teaspoons were given his attention. Reconstruction took two years and the Willow reopened as a tearoom in 1980 (having been closed since 1926). The street name Sauchiehall means 'lane of willows', hence the choice of a stylised willow motif.

Sharmanka Kinetic Gallery & Theatre   MECHANICAL THEATRE
(Map p106; ☎0141-552 7080; www.sharmanka .com; 103 Trongate; adult/child £8/free) Great fun for kids and often surprisingly moving for adults, this extraordinary mechanical thea-

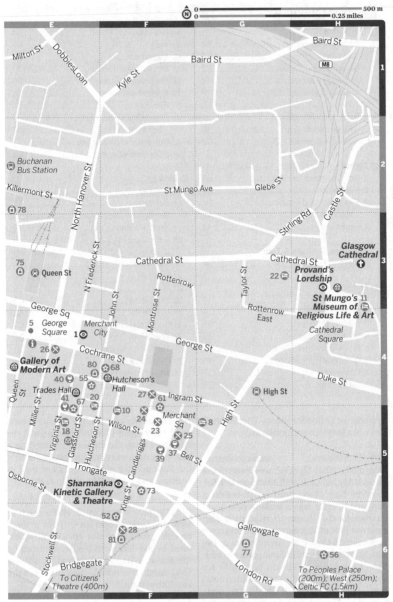

tre is located at the Trongate 103 arts centre. Originally from St Petersburg, it brings inanimate objects to life, as sculptured pieces of scrap and tiny carved figures perform humorous and tragic stories of the human spirit, set to haunting music. It's joyful, ironic theatre: inspirational one moment and macabre the next, but always colourful, clever and thought-provoking. Full performances are at 7pm Thursday and Sunday, and there are shorter daily performances (£5 with two kids free) from Wednesday to Sunday (check

Central Glasgow

by phone or online for times). The gallery is also open between performances.

FREE Lighthouse   MACKINTOSH BUILDING
(Map p106; ☏0141-221 6362; www.thelighthouse
.co.uk; 11 Mitchell Lane; ⊙10.30am-5pm Mon-Sat, noon-5pm Sun) Mackintosh's first building, designed in 1893, was a striking new headquarters for the *Glasgow Herald*. Tucked up a narrow lane off Buchanan St, it now serves as Scotland's Centre for Architecture & Design, with fairly technical temporary exhibitions (sometimes admission is payable for these), as well as the Mackintosh Interpretation Centre, a detailed (if slightly dry) overview of his life and work. On the top floor of the 'lighthouse', drink in great views over the rooftops and spires of the city centre.

City Chambers   TOWN HALL
(Map p106; www.glasgow.gov.uk; George Sq) The grand City Chambers, the seat of local government, were built in the 1880s at the high point of the city's wealth. The interior is even more extravagant than the exterior, and the chambers have sometimes been used as a movie location to represent the Kremlin or the Vatican. Free guided tours are held at 10.30am and 2.30pm Monday to Friday.

Tenement House   HISTORIC HOUSE
(NTS; Map p106; www.nts.org.uk; 145 Buccleuch St; adult/child £6/5; ⊙1-5pm Mar-Oct) For a time-capsule experience, visit this small apartment in the Tenement House, operated by the National Trust for Scotland. It offers a vivid insight into middle-class city life in the late 19th century.

FREE Royal Highland
Fusiliers Museum   MUSEUM
(Map p106; www.rhf.org.uk; 518 Sauchiehall St; ⊙9am-4pm Mon-Thu, to 3pm Fri) Charts the history of the Royal Highland Fusiliers, as well as previous regiments, from 1678 to the present. The walls are dripping with exhib-

GLASGOW SIGHTS

its, including uniforms, medals, pictures and other militaria. The wrought ironwork was designed by Mackintosh.

East End

The oldest part of the city, given a facelift in the 1990s, is concentrated around Glasgow Cathedral, to the east of the modern centre. It takes 15 minutes to walk from George Sq, but numerous buses pass nearby, including buses 11, 12, 36, 37, 38 and 42.

Glasgow Cathedral   CATHEDRAL
(HS; Map p106; www.historic-scotland.gov.uk; Cathedral Sq; ☉9.30am-5.30pm Mon-Sat, 1-5pm Sun Apr-Sep, closes 4.30pm Oct-Mar) An attraction that shouldn't be missed, Glasgow Cathedral has a rare timelessness. The dark, imposing interior conjures up medieval might and can send a shiver down the spine. It's a shining example of Gothic architecture, and, unlike nearly all Scotland's cathedrals, survived the turmoil of the Reformation mobs almost in-tact. Most of the current building dates from the 15th century.

Entry is through a side door into the **nave**, which is hung with regimental colours. The wooden roof above has been restored many times since its original construction, but some of the timber dates from the 14th century; note the impressive shields. Many of the cathedral's stunning, narrow windows of stained glass are modern; to your left is Francis Spear's 1958 work *The Creation*, which fills the west window.

The cathedral, divided by a late-15th-century stone choir screen, is decorated with seven pairs of figures representing the seven deadly sins. Beyond is the **choir**. The four stained-glass panels of the east window de-picting the Apostles (also by Francis Spear) are particularly evocative. At the northeast-ern corner is the entrance to the 15th-cen-tury **upper chapter house**, where Glasgow University was founded. It's now used as a sacristy.

The most interesting part of the cathedral, the **lower church**, is reached by a stairway. Its forest of pillars creates a powerful atmosphere around St Mungo's tomb (St Mungo founded a monastic community here in the 5th century), the focus of a famous medieval pilgrimage that was believed to be as meritorious as a visit to Rome.

Behind the cathedral, the **necropolis** stretches picturesquely up and over a green hill. The elaborate Victorian tombs of the city's wealthy industrialists make for an intriguing stroll, great views and a vague Gothic thrill.

TOP
CHOICE **St Mungo's Museum of Religious Life & Art** MUSEUM
(Map p106; www.glasgowmuseums.com; 2 Castle St; admission free; ⊙10am-5pm Tue-Thu & Sat, 11am-5pm Fri & Sun) Set in a reconstruction of the bishop's palace that once stood in the cathedral forecourt, this museum is an audacious attempt to capture the world's major religions in an artistic nutshell. A startling achievement, it presents the similarities and differences of how various religions approach common themes such as birth, marriage and death. The attraction is twofold: firstly, impressive art that blurs the lines between religion and culture; and secondly, the opportunity to delve into different faiths, an experience that can be as deep or shallow as you wish. There are three galleries, representing religion as art, religious life and, on the top floor, religion in Scotland. A Zen garden is outside.

FREE **Provand's Lordship** HISTORIC HOUSE
(Map p106; www.glasgowmuseums.com; 3 Castle St; ⊙10am-5pm Tue-Thu & Sat, 11am-5pm Fri & Sun) Near the cathedral is Provand's Lordship, the oldest house in Glasgow. A rare example of 15th-century domestic Scottish architecture, it was built in 1471 as a manse for the chaplain of St Nicholas Hospital. The ceilings and doorways are low, and the rooms are sparsely furnished with period artefacts, except for an upstairs room, which has been furnished to reflect the living space of an early-16th-century chaplain. The building's biggest draw is its authentic feel – if you ignore the tacky imitation-stone linoleum covering the ground floor.

FREE **People's Palace** MUSEUM
(www.glasgowmuseums.com; Glasgow Green; ⊙10am-5pm Tue-Thu & Sat, 11am-5pm Fri & Sun) Set in the city's oldest park, Glasgow Green, is the solid orange stone People's Palace. It is an impressive museum of social history, telling the story of Glasgow from 1750 to the present through creative, inventive displays, which are great for families – the kids will love the re-creation of a WWII air raid. The palace was built in the late 19th century as a cultural centre for Glasgow's East End. The attached greenhouse, the Winter Gardens,

---

GLASGOW IN...

Two Days

On your first day, hit the **East End** for **Glasgow Cathedral**, **St Mungo's Museum** and a wander through the hillside **necropolis**. Later take in one of the city's top museums: either the **Burrell Collection** or the **Kelvingrove**. As evening falls, head to trendy **Merchant City** for a stroll and dinner – **Café Gandolfi** maybe, or the latest trendy newcomer. Make sure you head to **Artá** for a pre- or post-meal drink. The next day, visit whichever museum you missed yesterday, and then it's Mackintosh time. **Glasgow School of Art** is his finest work: if you like his style, head to the West End for **Mackintosh House**. Hungry? Thirsty? Some of the city's best restaurants and bars are up this end of town, so you could make a night of it. Make sure to check out one of the numerous excellent music venues around the city.

Four Days

A four-day stay gives much better scope for getting to know the city in some depth. Spend a day along the Clyde – the **Riverside Museum** and the **Science Centre**. Plan your weekend around a night out at **Arches** or the legendary **Sub Club**, a day strolling the stylish city-centre clothing emporia, earthier shopping at the **Barras** flea market and a football game. Don't miss trying at least one of the city's classic curry houses.

THE GLASGOW BOYS

The great rivalry between Glasgow and Edinburgh has also played out in the art world. In the late 19th century a group of Glaswegian painters challenged the domineering artistic establishment in the capital. Up to this point, paintings were largely confined to historical scenes and sentimental visions of the Highlands. These painters – including Sir James Guthrie, EA Hornel, George Henry and Joseph Crawhall – experimented with colour and themes of rural life, shocking Edinburgh's conservative artistic society. Many of them went to study in Paris studios, and brought back a much-needed breath of European air into the Scottish art scene. Like Charles Rennie Mackintosh, the Glasgow Boys' work met with admiration and artistic recognition on the Continent.

The Glasgow Boys had an enormous influence on the Scottish art world, inspiring the next generation of Scottish painters – the Colourists. Their works can be seen in the Kelvingrove (p112) and Hunterian (p112) galleries as well as Broughton House in Kirkcudbright (p178) and the National Gallery of Scotland in Edinburgh (p62).

has tropical plants and is a nice spot for a coffee.

The Clyde

Once a thriving shipbuilding area, the Clyde sank into dereliction during the postwar era but is slowly being rejuvenated. A major campaign to redevelop Glasgow Harbour, involving the conversion of former docklands into shops and public areas, is under way – to find out more about this project see www.glasgowharbour.com.

There are several good attractions along the Clyde, but the walk along its banks still isn't all that it could be; it can feel bleak and impersonal, with oversized buildings dwarfing the humble pedestrian.

FREE Riverside Museum   MUSEUM

(www.glasgowmuseums.com; 100 Pointhouse Pl; ☺10am-5pm Mon-Thu & Sat, 11am-5pm Fri & Sun) The latest development along the Clyde is this visually impressive new museum, whose striking curved facades are the work of Iraqi architect Zaha Hadid. A transport museum forms the main part of the collection, featuring an excellent series of cars made in Scotland, plus assorted railway locos, trams, bikes (including the world's first pedal-powered bicycle from 1847) and model Clyde-built ships. An atmospheric recreation of a Glasgow shopping street from the early 20th century puts the vintage vehicles into a social context. The magnificent Tall Ship Glenlee (www.thetallship.com; adult/child £5/3; ☺10am-5pm Mar-Oct, to 4pm Nov-Feb), a beautiful three-master launched in 1896, is berthed alongside the museum. On board are displays about the ship's history, restoration

and shipboard life during its heyday. The Riverside is west of the centre at Glasgow Harbour; you can reach it on bus 100 from the north side of George Sq, or via the Clyde Clippers boat service. There's also a cafe.

Glasgow Science Centre   MUSEUM

(Map p114; ☎0141-420 5000; www.gsc.org.uk; 50 Pacific Quay; Science Mall adult/child £9.95/7.95, IMAX, tower or planetarium £2.50; ☺10am-5pm Wed-Sun) Scotland's flagship millennium project, the ultramodern Glasgow Science Centre, will keep the kids entertained for hours (that's middle-aged kids, too!). It brings science and technology alive through hundreds of interactive exhibits on four floors. Look out for the illusions (like rearranging your features through a 3-D head-scan) and the cloud chamber, which makes natural radiation visible. The museum consists of an egg-shaped titanium-covered IMAX theatre (phone for current screenings) and an interactive Science Mall with floor-to-ceiling windows – a bounty of discovery for young, inquisitive minds. There's also a rotating 127m-high observation tower; a planetarium, where the Scottish Power Space Theatre brings the night sky to life, and a Virtual Science Theatre, which treats visitors to a 3-D molecular journey. To get here, take Arriva bus 24 from Renfield St or First Glasgow bus 89 or 90 from Union St.

West End

With its trendy bars and nonchalant swagger, the West End is perhaps the most engaging area of Glasgow – it's as close as Glasgow gets to bohemian. From the centre, buses 9, 16 and 23 run towards Kelvingrove, 8, 11, and 16 to the university, and 20, 44 and 66 to Byres Rd (among others).

TOP CHOICE Kelvingrove Art Gallery & Museum

MUSEUM, GALLERY

(Map p114; www.glasgowmuseums.com; Argyle St; admission free; ☉10am-5pm Mon-Thu & Sat, 11am-5pm Fri & Sun; ☜) A magnificent stone building, this grand Victorian cathedral of culture has been revamped into a fascinating and unusual museum, with a bewildering variety of exhibits. You'll find fine art alongside stuffed animals, and Micronesian shark-tooth swords alongside a Spitfire plane, but it's not mix 'n' match: rooms are carefully and thoughtfully themed, and the collection is a manageable size. There's an excellent room of Scottish art, a room of fine French Impressionist works, and quality Renaissance paintings from Italy and Flanders. Salvador Dalí's superb *Christ of St John of the Cross* is also here. Best of all, nearly everything – including the paintings – has an easy-reading paragraph of interpretation next to it. You can learn a lot about art and more here, and it's excellent for children, with plenty for them to do and displays aimed at a variety of ages. There are free hour-long guided tours beginning at 11am and 2.30pm. Bus 17, among many others, runs here from Renfield St.

FREE Hunterian Museum

MUSEUM

(Map p114; www.hunterian.gla.ac.uk; University Ave; ☉10am-5pm Tue-Sat, 11am-4pm Sun) Housed in the glorious sandstone building of the university, which is in itself reason enough to pay a visit, this quirky museum contains the collection of a renowned one-time student of the university, William Hunter (1718–83). Hunter was primarily an anatomist and physician but, as one of those gloriously well-rounded Enlightenment figures, he interested himself in everything the world had to offer. Pickled organs in glass jars take their place alongside geological phenomena, potsherds gleaned from ancient brochs, dinosaur skeletons and a creepy case of deformed animals. The main halls of the exhibition, with their high vaulted roofs, are magnificent in themselves. A highlight is the 1674 *Map of the Whole World* in the World Culture section.

FREE Hunterian Art Gallery

GALLERY, MUSEUM

(Map p114; www.hunterian.gla.ac.uk; 82 Hillhead St; ☉10am-5pm Tue-Sat, 11am-4pm Sun) Across

the road from the Hunterian Museum, the bold tones of the Scottish Colourists (Samuel Peploe, Francis Cadell, JD Fergusson and Leslie Hunter) are well represented in this gallery, which also forms part of Hunter's bequest to the university. There are Sir William MacTaggart's Impressionistic Scottish landscapes and a gem by Thomas Millie Dow. There's also a special collection of James McNeill Whistler's limpid prints, drawings and paintings. Upstairs, in a section devoted to late-19th-century Scottish art, you can see works by several of the Glasgow Boys.

TOP CHOICE Mackintosh House

MACKINTOSH BUILDING

(Map p114; www.hunterian.gla.ac.uk; 82 Hillhead St; adult/concession £5/3; ☉10am-5pm Tue-Sat, 11am-4pm Sun) Attached to the Hunterian Art Gallery, this is a reconstruction of the first home that Charles Rennie Mackintosh bought with his wife, noted artist Mary Macdonald. It's fair to say that interior decoration was one of their strong points; the Mackintosh House is startling even today. The quiet elegance of the hall and dining room on the ground floor give way to a stunning drawing room. There's something otherworldly about the very mannered style of the beaten silver panels, the long-backed chairs and the surface decorations echoing Celtic manuscript illuminations. You wouldn't have wanted to be the guest that spilled a glass of red on this carpet.

Botanic Gardens

PARK

(Map p114; 730 Great Western Rd; ☉7am-dusk, glasshouse 10am-6pm summer, to 4.15pm winter) A marvellous thing about walking into these beautiful gardens is the way the noise of Great Western Rd suddenly recedes into the background. Amazingly, the lush grounds don't seem that popular with locals (except on sunny weekends) and away from the entrance you may just about have the place to yourself. The wooded gardens follow the riverbank of the River Kelvin and there are plenty of tropical species to discover. **Kibble Palace**, an impressive Victorian iron and glass structure dating from 1873, is one of the largest glasshouses in Britain; check out the herb garden, too, with its medicinal species. The gorgeous hilly grounds make the perfect place for a picnic lunch. There are also organised walks and concerts in summer – have a look at the noticeboard near the entrance to see what's on.

VISITING KELVINGROVE

Duration: Three hours

There are over a million objects in the museum's collection, but fortunately they've pared things down so you won't feel overwhelmed. Enter from either side and first admire the building's interior, with its high central hall, elaborate lamps and organ (recitals at 1pm).

The museum is divided into two wings, one focusing on Life (history, archaeology and natural history) and the other on Expression (art).

FIRST FLOOR

Start with the art: upstairs in the hall with the hanging heads. The Dutch room features Rembrandt's magnificent *Man in Armour,* with chiaroscuro techniques learned from Caravaggio. Hit the interactive screen and decide whom you think the painting represents.

The adjacent French gallery holds a fine Renoir portrait of his pupil Valentine Fray, and an early Van Gogh depicting his Glaswegian flatmate Alexander Reid. Nearby, Monet's *Vétheuil* offers a quintessential representation of both Impressionism and the French countryside; contrast it with the less ethereal landscape by Cézanne's located alongside. Dufy's famous canvas of *The Jetty at Trouville* also inhabits this room, as do works by many other masters.

The Scottish landscape gallery has some jaw-dropping depictions of Highland scenes. Standing in front of Gustave Doré's *Glen Massan* you can almost feel the drizzle and smell the heather. David Wilkie's *The Cottar's Saturday Night* is based on the poem by Robert Burns.

While you're up here, don't miss the paintings around the arcade. The collection's highlight, however, sits upstairs in the central atrium. Based on dreams, Salvador Dalí's *Christ of St John of the Cross* is arguably his greatest work. Forget ridiculous moustaches and Surrealist frippery: this is a serious, awesomely powerful painting. A sinewy man-god looks down through an infinity of sky and darkness to a simple fishing boat in Galilee (or Catalunya in this case). You could spend a while in front of this.

GROUND FLOOR

Downstairs, check out the **Art Discovery Centre**, aimed at kids but well worth a stroll, then head for the large room devoted to the Glasgow Boys. Inspired by Whistler, these artists broke with romanticism to pioneer a more modern style. Compare William Kennedy's grounded *Stirling Station* or the realism of James Guthrie's *A Funeral Service in the Highlands* with those misty Scottish landscapes upstairs. Also noteworthy in this space are John Lavery's famous theatrical portrait of Anna Pavlova, and EA Hornel's much-reproduced *The Coming of Spring*.

You've seen most of the paintings now, but there's still plenty left to discover. Try the room dedicated to interiors and designs of art deco and the Glasgow style. 'Margaret has genius, I have only talent', said Charles Rennie Mackintosh of his wife, and there's a good display of her work here, as well as that of her sister, Frances Macdonald.

The other side of the museum, dominated by a hanging Spitfire, has rooms with impressive carved stones from the Viking era, Egyptian grave goods and other archaeological finds. Suits of armour are cleverly placed in an exhibition about the human consequences of war, and there are some fine social history displays. The taxidermy animals downstairs are a reminder of the museum's Victorian past. Don't miss John Fulton's elaborate orrery, a working model of the solar system: you'll find it near the much-loved elephant (who is called Sir Roger, if you'd like to be introduced).

FREE **Fossil Grove** GEOLOGICAL SITE (Victoria Park, Dumbarton Rd; ⊙10am-4pm Apr-Sep) With sections of 350-million-year-old fossilised trees lying around just as they were found, Fossil Grove is an intriguing site. To get here, take bus 44 from the city centre to Victoria Park.

South Side

The south side is a tangled web of busy roads with a few oases giving relief from the

West End

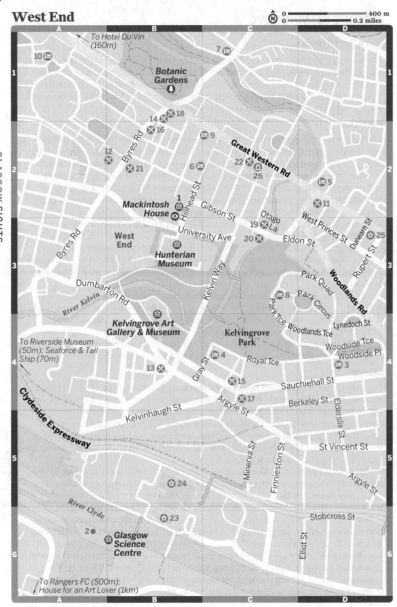

To Hotel Du Vin (160m)

Botanic Gardens

Great Western Rd

Mackintosh House

West End

Hunterian Museum

Dumbarton Rd

River Kelvin

Kelvingrove Art Gallery & Museum

To Riverside Museum (50m); Seaforce & Tall Ship (70m)

Kelvingrove Park

Clydeside Expressway

Woodlands Rd

River Clyde

Glasgow Science Centre

To Rangers FC (500m); House for an Art Lover (1km)

urban congestion. It does, however, contain some excellent attractions.

FREE **Burrell Collection** GALLERY
(www.glasgowmuseums.com; Pollok Country Park; ⊙10am-5pm Mon-Thu & Sat, 11am-5pm Fri & Sun) One of Glasgow's top attractions is the Burrell Collection. Amassed by wealthy industrialist Sir William Burrell before being donated to the city, it is housed in an outstanding museum, 3 miles south of the city centre. Burrell collected all manner of art

West End

from his teens to his death at 97, and this idiosyncratic collection of treasure includes everything from Chinese porcelain and medieval furniture to paintings by Degas and Cézanne. It's not so big as to be overwhelming, and the stamp of the collector lends an intriguing coherence.

Visitors will find their own favourite part of this museum, but the exquisite tapestry galleries are outstanding. Intricate stories capturing life in Europe are woven into staggering wall-size pieces dating from the 13th to 16th centuries.

Within the spectacular interior, carved-stone Romanesque doorways are incorporated into the structure so you actually walk through them. Floor-to-ceiling windows admit a flood of light, and enable the surrounding landscape outside to enhance the effect of the exhibits. It feels as if you're wandering in a huge tranquil greenhouse.

In springtime, it's worth spending a full day here and taking your time wandering in the beautiful park, studded with flowers. Once part of the estates of **Pollok House**,

which can be visited, the grounds have numerous picnic spots; if you're not heading further north, here's the place to see shaggy Highland cattle, as well as heavy horses.

Many buses pass the park gates (including buses 45, 47, 48 and 57 from the city centre), and there's a twice-hourly bus service between the gallery and the gates (a pleasant 10-minute walk). Alternatively catch a train to Pollokshaws West from Central station (four per hour; you want the second station on the line for East Kilbride or Kilmarnock).

FREE Scotland Street
School Museum   MACKINTOSH BUILDING
(www.glasgowmuseums.com; 225 Scotland St; ◎10am-5pm Tue-Thu & Sat, 11am-5pm Fri & Sun) Mackintosh's Scotland Street School seems a bit forlorn these days, on a windswept industrial street with no babble of young voices filling its corridors. Nevertheless it's worth a visit for its stunning facade and interesting museum of education that occupies the interior. Reconstructions of classrooms from various points in the school's

VISITING THE BURRELL COLLECTION

Duration: Two hours

The Burrell collection is of a manageable size, but the surrounding parkland is so lovely, you should come equipped for strolling and, if it's a fine day, bring a picnic. In the museum itself, start in the luminous main courtyard, which is dotted with Rodin bronzes, including an 1880 version of *The Thinker*, the fabulous *Eve After the Fall* and *The Age of Bronze*. Next, pass through the ornate portal; this 16th-century work was originally part of Hornby Castle in Yorkshire and is appropriate preparation for the eclectic nature of the collection.

As you pass through the portal, you are thrown back millennia in time to ancient Egypt. Admire the fine carvings and the delicate faience shawabtiu – mummylike figures that accompanied the deceased to the afterlife. Attic black- and red-figure vases are next; continuing along the windows you jump forward via Chinese porcelain to religious sculpture; look for the noteworthy *Lamentation over the Crucified Christ*, an early-16th-century German work by that most versatile and prolific of artists, Anonymous.

Also on the ground floor are recreated interiors of Hutton Castle, a small section on Islamic art, and the Burrell's superb collection of tapestries, which get regularly rotated.

Retrace your steps to the Greek vases, and head up the stairs to the small suite of rooms that make this gallery a must-see for art-lovers. First up are some wonderful 15th- and 16th-century Flemish paintings, mostly on wood, and beautifully restored. *Rest on the Flight into Egypt* stands out here, the title belied by the very European landscape in the background.

The rest of this assemblage of art is French. Burrell was an important patron of Edgar Degas, whose series of ballet paintings, snapshotlike *Woman With a Parasol*, and masterful portrait of his friend Edmond Duranty are highlights. A series of Manets showcases his versatility, while Géricault's horses are also to be admired. You can feel the French summer sun in Alfred Sisley's *Church at Noisy-le-Roi;* compare it with the more dreamlike landscape of Cézanne's almost tropical *Château de Médan*.

Pleasingly, there's good information provided on each painting and, downstairs, computers where you can browse the database of the collection.

lifetime, combined with grumbling headmaster and cleaner, will have older visitors recalling their own schooldays. It's right opposite Shields Rd subway station and there's also an OK cafe.

House for an Art Lover   MACKINTOSH BUILDING
(☑0141-353 4770; www.houseforanartlover.co.uk; Bellahouston Park, Dumbreck Rd; adult/child £4.50/3; ⊘10am-4pm Mon-Wed, 10am-1pm Thu-Sun) Although designed in 1901 as an entry in a competition run by a German magazine, the House for an Art Lover was not built until the 1990s. Mackintosh worked closely with his wife on the design and her influence is evident, especially in the rose motif. The overall effect of this brilliant architect's design is one of space and light. Buses 3, 9, 54, 55 and 56 all run here from the city centre; always ring ahead before making the journey, as the house may be booked for events.

Holmwood House   HISTORIC HOUSE
(NTS; www.nts.org.uk; 61-63 Netherlee Rd; adult/child £6/5; ⊘noon-5pm Thu-Mon Apr-Oct) An interesting building designed by Alexander 'Greek' Thomson, Holmwood House dates from 1857. Despite constant ongoing renovations, it's well worth a visit. Look for sun symbols downstairs and stars upstairs in this attractive house with its adaptation of classical Greek architecture. Cathcart is 4 miles south of the centre; get a train via Queen's Park or Neilston. Otherwise, take bus 44, 44A, 44D or 66 from the city centre. Follow Rhannan Rd for about 800m to find the house.

Scottish Football Museum   MUSEUM
(The Hampden Experience; www.scottishfootball museum.org.uk; Hampden Park; adult/child £6/3; ⊘10am-5pm Mon-Sat, 11am-5pm Sun) Football fans will love the Scottish Football Museum, which features exhibits on the history of the game in Scotland and the influence of

Scots on the world game. Football inspires an incredible passion in Scotland and the museum is crammed full of impressive memorabilia, including a cap and match ticket from the very first international football game (which took place in 1872 between Scotland and England, and ended 0-0). The museum's engrossing exhibits give insight into the players, the fans, the media and the way the game has changed over the last 140 years. You can also take a tour of the stadium (adult/child £6/3; combined ticket with museum £9/4.50), home ground of the national football side and of lesser league outfit Queens Park. The museum is at Hampden Park, off Aikenhead Rd. To get there, take a train to Mount Florida station or take bus 5, 31, 37 or 75 from Stockwell St.

North Side
The north side doesn't have much of interest for visitors, apart from a unique church that also happens to be the headquarters of the Rennie Mackintosh Society.

Mackintosh Church   MACKINTOSH BUILDING
(www.crmsociety.com; 870 Garscube Rd; adult/child £4/free; ⊙10am-5pm Mon, Wed & Fri Apr-Oct, to 4pm Nov-Mar) Now the headquarters of the Charles Rennie Mackintosh Society, this is the only one of Mackintosh's church designs to be built. It has excellent stained glass and relief carvings, and the wonderful simplicity and grace of the barrel-shaped design is particularly inspiring. Garscube Rd is the northern extension of Rose St in the city centre.

🏃 Activities
There are numerous green spaces within the city. **Pollok Country Park** surrounds the Burrell Collection and has several woodland trails. Nearer the centre of the city, the **Kelvin Walkway** follows the River Kelvin through Kelvingrove Park, the Botanic Gardens and on to Dawsholm Park.

Walking & Cycling
The **Clyde Walkway** extends from Glasgow upriver to the Falls of Clyde near New Lanark, some 40 miles away. The tourist office has a good leaflet pack detailing different sections of this walk. The 10-mile section through Glasgow has interesting parts, though modern buildings have replaced most of the old shipbuilding works.

Well-trodden, long-distance footpath **West Highland Way** begins in Milngavie, 8 miles north of Glasgow (you can walk to

Milngavie from Glasgow along the River Kelvin), and runs for 95 spectacular miles to Fort William.

There are several long-distance pedestrian/cycle routes that begin in Glasgow and follow off-road routes for most of the way. Check www.sustrans.org.uk for more details. The **Clyde–Loch Lomond route** traverses residential and industrial areas in a 20-mile ride from Bell's Bridge to Loch Lomond. This route continues to Inverness as part of the **Lochs and Glens National Cycle Route**.

The **Clyde to Forth cycle route** runs through Glasgow. One way takes you to Edinburgh via Bathgate, the other takes you via Paisley to Greenock and Gourock, the first section partly on roads. Another branch heads down to Irvine and Ardrossan, for the ferry to Arran. An extension via Ayr, Maybole and Glentrool leads to the Solway coast and Carlisle.

☞ Tours
City Sightseeing   BUS TOUR
(Map p106; ✆0141-204 0444; www.citysightseeing glasgow.co.uk; adult/child £11/5) These double-decker tourist buses run a circuit along the main sightseeing routes, starting near the tourist office on George Sq. You get on and off as you wish. A ticket, bought from the driver or in the tourist office, is valid for two consecutive days. All buses have wheelchair access and multilingual commentary.

Glasgow Taxis City Tour   TAXI TOUR
(✆0141-429 7070; www.glasgowtaxis.co.uk) If you're confident you can understand the driver's accent, a taxi tour is a good way to get a feel of the city and its sights. The 60-minute tour takes you around all the centre's important landmarks, with commentary. The standard tour costs £35 for up to five people.

Loch Lomond Seaplanes   SCENIC FLIGHTS
(Map p114; ✆0143-667 5030; www.lochlomondsea planes.com; Clyde River, Glasgow Science Centre; flights from £129) This set-up uses the Clyde as its runway and will take you on scenic flights over Glasgow and Loch Lomond, or even run you up to Oban.

Seaforce   BOAT TRIPS
(✆0141-221 1070; www.seaforce.co.uk; Riverside Museum) Departing from the Riverside Museum, Seaforce offers speedy all-weather powerboat jaunts along the Clyde. There's

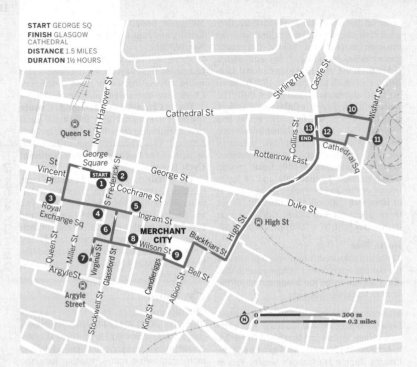

Walking Tour
Glasgow

❭ This stroll takes you to Glasgow Cathedral through trendy Merchant City, once headquarters for Glasgow industrialists.

The tourist office on ❶ **George Square** is a good starting point. The square is surrounded by imposing Victorian architecture: the old post office, the Bank of Scotland and the grandiose ❷ **City Chambers**. Statues include Robert Burns, James Watt, and, atop a Doric column, Sir Walter Scott.

Walk one block south down Queen St to the ❸ **Gallery of Modern Art**. This striking colonnaded building was once the Royal Exchange and now hosts some of the country's best contemporary art displays.

Walk east along Ingram St, ducking into the former Court House cells now housing the ❹ **Corinthian** bar for a glimpse of the extravagant interior, then continue on to ❺ **Hutcheson's Hall**. Built in 1805, this elegant building is now maintained by the National Trust for Scotland (NTS). Retrace your steps one block and continue south down Glassford St past ❻ **Trades Hall**, designed by Robert Adam in 1791 to house the trades guild. The exterior is best viewed from Garth St. Turn right into Wilson St and left along Virginia St, lined with the old warehouses of the Tobacco Lords; many of these have been converted into posh flats. The ❼ **Tobacco Exchange** became the Sugar Exchange in 1820.

Back on Wilson St, the ❽ **Sheriff Court** fills a whole block and was originally Glasgow's town hall. Continue east on Wilson St past Ingram Sq to ❾ **Merchant Square**, a covered courtyard that was once the city's fruit market but now bustles with cafes and bars.

Head up Albion St, then right into Blackfriars St. Emerging onto High St, turn left and follow it up to the ❿ **cathedral**. Behind the cathedral wind your way up through the ⓫ **Necropolis**, which offers great city views. On your way back check out the fabulous ⓬ **St Mungo's Museum of Religious Life & Art** and ⓭ **Provand's Lordship**.

a variety of trips, including a half-hour ride around central Glasgow (adult/child £12/6), an hour-long trip to the Erskine Bridge (£15/10) or four-hour rides to local wildlife hot spots (£50/35).

Waverley BOAT TRIPS
(Map p114; www.waverleyexcursions.co.uk; Clyde River, near Glasgow Science Centre; tickets £15-40; ☉Apr-Sep) The world's last ocean-going paddle steamer (built in 1947), cruises the Firth of Clyde from April to September; the website details days of departure. It serves several towns and the islands of Bute, Great Cumbrae and Arran. It departs from Glasgow Science Centre, among other places near Glasgow.

★ Festivals & Events

Not to be outdone by Edinburgh, Glasgow has some excellent festivals of its own.

Celtic Connections MUSIC
(www.celticconnections.com) Two-week music festival held in January.

Glasgow International Festival of Visual Art VISUAL ART
(www.glasgowinternational.org) Held in late April in even years, this festival features a range of innovative installations, performances and exhibitions around town.

Glasgow Jazz Festival JAZZ
(www.jazzfest.co.uk) Excellent festival held in June.

West End Festival ARTS
(www.westendfestival.co.uk) This music and arts event is Glasgow's biggest festival, running for three weeks in June.

Glasgow International Comedy Festival COMEDY
(www.glasgowcomedyfestival.com) Late March sees high-standard comedy acts tickle ribs around town.

Merchant City Festival ARTS
(www.merchantcityfestival.com) Lively street festival in the Merchant City quarter, with lots of performances and stalls. Late July.

Glasgow Film Festival FILM
(www.glasgowfilm.org) Ten-day film festival in February with screenings in various locations across the city.

World Pipe Band Championships PIPE BANDS
(www.rspba.org) Over 200 pipe bands; held in mid-August.

🛏 Sleeping

The city centre gets very rowdy at weekends, and accommodation options fill up fast, mostly with groups who will probably roll home boisterously some time after 3am. If you prefer an earlier appointment with your bed, you'll be better off in a smaller, quieter lodging, or in the West End. Booking ahead is essential at weekends and in July and August.

City Centre

TOP CHOICE **Brunswick Hotel** HOTEL ££
(Map p106; ☎0141-552 0001; www.brunswick hotel.co.uk; 106 Brunswick St; d £50-95; ☎☀) Some places have dour owners threatening lockouts if you break curfew. Then there's the Brunswick, which every now and then converts the whole hotel into a party venue,

---

GLASGOW FOR CHILDREN

Although Glasgow is a bigger, busier city than Edinburgh, it's an easy city to traverse with children due to its extensive public transport system and friendly locals. The city boasts excellent family attractions, including the Glasgow Science Centre (p111) and Sharmanka Kinetic Gallery & Theatre (p106), which both vie for the title of Glasgow's top child-friendly attraction. The Riverside Museum (p111) and the People's Palace (p110) are also recommended.

For suggestions for short-term child-care agencies, get in touch with the council-run Glasgow Childcare Information Service (☎0141-287 5223; chis@education.glasgow. gov.uk; 100 Morrison St). The KidsGlasgow (www.kidsglasgow.com) website lists upcoming events for children, as well as soft play areas and other recommendations.

Most parks in Glasgow have playgrounds for children. In the centre of town, the major shopping complexes like Buchanan Galleries (p135) and St Enochs are handy stops, with baby-changing facilities and shops and activities designed to keep the kids occupied for an hour or two.

THE GENIUS OF CHARLES RENNIE MACKINTOSH

Great cities have great artists, designers and architects contributing to the cultural and historical roots of their urban environment while expressing its soul and individuality. Charles Rennie Mackintosh was all of these. His quirky, linear and geometric designs have had almost as much influence on the city as have Gaudí's on Barcelona. Many of the buildings Mackintosh designed in Glasgow are open to the public, and you'll see his tall, thin, art nouveau typeface repeatedly reproduced.

Born in 1868, Mackintosh studied at the Glasgow School of Art. It was there that he met the also influential artist and designer Margaret Macdonald, whom he married; they collaborated on many projects and were major influences on each other's work. In 1896, when he was aged only 27, he won a competition for his design of the School of Art's new building, Mackintosh's supreme architectural achievement. The first section was opened in 1899 and is considered to be the earliest example of art nouveau in Britain. This building demonstrates his skill in combining function and style.

Although Mackintosh's genius was quickly recognised on the Continent, he did not receive the same encouragement in Scotland. His architectural career here lasted only until 1914, when he moved to England to concentrate on furniture design. He died in 1928, and it is only since the last decades of the 20th century that Mackintosh's genius has been widely recognised. For more about the man and his work, contact the Charles Rennie Mackintosh Society (☎0141-946 6600; www.crmsociety.com; 870 Garscube Rd, Mackintosh Church). Check its website for special events.

If you're planning to go CRM crazy, the **Mackintosh Trail ticket** (£16), available at the tourist office or any Mackintosh building, gives you a day's admission to all his creations as well as unlimited bus and subway travel.

To see another of Mackintosh's finest works, check out Hill House (p279), in Helensburgh.

---

with DJs in the lifts and art installations in the rooms. You couldn't ask for a more relaxed and friendly Merchant City base. The rooms are all stylish with a mixture of minimalism and rich, sexy colours. Compact and standard doubles will do if you're here for a night out, but king-size rooms are well worth the £10 upgrade. There's an excellent restaurant downstairs and occasional nightclub in the basement.

Malmaison HOTEL £££
(Map p106; ☎0141-572 1000; www.malmaison.com; 278 West George St; r/ste £160/345; ☎☒) Heavenly Malmaison is the ultimate in seductive urban accommodation. Cutting-edge but decadent and plush living at its best, this sassy sister of hospitality is superslinky and a cornerstone of faith in Glaswegian accommodation. Stylish rooms with their moody lighting have a dark, brooding tone, opulent furnishings and a designer touch. It's best to book online, as it's cheaper, and various suite offers can be mighty tempting.

Blythswood Square HOTEL £££
(Map p106; ☎0141-248 8888; www.blythswood square.com; 11 Blythswood Sq; r £150-290; @☎☒☒) In a gorgeous Georgian terrace, this elegant five-star offers plenty of inner-city luxury, with grey and cerise tweeds providing casual soft-toned style throughout. Grades of rooms go from standard to penthouse with corresponding increases in comfort; it's hard to resist the traditional 'classic' ones with windows onto the delightful square, but at weekends you'll have a quieter sleep in the new wing at the back. There's an excellent bar and superb restaurant, as well as a very handsome floorboarded and colonnaded salon space on the 1st floor that functions as an evening spot for cocktails. Other facilities include valet parking and a seductive spa complex.

Citizen M HOTEL ££
(Map p106; ☎0141-4049485; www.citizenm.com; 60 Renfrew St; r £70-120; @☎) This modern chain does away with some of the accoutrements of the standard hotel in favour of self-check-in terminals and minimalist, plasticky modern rooms with just two features: a big, comfortable king-sized bed and a decent shower with mood lighting. The idea is that guests make liberal use of the public areas, and why wouldn't you, with upbeat and supercomfortable designer furniture, a

24-hour cafe, and a table full of Macs to use. Prices vary widely according to demand.

Rab Ha's
INN ££

(Map p106; ☑0141-572 0400; www.rabhas.com; 83 Hutcheson St; r £69-89; 🛜) This Merchant City favourite is an atmospheric pub-restaurant with four stylish rooms upstairs. They are all quite distinct and colourful. Room 1 is the best and largest, but all are comfortable, and the location is great. The personal touches like fresh flowers, iPod docks, a big welcome and any-time breakfast make you feel special.

Indigo
HOTEL ££

(Map p106; ☑0141-226 7700; www.hotelindigoglasgow.com; 75 Waterloo St; d £99-169; @🛜) A successful conversion of an elegant city centre building by an American chain of boutique-style hotels has resulted in this satisfying option in the heart of things. It was once the power station for the first trams, but these days is surprisingly quiet for this downtown location. Rooms have been individually decorated to some extent, with mural-style artwork, great beds and free minibar (with better stuff in it as you go up the room grades). Space is good, and bathrooms have rainfall showers. Prices vary by demand; there are usually good deals on the website.

Artto
HOTEL ££

(Map p106; ☑0141-248 2480; www.arttohotel.com; 37 Hope St; s/d £75/90; 🛜) Right by the train station, this modish but affordable hotel has soft white, fawn, and burgundy tones in its compact but attractive rooms, located above a popular bar and eatery. Large windows make staying at the front appealing but, though the double glazing does a good job of subduing the street noise, light sleepers will be happier at the rear. Rates vary widely by the day, and there are room-only prices available.

Pipers Tryst Hotel
HOTEL ££

(Map p106; ☑0141-353 5551; www.thepipingcentre.co.uk; 30-34 McPhater St; s/d £50/65; 🛜) The name is no strategy to lure tartan tourists; this intimate, cosy hotel is in a noble building actually run by the adjacent bagpiping centre, and all profits going towards maintaining it. Cheery staff, great value and a prime city-centre location make this a cut above other places. Of the eight well-appointed rooms, Nos 6 and 7 are our faves; you won't have far to migrate after a night

of Celtic music and fine single malts in the snug bar-restaurant downstairs.

Euro Hostel
HOSTEL £

(Map p106; ☑0141-222 2828; www.euro-hostels.co.uk; 318 Clyde St; dm £17-20, s £29-40, d £36-52; @🛜) With hundreds of beds, this mammoth hostel is handily close to the station and centre. While it feels a bit institutional, it has excellent facilities, including en-suite dorms with lockers, internet access, a compact kitchen, breakfast and a laundry. Dorms range in size from four to 14 beds, and price varies on a daily basis. It's very popular with groups and has an instant social life, with snooker, pool, and a great downstairs bar on-site.

Grand Central Hotel
HOTEL ££

(Map p106; ☑0141-240 3700; www.thegrandcentralhotel.com; 99 Gordon St; s/d £89/109; @🛜) After a recent rejuvenation, this handsome Victorian hotel is back to its former glory. It's part of the central railway station, and some rooms even overlook the platforms. High ceilings, vast corridors stretching off into the distance and a fabulous ballroom are the highlights of this throwback to the golden age of rail. Decent modern bathrooms and spacious rooms – the executive ones are worth the upgrade – make this a far more comfortable pad for trainspotting than a level crossing in the drizzle.

Babbity Bowster
INN £

(Map p106; ☑0141-552 5055; www.babbitybowster.com; 16-18 Blackfriars St; s/d £45/60; 🅿) Smack bang in the heart of the trendy Merchant City, this lively, pleasant pub has simple rooms with sleek furnishings and a minimalist design (No 3 is a good one). Staying here is an excellent Glaswegian experience – the building's design is attributed to Robert

---

ℹ GLASGOW 2014

In late July and early August of 2014, Glasgow hosts the **20th Commonwealth Games** (www.glasgow2014.com), a 17-event jamboree that will involve athletes from some 70 countries. Events will be held in various locations, including Hampden Park, the SECC, and both the Celtic and Rangers football stadiums. Expect some improvements to the public transport system; equally, expect some disruptions to services in the lead-up to the event.

Adam. Unusually, room rates do not include breakfast – but that helps keep prices down.

Rennie Mackintosh
Art School Hotel
GUESTHOUSE ££

(Map p106; ☎0141-333 9992; www.rmghotels.com; 218 Renfrew St; s/d £50/68; ⍟) If you can book this place at one of its regularly discounted prices, it represents a good deal, as it's a block above Sauchiehall Street and a shortish walk to the museums of the West End too. The rooms are more stylish and comfortable than the rest of the string of guesthouses on this street and it feels better looked-after. Wi-fi doesn't reach the rooms.

Adelaide's
GUESTHOUSE ££

(Map p106; ☎0141-248 4970; www.adelaides.co.uk; 209 Bath St; standard s £37, s/d £55/69; @) Quiet and cordial, this is ideal for folk who want location at a reasonable price. It's an unusual place – a simple, friendly guesthouse on prestigious Bath St set in a historic church conversion and still Baptist-run, though there's not a hint of preachiness in the air. Tariffs include a continental breakfast, with cooked available for extra – and families are very welcome. Aim for the back to minimise weekend noise.

McLay's Guesthouse
B&B £

(Map p106; ☎0141-332 4796; www.mclays.com; 260 Renfrew St; s/d £28/48, with bathroom £36/56; @⍟) The string of cheapish guesthouses along the western end of Renfrew St are a mixed bag but offer a tempting location right by the Sauchiehall nightlife and a block or so from the College of Art. This is among the best of them, a solid choice with decent warm rooms and fair prices. It's sometimes a little cheaper via online booking agencies.

Merchant City Inn
HOTEL ££

(Map p106; ☎0141-552 2424; www.merchantcityinn.com; 52 Virginia St; s/d £50/80; @⍟⍟) Right in the heart of Merchant City alongside three of the city's key gay venues, this has snug rooms featuring pine fittings, wooden floors, and passable bathrooms. Rooms on the 2nd and 3rd floors have the better outlook. Continental breakfast provided.

East End

Cathedral House Hotel
HOTEL ££

(Map p106; ☎0141-552 3519; www.cathedralhousehotel.org; 28-32 Cathedral Sq; s/d £60/90; ℗⍟) Who said you had to get out of town for those Scottish Baronial mansions,

turrets and all? Right opposite the cathedral, this handy spot has eight individual rooms above an attractive bar and restaurant. The corner rooms – No 7 is the best – offer sumptuous beds and great views of St Mungo's and the Necropolis. Free private parking is a rarity in Glasgow too. The only catch is that the less mobile might struggle with the steep spiral stairs.

University of Strathclyde
Campus Village
UNIVERSITY ACCOMMODATION ££

(Map p106; ☎0141-553 4148; www.rescat.strath.ac.uk; Rottenrow East; s £42, without bathroom £33, d £57; ⊘mid-Jun–mid-Sep; ⍟) This uni opens its halls of residence to tourists over summer. The Campus Village, opposite Glasgow Cathedral, offers B&B accommodation in single rooms (there may be a few doubles available on request) at good prices. Cheaper, self-catering prices are also available.

West End

Glasgow SYHA
HOSTEL £

(Map p114; ☎0141-332 3004; www.syha.org.uk; 8 Park Tce; dm/tw £23/62; @⍟) Perched on a hill overlooking Kelvingrove Park in a charming town house, this place is one of Scotland's best official hostels. Dorms are mostly four to six beds with padlock lockers and all have their own en suite – very posh. The common rooms are spacious, plush and good for lounging about. There's no curfew, a good kitchen, and meals are available. The prices listed reflect maximums and are usually cheaper.

Hotel Du Vin
HOTEL £££

(One Devonshire Gardens; ☎0141-339 2001; www.hotelduvin.com; 1 Devonshire Gardens; r from £160, ste from £425; ℗@⍟⍟) This is traditionally Glasgow's favoured hotel of the rich and famous, and the patriarch of sophistication and comfort. A study in elegance, it's sumptuously decorated and occupies three classical sandstone terrace houses. There's a bewildering array of room types, all different in style and size. The hospitality is old-school courteous, and there's an excellent restaurant on-site with a wine selection exceeding 600 varieties. Breakfast is extra.

Embassy Apartments
APARTMENTS ££

(Map p114; ☎0141-946 6698; www.glasgowhotelsandapartments.co.uk; 8 Kelvin Dr; 1/2/4-person flat per night £60/80/99; ⍟) If you're after a self-catering option, it's hard to go past this elegant place both for facilities and location. Situated in the leafy West End on a quiet, exclusive street right on the edge of the Botanical Gardens, the studio-style apartments sleep one to seven people, have fully equipped kitchens and are sparkling clean. They're a particularly good option for couples and families with older kids. The apartments are available by the day, but prices drop for three- and seven-day rentals. Prices vary extensively according to demand.

Alamo Guest House   B&B ££
(Map p114; ☎0141-339 2395; www.alamoguest house.com; 46 Gray St; d/superior d £95/145, s/d without bathroom £55/74; @☎) The Alamo may not sound like a quiet, peaceful spot, but that's exactly what this great little place is. Opposite Kelvingrove Park, it feels miles from the hustle of the city, but the city centre and West End are within walking distance and several of the best museums and restaurants in town are close by. The decor is an enchanting mixture of antique furnishings and modern design, with excellent bathrooms, and the owners will make you very welcome. All rooms have DVD players and there's an extensive collection to borrow from. Breakfast is abundant but there's no full Scottish option.

Kirklee Hotel   HOTEL ££
(Map p114; ☎0141-334 5555; www.kirkleehotel. co.uk; 11 Kensington Gate; s/d £65/80; ☎) Want to spoil someone special? In a leafy neighbourhood, Kirklee is a quiet little gem that combines the luxury of a classy hotel with the warmth of staying in someone's home. The rooms are simply gorgeous, beautifully furnished and mostly look onto lush gardens. For families there is an excellent downstairs room with enormous en suite. This could be Glasgow's most beautiful street.

Amadeus Guest House   B&B £
(Map p114; ☎0141-339 8257; www.amadeusguest house.co.uk; 411 North Woodside Rd; s £26-36, d £48-60; ☎) Just off the bustle of Great Western Road, a minute's walk from the subway but on a quiet street by the riverside pathway, this B&B has compact bright rooms with cheerful cushions on the comfortable beds. There's a variety of room types, but prices are very good for all of them. Breakfast is continental.

Bunkum Backpackers   HOSTEL £
(Map p114; ☎0141-581 4481; www.bunkumglas gow.co.uk; 26 Hillhead St; dm/tw £14/36; P☎) A tempting budget headquarters for assaults on the eateries and pubs of the West End,

Bunkum Backpackers occupies a noble old Victorian terrace on a quiet street. The dorms are spacious – one exaggeratedly so – and the common room and kitchen are also large. There's no curfew but it's not a party hostel. Watch the street numbers; the place isn't well signposted. Slightly cheaper midweek.

Acorn Hotel   HOTEL ££
(Map p114; ☎0141-332 6556; www.glasgowhotel sandapartments.co.uk; 140 Elderslie St; s/d £60/87; @☎) Enjoying a peaceful location by a park, yet just a block from Sauchiehall St, this smart little place has rooms that are compact but boast stylish colours and comfortable beds.

Heritage Hotel   HOTEL ££
(Map p114; ☎0141-339 6955; www.theheritageho tel.net; 4 Alfred Tce, Great Western Rd; s/d £40/60; P☎) A stone's throw from all the action of the West End, this friendly hotel has an open, airy feel despite the rather dilapidated raised terrace it's located on. Generally, the rooms on the 1st and 2nd floors are a bit more spacious (No 21 is best of the doubles) and have a better outlook. The location and very fair prices set it apart.

Craigendmuir
Caravan & Camping   CAMPING £
(☎0141-779 4159; www.craigendmuir.co.uk; Campsie View; sites for 1/2 people £14.25/17.75; P) The nearest camping ground to town, Craigendmuir Park is about 800m from Stepps station. It has sites for caravans and tents and there are a few well-equipped chalets and holiday homes for weekly rental.

✗ Eating

Glasgow is the best place to eat in Scotland, with an excellent range of eateries. The West End is the culinary centre of the city, with Merchant City also boasting an incredible concentration of quality restaurants and cafes. Many Glasgow restaurants post offers on the internet (changing daily) at 5pm.co.uk. Note also that pubs and bars are always a good lunchtime option.

City Centre
Café Gandolfi   CAFE, BISTRO ££
(Map p106; ☎0141-552 6813; 64 Albion St; mains £11-15; ☺9am-11.30pm) In the fashionable Merchant City, this cafe was once part of the old cheese market. It's been pulling in the punters for years and attracts an interesting mix of diehard Gandolfers, the upwardly

mobile and tourists. It's an excellent, friendly bistro and upmarket coffee shop. Book a Tim Stead–designed, medieval-looking table in advance for well-prepared Scottish and Continental food. There's an expansion, specialising in fish, next door.

Brutti Ma Buoni   MEDITERRANEAN £

(Map p106; ☎0141-552 0001; www.brunswickho tel.co.uk; 106 Brunswick St; mains £7-11; ⏰11am-10pm; 🖐) If you like dining in a place that has a sense of fun, Brutti delivers – it's the antithesis of some of the pretentious places around the Merchant City. With dishes such as 'ugly but good' pizza and 'angry or peaceful' prawns, Brutti's menu draws a smile for its quirkiness and its prices. The Italian and Spanish influences give rise to tapaslike servings or full-blown meals, which are imaginative, fresh and frankly delicious.

Mussel Inn   SEAFOOD ££

(Map p106; ☎0141-572 1405; www.mussel-inn.com; 157 Hope St; mains £10-18) Airy and easygoing, this two-level eatery – a longtime Rose St favourite in Edinburgh – has recently opened in Scotland's largest city. It specialises in sustainable scallops, oysters, and mussels at affordable prices, served with a smile.

Lunch@Lily's   CAFE, CHINESE £

(Map p106; 103 Ingram St; mains £3-6; ⏰9.30am-4pm Mon-Sat) Don't be put off by the slightly sterile feel: Lily's is a top lunch spot fusing a creative blend of East and West. It's a unique cross between a Chinese bistro and chic cafe with made-to-order Chinese food (such as dumpling buns and mandarin-duck wraps) and standards like burgers and baked potatoes that are tarted up almost beyond recognition. The Chinese food is particularly outstanding – fresh, lively and served with fruits and salad.

Dakhin   INDIAN ££

(Map p106; ☎0141-553 2585; www.dakhin.com; 89 Candleriggs; mains £7-19) This south Indian restaurant breathes some fresh air into the city's curry scene. Dishes are from all over the south, and include dosas (thin rice-based crêpes) and a yummy variety of fragrant coconut-based curries. If you're really hungry, try a thali: Indian 'tapas'.

Arisaig   SCOTTISH ££

(Map p106; ☎0141-553 1010; www.arisaigrestau rant.co.uk; 1 Merchant Sq; mains £12-20) Located in the Merchant Sq building, a historical location converted into an echoing food court, Arisaig offers a good chance to try well-prepared Scottish cuisine at a fair price, with friendly service to boot. Candlelight and crisp linen makes for atmosphere despite the artificial situation, with both terrace and indoor seating.

The Chippy Doon the Lane   FISH & CHIPS £

(Map p106; www.thechippyglasgow.com; McCormick Lane, 84 Buchanan St; meals £6-11; ⏰noon-9.30pm) Don't be put off by its location in a down-at-heel alleyway off the shopping precinct: this is a cut above your average chip shop. Sustainable seafood is served in a chic space, all old-time brick, metal archways and jazz. Otherwise, chow down on your takeaway at the wooden tables in the lane or out on Buchanan St itself.

Where the Monkey Sleeps   CAFE £

(Map p106; www.monkeysleeps.com; 182 West Regent St; dishes £4-7; ⏰7am-5pm Mon-Fri) This funky little number in the middle of the business district is a perfect escape from the ubiquitous coffee chains. Laid-back and a little hippy, the bagels and panini – with names like Burn the Witch or Meathammer – are highlights, as are some very inventive dishes, such as the 'nuclear' beans, dripping with cayenne and Tabasco.

Red Onion   BISTRO ££

(Map p106; ☎0141-221 6000; www.red-onion.co.uk; 257 West Campbell St; mains £10-18; 🖐) This comfortable split-level bistro buzzes with contented chatter. French, Mediterranean and Asian touches add intrigue to the predominantly British menu, and a good-value fixed-price deal (2/3 courses £14/16) is available daily, though only for early diners at weekends.

Jamie's Italian   ITALIAN ££

(Map p106; ☎0141-404 2690; www.jamieoliver .com/italian/glasgow; 1 George Sq; mains £10-17; ⏰noon-11pm) Celebrity chef Jamie Oliver gives his take on regional Italian food in this buzzy eatery on George Sq. Though service is variable, there's a lot to like, with rustic designer red-metal chairs, a deli counter, and a menu using superior quality British produce in time-honoured Mediterranean ways. The antipasto planks are particularly good.

Wee Curry Shop   INDIAN £

(Map p106; ☎0141-353 0777; www.theweecurry shopglasgow.com; 7 Buccleuch St; 2-course lunch £5.20, dinner mains £6-12; ⏰lunch Mon-Sat, dinner daily) Great home-cooked curries. It's wise to book – it's a snug place with a big reputation, a limited menu and a sensational-value two-course lunch. Cash only.

Bar Soba
ASIAN FUSION ££

(Map p106; 0141-204 2404; www.barsoba.co.uk; 11 Mitchell Lane; mains £10-13) With seating around the edges of the room and candles flickering in windows there's a certain sense of intimacy in stylish and very friendly Bar Soba. You can eat in the plush downstairs restaurant, or in the bar. The food is Asian fusion and the laksas go down a treat – followed up of course by an irresistible chocolate brownie. Background beats are perfect for chilling and it's a good stop in the heart of the shopping zone for lunch, when all dishes are £8.

Mono
VEGETARIAN £

(Map p106; www.monocafebar.com; 12 Kings Ct, King St; mains £3-8; noon-9pm;) Combining vegetarian food with music, Mono is one of Glasgow's best vegetarian and vegan eateries. Monorail is in the same premises, which means you can browse through an indie record shop while waiting for your food to be prepared. The all-day bar menu serves classics such as a breakfast fry-up, while the main menu has a touch of flair and a Mediterranean influence. The lasagne is well worth ploughing through. Mono also makes a relaxing place for a coffee or a beer.

Willow Tearooms
CAFE £

(www.willowtearooms.co.uk; light meals £4-8; 9am-5pm Mon-Sat, 11am-5pm Sun) There are two separate locations for these famous tearooms, one on Buchanan St (Map p106; 97 Buchanan St) and one (also see under Sights) on Sauchiehall St (Map p106; 217 Sauchiehall St).

Both are re-creations of the tearooms designed by Charles Rennie Mackintosh in 1904. They back up their wonderful design elements with excellent bagels, pastries or, more splendidly, champagne afternoon teas (£20). At busy times the queues for a table can be long.

Bar 91
PUB £

(Map p106; www.bar91.co.uk; 91 Candleriggs; mains £6-9; meals noon-9pm Mon-Thu, to 5pm Fri-Sun) By day this happy, buzzy bar serves excellent meals, far better than your average pub food. Salads, pasta and burgers are among the many tasty offerings, and in summer tables spill out onto the sidewalk – ideal for some people-watching.

The Secret Space
POP-UP RESTAURANT

(Map p106; 0141-553 1010; www.secretspace glasgow.com; 1 Merchant Sq) We can't give you much of a review, and neither can we provide opening hours or price ranges, as this pop-up restaurant changes completely every six months. Situated on the upper deck of the Merchant Sq complex, it has an intriguing location and plenty of cachet in Glasgow already, so book ahead. Check the website for details.

Noodle Bar
DINER £

(Map p106; 482 Sauchiehall St; mains £7; noon-4am) The after-party option: large doses of late-night noodles with oodles of different combinations.

West End

There are numerous excellent restaurants in the West End. They cluster along Byres Rd and just off it, on Ashton Lane and Ruthven Lane. Gibson St and Great Western Rd also have plenty to offer.

TOP CHOICE The Ubiquitous Chip
SCOTTISH £££

(Map p114; 0141-334 5007; www.ubiquitouschip .co.uk; 12 Ashton Lane; 2-/3-course dinner £35/40, brasserie mains lunch £7-12, dinner £12-15) The original champion of Scottish produce, The Ubiquitous Chip has won lots of awards for its unparalleled Scottish cuisine, and for its lengthy wine list. Named to poke fun at Scotland's perceived lack of finer cuisine, it offers a French touch but resolutely Scottish ingredients, carefully selected and following sustainable principles. The elegant courtyard space offers some of Glasgow's highest-quality dining, while above and in the atmospheric pub, the cheaper brasserie menu doesn't skimp on quality but keeps things affordable. The cute 'Wee Pub' down the side alley offers plenty of drinking pleasure. There's always something going on at the Chip – check the website for upcoming events.

Stravaigin
SCOTTISH ££

(Map p114; 0141-334 2665; www.stravaigin.co.uk; 28 Gibson St; mains £10-18; 9am-11pm) Stravaigin is a serious foodie's delight, with a menu constantly pushing the boundaries of originality and offering creative culinary excellence. The cool contemporary dining space in the basement has booth seating, and helpful, laid-back waiting-staff to assist in deciphering the audacious menu. Entry-level

KARL BLACKWELL / GETTY IMAGES ©

WILL SALTER / GETTY IMAGES ©

1. Haggis (p460)

Scotland's national dish – made from the finely chopped lungs, heart and liver of a sheep, mixed with oatmeal and onion – is tastier than it sounds.

2. Beer (p462)

Scottish breweries produce a wide range of beers, and recent years have seen a huge rise in the number of specialist brewers and microbreweries.

3. Eating out in Edinburgh (p81)

Edinburgh has more restaurants per head of population than any other UK city.

4. Whisky (p463)

Scotch whisky is Scotland's best-known product and biggest export. The spirit has been distilled in Scotland at least since the 15th century.

has a buzzing two-level bar; you can also eat here. There are always plenty of menu deals and special culinary nights.

Mother India   INDIAN ££

(Map p114; ☎0141-221 1663; www.motherindia .co.uk; 28 Westminster Tce, Sauchiehall St; mains £8-14; ☻lunch Fri-Sun, dinner daily; ✏♠) Glasgow curry buffs are forever debating the merits of the city's numerous excellent south Asian restaurants, and Mother India features in every discussion. It may lack the trendiness of some of the up-and-comers but it's been a stalwart for years, and the quality and innovation on show is superb. It also makes a real effort for kids, with a separate menu.

The Butchershop   STEAKHOUSE £££

(www.butchershopglasgow.com; 1055 Sauchiehall St; steaks £16-30; ☻noon-10pm) Offering several different cuts of traceably sourced, properly aged beef, this is just about the best spot in Glasgow for a tasty, served-as-you-want-it steak; a perfect lunch venue after the Kelvingrove museum. There are seats out the front if the weather happens to be fine. There's also seafood on the menu, and decently-mixed cocktails.

Wau Cafe   MALAY £

(27 Old Dumbarton Rd; dishes £4-7; ☻1-10pm Mon-Thu & Sat, 2.30-10pm Fri) The Wau factor at this hole-in-the-wall Malaysian diner comes not just from the incredibly low prices but also the quality and authenticity of the dishes, which include noodles, laksas and curries as well as lesser-known delights.

The Left Bank   BISTRO ££

(Map p114; ☎0141-339 5969; www.theleftbank .co.uk; 33 Gibson St; mains £12-18; ☻9am-10pm Mon-Fri, 10am-10pm Sat & Sun; ✏♠) Huge windows fronting the street greet patrons to this outstanding eatery specialising in gastronomic delights and lazy afternoons. There are lots of little spaces filled with couches and chunky tables, reflecting a sense of intimacy. The large starter-menu can be treated like tapas, making it good for sharing. Lots of delightful creations use seasonal and local produce, with an eclectic variety of influences.

Heart Buchanan   CAFE, DELI £

(Map p114; www.heartbuchanan.co.uk; 380 Byres Rd; light meals £6-10; ☻9am-4pm Mon-Sat, 10am-6pm Sun) The famous West End deli – give your nose a treat and drop in – has a small cafe space next door. Break any or all of the 10 commandments to bag a table, then enjoy some of Glasgow's best breakfasts, a refreshing juice or milkshake, or regularly changing light-lunch options. If you failed in the table quest, the deli also does some of these meals to take away.

La Vallée Blanche   FRENCH £££

(Map p114; ☎0141-334 3333; www.lavalleeblanche .com; 360 Byres Rd; mains £16-21; ☻Tue-Sun) Cosy and romantic, this upstairs venue is a haven from Byres Rd and sets up a most worthwhile 'Auld Alliance', combining the best of Scottish produce with classical French flair. It's a prime venue for attempted seduction, or re-seduction, and neither the food nor the service will let you down.

Stravaigin II   SCOTTISH ££

(Map p114; ☎0141-334 7165; www.stravaigin2.com; 8 Ruthven Lane; lunch mains £7-13, dinner £10-16; ☻noon-11pm) Top service makes all feel welcome at this relaxed eatery just off Byres Rd. The menu changes regularly but always features a few surprises from around the globe. Slow-cooking features prominently in the preparation of both meat and vegetables, so expect those flavours to burst out at you. It's also got a legendary reputation for burgers, fish and chips and haggis, so there's something here for every appetite.

Konaki   GREEK ££

(Map p114; ☎0141-342 4010; www.konakitaverna .co.uk; 920 Sauchiehall St; mains £11-16; ☻lunch Mon-Sat, dinner daily) Not far from the Kelvingrove museum, Konaki is a friendly and unpretentious Greek restaurant that makes a great morning or evening pitta stop. The starters are a particular highlight of the authentic menu – in fact, ordering a whole lot of them to share is the most enjoyable way to eat. There are several Greek wines to accompany your meal; knock back a traditional thick coffee afterwards.

Òran Mór Brasserie   SCOTTISH ££

(Map p114; ☎0141-357 6226; www.oran-mor.co.uk; 731 Great Western Rd; mains £12-20; ☻noon-9pm Sun-Wed, to 10pm Thu-Sat) This temple to Scottish dining and drinking is a superb venue in an old church. Giving new meaning to the word 'conversion', the brasserie pumps out high-quality meals in a dark, Mackintosh-inspired space. The menu runs from burgers to more elaborate mains and, at the time of writing, there was a great-value two-course special for £13 from four until close.

Bay Tree Café

CAFE £

(Map p114; www.baytreecafe.com; 403 Great Western Rd; mains £6-10; ⊘9am-10pm Mon-Sat, to 9pm Sun; 🌐🍴) There are many good cafes in the two or three blocks around here, but the Bay Tree is still our favourite. With lots of vegan and vegetarian options, it has smiling staff, filling mains (mostly Middle Eastern and Greek), generous salads and a good range of hot drinks. The cafe is famous for its all-day breakfasts.

78 Cafe Bar

CAFE £

(www.the78cafebar.com; 10 Kelvinhaugh St; mains £5-8; ⊘noon-9pm; 🍴) More a comfortable lounge than your typical veggie restaurant, this offers cosy couch seating and reassuringly solid wooden tables, as well as an inviting range of ales. The low-priced vegan food includes hearty stews and curries, and there's regular live music in a very welcoming atmosphere.

Bothy

SCOTTISH ££

(Map p114; 📞0141-334 4040; www.g1group.co.uk; 11 Ruthven Lane; mains £11-18) This West End player, boasting a combo of modern design and comfy retro furnishings, blows apart the myth that Scottish food is stodgy and uninteresting. The Bothy dishes out traditional home-style fare with a modern twist. It's filling, but leave room for dessert. Lunch deals will get you away cheaper.

Firebird

BISTRO ££

(Map p114; www.firebirdglasgow.com; 1321 Argyle St; mains £8-13) A combined bar and bistro with a cheery feel, Firebird has zany artwork on its bright walls and, more importantly, quality nosh whisked under the noses of its patrons. Local flavours and Mediterranean highlights (mainly Italian and Spanish) are evident and organic produce is used wherever possible. Taste sensations range from wood-fired pizzas to a Moroccan chicken and chickpea salad.

Wudon

JAPANESE £

(Map p114; www.wudon-noodlebar.co.uk; 535 Great Western Rd; dishes £7-11; ⊘noon-11pm Mon-Sat, 12.30-10pm Sun) Sushi, fried noodles, and ramen soups in a clean, contemporary setting.

Drinking

Some of Britain's best nightlife is found in the din and sometimes roar of Glasgow's pubs and bars. There are as many different styles of bar as there are punters to guzzle in them.

City Centre

TOP CHOICE Artà

BAR

(Map p106; www.arta.co.uk; 13-19 Walls St; ⊘Thu-Sat 5pm-3am) This extraordinary place is so baroque that when you hear a Mozart concerto over the sound system, it wouldn't surprise you to see the man himself at the other end of the bar. Set in a former cheese market, it really does have to be seen to be believed. As its door slides open, Artà's opulent, candle-lit interior is revealed with its floor-to-ceiling velvet and red curtains revealing a staircase to the tapas bar and restaurant above, in a show of decadence that the Romans would have appreciated. Despite the luxury, it's got a relaxed, chilled vibe and a mixed crowd. The big cocktails are great.

Horse Shoe

PUB

(Map p106; www.horseshoebar.co.uk; 17 Drury St) This legendary city pub and popular meeting place dates from the late 19th century and is largely unchanged. It's a picturesque spot, with the longest continuous bar in the UK, but its main attraction is what's served over it – real ale and good cheer. Upstairs in the lounge is some of the best-value pub food (three-course lunch £4.25) in town.

Blackfriars

PUB

(Map p106; www.blackfriarsglasgow.com; 36 Bell St) Merchant City's most relaxed and atmospheric pub, Blackfriars' friendly staff and chilled-out house make it special. They take their cask ales seriously here, and there's a seating area with large windows that are great for people-watching.

Butterfly & The Pig

PUB

(Map p106; www.thebutterflyandthepig.com; 153 Bath St) A breath of fresh air along trendy Bath St, the piggery is a little offbeat, a little zany and makes you feel comfortable as soon as you plunge into its basement depths. The decor is eclectic with a retro feel and this adds to its familiarity. You get the feeling that patronising this place regularly would be rewarded with your favourite pint being poured just as you enter the doorway. There's a sizable menu of pub grub, and more refined fare in the tearoom upstairs.

Babbity Bowster

PUB

(Map p106; 16-18 Blackfriars St) In a quiet corner of Merchant City, this handsome spot is perfect for a tranquil daytime drink, particularly in the adjoining beer garden. Service is attentive, and the smell of sausages may tempt you to lunch; it also offers accommodation. This is one of the city centre's most charming pubs, in one of its noblest buildings.

Arches   BAR

(Map p106; www.thearches.co.uk; 253 Argyle St) A one-stop culture-entertainment fix, Arches doubles as a theatre showing contemporary, avant-garde productions and there's also a club. The hotel-like entrance belies the deep interior, which make you feel as though you've discovered Hades' bohemian underworld. The crowd is mixed – hiking boots are as welcome as Versace.

Corinthian   BAR

(Map p106; www.thecorinthianclub.co.uk; 191 Ingram St; ☎) A breathtaking domed ceiling and majestic chandeliers make Corinthian an awesome venue. Originally a bank and later Glasgow's High Court, this regal building's main bar has to be seen to be believed. Cosy wraparound seating and space to spare are complemented by a snug wine bar and a plush club downstairs in old court cells.

Drum & Monkey   PUB

(Map p106; www.mbplc.com; 93-95 St Vincent St) Dark wood and marble columns frame this attractive drinking emporium, peppered with church pews and leather lounge chairs. Its cosy and relaxing vibe makes you want to curl up in an armchair with a pint for the afternoon. Its central location makes it popular with businessfolk after work.

Bar 10   BAR

(Map p106; www.davantaverns.com; 10 Mitchell Lane) A tiny city treasure that will cause the canny Glasgow drinker to give you a knowing glance if you mention its name. As laidback as you could ask for in a hip city bar, the friendly, tuned-in staff complete the happy picture. It transforms from a quiet daytime bar to a happening weekend pub on Friday and Saturday nights. It also does decent, cheap panini, salads, and the like during the day.

West   BREWERY,

(www.westbeer.com; Binnie Pl; mains £9-12; ☺food 11.30am-9pm) A cavernous room with an airy, industrial feel on the edge of Glasgow Green, this brewery churns out beers brewed in strict accordance with the Reinheitsgebot – a traditional German beer purity law. Which basically means it's bloody good. Excellent German dishes accompany the amber fluid, such as bratwurst sausages, sauerkraut and

schnitzels. Migrate to the beer garden overlooking the People's Palace in summer. To get there, head to the People's Palace and you'll see it opposite, next to the bizarrely ornate facade of the former carpet factory.

MacSorley's   BAR

(Map p106; www.macsorleys.com; 42 Jamaica St) There's nothing better than a good horseshoe-shaped bar in Glasgow, and here the elegantly moulded windows and ceiling add a touch of class to this happy place, which offers live music every night and some excellent, inventive pub food. DJs from the nearby Sub Club also play sets here.

Nice 'n' Sleazy   BAR, CLUB

(Map p106; www.nicensleazy.com; 421 Sauchiehall St) On the rowdy Sauchiehall strip, students from the nearby School of Art make the buzz here reliably friendly. If you're over 35 you'll feel like a professor not a punter, but retro decor, a big selection of tap and bottled beers, 3am closing, and nightly alternative live music downstairs followed by a club at weekends make this a winner. There's also popular, cheap Tex-Mex food (dishes £5 to £7).

Tiki Bar & Kitsch Inn   BAR

(Map p106; www.tikibarglasgow.com; 214 Bath St) Hawaiian shirts, palms and leis provide an appropriate backdrop to colourful cocktails in this hedonistic and amiable basement bar. Upstairs, kitsch plays the relative straight man, though MAD magazine covers mean it's not all poker-faces. Order top-shelf spirits to watch the bar staff negotiate the ladder.

Pivo Pivo   BAR

(Map p106; 15 Waterloo St) Cavernous downstairs beer hall with beers aplenty – 100 varieties from 32 different countries, to be exact. Add to that an impressive array of vodka and schnapps, and it may be a while before you see daylight.

Moskito   BAR

(Map p106; www.moskitoglasgow.com; 200 Bath St) A stylish Bath St basement bar, Moskito is just the place to kick back in the booth seating, play pool and let the in-house DJs mellow you out with their deep beats and electronica.

Waxy O'Connors   PUB

(Map p106; www.waxyoconnors.co.uk; 46 West George St) This lager labyrinth with its fantasy-realm elven treehouse feel could be an

Escher sketch brought to life, and it's a cut above most Irish theme pubs.

West End

Hillhead Bookclub   BAR
(www.hillheadbookclub.com; 17 Vinicombe St) Atmosphere in spades is the call sign of this easygoing West End bar. An ornate wooden ceiling overlooks two levels of well-mixed cocktails, seriously cheap drinks, comfort food and numerous intriguing decorative touches. There's even a pingpong table in a cage.

Òran Mór   BAR
(Map p114; www.oran-mor.co.uk; 731 Great Western Rd) Now some may be a little uncomfortable with the thought of drinking in a church. But we say: the Lord giveth. Praise be and let's give thanks – a converted church, and an almighty one at that, is now a bar, restaurant and club venue. The bar feels like it's been here for years – all wood and thick, exposed stone giving it warmth and a celestial air. There's an excellent array of whiskies. The only thing missing is holy water on your way in.

Brel   BAR
(Map p114; www.brelbarrestaurant.com; 39 Ashton Lane) Perhaps the best on Ashton Lane, this bar can seem tightly packed, but there's a conservatory out the back so you can pretend you're sitting outside when it's raining, and when the sun does peek through there's a beer garden. They've got a huge range of Belgian beers, and they also do mussels and other Lowlands favourites.

Vodka Wodka   BAR
(Map p114; www.vodkawodka.co.uk; 31 Ashton Lane) Every vodka drinker's dream, Vodka Wodka has more varieties of the stealthy poison than you could possibly conquer in one sitting. Its brushed-metal bar dishes out the liquid fire to students during the day and groups of mid-20s in the evening.

Jinty McGuinty's   PUB
(Map p114; www.jintys.com; 23 Ashton Lane) This is a popular Irish theme pub with unusual booth seating and a literary hall of fame.

☆ Entertainment

Glasgow is Scotland's entertainment city, from classical music, fine theatres and ballet to cracking nightclubs pumping out state-of-the-art hip-hop, electro, or techno; to cheesy chart tunes and contemporary Scottish bands at the cutting edge of modern music.

To tap into the scene, check out *The List* (www.list.co.uk), an invaluable fortnightly events-guide available at newsagents and bookshops.

For theatre tickets, book directly with the venue. For concerts, a useful booking centre is **Tickets Scotland** (Map p106; ☑0141-204 5151; www.tickets-scotland.com; 237 Argyle St).

Nightclubs

Glasgow has one of Britain's biggest and best clubbing scenes, attracting devotees from afar. Glaswegians usually hit clubs after the pubs have closed, so many clubs offer discounted admission and cheaper drinks if you go before 10.30pm. Entry costs £5 to £10 (up to £25 for big events), although bars often hand out free passes. By law, clubs shut at 3am, so keep your ear to the ground to find out where the after parties are at.

Sub Club   NIGHTCLUB
(Map p106; www.subclub.co.uk; 22 Jamaica St) Saturdays at the Sub Club are one of Glasgow's legendary nights, offering serious clubbing with a sound system that aficionados usually rate as the city's best. The claustrophobic, last-one-in vibe is not for those faint of heart.

Arches   NIGHTCLUB
(Map p106; www.thearches.co.uk; 253 Argyle St) R-e-s-p-e-c-t is the mantra at the Arches. The Godfather of Glaswegian clubs, it has a design based around hundreds of arches slammed together, and is a must for funk and hip-hop freaks. It is one of the city's biggest clubs pulling top DJs, and you'll also hear some of the UK's up-and-coming turntable spinners. It's off Jamaica St.

Classic Grand   NIGHTCLUB
(Map p106; www.classicgrand.com; 18 Jamaica St) Rock, industrial, electronic, and powerpop grace the stage and the turntables at this unpretentious central venue. It doesn't take itself too seriously, drinks are cheap and the locals are welcoming.

Cathouse   NIGHTCLUB
(Map p106; www.cathouse.co.uk; 15 Union St; ⊙Thu-Sun) It's mostly rock, emo and metal at this long-standing indie, goth and alternative venue. There are two dance floors: upstairs is pretty intense with lots of metal and hard rock, downstairs is a little more tranquil.

Tunnel   NIGHTCLUB
(Map p106; www.tunnelglasgow.co.uk; 84 Mitchell St; ⊙Wed-Sun) Tunnel is a Glasgow classic with

GAY & LESBIAN GLASGOW

Glasgow has a vibrant gay scene, with the gay quarter found in and around the Merchant City (particularly Virginia, Wilson and Glassford Sts). The city's gay community has a reputation for being very friendly.

To tap into the scene, check out *The List* (www.list.co.uk), the free *Scots Gay* (www.scotsgay.co.uk) magazine and website. If you're in Glasgow in autumn check out Glasgay (☎0141-552 7575; www.glasgay.co.uk), a gay performing-arts festival, held around October/November each year.

Many straight clubs and bars have gay and lesbian nights. The following is just a selection of gay and lesbian pubs and clubs in the city:

» **AXM** (Map p106; www.axmgroup.co.uk; 80 Glassford St; ⊙10pm-3am Wed-Sun) This popular Manchester club has recently opened up in Glasgow with a makeover of what used to be Bennet's, a Pink Triangle legend. It's a cheery spot, not too scene-y, with all welcome.

» **Delmonica's** (Map p106; ☎0141-552 4803; 68 Virginia St; ⊙noon-midnight) In the heart of the Pink Triangle, this is a popular bar with a bit of a predatory feeling of people on the pull. It's packed on weekday evenings. Drop in here before heading to the adjacent Polo Lounge, as they often give out free passes.

» **FHQ** (Map p106; www.fhqbar.co.uk; 10 John St) Fashionable women-only location in the heart of the Pink Triangle.

» **Polo Lounge** (Map p106; 84 Wilson St; admission £3-6; ⊙to 3am Tue-Sun) Staff claim 'the city's best talent' is found here; a quick glance at the many glamour pusses – male and female – proves their claim. The downstairs club is packed on weekends; just the main bars open on other nights.

» **Underground** (Map p106; www.underground-glasgow.com; 6a John St) Downstairs on cosmopolitan John St, this bar sports a relaxed crowd and, crucially, a free jukebox. You'll be listening to indie rather than Abba here.

» **Speakeasy** (Map p106; www.speakeasyglasgow.co.uk; 10 John St; ⊙4pm-2am Mon-Thu, 4pm-3am Fri, noon-3am Sat, 12.30pm-2am Sun) Relaxed and friendly bar that starts out publike and gets louder with gay anthem DJs as the night progresses. Serves food until very late.

» **Waterloo Bar** (Map p106; 306 Argyle St) This traditional pub is Scotland's oldest gay bar. It attracts punters of all ages. It's very friendly and, with a large group of regulars, a good place to meet people away from the scene.

two spaces and a good variety of sounds. It's fairly dressy for Glasgow. Saturdays are great here, with hip-hop and R'n'B in one zone, and house in the other.

ABC　NIGHTCLUB, LIVE MUSIC
(O2 ABC; Map p106; www.o2abcglasgow.co.uk; 300 Sauchiehall St) Both nightclub and venue, this star of Sauchiehall has two large concert spaces and several attractive bars. It's a good all-rounder, with a variety of DJs playing every Thursday to Saturday. Punters scrub up fairly well here.

Buff Club　NIGHTCLUB
(Map p106; www.thebuffclub.com; 142 Bath Lane) Tucked away in a laneway behind the Bath Street bar strip, this club is open nightly and presents eclectic, honest music without dress pretensions. The sounds vary substantially depending on the night, and can range from hip-hop to disco via electronica. It's more down-to-earth than many Glasgow venues, and has seriously cheap drinks midweek.

Live Music

Glasgow is the king of Scotland's live-music scene. Year after year, touring musicians and travellers alike name Glasgow one of their favourite cities in the world to enjoy live music. Much of Glasgow's character is encapsulated in the soul and humour of its inhabitants, and the main reason for the city's musical success lies within its audience and the musical community it has bred and nurtured for years.

There are so many venues it's impossible to keep track of them all. Pick up a copy or check the website of the Gig Guide (www.gigguide.co.uk), available free in most pubs and venues, for the latest listings.

One of the city's premier live-music pub venues, the excellent King Tut's Wah Wah Hut (Map p106; ☎0141-221 5279; www.kingtuts.co.uk; 272a St Vincent St), hosts bands every night of the week. Oasis were signed after playing here.

Two bars to see the best, and worst, of Glasgow's newest bands are Brunswick Cellars (Map p106; 239 Sauchiehall St) and Classic Grand (p131). Several of the bars mentioned under Drinking are great for live music, including MacSorley's (p130) and Nice 'n' Sleazy (p130). The ABC (p132) is also a popular venue.

13th Note Café
LIVE MUSIC, CAFE

(Map p106; www.13thnote.co.uk; 50-60 King St) Cosy basement venue with small independent bands as well as weekend DJs and regular comedy and theatre performances. At street level the cafe does decent vegetarian food.

Barrowland
CONCERT VENUE

(Map p106; www.glasgow-barrowland.com; 244 Gallowgate) An exceptional old dancehall catering for some of the larger acts that visit the city.

Captain's
LIVE MUSIC

(Map p114; www.captainsrest.co.uk; 185 Great Western Rd) Variety of indie bands. Gigs nearly every night, and a Monday open-mic session.

Hydro
AUDITORIUM

(☎0141-248 3000; www.thehydro.com; Finnieston Quay) Not yet open at the time of writing, this slick new venue will provide a high-capacity Colosseum-shaped space for big-name bands.

Clyde Auditorium
AUDITORIUM

(Map p114; ☎0844 395 4000; www.secc.co.uk; Finnieston Quay) Also known as the Armadillo because of its bizarre shape, the Clyde adjoins the SECC auditorium and caters for big national and international acts.

SECC
AUDITORIUM

(Map p114; ☎0844 395 4000; www.secc.co.uk; Finnieston Quay) Adjoins Clyde Auditorium and hosts major national and international acts.

Cinemas

Glasgow Film Theatre
CINEMA

(Map p106; ☎0141-332 6535; www.glasgowfilm.org; 12 Rose St; adult/concession £7/5.50) This much-loved two-screener off Sauchiehall St screens art-house cinema and classics.

Cineworld
CINEMA

(Map p106; ☎0871-200 2000; www.cineworld.co.uk; 7 Renfrew St; adult £7-9) Mainstream films.

GLASGOW ENTERTAINMENT

LOCAL KNOWLEDGE

CINDY-LOU RAMSAY, TV CAMERA OPERATOR & PHOTOGRAPHER

Top photography spot? Pollok Park. The park is gorgeous and full of good walks. It also takes you to the Burrell Collection, which may not look like much from outside, but inside it's a calming, beautiful building, jam-packed with exhibits from all over the world.

Something special people might miss? The amazing architecture and statues, you have to look UP!

Glasgow in one word? Charismatic.

Favourite spots for live music? Barrowland (p133) and King Tut's Wah Wah Hut (p133). Barrowland is an old, tired-looking ballroom badly in need of a bit of a wee facelift, but you're guaranteed to get an unforgettable atmosphere; this is the reason that the biggest bands in the world continue to grace its stage. King Tut's is a much smaller venue for getting 'up close and personal' with some great bands.

And for clubbing? I like jumping about the dance floor at the Classic Grand (p131) on Jamaica St. You have two different floors to choose from with classic rock anthems on the main floor to more indie or pop-punk downstairs. It's great for rock chicks like myself or people fed up with the trendy, expensive dance clubs and you don't have to worry about being knocked back at the door for not wearing the right kind of clothes.

Pub for a pint and a read of the paper? Blackfriars (p129) in the Merchant City.

Typical local words? Blethering (chatting)! Glaswegians tend to do a lot of it, especially if you decide to ask them about their city!

Grosvenor Cinema
CINEMA

(☎0845-166 6002; www.grosvenorcafe.co.uk; Ashton Lane) Puts you in the heart of West End eating and nightlife for postshow debriefings.

Theatres & Concert Halls

Theatre Royal
OPERA, BALLET, THEATRE

(Map p106; ☎0844-871 7627; www.atgtickets.com; 282 Hope St) This is the home of Scottish Opera, and the Scottish Ballet often performs here as well. For advance bookings in person, head to the King's Theatre.

City Halls
CONCERT HALL

(Map p106; ☎0141-353 8000; www.glasgowconcerthalls.com; Candleriggs) In the heart of Merchant City, there are regular performances here by the Scottish Chamber Orchestra and the Scottish Symphony Orchestra. The adjacent Old Fruitmarket venue also has concerts.

Glasgow Royal Concert Hall
CONCERT HALL

(Map p106; ☎0141-353 8000; www.glasgowconcerthalls.com; 2 Sauchiehall St) A feast of classical music is showcased at this concert hall, the modern home of the Royal Scottish National Orchestra.

King's Theatre
THEATRE

(Map p106; ☎0844 871 7627; www.atgtickets.com; 297 Bath St) King's Theatre hosts mainly musicals; on rare occasions there are variety shows, pantomimes and comedies.

Citizens' Theatre
THEATRE

(☎0141-429 0022; www.citz.co.uk; 119 Gorbals St) This is one of the top theatres in Scotland and it's well worth trying to catch a performance here.

Tron Theatre
THEATRE

(Map p106; ☎0141-552 4267; www.tron.co.uk; 63 Trongate) Tron Theatre stages contemporary Scottish and international performances. There's also a good cafe.

Centre for Contemporary Arts
ARTS SPACE

(Map p106; www.cca-glasgow.com; 350 Sauchiehall St; ◷10am-midnight Mon-Sat) This is a chic venue making terrific use of space and light. It showcases the visual and performing arts, including movies, talks and galleries. There's a good cafe-bar here too.

Tramway
ARTS SPACE

(☎0845-330 3501; www.tramway.org; 25 Albert Dr) Tramway theatre and exhibition space attracts cutting-edge theatrical groups, the visual and performing arts, and a varied range of artistic exhibitions. It's very close to Pollokshields East train station.

Sport

Two football clubs – Rangers and Celtic – dominate the sporting scene in Scotland, having vastly more resources than other clubs and a long history (and rivalry). This rivalry is also along partisan lines, with Rangers representing Protestant supporters, and Celtic, Catholic. It's worth going to a game; both play in magnificent arenas with great atmosphere. Games between the two (four a year when in the same division) are fiercely contested, but tickets aren't sold to the general public; you'll need to know a season-ticket holder. Rangers are currently working their way back up after a financial meltdown which led to them re-forming as a new company and starting out in Division 3, the fourth tier of Scottish football, in 2012–13.

Celtic FC
FOOTBALL CLUB

(☎0871 226 1888; www.celticfc.net; Celtic Park, Parkhead) There are daily stadium tours (adult/child £8.50/5.50). Catch bus 61 or 62 from outside St Enoch centre.

Rangers FC
FOOTBALL CLUB

(☎0871 702 1972; www.rangers.co.uk; Ibrox Stadium, 150 Edmiston Dr) Tours of the stadium and trophy room run Friday to Sunday (£8/5.50 per adult/child). Take the subway to Ibrox station.

Shopping

Boasting the UK's largest retail phalanx outside London, Glasgow is a shopaholic's paradise. The 'Style Mile' around Buchanan St, Argyle St and Merchant City (particularly upmarket Ingram Street) is a fashion hub, while the West End has quirkier, more bohemian shopping options: Byres Rd is great for vintage clothing.

Barras
FLEA MARKET

(Map p106; www.glasgow-barrowland.com; btwn Gallowgate & London Rd; ◷10am-5pm Sat & Sun) Glasgow's flea market, the Barras on Gallowgate, is the living, breathing heart of the city in many respects. It has almost a thousand stalls and people come here just for a wander as much as for their shopping, which gives the place a holiday air. The Barras is notorious for selling designer frauds, so be cautious. Watch your wallet, too.

Italian Centre FASHION
(Map p106; 7 John St) Fashion junkies can procure relief at Emporio Armani here.

Mr Ben CLOTHING
(Map p106; www.mrbenretroclothing.com; Kings Ct, King St) This cute place is one of Glasgow's best destinations for vintage clothing, with a great selection of brands like Fred Perry, as well as more glam choices, on offer.

Buchanan Galleries SHOPPING CENTRE
(Map p106; www.buchanangalleries.co.uk; Royal Exchange Sq) Huge number of contemporary clothing retailers.

Princes Square FASHION
(Map p106; www.princessquare.co.uk; Buchanan St) Set in a magnificent 1841 renovated square. Beauty and fashion outlets including Vivienne Westwood.

Argyll Arcade JEWELLERY
(Map p106; www.argyll-arcade.com; Buchanan St) Splendid, jewellery-laden arcade.

Geoffrey (Tailor) Kiltmaker KILTS
(Map p106; www.geoffreykilts.co.uk; 309 Sauchiehall St) The place to head if you want to take some tartan home.

Tiso OUTDOOR
(Map p106; www.tiso.co.uk; 129 Buchanan St) Good for Munro baggers and other outdoor enthusiasts.

Adventure 1 OUTDOOR
(Map p106; www.adventure1.co.uk; 38 Dundas St) An excellent place to buy hiking boots.

Waterstone's BOOKSHOP
(Map p106; 0141-332 9105; www.waterstones.com; 153 Sauchiehall St; 8.30am-7pm Mon-Fri, 9am-7pm Sat, 10am-6pm Sun) A major bookshop; also sells guidebooks and street maps of Glasgow.

Caledonia Books BOOKSHOP
(Map p114; www.caledoniabooks.co.uk; 483 Great Western Rd) Characterful secondhand bookshop in the West End.

ⓘ Information

The List (www.list.co.uk; £2.20), available from newsagents, is Glasgow and Edinburgh's invaluable fortnightly guide to films, theatre, cabaret, music, clubs – the works. The excellent *Eating & Drinking Guide* (£5.95), published by *The List* every April, covers both Glasgow and Edinburgh.

Internet Access
Gallery of Modern Art (0141-229 1996; Royal Exchange Sq; 10am-5pm Mon-Wed & Sat, 10am-8pm Thu, 11am-5pm Fri & Sun) Basement library; free internet access. Bookings recommended.

Hillhead Library (348 Byres Rd; 10am-8pm Mon-Tue & Thu, 10am-5pm Wed, 9am-5pm Fri-Sat, noon-5pm Sun) Offers free internet terminals.

iCafe (www.icafe.uk.com; 250 Woodlands Rd; per hr £2; 10am-11pm) Sip a coffee and munch on a pastry while you check your emails on super-fast connections. Wi-fi too.

Mitchell Library (0141-287 2999; www.glasgowlife.org.uk; North St; 9am-8pm Mon-Thu, to 5pm Fri & Sat) Free internet access; bookings recommended.

Yeeh@ (48 West George St; per hr £2; 9.30am-7pm Mon-Fri, 11am-6pm Sat & Sun)

Medical Services
To see a doctor, visit the outpatients department at any general hospital.

Glasgow Dental Hospital (0141-211 9600; www.nhsggc.org.uk; 378 Sauchiehall St)
Glasgow Royal Infirmary (0141-211 4000; www.nhsggc.org.uk; 84 Castle St) Medical emergencies and outpatients facilities.
Western Infirmary (0141-211 2000; www.nhsggc.org.uk; Dumbarton Rd)

Money
There are numerous ATMs around the centre. The post office and the tourist office have bureaux de change.

Post
There are post offices in some supermarkets; some of these are open Sunday as well.
Glassford St Post Office (www.postoffice.co.uk; 59 Glassford St; Mon-Sat) The most central post office.

Tourist Information
Glasgow Information Centre (0141-204 4400; www.seeglasgow.com; 11 George Sq; 9am-5pm Mon-Sat) Excellent tourist office; makes local and national accommodation bookings (£4). Closes later and opens Sundays in summer.

Airport Tourist Office (0141-848 4440; Glasgow International Airport; 7.30am-5pm Mon-Sat, to 3.30pm Sun)

ⓘ Getting There & Away
Air
Ten miles west of the city, Glasgow International Airport (p489) handles international and

domestic flights. Glasgow Prestwick Airport (p489), 30 miles southwest of Glasgow, is used by **Ryanair** (www.ryanair.com) and some other budget airlines, with connections to the rest of Britain and Europe.

Bus

All long-distance buses arrive at and depart from **Buchanan bus station** (☑0141-333 3708; www.spt.co.uk; Killermont St), which has pricey lockers, ATMs and a cafe with wi-fi.

Your first port of call if you're looking for the cheapest fare should be **Megabus** (www.mega bus.com), which offers very cheap demand-dependent prices on many major bus routes, including to Edinburgh and London. The fare to London can be as little as £12 if you're lucky.

Scottish Citylink (☑0871-266 3333; www .citylink.co.uk) has buses to most major towns in Scotland, including the following:

Edinburgh (£6.80, 1¼ hours, every 15 minutes)

Stirling (£7.30, 45 minutes, at least hourly)

Perth (£11.20, 1½ hours, hourly)

Inverness (£27.50, 3½ hours, eight daily)

Aberdeen (£28.80, 2½ to three hours, hourly)

Oban (£17.50, three hours, four direct daily)

Fort William (£22, three hours, seven daily)

Portree, Isle of Skye (£39.40, 6¼ to seven hours, three daily)

Cairnryan/Stranraer (£17.50, 2½ hours, three daily connecting with Belfast ferry).

Some of the longer-distance services are designated Gold, with onboard services and amenities.

As well as Megabus, **National Express** (☑08717 81 81 81; www.nationalexpress.com) and **Greyhound** (☑0900 096 0000; www .greyhounduk.com) also run to London (£23 to £36, eight hours). Most of these services are overnight. The 10.30pm National Express service stops at Heathrow. It's often cheaper to buy in advance online.

National Express also runs daily to several English cities. Check Megabus and the National Express website for heavily discounted fares on these routes.

Car & Motorcycle

There are numerous car-rental companies; the big names have offices at Glasgow and Prestwick airports. Companies include the following:

Arnold Clark (☑0141-423 9559; www.arnold clarkrental.com; 43 Allison St)

Avis (☑0844 544 6064; www.avis.co.uk; 70 Lancefield St)

Europcar (☑0141-204 1072; www.europcar .co.uk; 1 Waterloo St)

Train

As a general rule, **Glasgow Central station** serves southern Scotland, England and Wales,

and **Queen St station** serves the north and east. Buses run between the two stations every 10 minutes. There are direct trains to London's Euston station; they're much quicker (advance purchase single £28 to £105, full fare £162, 4½ hours, more than hourly) and more comfortable than the bus.

Scotrail (☑08457 55 00 33; www.scotrail .co.uk) runs Scottish trains. Destinations include Edinburgh (£12.90, 50 minutes, every 15 minutes), Oban (£21.60, three hours, three to four daily), Fort William (£26.30, 3¾ hours, four to five daily), Dundee (£25.30, 1½ hours, hourly), Aberdeen (£45.20, 2½ hours, hourly) and Inverness (£79, 3½ hours, 10 daily, four on Sunday).

❶ Getting Around

To/From the Airport

There are buses every 10 or 15 minutes from Glasgow International Airport to Buchanan bus station via Central and Queen St stations (single/return £5/7.50). This is a 24-hour service. Another bus, the 747, heads to the West End. A taxi costs £20 to £25.

Bike

There are several places to hire a bike; the tourist office has a full list.

Alpine Bikes (www.alpinebikes.com; 6 St Georges Pl; per day £20; ⊙9.30am-5.30pm) Hardtail and roadbikes available.

Gear Bikes (☑0141-339 1179; www.gearbikes. com; 19 Gibson St; half/1/2 days £15/20/35) Decent hybrids. Open daily.

Boat

Clyde Clippers (www.clydeclippers.com; ⊙mid-May-late Oct) Runs a ferry service on the Clyde between the city centre and Braehead (£6.50 return), stopping at the Science Museum and the Riverside Museum (£3.25 return).

Car & Motorcycle

The most difficult thing about driving in Glasgow, as with most Scottish urban centres, is the confusing one-way system. For short-term parking (up to two hours) you've got a decent chance of finding something on the street, paying at the meters. Otherwise, multistorey car parks are probably your best bet.

Public Transport

BUS City bus services, mostly run by **First Glasgow** (☑0141-423 6600; www.firstglasgow. com), are frequent. You can buy tickets when you board buses but on most you must have the exact change. Short journeys in town cost £1.85; a day ticket (£4.50) is good value and is valid until 1am, when a night network starts. A weekly ticket is £15.50. The tourist office hands out the highly complicated SPT Bus Map, detailing all routes in and around the city.

TRAIN & UNDERGROUND There's an extensive suburban network of trains in and around Glasgow; tickets should be bought before travel if the station is staffed, or from the conductor if it isn't. There's also an underground line, the Subway, that serves 15 stations in the centre, west and south of the city (single £1.20, 10-ride pass £11). The train network connects with the Subway at Buchanan St station. The Discovery Ticket (£3.50) gives unlimited travel on the Subway for a day, while the Roundabout ticket gives a day's unlimited train and Subway travel for £6.

COMBINED TICKET The Daytripper ticket gives you a day's unlimited travel on buses, the Subway, rail and some ferries in the Glasgow region. It costs £10.70 for one or £19 for two. Two kids per adult are included free.

Taxi

There's no shortage of taxis and if you want to know anything about Glasgow, striking up a conversation with a cabbie is a good place to start.

You can pay by credit card with **Glasgow Taxis** (☏0141-429 7070; www.glasgowtaxis.co.uk) if you order by phone; most of its taxis are wheelchair accessible.

AROUND GLASGOW

Good transport connections mean it's easy to plan day trips out of Glasgow. There are some excellent sights along the southern shore of the Clyde, where the ghosts of shipbuilding haunt places like Greenock, and Paisley's magnificent abbey tells a tale of nobler architectural times. Other appealing destinations within easy reach of Glasgow include New Lanark, Helensburgh and Loch Lomond.

Inverclyde

The ghostly remains of once-great shipyards still line the banks of the Clyde west of Glasgow.

The only places worth stopping along the coast west of the city are Greenock and Gourock, although there are a couple of items of interest in the otherwise unprepossessing town of **Port Glasgow**, including the fine 16th-century Newark Castle (HS; www.historic-scotland.gov.uk; adult/child £4/2.40; ⊙9.30am-5.30pm Apr-Sep), which is still largely intact and has a spectacular position on the shores of the Clyde.

GREENOCK & GOUROCK
POP 57,500

Fused together these days, the towns of Gourock and Greenock were always warming sights to a Glasgow mariner's heart as their ships rounded the point from the Firth of Clyde into the river proper and thence to home. Gourock's firthside views are spectacular, and Greenock's historical buildings – despite the scrappy shopping complexes in its centre – invite a stop. In summer and on fine days, these become little resort towns for Glasgow families looking for a day out.

The McLean Museum & Art Gallery (☏01475 715624; www.inverclyde.gov.uk; 15 Kelly St; admission free; ⊙10am-5pm Mon-Sat) in the historic centre of Greenock is well worth checking out. There's quite an extensive collection, with displays charting the history of steam power and Clyde shipping. There's also a pictorial history of Greenock through the ages, while upstairs are very good temporary exhibitions and small displays from China, Japan and Egypt. The natural history section highlights the sad reality of species extinction in the modern world. There are free internet terminals here.

Greenock was the birthplace of **James Watt**, the inventor whose work on the steam engine was one of the key developments of the Industrial Revolution. A statue of him marks his birthplace; behind this looms the spectacular Italian-style **Victoria Tower** on the municipal buildings, constructed in 1886.

Sleeping & Eating

Tontine Hotel HOTEL ££
(☏01475-723316; www.tontinehotel.co.uk; 6 Ardgowan Sq; s/d £65/75, superior s/d £85/95; P☎) Spend the extra for the superior rooms at this noble hotel in the nicest part of Greenock. These spacious chambers are in the old part of the building, and have been recently refurbished, with good bathrooms. The standard rooms are good too, but just don't have the same appeal. Staff are very welcoming; book ahead in summer.

Spinnaker Hotel HOTEL ££
(☏01475-633107; www.spinnakerhotel.co.uk; 121 Albert Rd; s/d £48/78; ☎) The Spinnaker is a pub looking out on Gourock's great view across the firth to Dunoon. The appealing rooms have country-pine decor, are clean and spacious, and have large-screen TVs. Downstairs the comfy bar, popular with an older crowd enjoying the vistas, is laid-back and has ales on tap. Pub grub (mains £8 to £11) is also on offer.

SHIPBUILDING ON THE CLYDE

One of the earliest permanent Lower Clyde shipyards was established in 1711 by John Scott at Greenock. Initial construction was for small-scale local trade but by the end of the 18th century large ocean-going vessels were being built. As the market expanded, shipyards also opened at nearby Dumbarton and Port Glasgow.

The *Comet*, Europe's first steamship, was launched at Port Glasgow in 1812. By the 1830s and 1840s the Clyde had secured its position as the world leader in shipbuilding. Steel hulls came into use by the 1880s, allowing construction of larger ships with the latest and best engines.

In 1899 John Brown & Co, a Sheffield steelmaker, took over a Clydebank yard and by 1907 had become part of the world's largest shipbuilding conglomerate, producing ocean-going liners. Output from the Clyde shipyards steadily increased up to WWI and, with the advent of the war, there was huge demand for new shipping from both the Royal Navy and merchant navy.

During and after the war many small companies disappeared and shipbuilding giants, such as Lithgows Ltd, took their place. The depression years of the 1920s and 1930s saw many yards mothballed or closed. Another boom followed during WWII but these were to be the twilight years.

Many yards went into liquidation in the 1960s, and in 1972 Upper Clyde Shipbuilders was liquidated, causing complete chaos, a sit-in and a bad headache for Ted Heath's government.

Now the great shipyards of the Clyde are mostly derelict and empty. The remains of a once-mighty industry include just a handful of companies still operating along the Clyde.

Tribeca   BAR £

(www.tribecagreenock.tumblr.com; 2 Clyde Sq; mains £7-12) Just by the tower in the heart of Greenock, this spacious and popular modern bar does burgers and generous sandwiches plus a couple of more interesting dishes like braised oxcheek or pork belly.

ℹ Getting There & Away

Greenock is 27 miles west of Glasgow, and Gourock is 3 miles further west. The Glasgow–Greenock–Gourock leg of the Clyde to Forth pedestrian and cycle route follows an old train track for 10 miles. There are trains from Glasgow Central station (£5, 30 minutes, two to three per hour) and hourly buses stopping in both towns.

Gourock is an important ferry hub. **Argyll Ferries** (☑01475-650338; www.argyllferries.co.uk) has a passenger service for Dunoon (£4.10, 25 minutes, half hourly Monday to Saturday, hourly Sunday) on Argyll's Cowal peninsula. Gourock's train station is next to the CalMac terminal.

Clyde Marine Transport (☑0871-705 0888) runs a passenger-only ferry service to Kilcreggan (£2.35, 15 minutes, 11 to 15 daily Monday to Saturday, three Sunday); buy tickets on board.

Western Ferries (☑01369-704452; www .western-ferries.co.uk) also has a service (passenger/car £4.10/11.40, 20 minutes, two to three hourly) to Dunoon from McInroy's Point, 2 miles from the train station on the Irvine road; Scottish Citylink buses run to here.

WEMYSS BAY
POP 2500

Eight miles south of Gourock is Wemyss Bay (pronounced 'weemz'), where you can jump off a train and onto a ferry for Rothesay on the Isle of Bute. There are trains from Glasgow (£6.40, one hour, hourly). CalMac (☑0800 066 5000; www.calmac.co.uk) ferries to Rothesay connect with trains and cost £4.75/18.75 per passenger/car.

Blantyre
POP 17,300

Though technically part of Lanarkshire, Blantyre, the birthplace of David Livingstone, is an outlying suburb of Glasgow these days. It was founded as a cotton mill in the late 18th century. Livingstone, that zealous and pious doctor, missionary and explorer, was raised in a one-room tenement and worked in the mill by day from the age of 10, going to the local school at night. Amazingly for a time in which most mill-workers were barely able to write their names, he managed to get himself into university to study medicine.

The David Livingstone Centre (NTS; www .nts.org.uk; adult/child £6/5; ⊙10am-5pm Mon-Sat, 12.30-5pm Sun Apr-late Dec) tells the story of his life from his early days in Blantyre to the

30 years he spent in Africa, where he named the Victoria Falls on one of his numerous journeys. It's a good display and brings to life the incredible hardships of his missionary existence, his battles against slavery, and his famous meeting with Stanley. There's a child-friendly African wildlife feature and the grassy park the museum is set in makes a perfect picnic spot.

It's a 30-minute walk along the river to Bothwell Castle (HS; www.historic-scotland .gov.uk; adult/child £4/2.40; ☉9.30am-5.30pm Apr-Sep, to 4.30pm Sat-Wed Oct-Mar), regarded as the finest 13th-century castle in Scotland. The stark, roofless, red-sandstone ruins are substantial and, largely due to their beautiful green setting, romantic.

Trains run from Glasgow Central station to Blantyre (20 minutes, three hourly). Head straight down the hill from the station to reach the museum.

The Campsies & Strathblane

The beautiful Campsies reach an altitude of nearly 600m and lie just 10 miles north of Glasgow. The plain of the River Forth lies to the north; Strathblane and Loch Lomond are to the west.

One of several villages around the Campsies, attractive **Killearn** is known for its 31m-high obelisk, raised in honour of George Buchanan, James VI's tutor. Eight miles to the east, **Fintry** has carved itself a gorgeous spot deep in the Campsies on the banks of Endrick Water, which has an impressive 28m waterfall, the **Loup of Fintry**. In the west (on the West Highland Way) is **Drymen**, a pretty village with lots of character, popular due to its close proximity to Loch Lomond.

🏃 Activities

One of the best walks in the area is the ascent of spectacular Dumgoyne hill (427m) from Glengoyne distillery, about 2 miles south of Killearn. Allow at least one hour for the ascent of Dumgoyne. It will take another hour to Earl's Seat, and 1½ hours to return from there to the distillery. From Drymen, the Rob Roy Way (www.robroyway.com) is a great week's walk through Central Scotland's most beautiful lochlands to Pitlochry.

🛏 Sleeping & Eating

Elmbank   B&B £
(☎01360-661016; www.elmbank-drymen.co.uk; Stirling Rd, Drymen; d £54-65; ℗ ⑧) Just off the square, this welcoming, walker-friendly

---

WORTH A TRIP

PAISLEY

Once a proud weaving town, but these days effectively a southwestern suburb of Glasgow, Paisley gave its name to the funky patterned fabric. Though flanked by green countryside, it's not an engaging place, but it has an ace up its sleeve in the shape of the magnificent Paisley Abbey (www.paisleyabbey.org.uk; Abbey Close; admission free; ☉10am-3.30pm Mon-Sat), which is well worth the short trip from Glasgow to see.

This majestic Gothic building was founded in 1163 by Walter Fitzalan, the first high steward of Scotland and ancestor of the Stuart dynasty. A monastery for Cluny monks, it was damaged by fire during the Wars of Independence in 1306 but rebuilt soon after. Most of the nave is 14th or 15th century. The building was mostly a ruin from the 16th century until the 19th-century restoration, completed in 1928. Apart from the magnificent perspective down the nave, points of interest include royal tombs, some excellent 19th- and 20th-century stained glass, including three windows by Edward Burne-Jones, and the 10th-century Celtic **Barochan Cross**. A window commemorates the fact that William Wallace was educated by monks from this monastery.

If you've got time, at the western end of the High St there's the Paisley Museum (www.renfrewshire.gov.uk; High St; admission free; ☉11am-4pm Tue-Sat, 2-5pm Sun), which features paisley psychedelia! There are some marvellous exhibits, including contemporary displays of children in the modern world – it's worth at least a couple of hours. It also has collections of local and natural history, ceramics and 19th-century Scottish art.

Trains run from Glasgow's Central station to Paisley's Gilmour St station (10 minutes, eight per hour).

place has an interesting variety of rooms, including self-catering options. The friendly owner runs a relaxed ship and is flexible, so will happily do deals for singles and groups. The two rooms looking over the garden are absolutely fabulous on a sunny day.

Culcreuch Castle HOTEL ££
(☏01360-860555; www.culcreuch.com; Fintry; s/d from £83/116; P✿😊) Fancy a night in a 700-year-old castle? Parts of Culcreuch date to 1296 and the whole is a remarkably well-preserved historic building. The rooms vary substantially in size, price and comfort, and most look out onto the collage of greenery engulfing the surrounding estate. A little dowdy perhaps and popular with groups, but this place, with its period furnishings, has real character. There are also self-catering lodges a little removed from the castle itself, great for families; one is pet-friendly.

TOP CHOICE **The Inn at Kippen** INN ££
(☏01786-870500; www.theinnatkippen.co.uk; Fore Rd, Kippen; mains £11-17; ⊘meals noon-9pm; P✿😊) Though it doesn't promise a great deal from outside, this atmospheric and historic pub is one of the best places in the region to eat, and offers exceptional value for this quality of food. Elaborate, imaginative dishes are solidly grounded in British tradition with the odd exotic influence; everything is reliably delicious. There are also three gorgeous rooms (doubles from £85) available. Kippen is just off the A811 between Balfron and Stirling.

Clachan Inn PUB £
(www.clachaninndrymen.co.uk; The Square, Drymen; mains £9-10) One of several pubs in Scotland claiming the oldest inn title (opened 1734), this isn't as atmospheric as it could be – who thought a fruit machine was a good idea in an historic hostelry? Nevertheless, it serves a reliable menu of bar meals. Order the local malt, Glengoyne, for dessert.

❶ Getting There & Away

First bus 10 runs from Glasgow to Killearn regularly. There are frequent daily services (except Sunday) between Balfron and Drymen on First bus 8.

Southern Scotland

Best Places to Stay

» Corsewall Lighthouse Hotel (p184)

» Churches Hotel (p155)

» Kildonan Hotel (p164)

» Cornhill House (p159)

» Knockinaam Lodge (p185)

» Lochranza SYHA (p164)

Best Places to Eat

» Coltman's (p146)

» The Brodick Bar (p163)

» The Cobbles (p153)

» Beresford (p167)

Why Go?

Though wise folk are well aware of its charms, for many southern Scotland is just something to drive through on the way to northern Scotland. Big mistake. But it does mean there's breathing room here in summer, and peaceful corners.

Southern Scotland's proximity to England brought raiding and strife; grim borderland fortifications saw skirmishes aplenty. There was loot to be had in the Borders, where large prosperous abbeys ruled over agricultural communities. Regularly ransacked before their destruction in the Reformation, the ruins of these constructions, linked by cycling and walking paths, are among Scotland's most atmospheric historic sites.

The hillier west enjoys extensive forest cover between bustling market towns. The hills cascade down to sandy stretches of coastline blessed with Scotland's sunniest weather. It's the land of Robert Burns, whose verse reflected his earthy attitudes and active social life. Offshore, Arran is an island jewel offering top cycling, walking and scenery.

When to Go

Ayr

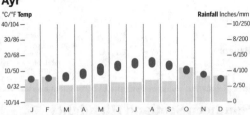

May If winter hasn't been too wet, lace the hiking boots and stride up Arran's hills.

Jun The perfect time to visit the region's numerous stately homes, with spectacular gardens in bloom.

Autumn Hit Galloway's forests to see red deer battling it out in the rutting season.

Southern Scotland Highlights

① Hiking or cycling between the noble ruins of the **Border Abbeys** (p152)

② Admiring 18th-century architectural genius at **Culzean Castle** (p170)

③ Pondering the tough old life on the England–Scotland frontier at desolate **Hermitage Castle** (p150)

④ Exploring charming, dignified **Kirkcudbright** (p178), and marvelling at the creative flair of its inhabitants

⑤ Learning some Lallans words from the Scottish Bard's verses at the **Robert Burns Birthplace Museum** (p169)

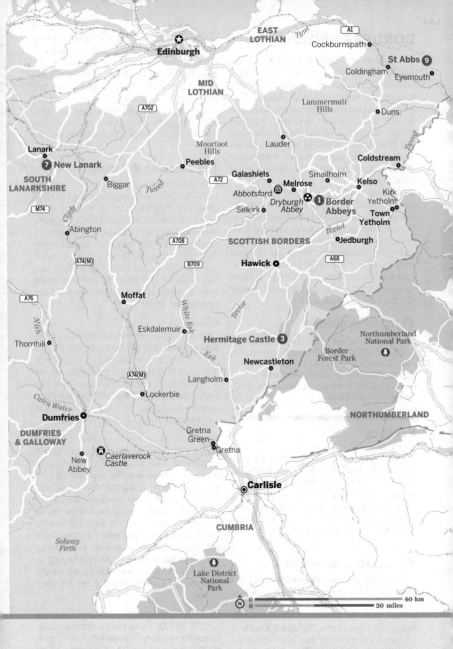

6 Whooshing down forest trails at the **7stanes mountain-biking hubs** (p181) near Glentrool

7 Marvelling at the radical social reform instituted in the mill community of **New Lanark** (p157)

8 Blowing away the cobwebs on the scenic, activity-packed **Isle of Arran** (p160)

9 Plunging the deeps off the picturesque fishing village of **St Abbs** (p156)

10 Browsing secondhand books at **Wigtown** (p182)

BORDERS REGION

The Borders is a distinctive region – centuries of war and plunder have left a battle-scarred landscape, encapsulated by the remnants of the great Border abbeys. Their wealth was an irresistible magnet during the Border wars, and they were destroyed and rebuilt numerous times. The monasteries met their scorched end in the 16th century and were never reconstructed. Today these massive stone shells are the region's finest attraction.

But there's more. Welcoming villages with ancient traditions pepper the countryside, one of the best cold-water diving sites in Europe is off the coast, and grandiose mansions await exploration. It's fine walking and cycling country too, the gentle hills lush with an artist's palette of shades of green. And don't miss Hermitage Castle; nothing encapsulates the region's turbulent history like this spooky stronghold.

❶ Getting Around

There's a good network of local buses. **First** (☎0870-8727271-602200; www.firstgroup.com), **Munro's** (☎01835-862253; www.munrosofjedburgh.co.uk) and **Perryman's** (☎01289-308719; www.perrymansbuses.com) are the main operators.

Peebles

POP 8065

With a picturesque main street set on a ridge between the River Tweed and the Eddleston Water, Peebles is one of the most handsome of the Border towns. Though it lacks a major sight, the agreeable atmosphere and good walking options in the rolling, wooded hills thereabouts will entice you to linger for a couple of days.

◉ Sights & Activities

If it's sunny, the **riverside walk** along the River Tweed has plenty of grassed areas ideal for a picnic, and there's a children's playground (near the main road bridge). A mile west of the town centre, **Neidpath Castle** is a tower house perched on a bluff above the river; it's closed for the foreseeable future but worth a look from the riverbank.

Two miles east of town off the A72, in **Glentress forest**, is one of the 7stanes mountain-biking hubs (p181), as well as osprey viewing and marked walking trails. A cafe (☎01721-721736; www.thehubinthefor est.co.uk) hires rigs and will put you on the right trail for your ability. These are some of Britain's best biking routes. There are also camping huts here (see www.glentress forestlodges.co.uk). In town, you can hire bikes to explore the region from Glentress Bikes (☎01721-729756; 20A Northgate; day hire £22).

🛏 Sleeping & Eating

Cringletie House   HOTEL £££
(☎01721-725750; www.cringletie.com; r £160-260, dinner £33; P@🛜🐾) Luxury without snobbery is this hotel's hallmark, and more power to them. To call it a house is being coy; it's an elegant baronial mansion, 2 miles north of Peebles on the A703, set in lush, wooded grounds. Rooms are plush and feature genteel elegance and linen so soft you could wrap a newborn in it. There's an excellent **restaurant** onsite.

Rowanbrae   B&B ££
(☎01721-721630; www.aboutscotland.co.uk/pee bles/rowanbrae.html; 103 Northgate; s/d £40/63; 🛜) A marvellously hospitable couple run this great B&B in a quiet cul-de-sac not far from the main street; you'll soon feel like you're staying with friends. There are three upstairs bedrooms, two with en suite, and an excellent guest lounge for relaxation.

Tontine Hotel   HOTEL, SCOTTISH ££
(☎01721-720892; www.tontinehotel.com; High St; s/d £60/110, mains £8-14; P🛜🐾) Glorious is the only word to describe the Georgian dining room here, complete with musicians' gallery, fireplace, and windows the like of which we'll never see again. It'd be worth it even if they served cat food on mouldy bread, but luckily the meals – ranging from pub classics like steak-and-ale pie to more ambitious fare – are tasty and backed up by very welcoming service. Rooms are decent too: there's a small supplement for river views.

Rosetta Holiday Park   CAMPING £
(☎01721-720770; www.rosettaholidaypark.co.uk; Rosetta Rd; tent site for 2 people £16; ☺Apr–Oct; P🐾) This camping ground, about 800m north of the town centre, has an exquisite green setting with lots of trees and grass. There are plenty of amusements for the kids, such as a bowling green and a games room.

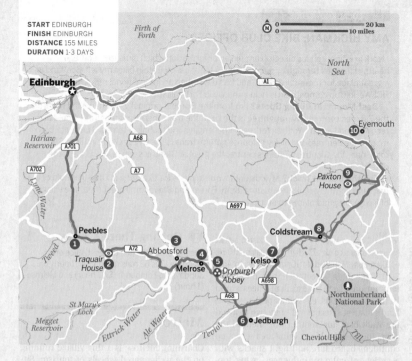

START EDINBURGH
FINISH EDINBURGH
DISTANCE 155 MILES
DURATION 1-3 DAYS

Driving Tour
Historic Sights

❯ This drive takes in several of the principal towns, ruins, castles and stately homes of the Borders region. You could do it in a long day, but to give yourself time to explore the historic buildings, better take two or three.

Starting in Edinburgh, head south on the A701 to ❶ **Peebles**; Rosslyn Chapel is an easy detour along the way. Stroll around Peebles, a typically attractive Borders town, then head east along the A72, deviating at Innerleithen to historic ❷ **Traquair House**, offering 10 centuries of history and great insights into the Jacobite cause and rebellions. Continue eastwards on the A72 pausing at ❸ **Abbotsford**, once the home of Sir Walter Scott. The pretty bijou village of ❹ **Melrose**, with its fabulous abbey, is a must-see and a good lunch stop. Turn south down the A68 to ❺ **Dryburgh Abbey**, perhaps the most evocative of the great Borders ruins.

Head on via the A68 to attractive ❻ **Jedburgh**, dominated by the skeleton of the third abbey. The turbulent history of these once-powerful communities tells of the constant strife in these frontier lands.

From Jedburgh, take the A698 northeast to ❼ **Kelso**, an historic market town and the location of the grandiose Floors Castle, the last and least intact of the abbey ruins. With several other historic buildings within easy striking distance, this makes an appealing stop for a night or two: the classical elegance of Mellerstain House and the grim Smailholm Tower are particularly worthwhile.

Beyond Kelso, the A698 brings you to ❽ **Coldstream**, which gives its name to the famous regiment once based here. Here, the road crosses the Tweed into England and leads eventually to the coast near Berwick-upon-Tweed. Head north and take the left turn to the magnificent 18th century ❾ **Paxton House**, just back over the border in Scotland. Continue north to ❿ **Eyemouth**, with a fascinating maritime history and excellent places to stay. Here, Gunsgreen House is another elegant Adam family mansion with an intriguing smuggling past. From here, it's an easy drive up the A1 through East Lothian and back to Edinburgh.

LOCAL KNOWLEDGE

AMY HICKMAN: BIKE CLUB OFFICER

I work in Edinburgh for bikeclub.org.uk, an organisation which aims to encourage healthy lifestyles through cycling, and I'm a fanatical mountain biker myself. Scotland is a great place for mountain biking, and has developed an international reputation – the UCI World Cup competition is held annually in Fort William.

Best Mountain Biking Spots? I'm from the Borders originally, so I'm biased towards the 7stanes centres – Kirroughtree is the best, the trails there are great fun. I would also recommend Laggan Wolftrax for really challenging and technical terrain. These are both man-made centres; one of my favourite natural trails is the Gypsy Glen circuit at Cardrona, near the Glentress 7stanes centre; the guys at Glentress can give you the route details.

Off the Beaten Track? My current favourite place for exploring is Fife – get hold of a map and go where looks interesting! Kelty Forest and Blairadam Forest (near the village of Kelty) are good places to start.

TOP CHOICE Coltman's   BISTRO, DELI ££

(www.coltmans.co.uk; 71 High St; mains £10-14; ⊙10am-5pm Mon-Wed, to 10pm Thu-Sat, to 4pm Sun) This main street deli has numerous temptations, such as excellent cheeses and Italian smallgoods, as well as perhaps Scotland's tastiest sausage roll - buy two to avoid the walk back for another one. Behind the shop, the good-looking dining area serves up confident bistro fare and light snacks with a variety of culinary influences, using top-notch local ingredients.

Sunflower Restaurant   FUSION ££

(☎01721-722420; www.thesunflower.net; 4 Bridgegate; lunches £6-9, dinner mains £12-16; ⊙lunch Mon-Sat, dinner Thu-Sat; ☑) The Sunflower, with its warm yellow dining room, is in a quiet spot off the main drag and has a reputation that brings diners from all over southern Scotland. It serves good salads for lunch and has an admirable menu in the evenings, with creative and elegant dishes that always include some standout vegetarian fare.

Cocoa Black   CAFE £

(www.cocoablack.com; 1 Cuddy Bridge; sweets £1.50-3; ⊙10am-5pm Mon-Sat, 11am-4.30pm Sun) Chocaholics should make a beeline for this friendly cafe, where exquisite cakes and other patisserie offerings will satisfy any cacao-focused cravings. They also run a school where you can learn to make them yourself.

ⓘ Information

Peebles Information Centre (☎01721-723159; www.visitscottishborders.com; High St; ⊙9am-5pm Mon-Sat) Open later and on Sundays in summer (Apr-Sep).

ⓘ Getting There & Away

The bus stop is beside the post office on Eastgate. Bus 62 runs half hourly (hourly on Sundays) to Edinburgh (£7, 1 hour) and Melrose (1 hour).

Melrose

POP 1656

Charming Melrose is a tiny village running on the well-greased wheels of tourism. Sitting at the feet of the three heather-covered Eildon Hills, Melrose has a classic market square and one of the great abbey ruins.

⊙ Sights

Melrose Abbey   RUINS

(HS; www.historic-scotland.gov.uk; adult/child £5.50/3.30; ⊙9.30am-5.30pm Apr-Sep, to 4.30pm Oct-Mar) Perhaps the most interesting of all the great Border abbeys, the red-sandstone Melrose Abbey was repeatedly destroyed by the English in the 14th century. The remaining broken shell is pure Gothic and the ruins are famous for their decorative stonework – see if you can glimpse the pig gargoyle playing the bagpipes on the roof. You can climb to the top for tremendous views.

The abbey was founded by David I in 1136 for Cistercian monks from Rievaulx Abbey in Yorkshire. It was rebuilt by Robert the Bruce, whose heart is buried here. The ruins date from the 14th and 15th centuries, and were repaired by Sir Walter Scott in the 19th century.

The adjoining **museum** has many fine examples of 12th- to 15th-century stonework and pottery found in the area. Note the impressive remains of the 'great drain' outside – a medieval sewerage system.

🏃 Activities

There are many attractive walks in the **Eildon Hills**, accessible via a footpath off Dingleton Rd (the B6359) south of Melrose, or via the trail along the River Tweed. The tourist office has details of local walks.

The **St Cuthbert's Way** long-distance walking path starts in Melrose, while the coast-to-coast **Southern Upland Way** passes through town. You can do a day's walk along St Cuthbert's Way as far as Harestanes (16 miles), on the A68 near Jedburgh, and then return to Melrose on the hourly Jedburgh–Galashiels bus. The **Tweed Cycle Way** also passes through Melrose.

✨ Festivals & Events

Melrose Rugby Sevens RUGBY
(www.melrose7s.com) In mid-April rugby followers fill the town to see the week-long competition.

Borders Book Festival BOOKS
(www.bordersbookfestival.org) Runs over four days in late June.

🛏 Sleeping

Townhouse TOP CHOICE HOTEL ££
(☎01896-822645; www.thetownhousemelrose.co.uk; Market Sq; s/d £90/126; 🅿🛜) The classy Townhouse exudes warmth and professionalism, and has some of the best rooms in town, tastefully furnished with attention to detail. There are two superior rooms (£140) that are enormous in size with lavish furnishings; the one on the ground floor in particular has an excellent en suite, which includes a jacuzzi. It's well worth the price.

Old Bank House TOP CHOICE B&B £
(☎01896-823712; www.oldbankhousemelrose.co.uk; 27 Buccleuch St; s/d £45/60; 🛜🐾) Right in the middle of town, this is a superb B&B in a charming old building. Art on the walls, spacious rooms, and a sumptuous breakfast room are complemented by a generous can-do attitude. A great Borders base.

Burts Hotel HOTEL ££
(☎01896-822285; www.burtshotel.co.uk; Market Sq; s/d £72/133; 🅿🛜🐾) Set in an early-18th-century house, and with an enviable reputation,

SOUTHERN SCOTLAND MELROSE

DON'T MISS

TRAQUAIR HOUSE

One of Scotland's great country houses, Traquair House (www.traquair.co.uk; adult/child/family £7.70/4/21; ⏰11am-5pm Easter-Sep, 11am-4pm Oct, 11am-3pm Sat & Sun Nov) has a powerful ethereal beauty, and wandering around here is like travelling back in time. Odd, sloping floors and a musty odour bestow a genuine feel, and parts of the building are believed to have been constructed long before the first official record of its existence in 1107. The massive tower house was gradually expanded over the next 500 years but has remained virtually unchanged since the 17th century.

The house has belonged to various branches of the Stuart family since the 15th century. The family's unwavering Catholicism and loyalty to the Stuart cause led to famous visitors like Mary, Queen of Scots, and Bonnie Prince Charlie, but also to numerous problems after the deposal of James II of England in 1688. The family's estate, wealth and influence were gradually whittled away, as life as a Jacobite became a furtive, clandestine affair.

One of Traquair's most interesting places is the concealed room where priests secretly lived and performed Mass up until 1829, when the Catholic Emancipation Act was finally passed. Other beautiful, time-worn rooms hold fascinating relics, including the cradle used by Mary for her son, James VI of Scotland (who also became James I of England), and fascinating letters from the Jacobite Earls of Traquair and their families, including one particularly moving one written from death row in the Tower of London.

The main gates to the house were locked by one earl in the 18th century, not to be opened until the day a Stuart king reclaimed the throne in London; meanwhile, you'll have to enter by a side gate.

In addition to the house, there's a garden maze, a small brewery producing the tasty Bear Ale, and a series of craft workshops.

Traquair is 1.5 miles south of Innerleithen, about 6 miles southeast of Peebles. Bus 62 runs from Edinburgh via Peebles to Innerleithen and on to Galashiels and Melrose.

Burts retains much of its period charm and has been run by the same couple for over 30 years. It would suit older visitors or families. Room No 5 is the best. They do appealing food too.

Braidwood B&B **££**
(01896-822488; www.braidwoodmelrose.co.uk; Buccleuch St; s £45, d £60-65; 🐕🖥) This popular option near the abbey is solid and comfortable. The bright rooms have a well-cared-for feel, and the twin room has great views. No singles are available in summer.

✗ Eating

Townhouse SCOTTISH **££**
(01896-822645; www.thetownhousemelrose.co.uk; Market Sq; mains £10-15) The brasserie and restaurant here turn out just about the best gourmet cuisine in town – the sister hotel Burt's, opposite, comes a close second – and offer decent value. There's some rich, elaborate, beautifully presented fare here, but for a lighter feed you can always opt for the range of creative lunchtime sandwiches.

Marmion's Brasserie SCOTTISH **££**
(01896-822225; www.marmionsbrasserie.co.uk; 5 Buccleuch St; mains £11-18; ⊙lunch & dinner Mon-Sat; 🖉) This atmospheric, oak-panelled niche serves snacks all day, but the lunch and dinner menus include gastronomic delights like local lamb, venison steaks, or pan-seared cod. The spicy bean lasagne is one of several more-than-token offerings for vegetarians. For lunch, the focaccias with creative fillings are a good choice.

Russell's CAFE **£**
(Market Sq; dishes £6-10; ⊙9.30am-5pm Tue-Sat, noon-5pm Sun) Solid wooden furniture and big windows looking out over the centre of Melrose make this stylish little tearoom a popular option. There's a large range of snacks and some more substantial lunch offerings, with daily specials. It's famous throughout the Borders for its excellent scones.

Cellar CAFE **£**
(17 Market Sq; mains £5-8; ⊙9.30am-4.30pm Mon-Sat) Drop into the Cellar for a caffeine hit. It's also a good spot for a glass of wine on the town square, as well as food platters and speciality cheeses.

❶ Information

Melrose Library (18 Market Sq; ⊙Mon-Fri) Free internet access.

Melrose Information Centre (01896-822283; www.visitscottishborders.com; Abbey St; ⊙10am-4pm Mon-Sat, noon-4pm Sun Apr-Oct) Located by the abbey.

❶ Getting There & Away

First buses run to/from Edinburgh (£6.80, 2¼ hours, hourly) via Peebles. Change in Galashiels (20 minutes) for more frequent Edinburgh services and for other Borders destinations.

Around Melrose

In the vicinity of Melrose are a couple of excellent attractions intimately connected with Sir Walter Scott.

◉ Sights

Dryburgh Abbey RUINS
(HS; www.historic-scotland.gov.uk; adult/child £5/3; ⊙9.30am-5.30pm Apr-Sep, 9.30am-4.30pm Oct-Mar) This is the most beautiful and complete of the Border abbeys, partly because the neighbouring town of Dryburgh no longer exists (another victim of the wars) and partly because it has a lovely site in a sheltered valley by the River Tweed, accompanied only by a symphony of birdsong. The abbey conjures up images of 12th-century monastic life more successfully than its counterparts in nearby towns. Dating from about 1150, it belonged to the Premonstratensians, a religious order founded in France. The pink-hued stone ruins were chosen as the burial place for Sir Walter Scott.

The abbey is 5 miles southeast of Melrose on the B6404, which passes the famous **Scott's View** overlooking the valley. You can hike there along the southern bank of the River Tweed, or take a bus to the nearby village of Newtown St Boswells.

Abbotsford HISTORIC HOUSE
(www.scottsabbotsford.co.uk; adult/child £8/4; ⊙9.30am-5pm Mon-Sat, 9.30am-5pm Sun Jun-Sep, 11am-4pm Sun Mar-Oct) Fans of Sir Walter Scott should visit this, his former residence. The inspiration he drew from the surrounding 'wild' countryside influenced many of his most famous works. A collection of Scott memorabilia is on display, including many personal possessions. At time of research a new visitor centre was being built.

The mansion is about 2 miles west of Melrose between the River Tweed and the B6360. Frequent buses run between Galashiels and Melrose; alight at the Tweed bank

SIR WALTER SCOTT

Sir Walter Scott (1771–1832) is one of Scotland's greatest literary figures. Born in Edinburgh, he moved to his uncle's farm at Sandyknowe in the Borders as a child. It was here, rambling around the countryside, that he developed a passion for historical ballads and Scottish heroes. After studying in Edinburgh he bought Abbotsford (p148), a country house in the Borders.

The Lay of the Last Minstrel (1805) was an early critical success. Further works earning him an international reputation included *The Lady of the Lake* (1810), set around Loch Katrine and the Trossachs. He later turned his hand to novels and was instrumental in the development of the historical fiction genre. His first novel, *Waverley* (1814), which dealt with the 1745 Jacobite rebellion, set the classical pattern of the historical novel. Other works included *Guy Mannering* (1815) and *Rob Roy* (1817).

Later in life Scott wrote obsessively to stave off bankruptcy. His works virtually single-handedly revived interest in Scottish history and legend in the early 19th century. Tourist offices stock a *Sir Walter Scott Trail* booklet, which will guide you to many places associated with his life in the Borders.

roundabout and follow the signposts (it's a 15-minute walk). You can also walk from Melrose to Abbotsford in an hour along the southern bank of the Tweed.

Selkirk

POP 5742

While the noisy throb of machinery no doubt once filled the river valleys below Selkirk, a prosperous mill town in the early 19th century, today it sits placidly and prettily atop its steep ridge. Naughty millworkers who fell foul of the law would have come face to face in court with Sir Walter Scott, who was sheriff here for three decades.

The helpful tourist office (☎01750-20054; www.visitscottishborders.com; Halliwell's Close; ⊙11am-4pm Mon-Sat, noon-3pm Sun Apr-Oct) is tucked away off Market Sq. Inside is Halliwell's House Museum (admission free), the oldest building (1712) in Selkirk. The museum charts local history with an engrossing exhibition, and the attached **Robson Gallery** has changing exhibitions.

Drop into Sir Walter Scott's Courtroom (Market Sq; admission free; ⊙11am-3pm Mon-Sat Apr-Oct), where there's an exhibition on his life and writings, plus a fascinating account of the courageous explorer Mungo Park (born near Selkirk) and his search for the River Niger.

🛏 Sleeping

Philipburn Country House Hotel   HOTEL **££**
(☎01750-20747; www.philipburnhousehotel.co.uk; s/d £100/130, luxury s/d £140/170; P❋🏠🐾) On the edge of town, this former dower house has a jazzy 21st-century look that hasn't ruined its historic features, as well as neat rooms and a snug bar and restaurant. The luxury rooms are great – some have a jacuzzi, while another is a split-level affair with a double balcony. There are room-only rates available and self-catering facilities in the separate **lodge** (single/double £100/130).

County Hotel   INN **££**
(☎01750-721233; www.countyhotelselkirk.co.uk; 1 High St; s/d £49/96; P❋🐾) Located in the centre of town, this is a former coaching inn with the odd Norwegian touch that has comfortable, modernized rooms. There's a stylish restaurant and lounge with original art and upmarket bar meals (£10 to £16). Room-only rates are also available for £7.50 less per person.

❶ Getting There & Away

First buses 95 and X95 run at least hourly between Hawick, Selkirk, Galashiels and Edinburgh (£7, two hours).

Hawick

POP 14,573

Straddling the River Teviot, Hawick (pronounced 'hoik') is the largest town in the Borders and has long been a major production centre for knitwear. There are several large outlets to buy jumpers and other woollens around town.

WORTH A TRIP

HERMITAGE CASTLE

Known as 'The Strength of Liddesdale', Hermitage Castle (HS; www.historic-scotland. gov.uk; adult/child £4/2.40; ⊙9.30am-5.30pm Apr-Sep) embodies the brutal history of the Scottish Borders. Desolate but proud, with massive squared stone walls, it looks more like a lair for orc raiding parties than a home for Scottish nobility, and is one of the bleakest and most stirring of the Border ruins.

Strategically crucial, the castle was the scene of many a dark deed and dirty deal with the English invaders, all of which rebounded heavily on the perfidious Scottish lord in question. Here, in 1338, Sir William Douglas imprisoned his enemy Sir Alexander Ramsay and deliberately starved him to death. Ramsay survived for 17 days by eating grain that trickled into his pit (which can still be seen) from the granary above. In 1566, Mary Queen of Scots famously visited the wounded tenant of the castle, Lord Bothwell. Fortified, he recovered to (probably) murder her husband, marry her himself, then abandon her months later and flee into exile.

The castle is about 12 miles south of Hawick on the B6357.

⊙ Sights

Heart of Hawick   VISITOR CENTRE
(www.heartofhawick.co.uk; Kirkstile) In the centre of town, three buildings form what is known as 'The Heart of Hawick'. A former mill now holds the tourist office (☑01450-373993; www. visitscottishborders.com; ⊙10am-5.30pm Mon-Thu, 10am-7pm Fri & Sat, noon-3.30pm Sun) and a cinema. Opposite, historic **Drumlanrig's Tower** is a solid stone mansion that was once a major seat of the Douglas clan. It now houses the Borders Textile Towerhouse (⊙10am-4.30pm Mon-Sat & noon-3pm Sun Apr-Oct, closed Tue & Sun Nov-Mar) that tells the story of the town's knitwear-producing history. Round the back of the tourist office, the Heritage Hub (⊙9.30am-1pm & 2-4.45pm Mon & Fri, to 7pm Tue-Thu, 10am-2pm Sat) is a state-of-the-art facility open to anyone wishing to trace their Scottish heritage or explore other local archives.

FREE Hawick Museum &
Art Gallery   MUSEUM, GALLERY
(☑01450-373457; Wilton Lodge Park; ⊙10am-noon & 1-5pm Mon-Fri, 2-5pm Sat & Sun Apr-Sep, noon-3pm Mon-Fri, 1-3pm Sun Oct-Mar) Across the river, this museum has an interesting collection of mostly 19th-century manufacturing and domestic memorabilia. There are usually a couple of temporary exhibitions on as well.

🛏 Sleeping & Eating

The Bank Guest House   B&B **££**
(☑01450-363760; www.thebankno12highst.com; 12 High St; d from £65; P �}) This posh boutique B&B in the centre of Hawick brings out the best in this solid 19th-century building with modish wallpapers and designer furniture and fabrics. Modern comforts like iPod docks and fully-functioning wifi, as well as numerous thoughtful extras, make this a great place to stay.

Damascus Drum   CAFE **£**
(www.damascusdrum.co.uk; 2 Silver St; light meals £3-7; ⊙10am-5pm Mon-Sat; ☑) The Middle East meets the Borders in this enticing cafe behind the tourist office. Patterned rugs and a second-hand bookshop make for a relaxing environment to enjoy breakfasts, bagels, burgers, and tasty Turkish-style meze options.

Sergio's   ITALIAN
(Sandbed; pizza & pasta £6-10; ⊙Tue-Sun) This well-established Italian restaurant near the river is a fine choice for pizza and pasta dishes or elaborate, if a little overpriced, mains. Go for the blackboard specials, which always include beautifully-prepared fish dishes.

ⓘ Getting Around

Rent hybrid bikes from **Borders Cycles** (☑01450-375976; www.borderscycles.com; cnr Howegate & Silver St; 1 day/6 days £18/72; ⊙Mon & Wed-Sat).

The half-hourly First buses 95 and X95 connect Hawick with Galashiels, Selkirk and Edinburgh (£7.20, two hours).

Jedburgh

POP 4090

Attractive Jedburgh, where many old buildings and wynds (narrow alleys) have been intelligently restored, invites exploration by foot. It's constantly busy with domestic tourists, but wander into some of the pretty side streets and you could hear a pin drop.

Sights

Jedburgh Abbey
RUINS

(HS; www.historic-scotland.gov.uk; Abbey Rd; adult/child £5.50/3.30; ⊙9.30am-5.30pm Apr-Sep, 9.30am-4.30pm Oct-Mar) Dominating the town skyline, Jedburgh Abbey was the first of the great Border abbeys to be passed into state care, and it shows – audio and visual presentations telling the abbey's story are scattered throughout the carefully preserved ruins (good for the kids). The red-sandstone ruins are roofless but relatively intact, and the ingenuity of the master mason can be seen in some of the rich (if somewhat faded) stone carvings in the nave. The abbey was founded in 1138 by David I as a priory for Augustinian canons.

FREE Mary, Queen of Scots House
HISTORIC HOUSE

(Queen St; ⊙10am-4.30pm Mon-Sat, 11am-4.30pm Sun Mar-Nov) Mary stayed at this beautiful 16th-century tower house in 1566 after her famous ride to visit the injured earl of Bothwell, her future husband, at Hermitage Castle. The interesting displays evoke the sad saga of Mary's life.

Activities

The tourist office sells some handy walking booklets for walks around the town, including sections of the **Southern Upland Way** or **Borders Abbeys Way**.

Festivals & Events

Jethart Callant's Festival
CULTURAL

(www.jethartcallantsfestival.com) For two weeks from late June this cavalcade recalls the perilous time when people rode out on horseback checking for English incursions.

Sleeping

Maplebank
B&B £

(☎01835-862051; maplebank3@btinternet.com; 3 Smiths Wynd; s/d £25/40; P) It's very pleasing to come across places like this, where it really feels like you're staying in someone's home. In this case, that someone is a bit like your favourite aunt: friendly, chaotic and generous. There's lots of clutter and it's very informal. The rooms are comfortable and large, and share a good bathroom. Breakfast (particularly if you like fruit, yoghurts, homemade jams and a selection of every-

thing) is much better than you get at most posher places.

Willow Court
B&B ££

(☎01835-863702; www.willowcourtjedburgh.co.uk; The Friars; d £80-86; P🕿) It seems inadequate to call this impressive option a B&B; it's more like a boutique hotel. Three impeccable rooms with elegant wallpaper, showroom bathrooms and great beds are complemented by a courteous professional welcome. Breakfast can include a grapefruit medley or smoked salmon, and you could spend hours in the conservatory lounge admiring the views over the garden and town.

Eating

The Clock Tower
BISTRO ££

(☎01835-869788; www.clocktowerbistro.co.uk; Abbey Pl; mains £9-15; ⊙Tue-Sat) Opposite the skeleton of the abbey, this place will put meat on your bones with its eclectic menu of upmarket bistro fare, drizzling truffle oil or Rioja jus over ingredients like tuna steaks, duck confit or west coast scallops. Prices are good for this level of food, though some of the flavours could be more adventurous.

Carters Rest
PUB ££

(Abbey Pl; mains £9-12; 🕿) Right opposite the abbey, here you'll find upmarket pub grub in an attractive lounge bar. The standard fare is fleshed out with an evening dinner menu featuring local lamb and other goodies. Portions are generous and served with a smile.

RIDING OF THE MARCHES

The Riding of the Marches, also known as the Common Riding, takes place in early summer in the major Borders towns. Like many Scottish festivals it has ancient origins, dating back to the Middle Ages when riders would be sent to the town boundary to check on the common lands. The colourful event normally involves extravagant convoys of horse riders following the town standard as it is paraded along a well-worn route. Festivities vary between towns but usually involve lots of singing, sport, pageants, concerts and plenty of whisky. If you want to zero in on the largest of the Ridings, head to Jedburgh for the Jethart Callant's Festival (p151).

WALKING & CYCLING IN SOUTHERN SCOTLAND

The region's most famous walk is the challenging 212-mile Southern Upland Way (www.southernuplandway.gov.uk). If you want a sample, one of the best bits is the three- to four-day section from St John's Town of Dalry to Beattock.

Another long-distance walk is the 62-mile St Cuthbert's Way (www.stcuthbertsway.info), inspired by the travels of St Cuthbert, a 7th-century saint who lived at Melrose Abbey. It crosses some superb scenery between Melrose and Lindisfarne (in England).

In Galloway the Pilgrims Way follows a 25-mile trail from Glenluce Abbey to the Isle of Whithorn.

The Borders Abbeys Way (p153) links all the great Border abbeys in a 65-mile circuit. For shorter walks and especially circular loops in the hills, the towns of Melrose, Jedburgh and Kelso all make ideal bases.

For baggage transfer on these walks, contact WalkingSupport (☎01896-822079; www.walkingsupport.co.uk). In early September, look out for the Scottish Borders Walking Festival (www.borderswalking.com), with nine days of walks for all abilities and an instant social scene.

With the exception of the main A-roads, traffic is sparse, which, along with the beauty of the countryside, makes this ideal cycling country.

The Tweed Cycle Route is a waymarked route running 62 miles along the beautiful Tweed Valley, following minor roads from Biggar to Peebles (22 miles), Melrose (25 miles), Coldstream (28 miles) and Berwick-upon-Tweed (19 miles). The 4 Abbeys Cycle Route is a 55-mile circuit of the Border abbeys. Local tourist offices have route maps; these and other routes are also detailed at www.cyclescottishborders.com.

For an island tour, the Isle of Arran offers excellent cycling opportunities. The 55-mile coastal road circuit (p162) is stunning and is worth splitting into two or three days.

Information

There's a free wi-fi zone around the centre, with especially strong signal in and around the tourist office.

Jedburgh Library (Castlegate; ⊘Mon-Fri) Free internet.

Jedburgh Information Centre (☎01835-863170; jedburgh@visitscotland.com; Murray's Green; ⊘9.15am-5pm Mon-Sat, 10am-4pm Sun) The head tourist office for the Borders region. Very helpful. Extended hours in summer. Closed Sunday November to March.

❶ Getting There & Away

Jedburgh has good bus connections to Hawick (25 minutes, roughly hourly, four on Sunday), Melrose (30 minutes, hourly Monday to Saturday, every two hours Sunday) and Kelso (25 minutes, hourly Monday to Saturday, four Sunday). Munro's runs buses from Jedburgh to Edinburgh (£7.10, two hours, hourly Monday to Saturday, five Sunday).

Kelso

POP 5116

Kelso, a prosperous market town with a broad, cobbled square flanked by Georgian buildings, has a cheery feel and an historic appeal. During the day it's a busy little place, but after 8pm you'll have the streets to yourself. The town has a lovely site at the junction of the Rivers Tweed and Teviot, and is one of the most enjoyable places in the Borders.

Sights

Floors Castle   CASTLE

(www.floorscastle.com; adult/child £8/4; ⊘11am-5pm May-Oct) Grandiose Floors Castle is Scotland's largest inhabited mansion, home to the Duke of Roxburghe, and overlooks the Tweed about a mile west of Kelso. Built by William Adam in the 1720s, the original Georgian simplicity was 'improved' in the 1840s with the addition of rather ridiculous battlements and turrets. Inside, view the vivid colours of the 17th-century Brussels tapestries in the drawing room and the intricate oak carvings in the ornate ballroom. It opens at 10.30am from June to September and is also open over Easter.

FREE Kelso Abbey   RUINS

(HS; www.historic-scotland.gov.uk; Bridge St; ⊘9.30am-6.30pm Apr-Sep, 9.30am-4.30pm Sat-Wed Oct-Mar) Once one of the richest abbeys in southern Scotland, Kelso Abbey was built by the Tironensians, an order founded at Tiron in Picardy and brought to the Borders around 1113 by David I. English raids in the 16th century reduced it to ruins, though what remains today is some of the finest surviving Romanesque architecture in Scotland.

Activities

The **Borders Abbeys Way** (www.bordersab beysway.com) links the great abbeys of Kelso, Jedburgh, Melrose and Dryburgh in a 65-mile circuit. The Kelso–Jedburgh section (12 miles) is a fairly easy walk, largely following the River Teviot between the towns. The tourist office has a free leaflet with a map and description of the route.

Less-ambitious walkers should leave the Square by Roxburgh St and take the signposted alley to **Cobby Riverside Walk**, a pleasant ramble along the river to Floors Castle (you have to rejoin Roxburgh St to gain admission to the castle).

Sleeping

TOP CHOICE **Old Priory** B&B ££

(01573-223030; www.theoldpriorykelso.com; 33 Woodmarket St; s/d £50/80; P⊗) The doubles in this atmospheric place are fantastic and the family room has to be seen to be believed; rooms are both sumptuous and debonair with gorgeous dark polished wood pieces. The good news extends to the garden – perfect for a coffee in the morning – and a comfortable sitting room. The huge windows flood the rooms with natural light.

TOP CHOICE **Edenbank House** B&B ££

(01573-226734; www.edenbank.co.uk; Stichill Rd; s/d £40/80; P⊗) Half a mile down the road to Stichill, this grand Victorian house (no sign) sits in spacious grounds where only the bleating of lambs in the green fields and birds in the garden break the silence. It's a fabulous place, with huge opulent rooms, lovely views over the fields, and incredibly warm, generous hospitality. Breakfast features homemade produce, and a laissez-faire attitude makes for an utterly relaxing stay. Call ahead.

Ednam House Hotel HOTEL ££

(01573-224168; www.ednamhouse.com; Bridge St; s/d from £85/125; P⊗) The genteel, Georgian Ednam House, touched with a quiet dignity, contains many of its original features, with fine gardens overlooking the river and an excellent restaurant, as well as a deli-bistro by the gates. It's very popular with fisher folk; during salmon season, from the end of August until November, the hotel is very busy. Rooms have charming old furniture; those with a river view cost more.

Central Guest House B&B £

(01890-883664; www.thecentralguesthousekel so.co.uk; s/d £30/45) A bargain in sometimes pricey Kelso and just on the central square. The owners live off-site, so call ahead first. The rooms are fine: spacious, with firm beds, new carpets and good bathrooms. Rates are room-only, but you get a fridge, toaster and microwave so you can create your own breakfast.

Eating & Drinking

TOP CHOICE **The Cobbles** PUB ££

(01573-223548; www.thecobblesinn.co.uk; 7 Bowmont St; bar mains £9-13; ⊗meals Tue-Sun) We've included the phone number for a reason: this inn off the main square is so popular you will need to book a table at weekends. It's cheery, very welcoming, warm, and serves excellent upmarket pub food in generous portions. Choose from the bar menu or the more upmarket dinner list (£21 for two courses). There's a decent wine selection and proper coffee, but the wise leave room for dessert too. The bar always has an interesting guest ale or two as well. A cracking place.

Oscar's BISTRO ££

(01573-224008; www.oscars-kelso.com; 33 Horsemarket; mains £10-16; ⊗dinner Wed-Mon) Posh comfort food and the work of local artists sit side by side in this likeable bar-restaurant-gallery in the centre of town. A list of excellent daily specials complements the more standard permanent selection. A wide choice of wines is available, and you can browse the exhibition space downstairs while you wait for your meal.

Information

Kelso Library (Bowmont St; ⊗Mon-Sat) Free internet access.

Kelso Information Centre (01573-223464; www.visitscottishborders.com; The Square; ⊗10am-4pm Mon-Sat Apr-Oct, plus 10am-2pm Sun late Jun-early Sep)

❶ Getting There & Away

There are nine buses daily (four on Sunday) to Berwick-upon-Tweed (50 minutes). Buses run to/from Jedburgh (25 minutes, up to 10 daily Monday to Saturday, four Sunday) and on to Hawick (one hour). There are also frequent services to Edinburgh (£6.90, two hours).

Around Kelso

The area around Kelso has two starkly contrasting historic buildings to visit, and the twin walkers' villages of Town and Kirk Yetholm.

◉ Sights

Smailholm Tower   TOWER
(HS; www.historic-scotland.gov.uk; adult/child £4.50/2.70; ⊙9.30am-5.30pm daily Apr-Sep, 9.30am-4.30pm Sat & Sun only Oct-Mar) Perched on a rocky knoll above a small lake, this narrow stone tower provides one of the most evocative sights in the Borders and keeps the bloody uncertainties of its history alive. Although the displays inside are sparse, the panoramic view from the top is worth the climb.

The nearby farm, Sandyknowe, was owned by Sir Walter Scott's grandfather. As Scott himself recognised, his imagination was fired by the ballads and stories he heard as a child at Sandyknowe, and by the ruined tower a stone's throw away.

The tower is 6 miles west of Kelso, a mile south of Smailholm village on the B6397. You pass through the farmyard to get to the tower. First bus 66 between Kelso and Galashiels stops in Smailholm village.

Mellerstain House   HISTORIC HOUSE
(www.mellerstain.com; adult/child £8.50/4; ⊙12.30-5pm Mon, Wed & Sun Apr-Oct) Finished in 1778, this is considered to be Scotland's finest Robert Adam–designed mansion. It is famous for its classic elegance, ornate interiors and plaster ceilings; the library in particular is outstanding. The upstairs bedrooms are less attractive, but have a peek at the bizarre puppet-and-doll collection in the gallery.

It's about 6 miles northwest of Kelso, near Gordon. First bus 66 between Kelso and Galashiels passes about a mile from Mellerstain House.

TOWN YETHOLM & KIRK YETHOLM
The twin villages of Town Yetholm and Kirk Yetholm, separated by Bowmont Water, are close to the English border, about 6 miles southeast of Kelso. Hill-walking centres, they lie at the northern end of the **Pennine Way** and on **St Cuthbert's Way** between Melrose and Lindisfarne (Holy Island) in Northumberland. There are several places to stay, including the excellent Border Hotel (⊉01573-420237; www.theborderhotel.com; The Green, Kirk Yetholm; s £50, d £80-90; ℗ 🛜 🌫), whose bar is a welcome one at the end of a long trek.

Bus 81 from Kelso runs up to seven times a day Monday to Saturday (three times on Sunday).

Coldstream
POP 1813

On a sweeping bend of the River Tweed, which forms the border with England, Coldstream is small and relatively hidden from the well-trodden Borders tourist beat.

◉ Sights

FREE Coldstream Museum   MUSEUM
(12 Market Sq; ⊙10am-4pm Mon-Sat, 2-4pm Sun Apr-Sep, 1-4pm Mon-Sat Oct) The proud history of the Coldstream Guards is covered in this museum. Formed in 1650 in Berwick as part of Oliver Cromwell's New Model Army, the regiment took its present name from the town in which it was stationed in 1659. The Guards played a significant part in the restoration of the monarchy in 1660 and saw service at Waterloo, at Sebastopol during the Crimean War, in the Boer War, at the Somme and Ypres in WWI, and at Dunkirk and Tobruk in WWII. It remains the oldest regiment in continuous existence in the British army.

🛏 Sleeping & Eating

Eastbraes B&B   B&B ££
(⊉01890-883949; www.eastbraes.co.uk; 100C High St; s/d £45/70) Trundling down the main street in Coldstream, you simply don't expect the view you get out the back of this welcoming place; an idyllic vista over a grassy garden and a picture-book bend in the Tweed beyond. A double and twin share a bathroom and there's one en suite double, which is simply enormous and comes with a separate sitting area.

Calico House   B&B ££
(⊉07985-249207; www.bedandbreakfast-luxury. co.uk; 44 High St; d/ste £80/100; ℗ 🛜) Set be-

hind a shop that churns out high-quality interior designs, this is a superb B&B with sumptuous rooms blessed with great views and attention to detail. Privacy from your hosts and value for money are two very strong points in this classy accommodation option. They prefer you to stay more than one night.

❶ Getting There & Away

Coldstream is on the busy A697 linking Newcastle with Edinburgh. There are nine buses daily Monday to Saturday (four on Sunday) between Kelso (20 minutes) and Berwick-upon-Tweed (20 to 40 minutes) via here.

Eyemouth

POP 3383

Eyemouth is a busy fishing port and popular domestic holiday destination. The harbour itself is very atmospheric – you may even spot seals frolicking in the water, as well as tourists frolicking around the boats, snapping pics of old fishing nets.

The community here suffered its greatest catastrophe in October 1881, when a storm destroyed the coastal fishing fleet, killing 189 fishermen, 129 of whom were locals.

◉ Sights

Eyemouth Maritime Centre MUSEUM
(www.worldofboats.org; Harbour Rd; adult/child £4.25/2.75; ☻10am-5pm) Situated right on Eyemouth's working fishing harbour, what was once the fish market has now been decked out to resemble an 18th-century man o' war. A changing yearly exhibition occupies most of the interior, drawing on the museum's large collection of well-loved wooden coastal craft. The museum guides are great for extra information.

Gunsgreen House MUSEUM
(www.gunsgreenhouse.org; adult/child £6/3.50; ☻11am-5pm Thu-Mon Apr-Sep) Standing proud and four-square across the harbour, this elegant 18th-century John Adam mansion was built on the profits of smuggling: Eyemouth was an important landing point for illegal cargoes arriving from northern Europe and the Baltic. The house has been beautifully restored to reflect its smuggling history and other aspects of its varied past. Both the house and the adjacent tower-like dovecote can be hired out as self-catering accommodation.

Eyemouth Museum MUSEUM
(www.eyemouthmuseum.org.uk; Manse Rd; adult/child £3/free; ☻10am-4pm Tue-Sat, noon-4pm Sun Apr-Oct) Captivating Eyemouth Museum has local history displays, particularly relating to the town's fishing heritage. Its centrepiece is the tapestry commemorating the 1881 fishing disaster.

☕ Sleeping & Eating

Churches Hotel HOTEL, SEAFOOD ££
(☎01890-750401; www.churcheshotel.com; Albert Rd; s/d £75/£95-120; ☻Mar-Oct; P ☑) This is a very stylish place set in an 18th-century building, with rooms exuding a cool and classic demeanour. Each room has a different theme but No 4, with its four-poster bed, and No 6, with huge windows overlooking the harbour, are our favourites. Little conveniences like bottled water, a DVD library and iPod docks are complemented by excellent personal service from the owners. The restaurant menu (mains £13 to £25) is blessed with the day's catch from the harbour – it's by far the best spot in town for fresh seafood. One of southern Scotland's standout establishments.

Bantry B&B ££
(Mackays; ☎01890-751900; www.mackaysofeyemouth.co.uk; 20 High St; s without bathroom £25, d ensuite £60; ☑) Plonked on top of the restaurant of the same name on the main drag, this B&B has redecorated and refurbished rooms with muted tones and a luxurious, modern feel, positioned right on the waterfront. Try to get room No 3 if you're after a double, as it's the only one with sea views. There's a fabulous deck with loungers and a summer hot tub, overlooking the lapping waves. Add £2.50 per person for continental breakfast, or £7.50 for the works.

Oblò BISTRO ££
(www.oblobar.com; 20 Harbour St; mains £8-14; ☻food 10am-9pm) For a meal pretty much anytime, find your way upstairs to this modern Mediterranean-fusion bar-bistro with comfy seating and a modish interior. It's just down from the tourist office, and it's got a great deck to lap up the sunshine. Try the local seafood.

❶ Information

Eyemouth Information Centre (☎018907-50678; eyemouth@visitscotland.com; Manse Rd; ☻10am-4pm Tue-Sat, noon-4pm Sun Apr-Oct) Very helpful; inside Eyemouth Museum near the harbour.

ℹ Getting There & Away

Eyemouth is 5 miles north of the Scotland-England border. Buses go to Berwick-upon-Tweed (15 minutes, frequent), which has a train station, and to Edinburgh (£10, 1¾ hours, seven daily Monday to Saturday, three Sunday).

South of Eyemouth

Five miles west of Berwick along the B6461, Paxton House (www.paxtonhouse.com; adult/child £8/3.50; ⊙11am-5pm mid-Mar-Oct, grounds 10am-sunset) is beside the River Tweed and surrounded by parkland and gardens. It was built in 1758 by Patrick Home for his intended wife, the daughter of Prussia's Frederick the Great. Unfortunately, she stood him up, but it was her loss; designed by the Adam family – brothers John, James and Robert – Paxon House is acknowledged as one of the finest 18th-century Palladian houses in Britain. It contains a large collection of Chippendale and Regency furniture, and its picture gallery houses paintings from the national galleries of Scotland. The nursery is a feature designed to provide insight into a child's 18th-century life. In the grounds are walking trails, an adventure playground, a campsite and a riverside museum on salmon fishing.

Coldingham & St Abbs

This picturesque area is fantastic for those who love the great outdoors. There's some of the UK's best diving here, as well as great cycling, walking, angling, and birdwatching. From the village of Coldingham, with its twisting streets, take the B6438 downhill to the small fishing village of St Abbs, a gorgeous, peaceful little community with a picture-perfect harbour nestled below the cliffs.

◉ Sights & Activities

FREE St Abbs Visitor Centre   MUSEUM
(www.stabbsvisitorcentre.co.uk; ⊙10am-5pm Tue-Sun Apr-Nov) This shiny new exhibition in St Abbs has interesting interactive displays on the oft-stormy history of this harbour village. Spoken reminiscenses from locals like a fisherman and lighthouse keeper are the highlight.

St Abb's Head National
Nature Reserve   NATURE RESERVE
(www.nts.org.uk) North of St Abbs, this 78-hectare reserve is an ornithologist's wonderland, with large colonies of guillemots, kittiwakes, herring gulls, fulmars, razorbills and some puffins. You get to the reserve by following the 2-mile circular trail that begins beside the Northfield Farm car park (£2) on the road just west of St Abbs. The clifftop walks here are spectacular, especially on sunny days. There's a good little nature exhibition (⊙11am-4pm Apr-Oct) in the Old Smiddy complex alongside.

Coldingham Bay   BEACH, SURFING
In Coldingham, a signposted turn-off to the east leads just under a mile down to away-from-it-all Coldingham Bay, which has a sandy beach and a clifftop walking trail to Eyemouth (3 miles). At St Vedas Surf Shop (☎018907-71679; www.stvedas.co.uk) you can hire surfboards and snorkelling gear; there's a hotel here that serves cheap food. Surfing lessons are also available.

Diving

The clear, clean waters around St Abbs form part of the St Abbs & Eyemouth Voluntary Marine Reserve (☎018907-71443; www.marine-reserve.co.uk), one of the best coldwater diving sites in Europe. The reserve is home to a variety of marine life, including grey seals, porpoises, and wolf-fish. Visibility is about 7m to 8m but has been recorded at 24m. Beds of brown kelp form a hypnotically undulating forest on the seabed.

Four dive boats operate out of St Abbs, run by Paul Crowe (☎018907-71945, 07710-961050; www.divestabbs.com), Paul O'Callaghan (☎077 80-980179, 018907-71525; www.stabbsdiving.com), Graeme Crowe (☎07803-608050, 018907-71766; www.stingrayboatcharters.co.uk) and Peter Gibson (☎018907-71681). You can charter them whole, or phone to book a spot on a boat; these cost around £15 per person.

To hire diving equipment and for tips on the best dive sites, drop by the excellent Scoutscroft (☎01890-771338; www.scoutscroft.co.uk) dive shop in Coldingham on the road to St Abbs. You can also hire equipment here and organise a boat dive. This professional set-up can kit you up with nitrox tanks and do a full range of IANTD courses. The St Abbs Visitor Centre can also provide diving advice. A guide to local dive sites costs £7.50.

🛏 Sleeping

Rock House   BUNKHOUSE, B&B ££
(☎01890-771945; www.divestabbs.com; dm/s/d £20/30/60) Right by the harbour in St Abbs, this is run by a friendly dive skipper; you can almost roll out of bed onto the boat. There's

a bunkhouse which is normally booked up by groups at the weekend, and a sweet B&B room that can sleep up to three. There's also a self-catering cottage.

❶ Getting There & Away

Bus 253 between Edinburgh and Berwick-upon-Tweed (seven daily Monday to Saturday, three Sunday) stops in Coldingham (some go to St Abbs on request). Bus 235 runs at least hourly to both from Eyemouth.

SOUTH LANARKSHIRE

South Lanarkshire combines a highly urbanised area south of Glasgow with scenically gorgeous country around the Falls of Clyde and the World Heritage–listed area of New Lanark, by far the biggest drawcard of the region. If you're roaring up to Scotland on the M74, there are some fine places to break your journey.

Lanark & New Lanark

POP 8253

Below the market town of Lanark, in an attractive gorge by the River Clyde, is the World Heritage Site of **New Lanark** – an intriguing collection of restored mill buildings and warehouses.

Once the largest cotton-spinning complex in Britain, it is better known for the pioneering social experiments of Robert Owen, who managed the mill from 1800. New Lanark is really a memorial to this enlightened capitalist. He provided his workers with housing, a cooperative store (the inspiration for the modern cooperative movement), the world's first nursery school for children, a school with adult-education classes, a sick-pay fund for workers and a social centre he called the New Institute for the Formation of Character. You'll need at least half a day to explore this site, as there's plenty to see, and appealing walks along the riverside. What must once have been a thriving, noisy, grimy industrial village, pumping out enough cotton to wrap the planet, is now a peaceful oasis with only the swishing of trees and the rushing of the River Clyde to be heard.

◉ Sights & Activities

 New Lanark Visitor Centre   MUSEUM
(www.newlanark.org; adult/child/family £8.50/6/24; ⊙10am-5pm Apr-Oct, 10am-4pm Nov-Mar) You need to buy a ticket to enter the main attractions. These include a huge working spinning mule, producing woollen yarn, and the **Historic Schoolhouse**, which contains an innovative, high-tech journey to New Lanark's past via a 3D hologram of the spirit of Annie McLeod, a 10-year-old mill girl who describes life here in 1820. The kids will love it as it's very realistic, although the 'do good for all mankind' theme is a little overbearing.

Included in your admission is entrance to a **millworker's house**, **Robert Owen's home** and exhibitions on 'saving New Lanark'. There's also a 1920s-style **village store**.

Falls of Clyde Wildlife Centre   NATURE CENTRE
(www.scottishwildlifetrust.co.uk; adult/child £2/1; ⊙10am-5pm Apr-Sep, 11am-5pm Oct-Mar) The wildlife centre is also by the river in New Lanarkm and features child-friendly displays focused on badgers, bats, peregrine falcons and other prominent species. In season, there's a live video feed of peregrines nesting nearby. Entry is a pound cheaper if you buy it together with the New Lanark Visitor Centre entrance. The centre also organises various activities in summer, including badger-watching (adult/child £8/4).

From the centre, you can walk through the beautiful nature reserve up to **Corra Linn** (30 minutes) and **Bonnington Linn** (one hour), two of the **Falls of Clyde** that inspired Turner and Wordsworth. You could return via the muddier path on the opposite bank, pass New Lanark, and cross the river a little further downstream to make a circular walk of it (three hours).

Craignethan Castle   CASTLE
(HS; www.historic-scotland.gov.uk; adult/child £4/2.40; ⊙9.30am-5.30pm Apr-Sep, 9.30am-4.30pm Sat & Sun Oct-Mar) This castle has a very authentic feel – it hasn't been restored beyond recognition – and it is located in a stunning, tranquil spot. You'll feel miles from anywhere, so bring a picnic and make a day of it.

With a commanding position above the River Nethan, this extensive ruin includes a virtually intact tower house and a **caponier** – a small gun emplacement with holes in the wall so men with handguns could pick off attackers. The chilly chambers under the tower house are quite eerie.

Craignethan is 5 miles northwest of Lanark. If you don't have your own transport, take an hourly Lanark–Hamilton bus to

Crossford, then follow the footpath along the northern bank of the River Nethan (20 minutes).

🛏 Sleeping & Eating

New Lanark makes a very relaxing, attractive place to stay.

TOP CHOICE New Lanark Mill Hotel HOTEL ££
(📞01555-667200; www.newlanarkmillhotel.co.uk; s/d £75/119; P@🖙🐾🐾) Cleverly converted from an 18th-century mill, this hotel is full of character and is a stone's throw from the major attractions. It has luxury rooms (only £10 extra for a spacious superior room), with contemporary art on the walls and views of the churning Clyde below, as well as self-catering accommodation in charming cottages (from £67). There are good facilities for the disabled here. The hotel also serves good meals (bar meals £10 to £17, restaurant mains £15 to £20).

New Lanark SYHA HOSTEL £
(📞01555-666710; www.syha.org.uk; dm/tw £18/45; ☺mid-Mar–mid-Oct; P@🖙) This hostel has a great location in an old mill building by the River Clyde, in the heart of the New Lanark complex. It has comfortable en suite dormitories and a really good downstairs common area. They do breakfasts and dinners and will also make a packed lunch. Closed between 10am and 4pm.

La Vigna ITALIAN ££
(📞01555-664320; www.lavigna.co.uk; 40 Wellgate; 3-course lunch/dinner £14/24; ☺lunch & dinner Mon-Sat, dinner Sun) This well established local favourite is a great spot, seemingly plucked from some bygone age with its quietly efficient service and, charmingly, a separate menu for ladies – without prices! The food is distinctly Italian, albeit using sound Scottish venison, beef, and fish, and there are also vegetarian options. The set-price lunch is fine value; the set dinner is available Monday to Thursday only.

ℹ Information

Lanark Information Centre (📞01555-661661; lanark@visitscotland.com; Ladyacre Rd; ☺10am-5pm) Close to the bus and train stations. Closed Sundays October to March.

ℹ Getting There & Around

Lanark is 25 miles southeast of Glasgow. Express buses from Glasgow run hourly from Monday to Saturday (one hour).

Trains also run between Glasgow Central station and Lanark (£6.20, 55 minutes, every 30 minutes, hourly on Sundays).

It's a pleasant walk to New Lanark, but there's also a half-hourly bus service from the train station (daily). If you need a taxi, call **Clydewide** (📞01555-663813; www.clydewidetaxis.co.uk).

Biggar

POP 2098

Biggar is a pleasant town in a rural setting dominated by Tinto Hill (712m). The town has a number of offbeat museums that give it a quirky appeal. It's also known for the nationalist, leftist poet Hugh MacDiarmid, who lived near here for nearly 30 years until his death in 1978.

👁 Sights & Activities

The **Biggar Museum Trust** (📞01899-221050; www.biggarmuseumtrust.co.uk) looks after most of the town's museums. It all relies on the goodwill of volunteers, so opening hours can be quite variable: it's worth ringing ahead if you've got a special interest in one of them.

Gladstone Court MUSEUM
(North Back Rd; adult/child £2.50/1.50; ☺11am-4.30pm Mon-Tue & Thu-Sat, 2-4.30pm Sun Apr-Oct) An intriguing indoor street museum with historic Victorian-era nook-and-cranny shops that you can pop into to steal a glimpse of the past. Don't miss the **old printing press** and the **Albion A2 Dogcart**, one of the oldest British cars still around.

Biggar Puppet Theatre THEATRE
(📞01899-220631; www.purvespuppets.com; Broughton Rd; seats £8; ☺11am-4.30pm Tue-Sat) A well-loved local institution that runs matinee shows every couple of days throughout the summer using miniature Victorian puppets and bizarre glow-in-the-dark modern ones over 1m high. Different shows are suitable for varying age groups, so inquire before you take along the kids. Check the website for performance times.

Moat Park Heritage Centre MUSEUM
(adult/child £2.50/1.50; ☺11am-4.30pm Mon-Sat, 2-4.30pm Sun Apr-mid-Oct) In a renovated church, the museum covers the history of the area through geological and archaeological displays.

Greenhill Covenanter's House MUSEUM
(adult/child £1.50/70p) An intelligently reconstructed farmhouse with 17th-century fur-

nishings and artefacts relating to the fascinating story of the local Covenanters, who valiantly defied the king to protect their religious beliefs. In theory it only opens the first Saturday of every month, but if you ask at nearby Moat Park Heritage Centre, they'll usually be able to arrange a visit. Lovely location by a stream.

Tinto Hill   HIKE

The hill dominates town. It is a straightforward ascent by the northern ridge from the car park, just off the A73 by Thankerton Crossroads. Look out for the Stone Age **fort** on your way up. Allow two hours for the return trip.

🛏 Sleeping & Eating

TOP CHOICE **Cornhill House**   HOTEL **££**

(📞01899-220001; www.cornhillhousehotel.com; s/d £80/110; 🅿🤶) Just off the A72 a couple of miles west of Biggar, this is a fabulous country hotel in a striking château-style building that offers artistic, opulent décor with not a hint of tartan. There are nine rooms (with more on the way), and they are huge, with loads of character and appealing furniture, like leather sofas or four-poster beds. There's also a good on-site restaurant.

School Green Cottage   B&B **££**

(📞01899-220388; isobel.burness@virgin.net; 1 Kirkstyle; s/d £35/60; 🤶) Just off the sometimes noisy main road in the centre of town, this is an upright little place with courteous homespun hospitality. The neat double and twin here are old fashioned but comfortable and the host's watercolours decorate the walls.

Fifty-Five   BRITISH **££**

(www.restaurantfiftyfive.com; 55 High St; mains £13; ⊙Tue-Sat; 🤶) A classier option than Biggar's decent pubs, this well-run restaurant features a handsome dining area with exposed stone, candlelight, posh glassware and inviting chairs. The short menu covers upmarket comfort food and a few more ambitious creations. There are good lunch specials.

ℹ Getting There & Away

Biggar is 33 miles southeast of Glasgow. There are hourly buses (three on Sunday) to/from Edinburgh and Lanark (30 minutes), where you can change for Glasgow. Other buses run to Peebles.

AYRSHIRE & ARRAN

Ayrshire is synonymous with golf and with Robert Burns – and there's plenty on offer here to satisfy both of these pursuits. Troon has six golf courses for starters, and there's enough Burns memorabilia in the region to satisfy even his most fanatic admirers.

This area's main drawcard, though, is the irresistible Isle of Arran. With a gourmet culinary scene, atmospheric watering holes, and the most varied and scenic countryside of the southern Hebridean islands, this easily accessible island shouldn't be missed.

The best way to appreciate the Ayrshire coastline is on foot: the Ayrshire Coastal Path (www.ayrshirecoastalpath.org) offers 100 miles of spectacular waterside walking.

North Ayrshire

LARGS
POP 11,241

On a sunny day, there are few places in southern Scotland more beautiful than Largs, where green grass meets the sparkling water of the Firth of Clyde. It's a resort-style waterfront town that harks back to seaside days in times of gentler pleasures, and the minigolf, amusements, old-fashioned eateries and bouncy castle mean you should get into the spirit, buy an ice cream, and go for a stroll around this slice of retro Scotland.

◉ Sights

Víkingar!   MUSEUM

(📞01475-689777; www.kaleisure.com; Greenock Rd; adult/child £4.50/3.50; ⊙10.30am-2.30pm Mar-Oct, weekends only Feb & Nov, to 3.30pm Jul & Aug; 🚼) The town's main attraction is a multimedia exhibition describing Viking influence in Scotland until its demise at the Battle of Largs in 1263. Tours with staff in Viking outfits run every hour, but check opening times beforehand as they change frequently. There's also a swimming pool and leisure centre. It's on the waterfront road just north of the centre. You can't miss it, as it's the only place with a longship outside.

🎉 Festivals

Viking Festival   HISTORIC

(www.largsvikingfestival.com) During the first week of September, this festival celebrates the Battle of Largs and the end of Viking political domination in Scotland.

📖 Sleeping & Eating

Brisbane House Hotel HOTEL ££

(☑01475-687200; www.brisbanehousehotel.com; 14 Greenock Rd; s/d £70/105, d/ste with sea view £135/150; P🗐🖧) We're not sure about the modern facade on this genteel old building, but the rooms are quite luxurious, and some – it's aimed at wedding parties – have jacuzzis and huge beds. It's on the waterfront, so paying the extra for a sea view will reward in fine weather, as the sun sets over Great Cumbrae opposite. There's a decent bar and restaurant downstairs and a comfortable contemporary feel. It's usually substantially cheaper via booking websites.

Glendarroch B&B ££

(☑01475-676305; www.glendarrochbedandbreakfast.co.uk; 24 Irvine Rd; s/d/f £40/65/80; P🗐) This B&B on the main road through town typifies Scottish hospitality – the rooms are well kept and the owner is friendly without being intrusive. If it's full, staff will probably ring around to try to find you something else.

Nardini's CAFE, BISTRO ££

(www.nardinis.co.uk; mains £8-16; ⊘9am-10pm; 🖨) Nothing typifies the old-time feel of Largs more than this giant art deco gelateria, well into its second century. The ice creams are decadently delicious, with rich flavours that'll have parents licking more than their fair share from the kids. There's also a cafe with outdoor seating, and a restaurant which does pizzas, pastas, and some surprisingly decent dishes like duck breast and delicious sardines on toast.

❶ Information

Largs Information Centre (☑01475-689962; www.ayrshire-arran.com; ⊘10.30am-3pm Mon-Sat Easter-Oct) At the train station, a block back from the waterfront on the main street.

❶ Getting There & Away

Largs is 32 miles west of Glasgow by road. There are very regular buses to Glasgow via Gourock and Greenock (45 minutes), and roughly one or two hourly to Ardrossan (30 minutes), Irvine (55 minutes) and Ayr (1¼ hours). There are trains to Largs from Glasgow Central station (£7.20, one hour, hourly).

ISLE OF GREAT CUMBRAE
POP 1200

Walking or cycling is the best way to explore this accessible, hilly island (it's only 4 miles long), ideal for a day-trip from Largs. **Millport** is the only town, strung out a long way around the bay overlooking neighbouring Little Cumbrae. The town boasts Britain's smallest cathedral, the lovely **Cathedral of the Isles** (College St; ⊘daylight hrs). Inside it's quite ornate, with a lattice woodwork ceiling and fragments of early Christian carved stones.

The island's minor roads have well-marked **walking** and **cycling** routes. Take the **Inner Circle route** up to the island's highest point, **Glaid Stone**, where you get good views of Arran and Largs, and even as far as the Paps of Jura on a clear day. You can walk between the ferry and the town via here in about an hour. There are several bike-hire places in Millport.

If you're staying overnight on the island there are several choices. Try the unusual **College of the Holy Spirit** (☑01475-530353; www.island-retreats.org; College St; s/d £40/69, with en suite £55/79; P🗐), next to the cathedral; there's a refectory-style dining room and a library.

Dancing Midge (www.thedancingmidge.com; 24 Glasgow St; light meals £3-7; ⊘9am-5pm; 🗐) is a cheerful seafront cafe providing healthy, tasty alternatives to the chippies in town. Food is freshly prepared (sandwiches, salads and soups) and the coffee is freshly brewed.

A very frequent **CalMac ferry** (www.calmac.co.uk) links Largs with Great Cumbrae (15 minutes; passenger/car return £4.90/21.05). Buses meet the ferries for the 3.5-mile journey to Millport.

Isle of Arran
POP 4800

Enchanting Arran is a jewel in Scotland's scenic crown. The island is a visual feast, and boasts culinary delights, cosy pubs (as well as its own brewery and distillery) and stacks of accommodation options. The variations in Scotland's dramatic landscape can all be experienced on this one small island, which is best explored by pulling on the hiking boots or jumping on a bicycle. Arran offers some challenging walks in the mountainous north, often compared to the Highlands, while the island's circular road is very popular with cyclists.

❶ Information

There are banks with ATMs in Brodick, the main town, where the Ardrossan ferry docks. Useful websites include www.ayrshire-arran.com, www.visit-isle-of-arran.eu and www.visitarran.com.

Isle of Arran

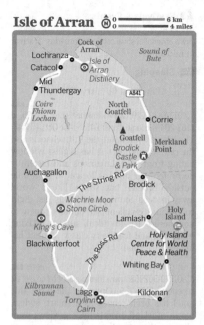

Arran Library (☑01770-302835; Brodick Hall, Brodick; ⏰10am-5pm Tue, 10am-7.30pm Thu & Fri, 10am-1pm Sat) Free internet access.

Brodick Information Centre (☑01770-303774; www.ayrshire-arran.com; Brodick; ⏰9am-5pm Mon-Sat) Efficient. Located by Brodick ferry pier; also open Sundays in July and August.

❶ Getting There & Away

CalMac (www.calmac.co.uk) runs a car ferry between Ardrossan and Brodick (passenger/car return £10.75/66, 55 minutes, four to six daily), and from April to late October also runs services between Claonaig on the Kintyre peninsula and Lochranza (passenger/car return £9.75/44, 30 minutes, seven to nine daily).

❶ Getting Around

Bicycle

Several places hire out bicycles.

Arran Adventure Company (☑01770-302244; www.arranadventure.com; Auchrannie Rd, Brodick; day/week £15/60) Good mountain bikes.

Boathouse (☑01770-302868; Brodick Beach; day/week £14/48) Will still hire even when closed in winter.

Sandwich Station (☑07810-796248; Lochranza; 2 hrs/day £6/15)

Car

For car hire, try **Arran Transport** (☑01770-302839; car rental half-/full day from £25/32) at the service station near the ferry pier.

Public Transport

Three to six buses daily go from Brodick pier to Lochranza (45 minutes), and many daily go from Brodick to Lamlash and Whiting Bay (30 minutes), then on to Kildonan and Blackwaterfoot. Pick up a timetable from the tourist office. An Arran Day Rider ticket costs £4.90 and permits travel anywhere on the island for a day (buy it from the driver).

BRODICK & AROUND

Most visitors arrive in Brodick, the beating heart of the island, and congregate along the coastal road to admire the town's long curving bay.

◉ Sights

Many of Brodick's attractions are just out of town, off the main road that runs north to Lochranza.

Brodick Castle & Park   CASTLE
(NTS; www.nts.org.uk; adult/child castle & park £11.50/8.50, park only £6.50/5.50; ⏰castle 11am-4.30pm Apr-Oct, park 9.30am-sunset year-round) Your first impression of this estate 2.5 miles north of Brodick will be of an animal morgue – you enter via the hunting gallery, which is wallpapered with prized deer heads. On the way to the formal dining room (with its peculiar table furnishings), note the intricacy of the fireplace in the library. The castle has more of a lived-in feel than some NTS properties, and only a small portion of the building is open to visitors. The extensive grounds, now a country park with various trails among the rhododendrons, justify the steep entry fee.

Arran Aromatics   SOAP FACTORY
(☑01770-302595; www.arranaromatics.com; ⏰9.30am-6pm) In Duchess Court is this popular visitor centre where you can purchase any number of scented items and watch the production line at work. The same people also run **Soapworks** (soapmaking from £7.50; ⏰10am-4pm), a fun little place where kids (and adults...) can experiment by making their own soaps, combining colours and moulds to make weird and wonderful creations.

Isle of Arran Brewery   BREWERY
(☑01770-302353; www.arranbrewery.com; tour £4; ⏰10am-5pm Mon-Sat, 12.30-5pm Sun Apr-Sep,

ℹ ARDROSSAN

An otherwise unremarkable coastal town, Androssan is the main ferry port for Arran. Trains leave Glasgow Central station (£6.70, 40 to 50 minutes, half-hourly) to connect with ferries.

10am-3.30pm Mon & Wed-Sat Oct-Mar) At the Cladach centre, this brewery produces the excellent quality Arran beers. Warning: Arran Dark is highly addictive. Tours run daily: call for times as they vary by season. There's a good **outdoors shop** here too, if you're heading up Goatfell.

🏃 Activities

Drop into the tourist office for **walking** and **cycling** suggestions around the island. The 55-mile circuit on the coastal road is popular with cyclists and has few serious hills – more in the south than the north. There are plenty of walking booklets and maps available and walking trails are clearly signposted around the island. Several leave from Lochranza, including the spectacular walk to the island's northeast tip, the **Cock of Arran**, and finishing in the village of Sannox (8 miles one-way).

The walk up and down **Goatfell** (the island's tallest peak) takes up to eight hours return, starting in Brodick. If the weather's fine, there are superb views to Ben Lomond and the coast of Northern Ireland. It can, however, be very cold and windy up there; take the appropriate maps (available at the tourist office), waterproof gear and a compass.

Arran Adventure Company OUTDOOR ACTIVITIES
(☎01770-302244; www.arranadventure.com; Auchrannie Rd; adult/teen/child £50/40/30; ☺Easter-Oct) This company offers loads of activities, and they run a different one each day, including gorge walking, sea kayaking, climbing, abseiling and mountain biking. All activities run for about three hours. Drop in to see what's available while you're around.

Auchrannie Resort RESORT
(☎01770-302234; www.auchrannie.co.uk) This huge resort complex offers a bit of everything and can make a good destination if you're looking for something to do in Brodick. As well as tennis courts and gym, it has a pool and spa area which nonguests can access for £4.60.

🎊 Festivals & Events

Arran Folk Festival FOLK MUSIC
(www.arranfolkfestival.com) A four-day festival in mid-June.

🛏 Sleeping

TOP CHOICE Kilmichael Country House Hotel HOTEL £££
(☎01770-302219; www.kilmichael.com; s £95, d £163-204, 4-course dinner £45; ☺Apr-Oct; P🐾🖥🐶) The island's best hotel, the Kilmichael is also the oldest building – it has a glass window dating from 1650. Luxurious and tastefully decorated, the hotel is located only a mile outside Brodick but seems like a world away in deep countryside. It has just eight rooms and excellent set dinners (open to nonguests). It's an ideal, utterly relaxing hideaway, and feels very classy without being overly formal.

The Douglas HOTEL £££
(☎01770-302968; www.thedouglashotel.co.uk; d/superior d £135/165) Opposite the ferry, this hotel has been reborn as a smart, stylish, haven of island hospitality. The views were already there, but the luxurious rooms make the most of them. There are numerous thoughtful touches like binoculars to admire the vistas, and the bathrooms are great. The downstairs bar and bistro are also recommended. Prices drop midweek and in winter.

Glenartney B&B ££
(☎01770-302220; www.glenartney-arran.co.uk; Mayish Rd; s/d £50/80; ☺late Mar-Sep; P🐾🖥🐶) Uplifting bay views and genuine, helpful hosts make this a cracking option. Airy, stylish rooms make the most of the natural light available at the top of the town. Cyclists will appreciate the bike wash, repair and storage facilities, while hikers can benefit from the drying rooms and expert trail advice. The owners make big efforts to be sustainable.

Belvedere Guest House B&B ££
(☎01770-302397; www.vision-unlimited.co.uk; Alma Rd; s £35, d £60-90; P🖥) Overlooking the town, bay and surrounding mountains, Belvedere has well-presented rooms and very welcoming hosts, who also offer reiki, healing and de-stressing packages. They provide excellent island information and there are good breakfasts with vegetarian choices.

Chalmadale B&B £££

(📞01770-302196; www.chalmadalebandb.co.uk; 7 Alma Park; s £35, d £60-70; 🅿🛜🍽) A little tough to find (ask for directions), this unsigned place is run by a genial, welcoming couple who make you feel right at home. There are just two rooms, both very comfortable; the larger one is en-suite and has great views over the bay.

Glen Rosa Farm CAMPING £

(📞01770-302380; www.arrancamping.co.uk; sites per adult/child £4/2; 🅿🍽) In a lush glen by a river, 2 miles from Brodick, this large place has plenty of nooks and crannies to pitch a tent. It's remote camping, with cold water and toilets only. To get there from Brodick head north, take String Rd, then turn right almost immediately on the road signed to Glen Rosa. After 400m, you'll see a white house on the left, where you book in; the campground is further down the road.

✗ Eating & Drinking

TOP CHOICE The Brodick Bar BRASSERIE ££

(Alma Rd; mains £9-19) Don't leave Brodick without dropping in here. The regularly changing menu chalked up on a blackboard brings a modern French flair to this Arran pub, with great presentation, efficient service and delicious flavour combinations. It's very buzzy on weekend evenings.

Creelers SEAFOOD

(📞01770-302810; www.creelers.co.uk; mains £12-20; ⊙Wed-Sun Apr-Sep) Creelers has been threatening to close for years, but seems to keep on opening every season so you might be lucky. Situated 1.5 miles north of Brodick, it's Arran's top choice for fresh seafood. It's rather no-frills inside, but the dishes - cured salmon, fish soup, fresh oysters, daily fish special - are delicious. It's not licensed, so bring a bottle.

Eilean Mòr CAFE ££

(www.eileanmorarran.com; Shore Rd; mains £9-12; ⊙meals 10am-9.30pm; 🛜) Upbeat and modern, this likeable little cafe-bar does tasty meals through the day, with pizzas and pastas featuring. It's not afraid to give them a Scottish twist – try the haggis ravioli.

Arran on a Plate SCOTTISH ££

(📞01770-303886; www.arranonaplate.com; Shore Rd; mains £9-15) Unprepossessing from the outside, this new restaurant makes up for it inside, with solicitous service, a striking

mural and great sunset views over the bay. Dishes focus on fresh seafood and are attractively presented if a little short on quantity.

Ormidale Hotel PUB £

(📞01770-302293; www.ormidalehotel.co.uk; Glen Cloy; mains £7-10; 🎣🍺) This hotel has decent bar food. Dishes change regularly, but there are always some good vegetarian options and daily specials. Quantities and value-for-money are high, and Arran beers are on tap.

🛍 Shopping

Island Cheese Co CHEESE

(www.islandcheese.co.uk; Duchess Ct, Home Farm) Anyone with a fetish for cheese should stop by this place where you can stock up on the famed local varieties. There are free samples.

CORRIE TO LOCHRANZA

The coast road continues north to the small, pretty village of Corrie, where one of the tracks up **Goatfell** starts. After **Sannox**, with a sandy beach and great views of the mountains, the road cuts inland. Heading to the very north, on the island's main road, visitors weave through lush glens flanked by Arran's towering mountain splendour.

Moderate walks here include the trail through **Glen Sannox**, which goes from the village of Sannox up the burn, a two-hour return trip.

The traditional stone **Corrie Hotel** (📞01770-810273; www.corriehotel.co.uk; Corrie; r per person £36, shared bathroom £32; 🅿🛜🍽) offers simple but comfortable rooms, several with great views, above a pub with a wonderful beer garden that scrapes the water's edge. Groups of four or more can reserve a bunkroom (£15 to £20 per person, bed only).

LOCHRANZA

The village of Lochranza has a stunning location in a small bay at the north of the island. On a promontory stand the ruins of the 13th-century **Lochranza Castle** (HS; www.historic-scotland.gov.uk; admission free; ⊙24hr), said to be the inspiration for the castle in *The Black Island*, Hergé's Tintin adventure. It's basically a draughty shell inside, with interpretative signs to help you decipher the layout.

Also in Lochranza is the **Isle of Arran Distillery** (📞01770-830264; www.arranwhisky.com; tours adult/child £6/free; ⊙10am-6pm mid-Mar–Oct), which produces a light, aromatic single malt. The tour is a good one; it's a small distillery, and the whisky-making process is thoroughly explained. More expensive tours (£15) include extra tastings. Opening hours are reduced in winter.

The Lochranza area bristles with red deer, who wander into the village unconcernedly to crop the grass on the golf course.

🛏 Sleeping & Eating

🏠 Lochranza SYHA HOSTEL £
(☎01770-830631; www.syha.org.uk; dm/d £19/50; ⊘mid Mar–Oct plus weekends year-round; P@⟨⟩) A recent refurbishment has made a really excellent hostel of what was always a charming place, with lovely views. The rooms are great, with chunky wooden furniture, key-cards, and lockers. Rainwater toilets, energy-saving heating solutions, and an excellent room for guests with disabilities show the thought that's gone into the redesign, while plush lounging areas, a kitchen you could run a restaurant out of, a laundry, a drying room, red deer in the garden and welcoming management combine to make this a top option. Internet access is unreliable and expensive.

Apple Lodge B&B ££
(☎01770-830229; s/d/ste £54/78/90; P) Once the village manse, this rewarding choice is dignified and hospitable. Rooms are individually furnished and very commodious. One has a four-poster bed, while another is a self-contained suite in the garden. The guest lounge is perfect for curling up with a good book, and courteous hosts mean you should book this one well ahead in summer. Dinner is available (£25).

Catacol Bay Hotel PUB £
(☎01770-830231; www.catacol.co.uk; r per person £30; P@⟨⟩) Genially run, and with a memorable position overlooking the water, this no-frills pub 2 miles south of Lochranza offers comfortable-enough rooms with shared bathroom and views to lift the heaviest heart. Unpretentious bar food comes out in generous portions, there's a Sunday lunch buffet (£13.25), and the beer garden is worth a contemplative pint or two as you gaze off across the water into the west.

Lochranza Hotel HOTEL ££
(☎01770-830223; www.lochranza.co.uk; s/d £58/94; P) The focus of the village, and the only place you can get an evening meal, this bastion of Arran hospitality has comfortable rooms decked out in pink. The showers are pleasingly powerful, and the double and twin at the front (room Nos 1 and 10) have super views. Rooms are a bit overpriced, but they get cheaper if you stay more than one night.

WEST COAST
On the western side of the island is the Machrie Moor Stone Circle, a pleasant 20 to 30 minute stroll from the parking area on the coastal road. There are actually several separate groups of stones of varying sizes, erected around 4000 years ago. You pass a Bronze Age burial cairn along the path.

Blackwaterfoot is the largest village on the west coast; it has a shop and hotel. You can walk to King's Cave from here, via Drumadoon Farm – Arran is one of several islands that claim the cave where Robert the Bruce had his famous arachnid encounter. This walk can easily be extended to the Machrie stones.

SOUTH COAST
The landscape in the southern part of the island is much gentler; the road drops into little wooded valleys, and it's particularly lovely around **Lagg**. There's a 10-minute walk from Lagg Hotel to Torrylinn Cairn, a chambered tomb over 4000 years old. **Kildonan** has pleasant sandy beaches, a gorgeous water outlook, a hotel, a campground and an ivy-clad ruined castle.

In **Whiting Bay** you'll find small sandy beaches and the Arran Art Gallery (☎01770-700250; www.arranartgallery.com; Shore Rd), which has exquisite landscape portraits of Arran. From Whiting Bay there are easy one-hour walks through the forest to the **Giant's Graves** and **Glenashdale Falls**, and back – keep an eye out for golden eagles and other birds of prey.

🛏 Sleeping & Eating

TOP CHOICE Kildonan Hotel HOTEL ££
(☎01770-820207; www.kildonanhotel.com; Kildonan; s/d/ste £75/99/135; P@⟨⟩☼) Luxurious rooms and a grounded attitude – dogs and kids are made very welcome – combine to make this one of Arran's best options. Oh, and it's right by the water, with fabulous views and seals basking on the rocks. The standard rooms are beautifully furnished and spotless, but the suites – with private terrace or small balcony – are superb. Other attractions include great staff, a bar serving good grub, a restaurant doing succulent

seafood, an ATM, book exchange, and laptops lent to guests if you didn't bring one. Applause.

Royal Arran Hotel   B&B **££**
(☑ 01770-700286; www.royalarran.co.uk; Shore Rd, Whiting Bay; s £55, d £95-110; P ☎) This personalised, intimate spot has just four rooms. The double upstairs is our idea of accommodation heaven – four-poster bed, big heavy linen, a huge room and gorgeous water views. Room No 1 downstairs is a great size and has a private patio. The hosts couldn't be more welcoming (except to kids under 12, who aren't permitted).

Lagg Hotel   HOTEL **££**
(☑ 01770-870255; www.lagghotel.com; Kilmory; s/d £48/85; P ☎☎) An 18th-century coach house, this inn has a beautiful location and is the perfect place for a romantic weekend away from the cares of modern life. Rooms are smart and up-to-date; grab a superior one (£95) with garden views. There's also a cracking beer garden, a fine bar with log fire and an elegant restaurant (mains £10 to £14).

Viewbank House   B&B **££**
(☑ 01770-700326; www.viewbank-arran.co.uk; Whiting Bay; s £30-33, d £60-76; P ☎☎) Appropriately named, this friendly place does indeed have tremendous views from its vantage point high above Whiting Bay. Rooms, of which there are a variety with and without bathroom, are tastefully furnished and well kept. It's well signposted from the main road. You can book an evening meal here (BYOB).

Sealshore Campsite   CAMPING **£**
(☑ 01770-820320; www.campingarran.com; sites per adult/child £6/3, per tent £1-4; P ☎) Living up to its name, this excellent small campsite is right by sea (and, happily, the Kildonan Hotel) with one of Arran's finest views from its grassy camping area. There's a good washroom area with heaps of showers, kitchen facilities, and the breeze keeps the midges away.

Coast   BISTRO **££**
(☑ 01770-700308; www.coastarran.co.uk; Shore Rd, Whiting Bay; mains £10-15; ⊙ lunch Thu-Tue, dinner Thu-Sat) This funky place decked out in suave red tones and with a sun-drenched conservatory on the water's edge serves grills, seafood and salads in the evening, with lighter offerings during the day. Opens Wed & Sun evenings in summer too.

LAMLASH

Lamlash is in a dazzling setting, strung along the beachfront. The bay was used as a safe anchorage by the navy during WWI and WWII.

Just off the coast is **Holy Island**, owned by the Samye Ling Tibetan Centre and used as a retreat, but day visits are allowed. Depending on the tides, the ferry (☑ 01770-600998; tomin10@btinternet.com; adult/child return £11/6) makes around seven trips a day from Lamlash (15 minutes) and runs between May and September. The same folk also run fun mackerel-fishing expeditions (£20 per person).

No dogs, bikes, alcohol or fires are allowed on the island. There's a good walk to the top of the hill (314m), taking two or three hours return. It is possible to stay on the island in accommodation belonging to the Holy Island Centre for World Peace & Health (☑ 01770-601100; www.holyisle.org; dm/s/d £28/47/72). Prices include full (vegetarian) board.

🛏 Sleeping & Eating

Glenisle Hotel   HOTEL, PUB **££**
(www.glenislehotel.com; Shore Rd; s/d £78/113; ☎) This stylish hotel in the heart of town offers plush rooms and cordial service. Upgrade to a superior room for the best views over the water. Downstairs is excellent pub food, with Scottish classics such as Cullen skink (soup made with smoked haddock, potato, onion and milk) and a good wine list.

Lilybank Guest House   B&B **££**
(☑ 01770-600230; www.lilybank-arran.co.uk; Shore Rd; s/d £50/80; P ☎) Built in the 17th century, Lilybank retains its heritage but has been refurbished for 21st-century needs. Rooms are clean and comfortable, with one adapted for disabled use. The front ones have great views over Holy Island. Breakfast includes oak-smoked kippers and other Arran goodies.

Drift Inn   PUB **£**
(Shore Rd; mains £8-10; ☋) There are few better places to be on the island on a sunny day than the beer garden at this child-friendly hotel, ploughing your way through an excellent bar meal while gazing over to Holy Island. There are traditional pub faves and genuine Angus beef burgers, with generous portions all round.

East Ayrshire

KILMARNOCK

In **Kilmarnock**, where Johnnie Walker whisky was blended from 1820 to 2012, is Dean Castle (☏01563-522702; www.deancastle.com; Dean Rd; admission free; ⊙11am-5pm daily Apr-Sep, 10am-4pm Wed-Sun Oct-Mar; ⚐), a 15-minute walk from the bus and train stations. The castle, restored in the first half of the 20th century, has a virtually windowless keep (dating from 1350) and an adjacent palace (1468) with a superb collection of medieval arms, armour, tapestries and musical instruments. The huge grounds are a good place for a stroll or a picnic, or you can eat at the visitor centre's tearoom, where snacks and light meals cost around £5. From Ayr there are frequent buses throughout the day.

South Ayrshire

AYR

POP 46,431

Ayr's long sandy beach has made it a popular family seaside resort since Victorian times, but it has struggled in the recent economic climate. Parts of the centre have a neglected air, though there are many fine Georgian and Victorian buildings, and it makes a convenient base for exploring this section of coast and exploring the area's Robbie Burns heritage.

◉ Sights

Most things to see in Ayr are Robert Burns-related. The bard was baptised in the Auld Kirk (Old Church; Map p168) off High St. The atmospheric cemetery here overlooks the river and is good for a stroll, offering an escape from the bustle of High St. Several of Burns' poems are set in Ayr; in 'Twa Brigs', Ayr's old and new bridges argue with one another. The Auld Brig (Old Bridge; Map p168) was built

in 1491 and spans the river just north of the church.

St John's Tower (Map p168; Eglinton Tce) is the only remnant of a church where a parliament was held in 1315, the year after the celebrated victory at Bannockburn. John Knox's son-in-law was the minister here, and Mary, Queen of Scots, stayed overnight in 1563.

✦ Festivals & Events

Burns an' a' That   CULTURAL
(www.burnsfestival.com) Held in Ayr in late May, this festival has a bit of everything, from wine-tasting to horseracing to concerts, some of it Burns-related.

⌸ Sleeping

⌸TOP
CHOICE 26 The Crescent   B&B ££
(Map p168; ☏01292-287329; www.26crescent.co.uk; 26 Bellevue Cres; s £53, d £75-93; ⚐) When the blossoms are out, Bellevue Cres is Ayr's prettiest street, and this is an excellent place to stay on it. The rooms are impeccable – an upgrade to the spacious four-poster room is a sound investment – but it's the warm welcome given by the hosts that makes this special. Numerous little extras, like iPod docks, Arran toiletries, bottled water in the rooms, and silver cutlery at breakfast, add appeal. B&B at its best.

Eglinton Guest House   B&B ££
(Map p168; ☏01292-264623; www.eglintonguesthouse.com; 23 Eglinton Tce; r per person £28; ⚐⚑) A short walk west of the bus station, this friendly family-run Georgian property has a range of traditional, tidy rooms. The location, between the beach and the town, is brilliant, and it offers great value, with comfortable beds and compact en suite bathrooms.

Belmont Guest House   B&B ££
(Map p168; ☏01292-265588; www.belmontguesthouse.co.uk; 15 Park Circus; s/d £40/60; ⚐) Com-

---

WORTH A TRIP

DUMFRIES HOUSE

A Palladian mansion designed in the 1750s by the Adam brothers, Dumfries House (☏01290-421742; www.dumfries-house.org.uk; adult/child £8.50/4; ⊙11am-3.30pm Sun-Fri Mar-Oct) is an architectural jewel: such is its significance that Prince Charles personally intervened to ensure its protection. It contains an extraordinarily well-preserved collection of Chippendale furniture and numerous objets d'art. Visits are by guided tour; book ahead by phone or internet. The once-daily Grand Tour (adult/child £12.50/4) also takes you to the bedrooms upstairs. The house is located 13 miles east of Ayr, near Cumnock. Buses from Ayr or Kilmarnock to Cumnock will drop you near the house.

THE SCOTTISH BARD

I see her in the dewy flowers,
I see her sweet and fair:
I hear her in the tuneful' birds,
I hear her charm the air:
There's not a bonnie flower that springs
By fountain, shaw, or green;
There's not a bonnie bird that sings,
But minds me o' my Jean.
Robert Burns, 'Of a' the Airts', 1788

Best remembered for penning the words of 'Auld Lang Syne', Robert Burns (1759–96) is Scotland's most famous poet and a popular hero; his birthday (25 January) is celebrated as Burns Night by Scots around the world.

Burns was born in 1759 in Alloway to a poor family, who scraped a living gardening and farming. At school he soon showed an aptitude for literature and a fondness for the folk song. He later began to write his own songs and satires. When the problems of his arduous farming life were compounded by the threat of prosecution from the father of Jean Armour, with whom he'd had an affair, he decided to emigrate to Jamaica. He gave up his share of the family farm and published his poems to raise money for the journey.

The poems were so well reviewed in Edinburgh that Burns decided to remain in Scotland and devote himself to writing. He went to Edinburgh in 1787 to publish a 2nd edition, but the financial rewards were not enough to live on and he had to take a job as a excise man in Dumfriesshire. Though he worked well, he wasn't a taxman by nature, and described his job as 'the execrable office of whip-person to the blood-hounds of justice'. He contributed many songs to collections, and a 3rd edition of his poems was published in 1793. A prodigious writer, Burns composed more than 28,000 lines of verse over 22 years. He died (probably of heart disease) in Dumfries in 1796, aged 37, having fathered more than a dozen children to several different women.

Burns wrote in Lallans, the Scottish Lowland dialect of English that is not very accessible to the Sassenach (Englishman) or foreigner; perhaps this was part of his appeal. He was also very much a man of the people, satirising the upper classes and the church for their hypocrisy.

Many of the local landmarks mentioned in the verse-tale 'Tam o' Shanter' can still be visited. Farmer Tam, riding home after a hard night's drinking in a pub in Ayr, sees witches dancing in Alloway churchyard. He calls out to the one pretty witch, but is pursued by them all, and has to reach the other side of the River Doon to be safe. He just manages to cross the Brig o' Doon, but his mare loses her tail to the witches.

The Burns connection in southern Scotland is milked for all it's worth and tourist offices have a *Burns Heritage Trail* leaflet leading you to every place that can claim some link with the bard. Burns fans should have a look at www.robertburns.org.

fortable, spacious rooms and some attractive original features make this Victorian town house a decent Ayr address. There's a good-value family room and a relaxed, laissez-faire attitude.

Heads of Ayr Caravan Park CAMPING £
(☎01292-442269; www.headsofayr.com; sites £20; ☺Mar-Oct) This caravan park is in a lovely, quiet location close to the beach. There are various caravans and chalets available to rent by the week or for a few days. From Ayr take the A719 south for about 5 miles.

✖ Eating & Drinking

Look out for the famous locally-made Mancini's ice-cream around town, often cited as Scotland's best. Their original outlet is the **Royal Café** at 11 New Road.

TOP CHOICE Beresford BISTRO ££
(Map p168; ☎01292-280820; www.theberesfordayr.co.uk; 22 Beresford Tce; mains £11-15; ☺meals 9am-9pm) Style and fun go hand in hand at this upbeat establishment serving afternoon martinis in teapots and luring churchgoing ladies with artisanal chocolates. The

Ayr

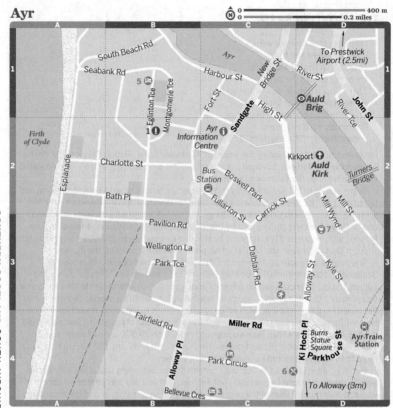

food is a creative fusion of influences based on solid local produce, with Ayrshire pork, west coast oysters, and Scottish lamb often featuring. Some dishes hit real heights, and are solidly backed by a wide choice of wines, with 10 available by the glass. Upstairs does pizzas and other Italian dishes. It stays open as a bar after the kitchen closes. Top service seals the deal.

Tam O'Shanter PUB

(Map p168; 01292 611684; 230 High St; mains £7-9) Opened in the mid-18th century and featured in the Burns poem whose name it now bears, this is an atmospheric old pub with traditional pub grub (served noon to 9pm).

ℹ Information

Carnegie Library (12 Main St; Mon-Sat) Offers fast, free internet access.

Ayr Information Centre (01292-290300; www.ayrshire-arran.com; 22 Sandgate; 9am-5pm Mon-Sat year-round, 10am-5pm Sun Easter-Aug) In the centre of town.

ℹ Getting There & Around

CYCLE

AMG Cycles (Map p168; 01292-287580; www.irvinecycles.co.uk; 55 Dalblair Rd; day/week-end/week £15/20/50) hires out bikes.

BUS

Ayr is 33 miles from Glasgow and is Ayrshire's major transport hub. There are very frequent express services to Glasgow (£5.60, one hour) via Prestwick Airport, as well as services to Stranraer (£7.80, two hours, four to eight a day), other Ayrshire destinations, and Dumfries (£6.20, 2¼ hours, five to seven a day).

TRAIN

There are at least two trains an hour that run between Ayr and Glasgow Central station (£7.50, 50 minutes), and some trains continue south from Ayr to Stranraer (£14.60, 1½ hours).

Ayr

Top Sights

Sights

Activities, Courses & Tours

Sleeping

Eating

Drinking

ALLOWAY

The pretty, lush village of Alloway (3 miles south of Ayr) should be on the itinerary of every Robert Burns fan – he was born here on 25 January 1759. Even if you haven't been seduced by Burnsmania, it's still well worth a visit, as the Burns-related exhibitions give a good impression of life in Ayrshire in the late 18th century.

Sights

Robert Burns Birthplace Museum MUSEUM
(NTS; www.nts.org.uk; adult/child £8/6; ⊙10am-5pm Oct-Mar, to 5.30pm Apr-Sep; ⊛) This impressive new museum has collected a solid range of Burns memorabilia, including manuscripts and possessions of the poet, like the pistols he packed in order to carry out his daily work as a taxman. There's good biographical information, and a series of displays that bring to life individual poems via background snippets, translations, and audiophones with recitations. Appropriately, the museum doesn't take itself too seriously: there's plenty of humour that the man himself surely would have approved of, and entertaining audio and visual performances will keep the kids amused.

The admission ticket also covers the atmospheric **Burns Cottage**, connected via a walkway to the Birthplace Museum. Born in the little box-bed in this cramped thatched dwelling, the poet spent the first seven years of his life here. It's an attractive display which gives you a context for reading plenty of his verse. Much-needed translation of some of the more obscure Scots farming terms he loved to use decorate the walls.

Alloway Auld Kirk CHURCH
Near the Birthplace Museum are the ruins of the kirk, the setting for part of 'Tam o' Shanter'. Burns' father, William Burnes (his son dropped the 'e' from his name), is buried in the kirkyard; read the poem on the back of the gravestone.

Burns Monument & Gardens GARDEN
The monument was built in 1823; the gardens afford a view of the 13th-century Brig o' Doon.

Sleeping

Brig O' Doon House HOTEL
(☎01292-442466; www.brigodoonhouse.com; s/d £85/120, restaurant 3-course dinner £25; ⓟ⚙) On the main road right by the monument and bridge, a charming ivy-covered facade conceals this romantic, rather luxurious hotel, which will appeal greatly to Burns fans. The heavyish decor of plaid carpets is relieved by slate-floored bathrooms; rooms are spacious and very comfortable, and there are also a couple of cottages – Rose, traditionally decorated, and Gables, more contemporary – across the way. Service is helpful, and there's a decent **restaurant**, but the place is often booked up by wedding parties at weekends.

❶ Getting There & Away

Various buses (including 58) operate regularly between Alloway and Ayr (10 minutes). Otherwise, walk or rent a bike and cycle here.

TROON
POP 14,766

Troon, a major sailing centre on the coast 7 miles north of Ayr, has excellent sandy beaches and six golf courses. The demanding championship Old Course at **Royal Troon** (☎01292-311555; www.royaltroon.com; Craigend Rd) is a classic of links golf. There are offers on its website; the standard green fee is £175, which includes a complimentary round at the Portland course.

Four miles northeast of Troon, **Dundonald Castle** (HS; www.historic-scotland.gov.uk; adult/child £3.50/1.50; ⊙10am-5pm Apr-Oct) commands impressive views and, in its main

WORTH A TRIP

IRVINE

Boat lovers should check out the Scottish Maritime Museum (☏01294-278283; www.scottishmaritimemuseum.org; Gottries Rd; adult/child £3.50/2.50; ☺10am-4pm Mon-Sat) in Irvine. In the massive **Linthouse Engine Shop** – an old hangar with a cast-iron framework – is an absorbing collection of boats and machinery. Your ticket also gives admission to the **boat shop**, with its wonderful works of art and huge kids activity area. Free guided tours leave from the boat shop – you'll go down to the pontoons where you can clamber over various ships, and visitors can also see a shipyard worker's restored flat. Ring to check opening hours, as it was being refurbished at time of last visit.

Further along the harbour road, make sure to drop into the wonderful Ship Inn (www.shipinnirvine.co.uk; 120 Harbour St; mains £7-9) It's the oldest pub in Irvine (1597), serves tasty bar meals (noon to 9pm) and has bucket-loads of character.

Irvine is 26 miles from Glasgow. There are frequent buses from Ayr (30 minutes) and Largs (45 minutes). Trains run to/from Glasgow Central station (£6.50, 35 minutes, half-hourly); the other way they go to Ayr (£3.70, 20 minutes, half-hourly).

hall, has one of the finest preserved barrel-vaulted ceilings in Scotland. It was the first home of the Stuart kings, built by Robert II in 1371, and reckoned to be the third most important castle in Scotland in its time, after Edinburgh and Stirling. The visitor centre below the castle has good information on prior settlements, and scale models of the castle and its predecessors. Buses running between Troon and Kilmarnock stop in Dundonald village.

❶ Getting There & Away

There are half-hourly trains to Ayr (10 minutes) and Glasgow (£6.90, 40 minutes).

P&O (☏0871 66 44 777; www.poirishsea.com) sails twice daily to Larne in Northern Ireland (£33 for passengers, up to £142 for a car and driver; two hours).

CULZEAN CASTLE

The Scottish National Trust's flagship property, magnificent Culzean Castle (NTS; ☏01655-884400; www.culzeanexperience.org; adult/child/family £15/11/36, park only adult/child £9.50/7; ☺castle 10.30am-5pm Apr-Oct, park 9.30am-sunset year round) (pronounced kull-*ane*) is one of the most impressive of Scotland's great stately homes. The entrance is a converted viaduct, and on approach the castle appears like a mirage, floating into view. Designed by Robert Adam, who was encouraged to exercise his romantic genius in its design, this 18th-century mansion is perched dramatically on the edge of the cliffs. Adam was the most influential architect of his time, renowned for his meticulous attention to detail and the elegant classical embellishments with which he decorated his ceilings and fireplaces.

The beautiful oval staircase here is regarded as one of his finest achievements. On the 1st floor, the opulence of the circular saloon contrasts violently with the views of the wild sea below. Lord Cassillis' bedroom is said to be haunted by a lady in green, mourning for a lost baby. Even the bathrooms are palatial.

There are also two ice houses, a swan pond, a pagoda, a re-creation of a Victorian vinery, an orangery, a deer park and an aviary. Wildlife in the area includes otters.

If you really want to experience the magic of this place, it's possible to stay in the castle (s/d from £140/225, Eisenhower ste s/d £250/375; Pⓟ🐱) from April to October. There's also a Camping & Caravanning Club (☏01655-760627; www.campingandcaravanningclub.co.uk; sites members/non-members £9.35/16.45; 🐱) at the entrance to the park, offering grassy pitches with great views.

❶ Getting There & Away

Culzean is 12 miles south of Ayr; buses from there (30 minutes, 11 daily Monday to Saturday) pass the park gates, from where it's a 20-minute walk through the grounds to the castle.

TURNBERRY
POP 200

Turnberry's Ailsa golf course (☏01655-334032; www.turnberry.co.uk) hosted the British Open in 2009 and is one of Scotland's most prestigious links courses, with spectacular views of Ailsa Craig offshore. You don't need a handicap certificate to play, just plenty of pounds – the standard green fee is £199. In summer though, you can take advantage of the after-3pm 'sunset' rate and go round for £95 a head.

Opposite the course, the super-luxurious Turnberry Resort (☎01655-331000; www.luxurycollection.com/turnberry; standard/deluxe r £350/400; P@🛜🐕🏊) offers everything you can think of, including kilted staff, an airstrip and helipad. As well as the luxurious rooms and excellent restaurant, there's a series of self-contained lodges. Rooms with sea views cost somewhat more.

KIRKOSWALD
POP 500

Just 2 miles east of Kirkoswald, by the A77, Crossraguel Abbey (HS; www.historic-scotland.gov.uk; adult/child £4/2.40; ⏱9.30am-5.30pm Apr-Sep) is a substantial ruin dating back to the 13th century that's good fun to explore. The renovated 16th-century gatehouse is the best part – you'll find decorative stonework and superb views from the top. Inside, if you have the place to yourself, you'll hear only the whistling wind – an apt reflection of the abbey's long-departed monastic tradition. Don't miss the echo in the chilly sacristy.

Stagecoach Western runs Ayr-to-Girvan buses via Crossraguel Abbey and Kirkoswald (35 minutes, hourly Monday to Saturday, every two hours Sunday).

AILSA CRAIG

The curiously shaped island of Ailsa Craig can be seen from much of southern Ayrshire. While its unusual blue-tinted granite – famous for making the best curling stones – has been used by geologists to trace the movements of the great Ice Age ice sheet, birdwatchers know Ailsa Craig as the world's second-largest gannet colony – around 10,000 pairs breed annually on the island's sheer cliffs.

To see the island close up you can take a cruise from Girvan on the MV Glorious (☎01465-713219; www.ailsacraig.org.uk; 7 Harbour St). It's possible to land if the sea is reasonably calm; a four-hour trip costs £20/15 per adult/child (£25 per person if you want three hours ashore).

Trains going to Girvan run approximately hourly (with only three trains on Sundays) from Ayr (30 minutes).

DUMFRIES & GALLOWAY

Some of the region's finest attractions lie in the gentle hills and lush valleys of Dumfries and Galloway. It's an ideal destination for families, as there's plenty on offer for the kids. Galloway Forest, with its sublime views, mountain-biking and walking trails, red deer, kites and other wildlife, is a highlight, as are the dream-like ruins of Caerlaverock Castle. Adding to the appeal of this enticing region is a string of southern Scotland's most idyllic towns, charming when the sun shines. And shine it does. Warmed by the Gulf Stream, this is the mildest region in Scotland, a phenomenon that has allowed the development of some famous gardens.

Dumfries
POP 31,146

Lovely, red-hued sandstone bridges crisscross pleasant Dumfries, bisected by the wide River Nith, with pleasant grassed areas along the river bank. Historically, Dumfries held a strategic position in the path of vengeful English armies. Consequently, although it has existed since Roman times, the oldest standing building dates from the 17th century. Plenty of famous names have passed through Dumfries: Robert Burns lived here and worked as a tax collector; JM Barrie, creator of Peter Pan, was schooled here; and the former racing driver David Coulthard also hails from the town.

👁 Sights

The red-sandstone bridges arching over the River Nith are the most attractive feature of the town: Devorgilla Bridge (Map p172) (1431) is one of the oldest bridges in Scotland. You can download a multilingual MP3 audio tour of the town at www.dumgal.gov.uk/audiotour.

FREE Burns House   MUSEUM
(Map p172; www.dumgal.gov.uk/museums; Burns St; ⏱10am-5pm Mon-Sat & 2-5pm Sun Apr-Sep, 10am-1pm & 2-5pm Tue-Sat Oct-Mar) This is a place of pilgrimage for Burns enthusiasts. It's here that the poet spent the last years of his life, and there are various possessions of his in glass cases, as well as manuscripts and, entertainingly, letters: make sure you have a read.

BUS PASS

A Megarider ticket costs £21 and gives you unlimited travel on Stagecoach buses within Dumfries and Galloway for a week - not a bad deal.

Dumfries

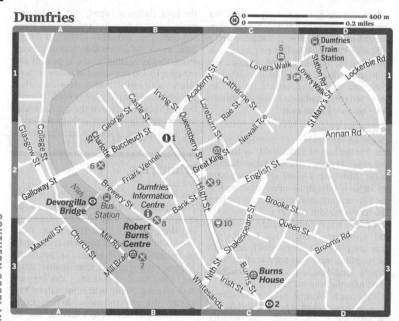

FREE **Robert Burns Centre** MUSEUM
(Map p172; www.dumgal.gov.uk/museums; Mill Rd; audiovisual presentation £2.20; ⊙10am-5pm Mon-Sat & 2-5pm Sun Apr-Sep, 10am-1pm & 2-5pm Tue-Sat Oct-Mar) A worthwhile Burns exhibition in an old mill on the banks of the River Nith. It tells the story of the poet and Dumfries in the 1790s. The optional audiovisual presentations give more background on Dumfries, and explain the exhibition's contents.

There are more Burns-related sights scattered throughout the town; you'll find Robert Burns' mausoleum (Map p172; St Michael's Kirk) in the graveyard at St Michael's Kirk (Map p172), where there's also a grisly account of his reburial on the information panel. At the top of High St is a statue (Map p172) of the bard.

Ellisland Farm MUSEUM
(www.ellislandfarm.co.uk; adult/child £4/free; ⊙10am-5pm Mon-Sat, 2-5pm Sun Apr-Sep, 10am-4pm Tue-Sat Oct-Mar) If you're not Burnsed out, you can head 6 miles northwest of town and visit the farm he leased. It still preserves some original features from when he and his family lived here, and there's a small exhibition. It's signposted off the A76 to Kilmarnock.

🛏 Sleeping

Hotels in central Dumfries are mundane, but luckily there are some excellent B&Bs in town.

Merlin B&B £
(Map p172; ☎01387-261002; 2 Kenmure Tce; s/d £35/60; 🔊) Beautifully located on the riverbank across a pedestrian bridge from the centre, this is a top place to hole up in Dumfries. So much work goes on behind the scenes here that it seems effortless: numerous small details and a friendly welcome make this a very impressive set-up. Rooms share a bathroom, and have super-comfy beds; the breakfast table is also quite a sight.

Ferintosh Guest House B&B ££
(Map p172; ☎01387-252262; www.ferintosh.net; 30 Lovers Walk; s £30-40, d £50-66; 🔊🐾) A Victorian villa opposite the train station, Ferintosh has sumptuous rooms done in individual themes. The whisky room is our fave, but no matter which you choose, there'll probably be a dram awaiting you on arrival. These people have the right attitude towards hospitality. The owner's artwork complements the decor and cyclists are welcomed with a shed and washing facilities out the back for bikes.

Dumfries

Torbay Lodge   B&B £।£
(Map p172; ☑01387-253922; www.torbaylodge.
co.uk; 31 Lovers Walk; s/d £29/60; ᴘ🖀) This
high-quality guesthouse has beautifully
presented bedrooms with big windows and
generously sized en suites (and a single
without); the good vibe is topped off by an
excellent breakfast.

✖ Eating & Drinking

 Hullabaloo   CAFE, BISTRO £।£
(Map p172; ☑01387-259679; www.hullabalooes
taurant.co.uk; Mill Rd; lunch mains £5-9, dinner
mains £10-15; ⊘lunch daily, dinner Tue-Sat) The
best eating option in Dumfries is this cosy
space upstairs at the Robert Burns Centre.
For lunch there's wraps, melts and ciabattas, but come dinner time it's inventive angles and interesting cuts and combinations.
There's a distinct Mediterranean flavour to
the regularly-changing specials, including
expertly-prepared fish dishes and appetizing vegetarian choices. Closed Sundays from
October to Easter.

Cavens Arms   PUB £
(Map p172; 20 Buccleuch St; mains £7-13; ⊘pub
daily, food Tue-Sun) Engaging staff, ten real
ales on tap, and a warm contented buzz
make this a legendary Dumfries pub. Generous portions of typical pub nosh backed

up by a long list of more adventurous daily
specials make it one of the town's most enjoyable places to eat too. If you were considering a move to Dumfries, you'd want to
make sure you lived within a block or two
of here.

One Bank St   CAFE £
(Map p172; ☑01387-279754; 1 Bank St; light meals
£4-7; ⊘10am-4pm Tue-Sat) This wee upstairs
room around the corner from the tourist
office (look for the sign on the street) does
gourmet rolls and sandwiches, with unique
flavours like stilton and pear. Toasted muf-
fins with appetizing fillings are another
sound option.

Kings   CAFE, BOOKSHOP
(Map p172; www.kingsonline.co.uk; 12 Queensberry
St; snacks £1-5) This buzzy cafe in the centre
of town doubles as a bookshop. It does tasty
fairtrade coffee, has big windows for ob-
serving Dumfries life passing by and serves
toothsome sweet things, breakfasts and
filled rolls.

Globe Inn   PUB
(Map p172; www.globeinndumfries.co.uk; 56 High
St) A traditional, rickety old nook-and-cranny pub down a narrow wynd off the main
pedestrian drag, this was reputedly Burns'
favourite watering hole, and scene of one
of his numerous seductions. It's got a great
atmosphere at weekends, created by its
welcoming locals and staff as much as the
numerous pictures of the 'ploughman poet'
himself.

❶ Information

Ewart Library (☑01387-253820; Catherine St;
⊘9.15am-7.30pm Mon-Wed & Fri, 9.15am-5pm
Thu & Sat) Free internet access.
Dumfries Information Centre (☑01387-
253862; www.visitdumfriesandgalloway.co.uk;
64 Whitesands; ⊘9.30am-5pm Mon-Sat year-
round, plus 11am-4pm Sun Jul–mid-Oct) Offers
plenty of information on the region.

❶ Getting There & Away
Bus
Local **buses** run regularly to Kirkcudbright (one
hour, hourly Monday to Saturday, six on Sunday)
and towns along the A75 to Stranraer (£7.80, 2¼
hours, eight daily Monday to Saturday, three on
Sunday).
   Bus 100/101 runs to/from Edinburgh (£7.50,
2¾ hours, four to seven daily), via Moffat and
Biggar.

SOUTHERN SCOTLAND DUMFRIES

WORTH A TRIP

WANLOCKHEAD

Even the phrase 'lead mining' has a sort of dulling effect on the brain, so you'd think it'd be a tough ask to make the subject interesting. But at the fabulous Hidden Treasures Museum of Lead Mining (www.leadminingmuseum.co.uk; Wanlockhead; adult/child £7.50/5.50; ⊙11am-4.30pm Apr-Jun & Sep, 10am-5pm Jul & Aug) at little Wanlockhead, signposted ten miles off the motorway northwest of Moffat, they pull it off. It's apparently Scotland's highest village, set amidst a striking landscape of treeless hills and burbling streams. The place is fascinating, and family-friendly, taking in a tour of a real mine, recreated miners' cottages, a remarkable 18th-century library, and a display on lead mining and other minerals. In summer, they also run gold-panning activities. The palpable enthusiasm and personableness of the staff bring the social history of the place alive. It's really rather special, and is one of our favourite museums in Scotland.

Buses running between Ayr and Dumfries stop in Sanquhar, from where there's a bus to Wanlockhead five times daily Monday to Saturday. Wanlockhead is also a stop on the Southern Upland Way walking route.

Train

There are trains between Carlisle and Dumfries (£9.70, 35 minutes, every hour or two), and direct trains between Dumfries and Glasgow (£14.50, 1¾ hours, eight daily Monday to Saturday). Services are reduced on Sundays.

South of Dumfries

CAERLAVEROCK

The ruins of Caerlaverock Castle (HS; www.historic-scotland.gov.uk; adult/child £5.50/3.30; ⊙9.30am-5.30pm Apr-Sep, 9.30am-4.30pm Oct-Mar), by Glencaple on a beautiful stretch of the Solway coast, are among the loveliest in Britain. Surrounded by a moat, lawns and stands of trees, the unusual pink-stoned triangular castle looks impregnable. In fact, it fell several times, most famously when it was attacked in 1300 by Edward I: the siege became the subject of an epic poem, 'The Siege of Caerlaverock'. The current castle dates from the late 13th century but, once defensive purposes were no longer a design necessity, it was refitted as a luxurious Scottish Renaissance mansion house in 1634. Ironically, the rampaging Covenanter militia sacked it a few years later. With nooks and crannies to explore, passageways and remnants of fireplaces, this castle is great for the whole family.

It's worth combining a visit to the castle with one to Caerlaverock Wetland Centre (www.wwt.org.uk; adult/child £7.30/3.60, free for WWT members; ⊙10am-5pm), a mile east. It protects 546 hectares of salt marsh and mud flats, the habitat for numerous birds, including barnacle geese. There are free,

daily wildlife safaris with experienced rangers, and a coffee shop that serves organic food.

From Dumfries, bus 6A runs several times a day (twice on Sunday) to Caerlaverock Castle. If you're travelling by car, take the B725 south.

RUTHWELL CROSS

Just off the B724, east of Caerlaverock, Ruthwell Church (⊙daylight hours) holds one of Europe's most important early Christian monuments. The 6m-high 7th-century Ruthwell Cross is carved top to bottom in New Testament scenes and is inscribed with a poem called 'The Dream of the Rood'; written in a Saxon runic alphabet, it's considered one of the earliest examples of English-language literature.

Bus 79 running between Dumfries and Carlisle stops by the church on request.

NEW ABBEY

The small, picturesque whitewashed village of New Abbey lies 7 miles south of Dumfries and has several worthwhile things to see and do.

⊙ Sights

Sweetheart Abbey RUINS
(HS; www.historic-scotland.gov.uk; adult/child £4/2.40; ⊙9.30am-5.30pm Apr-Sep, to 4.30pm Oct, 9.30am-4.30pm Sat-Wed Nov-Mar) The shattered, red-sandstone remnants of this 13th-century Cistercian abbey stand in stark contrast to the manicured lawns surrounding them. The abbey, the last of the major monasteries to be established in Scotland, was founded by Devorgilla of Galloway in 1273

in honour of her dead husband John Balliol (with whom she had founded Balliol College, Oxford). On his death, she had his heart embalmed and carried it with her until she died 22 years later. She and the heart were buried by the altar – hence the name.

National Museum of Costume MUSEUM
(www.nms.ac.uk; adult/child £4.50/2; ⊙10am-5pm Apr-Oct) On the edge of New Abbey, a historic house holds this museum, which gives an overview of what Scots have worn from Victorian times up to the postwar years, boosted by a feature exhibition each year. There are also picturesque gardens.

Mabie Farm Park FARM, RIDES
(www.mabiefarmpark.co.uk; adult/child/family £6.50/6/24; ⊙10am-5pm daily Apr-Oct, Sat & Sun Mar; 🚼) If your kids complaining about all the historic sights and Robert Burns, pack up the clan and get down to this spot, between Dumfries and New Abbey off the A710. It's a brilliantly-run complex with plenty of animals and activities for kids, including petting and feeding sessions, donkey rides, go-karting, slides, a soft play area, picnic spots... the list goes on – put a full day aside.

FREE **Mabie Forest Park** MOUNTAIN BIKING
(📞01387-270275; www.7stanesmountainbiking.com) Mabie Forest Park is one of southern Scotland's 7stanes mountain biking hubs, set among forested hills a couple of miles north of New Abbey. There are nearly 40 miles of trails for all levels; bike hire is also available.

🛏 Sleeping

Mabie House Hotel HOTEL ££
(📞01387-263188; www.mabiehousehotel.co.uk; s/d/ste £45/70/140; P🐶📶🐾) A couple of miles north of New Abbey, this welcoming country-house hotel is a great base, especially if you've got kids, as the farm park and mountain biking trails are on the doorstep. The rooms are stylish and luxurious, offering excellent comfort at a very fair price. In the garden are three cozy mini-huts which sleep four (£40), a good budget option for bikers or to give the younger generation some independence.

❶ Getting There & Away

To get to New Abbey, take Bus 372 from Dumfries.

Annandale & Eskdale

These valleys, in Dumfries & Galloway's east, form part of two major routes that cut across Scotland's south. Away from the highways, the roads are quiet and there are some interesting places to visit, especially if you're looking to break up a road trip.

GRETNA & GRETNA GREEN
POP 2705

Firmly on the coach tour circuit for its romantic associations, Gretna Green is on the outskirts of the town of Gretna, just across the river from Cumbria in England. Historically famous as a destination for eloping couples to get married, it's still one of Britain's most popular wedding venues.

The centre of the village is the Old Blacksmith's Shop (www.gretnagreen.com; exhibition

TYING THE KNOT IN GRETNA GREEN

The Marriage Act passed in England in 1754 suddenly required couples that did not have their parents' consent to be 21 years of age before they could marry. But cunning teenage sweethearts soon realized that the law didn't apply in Scotland, where a simple declaration in front of a pair of witnesses would suffice. As the first village in Scotland, Gretna Green's border location made it the most popular venue for eloping couples to get hitched.

Locals competed for the incoming trade, and marriages were performed by just about anyone who could round up a couple of witnesses from the nearest pub. One legendary Gretna vow-taker was the local blacksmith, who became known as the 'Anvil Priest'. In 1856 eloping was made more difficult when a law was passed obliging couples to have spent at least 3 weeks in Scotland prior to tying the knot, but Gretna Green remained popular. And it still is: some 5000 couples annually take or reaffirm their marriage vows in the village. If you want to get married over the famous anvil in the Old Blacksmith's Shop at Gretna Green, check out Gretna Green Weddings (www.gretnaweddings.co.uk).

adult/child £3.50/free; ☉9am-5pm Oct-Mar, to 5.30pm Apr-May, to 6.30pm Jun-Sep) complex, with a number of tourist shops and eateries as well as quite an entertaining multilingual exhibition on Gretna Green's history, with tales of intrigues, elopements, scoundrels, and angry parents arriving minutes too late. There's a recreation of a blacksmith's forge, a collection of handsome carriages and a few marriage rooms: you may well run into a modern-day wedding as you walk through.

Across the road, Smith's (☎01461-337007; www.smithsgretnagreen.co.uk; s/d £120/145; P🛜) is a large contemporary hotel with a reader-recommended restaurant (mains £12-19). Though the blocky exterior won't delight everybody, the interior is much more stylish. The rooms are decorated in a chic, restrained style with king-sized beds. Various grades are available; you'll get much cheaper rates booking online.

A mile away in Gretna, the very helpful tourist office (☎01461-337834; gretnatic@vis itscotland.com; Gretna Gateway; ☉10am-6pm Apr-Oct, 10am-4.30pm Nov-Mar) is a good first stop for information on Scotland if you're driving across from England.

Bus 79 between Dumfries (one hour) and Carlisle (35 minutes) stops in Gretna and Gretna Green (hourly Monday to Saturday, every two hours Sunday). Trains also run from Gretna Green to Dumfries and Carlisle.

MOFFAT
POP 2135

Moffat lies in wild, hilly country near the upper reaches of Annandale. It's really enjoyed by the older brigade and is a popular tourist-coach spot. The former spa town is a centre for the local wool industry, symbolised by the bronze ram statue on High St.

At Moffat Mill (☎01683-220134; www.ewm -store.co.uk; admission free; ☉9am-5pm), near the tourist office, there's a moribund weaving exhibition within a sizeable retail outlet selling woollens and other Scottish souvenirs. You can find some good specials on jumpers and the like. There's tourist information here too.

Groom's Cottage (☎01683-220049; Beattock Rd; d £65; P🛜) is a beautifully presented, self-contained nook with everything you could want for a comfortable stay. There are self-catering facilities (but breakfast is included). It has good privacy from the owner's residence, views over green fields and even an orthopaedic bed. It's a stylish job and very reasonably priced – weekly deals

are available too. Look for 'The Lodge' sign coming in from the M74 – it's on your right before you hit the town centre. This option is ideally suited to couples.

Flower-decked Buchan Guest House (☎01683-220378; www.buchanguesthouse.co.uk; Beechgrove; s/d £38/65; P🛜🍽) is in a quiet central street. There's a lovely garden and pleasant lounge overlooking the bowling green opposite. It's cyclist-friendly, with a bike garage out the back. The Moffat House Hotel (☎01683-220039; www.moffathouse.co.uk; High St; s/d £75/109; P🛜🍽) is a noble creeper-covered 18th-century mansion in the centre of town, offering comfortable beds in spacious rooms in the main building or an annexe in one of the wings.

There are several buses daily to Edinburgh, Glasgow and Dumfries.

LANGHOLM
POP 2311

The waters of three rivers – the Esk, Ewes and Wauchope – meet at Langholm, a gracious old town at the centre of Scotland's tweed industry. Most people come for fishing and walking in the surrounding moors and woodlands; check out the Langholm Walks website (www.langholmwalks.co.uk) for details.

Border House (☎013873-80376; www.bor der-house.co.uk; High St; s/d £30/60; P) is an excellent central accommodation option with large rooms (the downstairs double in particular), a lovely hostess and big sink-in-and-smile beds. You may get fresh handmade chocolates if a batch has just been made, but it was up for sale at time of research, so ring ahead.

Buses between Edinburgh and Carlisle pass through Langholm. There are frequent services to Lockerbie, where you can change to other routes.

ESKDALEMUIR

Surrounded by wooded hills, Eskdalemuir is a remote settlement 13 miles northwest of Langholm. About 1.5 miles further north is the Samye Ling Tibetan Centre (☎01387-373232; www.samyeling.org; camping/dm/s/d incl full board £15/24/37/57; P), the first Tibetan Buddhist monastery built in the West (1968). The colourful prayer flags and the red and gold of the temple itself are a striking contrast to the stark grey and green landscape. You can visit the centre during the day (donation suggested, cafe on site) or stay overnight in simple accommodation which includes full vegetarian board. There are also meditation courses and weekend workshops available. Reserve accommodation online, not by phone.

Bus 112 from Langholm/Lockerbie stops at the centre five times a day Monday to Saturday.

Castle Douglas & Around

POP 3671

Castle Douglas attracts a lot of day-trippers but hasn't been 'spruced up' for tourism. It's an open, attractive, well-cared-for town, with some remarkably beautiful areas close to the centre, such as the small Carlingwark Loch. The town was laid out in the 18th century by Sir William Douglas, who had made a fortune in the Americas.

◉ Sights & Activities

Threave Castle   CASTLE

(HS; www.historic-scotland.gov.uk; adult/child incl ferry £4.50/2.70; ◈9.30am-5pm Apr-Sep, to 4pm Oct) Two miles west of Castle Douglas, Threave Castle is an impressive tower on a small island in the River Dee. Built in the late 14th century, it became a principal stronghold of the Black Douglases, including the excellently named Archibald the Grim. It's now basically a shell, having been badly damaged by the Covenanters in the 1640s, but it's a romantic ruin nonetheless. It's a 15-minute walk from the car park to the ferry landing, where you ring a bell for the custodian to take you across to the island in a small boat. From the carpark, a 1.5 mile circular nature path gives you the chance to spot deer and ospreys, as well as waterbirds from hides. At dusk it's good for batwatching.

Loch Ken   WATER SPORTS

Stretching for 9 miles northwest of Castle Douglas between the A713 and A762, Loch Ken is a popular outdoor recreational area. The range of water sports includes windsurfing, sailing, canoeing, power-boating and kayaking. Back on land, off-road buggies can also be hired. **Galloway Activity Centre** (☑01644-420626; www.lochken.co.uk; ◈10am-5pm; ▣), on the eastern bank north of Parton village, runs a wide range of activities, and also provides equipment and hostel accommodation. Activities run in sessions of 1¼ hours; one session costs £16.50, and the price reduces substantially for further sessions. There are also walking trails and a

rich variety of bird life. The Royal Society for the Protection of Birds (RSPB) has a nature reserve (www.rspb.org.uk) on the western bank, north of Glenlochar.

Sulwath Brewery   BREWERY

(www.sulwathbrewers.co.uk; 209 King St; adult/child £3.50/free; ◈10am-6pm Mon-Sat) You can see traditional brewing processes at this main street alemakers. Tours only run twice a week, at 1pm on Monday and Friday, but the brewery functions as a sort of speakeasy where you can try the beers. Recommended is the Criffel, an India pale ale, and Knockendoch, a dark brew with a delicious taste of roasted malt.

⌷ Sleeping & Eating

Castle Douglas bills itself as a food town, and the main street is bristling with high-quality delis, butchers and cafés. Decent restaurants are scarcer however.

Douglas House   B&B ££

(☑01556-503262; www.douglas-house.com; 63 Queen St; s £39, d £70-85; ☜) A keen designer's eye is obviously present at this luxurious, attractively renovated B&B. Big beautiful bathrooms complement the light, stylish chambers, which include flatscreen digital TVs with inbuilt DVD players. The two upstairs doubles are the best, although the downstairs double is huge and has a king-size bed – you could sleep four in it! It was about to be taken over by new owners at the time of research.

Douglas Arms Hotel   HOTEL ££

(☑01556-502231; www.douglasarmshotel.com; 206 King St; s/d £55/95; ☜) Smack bang in the middle of town, Douglas Arms was originally a coaching inn, but these days has all the mod-cons to comfort the weary traveller. If you want to splash out, go for the honeymoon suite, which has a four-poster bed, jacuzzi and views over the main drag from a collage of windows. The lively bar serves scrumptious food (bar meals £8 to £12), although the atmosphere is a bit staid. The steak-and-ale pie, made with Galloway beef, is recommended.

The Craig   B&B ££

(☑01556-504840; www.thecraigcastledouglas. co.uk; 44 Abercromby Rd; s/d £38/60; ◈Feb-Oct; ▣☜) This solid old property is a fine B&B with a conscientious owner, large rooms and fresh fruit served up for breakfast. It's old-fashioned hospitality – genuine and very

SOUTHERN SCOTLAND CASTLE DOUGLAS & AROUND

comfortable. Would suit older visitors. It's on the edge of town on the road to New Galloway.

Lochside Caravan & Camping Site
CAMPING £

(☑01556-502949; www.dumgal.gov.uk/caravanand camping; Lochside Park; sites £16.50; ☺Mar-Oct; ℗⚽) Very central campsite attractively situated beside Carlingwark Loch; there's plenty of grass and fine trees providing shade.

Deli 173
TAKEAWAY £

(173 King St; baguettes £2-3; ☺8am-4pm Mon-Sat) For a truly awesome baguette drop into this fine-food deli. We recommend 'the Godfather'.

ℹ Information

Library (☑01556-502643; King St; ☺10am-7.30pm Mon-Wed & Fri, 10am-5pm Thu & Sat) Free internet access.

Castle Douglas Information Centre
(☑01556-502611; King St; ☺10am-5pm Mon-Sat Apr-Jun & Sep-Oct, 9.30am-6pm daily Jul & Aug) Located in a small park behind the library.

ℹ Getting There & Away

Buses pass through Castle Douglas roughly hourly en route to Dumfries (45 minutes) and Kirkcudbright (20 minutes); there are also regular connections to Stranraer, New Galloway and Ayr.

Kirkcudbright

POP 3447

Kirkcudbright (kirk-*coo*-bree), with its dignified streets of 17th- and 18th-century merchants' houses and appealing harbour, is the ideal base from which to explore the south coast. Look out for the nook-and-cranny wynds in the elbow of beautifully restored High St. With its architecture and setting, it's easy to see why Kirkcudbright has been an artists' colony since the late 19th century.

⦿ Sights & Activities

Broughton House
GALLERY

(NTS; www.nts.org.uk; 12 High St; adult/child £6/5; ☺noon-5pm Apr-Oct) The 18th-century Broughton House displays paintings by EA Hornel (he lived and worked here), one of the Glasgow Boys (p111). The library, with its wood panelling and stone carvings, is the most impressive room. Behind the house is a lovely Japanese-style garden (also open Monday to Friday in February and March).

MacLellan's Castle
CASTLE

(HS; www.historic-scotland.gov.uk; Castle St; adult/child £4/2.40; ☺9.30am-1pm & 2-5.30pm Apr-Sep) Near the harbour, this is a large, atmospheric ruin built in 1577 by Thomas MacLellan, then provost of Kirkcudbright, as his town residence. Inside look for the 'lairds' lug', a 16th-century hidey-hole designed for the laird to eavesdrop on his guests.

FREE **Tolbooth Art Centre**
EXHIBITION SPACE

(High St; ☺11am-5pm Mon-Sat, 2-5pm Sun) As well as catering for today's local artists, this centre has an exhibition on the history of the town's artistic development. The place is as interesting for the building itself as for the artistic works on display; it's one of the oldest and best-preserved tollbooths in Scotland, and there are interpretative signboards to explain its past. Reduced hours in winter.

FREE **Stewartry Museum**
MUSEUM

(St Mary St; ☺11am-5pm Mon-Sat, 2-5pm Sun) There's a certain charm to this higgledy-piggledy old-fashioned local history museum. There's everything from coronation teacups to lumps of local granite to stuffed fish. Reduced hours in winter.

Galloway Wildlife Conservation Park
ZOO

(www.gallowaywildlife.co.uk; Lochfergus Plantation; adult/child £7.50/5; ☺10am-5pm Feb-Nov, to 6pm summer) A mile from Kirkcudbright on the B727, this park is an easy walk from town, and you'll see red pandas, wolves, meerkats, monkeys, kangaroos, Scottish wildcats and many more creatures in a peaceful rural setting. An important role of the park is the conservation of rare and threatened species.

⚜ Festivals

Thursdays in high summer are Scottish theme nights, with music, dancing and more in the centre of town.

Kirkcudbright Jazz Festival
MUSIC

(www.kirkcudbrightjazzfestival.co.uk) In June, this is four days of swing, trad and dixie.

Wickerman Festival
MUSIC

(www.thewickermanfestival.co.uk) A diverse two-day music festival held in July on farmland a few miles southeast of town. From punk to reggae via indie rock, there's something for everyone. The festival climaxes with the burning of an enormous wickerman; much of the 1973 cult movie of the same name was filmed around this area.

🛏 Sleeping & Eating

Kirkcudbright has a swathe of good B&Bs, though single rooms are scarce. The **Kirkcudbright Bay Hotel** (☎01557-339544; www.kirkcudbrightbay.com; 25 St Cuthbert St) was getting a much-needed facelift by enthusiastic new owners when we last passed by, so should be worth checking out as a sleeping and eating option.

TOP CHOICE **Selkirk Arms Hotel**   HOTEL ££
(☎01557-330402;   www.selkirkarmshotel.co.uk; High St; s/d/superior d £84/110/130; P@�) What a haven of good hospitality this is. Superior rooms are excellent – wood furnishings and views over the back garden give them a rustic appeal. The **bistro** (mains £11-18) serves pricey but tasty pub nosh – the fish and chips come wrapped in the hotel newsletter – and the restaurant, **Artistas**, serves similar fare in a more refined atmosphere. Staff are happy to be there, and you will be too.

Greengate   B&B ££
(☎01557-331895; www.thegreengate.co.uk; 46 High St; s/d £60/80; �) The artistically inclined should snap up the one double room in this lovely place, which has both historic and current painterly connections.

Number One   B&B ££
(☎01557-330540; www.number1bedandbreakfast. co.uk; 1 Castle Gdns; s/d £65/80; �) Right by the castle, this tasteful spot offers high-end B&B with two very smart rooms, one with a great view of the fortress itself. In keeping with the town's artistic nature, there's a fine variety of canvases and watercolours on the walls. Solicitous hosts prepare great breakfasts and are happy to advise about walks in the area.

Anchorlee   B&B ££
(☎01557-330197; www.anchorlee.co.uk; 95 St Mary St; s/d £55/75; P�) This elegant residence on the main road is a comfortable haven of classic B&B. Welcoming hosts, cheerfully flowery rooms and a solid breakfast make staying here a pleasure.

Silvercraigs Caravan & Camping Site   CAMPING £
(☎01557-330123; www.dumgal.gov.uk/caravanand camping; Silvercraigs Rd; tent sites £10; ⊗Mar-Oct;

P) There are brilliant views from this camp ground; you feel like you're sleeping on top of the town. It's great for stargazing on clear nights, and there's good facilities, including a laundry.

🍴 **Castle Restaurant**   RESTAURANT ££
(☎01557-330569; www.thecastlerestaurant.net; 5 Castle St; mains £12-15; ⊗dinner Mon-Sat; 📶) The Castle Restaurant is the best place to eat in town and uses organic produce where possible. It covers a few bases with chicken, beef and seafood dishes on offer as well as tempting morsels for vegetarians.

ℹ Information

Check out www.kirkcudbright.co.uk and www. artiststown.org.uk for heaps of information on the town.

Kirkcudbright Information Centre (☎01557-330494; www.visitdumfriesandgalloway. co.uk; Harbour Sq; ⊗9.30am-5pm Mon-Sat, 11am-3pm Sun mid-Feb–Nov) Handy office with useful brochures detailing walks and road tours in the surrounding district. Extended hours in July and August.

ℹ Getting There & Away

Kirkcudbright is 28 miles southwest of Dumfries. Buses run hourly to Dumfries (one hour) via either Castle Douglas or Dalbeattie. Change at Gatehouse of Fleet for Stranraer.

Gatehouse of Fleet

POP 892

Gatehouse of Fleet is an attractive little town stretched along a sloping main street, in the middle of which sits an unusual castellated clock tower. The town lies on the banks of the Water of Fleet, off the beaten track, and is surrounded by partly wooded hills.

⊙ Sights

FREE **Mill on the Fleet Information Centre**   MUSEUM, TOURIST OFFICE
(www.millonthefleet.co.uk; High St; admission free; ⊗10am-5pm Apr-Oct) In the centre of town, in a converted 18th-century cotton mill, this centre has an exhibition on the history of the local industry and environment. The town was originally planned for the purpose of millworkers' accommodation. There's also tourist information, a cafe, a gallery and a likeably chaotic secondhand bookshop here.

Cardoness Castle CASTLE
(HS; www.historic-scotland.gov.uk; adult/child
£4/2.40; ⊙9.30am-5.30pm daily Apr-Sep, to
4.30pm Sat & Sun Nov-Mar) One mile southwest
on the A75, this well-preserved stronghold
was the home of the McCulloch clan. It's a
classic 15th-century tower house with great
views from the top.

🛏 Sleeping

TOP CHOICE Bobbin Guest House B&B **££**
(☎01557-814229; www.bobbinguesthouse.co.uk;
36 High St; s £35, d £60-70; ❂) Situated right
in the middle of town, this is a real home-
from-home with a variety of spacious, well-
appointed rooms with good en suite bathrooms. The welcome is exceptional.

Cally Palace Hotel HOTEL
(☎01557-814341; www.mcmillanhotels.co.uk; s/d
£137/234 dinner, bed & breakfast; P❂❂❂) On
the edge of town, in substantial grounds
that include a rather decent private golf
course, this 18th-century mansion is a
comfortable, upmarket hotel with various
grades of old-fashioned but commodious
rooms and numerous facilities including
tennis court, gym, heated indoor pool and
a well-regarded restaurant (jacket and tie
for gents). There are various offers including
unlimited golf on their website. B&B rates
are also available.

❶ Getting There & Away

Buses X75 and 500 between Dumfries (one
hour) and Stranraer (1¼ hours) stop here eight
times daily (three on Sunday). They stop in Castle Douglas and Newton Stewart. Further buses
run to Dumfries via Kirkcudbright.

Around Gatehouse

Ideal for families, Cream o' Galloway
(☎01557-815222; www.creamogalloway.co.uk;
visitor centre adult/child £2/4; incl all rides £10;
⊙10am-5pm mid-Mar–Oct, to 6pm Jul & Aug) is
the home of that delicious ice cream you'll
see all around the region, and offers a
plethora of activities and events. There are
4 miles of nature trails, an adventure playground for all ages, a 3-D maze, wildlife-
watching, a farm to explore and plenty of
ice cream to taste. There are also regular
events and special happenings. It's about
4 miles from Gatehouse off the A75 – signposted all the way. You can hire bikes from
here, as well.

Galloway Forest Park

South and northwest of the small town of
New Galloway is 300-sq-mile Galloway Forest Park, with numerous lochs and great
whale-backed, heather- and pine-covered
mountains. The highest point is **Merrick**
(843m). The park is criss-crossed by off-road
bike routes and some superb signposted
walking trails, from gentle strolls to long-
distance paths, including the **Southern Upland Way**. The park is very family focused;
look out for the booklet of annual events in
tourist offices.

The park is also a great place for **stargazing**; it's been named a Dark Sky Park by the
International Dark-Sky Association (www.
darksky.org).

The scenic 19-mile A712 (Queen's Way)
between New Galloway and Newton Stewart slices through the southern section of
the park.

On the shore of **Clatteringshaws Loch**,
6 miles west of New Galloway, is Clatteringshaws Visitor Centre (☎01671-402420; www.
forestry.gov.uk/scotland; ⊙10.30am-4.30pm Apr–
Oct, to 5.30pm Jul & Aug), featuring an exhibition on the area's flora and fauna. Pick up a
copy of the *Galloway Red Kite Trail* leaflet
here, which details a circular route through
impressive scenery that offers a good chance
to spot one of these majestic reintroduced
birds. From the visitor centre you can walk
to a replica of a Romano-British homestead,
and to **Bruce's Stone**, where Robert the
Bruce is said to have rested after defeating
the English at the Battle of Rapploch Moss
in 1307.

About a mile west of Clatteringshaws,
Raiders Rd is a 10-mile drive through
the forest with various picnic spots, child-
friendly activities and short walks marked
along the way. It costs £2 per vehicle; drive
slowly as there's plenty of wildlife about.

Further west is the **Galloway Red Deer
Range** where you can observe Britain's largest land-based beast. During rutting season
in autumn it's a bit like watching a bullfight
as snorting, charging stags compete for the
harem. During summer there are guided
ranger-led walks (adult/child £4/3).

Walkers and cyclists should head for
Glentrool in the park's west, accessed by
the forest road east from Bargrennan off the
A714, north of Newton Stewart. Located just
over a mile from Bargrennan is the Glentrool Visitor Centre (⊙10.30am-4.30pm Apr–

MOUNTAIN-BIKING HEAVEN

A brilliant way to experience southern Scotland's forests is by pedal power. The **7stanes** (stones) are seven mountain-biking centres around the region, featuring trails through some of the finest forest scenery you'll find in the country.

Glentrool is one of these centres; the **Blue Route** here is 5.6 miles in length and is a lovely ride climbing up to Green Torr Ridge overlooking Loch Trool. If you've more serious intentions, the **Big Country Route** is 36 miles of challenging ascents and descents that afford magnificent views of the Galloway Forest. It takes a full day and is not for wimps.

Another of the trailheads is at **Kirroughtree Visitor Centre**, 3 miles southeast of Newton Stewart. This centre offers plenty of singletrack at four different skill levels. You can hire also bikes here (www.thebreakpad.com). For more information on routes see www.7stanesmountainbiking.com.

Oct, to 5.30pm Jul & Aug), which has a cafe and stocks information on activities, including mountain biking. The road then winds and climbs up to **Loch Trool**, where there are magnificent views.

St John's Town of Dalry

St John's Town of Dalry is a charming village, hugging the hillside about 3 miles north of New Galloway on the A713. It's on the Water of Ken and gives access to the Southern Upland Way. It's also a good base for Galloway Forest Park.

Vine-engulfed Lochinvar Hotel (☎01644-430107; www.lochinvarhotel.co.uk; s/d £43/75; ✿🐾📶) an old hunting lodge built in the 1750s with a stately interior, has recently renovated rooms, some of them enormous, with good bathrooms and appealing vistas.

Walkers on the Southern Upland Way will appreciate Lodgings (☎01644-430015; www.thelodgings.co.uk; 26 Main St; r per person £25, with breakfast £30; 📶🐾). Its one room sleeps four or more, and there are self-catering facilties as well as an information office offering route advice.

Bus 521 runs twice daily (except Sunday) to Dumfries (55 minutes). Bus 520 connects Dalry with Castle Douglas (30 minutes, eleven daily Monday to Saturday); two services continue north to Ayr (1½ hours).

Newton Stewart

POP 3600

On the banks of the sparkling River Cree, Newton Stewart is at the heart of some beautiful countryside, and is popular with hikers and anglers. On the eastern bank, across the

bridge, is the older and smaller settlement of **Minnigaff**. With excellent accommodation and eating options, this makes a tempting base for exploring the Galloway Forest Park.

This is great angling country. For fishing gear and permits, as well as advice on landing the big one, drop into Galloway Angling Centre (☎01671-401333; www.gallowayangling.co.uk; 1 Queen St). You can also check out the very useful www.fishgalloway.co.uk.

🍴 Sleeping & Eating

Creebridge House Hotel HOTEL ££
(☎01671-402121; www.creebridge.co.uk; s/d/superior d £65/116/130; ✿🐾📶) This is a magnificent refurbished 18th-century mansion built for the Earl of Galloway. A maze inside, it has tastefully decorated rooms with modern furnishings and loads of character. Try to get a room overlooking the garden (No 7 is a good one). There's also good food here (mains £11 to £18).

Flowerbank Guest House B&B ££
(☎01671-402629; www.flowerbankgh.com; Millcroft Rd; s/d £40/60; ✿) This dignified 18th-century house is set in a magnificent landscaped garden in Minnigaff on the banks of the River Cree. The two elegantly furnished rooms at the front of the house are slightly more expensive (£66), but are spacious and have lovely garden views. It's a quiet, peaceful stop. Two-course dinners are £15.

Minnigaff SYHA HOSTEL £
(SYHA; ☎01671-402211; www.syha.org.uk; dm £17; ⊙Apr-Sep; ✿) This converted school is a well-equipped hostel with eight-bed dorms in a tranquil spot 800m north of the bridge, on the eastern bank. It's popular with outdoor enthusiasts, but you may just about have the place to yourself. Expect a lockout until 5pm.

Galloway Arms Hotel HOTEL, PUB **££**
(☑01671-402653; www.gallowayarmshotel.com;
54 Victoria St; s/d £39/75, mains £7-13; P🛈📶🍴)
There are decent rooms at this historic main
street pub; the best ones are upstairs. The
hotel is walker- and cyclist-friendly, with
bike storage and a drying room, while the
bar and restaurant churn out excellent local
fare: try the pork and apple burger.

ⓘ Information

Newton Stewart Information Centre
(☑01671-402431; www.visitdumfriesandgal
loway.com; Dashwood Sq; ⊘10am-4pm Tue-Sat
Apr-Oct)

ⓘ Getting There & Away

Buses stop in Newton Stewart (Dashwood Sq) on
their way to Stranraer (45 minutes) and Dumfries
(1½ hours); both run several times daily. There
are also connections to Ayr and Glasgow via Girvan. Frequent buses run south to the Machars.

The Machars

South of Newton Stewart, the Galloway Hills
give way to the softly rolling pastures of the
triangular peninsula known as the Machars.
The south has many early Christian sites
and the 25-mile Pilgrims Way walk.

Bus 415 runs every hour or so between Newton Stewart and Isle of Whithorn (one hour)
via Wigtown (15 minutes) and Whithorn.

WIGTOWN
POP 987

Little Wigtown, officially Scotland's National
Book Town, has more than a dozen bookshops offering an astonishingly wide selection of volumes, giving book enthusiasts
the opportunity to get lost here for days. A
major book festival (www.wigtownbookfestival.
com) is held here in late September.

⊙ Sights & Activities

Bookshop BOOKSHOP
(www.the-bookshop.com; 17 North Main St; ⊘9am-
5pm Mon-Sat) This bookshop claims to be
Scotland's largest secondhand bookshop,
and has a great collection of Scottish and
regional titles.

FREE Wigtown County
Buildings NATURE DISPLAY
(Market Sq; admission free; ⊘10am-5pm Mon, Thu
& Sat, 10am-7.30pm Tue, Wed & Fri, 2-5pm Sun)
Folk in this town love their resident ospreys.
It's a good conversation starter and if you'd

like to learn a bit more about the majestic
birds, and see a live CCTV link to a nearby
nest, drop by the Wigtown County Buildings
to check out its osprey exhibition.

Bladnoch Distillery DISTILLERY
(☑01988-402605; www.bladnoch.co.uk; Bladnoch; tours adult/child £3/free; ⊘9am-5pm Mon-
Fri, plus weekends Jul & Aug) Browsing books
can be thirsty work, so it's fortunate that
Bladnoch Distillery is just a couple of miles
away from Wigtown, in the village of Bladnoch. Ring for times of tours, which include
a dram. If you want a three-dram tasting,
it's a fiver.

Torhouse Stone Circle RUIN
Four miles west of Wigtown, off the B733,
this well-preserved ruin dates from the 2nd
millenium BC.

🛏 Sleeping & Eating

Hillcrest House B&B **££**
(☑01988-402018; www.hillcrest-wigtown.co.uk;
Station Rd; s £40-45, d £68-78; P🛈📶) Wow! That's
what we said when we saw the rooms in
Hillcrest House. A noble stone building in a
quiet part of town, the house features high
ceilings and huge windows; spend the extra
for one of the superior rooms, which have
stupendous views overlooking rolling green
hills and the sea beyond. This is all complemented by a ripper breakfast involving fresh
local produce.

ReadingLasses Bookshop Café CAFE **£**
(www.reading-lasses.com; 17 South Main St; mains
£6.50; ⊘10am-5pm Mon-Sat, also noon-5pm Sun
May-Oct; 🛈) This bookshop-cafe sells caffeine to prolong your reading time and does
a cracking smoked salmon salad sourced
locally. It specialises in books on the social
sciences and women's studies.

WHITHORN
POP 867

Whithorn has a broad, attractive High St
which is virtually closed at both ends (it
was designed to enclose a medieval market). There are few facilities in town, but
it's worth visiting because of its fascinating
history.

In 397, while the Romans were still in
Britain, St Ninian established the first
Christian mission beyond Hadrian's Wall in
Whithorn (pre-dating St Columba on Iona
by 166 years). After his death, **Whithorn
Priory**, the earliest recorded church in Scot-
land, was built to house his remains, and

Whithorn became the focus of an important medieval pilgrimage.

Today the ruined priory is part of the excellent Whithorn Trust Discovery Centre (www.whithorn.com; 45 George St; adult/child £4.50/2.25; ⊙10.30am-5pm Apr-Oct), which introduces you to the history of the town through a very informative audiovisual exhibition. There's an ongoing archaeological investigation here, and you can see the site of earlier churches. There's also a museum with some fascinating early Christian stone sculptures, including the **Latinus Stone** (c 450), reputedly Scotland's oldest Christian artefact. Learn about the influences their carvers drew on, from around the British Isles and beyond.

ISLE OF WHITHORN
POP 400

The Isle of Whithorn, once an island but now linked to the mainland by a causeway, is a curious place with an attractive natural harbour and colourful houses. The roofless 13th-century **St Ninian's Chapel**, probably built for pilgrims who landed nearby, sits on the windswept, evocative rocky headland. Around Burrow Head, to the southwest but accessed off the A747 before you enter the Isle of Whithorn, is **St Ninian's Cave**, where the saint went to pray.

Three hundred-year-old Dunbar House (☑01988-500336; http://dunbarhouse.herobo.com; Tonderghie Rd; s/d £23/40), overlooking the harbour, has two large, bright, perfect rooms that share a spotless bathroom. It's a bargain at this price, and cordially run. You can admire the view while tucking into your breakfast in the dining room.

The quayside Steam Packet Inn (☑01988-500334; www.steampacketinn.biz; Harbour Row; r per person £40, without bathroom £35; 🖋) is a popular pub with real ales, scrumptious bar meals (mains £7 to £11), a snug bar and comfy lodgings. Try to get a room at the front of the building as they have lovely views over the little harbour (No. 2 is a good one).

Stranraer

POP 10,851

The friendly but somewhat ramshackle port of Stranraer has seen its tourist mainstay, the ferry traffic to Northern Ireland, move up the road to Cairnryan. The town's still wondering what to do with itself, but there's lots to explore in the surrounding area.

◉ Sights

FREE St John's Castle   CASTLE
(George St; ⊙10am-1pm & 1.30-4.30pm Tue-Sat Jun-Sep) Worth a quick visit, St John's Castle is a tower built in 1510 by the Adairs of Kihilt, a powerful local family. The old stone cells carry a distinctly musty smell. There are displays and a couple of videos that trace its history and, from the top of the castle, superb views of Loch Ryan.

FREE Stranraer Museum   MUSEUM
(55 George St; ⊙10am-5pm Mon-Fri, 10am-1pm & 1.30-4.30pm Sat) This museum houses exhibits on local history and you can learn about Stranraer's polar explorers. The highlight is the carved stone pipe from Madagascar.

🍴 Sleeping & Eating

TOP CHOICE Balyett Farm   B&B, HOSTEL ££
(☑01776-703395; www.balyettbb.co.uk; Cairnryan Rd; dm/s £20/55, d £65-75; 🅿🛜) A mile north of town on the A77, Balyett has a super-welcoming host and lovely relaxing rooms in a tranquil setting; they are light, bright, clean as a whistle and boast lovely views over the surrounding country. Out the back is a self-catering cabin that sleeps five; it's a great space for a family but can also be used for beds on a dorm basis.

Ivy House   B&B £
(☑01776-704176; www.ivyhouse-ferrylink.co.uk; 3 Ivy Pl; s/d £30/50, s without bathroom £25; 🛜) This is a great guesthouse that does Scottish hospitality proud, with excellent facilities, tidy en suite rooms and a smashing breakfast. Nothing is too much trouble for the genial host, who always has a smile for their guests. The room at the back overlooking the churchyard is particularly light and quiet.

North West Castle Hotel   HOTEL ££
(☑01776-704413; www.northwestcastle.co.uk; s/d £80/120; 🅿🛜🏊🎱) Showing its age but still an enjoyable time-warp experience, this was formerly the home of Arctic explorer Sir John Ross. Rooms need a wee upgrade, but are comfortable enough: try for sea views. Service is excellent and here's the real pull: it was the first hotel in the world to have an indoor curling rink.

L'Aperitif   BISTRO ££
(☑01776-702991; www.laperitifstranraer.co.uk; London Rd; mains £10-14; ⊙Tue-Sat; 🛜) Purgatory at

WORTH A TRIP

CORSEWALL LIGHTHOUSE HOTEL

It's just you and the cruel sea out here at this fabulously romantic 200-year-old lighthouse (☎01776-853220; www.lighthousehotel.co.uk; d incl 5-course dinner £180-290; P☎), right at the tip of the peninsula, 13 miles northwest of Stranraer. On a sunny day, the water shimmers with light, and you can see Ireland, Kintyre, Arran and Ailsa Craig. But when the wind and rain beat in, it's just great to be cosily holed up in the snug bar-restaurant or snuggling under the covers in your room. Rooms in the lighthouse building itself are attractive if necessarily compact; chalets are also available.

dinnertime can look uncannily like Stranraer at times, so thank the powers that be for this cheerful local. It's definitely the town's best restaurant and is close to being its best pub too. Despite the name, dishes are more Italian than French, with great pastas alongside roasts, saltimbocca, and delicious appetisers featuring things like smoked salmon or greenlip mussels.

ℹ Information

Library (North Strand St; ◷9.15am-7.30pm Mon-Wed & Fri, to 5pm Thu & Sat) Free internet access.

Stranraer Information Centre (☎01776-702595; www.visitdumfriesandgalloway.com; 28 Harbour St; ◷10am-4pm Mon-Sat) Efficient and friendly.

ℹ Getting There & Away

Stranraer is 6 miles south of Cairnryan, which is on the eastern side of Loch Ryan. Bus 358 runs frequently between Stranraer and Ayr stopping in Cairnryan. For a taxi to Cairnryan (around £11), contact **McLean's Taxis** (☎01776-703343; 21 North Strand St; ◷24hr), just up from the tourist office.

Boat

P&O (☎0871 66 44 777; www.poferries.com) Runs six to eight fast ferries a day from Cairnryan to Larne (Northern Ireland). The crossing takes two hours; there's one Express service that takes just one hour.

Stena Line (☎08445-762762; www.stenaline.co.uk; passenger/car £28/110) Runs four to six ferries from Cairnryan to Belfast (2¾ hours).

Bus

Scottish Citylink buses run to Glasgow (£17.50, 2½ hours, three daily) and Edinburgh (£20, 4 hours, three daily).

There are also several daily local buses to Kirkcudbright and the towns along the A75, such as Newton Stewart (45 minutes, at least hourly) and Dumfries (£7.40, 2¼ hours, nine daily Monday to Saturday, three on Sunday).

Train

First Scotrail runs to/from Glasgow (£21.60, 2¼ hours, two to seven trains daily); it may be necessary to change at Ayr.

Around Stranraer

Magnificent **Castle Kennedy Gardens** (www.castlekennedygardens.co.uk; adult/child £5/1.50; ◷10am-5pm daily Apr-Oct, Sat & Sun only Feb-Mar), 3 miles east of Stranraer, are among the most famous in Scotland. They cover 30 hectares and are set on an isthmus between two lochs and two castles (Castle Kennedy, burnt down in 1716, and Lochinch Castle, built in 1864). The landscaping was undertaken in 1730 by the Earl of Stair, who used soldiers to do the work. Buses heading east from Stranraer stop at the gate on the main road; it's a pleasant 20-minute stroll from here to the entrance to the gardens.

Portpatrick

pop 585

Portpatrick is a charming port on the rugged west coast of the Rhinns of Galloway peninsula. It is a good base from which to explore the south of the peninsula, and it's the starting point for the **Southern Upland Way**. You can follow part of the way to Stranraer (9 miles). It's a clifftop walk, with sections of farmland and heather moor.

Harbour House Hotel (☎01776-810456; www.theharbourhousehotel.co.uk; 53 Main St; s/d £60/100; ☎☎) was formerly the customs house but is now a popular, friendly old pub. Some of the beautifully refurbished rooms have brilliant views over the harbour; there are also self-catering apartments out the back. The hotel is also a warm nook for a traditional bar meal (£7 to £10). There are various other hotels, seafood eateries and B&Bs along the harbourfront.

For a real dose of luxury, head 5 miles southeast to **Knockinaam Lodge** (☎01776-810471; www.knockinaamlodge.com; dinner, bed

& breakfast s £215-340, d £340-440; (P🛜❄), a former hunting lodge in a dramatic, secluded location with grassy lawns rolling down to a sandy cove. It's where Churchill plotted the endgame of WWII – you can stay in his suite – and it's a very romantic place to get away from it all. The excellent French-influenced cuisine (lunch/dinner £40/58) is backed up by a great range of wines and single malts, and breakfast features home-made jams.

Bus 367 runs to Stranraer (20 minutes, hourly Monday to Saturday, three Sunday).

South of Portpatrick

From Portpatrick, the road south to the Mull of Galloway passes coastal scenery that includes rugged cliffs, tiny harbours and sandy beaches. Dairy cattle graze on the greenest grass you've ever seen, and the warm waters of the Gulf Stream give the peninsula the mildest climate in Scotland.

This mildness is demonstrated at Logan Botanic Garden (www.rbge.org.uk/logan; adult/child £5.50/1; ⊘10am-4pm Sun Feb, 10am-5pm daily mid-Mar-Oct), a mile north of Port Logan, where an array of subtropical flora includes tree ferns and cabbage palms. The garden is an outpost of the Royal Botanic Garden in Edinburgh. **Port Logan** itself is a sleepy place with a decent pub and excellent sandy beach.

Further south, **Drummore** is a fishing village on the east coast. From here it's another 5 miles to the **Mull of Galloway**, Scotland's most southerly point. It's a spectacular spot, with windswept green grass and views of Scotland, England, the Isle of Man and Northern Ireland. The lighthouse (adult/child £2.50/1; ⊘10am-4pm Sat & Sun Easter-Oct, plus Mon Jul & Aug) here was built by Robert Stevenson, grandfather of the writer, in 1826. You can learn more about the Stevenson clan of lighthouse builders in the small exhibition (www.mull-of-galloway.co.uk; adult/child £2.50/1; ⊘10am-4pm Easter-Oct) at the lighthouse's base. The Mull of Galloway RSPB nature reserve, home to thousands of seabirds, has a visitor centre (www.rspb.org.uk; ⊘10am-5pm) with plenty of information on local species, and a cafe.

The former homes of the lightkeepers are available to stay in; check out www.ntsholidays.com.

Central Scotland

Best Places to Eat

» Peat Inn (p212)

» 63 Tay Street (p219)

» Vine Leaf (p211)

» Falls of Dochart Inn (p203)

Best Places to Stay

» Monachyle Mhor (p202)

» Milton Eonan (p225)

» Lake of Menteith Hotel (p200)

» Bunrannoch House (p226)

» Craigatin House (p228)

» Killiecrankie House Hotel (p229)

Why Go?

The country's historic roots are deeply embedded in central Scotland. Significant ruins and castles from the region's history pepper the landscape; key battles around Stirling shaped Scotland's fortunes; and Perth, the former capital, is where kings were crowned on the Stone of Destiny.

Arriving from Glasgow and Edinburgh, visitors begin to get a sense of the country further north as the Lowland belt gives way to Highland splendour. It is here that the majesty of Scotland's landscape unfolds in deep, dark, steely-blue lochs that reflect the silhouettes of soaring, sentinel-like craggy peaks on still days.

Whether in the big-tree country of Perthshire, the bare landscapes of Glenshee, or the green Fife coastline dotted with fishing villages, opportunities to enjoy the landscape abound: walking, cycling and mountaineering are all easy possibilities. The region also has some of the country's best pubs and eateries, which greet weary visitors at day's end.

When to Go
Stirling

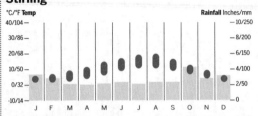

May If the weather's kind, it's a magical time for exploring before summer crowds arrive.

Aug Summer in Fife is a top time for coastal walks and crustacean feasts.

Dec–Mar Hit the slopes at Glenshee for the sight of Scottish crags blanketed with snow.

STIRLING REGION

Covering Scotland's wasplike waist, this region has always been a crucial strategic point dividing the Lowlands from the Highlands. For this reason Scotland's two most important independence battles were fought here, within sight of Stirling's hilltop stronghold. Separated by 17 years, William Wallace's victory over the English at Stirling Bridge, followed by Robert Bruce's triumph at Bannockburn, established Scottish nationhood. The region remains a source of much national pride.

Stirling's Old Town perches on a spectacular crag, and the castle is among Britain's most fascinating. Within easy reach, the dreamy Trossachs, home to Rob Roy and inspiration to Walter Scott, offer great walking and cycling in the eastern half of Scotland's first national park.

Stirling

POP 32,673

With an utterly impregnable position atop a mighty wooded crag (the plug of an extinct volcano), Stirling's beautifully preserved Old Town is a treasure trove of noble buildings and cobbled streets winding up to the ramparts of its dominant castle, which offer views for miles around. Clearly visible is the brooding Wallace Monument, a strange Victorian Gothic creation honouring the legendary freedom fighter of *Braveheart* fame. Nearby is Bannockburn, scene of Robert the Bruce's major triumph over the English.

The castle makes a fascinating visit, but make sure you also spend time exploring the Old Town and the picturesque path that encircles it. Below the Old Town, retail-minded modern Stirling doesn't offer the same appeal; stick to the high ground as much as possible and you'll love the place.

◉ Sights

Stirling Castle   CASTLE
(HS; Map p190; www.historic-scotland.gov.uk; adult/child £13/6.50; ◷9.30am-6pm Apr-Sep, to 5pm Oct-Mar) Hold Stirling and you control Scotland. This maxim has ensured that a fortress of some kind has existed here since prehistoric times. You cannot help drawing parallels with Edinburgh Castle, but many find Stirling's fortress more atmospheric – the location, architecture, historical significance and utterly commanding views

combine to make it a grand and memorable sight. This means it draws plenty of visitors, so it's advisable to visit in the afternoon; many tourists come on day trips, so you may have the castle to yourself by about 4pm.

The current castle dates from the late 14th to the 16th century, when it was a residence of the Stuart monarchs. The undisputed highlight of a visit is the fabulous, recently restored **Royal Palace**. The idea was that it should look brand new, just as when it was constructed by French masons under the orders of James V in the mid-16th century with the aim of impressing his new (also French) bride and other crowned heads of Europe. The suite of six rooms – three for the king, three for the queen – is a sumptuous riot of colour. Particularly notable are the fine fireplaces, the re-created painted oak discs in the ceiling of the king's audience chamber and the fabulous series of **tapestries** that have been painstakingly woven over many years. Based on originals in New York's Metropolitan Museum, they depict the hunting of a unicorn – an event ripe with Christian metaphor – and are utterly beautiful. Don't miss the palace exterior, studded with beautiful sculptures, or the **Stirling Heads Gallery** above the royal chambers. This has the original oak roundels – a real rogue's gallery of royals, courtiers and classical personalities. In the vaults beneath the palace is a kid-friendly **exhibition** on various aspects of castle life.

The other buildings surrounding the main castle courtyard are the vast **Great Hall**, built by James IV; the **Royal Chapel**, remodelled in the early 17th century by James VI and with the colourful original mural painting intact; and the King's Old Building. This is now home to the **Museum of the Argyll & Sutherland Highlanders** (donations appreciated), which traces the history of this famous regiment from 1794, including its famous defensive action in the Battle of Balaclava in 1854. Make sure you read the moving letters from the World Wars.

Until the last tapestry is completed, probably in late 2013, you can watch the weavers at work in the **Tapestry Studio** at the far end of the castle. It's fascinating to see. Other displays include the **Great Kitchens**, bringing to life the bustle and scale of the enterprise of cooking for the king and, near the entrance, the **Castle Exhibition**, which gives good background information on the

Central Scotland Highlights

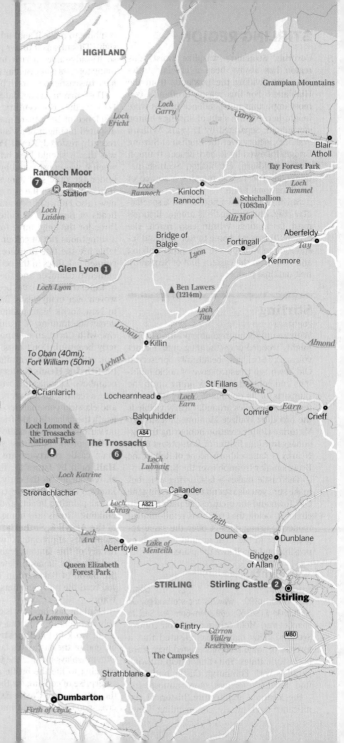

1 Opening your jaw in amazement at the epic splendour of the countryside of **Glen Lyon** (p225)

2 Admiring the views from magnificent **Stirling Castle** (p187), overlooking ancient independence battlefields

3 Pacing through historic **St Andrews** (p206) to the famous Old Course

4 Strutting with peacocks at noble **Scone Palace** (p216), where Scottish kings were crowned

5 Crunching local seafood in the picturesque fishing villages of the **East Neuk of Fife** (p213)

6 Exploring the lovely lochscapes and accessible walking and cycling routes in **the Trossachs** (p198)

7 Getting off the beaten track around Loch Rannoch and appreciating the bleak, end-of-the-road feel of **Rannoch Moor** (p225)

Stirling

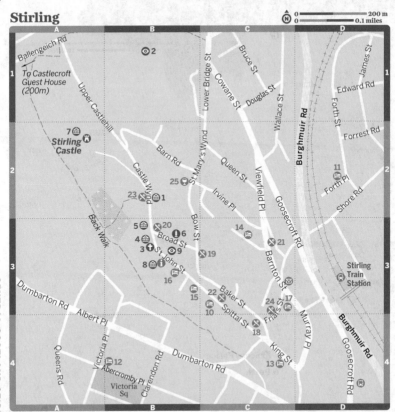

Stuart kings and updates on current archaeological investigations. The magnificent vistas from the **ramparts** are stirring.

Admission includes an audioguide, and free guided tours leave regularly from near the entrance. Tours (£2 extra, free for HS members) also run to **Argyll's Lodging**, at the top of Castle Wynd. Complete with turrets, this spectacular lodge is Scotland's most impressive 17th-century town house. It's the former home of William Alexander, Earl of Stirling and noted literary figure. It has been tastefully restored and gives an insight into lavish, 17th-century aristocratic life. There are four or five tours daily (you can't enter by other means).

Old Town
HISTORIC DISTRICT

Below the castle, the steep Old Town has a remarkably different feel to modern Stirling, its cobblestone streets packed with 15th- to 17th-century architectural gems. Its growth

began when Stirling became a royal burgh (about 1124), and in the 15th and 16th centuries rich merchants built their houses here.

Stirling has the best surviving **town wall** in Scotland. It was built around 1547 when Henry VIII of England began the 'Rough Wooing' – attacking the town in order to force Mary, Queen of Scots, to marry his son so the two kingdoms could be united. The wall can be explored on the **Back Walk**, which follows the line of the wall from Dumbarton Rd to the castle. You pass the town cemeteries (check out the **Star Pyramid**, an outsized affirmation of Reformation values dating from 1863), then the path continues around the back of the castle to Gowan Hill, where you can see the **Beheading Stone**, now encased in iron bars to prevent contemporary use.

Mar's Wark, on Castle Wynd at the head of the Old Town, is the ornate facade of a Renaissance town house commissioned in

Stirling

1569 by the wealthy Earl of Mar, regent of Scotland during James VI's minority.

The **Church of the Holy Rude** (Map p190; www.holyrude.org; St John St; admission free; ◷11am-4pm May-Sep) has been the town's parish church for 600 years and James VI was crowned here in 1567. The nave and tower date from 1456, and the church has one of the few surviving medieval open-timber roofs. Stunning stained-glass windows and huge stone pillars create a powerful effect.

Behind the church is **Cowane's Hospital** (Map p190; 49 St John St; admission free; ◷10.30am-3.30pm Apr-Oct), built as an almshouse in 1637 by the merchant John Cowane. The high vaulted hall was much modified in the 19th century.

The **Mercat Cross**, in Broad St, is topped with a unicorn (known as 'The Puggie') and was once surrounded by a bustling market. Nearby is the **Tolbooth**, built in 1705 as the town's administrative centre and renovated in 2001 to become an arts venue.

The **Old Town Jail** (Map p190; www.oldtown jail.com; St John St; adult/child £6.75/4.25; ◷10am-5pm Apr-Oct) is a great one for kids, as actors take you through the complex, portraying a cast of characters who illustrate the hardships of Victorian prison life in innovative, entertaining style.

National Wallace Monument   MONUMENT
(www.nationalwallacemonument.com; adult/child £8.25/5.25; ◷10am-5pm Apr-Jun, Sep & Oct, to 6pm Jul & Aug, 10.30am-4pm Nov-Mar) Towering over Scotland's narrow waist, this nationalist memorial is so Victorian Gothic it deserves circling bats and ravens. It commemorates the bid for Scottish independence depicted in the film *Braveheart*. From the visitor centre below, walk or shuttle-bus up the hill to the building itself. Once there, break the climb up the narrow staircase inside to admire Wallace's 66 inches of broadsword and see the man himself re-created in a 3-D audiovisual display. More staid is the marble pantheon of lugubrious Scottish heroes, but the view from the top over the flat, green gorgeousness of the Forth Valley, including the site of Wallace's 1297 victory over the English at Stirling Bridge, almost justifies the steep entry fee.

Buses 62 and 63 run from Murray Pl in Stirling to the tourist office, otherwise it's a half-hour walk from central Stirling. There's a cafe here.

Bannockburn   HISTORIC SITE
Though Wallace's heroics were significant, it was Robert the Bruce's defeat of the English on 24 June 1314 at Bannockburn, just outside Stirling, that eventually established lasting Scottish nationhood. Exploiting the marshy ground, Bruce won a great tactical victory against a much larger and better-equipped force, and sent Edward II 'homeward, tae think again', as the song 'Flower of Scotland' commemorates.

Stirling Castle

PLANNING YOUR ATTACK

Stirling's a sizeable fortress, but not so huge that you'll have to decide what to leave out – there's time to see it all. Unless you've got a working knowledge of Scottish monarchs, head to the **Castle Exhibition 1** first: it'll help you sort one James from another. That done, take on the sights at leisure. First, stop and look around you from the **ramparts 2**; the views high over this flat valley, a key strategic point in Scotland's history, are magnificent.

Next, head through to the back of the castle to the **Tapestry Studio 3**, if it is still functioning; seeing these skilful weavers at work is a highlight.

Track back towards the citadel's heart, stopping for a quick tour through the **Great Kitchens 4**; looking at all that fake food might make you seriously hungry, though. Then enter the main courtyard. Around you are the principal castle buildings. During summer there are events (such as Renaissance dancing) in the **Great Hall 5** – get details at the entrance. The **Museum of the Argyll & Sutherland Highlanders 6** is a treasure trove if you're interested in regimental history, but missable if you're not. Leave the best for last – crowds thin in the afternoon – and enter the sumptuous **Royal Palace 7**.

THE WAY UP & DOWN

If you have time, take the atmospheric Back Walk, a peaceful, shady stroll around the Old Town's fortifications and up to the castle's imposing crag-top position. Afterwards, wander down through the Old Town to admire its facades.

Museum of the Argyll & Sutherland Highlanders
The history of one of Scotland's legendary regiments – now subsumed into the Royal Regiment of Scotland – is on display here, featuring memorabilia, weapons and uniforms.

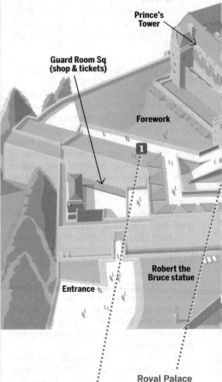

Prince's Tower

Guard Room Sq (shop & tickets)

Forework

Robert the Bruce statue

Entrance

Castle Exhibition
A great overview of the Stewart dynasty here will get your facts straight, and also offers the latest archaeological titbits from the ongoing excavations under the citadel. Analysis of skeletons has revealed surprising amounts of biographical data.

Royal Palace
The impressive new highlight of a visit to the castle is this recreation of the royal lodgings originally built by James V. The finely worked ceiling, ornate furniture and sumptuous unicorn tapestries dazzle.

DAVID ROBERTSON/ALAMY ©

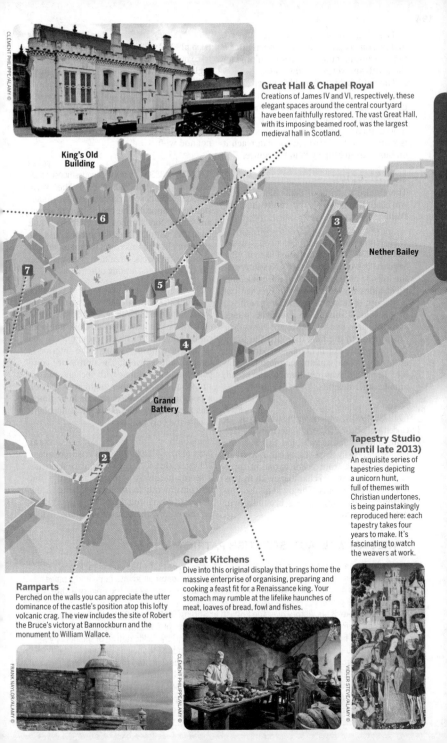

Great Hall & Chapel Royal
Creations of James IV and VI, respectively, these elegant spaces around the central courtyard have been faithfully restored. The vast Great Hall, with its imposing beamed roof, was the largest medieval hall in Scotland.

King's Old Building

Nether Bailey

6

7

5

4

3

Grand Battery

2

Tapestry Studio (until late 2013)
An exquisite series of tapestries depicting a unicorn hunt, full of themes with Christian undertones, is being painstakingly reproduced here: each tapestry takes four years to make. It's fascinating to watch the weavers at work.

Great Kitchens
Dive into this original display that brings home the massive enterprise of organising, preparing and cooking a feast fit for a Renaissance king. Your stomach may rumble at the lifelike haunches of meat, loaves of bread, fowl and fishes.

Ramparts
Perched on the walls you can appreciate the utter dominance of the castle's position atop this lofty volcanic crag. The view includes the site of Robert the Bruce's victory at Bannockburn and the monument to William Wallace.

The Bannockburn Heritage Centre (NTS; www.nts.org.uk) is due to reopen after a big refurbishment in spring 2014, in time for the 700th anniversary of the battle.

The battlefield itself (which never closes) will hopefully receive a bit of work too; at present, apart from a statue of the victor astride his horse and a misbegotten flag memorial, there's nothing to see. Bannockburn is 2 miles south of Stirling; you can reach it on bus 51 from Murray Pl in the centre.

🛏 Sleeping

There's also a string of B&Bs along Causewayhead Rd, between the centre and the Wallace Monument.

TOP CHOICE Castlecroft Guest House B&B ££

(☑01786-474933; www.castlecroft-uk.com; Ballengeich Rd; s/d £50/65; P@🕿) Nestling into the hillside under the back of the castle, this great hideaway feels like a rural retreat but is a short, spectacular walk from the heart of historic Stirling. The fabulous lounge and deck area boast extravagant views over green fields to the hills that gird the town, the rooms have excellent modern bathrooms and the welcome couldn't be more hospitable. Breakfast features homemade bread, among other delights.

Neidpath B&B £

(☑01786-469017; www.neidpath-stirling.co.uk; 24 Linden Ave; s/d £40/58; P🕿) Offering excellent value and a genuine welcome, this is a fine choice and easily accessed by car. A particularly appealing front room is one of three excellent modernised chambers with fridges and good bathrooms. The owners also run various self-catering options around town; details via the website.

Willy Wallace Backpackers Hostel HOSTEL £

(Map p190; ☑01786-446773; www.willywallacehostel.com; 77 Murray Pl; dm/tw £16/36; @🕿) This highly convenient central hostel is friendly, roomy and sociable. The colourful, spacious dormitories are clean and light, there's free tea and coffee, a good kitchen and a laissez-faire atmosphere. Other amenities include bicycle hire, laundry service and free internet and wi-fi.

Linden Guest House B&B ££

(☑01786-448850; www.lindenguesthouse.co.uk; 22 Linden Ave; d £60-80; P@🕿) The warm welcome and easy parking here offer understandable appeal. The rooms, two of which are great for families, have fridges and posh TVs with DVD and iPod dock, and the gleaming bathrooms could feature in ads for cleaning products. Breakfast features fresh fruit and kippers, among other choices.

Stirling SYHA HOSTEL £

(Map p190; ☑01786-473442; www.syha.org.uk; St John St; dm/tw £18.75/48; P@🕿) Right in the Old Town, this hostel has an unbeatable location and great facilities. Though its facade is that of a former church, the interior is modern and efficient. The dorms are compact but comfortable with lockers and en suite bathrooms; other highlights include a pool table, bike shed and, at busy times, cheap meals on offer. Lack of atmosphere can be the only problem.

Sruighlea B&B ££

(Map p190; ☑01786-471082; www.sruighlea.com; 27 King St; s/d £40/60; 🕿) This place feels like a secret hideaway – there's no sign – but it's conveniently located smack bang in the centre of town. You'll feel like a local staying here, and there are eating and drink-

---

WILLIAM WALLACE, SCOTTISH PATRIOT

William Wallace is one of Scotland's greatest heroes, a patriot whose exploits helped revive interest in Scottish history. Born in 1270, he was catapulted into fame and a place in history as a highly successful guerrilla commander who harassed the English invaders for many years.

In the wake of his victory over the English at Stirling Bridge in 1297, Wallace was knighted by Robert the Bruce and proclaimed Guardian of Scotland. However, it was only a short time before English military superiority and the fickle nature of the nobility's loyalties would turn against the defender of Scottish independence.

Disaster struck in July 1298 when King Edward's force defeated the Scots at the Battle of Falkirk. Wallace went into hiding and travelled throughout Europe to drum up support for the Scottish cause. Many of the Scottish nobility were prepared to side with Edward, and Wallace was betrayed after his return to Scotland in 1305, tried for treason at Westminster and hanged, beheaded and disembowelled at Smithfield, London.

ing places practically on the doorstep. It's a B&B that welcomes guests with the kind of warmth that keeps them returning.

Garfield Guesthouse
B&B **££**

(Map p190; ☎01786-473730; www.garfieldgh.com; 12 Victoria Sq; small/large d £65/70) Though close to the centre of town, Victoria Sq is a quiet oasis, with noble Victorian buildings surrounding a verdant swathe of lawn. The Garfield's huge rooms, bay windows, ceiling roses and other period features make it a winner. There's a great family room, and some rooms have views to the castle towering above.

Forth Guest House
B&B **££**

(Map p190; ☎01786-471020; www.forthguesthouse.co.uk; 23 Forth Pl; s/d £50/60; **P**🅿️🛜) Just a couple of minutes' walk from town, on the other side of the railway, this noble Georgian terrace offers attractive and stylish accommodation at a fair price. The rooms are very commodious, particularly the cute garret rooms with their coombed ceilings and good modern bathrooms. Substantially cheaper in low season.

Stirling Highland Hotel
HOTEL **£££**

(Map p190; ☎01786-272722; www.pumahotels.co.uk; Spittal St; r £130-190; **P**@🛜🏊) The unusual Stirling Highland Hotel is a sympathetic refurbishment of the old high school. The curious place still feels institutional in parts, but has great facilities that include pool, spa, gym, sauna and squash courts. It's very convenient for the castle and Old Town, service is helpful and the comfortably refitted rooms have decent beds, though they vary widely in size. Deluxe rooms offer the best views but aren't really worth the £50 upgrade. Prices are often lower than listed here.

Cairns Guest House
B&B **££**

(Map p190; ☎01786-479228; aquinn68@hotmail.co.uk; 12 Princes St; s/tw £35/60; 🛜) This central guest house gives decent value for simple comfort. The friendly, flexible, easygoing owners will offer discounts for stays of more than one night, or if you don't want breakfast.

Munro Guesthouse
B&B **££**

(Map p190; ☎01786-472685; www.munroguesthouse.co.uk; 14 Princes St; s/d/f £34/60/85; 🛜) Cosy and cheery, Munro Guesthouse is right in the centre of town, but located on a quiet side street. Things are done with a smile

here, and the smallish rooms are most inviting, particularly the cute attic ones. The breakfast is also better than the norm, with fruit salad on hand. There's easy (pay) parking opposite.

Colessio Hotel
HOTEL

(Map p190; ☎01786-448880; www.hotelcolessio.com; 33 Spittal St) This new luxury hotel and spa occupies an old hospital in the heart of the Old Town. It was still being built at time of research, but should be worth a look.

Witches Craig Caravan Park
CAMPSITE **£**

(☎01786-474947; www.witchescraig.co.uk; tent site for 1/2/2 plus car £9.50/11.50/18.50; ⊙Apr-Oct; **P**) In a brilliant spot, right at the foot of the Ochil Hills, which are just begging to be walked, Witches Craig is 3 miles east of Stirling by the A91.

🍴 Eating & Drinking

The Kitchen
BISTRO **££**

(Map p190; ☎01786-448833; www.thekitchenstirling.co.uk; 3 Friars St; mains £11-15) Likeable and laid-back on a central pedestrian street, this Stirling newcomer is doing things right. The small slate-floored dining area offers – in particular – excellent fish and seafood options with willing if slow service. It's worth booking ahead at weekends.

Portcullis
PUB **££**

(Map p190; ☎01786-472290; www.theportcullishotel.com; Castle Wynd; bar meals £8-12) Built in stone as solid as the castle that it stands below, this former school is just the spot for a pint and a pub lunch after your castle visit. With bar meals that would have had even William Wallace loosening his belt a couple of notches, a little beer garden and a cosy buzz indoors, it's well worth a visit; there are also rooms here (single/double £69/89).

🌿 Breá
CAFE **£**

(Map p190; www.breastirling.co.uk; 5 Baker St; mains £7-13; ⊙10am-9.30pm Tue-Sun; 🖭) Bringing a bohemian touch to central Stirling, this has pared-back contemporary decor and a short menu showcasing carefully sourced Scottish produce. Best in show is perhaps the pork burger with apple and black pudding – a huge thing with homemade bread.

Hermann's
AUSTRIAN, SCOTTISH **££**

(Map p190; ☎01786-450632; www.hermanns.co.uk; 58 Broad St; 2-course lunch/3-course dinner £13/22, mains £16-20) Solidly set on a corner above the Mercat Cross and below the castle, this elegant Scottish-Austrian restaurant is a reliable and popular choice. The solid, conservative decor is weirdly offset by magazine-style skiing photos, but the food doesn't miss a beat and ranges from Scottish favourites to gourmet schnitzel and spaetzle noodles. Vegetarian options are good, and quality Austrian wines provide an out-of-the-ordinary accompaniment.

Ibby's East India Company INDIAN £
(Map p190; www.eastindiastirling.co.uk; 7 Viewfield Pl; mains £7-10; ⊘5-11pm) This basement Indian restaurant is sumptuously decorated to resemble a ship's stateroom, with portraits of tea barons on the wall to conjure images of the days of the clippers. It offers dishes from all parts of India and you can BYO wine.

Mamma Mia ITALIAN ££
(Map p190; www.mammamiastirling.co.uk; 52 Spittal St; mains £12-17; ⊘5-10.30pm Mon-Sat) This Old Town split-level favourite has a short menu of southern Italian cuisine augmented by weekly specials, which are definitely worth going for. It shows a sure touch with sea bass and Scottish steaks alike, though it's hard not to feel the pasta dishes are a mite overpriced.

Darnley Coffee House CAFE £
(Map p190; ☑01786 474468; www.darnley.conn ectfree.co.uk; 18 Bow St; snacks £4-7; ⊘breakfast & lunch) Just down the hill from the castle, beyond the end of Broad St, this is a good pit stop for home baking and speciality coffees during a walk around the Old Town. The cafe is in the vaulted cellars of a 16th-century house where Darnley, lover and later husband of Mary, Queen of Scots, once stayed while visiting her.

Settle Inn PUB
(Map p190; ☑01786 474609; 91 St Mary's Wynd; ⊛) A warm welcome is guaranteed at Stirling's oldest pub (1733), a spot redolent with atmosphere, what with its log fire, vaulted back room and low-slung ceilings. Guest ales, atmospheric nooks for settling in for the night and a blend of local characters make it a classic of its kind.

❶ Information

Stirling Library (Corn Exchange Rd; ⊘Mon-Sat) Free internet access.

Stirling Community Hospital (☑01786-434000; Livilands Rd) South of the town centre.

Stirling Information Centre (☑01786-475019; www.visitscottishheartlands.com; St John St; ⊘10am-5pm)
At the entrance to the Old Town Jail below the castle.

❶ Getting There & Away

BUS The **bus station** (☑01786-446474) is on Goosecroft Rd. **Citylink** (☑0871 266 33 33; www.citylink.co.uk) offers a number of services to/from Stirling:

» **Dundee** £13, 1½ hours, hourly

» **Edinburgh** £7.50, one hour, hourly

» **Glasgow** £7, 40 minutes, hourly

» **Perth** £8.30, 50 minutes, at least hourly

Some buses continue to Aberdeen, Inverness and Fort William; more frequently a change will be required.

TRAIN First ScotRail (www.scotrail.co.uk) has services to/from a number of destinations, including the following:

» **Aberdeen** £43.30, 2¼ hours, hourly weekdays, every two hours Sunday

» **Dundee** £17.70, one hour, hourly weekdays, every two hours Sunday

» **Edinburgh** £7.70, 55 minutes, twice hourly Monday to Saturday, hourly Sunday

» **Glasgow** £8, 40 minutes, twice hourly Monday to Saturday, hourly Sunday

» **Perth** £11.70, 30 minutes, hourly weekdays, every two hours Sunday

Around Stirling

BRIDGE OF ALLAN
POP 5046

This upbeat former spa town, just 3 miles north of Stirling, has an open street plan, giving it a laid-back sense of space. It's a good alternative to staying in Stirling.

🛏 Sleeping & Eating

Adamo Hotel HOTEL ££
(☑01786-833268; www.adamohotels.com; 24 Henderson St; small s £70, d/ste £140/180, 2-course lunch/dinner £12.50/23.50; ⓟ⊛) The gorgeous, modern, plush rooms here have a dark and fuzzy decor that makes you want to get naked and have a good roll around. All rooms have car-wash showers, but only some come with a bath. The rooms are different sizes, so ask to see a selection. Ask about weekend specials, too, and even if you're not staying, drop in for lunch or dinner.

THE FALKIRK WHEEL

Scotland's canals were once vital avenues for goods transport, but the railway age left them to fall into dereliction. A millennium project restored two of Scotland's major canals, the Union and the Forth & Clyde. With a difference in level of 115ft, the two were once linked by an arduous series of 11 locks, but the construction of the unique Falkirk Wheel (www.thefalkirkwheel.co.uk; adult/child £7.95/4.95; ☉10am-5.30pm daily Mar-Oct, 11am-4pm Wed-Sun Nov-Feb) changed all that. Its rotating arms literally scoop boats up and lift them to the higher waterway – it's an engineering marvel that makes a compelling visit.

Boat trips leave every 40 minutes (hourly in winter) and travel into the wheel, which delivers you to the Union Canal high above. Boats then go through Roughcastle Tunnel before the return descent on the wheel. Anyone with an interest in engineering should not miss this boat ride – it's great for kids, too. There's also a visitor centre and cafe.

The Wheel is in Falkirk, a large town about 10 miles southeast of Stirling. Regular buses and trains link the two, and also connect Falkirk with Glasgow and Edinburgh.

Clive's   CAFE, DELI **££**
(www.clives.co.uk; 26 Henderson St; mains £9-15; ☉9am-9pm; 🛜) With a claim to 'sexy food', this little show pony also has a deli next door selling fresh local produce. The cafe has a very trendy vibe and seems to be the centre of the town's universe. Scrumptious treats drawing from several world cuisines won't break your budget.

ℹ Getting There & Away
You can walk to Bridge of Allan from Stirling in an hour. Frequent local buses from Stirling stop in Henderson St. Trains to Dunblane, Stirling, Glasgow and Edinburgh depart frequently from the station at the western end of Henderson St.

DUNBLANE
POP 7911

Dunblane, 5 miles northwest of Stirling, is a pretty town with a notable cathedral. It's difficult not to remember the horrific massacre that took place in the primary school in 1996, but happier headlines have come the town's way more recently with the rise of local tennis star Andy Murray.

Fabulous Dunblane Cathedral (HS; www.dunblanecathedral.org.uk; Cathedral Sq; admission free; ☉9.30am-5.30pm Mon-Sat Apr-Sep, 9.30am-4pm Mon-Sat & 2-4pm Sun Oct-Mar) is well worth a detour. It's a superb, elegant Gothic sandstone building. The lower parts of the walls date from Norman times, the rest mainly from the 13th to 15th centuries, though the bell tower stood alongside an earlier 12th-century structure. A 10th-century carved Celtic stone is at the nave's head, and a standing stone commemorates the town's slain children.

Just down from the cathedral, the musty old Leighton Library (www.leightonlibrary.co.uk; 61 High St; admission free; ☉11am-1pm Mon-Sat May-Sep), dating from 1684, is the oldest private library in Scotland. There are 4500 books in 90 languages.

You can walk to Bridge of Allan from Dunblane along Darn Rd in about an hour – it's an ancient path once used by monks. There are also frequent buses and trains from Stirling to Dunblane.

DOUNE
POP 1635

Doune is not far beyond Dunblane, on the road to Callander. Stop here to visit magnificent Doune Castle (HS; www.historic-scotland.gov.uk; adult/child £5/3; ☉9.30am-5.30pm Apr-Sep, to 4.30pm Oct-Mar, closed Thu-Fri Nov-Mar), one of the best-preserved 14th-century castles in Scotland. It was a favourite royal hunting lodge, but was also of great strategic importance because it controlled the route between the Lowlands and Highlands. Mary, Queen of Scots, stayed here, as did Bonnie Prince Charlie, who used it to imprison government troops. There are great **views** from the castle walls, and the lofty **gatehouse** is very impressive, rising nearly 30m. Some may recognise the castle from *Monty Python and the Holy Grail*.

Doune is 8 miles northwest of Stirling. First (www.firstgroup.com) buses every hour or two (30 minutes), less frequently on Sunday.

DOLLAR
POP 2877

Charming Dollar is about 11 miles east of Stirling in the lower Ochil Hills. Castle

Campbell (HS; www.historic-scotland.gov.uk; adult/child £5/3; ⊘9.30am-5.30pm Apr-Sep, to 4.30pm Oct, to 4.30pm Sat-Wed Nov-Mar) is a 20-minute walk up **Dollar Glen**, into the wooded hills above the town. It's a spooky old stronghold of the Dukes of Argyll and stands between two ravines; you can clearly see why it was known as 'Castle Gloom'. There's been a fortress of some kind on this site since the 11th century, but the present structure dates from the 15th century. The castle was sacked by Cromwell in 1654, but the tower is well preserved. From the little car park near the castle there's a great ramble with sweeping views over Castle Campbell and the surrounding country.

Regular buses run to Dollar from Stirling.

The Trossachs

The Trossachs region has long been a favourite weekend getaway, offering outstanding natural beauty and excellent walking and cycling routes within easy reach of the southern population centres. With thickly forested hills, romantic lochs and an increasingly interesting selection of places to stay and eat, its popularity is sure to continue, protected by its national-park status.

The Trossachs first gained popularity as a tourist destination in the early 19th century, when curious visitors came from all over Britain, drawn by the romantic language of Walter Scott's poem *Lady of the Lake*, inspired by Loch Katrine, and *Rob Roy*, about the derring-do of the region's most famous son.

In summer the Trossachs can be overburdened with coach tours, but many of these are day trippers – peaceful, long evenings

---

ⓘ **TROSSACHS TRANSPORT**

In a bid to cut public transport costs, 'Demand Responsive Transport' (DRT) now covers the Trossachs area. Sounds complex, but basically it means you get a taxi to where you want to go, for the price of a bus. There are various zones. Taxis run Monday to Saturday and should preferably be booked 24 hours in advance; call or text 0844-567 5670 between 7am and 7pm Monday to Saturday, or book online at www.aberfoylecoaches.com.

---

gazing at the reflections in the nearest loch are still possible. It's worth timing your visit not to coincide with a weekend.

ABERFOYLE & AROUND
POP 576

Crawling with visitors on most weekends and dominated by a huge car park, little Aberfoyle is a fairly uninteresting place, easily overwhelmed by day trippers. Callander or other Trossachs towns appeal more as places to stay, but Aberfoyle has lots to do close at hand. It's also a stop on the Rob Roy Way.

⊙ Sights & Activities

There are also some good (and not too busy) walking trails in the woods south of Loch Ard, west of town.

Inchmahome Priory   RUIN

(HS; www.historic-scotland.gov.uk; adult/child incl ferry £5/3; ⊘9.30am-5.30pm Apr-Sep, to 4.30pm Oct, last ferry to island 1hr before closing) From the **Lake of Menteith** (called lake not loch due to a mistranslation from Gaelic), 3 miles east of Aberfoyle, a ferry takes visitors to these substantial ruins. Mary, Queen of Scots, was kept safe here as a child during Henry VIII's 'Rough Wooing'. Henry attacked Stirling trying to force Mary to marry his son in order to unite the kingdoms.

FREE David Marshall

Lodge Visitor Centre   NATURE CENTRE

(www.forestry.gov.uk; car park £1-3; ⊘10am-4pm Oct-Mar, 10am-5pm Apr-Sep, to 6pm Jul & Aug) Half a mile north of Aberfoyle on the A821 is this nature centre in the Queen Elizabeth Forest Park, which has info about the many walks and cycle routes in and around the park. The Royal Society for the Protection of Birds (RSPB) has a display here on local bird life, the highlight being live video links to local osprey and buzzard nests. The centre is worth visiting solely for the views.

Several picturesque but busy waymarked trails start from here, ranging from a light 20-minute stroll to a nearby waterfall to a hilly 4-mile circuit. Also here, Go Ape! (www.goape.co.uk; adult/child £30/20; ⊘daily Apr-Oct, Wed-Mon Feb-Jun & Sep-Oct) will bring out the monkey in you on its exhilarating adventure course of long zip lines, swings and rope bridges through the forest.

Cycling   CYCLING

An excellent 20-mile circular cycle route links with the boat at Loch Katrine. From Aberfoyle, join the Lochs & Glens Cycle Way

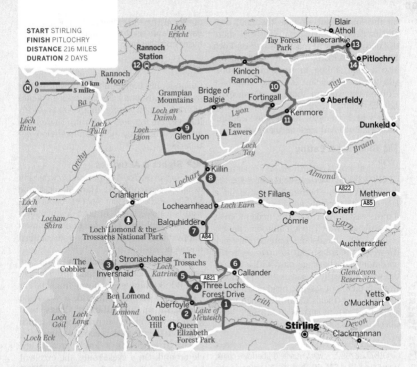

Driving Tour
Scenic Heartlands

> This drive takes in the best of the Trossachs region and some highlights of lovely Perthshire.

Head westwards from Stirling (A811), turning right at Arnprior (B8034), past scenic **1 Lake of Menteith**. Then head through **2 Aberfoyle** and along the B829, a beautiful drive past Loch Ard to the far tip of Loch Katrine and on down a rough road to the remotest banks of Loch Lomond at **3 Inversnaid**. From here you're going to have to retrace your route to Aberfoyle, but you might want to leave any passengers at Stronachlachar pier to get the 11.30am boat (April to October, also 3pm June to August) along Loch Katrine: you can pick them up later. They could also hike or bike the 12.5 miles.

Next take the A821 north past David Marshall Visitor Centre up to Dukes Pass. Off this road is the **4 Three Lochs Forest Drive**, a worthwhile 7.5-mile circuit (April to October, £2) through pine forest opening up to picturesque vistas. There are plenty of walks here to stretch your legs.

Next, turn left down to enchanting **5 Loch Katrine** (where you can pick up the strays), then head on to lovely **6 Callander**, a good overnight stop.

Leave Callander by the same road you entered, but keep straight on in Kilmahog, and on along Loch Lubnaig. Detour to **7 Balquhidder** to pay respects to Rob Roy's grave; you might continue down the single-track road to Monachyle Mhor for a coffee or posh lunch – the drive is worth it anyhow. Back on the main road, make for tranquil **8 Killin**, a great walking base.

From here, head for magnificent **9 Glen Lyon** via the remote, potholed road (unmarked on maps) through Glen Lochay. Take your time in one of Scotland's most majestic valleys before taking in **10 Fortingall** and **11 Kenmore**. Then head north again, and do the long loop around remote Loch Rannoch, making sure you get to the end of the road at **12 Rannoch Station**. Head back along the loch's north shore and on to Loch Tummel, the pass at **13 Killiecrankie** and, finally, pretty **14 Pitlochry**.

on the forest trail, or take the A821 over Duke's Pass. Following the southern shore of Loch Achray, you reach the pier on Loch Katrine. The 10.30am boat (p202); there's also a 2pm sailing in summer) can take you to Stronachlachar (one way with bike £16) on the western shore (or it's an extra 12 miles biking it along the northern shore), from where you can follow the beautiful B829 via Loch Ard back to Aberfoyle.

🛏 Sleeping & Eating

TOP CHOICE Lake of Menteith Hotel HOTEL £££
(☑01877-385258; www.lake-hotel.com; s £95-195, d £120-225; P 🛜) Soothingly situated on a lake (yes, it's the only non-loch in Scotland) 3 miles east of Aberfoyle, this makes a great romantic getaway. Though all rooms are excellent, with a handsome contemporary feel, it's worth the splash out to upgrade to the enormous 'lake heritage' ones with a view of the water: it really is a sensational outlook. Even if you're not staying, head down to the waterside bar (meals £8 to £10); there's also a good restaurant (mains £15 to £25) here. Check the website for packages.

Mayfield Guest House B&B £
(☑01877-382962; www.mayfield-aberfoyle.co.uk; Main St; s £40, d £55-60; P 🛜🐾) Nothing is too much trouble for the friendly hosts at this guest house. It has three compact, comfortable ground-floor rooms, all painted in cheerful colours and very well kept. It's bike and motorbike friendly, with a garage at the back.

Forth Inn PUB ££
(☑01877-382372; www.forthinn.com; Main St; mains £8-12; P 🛜🐾🐾) In the middle of the village, the solid Forth Inn is the lifeblood of the town, with locals and visitors alike queuing up for good, honest pub fare; the best bar meal in Aberfoyle. It also provides accommodation and beer, with drinkers spilling outside into the sunny courtyard. Single (£55) and double (£80 to £90) rooms are available, but they can be noisy at weekends.

ℹ Information

Aberfoyle Information Centre (☑01877-382352; www.visitscottishheartlands.com; Main St; ⊙10am-5pm Apr-Oct, 10am-4pm Nov-Mar) Large office with good selection of walking information.

ℹ Getting There & Away

First (www.firstgroup.com) has six daily buses (Monday to Saturday) from Stirling (40 min-

utes); you'll have to connect at Balfron on Sunday. There are also three Monday to Saturday buses from Glasgow.

CALLANDER
POP 2754

Callander has been pulling in the tourists for over 150 years, and has a laid-back ambience along its main thoroughfare that quickly lulls visitors into lazy pottering. There's also an excellent array of accommodation options here.

👁 Sights & Activities

The **Hamilton Toy Collection** (www.thehamiltontoycollection.co.uk; 111 Main St; adult/child £2/50p; ⊙10am-4.30pm Apr-Oct, opens noon Sun) is a powerhouse of 20th-century juvenile memorabilia, chock-full of dolls houses, puppets and toy soldiers. It's a guaranteed nostalgia trip.

The impressive **Bracklinn Falls** are reached by track and footpath from Bracklinn Rd (30 minutes each way from the car park). Also off Bracklinn Rd, a woodland trail leads up to **Callander Crags**, with great views over the surroundings; a return trip from the car park is about 4 miles.

The Trossachs is a lovely area to cycle around. On a cycle route, the excellent **Wheels Cycling Centre** (☑01877-331100; www.wheelscyclingcentre.com) has a wide range of hire bikes starting from £12/18 per half-/full day. To get there, take Bridge St off Main St, then turn right onto Invertrossachs Rd and continue for a mile.

🛏 Sleeping

TOP CHOICE Roman Camp Hotel HOTEL ££
(☑01877-330003; www.romancamphotel.co.uk; Main St; s/d/superior £100/155/195; P 🛜🐾) Callander's best hotel is centrally located but feels rural, set by the river in its own beautiful grounds, with birdsong the only sound. Its endearing features include a lounge with blazing fire and a library with a tiny secret chapel. It's an old-fashioned rabbit warren of a place with three grades of room; the standards are certainly luxurious, but the superior ones are even more appealing, with period furniture, excellent bathrooms, armchairs and a fireplace. The upmarket restaurant is open to the public. Reassuringly, the name refers not to toga parties but to a ruin in the adjacent fields.

Abbotsford Lodge B&B ££
(☑01877-330066; www.abbotsfordlodge.com; Stirling Rd; s/d £50/85; ⊙mid-Feb–mid-Dec; P 🛜)

This friendly Victorian house offers something different to the norm, with tartan and florals consigned to the bonfire, replaced by stylish, comfortable contemporary design that enhances the building's original features. Ruffled fabrics and ceramic vases with flower arrangements characterise the renovated rooms. There are fabulous superiors with bathrobes and big beds with great mattresses (£125) as well as cheaper top-floor rooms that share a bathroom (doubles £55), but have lovably offbeat under-roof shapes. It's on the main road on the eastern side of town.

Roslin Cottage B&B ££

(☎01877-339787; www.roslincottage.co.uk; Stirling Rd; s £40-50, d £60-70; P 🛜) A characterful cottage that's a haven of good hospitality holds three snug en suite rooms that make an enticing Trossachs base. They all have charm: we love the Kirtle room with the original 17th-century wall exposed. Other delights include a lovely big back garden, a log fire in the lounge and sociable chef-cooked breakfasts. It's on the right as you enter Callander from the east, before the petrol station.

Arden House B&B ££

(☎01877-330235; www.ardenhouse.org.uk; Bracklinn Rd; s/d £45/75; P 🛜) This elegant home has a woodsy, hillside location close to the centre but far from the crowds. The commodious rooms include a suite (£90) with great views. New owners will be in place by the time you read this, but it should definitely still be worth a look.

Callander Meadows B&B ££

(☎01877-330181; www.callandermeadows.co.uk; 24 Main St; s £45, d £75-85) Upstairs at this restaurant are three very appealing rooms, elegantly kitted out with dark-varnished furnishings and striped wallpaper (one has a four-poster bed).

White Shutters B&B £

(☎01877-330442; www.incallander.co.uk/whiteshutters.htm; 6 South Church St; s/d £24/42) A cute little house just off the main street, White Shutters offers pleasing rooms with shared bathroom and a friendly welcome. The mattresses aren't exactly new, but it's comfortable and offers great value for this part of the world.

Linley Guest House B&B ££

(☎01877-330087; www.linleyguesthouse.co.uk; 139 Main St; s/d £33/46, d ensuite £50) A spick-and-span B&B with bright rooms and helpful owners. The double en suite is worth the extra: it's beautifully appointed with a large window drawing in lots of natural light. Room-only rate available.

Eating & Drinking

Callander Meadows SCOTTISH ££

(☎01877-330181; www.callandermeadows.co.uk; 24 Main St; lunch £8.95, mains £11-18; ⊙Thu-Sun) Informal but smart, this well-loved restaurant in the centre of Callander occupies the two front rooms of a house on the main street. There's a contemporary flair for presentation and unusual flavour combinations, but a solidly British base underpins the cuisine, with things like mackerel, red cabbage, salmon and duck making regular and welcome appearances. There's a great daytime beer/coffee garden out the back, and the restaurant is also open on Mondays from April to September, and daily in high summer.

Poppies SCOTTISH ££

(☎01877-330329; www.poppies.com; Leny Rd; lunch mains £9-10, dinner mains £12-19; 🛜) This is the restaurant of a small main-road hotel, and offers high-class cuisine based on rigorously-sourced quality Scottish meat and fish in an elegant dining space. It's a friendly place whose atmosphere is more quiet clinks of cutlery than belches and belly-laughs. There's a good-value early-dining special.

Mhor Fish SEAFOOD ££

(☎01877-330213; www.mhor.net; 75 Main St; fish supper £6, mains £8-14; ⊙noon-9pm Tue-Sun) Both chip shop and fish restaurant, but wholly different, this endearing black-and-white-tiled cafe displays the day's fresh catch. You can choose how you want it cooked, whether pan-seared and accompanied by one of many good wines, or fried and wrapped in paper with chips to take away. The fish and seafood comes from sustainable stock, and includes oysters and other goodies. If they run out of fresh fish, they shut, so opening hours can be a bit variable.

Mhor Bread CAFE, BAKERY £

(www.mhor.net; 8 Main St; light meals £2-6; ⊙7am-5pm Mon-Sat, 8am-5pm Sun) Great bread for picnics is baked at this high-street spot, also a good stop for decent coffee and tasty pies and filled rolls.

Lade Inn PUB
(www.theladeinn.com; Kilmahog; 🍴) Callander's best pub isn't in Callander – it's a mile west of town. They pull a good pint here (the real ales here are brewed to a house recipe), and next door, the owners run a shop with a dazzling selection of Scottish beers. There's low-key live music here at weekends, but it shuts early midweek. The food at last visit was overpriced and mediocre.

ℹ Information

Loch Lomond & the Trossachs National Park Visitor Centre (☑01389-722600; www.lochlomond-trossachs.org; 52 Main St; ⊙9.30am-3.30pm Mon & Wed-Thu, 9.30am-4.30pm Tue & Fri) This place is a useful centre for specific information on the park. Closes half an hour for lunch.

Rob Roy & Trossachs Information Centre (☑01877-330342; www.visitscottishheart lands.com; Ancaster Sq; ⊙10am-5pm Apr-Oct, 10am-4pm Nov-Mar) This centre has heaps of info on the area. There's a 20-minute film on Rob Roy that costs £1.50.

ℹ Getting There & Away

First (☑0871 200 2233; www.firstgroup.com) operates buses from Stirling (45 minutes, hourly Monday to Saturday, every two hours Sunday), while **Kingshouse** (☑01877-384768; www.kingshousetravel.com) buses run from Killin (45 minutes, two to six daily). For Aberfoyle, get off a Stirling-bound bus at Blair Drummond safari park and cross the road. There are also **Citylink** (www.citylink.co.uk) buses from Edinburgh to Oban or Fort William via Callander (£15.60, 1¾ hours, two daily).

LOCHS KATRINE & ACHRAY

This rugged area, 6 miles north of Aberfoyle and 10 miles west of Callander, is the heart of the Trossachs. From April to October two **boats** (☑01877-376315; www.lochkatrine.com; Trossachs Pier; 1hr cruise adult/child £12/8) run cruises from Trossachs Pier at the eastern tip of Loch Katrine. One of these is the fabulous centenarian steamship *Sir Walter Scott*; check the website to see which boats depart when, as it's worth going on the veteran if you can. They run various one-hour afternoon sailings, and at 10.30am (and 2pm from June to August) there's a departure to Stronachlachar at the other end of the loch before returning (single/return adult £13/15.50, child £8/9.50, two hours return). From Stronachlachar (also accessible by car via Aberfoyle), you can reach the eastern shore of Loch Lomond at isolated Inversnaid. A tarmac path links Trossachs Pier with Stronachlachar, so you can also take the boat out and walk/cycle back (12.5 miles). At Trossachs Pier you can hire good bikes from Katrinewheelz (www.wheelscy clingcentre.com; hire per half-/full day from £8/12; ⊙daily Apr-Oct). It even has electric buggies (from £20) for the less mobile or inclined. Also at Trossachs Pier is Brenachoile Cafe (light meals £4-9, dinner £16.50; ⊙9am-10pm Apr-Oct), offering great views from the dining area and the garden, sandwiches and baked tatties during the day and a good-value three-course evening menu.

There are two good **walks** starting from nearby Loch Achray. The path to the rocky cone called **Ben A'an** (460m) begins at a car park just east of the Loch Katrine turn-off. It's easy to follow and the return trip is just under 4 miles (allow 2½ hours). A tougher walk is up rugged **Ben Venue** (727m) – there is a path all the way to the summit. Start walking from the signed car park just south of the Loch Katrine turn-off. The return trip is 7.5 miles – allow around five to six hours.

BALQUHIDDER & AROUND

North of Callander, you'll skirt past the shores of gorgeous Loch Lubnaig. Not as famous as some of its cousins, it's still well worth a stop for its sublime views of forested hills. In the small village of **Balquhidder** (ball-whidder), 9 miles north of Callander off the A84, there's a churchyard with **Rob Roy's grave**. It's an appropriately beautiful spot in a deep, winding glen in big-sky country. In the church is the 8th-century **St Angus' stone**, probably a marker to the original tomb of St Angus, an 8th-century monk who built the first church here.

Monachyle Mhor (☑01877-384622; www.mhor.net; d £195-265; ⊙Feb-Dec; P🔊🐕), 4 miles on, is a luxury hideaway with a fantastically peaceful location overlooking two lochs. It's a great fusion of country Scotland and contemporary attitudes to design and food. The rooms are superb and feature quirkily original decor, particularly the fabulous 'feature rooms'; you might get your own steam room or a wonderful double bathtub. The restaurant serves à la carte lunches and five-course dinners (£50), which are high in quality, sustainably sourced and deliciously innovative. Enchantment lies in its successful combination of top-class hospitality with a relaxed rural atmosphere; dogs and kids happily romp on the lawns, and no one

ROB ROY

Nicknamed Red ('*ruadh*' in Gaelic, anglicised to 'roy') for his ginger locks, Robert MacGregor (1671–1734) was the wild leader of the wildest of Scotland's clans. Although they had rights to the lands the clan occupied, these estates stood between powerful neighbours who had the MacGregors outlawed, hence their sobriquet, Children of the Mist. Incognito, Rob became a prosperous livestock trader, before a dodgy deal led to a warrant for his arrest.

A legendary swordsman, the fugitive from justice then became notorious for his daring raids into the Lowlands to carry off cattle and sheep. He was forever hiding from potential captors; he was twice imprisoned, but escaped dramatically on both occasions. He finally turned himself in and received his liberty and a pardon from the king. He lies buried in the churchyard at Balquhidder; his uncompromising epitaph reads 'MacGregor despite them'. His life has been glorified over the years due to Walter Scott's novel and the 1995 film. Many Scots see his life as a symbol of the struggle of the common folk against the inequitable ownership of vast tracts of the country by landed aristocrats.

looks askance if you come in flushed and muddy after a day's fishing or walking.

Local buses between Callander and Killin stop at the main road turn-off to Balquhidder, as do daily Citylink (www.citylink.co.uk) buses between Edinburgh and Oban/Fort William.

KILLIN
POP 666

A fine base for the Trossachs or Perthshire, this lovely village sits at the western end of Loch Tay and has a spread-out, relaxed sort of feel, particularly around the scenic **Falls of Dochart**, which tumble through the centre. On a sunny day people sprawl over the rocks by the bridge, pint or picnic in hand. Killin offers some fine walking around the town, and mighty mountains and glens close at hand.

🏃 Activities

Five miles northeast of Killin, **Ben Lawers** (1214m) rises above Loch Tay. Other routes abound; one rewarding **circular walk** heads up into the Acharn forest south of town, emerging above the treeline to great views of Loch Tay and Ben Lawers. The tourist office has walking leaflets and maps covering the area.

Glen Lochay runs westwards from Killin into the hills of Mamlorn. You can take a **mountain bike** up the glen; the scenery is impressive and the hills aren't too difficult. It's possible, on a nice summer day, to climb over the top of **Ben Challum** (1025m) and descend to Crianlarich, but it's hard work. A potholed road also connects Glen Lochay with Glen Lyon.

Killin is on the Lochs & Glens Cycle Way from Glasgow to Inverness. Hire bikes at Killin Outdoor Centre (☏01567-820652; www.killinoutdoor.co.uk; Main St; bike for 24hr £20; ⊙daily). It also hires out canoes and kayaks (from £20).

🛏 Sleeping & Eating

Fairview House   B&B **££**
(☏01567-820667; www.fairview-killin.co.uk; Main St; s £32, d £60-70; P🐾🛜) Very cosy rooms, all with en suite or private bathroom, and very fair prices characterise this handsome and cordial central guest house. There's a pleasant guest lounge, drying room and bike shed. The name doesn't lie; there are lovely perspectives over the surrounding hills from many of the rooms.

High Creagan   CAMPSITE **£**
(☏01567-820449; Aberfeldy Rd; tent/caravan sites per person £5/8; ⊙Mar-Oct) This place has a well-kept, sheltered campsite with plenty of grass set high on the slopes overlooking sparkling Loch Tay, 3 miles east of Killin. Kids under five years of age aren't allowed in the tent area as there's a stream running through it.

⌖ Falls of Dochart Inn   PUB **££**
(☏01567-820270; www.falls-of-dochart-inn.co.uk; mains £10-13; P🛜) In a prime position overlooking the falls, this is a terrific pub, a snug, atmospheric space with a roaring fire, personable service and really satisfying, great-value food, ranging from light meals to tasty, tender steaks and a couple of more advanced creations. The rooms (single/double from £60/80) are handsome but a few

glitches like poor heating let some of them down.

❶ Getting There & Away

Two daily **Citylink** (www.citylink.co.uk) buses between Edinburgh and Oban/Fort William stop here; two buses from Dundee to Oban also pass through. These buses stop in Crianlarich among other places. Kingshouse (p202) runs buses to Callander, where you can change to a Stirling service.

FIFE

Protruding like a serpent's head from Scotland's east coast, Fife (www.visitfife.com) is a tongue of land between the Firths of Forth and Tay. A royal history and atmosphere distinct from the rest of Scotland leads it to style itself as 'The Kingdom of Fife'.

Though overdeveloped southern Fife is commuter-belt territory, the eastern region's rolling green farmland and quaint fishing villages are prime turf for exploration and crab crunching, and the fresh sea air feels like it's doing a power of good. Fife's biggest attraction, St Andrews, has Scotland's most venerable university and a wealth of historic buildings. It's also, of course, the headquarters of golf and draws professionals and keen slashers alike to take on the Old Course – the classic links experience.

 Activities

The Fife Coastal Path (www.fifecoastalpath.co.uk) runs more than 80 miles, following the entire Fife coastline from the Forth Road Bridge to the Tay Bridge and beyond. It's well waymarked, picturesque and not too rigorous, though winds can buffet. It's easily accessed for shorter sections or day walks, and long stretches of it can also be tackled on a mountain bike.

❶ Getting Around

The main bus operator here is **Stagecoach Fife** (☑0871-2002233; www.stagecoachbus.com). For £7.50 you can buy a Fife Dayrider ticket, which gives unlimited travel around Fife on Stagecoach buses.

If you are driving from the Forth Road Bridge to St Andrews, a slower but much more scenic route than the M90/A91 is along the signposted **Fife Coastal Tourist Route**.

Culross

POP 500

An enchanting little town, Culross (koo-ross) is Scotland's best-preserved example of a 17th-century Scottish burgh: the National Trust for Scotland owns 20 of the town's buildings, including the palace. Small, red-tiled, whitewashed buildings line the cobbled streets, and the winding Back Causeway to the abbey is embellished with whimsical stone cottages.

As birthplace of St Mungo, Glasgow's patron saint, Culross was an important religious centre from the 6th century. The burgh developed, under laird George Bruce, by mining coal through extraordinary underwater tunnels. When mining was ended by flooding of the tunnels, the town switched to making linen and shoes.

Culross Palace (NTS; www.nts.org.uk; adult/child £9.50/7; ☺noon-5pm Thu-Mon Apr-May & Sep, noon-5pm daily Jun-Aug, noon-4pm Fri-Mon Oct) is more a large house than a palace, and features extraordinary decorative painted woodwork, barrel-vaulted ceilings and an interior largely unchanged since the early 17th century. The **Town House** (tourist office downstairs) and the **Study**, also completed in the early 17th century, are open to the public (via guided tour, included in palace admission), but the other NTS properties can only be viewed from the outside.

Ruined Culross Abbey (HS; www.historic-scotland.gov.uk; admission free; ☺9.30am-7pm Mon-Sat & 2-7pm Sun Apr-Sep, 9.30am-4pm Mon-Sat & 2-4pm Sun Oct-Mar), founded by the Cistercians in 1217, is on the hill in a lovely peaceful spot with vistas of the firth. Part of the ruins were converted into the parish

---

WORTH A TRIP

DEEP SEA WORLD

If the kids are tiring of historic buildings, a trip to Deep Sea World (www.deepseaworld.com; North Queensferry; adult/child £13/8.75; ☺10am-5pm Mon-Fri, 10am-6pm Sat & Sun) might make them feel more kindly towards Fife. Situated at North Queensferry, just by the Forth bridges, it's a blockbuster aquarium with all those 'respect' species like sharks and piranhas, as well as seals and touch pools with rays and other sea creatures. You can even arrange guided dives with sharks. It's a little cheaper if you pre-purchase tickets online.

church in the 16th century; it's worth a peek inside for the stained glass and the Gothic Argyll tomb.

Above a pottery workshop near the palace, **Biscuit Café** (www.culrosspottery.com; light meals £3-6; ⊙10am-5pm Mon-Sat, 11am-5pm Sun) has a tranquil little garden and sells coffee, tempting organic cakes and scones and tasty light meals.

Culross is 12 miles west of the Forth Road Bridge. **Stagecoach** (www.stagecoachbus.com) bus 78 runs to Culross from Dunfermline (25 minutes, hourly daily) and to Stirling (50 minutes, hourly Monday to Saturday).

Dunfermline

POP 39,229

Historic, monastic Dunfermline is Fife's largest population centre, sprawling eastwards through once-distinct villages. Its noble history is centred on evocative **Dunfermline Abbey** (HS; www.historic-scotland.gov.uk; St Margaret St; adult/child £3.70/2.20; ⊙9.30am-5.30pm daily Apr-Sep, to 4.30pm Oct, 9.30am-4.30pm Sat-Wed Nov-Mar), founded by David I in the 12th century as a Benedictine monastery. Dunfermline was already favoured by religious royals; Malcolm III married the exiled Saxon princess Margaret here in the 11th century, and both chose to be interred here. There were many more royal burials, none more notable than Robert the Bruce, whose remains were discovered here in 1818.

What's left of the abbey are the **ruins** of the impressive three-tiered refectory building, and the atmosphere-laden nave of the church, endowed with geometrically patterned columns and fine Romanesque and Gothic windows. It adjoins the 19th-century **church** (⊙May-Sep) where Robert the Bruce lies under the ornate pulpit.

Next to the refectory (and included in your abbey admission price) is **Dunfermline Palace**. Once the abbey guest house, it was converted for James VI, whose son, the ill-fated Charles I, was born here in 1600. Below stretches the bosky, strollable **Pittencrieff Park**.

The excellent **Abbot House Heritage Centre** (www.abbothouse.co.uk; Maygate; adult/child £4/free; ⊙9.30am-5pm Mon-Sat Mar-Oct, 10am-4pm Mon-Sat Nov-Feb), near the abbey, dates from the 15th century. History buffs could get lost for hours among the absorbing displays about the history of Scotland,

the abbey and Dunfermline. Entry includes a guided tour.

Dunfermline is a culinary desert, but the good folk at **Fresh** (2 Kirkgate; light meals £4-7; ⊙9am-5pm Mon-Sat, 10.30am-5pm Sun; 🛜), just up from the abbey, do decent sandwiches and coffee, as well as tasty daily specials based on deli produce. There's also wine, internet access, a gallery and book exchange.

There are frequent buses between Dunfermline and Edinburgh (£5.05, 40 minutes), Stirling (£9.95, 1¼ hours) and St Andrews (£9.95, 1¼ hours), and trains to/from Edinburgh (30 minutes).

Aberdour

POP 1690

It's worth stopping in this popular seaside town to ramble around impressive **Aberdour Castle** (HS; www.historic-scotland.gov.uk; adult/child £5/3; ⊙9.30am-5.30pm Apr-Sep, to 4.30pm Oct, 9.30am-4.30pm Sat-Wed Nov-Mar). Long a residence of the Douglases of Morton, the stately structure exhibits several architectural phases; it's worth purchasing the guidebook to better comprehend what you see. Most charming of all is the elaborate *doocot* (dovecote) in the garden. Be sure to pop into the beautiful Romanesque church of **St Fillan's**, next door to the castle.

It's difficult to imagine a more enchanting setting than that enjoyed by the **Forth View Hotel** (☎01383-860402; www.forthviewhotel.co.uk; Hawkcraig Point; s £45-65, d £65-95; ⊙Apr-Oct; 🅿🛜), a friendly B&B right on the water in a secluded location. The front rooms offer utterly fabulous views through huge windows across the firth to Edinburgh and the hospitality is most welcoming. Happily, there's also an excellent little seafood restaurant, **Room with a View** (www.roomwithaviewrestaurant.co.uk; lunch mains £10-13, dinner mains £14-19; ⊙lunch Wed-Sun, dinner Wed-Sat), in the front room. It's tough to find the place – part of its charm; follow signs for Silver Sands beach, go through the car park and down a steep narrow lane on the other side.

With real ales and good vegetarian choices on the menu, the family-run **Aberdour Hotel** (☎01383-860325; www.aberdourhotel.co.uk; 38 High St; s/d £65/85; 🅿🛜🐾) on the main road through town is not only a good place to stay, but also a tummy-warming meal stop (mains £8 to £12), and there's an emphasis on hearty, home-cooked food.

There are regular trains to Edinburgh (40 minutes) and Dundee (one hour) from Aberdour, as well as buses to nearby Dunfermline (40 minutes).

Kirkcaldy

POP 46,912

Kirkcaldy (ker-*caw*-dee) sprawls along the edge of the sea for several miles and has a rather shabby promenade with spectacular pounding surf on windy days. It's worth stopping in town to visit the excellent museum. Kirkcaldy is famous as the birthplace of 18th-century Enlightenment philosopher and economist Adam Smith, the man who features on the English £20 note.

A short walk east from the train and bus stations, you'll find the Kirkcaldy Museum & Art Gallery (War Memorial Gardens; admission free; ☺10.30am-5pm Mon-Sat, 2-5pm Sun), hopefully reopened after extensive remodelling. The kids will have a ball as there are plenty of hands-on attractions; there's also an impressive collection of **Scottish paintings** from the 18th to the 20th century, including work from the Scottish Colourists and the Glasgow Boys.

The tourist office (☎01592-267775; www.visitfife.com; 339 High St; ☺10am-5pm Mon-Sat Apr-Sep, 10am-4pm Mon-Sat Oct-Mar) is at the eastern end of the waterfront strip.

Frequent buses run to St Andrews (£5.60, one hour), Anstruther (1¼ hours) and Edinburgh (£5.60, one hour). Two to four trains an hour run to Edinburgh (£7.10, 45 minutes) and Dundee (£11.90, 40 minutes).

Falkland

POP 1183

Below the soft ridges of the Lomond Hills in the centre of Fife is the charming village of Falkland. Rising majestically out of the town centre is outstanding 16th-century Falkland Palace (NTS; www.nts.org.uk; adult/child £11.50/8.50; ☺11am-5pm Mon-Sat, 1-5pm Sun Mar-Oct), a country residence of the Stuart monarchs. Mary, Queen of Scots, is said to have spent the happiest days of her life 'playing the country girl in the woods and parks' at Falkland. The palace was built between 1501 and 1541 to replace a castle dating from the 12th century; French and Scottish craftspeople were employed to create a masterpiece of Scottish Gothic architecture. The **king's bedchamber** and the **chapel**, with its beautiful painted ceiling, have both been restored. Don't miss the prodigious 17th-century Flemish hunting **tapestries** in the hall. One feature of the royal leisure centre still exists: the oldest **royal tennis court** in Britain, built in 1539 for James V. It's in the grounds and still in use.

Falkland is 11 miles north of Kirkcaldy. Bus 36 travels between Glenrothes and Auchtermuchty via Falkland. From either of those two places there are regular connections to St Andrews and other Fife destinations. Buses continue on to Perth (one hour) more or less hourly.

St Andrews

POP 14,209

For a small place, St Andrews made a big name for itself, firstly as religious centre, then as Scotland's oldest university town. But its status as the home of golf has propelled it to even greater fame, and today's pilgrims arrive with a set of clubs. But it's a lovely place to visit even if you've no interest in the game, with impressive medieval ruins, stately university buildings, idyllic white sands and excellent accommodation and eating options.

The Old Course, the world's most famous, has a striking seaside location at the western end of town. It's a thrilling experience to stroll the hallowed turf.

History

St Andrews is said to have been founded by St Regulus, who arrived from Greece in the 4th century bringing the bones of St Andrew, Scotland's patron saint. The town soon grew into a major pilgrimage centre and St Andrews developed into the ecclesiastical capital of the country. The university, the first in Scotland, was founded in 1410.

Golf has been played here for more than 600 years; the game's governing body was founded here in 1754 and the imposing Royal & Ancient clubhouse was built 100 years later.

◉ Sights

St Andrews Cathedral   RUIN
(HS; Map p208; www.historic-scotland.gov.uk; The Pends; adult/child £4.50/2.70, incl castle £7.60/4.60; ☺9.30am-5.30pm Apr-Sep, to 4.30pm Oct-Mar) The ruins of this cathedral are all that's left of one of Britain's most magnificent medieval buildings. You can appreciate the scale and majesty of the edifice from the small sections

that remain standing. Although founded in 1160, it was not consecrated until 1318, but stood as the focus of this important pilgrimage centre until 1559, when it was pillaged during the Reformation.

St Andrew's supposed bones lie under the altar; until the cathedral was built, they had been enshrined in the nearby Church of St Regulus (Rule). All that remains of this church is **St Rule's Tower**, worth the climb for the view across St Andrews. There's also a **museum** with a collection of Celtic crosses and gravestones found on the site. The entrance fee only applies for the tower and museum; you can wander freely around the atmospheric ruins, a fine picnic spot.

St Andrews Castle   CASTLE
(HS; Map p208; www.historic-scotland.gov.uk; The Scores; adult/child £5.50/3.30, with cathedral £7.60/4.60; ☺9.30am-5.30pm Apr-Sep, to 4.30pm Oct-Mar) With dramatic coastline views, the castle is mainly in ruins, but the site itself is evocative. It was founded around 1200 as the bishop's fortified home. After the execution of Protestant reformers in 1545, other reformers retaliated by murdering Cardinal Beaton and taking over the castle. They spent almost a year holed up, during which they and their attackers dug a complex of **siege tunnels**; you can walk (or stoop) along their damp mossy lengths. A tourist office gives a good audiovisual introduction and has a small collection of Pictish stones.

The Scores   STREET
From the castle, the Scores follows the coast west down to the first tee at the Old Course. Family-friendly **St Andrews Aquarium** (Map p208; www.standrewsaquarium.co.uk; adult/child £8/6; ☺10am-5pm Mar-Oct, to 4.30pm Nov-Feb; 🐾) has a seal pool, rays and sharks from Scottish waters and exotic tropical favourites. Once introduced to our finny friends, you can snack on them with chips in the cafe.

Nearby, the **British Golf Museum** (Map p208; www.britishgolfmuseum.co.uk; Bruce Embankment; adult/child £6/3; ☺9.30am-5pm Mon-Sat, 10am-5pm Sun Apr-Oct, 10am-4pm Nov-Mar) has an extraordinarily comprehensive overview of the history and development of the game and the role of St Andrews in it. Favourite fact: bad players were formerly known as 'foozlers'. Interactive panels allow you to relive former British Opens (watch Paul Azinger snapping his putter in frustration), and

PLAYING THE OLD COURSE

Golf has been played at St Andrews since the 15th century. By 1457 it was so popular that James II placed a ban on it because it interfered with his troops' archery practice. Although it lies beside the exclusive, all-male-membership Royal & Ancient Golf Club, the Old Course (Map p208; ☑ info 466666; www.standrews.org.uk; Reservations Office, St Andrews Links Trust) is public.

You'll need to book in advance to play via St Andrews Links Trust (☑01334-466666; www.standrews.org.uk). Reservations open on the first Wednesday in September the year before you wish to play. No bookings are taken for Saturdays or the month of September.

Unless you've booked months in advance, getting a tee-off time is literally a lottery; enter the ballot at the caddie office (Map p208; ☑01334-466666) before 2pm two days before you wish to play (there's no Sunday play). Be warned that applications by ballot are normally heavily oversubscribed, and green fees are £150 in summer. Singles are not accepted in the ballot and should start queuing as early as possible on the day – 5am is good – in the hope of joining a group. You'll need a handicap certificate (24/36 for men/women). If your number doesn't come up, there are six other public courses in the area (book up to seven days in advance on 01334-466718, no handicap required), including the prestigious Castle Course (£120). Other summer green fees: New £70, Jubilee £70, Eden £40, Strathtyrum £25 and Balgove (nine-holer for beginners and kids) £12. There are various multiple-day tickets available. A caddie for your round costs £45 plus tip. If you play on a windy day, expect those scores to balloon: Nick Faldo famously stated, 'When it blows here, even the seagulls walk'.

Guided walks (£2.50) of the Old Course run Tuesday to Sunday in July and August, and hit famous landmarks such as the Swilcan Bridge and the Road Hole bunker. They run from outside the shop by the 18th green at 11am and 1.30pm and last 50 minutes. On Sunday, a three-hour walk (£5) takes you around the whole course. You are free to walk over the course on Sunday, or follow the footpaths around the edge at any time.

St Andrews

200 m
0.1 miles

North Sea

St Andrews Bay

Old Course

St Andrews Castle

St Andrews Cathedral

The Pends

North Castle St

South Castle St

Abbey St

South St

West Burn La

Butts Wynd

College St

Church St

Mercat Cross

Holy Trinity Church

Church Sq

Queen's Gdns

Market St

Bell St

Greyfriars Gdn

North St

Murray Park

Murray Pl

Playfair Tce

The Scores

Golf Pl

The Links

Pilmour Pl

Hope St

City Rd

Station Rd

St Mary's Pl

Doubledykes Rd

Kinburn Park

West Port (Old Gate)

Louden's Cl

Argyle St

To West Sands (250m)

To Old Course Hotel (450m);
Leuchars Train Station (5mi);
Dundee (13mi)

To New Hall (250m)

To David Russell Hall (700m)

To Meade B&B (400m)

To Abbey Cottage (400m)

1 2 3 4 5 6 7 8 9 10 11 12 13 14 15 16 17 18 19 20 21 22 23 24 25 26 27 28 29 30 31 32 33 34 35

St Andrews

⊚ Top Sights
Old Course		B1
St Andrews Castle		F2
St Andrews Cathedral		F3

⊚ Sights
1	British Golf Museum	B1
2	Royal & Ancient Golf Club	B1
3	St Andrews Aquarium	C1
4	St Andrews Cathedral Museum	F4
5	St Andrews Museum	A3
6	St Rule's Tower	G3

⊕ Activities, Courses & Tours
7	Caddie Office	B1
8	Fairways of St Andrews	B2
9	Old Course	B1
10	Spokes	E3

⊜ Sleeping
11	Aslar House	D3
12	Burness House	C2
13	Cameron House	C2
14	Five Pilmour Place	B2
15	Ogstons on North Street	C2
16	Lorimer House	C2
17	McIntosh Hall	B2
18	Old Fishergate House	F3
19	Six Murray Park	C2
20	St Andrews Tourist Hostel	C3

⊗ Eating
21	B Jannetta	E3
22	Balaka	B3
23	Doll's House	D3
	Grill House	(see 20)
24	Kerachers	E3
25	Seafood Restaurant	C1
26	The Café in the Square	D3
27	The Glass House	D3
28	The Tailend	C3
29	Vine Leaf	D4

⊝ Drinking
30	Central Bar	D3
31	Vic	C3
32	West Port	B4

⊕ Entertainment
33	Byre Theatre	E4
34	New Picture House	C2

⊜ Shopping
35	IJ Mellis	C4

there's a large collection of memorabilia from Open winners, both male and female.

Opposite the museum is the **Royal & Ancient Golf Club**, which stands proudly at the head of the Old Course (p207). Beside it stretches magnificent **West Sands** beach, made famous by the film *Chariots of Fire*.

🖉 **St Andrews Museum**　　MUSEUM
(Map p208; www.fifedirect.org.uk/museums; Doubledykes Rd; admission free; ⊙10am-5pm Apr-Sep, 10.30am-4pm Oct-Mar) Near the bus station, St Andrews Museum has interesting displays that chart the history of the town from its founding by St Regulus to its growth as an ecclesiastical, academic and sporting centre.

🏃 Activities

Apart from the obvious one – **golf** – the tourist office has a list of local **walks** and also sells OS maps. The Fife Coastal Path (p204) section between St Andrews and the East Neuk is fun, either on foot or mountain bike. Parts of the track can be covered by the tide, so check tide times before you go. The tourist office has a detailed map. All the East Neuk attractions are within easy **cycling** distance.

🎉 Festivals & Events

Open Championship　　GOLF
(www.theopen.com; ⊙Jul) One of international golf's four majors, this takes place in July. However, the tournament venue changes from year to year, and the Open only comes to St Andrews itself every five years (next in 2015) – check the website for future venues.

St Andrews Festival　　ARTS FESTIVAL
(www.standrewsfestival.co.uk; ⊙Nov) Five days of festivities leading up to St Andrews Day (30 November), the feast day of Scotland's patron saint. Celebrations include a festival of Scottish food and drink, and various arts events.

🛏 Sleeping

St Andrews' accommodation is overpriced and often heavily booked (especially in summer), so reserve in advance. Almost every house on super-central Murray Park and Murray Pl is a guest house.

TOP CHOICE **Abbey Cottage** B&B **££**

(☎01334-473727; coull@lineone.net; Abbey Walk; s £45, d £65-70; **P**🐾) You know you've strayed from B&B mainstream when your charming host's hobby is photographing tigers in the wild – don't leave without browsing her albums. This engaging spot sits below the town, surrounded by stone walls that enclose a rambling garden; it feels like you're staying in the country. There are three excellent rooms, all different, with patchwork quilts, sheepskins and antique furniture.

Fairways of St Andrews B&B **££**

(Map p208; ☎01334-479513; www.fairwaysofstandrews.co.uk; 8A Golf Place; s £80-120, d £90-150; 🐾) Just around the corner from golf's most famous 18th green, this is more of a boutique hotel than a B&B. There are just three super-stylish rooms; the best on the top floor is huge and has its own balcony with views over the Old Course.

Old Course Hotel HOTEL **£££**

(☎01334-474371; www.oldcoursehotel.co.uk; Old Station Rd; s with/without view £460/410, ste £745; **P**🐾) A byword for golfing luxury, this hotel is right alongside the famous 17th hole and has huge rooms, excellent service and a raft of facilities, including a spa complex. Fork out the extra £50 or so for a view over the Old Course. You can usually find better deals online than the rack rates we list here.

Five Pilmour Place B&B **££**

(Map p208; ☎01334-478665; www.5pilmourplace.com; 5 Pilmour Pl; s £78, d £120-160; @🐾) Just around the corner from the Old Course, this luxurious and intimate spot offers stylish, compact rooms with an eclectic range of styles as well as modern conveniences such as flatscreen TV and DVD player. The king-size beds are especially comfortable, and the lounge area is a stylish treat.

Aslar House B&B **££**

(Map p208; ☎01334-473460; www.aslar.com; 120 North St; s/d/ste £50/96/100; ☺Feb–mid-Nov; 🐾) The rooms are so impeccable at this place that it's frightening to imagine how much work goes on behind the scenes. The modern comforts don't detract from the house's historical features (including a whimsical turret room) but certainly add value. IPod docks, hair straighteners and DVDs in every room are complemented by fabulous new

bathrooms. The master suite is very spacious and a good small extra investment. No under-16s.

Cameron House B&B **££**

(Map p208; ☎01334-472306; www.cameronhouse-sta.co.uk; 11 Murray Park; s/d £45/90; 🐾) Beautifully decorated rooms and warm, cheerful hosts make this a real home away from home on this guest house–filled street. The two single rooms share a bathroom. Prices drop £10 per person outside peak season.

Six Murray Park B&B **££**

(Map p208; ☎01334-473319; www.sixmurraypark.co.uk; 6 Murray Park; s £50, d £80-90; 🐾) Enticing rooms with classy contemporary styling make this a most appealing option on this street bristling with guest houses.

Meade B&B B&B **££**

(☎01334-477350; annmeade10@hotmail.com; 6 Livingstone Cres; d £60-70; 🐾🐾) This welcoming gem, in a quiet street south of the centre, is run by a friendly family and their pets, including a portly marmalade cat and feisty black lab. There's just one double room, which is lovely, light and comfortable. You'll feel right at home.

Old Fishergate House B&B **££**

(Map p208; ☎01334-470874; www.oldfishergatehouse.co.uk; North Castle St; s/d £80/110; 🐾) This historic 17th-century town house, furnished with period pieces, is in a great location – the oldest part of town, close to the cathedral and castle. The two twin rooms are very spacious and even have their own sitting room and cushioned ledges on their window sills. On a scale of one to 10 for quaintness, we'd rate it about a 9½. Cracking breakfasts feature fresh fish and pancakes.

St Andrews Tourist Hostel HOSTEL **£**

(Map p208; ☎01334-479911; www.standrewshostel.com; St Marys Pl; dm £11-13; 🐾) Laid-back and central, this hostel, down the side of the Grill House restaurant, is a little hard to spot. Occupying a stately old building, it has high corniced ceilings, especially in the huge lounge, and a laissez-faire approach. The dorms could use new mattresses, but are clean and bright. There's a supermarket close by. Reception closed between 2pm and 5pm.

 University of St Andrews UNIVERSITY ACCOMMODATION **££**

(www.discoverstandrews.com; ☺Jun–Aug; **P**@🐾) When the university is out of session, three student residences open up as visitor accommodation. There's the hotel-style New Hall (☎01334-467000; s/d £61/89; P☎); self-catering apartments sleeping up to six at David Russell Hall (☎01334-467100; apt for 3/7 days £325/595); and budget rooms in the central McIntosh Hall (Map p208; ☎01334-467035; s/d £37.50/65). These prices are all good value for the standard of accommodation on offer.

Ogstons on North Street   HOTEL £££
(Map p208; ☎01334-473387; www.ogstonson northst.com; 127 North St; r £120-180; ☎) If you want to eat, drink and sleep in the same stylish place, this classy inn could be for you. Smartened-up rooms feature elegant contemporary styling and coolly beautiful bathrooms, some with spa. There are also DVD players, iPod docks, crisp white linen and large windows that give the rooms an airy feel. The Oak Rooms (serving lunch and dinner) is the place for meals and a read of the paper. The bar is perfect for a snug tipple, and the Lizard Lounge in the basement is a late-night bar that cranks up with live gigs and regular DJs.

Burness House   B&B ££
(Map p208; ☎01334-474314; www.burnesshouse. com; 1 Murray Park; d per person £32-45; ☺Mar-Nov; ☎) Rich, Asian-inspired fabrics, golf pictures and shiny new bathrooms.

Lorimer House   B&B ££
(Map p208; ☎01334-476599; www.lorimerhouse. com; 19 Murray Park; s £45-75, d £70-120; @☎) Smallish, sparklingly clean rooms with extra-comfy beds and a fab deluxe double on the top floor.

Cairnsmill Caravan Park   CAMPSITE £
(☎01334-473604; cairnsmill@aol.com; Largo Rd; tent without/with car £10/18, dm £18; ☺Apr-Oct; P☎☎☎☎) About a mile west of St Andrews on the A915, this campsite has brilliant views over the town. Facilities are good, though it's very caravan-heavy. There's also a simple bunkhouse.

✖ Eating

St Andrews has a great range of eating options. Places compete heavily for the student custom, so there are good deals to be had everywhere. Two great options for self-catering or picnic fare are the fine fishmonger Kerachers (Map p208; www.kerachers.com; 73 South St), and IJ Mellis (Map p208; www.mel lischeese.co.uk; 149 South St), with a wealth of cheeses you can smell halfway down the street.

TOP CHOICE **Vine Leaf**   SCOTTISH £££
(Map p208; ☎01334-477497; www.vineleafstand rews.co.uk; 131 South St; 2-course dinner £26.50; ☺dinner Tue-Sat; ✖) Classy, comfortable and well-established, the friendly Vine Leaf offers a changing menu of sumptuous Scottish seafood, game and vegetarian dishes. There's a huge selection within the set-price menu, all well presented, and an interesting, mostly old-world wine list. It's down a close off South St.

🍃 **Seafood Restaurant**   SEAFOOD £££
(Map p208; ☎01334-479475; www.theseafoodres taurant.com; The Scores; lunch/dinner £22/45) The Seafood Restaurant occupies a stylish glass-walled room, built out over the sea, with plush navy carpet, crisp white linen, an open kitchen and panoramic views of St Andrews Bay. It offers top seafood and an excellent wine list. Look out for its special winter deals.

Doll's House   SCOTTISH ££
(Map p208; ☎01334-477422; www.dolls-house. co.uk; 3 Church Sq; mains £13-15) With its high-backed chairs, bright colours and creaky wooden floor, the Doll's House blends a Victorian child's bedroom with modern stylings. The result is a surprising warmth and no pretensions. The menu makes the most of local fish and other Scottish produce, and the £6.95 two-course lunch is unbeatable value. The early evening two-course deal for £12.95 isn't bad, either.

The Glass House   ITALIAN, SCOTTISH ££
(Map p208; www.glasshouse-restaurant.co.uk; 80 North St; mains £7-15; ☺noon-9pm) Casual but comfortable, this restaurant offers plenty of light in its split-level, open kitchen dining area. The menu is basically Italian, with attractively presented pizzas and pastas popular with students. But a handful of daily specials offer more Scottish meat and game choices of notable quality.

The Café in the Square   CAFE £
(Map p208; 4 Church Sq; light meals £4-7; ☺10.30am-4.30pm Mon-Sat) Hidden away down the side of the library, this upbeat wee coffee stop also makes a good venue for a light lunch, with sandwiches, panini and salads and a couple of secluded picnic tables out the back.

WORTH A TRIP

THE PEAT INN

Six miles west of St Andrews in the village also called Peat Inn, this superb **restaurant** (☑01334-840206; www. thepeatinn.co.uk; 3-course lunch/dinner £19/40; ☺lunch & dinner Tue-Sat), backed by a commodious suite of rooms, makes a great gourmet break. The chef makes a great effort to source premium-quality Scottish produce and presents it in innovative ways that never feel pretentious or over-modern. The split-level **rooms** (s/d £150/195; ℗ ☎) look over the garden and fields beyond; breakfast is brought to your chamber to enjoy at your leisure. There are various all-inclusive offers available. To get there, head west from St Andrews on the A915 then turn right on the B940.

The Tailend
SEAFOOD £

(Map p208; www.tailendfishbar.co.uk; 130 Market St; fish & chips takeaway/eat in £6/10.50; ☺11.30am-10pm) Delicious fresh fish sourced from Arbroath, just up the coast, puts this a class above most chippies. It fries to order and it's worth the wait. The array of exquisite smoked delicacies at the counter will have you planning a picnic or fighting for a table in the licensed cafe out the back.

B Jannetta
ICE CREAM £

(Map p208; ☑01334-473285; www.jannettas.co.uk; 31 South St; 1/2 scoop cone £1.40/2; ☺Mon-Sat) B Jannetta is a St Andrews institution, offering 52 varieties of ice cream, from the weird (Irn-Bru sorbet) to the decadent (strawberries-and-champagne).

Balaka
BANGLADESHI ££

(Map p208; www.balaka.com; 3 Alexandra Pl; mains £8-14; ☺noon-3pm & 5pm-midnight Mon-Thu, noon-12.30am Fri & Sat, 5pm-midnight Sun; ☑) Long-established Bangladeshi restaurant with both standard choices and more inspiring discoveries – all delicious and seasoned with herbs the owners grow themselves. There's an interesting selection of fish cooked in the tandoor, and various cheap lunch and early dining deals.

Grill House
BISTRO ££

(Map p208; www.grillhouserestaurant.co.uk; St Mary's Pl; mains £8-12) This cheerful, sometimes boisterous restaurant offers something for every taste and bank balance, with a big selection ranging from Mexican, pizza and pasta to chargrilled salmon and quality steaks. The upbeat atmosphere and service are pluses, as is the £6 lunchtime deal.

Drinking

Central Bar
PUB

(Map p208; www.taylor-walker.co.uk; 77 Market St) Rather staid compared to some of the wilder student-driven drinking options, this likeable pub keeps it real with traditional features, an island bar, lots of Scottish beers, decent service and filling (if uninspiring) pub grub.

West Port
PUB

(Map p208; www.maclay.com; 170 South St; ☎) Just by the gateway of the same name, this sleek, modernised pub has several levels and a great beer garden out the back. Cheap cocktails rock the uni crowd, mixed drinks are above average and there's some OK bar food.

Vic
BAR

(Map p208; www.vicstandrews.co.uk; 1 St Mary's Pl) Warehouse chic meets medieval conviviality in this strikingly restored student favourite. Walls plastered with black-and-white pop culture give way to a handsome, high-ceilinged bar with sociable long tables down the middle and an eclectic assortment of seating. Other spaces include a more romantic bar, a dance floor and a smokers' deck. There are regular events.

Entertainment

There's always something on in the pubs around town during term.

Byre Theatre
THEATRE

(Map p208; ☑01334-475000; www.byretheatre. com; Abbey St) This theatre company started life in a converted cow byre in the 1930s, and now occupies a flashy premises making clever use of light and space.

New Picture House
CINEMA

(Map p208; www.nphcinema.co.uk; North St) Two-screen cinema showing current films.

Information

J&G Innes (www.jg-innes.co.uk; 107 South St) Plenty of local-interest books, such as Fife's history of burning witches.

Library (Church Sq; ☺9.30am-5pm Mon, Fri & Sat, to 7pm Tue-Thu) Free internet access – drop-in only; no bookings.

St Andrews Community Hospital (☎01334-465656; www.nhsfife.org; Largo Rd)

St Andrews Information Centre (☎01334-472021; www.visit-standrews.co.uk; 70 Market St; ☉9.15am-6pm Mon-Sat & 10am-5pm Sun Jul & Aug, 9.15am-5pm Mon-Sat Sep-Jun, plus 11am-4pm Sun Apr-Jun, Sep & Oct) Helpful staff with good knowledge of St Andrews and Fife.

❶ Getting There & Away

BUS All buses leave from the bus station on Station Rd. There are frequent services:

» **Anstruther** 40 minutes, regularly

» **Crail** 30 minutes, regularly

» **Dundee** 30 minutes, half-hourly

» **Edinburgh** £9.50, two hours, hourly

» **Glasgow** £9.95, 2½ hours, hourly

» **Stirling** £7.45, two hours, every two hours Monday to Saturday

TRAIN There is no train station in St Andrews itself, but you can take a train from Edinburgh (grab a seat on the right-hand side of the carriage for great firth views) to Leuchars (£12.60, one hour, hourly), 5 miles to the northwest. From here, buses leave regularly for St Andrews.

❶ Getting Around

To order a cab, call **Golf City Taxis** (☎01334-477788). A taxi between Leuchars train station and the town centre costs around £12.

Spokes (Map p208; ☎01334-477835; www.spokescycles.com; 37 South St; per half-/full day/week £8.50/13.50/60; ☉9am-5.30pm Mon-Sat) hires out mountain bikes.

East Neuk

This charming stretch of coast runs south from St Andrews to the point at Fife Ness, then west to Leven. Neuk is an old Scots word for corner, and it's certainly an appealing nook of the country to investigate, with picturesque fishing villages and pretty coastal walks; the Fife Coastal Path's most scenic stretches are in this area. It's easily visited from St Andrews, but also makes a very pleasant place to stay.

CRAIL
POP 1695

Pretty and peaceful, little Crail has a much-photographed stone-sheltered harbour surrounded by wee cottages with red-tiled roofs. You can buy lobster and crab from a kiosk

(☉lunch Sat & Sun) there. The benches in the nearby grassed area are perfectly placed for munching your al fresco crustaceans while admiring the view across to the Isle of May.

The village's history and involvement with the fishing industry is outlined in the Crail Museum (www.crailmuseum.org.uk; 62 Marketgate; admission free; ☉10am-1pm & 2-5pm Mon-Sat, 2-5pm Sun Jun-Sep, weekends only Apr & May), which also offers tourist information.

Eighteenth-century Selcraig House (☎01333-450697; www.selcraighouse.co.uk; 47 Nethergate; s/d £35/70; ☎⊛) is a characterful, well-run place with a variety of rooms. Curiously shaped top-floor chambers will appeal to the quirky, while the fantastic four-poster rooms will charm those with a taste for luxury and beautiful furnishings. Across the road from the museum, a lot of work has gone into making Hazelton Guest House (☎01333-450250; www.thehazelton.co.uk; 29 Marketgate North; s £45-50, d £70-85; ☉Mar-Oct; ☎) what it is. Attractively remodelled rooms make full use of the abundant natural light in this lovely old building. The super front rooms boast glorious views across to the Isle of May. Walkers and cyclists are well catered for.

Crail is 10 miles southeast of St Andrews. Stagecoach (www.stagecoachbus.com) bus 95 between Leven, Anstruther, Crail and St Andrews passes through Crail hourly every day (30 minutes to St Andrews).

ANSTRUTHER
POP 3442

Once among Scotland's busiest ports, cheery Anstruther has ridden the tribulations of the declining fishing industry better than some, and now has a very pleasant mixture of bobbing boats, historic streets and visitors ambling around the harbour grazing on fish and chips or contemplating a trip to the Isle of May.

◉ Sights

The displays at the excellent Scottish Fisheries Museum (www.scotfishmuseum.org; adult/child £6/free; ☉10am-5.30pm Mon-Sat & 11am-5pm Sun Apr-Sep, 10am-4.30pm Mon-Sat & noon-4.30pm Sun Oct-Mar) include the **Zulu Gallery**, which houses the huge, partly restored hull of a traditional Zulu-class fishing boat, redolent with the scent of tar and timber. Afloat in the harbour outside the museum lies the *Reaper*, a fully restored Fifie-class fishing boat built in 1902.

The mile-long **Isle of May**, 6 miles southeast of Anstruther, is a stunning nature reserve. Between April and July the intimidating cliffs are packed with breeding kittiwakes, razorbills, guillemots, shags and around 40,000 puffins. Inland are the remains of the 12th-century **St Adrian's Chapel**, dedicated to a monk who was murdered on the island by the Danes in 875.

The five-hour trip to the island on the **May Princess** (☎01333-311808; www.anstrutherpleasurecruises.co.uk; adult/child £22/11), including two to three hours ashore, sails almost daily from April to September. Buy tickets at the harbour kiosk at least an hour before departure. Departure times vary depending on the tide – check times by phone or via the website. There's also a faster boat, the 12-seater rigid-hull inflatable *Osprey*, which makes nonlanding circuits of the island (adult/child £20/12.50) and longer visits (£25/15).

🛏 Sleeping & Eating

TOP CHOICE **The Spindrift** B&B ££
(☎01333-310573; www.thespindrift.co.uk; Pittenweem Rd; s/d £60/80; P🅿🛜🐾) Arriving from the west, there's no need to go further than Anstruther's first house on the left, a redoubt of Scottish cheer and warm hospitality. The rooms are elegant, classy and extremely comfortable – some have views across to Edinburgh and one is like a ship's cabin, courtesy of the sea captain who once owned the house. There are DVD players and teddies for company, an honesty bar with characterful ales and malts and fine company from your hosts. Breakfast includes porridge once voted the best in the kingdom. Dinner (£23) is also available.

The Bank INN ££
(☎01333-310189; www.thebank-anstruther.co.uk; 23 High St; s/d £50/100; 🛜) Refitted rooms at this modernised central pub offer loads of space, big beds and great bathrooms. The building itself backs onto the river mouth, meaning pleasant views from many of the chambers. The bar is enticing, with tables out the back, though its proximity means you might be better off in the lower rooms (7 & 8) at weekends. Prices are usually substantially lower than we list here.

Crichton House B&B ££
(☎01333-310219; www.crichtonhouse.com; High St W; d £70-80; P🅿🛜) You'll spot this B&B on the right as you approach the centre of town

from the west. Sparklingly clean rooms with fresh fruit and slate-floored bathrooms are complemented by a cheery host and plenty of breakfast options. Enter via the wooden stairs at the side of the house.

Cellar Restaurant SEAFOOD £££
(☎01333-310378; www.cellaranstruther.co.uk; 24 East Green; 2-/3-course set dinner £35/40; ⊘lunch Fri & Sat, dinner Tue-Sat) Tucked away in an alley behind the museum, the Cellar is famous for its seafood and fine wines. Try the local crab, lobster or whatever delicacies they've brought in that day. Inside it's elegant and upmarket. Advance bookings are essential.

Dreel Tavern PUB £
(16 High St W; mains £8-11; 🚗) This charming old pub on the banks of the Dreel Burn has bucketloads of character and serves reliably tasty bar meals. Chow down in the outdoor beer garden in summer. There are also some top-quality cask ales.

🍴 **Wee Chippy** FISH & CHIPS £
(4 Shore St; fish supper £5.50) The Anstruther Fish Bar is one of Britain's best chippies, but we – and plenty of locals – reckon this one might be even better. The fish is of a very high quality and there's less of a queue too. Eat your catch by the water.

🛈 Information

Anstruther Information Centre (☎01333-311073; www.visitfife.com; Harbourhead; ⊘10am-5pm Mon-Sat, 11am-4pm Sun Apr-Oct) The best tourist office in East Neuk.

🛈 Getting There & Away

Stagecoach (www.stagecoachbus.com) bus 95 runs daily from Leven (more departures from St Monans) to Anstruther and on to St Andrews (40 minutes, hourly) via Crail.

AROUND ANSTRUTHER

A magnificent example of Lowland Scottish domestic architecture, **Kellie Castle** (NTS; www.nts.org.uk; adult/child/parking £9.50/7/3; ⊘castle 12.30-5pm Thu-Mon Apr-Oct, open daily Jun-Aug, gardens year-round 9.30am-6pm or dusk) has creaky floors, crooked little doorways and some marvellous works of art. It's set in a beautiful garden, and many rooms contain superb plasterwork, the Vine room being the most exquisite. The original part of the building dates from 1360; it was enlarged to its present dimensions around 1606.

The castle is 3 miles northwest of Pittenweem on the B9171. Bus 95 from St Andrews gets you closest – about 1.5 miles away. You can get straight to the castle by booking a Go-Flexi (☎01334-840340; www.go-flexi.org; £2) 'taxibus' from Anstruther.

Three miles north of Anstruther, off the B9131 to St Andrews, is Scotland's Secret Bunker (www.secretbunker.co.uk; adult/child/family £9.90/7/29; ⊙10am-6pm Apr-Oct). This fascinating Cold War relic was to be one of Britain's underground command centres and a home for Scots leaders in the event of nuclear war. Hidden 30m underground and surrounded by nearly 5m of reinforced concrete are the austere operation rooms, communication centre and dormitories. It's very authentic and uses artefacts from the period, which make for an absorbing exploration. The Scottish Campaign for Nuclear Disarmament (CND) has an exhibit, bringing home the realities of Britain's current nuclear Trident policy. The bunker is a gripping experience and highly recommended.

To get to the bunker, book a Go-Flexi 'taxibus' from Anstruther, or it's a standard taxi (£15 to £18) from St Andrews. Alternatively, jump off an X26 bus from Anstruther to St Andrews at the Drumrack crossroads and walk east for about 1.5 miles along the B940.

PITTENWEEM
POP 1747

Just a short stroll from Anstruther, Pittenweem is now the main fishing port on the East Neuk coast, and there are lively morning fish sales at the harbour. The village name means 'place of the cave', referring to St Fillan's Cave (Cove Wynd; adult/child £1/free), which was used as a chapel by a 7th-century missionary. The peaceful, atmospheric cave is protected by a locked gate, but a key is available from the chocolate shop at 9 High St, a great street to wander in itself, with galleries, cafes and craft shops.

Bus details for Pittenweem are as for Anstruther.

ST MONANS
POP 1450

This ancient fishing village just over a mile west of Pittenweem is named after another cave-dwelling saint who was probably killed by pirates. Apart from a picturesque historic **windmill** overlooking the sea, its main sight is the **parish church**, built in 1362 on the orders of a grateful King David II, who was rescued by villagers from a shipwreck in the Firth of Forth. It was burned by the English in 1544 but restored. The church has sweeping views of the firth, and the past echoes inside its cold, whitewashed walls.

St Monans Heritage Collection (5 West Shore; admission free; ⊙11am-1pm & 2-4pm Tue, Thu, Sat & Sun May-Oct), on the harbour, is a wonderful small gallery devoted to the history of the St Monans' fishing industry through a collection of 20th-century black-and-white photos and several artefacts. Most of the photos were taken by a local photographer and the collection changes regularly.

There are a couple of B&Bs in St Monans, but there are more options in nearby Anstruther. For eating, Craig Millar @16 West End (☎01333-730327; www.16westend.com; 16 West End; 2-course lunch/dinner £22/35; ⊙lunch & dinner Wed-Sun) is a comfortable, but classy, fishy stalwart on the harbour. The menu changes – bouillabaisse, Dover sole, scallops – but just swim with the tide. The menu details the provenance of these sustainable morsels. A lighter bite can be had at Harbour Howff (6 Station Rd; light meals £3-5; ⊙10am-4pm Tue-Fri, 11am-5pm Sat & Sun), a community-run cafe promoting healthy eating and serving excellent panini and fresh cakes.

Stagecoach (www.stagecoachbus.com) bus 95 runs daily from St Monans to St Andrews (50 minutes, at least hourly), via Anstruther.

ELIE & EARLSFERRY
POP 1500

These two attractive villages mark the southwestern end of East Neuk. There are great sandy beaches and good walks along the coast, and there's nothing better than a lazy summer Sunday in Elie, watching the local team play cricket on the strand below.

Elie Watersports (☎01333-330962; www.eliewatersports.com; ⊙May-Sep, ring ahead at other times), on the harbour at Elie, hires out windsurfers (per two hours £28), sailing dinghies (Lasers/Wayfarers per hour £20/25), canoes (per hour £12) and mountain bikes (per day £12), and provides instruction as well.

Ship Inn (www.ship-elie.com; mains £8-11; ⊞), down by Elie harbour, is a pleasant and popular place for a bar lunch. Seafood and Asian dishes feature on the menu and, on a sunny day, you can tuck in at an outside table, overlooking the wide sweep of the bay.

PERTHSHIRE & KINROSS

For sheer scenic variety, Perthshire is the pick of Scotland's regions and a place where everyone will find a special, personal spot – whether it's a bleak moor, snaking loch, postcard-perfect village or magnificent forest. Highlights are many: the enchanting valley of Glen Lyon strikes visitors dumb with its wild and remote beauty; stunning Loch Tay is nearby; and the River Tay runs east from here towards Dunkeld, with its cathedral among the most beautifully situated in the country.

Things begin sedately in the southeast corner with Perth itself, a fine country town with a fabulous attraction in lavish Scone Palace, and get gradually wilder as you move northwards and westwards, moving through wooded slopes and river-blessed valleys, culminating in the bleak expanse of Rannoch Moor.

Kinross & Loch Leven

POP 4681

Kinross, just off the M90, sits on the banks of pretty Loch Leven. Stretch your legs or take a bike on the **Loch Leven Heritage Trail** (www.lochlevenheritagetrail.co.uk), which runs 8 miles around three-quarters of the loch, with sightings of deer common, or head across to the island in its centre to visit evocative **Lochleven Castle** (HS; www.historic-scotland.gov.uk; adult/child incl boat £5/3; ⌚9.30am-5.30pm Apr-Sep, to 4.30pm Oct, last sailing 1hr before), which served as a fortress and prison from the late 14th century. Its most famous captive was Mary, Queen of Scots, who was incarcerated here in 1567. Her famous charms bewitched Willie Douglas, who managed to get hold of the cell keys to release her, then rowed her across to the shore. A bistro by the ferry dock, near the centre of Kinross, serves decent light meals and you can rent bikes here (£20 per day).

Nearby, on the main street, **Roxburghe Guest House** (☎01577-864521; www.roxburgheguesthouse.co.uk; 126 High St; s £45-65, d £65-75; P 📶) is welcoming home away from home with a good attitude and lovely garden. The owner is a professional masseuse and acupuncturist if you need any creases ironed out. It's a fair bit cheaper outside of high summer.

Citylink (www.citylink.co.uk) runs bus services between Perth (30 minutes, hourly) and Kinross. In the other direction buses go to Edinburgh (1½ hours, hourly).

T TIME

Scotland's biggest music festival, **T in the Park** (www.tinthepark.com) rocks this nook of the country over the second weekend in July. A major event, with six stages and top-name acts, it takes place on the former Balado airfield near Kinross. It's a three-day affair, with camping available from the night before. The park is off the A91, just west of junction 7 of the M90.

Perth

POP 43,450

Sedately arranged along the banks of the Tay, this former capital of Scotland is a most liveable place with large tracts of enticing parkland surrounding an easily managed centre. On its outskirts lies Scone Palace, a country house of staggering luxury built alongside the mound that was the crowning place of Scotland's kings. It's a must-see, but the town itself, ennobled by stately architecture, fine galleries and excellent restaurants, merits exploration, and is within easy striking distance of both Edinburgh and Glasgow.

Sights

Scone Palace PALACE
(www.scone-palace.co.uk; adult/child/family £10/7/30; ⌚9.30am-5pm Apr-Oct, closed 4.30pm Sat) 'So thanks to all at once and to each one, whom we invite to see us crowned at Scone.' This line from *Macbeth* indicates the importance of this place (pronounced 'skoon'), 2 miles north of Perth. The palace itself was built in 1580 on a site intrinsic to Scottish history. Here in 838, Kenneth MacAlpin became the first king of a united Scotland and brought the **Stone of Destiny**, on which Scottish kings were ceremonially invested, to Moot Hill. In 1296 Edward I of England carted the talisman off to Westminster Abbey, where it remained for 700 years before being returned to Scotland.

These days, however, Scone doesn't really conjure up ye olde days of bearded warrior-kings swearing oaths in the mist because the palace, rebuilt in the early 19th century, is a Georgian mansion of extreme elegance and luxury.

The visit takes you through a succession of sumptuous **rooms** filled with fine French furniture and noble artworks. There's an astonishing collection of porcelain and fine portraits, as well as a series of exquisite Vernis Martin papier mâché. Scone has belonged for centuries to the Murray family,

Earls of Mansfield, and many of the objects have fascinating history attached to them (friendly guides are on hand). Each room has comprehensive multilingual information; there are also panels relating histories of some of the Scottish kings crowned at Scone over the centuries.

Outside, peacocks – all named after a monarch – strut around the magnificent **grounds**, which incorporate woods, a butterfly garden and a maze.

Ancient kings were crowned on **Moot Hill**, topped by a chapel, next to the palace. It's said that the hill was created by bootfuls of earth, brought by nobles attending the coronations as an acknowledgement of the king's rights over their lands, although it's more likely the site of an ancient motte-and-bailey castle.

From Perth's centre, cross the bridge, turn left, and keep bearing left until you reach the gates of the estate (15 to 20 minutes' walking). From here, it's a half-mile to the palace. Various buses from town stop here roughly hourly; the tourist office has a printout. There's a good cafe at the palace.

FJD Fergusson Gallery
GALLERY

(Map p218; www.pkc.gov.uk; cnr Marshall Pl & Tay St; ☉10am-5pm Mon-Sat, plus 1-4.30pm Sun May-Sep) Beautifully set in the round waterworks building, this gallery exhibits much of the work of the Scottish Colourist JD Fergusson in a most impressive display. Fergusson spent time in Paris, and the influence of artists such as Matisse on his work is evident; his voluptuous female portraits against a tropical-looking Riviera background are memorable, as is the story of his lifelong relationship with noted Scottish dancer Margaret Morris.

FREE St John's Kirk
CHURCH

(Map p218; www.st-johns-kirk.co.uk; St John's St; ☉10am-4pm Mon-Sat, to 1pm Sun May-Sep) Daunting St John's Kirk, founded in 1126, is surrounded by cobbled streets and is still the centrepiece of the town. In 1559 John Knox preached a powerful sermon here that helped begin the Reformation, inciting a frenzied destruction of Scone abbey and other religious sites. Perth used to be known as St John's Town after this church; the football team here is still called St Johnstone.

FREE Perth Museum
MUSEUM

(Map p218; www.pkc.gov.uk; cnr George & Charlotte Sts; ☉10am-5pm Mon-Sat) The city's main mu-

seum is worth wandering through for the elegant neoclassical interior alone. There's a varied shower of exhibits, ranging from portraits of dour lairds to interesting local social history. A geological room provides more entertainment for the young, while there are often excellent temporary exhibitions.

Black Watch Museum
MUSEUM

(Map p218; www.theblackwatch.co.uk; Hay St; adult/child £5/2.50; ☉9.30am-5pm Mon-Sat, also 10am-4pm Sun Apr-Oct) Housed in a mansion on the edge of North Inch, this museum honours what was once Scotland's foremost regiment. Formed in 1725 to combat rural banditry, the Black Watch fought in numerous campaigns, re-created here with paintings, memorabilia and anecdotes. Little attempt at perspective is evident: there's justifiable pride in the regiment's role in the gruelling trench warfare of WWI, where it suffered nearly 30,000 casualties, but no sheepishness about less glorious colonial engagements, such as against the 'Fuzzy Wuzzies' of Sudan. In 2006 the Black Watch was subsumed into the new Royal Regiment of Scotland. There should be a cafe here by the time you read this.

🛏 Sleeping

Parklands
HOTEL ££

(Map p218; ☎01738-622451; www.theparklandshotel.com; 2 St Leonard's Bank; s/d £93/123; 🅿@🖳) Tucked away near the train station, this relaxing, recently renovated hotel sits amidst a lush hillside garden overlooking the parklands of South Inch. While the rooms – which vary in size and shape – conserve the character of this beautiful building, formerly the residence of the town's mayors, they also offer modern conveniences and plenty of style. There's an excellent restaurant and a

Perth

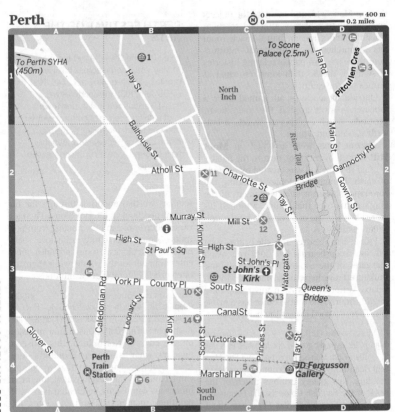

great terrace and garden area to lap up the Perthshire sun.

Pitcullen Guest House   B&B **££**
(Map p218; ☑01738-626506; www.pitcullen.co.uk; 17 Pitcullen Cres; s/d £50/70; P🖤) New owners have given this excellent place a much more contemporary look than other guest houses on this strip. Great-looking fabrics and modern styling give the light rooms an upbeat feel. Lots of thought has gone into making your stay more comfortable, resulting in things like fridges with free drinks in the rooms, plenty of plugs to make recharging easy and maps on the walls to help you plan the next stage of your journey.

Kinnaird Guest House   B&B **££**
(Map p218; ☑01738-628021; www.kinnaird-guesthouse.co.uk; 5 Marshall Pl; s £45, d £65-75; P🖤) The best of the handful of guest houses enjoying a privileged position across the road from the lovely South Inch parkland, this el-

egant old house has noble original features and boasts appealing, bright rooms with big beds. It's all impeccable, with nice touches like bathrobes and teddy bears on the beds. The owners are engaging and extremely helpful; breakfast features organic produce and quality bacon. The back rooms receive occasional train noise.

Comely Bank Cottage   B&B **££**
(Map p218; ☑01738-631118; www.comelybankcottage.co.uk; 19 Pitcullen Cres; d £60-70; P🖤) Pitcullen Cres is bristling with upmarket, flowery B&Bs. This is one of our favourites, a perfectly maintained family home offering large and commodious rooms with spacious bathrooms, and a solicitous owner who doesn't disappoint come breakfast time.

Heidl Guest House   B&B **££**
(Map p218; ☑01738-635031; www.heidl.co.uk; 43 York Pl; s £32, d £60-75; P🖤) Though it lacks a little character from outside, the Heidl is an excel-

Perth

lent guest house, and keen new owners have renovated the bright, light rooms, leaving them very spruce indeed. Most rooms come with excellent en suite bathrooms; those that don't have good private exterior bathrooms. Writer John Buchan (of *Thirty-Nine Steps* fame) was born in the house opposite.

Perth SYHA   HOSTEL £

(☑01738-877800; www.syha.org.uk; Crieff Rd; dm/tw £15/34) A 20-minute stroll from the centre, this summer hostel is set in a student residence at Perth College. The rooms are all en suite twins, with good share kitchens and common rooms. For some reason, there's a price jump for a week in July. Turn into the Brahan entrance on Crieff Rd, and the hostel is by the large car park. Numerous buses stop outside.

✕ Eating & Drinking

Perth has an exceptionally good dining scene.

TOP CHOICE **63 Tay Street**   SCOTTISH ££

(Map p218; ☑01738-441451; www.63taystreet.com; 63 Tay St; mains £13.50; ⊗Tue-Sat) Classy and warmly welcoming, this understated restaurant is Perth's best, featuring a lightly decorated dining area, excellent service and quality food. In a culinary Auld Alliance, French influence is applied to the best of Scottish produce to produce memorable game, seafood, beef and vegetarian plates. There are a couple of set menus available.

TOP CHOICE **Breizh**   BISTRO ££

(Map p218; ☑01738-444427; www.cafebreizh.co.uk; 28 High St; mains £8-14; ⊗9am-9.30pm Mon-Sat, 11am-9.30pm Sun) This warmly decorated bis-

tro – the place could define the word – is a treat. Dishes are served with real panache, and the salads, featuring all sorts of delicious ingredients, are a feast of colour, texture and subtle flavours. The blackboard meat and fish specials offer great value and a real taste of northwest France: breakfasts, galettes (Breton buckwheat crêpes), tasty wines... If you like quality food served in an unpretentious way, you'll love it here.

Deans@Let's Eat   SCOTTISH ££

(Map p218; ☑01738-643377; www.letseatperth.co.uk; 77 Kinnoull St; mains £15-20; ⊗Tue-Sat) A Perth favourite for splashing out on a special meal, this busy corner restaurant has a can-do attitude and an excellent line in fresh Scottish produce. Juicy scallops, fine Orkney beef, local venison or lamb may feature, but you can't really go wrong whatever you select. Browse the menu on the comfy couches with aperitif in hand, before being shown to your table. Recession-busting lunch and dinner set menus are a good way to graze here on a budget.

Pig'Halle   FRENCH ££

(Map p218; www.pighalle.co.uk; 38 South St; mains £10-15; ⊗Tue-Sun) A spacious bistro that presents the very best of pork products through traditional regional French cuisine. The sample platter of charcuterie is fabulous value, there are succulent mains and there's a decent selection of Gallic wines to accompany them. There are other dishes on the menu if pig ain't your thing, and a cheap early dinner deal.

Kerachers   SEAFOOD ££

(Map p218; ☑01738-449777; www.kerachers -restaurant.co.uk; 168 South St; 2-course dinner £24.50; ⊗dinner Tue-Sat) This classic seafood restaurant keeps things simple, combining fresh seafood with ingredients that add hints of flavour to complement but not overpower the dishes – a recipe for success!

Paco's
INTERNATIONAL **££**

(Map p218; www.pacos.co.uk; 3 Mill St; mains £8-14; ⊙4.30-10pm Sun-Thu, to 11pm Fri, noon-11pm Sat; ▣) Something of an institution, Paco's keeps Perthers coming back over and over, perhaps because it would take dozens of visits to even try half the menu. There's something for everyone: steaks, seafood, pizza, pasta and Mexican, all served in generous portions. The fountain-tinkled terrace is the place for a sunny day.

Twa Tams
PUB

(Map p218; www.myspace.com/thetwatams; 79 Scott St) Perth's best pub has a strange outdoor space with windows peering out onto the street, an ornate entrance gate and a large, cosy interior. There are regular events, including live music every Friday and Saturday night; it has a sound reputation for attracting talented young bands.

❶ Information

AK Bell Library (York Pl; ⊙9.30am-5pm Mon, Wed & Fri, to 8pm Tue & Thu, to 4pm Sat) Free internet; lots of terminals.

Perth Royal Infirmary (☑01738-623311; www. nhstayside.scot.nhs.uk; Taymount Tce) West of the town centre.

Perth Information Centre (☑01738-450600; www.perthshire.co.uk; West Mill St; ⊙daily Apr-Oct, Mon-Sat Nov-Mar) Efficiently run tourist office.

❶ Getting There & Away

BUS From the bus station, **Citylink** (www.city link.co.uk) operates buses to/from these cities:
Dundee £7, 40 minutes, hourly
Edinburgh £11, 1½ hours, hourly

Glasgow £11.20, 1¾ hours, hourly
Inverness £20, 2¾ hours, at least five daily
Stirling £8.30, 55 minutes, hourly

Further buses run from the Broxden Park & Ride on Glasgow Rd; this is connected regularly with the bus station by shuttle bus. These include **Megabus** (www.megabus.com) discount services to Aberdeen, Edinburgh, Glasgow, Dundee and Inverness.

Stagecoach (www.stagecoachbus.com) buses serve Perthshire destinations regularly, with reduced Sunday service. A Tayside Megarider ticket gives you seven days travel in Perth & Kinross and Dundee & Angus for £22. It also operates a Stirling service.

TRAIN Trains run between Perth and various destinations, including the following:
Edinburgh £14.50, 1¼ hours, at least hourly Monday to Saturday, every two hours Sunday
Glasgow £14.50, one hour, at least hourly Monday to Saturday, every two hours Sunday
Pitlochry £12.30, 40 minutes, two hourly, fewer on Sunday
Stirling £11.70, 30 minutes, one or two per hour

Strathearn

West of Perth, the wide strath (valley) of the River Earn was once a great forest where medieval kings hunted. The whole area is known as Strathearn, a very attractive region of undulating farmland, hills and lochs. The Highlands officially begin in the western section of Strathearn.

DUNNING
POP 900

If you think you've entered spooky country around here, you may just be right. On the way into Dunning, about a mile west of the town by the B8062, there's a strange **cross** on a pile of stones, etched with the words 'Maggie Wall burnt here 1657 as a witch'.

GLENEAGLES

Deep in rural Perthshire, near the town of Auchterarder, one of Scotland's most famous lodgings can be found: the Gleneagles Hotel (☑01764-662231; www.gleneagles.com; d £435-535; ᴘ@🛜🏊). Not your typical B&B, this is a no-holds-barred luxury spot with three championship golf courses, Andrew Fairlie at Gleneagles – often referred to as Scotland's best restaurant (open for dinner Tuesday to Saturday) – and a variety of extravagantly elegant rooms and suites designed to cope with anything from a serious romantic splash out to a royal family in exile. Despite the imposing building and kilted staff snapping to attention, it's welcoming to non-VIPs and family friendly to boot, with lots of activities available. There's Gleneagles train station to arrive sustainably; if not, limousine transfers are available. Check the website for deals. Gleneagles is the venue for the 2014 Ryder Cup.

The village is dominated by the 12th-century Norman tower of St Serfs Church (HS; www.historic-scotland.gov.uk; admission free; ⏰9.30am-5.30pm Apr-Sep), but most of the building dates from 1810. The main reason to come is the magnificent 9th-century **Dupplin Cross**, the finest Pictish cross known. Originally located near Forteviot (3 miles from Dunning), it's now the regal centrepiece here. The fascinating symbolism and artistic influences will be explained in superb detail by the warden. It's rare to get such detailed insight at these places, and you'll walk out feeling like you've learned something new.

Dunning is about 8 miles southwest of Perth. Stagecoach (☎01382-227201; www.stagecoachbus.com) bus 17 runs from Perth (40 minutes, eight Monday to Saturday, two Sunday).

CRIEFF
POP 6579

Elegant Crieff is an old resort-style town, as popular with tourists today as it was in Victorian times. It sits in a valley amid some glorious Perthshire countryside. With excellent eating and accommodation options, it's a fine base for exploring this part of the country.

◉ Sights

In the basement at the tourist office is a small but interesting free **exhibition** of the town stocks, the Drummond Cross (1400–1600) and a formidable 9th-century Pictish cross slab.

At noble old Glenturret Distillery, 1 mile north of town, the Famous Grouse Experience (www.thefamousgrouse.com; standard tour adult/child £8.95/7.50; ⏰9am-6pm, last tour 4.30pm Mar-Dec, 10am-5pm, last tour 3pm Jan & Feb) has a better-than-average tour that details the making of malt whisky and the blending process to create Famous Grouse. There's also a dizzying audiovisual that takes you on a grouse's flight around Scotland. Two tiny drams are included in the standard tour; more expensive tours offer more detailed tasting sessions.

🛏 Sleeping

Yann's   B&B ££
(☎01764-650111; www.yannsatglenearnhouse.com; Perth Rd; s/d £65/90; ⏰dinner Wed-Sun, lunch Sat & Sun; P🐾🏠) On the main road heading east out of town, this most welcoming establishment offers big light rooms with plenty of

THE LIBRARY OF INNERPEFFRAY

For anyone that loves books, the Innerpeffray Library (www.innerpeffraylibrary.co.uk; Innerpeffray; adult/child £5/free; ⏰10am-12.45pm & 2-4.45pm Wed-Sat, 2-4pm Sun Mar-Oct, by appointment only Nov-Feb), about 5 miles southeast of Crieff on the B8062, is a rare treat. Founded in 1680, it's Scotland's oldest free lending library, a living link to the Scottish Enlightenment with its beautiful collection of tomes dating back to the 16th century, including some marvellous, weighty Lonely-Planets-of-their-time. Best of all, the friendly librarians will get any of these ancient books out for you to browse: a magical experience. The library's lovely rural surrounds invite strolling and picnics.

understated style. The excellent restaurant (mains £12 to £15) serves French comfort food classics such as crêpes and coq au vin, with a contemporary flair.

Merlindale   B&B ££
(☎01764-655205; www.merlindale.co.uk; Perth Rd; d £75-85; ⏰Mar-Nov; P🏠) Georgian architecture meets generous hospitality at this excellent option at the eastern end of town. The four fabulous rooms all have individual character, and two have sumptuous bathrooms with free-standing tubs. Thoughtful touches abound.

Comrie Croft   HOSTEL £
(☎01764-670140; www.comriecroft.com; campsite per person £9, dm/s/d £18.50/23/40; P@🏠🐾) A rustic, hospitable place to stay with great facilities, Comrie Croft has a bit of everything: camping; a pleasant, airy hostel with plenty of bed space; and Sami-style tepees (£60 to £75) with wood stove that sleep up to four. Activities include mountain biking (bike hire available), fishing, walking, lots of games for the kids and plenty of places to just laze about. The Croft is 4 miles out of Crieff, on the A85 towards Comrie.

Comely Bank Guest House   B&B ££
(☎01764-653409; www.comelybankguesthouse.co.uk; 32 Burrell St; s with/without bathroom

£44/35, d £70; @⊙) Just down from the main street, Comely Bank is homelike and neat as a pin. The downstairs double is huge and could accommodate four at a pinch, while upstairs rooms are equally appealing and are still a good size.

Crieff Hydro　　　　　　　　　SPA HOTEL ££
(☑01764-655555; www.crieffhydro.com; Ferntower Rd; d dinner, bed & breakfast £168; P@⊙≋) This enormous spa hotel is nearly 150 years old, but apart from its monumental exterior it looks very different from its mannered Victorian past. It's attractively functional and really does have everything for a family holiday, from a cinema and gym to restaurants, activities and pools. It's exceptionally child friendly, with free daily childcare. Room rates vary substantially, so check the website: the above prices are a guide only. Its sister hotel, **Murraypark** (dinner, bed and breakfast d £110), is just around the corner, and offers a quieter, cheaper stay in a smaller, more couple-focused establishment (and you can still access all the leisure facilities at the Hydro).

✕ Eating & Drinking

Lounge　　　　　　　　　　　WINE BAR ££
(www.loungeincrieff.co.uk; 1 West High St; dishes £5-12; ⊙noon-9.30pm Mon-Sat) Enter the romantic interior of this stylish central newcomer for anything from a cup of tea, to good wines by the glass, to an interesting array of portions of Scottish seafood and other delights, designed to be shared tapas-style.

Delivino　　　　　　　　　　CAFE, ITALIAN £
(www.delivino.net; 6 King St; light meals £6-8; ⊙9am-6pm Mon-Thu, to 9pm Fri & Sat, noon-4pm Sun) Delivino is an elegant cafe just down from the square on the main street. It offers something for everyone, from Crieff ladies-who-lunch to a traveller looking for a light bite. An extensive selection of antipasti allows you to graze several flavours at a time, while delicious bruschettas and pizzas, accompanied by a glass of Italian red, make this central Crieff's best lunch option.

Gallery　　　　　　　　　　　BISTRO ££
(☑01764-653249; 13 Hill St; mains £12-16; ⊙dinner Tue-Sat) An inclusive atmosphere and lack of pretension accompany decent dishes featuring salmon, lamb, venison and the like in this cosy (too cosy if your neighbours are loud) restaurant just uphill from the main street. True to its name, works of local artists of varying quality adorn the walls.

Curly Coo Bar　　　　　　　　　　PUB
(47 High St) Crieff has bigger pubs, and busier ones, but you can't beat the welcome at this super-friendly main-street local. A fine selection of malts and good chat from the owner makes it the town's best boozer.

ℹ Information

Crieff Information Centre (☑01764-652578; www.perthshire.co.uk; ⊙daily Apr-Oct, Mon-Sat Nov-Mar) Most helpful. In a clocktower on the main street.

ℹ Getting There & Away

Hourly **Stagecoach** (www.stagecoachbus.com) buses link Crieff with Perth (45 minutes), less frequently on Sunday; and Stirling (50 minutes, four to 10 daily).

UPPER STRATHEARN

The Highland villages of **Comrie** and **St Fillans** in upper Strathearn are surrounded by forests and craggy, bare hilltops where deer and mountain hares live in abundance. St Fillans enjoys an excellent location at the eastern end of **Loch Earn**, which reflects the silhouettes of distant, towering peaks in its glittering waters.

In St Fillans, with utterly memorable loch views, the **Four Seasons Hotel** (☑01765-685333; www.thefourseasonshotel.co.uk; St Fillans; standard/superior d £122/144; ⊙Mar-Dec; P⊙≋) is a refined place with a touch of elegance, two beautifully appointed sitting rooms and a small characterful bar – great places to relax. There are boundless activities to choose from, including waterskiing, quad biking and pony trekking. The superior rooms – worth the upgrade – have the best vistas, and secluded bathrooms hidden in cupboards. There are also six chalets nestled in the slopes behind the hotel and a bistro, plus a noted fine-dining restaurant.

Comrie is 24 miles west of Perth, and St Fillans is about 5 miles further west. Buses run from Perth via Crieff to Comrie (20 minutes, roughly hourly Monday to Saturday, every two hours Sunday) and St Fillans (35 minutes, five daily Monday to Saturday).

West Perthshire

The jewel in central Scotland's crown, West Perthshire achieves a Scottish ideal with rugged, noble hills reflected in some of the nation's most beautiful lochs. Bring your hiking boots and camera and prepare to stay a few days.

ABERFELDY
POP 1895

Aberfeldy is the gateway to West Perthshire, and a good base: adventure sports, art and castles all feature here. It's a peaceful, pretty place on the banks of the Tay, but if it's moody lochs and glens you're after, you may want to push further into the region.

👁 Sights & Activities

The Birks of Aberfeldy, made famous by a Robert Burns poem, offer a great short walk from the centre of town, following a vigorous burn upstream past several picturesque cascades.

Dewar's World of Whisky   DISTILLERY
(www.dewarsworldofwhisky.com; tour adult/child £7/4; ⊙10am-6pm Mon-Sat & noon-4pm Sun Apr-Oct, 10am-4pm Mon-Sat Nov-Mar) At the eastern end of Aberfeldy, this home of the famous blend offers a good tour, fully 90 minutes long. After the usual overblown film, there's a museum section with audioguide, and an entertaining interactive blending session, as well as the tour of the whisky-making process. More expensive tours allow you to try venerable Aberfeldy single malts and others.

FREE The Watermill   GALLERY, BOOKSHOP
(www.aberfeldywatermill.com; Mill St; ⊙10am-5.30pm Mon-Sat, 11am-5.30pm Sun) An unusual attraction in the centre of town, incorporating a bookshop with a great Scottish collection, a gallery with contemporary works of art and a coffee shop. You could while away several hours in this old mill.

Castle Menzies   CASTLE
(www.menzies.org; adult/child £6/2.50; ⊙10.30am-5pm Mon-Sat, 2-5pm Sun Apr–mid-Oct) About 1.5 miles west of Aberfeldy, by the B846, Castle Menzies is the impressive restored 16th-century seat of the chief of the clan Menzies (*ming*-iss). The Z-plan tower house is magnificently located against a backdrop of Scottish forest. Inside it reeks of authenticity, despite extensive restoration work and is a highly recommended visit. Check out the fireplace in the dungeon-like kitchens and the gaudy great hall upstairs, with windows unfurling a ribbon of lush, green countryside extending into wooded hills beyond the estate. You'll get in for free if you share a surname with the castle.

Highland Safaris   WILDLIFE TOUR
(☎01887-820071; www.highlandsafaris.net; ⊙9am-5pm, closed Sun Nov-Jan; ⊛) This outfit, just past Castle Menzies, offers an ideal way to spot some wildlife or simply enjoy Perthshire's magnificent countryside. Standard trips include the 2½-hour Mountain Safari (adult/child £40/17.50), which includes a dram in the wilderness; and the Safari Trek (adult/child £60/45), which includes a walk in the mountains and a picnic.

You can hire mountain bikes here (per day £20), and for another £17.50 they'll drive you to the top of the hill and you make your own way down (a good option for walkers, too). Wildlife you may spot includes golden eagles, osprey and red deer. There's also gold panning for kids.

Splash   RAFTING
(☎01887-829706; www.rafting.co.uk; Dunkeld Rd; ⊙9am-9pm; ⊛) Splash offers family-friendly white-water rafting on the River Tay (adult/child £40/25) and more advanced adult trips on the Tummel (grade 3/4, June to September) and the Orchy (grade 3/5, October to March). It also offers pulse-racing descents on river bugs, canyoning trips (£45) and hires mountain bikes (per half-/full day £12/18).

🛏 Sleeping

Tigh'n Eilean Guest House   B&B ££
(☎01887-820109; www.tighneilean.com; Taybridge Dr; s/d £45/68; ℗🛜🐾) Everything about this property screams comfort. It's a gorgeous place overlooking the Tay, with individually designed rooms all creating a unique sense of space. One has a spa, while another is set on its own in a cheery yellow summer house in the garden, giving you a bit of privacy if that's your thing. The garden itself is fabulous, with hammocks to laze in in summer, and the riverbank is delightful, with birdsong above and ducks paddling below.

Balnearn Guest House   B&B ££
(☎01887-820431; www.balnearnhouse.com; Crieff Rd; s £45, d £65-80; ℗🛜) Balnearn is a sedate, refined and quite luxurious mansion near the centre of town, with space to spare. Most rooms have great natural light, and there's a particularly good family room downstairs. Breakfast has been lavishly praised by readers, and the attentive, cordial hosts are helpful while respecting your privacy.

ℹ Information

Aberfeldy Information Centre (☎01887-820276; The Square; ⊙Mon-Wed, Fri & Sat Nov-Mar, daily Apr-Oct) In an old church on the central square.

ⓘ Getting There & Away

Stagecoach (www.stagecoachbus.com) runs buses from Aberfeldy to Pitlochry (45 minutes, hourly Monday to Saturday, fewer on Sunday), Blairgowrie (1¼ hours, two daily Monday to Friday) and Perth (1¼ hours, hourly Monday to Saturday, one Sunday).

Local buses run a circular route from Aberfeldy through Kenmore, Fortingall and back to Aberfeldy three times each way on Monday, Thursday and Friday. There's also a service to Killin (one hour, two daily schooldays only), also via Kenmore.

KENMORE

Pretty Kenmore lies at Loch Tay's eastern end, 6 miles west of Aberfeldy, and is dominated by a church, clock tower and the striking archway of privately owned **Taymouth Castle**. On the loch is the fascinating Scottish Crannog Centre (☑01887-830583; www.crannog.co.uk; tours adult/child £7/5; ⊙10am-5.30pm Apr-Oct, to 4pm Sat & Sun Nov). A crannog, perched on stilts in the water, was a favoured form of defence-minded dwelling in Scotland from the 3rd millennium BC onwards. This one has been superbly reconstructed and the guided tour includes an impressive demonstration of fire making. It's an excellent attraction.

Kenmore is a good activity base, and Loch Tay Boat House (☑07923-540826; www.loch-tay.co.uk; Pier Rd; ⊙daily) can have you speeding off on a mountain bike (per half-/full day £15/20) or out on the loch itself, in anything from a canoe to a cabin cruiser that'll sleep a whole family.

The heart of the village, Kenmore Hotel (☑01887-830205; www.kenmorehotel.com; The Square; s/d £84/135; Ⓟ@🛜🐕) has a bar with a roaring fire and some verses scribbled on the chimneypiece by Robert Burns in 1787, when the inn was already a couple of centuries old. There's also a riverbank beer garden, great views from the modern restaurant and a wide variety of rooms, some across the road. They are rather staid, but comfortable and spacious; the nicest have bay windows and river views. Prices plummet in low season and midweek. There are also upmarket self-catering lodges available.

LOCH TAY

Serpentine and picturesque, long Loch Tay reflects the powerful forests and mountains around it. The bulk of mighty **Ben Lawers** (1214m) looms above and is part of a national nature reserve that includes the nearby **Tarmachan Range**.

The main access point for the ascent of Ben Lawers is the car park 1½ miles off the A827, 5 miles east of Killin. There's also an easier nature trail leaving from here.

There's good accommodation in Kenmore and Killin, as well as Culdees Bunkhouse (☑01887-830519; www.culdeesbunkhouse.co.uk; dm/tw/f £18/46/69; Ⓟ@🛜🐕), a wonderfully offbeat hostel with utterly majestic vistas: the whole of the loch stretches out before and below you. It's a quirky place you could get lost in, with compact, spotless dorms, lovable family rooms with the best views in Perthshire, and a range of cluttered, home-like lounging areas. It's a top spot to relax but also a fine base for hill walking or for mucking in with the volunteers who help run the sustainable farm here. It's half a mile above the village of Fearnan, 4 miles west of Kenmore.

FORTINGALL

Fortingall is one of the prettiest villages in Scotland, with 19th-century thatched cot-

BAG A MUNRO: BEN LAWERS

The ascent of Ben Lawers can take up to five hours (return): pack wet-weather gear, water and food. From the car park (£2), where a stone enclosure should have route maps, cross the road and follow the trail just uphill from you. After the boardwalk protecting a bog, cross a stile then fork left and ascend along the Edramucky burn (to the right). At the next rise, fork right and cross the burn. A few minutes later ignore the nature trail's right turn and continue ascending parallel to the burn's left bank for just over half a mile. Leave the protected zone by another stile and steeply ascend Beinn Ghlas's shoulder. Reaching a couple of large rocks, ignore a northbound footpath and continue zigzagging uphill. The rest of the ascent is a straightforward succession of three false summits. The last and steepest section alternates between erosion-sculpted rock and a meticulously crafted cobbled trail. Long views of majestic hillscapes, and even the North Sea and Atlantic Ocean, are your reward on a clear day.

tages in a very tranquil setting. The **church** has impressive wooden beams and a 7th-century **monk's bell**. In the churchyard, there's a 2000-year-old **yew** that was around when the Romans camped in the meadows by the River Lyon: popular if unlikely tradition says that Pontius Pilate was born here. Today the tree is a shell of its former self – at its zenith it had a girth of over 17m, but souvenir hunters have reduced it to two much smaller trunks.

Fortingall Hotel (☎01887-830367; www.fortingall.com; s/d £90/120; P☎☀), alongside, is a peaceful, old-fashioned country hotel with polite service and furnished with quiet good taste. The bedrooms are spotless with huge beds, modern bathrooms and thoughtful little extras. They look out over green meadows; in all, a perfect spot for doing very little except enjoying the clean air and excellent dinners.

GLEN LYON

This remote and stunningly beautiful glen runs for some 34 unforgettable miles of rickety stone bridges, Caledonian pine forest and sheer heather-splashed peaks poking through swirling clouds. It becomes wilder and more uninhabited as it snakes its way west, and is proof that hidden treasures still exist in Scotland. The ancients believed it to be a gateway to Faerieland, and even the most sceptical of people will be entranced by the valley's magic.

From Fortingall, a narrow road winds up the glen – another road from Loch Tay crosses the hills and reaches the glen halfway in, at **Bridge of Balgie**. The glen continues up to a dam (past a memorial to explorer Robert Campbell); bearing left here you can actually continue over a wild and remote road (unmarked on maps) to isolated **Glen Lochay** and down to Killin. **Cycling** through Glen Lyon is a wonderful way to experience this special place.

There's little in the way of attractions in the valley – the majestic and lonely scenery is the reason to be here – but at **Glenlyon Gallery** (www.glenlyongallery.co.uk; admission free; ☺10am-5pm Thu-Tue), in Bridge of Balgie, a selection of fine handmade pieces are for sale. Adjacent is the **Bridge of Balgie post office** (light meals £3-4; ☺8am-6pm Apr-Oct, closed Tue-Thu Nov-Mar, food served until 4pm), the best – the only – spot for supplies (limited), or sandwiches and soups (very tasty).

Milton Eonan (☎01887-866337; www.milton eonan.com; s/d £39/78; P☎☀) is a must for those seeking utter tranquillity in a glorious natural setting. On an effervescent stream where a historic watermill once stood, it's a working rare-breed croft that offers a romantic one-bedroom self-catering cottage (breakfast available for a little extra) at the bottom of the garden. It can sleep three at a pinch. The lively owners do packed lunches and evening meals (£20) using local and home-grown produce. After crossing the bridge at Bridge of Balgie, you'll see Milton Eonan signposted to the right.

There is no public transport in the glen.

LOCHS TUMMEL & RANNOCH

The route along Lochs Tummel and Rannoch is worth doing any way you can – by foot, bicycle or car. Hills of ancient birch and forests of spruce, pine and larch make up the fabulous **Tay Forest Park**. These wooded hills roll into the glittering waters of the lochs; a visit in autumn is recommended, when the birch trees are at their finest.

Queen's View Centre (www.forestry.gov.uk; ☺10am-6pm late Mar–mid-Nov) is at the eastern end of Loch Tummel. Despite the signage, the shop here is a shop and not an exhibition, so if you pay the parking fee (£2) it's for the magnificent viewpoint over the water and towards **Schiehallion** (1083m).

Waterfalls, towering mountains and a shimmering loch greet visitors in **Kinloch Rannoch**. It's a great base for cycle trips around **Loch Rannoch** and local walks, including the hike up Schiehallion, a relatively easy climb rewarded by spectacular views unobstructed by other hills, from Braes of Foss. See www.jmt.org/east-schiehallion-est ate.asp for more information.

Eighteen miles west, the road ends at romantic, isolated **Rannoch train station**, which is on the Glasgow–Fort William line. Beyond is desolate, intriguing **Rannoch Moor**, a winding, vaguely threatening peat bog stretching as far as the A82 and Glen Coe. There's a tearoom on the platform and a welcoming small hotel situated alongside.

There's no petrol in this area; the closest pumps are Aberfeldy, Pitlochry, and Blair Atholl.

🛏 Sleeping & Eating

TOP CHOICE **Bunrannoch House** B&B ££
(☎01882-632407; www.bunrannoch.co.uk; Kinloch Rannoch; s/d £45/90, with dinner £70/140; P☎☀) We've racked our brains, and can't come up with a place that offers better value or a better attitude in this part of Scotland.

This historic former shooting lodge is a short way from town but feels utterly isolated and makes a great away-from-it-all destination. The rooms – including a great family one, and lovely room 7 with skylight for stargazing – are all recently renovated with understated elegance and offer substantial comfort, but it's the friendly, generous, can-do hospitality that is so striking. Excellent meals (vegan/vegetarian diets catered for) feature the likes of pike fished from Loch Rannoch or locally stalked venison. Dinner for nonguests is £30.

Moor of Rannoch Hotel HOTEL **££**
(☎01882-633238; www.moorofrannoch.co.uk; Rannoch Station; s/d £62/102; ◎late Mar-Oct; 🐾) At the end of the road beside Rannoch train station, this is one of Scotland's most isolated places, but luckily this hotel is here to keep your spirits up if the solitude gets too much. No internet, no mobile reception, cosy rooms and great walks right from the doorstep – a magical getaway. They do good dinners here, and can make a pricey packed lunch.

Gardens B&B B&B **££**
(☎01882-632434; www.thegardensdunalastair. co.uk; s/d £40/80; P) Right off the beaten track between Kinloch Rannoch and Tummel Bridge, this place has just two rooms – a double and a twin. But what rooms they are: effectively suites, each with their own bathroom and sitting room. The conservatory space is great for soaking up the sun and contemplating the stunning view of Schiehallion. If you're looking for solitude and a touch of inspiring eccentricity, this is the place.

Loch Tummel Inn PUB **££**
(☎01882-634272; www.lochtummelinn.co.uk; dinner mains £10-17; ◎Tue-Sun) This old coaching inn is a snug spot for a decent feed from a menu ranging from pub classics to more ambitious meat and game dishes. The friendly bar has some good tap choices and is a top spot for a quiet pint at the outdoor tables with a marvellous view over Loch Tummel. The inn is about 3 miles from Queen's View and also has rooms.

❶ Getting There & Away

Broons Buses (☎01882-632331) operates a service between Kinloch Rannoch and Pitlochry (50 minutes, up to five a day Monday to Saturday) via Queen's View and Loch Tummel Inn.

ScotRail (www.scotrail.co.uk) runs two to four trains daily from Rannoch station north to Fort William (£9.40, one hour) and Mallaig, and south to Glasgow (£21.60, 2¾ hours).

Perth to Blair Castle

There are a number of major sights strung along the busy but scenic A9, the main route north to the Cairngorms and Inverness.

DUNKELD & BIRNAM
POP 1005

The Tay runs like a storybook river between the twin towns of Dunkeld and Birnam, nestled in the heart of Perthshire's big-tree country. As well as Dunkeld's lovely cathedral, there's much walking to be done in this area of magnificent forested hills. These same walks were one of the inspirations for Beatrix Potter to create her children's tales.

◉ Sights & Activities

Situated on the grassy banks of the Tay, **Dunkeld Cathedral** (HS; www.historic-scotland.gov. uk; High St; admission free; ◎9.30am-6.30pm Mon-Sat & 2-4.30pm Sun Apr-Sep, 9.30am-4pm Mon-Sat & 2-4pm Sun Oct-Mar) is one of the most beautifully sited cathedrals in Scotland. Don't miss it on a sunny day, as there are few lovelier places to be. Half the cathedral is still in use as a church; the rest is in ruins, and you can explore it all. It partly dates from the 14th century; the cathedral was damaged during the Reformation and burnt in the battle of Dunkeld (Jacobites vs Government) in 1689. The **Wolf of Badenoch**, a fierce 14th century noble who burned towns and abbeys to the ground in protest at his excommunication, is buried here - undeservedly - in a fine medieval tomb behind the wooden screen in the church.

If you're looking to entertain the kids for a few hours, drop by welcoming **Going Pottie** (www.goingpottie.com; Cathedral St; painting from £6; ◎10am-4pm Mon-Sat, 11am-4pm Sun) where they can get a paintbrush in their hand and create colourful ceramics. They're happy to look after them here while you go off to see the cathedral nearby.

Across the bridge is Birnam, made famous by *Macbeth*. There's not much left of Birnam Wood, but there is a small, leafy **Beatrix Potter Park** (the children's author, who wrote the evergreen story of *Peter Rabbit*, spent childhood holidays in the area). Next to the park, in the Birnam Arts Centre, is a small **exhibition** (www.birnamarts.com; Station

Rd; admission £1.50; ⊙10am-4.30pm Oct-Mar, to 5pm Apr-Sep) on Potter and her characters.

Loch of the Lowes Wildlife Centre (☎01350-727337; www.swt.org.uk; adult/child £4/50p; ⊙10am-5pm), 2 miles east of Dunkeld off the A923, has wildlife displays mostly devoted to the majestic osprey. There's also an excellent birdwatching hide (with binoculars provided), where you can see the birds nesting during breeding season.

🛏 Sleeping & Eating

Birnam Hotel HOTEL ££
(☎01350-728030; www.birnamhotel.com; Perth Rd; s/d/f £80/100/138; P🛜🐾) This grand-looking place with crow-stepped gables has tastefully fitted rooms – superiors (double £133) are substantially larger than the standards. Service is very welcoming. There's a fairly formal restaurant, as well as a livelier pub alongside serving creative bar meals.

TOP CHOICE **Taybank** PUB £
(☎01350-727340; www.thetaybank.com; Tay Tce; mains £5-9) Top choice for a sun-kissed pub lunch by the river is the Taybank, a regular meeting place and performance space for musicians of all creeds and a wonderfully open and welcoming bar. There's live music of some kind nightly, and the menu runs to burgers and various incarnations of stovies (stewed potato and onion with meat or other ingredients).

ℹ Information

Dunkeld's **tourist office** (☎01350-727688; www.perthshire.co.uk; The Cross; ⊙daily Apr-Oct, Fri-Sun Nov-Mar) has information on local trails and paths.

ℹ Getting There & Away

Dunkeld is 15 miles north of Perth. Trains and buses between Glasgow/Edinburgh and Inverness stop here. **Stagecoach** (www.stagecoachbus.com) also runs 10 buses daily (only one on Sunday) between Perth and Aberfeldy via Dunkeld. There are also services to Blairgowrie (30 minutes), twice daily Monday to Friday only.

PITLOCHRY
POP 2564

Pitlochry, with its air already smelling of the Highlands, is a popular stop on the way north and a convenient base for exploring northern central Scotland. On a quiet spring evening it's a pretty place with salmon jumping in the Tummel and good things brewing at the Moulin Hotel. In summer the main street can be a conga line of tour groups, but get away from that and it'll still charm you.

⊙ Sights

One of Pitlochry's attractions is its beautiful **riverside**; the River Tummel is dammed here, and you can watch salmon swimming (not jumping) up a **fish ladder** to the loch above.

Bell's Blair Athol Distillery DISTILLERY
(☎01796-482003; www.discovering-distilleries.com; Perth Rd; tour £6; ⊙daily Apr-Oct, Mon-Fri Nov-Mar) One of two distilleries around Pitlochry, this one is at the southern end of town. Tours focus on whisky making and the blending of this well-known drop. More detailed private tours give you greater insights and superior tastings.

FREE **Edradour Distillery** DISTILLERY
(☎01796-472095; www.edradour.co.uk; ⊙daily) This is proudly Scotland's smallest distillery and a great one to visit: you can see the whole process, easily explained, in one room. It's 2.5 miles east of Pitlochry, along the Moulin road, and it's a pleasant walk.

Explorers Garden GARDENS
(☎01796-484600; www.explorersgarden.com; Foss Rd; adult/child £4/1; ⊙10am-5pm Apr-Oct) At the Pitlochry Festival Theatre, this excellent garden commemorates 300 years of plant collecting and those who hunted down 'new' species. The whole collection is based on plants brought back to Scotland by Scottish explorers.

Heathergems CRAFTS
(☎01796-474391; www.heathergems.com; 22 Atholl Rd; ⊙9am-5.30pm Mon-Sat, 9.30am-5pm Sun Apr-Oct, 9am-5pm Mon-Sat Nov-Mar) Just behind the tourist office, Heathergems is a factory outlet of a most unusual and beautiful form of Scottish jewellery. The jewellery is made from natural heather stems, which are dyed and pressed to create colourful, original pieces. You can view the jewellery being made through windows into the workshop.

🎪 Festivals & Events

Étape CYCLING
(www.etapecaledonia.co.uk; ⊙May) Étape, an 81-mile charity cycling event, brings competitors of all standards onto the beautiful Highland roads around Pitlochry in mid-May. It's become a big deal; you'll have to prebook accommodation.

Enchanted Forest
LIGHT SHOW

(www.enchantedforest.org.uk; adult £12.50-15, child £7.50; ☺Oct) This spectacular sound-and-light show in a forest near Pitlochry is a major family hit.

🛏 Sleeping

TOP CHOICE Craigatin House
GUEST HOUSE ££

(☎01796-472478; www.craigatinhouse.co.uk; 165 Atholl Rd; s £75, d standard/deluxe £85/95; ☺mid-Jan–Oct; P@☎) Several times more tasteful than the average Pitlochry lodging, this noble house and garden is set back from the main road. Chic contemporary fabrics covering expansive beds offer a standard of comfort above and beyond the reasonable price; the rooms in the converted stable block are particularly inviting. A fabulous breakfast and lounge area gives perspectives over the lush garden. Breakfast choices include whisky-laced porridge, smoked-fish omelettes and apple pancakes. Kids not allowed.

Ashleigh
B&B £

(☎01796-470316; www.realbandbpitlochry.co.uk; 120 Atholl Rd; s/d £30/50; ☎) Genuine welcomes don't come much better than Nancy's, and her place on the main street makes a top Pitlochry pit stop. Three comfortable rooms share an excellent bathroom, and there's an open kitchen stocked with goodies where you make your own breakfast in the morning. A home away from home and a standout budget choice. She also has a good self-catering apartment with great views, available by the night.

Knockendarroch House
HOTEL ££

(☎01796-473473; www.knockendarroch.co.uk; Higher Oakfield; d dinner, bed & breakfast £188; P☎☺) Top of the town and boasting the best views, this genteel, well-run hotel has a range of luxurious rooms with huge windows that take advantage of the Highland light. The standard rooms have better views than the larger, slightly pricier superior ones. A couple of rooms have great little balconies, perfect for a sundowner. Meals are highly commended here.

Pitlochry Backpackers Hotel
HOSTEL £

(☎01796-470044; www.scotlands-top-hostels.com; 134 Atholl Rd; dm/tw/d £18/47/52; P@☎) Friendly, laid-back and very comfortable, this is a cracking hostel smack bang in the middle of town, with three- to eight-bed dorms that are in mint condition. There are also good-value en suite twins and doubles,

with beds, not bunks. Cheap breakfast and a pool table add to the convivial party atmosphere. No extra charge for linen.

Strathgarry
HOTEL ££

(☎01796-472469; www.strathgarryhotel.co.uk; 113 Atholl Rd; s/d £97/147, deluxe d £169; ☎) With a main street location, Strathgarry is a hotel-bar-cafe-restaurant that's all done pretty well. En suite rooms are snug and have luxurious touches – it's better value if you can grab one of its regularly discounted online offers rather than paying the rack rates listed here.

Tir Aluinn
B&B ££

(☎01796-473811; www.tiraluinn.co.uk; 10 Higher Oakfield Rd; s/d £35/70; P☎) Tucked away above the main street, this is a little gem of a place, with bright rooms with easy-on-the-eye furniture, and an excellent personal welcome. Breakfasts are excellent.

Pitlochry SYHA
HOSTEL £

(☎01796-472308; www.syha.org.uk; Knockard Rd; dm £18.50; ☺Mar-Oct; P@☎) Great location overlooking the town centre. Popular with families and walkers.

🍴 Eating & Drinking

TOP CHOICE Moulin Hotel
PUB ££

(☎01796-472196; www.moulinhotel.co.uk; bar mains £9-12) A mile away but a world apart, this atmospheric hotel was trading centuries before the tartan tack came to Pitlochry. With its romantic low ceilings, ageing wood and booth seating, the inn is a wonderfully atmospheric spot for a house-brewed ale or a portion of Highland comfort food: try the filling haggis or venison stew. A more formal restaurant (mains £12 to £16) serves equally delicious traditional fare, with excellent game and meat options. The hotel also has a variety of rooms (single/double £62/77) as well as a self-catering annexe. The best way to get here from Pitlochry is walking: it's a pretty uphill stroll through green fields, and an easy roll down the slope afterwards.

Fern Cottage
SCOTTISH, TURKISH ££

(www.ferncottagepitlochry.co.uk; Ferry Rd; mains £11-16; ☺10.30am-9pm; ☎) Just off the main road through town, this has plenty of atmosphere with its intimate candlelit tables, stone walls and creaky wooden floor. The menu combines Scottish favourites such as lamb and salmon with Eastern Mediterranean dishes such as moussaka, tsatziki and mixed meze plates to good effect. Outdoor tables are the spot for lunching if the weather's kind.

Port-na-Craig Inn BISTRO ££
(01796-472777; www.portnacraig.com; Port Na Craig; mains £12-17; ☺11am-8.30pm) Right on the river, this top little spot sits in what was once a separate hamlet. Delicious main meals are prepared with confidence and panache; there are also simpler sandwiches, kids' meals and light lunches. Or you could just sit out by the river with a pint and watch the anglers.

McKay's PUB
(www.mckayshotel.co.uk; 138 Atholl Rd) This is the place to go to meet locals and have a big night out. Live music at weekends, weekly karaoke and DJs make this Pitlochry's most popular place. The action moves from the spacious front bar (which serves food) to the boisterous dance floor out the back.

☆ Entertainment

Pitlochry Festival Theatre THEATRE
(01796-484626; www.pitlochry.org.uk; Foss Rd; tickets £26-35) This well-known and loved theatre has a summer season of several different plays daily except Sunday, from May to mid-October.

❶ Information
Computer Services Centre (www.computerservicescentre.co.uk; 23 Atholl Rd; ☺9.30am-5.30pm Mon-Fri, to 12.30pm Sat; ☎) Internet access opposite the tourist office.
Pitlochry Information Centre (01796-472215; www.perthshire.co.uk; 22 Atholl Rd; ☺daily Mar-Oct, Mon-Sat Nov-Feb) Good information on local walks.

❶ Getting There & Away
Citylink (www.citylink.co.uk) buses run roughly hourly to Inverness (£15.50, two hours), Perth (£10, 40 minutes), Edinburgh (£15.50, two to 2½ hours) and Glasgow (£15.70, 2¼ hours). **Megabus** (0871 266 3333; www.megabus.com) discount services also run these routes.

Stagecoach (www.stagecoachbus.com) runs to Aberfeldy (30 minutes, hourly Monday to Saturday, three Sunday), Dunkeld (25 minutes, up to 10 daily Monday to Saturday) and Perth (one hour, up to 10 daily Monday to Saturday).

Pitlochry is on the main railway from Perth (£12.30, 30 minutes, nine daily Monday to Saturday, five on Sunday) to Inverness.

❶ Getting Around
Escape Route (01796-473859; www.escape-route.co.uk; 3 Atholl Rd; bike hire per half-/full day from £16/24; ☺daily) rents out bikes; it's worth booking ahead at weekends.

PASS OF KILLIECRANKIE
Drop into the **Killiecrankie visitor centre** (NTS; 01796-473233; www.nts.org.uk; admission free, parking £2; ☺10am-5.30pm Apr-Oct) in this beautiful, rugged gorge, 3.5 miles north of Pitlochry. It has great interactive displays on the Jacobite rebellion and local flora and fauna. There's plenty to touch, pull and open – great for kids. There are some stunning walks into the wooded gorge, too; keep an eye out for red squirrels. Also here, **Highland Fling** (0845 366 5844; www.bungeejumpscotland.co.uk; £70, repeat jumps £30) offers breathtaking 40m jumps off the bridge over the gorge at weekends, plus Wednesday and Friday in summer.

Just near the pass, **Killiecrankie House Hotel** (01796-473220; www.killiecrankiehotel.co.uk; d standard/superior dinner, bed & breakfast £230/260; ☺Mar-Dec; P☎☺) offers faultless hospitality in a peaceful setting. There's interesting art exhibited on the walls, and rooms are elegant, relaxing retreats with views over the lovely gardens. The best aspects of Scottish country-house hospitality are here without the musty feel that sometimes goes with it. The food is also excellent. Two-night minimum stay at busy times; B&B rates are also sometimes available.

Local buses run between Pitlochry and Blair Atholl via Killiecrankie (10 minutes, three to seven daily).

BLAIR CASTLE & BLAIR ATHOLL
One of the most popular tourist attractions in Scotland, magnificent **Blair Castle** (01796-481207; www.blair-castle.co.uk; adult/child/family £9.50/5.70/25.75; ☺9.30am-5.30pm Apr-Oct, 10am-4pm Sat & Sun Nov-Mar) and the 108 square miles it sits on, is the seat of the Duke of Atholl, head of the Murray clan. It's an impressive white building set beneath forested slopes above the River Garry.

The original tower was built in 1269, but the castle has undergone significant remodelling since. Thirty rooms are open to the public and they present a wonderful picture of upper-class Highland life from the 16th century on. The **dining room** is sumptuous – check out the nine-pint wine glasses – and the **ballroom** is a vaulted chamber that's a virtual stag cemetery.

The current duke visits the castle every May to review the Atholl Highlanders, Britain's only private army.

1. Blair Castle (p229)

Magnificent Blair Castle, and the 108 square miles it sits on, is the seat of the Duke of Atholl, head of the Murray clan.

2. Balmoral Castle (p260)

Built for Queen Victoria in 1855, Balmoral Castle kicked off the revival of the Scottish Baronial style of architecture that characterises so many of Scotland's 19th-century country houses.

3. Eilean Donan Castle (p390)

Situated at the entrance to Loch Duich, Eilean Donan is one of Scotland's most evocative castles.

BRIAN LAWRENCE / GETTY IMAGES ©

UNIQUE LANDSCAPE / GETTY IMAGES ©

For a great cycle, walk or drive, take the stunning road to **Glenfender** from Blair Atholl village. It's about 3 miles on a long, winding uphill track to a farmhouse; the views of snowcapped peaks along the way are spectacular.

Atholl Arms Hotel (☎01796-481205; www.athollarms.co.uk; s/d £67/82; P🕸🛜🐾), near the castle, is a well-run place with darkish rooms with comfortably old-fashioned decor. The Bothy Bar here is the sibling pub of the Moulin Hotel in Pitlochry, snug with booth seating, low-slung roof, bucketloads of character and an enormous fireplace.

Blair Atholl is 6 miles northwest of Pitlochry, and the castle a further mile beyond it. Local buses run between Pitlochry and Blair Atholl (25 minutes, three to seven daily). Four buses a day (Monday to Saturday) go directly to the castle. There's a train station in the village, but not all trains stop here.

Blairgowrie & Glenshee

The route along the A93 through Glenshee is one of the most spectacular drives in the country. Meandering burns and soaring peaks splotched with blinding-white snow dwarf open-mouthed drivers. It's fantastic **walking** country in summer, and there's **skiing** in winter. **Blairgowrie** and **Braemar** are the main accommodation centres for the Glenshee resort, although there is a small settlement 5 miles south of the ski runs at **Spittal of Glenshee** with a couple of good sleeping options.

🏃 Activities

Glenshee Ski Resort   SNOW SPORTS
(☎01339-741320; www.ski-glenshee.co.uk; half-/full day lift pass £23/28) With 36 pistes Glenshee is one of Scotland's largest skiing areas. When the sun burns through the clouds after a good fall of snow, you'll be in a unique position to drink in the beauty of the country; the skiing isn't half bad either. The chairlift, which also opens in July and August for walkers and mountain bikers, can whisk you up to 910m, near the top of the **Cairnwell** (933m).

🛏 Sleeping & Eating

Dalmunzie House   HOTEL £££
(☎01250-885224; www.dalmunzie.com; s £105-145, d £165-235; P@🛜🐾) A noble estate with a dash of Antipodean hospitality thrown into the mix, this classy retreat lives up to the best Highland stereotypes: roaring fires, leather armchairs, antlers and decanters of malt. There are four classes of room, offering plenty of comfort (some with four-poster beds); the tower rooms are particularly spacious and worth the splash out. There's also a beautiful library set up to help research into Scottish forebears. Dinners (£45) in the restaurant are opulent affairs with three courses broken by a cleansing sorbet; there are money-saving rates, including dinner. As well as wonderful walks hereabouts, the property offers golf, tennis, fishing and other activities; bikes are also hired.

Spittal of Glenshee Hotel   HOTEL, HOSTEL ££
(☎01250-885215; www.spittalofglenshee.co.uk; dm/s/d £18/60/70; P🛜🐾) This ski-lodge-style place has a good-time atmosphere and simple, comfortable rooms that drop substantially in price outside of high summer and the snow season. There's a sociable bar and a bunkhouse (without cooking facilities).

Rosebank House   B&B ££
(☎01250-872912; colhotel@rosebank35.fsnet.co.uk; 42 Balmoral Rd; r per person £30; ☺Jan-Nov; P🛜) This fine Georgian property with great original features is a bargain. Good-sized rooms upstairs (rooms 2 and 4 are especially spacious) are well kept and have small but clean en suites, and there's a large front garden. The friendly owners have been running this for two decades and know how to take good care of their guests. They're walker, cyclist and skier friendly and well-priced four-course dinners (£17) are available.

ℹ Information

Blairgowrie Information Centre (☎01250-872960; www.perthshire.co.uk; 26 Wellmeadow; ☺daily Apr-Oct & Dec, Mon-Sat Nov & Jan-Mar) On the central square in Blairgowrie; has plenty of walking and skiing information.

ℹ Getting There & Away

Stagecoach (www.stagecoachbus.com) operates from Perth to Blairgowrie (50 minutes, three to eight daily). Buses also run from Dundee to Blairgowrie (50 minutes, hourly, less frequent on Sunday).

The only service from Blairgowrie to the Glenshee area, about 30 miles away, is Stagecoach bus 71, which runs twice on Wednesday and four times on Saturday to Spittal of Glenshee.

Around Blairgowrie

About 5 miles east of Blairgowrie, **Alyth** is a charming historic village with a small canal and exquisite stone bridges. Ask at Blairgowrie's tourist office for the *Walk Auld Alyth* leaflet. Perusing the displays on local history at Alyth Museum (www.pkc.gov.uk; Commercial St; admission free; ⊙1-5pm Wed-Sun May-Sep) is a fine way to pass an hour or so.

Alyth Hotel (☑01828-632447; www.alythhotel.com; 6 Commercial St; s/d £50/80, mains £8-12; ℗) is a classic town pub that has comfortable refurbished rooms. Try to get a room overlooking the square; room 1 is a good choice. The downstairs bar and restaurant is infinitely cosy with low-slung roof, stone walls and all manner of clutter giving it a homely feel.

Off the A94 and 8 miles east of Blairgowrie, **Meigle** is well worth the trip for those with a fascination for Pictish stones. The tiny Meigle Museum (HS; www.historic-scotland.gov.uk; adult/child £4/2.40; ⊙9.30am-12.30pm & 1.30-5.30pm Apr-Sep) has 26 beautiful carved works from the 7th to the 9th centuries, all found in the local area. Motifs range from propaganda for local strongmen to intricate geometric designs, biblical scenes and a whole menagerie of strange beasts. If the manager is there, she's a mine of information on the carvings and is happy to help you unravel some of the complex symbolism.

Northeast Scotland

Best Places to Stay

» Glen Clova Hotel (p246)
» 24 Shorehead (p257)
» Auld Kirk (p258)
» City Wharf Apartments (p252)

Best Places to Eat

» Tolbooth Restaurant (p257)
» Café 52 (p253)
» Metro (p239)
» Gathering Place (p262)

Why Go?

Many visitors pass by this corner of the country in their headlong rush to the tourist honeypots of Loch Ness and Skye. But they're missing out on a part of Scotland that's just as beautiful and diverse as the more obvious attractions of the west.

Within its bounds you'll find two of Scotland's four largest cities – Dundee, the city of jute, jam and journalism, cradle of some of Britain's favourite comic characters, and home to Captain Scott's Antarctic research ship, the *Discovery;* and Aberdeen, the granite city, an economic powerhouse fuelled by the riches of North Sea oil.

Angus is a region of rich farmland and scenic glens dotted with the mysterious stones left behind by the ancient Picts, while Aberdeenshire and Moray are home to the greatest concentration of Scottish Baronial castles in the country, and dozens of distilleries along the River Spey.

When to Go
Aberdeen

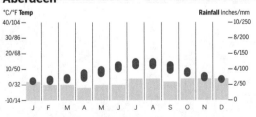

Jun/Jul Classic boats large and small fill Portsoy harbour for the Scottish Wooden Boat Festival.

Sep Braemar Gathering (Highland games); whisky and music festival in Dufftown.

Dec Spectacular fireball ceremony in Stonehaven on Hogmanay (New Year's Eve).

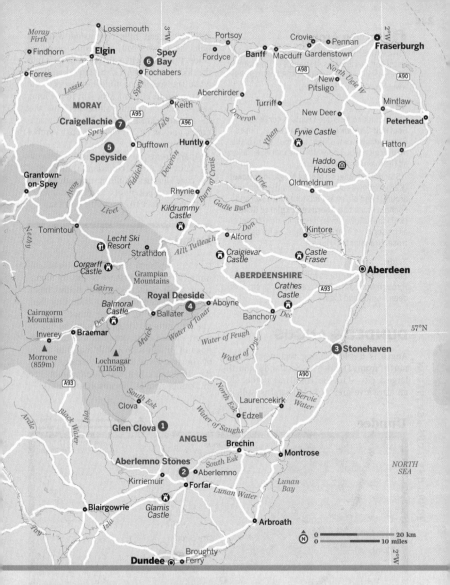

Northeast Scotland Highlights

1 Hiking through the hills around beautiful **Glen Clova** (p246)

2 Meditating on the meaning of the mysterious **Pictish stones** (p242) of Angus at Aberlemno

3 Tucking into the freshest of Scottish seafood at the **Tolbooth Restaurant** (p257) in Stonehaven

4 Exploring the hills, forests, castles and pretty villages of **Royal Deeside** (p258)

5 Being initiated into the mysteries of malt whisky on a Speyside **distillery tour** (p266)

6 Learning about the Moray Firth's bottlenose dolphins at the **Scottish Dolphin Centre** (p268) at Spey Bay

7 Sampling from 700-plus varieties of single malt in the Craigellachie Hotel's **Quaich Bar** (p266)

ⓘ Getting Around

You can pick up a **public transport map** from tourist offices and bus stations. For timetable information, call **Traveline** (☏0871 200 2233; www.travelinescotland.com).

Bus

The Dundee to Aberdeen route is served by **Scottish Citylink** (www.citylink.co.uk) buses. **Stagecoach** (www.stagecoachbus.com) is the main regional bus operator, with services linking all the main towns and cities.

Stagecoach offers a **Moray Megarider ticket** (£28) that gives seven days unlimited bus travel around Elgin as far as Findhorn, Dufftown and Fochabers, and an **Aberdeen Explorer ticket** (£41) that allows seven days unlimited travel on all its services in Aberdeenshire, as far as Montrose, Braemar and Huntly.

Train

The Dundee–Inverness railway line passes through Arbroath, Montrose, Stonehaven, Aberdeen, Huntly and Elgin.

DUNDEE & ANGUS

Angus is fertile farming region stretching north from Dundee – Scotland's fourth-largest city – to the Highland border. It's an attractive area of broad straths (valleys) and low, green hills contrasted with the rich, red-brown soil of freshly ploughed fields. Romantic glens finger their way into the foothills of the Grampian Mountains, while the scenic coastline ranges from the red-sandstone cliffs of Arbroath to the long, sandy beaches around Montrose. This was the Pictish heartland of the 7th and 8th centuries, and many interesting Pictish symbol stones survive here.

Apart from the crowds visiting Discovery Point in newly confident Dundee and the coach parties shuffling through Glamis Castle, Angus is a bit of a tourism backwater and a good place to escape the hordes.

Dundee

POP 144,000

London's Trafalgar Sq has Nelson on his column, Edinburgh's Princes St has its monument to Sir Walter Scott and Belfast has a statue of Queen Victoria outside City Hall. Dundee's City Sq, on the other hand, is graced – rather endearingly – by the bronze figure of Desperate Dan. Familiar to generations of British school children, Dan is one of the best-loved cartoon characters from the children's comic the *Dandy,* published by Dundee firm DC Thomson since 1937.

Dundee

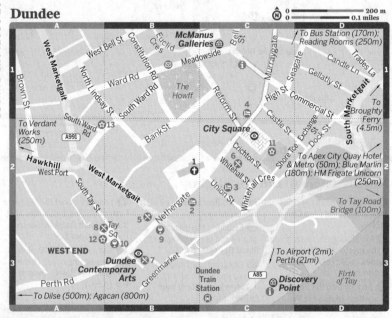

Dundee enjoys perhaps the finest location of any Scottish city, spreading along the northern shore of the Firth of Tay, and boasts tourist attractions of national importance in Discovery Point and the Verdant Works museum. Add in the attractive seaside town of Broughty Ferry, some lively nightlife and the Dundonians themselves – among the friendliest, most welcoming and most entertaining people you'll meet – and Dundee is definitely worth a stopover.

History

During the 19th century Dundee grew from its trading port origins to become a major player in the shipbuilding, whaling, textile and railway engineering industries. Dundonian firms owned and operated most of the jute mills in India (jute is a natural fibre used to make ropes and sacking), and the city's textile industry employed as many as 43,000 people – little wonder Dundee earned the nickname 'Juteopolis'.

Dundee is often called the city of the 'Three Js' – jute, jam and journalism. According to legend, it was a Dundee woman, Janet Keillor, who invented marmalade in the late 18th century; her son founded the city's famous Keillor jam factory. Jute is no longer produced, and when the Keillor factory was taken over in 1988 production was transferred to England. Journalism still thrives, however, led by the family firm of DC Thomson. Best known for children's comics, such as the *Beano,* Thomson is now the city's largest employer.

In the late 19th and early 20th centuries Dundee was one of the richest cities in the country – there were more millionaires per head of population here than anywhere else in Britain – but the textile and engineering industries declined in the second half of the 20th century, leading to high unemployment and urban decay.

In the 1960s and '70s Dundee's cityscape was scarred by ugly blocks of flats, office buildings and shopping centres linked by unsightly concrete walkways – the view as you approach across the Tay Road Bridge does not look promising – and most visitors passed it by. Since the mid-1990s, however, Dundee has reinvented itself as a tourist destination, and a centre for banking, insurance and new industries, while its waterfront is currently undergoing a major redevelopment. It also has more university students – one in seven of the population – than any other town in Europe, except Heidelberg.

⊙ Sights

Discovery Point   MUSEUM
(Map p236; www.rrsdiscovery.com; Discovery Quay; adult/child £8.25/5; ☺10am-6pm Mon-Sat, 11am-6pm Sun Apr-Oct, to 5pm Nov-Mar) The three masts of Captain Robert Falcon Scott's famous polar expedition vessel the **RRS Discovery** dominate the riverside to the south of the city centre. The ship was built in Dundee in 1900, with a wooden hull at least half a metre thick to survive the pack ice, and sailed for the Antarctic in 1901 where it spent two winters trapped in the ice. From 1931 on it was laid up in London where its condition steadily deteriorated, until it was rescued by the efforts of Peter Scott (Robert's son) and the Maritime Trust, and restored to its 1925 condition. In 1986 the ship was given a berth in its home port

NORTHEAST SCOTLAND DUNDEE

Dundee

of Dundee, where it became a symbol of the city's regeneration.

Exhibitions and audiovisual displays in the main building provide a fascinating history of both the ship and the Antarctic exploration, but *Discovery* itself – afloat in a protected dock – is the star attraction. You can visit the bridge, the galley and the mahogany-panelled officers' wardroom, and poke your nose into the cabins used by Scott and his crew.

A joint ticket that gives entry to both Discovery Point and the Verdant Works costs £13.50/8.50 per adult/child.

Verdant Works · · · · · · · · · · · · · MUSEUM

(www.verdantworks.com; West Henderson's Wynd; adult/child £8.25/5; ☺10am-6pm Mon-Sat, 11am-6pm Sun Apr-Oct; 10:30am-4.30pm Wed-Sun Nov-Mar) One of the finest industrial museums in Europe, the Verdant Works explores the history of Dundee's jute industry. Housed in a restored jute mill, complete with original machinery still in working condition, the museum's interactive exhibits and computer displays follow the raw material from its origins in India through to the manufacture of a wide range of finished products, from sacking to rope to wagon covers for the pioneers of the American West. The mill is 250m west of the city centre.

FREE McManus Galleries · · · · · · · MUSEUM

(Map p236; www.mcmanus.co.uk; Albert Sq; ☺10am-5pm Mon-Sat, 12.30-4.30pm Sun) Housed in a solid Victorian Gothic building designed by Gilbert Scott in 1867, the McManus Galleries is a city museum on a human scale – you can see everything there is to see, without feeling rushed or overwhelmed. The exhibits cover the history of the city from the Iron Age to the present day, including relics of the Tay Bridge Disaster and the Dundee whaling industry. Computer geeks will enjoy the Sinclair ZX81 and Spectrum (pioneering personal computers with a whole 16K of memory!) which were made in Dundee in the early 1980s.

HM Frigate Unicorn · · · · · · · · · · · MUSEUM

(www.frigateunicorn.org; Victoria Dock; adult/child £5.25/3.25; ☺10am-5pm Apr-Oct; noon-4pm Wed-Fri, 10am-4pm Sat & Sun Nov-Mar) Unlike the polished and much-restored *Discovery,* Dundee's other floating tourist attraction retains the authentic atmosphere of a salty old sailing ship. Built in 1824, the 46-gun *Unicorn* is the oldest British-built ship

still afloat – she was mothballed soon after launching and never saw action. By the mid-19th century sailing ships were outclassed by steam and the *Unicorn* served as a gun-powder store, then later as a training vessel. When it was proposed to break up the ship for scrap in the 1960s, a preservation society was formed. Wandering around the deck gives you an excellent impression of what it must have been like for the crew forced to live in such cramped conditions.

The *Unicorn* is berthed in Victoria Dock, just northeast of the Tay Road Bridge. The entry price includes a self-guided tour (also available in French and German).

FREE Dundee Contemporary Arts · · · · · · ARTS CENTRE

(Map p236; www.dca.org.uk; Nethergate; ☺11am-6pm Tue, Wed, Fri & Sat, 11am-8pm Thu, noon-6pm Sun) The focus for the city's emerging Cultural Quarter is Dundee Contemporary Arts, a centre for modern art, design and cinema. The galleries here exhibit work by contemporary UK and international artists, and there are printmakers' studios where you can watch artists at work, or even take part in craft demonstrations and workshops. There's also the Jute Cafe-Bar (p240).

Dundee Law · · · · · · · · · · · · · · · · · PARK

It's worth making the climb up Dundee Law (174m) for great views of the city, the two Tay bridges, and across to Fife. The **Tay Rail Bridge** – at just over 2 miles long, it was the world's longest when it was built – was completed in 1887 and replaced an earlier bridge whose stumps can be seen alongside. The original bridge collapsed during a storm in 1879 less than two years after it was built, in the infamous Tay Bridge Disaster, taking a train and 75 lives along with it. The 1.5-mile **Tay Road Bridge** was opened in 1966. Dundee Law is a short walk northwest of the city centre, along Constitution Rd.

City Square · · · · · · · · · · · · · · · · SQUARE

(Map p236) The heart of Dundee is City Sq, flanked to the south by the 1930s facade of **Caird Hall**, which was gifted to the city by a textile magnate and is now home to the City Chambers. A more recent addition to the square, unveiled in 2001, is a bronze statue of **Desperate Dan**, the lantern-jawed hero of children's comic the *Dandy* (he's clutching a copy in his right hand).

Pedestrianised High St leads west into Nethergate, flanked to the north by St

Mary's Church (Map p236; Nethergate). Most of the church dates from the 19th century, but the **Old Steeple** was built around 1460.

★ Festivals & Events

If you're around in late July, look out for the Dundee Blues Bonanza (www.dundee bluesbonanza.co.uk), a two-day festival of free blues, boogie and roots music.

🛏 Sleeping

Most of Dundee's city-centre hotels are business oriented and offer lower rates on weekends. B&Bs are concentrated along Broughty Ferry Rd and Arbroath Rd east of the city centre, and on Perth Rd to the west. If you don't fancy a night in the city, consider staying at the nearby seaside town of Broughty Ferry.

Accommodation in Dundee is usually booked solid when the Open golf tournament is staged at Carnoustie or St Andrews – check www.theopen.com for future dates and venues (it'll be in St Andrews in 2015).

Balgowan House   B&B **££**
(☏01382-200262; www.balgowanhouse.co.uk; 510 Perth Rd; s/d from £55/80; P🐾) Built in 1900 and perched in a prime location with stunning views over the Firth of Tay, Balgowan is a wealthy merchant's mansion converted into a luxurious guesthouse with three sumptuous en suite bedrooms. It's 2 miles west of the city centre, overlooking the university botanic gardens.

Apex City Quay Hotel   HOTEL **££**
(☏0845-365 0000; www.apexhotels.co.uk; 1 West Victoria Dock Rd; r from £72; P🐾🏊) Though it looks plain and boxy from the outside, the Apex overlooks the city's redeveloping waterfront and sports the sort of stylish, spacious, sofa-equipped rooms that make you want to lounge around all evening munching chocolate in front of the TV. If you can drag yourself away from your room, there are spa treatments, saunas and Japanese hot tubs to enjoy. The hotel is just east of the city centre, close to the HM Frigate Unicorn.

Errolbank Guest House   B&B **££**
(☏01382-462118; www.errolbank-guesthouse. com; 9 Dalgleish Rd; s/d £49/69; P) A mile east of the city centre, just north of the road to Broughty Ferry, Errolbank is a lovely Victorian family home with small but beautifully decorated en suite rooms set on a quiet street.

Dundee Backpackers   HOSTEL **£**
(Map p236; ☏01382-224646; www.hoppo.com; 71 High St; dm £18.50, s/tw from £25/40; @) Set in a beautifully converted historic building, with clean, modern kitchen, pool room, and an ideal location right in the city centre. Can get a bit noisy at night, but that's because it's close to pubs and nightlife.

Shaftesbury Hotel   HOTEL **££**
(☏01382-669216; www.shaftesburyhotel.net; 1 Hyndford St; s/d from £60/75; @🐾) The family-run, 12-room Shaftesbury is a Victorian mansion built for a jute baron and has many authentic period features, including a fine marble fireplace in the dining room. It's 1.5 miles west of the city centre, just off Perth Rd.

Aabalree   B&B **£**
(Map p236; ☏01382-223867; www.aabalree.com; 20 Union St; s/d £24/40) This is a pretty basic B&B – there are no en suites – but the owners are welcoming (don't be put off by the dark entrance) and it couldn't be more central, close to both train and bus stations. This makes it popular, so book ahead.

Grampian Hotel   HOTEL **£**
(☏01382-667785; www.grampianhotel.com; 295 Perth Rd; s/d from £55/70; P🐾) A small and welcoming hotel set in a restored Victorian town house with six spacious bedrooms (all en suite), just five minutes' walk from the West End.

Aauld Steeple Guest House   B&B **£**
(Map p236; ☏01382-200302; www.aauldsteeple guesthouse.co.uk; 94 Nethergate; s/d from £27/44; 🐾) Just as central as Aabalree, but a bit more comfortable, the Aauld Steeple has spacious double and family rooms, some with views of St Mary's Church. It does suffer a bit from street noise, though.

🍴 Eating

TOP CHOICE / **Metro**   BRASSERIE **££**
(☏0845-365 0002; www.apexhotels.co.uk/eat; Apex City Quay Hotel, 1 West Victoria Dock Rd; mains £11-22; ⏱lunch & dinner) Sleek, slate-blue banquettes, white linen napkins, black-clad staff and a view of Victoria Dock lend an air of sophistication to this stylish hotel brasserie, with a menu that ranges from steaks and burgers to Indian butter chicken curry. There's a three-course dinner menu for £22.50 (before 7pm).

Blue Marlin
SEAFOOD £££

(☎01382-221397; www.thebluemarlin.co.uk; City Quay; mains £20-25; ☺lunch & dinner Mon-Sat) The ongoing redevelopment of Dundee's former docks means that the setting for the city's best fish restaurant doesn't look too promising. But once inside, there is sleek and understated nautical-themed decor, and the chance to feast on the best of Scottish seafood.

Playwright
BISTRO ££

(Map p236; ☎01382-223113; www.theplaywright. co.uk; 11 Tay Sq; mains £23-26; ☺10am-midnight) Next door to the Dundee Rep Theatre, and decorated with photos of Scottish actors, this innovative cafe-bar and bistro serves a set lunch (two course £13), pre-theatre menu (£17/20 for two/three courses, 5pm to 6.30pm) and a gourmet à la carte menu that concentrates on fine Scottish produce with dishes such as saddle of lamb with celeriac dauphinoise.

Jute Café Bar
BISTRO ££

(Map p236; www.jutecafebar.co.uk; 152 Nethergate; mains lunch £8-12, dinner £10-19; ☺10.30am-midnight Mon-Sat, noon-midnight Sun) The industrial-chic cafe-bar in the Dundee Contemporary Arts centre serves excellent deli sandwiches and burgers, as well as more adventurous Mediterranean-Asian fusion cuisine. The early-bird menu (5pm to 6.30pm weekdays) offers a two-course dinner for £13.50. Tables spill out into the sunny courtyard in summer.

Agacán
TURKISH ££

(☎01382-644227; 113 Perth Rd; mains £11-18; ☺dinner Tue-Sun) With a charismatic owner, quirky decor and wonderfully aromatic Turkish specialities (İskender kebab is our favourite), it's no wonder that you have to book ahead at this colourful little restaurant, a 20-minute walk up Perth Rd from the centre. If you can't get a table, you can settle for takeaway.

Encore Bar & Brasserie
CAFE, BAR ££

(Map p236; ☎01382-206699; www.encoredundee.co.uk; Tay Sq; mains £10-16; ☺bar 11am-late, brasserie noon-3pm & 5-9pm Mon-Sat) The city's arty types hang out in this Continental-style cafe-bar and restaurant in the foyer at the Dundee Rep Theatre. The menu ranges from crayfish salad to wild mushroom and blue cheese puff pastry.

Parrot Café
CAFE £

(91 Perth Rd; mains £4-10; ☺10am-5pm Tue-Fri, 10am-4pm Sat) A cracking wee cafe with good coffee and tea, home baking like Mum used to make and a couple of hot lunch dishes. A mile west of the city centre, near the university.

Fisher & Donaldson
TEAROOM £

(Map p236; 12 Whitehall St; ☺6.30am-5pm Mon-Sat) There's an excellent tearoom in this upmarket bakery and patisserie, which sells traditional Dundee cake and less traditional Irn-Bru-flavoured cupcakes.

Deep Sea
FISH & CHIPS £

(Map p236; 81 Nethergate; mains £5-10; ☺9.30am-6.30pm Mon-Sat) Dundee's best fish and chips.

🍺 Drinking

Dundee has many lively pubs, especially in the West End and along West Port.

Speedwell Bar
PUB

(www.mennies.co.uk; 165-167 Perth Rd) Known to generations of Dundonians as 'Mennie's', this university district pub, 1½ miles west of the city centre, is the city's best preserved Edwardian bar, complete with acres of polished mahogany, real ale on tap and a choice of 150 malt whiskies.

Nether Inn
PUB

(Map p236; 134 Nethergate) This large, lounge-type bar with comfy couches, pool table and drink promos, is popular with students.

Social
BAR

(Map p236; www.socialdundee.co.uk; 10 South Tay St) A lively style bar and club with a separate dining area.

☆ Entertainment

Dundee's nightlife may not be as hot as Glasgow's, but there are lots of places to go – pick up a free what's-on guide from the tourist office, or check out the What's On section of www.dundee.com. Tickets for most events are on sale at the Dundee Contemporary Arts centre.

Caird Hall
MUSIC, COMEDY

(Map p236; www.cairdhall.co.uk; 6 City Sq; ☺box office 9am-4.30pm Mon-Fri, 9.30am-1.30pm Sat) The Caird Hall hosts regular concerts of classical music, as well as organ recitals, rock bands, dances, comedians, fetes and fairs. Check the website for details of coming events.

Dundee Rep Theatre
DRAMA

(Map p236; www.dundereptheatre.co.uk; Tay Sq; ☺box office 10am-6pm or start of performance) Dundee's main venue for the performing arts, the Rep is home to Scotland's only full-time repertory company and to the Scottish Dance Theatre.

Reading Rooms　　　　　CLUB, LIVE MUSIC
(www.readingroomsdundee.com; 57 Blackscroft; admission £5-8) Dundee's hippest venue is an arty, bohemian hang-out in a run-down former library that hosts some of Scotland's best indie club nights. Live gigs have ranged from island singer-songwriter Colin MacIntyre (aka Mull Historical Society) to Glasgow guitar band Franz Ferdinand and Ayrshire rockers Biffy Clyro.

Fat Sams　　　　　　　CLUB, LIVE MUSIC
(Map p236; www.fatsams.co.uk; 31 South Ward Rd; ☺11pm-late) Fat Sams has been around for more than 20 years but is still one of the city's most popular clubs, with regular live gigs, DJs and student nights pulling in a young crowd (including lots of students from St Andrews University).

ⓘ Information

Dundee Tourist Office (☑01382-527527; www.angusanddundee.co.uk; Discovery Point; ☺10am-5pm Mon-Sat, noon-4pm Sun Jun-Sep; 10am-4pm Mon-Sat Oct-May)

Ninewells Hospital (☑01382-660111; ☺casualty 24hr) At Menzieshill, west of the city centre.

ⓘ Getting There & Away

AIR Two and a half miles west of the city centre, **Dundee Airport** (www.hial.co.uk) has daily scheduled services to London City airport, Birmingham and Belfast. A taxi from the city centre to the airport takes ten minutes and costs £3.80.

BUS The bus station is northeast of the city centre. Some Aberdeen buses travel via Arbroath, others via Forfar.

Aberdeen £16, 1½ hours, hourly

Edinburgh £15, two hours, hourly, some change at Perth

Glasgow £15, two hours, hourly

London £40, 11 hours; National Express

Perth £7, 35 minutes, hourly

Oban £23, 3½ hours, two daily

TRAIN Trains from Dundee to Aberdeen travel via Arbroath and Stonehaven.

Aberdeen £27, 1¼ hours, twice an hour

Edinburgh £23, 1¼ hours, at least hourly

Glasgow £25, 1½ hours, hourly

ⓘ Getting Around

The city centre is compact and is easy to get around on foot. For information on local public transport, contact **Travel Dundee** (www.traveldundee.co.uk; Forum Shopping Centre, 92 Commercial St; ☺9.15am-4.55pm Mon-Fri, 10am-3.55pm Sat).

BUS City bus fares cost £1.10 to £2.10 depending on distance; buy your ticket from the driver (exact fare only – no change given).

CAR Rental agencies include:

Arnold Clark (☑01382-225382; www.arnoldclarkrental.com; East Dock St)

National Car Rental (☑01382-224037; www.nationalcar.co.uk; 45-53 Gellatly St)

TAXI **Discovery Taxis** (☑01382-732111)

Broughty Ferry

Dundee's attractive seaside suburb, known locally as 'The Ferry', lies 4 miles east of the city centre. It has a castle, a long, sandy beach and a number of good places to eat and drink. It's also handy for the golf courses at nearby Carnoustie.

ⓞ Sights

FREE **Broughty Castle Museum**　　　MUSEUM
(Castle Green; ☺10am-4pm Mon-Sat, 12.30-4pm Sun, closed Mon Oct-Mar) A 16th-century tower house that looms imposingly over the harbour, guarding the entrance to the Firth of Tay. There's a fascinating exhibit on Dundee's whaling industry, and the view from the top offers the chance of spotting seals and dolphins offshore.

🛏 Sleeping

Fisherman's Tavern　　　　　B&B **££**
(☑01382-775941; www.fishermanstavern.co.uk; 10-16 Fort St; s/d from £49/74; 🐾) A delightful 17th-century terraced cottage just a few paces from the seafront, the Fisherman's was converted into a pub in 1827. It now has 11 stylishly modern rooms, most with en suite, and an atmospheric pub.

Hotel Broughty Ferry　　　　HOTEL **££**
(☑01382-480027; www.hotelbroughtyferry.com; 16 W Queen St; s/d from £60/78; 🅿🛜🏊) It doesn't look like much from the outside, but this is the Ferry's swankiest place to stay, with 16 beautifully decorated bedrooms, a sauna, a solarium and a small heated pool. It's only a five-minute stroll from the waterfront.

PICTISH SYMBOL STONES

The mysterious carved stones that dot the landscape of eastern Scotland are the legacy of the warrior tribes who inhabited these lands 2000 years ago. The Romans occupied the southern half of Britain from AD 43 to 410, but the region to the north of the firths of Forth and Clyde – known as Caledonia – was abandoned as being too dangerous, and sealed off behind the ramparts of the Antonine Wall and Hadrian's Wall.

Caledonia was the homeland of the Picts, a collection of tribes named by the Romans for their habit of painting or tattooing their bodies. In the 9th century they were culturally absorbed by the Scots, leaving behind only a few archaeological remains, a scattering of Pictish place names beginning with 'Pit', and hundreds of mysterious carved stones decorated with intricate symbols, mainly in northeast Scotland. The capital of the ancient Southern Pictish kingdom is said to have been at Forteviot in Strathearn; Pictish symbol stones are found throughout this area and all the way up the eastern coast of Scotland into Sutherland and Caithness.

It is thought that the stones were set up to record Pictish lineages and alliances, but no-one is sure exactly how the system worked. They are decorated with unusual symbols, including z-rods (a lightning bolt?), circles (the sun?), double discs (a hand mirror?) and fantastical creatures, as well as figures of warriors on horseback, hunting scenes and (on the later stones) Christian symbols.

Local tourist offices provide a free leaflet titled the *Angus Pictish Trail*, which will guide you to the main Pictish sites in the area. The finest assemblage of stones in their natural outdoor setting is at **Aberlemno** (p244), and there are excellent indoor collections at St Vigeans Museum (p243) and the Meigle Museum (p233). The Pictavia (p247) interpretive centre at Brechin provides a good introduction to the Picts and is worth a look before you visit the stones.

The Pictish Trail by Anthony Jackson lists 11 driving tours, while *The Symbol Stones of Scotland* by the same author provides detail on the history and meaning of the stones.

Invermark House B&B £
(☎01382-739430; www.invermark.co.uk; 23 Monifieth Rd; s/d from £30/50; P ᯤ) Invermark is a grand Victorian villa set in its own grounds, built for a jute baron in the mid-19th century. There are five large en suite bedrooms and an elegant lounge and dining room with a view of the gardens.

Ashley House B&B ££
(☎01382-776109; www.ashleyhousebroughtyferry.com; 15 Monifieth Rd; per person £32-37; P ᯤ) This spacious and comfortable guesthouse has long been one of Broughty Ferry's best. Its four cheerfully decorated bedrooms come equipped with hotel-grade beds and DVD players; one has a particularly grand bathroom.

Eating & Drinking

Ship Inn PUB ££
(www.theshipinn-broughtyferry.co.uk; 121 Fisher St; mains £9-18; ⏲meals noon-2pm & 5-10.30pm Mon-Fri, noon-10.30pm Sat & Sun) The Ship Inn is a snug, wood-panelled, 19th-century pub on the waterfront, which serves top-notch dishes ranging from gourmet haddock and chips to venison steaks; you can eat in the upstairs restaurant, or down in the bar (bar meals £7 to £10). It's always busy, so get there early to grab a seat.

Fisherman's Tavern PUB £
(10-16 Fort St; mains £7-12; ⏲meals noon-2.30pm & 5-7.30pm) The Fisherman's – a maze of cosy nooks and open fireplaces in a 17th-century cottage – is a lively little pub where you can wash down smoked haddock fishcakes or steak and chips with a choice of Scottish ales.

Visocchi's CAFE £
(40 Gray St; mains £7-10; ⏲9.30am-5pm Tue, 9.30am-8pm Wed, Thu & Sun, 9.30am-1pm Fri & Sat) Visocchi's – a 70-year-old institution – is a traditional, family-run Italian cafe that sells delicious homemade ice cream, good coffee and a range of burgers, pizzas and pasta dishes.

Getting There & Away

City bus 5 and Stagecoach bus 73 run from Dundee High St to Broughty Ferry (20 minutes) several times an hour from Monday to Saturday, and hourly on Sunday.

There are five trains daily from Dundee (£1.20, five to ten minutes).

Glamis Castle & Village

Looking every inch the Scottish Baronial castle, with its roofline sprouting a forest of pointed turrets and battlements, Glamis Castle (www.glamis-castle.co.uk; adult/child £9.75/7.25; ☉10am-6pm Mar-Oct, 10.30am-4.30pm Nov & Dec, closed Jan-Feb) claims to be the legendary setting for Shakespeare's *Macbeth*. A royal residence since 1372, it is the family home of the earls of Strathmore and Kinghorne – the Queen Mother (born Elizabeth Bowes-Lyon; 1900–2002) spent her childhood at Glamis (pronounced 'glams') and Princess Margaret (the Queen's sister; 1930–2002) was born here.

The five-storey, L-shaped castle was given to the Lyon family in 1372, but was significantly altered in the 17th century. Inside, the most impressive room is the **drawing room**, with its vaulted plasterwork ceiling. There's a display of armour and weaponry in the haunted crypt, and frescoes in the chapel (also haunted). **Duncan's Hall** is named for the murdered King Duncan from *Macbeth* (though the scene actually takes place in Macbeth's castle in Inverness). The claimed Shakespeare connection is fictitious – the real Macbeth had nothing to do with the castle, and died long before it was built.

You can also look around the **royal apartments**, including the Queen Mother's bedroom. Hour-long guided tours depart every 15 minutes (last tour at 4.30pm, or 3.30pm in winter).

The Angus Folk Museum (NTS; Kirkwynd; adult/child £6/5; ☉10.30am-4.30pm Thu-Mon Jul

---

THE FORFAR BRIDIE

Forfar, the county town of Angus, is the home of Scotland's answer to the Cornish pasty: the famous **Forfar bridie**. A shortcrust pastry turnover filled with minced beef, onion and gravy, it was invented in Forfar in the early 19th century. If you fancy trying one, head for James McLaren & Son (☎01382-462762; 8 The Cross, Forfar; ☉8am-4.30pm Mon-Wed, Fri & Sat, 8am-1pm Thu), a family bakery bang in the centre of Forfar, which has been selling tasty, home-baked bridies since 1893.

& Aug, 11.30am-4.30pm Sat-Mon Apr-Jun, Sep & Oct), in a row of 18th-century cottages just off the flower-bedecked square in Glamis village, houses a fine collection of domestic and agricultural relics.

Glamis Castle is 12 miles north of Dundee. There are two to four buses a day from Dundee (35 minutes) to Glamis; some continue to Kirriemuir.

Arbroath

POP 22,800

Arbroath is an old-fashioned seaside resort and fishing harbour, home of the famous **Arbroath smokie** (a form of smoked haddock). The humble smokie achieved European Union 'Protected Geographical Indication' status in 2004 – the term 'Arbroath smokie' can be only be used legally to describe haddock smoked in the traditional manner within an 8km radius of Arbroath. No visit is complete without buying a pair of smokies from one of the many fish shops and eating them with your fingers while sitting beside the harbour. Yum.

◉ Sights

Arbroath Abbey   ABBEY
(HS; Abbey St; adult/child £5.50/3.30; ☉9.30am-5.30pm Apr-Sep, to 4.30pm Oct-Mar) The magnificent, red-sandstone ruins of Arbroath Abbey, founded in 1178 by King William the Lion, dominate the town centre. It is thought that Bernard of Linton, the abbot here in the early 14th century, wrote the famous Declaration of Arbroath in 1320, asserting Scotland's right to independence from England. You can climb to the top of one of the towers for a grand view over the town.

St Vigeans Museum   MUSEUM
(HS; ☎01241-878756; St Vigeans Lane; adult/child £4.50/2.70) About a mile north of the town centre, this cottage museum houses a superb collection of Pictish and medieval sculptured stones. The museum's masterpiece is the **Drosten Stone**, beautifully carved with animal figures and hunting scenes on one side, and an interlaced Celtic cross on the other (look for the devil perched on the top left corner). Phone ahead to check opening hours.

[FREE] **Signal House Museum**   MUSEUM
(Ladyloan; ☉10am-5pm Mon-Sat year-round, plus 2-5pm Sun Jul & Aug) This museum is housed in the elegant Signal Tower that was once

used to communicate with the construction team working on the Bell Rock Lighthouse 12 miles offshore. There are displays dedicated to Arbroath's maritime heritage and the Bell Rock Lighthouse, which was built between 1807 and 1811 by the famous engineer Robert Stevenson (grandfather of writer Robert Louis Stevenson).

🏃 Activities

The coast northeast of Arbroath consists of dramatic red-sandstone cliffs riven by inlets, caves and natural arches. An excellent **clifftop walk** (pick up a leaflet from the tourist office) follows the coast for 3 miles to the quaint fishing village of **Auchmithie**, which claims to have invented the Arbroath smokie.

If you fancy catching your own fish, the **Marie Dawn** (☑01241-873957) and **Girl Katherine II** (☑01241-874510) offer three-hour sea-angling trips (usually from 2pm to 5pm) out of Arbroath harbour for £15 per person, including tackle and bait.

🛌 Sleeping

Harbour Nights Guest House   B&B **££**
(☑01241-434343; www.harbournights-scotland.com; 4 The Shore; s/d from £45/60) With a superb location overlooking the harbour, five stylishly decorated bedrooms and a gourmet breakfast menu, Harbour Nights is our favourite place to stay in Arbroath. Rooms 2 and 3, with harbour views, are a bit more expensive (doubles £70 to £80), but well worth asking for when booking.

Old Vicarage   B&B **££**
(☑01241-430475; www.theoldvicaragebandb.co.uk; 2 Seaton Rd; s/d £55/80; ℗🤶) The three five-star bedrooms in this attractive Victorian villa have a pleasantly old-fashioned atmosphere, and the extensive breakfast menu includes Arbroath smokies. The house is on a quiet street close to the start of the clifftop walk to Auchmithie.

🍴 Eating

Gordon's Restaurant   SCOTTISH **£££**
(☑01241-830364; www.gordonsrestaurant.co.uk; Main St, Inverkeillor; 3-course lunch £28, 4-course dinner £48; ☉lunch Wed-Fri & Sun, dinner Tue-Sun) Six miles north of Arbroath, in the tiny and unpromising-looking village of Inverkeillor, lies this hidden gem – an intimate and rustic eatery serving gourmet-quality Scottish cuisine. There are five comfortable bedrooms (single/double from £85/110) for those who don't want to drive after dinner.

But'n'Ben Restaurant   SCOTTISH **££**
(☑01241-877223; www.butnbenauchmithie.co.uk; 1 Auchmithie; mains £8-17; ☉lunch & dinner Wed-Mon; 🍴) Above the harbour in Auchmithie, this cosy cottage restaurant with open fireplace, rustic furniture and sea-themed art serves the best of local seafood – the Arbroath smokie pancakes are recommended – plus great homemade cakes and desserts. Best to book.

Smithie's   CAFE **£**
(16 Keptie St; mains £3-6; ☉9.30am-4.30pm Mon-Fri, to 4pm Sat) Housed in a former butcher's shop, with hand-painted tiles and meat hooks on the ceiling, Smithie's is a great little neighbourhood deli and cafe serving Fairtrade coffee, pancakes, wraps and freshly made pasta – butternut squash and sage tortellini make a tasty change from macaroni cheese for a vegetarian lunch.

Sugar & Spice Tearoom   CAFE **£**
(www.sugarandspiceshop.co.uk; 9-13 High St; mains £6-12; ☉10am-5pm Mon-Thu, 10am-9pm Fri & Sat, noon-7pm Sun, longer hours Jun-Sep; 🍴) With its flounces, frills and black-and-white uniformed waitresses, this chintzy tearoom verges on the twee. However, the place is very child-friendly – there's an indoor play area and a play garden out the back – and

---

WORTH A TRIP

THE ABERLEMNO STONES

Five miles northeast of Forfar, on the B9134, are the mysterious **Aberlemno stones**, some of Scotland's finest Pictish symbol stones. By the roadside there are three 7th- to 9th-century slabs with various symbols, including the z-rod and double disc, and in the churchyard at the bottom of the hill there's a magnificent 8th-century stone displaying a Celtic cross, interlace decoration, entwined beasts and, on the reverse, scenes of the Battle of Nechtansmere (where the Picts vanquished the Northumbrians in 685). The stones are covered up from November to March; otherwise there's free access at all times.

the tea and scones are sublime. You can even try an Arbroath smokie, grilled with lemon butter.

ℹ Information

Visitor Centre & Tourist Office (☏01241-872609; Fishmarket Quay; ⊙9.30am-5.30pm Mon-Sat, 10am-3pm Sun Jun-Aug; 9am-5pm Mon-Fri, 10am-5pm Sat Apr, May & Sep, to 3pm Sat Oct-Mar) Beside the harbour.

ℹ Getting There & Away

BUS Bus 140 runs from Arbroath to Auchmithie (15 minutes, six daily Monday to Friday, three daily on Saturday and Sunday).

TRAIN Trains from Dundee to Arbroath (£5, 20 minutes, two per hour) continue to Aberdeen (£21, 55 minutes) via Montrose and Stonehaven.

Kirriemuir

POP 6000

Known as the Wee Red Town because of its close-packed, red-sandstone houses, Kirriemuir is famed as the birthplace of JM Barrie (1860–1937), writer and creator of the much-loved *Peter Pan*. A bronze statue of the 'boy who wouldn't grow up' graces the intersection of Bank and High Sts.

The tourist office is in the Gateway to the Glens Museum.

⊙ Sights

JM Barrie's Birthplace   MUSEUM
(NTS; 9 Brechin Rd; adult/child £6/5; ⊙11am-5pm Jul & Aug, noon-5pm Sat-Wed Apr-Jun, Sep & Oct) This is Kirriemuir's big attraction, a place of pilgrimage for Peter Pan fans from all over the world. The two-storey house where Barrie was born has been furnished in period style, and preserves Barrie's writing desk and the wash house at the back that served as his first 'theatre'.

Your ticket also gives admission to the **Camera Obscura** (adult/child Camera Obscura only £3.50/2.50; ⊙noon-5pm Mon-Sat, 1-5pm Sun Jul-Sep, Sat & Sun only Easter-Jun) on the hilltop northeast of the town centre, given to the town by Barrie himself.

Gateway to the Glens Museum   MUSEUM
(32 High St; admission free; ⊙10am-5pm Mon-Sat Apr-Sep, closed Thu 10am-noon Oct-Mar) The old Town House opposite the Peter Pan statue dates from 1604 and houses the Gateway to the Glens Museum, a useful introduction to local history, geology and wildlife for those planning to explore the Angus Glens.

✗ Eating

TOP CHOICE 88 Degrees   CAFE, DELI £
(17 High St; mains £3-6; ⊙9.30am-5pm Wed-Fri, 9.30am-4pm Sat, 10am-4pm Sun) This tiny deli serves the best cafe cuisine in the county – superb coffee (it's named for the ideal temperature of an espresso), delicious cakes and handmade chocolates. Breakfast (served till 10.30am) includes delicious omelettes made with free-range eggs.

🛍 Shopping

Star Rock Shop   CONFECTIONERY
(☏01575-572579; 27-29 Roods) For generations of local school kids, the big treat when visiting Kirriemuir was a trip to the Star Rock Shop. Established in 1833, it still specialises in traditional Scottish 'sweeties', arranged in colourful jars along the walls – including humbugs, cola cubes, pear drops, and the original Star Rock, still made to an 1833 recipe.

ℹ Getting There & Away

Stagecoach bus 20 runs from Dundee to Kirriemuir (£5.60, one hour, hourly Monday to Saturday, every two hours Sunday) via Glamis (20 minutes) and Forfar (25 minutes).

The Angus Glens

The northern part of Angus is bounded by the Grampian Mountains, where five scenic glens – Isla, Prosen, Clova, Lethnot and Esk – cut into the hills along the southern edge of the Cairngorms National Park. All have attractive scenery, though each glen has its own distinct personality: Glen Clova and Glenesk are the most beautiful, while Glen Lethnot is the least frequented. You can get detailed information on walks in the Angus Glens from the tourist office in Kirriemuir and from the Glen Clova Hotel in Glen Clova.

There is no public transport to the Angus Glens other than a limited school-bus service along Glen Clova; ask at the tourist office in Kirriemuir or Dundee for details.

GLEN ISLA

At Bridge of Craigisla at the foot of the glen is a spectacular, 24m waterfall called **Reekie Linn**; the name Reekie (Scottish for 'smoky') comes from the billowing spray that rises from the falls.

A 5-mile walk beyond the road end at Auchavan leads into the wild and mountainous upper reaches of the glen, where the

Caenlochan National Nature Reserve protects rare alpine flora on the high plateau.

GLEN PROSEN

Near the foot of Glen Prosen, 6 miles north of Kirriemuir, there's a good forest walk up to the **Airlie monument** on Tulloch Hill (380m); start from the eastern road, about a mile beyond Dykehead.

From Glenprosen Lodge, at the head of the glen, a 9-mile walk along the **Kilbo Path** leads over a pass between Mayar (928m) and Driesh (947m), and descends to Glendoll Lodge at the head of Glen Clova (allow five hours).

Prosen Hostel (☑01575-540238; www.prosenhostel.co.uk; per person £20; ☺year round; @) is an 18-bed bunkhouse with excellent facilities (including a red squirrel viewing area in the lounge). It's 7 miles up the glen, just beyond Prosen village, but there's no public transport.

GLEN CLOVA

The longest and loveliest of the Angus Glens stretches north from Kirriemuir for 20 miles, broad and pastoral in its lower reaches but growing narrower and craggier as the steep, heather-clad Highland hills close in around its head.

The minor road beyond the Glen Clova Hotel ends at a Forestry Commission car park at Glen Doll with a visitor centre (☺9am-6pm Apr-Sep, to 4.30 Oct-Mar) and **picnic area**, which is the trailhead for a number of strenuous **walks** through the hills to the north.

Jock's Road is an ancient footpath that was much used by cattle drovers, soldiers, smugglers and shepherds in the 18th and 19th centuries; 700 Jacobite soldiers passed this way during their retreat in 1746, en route to defeat at Culloden. From the car park the path strikes west along Glen Doll, then north across a high plateau (900m) before descending steeply into Glen Callater and on to Braemar (15 miles; allow five to seven hours). The route is hard going and should not be attempted in winter; you'll need OS 1:50,000 maps numbers 43 and 44.

An easier walk leads from Glen Doll car park to **Corrie Fee**, a spectacular glacial hollow in the edge of the mountain plateau (4.5 miles round trip, waymarked).

Glen Clova Hotel (☑01575-550350; www.clova.com; s/d from £60/90, bunkhouse per person £17; ℗) is a lovely old drover's inn near the head of the glen and a great place to get away from it all. As well as 10 comfortable, country-style, en suite rooms (one with a four-poster bed), it has a bunkhouse out the back, a rustic, stone-floored climbers' bar with a roaring log fire, and a bay-windowed restaurant (mains £9-16; ☺noon-8pm Sun-Thu, to 9pm Fri & Sat; ⊕) with views across the glen. The menu includes haggis, venison casserole and vegetarian lasagne, and there's a separate children's menu.

GLEN LETHNOT

This glen is noted for the **Brown & White Caterthuns** – two extraordinary Iron Age hill forts, defended by ramparts and ditches, perched on twin hilltops at its southern end. A minor road crosses the pass between the two summits, and it's an easy walk to either fort from the parking area in the pass; both are superb viewpoints. If you don't have a car, you can walk there from Brechin (6 miles) or from Edzell (5 miles).

GLENESK

The most easterly of the Angus Glens, Glenesk runs for 15 miles from Edzell to lovely **Loch Lee**, surrounded by beetling cliffs and waterfalls. Ten miles up the glen from Edzell is Glenesk Folk Museum (www.glenesketreat.co.uk; adult/child £2/1; ☺noon-6pm Apr–Oct), an old shooting lodge that houses a fascinating collection of antiques and artefacts documenting the local culture of the 17th, 18th and 19th centuries. It also has a tearoom, restaurant and gift shop, and has public internet access.

Five miles further on, the public road ends at **Invermark Castle**, an impressive ruined tower guarding the southern approach to the Mounth, a hill track to Deeside.

Edzell

POP 785

The picturesque village of Edzell, with its broad main street and grandiose monumental arch, dates from the early 19th century when Lord Panmure decided that the original medieval village, a mile to the west, spoiled the view from Edzell Castle. The old village was razed and the villagers moved to this pretty, planned settlement.

Lord Panmure's predecessors as owners of Edzell Castle (HS; adult/child £5/3; ☺9.30am-5.30pm Apr-Sep) were the Lindsay earls of Crawford, who built this 16th-century L-plan tower house. Sir David Lindsay, a cultured and well-travelled man, laid out the castle's beautiful **pleasance** in 1604 as a place of contemplation and learning. Unique in all of Scotland, this Renaissance walled garden is lined with niches for nesting birds and sculptured plaques illustrating the cardinal virtues, the arts and the planetary deities.

Two miles north of Edzell, the B966 to Fettercairn crosses the River North Esk at Gannochy Bridge. From the lay-by just over the bridge, a blue-painted wooden door in the stone wall gives access to a delightful footpath that leads along the wooded river gorge for 1.5 miles to a scenic spot known as the **Rocks of Solitude**.

Bus 29 or 29A from Brechin to Laurencekirk stops at Edzell (15 minutes, seven daily Monday to Friday, five on Saturday).

Brechin

POP 7200

The name of the local football team, Brechin City, proclaims this diminutive town's main claim to fame – as the seat of **Brechin Cathedral** (now demoted to a parish church) it has the right to call itself a city, albeit the smallest one in Scotland. Adjacent to the cathedral is a 32m-high **round tower** built around 1000 as part of a Celtic monastery. It is of a type often seen in Ireland, but one of only three that survive in Scotland. Its elevated doorway, 2m above the ground, has carvings of animals, saints and a crucifix.

Housed nearby in the 18th-century former town hall, court room and prison, Brechin Town House Museum (St Ninian's Sq; admission free; ☉10am-5pm Mon-Sat) records the history of the round tower, cathedral and town.

The town's (OK, city's) picturesque Victorian train station dates from 1897 and is now the terminus of the restored Caledonian Railway (www.caledonianrailway.com; 2 Park Rd), which runs heritage steam trains (£10 return) along a 3.5-mile stretch of track to Bridge of Dun. Trains run on Sunday from June to August, and on Saturday in July and August; check website for other dates. From Bridge of Dun, it's a 15-minute signposted walk to the House of Dun (NTS; adult/child £9.50/7; ☉11am-5pm Jul & Aug, noon-5pm Wed-Sun Apr-Jun, Sep & Oct), a beautiful Georgian country house built in 1730.

Adjoining Brechin Castle Centre (a gardening and horse-riding centre on the A90

just west of Brechin) is Pictavia (www.pictavia.org.uk; adult/child £3.25/2.25; ☉9am-5pm Mon-Sat, 10am-5pm Sun Apr-Oct, Sat & Sun only Nov-Mar), an interpretive centre telling the story of the Picts and explaining current theories about the mysterious carved symbol stones they left behind. It's worth making a trip here before going to see the Pictish stones at Aberlemno (p244).

❶ Getting There & Away

Scottish Citylink buses between Dundee and Aberdeen stop at Clerk St in Brechin. Stagecoach buses depart from South Esk St heading to Forfar (30 minutes, hourly), Aberlemno (15 minutes, six a day) and Edzell.

Bus 24 links Brechin and Stonehaven (55 minutes, at least three daily).

ABERDEENSHIRE & MORAY

Since medieval times Aberdeenshire and its northwestern neighbour Moray have been the richest and most fertile regions of the Highlands. Aberdeenshire is famed for its Aberdeen Angus beef cattle, its many fine castles and the prosperous 'granite city' of Aberdeen. Moray's main attractions are the Speyside whisky distilleries that line the valley of the River Spey and its tributaries.

Aberdeen

POP 197,300

Aberdeen is the powerhouse of the northeast, fuelled by the North Sea petroleum industry. Oil money has made the city as expensive as London and Edinburgh, and there are hotels, restaurants and clubs with prices to match the depth of oil-wealthy pockets. Fortunately, most of the cultural attractions, such as the excellent Maritime Museum and the Aberdeen Art Gallery, are free.

Known throughout Scotland as the granite city, much of the town was built using silvery-grey granite hewn from the now abandoned Rubislaw Quarry, at one time the biggest artificial hole in the ground in Europe. On a sunny day the granite lends an attractive glitter to the city, but when low, grey rain clouds scud in off the North Sea it can be hard to tell where the buildings stop and the sky begins.

Aberdeen

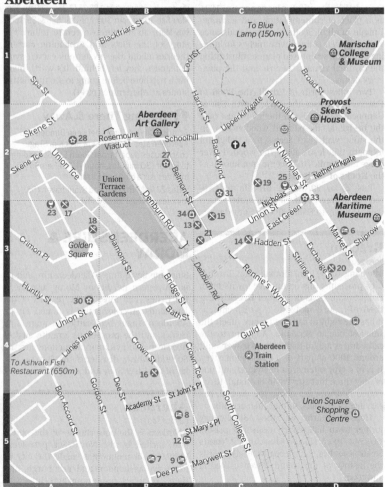

Royal Deeside is easily accessible to the west, Dunnottar Castle to the south, sandy beaches to the north and whisky country to the northwest.

History

Aberdeen was a prosperous trading and fishing port, centuries before oil became a valuable commodity. After the townspeople supported Robert the Bruce against the English at the Battle of Bannockburn in 1314, the king rewarded the town with land for which he had previously received rent. The rental income was used to establish the Common

Good Fund, to be spent on town amenities, a fund that survives to this day: it helped to finance Marischal College, the Central Library, the art gallery and the hospital, and also pays for the colourful floral displays that have won the city numerous awards.

The name Aberdeen is a combination of two Pictish-Gaelic words, *aber* and *devana*, meaning 'the meeting of two waters'. The area was known to the Romans, and was raided by the Vikings when it was already an important port trading in wool, fish, hides and fur. By the 18th century paper- and rope-making, whaling and textile manufacture were the

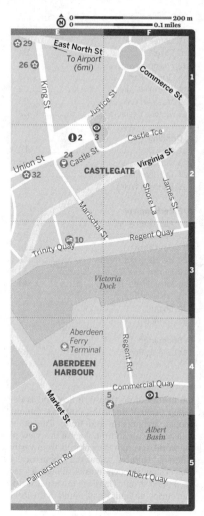

The oldest area is **Castlegate**, at the eastern end, where the castle once stood. When it was captured from the English for Robert the Bruce, the password used by the towns-people was 'Bon Accord', which is now the city's motto.

In the centre of Castle St stands the 17th-century Mercat Cross (Map p248), bearing a sculpted frieze of portraits of Stuart monarchs. The Baronial heap towering over the eastern end of Castle St is the Salvation Army Citadel (Map p248), which was modelled on Balmoral Castle.

On the northern side of Union St, 300m west of Castlegate, is St Nicholas Church (Map p248), the so-called 'Mither Kirk' (Mother Church) of Aberdeen. The granite spire dates from the 19th century, but there has been a church on this site since the 12th century; the early 15th-century **St Mary's Chapel** survives in the eastern part of the church.

FREE Aberdeen Maritime Museum MUSEUM
(Map p248; ☎01224-337700; www.aagm.co.uk; Shiprow; ⊙10am-5pm Tue-Sat, noon-3pm Sun) Overlooking the nautical bustle of Aberdeen harbour is the Maritime Museum. Centred on a three-storey replica of a North Sea oil production platform, it explains all you ever wanted to know about the petroleum industry. Other galleries, some situated in **Provost Ross's House**, the oldest building in the city and part of the museum, cover the shipbuilding, whaling and fishing industries. Sleek and speedy Aberdeen clippers were a 19th-century shipyard speciality, used by British merchants for the importation of tea, wool and exotic goods (opium, for instance) to Britain, and, on the return journey, the transportation of emigrants to Australia.

FREE Aberdeen Art Gallery ART MUSEUM
(Map p248; ☎01224-523700; www.aagm.co.uk; Schoolhill; ⊙10am-5pm Tue-Sat, 2-5pm Sun) Behind the grand facade of Aberdeen Art Gallery is a cool, marble-lined space exhibiting the work of contemporary Scottish and English painters, such as Gwen Hardie, Stephen Conroy, Trevor Sutton and Tim Ollivier. There are also several landscapes by Joan Eardley, who lived in a cottage on the cliffs near Stonehaven in the 1950s and '60s and painted tempestuous oils of the North Sea and poignant portraits of slum children. Among the Pre-Raphaelite works upstairs, look out for the paintings by Aberdeen artist

main industries, and in the 19th century it became a major herring-fishing centre.

Since the 1970s Aberdeen has been the main focus of the UK's offshore oil industry, home to oil company offices, engineering yards, a bustling harbour filled with supply ships, and the world's busiest civilian heliport. Unemployment rates, once among the highest in the country, are now among the lowest.

Sights & Activities
City Centre
Union St is the city's main thoroughfare, lined with solid, Victorian granite buildings.

NORTHEAST SCOTLAND ABERDEEN

Aberdeen

William Dyce (1806–64), ranging from religious works to rural scenes.

FREE **Marischal College & Museum**   MUSEUM
(Map p248; www.abdn.ac.uk/marischal_museum; Marischal College, Broad St; ⊗10am-5pm Mon-Fri, 2-5pm Sun) Marischal College, founded in 1593 by the 5th Earl Marischal, merged with King's College (founded 1495) in 1860 to create the modern University of Aberdeen. The huge and impressive facade in Perpendicular Gothic style – unusual in having such elaborate masonry hewn from notoriously hard-to-work granite – dates from 1906 and is the world's second-largest granite structure (after L'Escorial near Madrid). A recent renovation project saw the facade returned to it original silvery grey glory, and the building now houses Aberdeen City Council's new headquarters.

Founded in 1786, the **Marischal Museum** houses a fascinating collection of material donated by graduates and friends of the university over the centuries. In one room,

the history of northeastern Scotland is depicted through its myths, customs, famous people, architecture and trade. The other gallery gives an anthropological overview of the world, incorporating objects from vastly different cultures, arranged thematically (Polynesian wooden masks alongside gas masks and so on). There are the usual Victorian curios, an Inuit kayak found in the local river estuary in the 18th century and Inuit objects collected by whalers. At the time of research the museum was still closed to the public following renovation work; check the website for notice of its reopening.

FREE **Provost Skene's House**   HISTORIC BUILDING
(Map p248; www.aagm.co.uk; ⊗10am-5pm Mon-Sat) Surrounded by concrete and glass office blocks in what was once the worst slum in Aberdeen is this late-medieval turreted town house occupied in the 17th century by the provost (the Scottish equivalent of a mayor) Sir George Skene. It was also occupied for six weeks by the Duke of Cum-

berland on his way to Culloden in 1746. The tempera ceiling of the Painted Gallery with its religious symbolism, dating from 1622, is unusual for having survived the depredations of the Reformation. It's a period gem featuring earnest-looking angels, soldiers and St Peter with crowing cockerels.

Gordon Highlanders
Museum
MILITARY MUSEUM

(www.gordonhighlanders.com; St Lukes, Viewfield Rd; adult/child £5/2; ⊙10am-4pm Tue-Sat Feb-Nov) This excellent museum records the history of one of the British Army's most famous fighting units, described by Winston Churchill as 'the finest regiment in the world'. Originally raised in the northeast of Scotland by the 4th Duke of Gordon in 1794, the regiment was amalgamated with the Seaforths and Camerons to form the Highlanders regiment in 1994. The museum is about a mile west of the western end of Union St – take bus 14 or 15 from Union St.

Aberdeen Harbour

Aberdeen has a busy, working harbour crowded with survey vessels and supply ships servicing the offshore oil installations, and car ferries bound for Orkney and Shetland.

Fish Market
MARKET

(Map p248) From 4am until about 7:30am the colourful fish market on Albert Basin operates as it has done for centuries.

Aberdeen Harbour Cruise
BOAT TRIPS

(Map p248; ☑01475-721281; www.clydeclippers. com; Aberdeen Harbour; adult/child £8/4; ⊙daily Jul-Aug, Wed-Sun Jun & Sep) Offers 45-minute cruises around Aberdeen's bustling commercial harbour.

Aberdeen Beach

Just 800m east of Castlegate is a spectacular 2-mile sweep of clean, golden sand stretching between the mouths of the Rivers Dee and Don. At one time Aberdeen Beach was a good, old-fashioned British seaside resort, but the availability of cheap package holidays has lured Scottish holidaymakers away from its somewhat chilly delights. On a warm summer's day, though, it's still an excellent beach. When the waves are right, a small group of dedicated **surfers** ride the breaks at the south end.

The Esplanade sports several traditional seaside attractions, including Codona's Amusement Park (☑01224-595910; www. codonas.com; Beach Blvd; day pass £13; ⊙11am-

6pm Jul & Aug, check website rest of year, closed Nov-Easter), complete with stomach-churning waltzers, dodgems, a roller coaster, log flume and haunted house. The adjacent Sunset Boulevard (www.codonas.com; Beach Blvd; day pass £13; ⊙10am-midnight) is the indoor alternative, with tenpin bowling, dodgems, arcade games and pool tables.

Halfway between the beach and the city centre is Satrosphere (☑01224-640340; www. satrosphere.net; 179 Constitution St; adult/child £5.75/4.50; ⊙10am-5pm), a hands-on, interactive science centre.

You can get away from the funfair atmosphere by walking north towards the more secluded part of the beach. There's a **bird-watching hide** on the south bank of the River Don, between the beach and King St, which leads back south towards Old Aberdeen.

Buses 14 and 15 (eastbound) from Union St go to the beach; or you can walk from Castlegate in 10 minutes.

Old Aberdeen

Just over a mile north of the city centre is the district called Old Aberdeen. The name is misleading – although Old Aberdeen is certainly old, the area around Castlegate in the city centre is older still. This part of the city was originally called Aulton, from the Gaelic for 'village by the pool', and this was anglicised in the 17th century to Old Town.

Bus 20 from Littlejohn St (just north of Marischal College) runs to Old Aberdeen every 15 to 20 minutes.

King's College Chapel
HISTORIC BUILDING

(College Bounds; admission free; ⊙10am-3.30pm Mon-Fri) It was here that Bishop Elphinstone established King's College, Aberdeen's first university, in 1495. The 16th-century college chapel is easily recognised by its crown spire; the interior is largely unchanged since it was first built, with impressive stained-glass windows and choir stalls.

FREE Old Town House
VISITOR CENTRE

(☑01224-273650; www.abdn.ac.uk/oldtownhouse; High St; ⊙9am-5pm Mon-Sat) At the north end of High St, the Old Town House now houses a visitor centre with information and exhibits on the history of Old Aberdeen.

FREE St Machar's Cathedral
CATHEDRAL

(www.stmachar.com; The Chanonry; ⊙9am-5pm Mon-Sat Apr-Oct, 10am-4pm Nov-Mar) The 15th-century St Machar's Cathedral, with its massive twin towers, is a rare example of a fortified cathedral. According to legend, St Machar was ordered to establish a church where the river takes the shape of a bishop's crook, which it does just here. The cathedral is best known for its impressive **heraldic ceiling**, dating from 1520, which has 48 shields of kings, nobles, archbishops and bishops. Sunday services are held at 11am and 6pm.

🛌 Sleeping

There are clusters of B&Bs on Bon Accord St and Springbank Tce (both 400m southwest of the train station) and along Great Western Rd (the A93, a 25-minute walk southwest of the city centre). They're usually more expensive than the Scottish average and, with so many oil industry workers staying the night before flying offshore, single rooms are at a premium. Prices tend to be lower on weekends.

TOP
CHOICE **Globe Inn**   B&B ££
(Map p248; ☑01224-624258; www.the-globe-inn. co.uk; 13-15 North Silver St; s/d £70/75) This popular pub has seven appealing and comfortable guest bedrooms upstairs, done out in dark wood with burgundy bedspreads. There's live music in the pub on weekends so it's not a place for early-to-bed types, but the price vs location factor can't be beaten. No dining room, so breakfast is continental, served on a tray in your room.

City Wharf Apartments   APARTMENTS ££
(Map p248; ☑0845 094 2424; www.citywharfapart ments.co.uk; 19-20 Regent Quay; d from £105; 🛜) You can watch the bustle of Aberdeen's commercial harbour as you eat breakfast in one of these luxury serviced apartments, complete with stylish, fully equipped kitchen, champagne-stocked minibar and daily cleaning service. Available by the night or the week, with discounts for longer stays.

Brentwood Hotel   HOTEL ££
(Map p248; ☑01224-595440; www.brentwood-ho tel.co.uk; 101 Crown St; s £45-95, d £59-105; P🛜) The friendly and flower-bedecked Brentwood, set in a granite town house, is one of the most attractive hotels in the city centre. It's comfortable and conveniently located, but often busy during the week – weekend rates (Friday to Sunday) are much cheaper.

Butler's Guest House   B&B ££
(Map p248; ☑01224-212411; www.butlersguest house.com; 122 Crown St; s/d from £58/65; @🛜)

Just across the street from the Brentwood, Butler's is a cosy place with a big breakfast menu that includes fresh fruit salad, kippers and kedgeree as alternatives to the traditional fry-up (rates include a continental breakfast - cooked breakfast is £5 extra per person). There are cheaper rooms with shared bathrooms.

Aberdeen Douglas Hotel   HOTEL £££
(Map p248; ☑01224-582255; www.aberdeendou glas.com; 43-45 Market St; s/d from £65/75 weekend, £145/155 weekday; 🛜) You can't miss the grand Victorian facade of this historic landmark, which first opened its doors as a hotel in 1853. Now renovated, it offers classy modern rooms with polished woodwork and crisp white bedlinen, and is barely a minute's walk from the train station.

Simpson's Hotel   BOUTIQUE HOTEL ££
(☑01224-327777; www.simpsonshotel.co.uk; 59 Queen's Rd; r from £99; P🛜) Simpson's, a mile west of Union St, is a stylish boutique hotel decorated with a Mediterranean-Italian theme in shades of sand, terracotta and aqua. It's aimed at both business and private guests, and is totally wheelchair accessible. Cheapest rates on weekends.

Dunrovin Guest House   B&B ££
(☑01224-586081; www.dunrovinguesthouse.co.uk; 168 Bon Accord St; s/d from £45/70; P🛜) Dunrovin is a typical granite Victorian house with eight bedrooms; the upstairs rooms are bright and airy. The friendly owners will provide a veggie breakfast if you wish. Located 400m south of Union St.

Royal Crown Guest House   B&B ££
(Map p248; ☑01224-586461; www.royalcrown. co.uk; 111 Crown St; s £35-70, d £60-80; P🛜) The Royal Crown has eight small but nicely furnished bedrooms, and a top location only five minutes' walk from the train station (though up a steep flight of stairs).

Aberdeen Youth Hostel   HOSTEL £
(SYHA; ☑01224-646988; 8 Queen's Rd; dm £21; @🛜) This hostel, set in a granite Victorian villa, is a mile west of the train station. Walk west along Union St and take the right fork along Albyn Pl until you reach a roundabout; Queen's Rd continues on the western side of the roundabout.

Jurys Inn   HOTEL ££
(Map p248; ☑01224-381200; www.jurysinns.com; Union Sq, Guild St; r £75-155; 🛜) Stylish and

comfortable hotel right next to the train station.

Adelphi Guest House
B&B **££**

(☑01224-583078; www.adelphiguesthouse.com; 8 Whinhill Rd; s/d from £45/60; ◉) Located 400m south from western end of Union St.

Arden Guest House
B&B **££**

(Map p248; ☑01224-580700; www.ardenguest house.co.uk; 61 Dee St; s/d from £50/60) Close to the city centre.

✕ Eating

 Café 52
BISTRO **££**

(Map p248; ☑01224-590094; www.cafe52.net; 52 The Green; mains £12; ◉noon-midnight Mon-Sat, to 6pm Sun; ◉) This little haven of laid-back industrial chic – a high, narrow space lined with bare stonework, rough plaster and exposed ventilation ducts – serves some of the finest and most inventive cuisine in the northeast. Try starters such as baked black pudding with wine-poached pear, or mains like beef casserole with red wine and Moroccan spices.

Silver Darling
SEAFOOD **£££**

(☑01224-576229; www.thesilverdarling.co.uk; Pocra Quay, North Pier; 2-course lunch £20, dinner mains £22-29; ◉lunch Mon-Fri & dinner Mon-Sat year-round, lunch Sun Apr-Oct) The Silver Darling (an old Scottish nickname for herring) is housed in a former Customs office at the entrance to Aberdeen harbour, with picture windows overlooking the sea. Here you can enjoy fresh Scottish seafood prepared by a top French chef while you watch the porpoises playing in the harbour mouth. Bookings are recommended.

Moonfish Café
FRENCH **££**

(Map p248; ☑01224-644166; www.moonfish cafe.co.uk; 9 Correction Wynd; 2-/3-course dinner £24/29; ◉lunch & dinner Tue-Sat) The menu of this funky little eatery tucked away on a back street concentrates on good quality Scottish produce cooked with an international flair that draws its influences from cuisines all around the world, from simple smoked haddock with pea risotto, to nut-crusted skate wing with Peruvian potatoes (with chilli, onion and hard-boiled egg).

✒ Foyer
FUSION **££**

(Map p248; ☑01224-582277; www.foyerrestaurant. com; 82a Crown St; mains £12-18; ◉11am-10pm Tue-Sat; ✒) A light, airy space filled with blond wood and bold colours, Foyer is an art gallery as well as a restaurant and is run by a charity that fights youth homelessness and unemployment. The seasonal menu is a fusion of Scottish, Mediterranean and Asian influences, with lots of good vegetarian (and gluten- or dairy-free) options.

✒ Musa Art Cafe
MODERN SCOTTISH **££**

(Map p248; ☑01224-571771; www.musaaberdeen. com; 33 Exchange St; lunch mains £8-10, dinner £13-23; ◉noon-11pm Tue-Sat; ✒) The bright paintings on the walls match the vibrant furnishings and smart gastronomic creations at this great cafe-restaurant, set in a former church. As well as a menu that focuses on quality local produce cooked in a quirky way – think haggis-and-coriander spring rolls with chilli jam – there are Brewdog beers from Fraserburgh, and interesting music, sometimes live.

Fusion
FUSION **££**

(Map p248; ☑01224-652959; www.fusionbarbistro. com; 10 North Silver St; 2-/3-course dinner £23/28; ◉5.30-10pm Tue-Sat) This chic and trendy bar-bistro in the upmarket Golden Square district has a menu that is true to its name, blending Scottish west-coast mussels with creamy curry sauce and onion bread, and giving slow-roast pork belly the French-Spanish treatment by serving it with cassoulet and garnishing with chorizo and Serrano ham.

Beautiful Mountain
CAFE **£**

(Map p248; www.thebeautifulmountain.com; 11-13 Belmont St; mains £4-10; ◉7.30am-3.30pm Mon-Fri, 8am-4.30pm Sat, 10.30am-3.30pm Sun) This cosy cafe is squeezed into a couple of tiny rooms (seating upstairs), but serves all-day breakfasts and tasty sandwiches (smoked salmon, Thai chicken, pastrami) on sourdough, bagels, ciabatta and lots of other breads, along with exquisite espresso and consummate cappuccino. It's also open for dinner Thursday to Saturday, when the menu changes to tapas.

Sand Dollar Café
CAFE, BISTRO **£**

(☑01224-572288; www.sanddollarcafe.com; 2 Beach Esplanade; mains £4-10; ◉9am-9pm daily, closed 4-6pm Thu-Sat) A cut above your usual seaside cafe – on sunny days you can sit at the wooden tables outside and share a bottle of chilled white wine, and there's a tempting menu that includes pancakes with maple syrup, homemade burgers and chocolate brownie with Orkney ice cream. An evening bistro menu (mains £12 to £24, served from 6pm Thursday to Saturday) offers steak and seafood dishes. The cafe is on the esplanade, 800m northeast of the city centre.

Ashvale Fish Restaurant   FISH & CHIPS £

(www.theashvale.co.uk; 42-48 Great Western Rd; takeaway £4-7, mains £8-12; ⊘noon-11pm;) This is the flagship, 200-seat branch of the Ashvale, an award-winning fish-and-chip restaurant famed for its quality haddock. The Ashvale Whale – a 1lb fish fillet in batter (£12.75) – is a speciality; finish it off and you get a second one free (as if you'd want one by then!). There are branches in Elgin and Brechin. It's 300m southwest of the west end of Union St.

Granite Park   MODERN SCOTTISH ££

(Map p248; ✆01224-478004; www.granitepark. co.uk; 8 Golden Sq; mains £15-22; ⊘noon-11pm Mon-Sat) This smart new restaurant is the talk of the town, taking Scottish favourites such as venison, haddock and smoked salmon and giving them an Asian or Mediterranean twist. Best to book.

Coffee House   CAFE £

(Map p248; www.thecoffeehouseoffers.co.uk; 1 Gaelic Lane; mains £4-6; ⊘8am-8pm Mon-Fri, 9am-8pm Sat & Sun; ☏) A bright and appealing cafe with long refectory tables and benches, serving sandwiches on organic bread, soups, herbal teas and great cappuccinos.

Victoria Restaurant   CAFE £

(Map p248; 140 Union St; mains £6-9; ⊘9am-5pm Fri-Wed, 9am-6.30pm Thu) The Victoria, above the Jamieson & Carry jewellery shop, is a traditional, posh Scottish tearoom, with delicious fresh soups, salads and sandwiches. Breakfast served till 11.30am.

🍷 Drinking

Aberdeen is a great city for a pub crawl – it's more a question of knowing when to stop than where to start. There are lots of pre-club bars in and around Belmont St, with more traditional pubs scattered throughout the city centre.

Globe Inn   PUB

(Map p248; www.the-globe-inn.co.uk; 13-15 North Silver St) This lovely Edwardian-style pub with wood panelling, marble-topped tables and walls decorated with old musical instruments is a great place for a quiet lunchtime or afternoon drink. It serves good coffee as well as real ales and malt whiskies, and has live music (rock, blues, soul) Friday to Sunday. It's also got probably the poshest pub toilets in the country.

Prince of Wales   PUB

(Map p248; 7 St Nicholas Lane) Tucked down an alley off Union St, Aberdeen's best-known pub boasts the longest bar in the city, a great range of real ales and good-value pub grub. Quiet in the afternoons, but standing-room only in the evenings.

Old Blackfriars   PUB

(Map p248; www.old-blackfriars.co.uk; 52 Castlegate; ☏) One of the most attractive traditional pubs in the city, with a lovely stone and timber interior, stained-glass windows and a relaxed atmosphere – a great place for an afternoon pint.

Blue Lamp   PUB

(121 Gallowgate) A long-standing feature of the Aberdeen pub scene, the Blue Lamp is a favourite student hang-out – a cosy drinking den with good beer, good *craic* (lively conversation) and regular sessions of live jazz and standup comedy. The pub is 150m north of the city centre, along Broad St.

BrewDog   BAR

(Map p248; www.brewdog.com/bars/aberdeen; 17 Gallowgate) The flagship bar of northeast Scotland's most innovative craft brewery brings a bit of designer chic to Aberdeen's pub scene along with a vast range of guest beers from around the world.

☆ Entertainment

Cinemas

Belmont Cinema   CINEMA

(Map p248; www.picturehouses.co.uk; 49 Belmont St) The Belmont is a great little art-house cinema, with a lively programme of cult classics, director's seasons, foreign films and mainstream movies.

Clubs & Live Music

Check out what's happening in the club and live-music scene at local record shops – try One Up Records (Map p248; www.oneupmusic. co.uk; 17 Belmont St).

Snafu   CLUB, MUSIC

(Map p248; www.clubsnafu.com; 1 Union St) Aberdeen's coolest club – though admittedly there isn't much competition – cosy Snafu offers a wide range of rotating club nights and guest DJs, as well as a Tuesday night comedy club and live music gigs.

Tunnels
LIVE MUSIC

(Map p248; www.thetunnels.co.uk; Carnegie's Brae) This cavernous, subterranean club – the entrance is in a road tunnel beneath Union St – is a great live music venue, with a packed programme of up-and-coming Scottish bands. It also hosts regular DJ nights – check the website for the latest program.

O'Neill's
LIVE MUSIC

(Map p248; www.oneills.co.uk; 9 Back Wynd) Upstairs at O'Neill's you're guaranteed a wild night of pounding, hardcore Irish rock, indie and alternative tunes Friday to Sunday; downstairs is a (slightly) quieter bar packed with rugby types downing large quantities of Murphy's stout.

Theatre & Concerts

You can book tickets for most concerts and other events at the box office (Map p248; www.boxofficeaberdeen.com; ⊕9.30am-6pm Mon-Sat) next to the Music Hall (Map p248; Union St), the main venue for classical music concerts.

Lemon Tree Theatre
DRAMA, MUSIC

(Map p248; www.boxofficeaberdeen.com; 5 West North St) Hosts an interesting program of dance, music and drama, and often has live rock, jazz and folk bands playing. There are also children's shows, ranging from comedy to drama to puppetry.

His Majesty's Theatre
BALLET, OPERA

(Map p248; www.boxofficeaberdeen.com; Rosemount Viaduct) The main theatre in Aberdeen hosts everything from ballet and opera to pantomimes and musicals.

Aberdeen Arts Centre
DRAMA

(Map p248; www.aberdeenartscentre.org.uk; King St) Stages regular drama productions in its theatre, and changing exhibitions in its gallery.

ℹ Information

Aberdeen Royal Infirmary (☎01224-681818; www.nhsgrampian.org; Foresterhill) Medical services. About a mile northwest of the western end of Union St.

Aberdeen Tourist Office (☎01224-288828; www.aberdeen-grampian.com; 23 Union St; ⊕9am-6.30pm Mon-Sat, 10am-4pm Sun Jul & Aug; 9.30am-5pm Mon-Sat Sep-Jun) Handy for general information; has internet access too.

Books & Beans (www.booksandbeans.co.uk; 22 Belmont St; per 15min £1; ⊕8am-6pm)

Internet access; also Fairtrade coffee and secondhand books.

Main Post Office (St Nicholas Shopping Centre, Upperkirkgate; ⊕9am-5.30pm Mon-Sat)

ℹ Getting There & Away

Air

Aberdeen Airport (p489) is at Dyce, 6 miles northwest of the city centre. There are regular flights to numerous Scottish and UK destinations, including Orkney and Shetland, and international flights to the Netherlands, Norway, Denmark, Germany and France.

Stagecoach Jet bus 727 runs regularly from Aberdeen bus station to the airport (single £2.70, 35 minutes). A taxi from the airport to the city centre takes 25 minutes and costs £15.

Boat

Car ferries from Aberdeen to Orkney and Shetland are run by **Northlink Ferries** (www.northlinkferries.co.uk). The **ferry terminal** is a short walk east of the train and bus stations.

Bus

The **bus station** (Guild St) is next to Jurys Inn, close to the train station.

Braemar £10, 2¼ hours, every two hours; via Ballater and Balmoral

Dundee £16, 1½ hours, hourly

Edinburgh £28, 3¼ hour, hourly; change at Perth

Glasgow £28, three hours, hourly

Inverness £9, 3¾ hours, hourly; via Huntly, Keith, Fochabers, Elgin and Nairn

London £46, 12 hours, twice daily; National Express

Perth £22, two hours, hourly

Train

The **train station** is south of the city centre, next to the massive Union Square shopping mall.

Dundee £27, 1¼ hours, twice an hour

Edinburgh £45, 2½ hours, hourly

Glasgow £45, 2¾ hours, hourly

Inverness £28, 2¼ hour, eight daily

London King's Cross £140, eight hours, hourly; some direct, most change at Edinburgh

ℹ Getting Around

BUS The main city bus operator is **First Aberdeen** (www.firstaberdeen.com). Local fares cost from £1.10 to £2.40; pay the driver as you board the bus. A FirstDay ticket (adult/child £4.80/2.70) allows unlimited travel from the time of purchase until midnight on all First Aberdeen buses. Information, route maps and tickets are available from the **First Travel Centre** (47 Union St; ⊕8.45am-5.30pm Mon-Sat).

The most useful services for visitors are buses 16A and 19 from Union St to Great Western Rd (for B&Bs); bus 27 from the bus station to Aberdeen Youth Hostel and the airport; and bus 20 from Marischal College to Old Aberdeen.

CAR Car rental companies include:

Arnold Clark (☑01224-249159; www.arnold clarkrental.com; Girdleness Rd)

Enterprise Car Hire (☑01224-642642; www. enterprise.co.uk; 80 Skene Sq).

TAXI The main city-centre taxi ranks are at the train station and on Back Wynd, off Union St. To order a taxi, phone **ComCab** (☑01224-353535) or **Rainbow City Taxis** (☑01224-878787).

Around Aberdeen

HADDO HOUSE
Designed in Georgian style by William Adam in 1732, Haddo House (NTS; ☑0844 493 2179; adult/child £9.50/7; ☺tours 11am, 1.30pm & 3.30pm daily Jul & Aug, Fri-Mon Apr-Jun, Sep & Oct) is best described as a classic English stately home transplanted to Scotland. Home to the Gordon family, it has sumptuous Victorian interiors with wood-panelled walls, Persian rug–scattered floors and a wealth of period antiques. The beautiful grounds and terraced gardens are open all year (9am to dusk); guided tours of the house are best booked in advance.

Haddo is 19 miles north of Aberdeen, near Ellon. Buses run hourly Monday to Saturday from Aberdeen to Tarves/Methlick, stopping at the end of the Haddo House driveway; it's a mile-long walk from bus stop to house.

CASTLE FRASER
The impressive 16th- to 17th-century Castle Fraser (NTS; adult/child £9.50/7; ☺11am-5pm Jul & Aug, noon-5pm Thu-Sun Apr-Jun, Sep & Oct) is the ancestral home of the Fraser family. The largely Victorian interior includes the great hall (with a hidden opening where the laird could eavesdrop on his guests), the library, various bedrooms and an ancient kitchen, plus a secret room for storing valuables; Fraser family relics on display include needlework hangings and a 19th-century artificial leg. The 'Woodland Secrets' area in the castle grounds is designed as an adventure playground for kids.

The castle is 16 miles west of Aberdeen and 3 miles south of Kemnay. Buses from Aberdeen to Alford stop at Kemnay.

FYVIE CASTLE
Though a magnificent example of Scottish Baronial architecture, Fyvie Castle (NTS; adult/child £11/8; ☺11am-5pm Jul & Aug, noon-5pm Sat-Tue Apr-Jun, Sep & Oct) is probably more famous for its ghosts, which include a phantom trumpeter and the mysterious Green Lady. The castle's art collection includes portraits by Thomas Gainsborough and Sir Henry Raeburn. The grounds are open all year (9am to dusk).

The castle is 25 miles north of Aberdeen on the A947 towards Turriff. A bus runs hourly every day from Aberdeen to Banff and Elgin via Fyvie village, a mile from the castle.

STONEHAVEN
POP 9600

Originally a small fishing village, Stonehaven has been the county town of Kincardineshire since 1600 and is now a thriving family-friendly seaside resort. There's a tourist office (☑01569-762806; 66 Allardice St; ☺10am-7pm Mon-Sat, 1-5.30pm Sun Jul & Aug, 10am-1pm & 2-5.30pm Mon-Sat Jun & Sep, 10am-

---

SAND DUNES AND SAND TRAPS

Coastal sand dunes extend north from Aberdeen for more than 14 miles, one of the largest areas of dunes in the UK, and the most untouched by human activity. Forvie National Nature Reserve (www.nnr-scotland.org.uk/forvie; admission free; ☺24hrs) has wildlife hides and waymarked trails through the dunes to an abandoned medieval village where only the ruins of the church survive. The dunes form an important nesting and feeding area for birds – don't wander off the trails during the nesting season (April to August).

American tycoon Donald Trump sparked off a major controversy when he opened **Trump International Golf Links** in 2012, amid a 'protected' area of sand dunes just four miles south of Forvie. In Trump's own words: 'I have never seen such an unspoiled and dramatic sea side landscape'. However, the development has split the community between those who welcome the potential economic benefits, and those worried about the environmental damage.

1pm & 2-5pm Mon-Sat Apr, May & Oct) near Market Sq in the town centre.

👁 Sights & Activities

From the lane beside the tourist office, a boardwalk leads south along the shoreline to the picturesque cliff-bound **harbour**, where you'll find a couple of appealing pubs and the town's oldest building, the **Tolbooth**, built about 1600 by the Earl Marischal. It now houses a small museum (admission free; ⏰10am-noon & 2-5pm Mon & Thu-Sat, 2-5pm Wed & Sun) and a restaurant.

Open-Air Swimming Pool   SWIMMING
(📞01569-762134; www.stonehavenopenairpool. co.uk; adult/child £4.90/2.90; ⏰10am-7.30pm Mon-Fri, 10am-6pm Sat & Sun Jul–mid-Aug, 1-7.30pm Mon-Fri, 10am-6pm Sat & Sun Jun & late Aug) At the northern end of town is the swimming pool, an Olympic-size (50m), heated, sea-water pool in art deco style, dating from 1934. The pool is also open for 'midnight swims' from 10pm to midnight on Wednesday from the end of June to mid-August.

Dunnottar Castle   CASTLE
(📞01569-762173; www.dunnottarcastle.co.uk; adult/child £5/2; ⏰9am-6pm Apr-Oct, 10.30am-dusk Nov-Mar) A pleasant, 15-minute walk along the clifftops south of the harbour leads to the spectacular ruins of Dunnottar Castle, spread out across a grassy promontory rising 50m above the sea. As dramatic a film set as any director could wish for, it provided the backdrop for Franco Zeffirelli's *Hamlet*, starring Mel Gibson. The original fortress was built in the 9th century; the keep is the most substantial remnant, but the drawing room (restored in 1926) is more interesting.

Lady Gail 2   BOAT
(📞01569-765064; www.castlecharter.co.uk; adult/child £10/5) The Lady Gail 2 offers boat trips from the harbour to the nearby sea cliffs of Fowlsheugh nature reserve, which from May to July are home to around 160,000 nesting seabirds, including kittiwakes, guillemots, razorbills and puffins.

🎉 Festivals & Events

The town hosts several special events, including the famous Fireball Ceremony (www.stonehavenfireballs.co.uk) at Hogmanay (New Years Eve), when people parade along the High St at midnight swinging blazing fireballs around their heads, and the three-day Stonehaven Folk Festival (www.stone havenfolkfestival.co.uk) in mid-July.

🛏 Sleeping & Eating

TOP CHOICE 24 Shorehead   B&B ££
(📞01569-767750; www.twentyfourshorehead. co.uk; 24 Shorehead; s/d £55/70; @📶) Location makes all the difference, and the location of this former cooperage offering peaceful and very stylish B&B accommodation can't be beaten – it's the last house at the end of the road, overlooking the harbour, with lovely sea views. Using the binoculars provided, you can even spot seals from your bedroom. No credit cards.

Beachgate House   B&B ££
(📞01569-763155; www.beachgate.co.uk; Beachgate Lane; s/d £55/70; P) This luxurious modern bungalow is right on the seafront, just a few paces from the tourist office; two of its five rooms have sea views, as does the lounge/dining room.

TOP CHOICE Tolbooth Restaurant   SEAFOOD £££
(📞01569-762287; www.tolbooth-restaurant.co.uk; Old Pier; mains £18-22; ⏰lunch & dinner Tue-Sat, also Sun May-Sep) Set in a 17th-century building overlooking the harbour, and decorated with local art and crisp white linen, this is one of the best seafood restaurants in the region. Daily specials include dishes such as scallops with samphire risotto, artichokes and saffron foam. From Tuesday to Saturday you can get a two-/three-course lunch for £14/17. Reservations recommended.

Marine Hotel   PUB, SEAFOOD ££
(📞01569-762155; www.marinehotelstonehaven. co.uk; 9-10 The Shore; mains £11-20; ⏰food noon-2.30pm & 5.30-9pm Mon-Fri, noon-9pm Sat & Sun) A makeover with bare timber, slate and dove-grey paintwork has given this popular harbourside pub a boutique look; there are half a dozen real ales on tap, including Deuchars IPA and Timothy Taylor, and a bar-meals menu that includes fresh seafood specials.

Carron Restaurant   SCOTTISH ££
(📞01569-760460; www.carron-restaurant.co.uk; 20 Cameron St; mains £11-22; ⏰Tue-Sat) This beautiful art deco restaurant is a remarkable survivour from the 1930s, complete with bow-fronted terrace, iron fanlights, deco mirrors, player piano and original tiled toilets. The French- and Mediterranean-influenced menu makes the most of local produce, matching the elegance of the surroundings.

NORTHEAST SCOTLAND AROUND ABERDEEN

Boathouse Café CAFE
(☑01569-764666; Old Pier; mains £6-8; ⏱9.30am-4pm Mon-Fri, 9.30am-5pm Sat & Sun) Excellent coffee, cakes and light lunches, and an outdoor terrace with a view of the sea.

Ship Inn PUB, SEAFOOD
(☑01569-279722; www.shipinnstonehaven.com; 5 Shorehead; mains £9-18; ⏱lunch & dinner Mon-Fri, noon-9.45pm Sat & Sun) Real ales, pub grub and outdoor tables with a view of the harbour. More formal dining in the neighbouring Captain's Table restaurant.

❶ Getting There & Away
Stonehaven is 15 miles south of Aberdeen and is served by frequent **buses** travelling between Aberdeen (45 minutes, hourly) and Dundee (1½ hours). **Trains** to Dundee are faster (£14, 55 minutes, hourly) and offer a more scenic journey.

Deeside

The valley of the **River Dee** – often called **Royal Deeside** because of the royal family's long association with the area – stretches west from Aberdeen to Braemar, closely paralleled by the A93 road. From Deeside north to Strathdon is serious castle country – there are more examples of fanciful Scottish Baronial architecture here than anywhere else in Scotland.

The Dee, world famous for its **salmon fishing**, has its source in the Cairngorm Mountains west of Braemar, the starting point for long walks into the hills. The Fish-Dee website (www.fishdee.co.uk) has all you need to know about fishing on the river.

CRATHES CASTLE
The atmospheric, 16th-century Crathes Castle (NTS; ☑01330-844525; adult/child £10.50/7.50; ⏱10.30am-5pm Jun-Aug, to 4.30pm Sat-Thu Apr, May, Sep & Oct, to 3.45pm Sat & Sun Nov-Mar; ♿) is famous for its Jacobean painted ceilings, magnificently carved canopied beds and the 'Horn of Leys', presented to the Burnett family by Robert the Bruce in the 14th century. The beautiful formal **gardens** include 300-year-old yew hedges and colourful herbaceous borders. The castle is signposted off the A93.

BALLATER
POP 1450
The attractive little village of Ballater owes its 18th-century origins to the curative waters of nearby Pannanich Springs (now bottled commercially as Deeside Natural

Mineral Water) and its prosperity to nearby Balmoral Castle.

The **tourist office** (☑01339-755306; Station Sq; ⏱9am-6pm Jul & Aug, 10am-5pm Sep-Jun) is in the Old Royal Station. For internet access, go to Cybernaut (☑01339-755566; 2 Braemar Rd; per 15min £1; ⏱9am-5pm Mon-Fri, 10am-4pm Sat).

◉ Sights & Activities
When Queen Victoria travelled to Balmoral Castle she would alight from the royal train at Ballater's Old Royal Station (☑01339 755306; Station Sq; admission £2; ⏱9am-6pm Jul & Aug, 10am-5pm Sep-Jun). The station has been beautifully restored and now houses the tourist office, a cafe and a museum with a replica of Victoria's royal coach. Note the crests on the shop fronts along the main street proclaiming 'By Royal Appointment' – the village is a major supplier of provisions to Balmoral.

Also on Station Sq is Dee Valley Confectioners (☑01339-755499; www.dee-valley.co.uk; Station Sq; admission free; ⏱9am-noon & 2-4.30pm Mon-Thu Apr-Oct), where you can drool over the manufacture of traditional Scottish sweeties.

As you approach Ballater from the east the hills start to close in, and there are many pleasant **walks** in the surrounding area. The steep woodland walk up **Craigendarroch** (400m) takes just over one hour. **Morven** (871m) is a more serious prospect, taking about six hours, but offers good views from the top; ask at the tourist office for more info.

You can hire bikes from CycleHighlands (www.cyclehighlands.com; The Pavilion, Victoria Rd; bicycle hire per day £16; ⏱9am-6pm), which also offers guided bike rides and advice on local trails, and Cabin Fever (☑01339-54004; Station Sq; bicycle hire per 2hr £8; ⏱9am-6pm), which can also arrange pony trekking, quad-biking, clay-pigeon shooting or canoeing.

🍴 Sleeping & Eating
Accommodation here is fairly expensive and budget travellers usually continue to Braemar.

TOP CHOICE **Auld Kirk** HOTEL ££
(☑01339-755762; www.theauldkirk.com; Braemar Rd; s/d from £73/110; ℗🛜) Here's something a little out of the ordinary – a six-bedroom 'restaurant with rooms' housed in a converted 19th-century church. The interior blends original features with sleek modern decor,

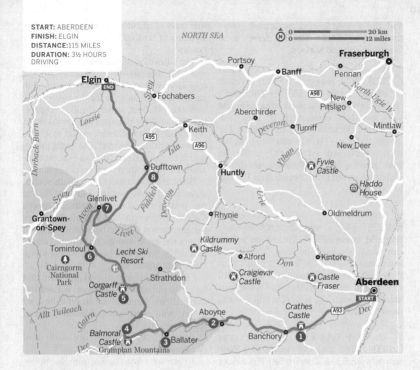

START: ABERDEEN
FINISH: ELGIN
DISTANCE: 115 MILES
DURATION: 3½ HOURS
DRIVING

Driving Tour
Deeside to Speyside

❯ This tour takes in the castles of Royal Deeside and the distilleries of Speyside, but plan ahead – realistically, you'll probably only have time to visit one castle and one distillery.

Head west out of **Aberdeen** on the A93 towards Banchory. Time your departure to arrive at ❶ **Crathes Castle** for opening time at 10.30am and spend an hour exploring.

Continue on the A93 through ❷ **Aboyne**, a good place for a coffee break at the **Black-Faced Sheep**; just beyond the village, you can watch gliders taking off at the Deeside Gliding Club. Alternatively, save your appetite for lunch at ❸ **Ballater**, a pretty village with royal associations and several good restaurants and cafes.

Stick to the A93 west of Ballater, which has better views than the minor road on the south of the river, to reach ❹ **Balmoral Castle**. You'll need at least two hours to make the most of a visit here, so plan accordingly. Now take the B976 northwards to join the A939.

The A939 **Cockbridge–Tomintoul road**, as it is known, is one of the wildest main roads in Britain. It follows the line of an 18th-century military road over high heather moors; its steep hills and swooping bends making it a magnet for motorcyclists. It passes the remote ❺ **Corgarff Castle** and reaches a height of 644m at the Lecht Ski Centre before dropping to the village of ❻ **Tomintoul**.

About a mile past Tomintoul turn right on the B9136 which leads to the classic Speyside village and distillery of ❼ **Glenlivet**; turn right and then left on the B9009 to ❽ **Dufftown**, the heart of Speyside whisky country. If time permits, take in a distillery tour (there are seven nearby), before heading north on the A941 to finish at **Elgin**.

and the stylish Scottish restaurant (two-/three-course dinner £29/36) serves local lamb, venison and seafood.

Green Inn
B&B ££

(☎01339-755701; www.green-inn.com; 9 Victoria Rd; B&B per person from £40; ℗) This lovely old house dotted with plush armchairs and sofas has three comfortable en suite bedrooms, but the accent is on fine dining. The menu includes French-influenced dishes such as roast quail with crayfish, truffle and wild mushrooms. A three-course dinner costs £43, served from 7pm till 9pm Tuesday to Saturday.

Habitat
HOSTEL £

(☎01339-753752; www.habitat-at-ballater.com; Bridge Sq; dm/tw £20/45) Tucked up a lane near the bridge over the River Dee, Habitat is an attractive and eco-friendly hostel with three eight-bed bunk rooms (with personal lockers and reading lamps), and a comfortable lounge with big, soft sofas and a wood-burning stove.

Old Station Cafe
CAFE ££

(☎01339-755050; Station Sq; mains £9-15; ⊙10am-5pm daily, plus 6.30-8.30pm Thu-Sat) The former waiting room at Queen Victoria's train station is now an attractive dining area with black-and-white floor tiles, basketwork chairs, and marble fireplace and table tops. Daily specials make good use of local produce, from salmon to venison, and good coffee and home-baked goods are available all day.

Rock Salt & Snails
CAFE £

(www.rocksaltandsnails.co.uk; 2 Bridge St; mains £4-7; ⊙10am-5pm Mon-Sat, 11am-5pm Sun) Great litte cafe serving excellent coffee, and lunch platters composed of locally sourced deli products (cheese, ham, salads etc).

❶ Getting There & Away

Bus 201 runs from Aberdeen to Ballater (£9.60, 1¾ hours, hourly Monday to Saturday, six on Sunday) via Crathes Castle, and continues to Braemar (30 minutes) every two hours.

BALMORAL CASTLE

Eight miles west of Ballater lies Balmoral Castle (☎01339-742334; www.balmoralcastle.com; adult/child £9/5; ⊙10am-5pm Apr-Jul, last admission 4pm), the Queen's Highland holiday home, screened from the road by a thick curtain of trees. Built for Queen Victoria in 1855 as a private residence for the royal family, it kicked off the revival of the Scottish Baronial style of architecture that characterises so many of Scotland's 19th-century country houses.

The admission fee includes an interesting and well thought-out audioguide, but the tour is very much an outdoor one through garden and grounds; as for the castle itself, only the ballroom, which displays a collection of Landseer paintings and royal silver, is open to the public. Don't expect to see the Queen's private quarters! The main attraction is learning about Highland estate management, rather than royal revelations.

You can buy a booklet that details several waymarked walks within Balmoral Estate; the best is the climb to **Prince Albert's Cairn**, a huge granite pyramid that bears the inscription 'To the beloved memory of Albert the great and good, Prince Consort. Erected by his broken hearted widow Victoria R. 21st August 1862'.

The massive pointy-topped mountain that looms to the south of Balmoral is **Lochnagar** (1155m), immortalised in verse by Lord Byron, who spent his childhood years in Aberdeenshire:

England, thy beauties are tame and domestic

To one who has roamed o'er the mountains afar.

O! for the crags that are wild and majestic:

The steep frowning glories of dark Lochnagar.

Balmoral is located beside the A93 at Crathie and can be reached by catching the Aberdeen–Braemar bus.

BRAEMAR
POP 400

Braemar is a pretty little village with a grand location on a broad plain ringed by mountains where the Dee Valley and Glen Clunie meet. In winter this is one of the coldest places in the country – temperatures as low as -29°C have been recorded – and during spells of severe cold hungry deer wander the streets looking for a bite to eat. Braemar is an excellent base for hill walking, and there's also skiing at nearby Glenshee.

The tourist office (☎01399-741600; The Mews, Mar Rd; ⊙9am-6pm Aug, 9am-5pm Jun, Jul, Sep & Oct, 10am-1.30pm & 2-5pm Mon-Sat, 2-5pm Sun Nov-May), opposite the Fife Arms Hotel, has lots of useful info on walks in the area. There's a bank with an ATM in the village centre, a couple of outdoor equipment shops

BRAEMAR GATHERING

There are Highland games in many Scottish towns and villages throughout the summer, but the best known is the Braemar Gathering (☎01339-755377; www.braemargathering. org; adult/child from £10/2), which takes place on the first Saturday in September. It's a major occasion, organised every year since 1817 by the Braemar Royal Highland Society. Events include Highland dancing, pipers, tug-of-war, a hill race up Morrone, tossing the caber, hammer- and stone-throwing and the long jump. International athletes are among those who take part.

These kinds of events took place informally in the Highlands for many centuries as tests of skill and strength, but they were formalised around 1820 as part of the rise of Highland romanticism initiated by Sir Walter Scott and King George IV. Queen Victoria attended the Braemar Gathering in 1848, starting a tradition of royal patronage that continues to this day.

and an Alldays (⊙7.30am-9pm Mon-Sat, 9am-6pm Sun) grocery store.

⊙ Sights & Activities

Just north of the village, turreted Braemar Castle (www.braemarcastle.co.uk; adult/child £6/3; ⊙10am-4pm Sat & Sun Easter-Oct, also Wed Jul–mid-Sep) dates from 1628 and served as a government garrison after the 1745 Jacobite rebellion. It was taken over by the local community in 2007, and now offers guided tours of the historic castle apartments.

An easy walk from Braemar is up **Creag Choinnich** (538m), a hill to the east of the village above the A93. The route is way-marked and takes about 1½ hours. For a longer walk (three hours) and superb views of the Cairngorms, head for the summit of **Morrone** (859m), southwest of Braemar. Ask at the tourist office for details of these and other walks.

You can hire mountain bikes from Braemar Mountain Sports (☎01339-741242; www. braemarmountainsports.com; 5 Invercauld Rd; ⊙9am-6pm) for £16 per 24 hours. They also rent skiing and mountaineering equipment.

🛏 Sleeping

TOP CHOICE Rucksacks Bunkhouse BUNKHOUSE £
(☎01339-741517; 15 Mar Rd; bothy £7, dm £12-15, tw £36; P@) An appealing cottage with a comfy dorm, and cheaper beds in an alpine-style bothy (shared sleeping platform for 10 people; bring your own sleeping bag). Extras include a drying room (for wet-weather gear), laundry and even a sauna (£10 an hour). Nonguests are welcome to use the internet (£3 per hour, 10.30am to 4.30pm), laundry and even the showers (£2). The friendly owner is a font of knowledge about the local area.

Clunie Lodge Guesthouse B&B ££
(☎01339-741330; www.clunielodge.com; Cluniebank Rd; r per person from £32; P🛜) A spacious Victorian villa set in beautiful gardens, the Clunie is a great place to relax after a hard day's hiking, with its comfortable residents lounge, bedrooms with views of the hills and red squirrels scampering through the neighbouring woods. There's a drying room and secure storage for bicycles.

Craiglea B&B ££
(☎01339-741641; www.craigleabraemar.com; Hillside Dr; d £72; P🛜) Craiglea is a homely B&B set in a pretty stone cottage with three en suite bedrooms. Vegetarian breakfasts are available and the owners can give advice on local walks.

Braemar Lodge Hotel HOTEL, BUNKHOUSE ££
(☎01339-741627; www.braemarlodge.co.uk; Glenshee Rd; dm from £12, s/d £75/120; P) This Victorian shooting lodge on the southern outskirts of Braemar has bags of character, not least in the wood-panelled Malt Room bar, which is as well stocked with mounted deer heads as it is with single-malt whiskies. There's a good restaurant with views of the hills, plus a 12-berth hikers' bunkhouse in the hotel grounds.

Braemar SYHA HOSTEL £
(☎01339-741659; 21 Glenshee Rd; dm £18; ⊙Feb-Oct; @) This hostel is housed in a grand former shooting lodge just south of Braemar viilage centre on the A93 to Perth. It has a comfy lounge with pool table, and a barbecue in the garden.

St Margarets B&B ££
(☎01339-741697; 13 School Rd; s/tw £32/54; 🛜) Grab this place if you can, but there's only

one room – a twin with a serious sunflower theme. The genuine warmth of the welcome is delightful.

Invercauld Caravan Club Site CAMPGROUND £
(✆01339-741373; tent sites £10, plus per person £7; ⊗late Dec-Oct) There is good camping here, or you can camp wild (no facilities) along the minor road on the east bank of the Clunie Water, 3 miles south of Braemar.

✕ Eating

TOP
CHOICE **Gathering Place** BISTRO ££
(✆01339-741234; www.the-gathering-place.co.uk; 9 Invercauld Rd; mains £15-19; ⊗dinner Tue-Sat) This bright and breezy bistro is an unexpected corner of culinary excellence, with a welcoming dining room and sunny conservatory, tucked below the main road junction at the entrance to Braemar village.

Taste CAFE £
(✆01339-741425; www.taste-braemar.co.uk; Airlie House, Mar Rd; mains £3-6; ⊗10am-5pm Mon-Sat; ⊕) Taste is a relaxed little cafe with armchairs in the window, serving soups, snacks, coffee and cakes.

❶ Getting There & Away

Bus 201 runs from Aberdeen to Braemar (£9.60, 2¼ hours, eight daily Monday to Saturday, five on Sunday). The 50-mile drive from Perth to Braemar is beautiful, but there's no public transport on this route.

INVEREY

Five miles west of Braemar is the tiny settlement of Inverey. Numerous mountain walks start from here, including the adventurous walk through the **Lairig Ghru** (p340) pass to Aviemore.

The **Glen Luibeg** circuit (15 miles, six hours) is a good day-walk. Start from the woodland car park 250m beyond the **Linn of Dee**, a narrow gorge at the road bridge about 1.5 miles west of Inverey, and follow the footpath and track to Derry Lodge and Glen Luibeg – there are beautiful remnants of the ancient Caledonian pine forest here. Continue westwards on a pleasant path over a pass into Glen Dee, then follow the River Dee back downstream to the linn. Take OS 1:50,000 map sheet number 43.

A good short walk (3 miles, 1½ hours) begins at the **Linn of Quoich** – a waterfall that thunders through a narrow slot in the rocks. Head uphill on a footpath on the east bank of the stream, past the impressive rock scenery of the **Punch Bowl** (a giant pothole), to a modern bridge that spans the narrow gorge, and return via an unsurfaced road on the far bank.

Strathdon Valley

The valley of the River Don, home to many of Aberdeenshire's finest castles, stretches westward from Kintore, 13 miles northwest of Aberdeen, taking in the villages of Kemnay, Monymusk, Alford (*ah*-ford) and tiny Strathdon. The A944 parallels the lower valley; west of Alford, the A944, A97 and A939 follow the river's upper reaches.

Stagecoach bus 220 runs from Aberdeen to Alford (1½ hours, seven a day Monday to Saturday, four on Sunday); bus 219 continues from Alford to Strathdon village (50 minutes, two daily Tuesday and Thursday, one on Saturday) via Kildrummy.

Craigievar Castle CASTLE
(NTS; adult/child £11.50/8.50; ⊗11am-5.30pm daily Jul & Aug, Fri-Tue only Apr-Jun & Sep) A superb example of the original Scottish Baronial style, Craigievar has managed to survive pretty much unchanged since its completion in the 17th century. The lower half is a plain tower house, the upper half sprouts corbelled turrets, cupolas and battlements – an extravagant statement of its builder's wealth and status. It's 6 miles south of Alford.

Kildrummy Castle CASTLE
(HS; ✆01975-571331; adult/child £4/2.40; ⊗9.30am-5.30pm Apr-Sep) Nine miles west of Alford lie the extensive remains of this 13th-century castle, former seat of the Earl of Mar and once one of Scotland's most impressive fortresses. After the 1715 Jacobite rebellion the earl was exiled to France and his castle fell into ruin.

Corgarff Castle CASTLE
(HS; ✆01975-651460; adult/child £5/3; ⊗9.30am-5.30pm daily Apr-Sep, 9.30am-4.30pm Sat & Sun Oct-Mar) In the wild upper reaches of Strathdon, near the A939 from Corgarff to Tomintoul, is the impressive fortress of Corgarff Castle. The tower house dates from the 16th century, but the star-shaped defensive curtain wall was added in 1748 when the castle was converted to a military barracks in the wake of the Jacobite rebellion.

ALFORD
POP 1925

Alford has a **tourist office** (✆01975-562052; Old Station Yard, Main St; ⊗10am-5pm Mon-Sat,

12.45-5pm Sun Jun-Aug, 10am-1pm & 2-5pm Mon-Fri, 10am-noon & 1.45-5pm Sat, 12.45-5pm Sun Apr, May & Sep), banks with ATMs and a supermarket.

The Grampian Transport Museum (01975-562292; www.gtm.org.uk; adult/child £9/free; 10am-5pm Apr-Sep, 10am-4pm Oct) houses a fascinating collection of vintage motorbikes, cars, buses and trams, including a Triumph Bonneville in excellent nick, a couple of Model T Fords (including one used by Drambuie), a Ferrari F40 and an Aston Martin V8 Mk II. Unusual exhibits include a 19th-century horse-drawn sleigh from Russia, a 1942 Mack snowplough and the Craigievar Express, a steam-powered tricycle built in 1895 by a local postman.

Next to the museum is the terminus of the narrow-gauge Alford Valley Steam Railway (01975-562811; www.alfordvalleyrailway.org.uk; adult/child £3/2; 11.30am-4pm Jul & Aug, Sat & Sun only Apr-Jun & Sep), a heritage line that runs from here to Haughton Country Park.

LECHT SKI RESORT

At the head of Strathdon the A939 – known as the **Cockbridge–Tomintoul road**, a magnificent rollercoaster of a route, much loved by motorcyclists – crosses the Lecht pass (637m) where there's a small skiing area with lots of short easy and intermediate runs. Lecht 2090 (www.lecht.co.uk) hires out skis, boots and poles for £20 a day; a one-day lift pass is £28.

In summer, the chairlift serves mountain-biking trails (day ticket £27); there are no bike-hire facilities though, so you'll need to bring your own.

Northern Aberdeenshire

North of Aberdeen, the Grampian Mountains fall away to rolling agricultural plains pocked with small, craggy volcanic hills. This fertile lowland corner of northeastern Scotland is known as Buchan, a region of traditional farming culture immortalised by Lewis Grassic Gibbon in his trilogy, *A Scots Quair*, based on the life of a farming community in the 1920s. The old Scots dialect called the Doric lives on in everyday use here – if you think the Glaswegian accent is difficult to understand, just try listening in on a conversation in Peterhead or Fraserburgh.

The Buchan coast alternates between rugged cliffs and long, long stretches of sand,

dotted with picturesque little fishing villages such as Pennan, where parts of the film *Local Hero* were shot.

FRASERBURGH
POP 12,500

Fraserburgh, affectionately known to locals as the Broch, is Europe's largest shellfish port. Like Peterhead's, Fraserburgh's fortune has been founded on the fishing industry and has suffered from its general decline. The harbour is still fairly busy, though, and is an interesting place to wander around; there are also good sandy **beaches** east of the town. There's a tourist office (01346-518315; www.visitfraserburgh.com; Saltoun Sq; 10am-1pm & 2-5pm Mon-Sat Apr-Oct), a supermarket and banks with ATMs.

The excellent Scottish Lighthouse Museum (01346-511022; www.lighthousemuseum.org.uk; Kinnaird Head; adult/child £5/2; 10am-5pm Wed-Mon, noon-5pm Tue Mar-Oct, 11.30am-4.30pm Wed-Sun Nov-Feb) provides a fascinating insight into the network of lights that have safeguarded the Scottish coast for over 100 years, and the men and women who built and maintained them (plus a sobering fact – that *all* the world's lighthouses are to be decommissioned by 1 January 2080). A guided tour takes you to the top of the old Kinnaird Head lighthouse, built on top of a converted 16th-century castle; the engineering is so precise that the 4.5-ton light assembly can be rotated by pushing with a single finger. The anemometer here measured the strongest wind speed ever recorded in the UK, with a gust of 123 knots (142mph) on 13 February 1989.

Buses 267 and 268 run to Fraserburgh from Aberdeen (1½ hours, every 30 minutes Monday to Saturday, hourly on Sunday) via Ellon.

PENNAN

Pennan is a picturesque harbour village tucked beneath red-sandstone cliffs, 12 miles west of Fraserburgh. The whitewashed houses are built gable-end to the sea, and the waves break just a few metres away on the other side of the village's only street.

The village featured in the 1983 film *Local Hero*, and fans of the film still come to make a call from the red telephone box that played a prominent part in the plot. However, the box in the film was just a prop, and it was only later that film buffs and locals successfully campaigned for a real one to be installed.

The interior of the village hotel, the **Pennan Inn**, also appeared in the film, though one of the houses further along the seafront to the east doubled for the exterior of the fictional hotel. The beach scenes were filmed on the other side of the country, at Camasdarach Beach in Arisaig.

Bus 273 from Fraserburgh to Banff stops at the Pennan road end (25 minutes, two a day, Saturday only), 350m south of (and a steep climb uphill from) the village.

HUNTLY
POP 4400

An impressive ruined castle and an attractive main square make this small town worth a stopover between Aberdeen and Elgin. The tourist office (☏01466-792255; The Square; ◷10am-5.30pm Mon-Sat, 10am-3pm Sun Jul & Aug, 10am-1pm & 2-5pm Mon-Sat Apr-Jun, Sep & Oct) is on the main square, next to a bank with an ATM.

Castle St (beside the Huntly Hotel) runs north from the town square to an arched gateway and tree-lined avenue that leads to 16th-century Huntly Castle (HS; adult/child £5/3; ◷9.30am-5.30pm Apr-Sep, 9.30am-4.30pm Sat-Wed Oct-Mar), the former stronghold of the Gordons on the banks of the River Deveron. Over the main door is a superb carving that includes the royal arms and the figures of Christ and St Michael.

Just off the A96, 3 miles northwest of Huntly, is the Peregrine WildWatch Centre (www.forestry.gov.uk/huntlyperegrines; adult/child £3/1; ◷10am-5pm Apr-Aug) where you can observe rare peregrine falcons, both live from a hide and via a remote camera monitoring their nest site.

🛏 Sleeping

There are a couple of hotels on the main square and a handful of B&Bs in the surrounding streets; the hospitable Hillview (☏01466-794870; www.hillviewbb.com; Provost St; s/d £30/50; P🖥) and its tasty breakfast pancakes are recommended.

If you want to spoil yourself, continue along the drive beyond the castle to the Castle Hotel (☏01466-792696; www.castleho tel.uk.com; s/d from £90/130; P🖥), a splendid 18th-century mansion set amid acres of parkland. It's comfortably old fashioned, with a grand wooden staircase, convoluted corridors, the odd creaky floorboard and rattling sash window, but must be among the most affordable country-house hotels in Scotland.

❶ Getting There & Away

Bus 10 from Aberdeen (1½ hours, hourly) to Inverness passes through Huntly. There are also regular trains from Aberdeen to Huntly (one hour, every two hours), continuing to Inverness.

Moray

The old county of Moray (*murr*-ree), centred on the county town of Elgin, lies at the heart of an ancient Celtic earldom and is famed for its mild climate and rich farmland – the barley fields of the 19th century once provided the raw material for the Speyside whisky distilleries, one of the region's main attractions for present-day visitors.

ELGIN
POP 21,000

Elgin's been the provincial capital of Moray for over eight centuries and was an important town in medieval times. Dominated by a hilltop monument to the 5th Duke of Gordon, Elgin's main attraction is its impressive ruined cathedral, where the tombs of the duke's ancestors lie.

◎ Sights

Elgin Cathedral   CATHEDRAL
(HS; King St; adult/child £5/3, joint ticket with Spynie Palace £6.70/4; ◷9.30am-5.30pm Apr-Sep, 9.30am-4.30pm Oct, 9.30am-4.30pm Sat-Wed Oct-Mar) Many people think that the ruins of Elgin Cathedral, known as the 'lantern of the north', are the most beautiful and evocative in Scotland. Consecrated in 1224, the cathedral was burned down in 1390 by the infamous Wolf of Badenoch, the illegitimate son of Robert II, following his excommunication by the Bishop of Moray. The octagonal chapter house is the finest in the country.

Elgin Museum   MUSEUM
(www.elginmuseum.org.uk; 1 High St; adult/child £4/1.50; ◷10am-5pm Mon-Fri, 11am-4pm Sat Oct) Palaeontologists and Pict lovers will enjoy Elgin Museum, where the highlights are its collections of fossil fish and Pictish carved stones.

Spynie Palace   HISTORIC BUILDING
(HS; adult/child £4/2.40; ◷9.30am-5.30pm Apr-Sep, 9.30am-4.30pm Sat & Sun Oct-Mar) This palace 2 miles north of Elgin was the residence of the medieval bishops of Moray until 1686. The massive tower house commands lovely views over Spynie Loch.

🛍 Shopping

Gordon & MacPhail
FOOD & DRINK

(www.gordonandmacphail.com; 58-60 South St; ⊙8.30am-5pm Mon-Sat) Gordon & MacPhail is the world's largest specialist malt-whisky dealer. Over a century old and offering around 450 different varieties, its Elgin shop is a place of pilgrimage for whisky connoisseurs, as well as housing a mouth-watering delicatessen.

Johnstons of Elgin
FASHION

(✆01343-554009; www.johnstonscashmere.com; Newmill; ⊙9am-5.30pm Mon-Sat, 11am-5pm Sun) Founded in 1797, Johnstons is famous for its cashmere woollen clothing, and is the only UK woollen mill that still sees the manufacturing process through from raw fibre to finished garment. There's a retail outlet and coffee shop, and free guided tours of the works.

🛌 Sleeping & Eating

Croft Guesthouse
B&B ££

(✆01343-546004; www.thecroftelgin.co.uk; 10 Institution Rd; s/d from £55/70; ℗) The Croft offers a taste of Victorian high society, set in a spacious mansion built for a local lawyer back in 1848. The house is filled with period features – check out the cast-iron and tile fireplaces – and the three large bedrooms are equipped with easy chairs and crisp bed linen.

Southbank Guest House
B&B ££

(✆01343-547132; www.southbankguesthouse.co.uk; 36 Academy St; s/d £55/75; ℗) The family-run, 12-room Southbank is set in a large Georgian town house in a quiet street south of Elgin's centre, just five minutes' walk from the cathedral and other sights.

Johnstons Coffee Shop
CAFE £

(Newmill; mains £5-7; ⊙10am-5pm Mon-Sat, 11am-4.30pm Sun; 🛜👶) The coffee shop at Johnstons woollen mill is the best place to eat in town, serving breakfast till 11.45am, hot lunches noon to 3pm (crepes with a range of fillings, inlcuding smoked salmon with cream cheese and dill), and cream teas.

Xoriatiki
GREEK ££

(✆01343-546868; 89 High St; mains £8-12; ⊙lunch & dinner Tue-Sat; 🍴) Likeable place that brings an authentic taste of Greece to Elgin at competitive prices. Access is via an alleyway off the main street.

Ashvale
FISH & CHIPS £

(11 Moss St; mains £6-13; ⊙10.45am-10pm) A branch of the famous Aberdeen fish-and-chip shop, sit in or takeaway.

ℹ Information

Post Office (Batchen St; ⊙8.30am-6pm Mon-Fri, 8.30am-4pm Sat)

Tourist Office (✆01343-562608; Elgin Library, Cooper Park; ⊙10am-5pm Mon-Sat, 10am-4pm Sun) Internet access upstairs.

ℹ Getting There & Away

The bus station is a block north of the High St, and the train station is 900m south of the town centre.

BUS Elgin is a stop on the hourly Stagecoach bus 10 service between Inverness (£9.50, one hour) and Aberdeen (£13, two hours). Bus 305 goes from Elgin to Banff and Macduff (£9, one hour), continuing to Aberdeen via Fyvie. Bus 336 goes to Dufftown (£4.30, 30 minutes, hourly Monday to Saturday).

TRAIN There are trains to **Aberdeen** (£17, 1½ hours, five a day) and **Inverness** (£12, 50 minutes, five a day).

DUFFTOWN
POP 1450

Rome may be built on seven hills, but Dufftown's built on seven stills, say the locals. Founded in 1817 by James Duff, 4th Earl of Fife, Dufftown is 17 miles south of Elgin and lies at the heart of the Speyside whisky-distilling region.

The **tourist office** (✆01340-820501; ⊙10am-1pm & 2-5.30pm Mon-Sat, 11am-3pm Sun Easter-Oct) is in the clock tower in the main square; the adjoining museum contains some interesting local items.

◉ Sights & Activities

With seven working distilleries nearby, Dufftown has been dubbed Scotland's malt-whisky capital. Ask at the tourist office for a **Malt Whisky Trail** (www.maltwhiskytrail.com) booklet, a self-guided tour around the seven stills plus the Speyside Cooperage.

Keith and Dufftown Railway
HERITAGE RAILWAY

(✆01340-821181; www.keith-dufftown-railway.co.uk; Dufftown Station; adult/child return £10/5) A line running for 11 miles from Dufftown to Keith sees trains hauled by 1950s diesel motor units running on weekends from June to September, plus Fridays in July and August. There are also two 1930s 'Brighton Belle' Pullman coaches, and a cafe housed in a 1957 British Railways cafeteria car.

Whisky Museum
MUSEUM

(✆01340-821097; www.dufftown.co.uk; 12 Conval St; ⊙1-4pm Mon-Fri May-Sep) As well as housing a selection of distillery memorabilia (try saying that after a few drams), the Whisky

BLAZE YOUR OWN WHISKY TRAIL

Visiting a distillery can be memorable, but only hardcore malthounds will want to go to more than two or three. Some are great to visit; others are depressingly corporate. The following are some recommendations.

Aberlour (☑01340-881249; www.aberlour.com; tours £12; ☺10am & 2pm daily Apr-Oct, by appointment Mon-Fri Nov-Mar) Has an excellent, detailed tour with a proper tasting session. It's on the main street in Aberlour.

Glenfarclas (☑01807-500257; www.glenfarclas.co.uk; admission £5; ☺10am-4pm Mon-Fri Oct-Mar, to 5pm Mon-Fri Apr-Sep, plus to 4pm Sat Jul-Sep) Small, friendly and independent, Glenfarclas is 5 miles south of Aberlour on the Grantown road. The last tour leaves 90 minutes before closing. The in-depth Connoisseur's Tour (Fridays only July to September) is £20.

Glenfiddich (www.glenfiddich.com; admission free; ☺9.30am-4.30pm daily year-round, closed Christmas & New Year) It's big and busy, but handiest for Dufftown and foreign languages are available. The standard tour starts with an overblown video, but it's fun, informative and free. An in-depth Connoisseur's Tour (£20) must be prebooked. Glenfiddich kept single malt alive during the dark years.

Macallan (☑01340-872280; www.themacallan.com; ☺9.30am-4.30pm Mon-Sat Easter-Oct, 11am-3pm Mon-Fri Nov-Mar) Excellent sherry-casked malt. Several small-group tours are available (last tour at 3.30pm), including an expert one (£20); all should be prebooked. Lovely location 2 miles northwest of Craigellachie.

Speyside Cooperage (☑01340-871108; www.speysidecooperage.co.uk; adult/child £3.50/2; ☺9am-4pm Mon-Fri) Here you can see the fascinating art of barrel-making in action. It's a mile from Craigellachie on the Dufftown road.

Spirit of Speyside (www.spiritofspeyside.com) This biannual whisky festival in Dufftown has a number of great events. It takes place in early May and late September; both accommodation and events should be booked well ahead.

Museum holds 'nosing and tasting evenings' where you can learn what to look for in a fine single malt (£10 per person; 8pm Wednesday in July and August).

You can then test your new-found skills at the nearby Whisky Shop (☑01340-821097; www.whiskyshopdufftown.co.uk; 1 Fife St), which stocks hundreds of single malts.

🛏 Sleeping & Eating

Craigellachie Hotel   HOTEL **££**
(☑08444 146 526; www.thecraigellachiehotel.com; Craigellachie; d from £75; P🐾) The Craigellachie has a wonderfully old-fashioned, hunting-lodge atmosphere, from the wood-panelled lobby to the opulent drawing room where you can sink into a sofa in front of the log fire. But the big attraction for whisky connoisseurs is the Quaich Bar, a cosy nook filled with green leather armchairs and lined with almost 700 varieties of single malt whisky.

The hotel is five miles northwest of Dufftown, overlooking the River Spey.

Davaar B&B   B&B **££**
(☑01340-820464; www.davaardufftown.co.uk; 17 Church St; s/d from £40/60) Just along the street opposite the tourist office, Davaar is a sturdy Victorian villa with three smallish but comfy rooms; the breakfast menu is superb, offering the option of Portsoy kippers instead of the traditional fry-up (which uses eggs from the owners' own chickens).

La Faisanderie   SCOTTISH **£££**
(☑01340-821273; The Square; mains £19-23; ☺noon-1.30pm & 5.30-8.30pm) This is a great place to eat, run by a local chef who shoots much of his own game. The interior is decorated in French *auberge* style with a cheerful mural and pheasants hiding in every corner. The three-course early-bird dinner menu (£19.50, from 5.30pm to 7pm) won't disappoint, but you can order à la carte as well.

SA Taste of Speyside   SCOTTISH **££**
(☑01340-820860; 10 Balvenie St; 2-/3-course dinner £19.50/22; ☺noon-9pm Tue-Sun Easter-Sep, noon-2pm & 6-9pm Tue-Sun Oct-Easter) This upmarket restaurant prepares traditional Scottish dishes using fresh local produce, including a challenging platter of smoked salmon, smoked venison, brandied chicken liver pâté, cured herring, a selection of Scot-

tish cheeses and homemade bread (phew!). A two-course lunch costs £11.

ℹ Getting There & Away

Buses link Dufftown to Elgin (50 minutes, hourly), Huntly, Aberdeen and Inverness.

On summer weekends, you can take a train from Aberdeen or Inverness to Keith, and then ride the Keith and Dufftown Railway to Dufftown.

TOMINTOUL
POP 320

This high-altitude (345m) village was built by the Duke of Gordon in 1775 on the old military road that leads over the Lecht pass from Corgarff, a route now followed by the A939 (usually the first road in Scotland to be blocked by snow when winter closes in). The duke hoped that settling the dispersed population of his estates in a proper village would help to stamp out cattle stealing and illegal distilling.

Tomintoul (tom-in-*towel*) is a pretty, stone-built village with a grassy, tree-lined main square, where you'll find the tourist office (☑01807-580285; The Square; ⊙9.30am-1pm & 2-5pm Mon-Sat Easter-Oct, plus 1-5pm Sun Aug); and, next door, the Tomintoul Museum (☑01807-673701; The Square; admission free; ⊙10am-5pm Mon-Sat Apr-Oct, plus 1-5pm Sun Jul & Aug), which has displays on a range of local topics.

The surrounding **Glenlivet Estate** (now the property of the Crown) has lots of **walking and cycling** trails – the estate's information centre (☑01479-870070; www.glenlivetestate.co.uk; Main St) distributes free maps of the area – and a spur of the **Speyside Way** long-distance footpath runs between Tomintoul and Ballindalloch, 15 miles to the north.

🛏 Sleeping & Eating

Accommodation for walkers includes the Tomintoul Youth Hostel (☑01807-580364; Main St; dm £15; ⊙May-Sep), housed in the old village school. The excellent Argyle Guest House (☑01807-580766; www.argyletomintoul.co.uk; 7 Main St; d/f £64/110) is a more comfortable alternative.

For something to eat, try the Clockhouse Restaurant (The Square; mains £10-13; ⊙lunch & dinner), which serves light lunches and bistro dinners made with fresh Highland lamb, venison and salmon.

ℹ Getting There & Away

There is a very limited bus service to Tomintoul from Elgin, Dufftown and Aberlour. Check with the tourist office in Elgin for the latest timetable.

BANFF & MACDUFF
COMBINED POP 7750

The handsome Georgian town of Banff and the busy fishing port of Macduff lie on either side of Banff Bay, separated only by the mouth of the River Deveron. Banff Links – 800m of clean golden sand stretching to the west – and Macduff's impressive aquarium pull in the holiday crowds.

The tourist office (☑01261-812419; Collie Lodge, High St; ⊙10am-5pm Mon-Sat, noon-5pm Sun Apr-Sep) is beside St Mary's car park in Banff.

◉ Sights

Duff House
ART GALLERY

(☑01261-818181; www.duffhouse.org.uk; adult/child £6.90/4.10; ⊙11am-5pm Apr-Oct, 11am-4pm Thu-Sun Nov-Mar) Duff House is an impressive baroque mansion on the southern edge of Banff. Built between 1735 and 1740 as the seat of the Earls of Fife, it was designed by William Adam and bears similarities to that Adam masterpiece, Hopetoun House (p96). Since being donated to the town in 1906 it has served as a hotel, a hospital and a POW camp, but is now an art gallery. One of Scotland's hidden gems, it houses a superb collection of Scottish and European art, including important works by Raeburn and Gainsborough.

Nearby Banff Museum (High St; admission free; ⊙10am-12.30pm Mon-Sat Jun-Sep) has award-winning displays on local wildlife, geology and history, and Banff silver.

Macduff Marine Aquarium
AQUARIUM

(www.macduff-aquarium.org.uk; 11 High Shore; adult/child £6.05/3.05; ⊙10am-5pm Mon-Sat & 11am-5pm Sun Apr-Oct, 11am-4pm Sat-Wed Nov-Mar; 🅰) The centrepiece of Macduff's aquarium is a 400,000L open-air tank, complete with kelp-coated reef and wave machine. Marine oddities on view include the brightly coloured cuckoo wrasse, the warty-skinned lumpsucker and the vicious-looking wolf fish.

🛏 Sleeping & Eating

Bryvard Guest House
B&B ££

(☑01261-818090; www.bryvardguesthouse.co.uk; Seafield St; s/d from £40/70; 🕿) The Bryvard is an imposing Edwardian town house close to the town centre, with four beautiful period-furnished bedrooms (two with en suite). Go for the 'McLeod' room, which has a four-poster bed and a sea view.

County Hotel
HOTEL ££

(☎01261-815353; www.thecountyhotel.com; 32 High St; s/d from £55/100; P) The County occupies an elegant Georgian mansion in the town centre, and is owned by a French chef – the hotel's bistro serves light meals (mains £6 to £10), while **Restaurant L'Auberge** offers the finest French cuisine (à la carte mains £29 to £35, three-course dinner £31).

Banff Links Caravan Park
CAMPSITE £

(☎01261-812228; tent/campervan from £10/15.50; ☺Apr-Oct) This campsite is beside the beach, 800m west of town.

❶ Getting There & Away

Bus 305 runs from Banff to Elgin (1½ hours, hourly) and Aberdeen (two hours), while bus 273 runs less frequently to Fraserburgh (one hour, twice on Saturday only).

PORTSOY
POP 1730

The pretty fishing village of Portsoy has an atmospheric **17th-century harbour** and a maze of narrow streets lined with picturesque cottages. An ornamental stone known as Portsoy marble – actually a beautifully patterned green-and-pale-pink serpentine – was quarried near Portsoy in the 17th and 18th centuries, and was reputedly used in the decoration of some rooms in the Palace of Versailles. Beside the harbour, the Portsoy Marble Shop & Pottery (Shorehead; ☺10am-5pm Apr-Oct) sells handmade stoneware and objects made from the local marble.

Each year on the last weekend in June or first weekend in July, Portsoy harbour is home to the Scottish Traditional Boat Festival (www.scottishtraditionalboatfestival. co.uk), a lively gathering of historic wooden sailing boats accompanied by sailing races, live folk music, crafts demonstrations, street theatre and a food festival.

The 12-room Boyne Hotel (☎01261-842242; www.boynehotel.co.uk; 2 North High St; s/d from £40/72) is a cosy and atmospheric place

to stay, while the Shore Inn (☎01261-842831; 49 Church St) is a characterful real-ale pub overlooking the harbour.

Portsoy is 8 miles west of Banff; the hourly bus between Elgin and Banff stops here.

FORDYCE
POP 150

This impossibly picturesque village lies about 3 miles southwest of Portsoy. The main attractions are the 13th-century **St Tarquin's Church**, with its extraordinary canopied Gothic tombs, and the impressive 16th-century tower house of **Fordyce Castle**. The castle isn't open to the public, but its whitewashed west wing provides atmospheric self-catering accommodation (☎01261-843722; www.fordycecastle.co.uk; per week £675-750, 3 nights in low season £400) for up to four people.

The nearby Joiner's Workshop & Visitor Centre (admission free; ☺10am-8pm Thu-Mon Jul & Aug, 1-6pm Fri-Mon Sep-Jun) has a collection of woodworking tools and machinery, and stages woodwork demonstrations by a master joiner.

FOCHABERS & AROUND
POP 1500

Fochabers sits beside the last bridge over the River Spey before it enters the sea. The town has a pleasant square, with a church and clock tower dated 1798, and a handful of interesting antique shops.

West of the bridge over the Spey is Baxters Highland Village (www.baxters.com; admission free; ☺10am-5pm), which charts the history of the Baxter family and their well-known brand of quality Scottish foodstuffs, founded in 1868. There's a factory tour with cookery demonstrations on weekdays, and a coffee shop.

Four miles north of Fochabers, at the mouth of the River Spey, is the tiny village of **Spey Bay**, the starting point for the Speyside Way long-distance footpath. It's also home to the Scottish Dolphin Centre

---

CULBIN FOREST

On the western side of Findhorn Bay is Culbin Forest (www.culbin.org.uk), a vast swathe of Scots and Corsican pine that was planted in the 1940s to stabilise the shifting sand dunes that buried the Culbin Estate in the 17th century. The forest is a unique wildlife habitat, supporting plants, birds and animals (such as the pine marten) that are normally found only in ancient natural pine woods.

The forest is criss-crossed by a maze of walking and cycling trails which lead to a fantastic beach near the mouth of Findhorn Bay, a great birdwatching spot. Check the website for more info, or pick up a leaflet from local tourist offices.

(www.wdcs.org/scottishdolphincentre; Tugnet Ice House, Spey Bay; admission free; ☉10.30am-5pm Apr-Oct) with an interesting display on the Moray Firth **dolphins**, which can occasionally be seen off the mouth of the river, and a pleasant cafe.

Fochabers is on the Aberdeen-to-Inverness bus route.

FINDHORN
POP 885

The attractive village of Findhorn lies at the mouth of the River Findhorn, just east of the Findhorn Bay nature reserve. It's a great place for **birdwatching**, **seal-spotting** and **coastal walks**.

Findhorn Heritage Centre (www.findhorn -heritage.co.uk; admission free; ☉2-5pm daily Jun-Aug, 2-5pm Sat & Sun May & Sep), housed in a former salmon-fisher's bothy at the northern end of the village, records the history of the settlement. The beach is just over the dunes north of the heritage centre – at low tide, you can see seals hauled out on the sandbanks off the mouth of the River Findhorn.

Hippies old and new should check out the Findhorn Foundation (www.findhorn.org; ☉visitor centre 10am-5pm Mon-Fri year-round, plus 1-4pm Sat Mar-Nov & 1-4pm Sun May-Sep), an international spiritual community founded in 1962. There's a small permanent population of around 150, but the community receives thousands of visitors each year. With no formal creed, the community is dedicated to cooperation with nature, 'dealing with work, relationships and our environment

---

SUENO'S STONE

The tidy town of Forres, 4 miles south of Findhorn, is famous for **Sueno's Stone**, a remarkable, 6.5m-high Pictish stone. It is the tallest and most elaborately carved Pictish stone in Scotland, dating from the 9th or 10th century, and is thought to depict a battle between the Picts and invading Scots or Vikings. It's protected from the elements by a huge plate-glass box, and is signposted from the main A96 Inverness-to-Elgin road at Forres.

---

in new and more fulfilling ways', and fostering 'a deeper sense of the sacred in everyday life'. Projects include an eco-village, a biological sewage-treatment plant and a wind-powered generator. Guided tours (£5) start from the visitor centre at 2pm on Monday, Wednesday, Friday and Saturday from April to November, and on Sunday as well from April to September, or you can take a self-guided tour with guidebook (£5).

There are two good places to eat: the Bakehouse (www.bakehousecafe.co.uk; mains £5-10; ☉10am-5pm), an organic bakery and cafe in the village centre, and the Blue Angel Cafe (www.blueangelcafe.co.uk; mains £3-9; ☉10am-5pm; 🐾🍴), an organic and vegetarian eatery in the Findhorn Foundation's eco-village.

Southern Highlands & Islands

Best Places to Stay

» Passfoot Cottage (p277)
» Argyll Hotel (p311)
» George Hotel (p285)

Best Places to Eat

» Café Fish (p308)
» Waterfront Fishouse Restaurant (p300)
» Starfish (p287)

Why Go?

From the rasping spout of a minke whale as it breaks the surface, to the 'krek-krek' of a corncrake, the coast and islands of southwest Scotland are filled with unusual wildlife experiences. You can spot otters tumbling in the kelp, watch sea eagles snatch fish from a lonely loch and thrill to the sight of dolphins riding the bow-wave of your boat.

Here, sea travel is as important as road and rail – dozens of ferries allow you to island-hop your way from the Firth of Clyde to Oban and beyond, via the whisky distilleries of Islay, the wild mountains of Jura and the scenic delights of diminutive Colonsay.

On fresh water too, passenger ferries, vintage steamboats, canoes and kayaks ply the lochs of Loch Lomond and the Trossachs National Park, amid some of Scotland's most beautiful and evocative scenery.

When to Go
Oban

°C/°F Temp — Rainfall Inches/mm

May Feis Ile (Islay Festival) celebrates traditional Scottish music and whisky.

Jun Roadsides and gardens become a blaze of colour with deep-pink rhododendron blooms.

Aug The best month of the year for whale watching off the west coast.

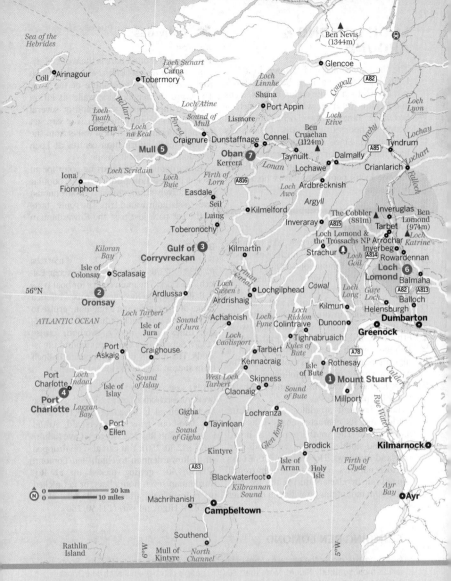

Southern Highlands & Islands Highlights

1 Staring in wonder at the magnificent marble-clad halls of **Mount Stuart** (p283)

2 Walking barefoot across the strand from Colonsay to Oronsay to visit the **medieval priory** (p296)

3 Riding a high-speed motorboat through the surging white water of the **Gulf of Corryvreckan** (p294)

4 Sitting by a log fire in the **Port Charlotte Hotel** (p292), sampling some of Islay's finest single malt whiskies

5 Whale watching in the waters off the west coast of **Mull** (p306)

6 Hiking the West Highland Way along the eastern shore of **Loch Lomond** (p272)

7 Tucking into a platter of fresh local langoustines at one of **Oban's seafood restaurants** (p300)

LOCH LOMOND & AROUND

The 'bonnie banks' and 'bonnie braes' of Loch Lomond have long been Glasgow's rural retreat – a scenic region of hills, lochs and healthy fresh air within easy reach of Scotland's largest city (Loch Lomond is within an hour's drive of 70% of Scotland's population). Since the 1930s Glaswegians have made a regular weekend exodus to the hills – by car, by bike and on foot – and today the loch's popularity shows no sign of decreasing.

Loch Lomond

Loch Lomond is the largest lake in mainland Britain and, after Loch Ness, perhaps the most famous of Scotland's lochs. Its proximity to Glasgow (20 miles away) means that the tourist honeypots of Balloch, Loch Lomond Shores and Luss get pretty crowded in summer. The main tourist focus is along the A82 on the loch's western shore, and at the southern end, around Balloch, which occasionally becomes a nightmare of jet skis and motorboats. The eastern shore, which is followed by the West Highland Way long-distance footpath, is a little quieter.

Loch Lomond straddles the Highland border and its character changes as you move north. The southern part is broad and island-studded, fringed by woods and Lowland meadows. However, north of Luss the loch narrows, occupying a deep trench gouged out by glaciers during the Ice Age, with 900m mountains crowding in on either side.

🏃 Activities

Walking

The big walk around here is the West Highland Way (www.west-highland-way.co.uk), which runs along the eastern shore of the loch. There are shorter lochside walks at Firkin Point on the western shore and at several other places around the loch. You can get further information on local walks from the national park information centres at Loch Lomond Shores and Balmaha.

Rowardennan is the starting point for an ascent of **Ben Lomond** (974m), a popular and relatively straighforward (if strenuous) five- to six-hour round trip. The route starts at the car park just past the Rowardennan Hotel.

Boat Trips

Sweeney's Cruises   BOAT TOUR

(☎01389-752376; www.sweeneyscruises.com; Balloch Rd, Balloch) The main centre for boat trips is Balloch, where Sweeney's Cruises offers a range of trips including a one-hour cruise to Inchmurrin and back (adult/child £8.50/5, five times daily), and a two-hour cruise (£15/8 departs 1pm and 3pm) around the islands. The quay is directly opposite Balloch train station, beside the tourist office.

Cruise Loch Lomond   BOAT TOUR

(www.cruiselochlomond.co.uk; Tarbet) Cruise Loch Lomond is based in Tarbet and offers two-hour trips to Inversnaid, Arklet Falls and Rob Roy MacGregor's Cave (adult/child £12.50/7.50). You can also be dropped off at Rowardennan to climb Ben Lomond (£14.50/7.50), getting picked up at Rowardennan seven hours later, or get picked up at Inversnaid after a 9-mile hike along the West Highland Way (£14.50/7.50).

CLIMBING BEN LOMOND

Standing guard over the eastern shore of Loch Lomond is Ben Lomond (974m), Scotland's most southerly Munro. More than 30,000 people climb the hill each year, most following the **Tourist Route** up and down from Rowardennan car park. It's a straightforward climb on a well-used and maintained path; allow about five hours for the 7 mile (11km) round trip.

The **Ptarmigan Route** is less crowded and has better views, following a narrow but clearly defined path up the western flank of Ben Lomond, directly overlooking the loch, to a curving ridge leading to the summit. You can then descend via the tourist route, making a satisfying circuit.

To find the start of the Ptarmigan path, head north along the loch shore trail for 600m from Rowardennan car park, past the youth hostel and Ardess Ranger Centre. Cross the bridge after Ben Lomond Cottage and immediately turn right along an unmarked path through the trees. The path is easy to follow from here on.

GAELIC & NORSE PLACE NAMES

Throughout the Highlands and islands the indigenous Gaelic language has left a rich legacy of place names. They're often intermixed with Old Norse names left by Viking invaders. The spelling is now anglicised, but the meaning is clear once you know what to look for. Here are a few more common Gaelic and Norse names and their meanings.

Gaelic Place Names

ach, auch – from *achadh* (field)

ard – from *ard* or *aird* (height, hill)

avon – from *abhainn* (river or stream)

bal – from *baile* (village or homestead)

ban – from *ban* (white, fair)

beg – from *beag* (small)

ben – from *beinn* (mountain)

buie – from *buidhe* (yellow)

dal – from *dail* (field or dale)

dow, dhu – from *dubh* (black)

drum – from *druim* (ridge or back)

dun – from *dun* or *duin* (fort or castle)

glen – from *gleann* (narrow valley)

gorm – from *gorm* (blue)

gower, gour – from *gabhar* (goat), eg Ardgour (height of the goats)

inch, insh – from *inis* (island, water-meadow or resting place for cattle)

inver – from *inbhir* (rivermouth or meeting of two rivers)

kil – from *cille* (church), eg Kilmartin (Church of St Martin)

kin, ken – from *ceann* (head), eg Kinlochleven (head of Loch Leven)

kyle, kyles – from *caol* or *caolas* (narrow sea channel)

more, vore – from *mor* or *mhor* (big), eg Ardmore (big height), Skerryvore (big reef)

strath – from *srath* (broad valley)

tarbert, tarbet – from *tairbeart* (portage), meaning a narrow neck of land between two bodies of water, across which a boat can be dragged

tay, ty – from *tigh* (house), eg Tyndrum (house on the ridge)

tober – from *tobar* (well), eg Tobermory (Mary's well)

Norse Place Names

a, ay, ey – from *ey* (island)

bister, buster, bster – from *bolstaor* (dwelling place, homestead)

geo – from *gja* (chasm)

holm – from *holmr* (small island)

kirk – from *kirkja* (church)

pol, poll, bol – from *bol* (farm)

quoy – from *kvi* (sheep fold, cattle enclosure)

sker, skier, skerry – from *sker* (rocky reef)

vig, vaig, wick – from *vik* (bay, creek)

voe, way – from *vagr* (bay, creek)

Loch Lomond & The Trossachs NP

0 ———— 5 km
0 ———— 2 miles

Balmaha Boatyard   BOAT TOUR
(www.balmahaboatyard.co.uk; Balmaha) The mailboat, run by Balmaha Boatyard, cruises from
Balmaha to the loch's four inhabited islands,
departing at 11.30am and returning at 2pm,
with a one-hour stop on Inchmurrin (£9/4.50
per adult/child). Trips depart daily (except Sunday) in July and August; on Monday, Thursday
and Saturday in May, June and September; and
Monday and Thursday only October to April .

Other Activities

The mostly traffic-free **Clyde and Loch
Lomond Cycle Way** links Glasgow to Balloch (20 miles), where it links with the **West
Loch Lomond Cycle Path**, which continues along the loch shore to Tarbet (10 miles).

You can rent **rowing boats** at Balmaha
Boatyard (p274) for £10/40 per hour/day
(£20/60 for a boat with outboard motor).
Lomond Adventure (☑01360-870218; www.
lomondadventure.co.uk) also rents out Canadian
canoes (£30 per day) and **sea kayaks** (£25).

Can You Experience (☑01389-756251;
www.canyouexperience.com; Loch Lomond Shores,
Balloch) rent out canoes (£12/17 per half-/full
hour) and bicycles (£13/17 per three hours/

full day), and offer a full-day **guided canoe safari** on the loch (adult/child £65/55).

ℹ Information

Balloch Tourist Office (☏0870 720 0607; Balloch Rd, Balloch; ⏱9.30am-6pm Jun-Aug, 10am-6pm Apr & Sep)

Balmaha National Park Centre (☏01389-722100; Balmaha; ⏱9.30am-4.15pm Apr-Sep)

National Park Gateway Centre (☏01389-751035; www.lochlomondshores.com; Loch Lomond Shores, Balloch; ⏱10am-6pm Apr-Sep, to 5pm Oct-Mar; 🛈)

Tarbet Tourist Office (☏0870-720 0623; Tarbet; ⏱10am-6pm Jul & Aug, to 5pm Easter-Jun, Sep & Oct) At the junction of the A82 and the A83.

ℹ Getting There & Away

Bus

First Glasgow (p136) buses 204 and 215 run from Argyle St in central Glasgow to Balloch and Loch Lomond Shores (1½ hours, at least two per hour).

Scottish Citylink (www.citylink.co.uk) coaches from Glasgow to Oban and Fort William stop at Luss (£8.20, 55 minutes, six daily), Tarbet (£8.20, 65 minutes) and Ardlui (£14.30, 1¼ hours).

Train

Glasgow to Balloch £4.70, 45 minutes, every 30 minutes

Glasgow to Arrochar & Tarbet £11, 1¼ hours, three or four daily

Glasgow to Ardlui £14, 1½ hours, three or four daily, continuing to Oban and Fort William

ℹ Getting Around

Pick up the useful **public transport booklet** (free), which lists timetables for all bus, train and ferry services in Loch Lomond and the Trossachs National Park, available from any tourist office or park information centre.

McColl's Coaches (www.mccolls.org.uk) bus 309 runs from Balloch to Balmaha (25 minutes, every two hours). An **SPT Daytripper ticket** (www.spt.co.uk/tickets) gives a family group unlimited travel for a day on most bus and train services in the Glasgow, Loch Lomond and Helensburgh area. Buy the ticket (£10.70 for one adult and one or two children, £19 for two adults and up to four children) from any train station or the main Glasgow bus station.

WESTERN SHORE

The town of **Balloch**, which straddles the River Leven where it flows from the southern end of Loch Lomond, is the loch's main population centre and transport hub. A Victorian resort once thronged by day-trippers transferring between the train station and the steamer quay, it is now a 'gateway centre' for Loch Lomond and the Trossachs National Park.

Loch Lomond Shores (www.lochlomond shores.com), a major tourism development a half-mile north of Balloch, sports a national park information centre plus various visitor attractions, outdoor activities and boat trips. In keeping with the times, the heart of the development is a large shopping mall. It's also home to the Loch Lomond Aquarium (www.sealife.co.uk; per person £13.20; ⏱10am-5pm), which has displays on the wildlife of Loch Lomond, an otter enclosure (housing short-clawed Asian otters, not Scottish ones), and a host of sea-life exhibits ranging from sharks to stingrays to sea turtles.

The vintage paddle steamer Maid of the Loch (www.maidoftheloch.com; admission free; ⏱11am-4pm Sat & 2-4pm Sun Easter-Aug), built in 1953, is moored here while undergoing restoration – you can nip aboard for a look around. It is hoped that her steam engines will be restored to working order in 2013.

Unless it's raining, give Loch Lomond Shores a miss and head for the little picture-postcard village of **Luss**. Stroll among the pretty cottages with roses around their doors (the cottages were built by the local laird in the 19th century for the workers on his estate), then pop into the Clan Colquhoun

---

LOCH LOMOND & THE TROSSACHS NATIONAL PARK

The importance of the Loch Lomond region was recognised when it became the heart of Loch Lomond & the Trossachs National Park (www.lochlomond-trossachs.org) – Scotland's first national park, created in 2002. The park extends over a huge area, from Balloch north to Tyndrum and Killin, and from Callander west to the forests of Cowal.

Coverage of the park is split between two chapters – the western part, around Loch Lomond, is here; the eastern part, centred around Callander and the Trossachs, is in the Central Scotland chapter.

LOCH LOMOND WATER BUS

From April to October a network of passenger ferries criss-crosses Loch Lomond, allowing you to explore the loch's hiking and biking trails using public transport (there are train services to Balloch, Arrochar and Tarbet and Ardlui, and buses to Luss and Balmaha). A Loch Lomond Water Bus (www.lochlomond-trossachs.org/waterbus) timetable is available from tourist offices, national park centres and online. Fares quoted are one-way.

Ferries to Rowardennan use a new jetty at the youth hostel; the old pier beside the Rowardennan car park is no longer in use. The ferry from Inverbeg to Rowardennan was not running at the time of research.

Arden to Inchmurrin Ferry (www.inchmurrin-lochlomond.com; per person return £4; ⊙Easter-Oct) On demand.

Ardlui to Ardleish Ferry (☎01307-704243; per person £3; ⊙9am-7pm May-Sep, to 6pm Apr & Oct) On demand; operated by Ardlui Hotel.

Balloch to Balmaha Ferry (www.sweeneyscruises.com; per person £7.50; ⊙Jul & Aug) Five daily.

Balloch to Luss Ferry (www.sweeneyscruises.com; per person £9; ⊙Jul & Aug)

Balmaha to Inchcailloch Ferry (☎01360-870214; per person £5; ⊙9am-8pm) On demand.

Balmaha to Luss Ferry (www.cruiselochlomond.co.uk; per person £7.50, bike £1; ⊙Apr-Oct) Four daily, calls at Inchcailloch island.

Inveruglas to Inversnaid Ferry (☎01877-386223; per person £5; ⊙Apr-Oct) On demand, except for one scheduled departure from Inveruglas daily at 4pm. Operated by Inversnaid Hotel; phone to book.

Rowardennan to Luss Ferry (www.cruiselochlomond.co.uk; per person £7; ⊙Apr-Oct) One daily. Departs Rowardennan at 9.30am; Luss at 4.15pm.

Tarbet to Inversnaid Ferry (www.cruiselochlomond.co.uk; per person £7; ⊙Apr-Oct) Three daily.

Tarbet to Rowardennan Ferry (www.cruiselochlomond.co.uk; per person £8; ⊙Apr-Oct) Departs Tarbet 8.45am, 10am and 4pm; Rowardennan at 10.45am and 4.45pm.

Visitor Centre (☎01436-860814; Shore Cottage, Luss; adult/child £1/free; ⊙10.30am-6pm Easter-Oct) for some background history before enjoying a cup of tea at the Coach House Coffee Shop.

🛏 Sleeping & Eating

TOP CHOICE Drover's Inn INN ££
(☎01301-704234; www.thedroversinn.co.uk; s/d from £42/83, bar meals £7-12; ⊙lunch & dinner; ℗) This is one howff (drinking den) you shouldn't miss – a low-ceilinged place with smoke-blackened stone, bare wooden floors spotted with candle wax, barmen in kilts and walls festooned with moth-eaten stags' heads and stuffed birds. There's even a stuffed bear and the desiccated husk of a basking shark.

The bar serves hearty hill-walking fuel such as steak-and-Guinness pie with mustard mash, and hosts live folk music on Friday and Saturday nights. We recommend this inn more as an atmospheric place to eat and drink than somewhere to stay – accommodation varies from eccentric, old-fashioned and rather run-down rooms in the old building (including a ghost in room 6), to more comfortable rooms (with en suite bathrooms) in the modern annexe across the road. Ask to see your room before taking it.

Loch Lomond SYHA HOSTEL £
(☎01389-850226; www.syha.org.uk; dm £19; ⊙Mar-Oct; ℗@🖨) Forget about roughing it, this is one of the most impressive hostels in the country – an imposing 19th-century country house set in beautiful grounds overlooking the loch. It's 2 miles north of Balloch and very popular, so book in advance in summer. And yes, it *is* haunted.

Ardlui Hotel
HOTEL ££

(☑01301-704243; www.ardlui.co.uk; Ardlui; s/d £55/95; P) This plush and comfy country-house hotel has a great lochside location, and a view of Ben Lomond from the breakfast room.

Coach House Coffee Shop
CAFE £

(mains £6-11; ☺10am-5pm; ☎♨☀) With its chunky pine furniture and deep, deep sofa in front of a rustic fireplace, the Coach House is one of the cosiest places to eat on Loch Lomond. The menu includes coffee and tea, home-baked cakes, scones, ciabattas and more-substantial offerings such as smoked salmon and prawns with Marie Rose sauce, and haggis with neeps and tatties (mashed potatoes and turnip).

EASTERN SHORE

The road along the loch's eastern shore passes through the attractive village of **Balmaha**, where you can hire boats or take a cruise on the mailboat. A short but steep climb from the village car park leads to the summit of **Conic Hill** (361m), a superb viewpoint (2.5 miles round trip, allow two to three hours).

There are several picnic areas along the lochside; the most attractive is at **Millarochy Bay** (1.5 miles north of Balmaha), which has a nice gravel beach and superb views across the loch to the Luss hills.

The road ends at **Rowardennan**, but the West Highland Way (p272) hiking trail continues north along the shore of the loch.

It's 7 miles to **Inversnaid**, which can be reached by road from the Trossachs, and 15 miles to **Inverarnan** on the main A82 road at the northern end of the loch.

🛏 Sleeping & Eating

From March to October, camping outside designated campsites is banned on the eastern shore of Loch Lomond between Drymen and Ptarmigan Lodge (just north of Rowardennan Youth Hostel). There are campsites at Millarochy, Cashel and Sallochy.

Oak Tree Inn
INN ££

(☑01360-870357; www.oak-tree-inn.co.uk; Balmaha; dm/s/d £30/60/75; P♨) An attractive traditional inn built in slate and timber, the Oak Tree offers luxurious guest bedrooms for pampered hikers, and two four-bed bunkrooms for hardier souls. The rustic restaurant dishes up hearty lunches and dinners (mains £9 to £12), such as steak-and-mushroom pie, and roast Arctic char with lime and chive butter, and cooks up an excellent bowl of Cullen skink (soup made with smoked haddock, potato, onion and milk).

⭐ TOP CHOICE Passfoot Cottage
B&B ££

(☑01360-870324; www.passfoot.com; Balmaha; per person £37.50; ☺Apr-Sep; ♨) Passfoot is a pretty little whitewashed cottage decked out with colourful flower baskets, with a lovely location overlooking Balmaha Bay. The bright bedrooms have a homely feel, and there's a cosy lounge with a wood-burning stove and loch view.

LOCH LOMOND'S ISLANDS

There are around 60 islands, large and small, in Loch Lomond. All except three are privately owned, and only two can be reached without your own boat or canoe.

Inchcailloch A nature reserve, owned by Scottish Natural Heritage. Reached by passenger ferry from Balmaha Boatyard (p274). The most easily accessible of the islands, with nature trails, toilets and a small campsite. See www.lochlomond-trossachs.org for details.

Inchmurrin Privately owned, reached by passenger ferry from Arden on the loch's western shore. Has walking trails, beaches, self-catering cottages and a restaurant that is open from Easter to October. See www.inchmurrin-lochlomond.com.

Inchconnachan Privately owned. Only accessible by boat or canoe. Was once the holiday home of Lady Arran, who introduced a number of wallabies in the 1940s. They bred successfully, and their descendants still roam wild on the island. The rare capercaillie (largest member of the grouse family) nests here too.

Island I Vow Privately owned. Only accessible by boat or canoe. The loch's most northerly island is home to a ruined castle, once a stronghold of Clan Macfarlane. Poet William Wordsworth visited in 1814 and found a hermit living in the castle's dungeon, inspiring his poem *The Brownie's Cell*.

Rowardennan Hotel

HOTEL ££

(☎01360-870273; www.rowardennanhotel.co.uk; Rowardennan; s/d £66/96; ☺lunch & dinner; P) Originally an 18th-century drovers' inn, the Rowardennan has two big bars (often crowded with rain-sodden hikers) and a good beer garden (often crowded with midges). It's a pleasant place to stay, with a choice of traditional hotel rooms and luxury self-catering lodges; food is served in the bar all day, from 7.30am to 9pm (mains £7 to £12).

Rowardennan SYHA

HOSTEL £

(☎01360-870259; www.syha.org.uk; Rowardennan; dm £17.50; ☺Mar-Oct) Housed in an attractive Victorian lodge, this hostel has a superb setting right on the loch shore, beside the West Highland Way.

Cashel Campsite

CAMPSITE £

(☎01360-870234; www.campingintheforest.co.uk; by Rowardennan; sites incl car £19, backpackers per person £6; ☺Mar-Oct) The most attractive campsite in the area is 3 miles north of Balmaha, on the loch shore.

CRIANLARICH & TYNDRUM

POP 350

Surrounded by spectacular hillscapes at the northern edge of the Loch Lomond & the Trossachs National Park, these villages are popular pitstops on the main A82 road and on the West Highland Way. Crianlarich has a train station and more community atmosphere than Tyndrum, but Tyndrum (*tyne*-drum), 5 miles up the road, has two stations, a bus interchange, petrol station, late-opening motorists' cafes and a flash tourist office (☎01838-400246; ☺10am-5pm Apr-Oct) – a good spot for route information and maps for ascents of Munros **Cruach Ardrain** (1046m), **Ben More** (1174m) and magnificent **Ben Lui** (1130m).

🛏 Sleeping & Eating

Crianlarich makes a more appealing base than Tyndrum: vehicles slow down through town and the views and food choice are better.

Tigh-na-Fraoch

B&B ££

(☎01838-400534; www.tigh-na-fraoch.com; Lower Station Rd, Tyndrum; per person £33; P) The name means 'house of the heather' in Gaelic, and Heather is the name of the owner – an alternative therapist who offers kinesiology and Indian head massages as well as three bright, clean and comfortable bedrooms, and a breakfast menu that includes (resident anglers' luck permitting) freshly caught trout as well as the usual bacon and eggs.

Crianlarich SYHA

HOSTEL £

(☎01838-300260; www.syha.org.uk; Station Rd, Crianlarich; dm £18; P@�) Well-run and comfortable, with a spacious kitchen, dining area and lounge, this is a real haven for walkers or anyone passing through Crianlarich. Dorms vary in size – there are some great en suite family rooms that should be prebooked – but all are clean and roomy.

Strathfillan Wigwams

CAMPGROUND, CABINS £

(☎01838-400251; www.wigwamholidays.com; sites per adult/child £8/3, wigwam d small/large £30/36, lodge d from £50; P@�) This charismatic place, 3 miles from Crianlarich and 2 miles from Tyndrum, is off the A82 and has 16 heated 'wigwams' – essentially wooden A-frame cabins with fridge and foam mattresses that can sleep four at a pinch. More upmarket are the self-contained lodges with their own bathroom and kitchen facilities. There's also camping with access to all facilities.

Crianlarich Hotel

HOTEL ££

(☎01838-300272; www.crianlarich-hotel.co.uk; d from £100; P�) At the junction in the middle of the village, this hotel has large rooms with appealingly comfortable beds and compact bathrooms – but we feel that they spent more on the reception area than the accommodation. It's good value in the low season. The bar meals (mains £10 to £13) are pricey, but served in a most elegant space, with haggis, venison and salmon available.

🍴 Real Food Café

CAFE £

(☎01838-400235; www.therealfoodcafe.com; Tyndrum; mains £5-9; ☺11am-9pm Sun-Thu, 11am-10pm Fri, 9am-9pm Sat; 🚼) Tyndrum is in the heart of Munro-bagging territory, and hungry hillwalkers throng the tables in this justifiably popular eatery. The menu looks familiar – with fish and chips, soups, salads and burgers – but the owners make an effort to source sustainably and locally, and the quality of the food shines through.

❶ Getting There & Away

Scottish Citylink (www.citylink.co.uk) runs several buses daily to Edinburgh, Glasgow, Oban and Skye from both villages.

Trains run to Tyndrum and Crianlarich from Fort William (£17, 1¾ hours, four daily Monday to Saturday, two on Sunday), Oban (£10, one hour, three or four daily) and Glasgow (£18, two hours, three or four daily).

Helensburgh

POP 16,500

With the coming of the railway in the mid-19th century, Helensburgh – named in the 18th century after the wife of Sir James Colquhoun of Luss – became a popular seaside retreat for wealthy Glaswegian families. Their spacious Victorian villas now populate the neat grid of streets that covers the hillside above the Firth of Clyde, but none can compare with the splendour of Hill House (NTS; ☎0844 493 2208; www.nts.org.uk; Upper Colquhoun St; adult/child £9.50/7; ◷1.30-5.30pm Apr-Oct). Built in 1902 for the Glasgow publisher Walter Blackie, it is perhaps architect **Charles Rennie Mackintosh's** finest creation – its timeless elegance feels as chic today as it no doubt did when the Blackies moved in a century ago.

Helensburgh has a ferry connection with Gourock via Kilcreggan, and a frequent train service to Glasgow (£5.60, 50 minutes, two per hour).

Arrochar

POP 650

The village of Arrochar has a wonderful location, looking across the head of Loch Long to the jagged peaks of the **Cobbler** (881m). The mountain takes its name from the shape of its north peak (the one on the right, seen from Arrochar), which looks like a cobbler hunched over his bench. The village has several hotels and shops, a bank and a post office.

If you want to **climb the Cobbler**, start from the roadside car park at Succoth near the head of Loch Long. A steep uphill hike through the woods is followed by an easier section as you head into the valley below the triple peaks. Then it's steeply uphill again to the saddle between the north and central peaks. The central peak to the left (south) is the highest point, but it's awkward to get to – scramble through the hole and along the ledge to reach the airy summit. The north peak to the right is an easy walk. Allow five to six hours for the 5-mile round trip.

There's good camping at Ardgartan Caravan & Campsite (☎01301-702293; www. campingintheforest.co.uk; Ardgartan; tent site plus

car & 2 people £19-26.50; ☜) at the foot of Glen Croe. Bicycle hire is also available.

The black-and-white, 19th-century Village Inn (☎01301-702279; www.villageinnarrochar.co.uk; s/d from £65/95, mains £7-13; ◷lunch & dinner; ℗☎) is a lovely spot for lunch, or just a pint of real ale – the beer garden has a great view of the Cobbler. There are 14 en suite bedrooms; the ones at the top end of the price range have four-poster beds and a view over the loch.

Citylink (www.citylink.co.uk) buses from Glasgow to Inveraray and Campbeltown call at Arrochar and Ardgartan (£10, 1¼ hours, three daily). There are also three or four trains a day from Glasow to Arrochar & Tarbet station (£11, 1¼ hours), continuing to Oban or Fort William.

SOUTH ARGYLL

Cowal

The remote Cowal peninsula is cut off from the rest of the country by the lengthy fjords of Loch Long and Loch Fyne – it's an area more accessible by boat than by car (there are ferries from Gourock to Dunoon in eastern Cowal, and from Tarbert to Portavadie in the west). It comprises rugged hills and narrow lochs, with only a few small villages; the scenery around Loch Riddon is particularly enchanting. The only town on the mainland is the old-fashioned holiday resort of Dunoon.

From Arrochar, the A83 to Inveraray loops around the head of Loch Long and climbs up Glen Croe. The pass at the head of the glen is called the **Rest and Be Thankful** – when the original military road through the glen was repaired in the 18th century, a stone was erected at the top inscribed 'Rest, and be thankful. This road was made, in 1748, by the 24th Regt...Repaired by the 93rd Regt. 1786'. A copy of the stone can be seen at the far end of the parking area at the top of the pass.

There's a Forest Enterprise visitor centre (☎01301-702432; admission free; ◷10am-5pm Apr-Oct) at the foot of the glen, with information on various walks on the Cowal peninsula.

As you descend Glen Kinglas on the far side of the Rest and be Thankful, the A815 forks to the left just before Cairndow; this

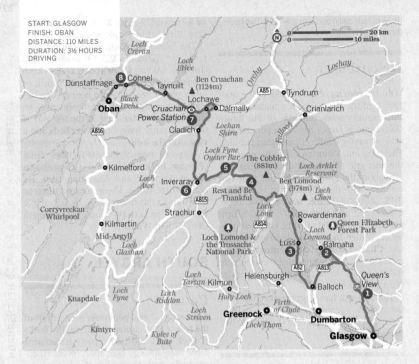

Driving Tour
Glasgow to Oban

❯ Leave Glasgow on the A81 (Garscube Rd then Maryhill Rd, from junction 16 on the M8) and continue on the A809 towards Drymen. About 5 miles beyond the city limits you will reach a parking area on the left, known as **❶ Queen's View** (one of many in Scotland named after Queen Victoria); pause for a bit to soak up this splendid panorama towards Loch Lomond and the Highland hills.

Continue to Drymen, and turn left along the minor road to **❷ Balmaha**, where you can hire a rowing boat for a splash on Loch Lomond, or spend an hour or so stretching your legs on a hike up Conic Hill. Return to Drymen and turn right on the A811 to Balloch, and then head north along the shores of Loch Lomond on the A82. The pretty village of **❸ Luss** is a good place to stop for lunch.

At Tarbet, keep straight on on the A83 to Arrochar with its grandstand view of the rocky peaks of the Cobbler, around the head of Loch Long and then up over the scenic mountain pass known as the **❹ Rest and Be Thankful**. A sweeping descent through Glen Kinglas leads to the salt waters of Loch Fyne, and the chance for another break at the **❺ Loch Fyne Oyster Bar** or **❻ Inveraray**.

Leave the main road here for the A819 north to Loch Awe, and some grand mountain scenery as the A85 squeezes along the lower slopes of Ben Cruachan; if the weather is wet, you can indulge in some underground sightseeing at **❼ Cruachan Power Station**.

The hills fall away beyond the Pass of Brander as you reach the shores of Loch Etive at Connel Bridge; if the tide is flowing, make a detour across the bridge to see the foaming **❽ Falls of Lora** before the final few miles to Oban.

is the main overland route into Cowal. From Glasgow, the most direct route is by ferry from Gourock to Dunoon.

DUNOON & AROUND

Like Rothesay on the Isle of Bute, Dunoon (population 9100) is a Victorian seaside resort that owes its existence to the steamers that once carried thousands of Glaswegians on pleasure trips 'doon the watter' in the 19th and 20th centuries. As with Rothesay, Dunoon's fortunes declined in recent decades when cheap foreign holidays stole its market – however, while the Bute resort appears to be recovering, Dunoon is still a bit down in the dumps.

The **tourist office** (☎01369-703785; www.visitcowal.co.uk; 7 Alexandra Pde; ☺9am-5.30pm Mon-Fri, 10am-5pm Sat & Sun Apr-Sep, 9am-5pm Mon-Thu, 10am-5pm Fri & 10am-4pm Sat & Sun Oct-Mar) is on the waterfront 100m north of the pier.

◉ Sights & Activities

The town's main attraction is still, as it was in the 1950s, strolling along the **promenade**, licking an ice-cream cone and watching the yachts at play in the Firth of Clyde. On a small hill above the seafront is a **statue of Highland Mary** (1763–86), who was one of the great loves of Robert Burns' life. She was born near Dunoon, but died tragically young; her statue gazes longingly across the firth to Burns' home territory in Ayrshire.

Benmore Botanic Garden   GARDENS
(www.rbge.org.uk; adult/child £5.50/1; ☺10am-6pm Apr-Sep, to 5pm Mar & Oct) This garden, 7 miles north of Dunoon, was originally planted in the 19th and early 20th centuries. It contains the country's finest collection of flowering trees and shrubs, including impressive displays of rhododendrons and azaleas, and is entered along a spectacular avenue of giant Californian redwoods planted in 1863. A highlight is the restored Victorian fernery, which is nestled in an unlikely fold in the crags. The cafe here (which stays open all year) is a nice place for lunch or a coffee.

✦ Festivals & Events

Cowal Highland Gathering   HIGHLAND GAMES
(www.cowalgathering.com; adult/child £13/2) Held in Dunoon in mid-August. The spectacular finale traditionally features 3000 bagpipers playing en masse.

Cowalfest   ARTS, OUTDOORS
(www.cowalfest.org) A 10-day arts and walking festival featuring art exhibitions, film screenings, guided walks and bicycle rides throughout the Cowal peninsula.

🛏 Sleeping & Eating

Dhailling Lodge   B&B ££
(☎01369-701253; www.dhaillinglodge.com; 155 Alexandra Pde; s/d £45/85; [P][@][☎]) You can experience some of Dunoon's former elegance at this large Victorian villa overlooking the bay about 0.75 miles north of the CalMac ferry pier. The owners are the essence of Scottish hospitality, and can provide excellent evening meals (per person £22).

Chatters   RESTAURANT ££
(☎01369-706402; www.chattersdunoon.co.uk; 58 John St; mains lunch £5-9, dinner £16-23; ☺lunch & dinner Wed-Sat) This pretty cottage restaurant has tartan sofas in the sitting room and tables in the tiny garden. It serves a mix of lunchtime snacks and brasserie dishes, and is famous for its open sandwiches and homemade puddings. Booking recommended.

❶ Getting There & Away

Dunoon is served by two competing ferry services from Gourock – the **CalMac** (www.calmac.co.uk) ferry is better if you are travelling on foot and want to arrive in the town centre.

There are three **Scottish Citylink** (☎0871-266 3333; www.citylink.co.uk) buses a day from Glasgow to Dunoon (£15, three hours, change at Inveraray).

TIGHNABRUAICH
POP 200

Sleepy little Tighnabruaich (tinna-*broo*-ach), a colony of seaside villas built by wealthy Glasgow families at the turn of the 20th century, is one of the most attractive villages on the Firth of Clyde. It was once a regular stop for Clyde steamers, and the old wooden pier is still occasionally visited by the paddle steamer *Waverley*.

The link with the sea continues in the **Tighnabruaich Sailing School** (www.tssargyll.co.uk; Carry Farm; ☺May-Sep), 2 miles south of Tighnabruaich. A five-day dinghy-sailing course costs £250, excluding accommodation.

The village is home to the **Royal an Lochan Hotel** (☎01700-811239; www.theroyalanlochan.co.uk; r £100-150; [P]), a local institution that has reverted from short-lived boutique hotel status to understated but luxurious elegance. Expect leather sofas, polished wood, fine bed linen and just a touch of tartan, with fantastic sea views from most bedrooms. The restaurant (mains £15 to £20) has a well-deserved reputation for good food prepared with fresh, locally sourced produce.

If all you want to do is fill up with good, hearty homemade grub, go for the mussels and chips at the Burnside Bistro (www.burnsidebistro.co.uk; mains £7-15; ◎9am-9pm) in the village centre, or a bar meal at the excellent Kames Hotel (☑01700-811489; kames-hotel.com; s/d from £50/90; mains £7-15; ◎lunch & dinner; P), a mile to the south.

Isle of Bute

POP 7350

The island of Bute lies pinched between the thumb and forefinger of the Cowal peninsula, separated from the mainland by a narrow, scenic strait known as the Kyles of Bute. The Highland Boundary Fault cuts through the middle of the island so that, geologically speaking, the northern half is in the Highlands and the southern half is in the central Lowlands – a metal arch on Rothesay's Esplanade marks the fault line.

The Isle of Bute Discovery Centre (☑01700-502151; www.visitscottishheartlands.com; Victoria St, Rothesay; ◎10am-6pm Mon-Fri, 9.30am-5pm Sat & Sun Jul & Aug, 10am-5pm daily Apr-Jun & Sep, shorter hours Oct-Mar) is in Rothesay's restored Winter Gardens.

The five-day Isle of Bute Jazz Festival (www.butejazz.com) is held over the first weekend of May.

ROTHESAY

From the mid-19th century until the 1960s, Rothesay – once dubbed the Margate of the Clyde – was one of the most popular holiday resorts in Scotland. Its Esplanade was bustling with day-trippers disembarking from the numerous steamers crowded around the pier, and its hotels were filled with elderly holidaymakers and convalescents taking advantage of the town's famously mild climate.

The fashion for foreign holidays that took off in the 1970s saw Rothesay's fortunes decline, and by the late 1990s it had become dilapidated and despondent. But in the last few years a nostalgia-fuelled resurgence of interest in Rothesay's holiday heyday has seen many of its Victorian buildings restored, the ferry terminal and harbour rebuilt and marinas constructed at Rothesay and Port Bannatyne. There's now a feeling of optimism in the air.

◉ Sights

Victorian Toilets   HISTORIC BUILDING
(Rothesay Pier; adult/child 20p/free) There aren't too many places where a public toilet would count as a tourist attraction, but Rothesay's Victorian toilets, dating from 1899, are a monument to lavatorial luxury – a disinfectant-scented temple of green and black marbled stoneware, glistening white enamel, glass-sided cisterns and gleaming copper pipes. The attendant will escort ladies into the hallowed confines of the gents for a look around when the facilities are unoccupied.

Rothesay Castle   CASTLE
(HS; www.historic-scotland.gov.uk; King St; adult/child £4.50/2.70; ◎9.30am-5.30pm Apr-Sep, to 4.30pm Sat-Wed Oct-Mar) The splendid ruins of 13th-century Rothesay Castle, with seagulls and jackdaws nesting in the walls, was once a favourite residence of the Stuart kings. It is unique in Scotland in having a circular plan, with four massive round towers. The landscaped moat, with its manicured turf, flower gardens and lazily cruising ducks, makes a picturesque setting.

Bute Museum   MUSEUM
(www.butemuseum.org; 7 Stuart St; adult/child £3/1; ◎10.30am-4.30pm Mon-Sat, from 2.30pm Sun Apr-Sep, 2.30-4.30pm Tue-Sat Oct-Mar) The most interesting displays in Bute Museum are those recounting the history of the famous Clyde steamers. Other galleries cover natural history, archaeology and geology; the prize exhibit is a stunning jet necklace found in a Bronze Age burial on the island.

🛏 Sleeping

Boat House   B&B ££
(☑01700-502696; www.theboathouse-bute.co.uk; 15 Battery Pl; s/d from £45/65; ☏) The Boat House brings a touch of class to Rothesay's guesthouse scene, with quality fabrics and furnishings and an eye for design that makes it feel a bit like a boutique hotel without the expensive price tag. Other features include sea views, a central location and a ground-floor room kitted out for wheelchair users.

Glendale Guest House   B&B ££
(☑01700-502329; www.glendale-guest-house.com; 20 Battery Pl; s/d/f from £35/60/90; P☏) Look out for the ornate, flower-bedecked facade on this beautiful Victorian villa, complete with pinnacled turret. All those windows

mean superb sea views from the front-facing bedrooms, the elegant, 1st-floor lounge and the breakfast room, where you'll find homemade smoked haddock fishcakes on the menu as well as the traditional fry-up.

Moorings
B&B £

(☑01700-502277; www.themoorings-bute.co.uk; 7 Mountstuart Rd; s/d from £37/55; P) The family-friendly Moorings is a delightful Victorian lodge with good sea views. It has an outdoor play area for kids and a high chair in the breakfast room. Vegetarian breakfasts are not a problem.

Roseland Caravan Park
CAMPSITE £

(☑01700-504529; www.roselandcaravanpark.co.uk; Roslin Rd; tent site & 2 people £10; ☺Apr-Oct) The island's only official campsite is a steep climb up the winding Serpentine Rd from the ferry terminal. There's a small but pleasant grassy area for tents amid the static caravans, and a handful of pitches for campervans.

✗ Eating

Waterfront Bistro
BISTRO ££

(www.thewaterfrontbistro.co.uk; 16 East Princes St; mains £8-16; ☺5.30-9pm Thu-Mon) Cheerful and informal, the wood-panelled Waterfront has a bistro menu that ranges from haddock and chips to venison in red-wine sauce, and grilled langoustines with garlic butter. Bottled real ale from the Arran Brewery complements the wine list. No bookings taken Easter to October – first come, first served.

Brechin's Brasserie
BRASSERIE ££

(☑01700-502922; www.brechins-bute.com; 2 Bridgend St; mains £12-15; ☺lunch Tue-Sat, dinner Fri & Sat) A friendly neighbourhood brasserie owned by jazz fan Tim (check out the sheet music and posters on the wall), Brechin's serves unpretentious but delicious dishes such as popeseye steak with Cafe de Paris butter, and local lamb shank with red-wine and rosemary sauce.

Pier at Craigmore
BISTRO ££

(Mount Stuart Rd; mains £7-14; ☺10.30am-4.30pm daily, 6.30-9.30pm Sat) Housed in the former waiting room of a Victorian pier on the eastern edge of town, the Craigmore is a neat little bistro with fantastic views. The lunch menu offers sandwiches, salads, homemade burgers and quiche, while Saturday dinner is more sophisticated, with seafood, steak and roast lamb. Unlicensed, but you can bring your own wine. No credit cards.

Musicker
CAFE £

(11 High St; mains £3-7; ☺9am-5pm) This cool little cafe, decked out in pale minty green, serves the best coffee on the island, alongside a range of sandwiches with imaginative fillings (haggis and cranberry, anyone?). It also sells music CDs (folk, world and country) and sports an old-fashioned jukebox.

AROUND ROTHESAY

Mount Stuart
HISTORIC BUILDING

(☑01700-503877; www.mountstuart.com; adult/child £11/6; ☺11am-5pm Apr-Oct, sometimes closed Sat afternoon) The Stuart Earls of Bute are direct descendants of Robert the Bruce, and have lived on the island for 700 years. Their family seat – Mount Stuart – is the finest neo-Gothic palace in Scotland, and one of the most magnificent stately homes in Britain, the first to have electric lighting, central heating and a heated swimming pool.

When a large part of the original house was destroyed by fire in 1877, the third Marquess of Bute, John Patrick Crichton-Stuart (1847–1900) – one of the greatest architecture patrons of his day, and the builder of Cardiff Castle and Castell Coch in Wales – commissioned Sir Robert Rowand Anderson to create a new one. The result, built in the 1880s and 1890s, and restored a hundred years later, is a byword for flamboyance.

The heart of the house is the stunning **Marble Hall**, a three-storey extravaganza of Italian marble that soars 25m to a dark-blue vault spangled with constellations of golden stars. Twelve stained-glass windows represent the seasons and the signs of the zodiac, with crystal stars casting rainbow-hued highlights across the marble when the sun is shining.

The design and decoration reflect the third marquess' fascination with astrology, mythology and religion, a theme carried over into the grand **Marble Staircase** beyond (where wall depict the six days of the Creation), and the lavishly decorated **Horoscope Bedroom**. Here the central ceiling panel records the positions of the stars and planets at the time of the marquess' birth on 12 September 1847.

Yet another highlight is the **Marble Chapel**, built entirely out of dazzling white Carrara marble. It has a dome lit to spectacular effect by a ring of ruby-red stained-glass windows – at noon on midsummer's day a shaft of blood-red sunlight shines directly onto the altar. It was here that Stella McCartney – daughter of ex-Beatle Sir Paul, and friend of the present marquess, former racing driver Johnny Dumfries – was married in 2003.

Mount Stuart is 5 miles south of Rothesay. Bus 90 runs from the bus stop outside the ferry terminal at Rothesay to Mount Stuart (15 minutes, hourly May to September). You can buy a special Mount Stuart day-trip ticket (adult/child £20/10) that includes return ferry and bus travel from Wemyss Bay ferry terminal (accessible by train from Glasgow) to Mount Stuart, as well as admission.

REST OF THE ISLAND

In the southern part of the island you'll find the haunting 12th-century ruin of **St Blane's Chapel**, set in a beautiful wooded grove, and a sandy beach at **Kilchattan Bay**.

There are more good beaches on the west coast. **Scalpsie Bay** is a 400m walk across a field from the parking area, and has a fantastic outlook to the peaks of Arran. You can often spot seals basking at low tide off Ardscalpsie Point, to the west.

Ettrick Bay is bigger, easier to reach, and has a tearoom, but it's not as pretty as Scalpsie.

There are lots of easy walks on Bute, including the **West Island Way**, a waymarked, 30-mile walking route from Kilchattan Bay to Port Bannatyne; map and details are available from the Isle of Bute Discovery Centre.

Cycling on Bute is excellent – the roads are well surfaced and fairly quiet. You can hire a bike from the Bike Shed (☑01700-505515; www.thebikeshed.org.uk; 23-25 East Princes St) for £10/15 per half-/full day.

Kingarth Trekking Centre (☑01700-831673; www.kingarthtrekkingcentre.co.uk; Kilchattan Bay) offers paddock rides for kids (£5; minimum age eight years), riding lessons (£20 per hour) and pony treks (£35 for two hours).

ⓘ Getting There & Away

BOAT **CalMac** (www.calmac.co.uk) car ferries serve Bute from Wemyss Bay in Ayrshire and Colintraive in Cowal.

Wemyss Bay to Rothesay passenger/car £4.75/18.75, 35 minutes, hourly

Colintraive to Rhubodach passenger/car £1.50/9.35, five minutes, every 15 to 20 minutes

BUS **West Coast Motors** (www.westcoastmotors.co.uk) buses run four or five times a week from Rothesay to Tighnabruaich and Dunoon via

the ferry at Colintraive. On Monday and Thursday a bus goes from Rothesay to Portavadie (via the Rhubodach–Colintraive ferry), where there's another ferry to Tarbert in Kintyre.

Inveraray

POP 700

You can spot Inveraray long before you get here – its neat, whitewashed buildings stand out from a distance on the shores of Loch Fyne. It's a planned town, built by the Duke of Argyll in Georgian style when he revamped his nearby castle in the 18th century. The **tourist office** (☑0845 225 5121; Front St; ⊙9am-6pm Jul & Aug, 10am-5pm Mon-Sat Apr-Jun, Sep & Oct, 10am-3pm Mon-Sat Nov-Mar) is on the seafront.

◉ Sights

Inveraray Castle　　　　　　　　　CASTLE
(☑01499-302203; www.inveraray-castle.com; adult/child £10/6.50; ⊙10am-5.45pm Apr-Oct) Inveraray Castle has been the seat of the Dukes of Argyll – chiefs of Clan Campbell – since the 15th century. The 18th-century building, with its fairytale turrets and fake battlements, houses an impressive armoury hall, its walls patterned with a collection of more than 1000 pole arms, dirks, muskets and Lochaber axes. The castle is 500m north of town, entered from the A819 Dalmally road.

Inveraray Jail　　　　　　　　　　MUSEUM
(☑01499-302381; www.inverarayjail.co.uk; Church Sq; adult/child £8.95/4.95; ⊙9.30am-6pm Apr-Oct, 10am-5pm Nov-Mar) At this award-winning, interactive tourist attraction you can sit in on a trial, try out a cell and discover the harsh tortures that were meted out to unfortunate prisoners. The attention to detail – including a life-sized model of an inmate squatting on a 19th-century toilet – more than makes up for the sometimes tedious commentary.

Inveraray Maritime Museum　　　MUSEUM
(☑01499-302213; www.inveraraypier.com; The Pier; adult/child £5/2.50; ⊙10am-5pm Apr-Oct; ♿) The *Arctic Penguin*, a three-masted schooner built in 1911 and one of the world's last surviving iron sailing ships, is permanently moored in Inveraray harbour, and houses a museum with interesting photos and models of the old Clyde steamers and puffers is often moored alongside.

🛏 Sleeping & Eating

TOP CHOICE **George Hotel** HOTEL ££
(☎01499-302111; www.thegeorgehotel.co.uk; Main St E; d from £75; ℗) The George Hotel boasts a magnificent choice of opulent rooms complete with four-poster beds, period furniture, Victorian roll-top baths and private jacuzzis (superior rooms cost £140 to £165 per double). The cosy wood-panelled bar, with its rough stone walls, flagstone floor and peat fires, is a delightful place for a bar meal (mains £8 to £16, open for lunch and dinner).

Claonairigh House B&B £
(☎01499-302160; www.argyll-scotland.demon.co.uk; Bridge of Douglas; s/d from £40/55; ℗@🛜) This grand 18th-century house, built for the Duke of Argyll in 1745, is set in 3 hectares of grounds on the bank of a river (salmon-fishing available). There are three homely en suite rooms, one with a four-poster bed, and a resident menagerie of dogs, ducks, chickens and goats. It's 4 miles south of town on the A83.

Inveraray SYHA HOSTEL £
(☎01499-302454; www.syha.org.uk; Dalmally Rd; dm £17; ☉Apr-Oct; @) To get to this hostel, housed in a comfortable, modern bungalow, go through the arched entrance on the seafront – it's set back on the left of the road about 100m further on.

Loch Fyne Oyster Bar SEAFOOD ££
(☎01499-600236; www.lochfyne.com; Clachan, Cairndow; mains £11-22; ☉9am-8pm) Located six miles northeast of Inveraray, this rustic-themed restaurant serves excellent seafood, although the service can be a bit hit and miss. It's housed in a converted byre, and the menu includes locally farmed oysters, mussels and salmon. The neighbouring shop sells packaged local seafood and other deli goods to take away, as well as bottled beer from the nearby Fyne Ales microbrewery.

❶ Getting There & Away

Scottish Citylink (www.citylink.co.uk) buses run from Glasgow to Inveraray (£11, 1¾ hours, six daily Monday to Saturday, two Sunday). Three of these buses continue to Lochgilphead and Campbeltown (£12, 2½ hours); while the others continue on to Oban (£10, 1¼ hours).

Crinan Canal

Completed in 1801, the picturesque Crinan Canal runs for 9 miles from Ardrishaig to Crinan allowing seagoing vessels – mostly yachts, these days – to take a short cut from the Firth of Clyde and Loch Fyne to the west coast of Scotland, avoiding the long and sometimes dangerous passage around the Mull of Kintyre. You can easily **walk or cycle** the full length of the canal towpath in an afternoon.

The canal basin at Crinan is the focus for the annual Crinan Classic Boat Festival (www.crinanclassic.com), usually held over the first weekend in July (though planned for early June in 2013), when traditional wooden yachts, motor boats and dinghies gather for a few days of racing, drinking and music.

The basin is overlooked by the Crinan Hotel (☎01546-830261; www.crinanhotel.com; Crinan; s/d incl dinner from £150/270 ; ℗), which boasts one of the west coast's most spectacular sunset views and one of Scotland's top seafood restaurants. You're paying for that view, and for the olde-worlde atmosphere – don't expect five-star luxury. You can also eat in the hotel's Crinan Seafood Bar (mains

---

RETURN OF THE BEAVER

Beavers have been extinct in Britain since the 16th century. But in 2009 they returned to Scotland, when a population of Norwegian beavers was released into the hill lochs of Knapdale in Argyllshire. In 2010 the beavers had their first offspring. The five-year Scottish Beaver Trial (www.scottishbeavers.org.uk) hopes to reveal whether the animals have a positive effect on habitat and biodiversity. If so, they could be introduced to other parts of the country.

Meanwhile, you can try and get a glimpse of them on the **Beaver Detective Trail**. It starts from the Barnluasgan forestry car park on the B8025 road to Tayvallich, about 1.5 miles south of the Crinan Canal. Rangers offer guided walks at 6pm on Tuesday and Saturday in summer.

£10-15, 4-course dinner £70; ⊘lunch & dinner) – the menu includes excellent local mussels with white wine, thyme and garlic.

The coffee shop (snacks £3-6; ⊘10am-5pm) on the western side of the canal basin at Crinan has great home-baked cakes and scones.

If you want to walk along the canal and take the bus back, bus 425 from Lochgilphead to Tayvallich stops at Cairnbaan, Bellanoch and Crinan Cottages (20 minutes, three or four daily Monday to Saturday).

Kilmartin Glen

In the 6th century, Irish settlers arrived in this part of Argyll and founded the kingdom of Dalriada, which eventually united with the Picts in 843 to create the first Scottish kingdom. Their capital was the hill fort of Dunadd, on the plain to the south of Kilmartin Glen.

This magical glen is the focus of one of the biggest concentrations of prehistoric sites in Scotland. Burial cairns, standing stones, stone circles, hill forts and cup-and-ring-marked rocks litter the countryside. Within a 6-mile radius of Kilmartin village there are 25 sites with standing stones and over 100 rock carvings.

⊙ Sights

Your first stop should be Kilmartin House Museum (☑01546-510278; www.kilmartin.org; Kilmartin; adult/child £5/2; ⊘10am-5.30pm Mar-Oct, 11am-4pm Nov-23 Dec), in Kilmartin village, a fascinating interpretive centre that provides a context for the ancient monuments you can go on to explore, alongside displays of artefacts recovered from various sites. The project was partly funded by midges – the curator exposed his body in Temple Wood on a warm summer's evening and was sponsored per midge bite!

The oldest monuments at Kilmartin date from 5000 years ago and comprise a linear cemetery of burial cairns that runs south from Kilmartin village for 1.5 miles. There are also ritual monuments (two stone circles) at Temple Wood, 0.75 miles southwest of Kilmartin. The museum bookshop sells maps and guides.

Kilmartin Churchyard contains some 10th-century Celtic crosses and lots of medieval grave slabs with carved effigies of knights. Some researchers have surmised that these were the tombs of Knights Templar who fled persecution in France in the 14th century.

The hill fort of Dunadd, 3.5 miles south of Kilmartin village, was the seat of power of the first kings of Dalriada, and may have been where the Stone of Destiny was originally located. The faint rock carvings of a wild boar and two footprints with an Ogham inscription may have been used in some kind of inauguration ceremony. The prominent little hill rises straight out of the boggy plain of the Moine Mhor Nature Reserve. A slippery path leads to the summit where you can gaze out on much the same view that the kings of Dalriada enjoyed 1300 years ago.

🛏 Sleeping & Eating

Kilmartin Hotel INN ££
(☑01546-510250; www.kilmartin-hotel.com; Kilmartin; s/d £40/65; P) Though the rooms here are a bit on the small side, this attractively old-fashioned hotel is full of atmosphere. There's a restaurant (mains £8 to £15) here too, and a whisky bar with real ale on tap where you can enjoy live folk music at weekends.

TOP CHOICE **Glebe Cairn Café** CAFE £
(☑01546-510278; mains £5-8; ⊘10am-5pm Mar-Oct, 11am-4pm Nov-Dec, closed Jan-Feb) The cafe in the Kilmartin House Museum has a lovely conservatory with a view across fields to a prehistoric cairn. Dishes include homemade Cullen skink, a Celtic cheese platter and hummus with sweet-and-sour beetroot relish. The drinks menu ranges from espresso to elderflower wine by way of Fraoch heather-scented ale.

❶ Getting There & Away

Bus 423 between Oban and Ardrishaig (four daily Monday to Friday, two on Saturday) stops at Kilmartin (£5, one hour and 20 minutes).

You can **walk or cycle** along the Crinan Canal from Ardrishaig, then turn north at Bellanoch on the minor B8025 road to reach Kilmartin (12 miles one way).

Kintyre

The Kintyre peninsula – 40 miles long and 8 miles wide – is almost an island, with only a narrow isthmus at Tarbert connecting it to the wooded hills of Knapdale. During the Norse occupation of the Western Isles, the Scottish king decreed that the Vikings could claim as their own any island they could circumnavigate in a longship. So in 1098 the wily Magnus Barefoot stood at the helm while his men dragged their boat across this neck of land, thus validating his claim to Kintyre.

TARBERT
POP 1500

The attractive fishing village and yachting centre of Tarbert is the gateway to Kintyre, and well worth a stopover for lunch or dinner, or a weekend visit for one of the local festivals. There's a tourist office (p404) here.

⊙ Sights & Activities

The picturesque harbour is overlooked by the crumbling, ivy-covered ruins of **Tarbert Castle**, built by Robert the Bruce in the 14th century. You can hike up to it via a signposted footpath beside the Loch Fyne Gallery (www.lochfynegallery.com; Harbour St; ⊙10am-5pm), which showcases the work of local artists.

Tarbert is the starting point for the 103-mile Kintyre Way (www.kintyreway.com), a walking route that runs the length of the peninsula to Southend at the southern tip. The first section, from Tarbert to Skipness (9 miles), makes a pleasant day-hike, climbing through forestry plantations to a high moorland plateau where you can soak up superb views to the Isle of Arran.

🎆 Festivals & Events

Scottish Series Yacht Races   SAILING
(www.scottishseries.com) Held over five days around the last weekend in May. The harbour is crammed with hundreds of visiting yachts.

Tarbert Seafood Festival   FOOD & DRINK
(www.seafood-festival.co.uk) First weekend in July; food stalls, cooking demonstrations, music, family entertainment.

Tarbert Music Festival   MUSIC
(www.tarbertmusicfestival.com) On the third weekend in September: live folk, blues, beer, jazz, rock, *ceilidhs* (evening of traditional Scottish entertainment), more beer...

🛏 Sleeping & Eating

There are plenty of B&Bs and hotels here, but be sure to book ahead during festivals and major events.

Knap Guest House   B&B **££**
(☑01880-820015; www.knapguesthouse.co.uk; Campbeltown Rd; s/d from £50/70; 📶) A flight of stairs lit by Edwardian stained glass leads to this 1st-floor flat with three spacious en suite bedrooms sporting an attractive blend of Scottish and Far Eastern decor. The welcome is warm, and there are great harbour views from the lounge (leather sofas, log fire and a small library) and breakfast room.

Springside B&B   B&B **££**
(☑01880-820413; www.scotland-info.co.uk/springside; Pier Rd; s/d £38/60; 🅿) You can sit in front of this attractive fisherman's cottage, which overlooks the entrance to the harbour, and watch the yachts and fishing boats come and go. There are four comfy rooms, three with en suite, and the house is just five minutes' walk from the village centre in one direction, and a short stroll from the Portavadie ferry in the other.

TOP CHOICE / Starfish   SEAFOOD **££**
(☑01880-820733; wwwstarfishtarbert.com; Castle St; mains £10-20; ⊙lunch & dinner Tue-Sun) Simple but stylish describes not only the decor in this friendly restaurant, but the dishes too. 'Scotch egg' scallops (wrapped in smoked salmon mousse and coated with crunchy crumbs) – who'd have thought of that? And local languoustines with garlic butter and homebaked bread are finger-licking scrumptious. It's worth a trip to Tarbert just to eat here. Best to book a table.

ⓘ Getting There & Away

BOAT CalMac (www.calmac.co.uk) operates a car ferry from **Tarbert to Portavadie** on the Cowal peninsula (passenger/car £4/18, 25 minutes, hourly).

Ferries to the islands of **Islay and Colonsay** depart from Kennacraig ferry terminal on West Loch Tarbert, 5 miles southwest of Tarbert.

BUS Tarbert is served by five **Scottish Citylink** (www.citylink.co.uk) coaches a day between Campbeltown and Glasgow (Glasgow to Tarbert £15, 3¼ hours; Tarbert to Campbeltown £7.10, 1¼ hours).

SKIPNESS
POP 100

The tiny village of Skipness is on the east coast of Kintyre, about 13 miles south of Tarbert, in a pleasant and quiet setting with great views of Arran. There's a post office and general store in the village.

Beyond the village rise the substantial remains of 13th-century Skipness Castle (HS; admission free; ⊙24hr, tower Apr-Sep only), a former possession of the Lords of the Isles.

It's a striking building, composed of dark-green local stone trimmed with contrasting red-brown sandstone from Arran. The tower house was added in the 16th century and was occupied until the 19th century. From the top you can see the roofless, 13th-century **St Brendan's Chapel** down by the shore. The kirkyard contains some excellent carved grave slabs.

Skipness Seafood Cabin (☑01880-760207; sandwiches £4, mains £6-10; ☺11am-7pm Sun-Fri late May-Sep), in the grounds of nearby Skipness House, serves tea, coffee and home baking, as well as local fish and shellfish dishes. In fine weather you can scoff the house special – crab sandwiches – at outdoor picnic tables with grand views of Arran.

Local **bus 448** runs between Tarbert and Skipness (35 minutes, two daily Monday to Saturday).

At Claonaig, 2 miles southwest of Skipness, there's a daily **car ferry** to Lochranza on the Isle of Arran (passenger/car £5.75/25.50, 30 minutes, seven to nine daily).

ISLE OF GIGHA
POP 120

Gigha (*ghee*-ah; www.gigha.org.uk) is a low-lying island, 6 miles long by about 1 mile wide, that's famous for its sandy beaches and mild climate – subtropical plants thrive in the island's **Achamore Gardens** (☑01583-505254; www.gigha.org.uk/gardens; Achamore House; admission free, donation requested; ☺dawn-dusk).

Locally made **Gigha cheese** is sold in many parts of Argyll – there are several varieties produced on the island, including pasteurised goat's-milk cheese and oak-smoked cheddar.

The island's limited accommodation includes **Post Office House** (☑01583-505251; www.gighastores.co.uk; d £50; ℗), a Victorian house at the top of the hill above the ferry slip with two self-catering cottages (it houses the island post office and shop as well). There's also the **Gigha Hotel** (☑01583-505254; www.gigha.org.uk/accom; r per person £50), 100m south of the post office, which serves bar meals, or if you're feeling peckish, four-course dinners. You can also eat at the **Boat House Café Bar** (☑01583-505123; mains £7-12; ☺lunch & dinner) near the ferry slip.

There's a single B&B, plus a range of **self-catering acoommodation** available (see www.gigha.org.uk for details). **Camping** is allowed on a grassy area beside the Boat House near the ferry slip – there's no charge but space is limited, so call the Boat House in advance to check availability.

CalMac (www.calmac.co.uk) runs a ferry from Tayinloan in Kintyre to Gigha (passenger/car return £6.90/25.50, 20 minutes, hourly Monday to Saturday, six on Sunday). Bicycles travel free.

You can **rent bikes** from Post Office House for £12 per day.

CAMPBELTOWN
POP 6000

Campbeltown, with its ranks of grey council houses, feels a bit like an Ayrshire mining town that's been placed incongruously on the shores of a beautiful Argyllshire harbour. It was once a thriving fishing port and whisky-making centre, but industrial decline and the closure of the former air-force base at nearby Machrihanish saw Campbeltown's fortunes decline.

But renewal is in the air – the spruced-up seafront, with its flower beds, smart Victorian buildings and restored art-deco cinema, lends the town a distinctly optimistic air.

The **tourist office** (☑01586-552056; The Pier; ☺9am-5.30pm Mon-Sat) is beside the harbour.

◉ Sights & Activities

There were once no fewer than 32 distilleries in the Campbeltown area, but most closed down in the 1920s. Today **Springbank Distillery** (☑ext 1 01586-551710; www.the-tastingroom.com; 85 Longrow; tours from £6.50; ☺tours 10am & 2pm Mon-Sat) is one of only three that now operate in town. It is also one of the very few distilleries in Scotland that distils, matures and bottles all its whisky on the one site.

One of the most unusual sights in Argyll is in a **cave** on the southern side of the island of **Davaar**, at the mouth of Campbeltown Loch. On the wall of the cave is an eerie **painting of the Crucifixion** by local artist Archibald MacKinnon, dating from 1887. You can walk to the island at low tide across a shingle bar called the Dhorlinn (allow at least 1½ hours for the round trip), but make sure you're not caught by a rising tide – check tide times with the tourist office before you set off.

Mull of Kintyre Seatours (☑07785 542811; www.mull-of-kintyre.co.uk; adult/child from £35/£25) operates two-hour, high-speed boat trips out of Campbeltown harbour to look for wildlife: seals, porpoises, minke whales, golden eagles and peregrine falcons live in the turbulent tidal waters and on the spectacular sea cliffs of the Mull of Kintyre. Book in advance by phone or at the tourist office.

The Mull of Kintyre Music Festival (☎01586-551053; www.mokfest.com), held in Campbeltown in late August, is a popular event featuring traditional Scottish and Irish music.

Opened in 2009, the nearby Machrihanish Dunes (p35) golf resort has won accolades around the world for the quality of its two golf courses and associated hotels. **Machrihanish Bay**, accessible from a car park on the A83, 5 miles northwest of Campbeltown, has a 3-mile-long sandy beach that is popular with surfers and windsurfers.

❶ Getting There & Away

AIR **Loganair/FlyBe** (www.loganair.co.uk) operates two flights daily, Monday to Friday, from Glasgow to Campbeltown (£51, 35 minutes).

BOAT **Kintyre Express** (☎01856-555895; www.kintyreexpress.com) operates a small, high-speed passenger ferry from Campbeltown to Ballycastle in Northern Ireland (£35 one way, two hours, three daily May to September, two weekly October to April). Tickets must be booked in advance.

BUS **Scottish Citylink** (www.citylink.co.uk) buses run from Campbeltown to Glasgow (£18.50, four hours, three daily) via Tarbert, Inveraray, Arrochar and Loch Lomond. It also runs to Oban (£19, four hours, three daily), changing at Inveraray.

MULL OF KINTYRE

A narrow winding road, about 18 miles long, leads south from Campbeltown to the **Mull of Kintyre**, passing some good **sandy beaches** near Southend. The name of this remote headland was immortalised in Paul McCartney's famous song – the former Beatle owns a farmhouse in the area. A **lighthouse** marks the spot closest to Northern Ireland, the coastline of which, only 12 miles away, is visible across the North Channel.

Isle of Islay

POP 3400

The most southerly island of the Inner Hebrides, Islay (*eye*-lah) is best known for its single malt whiskies, which have a distinctive smoky flavour. There are eight working distilleries here, all of which welcome visitors and offer guided tours.

Islay's whisky industry contributes approximately £480 million a year to the government in excise duty; that's about £140,000 for every man, woman and child on the island. Little wonder that the islanders complain about lack of government investment in the area.

With a list of more than 250 recorded bird species, Islay also attracts birdwatchers. It's an important wintering ground for thousands of white-fronted and barnacle geese. As well as the whisky and wildfowl, there are miles of sandy beaches, pleasant walking trails, and good food and drink.

There's a campsite and bunkhouse at Kintra, near Port Ellen, and a campsite and youth hostel in Port Charlotte. If you want to camp elsewhere, ask permission first. Camping is prohibited on the Ardtalla and Dunlossit estates on the eastern side of Islay.

🖝 Tours

Islay Wilderness Guide   BIRDWATCHING
(☎01496-850010; www.islaywildernessguide.co.uk; ⌖) Offers wild food foraging trips, and wildlife safaris by bike or on foot (£30/60 per half-/full day). There are also family bicycle safaris (two adults plus children £60 per half-day) teaching wild camping and cycle touring skills.

Islay Sea Safaris   BOAT TOUR
(☎01496-840510; www.islayseasafari.co.uk) Can arrange customised tours (£25 to £30 per person per hour) by sea from Port Ellen to visit some or all of Islay and Jura's distilleries in a single day, as well as birdwatching trips, coastal exploration and trips to Jura's remote west coast and the Corryvreckan whirlpool.

Islay Stalking   WILDLIFE WATCHING
(☎01496-850120; www.thegearach.co.uk) Here's your chance to stalk deer and other wildlife in the company of a gamekeeper, and shoot them – not with a gun but with a camera. Morning and evening photographic tours are £20/10 per adult/child.

✯ Festivals & Events

Fèis Ìle   MUSIC, WHISKY
(Islay Festival; www.theislayfestival.co.uk) A weeklong celebration of traditional Scottish music and whisky at the end of May. Events include *ceilidhs*, pipe-band performances, distillery tours, barbecues and whisky tastings.

Islay, Jura & Colonsay

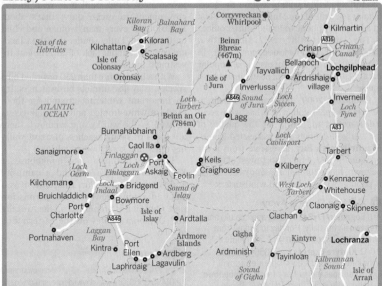

Islay Jazz Festival MUSIC
(☎01496-810262; www.islayjazzfestival.co.uk)
This three-day festival takes place over the second weekend in September. A varied line-up of international talent plays at various venues across the island.

ℹ Information

Islay Service Point (☎01496-810332; Jamieson St; ⊕9am-12.30pm & 1.30-5pm Mon-Fri)
Free internet access.

Islay Tourist Office (☎01496-810254; The Square, Bowmore; ⊕10am-5pm Mon-Sat, 2-5pm Sun Apr-Aug, shorter hr Sep-Mar)

MacTaggart Community CyberCafé
(☎01496-302693; www.islaycybercafe.co.uk; 30 Mansfield Pl, Port Ellen; per 30min £1; ⊕9am-10pm Mon & Wed-Sat, to 5pm Tue & Sun; ⓢ) Internet access.

ℹ Getting There & Away

There are two ferry terminals on the island, both served by ferries from Kennacraig in West Loch Tarbert – Port Askaig on the east coast, and Port Ellen in the south. Islay airport lies midway between Port Ellen and Bowmore.

AIR **Loganair/FlyBe** (www.loganair.co.uk) flies from Glasgow to Islay (£62 one way, 45 minutes, two or three flights daily Monday to Friday, one or two Saturday and Sunday).

Hebridean Air Services (☎0845 805 7465; www.hebrideanair.co.uk) operates flights (£65 one way, twice daily Tuesday and Thursday) from Connel Airfield (near Oban) to Colonsay (30 minutes) and Islay (40 minutes).

BOAT **CalMac** (www.calmac.co.uk) runs ferries from Kennacraig in West Loch Tarbert to Port Ellen (passenger/car £10.20/55, 2¼ hours, one to three daily) and Port Askaig (£10.20/55, two hours, one to three daily). On Wednesday only in summer the ferry continues from Port Askaig to Colonsay (£5.45/28, 1¼ hours) and on to Oban (£14.65/73, four hours).

ℹ Getting Around

BICYCLE You can hire bikes from **Bowmore Post Office** (per day £10), and from the house opposite the Port Charlotte Hotel.

BUS A bus service links Ardbeg, Port Ellen, Bowmore, Port Charlotte, Portnahaven and Port Askaig (limited service on Sunday). Pick up a copy of the *Islay & Jura Public Transport Guide* from the tourist office.

CAR **D & N MacKenzie** (☎01496-302300; Islay Airport) Car hire from £32 a day.

TAXI **Bowmore** (☎01496-810449); **Port Ellen** (☎01496-302155).

PORT ELLEN & AROUND

Port Ellen is the main point of entry for Islay. It has a Co-op Food minimarket (74

Frederick Cres; ⏰8am-8pm Mon-Sat, 12.30-7pm Sun), a pub and a bank (closed most afternoons and Wednesdays). There's an ATM in the Spar shop around the corner from the bank. While there's nothing to see in the town itself, the coast stretching northeast from Port Ellen is one of the loveliest parts of the island.

There are three **whisky distilleries** in close succession (check websites for tour times):

Laphroaig (www.laphroaig.com; tours £4.80; ⏰9.30am-5.30pm Mon-Fri, also 10am-4pm Sat & Sun Mar-Dec)

Lagavulin (www.discovering-distilleries.com; tours £6; ⏰9am-5pm Mon-Fri Apr-Oct, to 12.30pm Nov-Mar, plus 9am-5pm Sat & 12.30-4pm Sun Jul & Aug)

Ardbeg (www.ardbeg.com; tours from £4; ⏰10am-5pm Jun-Aug, 10am-4pm Mon-Fri Sep-May)

A pleasant **bike ride** leads past the distilleries to the atmospheric, age-haunted **Kildalton Chapel**, 8 miles northeast of Port Ellen. In the kirkyard is the exceptional late-8th-century **Kildalton Cross**, the only remaining Celtic high cross in Scotland (most surviving high crosses are in Ireland). There are carvings of biblical scenes on one side and animals on the other. There are also several extraordinary grave slabs around the chapel, some carved with swords and Celtic interlace patterns.

The kelp-fringed *skerries* (small rocky islands or reefs) of the **Ardmore Islands**, off the southeastern corner of Islay near Kildalton, are a wildlife haven and home to the second-largest colony of common seals in Europe.

🛏 Sleeping & Eating

TOP CHOICE Kintra Farm   CAMPSITE, B&B ££
(📞01496-302051; www.kintrafarm.co.uk; tent sites £4-10, plus per person £3, r per person £30-38; ⏰Apr-Sep) At the southern end of Laggan Bay, 3.5 miles northwest of Port Ellen, Kintra offers three bedrooms in a homely farmhouse B&B. There's also a basic but beautiful campsite on buttercup-sprinkled turf amid the dunes, with a sunset view across the beach.

Oystercatcher B&B   B&B ££
(📞01496-300409; www.islay-bedandbreakfast. com; 63 Frederick Cres; r per person £40; @🛜) If you like your breakfasts fishy, then this welcoming waterfront house is the place

for you – there's smoked haddock, smoked salmon and kippers on the menu, as well as the usual fry up. Bedrooms are small but comfortable and nicely decorated.

TOP CHOICE Old Kiln Café   CAFE £
(📞01496-302244; mains £5-10; ⏰10am-4pm daily Jun-Aug, Mon-Fri only Sep-Jun, lunch served from noon) Housed in the former malting kiln at Ardbeg Distillery, this well-run cafe serves hearty homemade soups, tasty light meals (try a panini sandwich with haggis and apple chutney, or a platter of smoked Islay beef, venison and pastrami); and a range of home-baked desserts, including traditional clootie dumpling (a rich steamed pudding filled with currants and raisins) with ice cream.

BOWMORE

The attractive Georgian village of Bowmore was built in 1768 to replace the village of Kilarrow, which just had to go – it was spoiling the view from the laird's house. Its centrepiece is the distinctive **Round Church** at the top of Main St, built in circular form to ensure that the devil had no corners to hide in.

Bowmore Distillery (📞01496-810671; www. bowmore.co.uk; School St; tours adult/child £6/ free; ⏰9am-5pm Mon-Fri, to noon Sat, plus 9am-5pm Sat Easter–mid-Sep & noon-4pm Sun Jul–mid-Sep) is the only distillery on the island that still malts its own barley. The standard tour (check website for times) includes a look at (and taste of) the germinating grain laid out in golden billows on the floor of the malting shed, and a free dram at the end; the two-hour Craftsman's Tour (£45 per person, book in advance) offers a more in-depth look at the process, and a chance to taste some rare bottlings.

Islay House Square, a collection of craft shops and studios 3 miles northeast of Bowmore at Bridgend, is home to Islay Ales (www.islayales.com; ⏰10.30am-5pm Mon-Sat), a microbrewery that produces a range of real ales, all bottled by hand. After a complimentary tour of the premises, you can taste the ales for free, and buy a bottle or two to drink outdoors or back home (the brewery doesn't have a bar licence). Our favourite is Saligo Ale, a refreshing, summery pale ale.

🛏 Sleeping & Eating

Harbour Inn   INN £££
(📞01496-810330; www.harbour-inn.com; The Square; s/d from £100/135; @🛜) The plush

seven-room Harbour Inn, smartly decorated with a nautical theme, is the poshest place in town. The restaurant (mains £18 to £25, open for lunch and dinner) has harbour views and serves fresh local oysters, lobster and scallops, Islay lamb and Jura venison.

Lambeth House
B&B ££

(☎01496-810597; lambethguesthouse@tiscali.co.uk; Jamieson St; s/d £60/90; @) A short stroll from the harbour, the Lambeth is a simple, good-value guesthouse with comfy en suite bedrooms. Breakfasts are excellent, and it also offers a two-course evening meal for £12.

Lochside Hotel
HOTEL ££

(☎01496-810244; www.lochsidehotel.co.uk; 19 Shore St; r per person from £60; ☎) The 10 en suite bedrooms at the Lochside are kitted-out with chunky pine furniture, including one room adapted for wheelchair users. The conservatory dining room provides sweeping views over Loch Indaal, and the bar boasts a range of more than 250 single malts, including many rare bottlings.

PORT CHARLOTTE

About 11 miles from Bowmore, on the opposite shore of Loch Indaal, is the attractive village of Port Charlotte. It has a general store (☺9am-12.30pm & 1.30-5.30pm Mon-Sat, 11.30am-1.30pm Sun) and post office.

Islay's long history is lovingly recorded in the Museum of Islay Life (☎01496-850358; www.islaymuseum.org; adult/child £3/1; ☺10am-5pm Mon-Sat, 2-5pm Sun Easter-Oct), housed in the former Free Church. Prize exhibits include an illicit still, 19th-century crofters' furniture and a set of leather boots once worn by the horse that pulled the lawnmower at Islay House (so it wouldn't leave hoof prints on the lawn!). There are also touch-screen computers displaying archive photos of Islay in the 19th and early 20th centuries.

The Islay Natural History Centre (www.islaynaturalhistory.org; adult/child £3/1.50; ☺10am-1pm Mon & Fri, 10.30am-4.30pm Tue-Thu May-Sep), next to the youth hostel, has displays explaining the island's natural history, with advice on where to see wildlife and lots of interesting hands-on exhibits for kids.

The Bruichladdich Distillery (☎01496-850190; www.bruichladdich.com; tours £5; ☺9am-5pm Mon-Fri & 10am-4pm Sat), at the northern edge of the village, reopened in 2001 with all its original Victorian equipment restored to working condition. Independently owned

and independently minded, Bruichladdich (brook-lah-day) produces an intriguing range of distinctive, very peaty whiskies. Call ahead to book a tour.

Sleeping & Eating

TOP CHOICE Port Charlotte Hotel
HOTEL £££

(☎01496-850360; www.portcharlottehotel.co.uk; s/d £105/180; ☺restaurant 6.30-9pm, bar meals noon-2pm & 5.30-8.30pm; P☎) This lovely old Victorian hotel has stylish, individually decorated bedrooms with sea views, and a candlelit restaurant (mains £16 to £27) serving local seafood (such as seared scallops with braised leeks and truffle cream sauce), Islay beef, venison and duck. The bar (bar meals £9 to £14) is well stocked with Islay malts and real ales, and has a nook at the back with a view over the loch towards the Paps of Jura.

Port Mor Campsite
CAMPSITE £

(☎01496-850441; www.islandofislay.co.uk; tent sites per adult/child £8/4; @☎) The sports field to the south of the village doubles as a campground – there are toilets, showers, laundry and a children's play area in the main building. Open all year.

Islay SYHA
HOSTEL £

(☎01496-850385; www.syha.org.uk; dm £17.50; ☺Apr-Oct; @☎) This modern and comfortable hostel is housed in a former distillery building with views over the loch.

Debbie's Minimarket
CAFE £

(☎01496-850319; ☺9am-5.30pm Mon-Sat; ☎) The village shop and post office at Bruichladdich doubles as a deli that stocks good wine and posh picnic grub, and also serves the best coffee on Islay – sit at one of the outdoor tables and enjoy an espresso with a sea view.

Croft Kitchen
CAFE £

(☎01496-850230; mains lunch £4-7, dinner £11-15; ☺snacks 10am-5pm, lunch noon-3pm, dinner 5.30-7.30pm) This laid-back little bistro serves as a cafe during the day and transforms into a restaurant serving quality meals in the evening.

PORTNAHAVEN

Six miles southwest of Port Charlotte the road ends at Portnahaven, another picturesque village that was purpose-built as a fishing harbour in the 19th century. A mile north of the village is the pretty little shell-sand beach of **Currie Sands**, with a lovely view of Orsay island.

The next inlet to the north of the beach is occupied by the world's first commercially viable, wave-powered electricity generating station, built on cliffs that are open to the Atlantic swell. The 500kW plant – known as the **Limpet** (Land-installed, marine-powered energy transformer) – provides enough electricity to power 200 island homes.

LOCH GRUINART & AROUND

Seven miles north of Port Charlotte is **Loch Gruinart Nature Reserve**, where you can hear corncrakes in summer and see huge flocks of migrating ducks, geese and waders in spring and autumn; there's a hide with wheelchair access. The nearby RSPB visitor centre (admission free; ⊙10am-5pm Apr-Oct, to 4pm Nov-Mar) offers two- to three-hour guided walks around the reserve (£3 per person, 10am Thursday April to October).

Kilchoman Distillery (☏01496-850011; www.kilchomandistillery.com; Rockfield Farm; tours £4.50; ⊙10am-5pm Mon-Fri, plus Sat Apr-Oct), 5 miles southwest of Loch Gruinart, is Islay's newest, going into production in 2005. The distillery grows its own barley on Islay, and the visitor centre explores the history of farmhouse distilling on the island. Its first single malt was released in 2010, and was so popular it sold out within days.

The cafe (mains £5-10; ⊙10am-5pm Mon-Fri, plus Sat Apr-Oct) at Kilchoman Distillery rustles up an excellent lunch – crusty brown rolls filled with hot-smoked salmon and dill mayo, and bowls of rich, smoky Cullen skink.

FINLAGGAN

Lush meadows swathed in buttercups and daisies slope down to reed-fringed Loch Finlaggan, the medieval capital of the Lords of the Isles. This bucolic setting, 3 miles southwest of Port Askaig, was once the most important settlement in the Hebrides, the central seat of power of the Lords of the Isles from the 12th to the 16th centuries. From the little island at the northern end of the loch the descendants of Somerled administered their island territories and entertained visiting chieftains in their great hall. Little remains now except the tumbled ruins of houses and a chapel, but the setting is beautiful and the history fascinating. A wooden walkway leads over the reeds and water lilies to the island, where information boards describe the remains.

Finlaggan Visitor Centre (www.finlaggan. com; adult/child £3/1; ⊙10.30am-4.30pm Mon-Sat & 1.30-4.30pm Sun Apr-Sep), in a nearby cottage (plus modern extension), explains the site's history and archaeology. The island itself is open at all times.

Buses from Port Askaig stop at the road's end, from where it's a 15-minute walk to the loch.

PORT ASKAIG & AROUND

Port Askaig is little more than a hotel, a shop (with ATM), a petrol pump and a ferry pier, set in a picturesque nook halfway along the Sound of Islay, the strait that separates the islands of Islay and Jura.

There are two distilleries within easy reach: Caol Ila Distillery (☏01496-840207; www.discovering-distilleries.com; tours from £6; ⊙9.15am-5pm Mon-Fri & 1.30-4.30pm Sat Apr-Oct, shorter hours in winter), pronounced 'cull *ee*-lah', 1 mile to the north, and Bunnahabhain Distillery (☏01496-840646; www.bunnahabhain. com; tours £6; ⊙9am-4.30pm Mon-Fri Mar-Oct, by appointment Nov-Feb), pronounced 'boo-na-*hah*-ven', 3 miles north of Port Askaig. Both enjoy wonderful locations with great views across to Jura.

The rooms at the Port Askaig Hotel (☏01496-840245; www.portaskaig.co.uk; s/d from £50/105; P), beside the ferry pier, seem pleasantly stuck in the 1970s, but the staff are warm and friendly, the breakfast is good and there's a great view of the Paps of Jura from the residents lounge. The beer garden is a popular spot to sit and watch the comings and goings at the quay.

Isle of Jura

POP 170

Jura lies off the coast of Argyll – long, dark and low like a vast Viking longship, its billowing sail the distinctive triple peaks of the Paps of Jura. A magnificently wild and lonely island, it's the perfect place to get away from it all – as George Orwell did in 1948. Orwell wrote his masterpiece *1984* while living at the remote farmhouse of Barnhill in the north of the island, describing it in a letter as 'a very un-get-at-able place'.

Jura takes its name from the Old Norse *dyr-a* (deer island) – an apt appellation, as the island supports a population of around 6000 red deer, outnumbering their human cohabitants by about 35 to one.

The community-run Jura Service Point (☏01496-820161; Craighouse; ⊙10am-1pm Mon-Fri;

☎), 400m north of the Jura Hotel, provides tourist information and free internet access. Jura Stores (www.jurastores.co.uk; Craighouse; ◷9am-1pm & 2-5pm Mon-Fri, 9am-1pm & 2-4.30pm Sat) is the island's only shop. There's no bank or ATM, but you can get cash on a debit card at the Jura Hotel.

◎ Sights

Apart from the superb wilderness walking and wildlife-watching, there's not a whole lot to do on the island except for visiting the Isle of Jura Distillery (☏01496-820385; www. isleofjura.com; Craighouse; tours free; ◷10am-4pm Mon-Fri, 10am-2pm Sat Apr-Sep, 11am-2pm Mon-Fri Oct-Mar) (call to book a tour) and the Feolin Study Centre (www.theisleofjura.co.uk; admission free; ◷9am-5pm), just south of the ferry slip at Feolin, which has a small exhibition on Jura's history and provides information on all aspects of the island's history, culture and wildlife.

The Jura Music Festival (www.juramu sicfestival.com) in late September offers a convivial weekend of traditional Scottish folk music. The other big event on the calendar is the Isle of Jura Fell Race (www.jurafellrace. org.uk) in late May, when around 250 hill runners converge on the island to race over the Paps.

There are regular **ceilidhs** held throughout the year where visitors are made very welcome; check the notice board outside Jura Stores for announcements.

⚡ Activities

There are few proper footpaths on Jura, but any off-the-beaten-path exploration will involve rough going through giant bracken, knee-deep bogs and thigh-high tussocks. Most of the island is occupied by deer-stalking estates, and access to the hills may be restricted during the stalking season (July to February); the Jura Hotel can provide details of areas to be avoided.

The only real trail is **Evans' Walk**, a stalkers' path that leads for 6 miles from the main road through a pass in the hills to a hunting lodge above the remote sandy beach at Glenbatrick Bay. The path leaves the road 4 miles north of Craighouse (just under a mile north of the bridge over the River Corran). The first 0.75 mile is hard going along an interwoven braid of faint, squelchy trails through lumpy bog; aim at or just left of the cairn on the near horizon.

THE SCOTTISH MAELSTROM

It may look innocuous on the map, but the Gulf of Corryvreckan – the 1km-wide channel between the northern end of Jura and the island of Scarba – is home to one of the three most notorious tidal whirlpools in the world (the others are the Maelstrom in Norway's Lofoten Islands, and the Old Sow in Canada's New Brunswick).

The tide doesn't just rise and fall twice a day, it flows – dragged around the earth by the gravitational attraction of the moon. On the west coast of Scotland, the rising tide – known as the flood tide – flows northwards. As the flood moves up the Sound of Jura, to the east of the island, it is forced into a narrowing bottleneck jammed with islands and builds up to a greater height than the open sea to the west of Jura. As a result, millions of tonnes of sea water pour westwards through the Gulf of Corryvreckan at speeds of up to 8 knots – an average sailing yacht is going fast at 6 knots.

The **Corryvreckan Whirlpool** forms where this mass of moving water hits an underwater pinnacle, which rises from the 200m-deep sea bed to within just 28m of the surface, and swirls over and around it. The turbulent waters create a magnificent spectacle, with white-capped breakers, standing waves, bulging boils and overfalls, and countless miniature maelstroms whirling around the main vortex.

Corryvreckan is at its most violent when a flooding spring tide, flowing west through the gulf, meets a westerly gale blowing in from the Atlantic. In these conditions, standing waves up to 5m high can form and dangerously rough seas extend more than 3 miles west of Corryvreckan, a phenomenon known as the Great Race.

You can see the whirlpool by making the long hike to the northern end of Jura (check tide times at Jura Hotel, and look under Activities for walk details), or by taking a boat trip from the Isle of Seil with Sea.fari (p303) or Sea Life Adventures (p303), or from Islay with Islay Sea Safaris (p289).

For more information, see www.whirlpool-scotland.co.uk.

The path firms up and is easier to follow after you cross a stream. On the descent on the far side of the pass, look out for wild orchids and sundew, and keep an eye out for adders basking in the sun. Allow six hours for the 12-mile round trip.

Another good walk is to a viewpoint for the **Corryvreckan Whirlpool**, the great tidal race between the northern end of Jura and the island of Scarba. From the northern end of the public road at Lealt you hike along a 4WD track past Barnhill to Kinuachdrachd Farm (6 miles). About 30m before the farm buildings a footpath forks left (there's an inconspicuous wooden signpost low down) and climbs up the hillside before traversing rough and boggy ground to a point 50m above the northern tip of the island. A rocky slab makes a natural grandstand for viewing the turbulent waters of the Gulf of Corryvreckan; if you have timed it right (check tide times at the Jura Hotel), you will see the whirlpool as a writhing mass of white water diagonally to your left and over by the Scarba shore. Allow five to six hours for the round trip (16 miles) from the road end.

Climbing the **Paps of Jura** is a truly tough hill-walk over ankle-breaking scree that requires good fitness and navigational skills (you'll need eight hours for the 11 long, hard and weary miles). A good place to start is by the bridge over the River Corran, 3 miles north of Craighouse. The first peak you reach is **Beinn a'Chaolais** (734m), the second is **Beinn an Oir** (784m) and the third is **Beinn Shiantaidh** (755m). Most people also climb **Corra Bheinn** (569m), before joining Evans' Walk to return to the road. If you succeed in bagging all four, you can reflect on the fact that the record for the annual Isle of Jura fell race is just three hours!

There are easier **short walks** (one or two hours) east along the coast from Jura House, and north along a 4WD track from Feolin. *Jura – A Guide for Walkers* by Gordon Wright (£2) is available from the tourist office in Bowmore, Islay.

Sleeping & Eating

Places to stay on the island are very limited, so book ahead – don't rely on just turning up and hoping to find a bed. Most of Jura's accommodation is in self-catering cottages that are let by the week (see www.juradevel opment.co.uk).

You can **camp** for free in the field below the Jura Hotel (ask at the bar first, and pop a donation in the bottle); there are toilets and hot showers (£1 coin) in the block behind the hotel. From July to February, check on the deer-stalking situation before **wild camping** elsewhere on the island (information available from the hotel).

Sealladh Na Mara   B&B **££**
(☎01496-820349; www.isleofjura.net; Knockrome; per person from £37) A modern croft house about 4 miles north of Craighouse, this place offers B&B in two cosy, IKEA-furnished bedrooms and a lovely guest lounge with a patio overlooking the sea. Evening meals can be provided, and there's also a self-catering two-bedroom chalet (from £200 a week).

Jura Hotel   HOTEL **££**
(☎01496-820243; www.jurahotel.co.uk; Craighouse; s/d from £50/78; ☺food served noon-2pm & 6.30-9pm. **P**) The 18-room Jura is the most comfortable place to stay on the island; ask for a room at the front with a view of the bay. The hotel also serves decent bar meals (£8 to £12) and the bar itself is a very sociable place to spend the evening.

🍴**Antlers**   BISTRO **££**
(☎01496-820496; Craighouse; mains £5-9, 2-/3-course dinner £25/29; ☺10am-6pm & 7-10pm Mon-Sat, 10am-4pm Sun Mar-Oct; ☎) This bistro makes the most of locally sourced produce, offering coffee, cakes, sandwiches and burgers during the day, and an unexpectedly classy menu at dinner time (booking essential) with dishes such as grilled local langoustines, and scallops with black pudding. Not licensed – £3 corkage.

❶ Getting There & Away

A **car ferry** shuttles between Port Askaig on Islay and Feolin on Jura (passenger/car/bicycle £1.35/7.60/free, five minutes, hourly Monday to Saturday, every two hours Sunday). There is no direct car-ferry connection to the mainland.

From April to September **Jura Passenger Ferry** (☎07768-450041; www.jurapassenger ferry.com) runs from Tayvallich on the mainland to Craighouse on Jura (£20, one hour, one or two daily except Wednesday). Booking recommended.

❶ Getting Around

BICYCLE You can hire bikes from **Jura Bike Hire** (☎07768 450000; Craighouse; per day £12.50) in Craighouse.

BUS The island's only **bus service** (☎01436-810200) runs between the ferry slip at Feolin and Craighouse (20 minutes, three or four a day), timed to coincide with ferry arrivals and departures. One or two of the runs continue north as far as Inverlussa.

Isle of Colonsay

POP 100

Legend has it that when St Columba set out from Ireland in 563, his first landfall was Colonsay. But on climbing a hill he found he could still see the distant coast of his homeland, and pushed on further north to found his monastery in Iona, leaving behind only his name (Colonsay means 'Columba's Isle').

Colonsay is a connoisseur's island, a little jewel-box of varied delights, none exceptional but each exquisite – an ancient priory, a woodland garden, a golden beach – set amid a Highland landscape in miniature: rugged, rocky hills, cliffs and sandy strands, machair and birch woods, even a trout loch. Here, hill walkers bag **McPhies** – defined as 'eminences in excess of 300ft' (90m) – instead of Munros. There are 22 in all; the supercompetitive will bag them all in one day.

The ferry pier is at **Scalasaig**, the main village, where you'll find a general store (⌚9am-1pm & 2-5.30pm Mon & Wed-Fri, 9am-1pm Tue & Sat), post office, public telephone and free internet access at the Service Point (⌚9.30am-12.30pm Mon-Fri). There isn't a tourist office, bank or ATM on the island. General information is available at the CalMac waiting room beside the ferry pier, and at www.colonsay.org.uk.

The tiny Colonsay Bookshop (☎01951-200375; Scalasaig; ⌚3-5.30pm Mon-Sat, from noon Wed & Sat), in the same building as the brewery, has an excellent range of books on Hebridean history and culture.

Sights & Activities

If the tides are right, don't miss the chance to walk across the half-mile of cockleshell-strewn sand that links Colonsay to the smaller island of Oronsay. Here you can explore the 14th-century ruins of **Oronsay Priory**, one of the best-preserved medieval priories in Scotland. There are two beautiful late 15th-century stone crosses in the kirkyard, but the highlight is the collection of superb 15th- and 16th-century carved grave slabs in the Prior's House; look for the ugly little devil trapped beneath the sword-tip of the knight on the right-hand side of the two horizontal slabs. The island is accessible on foot for about 1½ hours either side of low tide, and it's a 45-minute walk from the road-end on Colonsay to the priory. There are tide tables at the ferry terminal and the Colonsay Hotel.

The woodland Garden (☎01951-200211; www.colonsayestate.co.uk; Kiloran; admission free; ⌚dawn-dusk, walled garden 2-5pm Wed & noon-5pm Sat Easter-Sep) at Colonsay House, 1.5 miles north of Scalasaig, is tucked in an unexpected fold of the landscape and is famous for its outstanding collection of hybrid rhododendrons and unusual trees. There's a cafe in the formal walled garden beside the house.

There are good sandy beaches at several points around the coast, but **Kiloran Bay** in the northwest, a scimitar-shaped strand of dark golden sand, is outstanding. If there are too many people here for you, walk the 3 miles north to beautiful **Balnahard Bay**, accessible only on foot, bike or by boat; on the way, it's an easy climb to **Carnan Eoin** (143m), the highest point on the island.

Back at Scalasaig, the Colonsay Brewery (☎01951-200190; www.colonsaybrewery.co.uk; Scalasaig; ⌚3.30-5.30pm Mon, Wed, Fri & Sun) offers you the chance to have a look at how it produces its hand-crafted ales – the Colonsay IPA is a grand pint.

Kevin & Christa Byrne (☎01951-200320; byrne@colonsay.org.uk) offer two-hour minibus tours of the island (adult/child £12.50/7.50) on Tuesdays. There's also a regular 'Hidden Colonsay' walking tour (adult/child £12/7.50) every Saturday in summer; booking essential.

You can hire bikes from Archie McConnell (☎01951-200355; www.colonsaycottage.co.uk; Colnatarun Cottage, Kilchattan; per day £7.50) – book in advance and he can deliver to aerodrome or ferry pier.

Sleeping & Eating

Short-stay accommodation on Colonsay is limited and should be booked before coming to the island. **Wild camping** is allowed (no cars or campercans), as long as you abide by the provisions of the Scottish Outdoor Access Code (p30). See www.colonsay.org.uk for **self-catering** accommodation listings.

TOP CHOICE Colonsay Hotel HOTEL ££
(☎01951-200316; www.colonsayestate.co.uk; s/d from £70/100; P 🛜) This wonderfully laid-back hotel is set in an atmospheric old inn dating

from 1750, a short walk uphill from the ferry pier. The stylish **restaurant** (mains £11 to £20, open daily for breakfast, lunch and dinner) offers down-to-earth cooking using local produce as much as possible, from Colonsay oysters and lobsters to herbs and salad leaves from the Colonsay House gardens.

The bar is a convivial melting pot of locals, guests, hikers, cyclists and visiting yachties.

Backpackers Lodge   HOSTEL **£**
(✓01951-200312; www.colonsayestate.co.uk; Kiloran; dm £14-18, tw £40) Set in a former gamekeeper's house near Colonsay House, this lodge is about a 30-minute walk from the ferry terminal (you can arrange to be picked up at the pier). Rates include use of the tennis court at Colonsay House.

Island Lodges   SELF-CATERING **££**
(✓01343-890752; www.colonsayislandlodges. co.uk; chalet 2-night stay £160-260; 🛜) These comfortable and modern self-catering holiday chalets, sleeping from two to five people, are just a 10-minute walk from the ferry pier at Scalasaig. You can check last-minute availability on the website.

Pantry   CAFE **£**
(✓01951-200325; www.thecolonsaypantry.co.uk; Scalasaig; mains £5-9; ⊙10am-8pm Mon, 9am-8pm Tue-Sat, 3-8pm Sun Apr-Oct, shorter hr Nov-Mar; 🛜) This tearoom, close to the ferry pier, serves light meals, snacks and ice creams, and sells freshly baked loaves to take away.

❶ Getting There & Around

AIR **Hebridean Air Services** (✓0845 805 7465; www.hebrideanair.co.uk) operates flights from Oban Airport (at North Connel) to Colonsay (one way £65, twice daily Tuesday and Thursday; may be extended to Friday and Sunday), continuing to Islay (one way £25) for a connecting flight to Glasgow.

BOAT **Oban–Colonsay** From April to October the **CalMac** (www.calmac.co.uk) car ferry runs from Oban to Colonsay (passenger/car £14.35/73, 2¼ hours, one daily except Saturday). From November to March the ferry runs on Monday, Wednesday and Friday only.

Islay–Colonsay From April to October, on Wednesday only, the ferry from Kennacraig on the Kintyre peninsula to Islay's Port Askaig continues to Colonsay and on to Oban. A day-trip from Kennacraig or Port Askaig to Colonsay allows you seven hours on the island; the return fare from Port Askaig to Colonsay per passenger/car is £9.35/49.

BUS On Wednesdays, a **minibus service** (✓01951-200320; www.colonsay.org.uk/ walks.html; per person £8.50; ⊙departs ferry pier 12.15pm) aimed at day trippers makes two circuits of the island to meet the arriving and departing ferries – you can be dropped off/ picked-up at any point on the circuit.

OBAN & MULL

Oban
POP 8120

Oban is a peaceful waterfront town on a delightful bay, with sweeping views to Kerrera and Mull. OK, that first bit about peaceful is true only in winter; in summer the town centre is a heaving mass of humanity, its streets jammed with traffic and crowded with holiday-makers, day trippers and travellers headed for the islands. But the setting is still lovely.

There's not a huge amount to see in the town itself, but it's an appealingly busy place with some excellent restaurants and lively pubs, and it's the main gateway to the islands of Mull, Iona, Colonsay, Barra, Coll and Tiree.

◉ Sights

McCaig's Tower   HISTORIC BUILDING
(cnr Laurel & Duncraggan Rds; ⊙24hr) Crowning the hill above the town centre is the Victorian folly known as McCaig's Tower. Its construction was commissioned in 1890 by local worthy John Stuart McCaig, an art critic, philosophical essayist and banker, with the philanthropic intention of providing work for unemployed stonemasons.

To reach it on foot, make the steep climb up Jacob's Ladder (a flight of stairs) from Argyll St and then follow the signs. The views over the bay are worth the effort.

Oban Distillery   DISTILLERY
(✓01631-572004; www.discovering-distilleries.com; Stafford St; tour £7; ⊙9.30am-5pm Mon-Sat Easter-Oct, plus noon-5pm Sun Jul-Sep, closed Sat & Sun Nov-Dec & Feb-Easter, closed Jan) This distillery has been producing Oban single malt whisky since 1794. There are guided tours available (last tour begins one hour before closing time), but even without a tour, it's still worth a look at the small exhibition in the foyer.

FREE **War & Peace Museum**   MUSEUM
(✓01631-570007; www.obanmuseum.org.uk; Corran Esplanade; ⊙10am-6pm Mon-Sat, to 4pm Sun

May-Sep, to 4pm daily Mar, Apr, Oct & Nov) Military buffs will enjoy the little War & Peace Museum, which chronicles Oban's role in WWII as a base for Catalina seaplanes and as a marshalling area for Atlantic convoys.

Dunollie Castle & 1745 House CASTLE
(☑01631-570550; www.dunollie.org; Dunollie Rd; adult/child £3/free; ◷11am-4pm Tue-Sat, 1-4pm Sun) A pleasant 1-mile stroll along the coast road north of Corran Esplanade leads to Dunollie Castle, built by the MacDougalls of Lorn in the 13th century and unsuccessfully besieged for a year during the 1715 Jacobite rebellion. It's very much a ruin, but the nearby 1745 House – the seat of Clan MacDougall – is now a fascinating museum of local and clan history.

Pulpit Hill VIEWPOINT
An excellent viewpoint to the south of Oban Bay; the footpath to the summit starts to the right of Maridon House B&B on Dunuaran Rd.

🏃 Activities

A tourist-office leaflet lists local **bike rides**, which include a 7-mile Gallanach circular tour, a 16-mile route to the Isle of Seil and routes to Connel, Glenlonan and Kilmore. You can hire mountain bikes from Nevis Cycles (☑01631-566033; www.neviscycles.com; 87 George St; per day/half-day £20/12; ◷10am-5.30pm Tue-Sat).

Sea Kayak Oban (☑01631-565310; www.seakayakoban.com; Argyll St; ◷9am-5pm Mon, Tue, Sat & Sun, 10am-5pm Wed & Fri) has a well-stocked shop, and offers **sea-kayaking** courses, including a two-day intro for beginners (£160 per person). Also provides full equipment rental for experienced paddlers – you can trolley your kayak from the shop to the ferry terminal (kayaks carried free) to visit any of the islands.

Based at North Connel, sea-kayaking coach Rowland Woollven (☑01631-710417; www.rwoollven.co.uk) offers instruction for beginners and guided tours (£100 for a full day for one person, £60 per person for two or three people) for more experienced paddlers in the waters around Oban.

If you fancy exploring the underwater world, Puffin Adventures (☑01631-566088; www.puffin.org.uk; Port Gallanach) offers a 1½-hour **Try-a-Dive** package (£69) for complete beginners.

Various operators offer **boat trips** to spot seals and other marine wildlife, departing

Oban

from the North Pier slipway (adult/child £8/5.50); ask for details at the tourist office.

☞ Tours

City Sightseeing Oban BUS TOUR
(citysightseeingglasgow.co.uk/oban/oban.html; per person £8; ◷departs 11am & 2pm late May–late Sep) This 2½-hour open-top bus tour takes a spin around town before heading north to see the Falls of Lora, then south to the Isle of Seil and Easdale. It departs from the bus stop outside the train station. Ticket is valid 24 hours and can be used on all West Coast Motors buses (eg to Kilmartin and Lochgilphead).

Bowman's Tours BUS TOUR
(☑01631-566809; www.bowmanstours.co.uk; 1 Queens Park Pl) From April to October, Bowman's offers a Three Isles day trip (adult/child £55/27.50, 10 hours, daily) from Oban that visits Mull, Iona and Staffa. Note that

Oban

the crossing to Staffa is weather dependent. Bowman's also runs a circular coach tour around Mull (adult/child £20/10).

★ Festivals & Events

West Highland Yachting Week   SAILING
(☎01631-563309; www.whyw.co.uk) At the end of July/beginning of August, Oban becomes the focus of one of Scotland's biggest yachting events. Hundreds of yachts cram into the harbour and the town's bars are jammed with thirsty sailors.

Argyllshire Gathering   HIGHLAND GAMES
(☎01631-562671; www.obangames.com; adult/child £10/5) Held over two days in late August, this is one of the most important events on the Scottish highland-games calendar and includes a prestigious pipe-band competition. The main games are held at Mossfield Park on the eastern edge of town.

⌂ Sleeping

Despite having lots of B&B accommodation, Oban's beds can still fill up quickly in July and August so try to book ahead. If you can't find a bed in Oban, consider staying at Connel, 4 miles to the north.

Barriemore Hotel   B&B ££
(☎01631-566356; www.barriemore-hotel.co.uk; Corran Esplanade; s/d from £70/99; [P][❄]) The Barriemore enjoys a grand location, overlooking the entrance to Oban Bay. There are 13 spacious rooms here (ask for one with a sea view), plus a guest lounge with maga-

zines and newspapers, and plump Loch Fyne kippers on the breakfast menu.

Heatherfield House   B&B ££
(☎01631-562806; www.heatherfieldhouse.co.uk; Albert Rd; s/d from £38/88; [P][@][❄]) The welcoming Heatherfield House occupies a converted 1870s rectory set in extensive grounds and has six spacious rooms. If possible, ask for room 1, which comes complete with fireplace, sofa and a view over the garden to the harbour.

Kilchrenan House   B&B ££
(☎01631-562663; www.kilchrenanhouse.co.uk; Corran Esplanade; s/d £50/90; [P]) You'll get a warm welcome at the Kilchrenan, an elegant Victorian villa built for a textile magnate in 1883. Most of the rooms have views across Oban Bay, but rooms 5 and 9 are the best: room 5 has a huge freestanding bath tub, perfect for soaking weary bones.

Old Manse Guest House   B&B ££
(☎01631-564886; www.obanguesthouse.co.uk; Dalriach Rd; s/d from £65/80; [P][❄]) Set on a hillside above the town, the Old Manse commands great views over to Kerrera and Mull. The sunny, brightly decorated bedrooms have some nice touches (a couple of wine glasses and a corkscrew), and kids are made welcome with *Balamory* books, toys and DVDs.

Manor House   HOTEL £££
(☎01631-562087; www.manorhouseoban.com; Gallanach Rd; r £165-225; [P][❄]) Built in 1780 for the

Duke of Argyll as part of his Oban estates, the Manor House is now one of Oban's finest hotels. It has small but elegant Georgian-style rooms, a posh bar frequented by local and visiting yachties, and a fine restaurant serving Scottish and French cuisine. Children under 12 years are not welcome.

Kathmore Guest House
B&B **££**

(☑01631-562104; www.kathmore.co.uk; Soroba Rd; s £45-65, d £55-75; P☎) Warm and welcoming, the Kathmore combines traditional Highland hospitality and hearty breakfasts with a wee touch of boutique flair in its stylish bedspreads and colourful artwork. There's a comfortable lounge and outdoor deck where you can enjoy a pre- or post-prandial glass of wine on those long summer evenings.

Oban Backpackers Plus
HOSTEL **£**

(☑01631-567189; www.backpackersplus.com; Breadalbane St; dm/tw £20/49; @☎) This is a friendly place with a good vibe and a large and attractive communal lounge with lots of sofas and armchairs. Buffet breakfast is included in the price, plus there's free tea and coffee, a laundry service (£2.50) and powerful showers. Private rooms available in a separate building just around the corner.

Oban Caravan & Camping Park
CAMPSITE **£**

(☑01631-562425; www.obancaravanpark.com; Gallanachmore Farm; tent/campervan sites £15/17; ☉Apr-Oct; ☎) This spacious campground has a superb location overlooking the Sound of Kerrera, 2.5 miles south of Oban (bus twice a day). The quoted rate includes up to two people and a car; extra people stay for £2 each. A one-person tent with no car is £8. No prebooking – it's first-come, first-served.

Oban SYHA
HOSTEL **£**

(☑01631-562025; www.syha.org.uk; Corran Esplanade; dm/tw £19.50/46; P@☎) Oban's SYHA hostel is set in a grand Victorian villa on the Esplanade, 0.75 miles north of the train station. It was recently refurbished to a high standard with comfy wooden bunks, good showers and a lounge with great views across Oban Bay. The neighbouring lodge has three- and four-bedded rooms with en suite bathrooms.

Sand Villa Guest House
B&B **££**

(☑01631-562803; www.holidayoban.co.uk; Breadalbane St; r per person £28-33; P☎) Smart and stylish bedrooms. No credit cards.

Roseneath Guest House
B&B **££**

(☑01631-562929; www.roseneathoban.com; Dalriach Rd; s/d £45/74; P) Peaceful location with sea views.

Jeremy Inglis Hostel
HOSTEL **£**

(☑01631-565065; www.jeremyinglishostel.co.uk; 21 Airds Cres; dm/s from £15/22; ☎) More of an eccentric B&B than a hostel – most 'dorms' have only two or three beds, and are decorated with original artwork, books, flowers and cuddly toys.

✖ Eating

TOP CHOICE Waterfront Fishouse Restaurant
SEAFOOD **££**

(☑01631-563110; www.waterfrontoban.co.uk; Railway Pier; mains £11-20; ☉lunch & dinner; ☛) Housed on the top floor of a converted seamen's mission, the Waterfront's stylish, unfussy decor in burgundy and brown, with dark wooden furniture, does little to distract from the superb seafood freshly hauled ashore at the quay just a few metres away. The menu ranges from classic haddock and chips to fresh oysters, scallops and langoustines.

The lunch and early evening menu (5.30pm to 6.45pm) offers two courses for £10. Best to book for dinner.

TOP CHOICE Shellfish Bar
SEAFOOD **£**

(Railway Pier; mains £3-13; ☉9am-6pm) If you want to savour superb Scottish seafood without the expense of an upmarket restaurant, head for Oban's famous seafood stall – it's the green shack on the quayside near the ferry terminal. Here you can buy fresh and cooked seafood to take away – excellent prawn sandwiches (£2.95), dressed crab (£4.95) and fresh oysters for only 75p each.

Seafood Temple
SEAFOOD **£££**

(☑01631-566000; www.obanseafood.com; Gallanach Rd; mains £16-35; ☉lunch & dinner) Locally sourced seafood is the god that's worshipped at this tiny temple – a former park pavilion with glorious views over the bay. Oban's smallest restaurant serves up whole lobster cooked to order, baked crab with cheese and herb crust, plump langoustines and the 'Taste of Argyll' seafood platter (£70 for two people), which offers a taste of everything. Dinner is in two sittings, at 6.15pm and 8.30pm; bookings essential.

Cuan Mor   BISTRO ££
(☑01631-565078; www.cuanmor.co.uk; 60 George St; mains £9-14; ☺10am-midnight; 🛜🍴) This always-busy bar and bistro brews its own beer, and sports a no-nonsense menu of old favourites – from haddock and chips or homemade lasagne to sausage and mash with onion gravy – spiced with a few more-sophisticated dishes such as squat lobster carbonara, and a decent range of vegetarian dishes. And the sticky toffee pudding is not to be missed!

🖈 Ee'usk   SEAFOOD ££
(☑01631-565666; www.eeusk.com; North Pier; mains £13-20; ☺lunch & dinner) Bright and modern Ee'usk (it's how you pronounce *iasg*, the Gaelic word for 'fish') occupies Oban's prime location on the North Pier. Floor-to-ceiling windows allow diners on two levels to enjoy views over the harbour to Kerrera and Mull, while sampling a menu of locally caught seafood ranging from fragrant Thai fish cakes to langoustines with chilli and ginger.

A little pricey, perhaps, but both food and location are first class.

🖈 Waypoint Bar & Grill   SEAFOOD ££
(☑07840 650669; www.obanmarina.com; Oban Marina, Isle of Kerrera; mains £9-18; ☺lunch & dinner May-Sep) Join the yachting set for rustic, alfresco dining on the Isle of Kerrera, where a combination of wooden cabin, marquee and outdoor seating area offers the chance to feast on island-grown oysters and locally caught langoustines and scallops with a view back across the bay to Oban. A passenger ferry (p302) shuttles back and forth from Oban's North Pier to the marina.

Kitchen Garden   CAFE £
(☑01631-566332; www.kitchengardenoban.co.uk; 14 George St; mains £5-8; ☺9am-5.30pm Mon-Sat, 10am-4.30pm Sun) A deli packed with delicious picnic food. Also has a great little cafe above the shop – good coffee, scones, cakes, homemade soups and sandwiches.

Room 9   BISTRO ££
(☑01631-664200; www.room9oban.co.uk; 9 Craigard Rd; mains £14-17; ☺lunch & dinner) Highly rated local bistro that offers an alternative to seafood (though seafood is also on the menu), with excellent beef and chicken dishes.

Julie's Tearooms   CAFE £
(☑01631-565952; 37 Stafford St; mains £4-10; ☺10am-5pm Tue-Sat) Tea and scones, delicious Luca's ice cream and homemade soup with crusty bread.

Tesco   SUPERMARKET
(Lochside St; ☺8am-10pm Mon-Sat, 9am-6pm Sun) Self-caterers and campers can stock up here.

🍷 Drinking

Oban Chocolate Company   CAFE
(☑01631-566099; www.obanchocolate.co.uk; 34 Corran Esplanade; ☺10am-5pm Mon-Sat, 12.30-4pm Sun Easter-Sep, shorter hr in winter, closed Jan; 🖨) This shop specialises in hand-crafted chocolates (you can watch them being made) and also has a cafe serving excellent coffee and hot chocolate (try the chilli chocolate for a kick in the tastebuds), with big leather sofas in a window with a view of the bay. Open to 9pm Thursday to Saturday in July and August.

Lorne Bar   PUB
(www.thelornebar.co.uk; Stevenson St; 🛜) A traditional pub with a lovely old island bar, the Lorne serves Deuchars IPA and local Oban Brewery real ales, as well as above-average pub grub. Food is served from noon to 9pm, and there's a trad music session every Wednesday from 10pm.

Aulay's Bar   PUB
(☑01631-562596; www.aulaysbar.com; 8 Airds Cres) An authentic Scottish pub, Aulay's is cosy and low-ceilinged, its walls covered with old photographs of Oban ferries and other ships. It pulls in a mixed crowd of locals and visitors with its warm atmosphere and wide range of malt whiskies.

❶ Information

Fancy That (☑01631-562996; 112 George St; internet per 20 min £1; ☺9.30am-7pm Mon-Sat, 10am-5pm Sun)

Lorn & Islands District General Hospital (☑01631-567500; Glengallan Rd) Southern end of town.

Main Post Office (☑01631-510450; Lochside St; ☺8am-6pm Mon-Sat, 10am-1pm Sun) Inside Tesco supermarket.

Tourist Office (☑01631-563122; www.oban. org.uk; 3 North Pier; ☺9am-7pm Mon-Sat, 10am-5pm Sun May-Sep, 9am-5.30pm Mon-Sat Oct-Apr)

❶ Getting There & Away

The bus, train and ferry terminals are all grouped conveniently together next to the harbour on the southern edge of the bay.

Boat

CalMac (www.calmac.co.uk) ferries link Oban with the islands of **Mull**, **Coll**, **Tiree**, **Lismore**, **Colonsay**, **Barra** and **Lochboisdale** (South Uist). See the relevant island entries for details. Information and reservations for all CalMac ferry services are available at the **ferry terminal** (☑01631-562244; Railway Pier; ◷9am-6pm Mar-Oct) near the train station. Ferries to the **Isle of Kerrera** depart from a separate jetty, about 2 miles southwest of Oban town centre, or you can use the Oban Marina passenger ferry (p302) from Oban's North Pier.

Bus

Scottish Citylink (www.citylink.co.uk) operates intercity coaches to Oban, while **West Coast Motors** (www.westcoastmotors.co.uk) runs local and regional services. The bus terminal is outside the train station.

Glasgow (via Inveraray and Arrochar) £18, three hours, four daily

Perth (via Tyndrum and Killin) £16, three hours, twice daily

Fort William (via Appin and Ballachulish) £9.40, 1½ hours, three daily Monday to Saturday

Lochgilphead (via Kilmartin) £5, 1¾ hours, four daily Monday to Friday, two on Saturday

Campbeltown (change at Inveraray) £19, four hours, three daily

Train

Oban is at the terminus of a scenic route that branches off the West Highland line at Crianlarich. The train isn't much use for travelling north from Oban – to reach Fort William requires a detour via Crianlarich (3¾ hours). Take the bus instead.

Glasgow £22, three hours, three daily

Tyndrum £10, one hour, three daily

ⓘ Getting Around

Bus

West Coast Motors (p302) bus 417 makes two loops from the train station – north to Ganavan Sands via Oban Youth Hostel and south to the Kerrera ferry and Oban Caravan & Camping Park (hourly Monday to Saturday).

Car

Hazelbank Motors (☑01631-566476; www.obancarhire.co.uk; Lynn Rd; ◷8.30am-5.30pm Mon-Sat) hires out small cars per day/week from £40/225 including VAT, insurance and CDW (Collision Damage Waiver).

Taxi

There's a taxi rank outside the train station. Otherwise, call **Oban Taxis** (☑01631-564666).

Around Oban

ISLE OF KERRERA
POP 40

Some of the best **walking** in the area is on the island of Kerrera, which faces Oban across the bay. There's a 6-mile circuit of the island (allow three hours), which follows tracks or paths (use Ordnance Survey map 49) and offers the chance to spot wildlife such as Soay sheep, wild goats, otters, golden eagles, peregrine falcons, seals and porpoises. At **Lower Gylen**, at the southern end of the island, there's a **ruined castle**.

Kerrera Bunkhouse (☑01631-570223; www.kerrerabunkhouse.co.uk; Lower Gylen; dm £15) is a charming seven-bed bothy in a converted 18th-century stable near Gylen Castle, a 2-mile walk south from the ferry (keep left at the fork just past the telephone box). Booking ahead is recommended. You can get snacks and light meals at the neighbouring Tea Garden (☑01631-570223; Lower Gylen; ◷10.30am-4.30pm Wed-Sun Apr-Oct).

There's a daily passenger ferry (☑01631-563665; www.kerrera-ferry.co.uk) to Kerrera from Gallanach, about 2 miles southwest of Oban town centre, along Gallanach Rd (adult/child return £5/2.50, bicycle free, 10 minutes). From Easter to October it runs half-hourly from 10.30am to 12.30pm and 2pm to 6pm daily, plus 8.45am Monday to Saturday. From November to Easter there are five or six crossings a day.

You can also reach the island via the Oban Marina passenger ferry (per person £3 return; ◷every 30 min, 8am-11pm May-Sep) from Oban's North Pier.

ISLE OF SEIL
POP 500

The small island of Seil, 10 miles southwest of Oban, is best known for its connection to the mainland – the so-called **Bridge over the Atlantic**, designed by Thomas Telford and opened in 1793. The graceful bridge has a single stone arch and spans the narrowest part of the tidal Clachan Sound.

On the west coast of the island is the pretty conservation village of **Ellanbeich**, with its whitewashed cottages. It was built to house workers at the local slate quarries, but the industry collapsed in 1881 when the sea broke into the main quarry pit – the flooded pit can still be seen. The Scottish Slate Islands Heritage Trust (☑01852-300449; www.slateislands.org.uk; admission free; ◷10.30am-1pm & 2-5pm Apr-Oct) displays fascinating old photographs illustrating life in the village in the 19th and early 20th centuries.

Coach tours flock to the Highland Arts Studio (☎01852-300273; www.highlandarts. co.uk; Ellenbeich; admission free; ☺9am-7pm Apr-Sep, to 5pm Oct-Mar), a crafts and gift shop and a shrine to the eccentric output of the late 'poet, artist and composer' C John Taylor. Please, try to keep a straight face.

Just offshore from Ellanbeich is the small island of **Easdale**, which has more old slate-workers' cottages and the interesting Easdale Island Folk Museum (☎01852-300370; www. easdalemuseum.org; adult/child £2.25/50p; ☺11am-4.30pm Apr-Oct, to 5pm Jul & Aug). The museum has displays about the slate industry and life on the islands in the 18th and 19th centuries. Climb to the top of the island (a 38m peak!) for a great view of the surrounding area.

Anyone who fancies their hand at ducks and drakes should try to attend the World Stone-Skimming Championships (www. stoneskimming.com), held each year in Easdale on the last Sunday in September.

A short ferry trip from the south end of Seil takes you to the neighbouring **Isle of Luing**, a quiet backwater that has no real sights but is ideal for wildlife walks and easy-going bike rides.

BOAT TRIPS

From April to October Sea.fari Adventures (☎01852-300003; www.seafari.co.uk; Easdale Harbour; ☺Apr-Oct) runs exciting boat trips in high-speed rigid inflatable boats (RIBs) to the **Corryvreckan Whirlpool** (adult/child £38/29; call for the dates of 'Whirlpool Specials', when the tide is at its strongest) and the remote **Garvellach Islands** (£48/36). There are also 2½-hour **whale-watching trips** (£48/36), mostly in July and August, cruises to **Iona and Staffa** (£75/55) and a weekly day trip to **Colonsay** (£48/36).

Sea Life Adventures (☎01631-571010; www. sealife-adventures.co.uk) offers similar trips, but is based on the eastern side of the island and has a bigger, more comfortable boat.

ⓘ Getting There & Around

West Coast Motors (www.westcoastmotors. co.uk) bus 418 runs four times a day, except Sunday, from Oban to Ellanbeich (45 minutes) and on to North Cuan (one hour) for the **ferry** (☺per person/car £1.75/7 return, three minutes, every 30 minutes) to Luing.

Argyll & Bute Council (☎01631-562125) operates the daily passenger-only ferry service from Ellanbeich to Easdale island (£1.75 return, bicycles free, five minutes, every 30 minutes).

Isle of Mull

pop 2600

From the rugged ridges of Ben More and the black basalt crags of Burg to the blinding white sand, rose-pink granite and emerald waters that fringe the Ross, Mull can lay claim to some of the finest and most varied scenery in the Inner Hebrides, while the waters to the west of the island provide some of the best whale-spotting opportunities in Scotland. Add in two impressive castles, a narrow-gauge railway, the sacred island of Iona and easy access from Oban and you can see why it's sometimes impossible to find a spare bed on the island.

Despite the number of visitors who flock to the island, it seems to be large enough to absorb them all; many stick to the well-worn routes from Craignure to Iona or Tobermory, returning to Oban in the evening. Besides, there are plenty of hidden corners where you can get away from the crowds.

About two-thirds of Mull's population lives in and around Tobermory, the island's capital, in the north. Craignure, at the south-eastern corner, has the main ferry terminal and is where most people arrive. Fionnphort is at the far-western end of the long Ross of Mull peninsula, and is where the ferry to Iona departs.

☞ Tours

Bowman's Tours (☎01680-812313; www.bow manstours.co.uk) does day trips from Oban to Mull, Staffa and Iona by ferry and bus.

Gordon Grant Marine   BOAT TOURS (☎01681-700388; www.staffatours.com) Runs boat trips from Fionnphort to Staffa (adult/child £25/10, 2½ hours, daily April to October), and to Staffa and the Treshnish Isles (£45/20, five hours, Sunday to Friday May to July).

Mull Magic   WALKING TOURS (☎01688-301245; www.mullmagic.com) Offers guided walking tours in the Mull country-side (£37.50 to £47.50 per person) to spot eagles, otters, butterflies and other wildlife, as well as customised tours.

🎄 Festivals & Events

Mishnish Music Festival   MUSIC (☎01688-302383; www.mishnish.co.uk) Last weekend of April; three days of foot-stomping traditional Scottish and Irish folk music at Tobermory's favourite pub.

Mull, Coll & Tiree

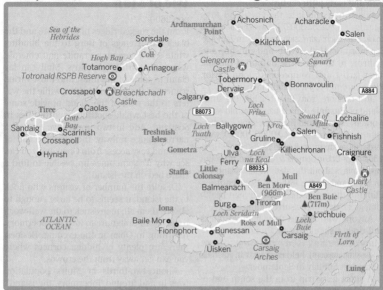

Mendelssohn on Mull
MUSIC

(www.mullfest.org.uk) A week-long festival of classical music in early July.

Mull Highland Games
HIGHLAND GAMES

(☏01688-302270; f.kirsop18@btinternet.com) Third Thursday in July; piping, highland dancing etc.

Tour of Mull Rally
CAR RALLY

(☏01254-826564; www.2300club.org) Part of the Scottish Rally Championship, with around 150 cars involved. Public roads are closed for parts of the early-October weekend.

ℹ Information

MEDICAL Dunaros Hospital (☏01680-300392) Has a minor injuries unit; the nearest casualty department is in Oban.

MONEY You can get cash using a debit card from the post offices in Salen and Craignure, or get cash back with a purchase from Co-op food stores.

Clydesdale Bank (Main St; ⊙9.15am-4.45pm Mon-Fri) The island's only bank and 24-hour ATM. No foreign exchange – you can change money at Tobermory tourist office.

POST Post Office (Main St; ⊙9am-1pm & 2-5.30pm Mon, Tue, Thu & Fri, 9am-1pm Wed & Sat) There are also post-office counters in Salen, Craignure and Fionnphort.

TOURIST INFORMATION Craignure Tourist Office (☏01680-812377; ⊙8.30am-5pm Mon-Sat, 10.30am-5pm Sun)

Mull Visitor & Information Centre (☏01688-302875; Ledaig, Tobermory; ⊙9am-5pm)

ℹ Getting There & Away

There are three **CalMac** (www.calmac.co.uk) car ferries linking Mull with the mainland.

Oban to Craignure (passenger/car £5.25/46.50, 40 minutes, every two hours) The shortest and busiest route – booking advised for cars.

Lochaline to Fishnish (£3.10/13.65, 15 minutes, at least hourly) On the east coast of Mull.

Tobermory to Kilchoan (£5/25.50, 35 minutes, seven daily Monday to Saturday) Links to the Ardnamurchan peninsula; from May to August there are also five sailings on Sunday.

ℹ Getting Around

BICYCLE You can hire bikes for around £10 to £15 per day from the following places.

Brown's Hardware Shop (☏01688-302020; www.brownstobermory.co.uk; Main St, Tobermory)

On Yer Bike (☏01680-300501; Salen) Easter to October only. Also has an outlet by the ferry terminal at Craignure.

BUS Public transport on Mull is fairly limited. Bowman's Tours (p303) is the main operator, connecting the ferry ports and the island's main villages.

Craignure to Tobermory (£7.30 return, one hour, four to seven daily Monday to Friday, three to five Saturday and Sunday)

Craignure to Fionnphort (£11 return, 1¼ hours, three daily Monday to Saturday, one Sunday)

Tobermory to Dervaig and Calgary (£4 return, three daily Monday to Friday, two on Saturday)

CAR Almost all of Mull's road network consists of single-track roads. There are petrol stations at Craignure, Fionnphort, Salen and Tobermory. **Mull Self Drive** (☎01680-300402; www.mull selfdrive.co.uk) rents small cars for £45/237 per day/week.

TAXI **Mull Taxi** (☎07760-426351; www.mull taxi.co.uk) is based in Tobermory, and has a vehicle that is wheelchair accessible.

CRAIGNURE & AROUND

There's not much to see at Craignure other than the ferry terminal and the hotel, so turn left and drive or cycle the 3 miles to Duart Castle (☎01680-812309; www.duartcastle.com; adult/child £5.50/2.75; ☉10.30am-5.30pm daily May–mid-Oct, 11am-4pm Sun-Thu Apr), a formidable fortress dominating the Sound of Mull (you can't miss it as you approach Craignure by ferry). The seat of the Clan Maclean, this is one of the oldest inhabited castles in Scotland – the central keep was built in 1360. It was bought and restored in 1911 by Sir Fitzroy Maclean and has damp dungeons, vast halls and bathrooms equipped with ancient fittings. A bus to the castle meets the 9.50am, 11.55am and 2pm ferries from Oban to Craignure.

On the way to Duart you'll pass Wings Over Mull (☎01680-812594; www.wingsovermull. com; Torosay; adult/child £4.50/1.50; ☉10.30am-5.30am Easter-Oct), a wildlife centre dedicated to birds of prey. The captive collection

WALKING ON MULL

More information on the following walks can be obtained from the tourist offices in Oban, Craignure and Tobermory.

Ben More

The highest peak on the island, and the only island Munro outside Skye, Ben More (966m) offers spectacular views of the surrounding islands. A trail leads up the mountain from Loch na Keal, by the bridge on the B8035 over the Abhainn na h-Uamha (the river is 8 miles southwest of Salen – see Ordnance Survey (OS) 1:50,000 map sheet 49, grid reference 507368). Return the same way or continue down the narrow ridge to the eastern top, A'Chioch, then descend to the road via Gleann na Beinn Fhada. The glen can be rather wet and there's not much of a path. The return trip is 6.5 miles; allow five to six hours.

Carsaig Arches

One of the most adventurous walks on Mull is along the coast west of Carsaig Bay to the natural rock formation of Carsaig Arches at Malcolm's Point. There's a good path below the cliffs most of the way from Carsaig, but it becomes a bit rough and exposed near the arches – the route climbs and then traverses a very steep slope above a vertical drop into the sea (not for the unfit or faint-hearted). You'll see spectacular rock formations on the way, culminating in the arches themselves. One, nicknamed the 'keyhole', is a freestanding rock stack; the other, the 'tunnel', is a huge natural arch. The western entrance is hung with curtains of columnar basalt – an impressive place. The return trip is 8 miles – allow three to four hours' walking time from Carsaig plus at least an hour at the arches.

Burg

At the tip of the remote Ardmeanach peninsula in western Mull there is a remarkable 50-million-year-old fossil tree preserved in the basalt lava flows of the cliffs. A 4WD track leads 4.5 miles from a parking area 400m beyond Tiroran House to a cottage at Burg; the last 2.5 miles to the tree is on a very rough coastal path. About 500m before the tree, a metal ladder allows you to climb down to the foreshore, which is only accessible at low tide – check tide times at Tobermory tourist office before setting off. Allow six to seven hours for the strenuous 14-mile round trip.

WATCHING WILDLIFE ON MULL

Mull's varied landscapes and habitats, from high mountains and wild moorland to wave-lashed sea cliffs, sandy beaches and seaweed-fringed skerries, offer the chance to spot some of Scotland's rarest and most dramatic wildlife, including eagles, otters, dolphins and whales.

Mull Wildlife Expeditions (☎01688-500121; www.torrbuan.com; null) offers full-day Land Rover tours of the island with the chance of spotting red deer, golden eagles, peregrine falcons, white-tailed sea eagles, hen harriers, otters and perhaps dolphins and porpoises. The cost (adult/child £43/40) includes pick-up from your accommodation or from any of the ferry terminals, a picnic lunch and use of binoculars. The timing of this tour makes it possible as a day-trip from Oban, with pick-up and drop-off at the Craignure ferry.

Sea Life Surveys (☎01688-302916; www.sealifesurveys.com; Ledaig) runs whale-watching trips from Tobermory harbour to the waters north and west of Mull. An all-day whale-watch (per person £80) gives up to seven hours at sea (not recommended for kids under 14), and has a 95% success rate for sightings. The four-hour Wildlife Adventure cruise is geared more towards children (£50/40 per adult/child).

Turus Mara (☎08000 85 87 86; www.turusmara.com) runs boat trips from Ulva Ferry in central Mull to Staffa and the Treshnish Isles (adult/child £50/25, 6½ hours), with an hour ashore on Staffa and two hours on Lunga, where you can see seals, puffins, kittiwakes, razorbills and many other species of seabird.

The RSPB (☎01680-812556; www.forestry.gov.uk/mullseaeagles) run escorted trips to a viewing hide in Glen Seilisdeir where you can watch white-tailed sea eagles. Tours (adult/child £6/3) leave at 10am and 1pm Monday to Friday, from the B8035 road about 1 mile north of Tiroran (advance booking essential, by phone or at the Craignure tourist office).

includes more than two dozen species, and there are daily displays of falconry and hawk handling.

🛌 Sleeping

To **camp** within walking distance of the ferry, turn left and walk south for five minutes to Shieling Holidays (☎01680-812496; www.shielingholidays.co.uk; tent site & 2 people £14.50, with car £17, dm £13; ⊘mid Mar-Oct; 🖥from Oban-Craignure), a well-equipped campsite with great views. Most of the permanent accommodation, including the hostel dorms and toilet block (dribbly showers), consists of 'cottage tents' made from heavy-duty tarpaulin, which gives the place a bit of a PVC-fetish feel.

Recommended B&Bs within 10 minutes' walk of the ferry include Pennygate Lodge (☎01680-812333; www.pennygatelodge.com; Craignure; s/d from £50/70; 🅿🛜), next to the Shieling Holidays entrance, and Dee-Emm B&B (☎01680-812440; www.dee-emm.co.uk; s/d £50/72; 🅿), a half-mile south of Craignure on the road towards Fionnphort.

TOBERMORY

POP 750

Tobermory, the island's main town, is a picturesque little fishing port and yacht-ing centre with brightly painted houses arranged around a sheltered harbour, with a grid-patterned 'upper town'. The village was the setting for the children's TV program *Balamory*, and while the series stopped filming in 2005 regular repeats mean that the town still swarms in summer with toddlers towing parents around looking for their favourite TV characters (frazzled parents can get a *Balamory* booklet from the tourist offices in Oban and Tobermory).

👁 Sights & Activities

The Hebridean Whale & Dolphin Trust's Marine Discovery Centre (☎01688-302620; www.whaledolphintrust.co.uk; 28 Main St; admission free; ⊘10am-5pm Mon-Fri, 11am-4pm Sun Apr-Oct, 11am-5pm Mon-Fri Nov-Mar) has displays, videos and interactive exhibits on whale and dolphin biology and ecology, and is a great place for kids to learn about sea mammals. It also provides information about volunteering and reporting sightings of whales and dolphins.

Sea Life Surveys (p306), based in the harbour building beside the main car park, runs whale-watching boat trips out of Tobermory harbour. At the time of research, the harbour building was undergoing reconstruction to house a new **marine educa-**

tion centre, with live tanks and interactive displays on fishing, fish-farming, diving and whale-watching.

Places to go on a rainy day include Mull Museum (01688-302603; www.mullmuseum.org.uk; Main St; admission by donation; 10am-4pm Mon-Fri Easter-Oct), which records the history of the island. There are interesting exhibits on crofting, and on the *Tobermory Galleon*, a ship from the Spanish Armada that sank in Tobermory Bay in 1588 and has been the object of treasure seekers ever since.

There's also An Tobar Arts Centre (01688-302211; www.antobar.co.uk; Argyll Tce; admission free; 10am-5pm Mon-Sat May-Sep, plus 2-5pm Sun Jul & Aug, 10am-4pm Tue-Sat Oct-Apr), an art gallery and exhibition space with a good vegetarian-friendly cafe and the tiny Tobermory Distillery (01688-302647; www.tobermorymalt.com; Ledaig; tour £3; 10am-5pm Mon-Fri Easter-Oct), established in 1798.

🛏 **Sleeping**

Tobermory has dozens of B&Bs, but the place can still be booked solid in July and August, especially at weekends.

TOP CHOICE Highland Cottage Hotel   BOUTIQUE HOTEL **£££**
(01688-302030; www.highlandcottage.co.uk; Breadalbane St; d £150-165; mid-Mar–Oct; P) Antique furniture, four-poster beds, embroidered bedspreads, fresh flowers and candlelight lend this small hotel (only six rooms) an appealingly old-fashioned cottage atmosphere, but with all mod cons including cable TV, full-size baths and room service. There's also an excellent fine-dining restaurant here.

Sonas House   B&B **££**
(01688-302304; www.sonashouse.co.uk; The Fairways, Erray Rd; s/d £110/125, apt from £90; P) Here's a first – a B&B with a heated, indoor 10m swimming pool! Sonas is a large, modern house that offers luxury B&B in a beautiful setting with superb views over Tobermory Bay; ask for the 'Blue Poppy' bedroom, which has its own balcony. There's also a self-contained studio apartment with double bed.

Cuidhe Leathain   B&B **££**
(01688-302504; www.cuidhe-leathain.co.uk; Salen Rd; r per person £40;) A handsome 19th-century house in the upper town, Cuidhe Leathain (coo-lane), which means Maclean's Corner, exudes a cosily cluttered Victorian atmosphere. The breakfasts will set you up for the rest of the day, and the owners are a fount of knowledge about Mull and its wildlife. Minimum two-night stay.

Harbour View   B&B **££**
(01688-301111; www.tobermorybandb.com; 1 Argyll Tce; per person £40-45;) This beautifully renovated fisherman's cottage is perched on the edge of Tobermory's 'upper town'. Exposed patches of original stone walls add a touch of character, while a new extension provides the family suite (two adjoining rooms with shared bathroom, sleeps four)

THAR SHE BLOWS!

The North Atlantic Drift – a swirling tendril of the Gulf Stream – carries warm water into the cold, nutrient-rich seas off the Scottish coast, resulting in huge blooms of plankton. Small fish feed on the plankton, and bigger fish feed on the smaller fish, and this huge seafood smorgasbord attracts large numbers of marine mammals, from harbour porpoises and dolphins to minke whales and even – though sightings are rare – humpback and sperm whales.

Scotland has cashed in on the abundance of minke whales off its coast by embracing **whale-watching**. There are now dozens of operators around the coast offering whale-watching boat trips lasting from a couple of hours to all day; some have whale-sighting success rates of 95% in summer.

While seals, porpoises and dolphins can be seen year-round, minke whales are migratory. The best time to see them is from June to August, with August being the peak month for sightings. The website of the Hebridean Whale & Dolphin Trust (www.whaledolphintrust.co.uk) has lots of information on the species you are likely to see, and how to identify them.

A booklet titled *Is It a Whale?* is available from tourist offices and bookshops, and provides tips on identifying the various species of marine mammal that you're likely to see.

with an outdoor terrace that enjoys breathtaking views across the harbour.

Tobermory Campsite CAMPSITE £
(☎01688-302624; www.tobermorycampsite.co.uk; Newdale, Dervaig Rd; tent sites per adult/child £7/3; ◷Mar-Oct) A quiet, family-friendly campground 1 mile west of town on the road to Dervaig. Credit/debit cards not accepted.

Tobermory SYHA HOSTEL £
(☎01688-302481; www.syha.org.uk; Main St; dm £17.50; ◷Mar-Oct; @🖢) Great location in a Victorian house right on the waterfront. Bookings recommended.

Eating & Drinking

Campers can stock up on provisions at the **Co-op supermarket** (33 Main St; ◷8am-8pm Mon-Sat, 12.30-7pm Sun), and the **Tobermory Bakery** (26 Main St; ◷9am-5pm Mon-Sat), which sells delicious, locally baked wholegrain bread, cakes, biscuits and pastries, as well as having a great deli counter.

Café Fish SEAFOOD ££
(☎01688-301253; www.thecafefish.com; The Pier; mains £10-22; ◷lunch & dinner) Seafood doesn't come much fresher than the stuff served at this warm and welcoming little restaurant overlooking Tobermory harbour – as its motto says, 'The only thing frozen here is the fisherman'! Langoustines and squat lobsters go straight from boat to kitchen to join rich Tuscan-style seafood stew, fat scallops, fish pie and catch-of-the-day on the daily-changing menu.

Also has freshly baked bread, homemade desserts and a range of Scottish cheeses on offer.

Fish & Chip Van FISH & CHIPS £
(☎01688-301109; www.tobermoryfishandchipvan.co.uk; Main St; mains £3-8; ◷12.30-9pm Mon-Sat Apr-Dec, plus Sun Jun-Sep, 12.30-7pm Mon-Sat Jan-Mar) If it's a takeaway you're after, you can tuck into some of Scotland's best gourmet fish and chips down on the waterfront. And where else will you find a chip van selling freshly cooked prawns and scallops?

MacGochan's PUB ££
(☎01688-302350; www.macgochans-tobermory.co.uk; Ledaig; mains £9-20; ◷lunch & dinner) A lively pub beside the car park at the southern end of the waterfront, MacGochan's does good bar meals (haddock and chips, steak pie, vegetable lasagne), and often has outdoor barbecues on summer evenings. There's a beer garden out front, and live music in the bar on weekends.

Mishnish Hotel PUB ££
(☎01688-302009; www.mishnish.co.uk; Main St; mains £11-20; ◷lunch & dinner; 🖢) 'The Mish' is a favourite hang-out for visiting yachties and a good place for a pint, or a meal at the pub's Mish-Dish restaurant. Wood-panelled and flag-draped, this is a good old traditional pub where you can listen to live folk music, toast your toes by the open fire, or challenge the locals to a game of pool.

Pier Café CAFE £
(The Pier; mains £5-8; ◷9am-5pm) A cosy wee corner with local art on the walls, tucked beneath Café Fish at the north end of the village, the Pier serves great coffee and breakfast rolls, plus tasty lunch dishes such as haddock and chips, lobster baguette, Malay peanut noodles and spicy Jamaican bean burger.

☆ Entertainment

Mull Theatre THEATRE
(☎01688-302828; www.mulltheatre.com; Salen Rd) One of Scotland's best-known touring companies, putting on shows all over Scotland. It is based at Druimfin, about a mile south of Tobermory, which is the venue for most of its Mull-based performances; check the website for details of the latest shows.

NORTH MULL

The road from Tobermory west to Calgary cuts inland, leaving most of the north coast of Mull wild and inaccessible. Just outside Tobermory a long, single-track road leads north for 4 miles to majestic **Glengorm Castle** (☎01688-302321; www.glengormcastle.co.uk; Glengorm; ◷10am-5pm Easter–mid-Oct) with views across the sea to Ardnamurchan, Rum and the Outer Hebrides. The castle outbuildings house an **art gallery** featuring the work of local artists, a **farm shop** selling local produce, and an excellent **coffee shop**. The castle itself is not open to the public, but you're free to explore the beautiful grounds.

The **Old Byre Heritage Centre** (☎01688-400229; www.old-byre.co.uk; Dervaig; adult/child £4/2; ◷10.30am-6.30pm Wed-Sun Apr-Oct) brings Mull's social and natural history to life through a series of tableaux and half-hour film shows. The prize for most bizarre exhibit goes to the 40cm-long model of a midge. The centre's tearoom serves good, inexpensive snacks, including homemade soup and clootie dumpling, and there's a kids' outdoor play area.

Mull's best (and busiest) silver-sand **beach**, flanked by cliffs and with views out to Coll and Tiree, is at **Calgary**, about 12 miles west of Tobermory. And yes – this is the place from which the more famous Calgary in Alberta, Canada, takes its name.

🛏 Sleeping & Eating

Achnadrish House APARTMENT **££**
(📞01688-400388; www.achnadrish.co.uk; Dervaig Rd; 1-bedroom apt per week £300, 3-bedroom apt per week £650; P 📶) Formerly a popular B&B, Achnadrish is a sympathetically restored shooting lodge that now offers self-catering accommodation in two units: the cute little one-bedroomed White Cabin (sleeps two), and the three-bedroom West Wing, a range of former servants' quarters, that sleeps six. Both have fully fitted kitchens, while the latter also has a large lounge with woodburning stove. The house is halfway between Tobermory and Calgary beach.

Calgary Farmhouse SELF-CATERING **££**
(📞01688-400256; www.calgary.co.uk; Calgary; 2-person apt per 3 nights £195; P 📶) This farmhouse complex offers eight fantastic self-catering properties (including apartments, cottages and a farmhouse, sleeping from two to eight people), beautifully designed and fitted out with timber furniture and woodburning stoves. The Hayloft (sleeps eight, £1200 a week in high season) includes a spectacular lounge/dining room with curved oak frames and locally produced art work.

Bellachroy HOTEL **££**
(📞01688-400314; www.bellachroyhotel.co.uk; Dervaig; s/d £75/100; P 📶) The Bellachroy is an atmospheric 17th-century droving inn with six plain but comfortable bedrooms. The bar is a focus for local social life and serves excellent meals (mains £11 to £19, plus kids' menu) based on fresh local produce: pork from a local Dervaig farm, lamb from Ulva, mutton from Iona, mussels from Inverlussa and Mull-landed seafood.

Dervaig Village Hall Hostel HOSTEL **£**
(📞01688-400491; www.mull-hostel-dervaig.co.uk; Dervaig; dm/q £15/55; P) Basic but very comfortable bunkhouse accommodation in Dervaig's village hall, with self-catering kitchen and sitting room.

FREE **Calgary Bay Campsite** CAMPSITE
(Calgary) You can camp for free at the southern end of the beach at Calgary Bay – keep to the area south of the stream. There are no facilities other than the public toilets across the road; water comes from the stream.

Glengorm Coffee Shop CAFE **£**
(www.glengormcastle.co.uk; Glengorm; mains £5-8; ⏰10am-5pm Easter-Oct) Set in a cottage courtyard in the grounds of Glengorm Castle, this cafe serves superb lunches (from noon to 4.30pm) – the menu changes daily, but includes sandwiches and salads (much of the salad veg is grown on the Glengorm estate), soups and specials such as curry-flavoured salmon fishcakes with mint and cucumber salad.

Calgary Farmhouse Tearoom CAFE **£**
(www.calgary.co.uk; mains £5-8; ⏰10.30am-4.30pm; P 📶) Just a few minutes' walk from the sandy beach at Calgary Bay, this tearoom serves soups, sandwiches, coffee and cake using fresh local produce as much as possible. There's also an art gallery and craft shop here. Open to 5.30pm in July and August.

CENTRAL MULL

The central part of the island, between the Craignure–Fionnphort road and the narrow isthmus between Salen and Gruline, contains the island's highest peak, **Ben More** (966m) and some of its wildest scenery.

The narrow B8035 road along the southern shore of Loch na Keal squeezes past some impressive cliffs before cutting south towards Loch Scridain. About 1 mile along the shore from Balmeanach, where the road climbs away from the coast, is **Mackinnon's Cave**, a deep and spooky fissure in the basalt cliffs that was once used as a refuge by Celtic monks. A big, flat rock inside, known as **Fingal's Table**, may have been their altar.

There's a very basic campsite (per person £3) at Killiechronan, 0.5 miles north of Gruline (toilets and water are a five-minute walk away), and plenty of **wild camping** on the south shore of Loch na Keal below Ben More.

SOUTH MULL

The road from Craignure to Fionnphort climbs through some wild and desolate scenery before reaching the southwestern part of the island, which consists of a long peninsula called the **Ross of Mull**. The Ross has a spectacular south coast lined with black basalt cliffs that give way further west to white-sand beaches and pink granite crags. The cliffs are highest at Malcolm's Point, near the superb **Carsaig Arches**.

The little village of **Bunessan** has a hotel, tearoom, pub and some shops, and is home to the Ross of Mull Historical Centre (☎01681-700659; www.romhc.org.uk; admission £2; ⊙10am-4pm Mon-Fri Easter-Oct), a cottage museum that houses displays on local history, geology, archaeology, genealogy and wildlife.

A minor road leads south from here to the beautiful white-sand bay of **Uisken**, with views of the Paps of Jura. You can camp beside the beach here (£1 per person; ask for permission at Uisken Croft), but there are no facilities.

At the western end of the Ross, 38 miles from Craignure, you'll find **Fionnphort** (*finn*-a-fort) and the ferry to Iona. The coast here is a beautiful blend of pink granite rocks, white sandy beaches and vivid turquoise sea.

Sleeping & Eating

TOP CHOICE Seaview B&B ££

(☎01681-700235; www.iona-bed-breakfast-mull.com; Fionnphort; d £70-80; P) Barely a minute's walk from the Iona ferry, the Seaview has five beautifully decorated bedrooms and a breakfast conservatory with grand views across to Iona. The owners – a semiretired fisherman and his wife – offer tasty three-course dinners (£23 per person, September to May only), often based around local seafood. Bike hire available for guests only.

Staffa House B&B ££

(☎01681-700677; www.staffahouse.co.uk; Fionnphort; s/d £53/76; P) This charming and hospitable B&B is packed with antiques and period features, and offers breakfast in a conservatory with a view of Iona. Solar panels top up the hot-water supply, and the hearty breakfasts and packed lunches (£6 to £8.50) make use of local and organic produce where possible.

Fidden Farm CAMPSITE £

(☎01681-700427; Fionnphort; tent sites per adult/child £6/3; ⊙Apr-Sep) A basic but beautifully situated campground, with views over pink granite reefs to Iona and Erraid. It's 1.25 miles south of Fionnphort.

Ninth Wave SEAFOOD £££

(☎01681-700757; www.ninthwaverestaurant.co.uk; Fionnphort; 4-course dinner £48; ⊙dinner Tue-Sun May-Oct) Based in a former croft 1 mile east of Fionnphort, this restaurant is owned and operated by a lobster fisherman and his Canadian wife. The daily menu makes use of locally landed shellfish and crustaceans, and vegetables and salad grown in the croft garden, served in a stylishly converted bothy. Advance booking essential.

Isle of Iona

POP 130

There are few more uplifting sights on Scotland's west coast than the view of Iona from Mull on a sunny day – an emerald island set in a sparkling turquoise sea. From the moment you step off the ferry you begin to appreciate the hushed, spiritual atmosphere that pervades this sacred island. Not surprisingly, Iona attracts a lot of day trippers, so if you want to experience the island's peace and quiet, the solution is to spend a night here. Once the crowds have gone for the day, you can wander in peace around the ancient graveyard where the early kings of Scotland are buried, attend an evening service at the abbey or walk to the top of Dun I and gaze south towards Ireland, as St Columba must have done so many centuries ago.

History

St Columba sailed from Ireland and landed on Iona in 563 before setting out to spread Christianity throughout Scotland. He established a monastery on the island and it was here that the *Book of Kells* – the prize attraction of Dublin's Trinity College – is believed to have been transcribed. It was taken to Kells in Ireland when Viking raids drove the monks from Iona.

The monks returned and the monastery prospered until its destruction during the Reformation. The ruins were given to the Church of Scotland in 1899, and by 1910 a group of enthusiasts called the Iona Community (www.iona.org.uk) had reconstructed the abbey. It's still a flourishing spiritual community that holds regular courses and retreats.

Sights & Activities

Head uphill from the ferry pier and turn right through the grounds of a ruined

WORTH A TRIP

ISLE OF STAFFA

Felix Mendelssohn, who visited the uninhabited island of Staffa in 1829, was inspired to compose his *Hebrides Overture* after hearing waves echoing in the impressive and cathedral-like **Fingal's Cave**. The cave walls and surrounding cliffs are composed of vertical, hexagonal basalt columns that look like pillars (Staffa is Norse for 'Pillar Island'). You can land on the island and walk into the cave via a causeway. Nearby **Boat Cave** can be seen from the causeway, but you can't reach it on foot. Staffa also has a sizable puffin colony, north of the landing place.

Northwest of Staffa lies a chain of uninhabited islands called the **Treshnish Isles**. The two main islands are the curiously shaped **Dutchman's Cap** and **Lunga**. You can land on Lunga, walk to the top of the hill and visit the shag, puffin and guillemot colonies on the west coast at **Harp Rock**.

Unless you have your own boat, the only way to reach Staffa and the Treshnish Isles is on an organised boat trip from Ulva, Fionnphort or Iona.

13th-century **nunnery** with fine cloistered gardens, and exit at the far end. Across the road is the Iona Heritage Centre (☑01681-700576; adult/child £2/free; ⊙10.30am-5pm Mon-Sat Apr-Oct), which covers the history of Iona, crofting and lighthouses; the centre's **coffee shop** serves delicious home baking.

Turn right here and continue along the road to **Reilig Oran**, an ancient cemetery that holds the graves of 48 of Scotland's early kings, including Macbeth, and a tiny Romanesque chapel. Beyond rises the spiritual heart of the island – Iona Abbey (HS; ☑01681-700512; adult/child £5.50/3.30; ⊙9.30am-5.30pm Apr-Sep, to 4.30pm Oct-Mar). The spectacular nave, dominated by Romanesque and early Gothic vaults and columns, contains the elaborate, white marble tombs of the 8th duke of Argyll and his wife. A door on the left leads to the beautiful Gothic cloister, where medieval grave slabs sit alongside modern religious sculptures. A replica of the intricately carved **St John's Cross** stands just outside the abbey – the massive 8th-century original is in the **Infirmary Museum** (around the far side of the abbey) along with many other fine examples of early Christian and medieval **carved stones**.

Continue past the abbey and look for a footpath on the left signposted **Dun I** (dunee). An easy walk of about 15 to 20 minutes leads to the highest point on Iona, with fantastic views in all directions.

Boat Trips

Alternative Boat Hire   BOAT TOUR
(☑01681-700537; www.boattripsiona.com; ⊙Mon-Thu Apr-Oct) Offers cruises in a traditional wooden sailing boat for fishing, birdwatch-

ing, picnicking or just drifting along admiring the scenery. Three-hour afternoon trips cost £20/9 per adult/child; on Wednesday there's a full day cruise (10am to 5pm, £40/18). Booking essential.

MV Iolaire   ISLAND TOUR
(☑01681-700358; www.staffatrips.co.uk) Three-hour boat trips to Staffa (adult/child £25/10), departing Iona pier at 9.45am and 1.45pm, and from Fionnphort at 10am and 2pm, with one hour ashore on Staffa.

MV Volante   WILDLIFE & FISHING TOURS
(☑01681-700362; www.volanteiona.com; ⊙Jun-Oct) Four-hour sea-angling trips (£50 per person including tackle and bait), as well as 1½-hour round-the-island wildlife cruises (adult/child £15/8) and 3½-hour whale-watching trips (per person £40).

🛏 Sleeping & Eating

TOP
CHOICE Argyll Hotel   HOTEL ££
(☑01681-700334; www.argyllhoteliona.co.uk; s/d from £66/99; ⊙Mar-Oct; @🐾) This cute little hotel has 16 snug rooms (a sea view costs rather a bit more – £140 for a double) and a country-house restaurant (☑01681-700334; www.argyllhoteliona.co.uk; mains £12-17; ⊙8-10am, 12.30-1.20pm & 7-8pm) with wooden fireplace and antique tables and chairs. The kitchen is supplied by a huge organic garden around the back, and the menu includes home-grown salads, local seafood and Scottish beef and lamb.

TOP
CHOICE Iona Hostel   HOSTEL £
(☑01681-700781; www.ionahostel.co.uk; dm per adult/child £20/17; ⊙check-in 4-7pm) This hostel

is set in an attractive, modern timber building on a working croft, with stunning views out to Staffa and the Treshnish Isles. Rooms are clean and functional, and the well-equipped lounge/kitchen area has an open fire. It's at the northern end of the island – to get here, continue along the road past the abbey for 1.5 miles (a 20- to 30-minute walk).

Tigh na Tobrach B&B £
(☏01861-700700; www.bandb-iona.co.uk; s/d £33/56) Comfortable B&B in modern house, with one family and one twin room. A short distance south of the ferry.

Cnoc-Oran Campsite CAMPSITE £
(☏01681-700112; www.ionaselfcateringaccommodation.co.uk; tent sites per adult/child £5/2.50; ☻Apr-Oct) Basic campsite about 1 mile west of the ferry.

Spar SUPERMARKET
(☻9am-5.30pm Mon-Sat, 11am-4.30pm Sun) Grocery store above the ferry slip.

❶ Information

To the left of the ferry slip **Finlay Ross Ltd** (www.finlayrossiona.co.uk; ☻9.30am-5pm Mon-Sat, 11.30am-4pm Sun) sells gifts, books and maps, hires out bikes and provides a laundry service.

POST There's a tiny post office on the right as you head uphill from the ferry.

TOURIST INFORMATION **Iona Community Council** (www.welcometoiona.com) There's no tourist office on the island, but a Community Council notice board at the top of the ferry slip lists accommodation and services.

❶ Getting There & Away

The passenger ferry from Fionnphort to Iona (£4.80 return, five minutes, hourly) runs daily. There are also various day trips available from Oban to Iona.

Isle of Tiree

POP 765

Low-lying Tiree (tye-ree; from the Gaelic tiriodh, meaning 'land of corn') is a fertile sward of lush, green machair liberally sprinkled with yellow buttercups, much of it so flat that, from a distance, the houses seem to rise out of the sea. It's one of the sunniest places in Scotland, but also one of the windiest – cyclists soon find that although it's flat, heading west usually feels like going uphill. One major benefit – the constant breeze keeps away the midges.

WHALE-WATCHING WISDOM: RUSSELL LEAPER

Russell Leaper works for the International Fund for Animal Welfare (IFAW), conducting scientific research to try and help reduce threats to whales around the world. He lives in Banavie, near Fort William.

How does Scotland's west coast compare in the league of world whale-watching spots? Rather like the weather, whale-watching in Scotland is less predictable than elsewhere. There is a good chance of seeing minke whales and harbour porpoises. Bottlenose and common dolphins are also seen regularly, and there is a small chance of seeing several other species of whales and dolphins. Basking sharks are also often seen on whale-watching trips. The whale-watching season tends to run from April to September because of the weather (they're easier to spot in calm conditions) but the whales may be around longer than this.

Are whale and dolphin numbers in Scottish waters rising, falling, or staying the same? We only have rather approximate estimates of numbers for a few species and almost no information on trends. The numbers of animals close to the coast varies from year to year but we don't really know how this relates to overall numbers. Unfortunately, Norway still kills several hundred minke whales a year from the same population that is watched around Scotland.

How can visitors ensure that their whale-watching activity has minimal impact on the whales? Scottish Natural Heritage has developed the Scottish Marine Wildlife Watching Code (www.marinecode.org). These are simple, common-sense measures to minimise disturbance. Feedback from customers is probably the most effective way of ensuring that operators stick to the code. You can contribute to minimising impact by knowing the code and telling the boat operator if they are not respecting it.

The surf-lashed coastline here is scalloped with broad, sweeping beaches of white sand, hugely popular with windsurfers and kite-surfers. Most visitors, however, come for the birdwatching, beachcombing and lonely coastal walks.

◉ Sights

In the 19th century Tiree had a population of 4500, but poverty and overcrowding – plus food shortages following the potato famine of 1846 – led the landowner, the Duke of Argyll, to introduce a policy of assisted emigration. Between 1841 and 1881, more than 3600 people left the island, many of them emigrating to Canada, the USA, Australia and New Zealand.

An Iodhlann (☎01879-220793; www.an iodhlann.org.uk; Scarinish; admission free; ☺9am-5pm Mon-Fri) is a historical and genealogical library and archive, where many of the estimated 38,000 descendants of Tiree emigrants come to trace their ancestry. The centre stages a summer exhibition (adult/child £3/free; ☺11am-5pm Tue-Fri Jul-Sep) on island life and history.

The picturesque harbour and hamlet of **Hynish**, near the southern tip of the island, was built in the 19th century to house workers and supplies for the construction of the Skerryvore Lighthouse, which stands 10 miles offshore. Skerryvore Lighthouse Museum (☎01879-220726; www.hebrideantrust. org; Hynish; admission free; ☺9am-5pm) occupies the old workshops beside the harbour; up the hill is the signal tower which was once used to communicate by semaphore with the lighthouse site.

For the best view on the island, walk up nearby **Ben Hynish** (141m), which is capped by a conspicuous radar station known locally as the Golf Ball.

✦ Activities

Reliable wind and big waves have made Tiree one of Scotland's top windsurfing venues. The annual Tiree Wave Classic (www. tireewaveclassic.co.uk) competition is held here in October.

Wild Diamond Watersports (☎01879-220399; www.wilddiamond.co.uk; Cornaig), based at Loch Bhasapoll in the northwest of the island, runs courses in windsurfing, kitesurfing, sand-yachting and stand-up paddleboarding, and rents out equipment. Six hours' equipment hire costs from £50, and a beginner's course (six hours over two days) costs £100 including gear. Sand-yachting on Gott Bay beach at low tide is £25 per hour.

Tiree Kitesurf & Kayak (☎07711 807976) operates out of a beach hut on Gott Bay (below the Tiree Lodge Hotel), renting kayaks (per hour £15), bikes, kitesurf gear and fishing tackle.

🛏 Sleeping & Eating

Most of the accommodation on the island is self-catering, so make sure you have booked a bed or campsite before arriving.

Scarinish Hotel   HOTEL ££
(☎01879-220308; www.tireescarinishhotel.com; Scarinish; s/d from £58/80; [P]) There's hospitality on tap at the Scarinish, with enthusiastic owners who go out of their way to make you feel welcome. The building is looking a little tired these days, but the rooms are crisp and clean, and the **restaurant** (mains £9 to £19) and traditional lean-to bar have a cosy atmosphere.

Kirkapol House   B&B ££
(☎01879-220729; www.kirkapoltiree.co.uk; Kirkapol; s/d £37/70; [P]) Set in a converted 19th-century church overlooking the island's biggest beach, the Kirkapol has six homely rooms and a big lounge with a leather sofa. It's 2 miles north of the ferry terminal.

Ceabhar   COTTAGE ££
(☎01879-220684; www.ceabhar.com; Sandaig; per week £850; [P]🐾📶) This snug cottage has a fantastic location at the western end of the island, looking out over the Atlantic towards the sunset; it can sleep up to eight people in five bedrooms. The owners are outdoor enthusiasts and can advise on kite-surfing, power-kiting and scuba diving. There's also a restaurant (mains £9-15; ☺dinner Wed-Sat Easter-Oct, plus Tue Jul & Aug) in a sunny conservatory with sea views.

Millhouse Hostel   HOSTEL £
(☎01879-220435; www.tireemillhouse.co.uk; Cornaig; dm/s/tw £15/30/36; [P]) Housed in a converted barn next to an old water mill, this small but comfortable hostel is 5 miles west from the ferry pier.

Balinoe Croft Campsite   CAMPSITE £
(☎01879-220399; www.wilddiamond.co.uk; Balinoe; tent sites per person £10-12; 📶) A sheltered site with full facilities in the southwest of the island, near Balemartine, with great views of Mull.

Farmhouse Cafe CAFE £

(☑01879-220107; Balemartine; mains £4.50-6.50; ☺11am-3.30pm Mon-Sat) A bright wee cafe with a view over sheep-scattered fields, and a menu of fresh sandwiches, tortilla wraps, nachos and baked potatoes, plus the best coffee on the island.

ⓘ Information

There's a **bank** (without ATM), **post office** and **Co-op supermarket** (☺8am-8pm Mon-Fri, 8am-6pm Sat, noon-6pm Sun) in Scarinish, the main village, 0.5 miles south of the ferry pier. You can get cash back with debit-card purchases at the Co-op.

Tourist information and internet access (per 15 min, £1.50) are available at the **Rural Centre** (☑01879-220677; Crossapol; ☺11am-4pm Mon-Sat; ☏) and An Iodhlann, but there is no accommodation booking service. For more information see www.isleoftiree.com.

ⓘ Getting There & Around

AIR **Loganair/FlyBe** (www.loganair.co.uk) flies from Glasgow to Tiree once daily (£64, 50 minutes).

Hebridean Air Services (☑0845 805 7465; www.hebrideanair.co.uk) operates flights from Connel Airfield (near Oban) to Tiree via Coll (one way from Oban/Coll £65/25, twice daily Monday and Wednesday).

BICYCLE & CAR You can rent bicycles (per day £10) and cars (per day £35) from **MacLennan Motors** (☑01879-220555; Gott) at the ferry pier. **Tiree Fitness** (☑01879-220421; www.tireefitness.co.uk; Sandaig) also rents bikes (per day £18) – much better quality than MacLennan's rusty old clunkers. Book in advance for delivery (£5) to ferry, airport or accommodation.

BOAT A **CalMac** (www.calmac.co.uk) car ferry runs from Oban to Tiree (passenger/car £18.50/95 return, four hours, one daily) via Coll, except on Wednesday and Friday when the boat calls at Tiree first (three hours 20 minutes). The one-way fare from Coll to Tiree (one hour) is £2.90/14.10 per passenger/car.

On Thursdays only, the ferry continues from Coll and Tiree to Barra in the Outer Hebrides (£7.85/39 one way, four hours).

TAXI **John Kennedy** (☑01879-220419)

Isle of Coll

POP 100

Rugged and low-lying, Coll is Tiree's less fertile and less populous neighbour. The northern part of the island is a mix of bare rock, bog and lochans (small lochs), while the south is swathed in golden shell-sand beaches and machair dunes up to 30m high.

The island's main attraction is the peace and quiet – empty beaches, bird-haunted coastlines and long walks along the shore. The biggest and most beautiful sandy beaches are at **Crossapol** in the south, and **Hogh Bay** and **Cliad** on the west coast.

In summer you may be lucky enough to hear the 'krek-krek' of the corncrake at the **RSPB Nature Reserve** at Totronald in the southwest of the island; there's an RSPB Visitor Centre (☑01879-230301; admission free; ☺24hr) here. From Totronald a sandy 4WD track runs north past the dunes backing Hogh Bay to the road at Totamore, allowing walkers and cyclists to make a circuit back to Arinagour rather than returning the way they came.

There are two ruined castles about 6 miles southwest of Arinagour, both known as **Breachachadh Castle**, built by the Macleans in medieval times.

At the time of research, a new community centre, An Cridhe (☑01879-230000; www.ancridhe.co.uk; Arinagour), was about to open. This will host exhibitions of art and photography, and provide a venue for music and entertainment.

⌂ Sleeping & Eating

Most accommodation on Coll is self-catering; only two places offer B&B, including Taigh-na-Mara (☑01879-230354; www.tighnamara.info; Arinagour; r per person £30-39; ☏) in Arinagour. You can **wild camp** for free on the hill above the Coll Hotel (no facilities); ask at the hotel first.

Coll Hotel HOTEL ££

(☑01879-230334; www.collhotel.com; Arinagour; s/d £65/120; P☏) The island's only hotel is an atmospheric old place. Its quirkily shaped rooms have white-painted, wood-panelled walls, and some have lovely views over the manicured hotel gardens and the harbour. The hotel also has a really good **restaurant** (mains £13 to £26) that serves a variety of dishes ranging from crab chowder to local lamb chops, langoustines and lobster.

Coll Bunkhouse HOSTEL £

(☑01879-230000; www.collbunkhouse.co.uk; Arinagour; dm/tw £19/46; ☏) The gorgeous, brand-new bunkhouse is just a 10- to 15-minute walk from the ferry pier.

**Garden House
Camping & Caravan Site** CAMPSITE £
(☎01879-230374; per adult/child £6/4; per car £2; ⏱Apr-Sep) Basic campsite with toilets and cold water only, 4.5 miles southwest of Arinagour. Dogs are not allowed.

Island Café CAFE ££
(www.firstportofcoll.com; mains £6-13; ⏱11am-2pm & 5-9pm Mon, Tue & Thu-Sat, noon-6pm Sun) This cheerful little cafe serves hearty, homemade meals such as sausage and mash with onion gravy, haddock and chips, and vegetarian cottage pie, accompanied by organic beer, wine and cider. Last orders for evening meals are at 7.30pm.

ℹ️ Information

Arinagour, 0.5 miles from the ferry pier, is the only village on Coll, and is home to the **Island Stores** (Arinagour; ⏱10am-5.30pm Mon & Fri, 10am-1pm Tue & Thu, 9am-5.30pm Wed, 9.30am-5pm Sat) grocery shop, a post office (with ATM), some craft shops and a petrol pump. There is no reliable mobile-phone signal on the island; there are payphones at the pier and in the hotel. For more information see www.visitcoll. co.uk.

ℹ️ Getting There & Around

AIR **Hebridean Air Services** (☎0845 805 7465; www.hebrideanair.co.uk) operates flights from Connel Airfield (near Oban) to Coll (£65 one way, twice daily Monday and Wednesday).

BIKE There is no public transport on Coll. Mountain bikes can be hired from the post office in Arinagour for £10 per day.

BOAT A **CalMac** (www.calmac.co.uk) car ferry runs from Oban to Coll (passenger/car £18.50/95 return, 2¾ hours, one daily) and continues to Tiree (one hour), except on Wednesday and Friday when the boat calls at Tiree first. The one-way fare from Coll to Tiree is £2.90/14.10 per passenger/car.

On Thursdays only, you can take a ferry from Coll and Tiree to Barra in the Outer Hebrides (£7.85/39 one way, four hours).

NORTH ARGYLL

Loch Awe

Loch Awe is one of Scotland's most beautiful lochs, with rolling forested hills around its southern end and spectacular mountains in the north. It lies between Oban and Inveraray and is the longest loch in Scotland –

about 24 miles long – but is less than 1 mile wide for most of its length. See www.loch -awe.com for more information.

At its northern end, Loch Awe escapes to the sea through the narrow **Pass of Brander**, where Robert the Bruce defeated the MacDougalls in battle in 1309. In the pass, by the A85, you can visit Cruachan power station (☎01866-822618; www.visitcruachan. co.uk; adult/child £6.50/2.50; ⏱9.30am-4.45pm Easter-Oct, 10am-3.45pm Mon-Fri Nov-Dec, Feb & Mar tours every 30min). Electric buses take you more than 0.5 miles inside Ben Cruachan, allowing you to see the pump-storage hydroelectric scheme which occupies a vast cavern hollowed out of the mountain.

Also at the northern end of Loch Awe are the scenic ruins of Kilchurn Castle (HS; admission free; ⏱9am-5pm Apr-Sep), built in 1440, which enjoys one of Scotland's finest settings; you can climb to the top of the four-storey castle tower. It's a 0.5 mile walk from the A85 road, just east of the bridge over the River Orchy.

Scottish Citylink (www.citylink.co.uk) buses from Glasgow to Oban go via Dalmally, Lochawe village and Cruachan power station. Trains from Glasgow to Oban stop at Dalmally and Lochawe village.

Connel & Taynuilt

Hemmed in by dramatic mountain scenery, **Loch Etive** stretches for 17 miles from Connel to Kinlochetive (accessible by road from Glencoe). At Connel Bridge, 5 miles north of Oban, the loch is joined to the sea by a narrow channel partly blocked by an underwater rock ledge. When the tide flows in and out – as it does twice a day – millions of tons of water pour through this bottleneck, creating spectacular white-water rapids known as the **Falls of Lora**. You can park near the north end of the bridge and walk back into the middle to have a look.

Dunstaffnage Castle (HS; ☎01631-562465; www.historic-scotland.gov.uk; adult/child £4/2.40; ⏱9.30am-5.30pm Apr-Sep, to 4.30pm Oct, closed Thu & Fri Nov-Mar), 2 miles west of Connel, looks like a schoolkid's drawing of what a castle should be – square and massive, with towers at the corners, perched on top of a rocky outcrop. It was built around 1260 and was captured by Robert the Bruce during the Wars of Independence in 1309. The haunted ruins of the nearby 13th-century **chapel** contain lots of Campbell tombs decorated with skull-and-crossbone carvings.

One of the region's most unusual historical sights is **Bonawe Iron Furnace** (HS; ☑01866-822432; www.historic-scotland.gov.uk; adult/child £4.50/2.70; ☉9.30am-5.30pm Apr-Sep), near Taynuilt. Dating from 1753, it was built by an iron-smelting company from the English Lake District because of the abundance of birchwood in the area. The wood was made into charcoal, which was needed for smelting the iron – to produce Bonawe's annual output of 700 tons of pig iron took 10,000 acres of woodland. A fascinating self-guided tour leads you around the various parts of the site.

From the jetty opposite the entrance to Bonawe, **Loch Etive Cruises** (☑01866-822430, 07721-732703; ☉Mar-Nov) runs boat trips to the head of Loch Etive and back two or three times daily (except Saturday) from Easter to Christmas. There are two-hour cruises (adult/child £10/8, departing 10am and noon) and three-hour cruises (£15/12, departing 2pm). You may spot eagles, otters, seals and deer, and at the head of the loch you can see the famous Etive slabs – dotted with rock climbers in dry weather. Bookings essential.

Buses between Oban and Fort William or Glasgow, and trains between Oban and Glasgow, all stop in Connel and Taynuilt.

Appin & Around

The Appin region, once ruled over by the Stewarts of Appin from their stronghold at Castle Stalker, stretches north from the rocky shores of Loch Creran to the hills of Glencoe.

The **Scottish Sea Life Sanctuary** (☑01631-720453; www.sealsanctuary.co.uk; Barcaldine; adult/child £13.20/10.80; ☉10am-4pm Mar-Oct, shorter hours Nov-Feb), 8 miles north of Oban on the shores of Loch Creran, provides a haven for orphaned seal pups. As well as the seal pools there are tanks with herrings, rays and flatfish, touch pools for children, an otter sanctuary and displays on Scotland's marine environment.

North of Loch Creran, at Portnacroish, there's a wonderful view of **Castle Stalker** perched on a tiny offshore island – Monty Python buffs will recognise it as the castle that appears in the final scenes of the film *Monty Python and the Holy Grail*. **Port Appin**, a couple of miles off the main road, is a pleasant spot with a passenger ferry to the island of Lismore.

Scottish Citylink (www.citylink.co.uk) buses between Oban and Fort William stop at the Sea Life Sanctuary and Appin village. You can hire bikes from Port Appin Bike, at the entrance to the village.

🛏 Sleeping & Eating

Ecopod Boutique Retreat   SELF-CATERING £££
(☑07725-409003; www.domesweetdome.co.uk; 2-person pod per week £1100; 🅿🐾) 'Glamping' (glamorous camping) has been all the rage in recent years, but the Ecopod Retreat takes things to a new level of luxury. Technically they're tents, but these geodesic structures cover 70 sq ft and include designer furniture, handmade kitchens, sheepskin rugs, gourmet hampers and private wooden decks complete with cedar hot tubs.

The sylvan setting is superb, nestled among rhododendrons and native birch woodland, with a stunning outlook over Loch Linnhe and Castle Stalker.

Pierhouse Hotel   HOTEL ££
(☑01631-730302; www.pierhousehotel.co.uk; Port Appin; s/d from £75/130; 🅿🐾) The delightfully quaint Pierhouse Hotel sits on the waterfront above the pier for the Lismore ferry, and has stylish modern rooms, a sauna and an excellent **restaurant** (mains £15-25; ☉lunch & dinner) that enjoys a view across the water to Lismore, and specialises in local seafood and game.

Lismore

POP 170

The first thing you notice about the island of Lismore is how green it is (the Gaelic name Lios Mor means 'Great Garden') – all lush grassland sprinkled with wildflowers, with grey blades of limestone breaking through the soil. And that's the secret – limestone is rare in the Highlands, but it weathers to a very fertile soil.

St Moluag's Centre (☑01631-760300; www.celm.org.uk; adult/child £3.50/free; ☉11am-4pm May-Sep, noon-3pm Apr, Oct & Nov) houses a fascinating exhibition on Lismore's history and culture; alongside stands a reconstruction of a crofter's cottage. The **Lismore Café** (☑01631-760020; www.isleoflismorecafe. com; mains £4-7; ☉11am-4pm Apr-Oct; 🐾) here has an outdoor deck with a stunning view of the mainland mountains. The centre is in the middle of the island – if you're walking from the Oban ferry, you can take a short cut by starting along the coastal path north of the pier at Achnacroish (2 miles by road, just over 1 mile by the path).

The romantic ruins of 13th-century **Castle Coeffin** have a lovely setting on the west coast, 1 mile from Clachan (follow the waymarked path). **Tirefour Broch**, a defensive tower with double walls reaching 4m in height, is directly opposite on the east coast.

There is very little short-stay accommodation on Lismore. However, there are several self-catering options advertised on www.isleoflismore.com.

Lismore is long and narrow – 10 miles long and just over 1 mile wide – with a road running almost its full length. **Clachan**, a scattering of houses midway between Achnacroish and Point, is the nearest the island has to a village. Lismore Stores (⊙9am-5.30pm Mon, Tue, Thu & Fri, to 1pm Wed & Sat), between Achnacroish and Clachan, is a grocery store and post office, and has internet access.

❶ Getting There & Around

BIKE **Lismore Bike Hire** (☎01631-760213) will deliver your bike to the ferry slip; hire costs £6/10 per half-/full day.

BOAT A **CalMac** (www.calmac.co.uk) car ferry runs from Oban to Achnacroish, with five sailings Monday to Saturday, two on Sunday (passenger/ car return £6.20/51, 50 minutes).

Argyll & Bute Council (www.argyll-bute.gov. uk) operates the passenger ferry from Port Appin to Point (£1.50, 10 minutes, hourly). Bicycles are carried for free.

TAXI **Lismore Taxi** (☎01631-730391)

Inverness & the Central Highlands

Best Places to Eat

» Lime Tree (p350)

» Contrast Brasserie (p324)

» The Cross (p344)

» Lochleven Seafood Cafe (p348)

» Old Forge (p358)

Best Places to Stay

» Rocpool Reserve (p323)

» Lime Tree (p349)

» Lovat (p335)

» Eagleview Guest House (p344)

» Trafford Bank (p323)

Why Go?

From the high, subarctic plateau of the Cairngorms to the rugged, rocky peaks of Glen Coe and Ben Nevis, the central mountain ranges of the Scottish Highlands are testimony to the sculpting power of ice and weather. Here the landscape is at its grandest, with soaring hills of rock and heather bounded by wooded glens and rushing waterfalls.

Not surprisingly, this part of the country is an adventure playground for outdoor sports enthusiasts. Aviemore, Glen Coe and Fort William draw hill walkers and climbers in summer, and skiers, snowboarders and ice climbers in winter. Inverness, the Highland capital, provides urban rest and relaxation, while nearby Loch Ness and its elusive monster add a hint of mystery.

From Fort William, base camp for climbing Ben Nevis, the Road to the Isles leads past the beaches of Arisaig and Morar to Mallaig, jumping-off point for the isles of Eigg, Rum, Muck and Canna.

When to Go
Inverness

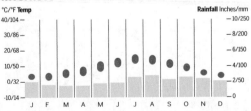

Apr–May The scenery is at its most spectacular, with snow lingering on the higher peaks.

Jun Fort William plays host to the UCI Mountain Bike World Cup, pulling in huge crowds of spectators.

Sep Ideal for hiking and hill walking: midges are dying off, but weather is still reasonably good.

❶ Getting Around

Pick up a free *Highlands & Islands Public Transport Map* at any tourist office. For timetable information, call **Traveline** (☑0871-200 2233; www.travelinescotland.com).

Bus

Scottish Citylink (☑0871 266 3333; www.citylink.co.uk) Runs buses from Perth to Inverness and from Glasgow to Fort William; links Inverness to Fort William along the Great Glen.

Stagecoach (www.stagecoachbus.com) The main regional bus company, with offices in Aviemore, Inverness and Fort William. Dayrider tickets are valid for a day's unlimited travel on Stagecoach buses in various regions, including Inverness (£3.20), Aviemore and around (£6) and Fort William (£2.60).

Train

Two railway lines serve the region: the Perth–Aviemore–Inverness line in the east, and the Glasgow–Fort William–Mallaig line in the west.

INVERNESS & THE GREAT GLEN

Inverness, one of the fastest growing towns in Britain, is the capital of the Highlands. It's a transport hub and jumping-off point for the central, western and northern Highlands, the Moray Firth coast and the Great Glen.

The Great Glen is a geological fault running in an arrow-straight line across Scotland from Fort William to Inverness. The glaciers of the last ice age eroded a deep trough along the fault line that is now filled by a series of lochs – Linnhe, Lochy, Oich and Ness. The glen has always been an important communication route – General George Wade built a military road along the southern side of Loch Ness in the early 18th century, and in 1822 the various lochs were linked by the Caledonian Canal to create a cross-country waterway. The modern A82 road along the glen was completed in 1933 – a date that coincides neatly with the first modern sightings of the Loch Ness Monster.

Inverness

POP 55,000

Inverness, the primary city and shopping centre of the Highlands, has a great location astride the River Ness at the northern end of the Great Glen. In summer it overflows with visitors intent on monster hunting at nearby Loch Ness, but it's worth a visit in its own right for a stroll along the picturesque River Ness, a cruise on Loch Ness, and a meal in one of the city's excellent restaurants.

Inverness was probably founded by King David in the 12th century, but thanks to its often violent history few buildings of real age or historical significance have survived – much of the older part of the city dates from the period following the completion of the Caledonian Canal in 1822. The broad and shallow River Ness, which flows a short 6 miles from Loch Ness into the Moray Firth, runs through the heart of the city.

◉ Sights & Activities

Ness Islands PARK

The main attraction in Inverness is a leisurely stroll along the river to the Ness Islands. Planted with mature Scots pine, fir, beech and sycamore, and linked to the river banks and each other by elegant Victorian footbridges, the islands make an appealing picnic spot.

They're a 20-minute walk south of the castle – head upstream on either side of the river (the start of the Great Glen Way), and return on the opposite bank. On the way you'll pass the red-sandstone towers of St Andrew's Cathedral (Map p322; 11 Ardross St), dating from 1869, and the modern Eden Court Theatre (p326), which hosts regular art exhibits, both on the west bank.

FREE **Inverness Museum & Art Gallery** MUSEUM

(Map p322; ☑01463-237114; www.inverness.highland.museum; Castle Wynd; ◷10am-5pm Tue-Sat Apr-Oct, Thu-Sat Nov-Mar) Inverness Museum & Art Gallery has wildlife dioramas, geological displays, period rooms with historic weapons, Pictish stones and contemporary Highland arts and crafts.

Victorian Market MARKET

(Map p322; www.invernessvictorianmarket.co.uk; Academy St; ◷9am-5pm) If the rain comes down, you could opt for a spot of retail therapy in the Victorian Market, a shopping mall that dates from the 1890s and has rather more charm than its modern equivalents.

Inverness Castle CASTLE

(Map p322; Castle St) The hill above the city centre is topped by the picturesque Baronial turrets of Inverness Castle, a pink-sandstone confection dating from 1847 that replaced a

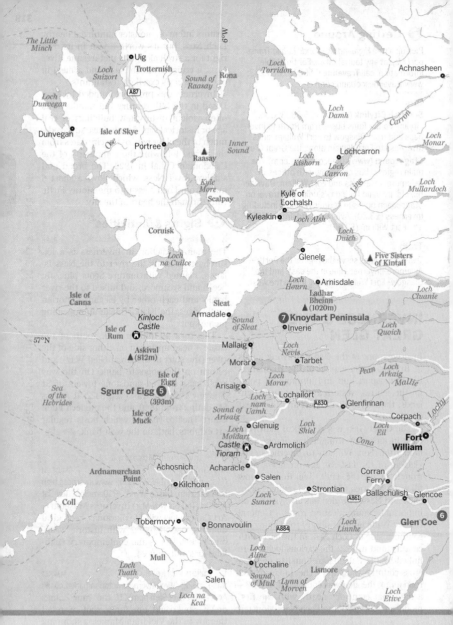

Inverness & the Central Highlands Highlights

1 Hiking among the hills, lochs and forests of beautiful **Glen Affric** (p328)

2 Wandering through the ancient Caledonian forest at **Rothiemurchus Estate** (p336)

3 Making it to the summit of **Ben Nevis** (p351) – and being able to see the view

4 Rattling your teeth loose on the championship downhill

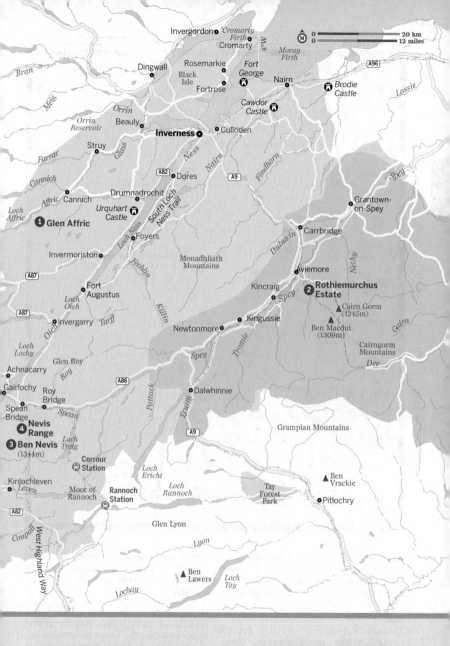

mountain-bike course at **Nevis Range** (p352)

5 Taking in the stunning panorama from the summit of the **Sgurr of Eigg** (p360)

6 Soaking up the scenery (when you can see it!) in moody but magnificent **Glen Coe** (p345)

7 Exploring the remote and rugged wilderness of the **Knoydart Peninsula** (p358)

Inverness

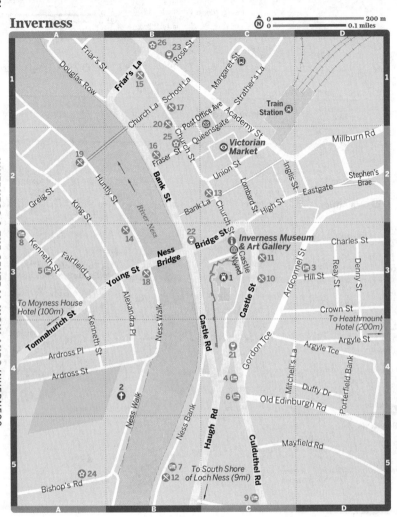

medieval castle blown up by the Jacobites in 1746; it serves today as the Sheriff's Court. It's not open to the public, but there are good views from the surrounding gardens.

👉 Tours

Jacobite Cruises　　　　　　BOAT TOUR
(☎01463-233999; www.jacobite.co.uk; Glenurquhart Rd; adult/child incl admission fee £29/22; ☉twice daily Jun-Sep, once daily Apr-May) Boats depart from Tomnahurich Bridge for a 1½-hour cruise along Loch Ness, followed by a visit to Urquhart Castle and a return to Inverness by coach. You can buy tickets at the tourist office and catch a free minibus to the boat. Other cruises and combined cruise/coach tours, from one to 6½ hours, are also available.

Happy Tours　　　　　　　WALKING TOUR
(www.happy-tours.biz) Offers 1¼-hour guided walks exploring the town's history and legends. Tours begin outside the tourist office at 11am, 1pm and 3pm daily. A tip is expected.

Inverness Taxis　　　　　　TAXI TOUR
(☎01463-222900; www.inverness-taxis.co.uk) Wide range of day tours to Urquhart Castle, Loch Ness, Culloden and even Skye. Fares

Inverval

Inverness

◎ Top Sights
Inverness Museum & Art Gallery.......... C3
Victorian Market C2

◎ Sights
1 Inverness Castle C3
2 St Andrew's Cathedral......................... B4

🛏 Sleeping
3 Ardconnel House D3
4 Bazpackers Backpackers Hotel........... C4
5 Bluebell House A3
Crown Hotel Guest House ....(see 3)
Glenmoriston Town House Hotel (see 12)
6 Inverness Student Hotel........................ C4
7 MacRae Guest House............................. B5
8 Mardon Guest House A3
9 Rocpool Reserve C5

✹ Eating
10 Café 1.. C3

11 Castle Restaurant C3
12 Contrast Brasserie................................. B5
13 Joy of Taste.. C2
14 Kitchen.. B3
15 Leakey's.. B1
16 Mustard Seed B2
17 Red Pepper... B1
18 Rocpool... B3
19 River House A2
20 Sam's Indian Cuisine............................. B1

◎ Drinking
21 Castle Tavern... C4
22 Johnny Foxes... B3
23 Phoenix B1

◎ Entertainment
24 Eden Court Theatre............................... A5
25 Hootananny.. B2
26 Ironworks... B1

per car (up to four people) range from £60 (two hours) to £240 (all day).

🛏 Sleeping

Inverness has a good range of backpacker accommodation, and also has several excellent boutique hotels. There are lots of guesthouses and B&Bs along Old Edinburgh Rd and Ardconnel St on the east side of the river, and on Kenneth St and Fairfield Rd on the west bank; all are within 10 minutes' walk of the city centre.

The city fills up quickly in July and August, so you should either prebook your accommodation or get an early start looking for somewhere to stay.

TOP CHOICE Trafford Bank   B&B ££
(🕿01463-241414; www.traffordbankguesthouse.
co.uk; 96 Fairfield Rd; d £110-125; **P**🛜) There's been lots of word-of-mouth love for this elegant Victorian villa, once home to a bishop, just a mitre-toss from the Caledonian Canal and 10 minutes' walk west from the city centre. The luxurious rooms include fresh fruit, bathrobes and fluffy towels – ask for the Tartan Room, which has a wrought-iron king-size bed and Victorian roll-top bath.

TOP CHOICE Rocpool Reserve   BOUTIQUE HOTEL £££
(Map p322; 🕿01463-240089; www.rocpool.com; Culduthel Rd; s/d from £175/210; **P**🛜) Boutique

chic meets the Highlands in this slick and sophisticated little hotel, where an elegant Georgian exterior conceals an oasis of contemporary cool. A gleaming white entrance hall lined with red carpet and contemporary art leads to designer rooms in shades of chocolate, cream and gold; expect lots of high-tech gadgetry in the more expensive rooms, ranging from iPod docks to balcony hot tubs with aquavision TV. A restaurant by Albert Roux completes the luxury package.

Ardconnel House   B&B ££
(Map p322; 🕿01463-240455; www.ardconnel
-inverness.co.uk; 21 Ardconnel St; r per person £35-40; 🛜) The six-room Ardconnel is one of our favourites – a terraced Victorian house with comfortable en suite rooms, a dining room with crisp white table linen, and a breakfast menu that includes Vegemite for homesick Antipodeans. Kids under 10 not allowed.

Ach Aluinn   B&B ££
(🕿01463-230127; www.achaluinn.com; 27 Fairfield Rd; r per person £25-35; **P**) This large, detached Victorian house is bright and homely, and offers all you might want from a B&B – private bathroom, TV, reading lights, comfy beds with two pillows each, and an excellent breakfast. Less than 10 minutes' walk west from the city centre.

Loch Ness Country House Hotel HOTEL £££
(☎01463-230512; www.lochnesscountryhouseho
tel.co.uk; Dunain Park, Loch Ness Rd; d from £169;
P✿) This sumptuous country-house hotel
offers traditional decor, featuring Victorian
four-poster beds, Georgian-style furniture
and Italian marble bathrooms, all set in
beautiful wooded grounds just five minutes'
stroll from the Caledonian Canal and River
Ness. The hotel is a mile southwest of Inverness on the A82 to Fort William.

Heathmount Hotel BOUTIQUE HOTEL ££
(☎01463-235877; www.heathmounthotel.com;
Kingsmills Rd; s/d from £75/115; P✿) Small
and friendly, the Heathmount combines a
popular local bar and restaurant with eight
designer hotel rooms, each one different,
ranging from a boldly coloured family room
in purple and gold to a slinky black velvet
four-poster double. Five minutes' walk east
of the city centre.

MacRae Guest House B&B ££
(Map p322; ☎01463-243658; joycemacrae@hot
mail.com; 24 Ness Bank; s/d from £45/64; P) This
pretty, flower-bedecked Victorian house on
the eastern bank of the river has smart,
tastefully decorated bedrooms (one is wheelchair accessible), and vegetarian breakfasts
are available. Minimum two-night bookings
in July and August.

Bazpackers Backpackers Hotel HOSTEL £
(Map p322; ☎01463-717663; www.bazpackershos
tel.co.uk; 4 Culduthel Rd; dm/tw £17/44; @✿) This
may be Inverness' smallest hostel (30 beds),
but it's hugely popular. It's a friendly, quiet
place – the main building has a convivial
lounge centred on a wood-burning stove,
and a small garden and great views (some
rooms are in a separate building with no
garden). The dorms and kitchen can be a bit
cramped, but the showers are great.

Inverness Student Hotel HOSTEL £
(Map p322; ☎01463-236556; www.scotlands-top
-hostels.com; 8 Culduthel Rd; dm £18; P@✿) Set
in a rambling old house with comfy beds
and views across the River Ness, this hostel
has a party atmosphere, and runs organised
pub crawls in town. It's a 10-minute walk
from the train station, just past the castle.

Inverness Millburn SYHA HOSTEL £
(SYHA; ☎01463-231771; www.syha.org.uk; Victoria Dr; dm £18; ☯Apr-Dec; P@✿) Inverness'
modern 166-bed hostel is 10 minutes' walk
northeast of the city centre. With its comfy

beds and flashy stainless-steel kitchen, some
reckon it's the best hostel in the country.
Booking is essential, especially at Easter, and
in July and August.

**Glenmoriston Town
House Hotel** BOUTIQUE HOTEL £££
(Map p322; ☎01463-223777; www.glenmoriston
townhouse.com; 20 Ness Bank; s/d from £120/165;
P✿) Luxurious boutique hotel on the banks
of the River Ness. Can organise golfing and
fishing for guests.

Crown Hotel Guest House B&B ££
(Map p322; ☎01463-231135; www.inverness-guest
house.info; 19 Ardconnel St; s/d from £36/56; P@)
Two of the six bedrooms are family rooms,
and there's a spacious lounge equipped with
games consoles, DVDs and board games.

Mardon Guest House B&B ££
(Map p322; ☎01463-231005; www.mardonguest
house.co.uk; 37 Kenneth St; r per person £30-38;
P✿) Friendly B&B with six cosy rooms (all
en suite), just five minutes' walk west from
the city centre.

Moyness House Hotel B&B ££
(☎01463-233836; www.moyness.co.uk; 6 Bruce
Gardens; d £77-105; P✿) Elegant Victorian
villa with a beautiful garden and peaceful
setting, 10 minutes' walk southwest of the
city centre.

Bluebell House B&B ££
(Map p322; ☎01463-238201; www.bluebell-house.
com; 31 Kenneth St; r per person £30-45; P✿)
Warm and welcoming hosts, top breakfasts,
close to city centre.

**Bught Caravan
Park & Campsite** CAMPSITE £
(☎01463-236920; www.invernesscaravanpark.
com; Bught Lane; site per person £8, campervan
£16; ☯Easter–mid-Oct) A mile southwest of
the city centre near Tomnahurich Bridge,
this camping ground is hugely popular with
backpackers.

Eating

TOP CHOICE **Contrast Brasserie** BRASSERIE ££
(Map p322; ☎01463-227889; www.glenmoris
tontownhouse.com/contrast.html; 22 Ness Bank;
mains £13-20) Book early for what we think
is the best restaurant in Inverness – a dining
room that drips designer style, with smiling
professional staff and truly delicious food.
Try scallops with chorizo bolognese, or pork
belly with mange tout salad and lemongrass

purée; 10 out of 10. And at £10 for a two-course lunch, or £15 for three-course early-bird dinner (5pm to 6.30pm), the value is unbeatable.

TOP CHOICE **Café 1**   BISTRO **££**
(Map p322; ✆01463-226200; www.cafe1.net; 75 Castle St; mains £10-23; ⊙noon-9.30pm Mon-Fri, noon-2.30pm & 6-9.30pm Sat) Café 1 is a friendly and appealing bistro with candlelit tables amid elegant blonde-wood and wrought-iron decor. There is an international menu based on quality Scottish produce, from Aberdeen Angus steaks to crisp sea bass with velvet crab risotto and chilli jam. Early-bird menu (one/two courses for £9/12.50) is served noon to 6.45pm weekdays, and noon to 2.30pm Saturday.

Rocpool   RESTAURANT **££**
(Map p322; ✆01463-717274; www.rocpoolrestaurant.com; 1 Ness Walk; mains £17-24; ⊙Mon-Sat) Lots of polished wood, navy-blue leather and crisp white linen lend a nautical air to this relaxing bistro, which offers a Mediterranean-influenced menu that makes the most of quality Scottish produce, especially seafood. The two-course lunch is £14.

Mustard Seed   BISTRO **££**
(Map p322; ✆01463-220220; www.mustardseedrestaurant.co.uk; 16 Fraser St; mains £11-16; ⊙lunch & dinner) The menu at this bright and bustling bistro changes weekly, but focuses on Scottish and French cuisine with a modern twist. Grab a table on the upstairs balcony if you can – it's the best outdoor lunch spot in Inverness, with a great view across the river. And a two-course lunch for £7 – yes, that's right – is hard to beat.

Joy of Taste   BRITISH
(Map p322; ✆01463-241459; www.thejoyoftaste.co.uk; 25 Church St; mains £12-17; ⊙lunch & dinner) Here's a novel concept – a restaurant run by a head chef and 25 volunteers who work a shift a week just for 'the love of creating a beautiful restaurant' (plus a share of the profits). And a very good job they're making of it, with a menu of classic British cuisine – from broccoli and stilton soup to lemon posset via Scottish sirloin – and a growing fan club of satisfied customers.

Sam's Indian Cuisine   INDIAN **££**
(Map p322; ✆01463-713111; 77-79 Church St; mains £8-15; ⊙noon-2pm & 5-11pm Mon-Wed, noon-11pm Thu-Sat, 12.30-11pm Sun) The stylish decor in Sam's is a cut above your average curry shop, and so is the food – lots of fresh and flavoursome spices and herbs make dishes such as *jeera* chicken (cooked with cumin seed) really zing. Wash it down with Indian Cobra beer.

River House   RESTAURANT **£££**
(Map p322; ✆01463-222033; www.riverhouseinverness.co.uk; 1 Greig St; mains £16-26; ⊙dinner Mon-Sat, lunch Fri & Sat) This is an elegant restaurant of the polished-wood and crisp-white-linen variety, serving the best of British venison, beef, lamb, duck and seafood.

Kitchen   MODERN SCOTTISH **££**
(Map p322; ✆01463-259119; www.kitchenrestaurant.co.uk; 15 Huntly St; mains £11-16; ⊙⊙) This spectacular glass-fronted restaurant offers a great menu and a view of the River Ness – try to get a table upstairs.

Castle Restaurant   CAFE **£**
(Map p322; ✆01463-230925; 41-43 Castle St; mains £6-13; ⊙9am-8.30pm) This is a classic old-fashioned cafe.

Red Pepper   CAFE **£**
(Map p322; ✆01463-237111; www.red-pepper-inverness.co.uk; 74 Church St; mains £2-4; ⊙7.30am-4.30pm Mon-Fri, 9am-4.30pm Sat) Cool coffee and sandwich place.

Leakey's   CAFE **£**
(Map p322; Greyfriars Hall, Church St; mains £3-5; ⊙10am-5.30pm Mon-Sat) Cosy cafe in an excellent secondhand bookshop.

🍷 Drinking

TOP CHOICE **Clachnaharry Inn**   PUB
(✆01463-239806; www.clachnaharryinn.co.uk; 17-19 High St) Just over a mile northwest of the city centre, on the bank of the Caledonian Canal just off the A862, this is a delightful old coaching inn (with beer garden out back) serving an excellent range of real ales and good pub grub.

Castle Tavern   PUB
(Map p322; ✆01463-718718; www.castletavern.net; 1-2 View Pl) With a tasty selection of real ales, this pub has a wee suntrap of a terrace out the front. It's a great place for a pint on a summer afternoon.

Phoenix   PUB
(Map p322; ✆01463-233685; 108 Academy St) This is the most traditional of the pubs in the city centre, with a mahogany horseshoe bar, a comfortable, family friendly lounge,

and good food at both lunchtime and in the evening. Real ales on tap include the rich and fruity Orkney Dark Island.

Johnny Foxes BAR
(Map p322; ☑01463-236577; www.johnnyfoxes. co.uk; 26 Bank St) Stuck beneath the ugliest building on the riverfront, Johnny Foxes is a big and boisterous Irish bar with a wide range of food served all day and live music nightly. Part of the premises, the **Den**, is a smart cocktail bar and club.

☆ Entertainment

Hootananny LIVE MUSIC
(Map p322; ☑01463-233651; www.hootananny. com; 67 Church St) Hootananny is the city's best live-music venue, with traditional folk-and/or rock-music sessions nightly, including big-name bands from all over Scotland (and, indeed, the world). The bar is well stocked with a range of beers from the local Black Isle Brewery.

Eden Court Theatre THEATRE
(Map p322; ☑01463-234234; www.eden-court. co.uk; Bishop's Rd) The Highlands' main cultural venue – with theatre, art-house cinema and conference centre – Eden Court stages a busy program of drama, dance, comedy, music, film and children's events, and has a good bar and restaurant. Pick up a program from the foyer or check the website.

Ironworks LIVE MUSIC, COMEDY
(Map p322; ☑0871 789 4173; www.ironworksvenue. com; 122 Academy St) With live bands (rock, pop, tribute) and comedy shows two or three times a week, the Ironworks is the town's main venue for big-name acts.

ⓘ Information

ClanLAN (22 Baron Taylor's St; per 30 minutes £1.50; ⊙10am-8pm Mon-Fri, 11am-8pm Sat, noon-5pm Sun)

Inverness tourist office (☑01463-252401; www.visithighlands.com; Castle Wynd; internet access per 20min £1 ; ⊙9am-6pm Mon-Sat, 9.30am-5pm Sun Jul & Aug, 9am-5pm Mon-Sat, 10am-4pm Sun Jun, Sep & Oct, 9am-5pm Mon-Sat Apr & May) Bureau de change and accommodation booking service; also sells tickets for tours and cruises. Opening hours limited November to March.

ⓘ Getting There & Away

Air

Inverness Airport (INV; ☑01667-464000; www.hial.co.uk) At Dalcross, 10 miles east of the city, off the A96 towards Aberdeen. There are scheduled flights to Amsterdam, Dusseldorf, London, Bristol, Manchester, Belfast, Stornoway, Benbecula, Orkney, Shetland and several other British airports.

Bus

Services depart from **Inverness bus station** (Margaret St).

London £45, 13 hours, one daily; more frequent services requiring a change at Glasgow. Operated by **National Express** (☑08717 81 81 78; www.gobycoach.com).

Aberdeen £9, 3¾ hours, hourly

Aviemore £5.50, 1¾ hours, three daily Monday to Friday; via Grantown-on-Spey

Edinburgh £28, 3½ to 4½ hours, hourly

Glasgow £28, 3½ to 4½ hours, hourly

Fort William £12, two hours, five daily

Portree £23, 3½ hours, four daily

Thurso £18.50, 3½ hours, two daily

Ullapool £12, 1½ hours, two daily except Sunday

If you book far enough in advance, **Megabus** (☑0871 266 3333; www.megabus.com) offers fares from £5.50 for buses from Inverness to Glasgow and Edinburgh, and £17 to London.

Train

Aberdeen £28, 2¼ hours, eight daily

Edinburgh £40, 3½ hours, eight daily

Glasgow £40, 3½ hours, eight daily

Kyle of Lochalsh £13, 2½ hours, four daily Monday to Saturday, two Sunday; one of Britain's great scenic train journeys

London £100, eight hours, one daily direct; others require a change at Edinburgh

Wick £13, four hours, four daily Monday to Saturday, one or two on Sunday; via Thurso

ⓘ Getting Around

To/From the Airport

Stagecoach Jet (www.stagecoachbus.com) Buses run from the airport to Inverness bus station (£3.30, 20 minutes, every 30 minutes).

Bicycle

Ticket to Ride (☑01463-419160; www.ticketto ridehighlands.co.uk; Bellfield Park; per day from £20) Hire mountain bikes, hybrids and tandems. Will deliver bikes free to local hotels and B&Bs.

Bus

City services and buses to places around Inverness, including Nairn, Forres, the Culloden battlefield, Beauly, Dingwall and Lairg, are operated by Stagecoach (p491). An Inverness City Dayrider ticket costs £3.30 and gives unlimited travel for a day on buses throughout the city.

Car
Focus Vehicle Rental (☎01667-461212; www.focusvehiclerental.co.uk; Inverness Airport) The big boys charge from around £50 per day, but Focus has cheaper rates starting at £35 per day.

Taxi
Highland Taxis (☎01463-222222)

Around Inverness

CULLODEN BATTLEFIELD
The Battle of Culloden in 1746, the last pitched battle ever fought on British soil, saw the defeat of Bonnie Prince Charlie and the end of the Jacobite dream when 1200 Highlanders were slaughtered by government forces in a 68-minute rout. The duke of Cumberland, son of the reigning king George II and leader of the Hanoverian army, earned the nickname 'Butcher' for his brutal treatment of the defeated Jacobite forces. The battle sounded the death knell for the old clan system, and the horrors of the Clearances soon followed. The sombre moor where the conflict took place has scarcely changed in the ensuing 260 years.

Culloden is 6 miles east of Inverness. Bus No 1 runs from Queensgate in Inverness to Culloden battlefield (30 minutes, hourly).

Culloden Visitor Centre   VISITOR CENTRE (NTS; www.nts.org.uk/culloden; adult/child £10/7.50; ⊙9am-6pm Apr-Sep, 9am-5pm Oct, 10am-4pm Nov-Mar) This impressive visitor centre presents detailed information about the Battle of Culloden in 1746, including the lead-up and the aftermath, with perspectives from both sides. An innovative film puts you on the battlefield in the middle of the mayhem, and a wealth of other audio presentations must have kept Inverness' entire acting community in business for weeks. The admission fee includes an audioguide for a self-guided tour of the battlefield itself.

FORT GEORGE
The headland guarding the narrows in the Moray Firth opposite Fortrose is occupied by the magnificent and virtually unaltered 18th-century artillery fortification of Fort George.

Fort George   FORTRESS (HS; ☎01667-462777; adult/child £6.90/4.10; ⊙9.30am-5.30pm Apr-Sep, to 4.30pm Oct-Mar) One of the finest examples of its kind in Europe, Fort George was established in 1748 as a base for George II's army of occupation in the Highlands – by the time of its completion in 1769 it had cost the equivalent of around £1 billion in today's money. The mile-plus walk around the ramparts offers fine views out to sea and back to the Great Glen. Given its size, you'll need at least two hours to do the place justice. The fort is off the A96 about 11 miles northeast of Inverness; no public transport runs to the fort.

NAIRN
POP 11,000
Nairn is a popular golfing and seaside resort with a good sandy beach.

The most interesting part of Nairn is the old fishing village of **Fishertown**, down by the harbour, a maze of narrow streets lined with picturesque cottages. Nairn Museum (☎01667-456791; www.nairnmuseum.co.uk; Viewfield House; adult/child £3/50p; ⊙10am-4.30pm Mon-Fri, to 1pm Sat Apr-Oct), a few minutes' walk from the tourist office, has displays on the history of Fishertown, as well as on local archaeology, geology and natural history.

You can spend many pleasant hours wandering along the **East Beach**, one of the finest in Scotland.

The big event in the town's calendar is the Nairn Highland Games (www.nairnhighlandgames.co.uk), held in mid-August, and in September there's the Nairn Book and Arts Festival (www.nairnfestival.co.uk).

🍴 Sleeping & Eating
Glebe End   B&B ££ (☎01667-451659; www.glebe-end.co.uk; 1 Glebe Rd; r per person £25-40; P🖥) It's people as much as place that make a good B&B, and the owners here are all you could wish for – helpful and welcoming. The house is lovely too, a spacious Victorian villa with home-away-from-home bedrooms and a sunny conservatory where breakfast is served.

Sunny Brae Hotel   HOTEL £££ (☎01667-452309; www.sunnybraehotel.com; Marine Rd; s £95, d from £130; P🖥) Beautifully decked out with fresh flowers and potplants, the Sunny Brae enjoys an enviable location with great views across the Moray Firth. The hotel restaurant specialises in Scottish produce cooked with Continental flair.

Boath House Hotel   HOTEL £££ (☎01667-454896; www.boath-house.com; Auldearn; s/d from £190/265; P) This beautifully restored Regency mansion, set in private woodland gardens 2 miles east of Nairn on the A96, is one of Scotland's most luxurious country-house hotels, and includes a spa offering holistic treatments and a Michelin-starred restaurant (six-course dinner £70).

Classroom GASTROPUB ££
(☏01667-455999; www.theclassroombistro.com; 1 Cawdor St; mains £15-23; ☺10am-midnight Mon-Sat, 11am-10.30pm Sun) Done up in an appealing mixture of modern and traditional styles – lots of richly glowing wood with designer detailing – the Classroom doubles as cocktail bar and gastropub with a tempting menu that goes from Cullen skink (soup made with smoked haddock, potato, onion and milk) to steak with red wine and mushroom sauce.

ℹ️ Information

Nairn has a tourist office (☏01667-452763; 62 King St; ☺Apr-Oct), banks with ATMs and a post office.

ℹ️ Getting There & Away

Buses run hourly (less frequently on Sunday) from Inverness to Aberdeen via Nairn. The town also lies on the Inverness–Aberdeen railway line; there are five to seven trains a day from Inverness (£6, 20 minutes).

CAWDOR CASTLE

Cawdor Castle (☏01667-404615; www.cawdor castle.com; adult/child £9.50/6; ☺10am-5.30pm May–Sep) was the 14th-century home of the Thanes of Cawdor, one of the titles prophesied by the three witches for the eponymous character of Shakespeare's *Macbeth*. Macbeth couldn't have lived here though, since the central tower dates from the 14th century (the wings were 17th-century additions) and he died in 1057. The castle is 5 miles southwest of Nairn.

Cawdor Tavern (www.cawdortavern.co.uk; bar meals £8-15; ☺lunch & dinner) in the nearby village is worth a visit, though it can be difficult deciding what to drink as it stocks more than 100 varieties of whisky. There's also good pub food, with tempting daily specials.

BRODIE CASTLE

Set in 70 hectares of parkland, Brodie Castle (NTS; ☏01309-641371; adult/child £9.50/7; ☺10.30am-5pm daily Jul & Aug, 10.30am-4.30pm Apr, 10.30am-4.30pm Sun-Thu May-Jun & Sep-Oct) has several highlights, including a library with more than 6000 peeling, dusty volumes. There are wonderful clocks, a huge Victorian kitchen and a 17th-century dining room with wildly extravagant moulded

plaster ceilings depicting mythological scenes. The Brodies have been living here since 1160, but the present structure dates mostly from 1567, with many additions over the years.

The castle is 8 miles east of Nairn. Stagecoach (p491) bus 10A or 11 from Inverness to Elgin stops at Brodie (35 minutes, hourly Monday to Saturday).

West of Inverness

BEAULY
POP 1160

Mary, Queen of Scots, is said to have given this village its name in 1564 when she exclaimed, in French: *'Quel beau lieu!'* (What a beautiful place!). Founded in 1230, the red-sandstone **Beauly Priory** is now an impressive ruin; a small information kiosk next door has information on the history of the priory.

The central Priory Hotel (☏01463-782309; www.priory-hotel.com; The Square; s/d £65/110; 🅿🛜) has bright, modern rooms and serves good bar meals. However, the best place for lunch is across the street at the Corner on the Square (www.corneronthesquare.co.uk; 1 High St; mains £5-7; ☺9am-5.30pm Mon-Sat, 11am-4.30pm Sun), a superb little delicatessen and cafe that serves breakfast (till 11.30am), daily lunch specials (noon to 4.30pm) and excellent coffee.

Buses 28 and 28A from Inverness run to Beauly (45 minutes, hourly Monday to Saturday, five on Sunday), and the town lies on the Inverness–Thurso railway line.

STRATHGLASS & GLEN AFFRIC

The broad valley of Strathglass extends about 18 miles inland from Beauly, followed by the A831 to **Cannich** (the only village in the area), where there's a grocery store and a post office.

Glen Affric, one of the most beautiful glens in Scotland, extends deep into the hills beyond Cannich. The upper reaches of the glen, now designated as Glen Affric National Nature Reserve (www.glenaffric. org), is a scenic wonderland of shimmering lochs, rugged mountains and native Scots pine, home to pine marten, wildcat, otter, red squirrel and golden eagle.

About 4 miles southwest of Cannich is **Dog Falls**, a scenic spot where the River Affric squeezes through a narrow, rocky gorge. A waymarked walking trail leads there easily from Dog Falls car park.

The road continues beyond Dog Falls to a parking area and picnic site at the eastern end of **Loch Affric** where there are several short walks along the river and the loch shore. The circuit of Loch Affric (10 miles, allow five hours) follows good paths right around the loch and takes you deep into the heart of some very wild scenery.

It's possible to walk all the way from Cannich to **Glen Shiel** on the west coast (35 miles) in two days, spending the night at the remote Glen Affric SYHA Hostel.

The minor road on the east side of the River Glass leads to the pretty little conservation village of **Tomich**, 3 miles southwest of Cannich, built in Victorian times as accommodation for estate workers. The road continues (unsurfaced for the last 2 miles) to a forestry car park, the starting point for a short (800m) walk to **Plodda Falls**. A restored Victorian viewing platform extends above the top of the falls like a diving board, giving a dizzying view straight down the cascade into a remote and thickly forested river gorge. Keep your eyes peeled for red squirrels and crossbills.

🛏 Sleeping & Eating

Kerrow House
B&B **££**

(☎01456-415243; www.kerrow-house.co.uk; Cannich; per person £35-43; **P**) This wonderful Georgian hunting lodge has bags of old-fashioned character – it was once the home of Highland author Neil M Gunn – and has spacious grounds with 3.5 miles of private trout fishing. It's a mile south of Cannich on the minor road along the east side of the River Glass.

Tomich Hotel
HOTEL **££**

(☎01456-415399; www.tomichhotel.co.uk; Tomich; s/d from £70/110; **P 🕸 �wimming pool**) About 3 miles southwest of Cannich on the southern side of the river, this Victorian hunting lodge has a blazing log fire, a Victorian restaurant, eight comfortable en suite rooms and – a bit of a surprise out here in the wilds – a small, heated indoor swimming pool.

Glen Affric SYHA
HOSTEL **£**

(☎bookings 0845 293 7373; www.syha.org.uk; Allt Beithe; dm £21.50; ☉Apr–mid-Sep) This remote and rustic hostel is set amid magnificent scenery at the halfway point of the cross-country walk from Cannich to Glen Shiel, 8 miles from the nearest road. Facilities are basic and you'll need to take all supplies with you. Book in advance. There is no phone at the hostel.

BCC Loch Ness Hostel
HOSTEL **£**

(☎01456-476296; www.bcclochnesshostel.co.uk; Glen Urquhart; s/d £25/45; **P 🕸**) Clean, modern, high-quality budget accommodation located halfway between Cannich and Loch Ness; advance booking recommended.

Cannich Caravan Park
CAMPSITE **£**

(☎01456-415364; www.highlandcamping.co.uk; sites per person £6, pods per person £13, plus per car £1; 🕸) Good, sheltered site, with option of wooden camping 'pods'. Mountain bikes for hire at £17 a day.

Glen Affric Bar
PUB **£**

(Cannich; mains £6-9; ☉11am-11pm; 🕸) This is a friendly hill-walkers' pub (walking guides are scattered around the place) serving cappuccino and bar meals as well as An Teallach real ale; it also has the only ATM for miles around.

❶ Getting There & Away

Stagecoach (p491) bus 17 runs from Inverness to Cannich (one hour, three a day Monday to Saturday) via Drumnadrochit; there are also three buses a day (except Sunday) from Cannich to Tomich (10 minutes).

Ross's Minibuses (www.ross-minibuses.co.uk) Operates a service from Inverness to the Glen Affric car park via Drumnadrochit and Cannich (1½ hours, once daily Monday, Wednesday and Friday only, July and August). It shuttles between Cannich and Glen Affric (30 minutes) twice more on the same days. Check the website for the latest timetables.

Black Isle

The Black Isle – a peninsula rather than an island – is linked to Inverness by the Kessock Bridge.

❶ Getting There & Away

Stagecoach (p491) buses 26 and 26A run from Inverness to Fortrose and Rosemarkie (30 to 40 minutes, twice hourly Monday to Saturday); half of them continue to Cromarty (one hour).

FORTROSE & ROSEMARKIE

At **Fortrose Cathedral** you'll find the vaulted crypt of a 13th-century chapter house and sacristy, and the ruinous 14th-century south aisle and chapel. **Chanonry Point**, 1.5 miles east, is a favourite dolphin-spotting lookout – there are one-hour **dolphin-watching cruises** (☎01381-622383; www.dolphintripsav och.co.uk; adult/child £13/9) departing from Avoch (pronounced 'auch'), 3 miles southwest.

LOCAL KNOWLEDGE

ERLEND & PAMELA TAIT: ARTISTS

Erlend and Pamela Tait are artists from Fortrose on the Black Isle. They exhibit internationally and you can see their work at www.erlendtait.com and www.pamelatait.co.uk.

Highland artists whose work you admire? *Erlend:* Tim Maclean, Michael Forbes, Allan MacDonald, Gordon Robin Brown, Shaun MacDonald, Jonathan Shearer, Kirstie Cohen.
Pamela: There's also Jennifer Houliston, Gerald Laing, Fin MacRae, Alex Dunn, Rosie Newman, Angus Mcphee and Alex Main.

Top Highland art galleries? Highland Institute for Contemporary Art (www.h-i-c-a. org), near Dores, **Browns Gallery** (www.brownsart.com) in Tain, **Moray Art Centre** (www.morayartcentre.org) in Findhorn and **Inverness Museum & Art Gallery** (p319).

Best secret spots? *Erlend:* The Black Isle is worth exploring – **Learnie Red Rock** for mountain biking, Groam House Museum (p330) for everything Pictish, Hugh Miller's Cottage & Museum (p330) for local geology and folklore. And the **Clootie Well** is a magical place where you hang a piece of your clothing to cure an ailment or bring you good luck.
Pamela: **Dogs Falls** over at Glen Affric, and there's a lovely wee walk at **Reelig Forest** near Beauly which has some of the tallest trees in Britain. You must visit the **Pirates Graveyard** in Cromarty followed by the Cromarty Bakery (p331) which sells the nicest bread ever, and great pies!

Good place for a drink? We both love the Anderson (p330) in Fortrose – it has the best selection of whiskies and beers, great food too, and is just a lovely pub to be in. Its worth making a special trip to the Anderson for Halloween, especially if you like dressing up and eating chillies! And for its pub quizzes at the end of each month, the Monday knitting night, the music sessions... we're positively spoilt living so close to such a great pub.

In Rosemarkie, the Groam House Museum (☏01381-620961; www.groamhouse.org.uk; High St; admission free; ☉11am-4.30pm Mon-Fri, 2-4.30pm Sat Apr-Oct, 2-4pm Sat only Nov) has a superb collection of Pictish stones engraved with designs similar to those on Celtic Irish stones.

From the northern end of Rosemarkie's High St, a short but pleasant signposted walk leads you through the gorges and waterfalls of the **Fairy Glen**.

Once you've worked up a thirst, retire to the bar at the Anderson Hotel (☏01381-620236; www.theanderson.co.uk; Union St) to sample its range of real ales (including Belgian beers and Somerset cider) and more than 200 single malt whiskies.

CROMARTY
POP 720

The pretty village of Cromarty at the northeastern tip of the Black Isle has lots of 18th-century red-sandstone houses, and a lovely green park beside the sea for picnics and games. An excellent walk, known as the **100 Steps**, leads from the north end of the village to the headland viewpoint of South Sutor (4 miles round trip).

The 18th-century Cromarty Courthouse (☏01381-600418; www.cromarty-courthouse.org.

uk; Church St; admission free; ☉noon-4pm Sun-Thu Apr-Sep) details the town's history using contemporary references. Kids will love the talking mannequins.

Near the courthouse is Hugh Miller's Cottage & Museum (www.hughmiller.org; Church St; adult/child £5.50/4.50; ☉noon-5pm daily Apr-Sep, Tue, Thu & Fri only Oct), the thatch-roofed birthplace of Hugh Miller (1802–56), a local stonemason and amateur geologist who later moved to Edinburgh and became a famous journalist and newspaper editor. The Georgian villa next door is home to a museum celebrating his life and achievements.

From Cromarty harbour, Ecoventures (☏01381-600323; www.ecoventures.co.uk; Cromarty Harbour; adult/child £24/18) runs 2½-hour boat trips into the Moray Firth to see bottlenose dolphins and other wildlife.

Also at the harbour, Sutor Creek (☏01381-600855; www.sutorcreek.co.uk; 21 Bank St; mains £7-18; ☉11am-9pm late May-Sep) is an excellent little cafe-restaurant serving wood-fired pizzas and fresh local seafood – we can recommend the Cromarty langoustines with garlic and chilli butter.

For something lighter, there's good tea and scones at The Pantry (1 Church St;

⊙10am-5pm Easter-Sep), or delicious filled rolls and savoury pies at the **Cromarty Bakery** (8 Bank St; ⊙9am-5pm Mon-Sat).

Loch Ness

Deep, dark and narrow, Loch Ness stretches for 23 miles between Inverness and Fort Augustus. Its bitterly cold waters have been extensively explored in search of Nessie, the elusive Loch Ness monster, but most visitors see her only in cardboard-cutout form at the monster exhibitions. The busy A82 road runs along the northwestern shore, while the more tranquil and picturesque B862 follows the southeastern shore. A complete circuit of the loch is about 70 miles – travel anticlockwise for the best views.

Activities

The 73-mile **Great Glen Way** (www.greatglen way.com) long-distance footpath stretches from Inverness to Fort William, where walkers can connect with the **West Highland Way**. It is described in detail in *The Great Glen Way,* a guide by Jacquetta Megarry and Sandra Bardwell.

The Great Glen Way footpath can also be ridden (strenuous!) by mountain bike, while the **Great Glen Mountain Bike Trails** at Nevis Range and Abriachan Forest offer challenging cross-country and downhill trails.

The new **South Loch Ness Trail** (www. visitlochness.com/south-loch-ness-trail), opened in 2011, links a series of footpaths and minor roads along the less-frequented southern side of the loch. The 28 miles from Loch Tarff near Fort Augustus to Torbreck on the

---

STRANGE SPECTACLE ON LOCH NESS

Highland folklore is filled with tales of strange creatures living in lochs and rivers, notably the kelpie (water horse) that lures travellers to their doom. The use of the term 'monster', however, is a relatively recent phenomenon, the origins of which lie in an article published in the *Inverness Courier* on 2 May 1933, entitled 'Strange Spectacle on Loch Ness'.

The article recounted the sighting of a disturbance in the loch by Mrs Aldie Mackay and her husband: 'There the creature disported itself, rolling and plunging for fully a minute, its body resembling that of a whale, and the water cascading and churning like a simmering cauldron.'

The story was taken up by the London press and sparked off a rash of sightings that year, including a notorious on-land encounter with London tourists Mr and Mrs Spicer on 22 July 1933, again reported in the *Inverness Courier*:

'It was horrible, an abomination. About 50 yards ahead, we saw an undulating sort of neck, and quickly followed by a large, ponderous body. I estimated the length to be 25 to 30 feet, its colour was dark elephant grey. It crossed the road in a series of jerks, but because of the slope we could not see its limbs. Although I accelerated quickly towards it, it had disappeared into the loch by the time I reached the spot. There was no sign of it in the water. I am a temperate man, but I am willing to take any oath that we saw this Loch Ness beast. I am certain that this creature was of a prehistoric species.'

The London newspapers couldn't resist. In December 1933 the *Daily Mail* sent Marmaduke Wetherall, a film director and big-game hunter, to Loch Ness to track down the beast. Within days he found 'reptilian' footprints in the shoreline mud (soon revealed to have been made with a stuffed hippopotamus foot). Then in April 1934 came the famous 'long-necked monster' photograph taken by the seemingly reputable Harley St surgeon Colonel Kenneth Wilson. The press went mad and the rest, as they say, is history.

In 1994, however, Christian Spurling – Wetherall's stepson, by then 90 years old – revealed that the most famous photo of Nessie ever taken was in fact a hoax, perpetrated by his stepfather with Wilson's help. Today, of course, there are those who claim that Spurling's confession is itself a hoax. And, ironically, the researcher who exposed the surgeon's photo as a fake still believes wholeheartedly in the monster's existence.

Hoax or not, there's no denying that the bizarre mini-industry that has grown up around Loch Ness and its mysterious monster since that eventful summer three-quarters of a century ago is the strangest spectacle of all.

fringes of Inverness can be done on foot, by bike or on horseback.

There's also the option of the Great Glen Canoe Trail (www.greatglencanoetrail.info), a series of access points, waymarks and informal campsites that allow you to travel the length of the glen by canoe or kayak.

The climb to the summit of **Meallfuarvonie** (699m), on the northwestern shore of Loch Ness, makes an excellent short hill walk: the views along the Great Glen from the top are superb. It's a 6-mile round trip, so allow about three hours. Start from the car park at the end of the minor road leading south from Drumnadrochit to Bunloit.

★ Festivals & Events

RockNess Music Festival   MUSIC
(www.rockness.co.uk) A vast lochside field at the village of Dores hosts this annual festival, a three-day smorgasbord of the best in Scottish and international DJs and bands. Recent headliners include Fat Boy Slim, Leftfield and The Strokes.

DRUMNADROCHIT
POP 800

Seized by monster madness, its gift shops bulging with Nessie cuddly toys, Drumnadrochit is a hotbed of beastie fever, with two monster exhibitions battling it out for the tourist dollar.

◉ Sights & Activities

Urquhart Castle   CASTLE
(HS; ☎01456-450551; adult/child £7.40/4.50; ☺9.30am-6pm Apr-Sep, to 5pm Oct, to 4.30pm Nov-Mar) Commanding a brilliant location 1.5

miles east of Drumnadrochit, with outstanding views (on a clear day), Urquhart Castle is a popular Nessie-watching hotspot. A huge visitor centre (most of which is beneath ground level) includes a video theatre (with a dramatic 'unveiling' of the castle at the end of the film) and displays of medieval items discovered in the castle.

The castle was repeatedly sacked and rebuilt (and sacked and rebuilt) over the centuries; in 1692 it was blown up to prevent the Jacobites from using it. The five-storey tower house at the northern point is the most impressive remaining fragment and offers wonderful views across the water. The site includes a huge gift shop and a restaurant, and is often very crowded in summer.

Loch Ness Centre & Exhibition   EXHIBITION
(☎01456-450573; www.lochness.com; adult/child £6.95/4.95; ☺9am-6pm Jul & Aug, to 5.30pm Jun, 9.30am-5pm Easter-May & Sep-Oct, 10am-3.30pm Nov-Easter) This Nessie-themed attraction adopts a scientific approach that allows you to weigh the evidence for yourself. Exhibits include the original equipment – sonar survey vessels, miniature submarines, cameras and sediment coring tools – used in various monster hunts, as well as original photographs and film footage of sightings. You'll find out about hoaxes and optical illusions, as well as learning a lot about the ecology of Loch Ness – is there enough food in the loch to support even one 'monster', let alone a breeding population?

WORTH A TRIP

DORES INN

While crowded tour coaches pour down the west side of Loch Ness to the hotspots of Drumnadrochit and Urquhart Castle, the narrow B862 road along the eastern shore is relatively peaceful. It leads to the village of Foyers, where you can enjoy a pleasant hike to the **Falls of Foyers**.

But it's worth making the trip just for the Dores Inn (☎01463-751203; www.thedores inn.co.uk; Dores; mains £9-13; ☺lunch & dinner; P☎), a beautifully restored country pub furnished with old church seating, local landscape paintings and fresh flowers. The menu specialises in quality Scottish produce, from haggis, neeps and *tatties* (potatoes), and haddock and chips, to steaks, scallops and seafood platters.

The pub garden enjoys a stunning view along the length of Loch Ness, and even has a dedicated monster-spotting vantage point. The nearby campervan, emblazoned with Nessie-Serry Independent Research, has been home to dedicated Nessie hunter Steve Feltham (www.haveyouseenityet.co.uk) since 1991; he sells clay models of the monster, and is a fund of fascinating stories about the loch.

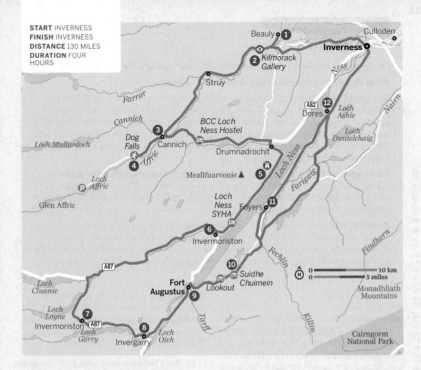

Driving Tour
A Loch Ness Circuit

❭ Head out of Inverness on the A862 to Beauly, arriving in time for breakfast at **1 Corner on the Square** in Beauly. Backtrack a mile and turn right on the A831 to Cannich, passing **2 Kilmorack Gallery**, which exhibits contemporary art in a converted church. The scenery gets wilder as you approach **3 Cannich**; turn right and follow the single-track road to the car park at **4 Dog Falls**. Take a stroll along the rushing river, or hike to the viewpoint (one hour round trip) for a glimpse of remote Glen Affric.

Return to Cannich and turn right on the A831 to Drumnadrochit, then right on the A82 past picturesque **5 Urquhart Castle** and along the shores of Loch Ness. At **6 Invermoriston**, pause to look at the old bridge, built by Telford in 1813, then head west on the A897 towards Kyle of Lochalsh; after 16 miles go left on the A87 towards Invergarry. You are now among some of the finest mountain scenery in the Highlands; as the road turns east above Loch Garry, stop at the famous **7 viewpoint** (layby on right,

not signposted). By a quirk of perspective, the lochs to the west appear to form the map outline of Scotland.

At **8 Invergarry**, turn left on the A82 to reach **9 Fort Augustus** and a late lunch at the Lovat or Lock Inn. Take the B862 out of town, following the line of General Wade's 18th-century military road, to another viewpoint at **10 Suidhe Chuimein**. A short (800m) walk up the well-worn path to the summit affords an even better panorama.

Ahead, you can choose the low road via the impressive **11 Falls of Foyers**, or stay on the the high road (B862) for more views; both converge on Loch Ness at the **12 Dores Inn**, where you can sip a pint with a view along Loch Ness, and even stay for dinner before returning to Inverness.

LOCAL KNOWLEDGE

ADRIAN SHINE

Leader of the Loch Ness Project, and designer of the Loch Ness Centre & Exhibition

What do you recommend seeing around Loch Ness?

Urquhart Castle If, having learned some of the inner secrets of the loch at the Loch Ness Centre & Exhibition (p332), you want to see it through new eyes, you cannot do better than visit Urquhart Castle (p332). Perched on a rocky promontory jutting into Loch Ness, its exhibits recount the castle's history from a vitrified Pictish fort to its role in the Scottish Wars of Independence. The view from the Grant Tower is truly breathtaking.

Fort Augustus Locks At the southern end of the loch there is a flight of locks on the Caledonian Canal (p335) built by the great engineer Thomas Telford. It is always interesting to watch vessels being worked up this 'staircase' of water. British Waterways have a fascinating exhibition halfway up.

Waterfall Walks Starting from the car park at Invermoriston, cross the road to find a magnificent waterfall, then go back to take the path down the river through a mature beech wood to the shores of the loch. There is another famous waterfall at Foyers on the southeastern shore of Loch Ness, and Divach Falls up Balmacaan Rd at Drumnadrochit.

Nessieland Castle Monster Centre
EXHIBITION

(www.nessieland.co.uk; adult/child £5.50/4; ⊙9am-8pm Jul & Aug, 10am-5.30pm Apr-Jun, Sep & Oct, 10am-4pm Nov-Mar) This attraction is a miniature theme park aimed squarely at the kids, though we suspect its main function is to sell you Loch Ness monster souvenirs.

Nessie Hunter
BOAT TOUR

(☏01456-450395; www.lochness-cruises.com; adult/child £15/10; ⊙Easter-Oct) One-hour monster-hunting cruises, complete with sonar and underwater cameras. Cruises depart from Drumnadrochit hourly (except 1pm) from 9am to 6pm daily.

🛏 Sleeping & Eating

Loch Ness Inn
INN ££

(☏01456-450991; www.staylochness.co.uk; Lewiston; s/d/f £89/102/145; P🐾) The Loch Ness Inn ticks all the weary traveller's boxes, with comfortable bedrooms (the family suite sleeps two adults and two children), a cosy bar pouring real ales from the Cairngorm and Isle of Skye breweries, and a rustic restaurant (mains £9 to £18) serving hearty, wholesome fare such as whisky-flambéed haggis and roast rump of Scottish lamb.

It's conveniently located in the quiet hamlet of Lewiston, between Drumnadrochit and Urquhart Castle.

Drumbuie Farm
B&B ££

(☏01456-450634; www.loch-ness-farm.co.uk; Drumnadrochit; per person from £30; ⊙Mar-Oct; P) Drumbuie is a B&B in a modern house on a working farm – the surrounding fields are full of sheep and highland cattle – with views over Urquhart Castle and Loch Ness. Walkers and cyclists are welcome.

Loch Ness Backpackers Lodge
HOSTEL £

(☏01456-450807; www.lochness-backpackers. com; Coiltie Farmhouse, East Lewiston; per person from £16; P) This snug, friendly hostel housed in a cottage and barn has six-bed dorms, one double and a large barbecue area. It's about 0.75 miles from Drumnadrochit, along the A82 towards Fort William; turn left where you see the sign for Loch Ness Inn, just before the bridge.

Loch Ness SYHA
HOSTEL £

(☏01320-351274; www.syha.org.uk; dm £18.50; ⊙Apr-Sep; @) This hostel is housed in a big lodge overlooking Loch Ness, and many dorms have loch views. It's located on the A82 road, 13 miles southwest of Drumnadrochit, and 4 miles northeast of Invermoriston. Buses from Inverness to Fort William stop nearby.

Borlum Farm
CAMPSITE £

(☏01456-450220; www.borlum.co.uk; sites per adult/child £6/4; ⊙Mar-Oct) Beside the main road 800m southeast of Drumnadrochit.

Fiddler's Coffee Shop & Restaurant
CAFE, RESTAURANT ££

(www.fiddledrum.co.uk; mains £8-17; ⊙11am-11pm; 🐾) The coffee shop does cappuccino and croissants, while the restaurant serves Highland fare such as venison casserole, and a wide range of Scottish beers. There's a whisky bar with huge range of single malts.

❶ Getting There & Away

Scottish Citylink (p319) and Stagecoach (p491) buses from Inverness run along the shores of Loch Ness (six to eight daily, five on Sunday); those headed for Skye turn off at Invermoriston. There are bus stops at Drumnadrochit (£6.20, 30 minutes), Urquhart Castle car park (£6.60, 35 minutes) and Loch Ness Youth Hostel (£8.60, 45 minutes).

FORT AUGUSTUS
POP 510

Fort Augustus, at the junction of four old military roads, was originally a government garrison and the headquarters of General George Wade's road-building operations in the early 18th century. Today it's a neat and picturesque little place, often overrun by tourists in summer.

◉ Sights & Activities

Caledonian Canal   CANAL

At Fort Augustus, boats using the Caledonian Canal are raised and lowered 13m by a 'ladder' of five consecutive locks. It's fun to watch, and the neatly landscaped canal banks are a great place to soak up the sun or compare accents with fellow tourists. The Caledonian Canal Heritage Centre (☏01320-366493; admission free; ⊙10am-5pm Apr-Oct), beside the lowest lock, showcases the history of the canal.

Clansman Centre   MUSEUM

(www.scottish-swords.com; ⊙10am-6pm Apr-Oct) This exhibition of 17th-century Highland life has live demonstrations of how to put on a plaid (the forerunner of the kilt) and how the claymore (Highland sword) was made and used. There is also a workshop where you can purchase handcrafted reproduction swords, dirks and shields.

Royal Scot   BOAT TOUR

(☏01320-366277; www.cruiselochness.com; adult/child £12.50/8; ⊙hourly 10am-4pm Apr-Oct, 1 & 2pm only Nov-Mar) One-hour cruises on Loch Ness accompanied by the latest high-tech sonar equipment so you can keep an underwater eye open for Nessie.

🛏 Sleeping & Eating

TOP CHOICE **Lovat**   HOTEL £££

(☏01456-459250; www.thelovat.com; Main Rd; d from £121; P🐾) A boutique-style makeover has transformed this former huntin'-and-shootin' hotel into a luxurious but ecoconscious retreat set apart from the tourist crush around the canal. The bedrooms are spacious and stylishly furnished, while the lounge is equipped with a log fire, comfy armchairs and grand piano.

There's an informal brasserie here, as well as a highly acclaimed restaurant (five-course dinner £45) which serves top-quality cuisine.

Morag's Lodge   HOSTEL £

(☏01320-366289; www.moragslodge.com; Bunoich Brae; dm/tw/f from £20/48/66; P@🐾) This large and well-run hostel is based in a big Victorian house with great views of Fort Augustus' hilly surrounds, and has a convivial bar with open fire. It's hidden away in the trees up the steep side road just north of the tourist office car park.

Lorien House   B&B ££

(☏01320-366736; www.lorien-house.co.uk; Station Rd; s/d £40/70) Lorien is a cut above your usual B&B – the bathrooms here come with bidets and the breakfasts with smoked salmon, and you can find a library of walking, cycling and climbing guides in the lounge.

Cumberland's Campsite   CAMPSITE £

(☏01320-366257; www.cumberlands-campsite.com; Glendoe Rd; sites per adult/child £8/3; ⊙Apr-Sep) Southeast of the village on the B862 towards Whitebridge; entrance beside Stravaigers Lodge.

Lock Inn   PUB ££

(Canal Side; mains £9-14; ⊙meals noon-8pm) A superb little pub right on the canal bank, the Lock Inn has a vast range of malt whiskies and a tempting menu of bar meals, which includes Orkney salmon, Highland venison and daily seafood specials; the house speciality is beer-battered haddock and chips.

❶ Information

There's an ATM and bureau de change in the post office beside the canal.

Fort Augustus tourist office (☏01320-366367; ⊙9am-6pm Mon-Sat & 9am-5pm Sun Easter-Oct) In the central car park.

❶ Getting There & Away

Scottish Citylink (p319) and Stagecoach (p491) buses from Inverness to Fort William stop at Fort Augustus (£10.20, one hour, six to eight daily Monday to Saturday, five on Sunday).

THE CAIRNGORMS

The Cairngorms National Park (www.cairn gorms.co.uk) encompasses the highest land-mass in Britain – a broad mountain plateau, riven only by the deep valleys of the Lairig Ghru and Loch Avon, with an average altitude of over 1000m and including five of the six highest summits in the UK. This wild mountain landscape of granite and heather has a sub-Arctic climate and supports rare alpine tundra vegetation and high-altitude bird species, such as snow buntings, ptarmigans and dotterels.

The harsh mountain environment gives way lower down to scenic glens softened by beautiful open forests of native Scots pine, home to rare animals and birds such as pine martens, wildcats, red squirrels, ospreys, capercaillies and crossbills.

This is prime hill-walking territory, but even couch potatoes can enjoy a taste of the high life by taking the Cairngorm Mountain Railway up to the edge of the Cairngorm plateau.

Aviemore

POP 2400

Aviemore is the gateway to the Cairngorms, the region's main centre for transport, accommodation, restaurants and shopping. It's not the prettiest town in Scotland by a long stretch – the main attractions are in the surrounding area – but when bad weather puts the hills off-limits, Aviemore fills up with hikers, cyclists and climbers (plus skiers and snowboarders in winter) cruising the outdoor-equipment shops or recounting their latest adventures in the cafes and bars. Add in tourists and locals and the eclectic mix makes for a lively little town.

Aviemore is on a loop off the A9 Perth–Inverness road; almost everything of note is to be found along the main drag, Grampian Rd. The train station and bus stop are towards the southern end.

The Cairngorm skiing area and funicular railway lie 9 miles southeast of Aviemore along the B970 (Ski Rd) and its continuation, past Coylumbridge and Glenmore.

◉ Sights

Strathspey Steam Railway   HERITAGE RAILWAY
(☑01479-810725; www.strathspeyrailway.co.uk; Station Sq; return ticket per adult/child £11.50/5.75) Strathspey Steam Railway runs steam trains on a section of restored line between Aviemore and Broomhill, 10 miles to the northeast, via Boat of Garten. There are four or five trains daily from June to September, and a more limited service in April, May, October and December.

An extension to Grantown-on-Spey is planned (see www.railstograntown.org); in the meantime, you can continue from Broomhill to Grantown-on-Spey by bus.

Rothiemurchus Estate   FOREST
(www.rothiemurchus.net) The Rothiemurchus Estate, which extends from the River Spey at Aviemore to the Cairngorm summit plateau, is famous for having Scotland's largest remnant of **Caledonian forest**, the ancient forest of Scots pine that once covered most of the country. The forest is home to a large population of red squirrels, and is one of the last bastions of the Scottish wildcat.

The **Rothiemurchus Estate visitor centre** (☑01479-812345; admission free; ⊙9am-5.30pm), a mile southeast of Aviemore along the B970, sells an *Explorer Map* detailing more than 50 miles of **footpaths** and **cycling trails**, including the wheelchair-accessible 4-mile trail around **Loch an Eilein**, with its ruined castle and peaceful pine woods.

Craigellachie
Nature Reserve   NATURE RESERVE
(www.nnr-scotland.org.uk/craigellachie; Grampian Rd; ♿) A trail leads west from Aviemore Youth Hostel and passes under the A9 into the Craigellachie Nature Reserve, a great place for short hikes across steep hillsides covered in natural birch forest. Look out for wildlife, including the peregrine falcons that nest on the crags from April to July. If you're very lucky, you may even spot a capercaillie.

🏃 Activities

Bothy Bikes   MOUNTAIN BIKING
(☑01479-810111; www.bothybikes.co.uk; Dalfaber; per half-/full day £16/20; ⊙9am-5.30pm) Located just outside Aviemore on the way to Cairngorm, this place rents out mountain bikes and can also advise on routes and trails; a good choice for beginners is the **Old Logging Way**, which runs from the hire centre to Glenmore, where you can make a circuit of Loch Morlich before returning. For experienced bikers, the whole of the Cairngorms is your playground. Booking recommended.

The Cairngorms

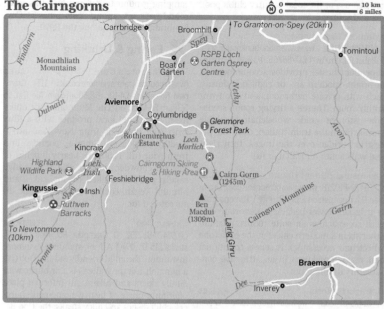

Rothiemurchus Fishery

FISHING

(☎01479-810703; www.rothiemurchus.net; Rothiemurchus Estate; ☉9am-5.30pm, to 9pm Jul & Aug) Cast for rainbow trout at this loch at the southern end of the village; buy permits (from £10 to £30 per day, plus £5 for tackle hire) at the Fish Farm Shop. If you're a fly-fishing virgin, there's a beginner's package, including tackle hire, one hour's instruction and one hour's fishing, for £39 per person.

For experienced anglers, there's also salmon and sea-trout fishing on the River Spey – a day permit costs around £20; numbers are limited, so it's best to book in advance.

Cairngorm Sled-Dog Centre

DOG SLEDDING

(☎07767-270526; www.sled-dogs.co.uk; Ski Rd) This outfit will take you on a 20-minute sled tour of local forest trails in the wake of a team of huskies (adult/child £50/35), or a three-hour sled-dog safari (£150 per person). The sleds have wheels, so snow's not necessary. There are also one-hour guided tours of the kennels (adult/child £8/4). The centre is 3 miles east of Aviemore, signposted off the road to Loch Morlich.

Alvie & Dalraddy Estate

QUAD BIKING

(☎01479-810330; www.alvie-estate.co.uk; Dalraddy Holiday Park; per person £42) Join a cross-country quad-bike trek at this estate, 3 miles south of Aviemore on the B9152 (call first).

Aviemore Highland Resort

LEISURE COMPLEX

(☎0844 879 9152; www.aviemorehighlandresort.com) This complex of hotels, chalets and restaurants to the west of Grampian Rd includes a swimming pool, gym, spa, videogame arcade and a huge, shiny shopping mall. The swimming pool and other leisure facilities are open to nonresidents.

🛏 Sleeping

Old Minister's House

B&B ££

(☎01479-812181; www.theoldministershouse.co.uk; Rothiemurchus; s/d £70/110; ℗🖂) This former manse dates from 1906 and has four rooms with a homely, country-farmhouse feel. It's in a lovely setting amid Scots pines on the banks of the River Druie, just 0.75 miles southeast of Aviemore.

Ardlogie Guest House

B&B ££

(☎01479-810747; www.ardlogie.co.uk; Dalfaber Rd; s/d from £40/60, bothy per 3 nights £165; ℗🖂) Handy for the train station, the five-room Ardlogie has great views over the River Spey towards the Cairngorms. There's also self-catering accommodation in the Bothy, a cosy, two-person timber cabin. Facilities include a boules pitch in the garden, and guests can get free use of the local country club's pool, spa and sauna.

Aviemore Bunkhouse
HOSTEL £

(☎01479-811181; www.aviemore-bunkhouse.com; Dalfaber Rd; dm/tw/f £17/55/65; P@🛜) This independent hostel provides accommodation in bright, modern six- or eight-bed dorms, each with private bathroom, and one twin/family room. There's a drying room, secure bike storage and wheelchair-accessible dorms. From the train station, cross the pedestrian bridge over the tracks, turn right and walk south on Dalfaber Rd.

Ravenscraig Guest House
B&B ££

(☎01479-810278; www.aviemoreonline.com; Grampian Rd; r per person £35-42; P🛜) Ravenscraig is a large, flower-bedecked Victorian villa with six spacious en suite rooms, plus another six in a modern chalet at the back (one wheelchair accessible). It serves traditional and veggie breakfasts in an attractive conservatory dining room.

Cairngorm Hotel
HOTEL ££

(☎01479-810233; www.cairngorm.com; Grampian Rd; s/d from £59/98; P🛜) Better known as 'the Cairn', this long-established hotel is set in the fine old granite building with the pointy turret opposite the train station. It's a welcoming place with comfortable rooms and a determinedly Scottish atmosphere, all tartan carpets and stags' antlers. There's live music on weekends, so it can get a bit noisy – not for early-to-bedders.

Hilton Coylumbridge
HOTEL ££

(☎01479-810661; www.coylumbridge.hilton.com; Coylumbridge; d from £110; P🛜🏊) This modern, low-rise Hilton, set amid the pine woods just outside Aviemore, is a wonderfully family-friendly hotel, with bedrooms for up to two adults and two children, indoor and outdoor play areas, a crèche and a baby-sitting service. The hotel is 1.5 miles east of Aviemore, on the road to Loch Morlich.

Aviemore SYHA
HOSTEL £

(☎01479-810345; www.syha.org.uk; 25 Grampian Rd; dm £18; P@🛜) Upmarket hostelling in a spacious, well-equipped building, five minutes' walk south of the village centre. There are four- and six-bed rooms, and a comfortable lounge with views of the mountains.

Rothiemurchus Camp & Caravan Park
CAMPSITE £

(☎01479-812800; www.rothiemurchus.net; Coylumbridge; sites per adult/child £9/2) The nearest camping ground to Aviemore is this year-round park set among Scots pines at Coylumbridge, 1.5 miles along the B970.

🍴 Eating & Drinking

⭐ TOP CHOICE Mountain Cafe
CAFE £

(www.mountaincafe-aviemore.co.uk; 111 Grampian Rd; mains £4-10; ⊗8.30am-5pm Tue-Thu, to 5.30pm Fri-Mon; 🚼) The Mountain Cafe offers freshly prepared local produce with a Kiwi twist (the owner is from New Zealand) – healthy breakfasts of muesli, porridge and fresh fruit (till 11.30am), hearty lunches of seafood chowder, burgers and imaginative salads, and homebaked breads, cakes and biscuits. Vegan, coeliac and nut-allergic diets catered for.

Ski-ing Doo
BISTRO ££

(☎01479-810392; 9 Grampian Rd; mains £7-12, steaks £15-17; 🛜🚼) A long-standing Aviemore institution, the child-friendly Ski-ing Doo (it's a pun…oh, ask the waiter!) is a favourite with family skiers and hikers. An informal place offering a range of hearty, homemade burgers, chilli dishes and juicy steaks; the Doo Below cafe-bar is open all day from noon.

Winking Owl
PUB

(Grampian Rd) Lively local pub, popular with hikers and climbers, serving a good range of real ales and malt whiskies.

Old Bridge Inn
PUB

(☎01479-811137; www.oldbridgeinn.co.uk; 23 Dalfaber Rd; 🛜) The Old Bridge has a snug bar, complete with roaring log fire in winter, and a cheerful, chalet-style restaurant (www.oldbridgeinn.co.uk; 23 Dalfaber Rd; mains £9-18; ⊗lunch & dinner, till 10pm Fri & Sat) at the back serving quality Scottish cuisine.

Café Mambo
CAFE, BAR

(The Mall, Grampian Rd; 🛜) The Mambo is a popular chill-out cafe in the afternoon, and turns into a clubbing and live-band venue in the evenings.

ℹ️ Information

There are ATMs outside the Tesco supermarket, and currency exchange at the post office and the tourist office, all located on Grampian Rd.

Aviemore tourist office (☎01479-810363; www.visitaviemore.com; The Mall, Grampian Rd; ⊗9am-6pm Mon-Sat, 9.30am-5pm Sun Jul & Aug, 9am-5pm Mon-Sat, 10am-4pm Sun Easter-Jun, Sep & Oct) Hours are limited from October to Easter.

Caffe Bleu (www.caffebleu.com; Grampian Rd; per 30min £1; 🛜) Free wi-fi. Next door to the tourist office.

ℹ️ Getting There & Away

Bus

Buses stop on Grampian Rd opposite the train station; buy tickets at the tourist office. Services include the following:

Edinburgh £24.40, 3¾ hours, three daily

Glasgow £24.40, 3¾ hours, three daily

Grantown-on-Spey 35 minutes, five daily weekdays, two Saturday; bus 33 via Carrbridge (15 minutes)

Inverness £5.50, 1¾ hours, three daily Monday to Friday; via Grantown-on-Spey

Perth £18, two hours, five daily

Train

The train station is on Grampian Rd.

Glasgow/Edinburgh £44, three hours, six daily

Inverness £11, 40 minutes, 12 daily

ℹ️ Getting Around

Bicycle

Several places in Aviemore, Rothiemurchus Estate and Glenmore have mountain bikes for hire. An off-road cycle track links Aviemore with Glenmore and Loch Morlich.

Bothy Bikes (📞01479-810111; www.bothy bikes.co.uk; Ski Rd; ⊙9am-5.30pm) Charges £20 a day for a quality bike with front suspension and disc brakes.

Bus

Bus 34 links Aviemore to Cairngorm car park (45 minutes, hourly) via Coylumbridge and Glenmore. A Strathspey Dayrider/Megarider ticket (£6.40/16) gives one/seven days unlimited bus travel from Aviemore as far as Cairngorm, Carrbridge and Kingussie (buy from the bus driver).

Around Aviemore

CAIRNGORM MOUNTAIN

Cairngorm Mountain
Railway   FUNICULAR RAILWAY
(📞01479-861261; www.cairngormmountain.org; adult/child return £9.95/6.50; ⊙10.20am-4pm May-Nov, 9am-4.30pm Dec-Apr) The region's most popular attraction is a funicular railway that will whisk you to the edge of the Cairngorm plateau (1085m) in just eight minutes. The bottom station is at the Coire Cas car park at the end of Ski Rd; at the top is an exhibition, a shop (of course) and a restaurant. Unfortunately, for environmental

and safety reasons, you're not allowed out of the top station in summer unless you book a 90-minute guided walk to the summit of Cairn Gorm (adult/child £15.95/10.50, twice a day May to October). Check the website for details.

Cairngorm Mountain   WINTER SPORTS
(www.cairngormmountain.org) Aspen or Val d'Isère it ain't, but with 19 runs and 23 miles of piste Cairngorm is Scotland's biggest ski area. A ski pass for one day is £31.50/19 for adults/under 16s. Ski or snowboard hire is around £22.50/16.50 per adult/child per day; there are lots of hire outlets at Coire Cas, Glenmore and Aviemore.

When the snow is at its best and the sun is shining you can close your eyes and imagine you're in the Alps; sadly, low cloud, high winds and horizontal sleet are more common. The season usually runs from December until the snow melts, which may be as late as the end of April, but snowfall here is unpredictable – in some years the slopes can be open in November, but closed for lack of snow in February. During the season the tourist office in Aviemore displays snow conditions and avalanche warnings. You can check the latest snow conditions at http://ski.visitscotland.com and www.winterhigh land.info.

LOCH MORLICH

Six miles east of Aviemore, Loch Morlich is surrounded by some 8 sq miles of pine and spruce forest that makes up the **Glenmore Forest Park**. Its attractions include a sandy beach (at the east end).

◉ Sights & Activities

The park's **visitor centre** at Glenmore has a small exhibition on the Caledonian forest and sells the *Glenmore Forest Park Map,* detailing local walks. The **circuit of Loch Morlich** (one hour) makes a pleasant outing; the trail is pram- and wheelchair-friendly.

🏆 **Glenmore Lodge**   ADVENTURE SPORTS
(www.glenmorelodge.org.uk) One of Britain's leading adventure sports training centres, offering courses in hill walking, rock climbing, ice climbing, canoeing, mountain biking and mountaineering. The centre's comfortable **B&B accommodation** (tw £54-74) is available to all, even if you're not taking a course, as is the indoor-climbing wall, gym and sauna.

MOUNTAIN WALKS IN THE CAIRNGORMS

The climb from the car park at the Coire Cas ski area to the summit of **Cairn Gorm** (1245m) takes about two hours (one way). From there, you can continue south across the high-level plateau to Ben Macdui (1309m), Britain's second-highest peak. This takes eight to 10 hours return from the car park and is a serious undertaking; it's for experienced and well-equipped walkers only.

The **Lairig Ghru trail**, which can take eight to 10 hours, is a demanding 24-mile walk from Aviemore through the Lairig Ghru pass (840m) to Braemar. An alternative to doing the full route is to make the six-hour return hike up to the summit of the pass and back to Aviemore. The path starts from Ski Rd, a mile east of Coylumbridge, and involves some very rough going.

Warning – the Cairngorm plateau is a sub-Arctic environment where navigation is difficult and weather conditions can be severe, even in midsummer. Hikers must have proper hill-walking equipment, and know how to use a map and compass. In winter it is a place for experienced mountaineers only.

Cairngorm Reindeer Centre WILDLIFE PARK
(www.cairngormreindeer.co.uk; adult/child £10/5) The warden here will take you on a tour to see and feed Britain's only herd of reindeer, who are very tame and will even eat out of your hand. Walks take place at 11am, plus another at 2.30pm from May to September, and 3.30pm Monday to Friday in July and August.

Loch Morlich
Watersports Centre WATER SPORTS
(www.lochmorlich.com; ☉9am-5pm May-Oct) This popular outfit rents out Canadian canoes (£19 an hour), kayaks (£7.50), sailboards (£16.50), sailing dinghies (£23) and rowing boats (£19), and also offers instruction.

🛏 Sleeping

Cairngorm Lodge SYHA HOSTEL £
(☎01479-861238; dm £18; ☉closed Nov & Dec; @⊛) Set in a former shooting lodge that enjoys a great location at the east end of Loch Morlich; prebooking is essential.

Glenmore Caravan &
Camping Site CAMPSITE £
(☎01479-861271; www.campingintheforest.co.uk; tent & campervan sites £23; ☉year-round) Campers can set up base at this attractive lochside site with pitches amid the Scots pines; rates include up to four people per tent/campervan.

ℹ Getting There & Away

Bus 34 links Aviemore with Glenmore.

KINCRAIG & GLEN FESHIE

The Highland Wildlife Park (☎01540-651270; www.highlandwildlifepark.org; adult/child £14/10; ☉10am-5pm Apr-Oct, to 6pm Jul & Aug, to 4pm Nov-Mar) near Kincraig, 6 miles southwest of Aviemore, features a drive-through safari park and animal enclosures offering the chance to view rarely-seen native wildlife, such as wildcats, capercaillies, pine martens, white-tailed sea eagles and red squirrels, as well as species that once roamed the Scottish hills but have long since disappeared, including wolves, lynx, wild boars, beavers and European bison. Visitors without cars get driven around by staff (at no extra cost). Last entry is two hours before closing. Stagecoach bus 32 runs from Aviemore to Kincraig (10 minutes, five daily Monday to Saturday).

At Kincraig the Spey widens into Loch Insh, home of the **Loch Insh Watersports Centre** (☎01540-651272; www.lochinsh.com; Kincraig; ☉8.30am-5.30pm), which offers canoeing, windsurfing, sailing, bike hire and fishing, as well as B&B accommodation. The food here is good, especially after 6.30pm when the lochside cafe metamorphoses into a cosy restaurant.

Beautiful, tranquil **Glen Feshie** extends south from Kincraig, deep into the Cairngorms, with Scots pine woods in its upper reaches surrounded by big, heathery hills. The 4WD track to the head of the glen makes a great mountain-bike excursion (25-mile round trip).

CARRBRIDGE
POP 540

Carrbridge, 7 miles northeast of Aviemore, is a good alternative base for exploring the region. It takes its name from the graceful old bridge (spotlit at night), built in 1717, over the thundering rapids of the Dulnain.

The **Landmark Forest Adventure Park** (01479-841613; www.landmarkpark.co.uk; adult/child £12.95/10.80; 10am-7pm mid-Jul–Aug, to 6pm Apr–mid-Jul, to 5pm or 6pm Sep-Mar), set in a forest of Scots pines, is a theme park with a difference; the theme is timber. The main attractions are the Ropeworx highwire adventure course, the Treetops Trail (a raised walkway through the forest canopy that allows you to view red squirrels, crossbills and crested tits), and the steam-powered sawmill.

Bus 34 runs from Inverness to Carrbridge (45 minutes, six daily Monday to Friday, three on Saturday) and onwards to Grantown-on-Spey (20 minutes) and Aviemore.

BOAT OF GARTEN

Boat of Garten is known as the Osprey Village because these rare and beautiful birds of prey nest nearby at the **RSPB Loch Garten Osprey Centre** (01479-831694; www.rspb.org.uk/lochgarten; Tulloch; adult/child £4/2.50; 10am-6pm Apr-Aug). The ospreys migrate here each spring from Africa and nest in a tall pine tree – you can watch from a hide as the birds feed their young. The centre is signposted about 2 miles east of the village.

There is good-quality hostel accommodation at **Fraoch Lodge** (01479-831331; www.scotmountain.co.uk/hostel; Deshar Rd; per person £21-23; P), while the **Boat Hotel** (01479-831258; www.boathotel.co.uk; s/d from £77/147; P) offers luxurious accommodation and a superb restaurant.

Boat of Garten is 6 miles northeast of Aviemore. The most interesting way to get here is on the Strathspey Steam Railway (p336).

Grantown-on-Spey

POP 2170

Grantown (*gran*-ton) is an elegant Georgian town on the banks of the Spey, a favoured haunt of anglers and the tweed-cap-and-green-wellies brigade. Thronged with tourists in summer, it reverts to a quiet backwater in winter. Most hotels can kit you out for a day of fly-fishing or put you in touch with someone who can.

🛏 Sleeping & Eating

Brooklynn   B&B ££
(01479-873113; www.woodier.com; Grant Rd; r per person £36-42; P) This beautiful Victorian villa features original stained glass and wood panelling, and seven spacious, luxurious rooms (all doubles have en suites). The food – dinner is available as well as breakfast – is superb, too.

Craggan Mill   RESTAURANT ££
(01479-872288; www.cragganmill.co.uk; mains £13-23; Wed-Mon) Housed in a restored 18th-century meal mill just south of Grantown-on-Spey on the A95 towards Aviemore, the Craggan is strong on rustic atmosphere and friendly service. The menu doesn't disappoint either, with expertly prepared Scottish seafood, lamb and beef.

Glass House   RESTAURANT £££
(01479-872980; Grant Rd; mains £18-22; noon-1.45pm Wed-Sat, 7-9pm Tue-Sat, 12.30-2pm Sun) Elegant but unpretentious restaurant famous for fresh, seasonal menus that focus on local produce.

Chaplin's Coffee House & Ice Cream Parlour   CAFE £
(High St; 9.30am-5pm Mon-Sat, 10am-4.30pm Sun) Traditional family cafe selling delicious homemade ice cream.

❶ Getting There & Away

Bus 34 runs from Inverness to Aviemore via Grantown-on-Spey (£8, 1¾ hours, six daily Monday to Friday, three on Saturday).

Kingussie & Newtonmore

The gracious old Speyside towns of Kingussie (kin-*yew*-see) and Newtonmore sit at the foot of the great heather-clad humps known as the Monadhliath Mountains. Newtonmore is best known as the home of the excellent Highland Folk Museum.

◉ Sights & Activities

FREE **Highland Folk Museum**   MUSEUM
(01540-673551; www.highlandfolk.museum; Kingussie Rd, Newtonmore; 10.30am-5.30pm Apr-Aug, 11am-4.30pm Sep & Oct) The open-air Highland Folk Museum comprises a collection of historical buildings and relics revealing many aspects of Highland culture and lifestyle. Laid out like a farming township, it has a community of traditional thatch-roofed cottages, a sawmill, a schoolhouse, a shepherd's bothy (hut) and a rural post office. Actors in period costume give demonstrations of woodcarving, spinning and peat-fire baking. You'll need at least two to three hours to make the most of a visit here.

1. Isle of Skye (p392)
The largest of Scotland's islands is a 50-mile-long smorgasbord of velvet moors, jagged mountains, sparkling lochs and towering sea cliffs.

2. Assynt (p382)
The otherwordly scenery of Assynt epitomises the wild magnificence of the northwest Highlands.

3. Loch Lomond (p272)
Loch Lomond is the largest lake in mainland Britain and, after Loch Ness, perhaps the most famous of Scotland's lochs.

FREE Laggan Wolftrax MOUNTAIN BIKING
(www.forestry.gov.uk/WolfTrax; Strathmashie Forest; ☺10am-6pm Mon, 9.30am-5pm Tue, Thu & Fri, 9.30am-6pm Sat & Sun) Ten miles southwest of Newtonmore, on the A86 road towards Spean Bridge, this is one of Scotland's top mountain-biking centres with purpose-built trails ranging from open-country riding to black-diamond downhills with rock slabs and drop-offs. Bike hire is available on-site, from £25 a day for a hardtail mountain bike to £50 for a full-suspension bike.

Ruthven Barracks RUIN
(HS; ☺24hr) Ruthven Barracks was one of four garrisons built by the British government after the first Jacobite rebellion of 1715, as part of a Hanoverian scheme to take control of the Highlands. Ironically, the barracks were last occupied by Jacobite troops awaiting the return of Bonnie Prince Charlie after the Battle of Culloden.

Learning of his defeat and subsequent flight, they set fire to the barracks before taking to the glens (the building is still roofless). Perched dramatically on a river terrace and clearly visible from the main A9 road near Kingussie, the ruins are spectacularly floodlit at night.

🛏 Sleeping & Eating

TOP CHOICE Eagleview Guest House B&B ££
(☎01540-673675; www.eagleviewguesthouse.co.uk; Perth Rd, Newtonmore; r per person £36-38; P@�☞) The family-friendly Eagleview is one of the nicest places to stay in the area, with beautifully decorated bedrooms, super-king-size beds, spacious bathrooms with power showers, and nice little touches such as wall-mounted flatscreen TVs, cafetières with real coffee on your hospitality tray and real milk rather than that yucky UHT stuff.

Homewood Lodge B&B ££
(☎01540-661507; www.homewood-lodge-kingussie.co.uk; Newtonmore Rd, Kingussie; r per person £25-30; P) This elegant Victorian lodge on the western outskirts of Kingussie offers double rooms with exquisite views of the Cairngorms – a nice way to wake up in the mornings! The owners are committed to recycling and energy efficiency, and have created a mini–nature reserve in the garden.

Hermitage B&B ££
(☎01540-662137; www.thehermitage-scotland.com; Spey St, Kingussie; s/d from £38/78; P�☞) The five-bedroom Hermitage is a lovely old house with plenty of character, filled with Victorian period features – ask for room 5, with double bed, Chesterfield sofa, and a view of the hills. The lounge has deep sofas ranged by a log fire, and there are good views of the Cairngorms from the breakfast room and garden.

TOP CHOICE The Cross RESTAURANT £££
(☎01540-661166; www.thecross.co.uk; Tweed Mill Brae, off Ardbroilach Rd, Kingussie; 3-course dinner £55; ☺dinner Tue-Sat, closed Jan; P) Housed in a converted water mill, the Cross is one of the finest restaurants in the Highlands. The intimate, low-raftered dining room has an open fire and a patio overlooking the stream, and serves a daily-changing menu of fresh Scottish produce accompanied by a superb wine list.

If you want to stay the night, there are eight stylish rooms (double or twin £110 to £140) to choose from.

❶ Getting There & Away

Bus
Kingussie and Newtonmore are served by Scottish Citylink (p319) buses:

Aviemore £7.20, 25 minutes, five to seven daily

Inverness £12.50, one hour, six to eight Monday to Saturday, three Sunday

Perth £15.20, 1¾ hours, five daily

Train
Kingussie's train station is at the southern end of town. Kingussie and Newtonmore are served by the following:

Edinburgh £44, 2½ hours, seven a day Monday to Saturday, two Sunday

Inverness £11, one hour, eight a day Monday to Saturday, four Sunday

WEST HIGHLANDS

This area extends from the bleak blanket-bog of the Moor of Rannoch to the west coast beyond Glen Coe and Fort William, and includes the southern reaches of the Great Glen. The scenery is grand throughout, with high and wild mountains dominating the glens. Great expanses of moor alternate with lochs and patches of commercial forest. Fort William, at the inner end of Loch Linnhe, is the only sizable town in the area.

Since 2007 the region has been promoted as Lochaber Geopark (www.lochabergeopark.org.uk), an area of outstanding geology and scenery.

Glen Coe

Scotland's most famous glen is also one of the grandest and, in bad weather, the grimmest. The approach to the glen from the east, watched over by the rocky pyramid of **Buachaille Etive Mor** – the Great Shepherd of Etive – leads over the Pass of Glencoe and into the narrow upper valley. The southern side is dominated by three massive, brooding spurs, known as the **Three Sisters**, while the northern side is enclosed by the continuous steep wall of the knife-edged Aonach Eagach ridge. The main road threads its lonely way through the middle of all this mountain grandeur, past deep gorges and crashing waterfalls, to the more pastoral lower reaches of the glen around Loch Achtriochtan and Glencoe village.

Glencoe was written into the history books in 1692 when the resident MacDonalds were murdered by Campbell soldiers in what became known as the Glencoe Massacre.

🏃 Activities

There are several short, pleasant walks around **Glencoe Lochan**, near the village. To get there, turn left off the minor road to the youth hostel, just beyond the bridge over the River Coe. There are three walks (40 minutes to an hour), all detailed on a signboard at the car park. The artificial lochan was created by Lord Strathcona in 1895 for his homesick Canadian wife Isabella and is surrounded by a North American–style forest.

A more strenuous hike, but well worth the effort on a fine day, is the climb to the **Lost Valley**, a magical mountain sanctuary still haunted by the ghosts of the murdered MacDonalds (only 2.5 miles round trip, but allow three hours). A rough path from the car park at Allt na Reigh (on the A82, 6 miles east of Glencoe village) bears left down to a footbridge over the river, then climbs up the wooded valley between Beinn Fhada and Gearr Aonach (the first and second of the Three Sisters). The route leads steeply up through a maze of giant, jumbled, moss-coated boulders before emerging – quite unexpectedly – into a broad, open valley with

an 800m-long meadow as flat as a football pitch. Back in the days of clan warfare, the valley – invisible from below – was used for hiding stolen cattle; its Gaelic name, Coire Gabhail, means 'corrie of capture'.

The summits of Glen Coe's mountains are for experienced mountaineers only. Details of hill-walking routes can be found in the Scottish Mountaineering Club's guidebook *Central Highlands* by Peter Hodgkiss, available in most bookshops and outdoor equipment stores in the area.

EAST OF THE GLEN

Glencoe Mountain Resort   OUTDOOR ACTIVITIES
(www.glencoemountain.com) A few miles east of Glen Coe proper, on the south side of the A82, is the car park and base station for the Glencoe Mountain Resort, where commercial skiing in Scotland first began back in 1956. The **Lodge Café-Bar** has comfy sofas where you can soak up the view through the floor-to-ceiling windows.

The chairlift (adult/child £10/5; ⊘9.30am-4.30pm Thu-Mon) continues to operate in summer – there's a grand view over the Moor of Rannoch from the top station – and provides access to a downhill mountain-biking track. In winter a lift pass costs £30 a day and equipment hire is £25 a day.

Two miles west of the ski centre, a minor road leads along peaceful and beautiful **Glen Etive**, which runs southwest for 12 miles to the head of Loch Etive. On a hot summer's day the River Etive contains many tempting pools for swimming in, and there are lots of good picnic sites.

Kings House Hotel   HOTEL, PUB ££
(⬛01855-851259; www.kingy.com; s/d £35/70; Ⓟ) The remote Kings House Hotel claims to be one of Scotland's oldest licensed inns, dating from the 17th century. It has long been a favourite meeting place for climbers, skiers and hill walkers – the rustic Climbers Bar (bar meals £8-12; ⊘11am-11pm) round the back is more relaxed than the lounge – and serves good pub grub and real ale.

The hotel lies on the old military road from Stirling to Fort William, and after the Battle of Culloden it was used as a Hanoverian garrison – hence the name.

GLENCOE VILLAGE
POP 360
The little village of Glencoe stands on the south shore of Loch Leven at the western end of the glen, 16 miles south of Fort William.

THE GLENCOE MASSACRE

Glen Coe – Gleann Comhann in Gaelic – is sometimes (wrongly) said to mean 'the glen of weeping', a romantic mistranslation that gained popularity in the wake of the brutal murders that took place here in 1692 (the true origin of the name is pre-Gaelic, its meaning lost in the mists of time).

Following the Glorious Revolution of 1688, in which the Catholic King James VII/II (VII of Scotland, II of England) was replaced on the British throne by the Protestant King William II/III, supporters of the exiled James – known as Jacobites, most of them Highlanders – rose up against William in a series of battles. In an attempt to quash Jacobite loyalties, King William offered the Highland clans an amnesty on the condition that all clan chiefs took an oath of loyalty to him before 1 January 1692.

Maclain, the elderly chief of the MacDonalds of Glencoe, had long been a thorn in the side of the authorities. Not only was he late in setting out to fulfil the king's demand, but he mistakenly went first to Fort William before travelling slowly through winter mud and rain to Inveraray, where he was three days late in taking the oath before the Sheriff of Argyll.

The secretary of state for Scotland, Sir John Dalrymple, decided to use the fact that Maclain had missed the deadline to punish the troublesome MacDonalds, and at the same time set an example to other Highland clans, some of whom had not bothered to take the oath.

A company of 120 soldiers, mainly from the Campbell territory of Argyll, were sent to the glen under cover of collecting taxes. It was a long-standing tradition for clans to provide hospitality to travellers and, since their commanding officer was related to Maclain by marriage, the troops were billeted in MacDonald homes.

After they'd been guests for 12 days, the government order came for the soldiers to 'fall upon the rebels the MacDonalds of Glencoe and put all to the sword under 70. You are to have a special care that the Old Fox and his sons do upon no account escape'. The soldiers turned on their hosts at 5am on 13 February, killing Maclain and 37 other men, women and children. Some of the soldiers alerted the MacDonalds to their intended fate, allowing them to escape; many fled into the snow-covered hills, where another 40 people perished in the cold.

The ruthless brutality of the incident caused a public uproar, and after an inquiry several years later Dalrymple lost his job. There's a monument to Maclain in Glencoe village, and members of the MacDonald clan still gather here on 13 February each year to lay a wreath.

Sights & Activities

Glencoe Folk Museum MUSEUM
(☎01855-811664; www.glencoemuseum.com; adult/child £3/free; ⊙10am-4.30pm Mon-Sat Easter-Oct) This small, thatched museum houses a varied collection of military memorabilia, farm equipment and tools of the woodworking, blacksmithing and slate-quarrying trades.

Glencoe Visitor Centre VISITOR CENTRE
(NTS; ☎01855-811307; www.glencoe-nts.org.uk; adult/child £6/5; ⊙9.30am-5.30pm Easter-Oct, 10am-4pm Thu-Sun Nov-Easter) About 1.5 miles east of Glencoe village is this modern facility with an ecotourism angle. The centre provides comprehensive information on the geological, environmental and cultural history of Glencoe via high-tech interactive and audiovisual displays, charts the history of mountaineering in the glen, and tells the story of the Glencoe Massacre in all its gory detail.

Lochaber Watersports WATER SPORTS
(☎01855-811931; www.lochaberwatersports.co.uk; Ballachulish; ⊙9.30am-5pm Apr-Oct) You can hire kayaks (£12 an hour), rowing boats (£22 an hour), motor boats (£30 an hour) and even a 10m sailing yacht complete with skipper (£150 for three hours, up to five people) here.

Sleeping

TOP CHOICE **Clachaig Inn** HOTEL, PUB ££
(☎01855-811252; www.clachaig.com; s/d from £70/92; P🐾📶🏊) The Clachaig has long been a favourite haunt of hill walkers and climbers.

As well as comfortable en suite accommodation, there's a smart, wood-panelled lounge-bar with lots of sofas and armchairs, mountaineering photos, and climbing magazines to leaf through.

Climbers usually head for the lively **Boots Bar** on the other side of the hotel – it has log fires, serves real ale and good pub grub (mains £9 to £18), and has live Scottish, Irish and blues music on Friday and Saturday night. It's 2 miles southeast of Glencoe village.

Glencoe Independent Hostel   HOSTEL £
(☏01855-811906; www.glencoehostel.co.uk; dm £13-16.50, bunkhouse £11.50-13.50; P@⊡☀) This handily located hostel, just 10 minutes' walk from the Clachaig Inn and 1.5 miles southeast of Glencoe village, is set in an old farmhouse with six- and eight-bed dorms, and a bunkhouse with another 16 bed spaces in communal, Alpine-style bunks. There's also a cute little wooden cabin that sleeps up to three (£20 to £24 per person per night).

Glencoe SYHA   HOSTEL £
(☏08155-811219; www.syha.org.uk; dm £21; P@☀) Very popular with hikers, though the atmosphere can be a little institutional. It's a 1.5-mile walk from the village along the minor road on the northern side of the river.

Invercoe Caravan & Camping Park   CAMPSITE £
(☏01855-811210; www.invercoe.co.uk; tent sites per person £8, campervan site £21) Our favourite official campground in Glencoe, this place has great views of the surrounding mountains and is equipped with antimidge machines and a covered area for campers to cook in.

✗ Eating

Glencoe Café   CAFE £
(☏01855-811168; www.glencoecafe.com; mains £4-7; ⊙10am-5pm) This friendly cafe is the hub of Glencoe village, serving breakfast fry-ups till 11.30am, light lunches based around local produce (think Cullen skink, smoked salmon quiche, venison burgers), and the best cappuccino in the glen.

Crafts & Things   CAFE £
(☏01855-811325; www.craftsandthings.co.uk; Annat; mains £3-6; ⊙9.30am-5pm Mon-Fri, to 5.30pm Sat & Sun; ⊞) Just off the main road between Glencoe village and Ballachulish, the coffee shop in this craft shop is a good spot for a lunch of homemade lentil soup with crusty rolls, ciabatta sandwiches, or just coffee and carrot cake. There are tables outdoors, and a box of toys to keep the little ones occupied.

❶ Getting There & Away

Scottish Citylink (p319) buses run between Fort William and Glencoe (£7.50, 30 minutes, eight daily) and from Glencoe to Glasgow (£20, 2½ hours, eight daily). Buses stop at Glencoe village, Glencoe Visitor Centre and Glencoe Mountain Resort.

Stagecoach (p491) bus 44 links Glencoe village with Fort William (35 minutes, hourly Monday to Saturday, three on Sunday) and Kinlochleven (25 minutes).

Kinlochleven

POP 900

Kinlochleven is hemmed in by high mountains at the head of beautiful Loch Leven, about 7 miles east of Glencoe village. The aluminium smelter that led to the town's development in the early 20th century has long since closed, and the opening of the Ballachulish Bridge in the 1970s allowed the main road to bypass it completely. Decline was halted by the opening of the West Highland Way, which now brings a steady stream of hikers through the village.

The final section of the **West Highland Way** stretches for 14 miles from Kinlochleven to Fort William. The village is also the starting point for easier walks up the glen of the River Leven, through pleasant woods to the **Grey Mare's Tail waterfall**, and harder mountain hikes into the **Mamores**.

🏃 Activities

Ice Factor   CLIMBING
(☏01855-831100; www.ice-factor.co.uk; Leven Rd; ⊙9am-10pm Tue & Thu, to 7pm Mon, Wed & Fri-Sun; ⊞) If you fancy trying your hand at ice-climbing, even in the middle of summer, head for the Ice Factor, the world's biggest indoor ice-climbing wall; a one-hour beginner's 'taster' session costs £30. There's also a rock-climbing wall, sauna and steam room, and a cafe and bar-bistro.

🛏 Sleeping & Eating

Blackwater Hostel   HOSTEL, CAMPSITE £
(☏01855-831253; www.blackwaterhostel.co.uk; Lab Rd; sites per person £7, dm/tw £15/35) This 40-bed hostel has spotless dorms with en suite bathrooms and TV, and a level, well-sheltered camping ground.

TOP CHOICE Lochleven

Seafood Cafe RESTAURANT ££

(☎01855-821048; www.lochlevenseafoodcafe. co.uk; mains £10-22; ☉noon-9pm Wed-Sun) This outstanding place serves superb shellfish freshly plucked live from tanks – oysters on the half shell, razor clams, scallops, lobster and crab – plus a daily fish special and some nonseafood dishes. For warm days, there's an outdoor terrace with a view across the loch to the Pap of Glencoe, a distinctive conical mountain.

❶ Getting There & Away

Stagecoach (p491) bus 44 runs from Fort William to Kinlochleven (50 minutes, hourly Monday to Saturday, three on Sunday) via Ballachulish and Glencoe village.

Fort William

POP 9910

Basking on the shores of Loch Linnhe amid magnificent mountain scenery, Fort William has one of the most enviable settings in the whole of Scotland. If it wasn't for the busy dual carriageway crammed between the town centre and the loch, and one of the highest rainfall records in the country, it would be almost idyllic. Even so, the Fort has carved out a reputation as 'Outdoor Capital of the UK' (www.outdoorcapital.co.uk), and its easy access by rail and bus makes it a good place to base yourself for exploring the surrounding mountains and glens.

Magical **Glen Nevis** begins near the northern end of the town and wraps itself around the southern flanks of **Ben Nevis** (1344m) – Britain's highest mountain and a magnet for hikers and climbers. The glen is also popular with movie makers – parts of *Braveheart, Rob Roy* and the *Harry Potter* movies were filmed there.

History

There is little left of the fort from which the town derives its name. The first castle here was constructed by General Monck in 1654 and called Inverlochy, but the meagre ruins by the loch are those of the fort built in the 1690s by General Mackay and named after King William II/III. In the 18th century it became part of a chain of garrisons (along with Fort Augustus and Fort George) that controlled the Great Glen in the wake of the Jacobite rebellions; it was pulled down in the 19th century to make way for the railway.

Originally a tiny fishing village called Gordonsburgh, the town adopted the name of the fort after the opening of the railway in 1901 (in Gaelic it is known as An Gearasdan, 'the garrison'). The juxtapostion of the railway and the Caledonian Canal saw the town grow into a major tourist centre. Its position has been consolidated in the last three decades by the huge increase in popularity of climbing, skiing, mountain biking and other outdoor sports.

◉ Sights

Jacobite Steam Train HERITAGE RAILWAY

(☎0844 850 4685; www.steamtrain.info; day return adult/child £32/18; ☉daily Jul & Aug, Mon-Fri mid-May–Jun & Sep-Oct) The Jacobite Steam Train, hauled by a former LNER K1 or LMS Class 5MT locomotive, travels the scenic two-hour run between Fort William and Mallaig, departing from Fort William train station in the morning and returning from Mallaig in the afternoon. There's a brief stop at Glenfinnan station, and you get 1½ hours in Mallaig.

Classed as one of the great railway journeys of the world, the route crosses the historic Glenfinnan Viaduct, made famous in the *Harry Potter* films – the Jacobite's owners supplied the steam locomotive and rolling stock used in the film.

West Highland Museum MUSEUM

(☎01397-702169; www.westhighlandmuseum.org. uk; Cameron Sq; ☉10am-5pm Mon-Sat Apr-Oct, 10am-4pm Mon-Sat Mar & Oct-Dec, closed Jan & Feb) This small but fascinating museum is packed with all manner of Highland memorabilia. Look out for the secret portrait of Bonnie Prince Charlie – after the Jacobite rebellions all things Highland were banned, including pictures of the exiled leader, and this tiny painting looks like nothing more than a smear of paint until viewed in a cylindrical mirror, which reflects a credible likeness of the prince.

Ben Nevis Distillery DISTILLERY

(☎01397-702476; www.bennevisdistillery.com; Lochy Bridge; guided tour adult/child £4/2; ☉9am-5pm Mon-Fri year round, plus 10am-4pm Sat Easter-Sep & noon-4pm Sun Jul & Aug) A tour of this distillery makes for a warming rainy day alternative to exploring the hills.

☞ Tours

Crannog Cruises WILDLIFE CRUISE

(☎01397-700714; adult/child £10/5; ☉four daily) Operates 1½-hour wildlife cruises on Loch

Linnhe, visiting a seal colony and a salmon farm.

Al's Tours
TAXI TOUR

(01397-700700; www.alstours.com) Taxi tours with driver-guide around Lochaber and Glencoe cost £80/195 for a half-/full day.

✹ Festivals & Events

UCI Mountain Bike
World Cup
MOUNTAIN BIKING

(www.fortwilliamworldcup.co.uk) In June, Fort William pulls in crowds of more than 18,000 spectators for this World Cup downhill mountain-biking event. The gruelling downhill course is at nearby Nevis Range ski area.

🛏 Sleeping

It's best to book well ahead in summer, especially for hostels.

TOP CHOICE Lime Tree
HOTEL ££

(01397-701806; www.limetreefortwilliam.co.uk; Achintore Rd; s/d from £80/110; P) Much more interesting than your average guesthouse, this former Victorian manse overlooking Loch Linnhe is an 'art gallery with rooms', decorated throughout with the artist-owner's atmospheric Highland landscapes. Foodies rave about the restaurant, and the gallery space – a triumph of sensitive design – stages everything from serious exhibitions (works by David Hockney and Andy Goldsworthy have appeared) to folk concerts.

Grange
B&B ££

(01397-705516; www.grangefortwilliam.com; Grange Rd; r per person £58-63; P) An exceptional 19th-century villa set in its own landscaped grounds, the Grange is crammed with antiques and fitted with log fires, chaise longues and Victorian roll-top baths. The Turret Room, with its window seat in the turret overlooking Loch Linnhe, is our favourite. It's 500m southwest of the town centre.

Crolinnhe
B&B £££

(01397-703795; www.crolinnhe.co.uk; Grange Rd; r £120-127; ☺Easter-Oct; P@) This grand 19th-century villa has a lochside location, beautiful gardens and sumptuous accommodation. A vegetarian breakfast is provided on request.

Calluna
APARTMENTS £

(01397-700451; www.fortwilliamholiday.co.uk; Heathercroft, Connochie Rd; dm/tw £16/36, 6- to 8-person apt per week £550; P☎) Run by well-known mountain guide Alan Kimber and wife Sue, the Calluna offers self-catering apartments geared to groups of hikers and climbers, but also takes individual travellers prepared to share; there's a fully equipped kitchen and an excellent drying room for your soggy hiking gear.

St Andrew's Guest House
B&B ££

(01397-703038; www.standrewsguesthouse.co.uk; Fassifern Rd; r per person £24-30; P☎) Set in a lovely 19th-century building that was once a rectory and choir school, St Andrew's retains period features, such as carved masonry, wood panelling and stained-glass windows. It has six spacious bedrooms, some with stunning views.

Glenlochy Apartments
APARTMENTS ££

(01397-702909; www.glenlochyguesthouse.co.uk; Nevis Bridge; 2-person apt per night £65, per week £380-490; P) Convenient for Glen Nevis, Ben Nevis and the end of the West Highland Way, the Glenlochy is a sprawling modern place with five modern apartments set in a huge garden beside the River Nevis, a pleasant place to sit on summer evenings.

Fort William Backpackers
HOSTEL £

(01397-700711; www.scotlands-top-hostels.com; Alma Rd; dm/tw £18/47; P@☎) A 10-minute walk from the bus and train stations, this lively and welcoming hostel is set in a grand Victorian villa, perched on a hillside with great views over Loch Linnhe.

Bank Street Lodge
HOSTEL £

(01397-700070; www.bankstreetlodge.co.uk; Bank St; dm/tw £16/52) Part of a modern hotel and restaurant complex, the Bank Street Lodge offers the most central budget beds in town, only 250m from the train station. It has kitchen facilities and a drying room.

No 6 Caberfeidh
B&B ££

(01397-703756; www.6caberfeidh.com; Fassifern Rd, 6 Caberfeidh; r per person £30-40; ☎) Friendly B&B; vegetarian breakfast on request.

Ashburn House
B&B ££

(01397-706000; www.highland5star.co.uk; Achintore Rd; r per person £45-55; P☎) Grand Victorian villa south of the centre; children under 12 not welcome.

Alexandra Hotel
HOTEL £££

(01397-702241; www.strathmorehotels.com; The Parade; s/d from £110/168; P☎) Large, traditional, family-oriented hotel bang in the middle of town.

✕ Eating & Drinking

TOP CHOICE **Lime Tree** RESTAURANT £££
(☎01397-701806; www.limetreefortwilliam.co.uk; Achintore Rd; 2-/3-course dinner £28/30; ⊙dinner daily, lunch Sun) Fort William is not over-endowed with great places to eat, but the restaurant at this small hotel and art gallery has put the UK's Outdoor Capital on the gastronomic map. The chef won a Michelin star in his previous restaurant, and turns out delicious dishes built around fresh Scottish produce such as seared saddle of Glenfinnan venison with red wine and rosemary jus.

Crannog Seafood Restaurant RESTAURANT ££
(☎01397-705589; www.crannog.net; Town Pier; mains £16-20) The Crannog has the best location in town – perched on the Town Pier, giving window-table diners an uninterrupted view down Loch Linnhe. Informal and unfussy, it specialises in fresh local fish, with three or four daily fish specials plus the main menu – though there are beef, poultry and vegetarian dishes, too. Two-course lunch £13.

Grog & Gruel RESTAURANT ££
(www.grogandgruel.co.uk; 66 High St; mains £7-13; ⊙bar meals noon-9pm, restaurant 5-9pm; P 🎧) Upstairs from the Grog & Gruel real-ale pub is a lively Tex-Mex restaurant, with a crowd-pleasing menu of tasty enchiladas, burritos, fajitas, burgers, steaks and pizza.

Café Mango ASIAN ££
(☎01397-701367; www.thecafemango.co.uk; 24-26 High St; mains £9-14; ⊙lunch & dinner; 🎧) Bright and modern restaurant serving fragrant Thai and spicy Indian dishes.

Sugar and Spice CAFE £
(☎01397-705005; 147 High St; mains £7-9; ⊙10am-5pm Mon-Sat, 6-9pm Thu-Sat; 🎧🍴) Enjoy what is probably the best coffee in town at this colourful cafe, just a few paces from the official finishing line of the West Highland Way. In the evening (Thursday to Saturday only) it serves authentic Thai dishes.

Ben Nevis Bar PUB
(☎01397-702295; 105 High St) The lounge here enjoys a good view over the loch, and the bar exudes a relaxed, jovial atmosphere where climbers and tourists can work off leftover energy jigging to live music (Thursday and Friday nights).

ℹ Information

Belford Hospital (☎01397-702481; Belford Rd) Opposite the train station.

Fort William tourist office (☎01397-703781; www.visithighlands.com; 15 High St; internet per 20min £1; ⊙9am-6pm Mon-Sat, 10am-5pm Sun Apr-Sep, limited hours Oct-Mar) Internet access.

Post Office (☎0845 722 3344; 5 High St)

ℹ Getting There & Away

Both bus and train station are next to the huge Morrisons supermarket, reached from the town centre via an underpass next to the Nevisport shop.

Bus

Scottish Citylink (p319) buses link Fort William with other major towns and cities. **Shiel Buses** (www.shielbuses.co.uk) service No 500 runs to Mallaig (1½ hours, three daily Monday to Friday only) via Glenfinnan (30 minutes) and Arisaig (one hour).

Edinburgh £33, 4½ hours, one daily direct, seven with a change at Glasgow; via Glencoe and Crianlarich

Glasgow £22, three hours, eight daily

Inverness £12, two hours, five daily

Oban £9.40, 1½ hours, three daily

Portree £28.60, three hours, four daily

Car

Easydrive Car Hire (☎01397-701616; www.easydrivescotland.co.uk; Unit 36a, Ben Nevis Industrial Estate, Ben Nevis Dr) Hires out small cars from £31/195 a day/week, including tax and unlimited mileage, but not Collision Damage Waiver (CDW).

Train

The spectacular **West Highland line** runs from Glasgow to Mallaig via Fort William. The overnight *Caledonian Sleeper* service connects Fort William and London Euston (£103 sharing a twin-berth cabin, 13 hours).

There's no direct rail connection between Oban and Fort William – you have to change at Crianlarich, so it's faster to use the bus.

Edinburgh £44, five hours; change at Glasgow's Queen St station

Glasgow £26.30, 3¾ hours, three daily, two on Sunday

Mallaig £11, 1½ hours, four daily, three on Sunday

ℹ Getting Around

Bike

Alpine Bikes (☎01397-704008; www.alpinebikes.com; 117 High St; ⊙9am-5.30pm Mon-Sat, 10am-5.30pm Sun) Rents out mountain bikes for £20/12 for a day/half-day.

Bus

The Fort Dayrider ticket (£3) gives unlimited travel for one day on Stagecoach bus services in the Fort William area. Buy from the bus driver.

Taxi

There's a taxi rank on the corner of High St and the Parade.

Around Fort William

GLEN NEVIS

You can walk the 3 miles from Fort William to scenic Glen Nevis in about an hour or so. The Glen Nevis tourist office (☎01397-705922; www.bennevisweather.co.uk; ☉9am-5pm Apr-Oct, shorter hours in winter) is situated 1.5 miles up the glen, and provides information on walking, weather forecasts, and specific advice on climbing Ben Nevis.

From the car park at the far end of the road along Glen Nevis, there is an excellent 1.5-mile walk through the spectacular Nevis Gorge to **Steall Meadows**, a verdant valley

dominated by a 100m-high bridal-veil waterfall. You can reach the foot of the falls by crossing the river on a wobbly, three-cable wire bridge – one cable for your feet and one for each hand – a real test of balance!

🛏 Sleeping & Eating

TOP CHOICE **Ben Nevis Inn** HOSTEL £
(☎01397-701227; www.ben-nevis-inn.co.uk; Achintee; dm £15.50; ☉noon-11pm daily Apr-Oct, Thu-Sun only Nov-Mar; 🅿) A good alternative to the youth hostel is this great barn of a pub (real ale and tasty bar meals available; mains £9 to £16), with a comfy 24-bed hostel downstairs. It's at the Achintee start of the path up Ben Nevis, and only a mile from the end of the West Highland Way. Food served noon to 9pm.

Achintee Farm HOSTEL, B&B £
(☎01397-702240; www.achinteefarm.com; Achintee; B&B s/d £60/78, hostel dm/tw £17/38; 🅿🅯) This attractive farmhouse offers excellent B&B accommodation and also has a small

---

CLIMBING BEN NEVIS

As the highest peak in the British Isles, Ben Nevis (1344m) attracts many would-be ascensionists who would not normally think of climbing a Scottish mountain – a staggering (often literally) 100,000 people reach the summit each year.

Although anyone who is reasonably fit should have no problem climbing Ben Nevis on a fine summer's day, an ascent should not be undertaken lightly. Every year people have to be rescued from the mountain. You will need proper walking boots (the path is rough and stony, and there may be soft, wet snowfields on the summit), warm clothing, waterproofs, a map and compass, and plenty of food and water. And don't forget to check the weather forecast (see www.bennevisweather.co.uk).

Here are a few facts to mull over before you go racing up the tourist track: the summit plateau is bounded by 700m-high cliffs and has a sub-Arctic climate; at the summit it can snow on any day of the year; the summit is wrapped in cloud nine days out of 10; in thick cloud, visibility at the summit can be 10m or less; and in such conditions the only safe way off the mountain requires careful use of a map and compass to avoid walking over those 700m cliffs.

The tourist track (the easiest route to the top) was originally called the Pony Track. It was built in the 19th century for the pack ponies that carried supplies to a meteorological observatory on the summit (now in ruins), which was manned continuously from 1883 to 1904.

There are three possible starting points for the tourist track ascent – Achintee Farm; the footbridge at Glen Nevis SYHA; and, if you have a car, the car park at Glen Nevis tourist office. The path climbs gradually to the shoulder at Lochan Meall an t-Suidhe (known as the Halfway Lochan), then zigzags steeply up beside the Red Burn to the summit plateau. The highest point is marked by a trig point on top of a huge cairn beside the ruins of the old observatory; the plateau is scattered with countless smaller cairns, stones arranged in the shape of people's names and, sadly, a fair bit of litter.

The total distance to the summit and back is 8 miles; allow at least four or five hours to reach the top, and another 2½ to three hours for the descent. Afterwards, as you celebrate in the pub with a pint, consider the fact that the record time for the annual Ben Nevis Hill Race is just under 1½ hours – up *and* down. Then have another pint.

hostel attached. It's at the start of the path up Ben Nevis.

Glen Nevis SYHA   HOSTEL £

(SYHA; ☎01397-702336; www.glennevishostel. co.uk; dm £21.50; @🛜) Large, impersonal and reminiscent of a school camp, this hostel is 3 miles from Fort William, right beside one of the starting points for the tourist track up Ben Nevis.

Glen Nevis Caravan & Camping Park   CAMPSITE £

(☎01397-702191; www.glen-nevis.co.uk; tent site £7, tent & car site £11, campervan £11.90, per person £3.20; ⊙mid-Mar–Oct) This big, well-equipped site is a popular base camp for Ben Nevis and the surrounding mountains. The site is 2.5 miles from Fort William, along the Glen Nevis road.

❶ Getting There & Away

Bus 41 runs from Fort William bus station up Glen Nevis to the Glen Nevis SYHA (10 minutes, two daily year round, five daily Monday to Saturday June to September) and on to the Lower Falls 3 miles beyond the hostel (20 minutes). Check at the tourist office for the latest timetable, which is liable to alteration.

NEVIS RANGE

Nevis Range   OUTDOORS

(☎01397-705825; www.nevisrange.co.uk; gondola return trip per adult/child £11.25/6.50; ⊙10am-5pm summer, 9am-5pm winter) The Nevis Range ski area, 6 miles north of Fort William, spreads across the northern slopes of Aonach Mor (1221m). The gondola that gives access to the bottom of the ski area at 655m operates year round (15 minutes each way). At the top there's a restaurant and a couple of hiking trails through nearby Leanachan Forest, as well as excellent mountain-biking trails.

During the **ski season** a one-day lift pass costs £30/18 per adult/child; a one-day package, including equipment hire, lift pass and two hours' instruction, costs £68.

Bus 41 runs from Fort William bus station to Nevis Range (15 minutes, five daily Monday to Saturday, three on Sunday, limited service October to April). Check at the tourist office for the latest timetable, which is liable to alteration.

Nevis Range Downhill & Witch's Trails   MOUNTAIN BIKING

(☎01397-705825; bike.nevisrange.co.uk; multitrip ticket £30, single £12.50; ⊙10.15am-3.45pm mid-May–mid-Sep) A world championship **down-**

hill mountain-bike trail – for experienced riders only – runs from the Snowgoose restaurant at the Nevis Range ski area to the base station; bikes are carried up on a rack on the gondola cabin. A multitrip ticket gives unlimited uplift for a day; full-suspension bike hire costs from £40/70 per single run/full day.

There's also a 4-mile **XC red trail** that begins at the Snowgoose, and the **Witch's Trails** – 25 miles of waymarked forest road and singletrack in the nearby forest, including a 5-mile world championship loop.

CORPACH TO LOCH LOCHY

Corpach lies at the southern entrance to the Caledonian Canal, 3 miles north of Fort William; there's a classic picture-postcard view of Ben Nevis from the mouth of the canal. Nearby is the award-winning Treasures of the Earth (☎01397-772283; www. treasuresoftheearth.co.uk; Corpach; adult/child £5/3; ⊙9.30am-7pm Jul-Sep, 10am-5pm Mar-Jun & Oct-Nov, shorter hours Dec-Feb) exhibition, a rainy-day diversion with a great collection of gemstones, minerals, fossils and other geological curiosities.

A mile east of Corpach, at Banavie, is **Neptune's Staircase**, an impressive flight of eight locks that allows boats to climb 20m to the main reach of the **Caledonian Canal**. The B8004 road runs along the west side of the canal to Gairlochy at the south end of Loch Lochy, offering superb views of Ben Nevis; the **canal towpath** on the east side makes a great walk or bike ride (6.5 miles).

From Gairlochy the B8005 continues along the west side of Loch Lochy to Achnacarry and the Clan Cameron Museum (☎01397-712480; www.clan-cameron.org; Achnacarry; adult/child £3.50/free; ⊙11am-5pm Jul & Aug, 1.30-5pm Easter-Jun & Sep–mid-Oct), which records the history of the clan and its involvement with the Jacobite rebellions, including items of clothing that once belonged to Bonnie Prince Charlie.

From Achnacarry the **Great Glen Way** continues along the roadless western shore of Loch Lochy, and a dead-end minor road leads west along remote but lovely **Loch Arkaig**.

There are a couple of backpacker hostels in Corpach. At Farr Cottage Lodge (☎01397-772315; www.farrcottage.com; Corpach; dm/tw £15/36; P@) bike hire is also available, while the folk at Blacksmiths Backpackers Hostel (☎01397-772467; www.highland -mountain-guides.co.uk; Corpach; dm £16.50; P)

THE CALEDONIAN CANAL

Running for 59 miles from Corpach, near Fort William, to Inverness via lochs Lochy, Oich and Ness, the Caledonian Canal links the east and west coasts of Scotland, avoiding the long and dangerous sea passage around Cape Wrath and through the turbulent Pentland Firth. Designed by Thomas Telford and completed in 1822 at a cost of £900,000 – a staggering sum then – the canal took 20 years to build, including 29 locks, four aqueducts and 10 bridges.

Conceived as a project to ease unemployment and bring prosperity to the Highlands in the aftermath of the Jacobite rebellions and the Clearances, the canal proved to be a commercial failure – the locks were too small for the new breed of steamships which came into use soon after its completion. But it proved to be a success in terms of tourism, especially after it was popularised by Queen Victoria's cruise along the canal in 1873. Today the canal is used mainly by yachts and pleasure cruisers, though in late 2010 a pilot scheme was introduced to assess the viability of using it to transport timber from local forestry plantations.

Much of the Great Glen Way (p331) follows the line of the canal; it can be followed on foot, by mountain bike or on horseback, and 80% of the route has even been done on mobility scooters. An easy half-day hike or bike ride is to follow the canal towpath from Corpach to Gairlochy (10 miles), which takes you past the impressive flight of eight locks known as **Neptune's Staircase**, and through beautiful countryside with grand views to the north face of Ben Nevis.

can organise courses in climbing, kayaking and other sports.

GLEN SPEAN & GLEN ROY

Near Spean Bridge, at the junction of the B8004 and A82, 2.5 miles east of Gairlochy, stands the **Commando Memorial**, which commemorates the WWII special forces soldiers who trained in this area.

Four miles further east, at Roy Bridge, a minor road leads north up **Glen Roy**, which is noted for its intriguing, so-called **parallel roads**. These prominent horizontal terraces contouring around the hillside are actually ancient shorelines formed during the last ice age by the waters of an ice-dammed glacial lake. The best viewpoint is at a car park just over 3 miles up Glen Roy, where there's an interpretation board explaining the landscape features you can see.

Ardnamurchan

Ten miles south of Fort William, a car ferry (car £7, bicycle & foot passenger free; ☉5 min, every 30min) makes the short crossing to Corran Ferry. The drive from here to Ardnamurchan Point (www.ardnamurchan. com), the most westerly point on the British mainland, is one of the most beautiful in the western Highlands, especially in late spring and early summer when much of the nar-

row, twisting road is lined with the bright pink and purple blooms of rhododendrons.

The road clings to the northern shore of Loch Sunart, going through the pretty villages of **Strontian** – which gave its name to the element strontium, first discovered in ore from nearby lead mines in 1790 – and **Salen**.

The mostly single-track road from Salen to Ardnamurchan Point is only 25 miles long, but it'll take you 1½ hours each way. It's a dipping, twisting, low-speed roller coaster of a ride through sun-dappled native woodlands draped with lichen and fern. Just when you're getting used to the views of the islands of Morvern and Mull to the south, it makes a quick detour to the north for a panorama over the islands of Rum and Eigg.

◉ Sights

Nádurra Visitor Centre WILDLIFE CENTRE
(☎01972-500209; www.nadurracentre.co.uk; Glenmore; adult/child £4.50/2.25; ☉10am-5.30pm Mon-Sat & 11am-5.30pm Sun Apr-Oct, 10am-4pm Tue-Fri & 11.30am-4pm Sun Nov-Mar; ⋈) This fascinating centre – midway between Salen and Kilchoan – was originally devised by a wildlife photographer and tries to bring you face to face with the flora and fauna of the Ardnamurchan peninsula. The Living Building exhibit is designed to attract local wildlife, with a mammal den that is occasionally

occupied by hedgehogs or pine martens, an owl nest-box, a mouse nest and a pond.

If the beasties are not in residence, you can watch recorded video footage of the animals. There's also seasonal live CCTV coverage of local wildlife, ranging from nesting herons to a golden eagle feeding site.

Ardnamurchan Lighthouse   HISTORIC BUILDING
(☑01972-510210; www.ardnamurchanlighthouse. com; Ardnamurchan Point; adult/child £3/1.70; ☺10am-5.30pm Apr-Oct; 🏛) The final 6 miles of road from Kilchoan to Ardnamurchan Point end at the 36m-high, grey granite tower of Ardnamurchan Lighthouse, built in 1849 by the 'Lighthouse Stevensons' – family of Robert Louis – to guard the westernmost point of the British mainland. There's a good tearoom, and the visitor centre will tell you more than you'll ever need to know about lighthouses, with lots of hands-on stuff for kids.

The guided tour (£6, every half-hour 11am to 4.30pm) includes a trip to the top of the lighthouse. But the main attraction here is the expansive view over the ocean – this is a superb sunset viewpoint, provided you don't mind driving back in the dark.

Kilchoan   VILLAGE
The scattered crofting village of Kilchoan, the only village of any size west of Salen, is best known for the scenic ruins of 13th-century Mingary Castle. The village has a **tourist office** (☑01972-510222; Pier Rd, Kilchoan; ☺8.30am-5pm Easter-Oct), a shop, a hotel and a campsite, and there's a ferry to Tobermory on the Isle of Mull.

🛏 Sleeping & Eating

Salen Hotel   INN ££
(☑01967-431661; www.salenhotel.co.uk; Salen; r £60; P) A traditional Highland inn with views over Loch Sunart, the Salen Hotel has three rooms above the pub (with sea views) and another three rooms (each with en suite) in a modern chalet out the back. The cosy lounge has a roaring fire and comfy sofa, and the bar meals, including seafood, venison and other game dishes, are very good.

Inn at Ardgour   INN ££
(☑01855-841225; www.ardgour.biz; Corran Ferry; d/f £110/140; P) This pretty, whitewashed coaching inn, draped in colourful flower baskets, makes a great place for a lunch break or overnight stop. The restaurant (mains £8

to £14) is set in the row of cottages once occupied by the Corran ferrymen, and serves traditional, homemade Scottish dishes.

Resipole Caravan Park   CAMPSITE £
(☑01967-431235; www.resipole.co.uk; Salen; sites £8, plus per person £3) An attractive coastal caravan park, 3 miles east of Salen.

Ardnamurchan Campsite   CAMPSITE £
(☑01972-510766; www.ardnamurchanstudycentre. co.uk; Kilchoan; site £2, plus per person £6; ☺May-Sep; P) Along the Ormsaig road, two miles west of Kilchoan village. Backpackers can also camp at the Kilchoan Hotel (a shorter walk from the ferry) – ask at the bar first.

Antler Tearoom   CAFE £
(Nádurra Visitor Centre, Glenmore; mains £5-8; ☺10am-5.30pm Mon-Sat & 11am-5.30pm Sun Apr-Oct, 10am-4pm Tue-Fri & 11.30am-4pm Sun Nov-Mar; 🏛) The cafe at this wildlife centre serves coffee, home baking and lunch dishes, ranging from fresh salads and sandwiches to daily specials such as prawns.

❶ Getting There & Away

Sheil Buses bus 502 runs from Fort William to Glenuig and Acharacle, continuing to Salen and Kilchoan on request (3¼ hours, one daily Monday to Saturday). There are ferries between Kilchoan and Tobermory.

Salen to Lochailort

The A861 road from Salen to Lochailort passes through the low, wooded hills of Moidart. A minor road (signposted Dorlin) leads west from the A861 at Shiel Bridge to a parking area looking across to the picturesque roofless ruin of 13th-century **Castle Tioram**. The castle sits on a tiny island in Loch Moidart, connected to the mainland by a narrow strand that is submerged at high tide (the castle's name, pronounced *chee*-ram, means 'dry'). It was the ancient seat of the Clanranald Macdonalds, but the Clanranald chief ordered it to be burned (to prevent it falling into the hands of Hanoverian troops) when he set off to fight with the Jacobites in the 1715 rebellion. A proposal by the owner to restore the castle was turned down by Historic Scotland; it is now closed to the public due to its unsafe condition.

As the A861 curls around the north shore of Loch Moidart you will see a line of three huge beech trees (and two obvious stumps) between the road and the shore. Known as the **Seven Men of Moidart** (four have been blown down by gales and replaced with saplings), they were planted in the late 18th century to commemorate the seven local men who accompanied Bonnie Prince Charlie from France and acted as his bodyguards at the start of the 1745 rebellion.

Road to the Isles

The 46-mile A830 road from Fort William to Mallaig is traditionally known as the Road to the Isles, as it leads to the jumping-off point for ferries to the Small Isles and Skye, itself a stepping stone to the Outer Hebrides. This is a region steeped in Jacobite history, having witnessed both the beginning and the end of Bonnie Prince Charlie's doomed attempt to regain the British throne in 1745–46.

The final section of this scenic route, between Arisaig and Mallaig, has been upgraded to a fast straight road. Unless you're in a hurry, opt instead for the more scenic old road (signposted Alternative Coastal Route).

Between the A830 and the A87 far to the north lie Knoydart and Glenelg – Scotland's 'Empty Quarter' – a rugged landscape of wild mountains and lonely sea lochs roughly 20 miles by 30 miles in size, mostly uninhabited and penetrated only by two minor roads (along Lochs Arkaig and Quoich). If you want to get away from it all, this is the place to go.

ⓘ Getting Around

Bus

Shiel Buses (www.shielbuses.co.uk) bus 500 runs to Mallaig (1½ hours, three daily Monday to Friday, one on Saturday) via Glenfinnan (30 minutes) and Arisaig (one hour).

Train

The Fort William–Mallaig railway line has four trains a day (three on Sunday), with stops at many points along the way, including Corpach, Glenfinnan, Lochailort, Arisaig and Morar.

GLENFINNAN
POP 100

Glenfinnan is hallowed ground for fans of Bonnie Prince Charlie; the monument here marks where he raised his Highland army. It is also a place of pilgrimage for steam train enthusiasts and Harry Potter fans – the famous railway viaduct features in the films, and is regularly traversed by the Jacobite Steam Train (p348).

◉ Sights & Activities

Glenfinnan Monument MONUMENT
This tall column, topped by a statue of a kilted Highlander, was erected in 1815 on the spot where the Young Pretender first raised his standard and rallied the Jacobite clans on 19 August 1745, marking the start of the ill-fated campaign that would end in disaster 14 months later. The setting, at the north end of Loch Shiel, is hauntingly beautiful.

Glenfinnan Visitor Centre VISITOR CENTRE
(NTS; adult/child £3.50/2.50; ⊙9.30am-5.30pm Jul & Aug, 10am-5pm Easter-Jun, Sep & Oct) This centre recounts the story of the '45, as the Jacobite rebellion of 1745 is known, when the prince's loyal clansmen marched and fought their way from Glenfinnan south via Edinburgh to Derby, then back north to final defeat at Culloden.

Glenfinnan Station Museum MUSEUM
(www.glenfinnanstationmuseum.co.uk; adult/child £1.50/75p; ⊙9am-5pm Jun–mid-Oct) This museum is dedicated to the great days of steam on the West Highland line. The famous 21-arch Glenfinnan Viaduct, just east of the station, was built in 1901, and featured in the movie *Harry Potter & the Chamber of Secrets*. A pleasant walk of around 0.75 miles east from the station (signposted) leads to a viewpoint for the viaduct and for Loch Shiel.

Loch Shiel Cruises BOAT TOUR
(☎07801-537617; www.highlandcruises.co.uk; ⊙Apr-Sep) Offers boat trips along Loch Shiel. There are one- to 2½-hour cruises (£10 to £18 per person) daily except Saturday and Wednesday. On Wednesday the boat goes the full length of the loch to **Acharacle** (£17/25 one way/return), calling at Polloch and Dalilea, allowing for a range of walks and bike rides using the forestry track on the eastern shore. The boat departs from a jetty near Glenfinnan House Hotel.

🛏 Sleeping & Eating

Sleeping Car Bunkhouse HOSTEL £
(☎01397-722295; www.glenfinnanstationmuseum.co.uk; Glenfinnan Station; dm £15; ⊙Jun–mid-Oct) Two converted railway carriages at Glenfinnan Station house this 10-berth bunkhouse and the atmospheric **Dining Car Tearoom** (snacks £2-5; ⊙9am-4.30pm Jun–mid-Oct), which serves scones with cream and jam and pots of tea. There are superb views of the mountains above Loch Shiel.

WORTH A TRIP

GLENUIG INN

Set on a peaceful bay on the Arisaig coast, halfway between Lochailort and Acharacle on the A830 road, the **Glenuig Inn** (☎01687-470219; www.glenuig.com; B&B s/d/q from £60/95/125, bunkhouse per person £25; P 📶) is a great place to get away from it all. As well as offering comfortable accommodation, good food (mains £10 to £20, served noon to 9pm), and real ale on tap, it's a great base for exploring Arisaig, Morar and the Loch Shiel area.

Apart from the countless hiking and biking options, **Rockhopper Sea Kayaking** (www.rockhopperscotland.co.uk; half-/full day £40/75) can take you on a guided kayak tour along the wild and beautiful coastline, starting and finishing at the inn.

Prince's House Hotel INN ££
(☎01397-722246; www.glenfinnan.co.uk; s/d from £75/115; P) A delightful old coaching inn from 1658, the Prince's House is a good place to pamper yourself – ask for the spacious, tartan-clad Stuart Room if you want to stay in the oldest part of the hotel. Note that only dinner, bed and breakfast rates (£175 to £240 a double) are available on weekends from Easter to October.

There's no documentary evidence that Bonnie Prince Charlie actually stayed here in 1745, but it was the only sizable house in Glenfinnan at that time, so...

ARISAIG & MORAR

The 5 miles of coast between Arisaig and Morar is a fretwork of rocky islets, inlets and gorgeous silver-sand beaches backed by dunes and machair, with stunning sunset views across the sea to the silhouetted peaks of Eigg and Rum. The **Silver Sands of Morar**, as they are known, draw crowds of bucket-and-spade holidaymakers in July and August, when the many camping grounds scattered along the coast are filled to overflowing.

Sights

Camusdarach Beach BEACH
Fans of the movie *Local Hero* still make pilgrimages to Camusdarach Beach, just south of Morar, which starred in the film as Ben's beach. To find it, look for the car park 800m north of Camusdarach campsite; from here, a wooden footbridge and a 400m walk through the dunes lead to the beach.

(The village that featured in the film is on the other side of the country, at Pennan.)

Arisaig Marine BOAT TOUR
(☎01687-450224; www.arisaig.co.uk; Arisaig Harbour; ⊙May-Sep) Runs cruises from Arisaig harbour to Eigg (£18 return, one hour, six a week), Rum (£25 return, 2½ hours, two or three a week) and Muck (£20 return, two hours, three a week). The trips include whale-watching, with up to an hour for close viewing.

Land, Sea & Islands Visitor Centre VISITOR CENTRE
(www.arisaigcentre.co.uk; Arisaig; ⊙10am-6pm Mon-Fri, 10am-4pm Sun) This centre in Arisaig village houses exhibits on the cultural and natural history of the region, plus a small but fascinating exhibition on the part played by the local area as a base for training spies for the Special Operations Executive (SOE, forerunner of MI6) during WWII.

Sleeping & Eating

There are at least a half-dozen camping grounds between Arisaig and Morar; all are open in summer only, and are often full in July and August, so book ahead. Some are listed on www.road-to-the-isles.org.uk.

Garramore House B&B ££
(☎01687-450268; r per person £25-35; P 🐾) Built as a hunting lodge in 1840, this house served as a Special Operations Executive HQ during WWII. Today it's a wonderfully atmospheric, child- and pet-friendly guesthouse set in lovely woodland gardens with resident peacocks and great views to the Small Isles and Skye. Garramore is signposted off the coastal road, 4 miles north of Arisaig village.

Camusdarach Campsite CAMPSITE £
(☎01687-450221; Arisaig; tent/campervan sites £8/12, plus per person £3; ⊙Mar-Oct; 📶) A small and nicely landscaped site with good facilities, only three minutes' walk from the *Local Hero* beach (via gate in northwest corner).

Old Library Lodge & Restaurant
SCOTTISH ££

(✆01687-450651; www.oldlibrary.co.uk; Arisaig; mains £10-16) The Old Library is a charming restaurant with rooms (B&B single/double £60/90) set in converted 200-year-old stables overlooking the waterfront in Arisaig village. The lunch menu concentrates on soups and freshly made sandwiches, while dinner is a more sophisticated affair offering local seafood, beef and lamb.

MALLAIG
POP 800

If you're travelling between Fort William and Skye, you may find yourself overnighting in the bustling fishing and ferry port of Mallaig. Indeed, it makes a good base for a series of day trips by ferry to the Small Isles and Knoydart.

◉ Sights & Activities

Loch Morar
LAKE

(www.lochmorar.org.uk) A minor road from Morar village, 2.5 miles south of Mallaig, leads to scenic 11-mile-long Loch Morar, which at 310m is the deepest body of water in the United Kingdom. Reputed to be inhabited by its own version of Nessie – Morag, the Loch Morar monster – the loch and its surrounding hills are the haunt of otters, wildcats, red deer and golden eagles.

A 5-mile-long, signposted footpath leads along the north shore of the loch from the road-end at Bracorina, three miles east of Morar village, to Tarbet on Loch Nevis, from where you can catch a passenger ferry (p358) back to Mallaig (departs 3.30pm).

Mallaig Heritage Centre
HERITAGE CENTRE

(✆01687-462085; www.mallaigheritage.org.uk; Station Rd; adult/child £2/free; ◔9.30am-4.30pm Mon-Fri, noon-4pm Sat & Sun) The village's rainy-day attractions are limited to this heritage centre, which covers the archaeology and history of the region, including the heart-rending tale of the Highland Clearances in Knoydart.

MV Grimsay Isle
BOAT TOUR

(✆07780-815158) The MV *Grimsay Isle* provides entertaining, customised sea-fishing trips and seal-watching tours (book at the tourist office).

⛺ Sleeping & Eating

Seaview Guest House
B&B ££

(✆01687-462059; www.seaviewguesthousemallaig.com; Main St; r per person £28-35; ◔Mar-Nov;

P) This comfortable three-bedroom B&B has grand views over the harbour, not only from the upstairs bedrooms but also from the breakfast room. There's also a cute little cottage next door that offers self-catering accommodation (www.selfcateringmallaig.com; one double and one twin room) for £350 to £450 a week.

Springbank Guest House
B&B £

(✆01687-462459; www.springbank-mallaig.co.uk; East Bay; r per person £30; P⚗) The Springbank is a traditional West Highland house with seven homely guest bedrooms, with superb views across the harbour to the Cuillin of Skye.

TOP CHOICE **Fish Market Restaurant**
SEAFOOD ££

(✆01687-462299; Station Rd; mains £9-21; ◔lunch & dinner) At least half-a-dozen signs in Mallaig advertise 'seafood restaurant', but this bright, modern, bistro-style place next to the harbour is our favourite, serving simply prepared scallops with smoked salmon and savoy cabbage, grilled langoustines with garlic butter, and fresh Mallaig haddock fried in breadcrumbs, as well as the tastiest Cullen skink on the west coast.

Upstairs is a coffee shop (mains £5-6; ◔11am-5pm) that serves delicious hot roast-beef rolls with horseradish sauce, and scones with clotted cream and jam.

Tea Garden
CAFE £

(✆01687-462764; www.mallaigbackpackers.co.uk; Harbour View; mains £6-12; ◔9am-6pm) On a sunny day the Tea Garden's terrace cafe, with its flowers, greenery and cosmopolitan backpacker staff, can feel more like the Med than Mallaig. The coffee is good, and the speciality of the house is a pint glass full of Mallaig prawns with dipping sauce (£12.50). From late May to September the cafe opens in the evening with a bistro menu.

Jaffy's
FISH & CHIPS £

(www.jaffys.co.uk; Station Rd; mains £4-8; ◔noon-2.30pm & 5-8pm daily May-Oct, Fri & Sat only Nov-Apr) Owned by a third-generation fish merchant's family, Mallaig's chippy serves superbly fresh fish and chips, as well as kippers, prawns and other seafood.

❶ Information

Mallaig has a **tourist office** (✆01687-462170; East Bay; ◔10am-5.30pm Mon-Fri, 10.15am-3.45pm Sat, noon-3.30pm Sun), a post office, a bank with ATM and a **Co-op supermarket** (◔8.00am-10pm Mon-Sat, 9am-9pm Sun).

❶ Getting There & Away

BOAT

Ferries run from Mallaig to the Small Isles, the Isle of Skye and Knoydart. See the relevant section for details.

BUS

Shiel Buses (p350) bus 500 runs from Fort William to Mallaig (1½ hours, three daily Monday to Friday, one on Saturday) via Glenfinnan (30 minutes) and Arisaig (one hour).

TRAIN

The West Highland line runs between Fort William and Mallaig (£11, 1½ hours) four times a day (three on Sunday).

Knoydart Peninsula

POP 70

The Knoydart peninsula is the only sizable area in Britain that remains inaccessible to the motor car, cut off by miles of rough country and the embracing arms of Lochs Nevis and Hourn – Gaelic for the lochs of Heaven and Hell. No road penetrates this wilderness of rugged hills – **Inverie**, its sole village, can only be reached by ferry from Mallaig, or on foot from the remote road's end at Kinloch Hourn (a tough 16-mile hike).

The main reasons for visiting are to climb the remote 1020m peak of **Ladhar Bheinn** (*laar*-ven), which affords some of the west coast's finest views, or just to enjoy the feeling of being cut off from the rest of the world. There are no shops, no TV and no mobile-phone reception (although there *is* internet access); electricity is provided by a private hydroelectric scheme – truly 'off the grid' living! For more information and full accommodation listings, see www.knoydart-foundation.com.

🛏 Sleeping & Eating

Knoydart Lodge   B&B **££**

(☏01687-460129; www.knoydartlodge.co.uk; Inverie; s/d £60/90; ☏) This must be some of the most spacious and luxurious B&B accommodation on the whole west coast, let alone in Knoydart. On offer are large, stylish bedrooms in a fantastic, modern timber-built lodge reminiscent of an alpine chalet. Gourmet evening meals are available on Wednesday and Saturday (£30 per person).

Knoydart Foundation Bunkhouse   HOSTEL **£**

(☏01687-462163; www.knoydart-foundation.com; Inverie; dm adult/child £15/10; @) A 15-minute walk east of the ferry pier.

Torrie Shieling   HOSTEL **£**

(☏01687-462669; torrie@knoydart.org; dm £15) A 20-minute walk to the west of the ferry pier.

Barisdale Bothy   BOTHY **£**

(☏01764-684946; www.barisdale.com; Barisdale; dm £3, tent sites per person £1) The Barisdale Bothy, 6 miles west of Kinloch Hourn on the footpath to Inverie, has sleeping platforms without mattresses – you'll need your own sleeping bag and foam mat.

Long Beach   CAMPSITE **£**

(Long Beach; per tent £4) Basic but beautiful campsite, a 10-minute walk east of the ferry; water supply and composting toilet, but no showers.

⬛ TOP CHOICE Old Forge   PUB, RESTAURANT **££**

(☏01687-462267; www.theoldforge.co.uk; mains £11-23; ☏🍴) The Old Forge is listed in the *Guinness Book of Records* as Britain's most remote pub. It's surprisingly sophisticated – as well as having real ale on tap, there's an Italian coffee machine for those wilderness lattes and cappuccinos, and the house special is a platter of langoustines with aioli dipping sauce.

In the evening you can sit by the fire, pint of beer in hand and join the impromptu *ceilidh* (an evening of traditional Scottish entertainment including music, song and dance) that seems to take place just about nightly.

❶ Getting There & Away

Bruce Watt Cruises (☏01687-462320; www.knoydart-ferry.co.uk; one way £11) Passenger ferry linking Mallaig to Inverie (45 minutes) twice daily Monday to Friday from mid-May to mid-September, and on Monday, Wednesday and Friday only the rest of the year (no weekend ferries). Taking the morning boat gives you four hours ashore in Knoydart before the afternoon return trip.

The afternoon sailing returns via Tarbet on the south side of Loch Nevis, allowing walkers to hike along the northern shore of Loch Morar to Tarbet and return by boat (£15 Tarbet–Mallaig; Monday and Friday only outside summer season). It's also possible to join the boat just for the cruise, without going ashore (£20 for Mallaig–Inverie–Tarbet–Mallaig).

Sea Bridge Knoydart (☏01687-462916; www.knoydartferry.com; one way £10; ☺Apr-Oct) This new passenger ferry service runs from Mallaig to Inverie four times daily in season (25 minutes), and will carry bikes, canoes and kayaks at no extra charge.

SMALL ISLES

The scattered jewels of the Small Isles – Rum, Eigg, Muck and Canna – lie strewn across the silvery-blue cloth of the Cuillin Sound to the south of the Isle of Skye. Their distinctive outlines enliven the glorious views from the beaches of Arisaig and Morar.

Rum is the biggest and boldest of the four, a miniature Skye of pointed peaks and dramatic sunset silhouettes. Eigg is the most pastoral and populous, dominated by the miniature sugarloaf mountain of the Sgurr. Muck is a botanist's delight with its wildflowers and unusual alpine plants, and Canna is a craggy bird sanctuary made of magnetic rocks.

If your time is limited and you can only visit one island, choose Eigg; it has the most to offer on a day trip.

ⓘ Getting There & Away

The main ferry operator is **CalMac** (www.calmac.co.uk), which operates the passenger-only ferry from Mallaig.

Canna £22.45 return, two hours, four a week

Eigg £12.10 return, 1¼ hours, five a week

Muck £18.40 return, 1½ hours, four a week

Rum £17.85 return, 1¼ hours, five a week

You can also hop between the islands without returning to Mallaig, but the timetable is complicated and it requires a bit of planning – you would need at least five days to visit all four. Bicycles are carried for free.

In summer Arisaig Marine (p356) operates day cruises from Arisaig harbour to Eigg (£18 return, one hour, five a week), Rum (£25 return, 2½ hours, two or three a week) and Muck (£20 return, two hours, three a week). The trips include whale-watching, with up to an hour for close viewing. Sailing times allow four or five hours ashore on Eigg, two or three hours on Muck or Rum.

Isle of Rum

POP 37

The Isle of Rum – the biggest and most spectacular of the Small Isles – was once known as the Forbidden Island. Cleared of its crofters in the early 19th century to make way for sheep, from 1888 to 1957 it was the private sporting estate of the Bulloughs, a nouveau-riche Lancashire family who made their fortune in the textile industry. Curious outsiders who ventured too close to the island were liable to find themselves staring down the wrong end of a gamekeeper's shotgun.

The island was sold to the Nature Conservancy in 1957 and has since been a reserve noted for its deer, wild goats, ponies, golden and white-tailed sea eagles, and a 120,000-strong nesting colony of Manx shearwaters. Its dramatic, rocky mountains, known as the Rum Cuillin for their similarity to the peaks on neighbouring Skye, draw hill walkers and climbers.

◎ Sights & Activities

Kinloch Castle CASTLE
(☑01687-462037; www.isleofrum.com; adult/child £7/3.50; ⊙guided tours daily Apr-Oct, to coincide with ferry times) When George Bullough – a dashing, Harrow-educated cavalry officer – inherited Rum along with half his father's fortune in 1891, he became one of the wealthiest bachelors in Britain. Bullough blew half his inheritance on building his dream bachelor pad – the ostentatious Kinloch Castle.

Bullough shipped in pink sandstone from Dumfriesshire and 250,000 tonnes of Ayrshire topsoil for the gardens, and paid his workers a shilling extra a day to wear tweed kilts – just so they'd look more picturesque. Hummingbirds were kept in the greenhouses and alligators in the garden, and guests were entertained with an orchestrion, the Edwardian equivalent of a Bose hi-fi system (one of only six that were ever made). Since the Bulloughs left, the castle has survived as a perfect time capsule of upper-class Edwardian eccentricity. The guided tour should not be missed.

Nature Trails WALKING
There's some great coastal and mountain walking on the island, including a couple of easy, waymarked nature trails in the woods around Kinloch. The first path on the left after leaving the pier leads to an **otter hide** (signposted).

Glen Harris is a 10-mile round trip from Kinloch, on a rough 4WD track – allow four to five hours' walking. The climb to the island's highest point, **Askival** (812m), is a strenuous hike and involves a bit of rock scrambling (allow six hours for the round trip from Kinloch).

You can hire bikes from the Craft Shop (☑01687-462744; http://rumbikehire.co.uk; per day/half-day £14/7) near Kinloch Castle.

Bullough Mausoleum
CEMETERY

The only part of the island that still belongs to the Bullough family is this mausoleum in Glen Harris. It's a miniature Greek temple that wouldn't look out of place on the Acropolis. Lady Bullough was laid to rest here, alongside her husband and father-in-law, in 1967, having died at the age of 98.

📤 Sleeping & Eating

Accommodation on Rum is strictly limited – at the time of research there was only the Castle Hostel and the campsite. Booking is essential for the hostel, though not for campers. There are also two bothies (unlocked cottages with no facilities, for the use of hikers) on the island, and wild camping is permitted.

Kinloch Castle Hostel
HOSTEL £

(☑01687-462037; www.isleofrum.com; dm £16, d £45-55; ☺Mar-Oct; ☎) The castle has 42 beds in 4- or 6-bed dorms and four double bedrooms in its rear wing. There's a communal self-catering kitchen, and also a small restaurant offering a cooked breakfast (£7.50) and dinner (£17.50) to guests (meals must be booked in advance). At the time of research the hostel's future was in doubt, but there are plans for a new bunkhouse to replace it.

Kinloch Village Campsite
CAMPSITE £

(☑01687-460328; www.isleofrum.com; sites per adult/child £5/2.50) Situated between the pier and Kinloch Castle, this basic campground has toilets, a water supply and hot showers. There are also two new wooden camping cabins (£20 for two persons), which must be booked in advance.

❶ Information

Kinloch, where the ferry lands, is the island's only settlement; it has a small **grocery shop** (☺5-7pm), post office and public telephone, and a **tourist office** (☺8.30am-5pm) near the pier where you can get information and leaflets on walking and wildlife. There's a **tearoom** (☺noon-6pm Mon-Sat Apr-Sep) in the village hall, with wi-fi and internet access. The hall itself is open at all times for people to shelter from the rain (or the midges!). For more information see www.isleofrum.com.

Isle of Eigg

POP 70

The Isle of Eigg made history in 1997 when it became the first Highland estate to be bought out by its inhabitants. The island is now owned and managed by the Isle of Eigg Heritage Trust (www.isleofeigg.org), a partnership among the islanders, Highland Council and the Scottish Wildlife Trust.

🏃 Activities

The island takes its name from the Old Norse *egg* (edge), a reference to the Sgurr of Eigg (393m), an impressive minimountain that towers over Galmisdale. Ringed by vertical cliffs on three sides, it's composed of pitchstone lava with columnar jointing similar to that seen on the Isle of Staffa and at the Giant's Causeway in Northern Ireland.

Sgurr of Eigg
HIKING

The climb to the summit (4.5 miles round trip; allow three to four hours) of the Sgurr of Eigg begins on the road that leads steeply uphill from the pier, which continues through the woods to a red-roofed cottage. Go through the gate to the right of the cottage and turn left; just 20m along the road a cairn on the right marks the start of a boggy footpath that leads over the eastern shoulder of the Sgurr, then traverses beneath the northern cliffs until it makes its way up onto the summit ridge.

On a fine day the views from the top are magnificent – Rum and Skye to the north, Muck and Coll to the south, Ardnamurchan Lighthouse to the southeast and Ben Nevis shouldering above the eastern horizon. Take binoculars – on a calm summer's day there's a good chance of seeing minke whales feeding down below in the Sound of Muck.

Uamh Fraing
CAVE

A shorter walk (2 miles; allow 1½ hours round trip, and bring a torch) leads west from the pier to the spooky and claustrophobic Uamh Fraing (Massacre Cave). Start as for the Sgurr of Eigg, but 800m from the pier turn left through a gate and into a field. Follow the 4WD track and fork left before a white cottage to pass below it. A footpath continues across the fields to reach a small gate in a fence; go through it and descend a ridge towards the shore.

The cave entrance is tucked inconspicuously down to the left of the ridge. The entrance is tiny – almost a hands-and-knees job – but the cave opens out inside and runs a long way back. Go right to the back, turn off your torch, and imagine the cave packed shoulder to shoulder with terrified men, women and children. Then imagine the panic as your enemies start piling firewood into the entrance. Almost the entire population of Eigg – around 400 people – sought refuge in this cave when the MacLeods of Skye raided the island in 1577. In an act of inhuman cruelty, the raiders lit a fire in the narrow entrance and everyone inside died of asphyxiation. There are more than a few ghosts floating around in here.

Grulin & Laig Beach Hikes   HIKING

Two good walks are to the deserted crofts of **Grulin** on the southwest coast (5 miles, two hours round trip), and north by the road to **Laig Beach** with its famous singing sands – the sand makes a squeaking noise when you walk on it (8 miles, three hours return).

You can get more information on island walks from the craft shop in An Laimhrig (p361).

🛏 Sleeping & Eating

All accommodation should be booked in advance. For a full listing of self-catering accommodation, see www.iselofeigg.org.

Lageorna   B&B ££

(☎01687-482405; www.lageorna.com; Cleadale; per person £60 incl dinner; 🛜) This converted croft house and lodge in the island's northwest is Eigg's most luxurious accommodation. Rooms are fitted with beautiful, locally made, 'driftwood-style' timber beds, and even have iPod docks (but no mobile-phone reception). Evening meals are part of the package, with the menu heavy on locally grown vegetables, seafood and venison.

Sandavore Bothy   BOTHY £

(☎01687-482480; www.eiggbreaks.co.uk; Galmisdale; per night £35) This tiny, one-room bothy, a 15-minute walk from the pier, has space for four people in one double bed and two bunk beds. It's a real Hebridean experience – accessible only on foot, limited electricity, cold running water only and an outside toilet (there are public showers down by the pier).

Glebe Barn   HOSTEL £

(☎01687-482417; www.glebebarn.co.uk; dm/tw £16/38; @🛜) Excellent bunkhouse accommodation in the middle of the island, with a smart, maple-floored lounge with central fireplace, modern kitchen, laundry, drying room and bright, clean dorms and bedrooms.

Sue Holland's Croft   CAMPSITE £

(☎01687-482480; www.eiggyurtingandcamping. co.uk; Cleadale; per tent £5, yurt £35-40; 🛜) This organic croft in the north of the island has a campsite with basic facilities, and also offers accommodation for two in a Mongolian yurt.

Galmisdale Bay   CAFE £

(www.galmisdale-bay.com; Galmisdale; mains £4-8; ⊙10am-5pm Mon-Sat & 11am-4.30pm Sun May-Sep, longer hours Oct-Apr) There's a good cafe-bar above the ferry pier. Winter opening hours coincide with ferry arrivals and departures.

ℹ Information

The ferry landing is at Galmisdale in the south. **An Laimhrig** (www.isleofeiggshop.co.uk; ⊙10am-5pm Mon-Wed & Fri, 11am-3pm Thu, 11am-5pm Sat, noon-1pm Sun May-Sep, shorter hours in winter) The building above the pier houses a grocery store, post office, craft shop and cafe. You can hire **bikes** (www. eiggadventures.co.uk; per day/half-day £14/9) here, too.

Isle of Muck

POP 30

The tiny island of **Muck** (www.isleofmuck. com), measuring just 2 miles by 1 mile, has exceptionally fertile soil, and the island is carpeted with wildflowers in spring and early summer. It takes its name from the Gaelic *muc* (pig), and pigs are still raised here.

Ferries call at the southern settlement of Port Mor. There's a **tearoom and craft shop** (⊙11am-4pm Jun-Aug, shorter hours May & Sep) above the pier, which also acts as a tourist office.

It's an easy 15-minute walk along the island's only road from the pier to the sandy beach at **Gallanach** on the northern side of the island. A longer and rougher hike (1½ hours round trip) goes to the top of **Beinn Airein** (137m) for the best views. Puffins nest on the cliffs at the western end of Camas Mor, the bay to the south of the hill.

The cosy six-bed **Isle of Muck Bunkhouse** (☎01687-462042; dm £12), with its oil-fired Rayburn stove, is just above the pier, as is the welcoming eight-room **Port Mor House Hotel** (☎01687-462365; hotel@ isleofmuck.com; per person incl dinner £60); rates include evening meals, which are also available to nonguests (£18, book in advance).

You can camp on the island for free – but ask at the craft shop first. For a full accommodation listings see www.isleofmuck.com.

Isle of Canna

POP 19

The island of Canna (www.theisleofcanna. co.uk) is a moorland plateau of black basalt rock, just 5 miles long and 1.25 miles wide; it was gifted to the National Trust for Scotland in 1981 by its owner, the Gaelic scholar and author John Lorne Campbell. **Compass Hill** (143m), at the northeastern corner, contains enough magnetite (an iron oxide mineral) to deflect the navigation compasses in passing yachts.

The ferry arrives at the hamlet of **A'Chill** at the eastern end of the island, where visiting yachtsmen have left extensive graffiti on the rock face south of the harbour. There's a tearoom and craft shop by the harbour, and a tiny post office in a hut. There is no mobile-phone reception.

You can walk to **An Coroghon**, just east of the ferry pier, a medieval stone tower perched atop a sea cliff, and continue to Compass Hill, or take a longer hike along the southern shore past Canna House (admission £5; ☻1-2pm Wed, 11am-noon & 4-5pm Sat Apr-Sep) (the former home of John Lorne Campbell) and an ornately decorated **early Christian stone cross**. In 2012 a *bullaun*, or 'cursing stone', with an inscribed cross was discovered nearby; these are common in Ireland, but this was the first to be found in Scotland.

Accommodation is very limited. Tighard (☏08444 932 242; www.tighard.com; per person £35-50; ☻May-Sep) is the only B&B (evening meals £25 to £30), and cafe-restaurant Gille Brighde (☏01687-460164; www.cannarestaurant.com; mains £8-18; ☻lunch Tue-Sat, dinner daily in summer; check website for other times) the only eating place. Check www.theisleofcanna. co.uk for self-catering accommodation. **Wild camping** is allowed.

Northern Highlands & Islands

Includes »

Best Places to Stay

» The Torridon (p388)
» Garenin Holiday Cottages (p408)
» Toravaig House Hotel (p397)
» The Ceilidh Place (p384)
» Tongue SYHA (p379)

Best Places to Eat

» The Albannach (p382)
» Captain's Galley (p376)
» Three Chimneys (p402)
» Badachro Inn (p387)
» Applecross Inn (p388)

Why Go?

Scotland's vast and melancholy soul is here: an epic land with a stark beauty that leaves an indelible imprint on the hearts of those who journey through it. Mist and mountains, rock and heather, and long, sun-blessed summer evenings are the pay-off for so many days of horizontal rain. It's simply magical.

Stone tells stories throughout. The chambered cairns of Caithness and the brochs of Sutherland are testament to the skills of prehistoric builders; cragtop castles and the broken walls of abandoned crofts tell of turbulent history.

Outdoors is the place to be, whatever the weather; there's nothing like comparing windburn or mud-ruined boots over a well-deserved dram by the crackling fire of a Highland pub. The landscape lends itself to activity, from woodland strolls to thrilling mountain-bike descents, from sea kayaking to Munro bagging, from beachcombing to birdwatching. Best are the locals, big-hearted and straight-talking; make it your business to get to know them.

When to Go?

Portree

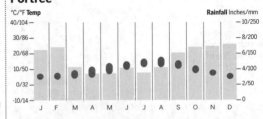

Jun Long evenings bathe achingly sublime landscapes in a dreamy light.

Jul The Hebridean Celtic Festival is a top time to experience the culture of the Outer Hebrides.

Sep Less busy than summer, the midges have gone and (if you're lucky) temperatures are still OK.

Northern Highlands & Islands Highlights

① Gorging on fresh, succulent seafood in the delightful town of **Ullapool** (p383), with its picture-perfect harbour

② Dipping your toes in the water at some of the world's most beautiful beaches on **Harris** (p409)and **Barra** (p414)

③ Shouldering the challenge of the **Cuillin Hills** (p398), with their rugged silhouettes brooding over the skyscape of Skye

④ Picking your jaw up off the floor as you marvel at the epic Highland scenery of the **far northwest** between Durness and Ullapool (p381)

⑤ Taking the trip out to **Cape Wrath** (p381), Britain's northwestern shoulder and gloriously remote

⑥ Relaxing in postcard-pretty **Plockton** (p389), where the Highlands meet the Caribbean

⑦ Launching yourself in a sea kayak to explore the otter-rich waters around the **Isle of Skye** (p392)

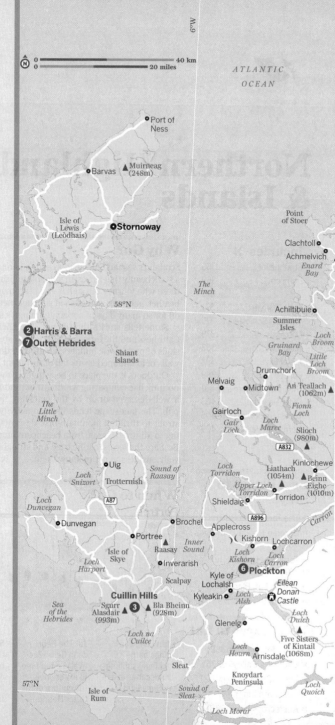

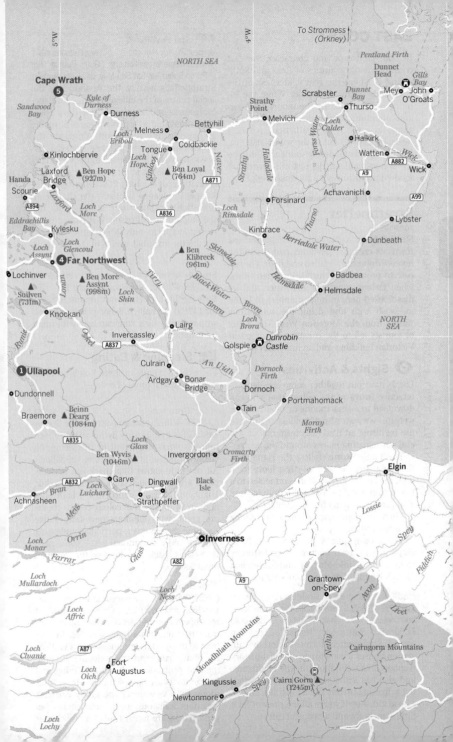

EAST COAST

In both landscape and character, the east coast of the old counties of Ross and Sutherland is where the real wilderness of the Highlands begins to unfold. While the interior is dominated by the mournful moor-and-mountain landscapes of Sutherland, along the coast great heather-covered hills heave themselves out of the wild North Sea. Rolling farmland drops suddenly into the icy waters, and small, historic towns are moored precariously on the coast's edge.

Strathpeffer

POP 900

Strathpeffer is a charming old Highland spa town, its creaking pavilions and grandiose hotels dripping with faded grandeur. The spa rose to prominence during Victorian times, when fashion-conscious gentlemen and ladies flocked here in huge numbers to bathe in, wash with and drink the sulphurous waters from the Morrison Well. The influx of tourists led to the construction of grand Victorian buildings and architectural follies.

◉ Sights & Activities

Locals have put together some excellent interactive **tours** of the village that you can download to a smartphone or tablet via the website www.strathpeffervillage.org.uk, or use by hiring an iPad (£2) from one of several participating places around the centre.

The **Eagle Stone** (follow the signs from the main drag) is well worth a look. It's a pre-7th-century Pictish stone connected to a figure from local history – the Brahan Seer, who predicted many future events.

There are many good signposted walking trails around Strathpeffer.

The Strathpeffer & District Pipe Band plays in the town square every Saturday from 8.30pm, mid-May to mid-September. There's Highland dancing and a festive air.

Highland Museum of Childhood   MUSEUM
(☑01997-421031; www.highlandmuseumofchild hood.org.uk; Old Train Station; adult/child £2.50/1.50; ◷10am-5pm Mon-Sat, 2-5pm Sun Apr-Oct) Strathpeffer's former Victorian train station houses a wide range of social-history displays about childhood in the Highlands, and also has activities for children, including a dressing-up box and a toy train. There's a good gift shop if you're after a present for a little somebody, and a peaceful cafe.

FREE Spa Pavilion & Upper Pump Room   MUSEUM, ARTS VENUE
(www.strathpefferpavilion.org; Golf Course Rd; ◷Pump Room Tue-Sat Sep-May, daily Jun-Aug) In Strathpeffer's heyday, the Pavilion was the social centre of the village, a venue for dances, lectures and concerts. These days it has been renovated as a performing-arts venue, and also holds a restaurant. Alongside, the Upper Pump Room has some splendid displays showing the bizarre lengths Victorians went to in the quest for a healthy glow, and exhibitions of local art. If you dare, you can sample the waters yourself; the chalybeate (iron-rich) spring water is delicious, but the sulphurous Morrison Well water is for strong stomachs only. Much more appetising are the artisanal sweets in the charming shop.

Square Wheels Cycles   BICYCLE HIRE
(☑01997-421000; www.squarewheels.biz; The Square; ◷Tue-Sun) Hires out mountain bikes for £12/20 per half-/full day; prices decrease with multiday hire. Staff can help with route information.

🛏 Sleeping & Eating

There are a couple of large hotels in town geared to coach tours of retirees.

TOP CHOICE Craigvar   B&B ££
(☑01997-421622; www.craigvar.com; The Square; s/d £50/86; P⊛) Luxury living with a refined touch is what you'll find in this delightful Georgian house in the heart of the village. All the little extras that mark out a classy place are here, such as a welcome drink, Highland-Belgian chocolates, bathrobes and fresh fruit. The colour-coded rooms are great, with fabulous new bathrooms; the Blue double has a particularly pleasing outlook and a sensational bed – you'll need to collapse back into it after the gourmet breakfast.

Coul House   HOTEL £££
(☑01997-421487; www.coulhouse.com; s/d £85/165; P@⊛⊛) At Contin, south of Strathpeffer on the A835, Coul House dates from 1821 but has a light, airy feel in contrast to many country houses of this vintage. It's family run, and the welcome is genuine and professional. Beautiful dining and lounge areas are complemented by elegant rooms with views over the lovely gardens; superiors look out to the mountains beyond. There are forest trails for walking or

mountain biking right on the doorstep and a good restaurant.

Red Poppy
BISTRO ££
(☎01997-423332; www.redpoppyrestaurant.co.uk; The Pavilion; mains £10-16; ☻11am-8pm Tue-Sat, lunch Sun) In the restored historical Victorian spa pavilion, Red Poppy is a much-needed dining option. There's a large selection of meals, including game dishes such as wild-boar steaks, and the dining is in elegant surrounds. It's a little cheaper at lunchtime.

❶ Getting There & Around

BUS **Stagecoach** (www.stagecoachbus.com) operates buses from Inverness to Strathpeffer (45 minutes, at least hourly Monday to Saturday, four on Sunday). The Inverness to Gairloch and Durness buses, plus some Inverness to Ullapool buses, also run via Strathpeffer.

Tain
POP 3500

Scotland's oldest royal burgh, Tain is a proud sandstone town that rose to prominence as pilgrims descended to venerate the relics of St Duthac, who is commemorated by the 12th-century ruins of **St Duthac's Chapel**, and St Duthus Church.

◉ Sights

Tain Through Time
MUSEUM
(☎01862-894089; www.tainmuseum.org.uk; Tower St; adult/child £3.50/2.50; ☻10am-5pm Mon-Fri Apr-Oct, also Sat Jun-Aug) Set in the grounds of St Duthus Church is Tain Through Time, an entertaining heritage centre with a colourful and educational display on St Duthac, King James IV and key moments in Scottish history. Another building focuses on the town's fine silversmithing tradition. Admission includes an audioguided walk around town.

Glenmorangie Distillery
DISTILLERY
(www.glenmorangie.com; tours £2.50; ☻10am-5pm Mon-Fri, plus to 4pm Sat & noon-4pm Sun Jun-Aug) Located on Tain's northern outskirts, Glenmorangie (emphasis on the second syllable) produces a fine light malt, which is subjected to a number of different cask finishes for variation. The tour is less in-depth than some but finishes with a free dram.

☐ Sleeping & Eating

Golf View House
B&B ££
(☎01862-892856; www.bedandbreakfasttain. co.uk; 13 Knockbreck Rd; s/d £50/70; P☻) Set

in an old manse in a secluded location just off the main road through town, this spot offers magnificent views over fields and water. The impeccable rooms are very cheerful and bright, and there's an upbeat feel to the place, with delicious breakfasts and welcoming hospitality. It's worth the extra fiver for a room with a view.

Royal Hotel
HOTEL ££
(☎01862-892013; www.royalhoteltain.co.uk; High St; s/d £50/85; ☎☻) So much the heart of town that the main street has to detour around it, the Royal Hotel has undergone a refurbishment that has left its good-sized rooms looking very spruce. For only a tenner more, you get a four-poster room in the old part of the hotel; these have a choice of colour schemes, and are well worth the upgrade. The restaurant is the best in town and bar meals are also decent.

❶ Getting There & Away

Stagecoach (p367) buses run to Tain (£8.50, 50 minutes, roughly hourly) from Inverness; three daily continue north as far as Thurso.

There are up to three trains daily to Inverness (£12.60, 1¼ hours) and Thurso (£15.40, 2¾ hours).

Portmahomack
POP 600

Portmahomack is a former fishing village in a flawless spot – right off the beaten track and gazing across the water at sometimes snowcapped peaks. The best place to enjoy the town is the grassy foreshore at the far end of Main St, near the little harbour.

The intriguing **Tarbat Discovery Centre** (☎01862-871351; www.tarbat-discovery.co.uk; Tarbatness Rd; adult/child £3.50/1; ☻10am-5pm Mon-Sat May-Sep, 2-5pm Mon-Sat Apr & Oct, also 2-5pm Sun Jun-Oct) has some excellent carved Pictish stones. The foundations of an Iron Age settlement were discovered around the village church; ongoing investigation revealed a Pictish monastery and evidence of production of illuminated manuscripts. The exhibition is excellent and includes the church's spooky crypt.

Seafood aficionados shouldn't miss the bright and cheerful **Oystercatcher Restaurant** (☎01862-871560; www.the-oystercatch er.co.uk; Main St; lunch mains £8-14, dinner mains £15-20; ☻lunch Thu-Sun, dinner Wed-Sat Apr-Oct). There's a bistro menu at lunchtime, where you can choose your serving size, and a classy brasserie evening menu with lots of lobster available, among other delights. It also offers three cosy rooms (single/double/superior double £45/77/108). The rates include what has to be the most amazing breakfast in Scotland, with numerous gourmet options.

Stagecoach Inverness (www.stagecoachbus.com) runs from Tain to Portmahomack (25 minutes, four to five Monday to Friday).

Bonar Bridge & Around

The A9 crosses the Dornoch Firth, on a bridge and causeway, near Tain. An alternative route goes around the firth via the tiny settlements of Ardgay, where you'll find a train station, and Bonar Bridge, where the A836 to Lairg branches west.

◉ Sights & Activities

Croick   HISTORIC SITE

From Ardgay, a single-track road leads 10 miles up Strathcarron to Croick, the scene of notorious evictions during the 1845 Clearances. You can still see the evocative messages scratched by refugee crofters from Glencalvie on the eastern windows of **Croick Church**.

Kyle of Sutherland Trails   MOUNTAIN BIKING

(☑01408-634063; www.forestry.gov.uk/cyclenorthhighland) Mountain bikers will find two networks of forest trails around Bonar Bridge. From the car park below the Carbisdale Castle hostel, there's a red and a blue trail (suitable for intermediate riders) with great views. At Balblair, 1 mile from Bonar Bridge off the Lairg road, 7 miles of black track will test expert bikers.

⌂ Sleeping

Carbisdale Castle SYHA   HOSTEL £

(☑01549-421232; www.syha.org.uk; dm/s/d £21/26/52; ⊙mid-Mar–Oct; P@🛜) This castle, 10 minutes' walk north of Culrain train station, was built in 1914 for the dowager duchess of Sutherland, but is now Scotland's biggest and most luxurious hostel, its halls studded with statues and dripping with opulence (advance bookings are highly recommended). Kick back in the superelegant library room or cook up a feast in the kitchen; catered meals (£12 for a three-course dinner) are also available. Mountain bikers coming off the trails can shower here for a small fee. At time of research the hostel

was closed for extensive refurbishment, so it may or may not be open by the time you read this: check the website.

ⓘ Getting There & Away

Trains running from Inverness to Thurso stop at Culrain (£15.20, 1½ hours, four Monday to Saturday, one Sunday), half a mile from Carbisdale Castle.

Lairg & Around

POP 900

Lairg is an attractive village, although the tranquillity can be rudely interrupted by the sound of military jets roaring overhead (Loch Shin valley is frequently used by the RAF for low-flying exercises). Located at the southern end of Loch Shin, it's the gateway to the remote mountains and loch-speckled bogs of central Sutherland.

SIGHTS & ACTIVITIES

Ferrycroft Visitor Centre   VISITOR CENTRE

(☑01549-402160; www.highland.gov.uk/ferrycroft; ⊙10am-4pm Apr-Oct; 🚼) On the opposite side of the the river from the town centre, this visitor centre has displays on local history, wildlife and a tourist information desk. A short walk leads from the centre to the **Ord Hut Circles and Chambered Cairns**, a collection of prehistoric roundhouses and tombs.

FREE Falls of Shin   WATERFALL

(☑01549-402231; www.fallsofshin.co.uk; ⊙10am-5pm year-round, 9am-7.30pm Jul & Aug; 🚼) Four miles south of Lairg, the picturesque Falls of Shin is one of the best places in the Highlands to see salmon leaping on their way upstream to spawn (June to September). The shop and cafe complex features an exhibition on salmon, as well as a bizarre kilted waxwork of Mohamed Al Fayed, who owns the surrounding Balnagown Estate. A short and easy footpath leads from the centre to a viewing terrace overlooking the waterfall. There are waymarked forest trails here, as well as a geocaching trail, an adventure playground and minigolf.

SLEEPING & EATING

Lairg Highland Hotel   HOTEL ££

(☑01549-402243; www.highland-hotel.co.uk; Main St; s £42-46, d £82-100; P🛜😺) The heart of the town, this friendly hotel offers surprisingly modern, stylish rooms that vary in colour scheme and size. It welcomes solo travellers,

THE RIGHT SIDE OF THE TRACKS

Scotland has some unusual hostels and Sleeperzzz.com (☑01408-641343; www.sleeperzzz.com; dm £15; ☺Mar–Sep; P) is one of them. Set in three caringly converted railway carriages, an old bus and a beautiful wooden caravan parked up in a siding by **Rogart** station, it has cute two-person bedrooms, kitchenettes and tiny lounges. The owners make an effort to run the hostel on sustainable lines, and there's a local pub that does food, as well as beautifully lonely Highland scenery in the vicinity. It's on the A839, 10 miles east of Lairg, but is also easily reached by train on the Inverness–Wick line (10% discount if you arrive this way or by bike).

walkers and cyclists, with a good lock-up cycle shed out the back. The attractive dining area offers up pub classics and a selection of Indian curries. There are discounts in low season, and for multinight stays.

GETTING THERE & AWAY

Trains from Inverness to Thurso stop at Lairg (£15.20, 1¾ hours) four times daily Monday to Saturday, and once on Sunday. Four buses run Monday to Saturday to Tain via Bonar Bridge and Ardgay (some stop at the Falls of Shin). Three buses run Monday to Friday to Helmsdale via Rogart and Golspie.

Dornoch

POP 1200

On the north shore of the Dornoch Firth, about 2 miles from the A9, this attractive old market town is one of the most pleasant settlements on the east coast. Dornoch is best known for its championship **golf course**, but there are some fine old buildings, including Dornoch Cathedral. Among other historical oddities, the last witch to be executed in Scotland was boiled alive in hot tar in Dornoch in 1722.

◉ Sights & Activities

If you've struck Dornoch on a sunny day, make sure you have a walk along its golden-sand **beach**, which stretches for miles. South of Dornoch, **seals** are often visible on the sandbars of Dornoch Firth.

FREE Dornoch Cathedral   CHURCH
(www.dornoch-cathedral.com; St Gilbert St; ☺9am-7pm or later) Consecrated in the 13th century, Dornoch Cathedral is an elegant Gothic edifice with an interior softly illuminated through modern stained-glass windows. It was restored in the late 1830s thanks to the generosity of Elizabeth, Duchess-Countess of Sutherland, whose husband – the controversional first Duke of Sutherland – lies in a sealed burial vault beneath the chancel. By the western door is the sarcophagus of Sir Richard de Moravia, who died fighting the Danes at the battle of Embo in the 1260s. Until he met his maker, the battle had been going rather well for him; he'd managed to slay the Danish commander with the unattached leg of a horse that was to hand.

Historylinks   MUSEUM
(www.historylinks.org.uk; The Meadows; adult/child £2.50/free; ☺10am-4pm daily Jun-Sep, Mon-Fri Apr, May & Oct, Wed & Thu only Nov-Mar; ⊞) Historylinks is a child-friendly museum with displays on local history.

Royal Dornoch   GOLF
(☑01862-810219; www.royaldornoch.com; Golf Rd; green fees £100-110) One of Scotland's most famous links courses, this was once described by Tom Watson as 'the most fun I have ever had on a golf course'. It's open to the public, and you can book a slot online. Twilight rates are the most economical way to get a game. A golf pass (www.dornochfirthgolf .co.uk) is available that will let you play several courses in the area at a good discount.

🛌 Sleeping & Eating

TOP CHOICE Dornoch Castle Hotel   HOTEL ££
(☑01862-810216; www.dornochcastlehotel.com; Castle St; s/d £73/123, superior/deluxe d £169/250; P🐾) This 16th-century former bishop's palace makes a wonderful place to stay, particularly if you upgrade to one of the superior rooms, which have views, space, malt whisky and chocolates on the welcome tray and, in some cases, four-poster bed; the deluxe rooms are unforgettable. Cheaper rooms (s/d £50/65) are also available in adjoining buildings.

Kyleview House   B&B ££
(☑01862-810999; www.kyleviewhouse.co.uk; Evelix Rd; s/d £55/80; P🐾) A bend-over-backwards host makes you feel truly welcome at this handsome stone house on the entrance road into town. Views over the

firth are complemented by superbly kept contemporary rooms with countless small touches that make for a memorable stay. Book ahead, as some of our readers head for the Highlands just so they can stay here.

2 Quail B&B **££**
(☑01862-811811; www.2quail.com; Castle St; s/d £80/100; ☎) Intimate and upmarket, 2 Quail offers a warm welcome on the main street. The tasteful, spacious chambers are full of old-world comfort, with sturdy metal bed frames, plenty of books and plump duvets. The downstairs guest lounge is an absolute delight. It's best to book ahead, especially in winter.

Trevose Guest House B&B **££**
(☑01862-810269; jamackenzie@tiscali.co.uk; Cathedral Sq; s/d £30/60; ☉Mar-Sep; ☎☎) First impressions deceive at Trevose Guest House, a lovely stone cottage right by the cathedral. It looks compact but actually boasts very spacious rooms with significant comfort and well-loved old wooden furnishings. Character oozes from every pore of the place and a benevolent welcome is a given.

Rosslyn Villa B&B **£**
(☑01862-810237; Castle St; s/d £20/40) On the main street, this place has old-fashioned charm and is run with gentle courtesy by the charming octogenarian owner. It's a real bargain: the rooms are comfortable, with reassuringly chunky old televisions and spotless en suite bathrooms. The four-poster double and guest lounge are particularly appealing. There's no breakfast included, but bring some bread to toast and eat it in the conservatory.

✖ Eating

Dornoch Castle Hotel SCOTTISH **£££**
(☑01862-810216; www.dornochcastlehotel.com; Castle St; mains from £18; ☉lunch & dinner) In the evening, toast your toes in the cosy bar before dining in style at this first-rate restaurant (three-course dinner £32.50), tucking into dishes featuring plenty of game and seasonal produce. Bar meals are also available during the day.

Luigi ITALIAN **£**
(www.luigidornoch.com; Castle St; light meals £5-8; ☉lunch daily, dinner Fri & Sat, dinner daily in summer) On the main drag, the clean lines of this contemporary Italian cafe make a clean break from the omnipresent heritage and history of this coastline. Ciabattas and

salads stuffed with tasty deli ingredients make it a good lunch stop; the more elaborate dinner mains (£12 to £18) usually include fine seafood choices.

Eagle Hotel PUB **£**
(☑01862-810008; www.eagledornoch.co.uk; Castle St; bar meals £8-10) Nobody on the streets of Dornoch after 7pm? You'll find most of them in this cosy, welcoming pub, which looks after its customers with good service and a wide-ranging menu of pizzas, pasta, burgers and pub classics.

ℹ Information

The **tourist office** (☑01862-810594; Castle St; ☉9am-12.30pm & 1.30-5pm Mon-Fri, also 10am-4pm Sat May-Aug & 10am-4pm Sun Jul-Aug) is next to Dornoch Castle Hotel.

ℹ Getting There & Away

There are buses roughly hourly from Inverness to Dornoch, with some services continuing north to Wick or Thurso.

Golspie

POP 1400

Golspie is a pretty little village that has benefited over the centuries from the proximity of Dunrobin Castle. There are good facilities and a pleasant beach: it's a congenial place to spend a day or two.

◉ Sights & Activities

Golspie is the starting point for some good walks. The classic local hike climbs steeply above the village to the summit of **Ben Bhraggie** (394m), which is crowned by a massive monument to the Duke of Sutherland, notorious for his leading role in the Highland Clearances.

Dunrobin Castle CASTLE
(☑01408-633177; www.dunrobincastle.co.uk; adult/child £9.50/5.50; ☉10.30am-4.30pm Mon-Sat, noon-4.30pm Sun Apr, May & Sep-mid-Oct, 10.30am-5.30pm Jun-Aug) One mile north of Golspie is magnificent Dunrobin Castle, the largest house in the Highlands. Although it dates back to 1275, most of what you see was built in French style between 1845 and 1850. One of the homes of the earls and dukes of Sutherland, it's richly furnished and offers an intriguing insight into the aristocratic lifestyle.

In spite of its beauty, Dunrobin inspires mixed feelings among local people. The castle was once the seat of the first Duke of Sutherland, notorious for his part in some of the cruellest episodes of the Highland Clearances. The duke's estate was once the largest privately owned area of land in Europe, covering 6070 square kilometres, and around 15,000 people were evicted from their homes to make way for sheep.

This classic fairy-tale castle is adorned with towers and turrets, but only 22 of its 187 rooms are on display, with hunting trophies much to the fore. The exhibits also include innumerable gifts from farm tenants (probably grateful they weren't victims of the Clearances).

Beautiful formal gardens, where impressive falconry displays take place two or three times a day, extend down to the sea. Also found in the gardens is the house's museum, which offers an eclectic mix of archaeological finds, natural-history exhibits, more non-PC animal remains and an excellent collection of Pictish stones found in Sutherland, including the fine pre-Christian Dunrobin Stone.

Highland Wildcat   MOUNTAIN BIKING
(www.highlandwildcat.com; Big Burn Car Park; car parking £5; ⊙dawn-dusk) The expert-only black trail at Highland Wildcat is famous among UK mountain bikers for having the highest single-track descent in the country (a 390m drop over 7km from the top of Ben Bhraggie almost to sea level). There's plenty for beginners and families too, with a scenic blue trail and some easy forest routes. No bike hire or other facilities.

🛏 Sleeping

Blar Mhor   B&B ££
(☎01408-633609; www.blarmhor.co.uk; Drummuie Rd; s/d/f £35/60/80; 🅿🛜❄) On the approach into Golspie from Dornoch is this excellent guest house with large, beautifully kept rooms with swish modern bathrooms in a towering Victorian mansion. There are beautifully landscaped gardens and the hosts, who'll brighten your stay with little extras like chocolates on the bed, are cheerful and helpful.

❶ Getting There & Away

Buses between Inverness and Thurso stop in Golspie. There are also trains from Inverness (£16.90, 2¼ hours, two or three daily) to Golspie and Dunrobin Castle.

Helmsdale
POP 900

Surrounded by hills with gorse that explodes mad-yellow in spring, this sheltered fishing town, like many other spots on this coast, was a major emigration point during the Clearances and also a booming herring port. It's surrounded by breathtaking, undulating coastline.

In the centre of town, the **Timespan Heritage Centre** (www.timespan.org.uk; Dunrobin St; adult/child £4/2; ⊙10am-5pm Mon-Sat, noon-5pm Sun Mar-Oct, 11am-4pm Sat & Sun, 2-4pm Tue Nov-Feb) has an impressive display covering local history (including the 1869 gold rush) and Barbara Cartland, the late queen of romance novels, who was a Helmsdale regular. There are also local art exhibitions, a geology garden and a cafe.

The River Helmsdale offers some of the best **salmon fishing** in the Highlands. Permits, tackle and advice can be obtained from the **Helmsdale Tackle Company** (☎01431-821372; www.helmsdalecompany.com; 15-17 Dunrobin St; ⊙9am-5pm Mon, Tue, Thu & Fri, to 12.45pm Wed & Sat).

🛏 Sleeping & Eating

🔝CHOICE **Bridge Hotel**   HOTEL ££
(☎01431-821100; www.bridgehotel.net; Dunrobin St; s/d £77/117; 🛜❄) Ideally located and exceptionally welcoming, this early 19th-century coaching inn is the smartest place to stay and the best place to eat in town. Proud of its Highland heritage, it displays a phalanx of antlers, even on the key fobs, part of the owner's eclectic collection that includes a huge array of wildlife prints. The guest lounge has to be seen to be believed: it's a who's who of the dead-deer world, but they all have their backstory – ask at reception. The rooms don't have the expected patina of age; they have wonderfully plush fabrics and a smart contemporary feel; there's a handsome suite that's ideal for families. The downstairs bar, with impressive whisky selection, and restaurant (April to mid-October only, closed Mondays) hum with good cheer and relaxed hospitality.

Helmsdale Hostel   HOSTEL £
(☎01431-821636; www.helmsdalehostel.co.uk; Stafford St; dm/tw/f £17.50/40/60; ⊙Apr-Sep; 🛜) This caringly run hostel is in very good nick and makes a cheerful, comfortable budget base for exploring Caithness. The dorm

berths are mostly cosy single beds rather than bunks, and the en suite rooms are great for families. The lofty kitchen-lounge space has a wood stove and good kitchen.

La Mirage   BISTRO £
(☑01431-821615; www.lamirage.org; 7 Dunrobin St; mains £7-12; ☺11am-8.45pm Mon-Sat, from noon Sun) Created in homage to Barbara Cartland by the larger-than-life late owner, this minor legend is a medley of pink flamboyance, faded celebrity photos and show tunes. The meals aren't gourmet – think chicken Kiev – but portions are huge and very tasty, especially the excellent fish and chips (also available to take away; eat 'em down on the pretty harbour).

❶ Getting There & Away
Buses from Inverness and Thurso stop in Helmsdale, as do trains (from Inverness £16.90, 2½ hours, two to three daily).

CAITHNESS
Once you pass Helmsdale, you are entering Caithness, a place of jagged gorse-and-grass-topped cliffs hiding tiny fishing harbours. This top corner of Scotland was once Viking territory, historically more connected to Orkney and Shetland than to the rest of the mainland. It's a magical and mystical land with an ancient aura, peopled by wise folk with long memories who are fiercely proud of their Norse heritage.

Helmsdale to Lybster
About 7 miles north of Helmsdale is **Badbea**, an abandoned crofting village. It was established during the Highland Clearances in the early 19th century, when people were evicted from their homes in the nearby glens. The village of **Dunbeath** has a spectacular setting in a deep glen – drop by the **Heritage Centre** (☑01593-731233; www.dunbeath-heritage.org.uk; The Old School; adult/child £2.50/free; ☺10am-5pm Sun-Fri Apr-Sep, 11am-3pm Mon-Fri Oct-Mar), which has a stone carved with runic graffiti, and a display on the work of Neil Gunn, whose wonderful novels evoke the Caithness of his boyhood.

Two miles north of Dunbeath is the **Laidhay Croft Museum** (☑0756 370 2321; www.laidhay.co.uk; adult/child £3.50/2.50; ☺10am-5pm Mon-Sat Jun-Sep), which recreates crofting life from the mid-1800s to WWII. At the

Clan Gunn Heritage Centre & Museum (☑01593-741700; www.clangunnsociety.org; adult/child £2.50/50p; ☺11am-1pm & 2-4pm Mon-Sat Jun-Sep) in Latheron, a mile past Laidhay, you'll learn that a Scot, not Christopher Columbus, discovered America – but you might take this claim with a pinch of salt!

Lybster & Around
Lybster is a purpose-built fishing village dating from 1810, with a stunning harbour area surrounded by grassy cliffs. In its heyday, it was Scotland's third-busiest port. Things have changed – now there are only a couple of boats – but there are several interesting prehistoric sites in the area.

◉ Sights & Activities

Waterlines   MUSEUM
(☑01593-721520; The Harbour; adult/child £2.50/50p; ☺11am-5pm May-Sep) At the picturesque harbour in Lybster, this has an exhibition on the town's fishing heritage and a popular downstairs cafe. In summer it operates a smokehouse (giving visitors a whiff of the kippering process).

Whaligoe Steps   HISTORIC SITE
At **Ulbster**, 5 miles north of Lybster on the A99, this staircase cut into the cliff face provides access to a tiny natural harbour ringed by vertical cliffs and echoing with the cackle of nesting fulmars. The path begins at the end of the minor road beside the telephone box, opposite the road signposted 'Cairn of Get'. There's a cafe at the top and a grassy area inviting picnics down below.

Cairn o'Get   HISTORIC SITE
The Cairn o'Get, a prehistoric burial cairn, is signposted off the road in Ulbster. It's a mile's boggy walk from the car park.

Achavanich Standing Stones   HISTORIC SITE
Five miles to the northwest of Lybster, on the minor road to Achavanich, just south of Loch Stemster, are the unsigned 30 Achavanich Standing Stones. In a desolate setting, these crumbling monuments of the distant past still capture the imagination with their evocative location.

Grey Cairns of Camster   HISTORIC SITE
Dating from between 4000 BC and 2500 BC, the Grey Cairns of Camster are burial chambers hidden in long, low mounds rising from an evocatively desolate stretch of moor. The

Long Cairn measures 60m by 21m. You can enter the main chamber, but must first crawl into the well-preserved Round Cairn, which has a corbelled ceiling.

From a turn-off a mile east of Lybster on the A99, the cairns are 4 miles north. From the site you can continue 7 miles north on this remote road to approach Wick on the A882.

Hill o'Many Stanes
HISTORIC SITE

The Hill o'Many Stanes, 2 miles beyond the Camster turn-off on the A99, is a curious, fan-shaped arrangement of 22 rows of small stones that probably date from around 2000 BC. Staggeringly, there were 600 in the original pattern. On a sunny day, the views from this hill are stunning.

ℹ️ Getting There & Away

Stagecoach buses between Thurso and Inverness run via Lybster and Dunbeath. There's also a coastal service from Wick to Helmsdale stopping at these places.

Wick

POP 7300

More gritty than pretty, Wick has been down on its luck since the collapse of the herring industry. It was once the world's largest fishing port for the 'silver darlings', but when the market dropped off after WWII, job losses were huge and the town hasn't totally recovered. These days Wick is an important local service centre and transport terminus. It's worth a look, particularly for its excellent museum, which puts everything in context, and its attractive, spruced-up harbour area.

⊙ Sights & Activities

A path leads a mile south from town to the ruins of 12th-century Old Wick Castle, with the spectacular cliffs of the **Brough** and the **Brig**, as well as **Gote o'Trams**, a little further south. In good weather, it's a fine coastal walk to the castle, but take care on the final approach. Three miles northeast of Wick is the magnificently located clifftop ruin of Castle Sinclair.

Wick Heritage Centre
MUSEUM

(☑01955-605393; www.wickheritage.org; 20 Bank Row; adult/child £4/50p; ⊙10am-5pm Mon-Sat Apr-Oct, last entry 3.45pm) Tracking the rise and fall of the herring industry, this great town museum displays everything from fishing equipment to complete herring boats. It's absolutely huge inside, and is crammed with memorabilia and extensive displays describing Wick's heyday in the mid-19th century.

The Johnston photographic collection is the museum's star exhibit. From 1863 to 1977, three generations of Johnstons photographed everything that happened around Wick, and the 70,000 photographs are an amazing portrait of the town's life. Prints of the early photos are for sale.

Old Pulteney Distillery
DISTILLERY

(☑01955-602371; www.oldpulteney.com; Huddart St; tours £5; ⊙10am-1pm & 2-4pm Mon-Fri Oct-Apr, 10am-4pm Mon-Sat May-Sep) Old Pulteney is the most northerly distillery on mainland Scotland and runs excellent tours twice a day, with more expensive visits available for aficionados. Old Pulteney whisky has a light, earthy character with a hint of sea air and sherry.

Caithness Seacoast
BOAT TOUR

(☑01955-609200; www.caithness-seacoast.co.uk) Wick's a boat town, and this outfit will take you out to sea to inspect the rugged coastline of the northeast. There are various options, from a half-hour jaunt (adult/child £17/11) to a three-hour trip down to Lybster and back (adult/child £45/35).

🛏️ Sleeping & Eating

Quayside
B&B £

(☑01955-603229; www.quaysidewick.co.uk; 25 Harbour Quay; s/d without breakfast £30/55; [P][🛜]) Quayside should be your first port of call for guest-house accommodation. The owners couldn't be more helpful – they've been in the business for many years and know what they're doing. Right by the harbour, it's handy for everything worth seeing in town. Spruce rooms have kitchenettes and can be taken at B&B or bed-only rates. There's a handy family room, and self-catering flats available, plus good facilities for cyclists and motorcyclists. Book ahead.

Mackays Hotel
HOTEL ££

(☑01955-602323; www.mackayshotel.co.uk; Union St; s/d £89/119; 🛜) The renovated Mackays is Wick's best hotel. Rooms vary in layout and size, so ask to see a few; prices drop if you're staying more than one night and walk-up prices are usually quite a bit lower than the rack rates we list here. On-site No 1 Bistro (Union St; mains £12-18) is a fine option for lunch or dinner. The 2.06m-long Ebenezer Pl, the world's shortest street, runs past one end of the hotel.

NORTHERN HIGHLANDS & ISLANDS WICK

Bord de l'Eau
FRENCH ££

(☏01955-604400; 2 Market St; mains £14-18; ☺lunch Tue-Sat, dinner Tue-Sun) This serene, relaxed French restaurant is the best place to eat in Wick. It overlooks the river and serves a changing menu of mostly meat and game French classics, backed up by daily fish specials. Starters are great value, and the pricier mains come with a huge assortment of vegetables, so you won't go hungry here. The conservatory dining room overlooking the river is lovely on a sunny evening.

❶ Information

Wick Information Centre (www.visithighlands .com; 66 High St; ☺9am-5.30pm Mon-Sat) Good selection of information; upstairs in McAllans Clothing Store.

Wick Carnegie Library (☏01955-602864; www.highland.gov.uk; Sinclair Tce; ☺Mon-Sat; 🛜) Free internet access.

❶ Getting There & Away

AIR Wick is a transport gateway to the surrounding area. **Flybe** (☏0871 700 2000; www.flybe .com) flies between Edinburgh and Wick airport once daily except Saturday. **Eastern Airways** (☏0870 366 9989; www.easternairways.com) flies to Aberdeen (three flights daily Monday to Friday).

BUS Stagecoach (www.stagecoachbus.com) and **Citylink** (☏0871 266 33 33; www.citylink .co.uk) operate buses to/from Inverness (£18.30, three hours, six daily) and Thurso (30 minutes, hourly). There's also connecting service to John O'Groats (40 minutes, two to three daily) for the passenger ferry to Burwick, Orkney; and to the Gills Bay ferry to St Margaret's Hope, Orkney.

TRAIN Trains service to Wick from Inverness (£18, 4¼ hours, four daily).

John O'Groats
POP 500

Though it's not the northernmost point of the British mainland (that's Dunnet Head), John O'Groats still serves as the end point of the 874-mile trek from Land's End in Cornwall, a popular if arduous route for cyclists and walkers, many of whom raise money for charitable causes. There's a passenger ferry from here to Orkney, and the settlement's spectacular setting is some consolation for the disappointment of finding that this famous destination is basically a car park surrounded by tourist shops.

◉ Sights & Activities

Duncansby Head
LOOKOUT

Two miles east, Duncansby Head provides a more solemn end-of-Britain moment, with a small lighthouse and 60m-high cliffs sheltering nesting fulmars. A 15-minute walk from here through a sheep paddock yields spectacular views of the sea-surrounded monoliths known as **Duncansby Stacks**.

🛏 Sleeping & Eating

There's a campsite and several B&Bs around town. At time of research, a series of wooden holiday chalets offering sensational views was being built, and the hotel, long in need of a loving hand, was being redeveloped into upmarket self-catering accommodation. Hit www.naturalretreats.co.uk to book. A licensed cafe was being built as part of the development. There are a couple of food outlets around the car park, and a hotel at the main-road intersection that serves meals.

Teuchters
B&B ££

(☏01955-611323; www.teuchtersbandb.co.uk; Gills; s/d £40/60; ℗🛜🐾) On the Thurso road, just by the Gills Bay ferry, 3 miles west of John O'Groats, this purpose-built B&B offers excellent rooms, plenty of space, modern comfort and stunning water views across to Stroma and Orkney. It has a lock-up shed for bikes and motorbikes.

❶ Information

John O'Groats Information Centre (☏01955-611373; www.visithighlands.com; ☺10am-5pm Apr-Oct) This tourist office has a fine selection of local novels and books about Caithness and the Highland Clearances.

❶ Getting There & Away

BOAT From May to September, a **passenger ferry** (☏01955-611353; www.jogferry.co.uk) shuttles across to Burwick in Orkney. Ninety-minute wildlife cruises to the island of Stroma or Duncansby Head cost £17 (late June to August).

BUS Stagecoach (www.stagecoachbus.com) runs buses between John O'Groats and Wick (40 minutes, two to three daily). There are also three to eight services Monday to Saturday to/from Thurso.

Mey

The **Castle of Mey** (www.castleofmey.org.uk; adult/child £10/5.50; ☺10.20am-5pm May–Sep, last admission to castle 4pm), a big crowd-puller for its Queen Mother connections, is about 6 miles west of John O'Groats, off the A836 to Thurso. The exterior may seem grand but inside it feels domestic and everything is imbued with the character of the late Queen Mum: from a surprisingly casual lounge area with TV showing her favourite show (*Dad's Army*, since you asked), to a photo of the corgis' evening meal – they didn't dine badly. The highlight is the genteel guided tour, with various anecdotes recounted by staff who once worked for her. Outside in the castle grounds there's a farm zoo, an unusual walled garden that's worth a stroll and lovely views over the Pentland Firth. The castle normally closes for a couple of weeks at the end of July for royal visits.

On the main road just near the castle, excellent The Hawthorns (☏01847-851710; www.thehawthornsbnb.co.uk; s/d £40/70; P🏠🐾) is a modern, easygoing B&B with a contemporary artistic flair, a genuine welcome and four very spruce, superspacious rooms with mini-fridges. There are good options for families here, and one room with disabled access.

Dunnet Head

Eight miles east of Thurso a minor road leads to dramatic Dunnet Head, the **most northerly point on the British mainland**, which beats John O'Groats hands down. There are majestic cliffs dropping into the turbulent Pentland Firth, inspiring views of the Orkney Islands, basking seals and nesting seabirds below, and a lighthouse built by Robert Louis Stevenson's granddad. Also on the headland, near the main road, is Mary-Ann's Cottage (adult/child £3/50p; ☺2-4.30pm Jun-Sep), well worth a visit. Mary-Ann lived in this 19th-century croft for nigh on a century, and in-depth guided tours take you round her humble but cosy farm and house: a fascinating back-in-time experience.

Just west, **Dunnet Bay** offers you one of Scotland's finest beaches, backed by high dunes, as well as Seadrift (☏01847-821531; admission free; ☺2pm-5pm May, Jun & Sep, 10.30-5pm Jul & Aug, closed Thu & Sat) – a small wildlife display and the base for local rangers, who organise walks in summer – and a caravan-dominated campsite (☏01847-821319; www.caravanclub.co.uk; members pitch £14.55; ☺Apr-Sep; P) backing the beach.

Thurso & Scrabster

POP 7700

Britain's most northerly mainland town, Thurso makes a handy overnight stop if you're heading west or across to Orkney. There's a pretty town beach, riverbank strolls and a good museum. Ferries cross from Scrabster, 2.5 miles west of Thurso, to Orkney.

◎ Sights

FREE Caithness Horizons   MUSEUM
(www.caithnesshorizons.co.uk; High St, Thurso; ☺10am-6pm Mon-Sat, also 11am-4pm Sun Apr-Sep) This museum brings much of the history and lore of Caithness to life through its excellent displays. A couple of fine Pictish cross-slabs greet the visitor downstairs; the main exhibition is a wide-ranging look at local history using plenty of audiovisuals – check out the wistful account of the now-abandoned island of Stroma for an emotional slice of social history. There's also a gallery space, an exhibition on the Dounreay nuclear reactor and a cafe.

🏃 Activities

Thurso is an unlikely surfing centre but the nearby coast has arguably the best and most regular surf on mainland Britain. There's an excellent right-hand reef break on the eastern side of town, directly in front of Lord Thurso's castle (closed to the public), and another shallow reef break 5 miles west at **Brimms Ness**. Pack a drysuit: this is no Hawaii. Thurso Surf (☏07590-419078; www.thursosurf.co.uk; lessons £35) gives lessons, normally on the beach at Dunnet Bay east of town.

Thurso's idyllic country Riverside Walk (Riverside) will make you feel miles away from town. It's a beautiful walk, taking about 45 minutes at a stroll, and is a very popular local pursuit in decent weather. You can also walk all the way to Scrabster (40 minutes) along cliffs for brilliant views. Take care in windy weather.

🛏 Sleeping

TOP CHOICE Pennyland House   B&B ££
(☏01847-891194; www.pennylandhouse.co.uk; s/d £60/70; P🏠) A super conversion of an historic house once lived in by the founder of the Boys' Brigade, this is Thurso's standout B&B choice. It offers phenomenal value

for this level of accommodation, with huge rooms named after golf courses: we especially loved St Andrews – so spacious, with a great chessboard-tiled bathroom. The hospitality is enthusiastic and most helpful, and there's an inviting breakfast space and terraced area with views over the water to Hoy.

Forss House Hotel
HOTEL ££

(☎01847-861201; www.forsshousehotel.co.uk; Forss; s/d/superior d £97/130/165; P🖨📶🐕) Tucked into a thicket of trees 4 miles west of Thurso is an old Georgian mansion offering elegant accommodation that has both character and style. Sumptuous upstairs rooms are preferable to basement rooms as they have lovely views of the garden. There are also separate, beautifully appointed suites in the garden itself, which provide both privacy and a sense of tranquillity. Thoughtful extras like a selection of CDs and books in every room add appeal. It's right alongside a beautiful salmon river – the hotel can sort out permits and equipment – and if you've had a chilly day in the waders, some 300 malt whiskies await in the hotel bar.

Waterside House
B&B £

(☎01847-894751; www.watersidehouse.org; 3 Janet St, Thurso; s £30, d £50-60; 📶🐕) Easy to find, and easy to park outside, this guest house (turn left just after the bridge coming into town) offers very spruce, recently made-over rooms with good en suites. There's a range of sizes, and the price is very reasonable. Breakfast choices include egg-and-bacon rolls, or takeaway if you've got an early ferry. No credit cards.

Murray House
B&B ££

(☎01847-895759; www.murrayhousebb.com; 1 Campbell St, Thurso; s/d/f £35/70/80; 📶) A solid 19th-century town house on a central corner, Murray House gives a good first impression with a genuine welcome. It continues with smart rooms with solid wooden furniture and modern bathrooms, two of which offer secluded sloping-ceiling spaces on the top floor. There's also an appealing lounge space. No credit cards.

Sandra's Hostel
HOSTEL £

(☎01847-894575; www.sandras-backpackers.co.uk; 24 Princes St, Thurso; dm/d/f £16/38/60; P@📶) In the heart of town above a chip shop, this reliable backpacker option offers appealing en suite dorms, mostly four-berthers, a spacious kitchen and traveller-friendly facilities

such as internet and help-yourself cereals and toast.

Thurso Hostel
HOSTEL £

(Ormlie Lodge; ☎01847-896888; ormlielodge@btconnect.com; Ormlie Rd, Thurso; s/d £15/25; P📶) This scruffy hostel is a students' hall of residence a few minutes' walk from the train station. It has a decent, if slightly ragged, range of budget accommodation. It's the place to go if you want a private room at a low price.

🍴 Eating

TOP CHOICE Captain's Galley
SEAFOOD £££

(☎01847-894999; www.captainsgalley.co.uk; Scrabster; 5-course dinner £47; ⊘dinner Tue-Sat) Right by the ferry terminal in Scrabster, Captain's Galley is a classy but friendly place offering a short, seafood-based menu that features local and sustainably sourced produce prepared in relatively simple ways, letting the natural flavours shine through. The chef picks the best fish off the local boats every day, and the menu describes exactly which boat and fishing grounds your morsel came from. Most rate it the best eatery in Caithness.

Holborn
BISTRO, PUB ££

(☎01847-892771; www.holbornhotel.co.uk; 16 Princes St, Thurso; bar meals £8-11, restaurant mains £12-20; 📶) A trendy, comfortable place decked out in light wood, the Holborn contrasts starkly with more traditional Thurso watering holes. Quality seafood – including delicious home-smoked salmon – is the mainstay of a short but solid menu at its **Red Pepper restaurant**, where desserts are excellent too. Its bar, Bar 16, is a modern space with couches and comfy chairs where bar meals are uncomplicated but decent.

Ferry Inn
PUB ££

(www.ferryinnscrabster.co.uk; Scrabster, Scrabster; mains £12-19, steaks £16-25; ⊘breakfast, lunch & dinner) Near the ferry dock in Scrabster, this traditional stone pub has rather ugly extensions, but these house the busy restaurant. It specialises in steaks – pick your size – and local haddock. We reckon it's a tad overpriced but the evening view over the harbour is great. Cheaper bar meals (£8 to £9) are downstairs, along with a pool table.

Cups
CAFE £

(www.cups-scrabster.co.uk; Scrabster; light meals £4-7; ⊘9am-7pm Mon-Sat, 10am-6pm Sun) Set in a converted chapel, it's all about teas and delicious home-baked scones and cakes at this little tearoom near the ferry. It also does good breakfast choices and a nice line in baked potatoes and sandwiches, going for classic flavour combinations but with high-quality local ingredients.

Le Bistro BISTRO **££**
(📞01847-893737; 2 Traill St, Thurso; lunch £6-10, dinner mains £11-17; ⊙Tue-Sat) This eatery buzzes with chatter on weekend evenings as locals of all ages chow down on its simple meat-and-carb creations. What it does, it does well: the respectably sized steaks come on a sizzling platter and service has a smile.

ℹ️ Information

Thurso Library (📞01847-893237; Davidson's Lane, Thurso; ⊙10am-6pm Mon & Wed, to 8pm Tue & Fri, to 1pm Thu & Sat) Free internet.

Thurso Information Centre (📞01847-893155; www.visithighlands.com; Riverside Rd, Thurso; ⊙daily Apr-Sep, Mon-Sat Oct) The future of Sunday opening was in doubt at time of research, so call to check.

ℹ️ Getting There & Around

It's a 2-mile walk from Thurso train station to the ferry port at Scrabster, or there are buses from Olrig St.

BUS From Inverness, Stagecoach/Citylink run to Thurso/Scrabster (£18.30, three hours, six daily). From Thurso, there are buses roughly hourly to Wick, as well as services every couple of hours to John O'Groats (one hour, Monday to Saturday). There's one bus on Tuesdays and Fridays westwards to Tongue via Bettyhill; it also runs some Saturdays.

TRAIN There are four daily train services from Inverness (£18, 3¾ hours), with connecting bus to Scrabster. Space for bicycles is limited, so book ahead.

NORTH & WEST COAST

Quintessential Highland country such as this, marked by single-track roads, breathtaking emptiness and a wild, fragile beauty, is a rarity on the modern, crowded, highly urbanised island of Britain. You could get lost up here for weeks – and that still wouldn't be enough time.

Thurso to Durness

It's 80 winding – and utterly spectacular – coastal miles from Thurso to Durness.

DOUNREAY & MELVICH
Ten miles west of Thurso is the **Dounreay nuclear power station**, which was the first in the world to supply mains electricity and is currently being decommissioned. The cleanup is planned to be finished by 2023; it's still a major employment source for the region.

WORTH A TRIP

DETOUR – FORSINARD & STRATHNAVER

Tough though it is to tear yourself away from the coast, we recommend plunging down the A897 just east of Melvich. After 14 miles you reach the railway at Forsinard. On the platform is the Forsinard Flows Visitor Centre (www.rspb.org.uk; admission free; ⊙9am-5.15pm Apr-Oct), a small free nature exhibition. There's a 1-mile trail here introducing you to the Flows peatland; 4 miles north of here is a 4-mile trail crossing golden plover and dunlin nesting grounds.

Once past the centre, you soon start to cross epic, lonely, peaty moorscapes that stir the heart with their desolate beauty. Take a right turn at the village of Kinbrace onto the B871, which covers more jaw-dropping scenery before bringing you to the village of Syre. Turn right up here to follow the Strathnaver valley back to the coast near Bettyhill. Strathnaver is famous for having been the site of some of the worst of the Clearances, and the Strathnaver Trail is a series of numbered points of interest along the valley relating to both this and several prehistoric sites.

Accommodation options on this lonely detour include Cornmill Bunkhouse (📞01641-571219; www.achumore.co.uk; dm £15; 🅿️), a comfortable modern hostel occupying a picturesque old mill on a working croft in the middle of nowhere; it's on the A897 4 miles south of the coast road. Turning left instead of right at Syre, you'll eventually reach the remote, upmarket Altnaharra Hotel (📞01549-411222; www.altnaharra.com; s/d/superior d £65/130/150; ⊙Mar-Dec; 🅿️🛜🐾).

Just beyond Dounreay, **Reay** has a shop and an interesting little harbour dating from 1830. **Melvich** overlooks a fine beach and there are great views from **Strathy Point** (a 2-mile drive from the coast road, then a 15-minute walk).

BETTYHILL
POP 500

The panorama of a sweeping, sandy beach backed by velvety green hills with bulbous, rocky outcrops makes a sharp contrast to the sad history of this area. Bettyhill is a crofting community of resettled tenant farmers kicked off their land during the Clearances. Just west of town, an enormous stretch of white sand flanks the River Naver as it meets the sea.

Strathnaver Museum (☏01641-521418; www.strathnavermuseum.org.uk; adult/child £2/50p; ☉10am-5pm Mon-Sat Apr-Oct), housed in an old church, tells the sad story of the Strathnaver Clearances through posters written by local kids. The museum contains memorabilia of Clan Mackay, croft-ing equipment and a 'St Kilda mailboat', a boat-shaped container that was used by St Kildans to send messages to the mainland. Outside the back door of the church is the **Farr Stone**, a fine carved Pictish cross-slab.

A good B&B option is friendly Farr Cottage (☏01641-521755; www.bettyhillbedand breakfast.co.uk; Farr; d £60; P🐾), a cute white house amid beautiful scenery a mile off the main road (follow signs to Farr). Dinner is offered here.

Bettyhill tourist office (☏01641-521244; www.visithighlands.com; ☉10.30am-4.30pm Mon-Thu, to 7.30pm Fri & Sat Apr-Oct) has information on the area and the cafe (☏01641-521244; mains £5-9; ☉10.30am-4.30pm Mon-Thu, to 7.30pm Fri & Sat Apr-Sep, 5-7.30pm Fri & Sat Oct-Mar) here serves home baking and light meals.

COLDBACKIE & TONGUE
POP 500

Coldbackie has outstanding views over sandy beaches, turquoise waters and off-shore islands. Only 2 miles further on is Tongue, with the evocative 14th-century

---

CROFTING & THE CLEARANCES

The wild and empty spaces up in these parts of the Highlands are among Europe's least populated zones, but this wasn't always so. Ruins of cottages in the most desolate areas are mute witnesses to one of the most heartless episodes of Scottish history: the High-land Clearances.

Up until the 19th century the most common form of farming settlement here was the *baile*, a group of a dozen or so families who farmed the land granted to them by the local chieftain in return for military service and a portion of the harvest. The arable land was divided into strips called *rigs*, which were allocated to different families by annual ballot so that each took turns at getting the poorer soils; this system was known as *runrig*. The families worked the land communally and their cattle shared the grazing land.

After Culloden, however, the king banned private armies and new laws made the clan chiefs actual owners of their traditional lands, often vast tracts of territory. With the prospect of unimagined riches allied to a depressing failure of imagination, the lairds decided that sheep were more profitable than agriculture and proceeded to evict tens of thousands of farmers from their lands. The Clearances forced these desperate folk to head for the cities in the hope of finding work or to emigrate to the Americas or southern hemisphere. Those who chose not to emigrate or move to the cities to find work were forced to eke a living from narrow plots of marginal agricultural land, often close to the coast. This was a form of smallholding that became known as crofting. The small patch of land barely provided a living and had to be supplemented by other work such as fish-ing and kelp-gathering. It was always precarious, as rights were granted on a year-by-year basis, so at any moment a crofter could lose not only the farm but also the house they'd built on it.

The economic depression of the late 19th century meant many couldn't pay their rent. This time, however, they resisted expulsion, instead forming the Highland Land Reform Association and their own political party. Their resistance led to several of their demands being acceded to by the government, including security of tenure, fair rents and eventu-ally the supply of land for new crofts. Crofters now have the right to purchase their farm-land and recent laws have abolished the feudal system, which created so much misery.

ruins of **Castle Varrich**, once a Mackay stronghold. To get to the castle, take the trail next to the Royal Bank of Scotland, near Ben Loyal Hotel – it's an easy stroll. Tongue has a shop, post office, bank and petrol station.

🛏 Sleeping & Eating

TOP CHOICE Tongue SYHA   HOSTEL **£**
(🖊01847-611789; www.syha.org.uk; Tongue; dm/tw £19/45; ☺Apr-Sep; **P**) In a wonderful spot right by the causeway across the Kyle of Tongue, a mile west of town, Tongue SYHA is the top budget option in the area, with clean, comfortably refitted dorms – some with views – a decent kitchen and cosy lounge. It's bright and helpful, and there's a lockable shed for bikes.

Cloisters   B&B **££**
(🖊01847-601286; www.cloistertal.demon.co.uk; Talmine; s/d £35/60; **P**🛜📶) Vying for the position of best-located B&B in Scotland, Cloisters has three en suite twin rooms and brilliant views over the Kyle of Tongue and offshore islands. Breakfast is in the artistically converted church alongside, and it can do evening meals at weekends. To get here from Tongue, cross the causeway and take the first turning on the right to Melness; Cloisters is a couple of miles down this road.

Tigh-nan-Ubhal   B&B **££**
(🖊01847-611281; www.tigh-nan-ubhal.com; Main St, Tongue; d £55-70; **P**🛜📶) At the junction of the A836 and A838, and within stumbling distance of two pubs, is this charming B&B. There are snug, loft-style rooms with plenty of natural light, but the basement double with spa is the pick of the bunch – it's the biggest en suite we've seen in northern Scotland. There's also accommodation in a caravan in the garden.

Tongue Hotel   HOTEL **££**
(🖊01847-611206; www.tonguehotel.co.uk; Tongue; s/d/superior d £75/110/120; **P**🛜) Tongue Hotel is a welcoming spot that offers attractive, roomy chambers in a former hunting lodge. It has a restaurant (temporarily closed at the time of research) and bar meals in the snug Brass Tap bar in the basement, a good spot to chat with locals or shelter from the weather.

Craggan Hotel   SCOTTISH **££**
(🖊01847-601278; www.thecraggan.co.uk; Melness; mains £11-20; ☺11am-9.15pm) On the side road to Melness, across the causeway from Tongue village, the Craggan Hotel doesn't look much from outside, but go in and you'll find smart, formal service and a menu ranging from exquisite burgers to classy game and seafood dishes, presented beautifully. It also does pizzas and curries to take away and the wine list's not bad for a pub either.

❶ Getting There & Away

One bus runs to Tongue Tuesday and Friday to/from Thurso. A postbus runs Monday to Saturday to Lairg. For Durness a bus runs schooldays from Talmine, stopping just west of the causeway across the kyle. It also goes on to Lairg.

TONGUE TO DURNESS
From Tongue it's 37 miles to Durness – the main road follows a causeway directly across the **Kyle of Tongue**, while the old road goes around the head of the kyle, with beautiful views of **Ben Loyal**. Continuing west, the road crosses a desolate moor to the northern end of freshwater **Loch Hope**. Beyond Loch Hope, as the main road descends towards the sea, there are stunning views over **Loch Eriboll**, Britain's deepest sea inlet and a shelter for ships during WWII.

Durness

POP 400

The scattered village of Durness (www.durness.org) is strung out along cliffs, which rise from a series of pristine beaches. It has one of the finest locations in Scotland. When the sun shines, the effects of blinding white sand, the cry of seabirds and the lime-coloured seas combine in a magical way.

There are shops, an ATM, petrol and plenty of accommodation options in Durness.

◉ Sights & Activities

Walking around the sensational sandy coastline is a highlight here, as is a visit to Cape Wrath. Durness' beautiful **beaches** include Rispond to the east, Sargo Sands below town and Balnakeil to the west; the sea offers scuba-diving sites complete with wrecks, caves, seals and whales. At **Balnakeil**, less than a mile beyond Durness, a craft village occupies what was once an early-warning radar station. A walk along the beach to the north leads to **Faraid Head**, where you can see puffin colonies in early summer. You can hire bikes from a shed on the square.

Smoo Cave   CAVE
A mile east of the village centre is a path, near the SYHA hostel, down to Smoo Cave.

The vast cave entrance stands at the end of an inlet, or geo, and a river cascades through its roof into a flooded cavern, then flows out to sea. From the vast main chamber, you can head through to a smaller flooded cavern where a waterfall sometimes cascades from the roof. There's evidence the cave was inhabited about 6000 years ago. You can also take a **boat trip** (adult/child £4/2.50; ⊘trips Apr-Sep) to explore a little further into the interior.

🛏 Sleeping & Eating

Mackays   HOTEL **££**
(☎01971-511202; www.visitdurness.com; d standard/deluxe £125/135; ⊘Easter-Oct; 🐾🏠) You really feel you're at the furthest corner of Scotland here, where the road turns through 90 degrees. But whether you're heading south or east, you'll go far before you find a better place to stay than this haven of Highland hospitality. With big beds and soft fabrics it's a romantic spot, and the restaurant presents local seafood and robust meat dishes. The same owners run **Croft 103** (☎01971-511202; www.croft103.com; Port na Con, Laid; per wk £1400; 🅿🏠), a stunning, modern self-catering option for couples 6 miles east, right on Loch Eriboll.

Lazy Crofter Bunkhouse   HOSTEL **£**
(☎01971-511202; www.durnesshostel.com; dm £16.50; 🏠) Lazy Crofter Bunkhouse is Durness' best budget accommodation. A bothy vibe gives it a Highland feel. The inviting dorms have plenty of room and lockers, and there's also a sociable shared table for meals and board games, and a great wooden deck with sea views, perfect for midge-free evenings.

Glengolly B&B   B&B **££**
(☎01971-511255; www.glengolly.com; d £64-70; ⊘Apr-Oct; 🅿🏠) This working croft provides comfortable rooms with good space in a traditional B&B atmosphere. Apart from the handy central location, there are other advantages: a superior breakfast menu, with smoked fish and fortified porridge options, and a chance to see a demonstration of the sheepdogs at work.

Sango Sands Oasis   CAMPSITE **£**
(☎01971-511222; www.sangosands.com; sites per adult/child £6.50/4; 🅿🏠) You couldn't imagine a better location for a campsite: great grassy areas on the edge of cliffs, descending to two lovely sandy beaches. Facilities are good and very clean and there's a pub next door. You can camp here free from November to March but don't complain about the cold.

Loch Croispol Bookshop   CAFE **£**
(www.scottish-books.net; light meals £5-9; ⊘10am-5pm Mon-Sat, to 4pm Sun) At this place you can feed your body and your mind. Set among books featuring all things Scottish are a few tables where you can enjoy an all-day breakfast, sandwiches and other scrumptious fare at lunch, such as fresh Achiltibuie salmon.

Smoo Cave Hotel   PUB **££**
(www.smoocavehotel.co.uk; mains £10-14; 🏠) Signposted off the main road at the eastern end of town, this no-frills local offers quality bar food in hefty portions. Haddock or daily seafood specials are an obvious and worthwhile choice; there's also a restaurant area with clifftop views.

Sango Sands Oasis   PUB **£**
(www.sangosands.com; mains £8-13) On the clifftops in the centre of town, this pub by the campsite offers some great views from its window tables. A cosy restaurant area does decent bar food in generous quantities.

🍫 **Cocoa Mountain**   CAFE **£**
(☎01971-511233; www.cocoamountain.co.uk; Balnakeil; hot chocolate £3.75, dozen truffles £9.50; ⊘9am-6pm high season, 10am-5pm low season) At the Balnakeil craft village, this upbeat cafe and chocolate maker offers handmade treats that include a chilli, lemongrass and coconut white-chocolate truffle, plus many more unique flavours. Tasty espresso and – of course – hot chocolate warm the cockles on those blowy horizontal-drizzle days.

❶ Information

Durness Community Building (1 Bard Tce; per 30min £1; 🏠) Coin-op internet access, opposite Mackays.
Durness Information Centre (☎01971-511368; www.visithighlands.com; ⊘daily Apr-Oct, 10am-12.30pm Tue & Thu Nov-Mar)

❶ Getting There & Away

From mid-May to September, one **bus** (☎01463-222444; www.decoaches.co.uk; ⊘May-Sep) runs Monday to Saturday from Durness to Inverness via Ullapool. You can take bikes on this service but they must be booked ahead. Another **bus** (www.thedurnessbus.com) heads daily Monday to Saturday to Lairg, which has a train station. On Saturday there's a service to either Inverness or Thurso.

Durness to Ullapool

Perhaps Scotland's most dramatic road trip, the 69 miles connecting Durness to Ullapool is a smorgasbord of dramatic scenery, almost too much to take in. From Durness to Rhiconich the road is almost all single track, passing through a broad heathered valley with the looming grey bulk of Foinaven and Arkle to the southeast. Heather gives way to a rockier landscape of Lewisian gneiss pockmarked with hundreds of small lochans, and gorse-covered hills prefacing the magnificent Torridonian sandstone mountains of Assynt and Coigach, including ziggurat-like Quinag, the distinctive sugarloaf of Suilven and pinnacled Stac Pollaidh. It's no wonder the area has been dubbed the Northwest Highlands Geopark (www.northwest-highlands-geopark.co.uk).

SCOURIE & HANDA ISLAND

Scourie (www.scourie.co.uk) is a pretty crofting community conveniently located halfway between Durness and Ullapool. A few miles north of Scourie Bay lies Handa Island (www.swt.org.uk), a nature reserve run by the Scottish Wildlife Trust. The island's western sea cliffs provide nesting sites for important breeding populations of seabirds. The boat (☑07775-625890; adult/child £12.50/5; ⊙outward sailings 9am-2pm Mon-Sat Apr-early Sep) to Handa leaves from Tarbet Pier, 5.5 miles north of Scourie.

If you're looking to spoil yourself, Scourie Lodge (☑01971-502248; www.scourielodge.co.uk; s/d £55/90; ⊙Apr-Oct; 🅿🐾), in a gorgeous building overlooking the bay, has old-style comfort and hospitality in a lovely setting. The welcoming owners have been doing this for two decades so they know a bit about guests' comfort. The rooms are traditionally styled and a good size. The separate 'coach house' twin is a lovely space. Best is the spectacular walled garden, a gloriously peaceful haven; the palm trees are proof of the Gulf Stream's good works. Cards aren't taken.

KYLESKU & LOCH GLENCOUL

Hidden from the main road on the shores of Loch Glencoul, the hamlet of Kylesku served as a ferry crossing on the route north from the beginning of the 19th century until it was made redundant by the beautiful **Kylesku Bridge** in 1984. There isn't much at Kylesku – just a few houses and a pub – but it's a good base for walks.

⊙ Sights & Activities

Eas a'Chuil Aluinn   WATERFALL
Five miles southeast of Kylesku, in wild and remote country beyond the head of Loch Glencoul, lies the 213m-high Eas a'Chuil Aluinn, Britain's highest waterfall. You can hike to the top of the falls from a parking area at a sharp bend in the main road 3

CAPE WRATH

Though its name actually comes from the Norse word for 'turning point', there is something daunting and primal about Cape Wrath, the remote northwestern point of the British mainland, crowned by a lighthouse (built by Robert Stevenson in 1828) and standing close to the seabird colonies of **Clo Mor**, Britain's highest coastal cliffs. Getting to Cape Wrath involves a boat ride (☑01971-511246; return adult/child £6/4, bicycle £2; ⊙Easter-Oct) – passengers and bikes only – across the Kyle of Durness (10 minutes), connecting with an optional minibus (☑07742-670196, 01971-511284; www.capewrath.org.uk; single/return £6/10; ⊙Easter-Oct) running 12 miles to the cape (40 minutes). This combination is a friendly but eccentric and sometimes shambolic service with limited capacity, so plan on waiting in high season, and ring before setting out to make sure the ferry is running. The ferry leaves from Keoldale pier, a couple of miles southwest of Durness, and runs two or more times daily from April to September. It's a spectacular ride or hike to Cape Wrath over bleak scenery occasionally used by the Ministry of Defence as a firing range. There's a cafe at the lighthouse serving soup and sandwiches.

An increasingly popular walking route is the Cape Wrath Trail (www.capewrathtrail.co.uk) which runs up here from Fort William (200 miles). It's unmarked, so you may want to do it guided – C-n-Do (www.cndoscotland.com) is one operator – or buy the *North to the Cape* guidebook (www.cicerone.co.uk).

miles south of Kylesku (6 miles round trip, allow five hours).

Kylesku Cruises BOAT TOUR
(☑07955 188352; www.kyleskucruises.co.uk; adult/child £20/10, or £10/5 for short cruise; ⊘May-Sep) From opposite the Kylesku Hotel, this little boat runs trips out to see the waterfall and local seal colonies.

🛏 Sleeping & Eating

TOP CHOICE Kylesku Hotel INN ££
(☑01971-502231; www.kyleskuhotel.co.uk; s £60-73, d £90-108, mains £10-19; ⊘Mar-Oct, food served noon-9pm; 🅿🖥) Run with pride and enthusiasm, this is a great place to stay, or to gorge yourself on delicious sustainable seafood in the convivial bar. Local langoustines and mussels are a speciality. There's a variety of rooms; the small extra charge for loch views is well worthwhile.

ACHMELVICH & AROUND

Not far south of Kylesku, a 30-mile detour on the narrow B869 rewards with spectacular views and fine beaches. From the lighthouse at Point of Stoer, a one-hour cliff walk leads to the **Old Man of Stoer**, a spectacular sea stack. On this stretch is the Clachtoll Beach Campsite (☑01571-855377; www.clachtollbeach campsite.co.uk; tent £8-10 plus per adult/child £3/1; ⊘Apr-Sep; 🅿🖥), a great coastal spot, and the Achmelvich Beach SYHA (☑01571-844480; www.syha.org.uk; dm/tw £18/44; ⊘Apr-mid-Sep), a whitewashed cottage set beside a great beach at the end of a side road. Dorms are simple, and there's a sociable common kitchen/eating area. There's a basic shop at the adjacent campsite or it's a 4-mile walk from Lochinver.

LOCHINVER & ASSYNT

With its otherworldly scenery of isolated peaks rising above a sea of crumpled, lochan-spattered gneiss, Assynt epitomises the wild magnificence of the northwest Highlands. The glaciers of the last ice age have sculpted the hills of Suilven (731m), Canisp (846m), Quinag (808m) and Ben More Assynt (998m) into strange and wonderful silhouettes.

Lochinver is the main settlement in the Assynt region. It's a busy little fishing port that's a popular port of call for tourists, with its laid-back atmosphere, good facilities, striking scenery and range of accommodation.

There's a supermarket in town, as well as a post office, bank (with an ATM) and petrol station.

🏄 Activities

NorWest Sea Kayaking KAYAKING
(☑01571-844281; www.norwestseakayaking.com) This outfit offers three-day introductory sea-kayaking courses and guided kayaking tours around the Summer Isles and in the Lochinver and Ullapool area. It also hires kayaks in Lochinver.

🛏 Sleeping & Eating

TOP CHOICE The Albannach HOTEL £££
(☑01571-844407; www.thealbannach.co.uk; Baddidarroch; s/d/ste with dinner £220/290/370; ⊘Tue-Sun Mar-Dec; 🅿🖥) One of the Highlands' top places to stay and eat, this hotel combines old-fashioned country-house elements – steep creaky stairs, stuffed animals, fireplaces and noble antique furniture – with strikingly handsome rooms that range from a sumptuous four-poster to more modern spaces with things like underfloor heating and, in one case, a private deck with outdoor spa. The restaurant serves a *table d'hôte* (they'll tailor it to your needs) that's famed throughout Scotland (£61 for non-residents); the welcoming owners grow lots of their own produce and focus on organic and local ingredients. Glorious views, spacious grounds and great walks in easy striking distance make this a perfect base.

Veyatie B&B ££
(☑01571-844424; www.veyatie-scotland.co.uk; Baddidarroch; s/d £45/78; ⊘Jan-Nov; 🅿🖥) This choice, at the end of the road across the bay, has perhaps the finest views of all, best enjoyed from the grassy garden or conservatory lounge on a sunny day. Readers rave about the breakfasts.

TOP CHOICE Lochinver Larder & Riverside Bistro CAFE, BISTRO ££
(☑01571-844356; www.lochinverlarder.co.uk; 3 Main St, Lochinver; pies £5, mains £10-16; ⊘10am-8.30pm) Serving as coffee shop, bistro and takeaway, the Larder offers an outstanding menu of inventive food made with local produce. The bistro turns out delicious seafood dishes in the evening, while the takeaway counter (open till 7pm) sells delicious Lochinver pies with a wide range of gourmet fillings: try the smoked haddock, or wild boar and apricot – very tasty indeed.

🛍 Shopping

Highland Stoneware CERAMICS
(www.highlandstoneware.com; Lochinver; ⊘Mon-Fri, plus Sat Easter-Oct) Using local landscapes

as inspiration, Highland Stoneware ensures you can relive the majesty of the northwest every time you look into the bottom of your teacup. Even better are the mosaics outside, especially the car. You can watch the potters at work here on weekdays.

❶ Information

Assynt Visitor Centre (☑01571-844654; www.assynt.info; Main St; ☺10am-5pm Mon-Sat Easter-Oct, also to 3pm Sun Jun-Aug) Has leaflets on hill walks in the area and a display on the story of Assynt, from wildlife and geology to clans, conflict and controversy.

COIGACH

The region to the south of Assynt, bounded on the east by the main A835 road from Ullapool to Ledmore Junction, is known as Coigach (www.coigach.com). A lone, single-track road penetrates this wilderness, leading through gloriously wild scenery to the remote settlements of Altandhu, Achiltibuie and Achininver. At the western end of Loch Lurgainn, a branch leads north to Lochinver, a scenic backroad so narrow and twisting that locals refer to it as the **Wee Mad Road**.

Coigach is a wonderland for walkers and wildlife enthusiasts, with a patchwork of sinuous silver lochs dominated by the isolated peaks of Cul Mor (849m), Cul Beag (769m), Ben More Coigach (743m) and Stac Pollaidh (613m). Ordnance Survey map sheet 15, *Loch Assynt*, charts this magical landscape in all its glory.

The main settlement in Coigach is the straggling township of **Achiltibuie**, 15 miles from the main road. With the gorgeous Summer Isles moored just off the coast, and the silhouettes of mountains skirting the bay, this village epitomises idyllic Scottish beauty.

◉ Sights & Activities

Stac Pollaidh   WALKING
Despite its diminutive size, Stac Pollaidh provides one of the most exciting hill walks in the Highlands, with some good scrambling on its narrow sandstone crest. Begin at the car park overlooking Loch Lurgainn, 5 miles west of the A835, and follow a clearly marked and well-made footpath around the eastern end of the hill to ascend from the far side; return by the same route (3 miles round trip, allow two to four hours).

Summer Isles Seatours   BOAT TOUR
(☑07927-920592; www.summerisles-seatours .co.uk; adult/child £25/15; ☺Mon-Sat May-Sep)

Three cruises daily to the Summer Isles from Achiltibuie, with time ashore on Tanera Mor, where the post office issues its own Summer Isles stamps.

🍽 Sleeping & Eating

TOP CHOICE ⟩ Summer Isles Hotel   HOTEL **£££**
(☑01854-622282; www.summerisleshotel.co.uk; Achiltibuie; s £115-175, d £155-220; ☺Easter-Oct; 🅿🛇🐾) The Summer Isles Hotel is a special place, with wonderfully romantic, commodious rooms – one is themed on Charlie Chaplin, who stayed here, others are suites in separate cottages – plus cracking views and a snug bar with convivial outdoor seating. The restaurant (dinner £58) is of high quality, with local lobster usually featuring, as well as the renowned cheese and dessert trolleys – and there's a great wine list considering you're in the middle of nowhere. It's the perfect spot for a romantic getaway or some quality time off life's treadmill.

Achininver SYHA   HOSTEL **£**
(☑01854-622482; www.syha.org.uk; Achininver; dm £18; ☺May-Aug) The rudimentary 20-bed Achininver hostel is designed for walkers and outdoor enthusiasts – you have to walk half a mile off the main road to reach it. Its remote, serene location has to be one of the best in the country.

❶ Getting There & Around

There are one to two daily buses Monday to Saturday from Ullapool to Badenscallie (half a mile from Achininver SYHA) and Achiltibuie (1½ hours).

Ullapool

POP 1300

The pretty port of Ullapool, on the shores of Loch Broom, is the largest settlement in Wester Ross and one of the most alluring spots in the Highlands, a wonderful destination in itself as well as a gateway to the Western Isles. Offering a row of whitewashed cottages arrayed along the harbour and special views of the loch and its flanking hills, the town has a very distinctive appeal. The harbour served as an emigration point during the Clearances, with thousands of Scots watching the loch recede behind them as the diaspora cast them across the world.

◉ Sights & Activities

Ullapool is a great centre for **walking**. Good walking books sold at the tourist office include *Walks in Wester Ross* (£2.95), or you can pick up a copy of the freebie guide to local woodland walks.

Ullapool Museum MUSEUM
(www.ullapoolmuseum.co.uk; 7 West Argyle St; adult/child £3.50/free; ☺10am-5pm Mon-Sat Apr-Oct) Housed in a converted Telford Parliamentary church, this museum relates the prehistoric, natural and social history of the town and Lochbroom area, with a particular focus on the emigration to Nova Scotia and other places. There's also a genealogy section if you want to trace your Scottish roots.

Seascape ISLANDS TOUR
(☎01854-633708; www.sea-scape.co.uk; adult/child £32/22) Runs two-hour tours out to the Summer Isles in an orange rigid inflatable boat (RIB).

Summer Queen BOAT TOUR
(☎07713-257219; www.summerqueen.co.uk; ☺Mon-Sat May-Sep) The stately *Summer Queen* takes you out (weather permitting) around **Isle Martin** (£20/10 per adult/child, two hours) or to the **Summer Isles** (£30/15, four hours), with a stop on Tanera Mor.

✦✦ Festivals

Ullapool Guitar Festival MUSIC
(www.ullapoolguitarfestival.com) Held in early October, this features a series of concerts and workshops over a weekend, with late-night club sessions and some high-quality musicians on show.

☷ Sleeping

Note that during summer Ullapool is very busy and finding accommodation can be tricky – book ahead.

TOP CHOICE West House B&B ££
(☎01854-613126; www.ullapoolaccommodation.net; West Argyle St; d £60-80; P🖤) Slap bang in the centre of Ullapool, this solid white house, which was once a manse, offers excellent rooms with contemporary style and great bathrooms. Breakfast is continental style: rooms come with a fridge stocked with fresh fruit salad, and quality cheeses, yoghurts, bread and juice so you can eat at your leisure in your own chamber. Most rooms have great views, as well as iPod docks and other conveniences. The owners also have tempting self-catering options in the Ullapool area.

TOP CHOICE The Ceilidh Place HOTEL ££
(☎01854-612103; www.theceilidhplace.com; 14 West Argyle St; s £55-68, d £136-158; P🖤😊) The Ceilidh Place is one of the more unusual and delightful places to stay in the Highlands. Rooms pleasingly go for character over modern conveniences and, rather than television, come with a selection of books chosen by Scottish literati, eclectic artwork and nice little touches like hot-water bottles. Best of all is the sumptuous lounge, with sofas, chaises longues and an honesty bar. The hotel, which includes a bookshop, is also a celebration of Scottish culture, with a capital C – we're talking literature and traditional music, not tartan and Nessie dolls. A great place.

TOP CHOICE Tamarin Lodge B&B ££
(☎01854-612667; www.tamarinullapool.com; The Braes; s/d £40/80; P🖤😊) The effortlessly elegant modern architecture in this hilltop house is noteworthy in its own right, but the glorious vistas over the hills opposite and water far below are unforgettable. All the rooms face the view – some have a balcony from which to admire it – and are very spacious, quiet and utterly relaxing, with unexpected features and gadgets. A great lounge with telescope and terrace provides another inviting space, while the benevolent hosts are a delight. Follow the sign for Braes a mile outside of town on the Inverness road.

Ullapool SYHA HOSTEL £
(☎01854-612254; www.syha.org.uk; Shore St; dm £19; ☺Apr-Oct; 🖤) You've got to hand it to the SYHA; it's chosen some very sweet locations for its hostels. This is as close to the water as it is to the town's best pub: about four seconds' walk. The front rooms have harbour views but the busy dining area and little lounge are also good spots for contemplating the water.

Point Cottage B&B ££
(☎01854-613702; www.ullapoolbedandbreakfast.co.uk; 22 West Shore St; d £70; P🖤) If you've just arrived by ferry, you've probably already admired Ullapool's line of shorefront cottages; this is one of them. Under keen new owners, this sports appealing renovated rooms with modern bathrooms and a very kindly welcome. It's got an optimistic, upbeat feel that chimes with the super views from all the chambers. Breakfast features blueberry pancakes, vegetarian sausages or smoked haddock, among other choices.

Woodlands   B&B **£**
(☑01854-612701; www.ullapoolbandb.com; 1a Pulteney St; d £55; ☺May-Sep; ℗🔊🛜) Excellent hospitality from the veteran but livewire owners makes this a top Ullapool option. There are just two comfortable rooms sharing a bathroom, and they don't take bookings much in advance. The breakfast is memorable, with your hosts making delicious bread, marmalade and jams from their own berries, plus they smoke their own fish out the back. A real treat.

Ceilidh Clubhouse   HOSTEL **£**
(☑01854-612103; West Lane; s/tw/f £22/38/66; ℗🛜) Opposite the Ceilidh Place, and under the same management, this annexe offers no-frills accommodation for walkers, journey people and staff. A big building, it has hostel-style rooms with sturdy bunks and basins. Though showers and toilets are a little institutional, the big bonus is that rooms are private: if you're woken by snores, at least they'll be familiar ones.

Broomfield Holiday Park   CAMPSITE **£**
(☑01854-612664; www.broomfieldhp.com; West Lane; tent sites £13-17; ☺Apr-Sep; ℗🔊🛜) Great grassy headland location, very close to centre. Midge-busting machines in action.

🍴 Eating & Drinking

Ceilidh Place   SCOTTISH **££**
(☑01854-612103; 14 West Argyle St; mains £10-16; ☺8am-9pm) The restaurant at the Ceilidh Place serves up inventive dishes that focus on fresh local seafood backed up by stews, pies and burgers. Presentation and quality are high, and it's an atmospheric place, cosy with outdoor seating, good wines by the glass and regular live music and events.

Ferry Boat Inn   PUB **££**
(☑01854-612366; www.ferryboat-inn.com; Shore St; mains £11-14) Known as the FBI, this character-laden waterfront inn is a little less traditional looking these days with its bleached wood and nonstained carpet, but it's still the place where locals and visitors mingle. Some dishes on the menu are a little bland, but a well-run dining room, quality ingredients and great presentation compensate.

Arch Inn   PUB **££**
(☑01854-612454; www.thearchinn.co.uk; West Shore St; mains £8-13; 🛜) There's pleasing pub food to be had at this shorefront establishment, where the cosy bar and restaurant area dishes up generously proportioned stews, steaks and fish and chips, as well as a couple of more advanced seafood plates. The outdoor tables right beside the lapping water are a top spot for a pint.

ℹ️ Information

Ullapool Bookshop (☑01854-612918; Quay St; ☺daily) Lots of books on Scottish topics and maps of the area. Internet access available at £1 per 15 minutes.

Ullapool Library (☑01854-612543; Mill St; ☺9am-5pm Mon-Fri plus 6-8pm Tue & Thu, closed Mon & Wed during holidays) Free internet access.

Ullapool Information Centre (☑01854-612486; ullapool@visitscotland.com; Argyle St; ☺daily Apr-Sep, Mon-Sat Oct)

ℹ️ Getting There & Around

Citylink (www.citylink.co.uk) has one to three daily buses from Inverness to Ullapool (£11.90, 1½ hours), connecting with the Lewis ferry.

Ullapool to Kyle of Lochalsh

Although it's less than 50 miles as the crow flies from Ullapool to Kyle of Lochalsh, it's more like 150 miles along the circuitous coastal road – but don't let that put you off. It's a deliciously remote region and there are fine views of beaches and bays backed by mountains all the way along.

If you're in a hurry to get to Skye, head inland on the A835 (towards Inverness) and catch up with the A832 further south, near Garve.

BRAEMORE & AROUND

Twelve miles southeast of Ullapool at Braemore, near the head of Loch Broom, the A832 doubles back towards the coast as it heads for Gairloch (the A835 continues southeast across the wild **Dirrie More** pass to Garve and Inverness, sometimes closed by snow in winter).

Just west of the junction, a car park gives access to the **Falls of Measach** ('ugly' in Gaelic), which spill 45m into the spectacularly deep and narrow **Corrieshalloch Gorge**. You can cross to the far side of the gorge on a swaying suspension bridge, and walk west for 250m to a viewing platform that juts out dizzyingly above a sheer drop. The thundering falls and misty vapours rising from the gorge are very impressive.

Sleeping & Eating

Badrallach CAMPSITE £

(☎01854-633281; www.badrallach.com; Badrallach; bothy per person/car £6/2.50, campsites per person/tent/car £4/2.50/2.50, r per person £40; P) Badrallach, 7 miles from the A832, is a friendly, sustainable croft that has a range of accommodation, including camping, a bothy, a self-catering cottage and B&B in a classic Airstream caravan, as well as boats and bikes for hire. It's the perfect place to get away from it all and enjoy the rural beauty of this region.

GAIRLOCH & AROUND

POP 1100

Gairloch is a group of villages (comprising Achtercairn, Strath and Charlestown) around the inner end of a loch of the same name. The surrounding area has beautiful sandy beaches, good trout fishing and bird-watching. Hill walkers also use Gairloch as a base for the Torridon hills and An Teallach.

⊙ Sights & Activities

The B8056 road runs along the southern shore of Loch Gairloch, past the cute little harbour of **Badachro**, to end at the gorgeous pink-sand beach of **Red Point** – a perfect picnic spot. Another coastal road leads north from Gairloch for 10 miles to the settlement of **Melvaig**. From here a private road (open to walkers and cyclists) continues for 3 miles to **Rua Reidh Lighthouse**.

Gairloch Heritage Museum MUSEUM

(www.gairlochheritagemuseum.org; Achtercairn; adult/child £4/1; ⊙10am-5pm Mon-Sat Apr-Oct) This museum has all sorts of interesting displays on life in the West Highlands from Pictish times to the present, including locally built fishing boats and a faithful recreation of a crofter's cottage.

Inverewe Garden GARDEN

(NTS; www.nts.org.uk; Poolewe; adult/concession £9.50/7; ⊙10am-3pm Nov-Mar, to 6pm Apr-Aug, to 4pm Sep & Oct) Six miles north of Gairloch, this splendid garden is a welcome splash of colour on an otherwise bleak stretch of coast. The climate here is warmed by the waters of the Gulf Stream, which allowed Osgood MacKenzie, a son of the laird of Gairloch, to create this exotic woodland garden in 1862. There are free guided tours on weekdays at 1.30pm (March to October). The cafe has great cakes.

FREE Gairloch Marine Wildlife Centre NATURE DISPLAY

(☎01445-712636; www.porpoise-gairloch.co.uk; Pier Rd, Charlestown; ⊙10am-4pm Easter-Oct) The Gairloch Marine Wildlife Centre has audiovisual and interactive displays, lots of charts and photos and knowledgeable staff. Cruises (☎01445-712636; www.porpoise gairloch.co.uk; adult/child £20/15) run from the centre and sail up to three times daily (weather permitting); during the two-hour trips you may see basking sharks, porpoises and minke whales. The crew collects data on water temperature and conditions, and monitors cetacean populations, so your fare is subsidising an important research project.

Hebridean Whale Cruises BOAT TOUR

(☎01445-712458; www.hebridean-whale-cruises.com; Pier Rd; cruises per hr £10-20) Based at the harbour, this set-up runs close-in trips to see seals, otters and seabirds, or trips further out to feeding grounds where you might see dolphins, minke whales or orca. It operates two boats, one a cabin cruiser, the other a zippy rigid inflatable.

Gairloch Trekking Centre HORSE RIDING

(☎01445-712652; www.gairlochtrekkingcentre.co.uk; Flowerdale Mains, Gairloch; ⊙Fri-Wed Mar-Oct) Offers riding lessons, pony trekking and guided treks in the ample grounds of Gailoch Estate.

Sleeping & Eating

Rua Reidh Lighthouse Hostel HOSTEL £

(☎01445-771263; www.ruareidh.co.uk; Melvaig; dm/d £13.50/38; P) Beyond Melvaig, 13 miles north of Gairloch (at the end of the road), this is an excellent hostel that will give you a taste of a lighthouse keeper's life. Buses from Gairloch run as far as Melvaig, then it's a 3-mile walk along the road to the lighthouse. En suite twins and doubles (£42 to £48) and family rooms are also available, as are breakfasts and dinners.

Gairloch View Guest House B&B ££

(☎01445-712666; www.gairlochview.com; Achtercairn; s/d £50/75; P🖤) The unique selling point of this unassuming modern house is a patio with a stunning view over the sea to Skye – a view you can enjoy from your breakfast table. The three bedrooms are comfortably furnished in classic country style, and the residents' lounge has satellite TV and a small library of books and games.

Wayside Guest House B&B ££
(📞01445-712008; issmith@msn.com; Strath; s/d £40/60; 🛜) Cosy and compact, this offers comfortable and welcoming accommodation in Strath, the spiritual heart of Gairloch. The spotless rooms come with either en suite bathroom or fabulous view; you decide what's more important.

Badachro Inn PUB ££
CHOICE
(📞01445-741255; www.badachroinn.com; Badachro; light meals £5-8, mains £11-16; 🅿) Set in an enchanting location, overlooking a sheltered yacht harbour at Badachro, 5 miles southwest of Gairloch, this old Highland inn serves real ales from the An Teallach brewery on Loch Broom, and platters of fresh local seafood: crab, scallops and langoustines, some landed at the pier right beside the inn. There are also tasty panini and sandwiches; eating out on the deck on a sunny day here is a real treat. The bar staff will recommend the potato wedges as a side dish – say yes!

Na Mara BISTRO ££
(www.namararestaurant.co.uk; Strath Sq; mains £7-14; ⊙3-8.30pm Thu-Tue) On the square in Strath, this brings a light, cheery smile to west-coast eating with its inclusive menu that starts at burgers, pastas and curries and includes steaks and seafood dishes in classic bistro style with a range of influences. Good value, but check opening times ahead.

Mountain Coffee Company CAFE £
(Strath Sq, Strath; light meals £3-6; ⊙9am-5pm, shorter hours in low season) More the sort of place you'd expect to find on the gringo trail in the Andes or a backpacker town in Southeast Asia, this offbeat and cosy spot is a shrine to all things mountaineering and travelling. It sells light meals, home baking and a range of decadent coffees and hot chocolates stuffed with sugary things. The conservatory is the place to lap up the sun, while the attached **Hillbillies Bookshop** is worth a browse.

❶ Information

Gairloch Information Centre (📞01445-712071; ⊙10am-4pm Mon-Sat, to 5pm plus 11am-4pm Sun Jun–mid-Sep) Set in the smart new wooden Gale Centre, on the main road through town, this has good walking pamphlets.

❶ Getting There & Away

Public transport to Gairloch is very limited. **Westerbus** (📞01445-712255) runs Monday to Saturday to/from Inverness, and Thursday to/from Ullapool.

LOCH MAREE & AROUND

Stretching for 12 miles between Poolewe and Kinlochewe, **Loch Maree** is often regarded as one of the most beautiful lochs in Scotland. At the southern end of the loch, tiny **Kinlochewe** makes a good base for outdoor activities. The **Beinn Eighe Visitor Centre** (📞01445-760254; www.nnr-scotland.org.uk/beinn eighe; admission free; ⊙10am-5pm Easter-Oct; ♿), a mile north of Kinlochewe, has interactive displays (good for kids, too) on local geography, ecology, flora and fauna, and provides information on local walking routes, including the **Beinn Eighe Mountain Trail**.

Kinlochewe Hotel (📞01445-760253; www. kinlochewehotel.co.uk; dm £14.50, s £50, d £90-98; 🅿🛜🐾) is a well-run, welcoming place that's very walker-friendly. As well as comfortable, spotless, new-looking rooms, there are nice features like a handsome lounge well stocked with books, a great bar with several real ales on tap and a thoughtful menu of locally sourced food. There's also a bunkhouse with one no-frills 12-bed dorm (BYO sleeping bag and towels), a decent kitchen and clean bathrooms.

TORRIDON & AROUND

The road southwest from Kinlochewe passes through **Glen Torridon**, amid some of the most beautiful scenery in Britain. Carved by ice from massive layers of the ancient sandstone that takes its name from the region, the mountains here are steep, shapely and imposing, whether flirting with autumn mists, draped in dazzling winter snows, or reflected in the calm blue waters of Loch Torridon on a summer day.

The road through the glen reaches the sea at spectacularly sited **Torridon** village, then continues westwards to lovely **Shieldaig**, which boasts an attractive main street of whitewashed houses right on the water, before turning south to Applecross, Lochcarron and Kyle of Lochalsh.

◉ Sights & Activities

The Torridon Munros – **Liathach** (1054m; pronounced 'lee-agakh', Gaelic for 'the Grey One'), **Beinn Eighe** (1010m; 'ben ay', 'the File') and **Beinn Alligin** (986m; 'the Jewelled Mountain') – are big, serious mountains for experienced hill walkers only. Though not technically difficult, their ascents are long and committing, often over rough and rocky terrain. Information is available at the NTS Countryside Centre (NTS; ☑01445-791221; www.nts.org.uk; Torridon Village; adult/child £3.50/2.50; ⊙10am-5pm Sun-Fri Easter-Sep) in Torridon; the NTS rangers also offer **guided mountain walks** (£25 per person, weekdays only, advance booking necessary) in July and August.

🛏 Sleeping & Eating

TOP CHOICE The Torridon HOTEL £££

(☑01445-791242; www.thetorridon.com; r standard/superior/master £220/275/425; ⊙closed Jan, closed Mon & Tue Nov, Dec, Feb & Mar; P@🀫🐾) If you prefer the lap of luxury to the sound of rain beating on your tent, head for the Torridon, a lavish Victorian shooting lodge with a romantic lochside location. Sumptuous contemporary rooms with awe-inspiring views, top bathrooms and a cheery stuffed Highland coo (cow) atop the counterpane couldn't be more inviting. Master suites are lavish in size and comfort, with a more classic decor and bay windows making the most of the panoramas. Service is excellent, with muddy boots positively welcomed, and dinners are sumptuous affairs, also open to nonresidents (£55). Friendly staff can organise any number of activities on land or water. This is one of Scotland's top country hotels, always luxurious but never pretentious.

Torridon Inn INN ££

(☑01445-791242; www.thetorridon.com; Annat; s/d/q £89/99/165; ⊙daily May-Oct, Thu-Sun Nov, Dec, Mar & Apr, closed Jan & Feb; P🀫🐾) Adjacent to the Torridon, this convivial but upmarket walkers' hang-out offers excellent modern rooms that vary substantially in size and layout, and a sociable bar offering all-day food. Rooms for groups up to six offer plenty of value.

Ferroch B&B ££

(☑01445-791451; www.ferroch.co.uk; Annat; s/d £70/92; P🀫) Just outside town, on the road to Shieldaig, this offers some of the most memorable vistas around from its pleasant garden and top-floor double. All the rooms are very spacious and comfortable, and it's a welcoming place, with a guest lounge with fire and music, afternoon tea served on the grass on a fine day and excellent breakfasts and dinners featuring homemade yoghurt, cheese and bread, among other goodies.

Torridon SYHA HOSTEL £

(☑01445-791284; www.syha.org.uk; Torridon Village; dm £18; ⊙Mar-Oct, plus weekends Nov-Feb;

P@🀫) The modern, boxy-looking Torridon hostel is in a magnificent location, surrounded by spectacular mountains. It's a very popular walking base, so book ahead in summer.

Tigh an Eilean Hotel HOTEL ££

(☑01520-755251; www.tighaneilean.co.uk; Shieldaig, Shieldaig; s/d £75/150; 🀫) With a lovely waterfront position, this offers old-style rooms that are comfortable but feel more than a little overpriced. The £45 dinner menu features competently presented local produce and shines on the seafood front and in its Scottish cheeses. There's also cheaper bar food in the sociable pub, which has waterside tables.

APPLECROSS
POP 200

The delightfully remote seaside village of Applecross feels more like an island retreat due to its isolation and the magnificent views of Raasay and the hills of Skye that set the pulse racing, particularly at sunset. On a clear day it's an unforgettable place, though the tranquil atmosphere isn't quite the same when the campsite and pub fill to the brim in school holidays.

The A896 heads here in 25 winding miles from Shieldaig, but more spectacular (accessed from further south on the A896) is the magnificent **Bealach na Ba** (626m; Pass of the Cattle), the third-highest motor road in the UK, and the longest continuous climb. Originally built in 1822, it climbs steeply and hair-raisingly via a couple of hairpin bends perched over sheer drops, with gradients up to 25%, then drops dramatically to the village with views ahead to Skye.

Mountain & Sea Guides (☑01250-744394; www.applecross.uk.com) runs short sea-kayaking, hill-walking and mountaineering excursions, as well as more serious expeditions.

🛏 Sleeping & Eating

TOP CHOICE Applecross Inn INN ££

(☑01520-744262; www.applecross.uk.com; Shore St; s/d £80/120; mains £9-17; ⊙food noon-9pm; P🀫🐾) The hub of the spread-out community is the Applecross Inn, the perfect shoreside location for a sunset pint. The inn is famous for its food – mostly daily blackboard specials that concentrate on local seafood and venison – and sports seven snug bedrooms, all with a view of the Skye hills and the sea.

Applecross Campsite
CAMPSITE **£**

(☑01520-744268; www.applecross.uk.com; campsites per adult/child £8/4, 2-person hut £38; ⊙Mar-Oct; ℗) You can pitch your tent at the Applecross Campsite, which offers green grassy plots, cute little wooden cabins and a good greenhouselike cafe.

LOCHCARRON
POP 1000

The appealing, whitewashed village of Lochcarron is a veritable metropolis in these parts, with good services and a long shoreline footpath at the loch's edge to walk off breakfast.

Old Manse (☑01520-722208; www.theoldmanselochcarron.com; Church St; s/d £40/65, tw with loch view £70; ℗ 🛜 🐾) is a top-notch Scottish guest house, beautifully appointed and in a prime lochside position. Rooms are simply gorgeous and the twin overlooking the water is larger and well worth the extra fiver. Take the road towards Strome.

On the main waterfront road through town, the excellent Rockvilla (☑01520-722379; www.therockvilla.com; Main St; r £70-79; ⊙Easter-Sep; 🛜) has very welcoming hosts and lovely modernised rooms with heaps of space and dreamy views over the water. The restaurant here is open to the public and serves good inventive bistro fare at fair prices.

PLOCKTON
POP 500

Idyllic little Plockton (www.plockton.com), with its perfect cottages lining a perfect bay, looks like it was designed as a film set. And it has indeed served as just that – scenes from *The Wicker Man* (1973) were filmed here, and the village became famous as the location for the 1990s TV series *Hamish Macbeth*.

With all this picture-postcard perfection, it's hardly surprising that Plockton is a tourist hot spot, crammed with day trippers and holidaymakers in summer. But there's no denying its appeal, with 'palm trees' (actually hardy New Zealand cabbage palms) lining the waterfront, a thriving small-boat sailing scene and several good places to stay, eat and drink. The big event of the year is the Plockton Regatta (www.plockton-sailing.com), a fortnight of boat races that culminates in a concert and ceilidh.

🏌 Activities

You can hire canoes and rowboats on the waterfront to explore the bay.

Calum's Seal Trips
WILDLIFE CRUISE

(☑01599-544306; www.calums-sealtrips.com; adult/child £9/5; ⊙Apr-Oct) Calum's Seal Trips runs seal-watching cruises – there are swarms of the slippery fellas just outside the harbour, and the trip comes with an excellent commentary. Trips leave daily at 10am, noon, 2pm and 4pm. You may even spot otters, and there's a longer dolphin-watching trip available.

🛏 Sleeping & Eating

The village has some excellent places to stay, but it's popular. Best to book ahead, especially if you plan to be here during regatta fortnight.

TOP CHOICE Plockton Hotel
HOTEL **££**

(☑01599-544274; www.plocktonhotel.co.uk; 41 Harbour St; s/d £90/130, cottage s/d £55/80, mains £8-16; 🛜) The black-painted Plockton Hotel is one of those classic Highland spots that manages to make everyone happy, whether it's thirst, hunger or fatigue that brings you knocking. The assiduously tended rooms are a delight, with excellent facilities and thoughtful touches like bathrobes. Those without a water view are consoled with more space and a balcony with rock-garden perspectives. Just down the way, the cottage offers simpler comfort. The cosy bar, or wonderful beer garden on a sunny day, are memorable places for a pint, and food ranges from sound-value bar meals to seafood platters and local langoustines brought in on the afternoon boat.

Plockton Station Bunkhouse
HOSTEL **£**

(☑01599-544235; mickcoe@btlnternet.com; dm £14; ℗🛜) Airily set in the former train station (the new one is opposite), Plockton Station Bunkhouse has cosy four-bed dorms, a garden and kitchen-lounge with plenty of light and good perspectives over the frenetic comings and goings (OK, that last bit's a lie) of the platforms below. It can get a bit cramped when there are lots of folk in. The owners also do good-value B&B (single/double £30/48) next door in the inaccurately named 'Nessun Dorma'.

Shieling
B&B **££**

(☑01599-544282; www.lochalsh.net/shieling; d £70; ⊙Easter-Oct) Slap bang by the sea, characterful Shieling is surrounded by an expertly trimmed garden and has two carpeted rooms with views and big beds. Next door is a historic thatched blackhouse (a low-walled stone cottage with a turf roof and earthen floor).

Duncraig Castle
B&B ££

(☎01599-544295; www.duncraigcastle.co.uk; d standard/superior £109/119; ℗) Duncraig Castle offers luxurious, offbeat hospitality, as long as stuffed animals don't offend you. It needs a bit of work still – the curiously ugly school building alongside is thankfully destined for removal – but ongoing improvements are in progress; at time of research it was closed for substantial renovation, but will be open by the time you read this. It's very close to Plockton but has its own train station.

TOP CHOICE Plockton Shores
SEAFOOD ££

(☎01599-544263; 30 Harbour St; mains lunch £9-18, dinner £11-22; ⊗cafe 9.30-5pm Mon-Sat & noon-5pm Sun, restaurant lunch daily & dinner Tue-Sun; ☑) This cafe-cum-restaurant sports a tempting menu of local seafood, including hand-dived scallops with lemon-and-basil dressing, squat lobster tails cooked in white wine and garlic, and a splendid platter of langoustines with paprika and garlic butter. There are also steaks, haggis and saddle of venison, and a small selection of tasty vegetarian dishes that are more than an afterthought.

Kyle of Lochalsh
POP 800

Before the controversial bridge, Kyle of Lochalsh was Skye's main ferry port. Visitors now tend to buzz through town, but Kyle has an intriguing attraction if you're interested in marine life.

⊙ Sights & Activities

Seaprobe Atlantis
BOAT TOUR

(☎0800 980 4846; www.seaprobeatlantis.com; adult/child from £13/7; ⊗Easter-Oct) A glass-hulled boat takes you on a spin around the kyle to spot seabirds, seals and maybe an otter or two. The basic trip includes entertaining commentary and plenty of beautiful jellyfish; longer trips also take in a WWII shipwreck. Book at the tourist office.

⊨ Sleeping & Eating

There's a string of B&Bs just outside of town on the road to Plockton.

Waverley
SCOTTISH ££

(☎01599-534337; www.waverleykyle.co.uk; Main St; mains £12-20; ⊗dinner Fri-Wed) This superb restaurant is an intimate place with excellent service; try the Taste of Land and Sea, combining Aberdeen Angus fillet steak with fresh local prawns, or one of several other reliably good fish options. Black-board specials offer a dinner deal if you eat before 7pm.

Buth Bheag
SEAFOOD £

(salads £3-5; ⊗10am-5pm Tue-Fri, to 2pm Sat) This tiny place by the water, near the tourist office, has great takeaway fresh seafood salads and rolls for a pittance. Munch them sitting by the harbour.

ℹ Information

Kyle of Lochalsh Information Centre

(☎01599-534276; ⊗daily Easter-Oct) Beside the main seafront car park; stocks information on Skye. Next to it is one of Scotland's most lavishly decorated public toilets.

ℹ Getting There & Away

Citylink buses run to Kyle three times daily from Inverness (£19.20, two hours) and Glasgow (£34.90, 5¾ hours).

The train route between Inverness and Kyle of Lochalsh (£20.50, 2½ hours, up to four daily) is one of Scotland's most scenic.

Kyle to the Great Glen

It's 55 miles southeast via the A87 from Kyle to Invergarry, which lies between Fort William and Fort Augustus, on Loch Oich.

EILEAN DONAN CASTLE

Photogenically sited at the entrance to Loch Duich, near Dornie village, Eilean Donan Castle (☎01599-555202; www.eileandonancastle.com; adult/child £6/5; ⊗9.30am-6pm Mar-Oct) is one of Scotland's most evocative castles, and must be represented in millions of photo albums. It's on an offshore islet, magically linked to the mainland by an elegant, stone-arched bridge. It's very much a re-creation inside, with an excellent introductory exhibition. Keep an eye out for the photos of castle scenes from the movie *Highlander*; there's also a sword used at the battle of Culloden in 1746. The castle was bombarded into ruins by government ships in 1719 when Jacobite forces were defeated at the Battle of Glenshiel. It was rebuilt between 1912 and 1932.

Citylink buses from Fort William and Inverness to Portree, on the Isle of Skye, will stop opposite the castle.

MADDENING MIDGES

Forget Nessie; the Highlands have a real monster. A voracious bloodsucking female fully 3mm long, known as *culicoides impunctatus*, or the Highland midge. The bane of campers and as much a symbol of Scotland as the kilt or dram, they drive sane folk to distraction as they descend in biting clouds.

Though normally vegetarian, the female midge needs a dose of blood in order to lay her eggs. And, like it or not, if you're in the Highlands between June and August, you just volunteered as a donor. Midges especially congregate near water, and are most active in the early morning, though squadrons also patrol in the late evening, around 10pm.

Repellents and creams are reasonably effective, though some walkers favour midge veils. Light-coloured clothing also helps. Pubs and campsites increasingly have midge-zapping machines. Check www.midgeforecast.co.uk for activity levels by area, but don't blame us: we've been eaten alive when the forecast said moderate too.

GLEN SHIEL & GLENELG

From Eilean Donan Castle, the A87 follows Loch Duich into spectacular **Glen Shiel**, with 1000m-high peaks soaring on either side of the road. Here in 1719, a Jacobite army was defeated by Hanoverian government forces. Among those fighting on the rebel side were clansmen led by the famous outlaw Rob Roy MacGregor, and 300 soldiers loaned by the king of Spain; the mountain above the battlefield is still called Sgurr nan Spainteach (Peak of the Spaniard).

At Shiel Bridge, home to a famous wild goat colony, a narrow side road goes over the Bealach Ratagain (pass) to Glenelg, where there's a community-run ferry to Skye. From the Bealach Ratagain, there are great views of the Five Sisters of Kintail peaks. From palindromic Glenelg round to the road-end at Arnisdale, the scenery becomes even more spectacular, with great views across Loch Hourn to the remote Knoydart peninsula. Along this road are two fine ruined Iron Age brochs – Dun Telve and Dun Troddan.

🏃 Activities

There are several good walks in the area, including the two-day, cross-country hike from Morvich to Cannich via scenic **Gleann Lichd** and Glen Affric SYHA (35 miles). A traverse of the **Five Sisters of Kintail** is a classic but seriously challenging hill-walking expedition, taking in three Munro summits; start at the parking area just east of the Glen Shiel battlefield and finish at Morvich (eight to 10 hours).

🛏 Sleeping & Eating

Ratagan SYHA   HOSTEL £
(☎01599-511243; www.syha.org.uk; Ratagan; dm £18.50; ☻mid-Mar–Oct; 🅿@🛜) This hostel has excellent facilities and a to-die-for spot on the south shore of Loch Duich. If you want a break from Munro bagging, this is the place. Cheap meals are on offer, and there's a licensed bar. Turn towards Glenelg from Shiel Bridge, then take the turning on the right to Ratagan. A bus runs Monday to Friday from Kyle of Lochalsh, otherwise it's a 2-mile walk from Shiel Bridge on the main road.

Kintail Lodge Hotel   INN, BOTHY ££
(☎01599-511275; www.kintaillodgehotel.co.uk; Shiel Bridge; dm/s/d £15/60/124; 🅿🛜) With 10 of the 12 fine rooms at this hotel facing the loch, you'd be unlucky not to get a decent outlook. Tasty bar meals (£9 to £16), including local venison and seafood, are available at lunch and dinner. There are also two bunkhouses with self-catering facilities, sleeping six people each; linen is £5.50 extra.

Glenelg Inn   INN ££
(☎01599-522273; www.glenelg-inn.com; Glenelg; mains £11-19; 🅿🐾) One of the Highlands' most picturesque places for a pint or a romantic away-from-it-all stay (doubles £120), the Glenelg Inn has tables in a lovely garden with cracking views of Skye. The elegant dining room and cosy bar area serves up posh fare, with the local catch always featuring. Service variable.

ℹ Getting There & Away

BOAT At Glenelg, a picturesque community-owned vehicle **ferry** (www.skyeferry.com; foot passenger/car with passengers £3/14; ☻10am-6pm Easter-mid-Oct) runs across to Kylerhea on Skye. This is a highly recommended way of reaching the island; it runs every 20 minutes and doesn't need booking.

BUS Citylink buses between Fort William or Inverness and Skye travel along the A87. A bus runs Monday to Friday from Kyle of Lochalsh to Arnisdale, via Shiel Bridge, Ratagan and Glenelg.

ISLE OF SKYE

POP 9900

The Isle of Skye (an t-Eilean Sgiathanach in Gaelic) takes its name from the old Norse *sky-a,* meaning 'cloud island', a Viking reference to the often-mist-enshrouded Cuillin Hills. It's the largest of Scotland's islands, a 50-mile-long smorgasbord of velvet moors, jagged mountains, sparkling lochs and towering sea cliffs. The stunning scenery is the main attraction, but when the mist closes in there are plenty of castles, crofting museums and cosy pubs and restaurants in which to retire.

Along with Edinburgh and Loch Ness, Skye is one of Scotland's top-three tourist destinations. However, the hordes tend to stick to Portree, Dunvegan and Trotternish – it's almost always possible to find peace and quiet in the island's further-flung corners. Come prepared for changeable weather: when it's fine it's very fine indeed, but all too often it isn't.

🏃 Activities

Walking

Skye offers some of the finest – and in places, the roughest and most difficult – walking in Scotland. There are many detailed guidebooks available, including a series of four walking guides by Charles Rhodes, available from the Aros Experience (p399) and the tourist office in Portree. You'll need Ordnance Survey (OS) 1:50,000 maps 23 and 32. Don't attempt the longer walks in bad weather or in winter.

Easy, low-level routes include: through **Strath Mor** from Luib (on the Broadford–Sligachan road) and on to Torrin (on the Broadford–Elgol road; allow 1½ hours, 4 miles); from **Sligachan to Kilmarie** via Camasunary (four hours, 11 miles); and from **Elgol to Kilmarie** via Camasunary (2½ hours, 6.5 miles). The walk from **Kilmarie to Coruisk** and back via Camasunary and the 'Bad Step' is superb but slightly harder (11 miles round trip, allow five hours). The Bad Step is a rocky slab poised above the sea that you have to scramble across; it's easy in fine, dry weather, but some walkers find it intimidating.

Skye Walking Holidays   WALKING
(☎01470-552213; www.skyewalks.co.uk; Duntulm Castle Hotel) Organises three-day guided walking holidays for £400 per person, including four nights of hotel accommodation.

Climbing

The Cuillin Hills is a veritable playground for rock climbers, and the two-day traverse of the Cuillin Ridge is the finest mountaineering expedition in the British Isles. There are several mountain guides in the area who can provide instruction and safely introduce inexperienced climbers to the more difficult routes.

Skye Guides   ROCK CLIMBING
(☎01471-822116; www.skyeguides.co.uk) A two-day introduction-to-rock-climbing course costs around £360, and a private mountain guide can be hired for around £200 a day (both rates apply for up to two clients).

Sea Kayaking

The sheltered coves and sea lochs around the coast of Skye provide water-lovers with magnificent sea-kayaking opportunities. The centres listed here can provide kayaking instruction, guiding and equipment hire for both beginners and experts. It costs around £35 to £40 for a half-day kayak hire with instruction.

Whitewave Outdoor Centre   KAYAKING
(☎01470-542414; www.white-wave.co.uk; 19 Linicro; ☺Mar-Oct) Provides kayaking instruction, guiding and equipment hire for both beginners and experts.

Skyak Adventures   KAYAKING
(☎01471-820002; www.skyakadventures.com; 29 Lower Breakish) Expeditions and courses to take both beginners and experienced paddlers to otherwise inaccessible places.

🚌 Tours

There are several operators who offer guided tours of Skye, covering history, culture and wildlife. Rates are from £150 to £200 for a six-hour tour for up to six people.

Skye Tours   BUS TOUR
(☎0800 980 4846; www.skye-tours.co.uk; adult/child £35/30; ☺Mon-Sat) Five-hour sightseeing tours of Skye in a minibus, departing from the tourist office car park in Kyle of Lochalsh (close to Kyle of Lochalsh train station).

Skye Light Images   4WD TOUR
(☎07909 706802; www.skyejeepsafaris.co.uk; ☺Oct-Easter) Offers 4WD winter safaris in the wilder areas of Skye with tuition on landscape and wildlife photography.

Skye & Outer Hebrides

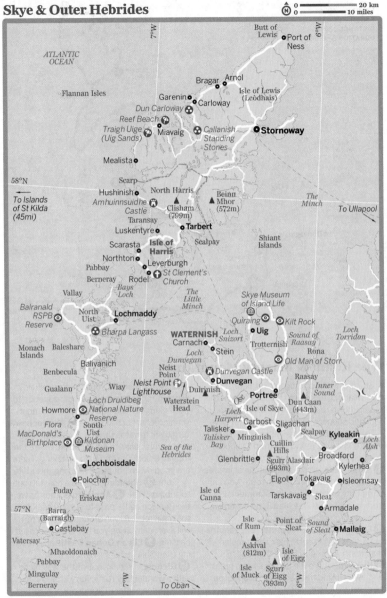

Skye & Outer Hebrides map:

- 0 — 20 km
- 0 — 10 miles

ATLANTIC OCEAN

Butt of Lewis • Port of Ness
Bragar • Arnol
Flannan Isles
Garenin • Carloway
Isle of Lewis (Leòdhais)
Dun Carloway
Reef Beach
Traigh Uige (Uig Sands) • Miavaig
Mealista •
Callanish Standing Stones
• **Stornoway**
58°N
Scarp
To Islands of St Kilda (45mi)
Hushinish • North Harris
Amhuinnsuidhe Castle
Clisham (799m)
Beinn Mhor (572m)
The Minch
To Ullapool
Taransay
Luskentyre • **Tarbert**
Scalpay
Shiant Islands
Isle of Harris
Scarasta
Northton • Leverburgh
Pabbay
Berneray • Rodel
St Clement's Church
Valley
Bays Loch
The Little Minch
Skye Museum of Island Life
Balranald RSPB Reserve
North Uist • **Lochmaddy**
Bharpa Langass
Quiraing • Kilt Rock
WATERNISH • **Uig**
Carnach • Loch Snizort
Sound of Raasay
Loch Torridon
Monach Islands
Baleshare
Stein
Trotternish
Rona
Benbecula
Balivanich
Loch Dunvegan
Old Man of Storr
Gualann
Wiay
Neist Point
Dunvegan Castle
Raasay
Neist Point Lighthouse
• Duirinish
• **Dunvegan**
• **Portree**
Inner Sound
Loch Druidibeg National Nature Reserve
Waterstein Head
Isle of Skye
Dun Caan (443m)
Howmore
South Uist
Loch Harport
Carbost • Sligachan
Flora MacDonald's Birthplace
Kildonan Museum
Talisker • Scalpay
Kyleakin
Talisker Bay
Minginish
Cuillin Hills
Loch Alsh
• **Lochboisdale**
Sea of the Hebrides
Glenbrittle
Sgurr Alasdair (993m)
Broadford
Kylerhea
• Polochar
Elgol • Tokavaig • Isleornsay
Fuday
Eriskay
Isle of Canna
Tarskavaig • Sleat
57°N
Barra (Barraigh)
• Armadale
Vatersay
• Castlebay
Isle of Rum
Point of Sleat
Sound of Sleat
• **Mallaig**
Mhaoldonaich
Pabbay
Askival (812m)
Isle of Eigg
Mingulay
Berneray
To Oban
Isle of Muck
Sgurr of Eigg (393m)

---

❶ Information

Internet Access

The Portree Information Centre (p395) also has internet access for £1 per 20 minutes.

Columba 1400 Community Centre (Staffin; per hr £1; ⏲10.30am-8pm Mon-Sat Apr-Oct)

Seamus's Bar (Sligachan Hotel; per 15min £1; ⏲11am-11pm)

Medical Services

Portree Community Hospital (☎01478-613200; Fancyhill) There's a casualty department and dental surgery here.

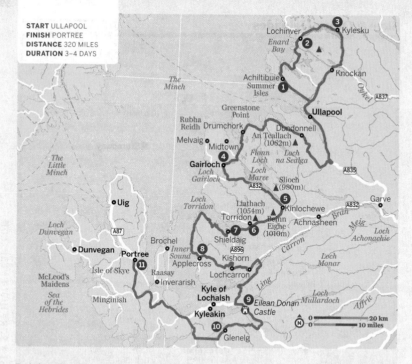

Driving Tour
Wee Roads & Mighty Mountains

> Starting in the photogenic harbour town of Ullapool, this drive takes in some of the lesser-known roads and the most majestic of Highland scenery, ending at the Isle of Skye.

Leave your bags in the hotel, because the first day is a long round trip from Ullapool. Head north, and take the left turn towards ❶ **Achiltibuie**, where after gaping at impressive lochside Stac Pollaidh en route, you can admire the outlook over the Summer Isles. From here, it's the Wee Mad Road, a narrow, tortuous but pretty drive north to ❷ **Lochinver**. From this pretty town, another minor road winds north past spectacular beaches at Achmelvich and Clachtoll to ❸ **Kylesku**, where the hotel makes a great lunch stop. Head back south to Ullapool on the main road, with classic northwestern scenery and things to see such as Inchnadamph Caves, Ardvreck Castle and Knockan Crag along the way.

The next day head inland along the A835 before taking the ❹ **Gairloch** turn-off, following the long, circuitous coast road with plenty of activity options from whale-watching trips to pacing a botanic garden to hill walking around one of Scotland's most scenic lochs, Loch Maree. At ❺ **Kinlochewe** turn back towards the coast, descending a spectacular pass to ❻ **Torridon**, where the rugged beauty is simply breathtaking. There are good overnight stops all along this route.

From ❼ **Shieldaig**, take the coastal route to sublime little ❽ **Applecross**, then brave the Bealach na Ba pass to get you back to the main road. A loop around Loch Carron will eventually bring you to the A87. Turn left, passing ❾ **Eilean Donan Castle** and, reaching Glen Shiel, take the right turn to ❿ **Glenelg**, a scenic, out-of-the-way place with a wonderfully rustic ferry crossing to Skye (not in winter). Disembark at Kylerhea and enjoy the vistas on one of the island's least-trafficked roads before hitting the A87 again. From here, ⓫ **Portree** is an easy drive, but numerous picturesque detours – to Sleet or Elgol for example – mean you might take a while to reach it yet.

Money

Only Portree and Broadford have banks with ATMs, and Portree's tourist office has a currency exchange desk.

Tourist Information

Broadford Information Centre (⌨01471-822361; car park, Broadford; ⏱9.30am-5pm Mon-Sat, 10am-4pm Sun Apr-Oct)

Dunvegan Information Centre (⌨01470-521581; 2 Lochside; ⏱10am-5pm Mon-Sat Jun-Oct plus 10am-4pm Sun Jul & Aug, 10am-5pm Mon-Fri Apr & May, limited opening hours Nov-Mar)

Portree Information Centre (⌨01478-612137; Bayfield Rd; internet per 20min £1; ⏱9am-6pm Mon-Sat, 10am-4pm Sun Jun-Aug, 9am-5pm Mon-Fri, 10am-4pm Sat Apr, May & Sep, limited opening hours Oct-Mar)

❶ Getting There & Away

BOAT Despite the bridge, there are still a couple of ferry links between Skye and the mainland. Ferries also operate from Uig on Skye to the Outer Hebrides.

Mallaig to Armadale (www.calmac.co.uk; per person/car £4.35/22.60) The Mallaig to Armadale ferry (30 minutes, eight daily Monday to Saturday, five to seven on Sunday) is very popular in July and August, so book ahead if you're travelling by car.

Glenelg to Kylerhea (www.skyeferry.co.uk; car with up to four passengers £14) Runs a tiny vessel (six cars only) on the short Kylerhea to Glenelg crossing (five minutes, every 20 minutes). The ferry operates from 10am to 6pm daily from Easter to October only (to 7pm June to August).

BUS Glasgow to Portree £40, seven hours, four daily

Glasgow to Uig £40, 7½ hours, two daily; via Crianlarich, Fort William and Kyle of Lochalsh

Inverness to Portree £23, 3½ hours, three daily

CAR & MOTORCYCLE The Isle of Skye became permanently tethered to the Scottish mainland when the Skye Bridge opened in 1995. The controversial bridge tolls were abolished in 2004 and the crossing is now free.

There are petrol stations at Broadford (open 24 hours), Armadale, Portree, Dunvegan and Uig.

❶ Getting Around

Getting around the island by public transport can be a pain, especially if you want to explore away from the main Kyleakin–Portree–Uig road. Here, as in much of the Highlands, there are only a few buses on Saturday, and only one Sunday service (between Kyle of Lochalsh and Portree).

BUS Stagecoach (p367) operates the main bus routes on the island, linking all the main villages and towns. Its **Skye Dayrider** ticket gives unlimited bus travel for one day for £7.50. For timetable info, call **Traveline** (⌨0871 200 2233).

TAXI Kyle Taxi Company (⌨01599-534323) You can order a taxi or hire a car from Kyle Taxi Company. Car hire costs from around £38 a day, and you can arrange for the car to be waiting at Kyle of Lochalsh train station.

Kyleakin (Caol Acain)

POP 100

Poor wee Kyleakin had the carpet pulled from under it when the Skye Bridge opened – it went from being the gateway to the island to a backwater bypassed by the main road. It's now a pleasant, peaceful little place, with a harbour used by yachts and fishing boats.

The community-run **Bright Water Visitor Centre** (⌨01599-530040; www.eileanban .org; The Pier; adult/child £1/free; ⏱10am-4pm Mon-Fri Easter-Sep) serves as a base for tours of **Eilean Ban** – the island used as a stepping stone by the Skye Bridge – where Gavin Maxwell (author of *Ring of Bright Water*) spent the last 18 months of his life in 1968–69, living in the lighthouse keeper's cottage. The island is now a nature reserve and tours (£7 per person) are available in summer (must be booked in advance). The visitor centre also houses a child-friendly exhibition on Maxwell, the lighthouse and the island's wildlife. Tour times were uncertain at the time of research – best call ahead to check.

There are two hostels and a couple of B&Bs in the village. The friendly **Skye Backpackers** (⌨01599-534510; www.skyeback packers.com; dm/tw £18/47) is our favourite, with even cheaper beds (£13) in caravans out back.

About 3 miles southwest of Kyleakin, a minor road leads southwards to **Kylerhea**, where there's a 1½-hour nature trail to a shorefront **otter hide**, where you stand a good chance of seeing these elusive creatures. A little further on is the jetty for the **car ferry to Glenelg** on the mainland.

A shuttle bus runs half hourly between Kyle of Lochalsh and Kyleakin (five minutes), and there are eight to 10 buses daily (except Sunday) to Broadford and Portree.

Broadford
(An T-Ath Leathann)

POP 1050

Broadford is a service centre for the scattered communities of southern Skye. The long, straggling village has a tourist office, a 24-hour petrol station, and a large Co-op supermarket (☺8am-10pm Mon-Sat, 9am-6pm Sun) with an ATM, a laundrette and a bank.

There are lots of B&Bs in and around Broadford and the village is well placed for exploring southern Skye by car.

Sleeping & Eating

Tigh an Dochais B&B ££
(☎01471-820022; www.skyebedbreakfast.co.uk; 13 Harrapool; per person from £40; P) A cleverly designed modern building, Tigh an Dochais is one of Skye's best B&Bs – a little footbridge leads to the front door, which is on the 1st floor. Here you'll find the breakfast room and lounge with double-height windows offering a stunning view of sea and hills; the bedrooms (downstairs) have spacious en suites and open onto an outdoor deck with that same wonderful view.

Broadford Hotel HOTEL ££
(☎01471-822204; www.broadfordhotel.co.uk; Torrin Rd; d £149; P☂) The Broadford Hotel is a glamorous and stylish retreat with luxury fabrics and designer colour schemes. There's a formal restaurant and the more democratic **Gabbro Bar** (mains £7-10; ☺food served noon-9pm), where you can enjoy a bar meal of smoked haddock chowder or steak pie washed down with Isle of Skye Brewery ale.

Berabhaigh B&B ££
(☎01471-822372; berabhaigh@freeuk.com; 3 Lime Park; r per person £34; ☺Mar-Oct; P) This is a lovely old croft house with bay views. It is located just off the main road, near Creelers.

Broadford Backpackers HOSTEL £
(☎01471-820333; www.broadfordbackpackers .co.uk; High Rd; dm/d £19/47) Friendly hostel set in a bright and modern building, 10 minutes' walk west of the Co-op supermarket in the village centre; take the road on the right, just past the pedestrian crossing outside the bank (signposted 'Hospital').

Luib House B&B ££
(☎01471-820334; www.luibhouse.co.uk; Luib; r per person £32; P) This is a large, comfortable and well-appointed B&B 6 miles north of Broadford.

Creelers SEAFOOD ££
(☎01471-822281; www.skye-seafood-restaurant .co.uk; Lower Harrapool; mains £12-17; ☺noon-9.30pm Mon-Sat Mar-Nov; ⏹) Broadford has several places to eat but one really stands out: Creelers is a small, bustling, no-frills restaurant that serves some of the best seafood on Skye; the house speciality is a rich, spicy seafood gumbo. Best to book ahead. If you can't get a table, nip around to the back door, where you'll find **Ma Doyle's Takeaway**, for fish and chips (£6) to go.

Sleat

If you cross over the sea to Skye on the ferry from Mallaig you arrive in Armadale, at the southern end of the long, low-lying peninsula known as Sleat (pronounced 'slate'). The landscape of Sleat itself is not exceptional, but it provides a grandstand for ogling the magnificent scenery on either side – take the steep and twisting minor road that loops through **Tarskavaig** and **Tokavaig** for stunning views of the Isle of Rum, the Cuillin Hills and Bla Bheinn.

ARMADALE

Armadale, where the ferry from Mallaig arrives, is little more than a store, a post office and a couple of houses. There are six or seven buses a day (Monday to Saturday) from Armadale to Broadford and Portree.

Sights & Activities

Museum of the Isles MUSEUM
(☎01471-844305; www.clandonald.com; adult/child £6.95/4.95; ☺9.30am-5.30pm Apr-Oct) Just along the road from the ferry pier is the part-ruined **Armadale Castle**, former seat of Lord MacDonald of Sleat. The neighbouring museum will tell you all you ever wanted to know about Clan Donald, as well as providing an easily digestible history of the Lordship of the Isles.

Prize exhibits include rare portraits of clan chiefs, and a wineglass that was once used by Bonnie Prince Charlie. The ticket also gives admission to the lovely **castle gardens**.

FREE Aird Old Church Gallery GALLERY
(☎01471-844291; www.airdoldchurchgallery.co.uk; Aird; ☺10am-5pm Mon-Sat Easter-Sep) At the end of the narrow road that leads southwest

from Armadale through Ardvasar village, this small gallery exhibits the powerful landscape paintings of Peter McDermott.

Sea.fari Adventures BOAT TOUR
(01471-833316; www.whalespotting.co.uk; adult/child £42/34; Easter-Sep) Sea.fari runs three-hour whale-watching cruises in a high-speed RIB. These trips have a high success rate for spotting minke whales in summer (an average of 180 sightings a year), with rarer sightings of bottlenose dolphins and basking sharks.

⏚ Sleeping & Eating

Flora MacDonald Hostel HOSTEL £
(01471-844272; www.skye-hostel.co.uk; The Glebe; dm/tw/q £16/42/72;) Rustic accommodation 3 miles north of the Mallaig–Armadale ferry, on a farm full of Highland cattle and Eriskay ponies.

Pasta Shed CAFE ££
(01471-844222; The Pier; mains £6-12; 9am-6pm) A cute little conservatory with some outdoor tables. Serves good seafood dishes, pizzas, fish and chips, crab salads and coffees – you can sit in or take away.

ISLEORNSAY

This pretty harbour, 8 miles north of Armadale, is opposite Sandaig Bay on the mainland, where Gavin Maxwell lived and wrote his much-loved memoir *Ring of Bright Water*. Gallery An Talla Dearg (admission free; 10am-6pm Mon-Fri, to 4pm Sat & Sun Apr-Oct) exhibits the works of artists who were inspired by Scottish landscapes and culture.

⏚ Sleeping & Eating

TOP CHOICE/ Toravaig House Hotel HOTEL ££
(01471-820200; www.skyehotel.co.uk; d £95-120;) This hotel, 3 miles south of Isleornsay, is one of those places where the owners know a thing or two about hospitality – as soon as you arrive you'll feel right at home, whether relaxing on the sofas by the log fire in the lounge or admiring the view across the Sound of Sleat from the lawn chairs in the garden.

The spacious bedrooms – ask for room 1 (Eriskay), with its enormous sleigh bed – are luxuriously equipped, from the rich and heavy bedlinen to the huge, high-pressure shower heads. The elegant **Islay** restaurant serves the best of local fish, game and lamb. After dinner you can retire to the lounge with a single malt and flick through the yachting magazines – you can even arrange

a day trip aboard the owners' 42ft sailing yacht.

Hotel Eilean Iarmain HOTEL £££
(01471-833332; www.eilean-iarmain.co.uk; s/d from £110/170;) A charming old Victorian hotel with log fires, a candlelit restaurant and 12 luxurious rooms, many with sea views. The hotel's cosy, wood-panelled **An Praban Bar** (mains £9-16) serves delicious, gourmet-style bar meals – try the haddock in beer batter, venison burger or vegetable cannelloni.

Elgol (Ealaghol)

On a clear day, the journey along the road from Broadford to Elgol is one of the most scenic on Skye. It takes in two classic postcard panoramas – the view of Bla Bheinn across **Loch Slapin** (near Torrin), and the superb view of the entire Cuillin range from **Elgol pier**.

Just west of Elgol is the **Spar Cave**, famously visited by Sir Walter Scott in 1814 and mentioned in his poem *Lord of the Isles*. The 80m-deep cave is wild, remote and filled with beautiful flowstone formations. It is a short walk from the village of Glasnakille, but the approach is over seaweed-covered boulders and is only accessible for one hour either side of low water. Check tide times and route information at Broadford tourist office, or ask at the tearoom in Elgol.

Bus 49 runs from Broadford to Elgol (40 minutes, three daily Monday to Friday, two Saturday).

✈ Activities

Bella Jane BOAT TOUR
(0800 731 3089; www.bellajane.co.uk; Apr-Oct) Bella Jane offers a three-hour cruise (adult/child £22/12, three daily) from Elgol harbour to the remote Loch na Cuilce, an impressive inlet surrounded by soaring peaks. On a calm day, you can clamber ashore here to make the short walk to Loch Coruisk in the heart of the Cuillin Hills. You get 1½ hours ashore and visit a seal colony en route.

Aquaxplore BOAT TOUR
(0800 731 3089; www.aquaxplore.co.uk; Apr-Oct) Runs 1½-hour high-speed boat trips from Elgol to an abandoned shark-hunting station on the island of **Soay** (adult/child £25/20), once owned by *Ring of Bright Water* author Gavin Maxwell. There are longer

trips (adult/child £48/38, four hours) to Rum, Canna and Sanday to visit breeding colonies of puffins, with the chance of seeing minke whales on the way.

Misty Isle   CRUISE
(☏01471-866288; www.mistyisleboattrips.co.uk; adult/child £18/7.50; ☺Apr-Oct) The pretty, traditional wooden launch *Misty Isle* offers cruises to Loch Coruisk with 1½ hours ashore (no Sunday service).

Cuillin Hills

The Cuillin Hills are Britain's most spectacular mountain range (the name comes from the Old Norse *kjöllen,* meaning 'keel-shaped'). Though small in stature (**Sgurr Alasdair**, the highest summit, is only 993m), the peaks are near-alpine in character, with knife-edge ridges, jagged pinnacles, scree-filled gullies and hectares of naked rock. While they are a paradise for experienced mountaineers, the higher reaches of the Cuillin are off limits to the majority of walkers.

The good news is that there are also plenty of good low-level hikes within the ability of most walkers. One of the best (on a fine day) is the steep climb from Glenbrittle campsite to **Coire Lagan** (6 miles round trip; allow at least three hours). The impressive upper corrie contains a lochan for bathing (for the hardy!), and the surrounding cliffs are a playground for rock climbers – bring your binoculars.

Even more spectacular, but much harder to reach, is **Loch Coruisk** (from the Gaelic Coir'Uisg, the Water Corrie), a remote loch ringed by the highest peaks of the Cuillin. Accessible by boat trip (p397) from Elgol, or via an arduous 5.5-mile hike from Kilmarie, Coruisk was popularised by Sir Walter Scott in his 1815 poem *Lord of the Isles.* Crowds of Victorian tourists and landscape artists followed in Scott's footsteps, including JMW Turner, whose watercolours were used to illustrate Scott's works.

There are two main bases for exploring the Cuillin – Sligachan to the north and Glenbrittle to the south.

🛏 Sleeping & Eating

Sligachan Hotel   HOTEL ££
(☏01478-650204; www.sligachan.co.uk; per person £65-75; P@🛜) The Slig, as it has been

known to generations of climbers, is a near village in itself, encompassing a luxurious hotel, a microbrewery, self-catering cottages, a bunkhouse, a campsite, a big barn of a pub (Seamus's Bar; p398) and an adventure playground.

Sligachan Bunkhouse   HOSTEL £
(☏01478-650458; www.sligachanselfcatering .co.uk; Sligachan Hotel; dm £16) Comfortable and modern bunkhouse opposite the Sligachan Hotel.

Sligachan Campsite   CAMPSITE £
(Sligachan Hotel; sites per person £5.50; ☺Apr-Oct) Across the road from the Sligachan Hotel is this basic campsite; be warned – this spot is a midge magnet. No bookings.

Glenbrittle SYHA   HOSTEL £
(☏01478-640278; dm £18; ☺Apr-Sep) Scandinavian-style timber hostel that quickly fills up with climbers on holiday weekends.

Glenbrittle Campsite   CAMPSITE £
(☏01478-640404; per adult/child incl car £7/4.50; ☺Apr-Sep) Excellent site, close to mountains and sea, with a shop selling food and outdoor kit; the midges can be diabolical, though.

Seamus's Bar   PUB £
(Sligachan Hotel; mains £8-10; ☺food served 11am-11pm; 🛜🍴) This place dishes up decent bar meals, including haggis, neeps and tatties, steak and ale pie and fish pie, and serves real ales from its own microbrewery. It also has a range of 200 malt whiskies in serried ranks above the bar. As well as the adventure playground outside, there are games, toys and a play area indoors.

Minginish

Loch Harport, to the north of the Cuillin, divides the Minginish Peninsula from the rest of Skye. On its southern shore lies the village of Carbost, home to the smooth, sweet and smoky Talisker malt whisky, produced at **Talisker Distillery** (☏01478-614308; www.dis covering-distilleries.com; guided tour £6; ☺9.30am-5pm Mon-Sat Apr-Oct, plus 11am-5pm Sun Jul & Aug, 10am-4.30pm Mon-Fri Nov-Mar). This is the only distillery on Skye; the guided tour includes a free dram. Magnificent **Talisker Bay**, 5 miles west of Carbost, has a sandy beach, sea stack and waterfall.

🛏 Sleeping & Eating

Old Inn   B&B, HOSTEL **££**

(✆01478-640205; www.theoldinnskye.co.uk; Carbost; s/d £48/76; P) The Old Inn is an atmospheric wee pub, offering accommodation in bright B&B bedrooms and an appealing chalet-style bunkhouse (from £15 per person). The bar is a favourite with walkers and climbers from Glenbrittle, and serves excellent pub grub (£9 to £13, noon to 10pm), from fresh oysters to haddock and chips. There's an outdoor patio at the back with great views over Loch Harport.

Skyewalker Independent Hostel   HOSTEL **£**

(✆01478-640250; www.skyewalkerhostel.com; Fiskavaig Rd, Portnalong; dm £13.50; @) Three miles northwest of Carbost, this hostel is housed in the old village school.

ℹ Getting There & Away

There are five buses a day on weekdays (one on Saturday) from Portree to Carbost via Sligachan.

Portree (Port Righ)

POP 1920

Portree is Skye's largest and liveliest town. It has a pretty harbour lined with brightly painted houses and there are great views of the surrounding hills. Its name (from the Gaelic for King's Harbour) commemorates James V, who came here in 1540 to pacify the local clans.

👁 Sights & Activities

Aros Experience   VISITOR CENTRE

(✆01478-613649; www.aros.co.uk; Viewfield Rd; sea eagle exhibition £4.75; ⏰9am-5.30pm; 🚸) On the southern edge of Portree, the Aros Experience is a combined visitor centre, book and gift shop, restaurant, theatre and cinema. The visitor centre offers a look at some fascinating, live CCTV images from local sea-eagle and heron nests, and a wide-screen video of Skye's impressive scenery (it's worth waiting for the aerial shots of the Cuillin).

The centre is a useful rainy-day retreat, with an indoor, soft play area for children.

MV Stardust   BOAT TOUR

(✆07798-743858; www.skyeboat-trips.co.uk; Portree Harbour; adult/child £15/9) MV *Stardust* offers one- to two-hour boat trips to the Sound of Raasay, with the chance to see seals, porpoises and – if you're lucky – white-tailed sea eagles. On Saturday there are longer cruises

to the Isle of Rona (£25 per person). You can also arrange to be dropped off for a hike on the Isle of Raasay and picked up again later.

🎆 Festivals & Events

Isle of Skye

Highland Games   HIGHLAND GAMES

(www.skye-highland-games.co.uk) These annual games are held in Portree in early August.

🛏 Sleeping

Portree is well supplied with B&Bs, but many of them are in bland, modern bungalows that, though comfortable, often lack character. Accommodation fills up fast in July and August so be sure to book ahead.

TOP CHOICE Ben Tianavaig B&B   B&B **££**

(✆01478-612152; www.ben-tianavaig.co.uk; 5 Bosville Tce; r £70-80; P🐾) A warm welcome awaits from the Irish-Welsh couple who run this appealing B&B bang in the centre of town. All four bedrooms have a view across the harbour to the hill that gives the house its name and breakfasts include free-range eggs and vegetables grown in the garden.

Peinmore House   B&B **££**

(✆01478-612574; www.peinmorehouse.co.uk; r £130-140; P🐾) Signposted off the main road about 2 miles south of Portree, this former manse has been cleverly converted into a guest house that is more stylish and luxurious than most hotels. The bedrooms and bathrooms are huge (one bathroom has an armchair in it!), as is the choice of breakfast (kippers and smoked haddock on the menu), and there are panoramic views to the Old Man of Storr.

Bosville Hotel   HOTEL **££**

(✆01478-612846; www.bosvillehotel.co.uk; 9-11 Bosville Tce; s/d from £130/138; 🐾) The Bosville brings a little bit of metropolitan style to Portree with its designer fabrics and furniture, flatscreen TVs, fluffy bathrobes and bright, spacious bathrooms. It's worth splashing out a bit for the 'premier' rooms, with leather recliner chairs from which you can lap up the view over the town and harbour.

Rosedale Hotel   HOTEL **££**

(✆01478-613131; www.rosedalehotelskye.co.uk; Beaumont Cres; s/d from £65/100; ⏰Easter-Oct; 🐾) The Rosedale is a cosy, old-fashioned hotel – you'll be welcomed with a glass of whisky or sherry when you check in – delightfully situated down by the waterfront. Its three converted fishermen's cottages are linked by a maze of narrow stairs and corridors, and the restaurant has a view of the harbour.

Woodlands
B&B ££

(☎01478-612980; www.woodlands-portree.co.uk; Viewfield Rd; r £68; P) A great location, with views across the bay, and unstinting hospitality make this modern B&B, a half-mile south of the town centre, a good choice.

Bayfield Backpackers
HOSTEL £

(☎01478-612231; www.skyehostel.co.uk; Bayfield; dm £17; @☎) Clean, central and modern, this hostel provides the best backpacker accommodation in town. The owner really makes you feel welcome, and is a fount of advice on what to do and where to go in Skye.

Torvaig Campsite
CAMPSITE £

(☎01478-612209; www.portreecampsite.co.uk; Torvaig; per adult/child £6/2; ☺Apr-Oct) An attractive, family-run campsite located 1.5 miles north of Portree, on the road to Staffin.

✕ Eating & Drinking

🍴 Café Arriba
CAFE £

(☎01478-611830; www.cafearriba.co.uk; Quay Brae; mains £4-8; ☺7am-10pm May-Sep, 8am-5.30pm Oct-Apr; ☑) Arriba is a funky little cafe, brightly decked out in primary colours and offering delicious flatbread melts (bacon, leek and cheese is our favourite) as well as the best choice of vegetarian grub on the island, ranging from a veggie breakfast fry-up to Indian-spiced bean cakes with mint yoghurt. Also serves excellent coffee.

TOP CHOICE Harbour View Seafood Restaurant
SEAFOOD ££

(☎01478-612069; www.harbourviewskye.co.uk; 7 Bosville Tce; mains £14-19; ☺lunch & 5.30-11pm Tue-Sun) The Harbour View is Portree's most congenial place to eat. It has a homely dining room with a log fire in winter, books on the mantelpiece and bric-a-brac on the shelves. And on the table, superb Scottish seafood, such as fresh Skye oysters, seafood chowder, king scallops, langoustines and lobster.

🍴 Sea Breezes
SEAFOOD ££

(☎01478-612016; www.seabreezes-skye.co.uk; 2 Marine Buildings, Quay St; mains £12-19; ☺lunch & dinner Apr-Oct) Sea Breezes is an informal, no-frills restaurant specialising in local fish and shellfish fresh from the boat – try the impressive seafood platter, a small mountain of langoustines, crab, oysters and lobster.

Early-bird menu (5pm to 6pm) offers two courses for £17. Book early, as it's often hard to get a table.

🍴 Bistro at the Bosville
BISTRO ££

(☎01478-612846; www.bosvillehotel.co.uk; 7 Bosville Tce; mains £9-20; ☺noon-2.30pm & 5.30-10pm; ☎) This hotel bistro sports a relaxed atmosphere, an award-winning chef and a menu that makes the most of Skye-sourced produce – including lamb, game, seafood, cheese, organic vegetables and berries – and adds an original twist to traditional dishes. The neighbouring **Chandlery Restaurant** (three-course dinner £44) offers a more up-market experience.

L'Incontro
CAFE

(The Green; ☺11am-11pm Mon-Sat) This adjunct to a popular pizza restaurant (upstairs beside the Royal Hotel) serves excellent Italian espresso, and also has an extensive range of Italian wines.

Isles Inn
PUB

(☎01478-612129; Somerled Sq; ☎) Portree's pubs are nothing special, but the Isles Inn is more atmospheric than most. The Jacobean bar, with its flagstone floor and open fires, pulls in a lively mix of young locals, backpackers and tourists.

Pier Hotel
PUB

(☎01478-612094; Quay St) You can almost guarantee a weekend singalong at this nautical-themed waterfront bar.

🛍 Shopping

Skye Batiks
GIFTS

(www.skyebatiks.com; The Green; ☺9am-6pm May-Sep, to 9pm Jul & Aug, to 5pm Mon-Sat Oct-Apr) Skye Batiks is a cut above your average gift shop, selling a range of interesting crafts such as carved wood, jewellery and batik fabrics with Celtic designs.

Isle of Skye Crafts@Over the Rainbow
GIFTS

(☎01478-612361; www.skyeknitwear.com; Quay Brae; ☺9am-5.30pm Mon-Sat, plus 11am-4pm Sun Apr-Oct) Crammed with colourful knitwear and cross-stitch kits, lambswool and cashmere scarves, plus all kinds of interesting gifts.

Isle of Skye Soap Co
COSMETICS

(☎01478-611350; www.skye-soap.co.uk; Somerled Sq; ☺9am-5.30pm Mon-Fri, to 5pm Sat) A sweet-smelling gift shop that specialises in handmade soaps and cosmetics made using natural ingredients and aromatherapy oils.

Carmina Gadelica   MUSIC
(☎01478-612585; Bank St; ☺9am-5.30pm Mon-Sat, to 9pm Jun-Aug) Browse the shelves for CDs of Gaelic music and books on local subjects.

❶ Getting There & Around

BICYCLE **Island Cycles** (☎01478-613121; www.islandcycles-skye.co.uk; The Green; ☺9am-5pm Mon-Sat) You can hire bikes here for £8.50/15 per half-/full day.

BUS The main bus stop is in Somerled Sq. There are seven Scottish Citylink buses every day from Kyle of Lochalsh to Portree (£6, one hour) and on to Uig.

Local buses (Monday to Saturday only) run from Portree to Broadford (40 minutes, at least hourly) via Sligachan (15 minutes); to Armadale (1¼ hours, connecting with the ferries to Mallaig); to Carbost (40 minutes, four daily); to Uig (30 minutes, six daily) and to Dunvegan Castle (40 minutes, five daily Monday to Friday, three on Saturday). There are also five or six buses a day on a circular route around Trotternish (in both directions), taking in Flodigarry (20 minutes), Kilmuir (1¼ hours) and Uig (30 minutes). Buses from the mainland also come through Portree.

Dunvegan (Dun Bheagain)

Skye's most famous historic building, and one of its most popular tourist attractions, is **Dunvegan Castle** (☎01470-521206; www.dunvegancastle.com; adult/child £9.50/5; ☺10am-5pm Apr-mid-Oct), seat of the chief of Clan MacLeod. It has played host to Samuel Johnson, Sir Walter Scott and, most famously, Flora MacDonald. The oldest parts are the 14th-century keep and dungeon but most of it dates from the 17th to 19th centuries.

In addition to the usual castle stuff – swords, silver and family portraits – there are some interesting artefacts, most famous being the Fairy Flag, a diaphanous silk banner that dates from some time between the 4th and 7th centuries. Bonnie Prince Charlie's waistcoat and a lock of his hair, donated by Flora MacDonald's granddaughter, share a room with Rory Mor's Drinking Horn, a beautiful 16th-century vessel of Celtic design that could hold 2.2L of claret. Upholding the family tradition, in 1956, John MacLeod – the 29th chief, who died in 2007 – downed the contents in one minute and 57 seconds 'without setting down or falling down'.

From the end of the minor road beyond Dunvegan Castle entrance, an easy 1-mile walk leads to the **Coral Beaches** – a pair of blindingly white beaches composed of the bleached exoskeletons of coralline algae known as *maerl*.

On the way to Dunvegan from Portree you'll pass Edinbane Pottery (☎01470-582234; www.edinbane-pottery.co.uk; ☺9am-6pm daily Easter-Oct, closed Sat & Sun Nov-Easter), one of the island's original craft workshops, established in 1971, where you can watch potters at work creating beautiful and colourful stoneware.

Duirinish & Waternish

The Duirinish peninsula to the west of Dunvegan, and Waternish to the north, boast some of Skye's most atmospheric hotels and restaurants, plus an eclectic range of artists' studios and crafts workshops. Portree tourist office provides a free booklet listing them all.

◉ Sights & Activities

The sparsely populated Duirinish peninsula is dominated by the distinctive flat-topped peaks of Helabhal Mhor (469m) and Helabhal Bheag (488m), known locally as **Mac Leod's Tables**. There are some fine walks from Orbost, including the summit of Helabhal Bheag (allow 3½ hours return) and the 5-mile trail from Orbost to **MacLeod's Maidens**, a series of pointed sea stacks at the southern tip of the peninsula.

It's worth making the long drive beyond Dunvegan to the west side of the Duirinish Peninsula to see the spectacular sea cliffs of **Waterstein Head** and to walk down to **Neist Point lighthouse** with its views to the Outer Hebrides.

🛏 Sleeping & Eating

TOP CHOICE **Red Roof Café**   CAFE ££
(☎01470-511766; www.redroofskye.co.uk; Glendale; mains £8-10; ☺11am-5pm Apr-Oct; Ⓟ🖧) Tucked away up a glen, a mile off the main road, this restored 250-year-old byre is a wee haven of home baking and home-grown grub. As well as great coffee and cake, there are lunch platters (noon to 3pm) of Skye seafood, game or cheese served with salad leaves and edible flowers grown just along the road. Add regular evening music gigs and you can see why this place is a local favourite.

TOP CHOICE **Three Chimneys**   MODERN SCOTTISH £££

(☎01470-511258; www.threechimneys.co.uk; Colbost; 3-course lunch/dinner £37/60; ☺lunch Mon-Fri mid-MarOct, dinner daily year-round; **P**) Halfway between Dunvegan and Waterstein, the Three Chimneys is a superb romantic retreat combining a gourmet restaurant in a candlelit crofter's cottage with sumptuous five-star rooms (double £295, dinner/B&B per couple £415) in the modern house next door. Book well in advance and note that children are not welcome in the restaurant in the evenings.

Stein Inn   PUB £

(☎01470-592362; www.steininn.co.uk; Stein; bar meals £8-12; ☺food noon-4pm & 6-9.30pm Mon-Sat, 12.30-4pm & 6.30-9pm Sun Easter-Oct; **P**) This old country inn dates from 1790 and has a handful of bedrooms (per person £37 to £55), all with sea views, a lively little bar and a delightful beer garden – a real suntrap on warm summer afternoons – beside the loch. The bar serves real ales from the Isle of Skye Brewery and does an excellent crab sandwich. Food is served in winter too, but call ahead to check.

Lochbay Seafood Restaurant   SEAFOOD £££

(☎01470-592235; www.lochbay-seafood-restaurant.co.uk; Stein; mains £14-23, lobster £30-42; ☺lunch & dinner Tue-Sat; **P**) Just along the road from the Stein Inn is one of Skye's most romantic restaurants, a cosy farmhouse kitchen with terracotta tiles and a wood-burning stove, and a menu that includes most things that either swim in the sea or live in a shell. Best to book ahead.

🛍 **Shopping**

Dandelion Designs   ARTS & CRAFTS

(www.dandelion-designs.co.uk; Captain's House, Stein; ☺11am-5pm Easter-Oct) At Stein on the Waternish Peninsula, Dandelion Designs is an interesting little gallery with a good range of colour and monochrome landscape photography, lino prints by Liz Myhill and a range of handmade arts and crafts.

Shilasdair Yarns   KNITWEAR

(www.theskyeshilasdairshop.co.uk; Carnach; ☺10am-6pm Apr-Oct) The couple who run this place, a few miles north of Stein, moved to Skye in 1971 and now raise sheep, hand-spin woollen yarn, and hand-dye a range of wools and silks using natural dyes. You can see the dyeing process and try hand-spinning in the exhibition area behind the studio, which sells finished knitwear as well as yarns.

Trotternish

The Trotternish Peninsula to the north of Portree has some of Skye's most beautiful – and bizarre – scenery. A loop road allows a circular driving tour of the peninsula from Portree, passing through the village of **Uig**, where the ferry to the Outer Hebrides departs. The following sights are described travelling anticlockwise from Portree.

◎ **Sights & Activties**

Old Man of Storr   ROCK FORMATION

The 50m-high, pot-bellied pinnacle of crumbling basalt known as the Old Man of Storr is prominent above the road 6 miles north of Portree. Walk up to its foot from the car park in the woods at the northern end of Loch Leathan (round trip 2 miles). This seemingly unclimbable pinnacle was first scaled in 1955 by English mountaineer Don Whillans, a feat that has been repeated only a handful of times since.

Quiraing   ROCK FORMATION

Staffin Bay is dominated by the dramatic basalt escarpment of the Quiraing: its impressive land-slipped cliffs and pinnacles constitute one of Skye's most remarkable landscapes. From a parking area at the highest point of the minor road between Staffin and Uig you can walk north to the Quiraing in half an hour.

Duntulm Castle   CASTLE

Right at the tip of the Trotternish Peninsula is the ruined MacDonald fortress of Duntulm Castle, which was abandoned in 1739, reputedly because it was haunted. The most famous spirit is the gibbering phantom of Hugh MacDonald, a local noble who was imprisoned in the dungeon for trying to seize Trotternish.

Skye Museum of Island Life   MUSEUM

(☎01470-552206; www.skyemuseum.co.uk; adult/child £2.50/50p; ☺9.30am-5pm Mon-Sat Easter-Oct) The peat-reek of crofting life in the 18th and 19th centuries is preserved in the thatched cottages, croft houses, barns and farm implements of the Skye Museum of Island Life. Behind the museum is Kilmuir Cemetery, where a tall Celtic cross marks the **grave of Flora MacDonald**; the cross was erected in 1955 to replace the original monument, of which 'every fragment was removed by tourists'.

Fairy Glen   NATURAL FORMATION

Just south of Uig, a minor road (signposted 'Sheader and Balnaknock') leads in a mile or so to the Fairy Glen, a strange and enchanting natural landscape of miniature conical hills, rocky towers, ruined cottages and a tiny roadside lochan.

🛏 Sleeping & Eating

Dun Flodigarry Hostel   HOSTEL £

(☎01470-552212; www.hostelflodigarry.co.uk; Flodigarry; dm/tw £17/38, campsite per person £9; P @) A bright and welcoming hostel that enjoys a stunning location above the sea, with views across Raasay to the mainland mountains. A nearby hiking trail leads to the Quiraing (2.5 miles away), and there's a hotel bar barely 100m from the door. You can also camp nearby and use all the hostel facilities.

Uig SYHA   HOSTEL £

(☎01470-542746; Uig; dm £17.50; ☺Apr-Sep; P @) Sociable hostel with fantastic sunset views over Uig Bay. You have to vacate the place between 10.30am and 5pm, even when it's raining!

Isle of Raasay

POP 160

Raasay (www.raasay.com) is the rugged, 10-mile-long island that lies off Skye's east coast. There are several good walks here, including one to the flat-topped conical hill of **Dun Caan** (443m). The Forestry Commission publishes a free leaflet (available from the tourist offices) with suggested walking trails.

The extraordinary ruin of **Brochel Castle**, perched on a pinnacle at the northern end of Raasay, was home to Calum Garbh MacLeod, an early 16th-century pirate.

Set in a rustic cottage high on the hill overlooking Skye, Raasay SYHA (☎01478-660240; Creachan Cottage; dm £18; ☺mid-May-Aug) is a fair walk from the ferry pier (2.5 miles) but is a good base for exploring the island. Raasay House (☎01478-660266; www .raasay-house.co.uk; s/d £79/89, dm £30, tent per person £6), currently undergoing a major renovation (but now open to the public), provides outdoor-activity courses, a campsite and hotel and bunkhouse accommodation.

A CalMac ferry (www.calmac.co.uk; passenger/car £7.25/39 return) runs from Sconser, on the road from Portree to Broadford, to the southern end of Raasay (15 minutes, hourly Monday to Saturday, twice daily Sunday). There are no petrol stations on the island.

OUTER HEBRIDES

POP 26.500

A professor of Spanish and a professor of Gaelic met at a conference and began discussing the relative merits of their respective languages. 'Tell me, ' said the Spanish professor, 'do you have a Gaelic equivalent for the Spanish phrase *mañana, mañana?*' The Hebridean professor thought for a while, then replied, 'No, I do not think that we have in the Gaelic a word that conveys such a pressing sense of urgency'.

An old joke perhaps, but one that hints at the slower pace of life you can expect to find in the Gaelic-speaking communities of the Western Isles, a place where the morning papers arrive in the afternoon and almost everything – in Lewis and Harris at least – closes down on Sunday.

The Western Isles, or Na h-Eileanan an Iar in Gaelic – also known as the Outer Hebrides – are a 130-mile-long string of islands lying off the northwest coast of Scotland. There are 119 islands in total, of which the five main inhabited islands are Lewis and Harris (two parts of a single island, although often described as if they are separate islands), North Uist, Benbecula, South Uist and Barra. The middle three (often referred to simply as 'the Uists') are connected by road-bearing causeways.

The ferry crossing from Ullapool or Uig to the Western Isles marks an important cultural divide – more than a third of Scotland's registered crofts are in the Outer Hebrides, and no less than 60% of the population are Gaelic speakers. The rigours of life in the old island blackhouses are still within living memory.

Religion still plays a prominent part in public and private life, especially in the Protestant north, where shops and pubs close their doors on Sundays and some accommodation providers prefer guests not to arrive or depart on the Sabbath. The Roman Catholic south is a little more relaxed about these things.

The name Hebrides is not Gaelic, and is probably a corruption of Ebudae, the Roman name for the islands. But the alternative derivation from the Norse *havbredey* ('isles at the edge of the sea') has a much more poetic ring, alluding to the broad vistas of sky and sea that characterise the islands' often bleak and treeless landscapes. But there is beauty here too, in the machair (grassy, wildflower-speckled dunes) and dazzling white-sand beaches, majesty in the rugged hills and sprawling lochs, and mystery in the islands' fascinating past. It's a past evidenced by neolithic standing stones, Viking place names, deserted crofts and folk memories of the Clearances.

If your time is limited, head straight for the west coast of Lewis with its prehistoric sites, preserved blackhouses and beautiful beaches. As with Skye, the islands are dotted with arts and crafts studios – the tourist offices can provide a list.

❶ Information

Internet Access
Barra Community Library (☎01871-810471; Community School; ☺9am-4.30pm Mon & Wed, 9am-4.30pm & 6-8pm Tue & Thu, 9am-3.30pm Fri, 10am-12.30pm Sat) Free internet access.

Stornoway Public Library (☎01851-708631; 19 Cromwell St; ☺10am-5pm Mon-Wed & Sat, to 6pm Thu & Fri) Free internet access.

Internet Resources
CalMac (www.calmac.co.uk) Ferry timetables.
Visit Hebrides (www.visithebrides.com)

Medical Services
Uist & Barra Hospital (☎01870-603603)
Western Isles Hospital (☎01851-704704; MacAulay Rd)

Money
There are banks with ATMs in Stornoway (Lewis), Tarbert (Harris), Lochmaddy (North Uist), Balivanich (Benbecula), Lochboisdale (South Uist) and Castlebay (Barra). Elsewhere, some hotels and shops offer cash-back facilities.

Tourist Information
Castlebay Information Centre (☎01871-810336; Main St, Castlebay; ☺9am-1pm & 2-5pm Mon-Sat, noon-4pm Sun Apr-Oct)

Lochboisdale Information Centre (☎01878-700286; Pier Rd; ☺9am-1pm & 2-5pm Fri-Mon & Wed, 9am-9.30pm Tue & Thu Apr-Oct)

Stornoway Information Centre (☎01851-703088; www.visithebrides.com; 26 Cromwell St; ☺9am-6pm & 8-9pm Mon, Tue & Thu, 9am-8pm Wed & Fri, 9am-5.30pm & 8-9pm Sat year-round)

Tarbert Tourist Office (☎01859-502011; Pier Rd, Tarbert; ☺9am-5pm Mon-Sat, plus 8-9pm Tue, Thu & Sat Apr-Oct)

❶ Getting There & Away

Air
There are airports at Stornoway (Lewis), Benbecula and Barra. There are flights to Stornoway from Edinburgh, Inverness, Glasgow and Aberdeen. There are also two flights a day (weekdays only) between Stornoway and Benbecula.

There are daily flights from Glasgow to Barra and Benbecula, and from Inverness to Benbecula. At Barra, the planes land on the hard-sand beach at low tide, so the timetable depends on the tides.

Eastern Airways (☎0870 366 9100; www.easternairways.com)

FlyBe/Loganair (☎01857-873457; www.loganair.co.uk)

Boat
Standard one-way fares:

CROSSING	DURATION (HOURS)	CAR	DRIVER/ PASSENGER
Ullapool– Stornoway	2¾	£43	£8.40
Uig– Lochmaddy	1¾	£26	£5.70
Uig–Tarbet	1½	£26	£5.70
Oban– Castlebay	4¾	£57	£12.60
Oban– Lochboisdale	6¾	£57	£12.60

There are two or three ferries a day to Stornoway, one or two a day to Tarbert and Lochmaddy, and one a day to Castlebay and Lochboisdale. You can also take the ferry from Lochboisdale to Castlebay (car/passenger £21.65/7.50, 1½ hours, one daily Monday, Tuesday and Thursday) and from Castlebay to Lochboisdale (one daily Wednesday, Friday and Sunday).

Advance booking for cars is essential in July and August; foot and bicycle passengers should have no problems. Bicycles are carried free.

❶ Getting Around
Despite their separate names, Lewis and Harris are actually one island. Berneray, North Uist, Benbecula, South Uist and Eriskay are all linked by road bridges and causeways. There are car ferries between Leverburgh (Harris) and Berneray; Tarbert (Harris) and Lochmaddy (North Uist); Eriskay and Castlebay (Barra); and Lochboisdale (South Uist) and Castlebay (Barra).

The local council publishes timetables of all bus, ferry and air services in the Outer Hebrides, available at tourist offices. Timetables can also be found online at www.cne-siar.gov.uk /travel.

Bicycle

Many visiting cyclists plan to cycle the length of the archipelago, but if you're one of them, remember that the wind is often strong (you may hear stories of people pedalling downhill and freewheeling uphill), and the prevailing direction is from the southwest – so south to north is usually the easier direction. There are few serious hills, except for a stiff climb on the main road just north of Tarbert.

Bikes can be hired for around £15 a day or £60 to £80 a week in Stornoway (Lewis), Uig (Lewis), Leverburgh (Harris), Howmore (South Uist) and Castlebay (Barra).

Harris Outdoor Adventure (☑07788 425157; www.harrisoutdoor.co.uk; Pier Rd, Leverburgh) Can deliver bikes to your accommodation.

Rothan Cycles (☑07740 364093; www.rothan. com; Howmore, South Uist) Offers a delivery and pick-up service at various points between Eriskay and Stornoway.

Bus

The bus network covers almost every village in the islands, with around four to six buses a day on all the main routes; however, there are no buses at all on Sunday. You can pick up timetables from tourist offices, or call **Stornoway bus station** (☑01851-704327) for information.

Car & Motorcycle

Apart from the fast, two-lane road between Tarbert and Stornoway, most roads are single track. The main hazard is posed by sheep wandering about or sleeping on the road. Petrol stations are far apart (almost all of those on Lewis and Harris are closed on Sunday), and fuel is about 10% more expensive than on the mainland.

There are petrol stations at Stornoway, Barvas, Borve, Uig, Breacleit (Great Bernera), Ness, Tarbert and Leverburgh on Lewis and Harris; Lochmaddy and Cladach on North Uist; Balivanich on Benbecula; Howmore, Lochboisdale and Daliburgh on South Uist; and Castlebay on Barra.

Cars can be hired from around £30 per day.

Arnol Motors (☑018510-710548; www.arnol motors.com; Arnol, Lewis; ◷Mon-Sat)

Lewis Car Rentals (☑01851-703760; www. lewis-car-rental.co.uk; 52 Bayhead St, Stornoway; ◷Mon-Sat)

Lewis (Leodhais)

POP 18,600

The northern part of Lewis is dominated by the desolate expanse of the Black Moor, a vast, undulating peat bog dimpled with glittering lochans, seen clearly from the Stornoway–Barvas road. But Lewis' finest scenery is on the west coast, from Barvas southwest

to Mealista, where the rugged landscape of hill, loch and sandy strand is reminiscent of the northwestern Highlands. The Outer Hebrides' most evocative historic sites – Callanish Standing Stones, Dun Carloway and Arnol Blackhouse Museum – are also to be found here.

The old blackhouses of this region may have been abandoned, but an increasing number are being restored as holiday homes. Most crofts still follow a traditional pattern dating back to medieval times, with narrow strips of land, designed to give all an equal share of good and bad soil, running from the foreshore (with its valuable seaweed, used as fertiliser), across the machair (the grassy sand dunes that provide the best arable land) to the poorer sheep-grazing land on hill or moor. Today few crofts are economically viable, so most islanders supplement their income with fishing, tweed-weaving and work on oil rigs and fish farms.

STORNOWAY (STORNABHAGH)

POP 6000

Stornoway is the bustling 'capital' of the Outer Hebrides and the only real town in the whole archipelago. It's a surprisingly busy little place, with cars and people swamping the centre on weekdays. Though set on a beautiful natural harbour, the town isn't going to win any prizes for beauty or atmosphere, but it's a pleasant enough introduction to this remote corner of the country. It's a bit of a ghost town on Sundays, especially from 11am to 12.30pm, when almost everyone is at church.

◉ Sights

FREE **An Lanntair Art Centre** ARTS CENTRE
(☑01851-703307; www.lanntair.com; Kenneth St; ◷10am-9pm Mon-Wed, to 10pm Thu, to midnight Fri & Sat) The modern, purpose-built An Lanntair Art Centre, complete with art gallery, theatre, cinema and restaurant, is the centre of the town's cultural life; it hosts changing exhibitions of contemporary art and is a good source of information on cultural events.

FREE **Museum nan Eilean** MUSEUM
(☑01851-703773; Francis St; ◷10am-5.30pm Mon-Sat, shorter hours in winter) This museum strings together a loose history of the Outer Hebrides from the earliest human settlements some 9000 years ago to the 20th century, exploring traditional island life and the changes inflicted by progress and technology.

KEEPING THE SABBATH

Religion still plays a major role in island life, especially on predominantly Protestant Lewis and Harris, where the Sabbath is still widely observed by members of the 'free churches'.

The Calvinist Free Church of Scotland (known as the 'Wee Frees') and the even more fundamentalist Free Presbyterian Church of Scotland (the 'Wee Wee Frees'), which split from the established Church of Scotland in 1843 and 1893 respectively, are deeply conservative, permitting no ornaments, organ music or choirs in church. Their ministers deliver uncompromising sermons (usually in Gaelic) from central pulpits and precentors lead the congregation in unaccompanied but fervent psalm singing. Visitors are welcome to attend services, but due respect is essential.

The Protestants of the Outer Hebrides have succeeded in maintaining a distinctive fundamentalist approach to their religion, with Sunday being devoted largely to religious services, prayer and Bible reading. On Lewis and Harris, the last bastion of Sabbath observance in the UK, almost everything closes down on a Sunday. In fact, Stornoway must be the only place in the UK to suffer a Sunday rush hour as people drive to church around 10.30am; it's then a ghost town for an hour and a half until the services are over. But a few cracks have begun to appear.

There was outrage when British Airways/Loganair introduced Sunday flights from Edinburgh and Inverness to Stornoway in 2002, with members of the Lord's Day Observance Society spluttering that this was the thin end of the wedge. They were probably right – in 2003 a Stornoway petrol station began to open on a Sunday, and now does a roaring trade in Sunday papers and takeaway booze. Then in 2006 the CalMac ferry from Berneray to Leverburgh in Harris started a Sunday service, despite strong opposition from the residents of Harris (ironically, they were unable to protest at the ferry's arrival, as that would have meant breaking the Sabbath).

Lews Castle
CASTLE

The Baronial mansion across the harbour from Stornoway town centre was built in the 1840s for the Matheson family, then owners of Lewis. The beautiful wooded grounds, criss-crossed with walking trails, are open to the public and host the Hebridean Celtic Festival (p406).

The castle was gifted to the community by Lord Leverhulme in 1923 and was home to the local college for 40 years, but has lain empty since 1997 (the college now occupies modern buildings in the castle grounds); it is now slated for development as a museum and hotel.

Lewis Loom Centre
EXHIBITION

(☎01851-704500; 3 Bayhead; adult/child £1/50p; ☉9.30am-5.30pm Mon-Sat) This centre houses an exhibition on the history of Harris Tweed; the 40-minute guided tour (£2.50 extra) includes spinning and weaving demonstrations.

✦ Festivals

Hebridean Celtic Festival   MUSIC FESTIVAL

(www.hebceltfest.com) A four-day extravaganza of folk/rock/Celtic music held in the second half of July.

⮡ Sleeping

Hal o' the Wynd   B&B ££

(☎01851-706073; www.halothewynd.com; 2 Newton St; s/d from £45/60) Touches of tartan and Harris Tweed lend a tradtional air to this welcoming B&B, conveniently located directly opposite the ferry pier. Most rooms have views over the harbour to Lews Castle.

Braighe House   B&B ££

(☎01851-705287; www.braighehouse.co.uk; 20 Braighe Rd; s/d from £95/130; Ⓟ) This spacious and comfortable guest house, 3 miles east of the town centre on the A866, has stylish, modern bedrooms and a great seafront location. Good bathrooms with powerful showers, hearty breakfasts and hospitable owners round off the perfect package.

Park Guest House   B&B ££

(☎01851-702485; www.theparkguesthouse.co.uk; 30 James St; s/d from £58/110; @) A charming Victorian villa with a conservatory and eight luxurious rooms (mostly en suite), the Park Guest House is comfortable and central and has the advantage of an excellent restaurant specialising in Scottish seafood, beef and game (plus one or two vegetarian dishes). Rooms overlooking the main road can be noisy on weekday mornings.

Royal Hotel
HOTEL ££

(☎01851-702109; www.royalstornoway.co.uk; Cromwell St; s/d £87/133; P🛜) The 19th-century Royal is the most appealing of Stornoway's hotels – the rooms at the front retain period features such as wood panelling, and enjoy a view across the harbour to Lews Castle. Ask to see your room first, though, as some are a bit cramped.

Heb Hostel
HOSTEL £

(☎01851-709889; www.hebhostel.co.uk; 25 Kenneth St; dm £16; @🛜) The Heb is a friendly, easygoing hostel close to the ferry, with comfy wooden bunks, a convivial living room with peat fire and a welcoming owner who can provide all kinds of advice on what to do and where to go.

Laxdale Holiday Park
CAMPSITE £

(☎01851-703234; www.laxdaleholidaypark.com; 6 Laxdale Lane; tent sites £7-9, plus per person £3.50; ⊘Apr-Oct; 🛜) This campsite, 1.5 miles north of town off the A857, has a sheltered woodland setting, though the tent area is mostly on a slope – get there early for a level pitch. There's also a bunkhouse (£15.50 per person) that stays open year-round.

✖ Eating

🔼TOP CHOICE Digby Chick
BISTRO £££

(☎01851-700026; www.digbychick.co.uk; 5 Bank St; mains £18-24, 2-course lunch £12.50; ⊘lunch & dinner Mon-Sat) A modern restaurant that dishes up bistro cuisine such as haddock and chips, slow-roast pork belly or spiced cauliflower and spinach fritter at lunchtime, the Digby Chick metamorphoses into a candlelit restaurant in the evening, serving dishes such as grilled langoustines, seared scallops, venison and steak. Three-course early-bird menu (5.30pm to 6.30pm) for £18.

An Lanntair Art Centre Café
BISTRO ££

(Kenneth St; mains lunch £6-10, dinner £8-16; ⊘cafe 10am-late, lunch & dinner Mon-Sat; 🛜♿) The stylish and family-friendly restaurant at the art centre serves a broad range of freshly prepared dishes, from tasty bacon rolls at breakfast to burgers, baguettes or fish and chips for lunch, and Thai curry, beef-and-Guinness pie or nut roast for dinner.

Thai Café
THAI £

(☎01851-701811; www.thai-cafe-stornoway.co.uk; 27 Church St; mains £5-8; ⊘noon-2.30pm & 5.30-11pm Mon-Sat) Here's a surprise – authentic, inexpensive Thai food in the heart of Stornoway. This spick-and-span little restaurant has a genuine Thai chef and serves some of the most delicious, best-value Asian food in the Hebrides. If you can't get a table, it does takeaway.

❶ Information

Baltic Bookshop (☎01851-702802; 8-10 Cromwell St; ⊘9am-5.30pm Mon-Sat) Good for local history books and maps.

Sandwick Rd Petrol Station (☎01851-702304; Sandwick Rd) The only shop in town that's open on a Sunday (from 10am to 4pm); the Sunday papers arrive around 2pm.

❶ Getting There & Around

The bus station is on the waterfront, next to the ferry terminal (left-luggage desk, 90p per piece). Bus W10 runs from Stornoway to Tarbert (£4.30, one hour, four or five daily Monday to Saturday) and Leverburgh (£6, two hours).

The Westside Circular bus W2 runs a circular route from Stornoway through Callanish, Carloway, Garenin and Arnol; the timetable means you can visit one or two of the sites in a day.

BUTT OF LEWIS (RUBHA ROBHANAIS)

The Butt of Lewis (no snickering, please) – the extreme northern tip of the Hebrides – is windswept and rugged, with a very imposing lighthouse, pounding surf and large colonies of nesting fulmars on the high cliffs. There's a bleak sense of isolation here, with nothing but the grey Atlantic between you and Canada.

Just before the turn-off to the Butt at Eoropie (Eoropaidh), you'll find **St Moluag's Church** (Teampull Mholuidh), an austere, barnlike structure believed to date from the 12th century but still used by the Episcopal Church. The main settlement here is **Port of Ness** (Port Nis), which has an attractive harbour. To the west of the village is the sandy beach of **Traigh**, which is popular with surfers and has a kids' adventure playground nearby.

ARNOL

One of Scotland's most evocative historic buildings, the Arnol Blackhouse (HS; ☎01851-710395; adult/child £3.25/free; ⊘9.30am-5.30pm Mon-Sat Apr-Sep, to 4.30pm Mon-Sat Oct-Mar, last admission 30min before closing) is not so much a museum as a perfectly preserved fragment of a lost world. Built in 1885, this traditional blackhouse – a combined byre, barn and home – was inhabited until 1964 and has not been changed since the last inhabitant moved out. The staff faithfully rekindle the central peat fire every morning so you can experience the distinctive peat-reek; there's no chimney, and the smoke finds its own way out through the turf roof, windows and door – spend too long inside and you might feel like you've been kippered! The museum is just off the A858, about 3 miles west of Barvas.

At nearby **Bragar**, a pair of whalebones forms an arch by the road, with the rusting harpoon that killed the whale dangling from the centre.

GARENIN (NA GEARRANNAN)

The picturesque and fascinating **Gearrannan Blackhouse Village** is a cluster of nine restored thatch-roofed blackhouses perched above the exposed Atlantic coast. One of the cottages is home to the Blackhouse Museum (☑01851-643416; www.gearrannan.com; adult/child £2.70/1; ⊘9.30am-5.30pm Mon-Sat Apr-Sep), a traditional 1955 blackhouse with displays on the village's history, while another houses the Taigh an Chocair Cafe (mains £3-6; ⊘9.30am-5.30pm Mon-Sat).

The other blackhouses in the village are let out as self-catering holiday cottages (☑01851-643416; www.gearrannan.com; 2-person cottages £199 for 3 nights), offering the chance to stay in a unique and luxurious modernised blackhouse with attached kitchen and lounge. There's a minimum five-night stay from June to August.

CARLOWAY (CARLABAGH)

Dun Carloway (Dun Charlabhaigh) is a 2000-year-old, dry-stone broch, perched defiantly above a beautiful loch with views to the mountains of North Harris. The site is clearly signposted along a minor road off the A858, a mile southwest of Carloway village. One of the best-preserved brochs in Scotland, its double walls (with internal staircase) still stand to a height of 9m and testify to the engineering skills of its Iron Age architects.

The tiny, turf-roofed Doune Broch Centre (☑01851-643338; admission free; ⊘10am-5pm Mon-Sat Apr-Sep) nearby has interpretative displays and exhibitions about the history of the broch and the life of the people who lived there.

CALLANISH (CALANAIS)

The **Callanish Standing Stones**, 15 miles west of Stornoway on the A858 road, form one of the most complete stone circles in Britain. It is one of the most atmospheric prehistoric sites anywhere; its ageless mystery, impressive scale and undeniable beauty leave a lasting impression. Sited on a wild and secluded promontory overlooking Loch Roag, 13 large stones of beautifully banded gneiss are arranged, as if in worship, around a 4.5m-tall central monolith. Some 40 smaller stones radiate from the circle in the shape of a cross, with the remains of a chambered tomb at the centre. Dating from 3800 to 5000 years ago, the stones are roughly contemporary with the pyramids of Egypt.

The nearby Calanais Visitor Centre (☑01851-621422; www.callanishvisitorcentre.co.uk; admission free, exhibition £2.50; ⊘10am-9pm Mon-Sat Apr-Sep, to 4pm Wed-Sat Oct-Mar; P) is a tour de force of discreet design. Inside is a small exhibition that speculates on the origins and purpose of the stones, and an excellent cafe (mains £5-7).

If you plan to stay the night, you have a choice of Eshcol Guest House (☑01851-621357; www.eshcol.com; 21 Breascleit; r per person £43; P) and neighbouring Loch Roag Guest House (☑01851-621357; www.lochroag.com; 22a Breascleit; r per person £40-55; P), half a mile north of Callanish. Both are modern bungalows with the same friendly owner, who is very knowledgeable about the local area.

GREAT BERNERA

This rocky island is connected to Lewis by a bridge built by the local council in 1953 – the islanders had originally planned to destroy a small hill with explosives and use the material to build their own causeway. On a sunny day, it's worth making the long detour to the island's northern tip for a picnic at the perfect little sandy beach of **Bosta** (Bostadh).

In 1996 archaeologists excavated an entire Iron Age village at the head of the beach. Afterwards, the village was reburied for protection, but a reconstruction of an Iron Age house (☑01851-612331; Bosta; adult/child £2.50/50p; ⊘noon-4pm Mon-Fri May-Sep) now sits nearby. Stand around the peat fire, with strips of mutton being smoked above, while the custodian explains the domestic arrangements – truly fascinating, and well worth the trip.

There are five buses a day between Stornoway and the hamlet of Breacleit (one hour, Monday to Saturday) on Great Bernera; two or three a day will continue to Bosta on request. Alternatively, there's a signposted 5-mile **coastal walk** from Breacleit to Bosta.

MIAVAIG (MIAGHAIG) & MEALISTA (MEALASTA)

The B8011 road (signposted Uig, on the A858 Stornoway–Callanish road) from Garrynahine to Timsgarry (Timsgearraidh) meanders through scenic wilderness to some of Scotland's most stunning beaches. At **Miavaig**, a loop road detours north through the Bhaltos Estate to the pretty, mile-long white strand of **Reef Beach**; there's a basic campsite (per person £2) in the machair behind the beach.

From April to September, SeaTrek (☎01851-672469; www.seatrek.co.uk; Miavaig Pier) runs two-hour boat trips (adult/child £35/25, Monday to Saturday) in a high-speed RIB to spot seals and nesting seabirds. In June and July it also runs more adventurous, all-day trips (£90 per person, two per month) in a large motor boat to the **Flannan Isles**, a remote group of tiny, uninhabited islands 25 miles northwest of Lewis. Puffins, seals and a ruined 7th-century chapel are the main attractions, but the isles are most famous for the mystery of the three lighthouse keepers who disappeared without trace in December 1900. There's also a 12-hour round trip to remote **St Kilda** (£180, once or twice weekly, May to September, weather permitting).

From Miavaig the road continues west through a rocky defile to Timsgarry and the vast, sandy expanse of **Traigh Uige** (Uig Sands). The famous 12th-century **Lewis chess pieces**, made of walrus ivory, were discovered in the sand dunes here in 1831. Of the 78 pieces, 67 are in the British Museum in London, with 11 in Edinburgh's National Museum of Scotland (p58); you can buy replicas at various outlets on the isle of Lewis.

There's a very basic campsite (per person £2) on the south side of the bay (signposted 'Ardroil Beach'; toilet only, no showers) and a superb guest house, Baile-na-Cille (☎01851-672242; www.bailenacille.co.uk; Timsgarry, Uig; per person £55), on the north side.

At the southwestern end of Traighe Uig is Auberge Carnish (☎01851-672459; www.aubergecarnish.co.uk; Carnais; s/d from £85/120), a beautifully designed timber building that houses a luxury B&B and restaurant with a stunning outlook over the sands.

The minor road that continues south from Timsgarry to **Mealista** passes a few smaller, but still spectacular, white-sand and boulder beaches on the way to a remote dead end; on a clear day you can see St Kilda on the horizon.

Harris (Na Hearadh)

POP 2000

Harris, to the south of Lewis, is the scenic jewel in the necklace of islands that comprise the Outer Hebrides. It has a spectacular blend of rugged mountains, pristine beaches, flower-speckled machair and barren rocky landscapes. The isthmus at Tarbert splits Harris neatly in two: North Harris is dominated by mountains that rise forbiddingly above the peat moors to the south of Stornoway – Clisham (799m) is the highest point. South Harris is lower-lying, fringed by beautiful white-sand beaches in the west and a convoluted rocky coastline to the east.

Harris is famous for Harris Tweed, a high-quality woollen cloth still hand-woven in islanders' homes. The industry employs around 400 weavers; staff at Tarbert tourist office can tell you about weavers and workshops you can visit.

TARBERT (AN TAIRBEART)

POP 480

Tarbert is a harbour village with a spectacular location, tucked into the narrow neck of land that links North and South Harris. It has ferry connections to Uig on Skye.

Village facilities include a petrol station, bank, ATM and two general stores.

🛏 Sleeping & Eating

Hotel Hebrides   HOTEL **££**
(☎01859-502364; www.hotel-hebrides.com; Pier Rd; s/d from £50/130; ⑨) The location and setting don't look promising – a nondescript new building squeezed between ferry pier and car park – but this modern establishment brings a dash of urban glamour to Harris, with flashy fabrics and wall coverings, luxurious towels and toiletries, and a stylish restaurant and lounge bar.

Harris Hotel   HOTEL **££**
(☎01859-502154; www.harrishotel.com; s/d from £65/98; P@⑨) Run since 1903 by four generations of the Cameron family, Harris Hotel is a 19th-century sporting hotel, originally built for deer stalkers visiting the North Harris Estates. It has spacious, comfy rooms and a good restaurant; look out for JM Barrie's initials scratched on the dining-room window (the author of *Peter Pan* visited in the 1920s).

The hotel is on the way out of the village, on the road north towards Stornoway.

Tigh na Mara   B&B £

(☑01859-502270; www.tigh-na-mara.co.uk; East Tarbert; per person £25-30; **P**) Excellent-value B&B (though the single room is a bit cramped) just five minutes from the ferry – go up the hill above the tourist office and turn right. The owner bakes fresh cakes every day, which you can enjoy in the conservatory with a view over the bay.

First Fruits   CAFE £

(☑01880-502439; Pier Rd; mains £3-10; ⊙10am-4pm Mon-Sat Apr-Sep) This is a cosy little cottage tearoom near the tourist office – handy while you wait for a ferry.

NORTH HARRIS

Magnificent North Harris is the most mountainous region of the Outer Hebrides. There are few roads here, but many opportunities for climbing, walking and birdwatching.

The B887 leads west, from a point 3 miles north of Tarbert, to **Hushinish**, where there's a lovely silver-sand beach. Along the way the road passes an **old whaling station**, one of Lord Leverhulme's failed development schemes, and the impressive shooting lodge of **Amhuinnsuidhe Castle**, now an exclusive hotel. Between the two, at Miavaig, a parking area and gated track gives hikers access to a **golden-eagle observatory**, a 1.3-mile walk north from the road.

Just northwest of Hushinish is the uninhabited island of **Scarp**, the scene of bizarre attempts to send mail by rocket in 1934, a story that was recounted in the movie *The Rocket Post* (2001), which was shot in Harris.

Rhenigidale Crofters' Hostel (www.gatliff.org.uk; Rhenigidale; dm adult/child £12/7) can be reached on foot from Tarbert (6 miles, allow three hours). It's an excellent walk, but take all the necessary supplies for a mountain hike (map, compass, protective clothing etc). Take the road towards Kyles Scalpay for 2 miles and, at a bend in the road just beyond Laxdale Lochs, veer off to the left on a signposted track across the hills (marked on Ordnance Survey maps). The hostel is a small white cottage standing above the road on the eastern side of the glen; the warden lives in the house closest to the shore.

The remote hamlet of Rhenigidale can also be reached by road; bus W11 (request service) will take you there from Tarbert (30 minutes, two a day Monday to Saturday), but you'll have to book in advance (01859-502871).

SOUTH HARRIS

The west coast of South Harris has some of the most beautiful beaches in Scotland. The blinding white sands and turquoise waters of **Luskentyre** and **Scarasta** would be major holiday resorts if they were transported to somewhere with a warm climate; as it is, they're usually deserted.

The **east coast** is a complete contrast to the west – a strange, rocky moonscape of naked gneiss pocked with tiny lochans, the bleakness lightened by the occasional splash of green around the few crofting communities. Film buffs will know that the psychedelic sequences depicting an alien landscape in *2001: A Space Odyssey* were shot from an aircraft flying low over the east coast of Harris.

The narrow, twisting road that winds its way along this coast is known locally as the **Golden Road**, because of the vast amount of money it cost per mile. It was built in the 1930s to link all the tiny communities known as 'The Bays'.

◉ Sights & Activities

Seallam! Visitor Centre   VISITOR CENTRE

(www.seallam.com; Northton; adult/child £2.50/2; ⊙10am-5pm Mon-Sat) The culture and landscape of the Hebrides are celebrated in the fascinating exhibition at Seallam! Visitor Centre. *Seallam* is Gaelic for 'Let me show you'. The centre, which is in Northton, just south of Scarasta, also has a genealogical research centre for people who want to trace their Hebridean ancestry.

FREE **St Clement's Church**   HISTORIC BUILDING

(Rodel) At the southernmost tip of the east coast of Harris stands the impressive 16th-century St Clement's Church, built by Alexander MacLeod of Dunvegan between the 1520s and 1550s, only to be abandoned after the Reformation. The fortified construction leaves little doubt that the church was built in troubled times.

There are several fine **tombs** inside the echoing stone hall, including the cenotaph of Alexander MacLeod, carved with hunting scenes, a castle, a birlinn (the traditional longboat of the islands) and various saints, including St Clement clutching a skull.

Leverburgh   VILLAGE

(An t-Ob; www.leverburgh.co.uk) The village of Leverburgh is named after Lord Leverhulme (creator of Sunlight Soap, and founder of Unilever), who bought Lewis and Harris in

1918. He had grand plans for An t-Ob, as Leverburgh was then known – it was to be a major fishing port with a population of 10,000 – but the plans died with him in 1925 and the village reverted to a sleepy backwater.

Kilda Cruises BOAT TOUR
(☎01859-502060; www.kildacruises.co.uk; Leverburgh Pier; per person £190; ⏲Apr-Sep) Operates 12-hour day trips to St Kilda (three hours each way, with six hours ashore; weather dependent), as well as customised cruises. Must be booked in advance.

Sleeping & Eating

Carminish Guest House B&B ££
(☎01859-520400; www.carminish.com; 1a Strond, Leverburgh; s/d £55/75; P 📶) One of the few B&Bs in Harris that is open all year, the welcoming Carminish is a modern house with three comfy bedrooms. There's a view of the ferry from the dining room, and lots of nice little touches such as handmade soaps, a carafe of drinking water in the bedroom and individual reading lamps above the beds.

Sorrel Cottage B&B ££
(☎01859-520319; www.sorrelcottage.co.uk; 2 Glen, Leverburgh; s/d from £45/70; 🐾) Sorrel Cottage is a pretty crofter's house, about 1.5 miles west of the ferry at Leverburgh. Evening meals can be provided (£18 a head), and vegetarians and vegans are happily catered for. Bike hire available.

Rodel Hotel INN ££
(☎01859-520210; www.rodelhotel.co.uk; Rodel; s/d from £79/130; P) Don't be put off by the rather grey and grim-looking exterior of this remote hotel – the interior has been refurbished to a high standard and offers four large, luxurious bedrooms; the one called Iona (a twin room) has the best view, across the little harbour towards Skye.

The hotel **restaurant** (mains £11-19; ⏲5.30-9.30pm) serves delicious local seafood and game, with dishes such as local scallops with a white wine and cream sauce.

Am Bothan HOSTEL £
(☎01859-520251; www.ambothan.com; Ferry Rd, Leverburgh; dm £20; P 📶) An attractive, chalet-style hostel, Am Bothan has small, neat dorms and a great porch where you can enjoy morning coffee with views over the creek. The hostel offers bike hire and can arrange wildlife-watching boat trips.

Lickisto Blackhouse Camping CAMPSITE £
(☎01859-530485; www.freewebs.com/vanvon; Liceasto; tent sites per adult/child £12/6, yurts £70) Remote and rustic campsite on an old croft, with pitches set among heather and outcrops with chickens running wild. Campers can use a communal kitchen/lounge in a converted blackhouse, and there's a yurt with double futon and gas stove (no electricity). Bus W13 from Tarbert to Leverburgh stops at the entrance.

Skoon Art Café CAFE £
(☎01859-530268; www.skoon.com; Geocrab; mains £4-7; ⏲10am-4.30pm Tue-Sat Mar-Oct, noon-4pm Wed-Sat Nov-22 Dec, lunch served 11am-4pm) Set halfway along the Golden Road, this neat little art gallery doubles as an excellent cafe serving delicious homemade soups, sandwiches, cakes and desserts (try the marmalade and ginger cake).

Getting There & Around

A **CalMac** (www.calmac.co.uk) car ferry zigzags through the reefs of the Sound of Harris from Leverburgh to Berneray (pedestrian/car £6.95/31.50, 1¼ hours, three or four daily Monday to Saturday).

There are two to four buses a day (except Sunday) from Tarbert to Leverburgh; W10 takes the main road along the west coast, while W13 winds along the Golden Road on the east.

Berneray (Bearnaraigh)

POP 140

Berneray was linked to North Uist by a causeway in 1998, but that hasn't altered the peace and beauty of the island. The **beaches** on its west coast are some of the most unspoilt in Britain, and seals and otters can be seen in Bays Loch on the east coast.

The basic but atmospheric **Gatliff Hostel** (www.gatliff.org.uk; dm adult/child £12/7, camping per person £7), housed in a pair of restored blackhouses right by the sea, is the place to stay. You can camp outside, or on the grass above the gorgeous beach just to the north.

In summer snacks are available at the **Lobster Pot** (⏲9am-5.30pm Mon-Sat), the tearoom attached to Ardmarree Stores (a grocery shop near the causeway). The **Nurse's Cottage** (www.isleofberneray.com; ⏲11am-3pm Mon-Fri Jun-Aug) provides tourist information.

Bus W19 runs from Berneray (Gatliff Hostel and Harris ferry) to Lochmaddy (30 minutes, six daily Monday to Saturday). There are ferries to Leverburgh (Harris).

North Uist (Uibhist A Tuath)

POP 1550

North Uist, an island half-drowned by lochs, is famed for its trout fishing but also has some magnificent beaches on its north and west coasts. For birdwatchers this is an earthly paradise, with regular sightings of waders and wildfowl ranging from red-shank to red-throated diver to red-necked phalarope. The landscape is less wild and mountainous than Harris but it has a sleepy, subtle appeal.

Little Lochmaddy is the first village you hit after arriving on the ferry from Skye. There's a tourist office, a couple of stores, a bank with an ATM, a petrol station, a post office and a pub.

◉ Sights

Balranald Nature Reserve   WILDLIFE RESERVE
Birdwatchers flock to this Royal Society for the Protection of Birds (RSPB) nature reserve, 18 miles west of Lochmaddy, in the hope of spotting the rare red-necked phalarope or hearing the distinctive call of the corncrake. There's a visitor centre (admission free; ⊘9am-6pm Apr-Aug) with a resident warden who offers 1½-hour guided walks (£5, depart visitor centre 10am Tuesday, May to August).

Taigh Chearsabhagh   ARTS CENTRE, MUSEUM
(☑01876-500293; http://taigh-chearsabhagh.org; Lochmaddy; arts centre free, museum £3; ⊘10am-4pm Mon-Sat) Taigh Chearsabhagh is a museum and arts centre that preserves and displays the history and culture of the Uists, and is also a thriving community centre, post office and meeting place. The centre's **cafe** (mains £3 to £7) dishes up homemade soups, sandwiches and cakes.

Bharpa Langass & Pobull Fhinn   HISTORIC SITES
A waymarked circular path beside the Langass Lodge Hotel (just off the A867, 6 miles southwest of Lochmaddy) leads to the chambered Neolithic burial tomb of **Bharpa Langass** and the stone circle of **Pobull Fhinn** (Finn's People); both are reckoned to be around 5000 years old. There are lovely views over the loch, where you may be able to spot seals and otters.

🛌 Sleeping & Eating

Tigh Dearg Hotel   HOTEL ££
(☑01876-500700; www.tighdearghotel.co.uk; Lochmaddy; s/d from £99/110; ℙ🛜) It looks a little

---

WORTH A TRIP

ST KILDA

St Kilda (www.kilda.org.uk) is a collection of spectacular sea stacks and cliff-bound islands about 45 miles west of North Uist. The largest island, Hirta, measures only 2 miles by 1 mile, with huge cliffs along most of its coastline. Owned by National Trust for Scotland (NTS), the islands are a Unesco World Heritage Site and are the biggest seabird nesting site in the North Atlantic. They are home to more than a million birds.

In addition to watching the bird life, visitors can explore the remains of the settlement at Village Bay, where there's a ranger's office and small museum, and climb to the island's highest point.

History

Hirta was inhabited by a Gaelic-speaking population of around 200 until the 19th century, when the arrival of church missionaries and tourists began the gradual breakdown of St Kilda's traditional way of life. By the 1920s disease and emigration had seen the islands' economy collapse, and the 35 remaining islanders were evacuated, at their own request, in 1930. The people had survived here by keeping sheep, fishing, growing a few basic crops such as barley, and climbing the cliffs barefoot to catch seabirds and collect their eggs. Over the centuries this resulted in a genetic peculiarity – St Kilda men had unusually long big toes.

Getting There & Away

Boat tours to St Kilda are a major undertaking, and depend on the weather – day trips are 12-hour affairs, involving a minimum three-hour crossing each way, often in rough seas. Tour operators include Kilda Cruises (p411) and SeaTrek (p409).

like a hostel from the outside but the 'Red House' (as the name translates) is actually Lochmaddy's most luxurious accommodation, with nine designer bedrooms, a lounge with leather sofas around an open fire, a gym and even a sauna. There's a good restaurant too, with sea views from the terrace.

Old Courthouse B&B **££**
(✆01876-500358; oldcourthouse@googlemail. com; Lochmaddy; r per person from £30; 🅿) This Georgian-style villa is within walking distance of the ferry, on the road that leads to Uist Outdoor Centre. It's a bit worn around the edges but full of character, with traditional porridge for breakfast, homemade marmalade, and kippers on the menu.

Langass Lodge Hotel HOTEL **££**
(✆01876-580285; www.langasslodge.co.uk; Locheport; s/d from £75/109; 🅿🛜) The delightful Langass Lodge Hotel is a former shooting lodge set in splendid isolation overlooking Loch Langais. Refurbished and extended, it now offers a dozen appealing rooms, many with sea views, and one of the Hebrides' best restaurants (2-/3-course dinner £30/36), noted for its fine seafood and game.

❶ Getting There & Around

Buses from Lochmaddy to Berneray, Langass, Clachan na Luib, Benbecula and Lochboisdale run five or six times a day Monday to Saturday.

Benbecula (Beinn Na Faoghla)

POP 1200
Benbecula is a low-lying island with a flat, lochan-studded landscape that's best appreciated from the summit of **Rueval** (124m), the island's highest point. There's a path around the south side of the hill (signposted from the main road; park beside the landfill site) said to be the route taken to the coast by Bonnie Prince Charlie and Flora MacDonald during the prince's escape in 1746.

The control centre for the Ministry of Defence's Hebrides Missile Range (located on the northwestern tip of South Uist) is the island's main source of employment, and Balivanich (Baile a'Mhanaich) – looking like a corner of a Glasgow housing estate planted incongruously on the machair – is the commercial centre serving the staff and their families.

The village has a bank with an ATM, a post office, a large Co-op supermarket (☺8am-8pm Mon-Sat, 11am-6pm Sun) and a

petrol station (open on Sunday). It is also the location of **Benbecula airport**.

South Uist (Uibhist A Deas)

POP 1900
South Uist is the second-largest island in the Outer Hebrides and saves its choicest corners for those who explore away from the main north–south road. The low-lying west coast is an almost unbroken stretch of white-sand beach and flower-flecked machair – a new waymarked hiking trail, the **Machair Way**, follows the coast – while the multitude of inland lochs provide excellent trout fishing. The east coast, riven by four large sea lochs, is hilly and remote, with spectacular **Beinn Mhor** (620m) the highest point.

Driving south from Benbecula you cross from the predominantly Protestant northern half of the Outer Hebrides into the mostly Roman Catholic south, a religious transition marked by the granite statue of **Our Lady of the Isles** on the slopes of Rueval (the hill with the military radomes on its summit) and the presence of many roadside shrines.

The ferry port of **Lochboisdale** is the island's largest settlement, with a tourist office, a bank with an ATM, a grocery store and a petrol station.

◉ Sights & Activties

Loch Druidibeg National Nature Reserve WILDLIFE RESERVE
The northern part of the island is mostly occupied by the watery expanses of Loch Bee and Loch Druidibeg. Loch Druidibeg National Nature Reserve is an important breeding ground for birds such as dunlin, redshank, ringed plover, greylag goose and corncrake; you can take a 5-mile self-guided walk through the reserve.

Pick up a leaflet from the Scottish Natural Heritage office on the main road beside the loch.

Kildonan Museum MUSEUM
(✆01878-710343; www.kildonanmuseum.co.uk; Kildonan; adult/child £2/free; ☺10am-5pm Apr-Oct) Six miles south of Howmore, Kildonan Museum explores the lives of local crofters through its collection of artefacts – an absorbing exhibition of black-and-white photography and first-hand accounts of harsh Hebridean conditions.

There's also an excellent tearoom (mains £3-8; ☺11am-4pm) and craft shop.

Amid Milton's ruined blackhouses, half a mile south of the museum, a cairn marks the site of **Flora MacDonald's birthplace**.

🛏 Sleeping & Eating

TOP CHOICE **Polochar Inn** INN **££**
(☏01878-700215; www.polocharinn.com; Polochar; s/d from £70/90; 🅿) Run by local sisters Morag McKinnon and Margaret Campbell, this 18th-century inn has been transformed into a stylish, welcoming hotel with a stunning location looking out across the sea to Barra. The excellent restaurant and bar menu (mains £8 to £17) includes fish chowder, local salmon and Uist lamb.

Polochar is 7 miles southwest of Lochboisdale, on the way to Eriskay.

Wireless Cottage B&B **£**
(☏01878-700660; www.wirelesscottage.co.uk; Lochboisdale; per person £25) This pretty little cottage, whic once housed the local telephone exchange, is now a welcoming and good-value B&B a short (300m) walk from the ferry, with just two bedrooms (one double, one family).

Lochside Cottage B&B **££**
(☏01878-700472;www.lochside-cottage.co.uk;Loch boisdale; r per person £30; 🅿🛜) Lochside Cottage is a friendly B&B, 1.5 miles west of the ferry, and has rooms with views and a sun lounge barely a fishing-rod's length from its own trout loch.

Tobha Mor Crofters' Hostel HOSTEL **£**
(www.gatliff.org.uk; Howmore; dm adult/child £12/7) Atmospheric hostel housed in a restored thatched blackhouse, about 6 miles south of Loch Druidibeg.

ℹ Getting There & Around

CalMac (www.calmac.co.uk) ferries run between Lochmaddy and Uig (Skye), and Lochboisdale and Oban.

Bus W17 runs about four times a day (not Sunday) between Berneray and Eriskay via Lochmaddy, Balivanich and Lochboisdale. The trip from Lochmaddy to Lochboisdale (£4.70) takes one hour 40 minutes.

Eriskay (Eiriosgaigh)

POP 170

In 1745 Bonnie Prince Charlie first set foot in Scotland on the west coast of Eriskay, on the sandy beach (immediately north of the ferry terminal) still known as **Prince's Strand** (Coilleag a'Phrionnsa).

More recently the SS *Politician* sank just off the island in 1941. The islanders salvaged much of its cargo of around 250,000 bottles of whisky and, after a binge of dramatic proportions, the police intervened and a number of the islanders landed in jail. The story was immortalised by Sir Compton Mackenzie in his comic novel *Whisky Galore,* later made into a famous film.

A CalMac (p411) car ferry (pedestrian/car £7.50/21.65, 40 minutes, four or five daily) links Eriskay with Ardmhor at the northern end of Barra.

Barra (Barraigh)

POP 1150

With its beautiful **beaches**, wildflower-clad dunes, rugged little hills and strong sense of community, diminutive Barra – just 14 miles in circumference – is the Outer Hebrides in miniature. For a great view of the island, walk up to the top of **Heaval** (383m), a mile northeast of Castlebay.

Castlebay (Bagh a'Chaisteil), in the south, is the largest village. There's a tourist office (p404), a bank with an ATM, a post office and two grocery stores.

⦿ Sights

Kisimul Castle CASTLE
(HS; ☏01871-810313; Castlebay; adult/child incl ferry £5/3; ⏱9.30am-5.30pm Apr-Sep) Castlebay takes its name from the island fortress of Kisimul Castle, first built by the MacNeil clan in the 11th century. A short boat trip (weather permitting) takes you out to the island, where you can explore the fortifications and soak up the view from the battlements.

The castle was restored in the 20th century by American architect Robert MacNeil, who became the 45th clan chief; he gifted the castle to Historic Scotland in 2000 for an annual rent of £1 and a bottle of whisky (Talisker single malt, if you're interested).

Traigh Mor BEACH
This vast expanse of firm golden sand (the name means 'Big Strand') serves as Barra's airport (a mile across at low tide, and big enough for three 'runways'), the only beach airport in the world that handles scheduled flights. Watching the little Twin Otter aircraft come and go is a popular spectator sport.

In between flights, locals gather cockles, a local seafood speciality, from the sands.

Barra Heritage Centre
HERITAGE CENTRE

(☎01871-810413; www.barraheritage.com; Castlebay; adult/child £3/1; ☉10.30am-4.30pm Mon-Sat Apr-Oct) This heritage centre has Gaelic-themed displays about the island, local art exhibitions and a tearoom.

🛏 Sleeping & Eating

Accommodation on Barra is limited, so make a reservation before committing to a night on the island. Wild camping (on foot or by bike) is allowed almost anywhere; campervans and car campers are restricted to official sites – check www.isleofbarra.com for details.

Castlebay Hotel
HOTEL ££

(☎01871-810223; www.castlebayhotel.com; Castlebay; s/d from £60/102; P) The Castlebay Hotel offers spacious bedrooms decorated with a subtle tartan motif – it's worth paying a bit extra for a sea view – and there's a comfy lounge and conservatory with grand views across the harbour to the islands south of Barra.

The hotel bar is the hub of island social life, with regular sessions of traditional music, and the restaurant specialises in local seafood and game (rabbit is often on the menu).

Tigh na Mara
B&B ££

(☎01871-810304; www.tighnamara-barra.co.uk; Castlebay; per person from £35; ☉Apr-Oct; 🛜) A lovely cottage B&B with a brilliant location just above the ferry pier, looking out over the bay and Kisimul Castle. Ask for the en suite double bedroom with bay view.

Dunard Hostel
HOSTEL £

(☎01871-810443; www.dunardhostel.co.uk; Castlebay; dm/tw from £16/36; P) Dunard is a friendly, family-run hostel just five minutes' walk from the ferry terminal. The owners can organise sea-kayaking tours for £35/65 a half-/full day.

Borve Camping and Caravan Site
CAMPSITE £

(www.barracamping.co.uk; Borve; 2-person tents £8, campervans £18; ☉Apr-Oct) An attractive campsite on the west coast of the island, close to Barra's best sandy beaches.

The Deck
CAFE £

(Castlebay; mains £4-6; ☉10am-6pm Mon-Sat, noon-5pm Sun) There are only outdoor seats at this cafe (attached to a toffee factory) on a wooden deck overlooking the bay, but it's worth waiting for a fine day to sample the freshly baked scones, homemade cakes and smoked-salmon sandwiches with dill and mustard dressing.

ℹ Getting There & Around

AIR There are two daily flights from Glasgow to Barra airport.

BOAT Ferries run from Castlebay to Oban, and Ardmhor to Eriskay; see p404 for details.

BICYCLE You can hire bikes from Island Adventures (☎01871-810284; Castlebay), at the east end of Castlebay.

BUS Bus W32 makes a circuit of the island up to five times daily (not Sunday), and also connects with the ferry at Ardmhor and flights at the airport.

Orkney & Shetland Islands

Why Go?

Up here at Britain's top end it can feel more Scandinavian than Scottish, and no wonder. For the Vikings, the jaunt across the North Sea from Norway was as easy as a stroll down to the local mead hall and they soon controlled these windswept, treeless archipelagos, laying down longhouses alongside stony remains of ancient prehistoric settlements.

Though they are not as scenically splendid as Skye, say, an ancient magic hovers in the air above the Orkney and Shetland Islands, endowing them with an allure that lodges firmly in the soul. It's in the misty seas, where seals, whales and porpoises patrol lonely coastlines; it's in the air, where squadrons of seabirds wheel above huge nesting colonies; and it's on land, where standing stones catch late summer sunsets and strains of folk music disperse in the air before the wind gusts shut the pub door. Make the journey; open that door.

Best Places to Stay

» Scalloway Hotel (p440)
» Brinkies Guest House (p429)
» Albert Hotel (p421)
» Linkshouse (p428)
» West Manse (p434)
» Almara B&B (p443)

Best Places to Eat

» Creel (p426)
» Foveran (p422)
» Hay's Dock (p437)

When to Go
Lerwick

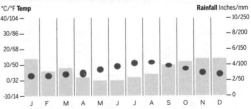

Jan Shetlands' Up Helly Aa festival, for horned helmets and burning Viking ships on the beach.

Jun Orkney rocks to the St Magnus Festival: book accommodation ahead.

Jul Take advantage of the summer sunlight and Britain's longest daylight hours.

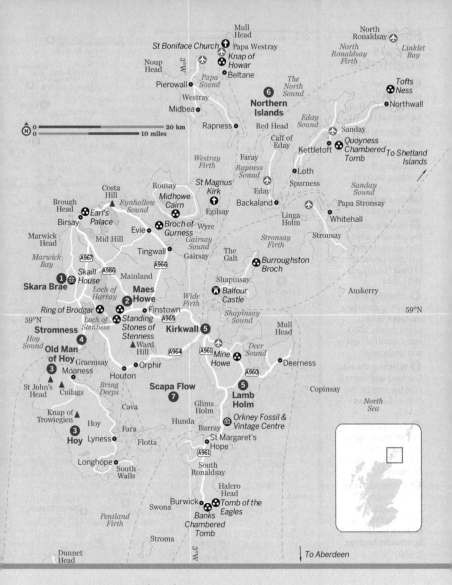

Orkney Islands Highlights

❶ Shaking your head in astonishment at **Skara Brae** (p427), a village of prehistoric perfection that pre-dates the pyramids

❷ Plunging down the passageway into spooky **Maes Howe** (p426), an enormous Stone Age tomb livened up by some bawdy Viking graffiti

❸ Exploring the scenic majesty of **Hoy** (p430) and – for serious rock climbers – scaling the Old Man there

❹ Pacing the stone-flagged main street of **Stromness** (p428), as salty a fishing town as you'll ever find

❺ Admiring the magnificent cathedral at **Kirkwall** (p420)

and the much humbler Italian Chapel at **Lamb Holm** (p424)

❻ Island-hopping the **Northern Islands** (p431) of Orkney, where azure waters lap against glittering beaches

❼ Diving the sunken warships of **Scapa Flow** (p425)

Shetland Islands Highlights

1 Discovering your inner Viking at Shetland's **Up Helly Aa festival** (p436)

2 Capering with puffins, spotting offshore orcas or dodging dive-bombing skuas in one of Shetland's fabulous **nature reserves** (p444)

3 Blowing away the cobwebs amid the raw, desolate and beautiful landscapes of **Unst** (p445) and **Yell** (p444)

4 Checking out Shetland's absorbing **museum** (p436), which details 5000 years' worth of history and landscapes

5 Watching the wild Shetland weather roll in to the spectacular cliffs of **Eshaness** (p443)

6 Exploring the islands' many layers of history at the ancient sights around **Sumburgh** (p442)

7 Taking advantage of the offbeat accommodation in a no-frills camping **böd** or a romantic **lighthouse cottage** (p440)

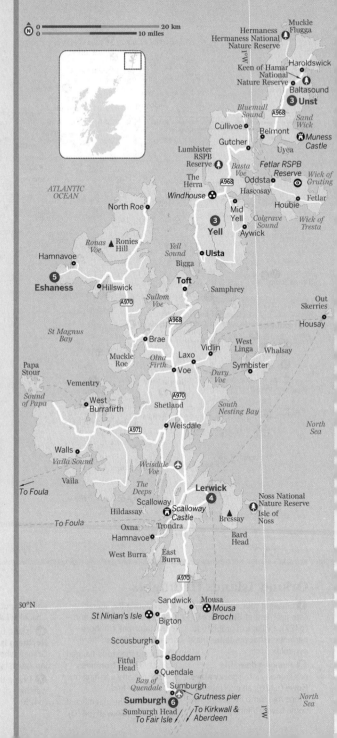

ORKNEY ISLANDS

There's a magic to the Orkney Islands that you begin to feel as soon as the Scottish mainland slips astern. Only a few short miles of ocean separate Stromness from Scrabster, but the Pentland Firth is one of Europe's most dangerous waterways, a graveyard of ships that adds an extra mystique to these islands shimmering in the sea mists.

An archipelago of mostly flat, green-topped islands stripped bare of trees by Atlantic gales and ringed with red sandstone cliffs, its heritage dates back to the Vikings whose influence is still strong today. Famed for its ancient standing stones and prehistoric villages, for sublime sandy beaches and spectacular coastal scenery, it's a region whose ports tell of lives shared with the blessings and rough moods of the sea, and a destination where seekers can find melancholy wrecks of warships and the salty clamour of remote seabird colonies.

☞ Tours

Orkney Island Holidays　　GUIDED TOURS
(☑01856-711373; www.orkneyislandholidays.com) Based on Shapinsay, with guided tours of archaeological sites, birdwatching and wildlife trips, and excursions to other islands. One-week, all-inclusive packages cost £1095.

Orkney Archaeology Tours　　GUIDED TOURS
(☑01856-721450; www.orkneyarchaeologytours. co.uk) Runs private half- (£160 for up to four) and full-day (£240) tours with an archaeologist guide.

Wildabout Orkney　　GUIDED TOURS
(☑01856-877737; www.wildaboutorkney.com) Operates tours covering Orkney's history, ecology, folklore and wildlife. Day trips operate year-round and cost £49, with pick-ups in Stromness and Kirkwall.

John O'Groats Ferries　　BUS TOUR
(☑01955-611353; www.jogferry.co.uk; ⊘May-Sep) If you're in a hurry, this operator runs a one-day tour of the main sites for £52, including the ferry from John O'Groats. You can do the whole thing as a long day trip from Inverness.

❶ Getting There & Away

Air

Flybe (☑0871 700 2000; www.flybe.com) flies daily from Kirkwall to Aberdeen, Edinburgh, Glasgow, Inverness and Sumburgh (Shetland). In summer it also serves Bergen (Norway).

Boat

During summer, book car spaces ahead. Fares vary according to season (low to peak fares are quoted here).

FROM SCRABSTER, SHETLANDS & ABERDEEN **Northlink Ferries** (☑0845 6000 449; www.northlinkferries.co.uk) operates ferries from Scrabster to Stromness (passenger £16 to £19, car £50 to £55, 1½ hours, two to three daily), from Aberdeen to Kirkwall (passenger £20 to £30, car £75 to £104, six hours, three or four weekly) and from Kirkwall to Lerwick (passenger one way £16 to £23, car one way £58 to £96, six to eight hours, three or four a week) on the Shetland Islands.

FROM GILLS BAY **Pentland Ferries** (☑0800 688 8998, 01856-831226; www.pentlandferries. co.uk) boats leave from Gills Bay, about 3 miles west of John O'Groats, and head to St Margaret's Hope on South Ronaldsay (passenger/car £14/33, one hour). There are three to four crossings daily.

FROM JOHN O'GROATS From May to September, John O'Groats Ferries (p374) operates a passenger-only service from John O'Groats to Burwick, on the southern tip of South Ronaldsay (one way/return £20/30). A bus to Kirkwall meets the ferry (all-included return from John O'Groats to Kirkwall is £32). There are two to three departures daily.

Bus

Citylink (☑0871 266 33 33; www.citylink.co.uk) runs daily from Inverness to Scrabster, connecting with the Stromness ferries.

John O'Groats Ferries (www.jogferry.co.uk) operates the summer-only Orkney bus service from Inverness to Kirkwall. Tickets (one way/return £38/52, five hours) include bus–ferry–travel from Inverness to Kirkwall. There are two buses daily from June to early September.

❶ Getting Around

The *Orkney Transport Guide*, a detailed schedule of all bus, ferry and air services around and to/from Orkney, is available free from tourist offices.

The largest island, Mainland, is linked by causeways to Burray, South Ronaldsay, Lamb Holm and Glims Holm; other islands are reached by air and ferry.

Air

Loganair (☑01856-873457; www.loganair. co.uk) operates interisland flights from Kirkwall. See individual islands for details.

Bicycle

Various locations on Mainland hire bikes, including **Cycle Orkney** (Map p422; ☑01856-875777; www.cycleorkney.com; Tankerness Lane, Kirkwall; per day £15; ⊘Mon-Sat; ⓐ) and **Orkney**

Cycle Hire (☐01856-850255; www.orkneycy clehire.co.uk; 54 Dundas St, Stromness; per day £8.50-10).

Boat

Orkney Ferries (☐01856-872044; www. orkneyferries.co.uk) operates car ferries from Mainland to the islands. See individual islands for details.

Bus

Stagecoach (☐01856-870555; www.stage coachbus.com) Runs buses on Mainland and connecting islands. Most don't operate on Sunday. Dayrider (£7.75) and 7-Day Megarider (£17) tickets allow unlimited travel.

Car

Small-car rates begin at around £34/175 per day/week, although there are specials for as low as £28 per day.

Drive Orkney (☐01856-877551; www.driveork ney.com; Garrison Rd, Kirkwall, Kirkwall)

Norman Brass Car Hire (☐01856-850850; www.stromnesscarhire.co.uk; North End Rd, Stromness, Stromness) At the Blue Star Garage.

Orkney Car Hire (☐01856-872866; www. orkneycarhire.co.uk; Junction Rd, Kirkwall, Kirkwall)

WR Tullock (☐01856-875500; www.orkney carrental.co.uk; Castle St, Kirkwall, Kirkwall)

Kirkwall

POP 6200

The capital of Orkney is a bustling market town, set back from a wide bay. Kirkwall's long, winding, paved main street and twisting wynds (lanes) are very atmospheric, and the town has a magnificent cathedral. Founded in the early 11th century, when Earl Rognvald Brusson established his kingdom here, the original part of Kirkwall is one of the best examples of an ancient Norse town.

◉ Sights

FREE **St Magnus Cathedral** CATHEDRAL
(Map p422; ☐01856-874894; www.stmagnus.org; Broad St; ◎9am-6pm Mon-Sat, 2-6pm Sun Apr-Sep, 9am-1pm & 2-5pm Mon-Sat Oct-Mar) Founded in 1137 and constructed from local red sandstone, fabulous St Magnus Cathedral is Kirkwall's centrepiece. The powerful atmosphere of an ancient faith pervades the impressive interior. Lyrical and melodramatic epitaphs of the dead line the walls and emphasise the serious business of 17th- and 18th-century bereavement.

Earl Rognvald Brusason commissioned the cathedral in the name of his martyred uncle, Magnus Erlendsson, who was killed by Earl Hakon Paulsson on Egilsay in 1117. Work began in 1137, but the building is actually the result of 300 years of construction and alteration.

Earl's Palace & Bishop's Palace RUINS
(HS; Map p422; ☐01856-871918; www.historic -scotland.gov.uk; Watergate; adult/child £4.50/2.70; ◎9.30am-5.30pm Apr-Sep, to 4.30pm Oct) These two ruined palaces are worth poking around. The more intriguing, the Earl's Palace, was once known as the finest example of French Renaissance architecture in Scotland. One room features an interesting history of its builder, Earl Patrick Stewart, who was executed in Edinburgh for treason. He started construction in about 1600, but ran out of money and it was never completed.

The **Bishop's Palace** (HS; Map p422; incl in Earl's Palace admission) was built in the mid-12th century to provide comfortable lodgings for Bishop William the Old. There's a good view of the cathedral from the tower, and a plaque showing the different phases of the cathedral's construction.

FREE **Orkney Museum** MUSEUM
(Map p422; ☐01856-873191; www.orkney.gov. uk; Broad St; ◎10.30am-5pm Mon-Sat May-Sep, 10.30am-12.30pm & 1.30-5pm Mon-Sat Oct-Apr) Opposite St Magnus Cathedral, in a former merchant's house, is this labyrinthine display. It has an overview of Orcadian history and prehistory, including Pictish carvings and a display on the Ba' (p421). Most engaging are the last rooms, covering 19th- and 20th-century social history.

TOP CHOICE **Highland Park Distillery** DISTILLERY
(☐01856-874619; www.highlandpark.co.uk; Holm Rd; tour adult/child £6/free; ◎daily May-Aug, Mon-Fri Sep-Apr) South of the centre, this distillery, where they malt their own barley, is great to visit. You can see the barley and the peat kiln used to dry it on the excellent, well-informed hour-long tour (hourly May to August, and weekdays at 2pm and 3pm September to April). The standard 12-year-old is a soft, balanced malt, great for novices and aficionados alike; the 18-year-old is among the world's finest drams. This and older whiskies can be tasted on more specialised tours (£35 and £75), which you can prearrange.

THE BA'

Every Christmas Day and New Year's Day, Kirkwall holds a staggering spectacle: a crazy ball game known as The Ba'. Two enormous teams, the Uppies and the Doonies, fight their way, no holds barred, through the streets, trying to get a leather ball to the other end of town. The ball is thrown from the Market Cross outside the St Magnus Cathedral to the waiting crowd; the Uppies' objective is to get the ba' to the corner of Main St and Junction Rd, the Doonies must get it to the water. Violence, skulduggery, and other stunts are common and the event, fuelled by plenty of strong drink, can last for hours.

✦ Festivals & Events

St Magnus Festival ARTS, MUSIC
(☎01856-871445; www.stmagnusfestival.com) A colourful celebration of music and the arts in June.

🛏 Sleeping

TOP CHOICE Albert Hotel HOTEL ££
(Map p422; ☎01856-876000; www.alberthotel. co.uk; Mounthoolie Lane; s/d £96/133; 🛜) Stylishly refurbished in plum and grey, this central but peaceful hotel is Kirkwall's finest address. Comfortable contemporary rooms in a variety of categories sport superinviting beds and smart bathrooms. A great Orkney base, but you may end up spending more time in the excellent Bothy Bar downstairs. Walk-in prices are usually somewhat lower than these rack rates.

Lynnfield Hotel HOTEL ££
(☎01856-872505; www.lynnfieldhotel.co.uk; Holm Rd; s £85-95, d £110-150; 🅿🛜🐾) South of the centre, this sizeable yet intimate hotel is run with a professional, but warmly personal, touch. Rooms are individually decorated, and feature extremely handsome furniture and plenty of character. Deluxe rooms feature enormous bathrooms and opulent four-poster beds; others might showcase a jacuzzi or antique writing desk. The public areas include a cosy dark-wood drawing room and a large, well-regarded restaurant (dinner mains £16 to £19).

Orcades Hostel HOSTEL £
(☎01856-873745; www.orcadeshostel.com; Muddisdale Rd; dm/s/d £18/40/50; 🅿@🛜) Book ahead to get a bed in this cracking hostel on the western edge of town. It's a guesthouse conversion so there's a very smart kitchen and lounge area, and great-value doubles. Comfortable dorms with just four bunks make for sound sleeping, and young, enthusiastic owners give the place plenty of spark.

2 Dundas Crescent B&B ££
(Map p422; ☎01856-874805; www.twodundas. co.uk; 2 Dundas Cres; s/d £40/75; 🅿🛜) This former manse is a magnificent building that has four enormous rooms blessed with large windows and sizeable beds. There are plenty of period features, but the en suite bathrooms are not among them: they're sparklingly new, and one has a free-standing bathtub. Both the welcome and the breakfast will leave you more than satisfied.

Ayre Hotel HOTEL ££
(Map p422; ☎01856-873001; www.ayrehotel.co.uk; Ayre Rd; s/d £80/112; 🅿🛜🐾) Right on the waterfront, this 200-year-old hotel has been recently renovated, leaving its low-ceilinged, large-bedded rooms looking very spruce. It's definitely worth paying the extra few pounds to grab one with a sea view.

Karrawa Guest House GUESTHOUSE ££
(☎018356-871100; www.karrawaguesthouseorkney. co.uk; Inganess Rd; s/d £50/64) In a peaceful location on the southeastern edge of Kirkwall, this enthusiastically run guesthouse offers significant value for its well-kept modern double rooms with comfortable new mattresses. Breakfast is generously proportioned.

Shore INN ££
(Map p422; ☎01856-872200; www.theshore.co.uk; 6 Shore St; s/d £67/92; 🛜) Smart contemporary rooms with a light Scandinavian touch above a lively harbourfront bar and restaurant. Those at the front are larger and (slightly) costlier. Breakfast extra.

Lerona B&B ££
(☎01856-874538; Cromwell Cres; s/d £40/66; 🅿) Guests come first here, but the wee folk – a battalion of garden gnomes and clans of dolls with lifelike stares – are close behind. The rooms are a good size, and the friendly owners make you feel very much at home. It's cheaper if you stay more than one night. Head east along the waterfront from the centre; Cromwell Crescent comes off this road.

Kirkwall

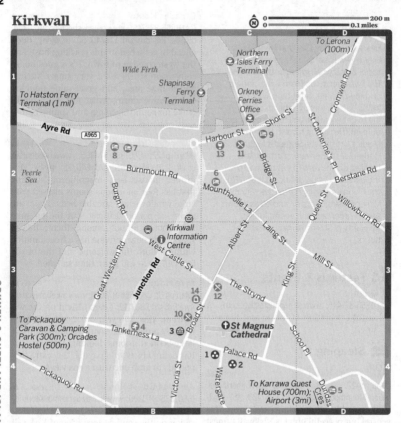

Peedie Hostel   HOSTEL **£**

(Map p422; ☎01856-875477; www.peediehostel.
yolasite.com; Ayre Rd; dm/s/d £15/20/30) Nestling into a corner at the end of the Kirkwall
waterfront, this cute hostel set in former
fisherfolk's cottages squeezes in all the necessary features for a comfortable stay. Despite the compact appearance, the dorms
actually have plenty of room – and there are
three tiny kitchens so you should find some
elbow room. A separate 'bothy' sleeps four
and costs £60.

Pickaquoy Caravan &
Camping Park   CAMPGROUND **£**

(☎01856-879900; www.pickaquoy.co.uk; Muddisdale Rd; sites per person £6.95, 2-3 people £13.50;
☺Apr-Oct; P🐾🛜🐕) No view, but plenty of
grass and excellent modern facilities. If the
office is unattended, check in at the nearby
Pickaquoy leisure centre.

Eating & Drinking

TOP
CHOICE **Foveran**   ORCADIAN **££**

(☎01856-872389; www.thefoveran.com; St Ola;
mains £14-23; ☺dinner) Three miles from Kirkwall on the Orphir road, this is one of Orkney's best dining options, but surprisingly affordable for the quality on offer. In a tranquil
location with a cosy eating area overlooking
the sea, it's at its best presenting classic Orcadian ingredients – the steak with haggis and
whisky sauce is feted throughout the region,
while the North Ronaldsay lamb comes with
meat from four different cuts and is deliciously tender. A medley of toothsome vegetables accompanies the mains, and interesting wines complement the dishes. If you like
the spot – and why wouldn't you? – there are
rooms available (single/double £78/116).

Reel   CAFE **£**

(Map p422; www.wrigleyandthereel.com; Albert St;
sandwiches £3-4; ☺9am-6pm) Part music shop

Kirkwall

and part cafe, Kirkwall's best coffee-stop sits alongside St Magnus Cathedral, and bravely puts tables outside at the slightest threat of sunshine. It's a relaxed spot that's good for morning-after debriefing, as well as lunchtime panini and musically named sandwiches (as well as its cheese one: Skara Brie). It's a centre for local folk musicians, with regular evening sessions.

Shore GASTROPUB ££
(Map p422; www.theshore.co.uk; 6 Shore St; restaurant mains £12-18; ⊙food 8am-9.30pm; ☜) This popular harbourside eatery brings the gastropub concept to Kirkwall, offering bar meals combined with more adventurous fare in the restaurant section. It's run with a customer-comes-first attitude, and the seafood is especially good.

Kirkwall Hotel PUB, SCOTTISH ££
(Map p422; ☎01856-872232; www.kirkwallhotel. com; Harbour St; mains £8-16) This grand old hotel on the waterfront is one of Kirkwall's best dining places. The elegant bar and eating area packs out; it's a favourite spot for an evening out with the clan. There's a fairly standard pub-food list that's complemented by a seasonal menu featuring local seafood and meat – the lamb is delicious.

Judith Glue Real Food Cafe CAFE £
(Map p422; www.judithglue.com; 25 Broad St; light meals £4-9; ⊙9am-10pm Mon-Sat, 10am-10pm Sun Jun-Sep, to 6pm Oct-May) At the back of a lively craft shop opposite the cathedral, this cafe serves toothsome sandwiches and salads, as well as daily specials and succulent seafood platters. There's an emphasis on sustainable

and organic ingredients, but put the feel-good factor aside for a moment to fight for a table.

Bothy Bar PUB £
(Map p422; ☎01856-876000; www.alberthotel. co.uk; Mounthoolie Lane; mains £7-10) In the Albert Hotel, the Bothy looks very smart these days with its modish floor and B&W photos of old-time Orcadian farming, but its low tables provide the customary cheer and sustaining food: think sausages, haddock and stews – good pub grub.

Helgi's PUB
(Map p422; www.helgis.co.uk; 14 Harbour St; ☜) There's a traditional cosiness about this place, but the decor has moved beyond the time-honoured beer-soaked carpet to a comfortable contemporary slate floor and quotes from the *Orkneyinga Saga* plastering the walls. It's more find-a-table than jostle-at-the-bar and serves cheerful, well-priced comfort food (mains £7 to £10). Take your pint upstairs for quiet harbour contemplation.

🔒 Shopping

Kirkwall has some gorgeous jewellery and crafts along Albert St. Try the Longship (Map p422; ☎01856-888790; www.olagoriejewel lery.com; 7 Broad St; ⊙9am-5.30pm Mon-Sat) for Orkney-made crafts and gifts and exquisite designer jewellery.

ℹ Information

Balfour Hospital (☎01856-888000; www.ohb. scot.nhs.uk; New Scapa Rd) Follow Junction

Road south out of town and you'll see it on your right.

Orkney Library (☎01856-873166; 44 Junction Rd; ⊗9.15am-5pm Tue-Sat, to 7pm Mon & Thu) Free Internet.

Kirkwall Information Centre (☎01856-872856; www.visitorkney.com; West Castle St; ⊗9am-6pm daily May-Sep, 9am-5pm Mon-Fri & 10am-4pm Sat Oct-Apr) Has a good range of publications on Orkney.

❶ Getting There & Away

AIR Flybe (p419) and Loganair (p419) services use **Kirkwall Airport** (www.hial.co.uk), located a few miles east of town.

BOAT Ferries to the Northern Islands depart from the town harbour; however, ferries to Aberdeen and Shetland use the Hatston terminal, 1 mile northwest.

BUS Bus X1 runs direct from Kirkwall to Stromness (30 minutes, hourly, seven Sunday); bus 2 runs to Orphir and Houton (20 minutes, four or five Monday to Saturday); bus 6 runs from Kirkwall to Evie (30 minutes, three to five daily Monday to Saturday) and to Tingwall to connect with the ferry to Rousay. All services leave from the **bus station** (West Castle St).

East Mainland to South Ronaldsay

After the sinking of the battleship HMS *Royal Oak* by a German U-boat in 1939, Winston Churchill had vast causeways of concrete blocks erected across the channels on the eastern side of Scapa Flow, linking Mainland to the islands of Lamb Holm, Glims Holm, Burray and South Ronaldsay. The Churchill Barriers, as they became known, flanked by the rusting wrecks of the blockships, now support the main road from Kirkwall to Burwick.

❶ Getting There & Away

Bus 3 from Kirkwall runs to Deerness in East Mainland (30 minutes, three to five Monday to Saturday), with some buses calling at Tankerness. There are buses from Kirkwall to South Ronaldsay's St Margaret's Hope (30 minutes, almost hourly Monday to Saturday).

EAST MAINLAND

At Tankerness is the mysterious Iron Age site of Mine Howe (☎01865-861234; www.minehowe.com; adult/child £4/2; ⊗10am-4pm daily Jun-Aug, 11am-3pm Tue & Fri Sep & May), an eerie underground construction, the function of which is unknown. In the centre

of an earthen mound ringed by a ditch, a claustrophobic, precarious flight of narrow steps descends steeply to a stone-lined chamber about 1.5m in diameter and 4m high. Archaeologists from TV's *Time Team* concluded that it may have had some ritual significance, perhaps as a shrine.

LAMB HOLM

On tiny Lamb Holm, the Italian Chapel (☎01865-781268; admission free; ⊗9am-dusk) is all that remains of a POW camp that housed the Italian soldiers who worked on the Churchill Barriers. They built the chapel in their spare time, using two Nissen huts, scrap metal and their considerable artistic and decorative skills. It's an extraordinary monument to human ingenuity.

Alongside is the enthusiastic little shop of the Orkney Wine Company (☎01856-878700; www.orkneywine.co.uk; ⊗Mon-Sat Mar-Dec, plus Sun Apr-Sep), which produces handmade wines made from berries, flowers and vegetables. Try some strawberry-rhubarb wine or carrot-and-malt-whisky liqueur – unusual flavours but surprisingly addictive.

BURRAY
POP 360

The small island of Burray has a fine beach at Northtown on the east coast, where you may see seals.

◉ Sights

Orkney Fossil & Vintage Centre   MUSEUM
(☎01865-731255; www.orkneyfossilcentre.co.uk; adult/child £4/2.50; ⊗10am-5pm mid-Ap–Sep) The Orkney Fossil & Vintage Centre has a quirky collection of household and farming relics, 360-million-year-old Devonian fish fossils found locally and galleries devoted to the world wars, including a display on the Churchill Barriers. There's an excellent coffee shop here. It's on the left half a mile after crossing to Burray, coming from Kirkwall.

🛏 Sleeping & Eating

Sands Hotel   HOTEL ££
(☎01856-731298; www.thesandshotel.co.uk; s/d/ste £90/115/165; P🐾) This is a spiffy, refurbished 19th-century herring station, right on the pier in Burray village. Very modern rooms have stylish furnishings, and all have great water views. Families and groups should consider a suite: two-level self-contained flats that sleep four and have a kitchen. There's a good restaurant with a genteel nautical feel.

DIVING SCAPA FLOW

One of the world's largest natural harbours, Scapa Flow has been in near-constant use by various fleets from the Vikings onwards. After WWI, 74 German ships were interned here; when the terms of the armistice included a severely reduced German navy, Admiral von Reuter, who was in charge of the fleet, decided to take matters into his own hands. A secret signal was passed from ship to ship and the British watched incredulously as every German ship began to sink. Fifty-two of them went to the bottom, with the rest left aground in shallow water.

Most were salvaged, but seven vessels remain to attract divers. There are three battleships – the *König*, the *Kronprinz Wilhelm* and the *Markgraf* – all of which weigh over 25,000 tonnes. The first two were subjected to blasting for scrap metal, but the *Markgraf* is undamaged and considered one of Scotland's best dives.

Numerous other ships rest on the sea bed in Scapa Flow. HMS *Royal Oak*, sunk by a German U-boat in October 1939 with the loss of 833 crew, is an official war grave – diving here is prohibited.

It's worth prebooking your diving excursion far in advance. Scapa Scuba (☑01856-851218; www.scapascuba.co.uk; Dundas St, Stromness; 2 guided dives £140) is an excellent operator.

SOUTH RONALDSAY
POP 850

South Ronaldsay's main village, pristine St Margaret's Hope was named after the Maid of Norway, who died here in 1290 on the way from her homeland to marry Edward II of England (strictly a political affair: Margaret was only seven years old). The ferry from Gills Bay on mainland Scotland docks here, while the passenger ferry from John O'Groats lands at Burwick, at the island's southern tip.

◉ Sights & Activities

Tomb of the Eagles   ARCHAEOLOGICAL SITE
(☑01865-831339; www.tomboftheeagles.co.uk; Liddel; adult/child £6.80/2; ☺9.30am-5.30pm Apr-Oct, 10am-noon Mar, by arrangement Nov-Feb) Near Burwick, this is the result of a local farmer finding two significant archaeological sites on his land. The first is a Bronze Age stone building with a firepit, indoor well, and plenty of seating; a communal cooking site or the original Orkney pub? Beyond, in a spectacular clifftop position, the Neolithic tomb (wheel yourself in prone on a trolley) is an elaborate stone construction which held the remains of up to 340 people who died some five millennia ago. Before you head out to the sites, an excellent personal explanation is given to you at the visitor centre; you meet a few spooky skulls and can handle some of the artefacts found. It's about a mile's airy walk to the tomb from the centre.

Banks Chambered Tomb   ARCHAEOLOGICAL SITE
(Tomb of the Otters; www.bankschamberedtomb. co.uk; Cleat; adult/child £5/free; ☺10am-5pm Apr-Oct) Accidentally discovered recently while making a car park for the adjacent bistro, this 5000-year-old chambered tomb is still being investigated but has yielded a vast quantity of human bones, well preserved thanks to the saturation of the earth. The tomb is dug into bedrock and makes for an atmospheric if claustrophobic visit. The guided tour from the guy who found it mixes homespun archaeological theories with astute observations. You can handle stones and bones that have been found, including the remains of otters, who presumably used this as a den in between burial ceremonies. Follow signs for Tomb of the Eagles.

Orkney Marine Life Aquarium   AQUARIUM
(☑01856-831700; www.orkneymarinelife.co.uk; Grimness; adult/child £6/4.25; ☺10am-6pm Apr-Oct) This aquarium showcases the fascinating collection of marine animals found in Scapa Flow and Orcadian coastal waters. There's a rock pool that allows up-close-and-personal inspections of local creatures – great for kids. Injured seals that have been nursed back to health can be viewed in open-air pools. Turn left off the A961 just after crossing to South Ronaldsay, coming from Kirkwall.

Pettlandsseker   BOAT TRIPS
(☑01856-831605; www.boattrips-orkney.co.uk; Burwick Harbour; adult/child £30/15; ☺Apr-Oct) Runs three-hour trips in ex–Royal National Lifeboat Institution lifeboats to bird- and seal-rich islets in the Pentland Firth.

📖 **Sleeping & Eating**

TOP
CHOICE **Bankburn House**   B&B **££**

(📞01856-831310; www.bankburnhouse.co.uk; s/d £45/70, with shared bathroom £40/59; P@🛜🐕) This large rustic house does everything right, with smashing rooms of a great size, and engaging owners who put on quality breakfasts and take pride in thinking of new innovations to further improve guests' comfort levels. There's a huge stretch of lawn out the front, which overlooks the town and bay – perfect for sunbathing on shimmering Orkney summer days. Listed prices are for one-night stays; things drop substantially after that, so, for example, for three nights you'll only pay £52 per night for the double en suite: an absolute bargain. It's on the A961, just outside St Margaret's Hope.

St Margaret's Hope Backpackers   HOSTEL **£**

(📞01856-831225;   www.orkneybackpackers.com; dm £14; P) Just a stroll from the Gills Bay ferry, this hostel is a lovely stone cottage offering small, simple rooms with up to four berths – great for families. There's a lounge, kitchen, laundry and good, hot showers. It's an excellent set-up and you can use the adjacent cafe's wi-fi. Book in at the Trading Post shop next door.

TOP
CHOICE **Creel**   SEAFOOD **£££**

(📞01856-831311; www.thecreel.co.uk; Front Rd, St Margaret's Hope; 2/3-course dinner £33/40; ⊙dinner Wed-Sun Apr–mid-Oct; 🛜) On the waterfront in an unassuming house, on unpretentious wooden tables, some of Scotland's best seafood has been served up for well over 20 years. Upstairs, three most comfortable **rooms** (singles/doubles £75/110) face the spectacular sunset over the water. Wooden ceilings and plenty of space give them an airy feel. It was up for sale at the time of research, so fingers crossed.

Skerries Bistro   SEAFOOD **£**

(📞01856-831605; www.skerriesbistro.co.uk; Cleat; mains £7-14; ⊙Apr-Oct) Helpful and friendly, this little bistro occupies a lovely sun-drenched conservatory near the island's southern tip. Meals range from soups and sandwiches to delicious seafood platters at knockdown prices, and daily fish and shellfish specials. It's all delicious. Dinner should be booked ahead. It also has self-catering cottages available at this beautiful spot.

West & North Mainland

This part of the island is sprinkled with outstanding prehistoric monuments: the journey up to Orkney is worth it for these alone. It would take the best part of a day to see all of them – if pushed for time, visit Skara Brae then Maes Howe, but book your visit to the latter in advance.

MAES HOWE

Egypt has pyramids, Scotland has Maes Howe (HS; 📞01856-761606; www.historic-scotland.gov.uk; adult/child £5.50/3.30; ⊙tours hourly 10am-4pm). Constructed about 5000 years ago, it's an extraordinary place, a stone-age tomb built from enormous sandstone blocks, some of which weighed many tons and were brought from several miles away. Creeping down the long stone passageway to the central chamber, you feel the indescribable gulf of years that separate us from the architects of this mysterious place. Though nothing is known about who and what was interred here, the scope of the project suggests it was a structure of great significance.

In the 12th century, the tomb was broken into by Vikings searching for treasure. A couple of years later, another group sought shelter in the chamber from a blizzard that lasted three days. While they waited out the storm, they carved runic graffiti on the walls. As well as the some-things-never-change 'Olaf was 'ere' and 'Thorni bedded Helga', there are also more intricate carvings, including a particularly fine dragon and a knotted serpent.

Buy tickets in Tormiston Mill, on the other side of the road. Entry is by 45-minute guided tours that leave on the hour. Make sure to reserve your tour-slot ahead by phone. Due to the oversized groups, guides tend to only show a couple of the Viking inscriptions, but they'll happily show more if asked.

ℹ️ **ORKNEY EXPLORER PASS**

The **Orkney Explorer Pass** covers all Historic Scotland sites in Orkney, including big ticket items such as Maes Howe, Skara Brae, the Broch of Gurness, the Brough of Birsay and the Bishop's Palace and Earl's Palace in Kirkwall; it costs £17/10 per adult/child.

STANDING STONES OF STENNESS

Within sight of Maes Howe, four mighty stones (HS; www.historic-scotland.gov.uk; admission free; ☉24hr) remain of what was once a circle of 12. Research suggests they were perhaps erected as long ago as 3300 BC, and they impose by their sheer size; the tallest measures 5.7m. The narrow strip of land they're on, the Ness of Brodgar, separates the Harray and Stenness lochs and was the site of a large settlement, inhabited throughout the Neolithic period (3500–1800 BC). A short walk to the east are the excavated remains of **Barnhouse Neolithic Village**, thought to have been inhabited by the builders of Maes Howe. Don't skip this: it brings the area to life.

RING OF BRODGAR

A mile north of Stenness is this wide circle of standing stones (HS; www.historic-scotland. gov.uk; admission free; ☉24hr), some over 5m tall. The last of the three Stenness monuments to be built (2500–2000 BC), it remains a most atmospheric location. Twenty-one of the original 60 stones still stand among the heather. On a grey day with dark clouds thudding low across the sky, the stones are a spine-tingling sight. Free guided tours leave from the car park at 1pm from June to August (Thursdays only rest of year).

ORKNEY FOLKLORE & STORYTELLING VISITOR CENTRE

Located between Brodgar and Skara Brae, this offbeat centre (☎01856-841207; www.ork neyattractions.com; P) focuses on the islands' folkloric tradition. The best way to experience it is on one of its atmospheric storytelling evenings, **Peatfire Tales of Orkney** (Sunday, Tuesday and Friday at 8.30pm March to October, adult/child £10/6) where local legends are told with musical accompaniment around a peat fire. It also runs interesting guided walks of the coastline and of Stromness (£7) and offers B&B. The building, Via House (☎01856-841207; www. orkneyattractions.com; s/d £26/52; P🛜❄), is characterful and a bit chaotic; this could make a relaxing away-from-it-all retreat, with great starwatching on clear nights and opportunities for various workshops for adults and children.

SKARA BRAE & SKAILL HOUSE

A visit to extraordinary Skara Brae (HS; www.historic-scotland.gov.uk; joint ticket with Skaill House adult/child £6.90/4.10; ☉9.30am-5.30pm Apr-Sep, to 4.30pm Oct-Mar), one of the world's

most evocative prehistoric sites, offers the best opportunity in Scotland for a glimpse of Stone Age life. Idyllically situated by a sandy bay 8 miles north of Stromness, and predating Stonehenge and the pyramids of Giza, Skara Brae is northern Europe's best-preserved prehistoric village.

Even the stone furniture – beds, boxes and dressers – has survived the 5000 years since a community lived and breathed here. It was hidden until 1850, when waves whipped up by a severe storm eroded the sand and grass above the beach, exposing the houses underneath. There's an excellent interactive exhibit and short video, arming visitors with facts and theory, which will enhance the impact of the site. You then enter a reconstructed house, giving the excavation, which you head on to next, more meaning. The official guidebook, available from the visitors centre, includes a good self-guided tour.

The joint ticket also gets you into Skaill House (HS; ☉Apr-Sep), a mansion built for the bishop in 1620. It's a bit anticlimactic catapulting straight from the Neolithic to the 1950s decor, but you can see a smart hidden compartment in the library as well as the bishop's original 17th-century four-poster bed.

Buses run to Skara Brae from Kirkwall and Stromness a few times weekly in summer, but not all are useful to visit the site. It's possible to walk along the coast from Stromness to Skara Brae via Yesnaby Sea Stacks and the Broch of Borwick (9 miles).

BIRSAY

The small village of Birsay is 6 miles north of Skara Brae.

Sights & Activities

FREE **Earl's Palace** RUINS

(⊘24hr) The ruins of this palace, built in the 16th century by the despotic Robert Stewart, earl of Orkney, dominate the village of Birsay. Today it's a mass of half walls and crumbling columns that look like dilapidated chimney stacks. Nevertheless, the size of the palace is impressive, matching the reputed ego and tyranny of its former inhabitant.

Brough of Birsay ARCHAEOLOGICAL SITE

(HS; www.historic-scotland.gov.uk; adult/child £4/2.40; ⊘9.30am-5.30pm mid-Jun–Sep) At low tide (check tide times at the shop in Earl's Palace (p428) you can walk out to this windswept island, site of extensive Norse ruins, including a number of longhouses and the 12th-century **St Peter's Church**. There's also a replica of a Pictish stone which was found here, carved with an eagle and human figures. St Magnus was buried here after his murder on Egilsay in 1117, and the island was long a place of pilgrimage. The attractive lighthouse has fantastic views along the coast.

Sleeping

TOP CHOICE **Linkshouse** B&B ££

(☎01856-721221; www.ewaf.co.uk; Birsay village; s/d £55/90; ⊘Mar-Oct; P🅿🅿) One of the Orkney Islands' most charming B&Bs, this is a welcoming stone house near the sea. The beautiful rooms – one with comforting sloping ceiling, one with a toilet that has wonderful vistas – have been recently renovated and it's all looking fabulous. Original art and handsome furniture grace them and the lounge, where a little gazebo lets you contemplate the scenery, or browse the books, maps and sherry kept here.

Breakfast here is a treat, served on gorgeous crockery with standout fish and vegetarian options changing daily – pancakes with blueberries and crème fraîche, anyone?

Birsay Hostel HOSTEL, CAMPGROUND £

(☎after hrs 01856-721470, office hrs 01856-873535; www.orkney.gov.uk; sites per 4 people £6.25-9.95, dm/tw £15.60/43; P🅿) Birsay makes a lovely, peaceful place to stay amid the Orkney countryside. Birsay Hostel is a former activity centre and school that now has dorms that vary substantially in spaciousness – go for one of the two- or four-bedded ones. There's a big kitchen and a grassy camping area. It's on the A967 south of Birsay village.

EVIE

On an exposed headland at Aikerness, a 1.5-mile walk northeast from the straggling village of Evie, you'll find the **Broch of Gurness** (HS; www.historic-scotland.gov.uk; adult/child £5/3; ⊘9.30am-12.30pm & 1.30-5.30pm Apr-Sep, to 4.30pm Oct), a fine example of the drystone fortified towers that were both status symbol for powerful farmers and useful protection from raiders some 2200 years ago. The imposing entranceway and sturdy stone walls – originally 10m high – are impressive; inside you can see the hearth and where a mezzanine floor would have fitted. Around the broch are a number of well-preserved outbuildings, including a curious shamrock-shaped house. The visitor centre has some interesting displays on the culture that built these remarkable fortifications.

Wee Eviedale Campsite (☎01856-751270; www.creviedale.orknet.co.uk; sites £5-9; ⊘Apr-Sep; P🅿), at the northern end of the village, has a good grassed area for tent camping, with picnic tables. Self-catering accommodation is available next door at three excellent, renovated farm cottages with wi-fi (per week £320 to £350).

Stromness

POP 1609

This appealing grey-stone port has a narrow, elongated, flagstone-paved main street and tiny alleys leading down to the waterfront between tall stone houses. It lacks Kirkwall's size but makes up for that with bucketloads of character, having changed little since its heyday in the 18th century, when it was a busy staging post for ships avoiding the troublesome English Channel during European wars. Stromness is ideally located for trips to Orkney's major prehistoric sites.

Sights

The main recreation in Stromness is simply strolling up and down the narrow, atmospheric main street, where cars and pedestrians move at the same pace. You can download an audioguide to the town (www.visitorkney.com/stromness), or pick up a portable player from the tourist office.

Stromness Museum MUSEUM

(☎01856-850025; www.orkneycommunities.co.uk/stromnessmuseum; 52 Alfred St; adult/child £4.50/1; ⊘10am-5pm Apr-Sep, 11am-3.30pm Mon-Sat Oct-Mar) A superb museum full of knickknacks from maritime and natural-history exhibitions covering whaling, the Hudsons Bay Company and the sunk German fleet. You can happily nose around for a couple of hours. Across the street is the house where local poet and novelist George Mackay Brown lived.

FREE Pier Arts Centre GALLERY
(☑01856-850209; www.pierartscentre.com; 30 Victoria St; ⊙10.30am-5pm Tue-Sat) Resplendently redesigned, this gallery has really rejuvenated the Orkney modern-art scene with its sleek lines and upbeat attitude. It's worth a look as much for the architecture as its high-quality collection of 20th-century British art and the changing exhibitions.

★☆ Festivals & Events

Orkney Folk Festival MUSIC
(☑01856-851331; www.orkneyfolkfestival.com) A four-day event in late May, with folk concerts, *ceilidhs* and casual pub sessions. Stromness packs out, and late-night buses from Kirkwall are laid on. Book ahead for event tickets and accommodation.

🛌 Sleeping

TOP CHOICE Brinkies Guest House B&B ££
(☑01856-851881; www.brinkiesguesthouse.co.uk; s/d £60/70; P🐾🌐) Just a short walk from the centre, but with a lonely, king-of-the-castle position overlooking the town and bay, this exceptional place offers five-star islander hospitality. Compact modern rooms are handsome, stylish and comfortable, public areas are done out most attractively in wood, but above all it's the charming owner's flexibility and can-do attitude that makes this so special. Breakfast is 'continental Orcadian' – a stupendous array of quality local cheese, smoked fish and homemade bere bannocks. Want a lie-in? No problem, saunter down at 10am. Don't want breakfast? How about packed lunch instead? Take Outertown Rd off Back Rd, turn right on to Brownstown Rd, and keep going.

Miller's House B&B ££
(☑01856-851969; www.millershouseorkney.com; 13 John St; s/d from £50/65; ⊙Easter-Oct) Miller's House is a historic Stromness residence with a wonderful 1716 stone doorway. There are two delightful en suite bedrooms where you can smell the cleanliness, and there's plenty of light and an optimistic feel. Showers hit the spot, there are fridges in the rooms and exceptional breakfasts include vegetarian options and daily baked bread.

Hamnavoe Hostel HOSTEL £
(☑01856-851202; www.hamnavoehostel.co.uk; 10a North End Rd; dm/s/tw £17/20/34; 🛜) This well-equipped hostel is efficiently run and boasts excellent facilities, including a fine kitchen and a lounge room with great perspectives over the water. The dorms are very commodious, with duvets, decent mattresses and reading lamps, and the showers are good. Ring ahead as the owner lives off-site.

Ferry Inn INN ££
(☑01856-850280; www.ferryinn.com; 10 John St; s £40-50, d £70-85; 🛜) With a wide variety of rooms divided between the pub itself and a guesthouse opposite, the Ferry is a useful accommodation option in Stromness, which can fill up fast. New owners have renovated the chambers, and they are mostly a good size, with attractive modern decor and OK bathrooms.

Brown's Hostel HOSTEL £
(☑01856-850661; www.brownsorkney.com; 45 Victoria St; dm £16, s & d per person £18-20; @🛜) On the main street, this sociable place has cramped but cosy dorms (the upstairs ones are a pound more but have more space) as well as small private rooms. Life centres on its inviting common area, where you can browse the internet for free or swap pasta recipes in the open kitchen. There are overflow rooms in a house up the street, with self-catering options available. Cycle shed.

Stromness Hotel HOTEL ££
(☑01856-850298; www.stromnesshotel.com; 15 Victoria St; s/d £59/106; P🛜) Proudly surveying the main street and harbour, this lofty Victorian hotel is a reminder of the way things used to be, with its posh revolving door and imposing facade. The pink-hued rooms are spacious and have a certain charm, though a few quirks (uneven floors, old-fashioned fittings, generator noise in some rooms) let the overall package down a bit. The claustrophobic lift means your suitcase'll have to find its own way up.

Ness Caravan & Camping Park CAMPGROUND £
(☑01856-873535; www.orkney.gov.uk; Ness Rd; sites for 4 people £7-10.85; ⊙Apr-Sep; P) This breezy, fenced-in campground overlooks the bay at the southern end of town and is as neat as a pin.

✗ Eating & Drinking

Hamnavoe Restaurant   SEAFOOD ££
(☑01856-850606; 35 Graham Pl; mains £15-22; ⊙dinner Tue-Sun Apr-Oct) Tucked away off the main street, this Stromness favourite specialises in excellent local seafood backed up by professional service. There's always something good off the boats, and the chef prides himself on his lobster. Booking is a must. It usually opens weekends in the winter months.

Stromness Hotel   SCOTTISH, PUB ££
(☑01856-850298; www.stromnesshotel.com; 15 Victoria St; restaurant mains £8-15; ☏) This central hotel does excellent seafood dishes fused with tastes of the Orient, and there are vegetarian options. There's a lounge bar with harbour views, or the earthier, convivial Flattie Bar downstairs.

Ferry Inn   PUB £
(☑01856-850280; www.ferryinn.com; 10 John St; mains £8-18; ⊙food 7.15am-9.30pm; ☏) Every port has its pub, and in Stromness it's the Ferry. Convivial and central, it warms the cockles with folk music, local beers and characters, and pub food that's unsophisticated but generously proportioned and good value. At the time of research, you were better sticking to the bar menu rather than the overpriced dinner offerings.

❶ Information

Stromness Library (☑01856-850907; Alfred St; ⊙2-7pm Mon-Thu, 2-5pm Fri, 11am-5pm Sat) Free internet access.
Stromness Information Centre (☑01856-850716; www.visitorkney.com; Ferry Rd; ⊙10am-4pm Mon-Sat Apr-May & Sep-Oct, 9am-5pm daily Jun-Aug) In the ferry terminal.

❶ Getting There & Around

BOAT Northlink Ferries (p419) runs services from Stromness to Scrabster on the mainland.
BUS Bus X1 runs regularly to Kirkwall (30 minutes) and on to St Margaret's Hope.

Hoy

POP 270

Orkney's second-largest island, Hoy (meaning 'High Island'), got the lion's share of the archipelago's scenic beauty. Shallow turquoise bays lace the east coast and massive seacliffs guard the west, while peat and moorland cover Orkney's highest hills. Much of the north is a bird reserve, with breeding seabirds. The ferry service from Mainland gets very busy in summer – book ahead.

◉ Sights & Activities

Old Man of Hoy   ROCK FORMATION
Hoy's best-known sight is this spectacular 137m-high rock stack that juts improbably from the ocean off the tip of an eroded headland. It's a tough ascent for experienced climbers only but a great walk from Moaness or Rackwick. You can see the Old Man as you pass on the Scrabster–Stromness ferry.

Scapa Flow Visitor Centre   MUSEUM
(☑01856-791300; www.orkney.gov.uk; admission by donation; ⊙9am-4.30pm Mon-Fri Mar-Oct, plus Sat May-Oct & Sun May-Sep) Lyness, on the eastern side of Hoy, was an important naval base during both world wars, when the British Grand Fleet was based in Scapa Flow. This fascinating museum and photographic display, located in an old pumphouse that once fed fuel to the ships, is a must-see for anyone interested in Orkney's military history.

Take your time to browse the exhibits about WWI and WWII, and have a look at the folders of supplementary information: the letters home from a seaman lost when the HMS *Royal Oak* was torpedoed are particularly moving.

🛏 Sleeping & Eating

Stromabank Hotel   HOTEL, PUB ££
(☑01856-701494; www.stromabank.co.uk; s/d £42/64; ⊙lunch Sat & Sun, dinner Fri-Wed Jun-Aug, lunch Sun, dinner Sat & Sun Sep-May) Perched on the hill above Longhope, the small atmospheric Stromabank has very acceptable, refurbished en suite rooms, as well as an attractive bar, offering tasty home-cooked meals (£6 to £10) using lots of local produce.

Wild Heather   B&B £
(☑01856-791098; www.wildheatherbandb.co.uk; Lyness; s/d £38/60; ℗) Turn right from the ferry to reach this great place right on the bay. Plenty of thoughtful extras add value, and evening meals and cycle storage are available.

Hoy Centre   HOSTEL £
(☑office hrs only 01856-873535; www.orkney.gov. uk; dm/f £17/41; ℗) This clean, bright hostel has an enviable location, around 15 minutes' walk from Moaness Pier, at the base of the rugged Cuilags. Rooms are all en suite and include family options.

ℹ️ Getting There & Away

Orkney Ferries (p420) runs a passenger and bike ferry (adult £4.15, 30 minutes, two to six daily) between Stromness and Moaness at the north end of Hoy.

There's also a frequent car ferry to Lyness (on Hoy) from Houton on Mainland (passenger/car £4.15/13.20, 40 minutes, up to seven daily Monday to Friday, two or three Saturday and Sunday); cars must be booked in advance. Sunday service is May to September only.

Northern Islands

The group of windswept islands north of Mainland provides a refuge for migrating birds and a nesting ground for seabirds. Some of the islands are also rich in archaeological sites, but it's the beautiful scenery, with wonderful white-sand beaches and azure seas, that's the main attraction. Most islands are home to traditional Orcadian communities that give a real sense of what Orkney was like before the modern world infringed upon island life.

The tourist offices in Kirkwall and Stromness have the useful *Islands of Orkney* brochure with maps and details of these islands. Note that the 'ay' at the end of each island name (from the Old Norse for 'island') is pronounced 'ee' (Shapinsay is pronounced 'shap-in-*see*').

ℹ️ Getting There & Away

Orkney Ferries (☎01856-872044; www.orkneyferries.co.uk) and **Loganair** (☎01857-873457; www.loganair.co.uk) enable you to make day trips to many of the islands from Kirk-

wall on most days of the week (North Ronaldsay services run only on Friday). That said, it's really best to stay and soak up the slow, easy pace of life.

SHAPINSAY
POP 300

Just 20 minutes by ferry from Kirkwall, Shapinsay is an intensively cultivated island with a fine castle and good beaches along its western edge.

◉ Sights & Activities

Balfour Castle   CASTLE
(www.balfourcastle.co.uk; tours £20) Completed in 1848 in the turreted Scottish Baronial style, Balfour Castle dominates the southern end of the island. It's only open for guided tours; these run on Sundays in August and must be booked in advance. The price includes admission to the castle and afternoon tea.

FREE **Burroughston Broch**   ARCHAEOLOGICAL SITE
(admission free; ⊙24hr) About 4 miles from the pier, at the far northeastern corner of the island is Iron Age Burroughston Broch, one of the best-preserved brochs (defensive towers) in Orkney.

ℹ️ Getting There & Away

Orkney Ferries (p420) operates a ferry from Kirkwall (passenger/car £4.15/13.20, 25 minutes). Services are limited in winter.

ROUSAY
POP 210

Off the north coast of Mainland, Rousay makes a great day trip, but you'll feel like

---

LOCAL KNOWLEDGE

JOHN BAIN: INTERISLAND PILOT

Best time to visit? The summer, but it's the busiest. Not a lot of visitors like the climate in winter, and a lot of places close down. Ferries are less frequent; you don't have the same chances to move around. But you do get some beautiful winter days.

Ferry or plane? If you've got time, experience both. I'm biased but I would say that from the aircraft you see more, and you can fit more into your trip. You can see nearly all the main islands in a few days.

Most beautiful island? Oh, no – I'd get hung, drawn, and quartered if I picked just one! I live up on North Mainland and look out on the islet of Eynhallow every morning. The stories say that's where strange folk, the Finmen, lived. That's one of the great things about Orkney, the storytelling. Go to a storytelling night, you'll be hooked.

A rainy day? Stay home! No, go round the craft shops in Kirkwall. And the town's got some good pubs, like Helgi's, for a quiet drink.

Favourite out-of-the-way spot? The Brough of Birsay. Go up there for a picnic.

Local Words? Peedie – it means little. It's a very common word on the islands.

staying longer. This hilly island is famous for its numerous archaeological sites, earning it the nickname 'Egypt of the North' (perhaps pushing it a *bit* too far).

◉ Sights & Activities

You can **hire a bike** at Trumland Farm (p432) and take on the winding, hilly 14-mile circuit of the island. It's also possible to **walk** from the ferry pier to Midhowe Broch, taking in all the main historic sites (12 miles return, allow six hours).

FREE Prehistoric Sites   ARCHAEOLOGICAL SITES
(HS; www.historic-scotland.gov.uk; ◷24hr) The major archaeological sites are clearly labelled from the road ringing the island. Heading west from the ferry, you soon come to **Taversoe Tuick**, an intriguing burial cairn constructed on two levels, with separate entrances – perhaps a joint tomb for different families; a semidetached solution in posthumous housing. Squeeze into the cairn to explore both levels, but there's not much space. Not far beyond are two other significant cairns; **Blackhammer**, then **Knowe of Yarso**, the latter a fair walk up the hill but with majestic views.

Six miles from the ferry, mighty **Midhowe Cairn** has been dubbed the 'Great Ship of Death'. Built around 3500 BC and enormous in size, it's divided into compartments, in which the remains of 25 people were found. Covered by a protective stone building, it's nevertheless a memorable sight. Next to it, **Midhowe Broch**, the sturdy stone lines of which echo the striations of the rocky shoreline, is a muscular Iron Age fortified compound with a mezzanine floor. The sites are by the water, a 10-minute walk downhill from the main road.

⌔ Sleeping & Eating

Taversoe Hotel   HOTEL **££**
(☎01856-821325; www.taversoehotel.co.uk; s/d £45/75; P) About 2 miles west from the ferry pier, the island's only hotel is a low-key place, with neat, simple doubles with water vistas that share a bathroom and a twin with en suite bathroom but no view. The best views, however, are from the dining room, which serves good-value meals. The friendly owners will pick you up from the ferry.

⌔ Trumland Farm Hostel   HOSTEL **£**
(☎01856-821252; trumland@btopenworld.com; sites £5, dm £10, bedding £2; P) An easy stroll from the ferry (turn left at the main road), this organic farm has a wee hostel with rather cramped six-bed dorms and a pretty little kitchen and common area. You can pitch tents outside and use the facilities; there's also a well-equipped self-catering cottage available that sleeps three (£60 to £100).

❶ Getting There & Around

BOAT A small **ferry** (☎01856-751360; www.orkneyferries.co.uk) connects Tingwall on Mainland with Rousay (passenger/bicycle/car return £9.30/2/26.40, 30 minutes, up to six daily) and the nearby islands of Egilsay and Wyre. Vehicle bookings are compulsory.

BICYLE Bikes can be hired for £7 per day from Trumland Farm (see below).

TAXI **Rousay Tours** (☎01856-821234; www.rousaytours.co.uk; tours adult/child £17.50/5.50) offers taxi service and guided tours of the island, including wildlife-spotting (seals and otters) and visits to the prehistoric sites.

STRONSAY
POP 343

Stronsay attracts walkers and cyclists for its lack of serious inclines and the beautiful landscapes of its four curving bays. You can spot wildlife here: chubby seals basking on the rocks, puffins and other seabirds.

⌔ Sleeping & Eating

Stronsay Hotel   HOTEL **££**
(☎01857-616213; www.stronsayhotelorkney.co.uk; s/d £38/76; ▣▦) The island's watering hole is near the ferry and has immaculate refurbished rooms. There's also recommended pub grub (mains from £7) in the bar, with excellent seafood (including paella and lobster) in particular. There are good deals for multinight stays.

❶ Getting There & Away

AIR Loganair (p431) flies from Kirkwall to Stronsay (£37 one way, 20 minutes, one or two daily Monday to Saturday).

BOAT A **ferry** (☎01856-872044; www.orkneyferries.co.uk) links Kirkwall with Stronsay (passenger/car £8.10/19.15, 1½ hours, two to three daily) and Eday.

EDAY
POP 121

This slender island was extensively cut for peat to supply the surrounding islands. The interior is hilly and covered in peat bog, while the coast and the north of the island are low-lying and green.

Sights & Activities

FREE Eday Heritage &
Visitor Centre   MUSEUM
(☏01857-622283; www.visiteday.com; ⊘9am-
5.30pm daily May-Sep, 10am-5pm Sat Oct-Apr) Has
a range of local history exhibits, as well as
an audiovisual about tidal energy initiatives.

Eday Minibus Tour   GUIDED TOUR
(☏01857-622206; tours adult/child £13.50/11.50)
Offers taxi service 2¼-hour guided tours
from the ferry pier on Monday, Wednesday
and Friday from May to August.

Sleeping & Eating

Eday Hostel   HOSTEL £
(☏07977-281084; dm £15; Ⓟ@) Four miles north
of the ferry pier, this recently renovated, community-run hostel is an excellent place to stay.
You can camp alongside too at no cost.

Getting There & Away

AIR There are two flights from Kirkwall (one
way £37, 30 minutes) to London airport – that's
London, Eday – on Wednesday only.
BOAT Ferries sail from Kirkwall, usually via Stronsay or Sanday (passenger/car
£8.10/19.15, two hours, two to three daily).

SANDAY
POP 478

Aptly named, blissfully quiet flat Sanday is
ringed by Orkney's best beaches – with daz-
zling-white sand of the sort you'd expect in
the Caribbean.

At the tip of the headland east of the main
village of Kettletoft is **Quoyness chambered tomb** (admission free; ⊘24hr), similar
to Maes Howe and dating from the 3rd
millennium BC. It has triple walls, a main
chamber and six smaller cells.

Beyond the loch at the northeastern tip of
the island is **Tofts Ness** (admission free; ⊘24
hr), a largely unexcavated funerary complex
with some 500 prehistoric burial mounds
and the remains of an Iron Age roundhouse.

Sleeping & Eating

Belsair   B&B, PUB £
(☏01857-600206; www.belsairsanday.co.uk; r per
person £30; ☎) Overlooks the harbour in Kettletoft village with tidy en suite rooms that
are good value. Bar meals all day feature Orcadian produce.

**Ayre's Rock Hostel &
Campsite**   HOSTEL, CAMPGROUND £
(☏01857-600410; www.ayres-rock-sanday-orkney.
co.uk; 1-/2-person tent sites £5/7, huts £20, dm/s

£13.50/18; Ⓟ@) Cosy hostel sleeping eight
in the outbuildings of a farm. There's a craft
shop and chip shop on-site, breakfasts and
dinners are available, and you can also pitch
a tent or sleep in a camping hut. It's on the
west coast, 6 miles north of the ferry pier.
Hosts can organise car and bike hire.

Getting There & Around

AIR There are flights from Kirkwall to Sanday
(one way £37, 20 minutes, once or twice daily
Monday to Saturday).
BOAT Ferries run from Kirkwall (passenger/car
£8.10/19.15, 1½ hours), with a link to Eday. A bus
meets the boat.

WESTRAY
POP 563

If you've time to visit only one of Orkney's
Northern Islands, make Westray the one.
The largest of the group, it has rolling farmland, handsome sandy beaches, great coastal
walks and several appealing places to stay.

Sights & Activities

FREE Noup Head   NATURE RESERVE
The Royal Society for the Protection of Birds
(RSPB) reserve at Noup Head, at Westray's
northwestern tip is a dramatic area of sea
cliffs with vast numbers of breeding seabirds
from April to July. You can walk to Noup
Head along the clifftops from a parking area,
passing the impressive chasm of Ramni Geo,
and return via the lighthouse access road (4
miles, allow two to three hours).

Westray Heritage Centre   HERITAGE CENTRE
(☏01857-677414; www.westrayheritage.co.uk; Pierowall; adult/child £2.50/50p; ⊘11.30am-5pm Mon,
10am-noon & 2-5pm Tue-Sat, 1.30-5.30pm Sun May-
Sep) This has displays on local history, nature dioramas, and archaeological finds, including the famous 5000-year-old 'Westray
Wife'. The sandstone figurine is the oldest
depiction of the human form yet found in
Scotland.

FREE Noltland Castle   CASTLE
(⊘24 hr) A half-mile west of Pierowall stand
the ruins of this tower house, built by Gilbert Balfour, aide to Mary, Queen of Scots.
The castle bristles with shot holes, part of
the defences of the deceitful Balfour, who
plotted to murder Cardinal Beaton and, after being exiled, the king of Sweden.

Westraak   GUIDED TOUR
(☏01857-677777; www.westraak.co.uk; Quarry Rd,
Pierowall) Runs informative and engaging

trips around the island, covering everything from Viking history to puffin mating habits.

Sleeping & Eating

TOP CHOICE **West Manse** B&B £

(☏01857-677482; www.westmanse.co.uk; Westside; r £20 per person; P🐾) No timetables reign at this imposing house with arcing coastal vistas; make your own breakfast when you feel like it. Your welcoming hosts have introduced a raft of green solutions for heating, fuel and more. Kids will love this unconventional place, while art exhibitions, cooking classes, venerably comfortable furniture and clean air are drawcards for parents.

The Barn HOSTEL, CAMPGROUND £

(☏01857-677214; www.thebarnwestray.co.uk; Pierowall; sites £5 plus per person £1.50, dm £17; P) This excellent, intimate, modern 13-bed hostel is an Orcadian gem. It's heated throughout and has an inviting lounge, complete with DVD collection. The price includes bed linen, shower and pristine kitchen facilities; local advice comes free. There's also a camp ground on-site complete with laundry and campers' kitchen.

No 1 Broughton B&B ££

(☏01857-677726; www.no1broughton.co.uk; s/d £35/60; P) This solid pinkish house sits right on Pierowall Bay and offers a very comfortable B&B with unusual extras, such as original artworks on the walls and a sauna. There are three spacious rooms and a conservatory breakfast room, where you can feel the sun but not that nasty wind.

Bis Geos GUESTHOUSE £

(☏01857-677420; www.bisgeos.co.uk; per week from £310; P) Stunning views at this spectacular self-catering option between Pierowall and Noup Head.

Pierowall Hotel PUB £

(☏01857-677472; www.pierowallhotel.co.uk; mains £8-10) The heart of this island community, the local pub is famous throughout Orkney for its popular fish and chips – whatever has turned up in the day's catch by the hotel's boats is displayed on the blackboard. There are also some curries available, but the sea is the way to go here.

❶ Getting There & Around

AIR There are daily flights from Kirkwall to Westray (one way £37, 20 minutes).

BOAT A ferry (p420) links Kirkwall with Rapness (passenger/car £8.10/19.15, 1½ hours, daily). A bus to the main town, Pierowall, meets the ferry.

PAPA WESTRAY
POP 65

Known locally as Papay, this exquisitely peaceful, tiny island (4 miles by 1 mile) attracts superlatives. It is home to Europe's oldest domestic building – built about 5500 years ago – the **Knap of Howar** (☉24 hr), and to Europe's largest colony of arctic terns. Even the two-minute hop from Westray airfield is featured in *Guinness World Records* as the world's shortest scheduled air service. The island was the cradle of Christianity in Orkney – **St Boniface Church** (☉24 hr) was founded in the 8th century, though most of it dates to the 12th century.

Sleeping & Eating

Beltane Guest House & Hostel GUESTHOUSE, HOSTEL £

(☏01857-644224; www.papawestray.co.uk; dm/s/d £15/25/35; P) Owned by the local community co-op, this comprises a 20-bed hostel and a guesthouse with four simple and immaculate rooms with en suite and self-catering kitchen access. It's just over a mile north of the ferry. You can camp here (£5) and lunch and dinner are served.

❶ Getting There & Away

AIR There are daily flights to Papa Westray (£18, 15 minutes) from Kirkwall, and a special £21 return fare if you stay overnight. Some of the Kirkwall flights go via Westray (£17, 2 minutes) or North Ronaldsay (£17, 10 minutes).

BOAT A passenger-only ferry runs from Pierowall on Westray to Papa Westray (£4.05, 25 minutes, three to six daily in summer); the crossing is free if you travel direct from the Rapness ferry from Westray. From October to April the boat sails by arrangement (☏01857-677216).

NORTH RONALDSAY
POP 70

North Ronaldsay is a real outpost surrounded by rolling seas and big skies. Delicious peace-and-quiet and excellent birdwatching lure visitors. There are enough semiferal sheep to seize power, but a 13-mile drystone wall running around the island keeps them off the grass; they make do with seaweed, which gives their meat a unique flavour.

◉ Sights & Activities

North Ronaldsay Tour GUIDED TOUR

(☏07703 112224; adult/child £4/2) Offers excellent tours of one of North Ronaldsay's two lighthouses and the **Woollen Mill** (adult/child £4/2, combined lighthouse & mill ticket £6/3).

🛏 Sleeping

Observatory Guest House HOSTEL, CAMPGROUND **££**
(☎01857-633200; www.nrbo.co.uk; sites £4.50, dm/s/d £15.50/36/72; **P@**🐾) Powered by wind and solar energy, this offers first-rate accommodation and ornithological activities next to the ferry pier. There's a cafe-bar with lovely coastal views and convivial communal dinners (£13.50) in a sun-kissed (sometimes) conservatory; if you're lucky, local lamb might be on the menu. You can also camp here.

ⓘ Getting There & Away

AIR There are two or three daily flights to North Ronaldsay (£18, 20 minutes) from Kirkwall. The £21 return offer is great value.

BOAT A ferry runs from Kirkwall on Tuesday and Friday (passenger/car £8.10/19.15, 2½ hours).

SHETLAND ISLANDS

Adrift in the North Sea and close enough to Norway geographically and historically to make nationality an ambiguous concept here, the Shetland Islands are Britain's most northerly outpost. There's a Scandinavian lilt to the local accent, and streets named King Haakon or St Olaf remind that Shetland was under Norse rule until 1469, when it was gifted to Scotland as the dowry of a Danish princess. The setting of this archipelago of mighty, wind-ravaged clumps of brown and green earth rising from the North Sea is still uniquely Scottish though, with deep, naked glens flanked by steep hills, sky-blue lochs and (of course) sheep on the roads.

One of the great attractions of Shetland is the birdlife; it's worth packing binoculars even if you're not fanatical about it.

ⓘ Getting There & Away
Air
The oil industry ensures that air connections are good. The main airport (p489) is at Sumburgh, 25 miles south of Lerwick. **Flybe** (☎0871 700 2000; www.flybe.com) runs daily services to Aberdeen, Kirkwall, Inverness, Edinburgh and Glasgow, and also twice-weekly summer services to Bergen (Norway).

Boat
Northlink Ferries (☎0845 600 0449; www.northlinkferries.co.uk; 🐾) runs daily overnight

ⓘ ONLINE SHETLAND

The excellent website www.visit.shetland.org has good info on accommodation, activities, and more.

car ferries between Aberdeen and Lerwick (passenger one-way £25 to £38, car £101 to £136, 12 to 15 hours), stopping three to four times a week at Kirkwall, Orkney. With a basic ticket you can sleep in recliner chairs or in the bar area. It's £31 for a berth in a shared cabin and up to £129 for a comparatively luxurious double cabin. There's a cafe, bar, restaurant and cinema on-board as well as slow wi-fi.

ⓘ Getting Around
Air
Interisland flights are operated by **DirectFlight** (☎01595-840246; www.directflight.co.uk), and depart from Tingwall airport, 6.5 miles northwest of Lerwick.

Boat
Ferry services link Mainland to the various inhabited islands, mostly run by **Shetland Islands Council** (www.shetland.gov.uk/ferries).

Bicycle
You can hire bikes from several places, including Grantfield Garage (p435) (per day/week £12.50/50) in Lerwick.

Bus
An extensive network of bus services radiate from Lerwick's **Viking bus station** (☎01595-694100; Commercial Rd) to all corners of Mainland, and on (via ferry) to the islands of Yell and Unst. Schedules aren't great for day tripping from Lerwick.

Car & Motorcycle
Shetland's broad, well-made roads (think 'oil money') seem like motorways after Orkney's winding lanes. Car hire is fuss-free, and they'll bring your vehicle to whatever transport terminal you arrive at. Prices start at around £20/110 for a day/week but are more usually around £30 a day.

Bolts Car Hire (☎01595-693636; www.boltscarhire.co.uk; 26 North Rd, Lerwick) Also has an office at Sumburgh airport.

Grantfield Garage (☎01595-692709; www.grantfieldgarage.co.uk; North Rd, Lerwick) The cheapest. A short walk towards town from the Lerwick ferry.

Star Rent-a-Car (☎01595-692075; www.starrentacar.co.uk; 22 Commercial Rd, Lerwick) Opposite the bus station. Has an office at Sumburgh airport.

Lerwick

POP 6830

Built on the herring trade, Lerwick is Shetland's only real town, home to a third of the islands' population and dug into the hills overlooking Bressay Sound. It has a solidly maritime feel, with aquiline oilboats competing for space in the superb natural harbour with the dwindling fishing fleet. The water's clear blue tones makes wandering along atmospheric Commercial St a delight, and the excellent museum provides all the cultural background.

◉ Sights

TOP CHOICE **Shetland Museum** MUSEUM
(☎01595-695057; www.shetland-museum.org.uk; Hay's Dock; admission free; ☻10am-5pm Mon-Sat, noon-5pm Sun) This modern museum is an impressive recollection of 5000 years' worth of culture, people and their interaction with this ancient landscape. Comprehensive but never dull, the display covers everything from the archipelago's geology to its fishing industry, via a great section on local mythology – find out about the scary *nyuggles* (ghostly horses), or use the patented machine for detecting *trows* (fairies). Pictish carvings and replica jewellery are among the finest pieces here; the museum also includes a working lighthouse mechanism, small art gallery, and a boat-building workshop, where you can watch carpenters restoring and re-creating traditional Shetland fishing vessels. There's also an archive here for tracing your Shetland ancestry.

FREE **Böd of Gremista** MUSEUM
(☎01595-695057; www.shetlandtextilemuseum.com; Gremista Rd; ☻noon-4pm Tue-Sat May–mid-Sep) This house was once a fish-curing station, and also the birthplace of Arthur Anderson, who founded P&O. The friendly custodian will show you around two rooms restored to how they were 200 years ago, as well as an exhibit on the history of the whitefish industry. The building also houses displays on the knitted and woven textiles and patterns that take their name from the islands. The *böd* (fishing booth) is a mile north of the town centre.

FREE **Clickimin Broch** ARCHEOLOGICAL SITE
This fortified site, just under a mile southwest of the town centre, was occupied from the 7th century BC to the 6th century AD. It's impressively large, and its setting on a small loch gives it a feeling of being removed from the present day.

FREE **Fort Charlotte** FORTRESS
(Charlotte St; ☻9.30am-sunset) Built in 1781, this occupies the site of an earlier fortification built in 1665 to protect the harbour from the Dutch navy. The five-sided fortress never saw action, but today houses local volunteer units and provides excellent views over the harbour.

TOURS

Shetland Geotours TOURS
(☎01595-859218; www.shetlandgeotours.com; per person from £45) Runs daily excursions and guided walks, focusing on history and archaeology, but including some nature-watching.

✦ Festivals & Events

Shetland Folk Festival MUSIC
(www.shetlandfolkfestival.com) Held in late April or early May.

⌂ Sleeping

Lerwick has very average hotels but excellent B&B choices. It fills year-round, so book ahead.

TOP CHOICE **Alder Lodge Guest House** B&B ££
(☎01595-695705; www.alderlodgeguesthouse.com; 6 Clairmont Pl; s £40-50, d £75; ℗⏍) This stone former bank is a delightful place to stay. Imbued with a sense of space and light, the rooms are large and very well furnished,

---

UP HELLY AA!!

Shetland's long Viking history has rubbed off in more ways than just street names and square-shouldered locals. Most villages have a fire festival, a continuation of Viking midwinter celebrations of the rebirth of the sun. The most spectacular happens in Lerwick.

Up Helly Aa (www.uphellyaa.org) takes place on the last Tuesday in January. Squads of *guizers* dress in Viking costume and march through the streets with blazing torches, dragging a replica longship, which they then surround and burn, bellowing out Viking songs from behind bushy beards.

with good en suites, fridges and DVD player. Excellent hosts really make the effort to help you feel at home, and do a great breakfast, with a smoked fish option and special diets catered for. There is also a self-catering house nearby.

Fort Charlotte Guesthouse   B&B ££
(☏01595-692140; www.fortcharlotte.co.uk; 1 Charlotte St; s £30-35, d £65; ☎☀) Sheltering under the fortress walls, this friendly place offers summery en suite rooms, including great singles. Views down the pedestrian street are on offer in some; sloping ceilings and oriental touches add charm to others. There's a bike shed and local salmon for breakfast. Very popular; book ahead.

Isleburgh House Hostel   HOSTEL £
(☏01595-745100; www.isleburgh.org.uk; King Harald St; dm/tw £17/34; ⊙Apr-Sep; P@☎) This typically grand Lerwick mansion houses an excellent hostel, with comfortable dorms, a shop, a laundry, a cafe and an industrial kitchen. Electronic keys offer excellent security and no curfew. It's wise to book ahead, and ask about winter availability as it sometimes opens for groups.

Woosung   B&B £
(☏01595-693687; conroywoosung@hotmail.com; 43 St Olaf St; s £25-35, d £46-50; ☎☀) A budget gem in the heart of Lerwick B&B-land, this has a wise and welcoming host, and comfortable, clean, good-value rooms that share a bathroom. The solid stone house dates from the 19th century, built by a clipper captain who traded tea out of the Chinese port it's named after.

Kveldsro House Hotel   HOTEL ££
(☏01595-692195; www.shetlandhotels.com; Greenfield Pl; s/d £105/130; P☎) Lerwick's best hotel overlooks the harbour and has a quiet but central setting. It's a dignified small set-up that will appeal to older visitors or couples. All doubles cost the same, but some are markedly better than others, with four-poster beds or water views. Rooms 415 and 417 have striking harbour vistas; if you're after a twin, try lovely 413. All boast new stylish bathrooms and iPod docks.

Brentham House   B&B ££
(☏01950-460201; www.brenthamhouse.com; 7 Harbour St; s/d/ste £60/75/120; ☎) This staffless place – pick up the keys from the restaurant on the corner – offers attractive rooms with great bathrooms and harbour views.

There's a posh self-catering apartment also. Continental breakfast is left in the fridge in your room.

Eddlewood Guest House   B&B ££
(☏01595-692772; chornby2@tiscali.co.uk; 8 Clairmont Pl; s/d £40/70; ☎☀) Cheerfully run, this sound selection has spacious, very well-kept en suite rooms, some with limited sea views. The beds offer plenty of space to stretch out in, and the showers might just be Shetland's finest.

Clickimin Caravan & Camp Site   CAMPGROUND £
(☏01595-741000; www.srt.org.uk; South Lochside; sites per small/large tent £8.80/11.90; P☎☀☀) Clickimin is a small and tidy park with good grassy sites overlooking a small loch. There's a laundry and shower block, and there's a leisure centre with pool and more as part of the complex. It's on the main A970 road in the west of town.

✖ Eating

Hay's Dock   CAFE, RESTAURANT ££
(☏01595-741569; www.haysdock.co.uk; Hay's Dock; mains lunch £6-11, dinner £11-20; ⊙lunch daily, dinner Tue-Sat; ☎) The upstairs cafe-restaurant in the Shetland Museum sports a wall of picture windows and a fairweather balcony that overlooks the harbour. Clean lines and pale wood recall Scandinavia, but the menu relies on carefully selected local and Scottish produce. Lunch ranges from delicious fish and chips to chowder, while the evening menu concentrates on seafood and steak.

Monty's Bistro   BRITISH ££
(☏01595-696555; www.montys-shetland.co.uk; 5 Mounthooly St; mains lunch £8-9, dinner £14-17; ⊙lunch Tue-Sat, dinner Mon-Sat) Though well hidden away behind the tourist office, Monty's is far from a secret and Shetlanders descend on its wee wooden tables with alacrity. The upstairs dining room is fragrant with aromas of things like Gressingham duck and local mussels from the short, quality menu, and the wine list has some welcome old friends.

Peerie Shop Cafe   CAFE £
(☏01595-692816; www.peerieshopcafe.com; Esplanade; light meals £2-7; ⊙9am-6pm Mon-Sat) If you've been craving proper espresso since leaving the mainland, head to this gem, with art exhibitions, wire-mounted halogens and industrial-gantry chic. Newspapers,

Lerwick

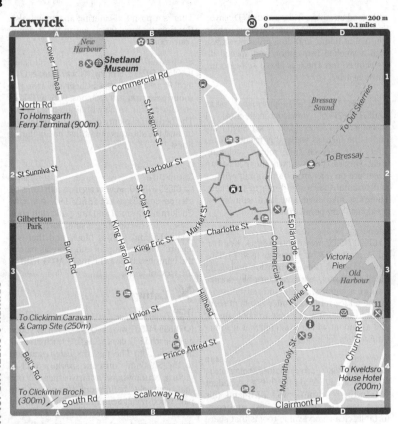

scrumptious cakes and sandwiches, hot chocolate that you deserve after that blasting wind outside, and – more rarely – outdoor seating give everyone a reason to be here.

Queen's Hotel SCOTTISH **££**
(☏01595-692826; www.kgqhotels.co.uk; Commercial St; mains £10-16; ☏) The dining room in this slightly run-down hotel wins marks for its harbour views – book one of the window tables. Portions are generous, and the seafood is good. There are options for vegetarians.

Fort Café CAFE, TAKEAWAY **£**
(☏01595-693125; 2 Commercial St; fish & chips £6-8; ⊙11am-10.30pm Mon-Fri, 11am-7pm Sat, 4-10.30pm Sun) Lerwick's salty air often creates fish-and-chip cravings. Eat in (until 8pm), or munch down on the pier if you don't mind the seagulls' envious stares.

🍷 Drinking & Entertainment

Shetland Fiddlers Society plays around town, and it's worth attending a session – enquire at the tourist office. Look out for **Mareel** (www.shetlandarts.org), a new arts venue near the museum.

Captain Flint's PUB
(2 Commercial St; ⊙11am-1am) This lively bar – by some distance Lerwick's best – throbs with happy conversation and has a distinctly nautical, creaky-wooden feel. There's a cross-section of young 'uns, tourists, boat folk and older locals. There's live music some nights and a pool table upstairs.

🛍 Shopping

Best buys are the woollen cardigans and sweaters for which Shetland is world-famous. Check www.shetlandsartsandcrafts. co.uk for craft outlets around the islands, or

Lerwick

◉ Top Sights
Shetland Museum.................................A1

◉ Sights
1 Fort Charlotte.....................................C2

◉ Sleeping
2 Alder Lodge Guest House....................C4
3 Brentham House.................................C2
Eddlewood Guest House ....(see 2)
4 Fort Charlotte Guesthouse.................C2
5 Isleburgh House Hostel......................B3
6 Woosung...B4

◉ Eating
7 Fort Café..C2
8 Hay's Dock...A1
9 Monty's Bistro....................................D4
10 Peerie Shop Cafe..............................C3
11 Queen's Hotel D3

◉ Drinking
12 Captain Flint's..................................D3

◉ Entertainment
13 Mareel B1

grab the Shetland Craft Trail brochure from the tourist office.

ℹ Information

There are several free wi-fi networks around the centre.

Gilbert Bain Hospital (☎01595-743000; www.shb.scot.nhs.uk/; South Rd)

Shetland Library (☎01595-693868; Lower Hillhead; ⊙9am-8pm Mon & Thu, to 5pm Tue, Wed, Fri & Sat) Free internet.

Lerwick tourist office (cnr Commercial St & Mounthooly St) Helpful, with a good range of books and maps and a comprehensive brochure selection.

ℹ Getting There & Away

BOAT Northlink Ferries (p435) services dock at **Holmsgarth terminal**, a 15-minute walk northwest from the town centre.

BUS From Viking bus station (p435), buses service various corners of the archipelago, including regular services to/from Sumburgh Airport.

GETTING AROUND

Allied Taxis   TAXI
(☎01595-690069; www.shetlandtaxis.co.uk) The main Shetland taxi company. You can arrange bespoke tours around the islands with them.

Bressay & Noss

POP 350

These islands lie across Bressay Sound just east of Lerwick. Bressay (*bress*-ah) has some interesting walks, especially along the cliffs and up **Ward Hill** (226m), which has good

views of the islands. Much smaller Noss, east of Bressay, is a nature reserve.

◉ Sights & Activities

Isle of Noss   NATURE RESERVE
(☎0800-107 7818; www.nnr-scotland.org.uk/noss; boat adult/child £3/1.50; ⊙10am-5pm Tue, Wed & Fri-Sun May-Aug) Little Noss, 1.5 miles wide, lies 150m east of Bressay. The high seacliffs on its east coast provide nesting sites for more than 100,000 pairs of breeding seabirds, while the inland heath supports 400 pairs of great skua.

Access is by dinghy from Bressay; if you see a red flag on Noss from the car park above the boat dock, it's not running. Phone in advance to check. Walking anticlockwise around Noss is an easier hike with better cliff viewing. There's a small visitor centre by the boat dock.

Seabirds & Seals   CRUISE
(☎07595-540224; www.seabirds-and-seals.com; adult/child £45/25; ⊙10am & 2pm mid-Apr–mid-Sep) Runs three-hour wildlife cruises (10am and 2pm) around Bressay and Noss, departing from Lerwick. Includes an underwater viewing session. Trips run year-round, weather permitting; book by phone or at Lerwick tourist office.

🛏 Sleeping & Eating

Northern Lights Holistic Spa   B&B ££
(☎01595-820257; www.shetlandspa.com; Uphouse; s/d £70/120; ℗⑤) Offering huge colourful rooms and marvellous views back over the sound towards Lerwick, this unusual place is appealingly decorated with Asian art. Room rates include use of the sauna, steam room and jacuzzi; massage

OFFBEAT ACCOMMODATION

Shetland offers intriguing options for getting off the beaten accommodation track. There's a great network of *böds* – simple rustic cottages or huts with peat fires. They cost £10 per person, or £8 for the ones without electricity, and are available from March to October. Contact and book via **Shetland Amenity Trust** (☎01595-694688; www.camping -bods.com).

The same organisation runs three **Lighthouse Cottages** (☎01595-694688; www.shetlandlighthouse.com), commanding dramatic views of rugged coastline: one at Sumburgh (under renovation until 2014), one on the island of Bressay near Lerwick, and one at Eshaness. Sleeping six to seven, the cottages cost from £190 to £290 for a three-night booking in high season.

treatments are available. Elaborate dinners (£35) are served in an attractive space. Follow signs for Uphouse and it's the big yellow building on your right near the crest of the hill.

Maryfield House Hotel   PUB ££
(☎01595-820207; s/d £38.50/77; P⌨) Near the ferry, this is friendly and provides comfortable-enough accommodation and tasty fishy bar meals (£7 to £9).

❶ Getting There & Away

Ferries (passenger/car return £4.30/10, seven minutes, frequent) link Lerwick and Bressay. It's then a 2.5-mile walk or bike ride across the island to reach the crossing point to Noss.

Central & West Mainland

SCALLOWAY
POP 812

Surrounded by bare, rolling hills, Scalloway (*scall*-o-wah) – Shetland's former capital – is a busy fishing and yachting harbour with a thriving seafood-processing industry. It's on the west coast 6 miles from Lerwick.

There are pretty beaches and pleasant walks on the islands of Trondra and East and West Burra, linked by bridges just south of Scalloway.

◉ Sights & Activities

Scalloway Museum   MUSEUM
(www.shetlandheritageassociation.com; Castle St; adult/child £3/1; ⊙11am-4pm Mon-Sat, 2-4pm Sun May-Sep; ⊕) This enthusiastic new museum has an excellent display on Scalloway life and history, with prehistoric finds, witch-burnings and local lore all featuring. There's a detailed section on the Shetland Bus, and a fun area for kids.

FREE **Scalloway Castle**   CASTLE
(HS; www.historic-scotland.co.uk) The town's most prominent landmark is Scalloway Castle, built around 1600 by Earl Patrick Stewart. The turreted and corbelled tower house is fairly well preserved. If it's locked, get keys from the Scalloway Museum or Scalloway Hotel on Main St.

Shetland Bus Memorial   MONUMENT
(Main St) During WWII a fleet of small boats – the Shetland Bus – shuttled from Scalloway to occupied Norway, carrying agents, wireless operators and military supplies for the resistance movement, and returning with refugees, recruits for the Free Norwegian forces and Christmas trees for treeless Shetland. The memorial is a moving tribute, built of stones from both countries.

⌖ Sleeping & Eating

TOP CHOICE **Scalloway Hotel**   HOTEL ££
(☎01595-880444; www.scallowayhotel.com; Main St; s/d/superior £75/110/150; P⌨) One of Shetland's best, this energetically run waterfront place has very stylish rooms featuring sheepskins, local tweeds and other fabrics and views over the harbour. Some are larger than others; the best is the fabulous superior, with handmade furniture, artworks and a top-of-the-line mattress on its four-poster bed. The restaurant (mains £14 to £23) is especially good for quality seafood. Excellent Scottish cheeses round off your meal.

❶ Getting There & Away

Buses run from Lerwick (25 minutes, roughly hourly Monday to Saturday, two Sunday) to Scalloway, stopping on Main St.

South Mainland

From Lerwick, the main road south winds 25 miles down the eastern side of this long, narrow, hilly tail of land to Sumburgh Head. The waters lapping against the cliffs are an inviting turquoise in many places – if it weren't for the raging Arctic gales, you might be tempted to have a dip.

SANDWICH & AROUND

Opposite scattered Sandwich, where you cross the 60-degree latitude line, is the small isle of Mousa, an RSPB reserve protecting some 7000 breeding pairs of storm petrels. It's also home to rock-basking seals and impressive **Mousa Broch**, the best preserved of the northern fortifications. Rising to 13m, it's an imposing structure, typically double-walled, and with a spiral staircase to access a 2nd floor. It features in Viking sagas as a hideout for eloping couples.

◉ Sights & Activities

Mousa Boat Trips   BOAT TOURS
(☎07901-872339; www.mousa.co.uk) From April to mid-September, this operator runs daily boat trips to Mousa (adult/child return £15.50/7, 15 minutes) from Sandwich, allowing three hours ashore on the island. It also offers night trips to view the petrels (see website for dates).

❶ Getting There & Away

There are buses between Lerwick and Sandwich (25 minutes, four to eleven daily).

BIGTON & AROUND

Three buses from Lerwick (not Sunday) stop in Bigton on the west coast, but it's another couple of miles to the largest shell-and-sand tombolo (narrow isthmus) in Britain. Walk across the tombolo to beautiful, emerald-capped **St Ninian's Isle**, where you'll find the ruins of a 12th-century church, beneath which are traces of an earlier Pictish church. During excavations in 1958, Pictish treasure, consisting of 27 silver objects probably dating from AD800, was found. They're now kept in the Museum of Scotland in Edinburgh, with replicas in Lerwick's Shetland Museum.

BODDAM & SCOUSBURGH

From small Boddam a side road leads to the Shetland Crofthouse Museum (☎01950-460557; www.shetlandheritageassociation.com; admission free; ☉10am-1pm & 2-5pm May-Sep). Built in 1870, this former dwelling has been restored, thatched and furnished with 19th-century furniture and utensils. The Lerwick–Sumburgh bus stops right outside.

West of Boddam, Scousburgh sits placidly above Shetland's best beach, gloriously white **Scousburgh Sands**. Nearby is the Spiggie Hotel (☎01950-460409; www.thespiggiehotel.co.uk; s/d £55/120, self-catering s/d from £70/80; Ⓟ🛜), with compact rooms, self-catering annexes and tasty seafood and bar meals (lunch Wednesday to Sunday, dinner daily). The rooms and dining room boast great views down over the local loch.

ORKNEY & SHETLAND ISLANDS SOUTH MAINLAND

WESTERN ISLANDS

Visible a mile offshore in West Mainland is the island of **Papa Stour** (pop 23), home to huge colonies of auks, terns and skuas. Buckled volcanic strata have been wonderfully eroded by the sea to produce dramatic caves, arches and stacks. There's limited self-catering accommodation, and a small campsite by the ferry pier. The island is served by Tuesday-only flights (p435) from Tingwall airport (return £39), with a day return possible, and a ferry (☎01595-745804; www.shetland.gov.uk/ferries/) from West Burrafirth (passenger return £8.20, car and driver return £10, 40 minutes, daily except Tuesday and Thursday).

Fifteen miles out in the Atlantic Ocean stands remote, windswept **Foula**. It's known as Britain's most isolated community, with just 30 human inhabitants, a handful of Shetland ponies and 1500 sheep, plus 500,000 seabirds, including the rare Leach's petrel and Manx shearwater, and the world's largest colony of great skuas. There's no shop, and accommodation is very limited – Leraback (☎01595-753226; B&B incl dinner per person £35; Ⓟ) offers B&B and evening meals.

DirectFlight (p435) flies to Foula from Tingwall airport four days a week. From March to mid-October there are two flights a day three days a week, allowing you to make a day trip, with six to seven hours spent on the island. There are two passenger ferries (☎01595-840208; www.bkmarine.co.uk) per week (on Tuesday and Thursday, car/driver and car single £4.10/19.10) year-round, departing from Walls; bookings are essential. There's also Saturday service from May to September, plus fortnightly service from Scalloway. You can also visit Foula on a day trip from Scalloway harbour with Cycharters (☎01595-696598; www.cycharters.co.uk).

DON'T MISS

SEA KAYAKING IN SHETLAND

Paddling is a top way to explore Shetland's tortuous coastline, and allows you to get up close to seals and bird life without scaring them away. Sea Kayak Shetland (☑01595-840272; www. seakayakshetland.co.uk; beginner session/half-day/day £25/40/70) is a reliable and professional operator that caters for beginners and experts alike, offering guided kayaking trips from various points around Shetland.

SUMBURGH

With sea cliffs and grassy headlands jutting out into sparkling blue waters, Sumburgh is one of the most scenic places to stay on the island. There's a tourist office open daily at Sumburgh airport.

◎ Sights

TOP CHOICE Old Scatness   ARCHAEOLOGICAL SITE
(☑01950-461869; www.shetland-heritage.co.uk; adult/child £5/4; ⊙10am-5pm Sun-Thu late May-Aug; ▣) This dig brings Shetland's prehistoric past vividly to life; it's a must-see for archaeology buffs, but fun for kids, too. Clued-up guides in Iron Age clothes show you around the site, which is still being excavated – it has provided important clues on the Viking takeover and the dating of these northern Scottish sites.

There's an impressive broch from around 300 BC, roundhouses and later wheelhouses. Best of all is the reconstruction of one of these, complete with smoky peat fire and working loom.

Jarlshof   ARCHAEOLOGICAL SITE
(HS; ☑01950-460112; www.historic-scotland.gov. uk; adult/child £5.30/3.30; ⊙9.30am-5.30pm Apr-Sep, 9.30am-4.30pm Oct-Mar) Old and new collide here, as Sumburgh airport lies only a few metres from this picturesque and instructive archaeological site. Various periods of occupation from 2500 BC to AD 1500 can be seen, and the complete change that occurred upon the Vikings' arrival is obvious: their rectangular longhouses present a marked contrast to the brochs, roundhouses and wheelhouses that preceded them.

Atop the site is the 16th-century Old House, named 'Jarlshof' in a novel by Sir Walter Scott. There's an informative audio tour included with admission.

Sumburgh Head   BIRDWATCHING
(www.rspb.org.uk) At the end of the island, these spectacular cliffs offer a good chance to get up close to puffins and see huge nesting colonies of fulmars, guillemots and razorbills. If you're lucky, you might spot dolphins or orcas; the car-park noticeboard documents recent sightings.

⌑ Sleeping & Eating

Another option is the Sumburgh Lighthouse cottage (p440), due to re-open after extensive renovation in 2014.

Sumburgh Hotel   HOTEL ££
(☑01950-460201; www.sumburghhotel.com; s/d £75/90; ▣@➎) A reliable country-style hotel. Rooms have been recently renovated and feature soft duvets, attractive colour schemes and big towels. Larger sea-view rooms looking out to Fair Isle cost a tenner more. This is a great location for birdwatching at Sumburgh Head or for convenience to the airport, though the food has dipped. A mile up the road is a cheaper lodge (single/double £45/65) wth simpler en suite rooms.

Betty Mouat's Camping Böd   BÖD £
(☑01595-694688; www.camping-bods.com; Dunrossness; dm £10; ⊙Mar-Oct; ▣) This is a simple and comfortable hostel run by the Shetland Amenity Trust, with peat fire (£5 a bag), power and decent hot-water bathrooms.

❶ Getting There & Away

To get to Sumburgh from Lerwick, take the airport bus (45 minutes, four to seven daily).

North Mainland

Northern Mainland is very photogenic – jumbles of cracked, peaty brown hills, blending with grassy pastureland, extend like bony fingers of land into numerous lochs and out into the wider, icy, grey waters of the North Sea.

VOE

Lower Voe is a pretty collection of buildings beside a tranquil bay on Olna Firth.

In previous incarnations, Sail Loft (☑01806-588327; www.camping-bods.co.uk; dm £10), by the pier, was a fishing shed and knitwear factory, but it's now a camping böd, with power, coin-operated showers and fuel for sale. Opposite, welcoming Pierhead

Restaurant & Bar (☏01806-588332; Lower Voe; mains £8-16) has hearty home cooking supplemented by daily local seafood specials. Eat in the convivial bar or the upstairs restaurant.

Buses go from Lerwick to Voe (35 minutes, four to six daily Monday to Saturday).

BRAE & AROUND

Accommodation is the reason to stop in Brae; there are several guesthouses. Book in advance, as they mainly cater to oil workers.

🛏 Sleeping & Eating

TOP CHOICE **Busta House Hotel** HOTEL **££**
(☏01806-522506; www.bustahouse.com; s/d £99/115; P🐕📶🐾) Genteel, characterful Busta House has a long, sad history and inevitable rumours of a (friendly) ghost. Built in the late 18th century (though the oldest part dates from 1588), its refurbished rooms – all individually decorated and named after islands in Shetland – are compact but retain a classy but homely charm. Rooms with sea views and/or four-poster bed cost a bit more. There are excellent dinners with local produce for £35.

❶ Getting There & Away

Buses from Lerwick to Eshaness and North Roe stop in Brae (35 minutes, four to six daily Monday to Saturday).

ESHANESS & HILLSWICK

Eleven miles northwest of Brae the road ends at the red basalt cliffs of Eshaness, which form some of the most impressive, wild coastal scenery in Shetland. When the wind subsides there is superb walking and panoramic views from the lighthouse on the headland.

A mile east, a side road leads to Tangwick Haa Museum (☏01806-503389; admission free; ⊙11am-5pm mid-Apr–Sep), in a restored 17th-century house. The wonderful collection of ancient black-and-white photos capture the sense of community here.

The waterside village of Hillswick makes an appealing accommodation base.

🛏 Sleeping & Eating

TOP CHOICE **Almara B&B** B&B **££**
(☏01806-503261; www.almara.shetland.co.uk; s/d £30/60; P📶) Follow the puffin signpost a mile short of Hillswick to find the most wonderful welcome in Shetland. With sweeping views over the bay, this house has a great lounge, unusual features in the excellent rooms and bathrooms (including thoughtful extras such as USB chargers) and a good eye on the environment. You'll feel completely at home and appreciated; this is B&B at its best.

St Magnus Bay Hotel HOTEL **££**
(☏01806-503372; www.stmagnusbayhotel.co.uk; s/d £70/95; P📶) This hotel in the centre of Hillswick occupies a wonderful wooden mansion built in 1896. The personable owners are involved in an ongoing renovation process to return it to former glories, so availability of rooms is variable, but if you can grab a renovated one, they are great. There's a sauna for guest use, and a sociable bar serving food (mains £7 to £10).

Johnnie Notions Camping Böd BÖD **£**
(☏01595-694688; www.camping-bods.co.uk; dm £8; ⊙Apr-Sep) There are four spacious berths in this cute wee stone *böd* with its challengingly low door. It's very basic; there are no showers or electricity. This was the birthplace of Johnnie 'Notions' Williamson, an 18th-century blacksmith who inoculated several thousand people against smallpox using a self-devised serum. The *böd* is 3.5 miles east of Eshaness.

ORKNEY & SHETLAND ISLANDS NORTH MAINLAND

WORTH A TRIP

FAIR ISLE

Halfway to Orkney, Fair Isle is one of Scotland's most remote inhabited islands, best known for its patterned knitwear, still produced in the island's cooperative, but also for birdwatching. Smart Fair Isle Lodge & Bird Observatory (☏01595-760258; www. fairislebirdobs.co.uk; s/d with full board £65/120; ⊙May-Oct; P@📶) offers good en suite rooms. Rates are full board, and there are free guided walks and other bird-related displays and activities. From Tingwall, DirectFlight (p435) operates flights to Fair Isle (£62.50 return, 25 minutes, three on Monday, two Wednesday to Friday, one on Tuesday and Saturday, fewer in winter). Ferries sail from Grutness (near Sumburgh) with the odd one from Lerwick (one-way per person/car and driver £4.10/19.10, three hours), running on Tuesday and Saturday year-round plus Thursday from May to early October.

Braewick Cafe & Caravan Park CAMPGROUND £
(☎01806-503345; www.eshaness.shetland.co.uk; sites for 1/2/wigwams £5/7/36; ☺10am-5pm Mar-Oct; 🅿) Decent tent pitches and tasty light meals served in a cafe (Thursday to Monday, dishes £3 to £10), with stunning views over St Magnus Bay and its weird and wonderful rock formations, are on offer here. Much of the food is sourced from the owners' croft next door. It also has 'wigwams' – wooden huts with fridge and kettle that sleep four (six at a pinch). It's at Braewick on the road between Hillswick and Eshaness.

❶ Getting There & Away

Buses from Lerwick (once daily Monday to Saturday, evening departure) run to Hillswick (1¼ hours), Eshaness (1½ hours) and North Roe (1½ hours). There's also a morning bus Monday to Saturday from Brae to Hillswick.

The North Isles

Yell, Unst and Fetlar make up the North Isles, connected to each other by ferry.

YELL
POP 957

Yell if you like but nobody will hear; the desolate peat moors here are typical Shetland scenery, though the bleak landscape has an undeniable appeal.

◉ Sights & Activities

Lumbister RSPB Reserve NATURE RESERVE
(www.rspb.org.uk) At this nature reserve red-throated divers, merlins, skuas and other bird species breed. The area is home to a large otter population, too, best viewed around Whale Firth, where you may also spot common and grey seals.

Windhouse RUINS
Northwest of the small settlement of Mid Yell, on the hillside above the main road, stand the reputedly haunted ruins of Windhouse, dating from 1707. It's been uninhabited since the 1920s, although there are plans to refurbish it. Look out for the Lady in Silk, the most famous of the ruins' several ghostly presences.

FREE **Old Haa Museum** MUSEUM
(☎01957-702431; ☺10am-4pm Tue-Thu & Sat, 2-5pm Sun Apr-Sep) This has a medley of curious objects (pipes, piano, doll-in-cradle, tiny bibles, ships in bottles and a sperm-whale jaw) as well as an archive of local history, and a tearoom. It's in Burravoe, 4 miles east of the southern ferry terminal in Ulsta.

🛏 Sleeping & Eating

Lots of excellent self-catering cottages are dotted around the island; check www.visit shetland.com for options.

Pinewood House B&B £
(www.pinewoodhouseshetland.co.uk; Aywick; s/d £30/60; 🅿🛜) Next to Aywick shop, this three-roomer boasts glorious water views from the lounge and bedrooms, and offers a warm welcome and optional evening meals.

Windhouse Lodge Camping Böd BÖD £
(☎01957-702475; www.camping-bods.co.uk; Mid Yell; dm £10) Below the haunted ruins of Windhouse, on the A968, you'll find this well-kept, clean, snug camping *böd* with

---

WILDLIFE-WATCHING IN SHETLAND

For birdwatchers, Shetland is paradise – a stopover for migrating Arctic species, it hosts vast seabird breeding colonies.

Of the 24 seabird species that nest in the British Isles, 21 are found here; June is the height of the breeding season. Every bird has its own name here: rain geese are red-throated divers, bonxies are great skuas, and alamooties are storm petrels. The RSPB (p482) maintains several reserves around the islands. There are National Nature Reserves at **Hermaness** (where you can't fail to be entertained by the clownish antics of the almost tame puffins), **Keen of Hamar** and **Noss**. **Fair Isle** also supports large seabird populations.

But keep an eye on the sea itself: killer whales are regularly sighted (as are other cetaceans), as well as sea otters. A useful website for all species is www.nature-shetland. co.uk, which details latest sightings.

Held over a week in early July, the Shetland Nature Festival (www.shetlandnature festival.co.uk) has guided walks, talks, boat trips, open days and art and photography workshops celebrating Shetland's wildlife and geology.

power and a pot-belly stove to warm your toes. Book via phone or the website.

Wind Dog Café
CAFE £

(📞01957-744321; www.winddogcafe.co.uk; Gutcher; mains £2-5; ⊙9am-6pm; 🛜) This eclectic cafe wins no prizes for decor – think Portakabin-meets–charity shop – but makes up for it with a warm atmosphere and good-value homemade nosh: cheap burgers, baked potatoes, soups and all-day fry-ups. Books to read and jigsaws to finish are great if the rain is pelting down.

❶ Getting There & Away

BOAT Yell is connected with Mainland by **ferries** (📞01595-745804; www.shetland.gov.uk/ferries) between Toft and Ulsta (passenger return £4.30, car and driver return £10, 20 minutes, frequent). It's wise to book in summer.

BUS Three buses run Monday to Saturday from Lerwick to Yell and on to Unst, crossing on the ferries. Connecting buses serve other parts of the island.

UNST
POP 1100

You're fast running out of Scotland once you cross to Unst, a rugged island of ponies and seabirds. Britain's most northerly inhabited island is prettier than Yell, with bare, velvety smooth hills and clusters of settlements that cling to their waterside locations, fiercely resisting the buffeting winds.

◉ Sights & Activities

There's a picturesque ruined tower-house castle at Muness, in the southeastern corner of the island.

TOP CHOICE Hermaness
Nature Reserve
NATURE RESERVE

Unst's stellar attraction is marvellous Hermaness headland, where a 4.5-mile round walk from the reserve entrance takes you to cliffs where gannets, fulmars and guillemots nest, and numerous puffins frolic. The path is guarded by a small army of great skuas who nest in the nearby heather, and dive-bomb at will if they feel threatened. They're damn solid birds too, but don't usually make contact. From the cliffs, you can see Britain's most northerly point, the rocks of Out Stack, and Muckle Flugga, with its lighthouse built by Robert Louis Stevenson's uncle. For tips on wildlife-watching duck into **Hermaness Visitor Centre** (📞01595-711278; admission free; ⊙9am-5pm Apr–mid-Sep), near the reserve's entrance, with its poignant story about long-

time resident Albert Ross. From here, **boat trips** (📞01806-522447; www.muckleflugga.co.uk; ⊙Tue, Thu, Sat Jun-Sep) run to Muckle Flugga.

TOP CHOICE Unst Bus Shelter
LANDMARK

(www.unstbusshelter.shetland.co.uk) At the turnoff from the main road to Littlehamar, just past Baltasound, is Britain's most impressive bus stop. Enterprising locals, tired of waiting in discomfort, have installed armchairs, novels, flowers, a telly, and a visitors' book to sign. The colour scheme changes yearly.

Unst Heritage Centre
HERITAGE CENTRE

(📞01957-711528; Haroldswick; adult/child £3/free, with Unst Boat Haven £5; ⊙11am-5pm May-Sep) This heritage centre houses a modern museum with a history of the Shetland pony and a re-creation of a croft house.

Unst Boat Haven
MUSEUM

(📞01957-711528; Haroldswick; adult/child £3/free, with Unst Heritage Centre £5; ⊙11am-5pm May-Sep) This large shed is a boaty's delight, packed with a beautifully cared for collection of Shetland rowing and sailing boats, all with a backstory. Old photos and maritime artefacts speak of the glory days of Unst fishing.

🛏 Sleeping & Eating

TOP CHOICE Gardiesfauld Hostel
HOSTEL £

(📞01957-755279; www.gardiesfauld.shetland.co.uk; 2 East Rd, Uyeasound; tent & 2 people £6, dm £13; ⊙Apr-Sep; Ⓟ) This 35-bed hostel is very clean, has most spacious dorms with lockers, family rooms, a garden, an elegant lounge and a wee conservatory dining area with great bay views. You can camp here too. The bus stops right outside. Bring 20p pieces for the shower.

Saxa Vord
HOSTEL £

(📞01957-711711; www.saxavord.com; Haroldswick; s/d £19.50/39; ⊙late May-early Sep; Ⓟ🛜) This former RAF base is not the most atmospheric lodging, but the barracks-style rooms offer great value. The restaurant dishes out reasonable local food, and there's a bar – Britain's northernmost, by our reckoning – and a friendly, helpful atmosphere. Self-catering holiday houses (£485 per week) are good for families and available year-round.

Prestegaard
B&B ££

(📞01957-755234; prestegaard@postmaster.co.uk; Uyeasound; s/d £30/56; ⊙May-Sep; Ⓟ🛜) This solid old manse near the water makes a great base. Rooms are spacious and comfy, with sea views and separate (but private) bathroom – we particularly like the upstairs one. The breakfast room with Up Helly Aa shields and axes on the wall will bring out the Viking in you, and the kindly owner is helpful. Continental breakfast only.

Baltasound Hotel   HOTEL, PUB ££
(☎01957-711334; www.baltasound-hotel.shetland.co.uk; Baltasound; s/d £52.50/85; P🖰) Brightly decorated, commodious rooms – some bigger than others – inside the building are complemented by wooden chalets arrayed around the lawn. There's also a lovely country outlook, and bar meals (mains £6 to £12) in a dining room dappled by the evening sun.

❶ Getting There & Around

Hire **bikes** (www.unstcyclehire.co.uk; Haroldswick; per day/wk £7.50/40) in the chocolate shop at the Saxa Vord complex in Haroldswick.

BOAT Unst is connected with Yell and Fetlar by a small ferry (p445) between Gutcher and Belmont (free, 10 minutes, frequent).

BUS Three buses a day (except Sunday) run from Lerwick to Unst (2½ hours), via the ferries. There are also services around Unst itself.

FETLAR
POP 90

At just 5 miles by 2 miles, Fetlar is the smallest but most fertile of the North Isles. Its name is derived from the Viking term for 'fat land'.

◉ Sights & Activities

There's great birdwatching – Fetlar is home to three-quarters of Britain's breeding population of red-necked phalaropes, which nest around the **Loch of Funzie** (pronounced 'finnie') in the southeast of the island. From April to October, you can view them from an RSPB hide in the nearby marshes.

Excellent **Fetlar Interpretive Centre** (☎01957-733206; www.fetlar.com; adult/child £2/free; ⊙11am-4pm Mon-Fri, 12.30-4pm Sat & Sun May-Sep) has photos, audio recordings and videos on the island and its history. You'll find it right in the middle of the island – look out for the colourful mural.

There are several scenic walks around the island, including the hike around the Lamb Hoga headland, beginning at **Tresta Beach**, about a mile west of Houbie.

🛏 Sleeping

Small **Fetlar Campsite** (☎01957-733227; sites £5-9; ⊙May-Sep), 2.5 miles from the ferry, overlooks the beach at Tresta and has great facilities. Run by the same people is friendly **Gord B&B** (☎01957-733227; nicboxall@gord.shetland.co.uk; r per person incl dinner £50; P), with terrific sea views and two twin rooms and one double, all with en suite. There's also a camping böd (p440) (powered) by the water, handily close to the Loch of Funzie.

❶ Information

There's no petrol on Fetlar, but there's a part-time shop in Houbie, the main village.

❶ Getting There & Away

Five to 10 daily free ferries (p445) connect Fetlar with Gutcher on Yell and Belmont on Unst.

Understand
Scotland

population per sq mile

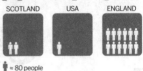

SCOTLAND · USA · ENGLAND

🧍 ≈ 80 people

Scotland Today

Scottish Politics

Although an integral part of Great Britain since 1707, Scotland has maintained a separate and distinct identity throughout the last 300 years. The return of a devolved Scottish parliament to Edinburgh in 1999 marked a growing confidence and pride in the nation's achievements.

The first decade of devolution saw Scottish politics diverge significantly from the Westminster way. Policies that have been applied in Scotland but not the rest of the UK include free long-term care for the elderly, the abolition of tuition fees for university students and higher pay for teachers.

The Scottish National Party (SNP), which had led a minority government in Edinburgh since 2007, surprised the nation in the 2011 elections with a landslide victory in the Scottish parliament, winning 69 out of 129 seats. Suddenly the question of Scotland breaking away from the United Kingdom was all over the news.

The election of a Conservative/Liberal Democrat coalition government in Westminster in 2010 only served to heighten the political difference between Scotland and the rest of the UK – only one of Scotland's 59 constituencies returned a Conservative MP, while the Labour Party (which was defeated in Westminster) increased its share of the Scottish vote.

The SNP has pledged to hold a referendum in the autumn of 2014 on whether Scotland should have full independence. Current opinion polls suggest that at least two-thirds of Scots are happy with the status quo, but with the state of the UK economy, who knows what might happen a few years down the line.

» Highest point: Ben Nevis (1344m)

» Annual whisky export: 1 billion bottles

» Value of haggis sold for Burns Night: £1.2 million

» Number of times Scotland has won the football World Cup: 0

Renewable Energy

One of the central planks of the SNP's vision for an independent Scotland is its energy policy. The party leader, Alex Salmond, has said that

Top Books

Raw Spirit (Iain Banks) An enjoyable jaunt around Scotland in search of the perfect whisky.
Mountaineering in Scotland (WH Murray) Classic account of hiking in Scotland in the 1930s, when just getting to Glen Coe was an adventure in itself.

Adrift in Caledonia (Nick Thorpe) An insightful tale of hitchhiking around Scotland on a variety of vessels.
The Poor Had No Lawyers (Andy Wightman) A fascinating analysis of who owns land in Scotland and how they got it.

Classic DVDs

Tutti Frutti Iconic 1980s TV series about a fading rock band's last tour, with Robbie Coltrane and Emma Thompson.
The Maggie Classic 1950s Ealing comedy about the crew of a puffer on the west coast of Scotland.

belief systems
(% of population)

43 Church of Scotland

28 Nonreligious

16 Roman Catholic

6.8 Other Christian

1.2 Other
0.8% Islamic
0.1% Buddhist
0.1% Sikh
0.1% Jewish
0.1% Hindu

if Scotland were 100 people

98 would be white
1 would be South Asian
1 would be other

---

he wants the country to be the 'Saudi Arabia of renewable energy' – becoming self-sufficient in energy by 2020, and a net exporter of 'clean' electricity.

In the first half of the 20th century the Scottish Highlands were one the first regions in the world to develop hydroelectric power on a large scale, and in the last decade, wind turbines have sprung up all over the place. By 2009, renewables provided 27% of Scotland's energy consumption, a figure that rose to 35% in 2011; the government's target is to reach 100% by 2020.

However, the future of Scotland's energy industry lies not on land, but in the sea: Scotland has access to 25% of Europe's available tidal energy, and 10% of its wave power. The country is at the leading edge of developing wave, tidal and offshore wind power, and in 2012 the waters around Orkney and the Pentland Firth were designated as a Marine Energy Park.

Development vs Conservation

In 2010 the Scottish government gave the go-ahead to a 135-mile, high-voltage overhead power line from Beauly (near Inverness) to Denny in Stirlingshire, to connect wind- and marine-generated electricity from the north to the heart of the national grid. It will be carried on 600 giant pylons marching through some of the Highlands' most scenic areas, including Strathglass, Fort Augustus and Bridge of Tummel.

Supporters point out that the scheme also involves the removal of almost 60 miles of low-voltage pylons from the Cairngorms National Park; opponents claim that a seabed cable, while more expensive, would be a better alternative. The debate reflects a larger tension that exists across the Highlands and Islands – between those keen to develop the region's resources and conservationists who want to keep the area unspoiled.

Along with Wales and England, Scotland is part of Great Britain. Throw in Northern Ireland and you have the United Kingdom. It's OK to talk about Scotland's inhabitants as Scottish or British – but *never* English!

Vital Stats

» Population: 5.2 million
» Area: 78,722 sq km
» First Minister: Alex Salmond (SNP)
» GVA per capita: £19,744 (2009)
» Inflation: 2.4% (2012)
» Unemployment: 8.1% (2012)

Scottish Media

» *Caledonian Mercury* (www.caledonianmercury.com)
» *Herald* (www.heraldscotland.com)
» *Scotsman* (www.scotsman.com)
» *Press & Journal* (www.pressandjournal.co.uk)

Internet Radio

BBC Radio Scotland (www.bbc.co.uk/radioscotland) Find out what's hitting the headlines by listening to *Good Morning Scotland* from 6am weekdays.

History

For a geographically isolated place, Scotland has had a substantial share of incursions, immigrations and territorial struggles, and has been subjected to influences from the Romans, the Norse lands, Ireland, France and, of course, England.

From the decline of the Vikings onwards, Scottish history has been predictably and often violently bound to that of its southern neighbour. Battles and border raids were commonplace until shared kingship, then political union, drew the two together. Even then, Jacobite risings asserted a widely felt desire for freedom, which was finally partially realised with the devolution of the late 20th century.

Scotland's misty prehistory has left outstanding monuments, particularly in the northern islands, but the first outside reference to northern Britain's inhabitants comes with the Romans, whose struggles with the Picts caused the construction of two massive walls to keep them out.

If the Roman presence pushed formerly disparate tribes into union, the Vikings did the same. Their incursions led the Scots kingdom of Dalriada and the Pictish kingdom to unite, forming Scotland.

Once Viking power was broken, a familiar story of strong and weak monarchs, political intrigues and dynastic struggles played out over the centuries. The Wars of Independence freed Scotland from English interference and set up William Wallace and Robert the Bruce as heroes.

The Stewart line established Scotland as a major European player in Renaissance politics and art, but once James VI inherited the kingship of England, royal attention was focused south of the border and, as fleets plied the seas to far-flung new colonies, Scotland was left behind. Political union in the early 18th century was born of pragmatism and widely resented. This, and the ousting of the Catholic King James in favour of his Dutch Protestant son-in-law led to widespread anger, and the Jacobite rebellions of the 18th century attempted to wrest power back by trying to put James' son and then grandson, Bonnie Prince Charlie, on the throne.

Top Prehistoric Sights

» Jarlshof, Shetland

» Skara Brae, Orkney

» Maes Howe, Orkney

» Kilmartin Glen, Argyll

» Callanish, Lewis

» Tomb of the Eagles, Orkney

» Scottish Crannog Centre, Kenmore

TIMELINE	4000 BC	2200 BC	AD 43
	Neolithic farmers move to Scotland from mainland Europe; sites from these ancient days dot Scotland, with the best concentrated in Orkney.	Beaker culture arrives in Scotland. The Bronze Age produces swords and shields. Construction of hill forts, crannogs and mystifying stone circles.	Claudius begins the Roman conquest of Britain, almost a century after Julius Caesar first invaded. By AD 80 a string of forts is built from the Clyde to the Forth.

Defeat at Culloden spelled the end of these dreams, and of the clan system. The Highlands had been ruled as a nation apart by clan leaders who now, stripped of power but possessed of vast lands, evicted their crofters in favour of estate-style sheep farming. This brutal period, the Clearances, left the Highlands an empty wilderness and forced hundreds of thousands to a precarious coastal life or emigration. Those who sought the cities were the fuel for the Industrial Revolution, building a spine of heavy industry across southern Scotland that lasted through to the late 20th century.

However, the 18th century also had a nobler legacy. The Scottish Enlightenment was a period of rich cultural and intellectual flowering that turned the eyes of all Europe on this northern outpost. The thinkers David Hume and Adam Smith, the poet Robert Burns and the architect Robert Adam are just a few of the many Scots who are still considered giants in their respective fields. They built a tradition of Scottish intellectualism and literature that has also continued to the present day.

Early Days

Hunters and gatherers have left fragments of evidence of the earliest human habitation in Scotland. These early people came in waves from northern Europe and Ireland as glaciers retreated in the wake of the last Ice Age around 10,000 BC.

The Neolithic was similarly launched by arrivals from mainland Europe. Scotland's Stone Age has left behind an astonishing diary of human development: Caithness, Orkney and Shetland have some of the world's best-preserved prehistoric villages, burial cairns and standing stones. Further south, crannogs (round structures built on stilts over a loch) were a favoured form of defensible dwelling through the Bronze Age.

The Iron Age saw the construction of a remarkable series of defence-minded structures of a different sort. Brochs (again a northeastern island development) were complex, muscular stone fortresses, some of which still stand well over 10m high.

Romans & Picts

The Roman invasion of Britain began in AD 43, almost a century after Julius Caesar first invaded. However, the Roman onslaught ground to a halt in the north, not far beyond the present-day Scottish border. Between AD 78 and 84, the Roman Governor Agricola marched northwards and spent several years trying to subdue the wild tribes the Romans called the Picts (from the Latin *pictus,* meaning 'painted'). By the 2nd century Emperor Hadrian, tired of fighting the tribes in the north, decided to cut his losses and built the wall (AD 122–28) that bears his name across northern England. Two decades later Hadrian's successor, Antoninus Pius, invaded Scotland again and built a turf rampart, the Antonine Wall, between the

---

Some Top Pictish Stones

» St Vigeans Museum, Arbroath

» Aberlemno Stones, Angus

» Dupplin Cross, Dunning

» Groam House Museum, Rosemarkie

» Meigle Museum, Meigle

» Inverness Museum, Inverness

» Tarbat Discovery Centre, Portmahomack

» Elgin Museum, Elgin

142	397	5th century	Early 500s
Building of Antonine Wall marks the northern limit of the Roman Empire. It is patrolled for about 40 years, but after this the Romans decide northern Britain is too difficult to conquer.	The first Christian mission beyond Hadrian's Wall, in Whithorn, is initiated by St Ninian. The earliest recorded church in Scotland is built to house his remains.	Roman soldiers stationed in Britain are recalled to Rome as the Empire faces attack from barbarian tribes. The last Romans depart and Emperor Honorius tells Britons to fend for themselves.	A Celtic tribe, the Scots, cross the sea from northern Ireland and establish a kingdom in Argyll called Dalriada.

ST COLUMBA

Firth of Forth and the River Clyde. In northern Britain, the Romans found they had met their match.

Little is known about the Picts, who inhabited northern and eastern Scotland. The Roman presence had probably helped to forge disparate Celtic tribes into a unified group; we can assume they were fierce fighters given the trouble the hardy Roman army had with them. The main material evidence of their culture is their fabulous carved symbol stones, found in many parts of eastern Scotland.

Eventually the Romans left Britain and at this time there were at least two indigenous peoples in the northern region of the British Isles: the Picts in the north and east, and the Britons in the southwest. A new group, the Celtic Scots probably arrived around AD 500, crossing from Northern Ireland and establishing a kingdom called Dalriada at Argyll. St Ninian was the earliest recorded bringer of Christianity to the region, establishing a mission in Whithorn in Scotland's southwest. In the 6th century, St Columba, Scotland's most famous missionary, resumed St Ninian's work. According to legend, Columba was a scholar and a soldier-priest who went into exile after involvement in a bloody battle. After fleeing Ireland in 563 he established a monastery on Iona, and also travelled to the northeast to take his message to the Picts.

The First Kings of Scotland

St Columba was a man of fixed ideas. After arriving on Iona he promptly set about banishing women and cows as he believed 'where there is a cow there is a woman, and where there is a woman there is mischief.' His manner of living was austere – he slept on the bare floor with a stone for a pillow.

The Picts and Scots were drawn together by the threat of a Norse invasion and by the combination of political and spiritual power from their common Christianity. Kenneth MacAlpin, first king of a united Scotland, achieved power using a mixture of blood ties and diplomacy. He set his capital in Pictland at Scone and brought to it the sacred Stone of Destiny, used in the coronation of Scottish kings.

Nearly two centuries later, Kenneth MacAlpin's great-great-great-grandson, King Malcolm II (r 1005–18), defeated the Northumbrian Angles, a Germanic tribe who had settled in eastern England, at the Battle of Carham (1018) bringing Edinburgh and Lothian under Scottish control and extending Scottish territory as far south as the Tweed.

But the Highland clans, inaccessible in their glens, remained a law unto themselves for another 700 years. A cultural and linguistic divide grew up between the Gaelic-speaking Highlanders and the Lowlanders who spoke the Scots tongue.

Robert the Bruce & William Wallace

When Alexander III fell to his death in Fife in 1286, there followed a dispute over the succession. There were no less than 13 claimants, but in the end it came down to a choice of two: Robert de Brus, lord of Annandale, and John Balliol, lord of Galloway. King Edward I of England was asked

» Iona Abbey

6th century	685	780
St Columba establishes a Christian mission on Iona. By the late 8th century the mission is responsible for the conversion of most of pagan Scotland.	The Pictish king Bridei defeats the Northumbrians at Nechtansmere in Angus, an against-the-odds victory that sets the foundations for Scotland as a separate entity.	From the 780s onwards, Norsemen in longboats from Scandinavia begin to pillage the Scottish coast and islands, eventually taking control of Orkney, Shetland and the Western Isles.

DANITA DELIMONT / GETTY IMAGES ©

to arbitrate. He chose Balliol, whom he thought he could manipulate more easily.

Seeking to tighten his feudal grip on Scotland, Edward – known as the 'Hammer of the Scots' – treated the Scots king as his vassal rather than his equal. The humiliated Balliol finally turned against him and allied Scotland with France in 1295, thus beginning the enduring 'Auld Alliance' and ushering in the Wars of Independence.

Edward's response was bloody. In 1296 he invaded Scotland and Balliol was incarcerated in the Tower of London; in another blow to Scots pride, Edward I removed the Stone of Destiny from Scone and took it back to London.

Enter William Wallace. Bands of rebels were attacking the English occupiers and Wallace led one such band to defeat the English at Stirling Bridge in 1297. After Wallace's execution, Robert the Bruce, grandson of Robert de Brus, the lord of Annandale, saw his chance, defied Edward (whom he had previously aligned himself with), murdered his rival John Comyn and had himself crowned king of Scotland at Scone in 1306. Bruce mounted a campaign to drive the English out of Scotland but suffered repeated defeats. Persistence paid off and he went on to secure an illustrious victory over the English at Bannockburn, enshrined in Scottish legend as one of the finest moments in the country's history.

Scottish independence was eventually won in 1328 and Robert the Bruce was finally crowned king, though he died the next year. Wars with England and civil strife continued, however. In 1371 Robert the Bruce's grandson, Robert II, acceded to the throne, founding the Stewart (Stuart) dynasty, which was to rule Scotland and, in time, the rest of Britain, until 1707.

The Renaissance

James IV (r 1488–1513) married the daughter of Henry VII of England, the first of the Tudor monarchs, thereby linking the two royal families through 'the Marriage of the Thistle and the Rose.' This didn't prevent

Robert the Bruce Trail

» Melrose Abbey

» Scone Palace

» Bannockburn

» Arbroath Abbey

» Dunfermline Abbey

THE DECLARATION OF ARBROATH

During the Wars of Independence, a group of Scottish nobles sent a letter to Pope John XXII requesting support for the cause of Scottish independence. Having railed against the tyranny of England's Edward I and sung the praises of Robert the Bruce, the declaration famously states: 'For so long as a hundred of us remain alive, we will yield in no least way to English dominion. For we fight, not for glory nor for riches nor for honours, but only and alone for freedom, which no good man surrenders but with his life.' The Pope initially supported the Scottish cause but English lobbying changed his mind.

848	1040	1263	1296
Kenneth MacAlpin unites the Scottish and Pictish thrones, thus uniting Scotland north of the Firth of Forth into a single kingdom.	Macbeth takes the Scottish throne after defeating Duncan in battle. This, and the fact that he was later killed by Duncan's son Malcolm, are the only parallels to the Shakespeare version.	Norse power, which controlled the entire western seaboard, is finally broken at the Battle of Largs, which marks the retreat of Viking influence and eventually the handing back of the western isles to Scotland.	King Edward I marches on Scotland with an army of 30,000 men, razing ports, butchering citizens and capturing the castles of Berwick, Edinburgh, Roxburgh and Stirling.

the French from persuading James to go to war with his in-laws, and he was killed at the Battle of Flodden in 1513, along with 10,000 of his subjects. Renaissance ideas, in particular Scottish poetry and architecture flourished during James IV's reign.

Mary, Queen of Scots & the Reformation

In 1542 King James V, childless, lay on his deathbed broken-hearted, it is said, after his defeat by the English at Solway Moss. Then news came that his wife had given birth to a baby girl. Fearing the end of the Stewart dynasty, and recalling its origin through Robert the Bruce's daughter, James sighed, 'It cam' wi' a lass, and it will gang wi' a lass.' He died shortly thereafter, leaving his week-old daughter, Mary, to inherit the throne as Queen of Scots.

She was sent to France when she was young and Scotland was ruled by regents, who rejected overtures from Henry VIII of England urging them to wed the infant queen to his son. Furious Henry sent his armies to take vengeance on the Scots. The 'Rough Wooing', as it was called, failed

---

THE LORDS OF THE ISLES

In medieval times, when overland travel through the Scottish Highlands was slow, difficult and dangerous, the sea lochs, firths (estuaries), kyles (narrow sea channels) and sounds of the west coast were the motorways of their time. Cut off from the rest of Scotland, but united by these sea roads, the west coast and islands were a world – and a kingdom – unto themselves.

Descended from the legendary Somerled (a half-Gaelic, half-Norse warrior of the 12th century), the chiefs of Clan Donald claimed sovereignty over this watery kingdom. It was John Macdonald of Islay who first styled himself Dominus Insularum (Lord of the Isles) in 1353. He and his descendants ruled their vast territory from their headquarters at Finlaggan in Islay, backed up by fleets of swift *birlinns* and *nyvaigs* (Hebridean galleys), an intimate knowledge of the sea routes of the west and a network of coastal castles, which included Skipness, Dunstaffnage, Duart, Stalker, Dunvegan and Kisimul.

Clan Donald held sway over the isles, often in defiance of the Scottish kings, from 1350 to 1493. At its greatest extent, in the second half of the 15th century, the Lordship of the Isles included all the islands on the west coast of Scotland, the west-coast mainland from Kintyre to Ross-shire, and the Antrim coast of northern Ireland. But in a greedy grab for territory, Clan Donald finally pushed its luck too far. John MacDonald made a secret pact with the English king Edward IV to divide Scotland between them. When this treason was discovered 30 years later, the Lordship was forfeited to King James IV of Scotland, and the title has remained in possession of the Scottish, and later British, royal family ever since. Lord of the Isles is one of the many titles held today by Prince Charles, heir to the British throne.

1298–1305	1314	1328	1410
William Wallace is proclaimed Guardian of Scotland in 1298. After Edward's force defeats the Scots at the Battle of Falkirk, Wallace resigns as guardian and goes into hiding, but is fatally betrayed after his return in 1305.	Robert the Bruce wins a famous victory over the English at the Battle of Bannockburn – a victory which would turn the tide in favour of the Scots for the next 400 years.	Continuing raids on northern England force Edward III to sue for peace and the Treaty of Northampton gives Scotland its independence, with Robert I, the Bruce, as king.	One of Europe's most venerable educational institutions, The University of St Andrews, is founded.

to win hearts and minds and in 1558 Mary was married to the French dauphin and became queen of France as well as Scotland.

While Mary was in France, being raised as a Roman Catholic, the Reformation tore through Scotland, to where, following the death of her sickly husband, the 18-year-old returned in 1561. She was formally welcomed to her capital city and held a famous audience with John Knox. The great reformer harangued the young queen and she later agreed to protect the budding Protestant Church in Scotland while continuing to practise as a Catholic privately.

She married Lord Darnley in the Chapel Royal at Holyrood and gave birth to a son (later James VI) in 1565. Any domestic bliss was short-lived and, in a scarcely believable train of events, Darnley was involved in the murder of Mary's Italian secretary Rizzio (rumoured to be her lover), before he himself was murdered, probably by Mary's new lover and third-husband-to-be, the earl of Bothwell.

The Scots had had enough; Mary's enemies – an alliance of powerful nobles – finally confronted her at Carberry Hill, east of Edinburgh, and Mary was forced to abdicate in 1567 and thrown into prison at Castle Leven. She managed to escape, and met her enemies in battle at Langside but was forced to flee to England after being defeated. There, she was imprisoned for 19 years by Queen Elizabeth I before finally being executed in 1587.

Her son James VI (r 1567–1625) had meanwhile been crowned at Stirling, and a series of regents ruled in his place. In England, Elizabeth died childless, and the English, desperate for a male monarch, soon turned their attention north. James VI of Scotland became James I of England and moved his court to London. His plan to politically unite the two countries, however, failed. For the most part, the Stewarts (Stuarts) ignored Scotland from then on.

Union with England

Civil war and religious conflict in the 17th century left the country and its economy ruined. Scotland couldn't compete in this new era of European colonialism and, to add to its woes, during the 1690s famine killed up to a third of the population in some areas. Anti-English feeling ran high: the Protestant king William, who had replaced the exiled Catholic James VII/II to the chagrin of many in Scotland, was at war with France and was using Scottish soldiers and taxes – many Scots, sympathetic to the French, disapproved. This feeling was exacerbated by the failure of an investment venture in Panama (the so-called Darien Scheme, designed to establish a Scottish colony in the Americas), which resulted in widespread bankruptcy in Scotland.

The failure of the Darien Scheme made it clear to the wealthy Scottish merchants and stockholders that the only way they could gain access

Mary Queen of Scots by Antonia Fraser is the classic biography of Scotland's ill-starred queen, digging deep behind the myths to discover the real woman caught up in the labyrinthine politics of the period.

MARY, QUEEN OF SCOTS

1468–69	1488–1513	1513	1603
Orkney and then Shetland are mortgaged to Scotland as part of a dowry from Danish King Christian I, whose daughter is to marry the future King James III of Scotland.	The Scottish Renaissance produces an intellectual climate that encourages Protestantism, a reaction against the perceived wealth and corruption of the medieval Roman Catholic Church.	James IV invades northern England and is soundly defeated in Northumberland at the Battle of Flodden. It marks a watershed in war history, with artillery on the upswing and archery on the way out.	James VI of Scotland inherits the English throne in the so-called Union of the Crowns, becoming James I of Great Britain.

to the lucrative markets of developing colonies was through union with England. The English parliament favoured union through fear of Jacobite sympathies in Scotland being exploited by its enemies, the French.

On receiving the Act of Union in Edinburgh, the chancellor of Scotland, Lord Seafield – leader of the parliament that the Act of Union abolished – is said to have murmured under his breath, 'Now there's an end to an auld sang'. Robert Burns later castigated the wealthy politicians who engineered the union in characteristically stronger language: 'We're bought and sold for English gold – such a parcel of rogues in a nation!'

> Jacobite, a term derived from the Latin for 'James', is used to describe the political movement committed to the return of the Catholic Stuart kings to the thrones of England and Scotland.

The Jacobites

The Jacobite rebellions of the 18th century sought to displace the Hanoverian monarchy (chosen by the English parliament in 1701 to succeed the house of Orange) and restore a Catholic Stuart king to the British throne.

James Edward Stuart, known as the Old Pretender, was the son of James VII/II. With French support he arrived in the Firth of Forth with a fleet of ships in 1708, causing panic in Edinburgh, but was seen off by English men-of-war.

The earl of Mar led another Jacobite rebellion in 1715 but proved an ineffectual leader better at propaganda than warfare. His campaign fizzled out soon after the inconclusive Battle of Sheriffmuir.

The Old Pretender's son, Charles Edward Stuart, better known as Bonnie Prince Charlie or the Young Pretender, landed in Scotland for the final uprising. He had little military experience, didn't speak Gaelic and had a shaky grasp of English. Nevertheless, supported by an army of Highlanders, he marched southwards and captured Edinburgh, except for the castle, in September 1745. He got as far south as Derby in England, but success was short-lived; an Hanoverian army led by the duke of Cumberland harried him all the way back to the Highlands, where Jacobite dreams were finally extinguished at the Battle of Culloden in 1746.

> Bonnie Prince Charlie's flight after the Battle of Culloden is legendary. He lived in hiding in the remote Highlands and islands for months before being rescued by a French frigate. His narrow escape from Uist to Skye, dressed as Flora MacDonald's maid, is the subject of the 'Skye Boat Song'.

Although a heavily romanticised figure, Bonnie Prince Charlie was partly responsible for the annihilation of Highland culture, given the crackdown following his doomed attempt to recapture the crown. After returning to France he gained a reputation for drunkenness and mistreatment of mistresses. France had serious plans to invade Britain during the mid-18th century, but eventually ceased to regard the prince as a serious character.

The Highland Clearances

In the aftermath of the Jacobite rebellions, Highland dress, the bearing of arms and the bagpipes were outlawed. The Highlands were put under military control and private armies were banned.

1692	1707	1745–46
The Massacre of Glencoe causes further rifts between those clans loyal to the crown and those loyal to the old ways.	Despite popular opposition, the Act of Union, which brings England and Scotland under one parliament, one sovereign and one flag, takes effect on 1 May.	The culmination of the Jacobite rebellions: Bonnie Prince Charlie lands in Scotland, gathers an army and marches south. Though he gains English territory, he is eventually defeated at the Battle of Culloden.

DOUGHOUGHTON / ALAMY ©

» Culloden memorial

The clansmen, no longer of any use as soldiers and uneconomical as tenants, were evicted from their homes and farms by the Highland chieftains to make way for the flocks of sheep. A few stayed to work the sheep farms; many more were forced to seek work in the cities, or to eke a living from crofts (smallholdings) on poor coastal land. Men who had never seen the sea were forced to take to boats to try their luck at herring fishing, and many thousands emigrated – some willingly, some under duress – to the developing colonies of North America, Australia and New Zealand.

If you do much walking in the Highlands and islands, you are almost certain to come across a pile of stones among the bracken, all that remains of a house or cottage. Look around and you'll find another, and another, and soon you'll realise that this was once a crofting settlement. It's one of the saddest sights you'll see in Scotland – this emptiness, where once there was a thriving community.

John Prebble's wonderfully written book *The Highland Clearances* tells the terrible story of how the Highlanders were driven out of their homes and forced into emigration.

The Scottish Enlightenment

During the period known as the Scottish Enlightenment (roughly 1740–1830) Edinburgh became known as 'a hotbed of genius.' The philosophers David Hume and Adam Smith and the sociologist Adam Ferguson emerged as influential thinkers, nourished on generations of theological debate. Medic William Cullen produced the first modern pharmacopoeia, chemist Joseph Black advanced the science of thermodynamics and geologist James Hutton challenged long-held beliefs about the age of the Earth.

After centuries of bloodshed and religious fanaticism, people applied themselves with the same energy and piety to the making of money and the enjoyment of leisure. There was a revival of interest in Scottish history and literature. The writings of Sir Walter Scott and the poetry of Robert Burns achieved lasting popularity.

The Industrial Revolution

The development of the steam engine ushered in the Industrial Revolution. Glasgow, deprived of its lucrative tobacco trade following the American War of Independence (1776–83), developed into an industrial powerhouse, the 'second city' of the British Empire (after London). Cotton mills, iron and steelworks, chemical works, shipbuilding yards and heavy-engineering works proliferated along the River Clyde in the 19th century, powered by the coal mines of Lanarkshire, Ayrshire, Fife and Midlothian.

The Clearances and the Industrial Revolution had shattered the traditional rural way of life, and though manufacturing cities and ports thrived in these decades of Empire, the wealth was generated for a select

Most clan tartans are in fact a 19th-century invention (long after the demise of the clan system) partly inspired by the writings of Sir Walter Scott.

1740s–1830s	Late 1700s	1890–1910	1914–1932
Following the loss of the Scottish parliament in 1707, Edinburgh declines in political importance, but its cultural and intellectual life flourishes during a period known as the Scottish Enlightenment.	Scotland flourishes during the Industrial Revolution, becoming a world leader in the production of textiles, iron, steel and coal – and above all in shipbuilding and marine engineering.	The 'Glasgow Boys' bring European influence and international recognition to Scottish art, breaking away from the Edinburgh mainstream.	Scottish industry slumps during WWI and collapses in its aftermath in the face of new Eastern production and the Great Depression. About 400,000 Scots emigrate between 1921 and 1931.

few by an impoverished many. Deep poverty forced many into emigration and others to their graves. The depopulation was exacerbated by WWI, which took a heavy toll on Scottish youth. The ensuing years were bleak and marked by labour disputes.

War & Peace

Between 1904 and 1931 around one million people emigrated from Scotland to begin a new life in North America and Australasia.

Scotland largely escaped the trauma and devastation wrought by WWII on the industrial cities of England (although Clydebank was heavily bombed over a couple of days). Indeed, the war brought a measure of renewed prosperity to Scotland as the shipyards and engineering works geared up to supply the war effort. But the postwar period saw the collapse of shipbuilding and heavy industry, on which Scotland had become over reliant.

After the discovery of North Sea oil off the Scottish coast, excitement turned to bitterness for many Scots, who felt that revenues were being siphoned off to England. This issue, along with takeovers of Scots companies by English ones (which then closed the Scots operation, asset-stripped and transferred jobs to England), fuelled increasing nationalist sentiment in Scotland. The Scottish National Party (SNP) developed into a third force (later, a second as they eclipsed the Conservatives, and the first as they won power from the Labour Party) in Scottish politics.

Devolution

A well-presented and easily absorbed introduction to Scottish history can be found at www.bbc.co.uk/history/scottishhistory. The accompanying images of historical sites help bring it to life.

In 1979 a referendum was held on whether to set up a directly elected Scottish Assembly. Fifty-two per cent of those who voted said 'yes' to devolution, but Labour Prime Minister James Callaghan decided that everyone who didn't vote should be counted as a 'no'. By this reasoning, only 33% of the electorate had voted 'yes', so the Scottish Assembly was rejected.

From 1979 to 1997 Scotland was ruled by a Conservative government in London for which the majority of Scots hadn't voted. Separatist feelings, always present, grew stronger. Following the landslide victory of the Labour Party in May 1997, another referendum was held on the creation of a Scottish parliament. This time the result was overwhelmingly and unambiguously in favour.

Elections to the new parliament took place on 6 May 1999 and the Scottish parliament convened for the first time on 12 May in Edinburgh, with Labour's Donald Dewar, who died in office the very next year, becoming First Minister. Labour held power until 2007, when the pro-independence Scottish National Party formed government. They were overwhelmingly re-elected in 2011 and have continued to press for independence.

1941–45	1970s	1999–2004	2012
Clydebank is blitzed by German bombers in 1941 with 1200 deaths; by 1945 one out of four males in the workforce is employed in heavy industries to support the war effort.	The discovery of oil and gas in the North Sea brings new prosperity to Aberdeen and the surrounding area, and also to the Shetland Islands.	Scottish parliament is convened for the first time on 12 May 1999. After scandals and huge expenses, a stunning new parliament building is opened in Edinburgh by Queen Elizabeth II in October of 2004.	The Scottish Government announces a referendum on full independence to be held in 2014.

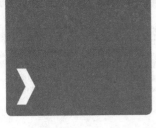

The Scottish Larder

Traditional Scottish cookery is all about basic comfort food: solid, nourishing fare, often high in fat, that will keep you warm on a winter's day spent in the fields or out fishing, and sweet treats to come home to in the evening.

But a new culinary style known as Modern Scottish has emerged over the last two decades. It's a style that should be familiar to fans of Californian Cuisine and Mod Oz. Chefs take top-quality Scottish produce – from Highland venison, Aberdeen Angus beef and freshly landed seafood, to root vegetables, raspberries and Ayrshire cheeses – and prepare it simply, in a way that enhances the natural flavours, often adding a French, Italian or Asian twist.

Scotland's traditional drinks – whisky and beer – have also found a new lease of life in recent years, with single malts being marketed like fine wines, and a new breed of microbreweries springing up all over the country.

Popular Scottish TV chef Nick Nairn's book *Wild Harvest* contains over 100 recipes based on the use of fresh, seasonal Scottish produce.

Breakfast, Lunch & Dinner

Haggis may be the national dish for which Scotland is most famous, but when it comes to what Scottish people actually cook and eat most often, the hands-down winner has to be mince and tatties (potatoes). Minced beef, browned in the pan and then stewed slowly with onion, carrot and gravy, is served with mashed potatoes (with a splash of milk and a knob of butter added during the mashing) – it's tasty, warming and you don't even have to chew.

The Full Scottish

Surprisingly few Scots eat porridge for breakfast – these days a cappuccino and a croissant is just as likely – and even fewer eat it in the traditional way; that is, with salt to taste, but no sugar. The breakfast offered in a B&B or hotel usually consists of fruit juice and cereal or muesli, followed

---

PRICE BANDS

Eating choices are flagged with price indicators, based on the cost of an average main course from the dinner menu.

» **£** Budget place where a main dish is less than £9

» **££** Midrange; mains are £9 to £18

» **£££** Top end; mains are more than £18

Lunch mains are often cheaper than dinner mains, and many places offer an 'early bird' special with lower prices (usually available between 5pm and 7pm).

by a choice of bacon, sausage, black pudding (a type of sausage made from dried blood), grilled tomato, mushrooms and a fried egg or two.

Fish for breakfast may sound strange, but was not unusual in crofting (smallholding) and fishing communities where seafood was a staple; many hotels still offer grilled kippers (smoked herrings) or smoked haddock (poached in milk and served with a poached egg) for breakfast – delicious with lots of buttered toast.

Broth, Skink & Bree

Scotch broth, made with mutton stock, barley, lentils and peas, is nutritious and tasty, while cock-a-leekie is a hearty soup made with chicken and leeks. Warming vegetable soups include leek and potato soup, and lentil soup (traditionally made using ham stock – vegetarians beware!).

Seafood soups include the delicious Cullen skink, made with smoked haddock, potato, onion and milk, and *partan bree* (crab soup).

Surf & Turf

It is illegal to import haggis into the USA, as the US government has declared that sheep lungs are unfit for human consumption.

Steak eaters will enjoy a thick fillet of world-famous Aberdeen Angus beef, and beef from Highland cattle is much sought after. Venison, from the red deer, is leaner and appears on many menus. Both may be served with a wine-based or creamy whisky sauce. Then there's haggis, Scotland's much-maligned national dish...

Scottish salmon is famous worldwide, but there's a big difference between the now-ubiquitous farmed salmon and the leaner, more expensive, wild fish. Also, there are concerns over the environmental impact of salmon farms on the marine environment.

Smoked salmon is dressed with a squeeze of lemon juice and eaten with fresh brown bread and butter. Trout – whether wild, rod-caught brown trout or farmed rainbow trout – is delicious fried in oatmeal.

As an alternative to kippers you may be offered Arbroath smokies (lightly smoked fresh haddock), traditionally eaten cold. Herring fillets fried in oatmeal are good, if you don't mind picking out a few bones. Mackerel pâté and smoked or peppered mackerel (both served cold) are also popular.

Juicy langoustines (also known as Dublin Bay prawns), crabs, lobsters, oysters, mussels and scallops are also widely available.

Clootie & Cranachan

Traditional Scottish puddings are irresistibly creamy, high-calorie concoctions. Cranachan is whipped cream flavoured with whisky, and mixed

HAGGIS – SCOTLAND'S NATIONAL DISH

Scotland's national dish is often ridiculed by foreigners because of its ingredients, which admittedly don't sound promising – the finely chopped lungs, heart and liver of a sheep, mixed with oatmeal and onion and stuffed into a sheep's stomach bag. However, it actually tastes surprisingly good.

Haggis should be served with *champit tatties* and *bashed neeps* (mashed potatoes and turnips), with a generous dollop of butter and a good sprinkling of black pepper.

Although it's eaten year-round, haggis is central to the celebrations of 25 January, in honour of Scotland's national poet, Robert Burns. Scots worldwide unite on Burns Night to revel in their Scottishness. A piper announces the arrival of the haggis and Burns' poem *Address to a Haggis* is recited to this 'Great chieftan o' the puddin-race'. The bulging haggis is then lanced with a dirk (dagger) to reveal the steaming offal within, 'warm, reekin, rich'.

Vegetarians (and quite a few carnivores, no doubt) will be relieved to know that veggie haggis is available in some restaurants.

SSSSSSMOKIN'!

Scotland is famous for its smoked salmon, but there are many other varieties of smoked fish – plus smoked meats and cheeses – to enjoy. Smoking food to preserve it is an ancient art that has recently undergone a revival, but this time it's more about flavour than preservation.

There are two parts to the process – first the cure, which involves covering the fish in a mixture of salt and molasses sugar, or soaking it in brine; and then the smoke, which can be either cold smoking (at less than 34°C), which results in a raw product, or hot smoking (at more than 60°C), which cooks it. Cold-smoked products include traditional smoked salmon, kippers and Finnan haddies. Hot-smoked products include *bradan rost* ('flaky' smoked salmon) and Arbroath smokies.

Arbroath smokies are haddock that have been gutted, beheaded and cleaned, then salted and dried overnight, tied together at the tail in pairs, and hot-smoked over oak or beech chippings for 45 to 90 minutes. Finnan haddies (named after the fishing village of Findon in Aberdeenshire) are also haddock, but these are split down the middle like kippers, and cold smoked.

Kippers (smoked herring) were invented in Northumberland, in northern England, in the mid-19th century, but Scotland soon picked up the technique, and both Loch Fyne and Mallaig were famous for their kippers.

There are dozens of modern smokehouses scattered all over Scotland, many of which offer a mail-order service as well as an on-site shop; here are a few recommended ones:

» **Hebridean Smokehouse** (☎01876-580209; www.hebrideansmokehouse.com; Clachan, North Uist; ⊗8am-5.30pm Mon-Fri, 9am-5pm Sat) Peat-smoked salmon and sea trout.

» **Inverawe Smokehouse & Fishery** (☎0844 8475 49; www.smokedsalmon.co.uk; Inverawe, nr Oban; admission free; ⊗8am-5.30pm Mar-Oct) Delicate smoked salmon, plump juicy kippers.

» **Marrbury Smokehouse** (☎01671-840241; www.visitmarrbury.co.uk; Carsluith Castle, Dumfries & Galloway; ⊗11am-4pm Thu & Fri, 10am-2pm Sat) Supplier to Gleneagles Hotel and other top restaurants.

» **Loch Duart Artisan Smokehouse** (☎01870-610324; www.lochduartsmoked salmon.com; Lochcarnan, South Uist; ⊗9am-5pm Mon-Fri) Famous for its flaky, hot-smoked salmon.

with toasted oatmeal and raspberries. Atholl brose is a mixture of cream, whisky and honey, flavoured with oatmeal. Clootie dumpling is a rich steamed pudding filled with currants and raisins.

Vegetarians & Vegans

Scotland has the same proportion of vegetarians as the rest of the UK – around 8% to 10% of the population – and vegetarianism has moved away from the hippie-student image of a few decades ago and is now firmly in the mainstream. Even the most remote Highland pub usually has at least one vegetarian dish on the menu, and there are many dedicated vegetarian restaurants in the cities. If you get stuck, there's almost always an Italian or Indian restaurant where you can get meat-free pizza, pasta or curry. Vegans, though, may find the options a bit limited outside of Edinburgh and Glasgow.

One thing to keep in mind is that lentil soup, a seemingly vegetarian staple of Scottish pub and restaurant menus, is traditionally made with ham stock.

A Caledonian Feast by Annette Hope is a fascinating and readable history of Scottish cuisine, providing a wealth of historical and sociological background.

Eating with Kids

Following the introduction of the ban on smoking in public places in 2006, many Scottish pubs and restaurants have had to broaden their appeal by becoming more family friendly. As a result, especially in the cities and more popular tourist towns, many restaurants and pubs now have family rooms and/or play areas.

In this guide we have indicated restaurants that offer children's menus, high chairs and other child-friendly facilities with a family-friendly icon.

You should be aware that children under the age of 14 are not allowed into the majority of Scottish pubs, even those that serve bar meals; even in family-friendly pubs (those in possession of a Children's Certificate), under-14s are only allowed in between 11am and 8pm, and must be accompanied by an adult aged 18 or above.

Cookery Courses

There are two principal places that offer courses in Scottish cookery. **Kinloch Lodge Hotel** (☎01471-833333; www.claire-macdonald.com) is located in Kinloch on the Isle of Skye. Here, cookery demonstrations using fresh, seasonal Scottish produce are given by Lady Claire Macdonald, author of *Scottish Highland Hospitality* and *Celebrations*.

Nairns Cook School (☎01877-389900; www.nairnscookschool.com) in Aberdeen offers two-day courses in modern Scottish cooking at the school owned by Scotland's top TV chef, Nick Nairn, author of *Wild Harvest* and *Island Harvest*.

What Are Ye Drinkin'?

A Pint...

Scottish breweries produce a wide range of beers. The market is dominated by multinational brewers such as Scottish & Newcastle, but smaller local breweries generally create tastier brews, some of them very strong. The aptly named Skull Splitter from Orkney is a good example, at 8.5% alcohol by volume.

Many Scottish beers use old-fashioned shilling categories to indicate strength (the number of shillings was originally the price per barrel; the stronger the beer, the higher the price). The usual range is from 60 to 80 shillings (written 80/-). You'll also see IPA, which stands for India Pale Ale, a strong, hoppy beer first brewed in the early 19th century for export to India (the extra alcohol meant that it kept better on the long sea voyage).

Draught beer is served in pints (usually costing from £2.20 to £3.50) or half pints; alcoholic content generally ranges from 3% to 6%. What the English call bitter, Scots call heavy, or export. Caledonian 80/-, Maclays 80/- and Belhaven 80/- are all worth trying, but Deuchar's IPA from Edinburgh's Caledonian Brewery is our favourite.

SCOTTISH ALES

The increasing popularity of real ales and a backlash against the bland conformity of globalised multinational brewing conglomerates has seen a huge rise in the number of specialist brewers and microbreweries springing up all over Scotland. They take pride in using only natural ingredients, and many try to revive ancient recipes, such as heather- and seaweed-flavoured ales.

These beers are sold in pubs, off-licences and delicatessens. Here are a few of our favourites:

» **Black Isle Brewery** (www.blackislebrewery.com; Old Allangrance) Range of organic beers.

» **Cairngorm Brewery** (☎01479-812222; www.cairngormbrewery.com; Dalfaber Industrial Estate) Creator of multi-award-winning Trade Winds ale.

» **Colonsay Brewery** (www.colonsaybrewery.co.uk) Produces lager, 80/- and IPA.

Top 10 Seafood Restaurants

» Ondine, Edinburgh

» Café Fish, Tobermory

» Waterfront Fishouse Restaurant, Oban

» Silver Darling, Aberdeen

» Tolbooth Restaurant, Stonehaven

» Lochleven Seafood Cafe, Kinlochleven

» Seafood Restaurant, St Andrews

» Mhor Fish, Callander

» Starfish, Tarbert

» Seafood Temple, Oban

The website www.scottishbrewing.com has a comprehensive list of Scottish breweries, both large and small.

» **Islay Ales** (p291) Refreshing and citrusy Saligo Ale.

» **Orkney Brewery** (☎01667-404555; www.sinclairbreweries.co.uk) Famous for its rich, chocolatey Dark Island ale, and the dangerously strong Skull Splitter.

» **Traquair House Brewery** (www.traquair.co.uk; Traquair House) Traquair House Ale, at 7.2% alcohol, is rich, dark and strong.

» **Williams Bros** (www.fraoch.com; New Alloa Brewery) Produces historic beers flavoured with heather flowers, seaweed, Scots pine and elderberries.

...Or a Wee Dram?

Scotch whisky (always spelt without an 'e' – whiskey with an 'e' is Irish or American) is Scotland's best-known product and biggest export. The spirit has been distilled in Scotland at least since the 15th century.

As well as whiskies, there are whisky-based liqueurs such as Drambuie. If you must mix your whisky with anything other than water, try a whisky-mac (whisky with ginger wine). After a long walk in the rain there's nothing better to put a warm glow in your belly.

At a bar, older Scots may order a 'half' or 'nip' of whisky as a chaser to a pint or half pint of beer (a 'hauf and a hauf'). Only tourists ask for 'Scotch' – what else would you be served in Scotland? The standard measure in pubs is either 25mL or 35mL.

Scotland's most famous soft drink is Barr's Irn Bru: a sweet fizzy drink, radioactive orange in colour, that smells like bubble gum and almost strips the enamel from your teeth. Many Scots swear by its restorative effects as a cure for a hangover.

HOW TO BE A MALT WHISKY BUFF

'Love makes the world go round? Not at all! Whisky makes it go round twice as fast.'
Whisky Galore, Compton Mackenzie (1883–1972)

Whisky tasting today is almost as popular as wine tasting was in the yuppie heyday of the late 1980s. Being able to tell your Ardbeg from your Edradour is de rigueur among the whisky-nosing set, so here are some pointers to help you impress your friends.

What's the difference between malt and grain whiskies?

Malts are distilled from malted barley – that is, barley that has been soaked in water, then allowed to germinate for around 10 days until the starch has turned into sugar – while grain whiskies are distilled from other cereals, usually wheat, corn or unmalted barley.

So what is a single malt?

A single malt is a whisky that has been distilled from malted barley and is the product of a single distillery. A pure (vatted) malt is a mixture of single malts from several distilleries, and a blended whisky is a mixture of various grain whiskies (about 60%) and malt whiskies (about 40%) from many different distilleries.

Why are single malts more desirable than blends?

A single malt, like a fine wine, somehow captures the essence of the place where it was made and matured – a combination of the water, the barley, the peat smoke, the oak barrels in which it was aged and (in the case of certain coastal distilleries) the sea air and salt spray. Each distillation varies from the one before, like different vintages from the same vineyard.

How should a single malt be drunk?

Either neat, or preferably with a little water added. To appreciate the aroma and flavour to the utmost, a measure of malt whisky should be cut (diluted) with one-third to two-thirds as much spring water (still, bottled spring water will do). Ice, tap water and (God forbid) mixers are for philistines. Would you add lemonade or ice to a glass of Chablis?

Where can I learn more?

If you're serious about spirits, the Scotch Malt Whisky Society (☎0131-554 3451; www.smws.com) has branches all around the world. Membership of the society costs from £110 for the first year (£57 a year thereafter) and includes use of members' rooms in Edinburgh and London.

TOP 10 SINGLE MALT WHISKIES – OUR CHOICE

After a great deal of diligent research (and not a few sore heads), Lonely Planet's *Scotland* authors have selected their 10 favourite single malts from across the country.

» **Ardbeg** (p291) (Islay) The 10-year-old from this noble distillery is a byword for excellence. Peaty but well balanced. Hits the spot after a hill walk.

» **Bowmore** (p291) (Islay) Smoke, peat and salty sea air – a classic Islay malt. One of the few distilleries that still malts its own barley.

» **Bruichladdich** (p292) (Islay) A visitor-friendly distillery with a quirky, innovative approach – famous for very peaty special releases such as Moine Mhor.

» **Glendronach** (Speyside) Only sherry casks are used here, so the creamy, spicy result tastes like grandma's Christmas trifle.

» **Highland Park** (p420) (Orkney) Full and rounded, with heather, honey, malt and peat. Award-winning distillery tour.

» **Isle of Arran** (p163) (Arran) One of the newest of Scotland's distilleries, offering a lightish, flavoursome malt with flowery, fruity notes.

» **Macallan** (p266) (Speyside) The king of Speyside malts, with sherry and bourbon finishes. Distillery set amid waving fields of Golden Promise barley.

» **Springbank** (p288) (Campbeltown) Complex flavours – sherry, citrus, pear drops, peat – with a salty tang. The entire production process from malting to bottling takes place on site.

» **Talisker** (p398) (Skye) Brooding, heavily peaty nose balanced by a satisfying sweetness from this lord of the isles. Great postdinner dram.

» **The Balvenie** (Speyside) Rich and honeyed, this Speysider is liquid gold for those with a sweet tooth.

Scottish Culture

Arts

The notion of 'the Scottish arts' often conjures up cliched images of bagpipe music, incomprehensible poetry and romanticised paintings of Highland landscapes. But Scottish artists have given the world a wealth of unforgettable treasures, from the songs and poems of Robert Burns and the novels of Walter Scott, to the paintings of David Wilkie and the architecture of Charles Rennie Mackintosh.

Literature

Scotland has a long and distinguished literary history, from the days of the medieval makars ('makers' of verses, ie poets) to the modern 'rat pack' of Iain Banks, Irvine Welsh and Ian Rankin.

BURNS & SCOTT

Scotland's best-loved and most famous literary figure is, of course, Robert Burns (1759–96). His works have been translated into dozens of languages and are known the world over.

In 1787 Burns was introduced to a 16-year-old boy at a social gathering in the house of an Edinburgh professor. The boy grew up to be Sir Walter Scott (1771–1832), Scotland's greatest and most prolific novelist. The son of an Edinburgh lawyer, Scott was born in Guthrie St (off Chambers St; the house no longer exists) and lived at various New Town addresses before moving to his country house at Abbotsford. Scott's early works were rhyming ballads, such as *The Lady of the Lake,* and his first historical novels – Scott effectively invented the genre – were published anonymously. He almost single-handedly revived interest in Scottish history and legend in the early 19th century, and was largely responsible for organising King George IV's visit to Scotland in 1822 (the first visit to Scotland of a reigning British monarch since 1650; the king had his portrait painted whilst wearing Highland dress, kicking off an obsession with tartanry among the upper and middle classes). Plagued by debt in later life, he wrote obsessively – to the detriment of his health – in order to make money, but will always be best remembered for classic tales such as *Waverley, The Antiquary, The Heart of Midlothian, Ivanhoe, Redgauntlet* and *Castle Dangerous.*

RLS & SHERLOCK HOLMES

Along with Scott, Robert Louis Stevenson (1850–94) ranks as Scotland's best-known novelist. Born at 8 Howard Pl in Edinburgh into a family of famous lighthouse engineers, Stevenson studied law at Edinburgh University but was always intent on pursuing the life of a writer. An inveterate traveller, but dogged by ill health, he finally settled in Samoa in 1889, where he was loved by the local people and known as 'Tusitala' – the teller of tales. Stevenson is known and loved around the world for those

THE SCOTTISH LANGUAGE

Scottish Gaelic (*Gàidhlig* – pronounced 'gallic' in Scotland) is spoken by about 80,000 people in Scotland, mainly in the Highlands and islands, and by many native speakers and learners overseas. It is a member of the Celtic branch of the Indo-European family of languages, which has given us Gaelic, Irish, Manx, Welsh, Cornish and Breton.

Gaelic culture flourished in the Highlands until the 18th century and the Jacobite rebellions. After the Battle of Culloden in 1746 many Gaelic speakers were forced from their ancestral lands; this 'ethnic cleansing' by landlords and governments culminated in the Highland Clearances of the 19th century. Although still studied at academic level, the spoken language declined, being regarded as little more than a mere 'peasant' language of no modern significance.

It was only in the 1970s that Gaelic began to make a comeback with a new generation of young enthusiasts who were determined that it should not be allowed to die. After two centuries of decline, the language is now being encouraged through financial help from government agencies and the EU. Gaelic education is flourishing at every level from play-groups to tertiary institutions. This rediscovered knowledge is flowing on into the fields of music, literature, cultural events and broadcasting, and people from all over Scotland, and indeed worldwide, are beginning to appreciate their Gaelic heritage.

tales: *Kidnapped, Catriona, Treasure Island, The Master of Ballantrae* and *The Strange Case of Dr Jekyll and Mr Hyde*. The Writers' Museum (p55) in Edinburgh celebrates the work of Burns, Scott and Stevenson.

Sir Arthur Conan Doyle (1859-1930), the creator of Sherlock Holmes, was born in Edinburgh and studied medicine at Edinburgh University. He based the character of Holmes on one of his lecturers, the surgeon Dr Joseph Bell, who had employed his forensic skills and powers of deduction on several murder cases in Edinburgh. There's a fascinating exhibit on Dr Bell in Edinburgh's Surgeons' Hall Museums. Conan Doyle's four novels and 56 short stories have spawned an industry that has produced no fewer than 211 films (the *Guinness Book of World Records* lists Holmes as the 'most portrayed movie character'), countless TV programs and a Broadway musical.

MACDIARMID TO MURIEL SPARK

Scotland's finest modern poet was Hugh MacDiarmid (born Christopher Murray Grieve; 1892-1978). Originally from Dumfriesshire, he moved to Edinburgh in 1908, where he trained as a teacher and a journalist, but spent most of his life in Montrose, Shetland, Glasgow and Biggar. His masterpiece is 'A Drunk Man Looks at the Thistle', a 2685-line Joycean monologue.

Born in Edinburgh, Norman MacCaig (1910-96) is widely regarded as the greatest Scottish poet of his generation. A primary school teacher for almost 40 years, MacCaig wrote poetry that is witty, adventurous, moving and filled with sharp observation; poems such as 'November Night, Edinburgh' vividly capture the atmosphere of his home city.

The poet and storyteller George Mackay Brown (1921–96) was born in Stromness in the Orkney Islands, and lived there almost all his life. Although his poems and novels are rooted in Orkney, his work, like that of Burns, transcends local and national boundaries. His novel *Greenvoe* (1972) is a warm, witty and poetic evocation of everyday life in an Orkney community; his last novel, *Beside the Ocean of Time*, a wonderfully elegiac account of remote island life, was published in 1994.

Lewis Grassic Gibbon (born James Leslie Mitchell; 1901–35) was another Scots writer whose novels vividly capture a sense of place – in this case the rural northeast of Kincardineshire and Aberdeenshire. His most famous work is the trilogy of novels called *A Scots Quair*.

Dame Muriel Spark (1918-2006) was born in Edinburgh and educated at James Gillespie's High School for Girls, an experience that provided material for perhaps her best-known novel, *The Prime of Miss Jean Brodie,* a shrewd portrait of 1930s Edinburgh. Dame Muriel was a prolific writer; her last novel, *The Finishing School,* published in 2004, was her 22nd.

THE CONTEMPORARY SCENE
The most widely known Scots writers today include the award-winning James Kelman (1946-), Iain Banks (1954-), Irvine Welsh (1961-) and Ian Rankin (1960-). The grim realities of modern Glasgow are vividly conjured in Kelman's short story collection *Not Not While the Giro;* his controversial novel *How Late It Was, How Late* won the 1994 Booker Prize.

The novels of Irvine Welsh, who grew up in Edinburgh's working-class district of Muirhouse, describe a very different world from that inhabited by Miss Jean Brodie: the modern city's underworld of drugs, drink, despair and violence. Best known for his debut novel *Trainspotting,* Welsh's most accomplished work is probably *Marabou Stork Nightmares,* in which a soccer hooligan, paralysed and in a coma, reviews his violent and brutal life.

Ian Rankin's Edinburgh-based crime novels, featuring the hard-drinking, introspective Detective Inspector John Rebus, are sinister, engrossing mysteries that explore the darker side of Scotland's capital city. Rankin's novels are filled with sharp dialogue, telling detail and three-dimensional characters; he has a growing international following (his books have been translated into 22 languages). Rankin seems to improve with every book – the final Rebus novel, *Exit Music* (2007), is one of his best. In *The Complaints* (2009) and *The Impossible Dead* (2011) he created a new and completely different character, Malcolm Fox, a cop who investigates other cops.

Music

TRADITIONAL MUSIC
Scotland has always had a strong folk tradition. In the 1960s and 1970s Robin Hall and Jimmy MacGregor, the Corries and the hugely talented Ewan McColl worked the pubs and clubs up and down the country. The Boys of the Lough, headed by Shetland fiddler Aly Bain, was one of the first professional bands to promote the traditional Celtic music of Scotland and Ireland. It has been followed by the Battlefield Band, Runrig (who write songs in Gaelic), Alba, Capercaillie and others.

The Scots folk songs that you will often hear sung in pubs and at *ceilidhs* (evenings of traditional Scottish entertainment, including music, song and dance) draw on Scotland's rich history. A huge number of them relate to the Jacobite rebellions in the 18th century and, in particular, to Bonnie Prince Charlie – 'Hey Johnnie Cope', the 'Skye Boat Song' and 'Will Ye No Come Back Again', for example – while others relate to the Covenanters and the Highland Clearances.

In recent years there has been a revival in traditional music, often adapted and updated for the modern age. Bands such as Runrig pioneered with their own brand of Celtic rock, while Shooglenifty blend Scottish folk music with anything from indie rock to electronica, producing a hybrid that has been called 'acid croft'.

But perhaps the finest modern renderings of traditional Scottish songs come from singer-songwriter Eddi Reader, who rose to fame with the band Fairground Attraction and their 1988 No 1 hit 'Perfect'. Since then her solo career has combined original songwriting with performances of traditional Scottish folk songs – her album *Eddi Reader Sings*

Six Essential Scottish Novels

» *Waverley* (Sir Walter Scott, 1814)

» *The Silver Darlings* (Neil M Gunn, 1941)

» *A Scots Quair* (Lewis Grassic Gibbon, trilogy 1932–4)

» *The Prime of Miss Jean Brodie* (Muriel Spark, 1961)

» *Greenvoe* (George Mackay Brown, 1972)

» *Trainspotting* (Irvine Welsh, 1993)

The Living Tradition is a bimonthly magazine covering the folk and traditional music of Scotland and the British Isles, as well as Celtic music, with features and reviews of albums and live gigs. See also www.folkmusic.net.

the Songs of Robert Burns (2003, re-released with extra tracks in 2009) is widely regarded as one of the best interpretations of Burns' works.

BAGPIPES

Bagpipe music may not be to everyone's taste, but Scotland's most famous instrument has been reinvented by bands like the Red Hot Chilli Pipers, who use pipes, drums, guitars and keyboards to create rock versions of trad tunes that have been christened, tongue firmly in cheek, as 'Jock 'n' Roll'. They feature regularly at festivals throughout the country.

The bagpipe consists of a leather bag held under the arm, kept inflated by blowing through the blowstick; the piper forces air through the pipes by squeezing the bag with the forearm. Three of the pipes, known as drones, play a constant note (one bass, two tenor) in the background. The fourth pipe, the chanter, plays the melody.

Highland soldiers were traditionally accompanied into battle by the skirl of the pipes, and the Scottish Highland bagpipe is unique in being the only musical instrument ever to be classed as a weapon. The playing of the pipes was banned – under pain of death – by the British government in 1747 as part of a scheme to suppress Highland culture in the wake of the Jacobite uprising of 1745. The pipes were revived when the Highland regiments were drafted into the British Army towards the end of the 18th century.

The Traditional Music & Song Association (www.tmsa.org.uk) website has listings of music, dance and cultural festivals around Scotland.

CEILIDHS

The Gaelic word *ceilidh* (*kay*-lay) means 'visit'. A *ceilidh* was originally a social gathering in the house after the day's work was over, enlivened with storytelling, music and song. These days, a *ceilidh* means an evening of traditional Scottish entertainment including music, song and dance. To find one, check the village noticeboard, or just ask at the local pub; visitors are always welcome to join in.

ROCK & POP

It would take an entire book to list all the Scottish artists and bands that have made it big in the world of rock and pop. From Glasgow-born King of Skiffle, Lonnie Donegan, in the 1950s, to the Glasgow-bred darlings of guitar-pop Franz Ferdinand today, the roll call is long and impressive.

The '90s saw the emergence of three bands that took the top three places in a vote for the best Scottish band of all time – melodic indie-pop songsters Belle and Sebastian, like-Oasis-only-better Brit-rock band Travis, and indie rockers Idlewild, who opened for the Rolling Stones in 2003.

The bespectacled twin brothers Craig and Charlie Reid from Auchtermuchty in Fife, better known as the Proclaimers, produced a new album in 2009 *(Notes and Rhymes)*, which is as passionate and invigorating as the songs that first made them famous back in the late '80s, 'Letter From America', and 'I'm Gonna Be (500 Miles)'.

Scottish artists who have made an impression in recent years include award-winning Glasgow band Glasvegas, who played the Lollapalooza festival in Chicago in 2009; Ayrshire rockers Biffy Clyro; and the darlings of indie rock, the View.

The airwaves have been awash with female singer-songwriters in recent years, but few are as gutsy and versatile as Edinburgh-born, St Andrews–raised KT Tunstall. Although she's been writing and singing since the late 1990s, it was her 2005 debut album *Eye to the Telescope* that introduced her to a wider audience. And then there's Glasgow-born Amy Macdonald, who was only 20 years old when her first album *This is the Life* (2007) sold 3 million copies; her second, *A Curious Thing*, was released in 2010.

Scottish Pop Playlist

» Franz Ferdinand: 'Take Me Out'

» KT Tunstall: 'Suddenly I See'

» The Proclaimers: 'Letter from America'

» The View: 'Same Jeans'

» Biffy Clyro: 'Bubbles'

» Amy Macdonald: 'This is the Life'

» Runrig: 'Loch Lomond'

» The Rezillos: 'Top of the Pops'

» Simple Minds: 'Don't You (Forget About Me)'

» Texas: 'Say What You Want'

Painting

MONARCH OF THE GLEN

If asked to think of a Scottish painting, most people probably picture *Monarch of the Glen,* a romanticised portrait of a magnificent Highland red deer stag by Sir Edwin Landseer (1802–73). Landseer was not a Scot but a Londoner, though he did spend a lot of time in Scotland, leasing a cottage in Glen Feshie and visiting the young Queen Victoria at Balmoral to tutor her in drawing and etching.

CLASSICAL PORTRAITISTS

Perhaps the most famous Scottish painting is the portrait *Reverend Robert Walker Skating on Duddingston Loch* by Sir Henry Raeburn (1756–1823), in the National Gallery of Scotland. This image of a Presbyterian minister at play beneath Arthur's Seat, with all the poise of a ballerina and the hint of a smile on his lips, is a symbol of Enlightenment Edinburgh, the triumph of reason over wild nature.

Scottish portraiture reached its peak during the Scottish Enlightenment in the second half of the 18th century with the paintings of Raeburn and his contemporary Allan Ramsay (1713–84). You can see many fine examples of their work in the Scottish National Portrait Gallery. At the same time, Alexander Nasmyth (1758–1840) emerged as an important landscape painter whose work had an immense influence on the Scottish art of the 19th century. One of the greatest artists of the 19th century was Sir David Wilkie (1785–1841), whose genre paintings depicted scenes of rural Highland life.

THE SCOTTISH COLOURISTS

In the early 20th century the Scottish painters most widely acclaimed outside of the country were the group known as the Scottish Colourists – SJ Peploe (1871–1935), Francis Cadell (1883–1937), Leslie Hunter (1877–1931) and JD Fergusson (1874–1961) – whose striking paintings drew on French post-Impressionist and Fauvist influences. Peploe and Cadell, active in the 1920s and 1930s, often spent the summer painting together on the Isle of Iona, and reproductions of their beautiful landscapes and seascapes appear on many a print and postcard. Aberdeen Art Gallery, Kirkcaldy Museum & Art Gallery and the JD Fergusson Gallery in Perth all have good examples of their work.

THE EDINBURGH SCHOOL

In the 1930s a group of modernist landscape artists called themselves the Edinburgh School. Chief among them were William Gillies (1898–1978), Sir William MacTaggart (1903–81) and Anne Redpath (1895–1965). Following WWII, artists such as Alan Davie (1920–) and Sir Eduardo Paolozzi (1924–2005) gained international reputations in abstract expressionism and pop art. The Dean Gallery in Edinburgh has a large collection of Paolozzi's work.

CONTEMPORARY ARTISTS

Among contemporary Scottish artists the most famous – or infamous – are Peter Howson and Jack Vettriano. Howson (1958–), best known for his grim portraits of Glasgow down-and-outs and muscular workers, hit the headlines when he went to Bosnia as an official war artist in 1993 and produced some disturbing and controversial works. *Croatian and Muslim,* an uncompromising rape scene, sparked a debate about what was acceptable in a public exhibition of art. More recently his nude portraits of pop icon Madonna garnered even more press. His work is much sought after and collected by celebrities such as David Bowie and Madonna

Despite dodgy Scottish accents from Liam Neeson and Jessica Lange, *Rob Roy* is a witty and moving cinematic version of Sir Walter Scott's tale of the outlaw MacGregor.

FILM

herself. You can see examples of Howson's work at Aberdeen Art Gallery and Glasgow's Gallery of Modern Art.

Jack Vettriano (1954–) was formerly a mining engineer, but now ranks as one of Scotland's most commercially successful artists. An entirely self-taught painter, his work – realistic, voyeuristic, occasionally sinister and often carrying a powerful erotic charge – has been compared to that of the American painters Edward Hopper and Walter Sickert. You can see reproductions of his work in coffee-table books and posters, but not in any Scottish art gallery. The Scottish art establishment looks down its nose at him, despite – or perhaps because of – the enormous popularity of his work.

Cinema

Perthshire-born John Grierson (1898–1972) is acknowledged around the world as the father of the documentary film. His legacy includes the classic *Drifters* (about the Scottish herring fishery) and *Seaward the Great Ships* (about Clyde shipbuilding). Filmmaker Bill Douglas (1934–91), the director of an award-winning trilogy of films documenting his childhood and early adult life, was born in the former mining village of Newcraighall just south of Edinburgh.

Glasgow-born writer-director Bill Forsyth (1946–) is best known for *Local Hero* (1983), a gentle comedy about an oil magnate seduced by the beauty of the Highlands, and *Gregory's Girl* (1980), about an awkward teenage schoolboy's romantic exploits. The directing credits of Gillies MacKinnon (1948–), another Glasgow native, include *Small Faces* (1996), *Regeneration* (1997) and *Hideous Kinky* (1998). Michael Caton-Jones (1958–), director of *Memphis Belle* (1990) and *Rob Roy* (1995), was born in West Lothian and is a graduate of Edinburgh University.

In the 1990s the rise of the director-producer-writer team of Danny Boyle (English), Andrew Macdonald and John Hodge (both Scottish) – who wrote the scripts for *Shallow Grave* (1994), *Trainspotting* (1996) and *A Life Less Ordinary* (1997) – marked the beginnings of what might be described as a home-grown Scottish film industry. Writer and director David McKenzie hit the headlines in 2003 with *Young Adam*, which starred Ewan McGregor and Tilda Swinton, and won BAFTAs for best actor, best actress, best director and best film. McKenzie more recently gave us *Hallam Foe* (2007) and *Perfect Sense* (2011).

Other Scottish directorial talent includes Kevin Macdonald, who made *Touching the Void* (2003), *The Last King of Scotland* (2006) and *State of Play* (2009), and Andrea Arnold, who directed *Red Road* (2006) and the BAFTA-winning *Fish Tank* (2009).

SCOTTISH ACTORS

Scotland's most famous actor is, of course, Sir Sean Connery (1930–), the original and arguably best James Bond, and star of dozens of other hit films including *Highlander* (1986), *The Name of the Rose* (1986), *Indiana Jones and the Last Crusade* (1989), *The Hunt for Red October* (1990) and *The League of Extraordinary Gentlemen* (2003). Connery started life as 'Big Tam' Connery, sometime milkman and brickie, born in a tenement in Fountainbridge, Edinburgh.

Other Scottish actors who have achieved international recognition include Robert Carlyle, who starred in *Trainspotting* (1996), *The Full Monty* (1997) – the UK's most commercially successful film – *The World Is Not Enough* (1999) and *28 Weeks Later* (2007); Ewan McGregor, who appeared in *Trainspotting,* the most recent Star Wars films, *Angels and Demons* (2009) and *The Ghost* (2010); and Kelly Macdonald, yet another

Top Five Scottish Films

» *The 39 Steps* (1935)

» *Whisky Galore!* (1949)

» *Local Hero* (1983)

» *Rob Roy* (1995)

» *Trainspotting* (1996)

For a guide to Scottish film locations check out www.scotlandthe movie.com.

Trainspotting alumna who went on to appear in *Gosford Park* (2001), *No Country for Old Men* (2007) and voiced heroine Merida in *Brave* (2012).

It's less widely known that Scotland produced some of the stars of silent film, including Eric Campbell (the big, bearded villain in Charlie Chaplin's films) and Jimmy Finlayson (the cross-eyed character in Laurel and Hardy films); in fact, English-born Stan Laurel grew up and made his acting debut in Glasgow.

Architecture

There are interesting buildings all over Scotland, but Edinburgh has a particularly rich heritage of 18th- and early-19th-century architecture, and Glasgow is noted for its superb Victorian buildings.

Prehistoric

The northern islands of Scotland have some of the best surviving examples of prehistoric buildings in Europe. The best known are the stone villages of Skara Brae (from 3100 BC) in Orkney, and Jarlshof (from 1500 BC) in Shetland. The characteristic stone defensive towers known as brochs that can be seen in the north and west, including Glenelg (south of Kyle of Lochalsh), Dun Carloway (Lewis) and Mousa (Shetland), are thought to date from the Iron Age (2nd century BC to 1st century AD).

Romanesque (12th Century)

The Romanesque style – with its characteristic round arches and chevron decoration – was introduced to Scotland via the monasteries that were founded during the reign of David I (1124–53). Good examples survive in Dunfermline Abbey, and St Magnus Cathedral in Kirkwall.

Gothic (12th to 16th Centuries)

The more elaborate Gothic style – tall, pointed arches, ornate window tracery and ribbed vaulting – was adapted by the monastic orders. Examples of Early Gothic architecture can be seen in the ruins of the great Border abbeys of Jedburgh and Dryburgh, at Holyrood Abbey in Edinburgh and in Glasgow Cathedral. The more decorative Middle and Late Gothic styles appear in Melrose Abbey, the cathedrals of Dunkeld and Elgin, and the parish churches of Haddington and Stirling.

Post-Reformation (16th & 17th Centuries)

After the Reformation many abbeys and cathedrals were damaged or destroyed, as the new religion frowned on ceremony and ornament.

During this period the old style of castle, with its central keep and curtain wall such as at Dirleton Castle, was superseded by the tower house. Good examples include Castle Campbell, Loch Leven Castle and Neidpath Castle. The Renaissance style was introduced in the royal palaces of Linlithgow and Falkland.

Georgian (18th & Early 19th Centuries)

The leading Scottish architects of the 18th century were William Adam (1684–1748) and his son Robert Adam (1728–92), whose revival of classical Greek and Roman forms influenced architects throughout Europe. Among the many neoclassical buildings they designed are Hopetoun House, Culzean Castle and Edinburgh's Charlotte Sq, possibly the finest example of Georgian architecture anywhere.

The New Town of Edinburgh, and other planned towns such as Inveraray (Argyll) and Blair Atholl (Perthshire), are characterised by their elegant Georgian architecture.

Top Prehistoric Sites

» Kilmartin Glen
» Skara Brae
» Broch of Gurness
» Callanish
» Maes Howe

Best Gothic Abbeys

» Jedburgh Abbey
» Dryburgh Abbey
» Melrose Abbey
» Sweetheart Abbey
» Inchcolm Abbey
» Oronsay Priory

TARTAN

This distinctive checked pattern, traditionally associated with the kilt, has become the definitive symbol of Scotland, inspiring skirts, scarves, blankets, ties, key-fobs and a thousand other souvenirs. The pattern is thought to date back to at least the Roman period, though it is romantically associated with the Gaels, who arrived from Ireland in the 6th century. What is certain is that a tartan plaid had become the standard uniform of Highlanders by the start of 18th century. Following the Battle of Culloden in 1746, the Disarming Act banned the wearing of Highland dress in an attempt to undermine clan solidarity.

In the 19th century, tartan got caught up in the cult of so-called 'Balmorality' – Queen Victoria's patronage of Scottish culture – and many of the setts (tartan patterns) now associated with particular clans were created out of thin air by a pair of brothers known as the Sobieski Stuarts, who claimed descent from Bonnie Prince Charlie. The brothers' setts were based on a 'lost' document dating back to the 15th century and they published a hugely successful book of invented tartans, *The Costume of the Clans*, which became established as the genuine tartans of many Highland clans before their elaborate fraud was exposed. Today every clan, and indeed every football team, has one or more distinctive tartans, though few date back more than 150 years.

You can search for your own clan tartan at www.tartansauthority.com.

Victorian (Mid- to Late-19th Century)

Alexander 'Greek' Thomson (1817–75) changed the face of 19th-century Glasgow with his neoclassical designs. Masterpieces such as the Egyptian Halls and Caledonia Rd Church in Glasgow combine Egyptian and Hindu motifs with Greek and Roman forms.

In Edinburgh, William Henry Playfair (1790–1857) continued Robert Adam's neoclassical tradition in the Greek temples of the National Monument on Calton Hill, the Royal Scottish Academy and the National Gallery of Scotland, before moving on to the neo-Gothic style in Edinburgh University's New College on The Mound.

Scotland's Castles by Chris Tabraham is an excellent companion for anyone touring Scottish castles – a readable, illustrated history detailing how and why they were built.

The 19th-century boom in country-house building was led by architects William Burn (1789–1870) and David Bryce (1803–76). The resurgence of interest in Scottish history and identity, led by writers such as Sir Walter Scott, saw architects turn to the towers, pointed turrets and crow-stepped gables of the 16th century for inspiration. The Victorian revival of the Scottish Baronial style, which first made an appearance in 16th-century buildings such as Craigievar Castle, produced many fanciful abodes such as Balmoral Castle, Scone Palace and Abbotsford.

The 20th Century

CASTLES

Scotland's best known 20th-century architect and designer is Charles Rennie Mackintosh (1868–1928), one of the most influential exponents of the art-nouveau style. His finest building is the Glasgow School of Art (1896), which still looks modern more than a century after it was built. The art-deco style of the 1930s made little impact in Scotland; the few examples include St Andrews House in Edinburgh and the beautifully restored Luma Tower in Glasgow.

During the 1960s Scotland's larger towns and cities suffered badly under the onslaught of the motor car and the unsympathetic impact of large-scale, concrete building developments. However, modern architecture discovered a new confidence in the 1980s and 1990s, exemplified by the impressive gallery housing the Burrell Collection in Glasgow and the stunning modern buildings lining the banks of Glasgow's River Clyde.

Scotland's most controversial new structure is the Scottish parliament building (p57) in Edinburgh.

Sport

Football

Football (soccer) in Scotland is not so much a sport as a religion, with thousands turning out to worship their local teams on Wednesdays and weekends throughout the season (August to May). Sacred rites include standing in the freezing cold of a February day, drinking hot Bovril and eating a Scotch pie as you watch your team getting gubbed.

Scotland's top 10 clubs play in the **Scottish Premier League** (www. scotprem.com), but two teams – Glasgow Rangers and Glasgow Celtic – have dominated the competition. On only 18 occasions since 1890 has a team other than Rangers or Celtic won the league; the last time was when Aberdeen won in 1985.

However, Rangers made headlines in 2012 when they were forced into liquidation over a tax dispute and kicked out of the SPL; they had to begin the 2012/13 season in the Third Division. It looks like Celtic will have an easy run while their traditional rivals claw their way back into the SPL.

Rugby Union

Traditionally, football was the sport of Scotland's urban working classes, while rugby union (www.scottishrugby.org) was the preserve of agricultural workers from the Borders and middle-class university graduates. Although this distinction is breaking down – rugby's popularity soared after the 1999 World Cup was staged in the UK, and the middle classes have invaded the football terraces – it persists to some extent.

Each year, starting in January, Scotland takes part in the Six Nations Rugby Union Championship. The most important fixture is the clash against England for the Calcutta Cup – it's always an emotive event; Scotland has won three times and drawn once in the last 10 years.

At club level, the season runs from September to May, and among the better teams are those from the Borders such as Hawick, Kelso and Melrose. At the end of the season, teams play a rugby sevens (seven-a-side) variation of the 15-player competition.

Golf

Scotland is the home of golf (www.scottishgolfunion.org). The game was probably invented here in the 12th century, and the world's oldest documentary evidence of a game being played (dating from 1456) was on Bruntsfield Links in Edinburgh.

Today, there are more than 550 golf courses in Scotland – that's more per capita than in any other country. The sport is hugely popular and much more egalitarian than in other countries, with lots of affordable, council-owned courses. There are many world-famous courses too, from Muirfield in East Lothian and Turnberry and Troon in Ayrshire, to St Andrews' Old Course in Fife. For more, see p33.

Highland Games

Highland games are held in Scotland throughout the summer, and not just in the Highlands. You can find dates and details of Highland games held all over the country on the website VisitScotland (www.visitscotland. com) – follow the links What to See & Do/What's On/Highland Games.

The traditional sporting events are accompanied by piping and dancing competitions and attract locals and tourists alike. Some events are peculiarly Scottish, particularly those that involve trials of strength: tossing the caber (heaving a tree trunk into the air), throwing the hammer and putting the stone. Major Highland games are staged at Dunoon, Oban and Braemar.

Shinty (*camanachd* in Gaelic) is a fast and physical ball-and-stick sport similar to Ireland's hurling, with more than a little resemblance to clan warfare. It's an indigenous Scottish game played mainly in the Highlands, and the most prized trophy is the Camanachd Cup. For more information, see www.shinty.com.

Wild Scotland

Visitors revel in the solitude and dramatic scenery encompassing so much of rural Scotland. Soaring peaks with veins of snow trickling down their summits, steely blue lochs, deep inlets, forgotten beaches and surging peninsulas are a taste of the astonishing natural diversity. The best wildlife in Britain – from the emblematic osprey to the red deer, its bellow reverberating among large stands of native forest – is found throughout the wild places of Scotland. Large chunks of land moored just offshore, or miles out into the raging northern Atlantic Ocean, are havens for species hunted to extinction centuries ago in habitats further south. Cetaceans patrol the seas, and the remote archipelagos of the northeast are havens for seabird breeding colonies of extraordinary magnitude.

Scotland accounts for one-third of the British mainland's surface area, but it has a massive 80% of Britain's coastline and only 10% of its population.

The Land

Scotland's mainland divides neatly into thirds. The Southern Uplands, ranges of grassy rounded hills divided by wide valleys and bounded by fertile coastal plains, form the southern border to the central Lowlands. The geological divide – the Southern Uplands Fault – runs in a line from Girvan (Ayrshire) to Dunbar (East Lothian).

The central Lowlands lie in a broad band stretching from Glasgow and Ayr in the west to Edinburgh and Dundee in the east. This area is underlaid by sedimentary rocks, including the beds of coal and oil shale that fuelled Scotland's Industrial Revolution. Though it's only a fifth of the nation by land area, most of the country's industry, its two largest cities and 80% of the population are concentrated here.

Some 90% of Britain's surface fresh water is found in Scotland, and Loch Lomond is Britain's biggest body of fresh water.

Another great geological divide – the Highland Boundary Fault – runs from Helensburgh in the west to Stonehaven on the east coast, and marks the southern edge of the Scottish Highlands. These hills – most of their summits reach to around the 900m to 1000m mark – were deeply scoured by glaciers during the last Ice Age, creating a series of deep, U-shaped valleys: the long, narrow sea lochs that today are such a feature of Highland scenery. The Highlands form 60% of the Scottish mainland, and are cut in two by the Great Glen, a rift valley running southwest to northeast.

Despite their pristine beauty, the wild, empty landscapes of the western and northern Highlands are artificial wildernesses. Before the Highland Clearances many of these empty corners of Scotland supported sizeable rural populations.

Offshore, some 800 islands are concentrated in four main groups: the Shetland Islands, the Orkney Islands, the Outer Hebrides and the Inner Hebrides.

LOCH LOMOND

The Water

It rains a lot in Scotland – some parts of the western Highlands get over 4.5m of it a year – so it's not surprising there's plenty of water about.

WINDING BACK THE CLOCK

Over the centuries many animal species have disappeared from Scotland, hunted into oblivion or left in the lurch after the destruction of their habitat or food supply. As a means of increasing biodiversity, there's a strong case for bringing some of them back. Though it has detractors, reintroduction of species has been implemented successfully in several instances. The red kite and the majestic white-tailed sea eagle, absent from Britain since the 19th century, are now soaring Scottish skies again. The European beaver was released in a trial in 2009, a move opposed by some campaigners, who felt beavers might negatively impact the forests or water quality; the situation is being carefully monitored.

But the mildly controversial beaver pales beside events at one Highland estate: the owner has already shipped in elk (moose), and wants to go for wolves next.

Around 3% of Scotland's land surface is fresh water; the numerous lochs, rivers and burns (streams) form the majority of this, but about a third is in the form of wetlands: the peat bogs and fens (mires) that form a characteristic Highland and island landscape.

But it's salt water that really shapes the country. Including the islands, there's over 10,000 miles of Scottish shoreline: tortuous, complex, coastline that doubles back on itself at the slightest opportunity.

Wildlife

Scotland's wildlife is one of its big attractions, and the best way to see it is to get out there. Pull on the boots and sling on the binoculars, go quietly and see what you can spot. Many species that have disappeared from, or are rare in, the rest of Britain survive here.

Animals

While the Loch Ness monster still hogs headlines, Scotland's wild places harbour a wide variety of animals. Britain's largest land animal, the red deer, is present in numbers, as is the more common roe deer. You'll see them if you spend any time in the Highlands: some are quite content to wander down the village street in the evening and crop at the lawns.

Otters are found in most parts of Scotland, around the coast and along salmon and trout rivers. The best places to spot them are in the northwest, especially in Skye and the Outer Hebrides. The piers at Kyle of Lochalsh and Portree are otter hotspots, as the otters have learned to scavenge from fishing boats.

Scotland is home to 75% of Britain's red-squirrel population; they've been pushed out in most of the rest of the country by the dominant greys, native to North America. The greys often carry a virus that's lethal to the reds, so measures are in place to try to prevent their further encroachment.

Other small mammals include the Orkney vole and various bats, as well as stoats and weasels. The blue mountain hare dwells in high mountain environments, and swaps a grey-brown summer coat for a pure-white winter one.

Rarer beasts that were slaughtered to the point of near-extinction in the 19th century include pine martens, polecats and wildcats. Populations of these are small and remote, but are slowly recovering thanks to their protected status and greater awareness.

Of course, most animals you'll see will be in fields or getting in your way on single-track roads. Several indigenous sheep varieties are still around, smaller and stragglier than the purpose-bred supermodels to which we're accustomed. Other emblematic domestic animals include

One of the best-loved pieces of Scottish wildlife writing is *Ring of Bright Water* by Gavin Maxwell, in which the author describes life on the remote Glenelg peninsula with his two pet otters in the 1950s.

JOURNEY OF THE SALMON

One of Scotland's most thrilling sights is the salmon's leap up a fast-flowing cascade, resolutely returning to the very river of its birth several years before. The salmon's life begins in early spring, hatching in a stretch of fresh water in some Scottish glen. Called fry at this stage and only an inch long, it stays for a couple of years, growing through the 'parr' stage to become smolt, when it heads out to sea.

Its destination could be anywhere in the North Atlantic, but it eventually, sometimes after several years, returns home – scientists think it may use the Earth's magnetic field to navigate – to reproduce. Arriving all through the year, but most commonly in late spring, salmon regain strength after the arduous journey and spawn in late autumn. That job done, the salmon normally dies and the cycle begins anew.

Scotland's most famous salmon rivers are the Tweed, the Tay, the Dee, and the Spey, though you'll see them in many smaller rivers throughout the country.

the Shetland pony and gentle Highland cow with its horns and shaggy reddish-brown coat and fringe.

The waters off Scotland's north and west coasts are rich in marine mammals. Dolphins and porpoises are fairly common, and in summer minke whales are regular visitors. Orcas, too, are regularly sighted around Shetland and Orkney. Seals are widespread. Both the Atlantic grey (identified by its Roman nose) and the common seal (with a face like a dog) are easily seen along the coasts and, especially, the islands.

Birds

Scotland has an immense variety of birds. For birdwatchers, the Shetland Islands are paradise. Twenty-one of the British Isles' 24 seabird species are found here, breeding in huge colonies, and being entertained by the puffins' clownish antics is a highlight.

Large numbers of grouse – a popular game bird – graze the heather on the moors. The ptarmigan (a type of grouse) is a native of the hills, seldom seen below 700m, with the unusual feature of having feathered feet. It is the only British bird that plays the Arctic trick of changing its plumage from mottled brown in summer to dazzling white in winter, to blend in with the snowfields. In heavily forested areas you may see capercaillie, a black, turkey-like bird and the largest member of the grouse family. Millions of greylag geese winter on Lowland stubble fields.

News on endangered Scottish birds has generally been positive in the last couple of decades. The Royal Society for the Protection of Birds (RSPB; www.rspb.org.uk) is active here, and has overseen several success stories. As well as the reintroduction of species, the population of several precariously placed bird species has stabilised.

The majestic osprey (absent for most of the 20th century) nests in Scotland from mid-March through to September, after migrating from West Africa. There are around 200 breeding pairs and you can see nesting sites throughout the country, including at Loch Garten and Loch of the Lowes. Other birds of prey, such as the golden eagle, buzzards, peregrine falcon and hen harrier, are now protected and their populations are slowly recovering.

The habitat of the once-common corncrake was almost completely wiped out by modern farming methods but farmers now mow in corncrake-friendly fashion and numbers have recuperated. Listen for its distinctive call – like a thumbnail drawn along the teeth of a comb – in the Uists and at Loch Gruinart Nature Reserve on Islay.

A beautifully written book about Scotland's wildlife, penned by a man who lived and breathed alongside the country's critters in a remote part of the Highlands, is *A Last Wild Place* by Mike Tomkies.

Plants & Trees

Although the thistle is Scotland's national flower, more characteristic are the Scottish bluebell (harebell), carpeting native woodlands in spring; and heather, the tiny pink and purple flowers of which emerge on the moors in August. Vivid pink rhododendrons are introduced but grow vigorously, and bright yellow gorse also flowers in May and June.

Only 1% of Scotland's ancient woodlands, which once covered much of the country, survive, and these are divided into small parcels across the land. Managed regeneration forests are slowly covering more of the landscape, especially in the Highlands. Some 5000 sq miles (1.3 million hectares) of tree cover (17% of the land area) now exists; not a huge figure, but an improvement on what it was. About one-third of this is controlled by the government's **Forestry Commission** (www.forestry.gov. uk), which, as well as conducting managed logging, dedicates large areas to sustainable recreational use. The vast majority of this tree cover is coniferous, and there's a plan to increase it to 25% of land area by 2050.

WILD SCOTLAND

Seventeen per cent of Scotland is forested, compared with England's 7%, Finland's 74% and a worldwide average of 30%.

National Parks

Scotland has two national parks – Loch Lomond & the Trossachs (p275) and the Cairngorms (p336). But national parks are only part of the story. There's a huge range of protected areas with a bewildering array of 25 distinct classifications. Forty-seven National Nature Reserves (www.nnr -scotland.org.uk) span the country, and there are also marine areas under various levels of protection.

Environmental Issues

Scotland's abundance of wind and water means the government hasn't had to look far for sources of renewable energy. The grand plan is to generate 100% of the country's energy needs from renewable sources by 2020, and things look to be on track. Scotland has been a European leader in the development of wind technology – wind farms now dot the hills and firths (estuaries), and the near-constant breeze in some areas means record-breaking output from some turbines.

The problem is, although everyone agrees that wind power is clean and economical, there's a powerful NIMBY (not in my back yard) element who don't want the windmills spoiling their view. And it's not just the whirring blades, of course. A remote Highland wind farm is all very well, but the power lines trailing all the way down to the south have a significant visual and environmental impact.

One of Scotland's major goals over the last decade or so has been to halt a worrying decline in biodiversity on land, in the air and in the sea. You can see progress reports on the Scottish Natural Heritage website (www.snh. gov.uk) but a huge threat to existing species is, of course, climate change.

Sustainable Scotland (www. sustainable -scotland.net/ climatechange) is a local govern- ment initiative to combat climate change and address sus- tainability in Scotland. Learn about community efforts to tackle a global problem.

OH FLOWERS OF SCOTLAND

As much as the untamed wildness of Scotland fills the spirit, another of the country's delights is a more managed beauty, in the shape of its numerous gardens, which emerge from harsh winter with a riotous explosion of colour in spring and summer. In the 19th century, every castle and stately home worth its salt had a planned garden in the grounds, and the warmer parts – the southwest, the Aberdeen and Moray area and the Gulf Stream–warmed northwest coast – are absolutely studded with them.

From royal roses at Balmoral (p260) to unlikely subtropical species at Inverewe (p386), there's a great deal more than anyone could reasonably expect at these lati- tudes. The National Trust for Scotland (p483) manages many of the finest gardens; its website is a good first stop to plan a route through the blooms.

Scottish Environment LINK (www.scotlink.org), the umbrella body for Scotland's voluntary environmental organisations, includes 36 bodies committed to environmental sustainability.

A rise of a few degrees across the north would leave plenty of mountain plants and creatures with no place to go; it's already been speculated that the steady decline in Scotland's seabird population since the early '90s has been partly caused by a temperature-induced decrease in certain plankton species.

But the main cause of the worrying level of some fish stocks is clear: we've eaten them all. In 2010 the Marine (Scotland) Act was passed. It's a compromise solution that tries to both protect vulnerable marine areas and stocks and sustain the flagging fishing industry. It may well be too little, too late.

Survival Guide

Directory A–Z

Accommodation

Scotland provides a comprehensive choice of accommodation to suit all visitors.

For budget travel, the options are campsites, hostels and cheap B&Bs. In highland areas you'll find bothies – simple walkers' hostels and shelters – and in the Shetlands there are *böds* (characterful but basic shared accommodation).

Above this price level is a plethora of comfortable B&Bs and guesthouses (£25 to £40 per person per night). Midrange hotels are present in most places, while in the higher price bracket (£65-plus per person a night) there are some superb hotels, the most interesting being converted castles and mansions, or chic designer options in cities.

If you're travelling solo, expect to pay a supplement in hotels and B&Bs, meaning you'll often be forking over 75% of the price of a double for your single room.

Almost all B&Bs, guesthouses and hotels (and even some hostels) include breakfast in the room price.

Prices increase over the peak tourist season (June to September) and are at their highest in July and August. Outside of these months, and particularly in winter, special deals are often available at guesthouses and hotels.

If you're going to be in Edinburgh in August (festival month) or at Hogmanay (New Year), book as far in advance as you can – a year if possible – as the city will be packed.

Tourist offices have an accommodation booking service (£4), which can be handy over summer. However, note that they can only book the ever-decreasing number of places that are registered with **VisitScotland** (☑0845 859 1006; www.visitscotland.com/accommodation). There are many other fine accommodation options that, mostly due to the hefty registration fee, choose not to register with the tourist board. Registered places tend to be a little pricier than nonregistered ones. Visit Scotland's star system is based on a rather arbitrary set of criteria, so don't set too much store by it.

Accommodation Price Indicators

Prices in this book always include breakfast unless otherwise noted, except for hostel and campground accommodation. Accommodation choices are flagged with price indicators, based on the cheapest accommodation for two people in high season:

£	up to £60
££	from £60 to £130
£££	£130 and over

B&Bs & Guesthouses

B&Bs are a Scottish institution. At the bottom end you get a bedroom in a private house, a shared bathroom and a fry-up (juice, coffee or tea, cereal and cooked breakfast – bacon, eggs, sausage, baked beans and toast). Midrange B&Bs have en suite bathrooms, TVs in each room and more variety (and healthier options) for breakfast. Almost all B&Bs provide hospitality trays (tea- and coffee-making facilities) in bedrooms. B&B options range from urban houses to pubs and farms.

Guesthouses, often large converted private houses, are an extension of the B&B concept. They are normally larger and less personal than B&Bs.

BOOK YOUR STAY ONLINE

For more accommodation reviews by Lonely Planet authors, check out http://hotels.lonelyplanet.com. You'll find independent reviews, as well as recommendations on the best places to stay. Best of all, you can book online.

Camping & Caravan Parks

Free 'wild' camping became a legal right under the Land Reform Bill. However, campers are obliged to camp on unenclosed land, in small numbers and away from buildings and roads.

Commercial camping grounds are geared to caravans and vary widely in quality. There are numerous campsites across Scotland; VisitScotland has a free map, available at tourist offices, showing a good selection of them.

Homestays & Hospitality Exchange

A convenient and increasingly popular holiday option is to join an international house-exchange organisation. You sign up for a year and place your home on a website giving details of what you're looking for, where and for how long. You organise the house swap yourself with people in other countries and arrange to swap homes, rent free, for an agreed period. Shop around, as registration costs vary between organisations. Check out **Home Link International** (www.homelink.org.uk) and **Home Base Holidays** (www.home base-hols.com) for starters.

Organisations such as **Hospitality Club** (www.hos pitalityclub.org) put people in contact for more informal free accommodation offers – a bit like blind-date couch-surfing. Even if you're not comfortable crashing in a stranger's house, these sites are a great way to meet locals just to go out for a pint or two.

Hostels

Numerous hostels offer cheap accommodation and in Scotland the standard of facilities is generally very good. The more upmarket hostels have en suite bathrooms in their dorms, and all manner of luxuries that give them the feel of hotels, if it weren't for the bunk beds.

PRACTICALITIES

» Leaf through Edinburgh's *Scotsman* newspaper or Glasgow's *Herald;* the latter is over 225 years old.

» Have a giggle at rival tabloids the *Daily Record* and the *Scottish Sun,* or try the old-fashioned *Sunday Post* for a nostalgia trip.

» BBC Radio Scotland (AM 810kHz, FM 92.4-94.7MHz) provides a Scottish point of view.

» Watch BBC1 Scotland, BBC2 Scotland and ITV stations STV or Border. Channel Four and Five are nationwide channels with unchanged content for Scotland.

» Use the metric system for weights and measures, with the exception of road distances (in miles) and beer (in pints). The pint is 570mL, more than the US version.

» In Scotland you can't smoke in any public place with a roof and at least half enclosed. That means pubs, bus shelters, restaurants and hotels – basically, anywhere you might want to.

Hostels have facilities for self-catering, and many provide internet access and can usually arrange activities and tours.

INDEPENDENT & STUDENT HOSTELS

There are a large number of independent hostels, most with prices around £12 to £18. Facilities vary considerably. The free *Scottish Independent Hostels* guide (www.hostel-scotland.co.uk), available from tourist offices, lists over 100 hostels in Scotland, mostly in the north.

SCOTTISH YOUTH HOSTEL ASSOCIATION

The **SYHA** (SYHA; ☎0845-293 7373; www.syha.org.uk) has a network of decent, reasonably priced hostels and produces a free booklet available from SYHA hostels and tourist offices. There are more than 60 to choose from around the country, ranging from basic walkers' digs to mansions and castles. You've got to be an HI member to stay, but nonmembers can pay a £2 supplement per night that goes towards the £10 membership fee. Prices vary according to the month, but average around £16 to £18 per adult in high season.

Most SYHA hostels close from mid-October to early March but can be rented out by groups.

Hotels

There are some wonderfully luxurious places, including rustic country-house hotels in fabulous settings, and castles complete with crenellated battlements, grand staircases and the obligatory rows of stag heads. Expect all the perks at these places, often including a gym, a sauna, a pool and first-class service. Even if you're on a budget, it's worth splashing out for a night at one of the classic Highland hotels, which are the hubs of the local community, including the local pub and restaurant.

In the cities, dullish chain options dominate the mid-range category, though there are some quirkier options to be had in Glasgow and Edinburgh.

Increasingly, hotels use an airline-style pricing system, so it's worth booking well ahead to take advantage of the cheapest rates. The website www.money-

SELF-CATERING IN SCOTLAND

Self-catering accommodation is very popular in Scotland and staying in a house in a city or cottage in the country gives you an opportunity to get a feel for a region and its community. The minimum stay is usually one week in the summer peak season, and three days or less at other times.

Accommodation of this type varies very widely, from rustic one-bedroom cottages with basic facilities and sheep cropping the grass outside to castles, historic houses and purpose-built designer retreats with every mod-con.

We've only listed limited self-catering options. The best place to start looking for this kind of accommodation is the website of **VisitScotland** (☎0845 859 1006; www.visitscotland.com/accommodation), which lists numerous options all over Scotland. These also appear in the regional accommodation guides available from tourist offices. A quick internet search will reveal many websites listing thousands of self-catering places all across the country.

Expect a week's rent for a simple two-bedroom cottage to cost from £180 in winter, and up to £300 or more July to September.

The following are other places to search:

Embrace Scotland (Association of Scotland's Self-Caterers; ☎01866-822522; www.embracescotland.com) Association of self-catering properties with a searchable database of over 2500 across Scotland.

LHH Scotland (☎01381-610496; www.lhhscotland.com) Has an upmarket portfolio of mostly larger houses and mansions, including some castle options.

Cottages and Castles (☎01738-451610; www.cottages-and-castles.co.uk) Offers a wide range of self-catering accommodation, as the name suggests.

Cottage Guide (www.cottageguide.co.uk) Lots of Scottish cottages to browse online.

NTS Holidays (☎0131-243 9331; www.nts.org.uk/holidays) The National Trust for Scotland has an excellent portfolio of upmarket accommodation, including historic houses, lighthouse cottages and more.

Ecosse Unique (☎01835-822277; www.uniquescotland.com) Offers holiday homes all over the country.

Landmark Trust (☎01628-825925; www.landmarktrust.org.uk) A building-preservation charity that restores historic buildings and rents them out as accommodation.

---

savingexpert.com has a good guide to finding cheap hotel rooms.

Try these online discount sites:

» www.hotels.com
» www.booking.com
» www.lastminute.com
» www.laterooms.com

University Accommodation

Many Scottish universities offer their student accommodation to visitors during the holidays. Most rooms are comfy, functional single bedrooms, some with shared bathroom, but there are also twin and family units, self-contained flats and shared houses. Full-board, half-board, B&B and self-catering options are often available. Rooms are usually let out from late June to mid-September.

Activities

Scotland is a brilliant place for outdoor recreation and has something to offer everyone, from those who enjoy a short stroll to full-on adrenalin junkies. Although hiking (see p29), golf (see p33), fishing and cycling are the most popular activities, there is an astonishing variety of things to do.

Most activities are well organised and have clubs and associations that can give visitors invaluable information and, sometimes, substantial discounts. **Visit Scotland** (www.visitscotland.com) has information on most activities. Its website has useful pages on fishing, golf, skiing, cycling and adventure sports. They also produce a good booklet, *Active in Scotland*, available at tourist offices.

Some other useful sources:

Birdwatching The **Royal Society for the Protection of Birds** (RSPB; ☎01950-460800; www.rspb.org.uk) should be any birdwatcher's first port of call. The **Scottish Wildlife Trust** (www.

swt.org.uk) manages several nature reserves, and the **Scottish Ornithologists' Club** (www.the-soc.org.uk) website has a useful section on where to watch birds.

Cycling There are many excellent routes throughout the country. **Sustrans** (www.sustrans. org.uk) is the first place to go for more information. For mountain-biking, check out the **7Stanes website** (www.7stanesmountainbike. com) if you're going to be in the south of the country.

Fishing Seasons and permits vary according to locality. Permits can usually be obtained at the local tackle shop. **VisitScotland** (www.visitscotland.com) produces a useful magazine, *Fishing in Scotland*, available free in tourist offices. Their website also has some useful information on permits and seasons.

Business Hours

In the Highlands and islands Sunday opening is restricted, and it's common for there to be little or no public transport.

Opening hours are as follows:

Banks 9.30am to 4pm or 5pm Monday to Friday; some are open 9.30am to 1pm Saturday.

Nightclubs 9pm or 10pm to 1am, 2am or later. Often only open Thursday to Saturday.

Post offices 9am to 6pm Monday to Friday, 9am to 12.30pm Saturday (main branches to 5pm Saturday).

Pubs & Bars 11am to 11pm Monday to Thursday, 11am to 1am Friday and Saturday, 12.30pm to 11pm Sunday; lunch is served noon to 2.30pm, dinner 6pm to 9pm daily.

Shops 9am to 5.30pm (or 6pm in cities) Monday to Saturday, and often 11am to 5pm Sunday.

Restaurants Lunch noon to 2.30pm, dinner 6pm to 9pm

or 10pm; in small towns and villages the chippy (fish-and-chip shop) is often the only place to buy cooked food after 8pm.

Children

Scotland offers a range of child-friendly accommodation and family activities.

It's worth asking in tourist offices for local family-focused publications. *The List* magazine (available at newsagents and bookshops) has a section on children's activities and events in and around Glasgow and Edinburgh.

The **National Trust for Scotland** (NTS; ☎0844-493 2100; www.nts.org.uk) and **Historic Scotland** (HS; ☎0131-668 8999; www.historic -scotland.gov.uk) organize family-friendly activities at their properties throughout the summer.

Children are generally well received around Scotland, and every area has some child-friendly attractions and B&Bs. Even local museums usually make an effort with an activity sheet or child-focused information panels.

A lot of pubs are family-friendly and some have great beer gardens where kids can run around and exhaust themselves while you have a quiet pint. However, be aware that many Scottish pubs, even those that serve bar meals, are forbidden by law to admit children under 14; even in family-friendly pubs (ie those in possession of a Children's Certificate), under-14s are only admitted between 11am and 8pm, and only when accompanied by an adult.

Children under a certain age can often stay free with their parents in hotels, but be prepared for hotels and B&Bs (normally upmarket ones) that won't accept children; call ahead to get the low-down. More hotels and guesthouses these days provide child-friendly fa-

cilities, including cots. Many restaurants (especially the larger ones) have highchairs and decent children's menus available.

Breastfeeding in public is accepted and is actively encouraged by government campaigns.

The larger car-hire companies can provide safety seats for children, but they're worth booking well ahead.

See also Lonely Planet's *Travel with Children*, by Brigitte Barta et al.

Customs Regulations

Travellers arriving in the UK from other EU countries don't have to pay tax or duty on goods for personal use, and can bring back as much EU duty-paid alcohol and tobacco as they like. However, if you bring in more than the following, you'll probably be asked some questions: 800 cigarettes, 400 cigarillos, 200 cigars, 1kg of smoking tobacco, 10L of spirits, 20L of fortified wine (eg port or sherry), 90L of wine and 110L of beer. Those under 17 years cannot import any alcohol or tobacco. Check the website of **HM Customs and Excise** (www.hmrc.gov.uk) for further details.

Travellers from outside the EU can bring in, duty-free:

» 200 cigarettes *or* 100 cigarillos *or* 50 cigars *or* 250g of tobacco

» 16L of beer

» 4L of non-sparkling wine

» 1L of spirits *or* 2L of fortified wine or sparkling wine

» £390 worth of all other goods, including perfume, gifts and souvenirs.
Anything over this limit must be declared to customs officers on arrival.

Discount Cards

Historic Sites

Membership of Historic Scotland (HS) and the National

Trust for Scotland (NTS) is worth considering, especially if you're going to be in Scotland for a while. Both are nonprofit organisations dedicated to the preservation of the environment, and both care for hundreds of spectacular sites. You can join up at any of their properties.

Historic Scotland (HS; ☎0131-668 8999; www.historic-scotland.gov.uk) A nonprofit organisation that cares for hundreds of sites of historical importance. A year's membership costs £46.50/86.50 per adult/family, and gives free entry to HS sites (half-price entry to sites in England and Wales). Also offers a short-term Explorer membership – three days out of five for £28, seven days out of 14 for £37.

National Trust for Scotland (NTS; ☎0844-493 2100; www.nts.org.uk) NTS looks after hundreds of sites of historical, architectural or environmental importance. A year's membership, costing £49/84 for an adult/family, offers free access to all NTS and National Trust properties (in the rest of the UK).

Hostel Cards

If travelling on a budget, membership of the **Scottish Youth Hostel Association/ Hostelling International** (SYHA; ☎0845-293 7373; www. syha.org.uk) is a must (annual membership over/under 16 years is £10/free, life membership is £100).

Senior Cards

Discount cards for those over 60 years are available for train travel.

Student & Youth Cards

The most useful card is the **International Student Identity Card** (ISIC; www. isic.org), which displays your photo. This can perform wonders, including producing discounts on entry to attractions and on many forms of transport.

There's a global industry in fake student cards, and many places now stipulate a maximum age for student discounts or substitute a 'youth discount' for 'student discount'. If under 26 but not a student, you can apply for the Euro/26 card, which goes by various names in different countries, or an International Youth Travel Card (IYTC), also issued by ISIC. These cards are available through student unions, hostelling organisations or youth travel agencies.

Electricity

230V/50Hz

Embassies & Consulates

Be aware that the Australian consulate in Edinburgh does not provide notarial services; travellers in need of these should contact the **Australian High Commission** (☎020-7379 4334; www. uk.embassy.gov.au) in London instead.

Food

In this guide eating choices are flagged with price indicators, based on the cost of an average main course from the dinner menu:

£	up to £9
£££	from £9 to £18
£££	£18 and over

Note though that lunch mains are often cheaper than dinner mains, and many places offer an 'early bird' special with lower prices (usually available between 5pm and 7pm).

Gay & Lesbian Travellers

Although many Scots are fairly tolerant of homosexuality, couples overtly displaying affection away from acknowledged 'gay' venues or districts may encounter hostility.

Edinburgh and Glasgow have small but flourishing gay scenes. The website and monthly magazine *Scotsgay* (www.scotsgay.co.uk) keeps gays, lesbians and bisexuals informed about gay-scene issues.

Health

» If you're an EU citizen, a European Health Insurance Card (EHIC) – available from health centres or, in the UK, post offices – covers you for most medical care. An EHIC will not cover you for non-urgent cases, or emergency repatriation.

» Citizens from non-EU countries should find out if there is a reciprocal arrangement for free medical care between their country and the UK.

» If you do need health insurance, make sure you get a policy that covers you for the worst possible scenarios, including emergency flights home.

» No jabs (vaccinations) are required to travel to Scotland

CONSULATES IN SCOTLAND

Most foreign diplomatic missions are in London, but many countries also have consulates in Edinburgh:

Australia	0131-538 0582	www.uk.embassy.gov.au	5 Mitchell St, Edinburgh
Canada	07702-359 916	www.canadainternational.gc.ca	5 St Margaret's Rd, Edinburgh
Denmark	0131-220 0300	www.amblondon.um.dk	48 Melville St, Edinburgh
France	0131-225 7954	www.ambafrance-uk.org	11 Randolph Cres, Edinburgh
Germany	0131-347 9877	www.edinburgh.diplo.de	16 Eglinton Cres, Edinburgh
Ireland	0131-226 7711	www.irishconsulatescotland.co.uk	16 Randolph Cres, Edinburgh
Japan	0131-225 4777	www.edinburgh.uk.emb-japan.go.jp	2 Melville Cres, Edinburgh
Netherlands	0131-510 0323	www.netherlands-embassy.org.uk	127 George St, Edinburgh
New Zealand	0131-222 8109	www.nzembassy.com	22 Hailes Grove, Edinburgh
USA	0131-556 8315	www.usembassy.org.uk	3 Regent Tce, Edinburgh

» The most painful problems facing visitors to the Highlands and islands are midges (p15).

Insurance

This not only covers you for medical expenses, theft or loss, but also for cancellation of, or delays in, any of your travel arrangements.

Lots of bank accounts give their holders automatic travel insurance – check if this is the case for you.

Always read the small print carefully. Some policies specifically exclude 'dangerous activities', such as scuba diving, motorcycling, skiing, mountaineering and even trekking.

There's a variety of policies and your travel agent can give recommendations. Make sure the policy includes health care and medication in the countries you may visit on your way to/from Scotland.

You may prefer a policy that pays doctors or hospitals directly rather than forcing you to pay on the spot and claim the money back later. If you have to claim later, make sure you keep all related documentation. Some policies ask you to call back (reverse charges) to a centre in your home country where an immediate assessment of your problem is made.

Not all policies cover ambulances, helicopter rescue or emergency flights home. Most policies exclude cover for pre-existing illnesses.

Worldwide travel insurance is available at www.lonelyplanet.com/travel_services. You can buy, extend and claim online anytime – even if you're already on the road.

Internet Access

If you're travelling with a laptop, you'll find a wide range of places offering a wi-fi connection. These range from cafes to B&Bs and public spaces.

We've indicated accommodation and eating and drinking options that have wi-fi with the 🛜 symbol in the text. Wi-fi is often free, but some places (typically, upmarket hotels) charge.

There are some increasingly good deals on pay-as-you-go mobile internet from mobile network providers.

If you see the symbol @, then the place has an internet terminal.

If you don't have a laptop, the best places to check email and surf the internet are public libraries – nearly all of which have at least a couple of computer terminals devoted to the internet, and they are free to use, though there's often a time limit.

Internet cafes also exist in the cities and larger towns and are generally good value, charging approximately £2 to £3 per hour.

Many of the larger tourist offices across the country also have internet access.

Language Courses

Scotland is a popular place to learn English, and there are numerous places to do it. Dedicated language academies offer intensive tuition at a price and can also arrange accommodation in residences or with local families. Much cheaper are colleges, some of which even offer free English classes for foreigners.

A good resource to start you off is the **English UK Scotland website** (www .englishukscotland.com), which has details of many colleges and language schools, mostly in Edinburgh and Glasgow.

Legal Matters

The 1707 Act of Union preserved the Scottish legal system as separate from the law in England and Wales.

Police have the power to detain, for up to six hours, anyone suspected of having committed an offence punishable by imprisonment (including drugs offences).

If you need legal assistance, contact the **Scottish Legal Aid Board** (☑0845-122 8686; www.slab.org.uk; 44 Drumsheugh Gardens, Edinburgh).

Possession of a small amount of cannabis is punishable by a fine, but possession of a larger amount of cannabis, or any amount of harder drugs, is much more serious, with a sentence of up to 14 years in prison. Police have the right to search anyone they suspect of possessing drugs.

Travellers should note that they can be prosecuted under the law of their home country regarding age of consent, even when abroad.

Maps

If you're about to tackle Munros, you'll require maps with far greater detail than the maps in this guide, or the ones supplied by tourist offices. The Ordnance Survey (OS) caters to walkers, with a wide variety of maps at 1:50,000 and 1:25,000 scales. Alternatively, look out for the excellent walkers' maps published by Harveys; they're at scales of 1:40,000 and 1:25,000.

Money

The British currency is the pound sterling (£), with 100 pence (p) to a pound. 'Quid' is the slang term for pound.

Three Scottish banks issue their own banknotes, meaning there's quite a variety of different notes in circulation. They are legal currency in England too, but you'll sometimes run into problems changing them. They are also harder to exchange once you get outside the UK.

Euros are accepted in Scotland only at some major tourist attractions and a few upmarket hotels – it's always better to have sterling cash.

ATMs

ATMs (called cashpoints in Scotland) are widespread and you'll usually find at least one in small towns and villages. You can use Visa, MasterCard, Amex, Cirrus, Plus and Maestro to withdraw cash from ATMs belonging to most banks and building societies in Scotland.

Cash withdrawals from some ATMs may be subject to a small charge, but most are free. If you're not from the UK, your home bank will likely charge you for withdrawing money overseas; it pays to be aware of how much, as it may be much better to withdraw larger amounts less often.

Credit Cards

Visa and MasterCard cards are widely recognised, although many places will charge a small amount for accepting them. Charge cards such as Amex and Diners Club may not be accepted in smaller establishments. Many smaller B&Bs do not take cards.

Moneychangers

Be careful using bureaux de change; they may offer good exchange rates but frequently levy outrageous commissions and fees. The best-value place to change money in the UK is at post offices, but only the ones in larger towns and cities offer this service. Larger tourist offices also have exchange facilities.

Tipping

Tip 10% in sit-down restaurants, but not if there's already a service charge on the bill.

In very classy places they may expect closer to 15%.

Service is at your discretion: even if the charge is added to the bill, you don't have to pay it if you feel service has been poor.

Don't tip in pubs: if the service has been exceptional over the course of an evening, you can say, 'have one for yourself'.

Taxis are expensive, and locals rarely tip; round up to the nearest pound.

Public Holidays

Although bank holidays are general public holidays in the rest of the UK, in Scotland they only apply to banks and some other commercial offices.

Scottish towns normally have four days of public holiday, which they allocate themselves; dates vary from year to year and from town to town. Most places celebrate St Andrew's Day (30 November) as a public holiday.

General public holidays:

New Year 1 & 2 January

Good Friday March or April

Christmas Day 25 December

Boxing Day 26 December

Telephone

The famous red telephone boxes are a dying breed now, surviving mainly in conservation areas. You'll mainly see two types of phone booths in Scotland: one takes money (and doesn't give change), while the other uses prepaid phonecards and credit cards. Some phones accept both coins and cards. Payphone cards are widely available.

The cheapest way of calling internationally is via the internet, or by buying a discount call card; you'll see these in newsagents, along with tables of countries and the number of minutes you'll get for your money.

Mobile Phones

Codes for mobile phones usually begin with 07. The UK uses the GSM 900/1800 network, which covers the rest of Europe, Australia and New Zealand, but isn't compatible with the North American GSM 1900. Most modern mobiles, however, can function on both networks – check before you leave home.

International roaming charges can be prohibitively high, though, and you'll probably find it cheaper to get a UK number. This is easily done by buying a SIM card (around £10 including calling credit) and sticking it in your phone. Your phone may be locked to your home network, however, so you'll have to either get it unlocked, or buy a pay-as-you-go phone along with your SIM card (around £50).

Pay-as-you-go phones can be recharged by buying vouchers from shops.

Phone Codes & Useful Numbers

Dialling the UK Dial your country's international access code then 44 (the UK country code), then the area code (dropping the first 0) followed by the telephone number.

Dialling out of the UK The international access code is 00; dial this, then add the code of the country you wish to dial.

Making a reverse-charge (collect) international call Dial 155 for the operator. It's an expensive option, but not for the caller.

Area codes in Scotland Begin with 01xxx, eg Edinburgh 0131, Wick 01955.

Directory Assistance There are several numbers; 118500 is one.

Mobile phones Codes usually begin with 07.

Free calls Numbers starting with 0800 are free; calls to 0845 numbers are charged at local rates.

Time

Scotland is on GMT/UTC. The clocks go forward for 'summer time' one hour at the end of March, and go back at the end of October. The 24-hour clock is used for transport timetables, but plenty of folk still struggle to get the hang of it.

Time difference between Scotland & major cities

Paris, Berlin, Rome	1hr ahead of Scotland
New York	5hr behind
Sydney	9hr ahead Apr-Sep, 10hr Oct, 11hr Nov-Mar
Los Angeles	8hr behind
Mumbai	5½hr ahead, 4½hr Mar-Oct
Tokyo	9hr ahead, 8hr Mar-Oct

Tourist Information

The Scottish Tourist Board, known as **VisitScotland** (☑0845-225 5121; www.visitscotland.com; Ocean Point One, 94 Ocean Dr), deals with inquiries made by post, email and telephone. You can request, online and by phone, for regional brochures be posted out to you.

Most larger towns have tourist offices ('information centres') that open 9am or 10am to 5pm Monday to Friday, and on weekends in summer. In small places, particularly in the Highlands, tourist offices only open from Easter to September.

If you want to email a tourist office, it's townname@visitscotland.com.

Travellers with Disabilities

Travellers with disabilities will find Scotland a strange mix of accessibility and inaccessibility. Most new buildings are accessible to wheelchair users, so modern hotels and tourist attractions are fine. However, most B&Bs and guesthouses are in hard-to-adapt older buildings, which means that travellers with mobility problems may pay more for accommodation. Things are constantly improving, though.

It's a similar story with public transport. Newer buses have steps that lower for easier access, as do trains, but it's wise to check before setting out. Tourist attractions usually reserve parking spaces near the entrance for drivers with disabilities.

Many places such as ticket offices and banks are fitted with hearing loops to assist the hearing-impaired; look for a posted symbol of a large ear.

A few tourist attractions, such as Glasgow Cathedral, have Braille guides or scented gardens for the visually impaired.

VisitScotland produces the guide *Accessible Scotland* for wheelchair-bound travellers, and many tourist offices have leaflets with accessibility details for their area. Regional accommodation guides have a wheelchair-accessible criterion.

Many regions have organisations that hire wheelchairs; contact the local tourist office for details. Many nature trails have been adapted for wheelchair use.

For more information:

Disabled Persons Railcard (www.disabledpersons-railcard.co.uk) Discounted train travel.

Tourism for All (☎0845-124 9971; www.tourismforall.org.uk) Publishes regional information guides for travellers with disabilities and can offer general advice.

Royal Association for Disability & Rehabilitation (Radar; ☎020-7250 3222; www.radar.org.uk; 12 City Forum, 250 City Rd, London) This is an umbrella organisation for voluntary groups for people with disabilities.

Visas

» If you're a citizen of the EEA (European Economic Area) nations or Switzerland, you don't need a visa to enter or work in Britain – you can enter using your national identity card.

» Visa regulations are always subject to change, so it's essential to check with your local British embassy, high commission or consulate before leaving home.

» Currently, if you're a citizen of Australia, Canada, New Zealand, Japan, Israel, the USA and several other countries, you can stay for up to six months (no visa required), but are not allowed to work.

» Nationals of many countries, including South Africa, will need to obtain a visa: for more info, see www.ukvisas.gov.uk.

» The Youth Mobility Scheme, for Australian, Canadian, Japanese, Monegasque, New Zealand, South Korean and Taiwanese citizens aged 18 to 31, allows working visits of up to two years, but must be applied for in advance.

» Commonwealth citizens with a UK-born parent may be eligible for a Certificate of Entitlement to the Right of Abode, which entitles them to live and work in the UK.

» Commonwealth citizens with a UK-born grandparent could qualify for a UK Ancestry Employment Certificate, allowing them to work full time for up to five years in the UK.

» British immigration authorities have always been tough; dress neatly and carry proof that you have sufficient funds with which to support yourself. A credit card and/or an onward ticket will help.

Women Travellers

Solo women travellers are likely to feel safe for the most part in Scotland.

The contraceptive pill is available only on prescription; however, the 'morning-after' pill (effective against conception for up to 72 hours after unprotected sexual intercourse) is available over the counter at chemists.

Transport

GETTING THERE & AWAY

Flights, tours and rail tickets can be booked online at lonelyplanet.com/bookings.

Air

There are direct flights to Scottish airports from England, Wales, Ireland, the USA, Canada, Scandinavia and several countries in Western and central Europe. From elsewhere, you'll probably have to fly into a European hub and catch a connecting flight to a Scottish airport – London, Amsterdam, Frankfurt and Paris have the best connections. If flying from North America, it's worth looking at Icelandair, which often has good deals to Glasgow via Reykjavik.

Airports & Airlines

Scotland has four main international airports: Aberdeen, Edinburgh, Glasgow and Glasgow Prestwick. A few short-haul international flights land at Inverness and Sumburgh, while London is the main UK gateway for long-haul flights.

Aberdeen Airport (ABZ; www.aberdeenairport.com) Aberdeen Airport is at Dyce, 6 miles northwest of the city centre. There are regular flights to numerous Scottish and UK destinations, including Orkney and Shetland, and international flights to some European countries.

Edinburgh Airport (EDI; www.edinburghairport.com) Scotland's busiest airport, 5 miles west of the city.

Glasgow International Airport (GLA; www.glasgow airport.com) Ten miles west of the city, Glasgow International Airport handles domestic traffic and international flights.

Glasgow Prestwick Airport (PIK; www.glasgowprest wick.com) Glasgow Prestwick Airport, 30 miles southwest of Glasgow, is used by Ryanair and some other budget airlines, with many connections to the rest of Britain and Europe.

Inverness Airport (INV; ☎01667-464000; www.hial. co.uk) At Dalcross, 10 miles east of the city, off the A96 towards Aberdeen. There are scheduled flights to Amsterdam, Dusseldorf, London, Bristol, Manchester, Belfast, Stornoway, Benbecula, Orkney, Shetland and several other British airports.

London Gatwick (LGW; www.gatwickairport.com) London's second long-haul airport.

London Heathrow (LHR; www.heathrowairport.com) Britain's principal international airport.

Sumburgh Airport (LSI; ☎01950-461000; www.hial. co.uk) Shetland's main airport is at Sumburgh, which is 25 miles south of Lerwick. There are daily services to Aberdeen, Kirkwall, Inverness, Edinburgh

---

CLIMATE CHANGE & TRAVEL

Every form of transport that relies on carbon-based fuel generates CO_2, the main cause of human-induced climate change. Modern travel is dependent on aeroplanes, which might use less fuel per kilometre per person than most cars but travel much greater distances. The altitude at which aircraft emit gases (including CO_2) and particles also contributes to their climate change impact. Many websites offer 'carbon calculators' that allow people to estimate the carbon emissions generated by their journey and, for those who wish to do so, to offset the impact of the greenhouse gases emitted with contributions to portfolios of climate-friendly initiatives throughout the world. Lonely Planet offsets the carbon footprint of all staff and author travel.

and Glasgow, and to Bergen (Norway) in summer.

Land

Bus

Buses are usually the cheapest way to get to Scotland from other parts of the UK. The main operators:

Megabus (☎0871 266 3333; www.megabus.com) One-way fares from London to Glasgow from as little as £5 if you book well in advance (up to 12 weeks).

National Express (☎08717 818178; www.nationalexpress. com) Regular services from London and other cities in England and Wales to Glasgow and Edinburgh.

Scottish Citylink (☎0871 266 3333; www.citylink.co.uk) Daily service between Belfast and Glasgow and Edinburgh via Cairnryan ferry.

Car & Motorcycle

Drivers of EU-registered vehicles will find bringing a car or motorcycle into Scotland fairly easy. The vehicle must have registration papers and a nationality plate, and you must have insurance. The International Insurance Certificate (Green Card) isn't compulsory, but it is excellent proof that you're covered. If driving from mainland Europe via the Channel Tunnel or ferry ports, head for London and follow the M25 orbital road to the M1 motorway, then follow the M1 and M6 north.

Train

Travelling to Scotland by train is faster and usually more comfortable than the bus, but more expensive. Taking into account check-in and travel time between city centre and airport, the train is a competitive alternative to air travel on the London-to-Edinburgh route.

East Coast (☎08457 225 111; www.eastcoast.co.uk) Trains between London Kings Cross and Edinburgh (four hours, every half hour).

Eurostar (☎outside UK +44 1233-617575, within UK 08432 186 186; www.eurostar.com) You can travel from Paris or Brussels to London in around two hours on the Eurostar service. From St Pancras it's a quick and easy change to Kings Cross or Euston for trains to Edinburgh or Glasgow. Total journey time from Paris to Edinburgh is about eight hours.

First ScotRail (☎08457 55 00 33; www.scotrail. co.uk) Runs the *Caledonian Sleeper*, an overnight service connecting London Euston with Edinburgh, Glasgow, Stirling, Perth, Dundee, Aberdeen, Fort William and Inverness.

National Rail Enquiry Service (☎08457 48 49 50; www.nationalrail.co.uk) Time-table and fares info for all UK trains.

Virgin Trains (☎08719 774 222; www.virgintrains.co.uk) Trains between London Euston and Glasgow (4½ hours, hourly).

TRAIN FARES

The complex British train ticketing system rewards advance planning, particularly on long routes. A one-way fare from London to Edinburgh, for example, can cost over £150, but a fare purchased well in advance, at off-peak times, can be as low as £30. Regional fares in Scotland have a lot less variation. In this book we have quoted fares that fall somewhere between the cheapest and most expensive options.

GETTING AROUND

Public transport in Scotland is generally good, but it can be costly compared with other European countries. Buses are usually the cheapest way to get around, but also the slowest. With a discount pass, trains can be competitive; they're also quicker and often take you through beautiful scenery.

Traveline (☎0871 200 2233; www.travelinescotland. com) provides timetable info for all public-transport services in Scotland, but can't provide fare information or book tickets.

Air

Most domestic air services are geared to business needs, or are lifelines for remote island communities. Flying is a pricey way to cover relatively short distances, and only worth considering if you're short of time and want to visit the Hebrides, Orkney or Shetland.

Airlines in Scotland

Eastern Airways (☎0870 366 9100; www.easternairways. com) Flies from Aberdeen to Stornoway and Wick.

Flybe/Loganair (☎0871 700 2000; www.loganair.co.uk) The main domestic airline in Scotland, with flights from Glasgow to Barra, Benbecula, Campbeltown, Islay, Kirkwall, Sumburgh, Stornoway and Tiree; from Edinburgh to Kirkwall, Sumburgh, Stornoway and Wick; from Aberdeen to Kirkwall and Sumburgh; and from Inverness to Kirkwall, Benbecula, Stornoway and Sumburgh. It also operates inter-island flights in Orkney, and from Benbecula to Barra and Stornoway.

Hebridean Air (☎0845 805 7465; www.hebrideanair.co.uk) Flies from Connel airfield near Oban to the islands of Coll, Tiree, Colonsay and Islay.

FERRY LINKS WITH NORTHERN IRELAND

Car-ferry links between Northern Ireland and Scotland are operated by **Stena Line** (☑08445-762762; www.stenaline.co.uk; passenger/car £28/110) and **P&O** (☑0871 66 44 777; www.poferries.com). Stena Line travels the Belfast–Cairnryan route and P&O Irish Sea the Larne–Troon and Larne–Cairnryan routes.

The prices in the table are a guide only; fares are often less than quoted here.

CROSSING	DURATION	FREQUENCY	FARE PASSENGER/ CAR (£)
Belfast– Cairnryan	2¾ hr	4-6 daily	28/110
Larne– Cairnryan	2hr (1hr express)	5-8 daily (incl 1 express daily late Mar-Sep)	26/108
Larne– Troon	2hr	2 daily (late Mar–Sep)	33/109

Bicycle

Scotland is a compact country, and travelling around by bicycle is a perfectly feasible proposition if you have the time. Indeed, for touring the islands a bicycle is both cheaper (for ferry fares) and more suited to their small sizes and leisurely pace of life. For more information, see http://active.visitscotland.com and the **Sustrans** (www.sustrans.org.uk) webpage.

Boat

Other smaller ferry companies are mentioned in the regional chapters.
Caledonian MacBrayne (CalMac; ☑0800 066 5000; www.calmac.co.uk) Serves the west coast and islands. Comprehensive timetable booklet available from tourist offices. **CalMac Island Hopscotch** offers more than two dozen tickets, giving reduced fares for various combinations of crossings; these are listed on the website and in the CalMac timetable booklet. **Island Rover** tickets allow unlimited ferry travel for £55/79 for a foot passenger for eight/15 days, plus £259/388 for a car or £130/195 for a motorbike. Bicycles travel free with foot passengers' tickets.
Northlink Ferries (☑0845 600 0449; www.northlinkferries.co.uk) Ferries from Aberdeen and Scrabster (near Thurso) to Orkney, from Orkney to Shetland and from Aberdeen to Shetland.

Bus

Scotland is served by an extensive bus network that covers most of the country. In remote areas, however, services are more geared to the needs of locals (getting to school or the shops in the nearest large town) and may not be well timed for visitors.
First (www.firstgroup.com) Operates local bus routes in Aberdeen, Greater Glasgow, Edinburgh and southeast Scotland.
Royal Mail Postbus (www.royalmail.com) Minibuses, or sometimes four-seater cars, driven by postal workers delivering and collecting the mail – there are no official stops, and you can hail a postbus anywhere on its route. Although services have been cut severely in recent years, it's still the only public transport in some remote parts of Scotland.
Scottish Citylink (☑0871 266 3333; www.citylink.co.uk) National network of comfy, reliable buses serving all main towns. Away from main roads, you'll need to switch to local services.

Bus Passes

Holders of a **National Entitlement Card** (www.entitlementcard.org.uk), available to seniors and disabled people who are Scottish citizens, get free bus travel throughout the country. The youth version, for 11- to 26-year-olds, gives discounted travel, and SYHA members receive a 20% discount on Scottish Citylink services. Students do, too, by registering online.

The **Scottish Citylink Explorer Pass** offers unlimited travel on Scottish Citylink (and selected other bus routes) services within Scotland for any three days out of five (£39), any five days out of 10 (£59) or any eight days out of 16 (£79). Also gives discounts on various regional bus services, on Northlink and CalMac ferries, and in SYHA hostels. Can be bought in the UK by both UK and overseas citizens.

Car & Motorcycle

Scotland's roads are generally good and far less busy than in England, so driving's more enjoyable. However, cars are nearly always inconvenient in city centres.

Motorways (designated 'M') are toll-free dual carriageways, limited mainly to central Scotland. Main roads ('A') are dual or single carriageways and are sometimes clogged up with slow-moving trucks or caravans; the A9 from Perth to Inverness is notoriously busy.

Life on the road is more relaxed and interesting on the secondary roads (designated 'B') and minor roads (undesignated), although in the Highlands and islands there's the added hazard of suicidal sheep wandering onto the road (be particularly wary of lambs in spring).

At around £1.45 per litre (equivalent to around US$9 per US gallon), petrol's expensive by American or Australian standards; diesel is about 3p per litre more expensive. Prices tend to rise as you get further from the main centres and are more than 10% higher in the Outer Hebrides. In remote areas petrol stations are widely spaced and sometimes closed on Sunday.

Driving Licence

A non-EU licence is valid in Britain for up to 12 months from time of entry into the country. If bringing a car from Europe, make sure you're adequately insured.

Hire

Car hire in the UK is competitively priced by European standards, and shopping around online can unearth some great deals, which can drop to as low as £12 per day for an extended hire period. Hit comparison sites like **Kayak** (www.kayak.com) or **Kelkoo** (www.kelkoo.com) to find some of the best prices.

The minimum legal age for driving is 17 but to rent a car, drivers must usually be aged 23 to 65 – outside these limits special conditions or insurance requirements may apply.

If planning to visit the Outer Hebrides, Orkney or Shetland, it'll often prove cheaper to hire a car on the islands, rather than pay to take a hire car across on the ferry.

The main international hire companies:

Avis (www.avis.co.uk)

Budget (www.budget.co.uk)

Europcar (www.europcar. co.uk)

Hertz (www.hertz.co.uk)

Road Rules

The *Highway Code*, widely available in bookshops, details all UK road regulations. Vehicles drive on the left. Front seatbelts are compulsory; if the back seat has belts, they must be worn too. The speed limit is 30mph in built-up areas, 60mph on single carriageways and 70mph on dual carriageways. Give way to your right at roundabouts (traffic already on the roundabout has right of way). Motorcyclists must wear helmets.

It is a criminal offence to use a hand-held mobile phone or similar device while driving; this includes while you are stopped at traffic lights, or stuck in traffic, when you can expect to be moving again at any moment.

The maximum permitted blood-alcohol level when driving is 80mg/100mL (35mg per 100mL of breath); this is slightly higher than in many other countries.

Traffic offences (illegal parking, speeding etc) usually incur a fine for which you're allowed 30 to 60 days to pay. In Glasgow and Edinburgh the parking inspectors are numerous and without mercy – never leave your car around the city centres without a valid parking ticket, as you risk a hefty fine.

Hitching

Hitching is never entirely safe in any country and we don't recommend it. Travellers who hitch take a small but potentially serious risk. However, many people choose to hitch, and the advice that follows should help to make their journeys as fast and safe as possible.

Hitching is fairly easy in Scotland, except around big cities and built-up areas, where you'll need to use public transport. Although the northwest is more difficult because there's less traffic, waits of over two hours are unusual (except on Sunday in 'Sabbath' areas). On some islands, where public transport is infrequent, hitching is so much a part of getting around that local drivers may stop and offer you lifts without you even asking.

It's against the law to hitch on motorways or their

ROAD DISTANCES (MILES)

	Aberdeen	Dundee	Edinburgh	Fort William	Glasgow	Inverness	Kyle of Lochalsh	Mallaig	Oban	Scrabster	Stranraer
Dundee	70										
Edinburgh	129	62									
Fort William	165	121	146								
Glasgow	145	84	42	104							
Inverness	105	131	155	66	166						
Kyle of Lochalsh	188	177	206	76	181	82					
Mallaig	189	161	180	44	150	106	34				
Oban	180	118	123	45	94	110	120	85			
Scrabster	218	250	279	185	286	119	214	238	230		
Stranraer	233	171	120	184	80	250	265	232	178	374	
Ullapool	150	189	215	90	225	135	88	166	161	125	158

SINGLE-TRACK ROADS

In many country areas, and especially in the Highlands and islands, you will find single-track roads that are only wide enough for one vehicle. Passing places (usually marked with a white diamond sign, or a black-and-white striped pole) are used to allow oncoming traffic to get by. Remember that passing places are also for overtaking – pull over to let faster vehicles pass if necessary. It's illegal to park in passing places.

immediate slip roads; make a sign and use approach roads, nearby roundabouts or service stations.

Tours

There are lots of companies in Scotland offering all kinds of tours, including historical, activity-based and backpacker tours. It's a question of picking the tour that suits your requirements and budget.

Haggis Adventures (☏0131-557 9393; www.hag gisadventures.com)
Offers backpacker tours, with longer options taking in the Outer Hebrides or Orkney.

Heart of Scotland Tours (☏01828-627799; www.hear tofscotlandtours.co.uk) Specialises in mini-coach day tours of central Scotland and the Highlands, departing from Edinburgh.

Hebridean Island Cruises (☏01756-704700; www.heb ridean.co.uk) Luxury small-boat cruises around the west coast, Outer Hebrides and northern islands.

Macbackpackers (☏0131-558 9900; www.macbackpack ers.com) Minibus tours for backpackers, using hostel accommodation, from Edinburgh to Loch Ness, Skye, Fort William, Glencoe, Oban and Stirling.

Mountain Innovations (☏01479-831331; www. scotmountain.co.uk) Guided activity holidays and courses in the Highlands: walking,

mountain biking and winter mountaineering.

Rabbie's (☏0131-226 3133; www.rabbies.com) One- to five-day tours of the Highlands in 16-seat minibuses with professional driver/guide.

Scot-Trek (☏0141-334 9232; www.scot-trek.co.uk) Guided walks for all levels; ideal for solo travellers wanting to link up with others.

Timberbush Tours (☏0131-226 6066; www.timberbush -tours.co.uk) Comfortable small-group minibus tours around Scotland, with Glasgow and Edinburgh departures.

Train

Scotland's train network extends to all major cities and towns, but the railway map has a lot of large, blank areas in the Highlands and the Southern Uplands where you'll need to switch to bus or car. The West Highland line from Glasgow to Fort William and Mallaig, and the Inverness to Kyle of Lochalsh line, offer two of the world's most scenic rail journeys.

ScotRail (☏08457 55 00 33; www.scotrail.co.uk) Operates most train services in Scotland; website has downloadable timetables.

Costs & Reservations

Train travel is more expensive than bus, but usually more comfortable: a standard return from Edinburgh to Inver-

ness is about £62 compared with £28 on the bus.

Reservations are recommended for intercity trips, especially on Fridays and public holidays. For shorter journeys, just buy a ticket at the station before you go. On certain routes, including the Glasgow–Edinburgh express, and in places where there's no ticket office at the station, you can buy tickets on the train.

Children under five travel free; those five to 15 usually pay half-fare.

Bikes are carried free on all ScotRail trains but space is sometimes limited. Bike reservations are compulsory on certain train routes, including the Glasgow–Oban–Fort William–Mallaig line and the Inverness–Kyle of Lochalsh line; they are recommended on many others. You can make reservations for your bicycle from eight weeks to two hours in advance at main train stations, or when booking tickets by phone (0845 755 0033).

There are several types of ticket. In general, the further ahead you can book the cheaper your ticket will be.

Advance Purchase Book by 6pm on the day before travel; cheaper than Anytime.

Anytime Buy any time and travel any time, with no restrictions.

Off Peak There are time restrictions (you're not usually allowed to travel on a train that leaves before 9.15am); relatively cheap.

Discount Cards

Discount railcards are available for people aged 60 and over, for people aged 16 to 25 (or mature full-time students), and for those with a disability. The **Senior Railcard** (www.senior-railcard. co.uk; £28), **Young Persons Railcard** (16-25 Railcard; www.16-25railcard.co.uk; £28) and **Disabled Persons Railcard** (www.disabledpersons -railcard.co.uk; £20) are each valid for one year and give one-third off most train fares in Scotland, England and Wales. Fill in an application at any major train station. You'll need proof of age (birth certificate, passport or driving licence) for the Young Persons and Senior Railcards (proof of enrolment for mature-age students) and proof of entitlement for the Disabled Persons Railcard.

Train Passes

ScotRail has a range of good-value passes for train travel. You can buy them online or by phone or at train stations throughout Britain. Note that Travelpass and Rover tickets are not valid for travel on certain (eg commuter) services before 9.15am weekdays.

Central Scotland Rover Covers train travel between Glasgow, Edinburgh, North Berwick, Stirling and Fife; costs £35 for three days' travel out of seven.

Freedom of Scotland Travelpass Gives unlimited travel on all Scottish train services (some restrictions), all CalMac ferry services and on certain Scottish Citylink coach services (on routes not covered by rail). It's available for four days' travel out of eight (£129) or eight days out of 15 (£173).

Highland Rover Allows unlimited train travel from Glasgow to Oban, Fort William and Mallaig, and from Inverness to Kyle of Lochalsh, Aviemore, Aberdeen and Thurso. It also gives free travel on the Oban/Fort William to Inverness bus, on the Oban–Mull and Mallaig–Skye ferries, and on buses on Mull and Skye. It's valid for four days' travel out of eight (£79).

Glossary

For a glossary of Scottish place names, see the boxed text, p273.

bag – reach the top of (as in to 'bag a couple of peaks' or '*Munro* bagging')

bailey – the space enclosed by castle walls

birlinn – Hebridean galley

blackhouse – low-walled stone cottage with thatch or turf roof and earth floors; shared by both humans and cattle and typical of the Outer Hebrides until the early 20th century

böd – once a simple trading booth used by fishing communities, today it refers to basic accommodation for walkers etc

bothy – hut or mountain shelter

brae – hill

broch – defensive tower

burgh – town

burn – stream

cairn – pile of stones to mark path or junction; also peak

camanachd – Gaelic for *shinty*

ceilidh (*kay*-lay) – evening of traditional Scottish entertainment including music, song and dance

Celtic high cross – a large, elaborately carved stone cross decorated with biblical scenes and Celtic interlace designs dating from the 8th to 10th centuries

chippy – fish-and-chip shop

Clearances – eviction of Highland farmers from their land by *lairds* wanting to use it for grazing sheep

Clootie dumpling – rich steamed pudding filled with currants and raisins

close – entrance to an alley

corrie – circular hollow on a hillside

craic – lively conversation

craig – exposed rock

crannog – an artificial island in a *loch* built for defensive purposes

crofting – smallholding in marginal agricultural areas following the Clearances

Cullen skink – soup made with smoked haddock, potato, onion and milk

dene – valley

dirk – dagger

dram – a measure of whisky

firth – estuary

gloup – natural arch

Hogmanay – Scottish celebration of New Year's Eve

howff – pub or shelter

HS – Historic Scotland

kyle – narrow sea channel

laird – estate owner

linn – waterfall

loch – lake

lochan – small *loch*

machair – grass- and wildflower-covered dunes

makar – maker of verses

Mercat Cross – a symbol of the trading rights of a market town or village, usually found in the centre of town and usually a focal point for the community

motte – early Norman fortification consisting of a raised, flattened mound with a keep on top; when attached to a *bailey* it is known as a motte-and-bailey

Munro – mountain of 3000ft (914m) or higher

Munro bagger – a hill walker who tries to climb all the *Munros* in Scotland

NNR – National Nature Reserve, managed by the *SNH*

NTS – National Trust for Scotland

nyvaig – Hebridean galley

OS – Ordnance Survey

Picts – early inhabitants of north and east Scotland (from Latin *pictus*, or 'painted', after their bodypaint decorations)

provost – mayor

RIB – rigid inflatable boat

rood – an old Scots word for a cross

RSPB – Royal Society for the Protection of Birds

Sassenach – from Gaelic 'Sasannach': anyone who is not a Highlander (including Lowland Scots)

shinty – fast and physical ball-and-stick sport similar to Ireland's hurling

SMC – Scottish Mountain-eering Club

SNH – Scottish Natural Her-itage, a government organisa-tion directly responsible for safeguarding and improving Scotland's natural heritage

sporran – purse worn around waist with the kilt

SSSI – Site of Special Scientific Interest

SYHA – Scottish Youth Hostel Association

wynd – lane

behind the scenes

SEND US YOUR FEEDBACK

We love to hear from travellers – your comments keep us on our toes and help make our books better. Our well-travelled team reads every word on what you loved or loathed about this book. Although we cannot reply individually to postal submissions, we always guarantee that your feedback goes straight to the appropriate authors, in time for the next edition. Each person who sends us information is thanked in the next edition – the most useful submissions are rewarded with a selection of digital PDF chapters.

Visit **lonelyplanet.com/contact** to submit your updates and suggestions or to ask for help. Our award-winning website also features inspirational travel stories, news and discussions.

Note: We may edit, reproduce and incorporate your comments in Lonely Planet products such as guidebooks, websites and digital products, so let us know if you don't want your comments reproduced or your name acknowledged. For a copy of our privacy policy visit lonelyplanet.com/privacy.

OUR READERS

Many thanks to the travellers who used the last edition and wrote to us with helpful hints, useful advice and interesting anecdotes:

Monica Bandettini, Pat Bates, Sven Berger, Morag & Gordon Brown, Martha Bryce, Emma Clark, Ian Dobie, Alec Drew, Candace Driskell, Margaretanne Dugan, Stefano Friani, Anna Galuszka, Ian Gartshore, Sandie Geddes, Rich Gernand, Pj Henry, Jon Hollingworth, Yvonne Jansen, Irfan Khokhar, Johnny Long, Ka Lun Tam, Gordon Mackenzie, Ronald Mackenzie, Eweb Mackinnon, James Maclean, Liisa Macnaughton, Ellen Mclaughlin, Karen Mickan, Tony Millar, Heather Monell, Monia Montis, Ngaire Moore, Helen Moye, D Olivier, Lotte Oostebrink, Dener Pereira, Stephen Rawlinson, Michal Rudziecki, Joanne Soe, Sharon Sullivan, John Tindal, J Wheatley, Tony Wheeler

AUTHOR THANKS

Neil Wilson

Many thanks to all the helpful and enthusiastic staff at TICs throughout the country, and to the many travellers I met on the road who chipped in with advice and recommendations. Thanks also to Carol Downie, and to Andrew Henderson, Steven Fallon, Russell Leaper, Adrian Shine, Erlend Tait and Pamela Tait. Finally, thanks to coauthor Andy and to the ever-helpful and patient editors and cartographers at Lonely Planet.

Andy Symington

Many thanks are due across the country, but particularly to ever-reliable and true friend Jenny Neil, and to Juliette and David Paton for guaranteed warm and over-generous hospitality. Gratitude goes also to my mother for visiting me in the remote Highlands, to Jose Eliseo Vázquez González for navigational assistance, to Harry Wycherley for the audiovisual side, to Eleanor Hamilton, Cindy-Lou Ramsay, John Bain and Riika Åkerlind. Applause to helpful tourist-office staff and cabbies, big thanks to Neil for coordinating, and cheers to Cliff and the LP team for a top organising job. And to Elena, at my side even when I'm far away: *gracias profundas amor*.

ACKNOWLEDGMENTS

Climate map data adapted from Peel MC, Finlayson BL & McMahon TA (2007) 'Updated World Map of the Köppen-Geiger Climate Classification', *Hydrology and Earth System Sciences*, 11, 163344.

Illustrations pp50-1, pp98-9 and pp192-3 by Javier Zarracina.

Cover photograph: Glen Coe, Scotland; Giovanni Simeone/4Corners ©

This Book

This 7th edition of Lonely Planet's *Scotland* guidebook was researched and written by Neil Wilson and Andy Symington. The previous edition was also written by Neil Wilson and Andy Symington. The 5th edition was written by Neil Wilson and Alan Murphy.

This guidebook was commissioned in Lonely Planet's London office, and produced by the following:

Commissioning Editors Clifton Wilkinson, Katie O'Connell

Coordinating Editor Kate Whitfield

Coordinating Cartographer Xavier Di Toro

Coordinating Layout Designer Carlos Solarte

Managing Editors Brigitte Ellemor, Angela Tinson

Managing Cartographers Shahara Ahmed, Anita Banh, Anthony Phelan

Managing Layout Designer Chris Girdler

Assisting Editors Andrew Bain, Jackey Coyle, Kate Evans, Justin Flynn, Samantha Forge, Gabrielle Innes, Christopher Pitts, Luna Soo

Cover Research Naomi Parker

Internal Image Research Louise Beanland, Aude Vauconsant

Thanks to Dan Austin, Kate Chapman, Ryan Evans, Larissa Frost, Tobias Gattineau, Jouve India, Asha Ioculari, Evan Jones, Trent Paton, Raphael Richards, Averil Robertson, Silvia Rosas, Fiona Siseman, Andrew Stapleton, Gerard Walker, Danny Williams

BEHIND THE SCENES

index

how to use this book

These symbols will help you find the listings you want:

- 👁 Sights
- 🐾 Beaches
- 🏃 Activities
- 🥢 Courses
- 👆 Tours
- 🎊 Festivals & Events
- 🛏 Sleeping
- ✕ Eating
- 🍷 Drinking
- ☆ Entertainment
- 🛍 Shopping
- ℹ Information/Transport

These symbols give you the vital information for each listing:

- ☎ Telephone Numbers
- ◷ Opening Hours
- P Parking
- ⊖ Nonsmoking
- ✳ Air-Conditioning
- @ Internet Access
- 🛜 Wi-Fi Access
- ⊠ Swimming Pool
- ◩ Vegetarian Selection
- ⊡ English-Language Menu
- ⊕ Family-Friendly
- ⊛ Pet-Friendly
- 🚍 Bus
- 🚢 Ferry
- Ⓜ Metro
- Ⓢ Subway
- 🚋 Tram
- 🚆 Train

Reviews are organised by author preference.

Look out for these icons:

TOP CHOICE	Our author's recommendation
FREE	No payment required
🍃	A green or sustainable option

Our authors have nominated these places as demonstrating a strong commitment to sustainability – for example by supporting local communities and producers, operating in an environmentally friendly way, or supporting conservation projects.

Map Legend

Sights
- 🟢 Beach
- 🔵 Buddhist
- 🔴 Castle
- 🟠 Christian
- 🟣 Hindu
- 🔵 Islamic
- 🟢 Jewish
- 🟠 Monument
- 🏛 Museum/Gallery
- 🟢 Ruin
- 🟢 Winery/Vineyard
- 🟢 Zoo
- 🔵 Other Sight

Activities, Courses & Tours
- 🟢 Diving/Snorkelling
- 🟢 Canoeing/Kayaking
- 🟠 Skiing
- 🟠 Surfing
- 🔵 Swimming/Pool
- 🟠 Walking
- 🔵 Windsurfing
- 🟢 Other Activity/Course/Tour

Sleeping
- 🛏 Sleeping
- 🛏 Camping

Eating
- ✕ Eating

Drinking
- 🟢 Drinking
- ⊖ Cafe

Entertainment
- 🟢 Entertainment

Shopping
- 🟠 Shopping

Information
- 🟢 Post Office
- ℹ Tourist Information

Transport
- ✈ Airport
- ⊗ Border Crossing
- 🚍 Bus
- 🚠 Cable Car/Funicular
- 🚲 Cycling
- ⊖ Ferry
- 🚝 Monorail
- P Parking
- Ⓢ S-Bahn
- 🚕 Taxi
- 🚆 Train/Railway
- 🚋 Tram
- Ⓣ Tube Station
- Ⓤ U-Bahn
- Ⓜ Underground Train Station
- ● Other Transport

Routes
- Tollway
- Freeway
- Primary
- Secondary
- Tertiary
- Lane
- Unsealed Road
- Plaza/Mall
- Steps
- ⊐⊏ Tunnel
- Pedestrian Overpass
- Walking Tour
- Walking Tour Detour
- Path

Boundaries
- –––– International
- –– State/Province
- –– Disputed
- ––– Regional/Suburb
- Marine Park
- Cliff
- Wall

Population
- ✪ Capital (National)
- ◉ Capital (State/Province)
- ● City/Large Town
- ● Town/Village

Geographic
- 🏠 Hut/Shelter
- 🔆 Lighthouse
- 🔭 Lookout
- ▲ Mountain/Volcano
- 🌴 Oasis
- 🟢 Park
-)(Pass
- 🟢 Picnic Area
- 🟢 Waterfall

Hydrography
- River/Creek
- Intermittent River
- Swamp/Mangrove
- Reef
- Canal
- Water
- Dry/Salt/Intermittent Lake
- Glacier

Areas
- Beach/Desert
- Cemetery (Christian)
- Cemetery (Other)
- Park/Forest
- Sportsground
- Sight (Building)
- Top Sight (Building)

OUR STORY

A beat-up old car, a few dollars in the pocket and a sense of adventure. In 1972 that's all Tony and Maureen Wheeler needed for the trip of a lifetime – across Europe and Asia overland to Australia. It took several months, and at the end – broke but inspired – they sat at their kitchen table writing and stapling together their first travel guide, *Across Asia on the Cheap*. Within a week they'd sold 1500 copies. Lonely Planet was born.

Today, Lonely Planet has offices in Melbourne, London and Oakland, with more than 600 staff and writers. We share Tony's belief that 'a great guidebook should do three things: inform, educate and amuse'.

OUR WRITERS

Neil Wilson ·

Coordinating Author; Edinburgh, Northeast Scotland, Southern Highlands & Islands, Inverness & the Central Highlands, Northern Highlands & Islands Neil was born in Scotland and, save for a few years spent abroad, has lived here most of his life. A lifelong enthusiasm for the great outdoors has inspired hiking, biking and sailing expeditions to every corner of the country. On his latest research trip he mountain-biked at Laggan Wolftrax, went canoeing on Loch Lomond, hiked up Eaval on Uist and Carnan Eoin on Colonsay, and drank too many BrewDog beers. Neil has been a full-time author since 1988 and has written about 60 guidebooks for various publishers, including Lonely Planet's guide to his home town of Edinburgh. Neil also wrote Plan Your Trip, the Walking in Scotland, Scotland Today, Scottish Larder and Scottish Culture chapters, and the Skye and Outer Hebrides sections of the Northern Highlands & Islands chapter.

Read more about Neil at:
lonelyplanet.com/members/neilwilson

Andy Symington

Glasgow, Southern Scotland, Central Scotland, Northern Highlands & Islands, Orkney & Shetland Islands Andy's Scottish forebears make their presence felt in a love of malt, a debatable ginger colour to his facial hair and a love of wild places. From childhood slogs up the M1 he graduated to making dubious road trips around the firths in a disintegrating Mini Metro and thence to peddling whisky in darkest Leith. While living there, he travelled widely around the country in search of the perfect dram, and, now resident in Spain, continues to visit very regularly. Andy also wrote the Golf, History, Wild Scotland, Directory and Transport chapters, and the East Coast, Caithness and North & West Coast sections of the Northern Highlands & Islands chapter.

Read more about Andy at:
lonelyplanet.com/members/andy_symington

Published by Lonely Planet Publications Pty Ltd
ABN 36 005 607 983
7th edition – March 2013
ISBN 978 1 74179 960 6
© Lonely Planet 2013 Photographs © as indicated 2013
10 9 8 7 6 5 4 3 2 1
Printed in China